Macroeconomics

The Pearson Series in Economics

Abel/Bernanke/Croushore
*Macroeconomics**

Bade/Parkin
*Foundations of Economics**

Berck/Helfand
The Economics of the Environment

Bierman/Fernandez
Game Theory with Economic Applications

Blanchard
*Macroeconomics**

Blau/Ferber/Winkler
The Economics of Women, Men and Work

**Boardman/Greenberg/Vining/
Weimer**
Cost-Benefit Analysis

Boyer
Principles of Transportation Economics

Branson
Macroeconomic Theory and Policy

Brock/Adams
The Structure of American Industry

Bruce
Public Finance and the American Economy

Carlton/Perloff
Modern Industrial Organization

Case/Fair/Oster
*Principles of Economics**

Caves/Frankel/Jones
World Trade and Payments: An Introduction

Chapman
*Environmental Economics: Theory,
Application, and Policy*

Cooter/Ulen
Law & Economics

Downs
An Economic Theory of Democracy

Ehrenberg/Smith
Modern Labor Economics

Ekelund/Ressler/Tollison
*Economics**

Farnham
Economics for Managers

Folland/Goodman/Stano
The Economics of Health and Health Care

Fort
Sports Economics

Froyen
Macroeconomics

Fusfeld
The Age of the Economist

Gerber
*International Economics**

Gordon
*Macroeconomics**

Greene
Econometric Analysis

Gregory
Essentials of Economics

Gregory/Stuart
*Russian and Soviet Economic Performance
and Structure*

Hartwick/Olewiler
The Economics of Natural Resource Use

Heilbroner/Milberg
The Making of the Economic Society

Heyne/Boettke/Prychitko
The Economic Way of Thinking

Hoffman/Averett
*Women and the Economy: Family, Work,
and Pay*

Holt
Markets, Games and Strategic Behavior

Hubbard/O'Brien
*Economics**

*Money, Banking, and the Financial System**

Hughes/Cain
American Economic History

Husted/Melvin
International Economics

Jehle/Reny
Advanced Microeconomic Theory

Johnson-Lans
A Health Economics Primer

Keat/Young
Managerial Economics

Klein
Mathematical Methods for Economics

Krugman/Obstfeld/Melitz
*International Economics: Theory & Policy**

Laidler
The Demand for Money

Leeds/von Allmen
The Economics of Sports

Leeds/von Allmen/Schiming
*Economics**

Lipsey/Ragan/Storer
*Economics**

Lynn
*Economic Development: Theory and Practice
for a Divided World*

Miller
*Economics Today**

Understanding Modern Economics

Miller/Benjamin
The Economics of Macro Issues

Miller/Benjamin/North
The Economics of Public Issues

Mills/Hamilton
Urban Economics

Mishkin
*The Economics of Money, Banking, and
Financial Markets**

*The Economics of Money, Banking, and
Financial Markets, Business School Edition**

*Macroeconomics: Policy and Practice**

Murray
Econometrics: A Modern Introduction

Nafziger
The Economics of Developing Countries

O'Sullivan/Sheffrin/Perez
*Economics: Principles, Applications and Tools**

Parkin
*Economics**

Perloff
*Microeconomics**

*Microeconomics: Theory and Applications
with Calculus**

**Perman/Common/
McGilvray/Ma**
*Natural Resources and Environmental
Economics*

Phelps
Health Economics

Pindyck/Rubinfeld
*Microeconomics**

**Riddell/Shackelford/Stamos/
Schneider**
*Economics: A Tool for Critically
Understanding Society*

Ritter/Silber/Udell
*Principles of Money, Banking & Financial
Markets**

Roberts
*The Choice: A Fable of Free Trade and
Protection*

Rohlf
Introduction to Economic Reasoning

Ruffin/Gregory
Principles of Economics

Sargent
Rational Expectations and Inflation

Sawyer/Sprinkle
International Economics

Scherer
Industry Structure, Strategy, and Public Policy

Schiller
*The Economics of Poverty and
Discrimination*

Sherman
Market Regulation

Silberberg
Principles of Microeconomics

Stock/Watson
Introduction to Econometrics

Introduction to Econometrics, Brief Edition

Studenmund
*Using Econometrics:
A Practical Guide*

Tietenberg/Lewis
*Environmental and Natural Resource
Economics*

Environmental Economics and Policy

Todaro/Smith
Economic Development

Waldman
Microeconomics

Waldman/Jensen
Industrial Organization: Theory and Practice

Weil
Economic Growth

Williamson
Macroeconomics

*denotes  titles   Log onto www.myeconlab.com to learn more

Case Studies and Boxes of Special Interest

Summarizing the Core Concepts

Students learn best when they attend lectures and keep up with their reading and assignments... but learning shouldn't end when class is over.

MyEconLab Picks Up Where Lectures and Office Hours Leave Off

Instructors choose MyEconLab:

"MyEconLab offers them a way to practice every week. They receive immediate feedback and a feeling of personal attention. As a result, my teaching has become more targeted and efficient."

—Kelly Blanchard, Purdue University

"Students tell me that offering them MyEconLab is almost like offering them individual tutors."

—Jefferson Edwards, Cypress Fairbanks College

"Chapter quizzes offset student procrastination by ensuring they keep on task. If a student is having a problem, MyEconLab indicates exactly what they need to study."

—Diana Fortier, Waubonsee Community College

Students choose MyEconLab:

In a recent study, 87 percent of students who used MyEconLab regularly felt it improved their grade.

"It was very useful because it had EVERYTHING, from practice exams to exercises to reading. Very helpful."

—student, Northern Illinois University

"It was very helpful to get instant feedback. Sometimes I would get lost reading the book, and these individual problems would help me focus and see if I understood the concepts."

—student, Temple University

"I would recommend taking the quizzes on MyEconLab because they give you a true account of whether or not you understand the material."

—student, Montana Tech

Macroeconomics

Twelfth Edition

Robert J. Gordon

Stanley G. Harris Professor in the Social Sciences
Northwestern University

Addison-Wesley

Boston   Columbus   Indianapolis   New York   San Francisco   Upper Saddle River
Amsterdam   Cape Town   Dubai   London   Madrid   Milan   Munich   Paris   Montréal   Toronto
Delhi   Mexico City   São Paulo   Sydney   Hong Kong   Seoul   Singapore   Taipei   Tokyo

Editorial Director:	Sally Yagan	Cover Designer:	Christina Gleason
Editor-in-Chief:	Donna Battista	Executive Media Producer:	Melissa Honig
Executive Editor:	David Alexander	MyEconLab Content Lead:	Noel Lotz
Editorial Project Manager:	Lindsey Sloan	Image Manager:	Rachel Youdelman
Senior Managing Editor:	Nancy Fenton	Text Design, Production Coordination, Photo Research, Composition, and Illustrations:	Integra
Supplements Coordinator:	Alison Eusden		
Director of Marketing:	Patrice Jones	Printer/Binder:	RR Donnelley/Harrisonburg
Senior Marketing Manager:	Lori DeShazo	Cover Printer:	RR Donnelley/Harrisonburg
Marketing Assistant:	Kimberly Lovato	Text Font:	10/12 Palatino
Senior Manufacturing Buyer:	Carol Melville		
Senior Art Director:	Jonathan Boylan		

Cover image: © Collier Campbell Lifeworks/CORBIS

Photo credits: page **v** photo of Robert J. Gordon by Julie P. Gordon; Chapter 2, page **27**: U.S. Department of Commerce; Chapter 5, page **135**: Everett Collection/SuperStock; page **153**: Fotosearch/SuperStock; Chapter 8, page **249**: A. H. C./AGE Fotostock; Chapter 10, page **323**: Robert Kradin/AP Images; page **325**: MGM/The Kobal Collection; Chapter 11, page **366**: Rob Crandall/The Image Works; Chapter 12, page **404**: Iain Masterton/Alamy; page **405**: Eye Ubiquitous/SuperStock; page **407**: Holton Collection/SuperStock; Chapter 13, page **437**: AFP/Getty Images; page **440**: Digital Vision; Chapter 14, page **454**: VisionsofAmerica/Joe Sohm; page **474**: Medioimages/Photodisc; Chapter 15, page **492**: Bachrach/Getty Images; page **498**: Caro/Alamy; Chapter 16, page **528**: Dmitry Kalinovsky/Shutterstock; page **534**: ClassicStock/Alamy; Chapter 17, page **545** top: Chuck Nacke/Alamy; page **545** bottom: Che Qingjiu/Imaginechina/AP Images; page **546**: Charles Bennett/AP Images; Chapter 18, page **591**: Directphoto/Alamy.

Many of the designations used by manufacturers and sellers to distinguish their products are claimed as trademarks. Where those designations appear in this book, and Addison-Wesley was aware of a trademark claim, the designations have been printed in initial caps or all caps.

Library of Congress Cataloging-in-Publication Data

Gordon, Robert J. (Robert James),
   Macroeconomics/Robert Gordon.—12th ed.
     p. cm.
   Includes index.
   ISBN 978-0-13-801491-9 (student)
   1. Macroeconomics.   I. Title.
   HB172.5 G67 2012
   339–dc22

                   2011006181

ISBN-13   978-0-13-801491-9
ISBN-10   0-13-801491-4

2 3 4 5 6 7 8 9 10—V056—15 14

Addison-Wesley is an imprint of

PEARSON

www.pearsonhighered.com

About the Author

Robert J. Gordon

Robert J. Gordon is Stanley G. Harris Professor in the Social Sciences and Professor of Economics at Northwestern University. He did his undergraduate work at Harvard and then attended Oxford University in England on a Marshall Scholarship. He received his Ph.D. in 1967 at M.I.T. and taught at Harvard and the University of Chicago before coming to Northwestern in 1973, where he has taught for 38 years and was chair of the Department of Economics from 1992 to 1996.

Professor Gordon is one of the world's leading experts on inflation, unemployment, and productivity growth. His recent work on the rise and fall of the New Economy, the U.S. productivity growth revival, and the recent stalling of European productivity growth has been widely cited. He is the author of *The Measurement of Durable Goods Prices,* which has become known as the definitive work showing that government price indexes substantially overstate the rate of inflation. His book of collected essays, *Productivity Growth, Inflation, and Unemployment,* was published in 2004. He is editor of *Milton Friedman's Monetary Framework: A Debate with His Critics, The American Business Cycle,* and *The Economics of New Goods.* In addition, he is the author of more than 100 scholarly articles and more than 60 published comments on the research of others. In addition to his main field of macroeconomics, he is also a frequently quoted expert and author on the airline industry and is the founder and president of an Internet chat group on airline management.

Gordon is a Research Associate of the National Bureau of Economic Research and since 1978 a member of its Business Cycle Dating Committee, a Research Fellow of the Centre for Economic Policy Research (London), a Research Fellow of OFCE in Paris, a Guggenheim Fellow, a Fellow of the American Academy of Arts and Sciences, and a Fellow of the Econometric Society. He has served as the co-editor of the *Journal of Political Economy* and as an elected at-large member of the Executive Committee of the American Economic Association. He serves currently as advisor to the Brookings Panel on Economic Activity and on the economic advisory panel of the Bureau of Economic Analysis. He has served as a member of the Technical Panel on Assumptions and Methods of the Social Security Administration and on the national "Boskin Commission" to assess the accuracy of the U.S. Consumer Price Index.

Gordon lives in Evanston, Illinois, with his wife, Julie, and their two dogs, Lucky and Toto (see the box on p. 325 for more about Toto).

with love, for Julie

Brief Contents

Contents

Preface

As in previous editions this book begins with business cycles, unemployment, and inflation. Experience teaches us that students want to understand what is happening today, and particularly why the Global Economic Crisis occurred and why the unemployment rate was above 9 percent during the first two years of the economic recovery. The curiosity of students about what is wrong with today's economy engages them with the subject matter, in no small measure because they know that the economy will influence their job prospects after graduation. This book provides an immediate payoff to that curiosity within the first few chapters by placing its treatment of business cycles first. The economics of long-term growth are important but should come later, after students learn about the models, answers, and puzzles surrounding business cycles.

What's New in This Edition?

- **The book's organization is an ideal home for systematic treatment of the Global Economic Crisis,** the single most important macroeconomic event since the Great Depression. It poses a challenge for intermediate macro instructors whose students will be expecting answers, not only about the causes of the Crisis but also the reasons why the recovery has been so slow. Fortunately, the structure of previous editions allows the treatment of the Crisis and recovery to fit seamlessly into the existing organization. Chapter 4 on the *IS-LM* model has always ended with sections on "strong and weak effects of monetary and fiscal policy" (pp. 102–06 in this edition).

- **The new Chapter 5, "Financial Markets, Financial Regulation, and Economic Instability,"** introduces the concepts relevant to the housing bubble and financial market meltdown, including risk, leverage, securitization, and bubbles. Balance sheets are introduced to contrast traditional banks with the "wild west" of finance in which loans are financed not from deposits but by borrowing. The post-2001 housing bubble is compared with the stock market bubble of 1927–29 that led to the Great Depression.

- **Financial market concepts are integrated into the *IS-LM* analysis of monetary policy weakness.** The "zero lower bound" is interpreted as a horizontal *LM* curve lying along the horizontal axis to the left of full employment, and the economy's problem is portrayed as a leftward shift in the *IS* curve that pushes its full-employment equilibrium interest rate into negative territory, below the zero lower bound. In addition to shifting leftward, the *IS* curve becomes steeper, i.e., less sensitive to interest rate changes, due to the effect of the post-bubble "hangover" on demand (foreclosures and excess consumer debt) and on supply (too many unsold houses and condos).

- **Term premium and risk premium add to the Fed's problem and motivate quantitative easing.** The traditional textbook focus on a single short-term interest rate is supplemented by the government bond rate, which exceeds the short-term rate by the term premium. And the corporate bond rate relevant for the borrowing of business firms exceeds the government bond rate by the risk premium. These two premiums provide the context for the new concept "quantitative easing" as the attempt by the Fed, hamstrung by the zero lower bound for the short rate, to reduce the term premium and/or the risk premium.

- **Bank and Federal Reserve balance sheets.** A colorful graph shows not only the now-familiar explosion of the Fed's assets in 2008–11 but also the counterpart of that explosion on the liability side, that is, the emergence of more than $1 trillion of excess reserves. A comparison shows that excess reserves were about the same share of GDP in 2009–10 as in 1938–39, one of many comparisons in the book of the Global Economic Crisis and the Great Depression.

- **Chapter 6 asks, "Can fiscal policy come to the rescue?"** It includes material from the previous edition on the deficit-GDP and debt-GDP ratios, the structural deficit, automatic stabilizers vs. discretionary policy, and stability conditions to avoid a long-term explosion of the debt-GDP ratio. The debate about the Obama stimulus motivates a new section that explains why fiscal multipliers are so different for alternative types of policies and why it is so difficult to design a stimulus program (e.g., multipliers of tax cuts may be small, "shovel-ready" projects may not be available in sufficient numbers). A unique set of graphs compares fiscal policy in 1933–41 with 2005–10.

- **The twin concepts of the "output gap" and the "unemployment gap" are introduced in the first chapter.** Students become familiar from the outset with the concept of an aggregate demand shock. Charts in several chapters compare aspects of output and labor-market behavior in the 1980–86 and 2006–11 cycles, and students learn about the stark difference in the causes and cures of the two largest postwar cycles.

- **New "Global Economic Crisis Focus" in-text mini-boxes.** A new pedagogical tool uses the reality of the Crisis and its aftermath to energize student learning throughout the book. Sprinkled throughout many chapters, at a rate of roughly two or three per chapter, are small in-text boxes of one or two paragraphs called "Global Economic Crisis Focus." These are used not just to reinforce the teaching of the causes and cures of the Crisis itself, but also to provide the student with a jolt that emphasizes "a basic concept about which you are reading right now is directly relevant to understanding the Crisis." Just within the first three chapters, including the introductory and measurement chapters, there are seven of these focus mini-boxes.

- **"International Perspective" boxes.** In addition to these mini-boxes, every chapter in the book has one or more topic boxes, usually appearing as a two-page spread on a left and right page. Continuing the tradition from previous editions, some of these are called "International Perspective Box" and highlight differences among countries. In this edition all of these "IP" boxes have been updated to provide new material relevant to understanding the Crisis.

- **New "Understanding the Global Economic Crisis" topic boxes.** Several new topic boxes are directly relevant to explanations of the Global Economic Crisis. An example in an early chapter is "How Changes in Wealth Affect Consumer Spending" (pp. 62–63), which traces the aftermath of the housing and stock market debacles for household assets, liabilities, net worth, and the household saving rate. Another example in Chapter 5 (pp. 134–35) is "Two Bubbles: 1927–29 in the Stock Market Versus 2000–06 in the Housing Market."

- **Theoretical treatment has been simplified.** Numerical examples have been removed from the graphs in Chapter 3 and 4 on the Keynesian 45-degree model and the *IS-LM* model; this simplifies the exposition while still allowing numerical examples both within the text itself and also in the end-of-chapter questions and problems. The derivation of the short-run aggregate supply *(SAS)* curve in Chapter 8 (previous Chapter 7) has been simplified to eliminate graphs showing the demand for and supply of labor.

- **Sections have been moved to improve the book's organization.** The introduction to financial institutions has been moved from Chapter 13 to the new Chapter 5. Material on the debt-GDP ratio and the solvency condition has been moved from the previous Chapter 12 to the new Chapter 6. To make room for new content on the Crisis, the last half of the previous Chapter 12 (supply-side economics and Social Security) has been deleted.

- **Unique custom-made graphs.** This book's tradition continues of providing unique data graphs that go far beyond the standard graphs that other textbooks download from government data Web sites. From the beginning of Chapter 1, students view custom graphs illustrating the concepts of the output and unemployment gaps, the disparate behavior of unemployment and productivity growth since 2007 for Europe versus the United States, and the comparison of the zero-lower-bound periods in the United States in the late 1930s and since 2009. Unique graphs include the price level versus the output gap in the Great Depression, the real and nominal prices of oil compared with the overall inflation rate, the actual and natural rates of unemployment, the failure of convergence of many poor countries, and many others.

Guiding Principles of the Text

This text has been guided by five organizing principles since its inception, and the Twelfth Edition develops them further.

1. **Macro questions have answers.** The use of traditional macro models can be enormously fruitful in developing answers to macro puzzles. Unlike other texts, this book introduces the natural level of output and natural rate of unemployment in the first few pages of Chapter 1. Students learn from the beginning that the output and unemployment gaps move in opposite directions and that to understand why output is so low is the same as understanding why unemployment is so high. Similarly, the fully developed dynamic inflation model of Chapter 9 shows that we have a solid answer to the puzzle of why inflation was so high in the 1970s and so low in the 1990s.

When an economic model fails, this is not swept under the rug but rather is used to highlight what the model misses, as in the lively treatment in Chapter 11 of "Puzzles That Solow's [Growth] Theory Cannot Explain" (see pp. 372–77). The Solow failure opens the way to a unique treatment of the debate between the new institutional economics versus the exponents of a tropical geography explanation for the failure of poor countries to converge to the income level of rich countries (pp. 398–408).

2. **Up-front treatment of business cycles and inflation.** Students come to the macro classroom caring most about today's economy, starting with how they and their family members can avoid unemployment. Responding to this basic curiosity of students, a core principle of this book is that students should be taught about business cycles first, instead of beginning the text with the dry abstractions of classical economics and growth theory. Accordingly, this text introduces the *IS-LM* model immediately after the first two introductory chapters, with a goal in each edition of having the *IS* and *LM* curves cross by p. 100 (it happens on p. 95 of this edition). An integrated treatment links the standard monetary and fiscal policy multipliers with the cases when monetary and fiscal policy could be weak or strong. This is immediately followed by the new Chapter 5 that creates links between the *IS-LM* framework and the new analysis of balance sheets, leverage, securitization, and bubbles.

   After a comprehensive chapter on international economics and exchange rates, the *AS-AD* model then allows an in-depth treatment of the Great Depression and its similarities and differences with the recent Global Economic Crisis. The static *AS-AD* model then flows naturally into the dynamic version of the *AS-AD* model, called the *SP* (for short-run Phillips curve) and *DG* (for demand growth) model. The treatment in this textbook allows us to explain why both inflation and unemployment were both so high in the 1970s and so low in the late 1990s; this is a parallel overlooked by most other competing intermediate macro texts. By the end of Chapter 9, students have learned the core theory of business cycles and inflation, and the text then turns to growth theory, the puzzles that Solow's theory cannot explain, and the big issues of economic growth and the non-convergence of so many poor countries.

3. **Integration of models.** The challenge many instructors face is that most intermediate macro texts overload the simple models, offering a new model every chapter or two without telling students how the models connect and work together. This book adopts the core distinction between short-run macro, devoted to explaining business cycles and their prevention, and long-run macro, dedicated to explaining economic growth.

   This text is unique in its cohesive presentation of the macro concepts. The aggregate demand curve is explicitly derived from the *IS-LM* model (pp. 231–36), and then the short-run Phillips Curve is explicitly derived from the short-run aggregate supply curve (pp. 267–70). In discussing the biggest question of economic growth—why so many nations are still so poor—the text provides an integration of the production function in the Solow growth theory with the added elements of human capital, political capital (i.e., legal systems and property rights), geography, and infrastructure (pp. 398–408).

4. **Simple graphs can convey important research results.** The graphs in this book go beyond those in the typical macro textbook in several dimensions, including the use of original data, the double-stacking of graphs plotting related concepts (see pp. 266 and 284), the extensive use of shading between

lines to convey concepts like a positive and negative output gap, and the integrated use of color.

5. **The economy is open from the start.** Students come to their macroeconomics classroom concerned about the open economy. They carry iPhones made in China, and they worry about whether their future jobs will be outsourced to India and whether a further slump in the dollar will make future trips to Europe unaffordable. This text avoids the false distinction between the closed and open economy. As early as pp. 34–35, the linkage between saving, investment, government budget, and foreign lending or borrowing is emphasized by the label "magic equation" to dramatize the importance of a basic accounting identity. In the *IS-LM* model of aggregate demand, net exports can be a source of instability from the start. Fiscal deficits can be financed by foreign borrowing, but international crowding out and growing international indebtedness reduce the future standard of living.

Pedagogy

The Use of Color

The graphs in the Twelfth Edition continue to use consistent colors to connect macro concepts and discussions, thereby strengthening conceptual ties throughout the text.

The supply curve of money, the *LM* curve, and plots of short-term interest rates are always shown in green. Government expenditures are red, and revenues are green; a government surplus is shown by green shading and a deficit by red shading. The government debt and long-term interest rates appear in purple. Data on inflation and the *AD* curve are plotted in orange. The *SAS* and *SP* curves are plotted in blue. Long-run "natural" concepts like natural real GDP, the natural rate of unemployment, the *LAS* curve, and the *LP* curve are all plotted in black.

Color is also used consistently for country-specific data. The U.S. is always red, the U.K. (or EU) is blue, Canada is gray, Japan is orange, Germany is black, France is purple, and Italy is green.

Continuing Pedagogical Features

The Twelfth Edition retains the main pedagogical features of the previous editions that aid student understanding.

- *Key terms* are introduced in bold type, defined in the margin, and listed at the end of each chapter.

- *Self-Test questions* appear at intervals within each chapter, so that students can immediately determine whether they understand what they have read. Answers are provided at the end of every chapter.

- *Learning About Diagrams boxes.* Each of these boxes covers on a single page every aspect of the key schedules—*IS, LM, AS, AD,* and *SP*—and discusses why they slope as they do, what makes them rotate and shift, and what is true on and off the curves. There are also summary boxes, including one summarizing all the sources of negative demand shocks in 2007–09 and another summarizing the different effects of monetary and fiscal policy in an open economy.

- *End-of-chapter elements* include a summary, a list of key terms, a revised and expanded set of questions and problems, and answers to the self-test questions.

- The *Glossary* at the end of the book lists definitions to every key term, with a cross-reference to the sections where they are first introduced.

- *Data Appendixes* provide annual data for the U.S. back to 1875, quarterly data for the U.S. back to 1947, and annual data since 1960 for other leading nations. This data can now be downloaded from the book's Companion Website for use in your course. Appendix C lists data sources and Web sites that offer the latest data on key macroeconomic variables.

- *Data diagrams* have been replotted electronically to ensure accuracy, and include annual and quarterly data to the end of 2010.

Supplements

With each edition, the supplements get more robust with the aim of helping you to prepare your lectures and your students to master the material.

- *MyEconLab.* This powerful assessment and tutorial system works hand-in-hand with *Macroeconomics*. MyEconLab includes comprehensive home-work, quiz, test, and tutorial options, where instructors can manage all assessment needs in one program. Here are the key features of MyEconLab:
  - Select end-of-chapter Questions and Problems, including algorithmic, graphing, and numerical, are available for student practice, or instruc-tor assignment.
  - Test Item File questions are available for assignment as homework.
  - The Custom Exercise Builder allows instructors the flexibility of creat-ing their own problems for assignment.
  - The powerful Gradebook records each student's performance and time spent on the Tests and Study Plan and generates reports by student or chapter.

  Visit **www.myeconlab.com** for more information and an online demonstra-tion of instructor and student features. MyEconLab content has been cre-ated through the efforts of Melissa Honig, Executive Media Producer, and Noel Lotz, Content Lead.

- *Online Instructor's Manual.* Subarna Samanta of the College of New Jersey revised the manual for this edition, providing chapter outlines, chapter overviews, a discussion of how the Twelfth Edition differs from the Eleventh Edition, and answers to the end-of-chapter questions and problems. The manual is available for download as PDF or Word files on the Instructor's Resource Center (www.pearsonhighered .com/irc).

- *Online Test Item File.* Completely revised by Mihajlo Balic of Palm Beach Community College, the Online Test Item File offers more than 2,000 questions specific to the book. It is available in Word format on the Instructor's Resource Center.

- *Online Computerized Test Bank.* The Computerized Test Bank reproduces the Test Item File material in the TestGen software that is available for Windows and Macintosh. With TestGen, instructors can easily edit existing questions, add questions, generate tests, and print the tests in a variety of formats. It is available in both Mac and PC formats on the Instructor's Resource Center.

- *Online PowerPoint with Art, Figures, and Lecture Notes.* PowerPoint presentations, revised by Richard Stahnke of Bryn Mawr College, contain the figures and tables in the text, as well as new lecture notes that correspond with the information in each chapter. The PowerPoint presentations are available on the Instructor's Resource Center.

- *Companion Website.* The open-access Web site http://www.pearsonhighered.com/gordon/ offers the following resources:

- The Data Appendixes from the text are available for download, as is the robust data set created explicitly for the text that includes the historical data and natural level of output.

- Excel®-based problems, written by David Ring of SUNY College at Oneonta, offer students one to two questions per chapter using the Excel program and data. Solutions to all Excel-based problems are available on the Instructor's Resource Center.

Acknowledgments

I remain grateful to all those who have given thoughtful comments on this book over the years. In recent years, these colleagues include:

Terence J. Alexander, *Iowa State University*
Mihajlo Balic, *Palm Beach Community College*
Jeffrey H. Bergstrand, *University of Notre Dame*
William Branch, *University of California, Irvine*
John P. Burkett, *University of Rhode Island*
Henry Chen, *University of West Florida*
Andrew Foshee, *McNeese State University*
Donald E. Frey, *Wake Forest University*
John Graham, *Rutgers University*
Luc Hens, *Vesalius College, Vrije Universiteit Brussel*
Tracy Hofer, *University of Wisconsin, Stevens Point*
Brad R. Humphreys, *University of Illinois, Urbana-Champaign*
Alan G. Isaac, *American University*
Thomas Kelly, *Baylor University*
Barry Kotlove, *Edmonds Community College*
Philip Lane, *Fairfield University*
Sandeep Mazumder, *Wake Forest University*
Ilir Miteza, *University of Michigan, Dearborn*
Gary Mongiovi, *St. John's University*
Jan Ondrich, *Syracuse University*
Chris Papageorgiou, *International Monetary Fund*
Walter Park, *American University*
Prosper Raynold, *Miami University, Oxford*
Michael Reed, *University of Kentucky*
Kevin Reffett, *WP Cary School of Business, ASU*
Charles F. Revier, *Colorado State University*

David Ring, *State University of New York, Oneonta*
Wayne Saint Aubyn Henry, *University of the West Indies*
Subarna K. Samanta, *The College of New Jersey*
Richard Sheeham, *University of Notre Dame*
William Doyle Smith, *University of Texas, El Paso*
Richard Stahnke, *Bryn Mawr College*
Manly E. Staley, *San Francisco State University*
Mark Thoma, *University of Oregon*
David Tufte, *Southern Utah University*
Kristin Van Gaasbeck, *California State University, Sacramento*
Anne Ramstetter Wenzel, *San Francisco State University*
Henry Woudenberg, *Kent State University*

An expanded set of questions and problems was provided by David Ring of SUNY at Oneonta. In addition, the book contains a great deal of data, some of it originally created for this book, both in the text and the Data Appendix. Geoffrey Bery with speed, accuracy, and frequent intiative created all the data, tables and graphs, as well as the Data Appendix.

Many thanks go to the staff at Addison-Wesley. I am extremely grateful to David Alexander for suggesting and then implementing the development of the Twelfth Edition. Lindsey Sloan handled her role as assistant editor with enthusiasm and accuracy. The final stages of handling proofs and other pre-publication details were managed efficiently, with tact and courtesy, by Nancy Fenton of Pearson and Allison Campbell of Integra. Thanks to Lori DeShazo, the marketing manager, and to Kimberly Lovato, the marketing assistant for this title, for their marketing efforts.

Finally, thanks go to my wife, Julie, for her patience at the distractions not just of writing the revised edition but also of the endless extra weeks of proofreading. A real bonus of modern technology for our household is the conversion of this revision to electronic editing, which allows my corrections to be made on the computer screen and then instantly e-mailed to the publisher. That has eliminated the role both of Fed Ex and of vast piles of paper in the revision process, which has been a great relief for me and especially to Julie. As always, her unfailing encouragement and welcome diversions made the book possible.

Robert J. Gordon
Evanston, IL
February 2011

What Is Macroeconomics?

Business will be better or worse.
—Calvin Coolidge, 1928

1-1 How Macroeconomics Affects Our Everyday Lives

Macroeconomics is concerned with the big economic issues that determine your own economic well-being as well as that of your family and everyone you know. Each of these issues involves the overall economic performance of the nation rather than whether one particular individual earns more or less than another.

> **Macroeconomics** is the study of the major economic totals, or aggregates.

The nation's overall macroeconomic performance matters, not only for its own sake but because many individuals experience its consequences. The **Global Economic Crisis** that began in late 2007 has created enormous losses of income and jobs for millions of American families. Not only were almost 15 million people unemployed in late 2010, but many more have given up looking for jobs, have been forced to work part-time instead of full-time, or have experienced pay cuts or furlough days when they have not been paid. By one estimate, more than half of American families since 2007 have experienced the job loss of a family member, a pay cut, or being forced to work part-time instead of full-time.

> The **Global Economic Crisis** is the crisis that began in 2007 that simultaneously depressed economic activity in most of the world's economies.

Macroeconomic performance can also determine whether inflation will erode the value of family savings, as occurred in the 1970s when the annual inflation rate reached 10 percent. Today's students also care about economic growth, which will determine whether in their future lives they will have a higher standard of living than their parents do today.

The "Big Three" Concepts of Macroeconomics

Each of these connections between the overall economy and the lives of individuals involves a central macroeconomic concept introduced in this chapter—unemployment, inflation, and economic growth. The basic task of macroeconomics is to study the causes of good or bad performance of these three concepts, why each matters to individuals, and what (if anything) the government can do to improve macroeconomic performance. While there are numerous other important macroeconomic concepts, we start by focusing just on these, which are the "Big Three" concepts of macroeconomics:

1. The **unemployment rate.** The higher the overall unemployment rate, the harder it is for each individual who wants a job to find work. College seniors who want permanent jobs after graduation are likely to have fewer job offers if the national unemployment rate is high, as in 2009–10, than low, as

> The **unemployment rate** is the number of persons unemployed (jobless individuals who are actively looking for work or are on temporary layoff) divided by the total of those employed and unemployed.

in 2005–2007. All adults fear a high unemployment rate, which raises the chances that they will be laid off, be unable to pay their bills, have their cars repossessed, lose their health insurance, or even lose their homes through mortgage foreclosures. In "bad times," when the unemployment rate is high, crime, mental illness, and suicide also increase. The widespread consensus that unemployment is the most important macroeconomic issue has been further highlighted by the dismal labor market of 2009–10, when fully half of the unemployed were jobless for more than six months. And the recognized harm created by high unemployment is nothing new. Robert Burton, an English clergyman, wrote in 1621 that "employment is so essential to human happiness that indolence is justly considered the mother of misery."

The **inflation rate** is the percentage rate of increase in the economy's average level of prices.

2. The **inflation rate.** A high inflation rate means that prices, on average, are rising rapidly, while a low inflation rate means that prices, on average, are rising slowly. An inflation rate of zero means that prices remain essentially the same, month after month. In inflationary periods, retired people, or those about to retire, lose the most, since their hard-earned savings buy less as prices go up. Even college students lose as the rising prices of room, board, and textbooks erode what they have saved from previous summer and after-school jobs. While a high inflation rate harms those who have saved, it helps those who have borrowed. Great harm comes from this capricious aspect of inflation, taking from some and giving to others. People want their lives to be predictable, but inflation throws a monkey wrench into individual decision making, creating pervasive uncertainty.

Productivity is the aggregate output produced per hour.

3. **Productivity** growth. "Productivity" is the aggregate output per hour of work that a nation produces in total goods and services; it was about $61 per worker-hour in the United States in 2010. The faster aggregate productivity grows, the easier it is for each member of society to improve his or her standard of living. If productivity were to grow at 3 percent from 2010 to the year 2030, U.S. productivity would rise from $61 per worker-hour to $111 per worker-hour. When multiplied by all the hours worked by all the employees in the country, this extra $50 per worker-hour would make it possible for the nation to have more houses, cars, hospitals, roads, schools, and to combat greenhouse gas emissions that worsen global warming.

But if the growth rate of productivity were zero instead of 3 percent, U.S. productivity would remain at $61 in the year 2030. To have more houses and cars, we would have to sacrifice by building fewer hospitals and schools. Such an economy, with no productivity growth, has been called the "zero-sum society," because any extra good or service enjoyed by one person requires that something be taken away from someone else. Many have argued that the achievement of rapid productivity growth and the avoidance of a zero-sum society form the most important macroeconomic challenge of all.

The first two of the "Big Three" macroeconomic concepts, the unemployment and inflation rates, appear in the newspaper every day. When economic conditions are poor—as in 2009–10—daily headlines announce that one large company or another is laying off thousands of workers. In the past, sharp increases in the rate of inflation have also made headlines, as when the price of gasoline jumped during 2006–08. The third major concept, productivity growth, has received widespread attention since 1995 as a source of an improving American standard of living compared to that in Europe and Japan.

Macroeconomic concepts also play a big role in politics. Incumbent political parties benefit when unemployment and inflation are relatively low, as in the landslide victories of Lyndon Johnson in 1964 and Richard Nixon in 1972. Incumbent presidents who fail to gain reelection often are the victims of a sour economy, as in the cases of Herbert Hoover in 1932, Jimmy Carter in 1980, and more recently George W. Bush in 2008. The defeat of Al Gore by George W. Bush in 2000 was an exception since the strong economy of 2000 should have helped Gore's incumbent Democratic party win the presidency.

GLOBAL ECONOMIC CRISIS FOCUS

What Makes It Unique?

The Global Economic Crisis that started in 2008 is by most measures the most severe downturn since the Great Depression of the 1930s. Its severity is most apparent in the high level of the unemployment rate (10 percent) reached in 2009–10, in the relatively long duration of unemployment suffered by those who lost their jobs, and in the prediction that the unemployment rate would not return to its normal level of around 5 percent until perhaps 2015 or 2016. Thus, of our three big macro concepts, the Global Economic Crisis mainly affected the unemployment rate, while the inflation rate remained low and productivity growth was relatively robust.

1-2 Defining Macroeconomics

How Macroeconomics Differs from Microeconomics

Most topics in economics can be placed in one of two categories: macroeconomics or microeconomics. *Macro* comes from a Greek word meaning large; *micro* comes from a Greek word meaning small. Put another way, macroeconomics deals with the totals, or **aggregates,** of the economy, and microeconomics deals with the parts. Among these crucial economic aggregates are the three central concepts introduced on pp. 1–2.

An **aggregate** is the total amount of an economic magnitude for the economy as a whole.

Microeconomics is devoted to the relationships among the different *parts* of the economy. For example, in micro we try to explain the wage or salary of one type of worker in relation to another. For example, why is a professor's salary more than that of a secretary but less than that of an investment banker? In contrast, macroeconomics asks why the total income of all citizens rises strongly in some periods but declines in others.

Economic Theory: A Process of Simplification

Economic theory helps us understand the economy by *simplifying complexity.* Theory throws a spotlight on just a few key relations. Macroeconomic theory examines the behavior of aggregates such as the unemployment rate and the inflation rate while ignoring differences among individual households. It studies the causes and possible cures of the Global Economic Crisis at the level of individual nations, instead of trying to explain why some individuals are more prone than others to losing their jobs.

It is this process of simplification that makes the study of economics so exciting. By learning a few basic macroeconomic relations, you can quickly learn how to sift out the hundreds of irrelevant details in the news in order to focus on the few key items that foretell where the economy is going. You also will begin to understand which national and personal economic goals can be attained and which are "pie in the sky." You will learn when it is fair to credit a president for strong economic performance or blame a president for poor performance.

1-3   Actual and Natural Real GDP

We have learned that the "Big Three" macroeconomic concepts are the unemployment rate, the inflation rate, and the rate of productivity growth. Linked to each of these is the total level of output produced in the economy. The higher the level of output, the lower the unemployment rate. The higher the level of output, the faster tends to be the rate of inflation. Finally, for any given number of hours worked, a higher level of output automatically boosts output per hour, that is, productivity.

Gross domestic product is the value of all currently produced goods and services sold on the market during a particular time interval.

The official measure of the economy's total output is called **gross domestic product** and is abbreviated GDP. As you will learn in Chapter 2, real GDP includes all currently produced goods and services sold on the market within a given time period and excludes certain other types of economic activity. As you will also learn, the adjective "real" means that our measure of output reflects the quantity produced, corrected for any changes in prices.

Actual real GDP is the value of total output corrected for any changes in prices.

Actual real GDP is the amount an economy actually produces at any given time. But we need some criterion to judge the desirability of that level of actual real GDP. Perhaps actual real GDP is too low, causing high unemployment. Perhaps actual real GDP is too high, putting upward pressure on the inflation rate. Which level of real GDP is desirable, neither too low nor too high? This intermediate compromise level of real GDP is called "natural," a level of real GDP in which there is no tendency for the rate of inflation to rise or fall.

Figure 1-1 illustrates the relationship between actual real GDP, natural real GDP, and the rate of inflation. In the upper frame the red line is actual real GDP. The lower frame shows the inflation rate. The thin dashed vertical lines connect the two frames. The first dashed vertical line marks time period t_0. Notice in the bottom frame that the inflation rate is constant at t_0, neither speeding up nor slowing down.

Natural real GDP designates the level of real GDP at which the inflation rate is constant, with no tendency to accelerate or decelerate.

By definition, **natural real GDP** is equal to actual real GDP when the inflation rate is constant. Thus, in the upper frame, at t_0 the red actual real GDP line is crossed by the black natural real GDP line. To the right of t_0, actual real GDP falls below natural real GDP, and we see in the bottom frame that inflation slows down. This continues until time period t_1, when actual real GDP once again is equal to natural real GDP. Here the inflation rate stops falling and is constant for a moment before it begins to rise.

This cycle repeats itself again and again. *Only when actual real GDP is equal to natural real GDP is the inflation rate constant.* For this reason, natural real GDP is a compromise level to be singled out for special attention. During a period of low actual real GDP, designated by the blue area, the inflation rate slows down. During a period of high actual real GDP, designated by the shaded red area, the inflation rate speeds up.

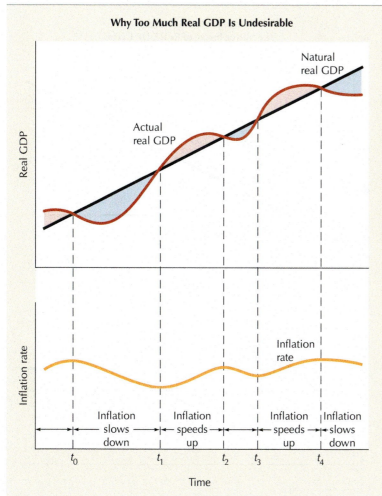

Why Too Much Real GDP Is Undesirable

Figure 1-1 **The Relation Between Actual and Natural Real GDP and the Inflation Rate**

In the upper frame the solid black line shows the steady growth of natural real GDP—the amount the economy can produce at a constant inflation rate. The red line shows the path of actual real GDP. In the blue region in the top frame, actual real GDP is below natural real GDP, so the inflation rate, shown in the bottom frame, slows down. In the region designated by the red area, actual real GDP is above natural real GDP, so in the bottom frame inflation speeds up.

Unemployment: Actual and Natural

When actual real GDP is low, many people lose their jobs, and the unemployment rate is high, as shown in Figure 1-2. The top frame duplicates Figure 1-1 exactly, comparing actual real GDP with natural real GDP. The blue line in the bottom frame is the actual percentage unemployment rate, the first of the three central concepts of macroeconomics. The thin vertical dashed lines connecting the upper frame and lower frame show that whenever actual and natural real GDP are equal in the top frame, the actual unemployment rate is equal to the **natural rate of unemployment** in the bottom frame.

The definition of the natural rate of unemployment corresponds exactly to natural real GDP, describing a situation in which there is no tendency for the inflation rate to change. When the actual unemployment rate is high, actual real GDP is low (shown by blue shading in both frames), and the inflation rate slows down. In periods when actual real GDP is high and the economy prospers, the actual unemployment rate is low (shown by red shading in both frames) and the inflation rate speeds up. It is easy to remember the mirror-image behavior of real GDP and the unemployment rate. We use the shorthand

The **natural rate of unemployment** designates the level of unemployment at which the inflation rate is constant, with no tendency to accelerate or decelerate.

Figure 1-2 The Behavior Over Time of Actual and Natural Real GDP and the Actual and Natural Rates of Unemployment

When actual real GDP falls below natural real GDP, designated by the blue shaded areas in the top frame, the actual unemployment rate rises above the natural rate of unemployment as indicated in the bottom frame. The red shaded areas designate the opposite situation. When we compare the blue shaded areas of Figures 1-1 and 1-2, we see that the time intervals when unemployment is high (1–2) also represent time intervals when inflation is slowing down (1–1). Similarly, the red shaded areas represent time intervals when inflation is speeding up and unemployment is low.

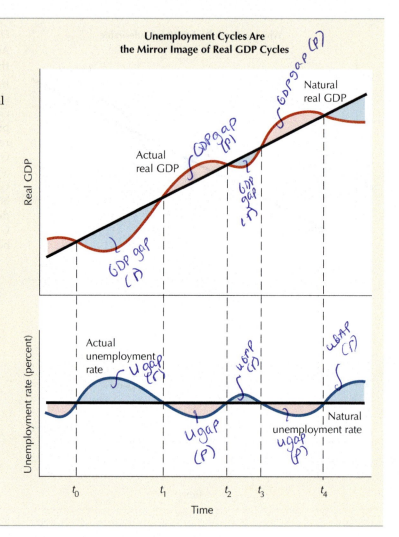

The **GDP gap** is the percentage difference between actual real GDP and natural real GDP. Another name for this concept is the "output gap."

The **unemployment gap** is the difference between the actual unemployment rate and the natural rate of unemployment.

label **GDP gap** for the percentage difference between actual real GDP and natural real GDP. We use the parallel shorthand label **unemployment gap** for the difference between the actual unemployment rate and the natural rate of unemployment. In recessions when the GDP gap is negative, the unemployment gap is positive, and both of the gaps are represented by the blue shaded areas in Figure 1-2. In highly prosperous periods like the late 1990s, the GDP gap is positive and the unemployment gap is negative, as indicated by the red shaded areas in Figure 1-2. Another name for the GDP gap is the "output gap."

Figures 1-1 and 1-2 summarize a basic dilemma faced by government policymakers who are attempting to achieve a low unemployment rate and a low inflation rate at the same time. If the inflation rate is high, lowering it requires a decline in actual real GDP and an increase in the actual unemployment rate. This happened in the early 1980s, when inflation was so high that the government deliberately pushed unemployment to its highest level since the 1930s. If, to the contrary, the policymaker attempts to provide jobs for everyone and keep the actual unemployment rate low then the inflation rate will speed up, as occurred in the 1960s and late 1980s.

Real GDP and the Three Macro Concepts

The total amount that the economy produces, actual real GDP, is closely related to the three central macroeconomic concepts introduced earlier in this chapter. First, as we see in Figure 1-2, the *difference* between actual and natural real GDP moves inversely with the *difference* between the actual and natural unemployment rates. When actual real GDP is high, unemployment is low, and vice versa.

The second link is with inflation, since inflation tends to speed up when actual real GDP is higher than natural real GDP (as in Figure 1-1). The third link is with productivity, which is defined as actual real GDP per hour; data on actual real GDP are required to calculate productivity.

Each of these links with the central macroeconomic concepts requires that actual real GDP be compared with *something else* in order to be meaningful. It must be compared to natural real GDP to provide a link with unemployment and inflation, or it must be divided by the number of hours worked to compute productivity. Actual real GDP by itself, without any such comparison, is not meaningful, which is why it is not included on the list of the three major macro concepts.

 SELF-TEST

1. When actual real GDP is above natural real GDP, is the actual unemployment rate above, below, or equal to the natural unemployment rate?
2. When actual real GDP is below natural real GDP, is the actual unemployment rate above, below, or equal to the natural unemployment rate?
3. When the actual unemployment rate is equal to the natural rate of unemployment, is the actual rate of inflation equal to the natural rate of inflation?

1-4 Macroeconomics in the Short Run and Long Run

Macroeconomic theories and debates can be divided into two main groups: (1) those that concern the "short-run" stability of the economy, and (2) those that concern its "long-run" growth rate. Much of macroeconomic analysis concerns the first group of topics involving the short run, usually defined as a period lasting from one year to five years, and focuses on the first two major macroeconomic concepts introduced in Section 1-1, the unemployment rate and the inflation rate. We ask why the unemployment rate and the inflation rate over periods of a few years are sometimes high and sometimes low, rather than always low as we would wish. These ups and downs are usually called "economic fluctuations" or **business cycles.** Much of this book concerns the causes of these cycles and the efficacy of alternative government policies to dampen or eliminate the cycles.

Business cycles consist of expansions occurring at about the same time in many economic activities, followed by similarly general recessions and recoveries.

The other main topic in macroeconomics concerns the long run, which is a longer period ranging from one decade to several decades. It attempts to explain the rate of productivity growth, the third key concept introduced in Section 1-1, or more generally, **economic growth.** Learning the causes of growth helps us predict whether successive generations of Americans will be better off than their predecessors, and why some countries remain so poor in a world

Economic growth is the topic area of macroeconomics that studies the causes of sustained growth in real GDP over periods of a decade or more.

where other countries by contrast are so rich. The remarkable achievement of China in achieving economic growth of 8 to 9 percent per year consistently over the past three decades raises a new question about economic growth—how long will it take the Chinese economy to catch up to the American level of real GDP per person?

The Short Run: Business Cycles

The main short-run concern of macroeconomists is to minimize fluctuations in the unemployment and inflation rates. This requires that fluctuations in real GDP be minimized.

Figure 1-3 contrasts two imaginary economies: "Volatilia" in the left frame and "Stabilia" in the right frame. The black "natural real GDP" lines in both frames are *absolutely identical.* The two economies differ only in the size of their business cycles, shown by the size of their GDP gap, which is simply the difference between actual and natural real GDP shown by blue and red shading.

In the left frame, Volatilia is a macroeconomic hell, with severe business cycles and large gaps between actual and natural real GDP. In the right frame, Stabilia is macroeconomic heaven, with mild business cycles and small gaps between actual and natural real GDP. All macroeconomists prefer the economy depicted by the right-hand frame to that depicted by the left-hand frame. But the debate between macro schools of thought starts in earnest when we ask how to achieve the economy of the right-hand frame. Active do-something policies? Do-nothing, hands-off policies? There are economists who support each of these alternatives, and more besides. But everyone agrees that Stabilia

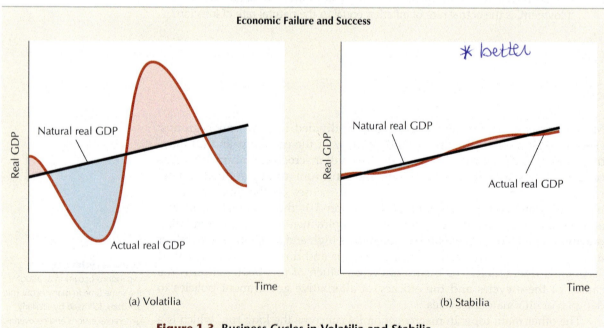

Figure 1-3 Business Cycles in Volatilia and Stabilia

The left frame shows the huge business cycles in a hypothetical nation called Volatilia. Short-run macroeconomics tries to dampen business cycles so that the path of actual real GDP is as close as possible to natural real GDP, as shown in the right frame for a nation called Stabilia.

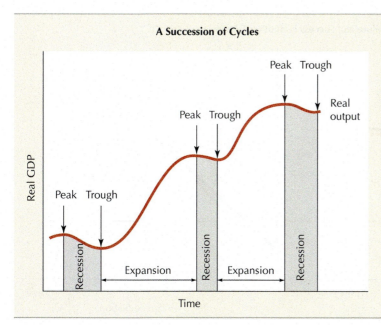

A Succession of Cycles

Figure 1-4 Basic Business-Cycle Concepts
The real output line exhibits a typical succession of business cycles. The highest point reached by real output in each cycle is called the *peak* and the lowest point the *trough*. The *recession* is the period between peak and trough; the *expansion* is the period between the trough and the next peak.

is a more successful economy than Volatilia. To achieve the success of Stabilia, Volatilia must find a way to eliminate its large real GDP gap.

The hallmark of business cycles is their pervasive character, which affects many different types of economic activity at the same time. This means that they occur again and again but not always at regular intervals, nor are they the same length. Business cycles in the past have ranged in length from one to twelve years.[1] Figure 1-4 illustrates two successive business cycles in real output. Although a simplification, Figure 1-4 contains two realistic elements that have been common to most real-world business cycles. First, the expansions last longer than the recessions. Second, the two business cycles illustrated in the figure differ in length.

The Long Run: Economic Growth

For a society to achieve an increasing standard of living, total output per person must grow, and such economic growth is the long-run concern of macroeconomists. Look at Figure 1-5, which contrasts two economies. Each has mild business cycles, like Stabilia in Figure 1-3. But in Figure 1-5, the left frame presents a country called "Stag-Nation," which experiences very slow growth in real GDP. In contrast, the right-hand frame depicts "Speed-Nation," a country with very fast growth in real GDP. If we assume that population growth in each country is the same, then growth in output per person is faster in Speed-Nation. In Speed-Nation everyone can purchase more consumer goods, and there is plenty of output left to provide better schools, parks, hospitals, and other public services. In Stag-Nation people must constantly face debates, since more money for schools or parks requires that people sacrifice consumer goods.

---

[1] A comprehensive source for the chronology of and data on historical business cycles, as well as research papers by distinguished economists, is Robert J. Gordon, ed., *The American Business Cycle: Continuity and Change* (Chicago: University of Chicago Press, 1986). An up-to-date chronology and a discussion of the 2007–09 recession can be found at www.nber.org/cycles/cyclesmain.html.

Economic Failure and Success in Another Dimension

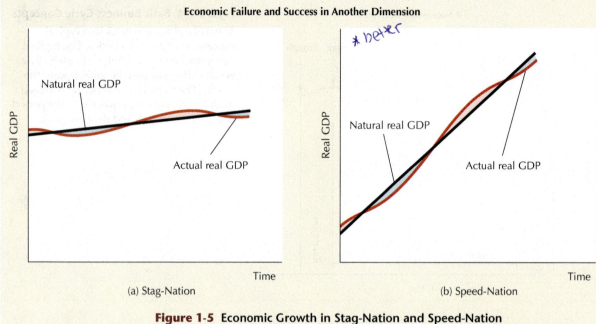

(a) Stag-Nation   (b) Speed-Nation

Figure 1-5 Economic Growth in Stag-Nation and Speed-Nation

In both frames the business cycle has been tamed, but in the left frame there is almost no economic growth, while economic growth in the right frame is rapid. For Speed-Nation there can be more of everything, while Stag-Nation in the left frame is a "zero-sum society," in which an increase in one type of economic activity requires that another economic activity be cut back.

Over the past decade, countries like Stag-Nation include Germany, Italy, and Japan. Countries like Speed-Nation include China and India. The United States has been between these extremes.

How do we achieve faster economic growth in output per person? In Chapters 11 and 12 we study the sources of economic growth and the role of government policy in helping to determine the growth in America's future standard of living, as well as the reasons why some countries remain so poor.

◆ SELF-TEST

Indicate whether each item in the following list is more closely related to short-run (business cycle) macro or to long-run (economic growth) macro:

1. The Federal Reserve reduces interest rates in a recession in an attempt to reduce the unemployment rate.

2. The federal government introduces national standards for high school students in an attempt to raise math and science test scores.

3. Consumers cut back spending because news of layoffs makes them fear for their jobs.

4. The federal government gives states and localities more money to repair roads, bridges, and schools.

◆ 1-5 CASE STUDY

How Does the Global Economic Crisis Compare to Previous Business Cycles?

This section examines U.S. macroeconomic history since the early twentieth century. You will see that unemployment in the past four decades did not come close to the extreme crisis levels of the 1930s.

Real GDP

Figure 1-6 is arranged just like Figure 1-2. But whereas Figure 1-2 shows hypothetical relationships, Figure 1-6 shows the actual historical record. In the top frame the solid black line is natural real GDP, an estimate of the amount the economy could have produced each year without causing acceleration or deceleration of inflation.

The red line in the top frame plots actual real GDP, the total production of goods and services each year measured in the constant prices of 2005. Can you pick out those years when actual and natural real GDP are roughly equal? Some of these years were 1900, 1910, 1924, 1964, 1987, 1997, and 2007.

In years marked by blue shading, actual real GDP fell below natural real GDP. A maximum deficiency occurred in 1933, when actual real GDP was only 64 percent of natural GDP; about 35 percent of natural real GDP was thus "wasted," that is, not produced. In some years actual real GDP exceeded natural real GDP, shown by the shaded red areas. The largest red area occurred during World War II in 1942–45.

Unemployment

In the middle frame of Figure 1-6, the blue line plots the actual unemployment rate. By far the most extreme episode was the Great Depression, when the actual unemployment rate remained above 10 percent for ten straight years, 1931–40. The black line in the middle frame of Figure 1-6 displays the natural rate of unemployment, the minimum attainable level of unemployment that is compatible with avoiding an acceleration of inflation. The red shaded areas mark years when actual unemployment fell below the natural rate, and the blue shaded areas mark years when unemployment exceeded the natural rate.

Notice now the relationship between the top and middle frames of Figure 1-6. The blue shaded areas in both frames designate periods of low production, low real GDP, and high unemployment, such as the Great Depression of the 1930s. The red shaded areas in both frames designate periods of high production and high actual real GDP, and low unemployment, such as World War II and other wartime periods. ◆

GLOBAL ECONOMIC CRISIS FOCUS
How It Differs from 1982–83

The bottom frame of Figure 1-6 magnifies the middle frame by starting the plot in 1970 instead of 1900. Over the past four decades there have been three big recessions with unemployment reaching its peak in 1975, then 1982–83, and most recently in 2009–10. The recent episode of high unemployment is more serious

(continued)

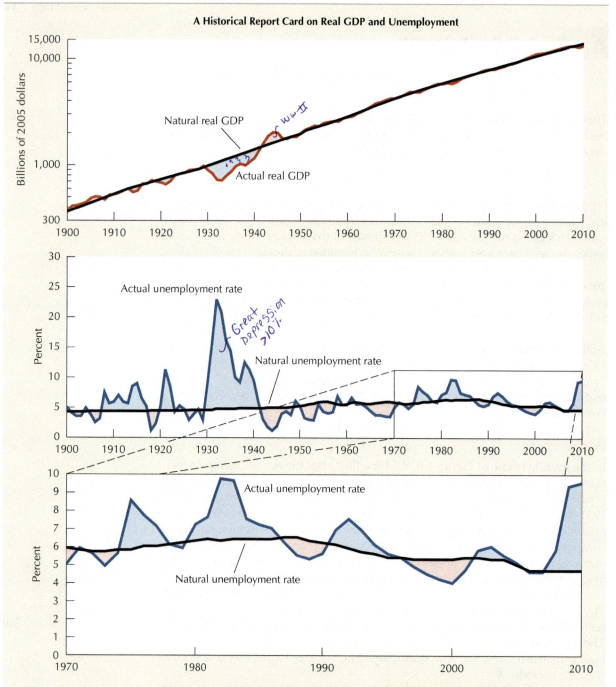

Figure 1-6 Actual and Natural GDP and Unemployment, 1900–2010

A historical report card for two important economic magnitudes. In the top frame the black line indicates natural real GDP. The red line shows actual real GDP, which was well below natural real GDP during the Great Depression of the 1930s and well above it during World War II. In the middle frame the black line indicates the natural rate of unemployment, and the blue line indicates the actual unemployment rate. Actual unemployment was much higher during the Great Depression of the 1930s than at any other time during the century. The bottom frame magnifies the middle frame to focus on unemployment since 1970. There we see that the 2009–10 levels of high unemployment were equivalent to 1982–83. However, the increase in unemployment was greater in 2007–10 than in 1980–82 since that economy started from a lower unemployment rate.

Sources: See Appendix A-1 and C-4.

and harmful than in 1982–83 for several reasons. Notice that the unemployment rate dropped sharply from 1983 to 1984, while the decline in the unemployment rate in 2011–12 is forecast to be very slow. In the recent episode a larger share of the unemployed have been without jobs for six months or more, and a much larger share of the labor force than in 1982–83 has been forced to work on a part-time basis rather than their desired full-time status.

1-6 Macroeconomics at the Extremes

Most of macroeconomics treats relatively normal events. Business cycles occur, and unemployment goes up and down, as does inflation. Economic growth registers faster rates in some decades than in others. Yet there are times when the economy's behavior is anything but normal. The normal mechanisms of macroeconomics break down, and the consequences can be dire. Three examples of unusual macroeconomic behavior involving our "Big Three" concepts are the Great Depression of the 1930s, the German hyperinflation of the 1920s, and the stark difference in economic growth between two Asian nations over the past 50 years.

Unemployment in the Great Depression, 1929–40

The first of our "Big Three" macroeconomic concepts is the unemployment rate. The most extreme event involving unemployment in recorded history was the Great Depression of the 1930s. As is clearly visible in Figure 1-6 in the previous section, real GDP collapsed between 1929 and 1933, and the unemployment rate soared. A closer look at the decade of the 1930s is provided in Figure 1-7. For contrast with the 1930s, the blue line displays the unemployment rate from 1998 to 2010. The unemployment rate during the Great Depression behaved quite differently, as shown by the purple line, soaring from 3.2 percent in 1929 to 25.2 percent in 1933, and never falling below 10 percent until 1941. By 2010 the unemployment rate had reached 9.5 percent, almost as high as it was in 1941.

In the United States, the Great Depression caused many millions of jobs to disappear. College seniors could not find jobs. Stories of job hunting were unbelievable but true. For example, men waited all night outside Detroit employment offices so they would be first in line the next morning. An Arkansas man walked 900 miles looking for work. So discouraged were Americans of finding jobs that for the first (and last) time in American history, there were more emigrants than immigrants. In fact, there were 350 applications per day from Americans who wanted to settle in Russia. Since there was no unemployment insurance, how did people live when there were no jobs? Wedding rings were sold, furniture pawned, life insurance borrowed against, and money begged from relatives. Millions with no resources moved aimlessly from city to city, sometimes riding on freight cars; some cities tried to keep the wanderers out with barricades and shotguns.[2]

The Great Depression affected most of the industrialized world but was most serious in the United States and in Germany. The Great Depression in Germany led directly to Hitler's takeover of power in 1933 and indirectly

---

[2] Details in this paragraph are from William Manchester, *The Glory and the Dream: A Narrative History of America, 1932–72* (Boston: Little-Brown, 1973), pp. 33–35.

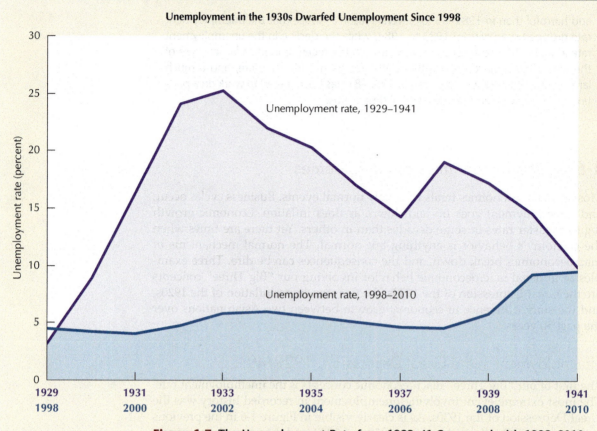

Figure 1-7 **The Unemployment Rate from 1929–41 Compared with 1998–2010**
The blue line displays the unemployment rate from 1998 to 2010, when the unemployment rate ranged from 4 percent in 2000 to 10 percent in 2010. In contrast the purple line exhibits the unemployment rate during the Great Depression; this never fell below 14 percent the ten years from 1931 to 1940.

Source: Bureau of Labor Statistics. See Appendix C-4.

caused the 50 million deaths of World War II. What caused the disastrous depression and what could have been done to avoid it? We need to study basic macroeconomics first, and then we will examine the causes of the Great Depression in Chapters 5 and 8.

The German Hyperinflation of 1922–23

A *hyperinflation* can be defined as an inflation raging at a rate of 50 percent or more *per month*. If a Big Mac cost $2 in January, a 50 percent monthly inflation would raise the price to $3 in February, $4.50 in March, $6.75 in April, and onward until it reached $173 in December! There were several examples of hyperinflation in the twentieth century, most of them involving the experience of European countries after World Wars I and II. The best known is the German hyperinflation, which proceeded at 322 percent per month between August 1922 and November 1923; in its final climactic days in October 1923, the inflation rate was 32,000 percent per month! Figure 1-8 displays the German price level from 1920 to 1923. The price

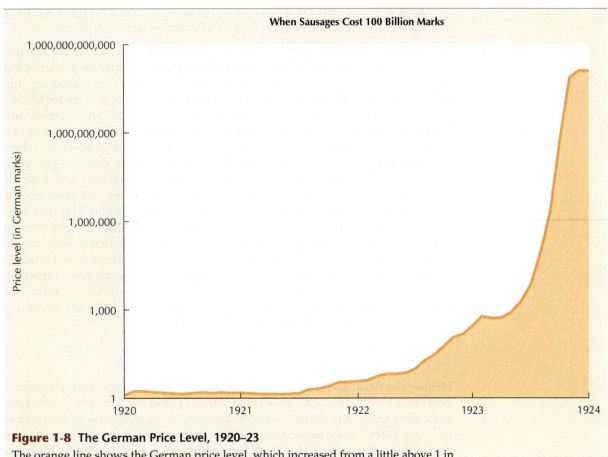

When Sausages Cost 100 Billion Marks

Figure 1-8 The German Price Level, 1920–23

The orange line shows the German price level, which increased from a little above 1 in 1920 and 1921 to 550 at the end of 1922 and to 100,000,000,000 in November 1923.

level goes from slightly above 1.0 in 1920 and early 1921 to 550 by the end of 1922 and about 100,000,000,000 at the end of 1923.

The basic cause of the German hyperinflation was the Versailles Peace Treaty, which ended World War I and required payment of massive reparations by Germany to Britain and France. The Germans were unwilling to obtain funds to pay the reparations by raising taxes, so instead they ran huge government budget deficits financed by printing paper money. When people realized the implications of these deficits, they became less willing to hold money; it was both the rapid increase in the supply of money and the ever-declining demand for money that combined to fuel the hyperinflation.[3]

The inflation decimated the savings of ordinary Germans. A farmer who sold a piece of land for 80,000 marks as a nest egg for his old age could barely buy a sandwich with the money a few years later. Elderly Germans can still recall the days in 1923 when:

> People were bringing money to the bank in cardboard boxes and laundry baskets. As we no longer could count it, we put the money on scales and weighed it. I can still see my brothers coming home Saturdays with heaps of paper money. When the

---

[3] Data from Philip Cagan, "The Monetary Dynamics of Hyperinflation," in Milton Friedman, ed., *Studies in the Quantity Theory of Money* (Chicago: University of Chicago Press, 1956), Table 1, p. 26.

shops reopened after the weekend they got no more than a breakfast roll for it. Many got drunk on their pay because it was worthless on Monday.[4]

Just as the Great Depression helped to create resentments about the existing government that turned voters to Hitler's Nazi party, so bitter memories of lost savings in the hyperinflation ten years earlier added to Hitler's growing support. Very rapid inflation is not an ancient artifact lacking relevance for today.

Throughout the 1980s and 1990s several Latin American countries suffered from inflation rates of 1,000 percent per year or more. Recently, a devastating inflation broke out in the southern African nation of Zimbabwe, where the inflation rate in October 2008 reached 210 billion percent per year! Because the government failed to raise the wages of teachers and hospital workers by even remotely the percentage by which prices had gone up, the nation in 2007–09 was in a state of collapse, with schools and hospitals closing down. So severe was the hyperinflation that in early 2009 the government cut 12 zeros off all types of currency and all prices, so that people would trade in a banknote marked 1,000,000,000,000 and receive a new banknote marked 1. In this chaotic environment more and more citizens turned to using currencies of other countries, particularly the South African Rand. We return in Chapter 10 to the sad story of Zimbabwe, which has become a poster child of macroeconomic mismanagement.

Fast and Slow Growth in Asia

Neither the Great Depression nor the German hyperinflation had any significant effect on the American or German standard of living a decade or two later. For effects that really matter over the decades, we need to look at the third of our "Big Three" macroeconomic concepts: productivity growth. Differences in growth rates that may appear small can compound over the decades and create enormous differences in the standard of living of any economic unit, from individuals to nations. A classic example of the importance of rapid growth is illustrated in Figure 1-9, which displays real GDP per capita in South Korea and the Philippines over the period 1960 to 2010.

In 1960, real GDP per capita in the Philippines was actually 20 percent higher than in South Korea. But between 1960 and 2010, real GDP per capita grew at 5.6 percent per year in South Korea compared to only 1.4 percent in the Philippines. Figure 1-9 shows the wide gap that opened up between the Korean and Philippine standards of living, with 2010 values of only $4,357 for the Philippines and $30,175 for South Korea. As a result of its superior economic growth record, the average Korean in 2010 could save or consume almost seven times as much as the average citizen of the Philippines. Stated another way, the Korean could consume everything enjoyed by the Philippine citizen and then have almost six times as much left over. This extra output in Korea is shown by the orange shading in Figure 1-9.

The outstanding achievement of South Korea has been duplicated in several other countries in East Asia, notably Hong Kong, Singapore, and Taiwan, and more recently by China. What secrets have the Koreans learned about economic growth that the Philippine government and population have not learned? The story of growth successes and failures is a fascinating one that awaits us in Chapters 11 and 12.

---

[4] Alice Siegert, "When Inflation Ruined Germany," *Chicago Tribune*, November 30, 1974.

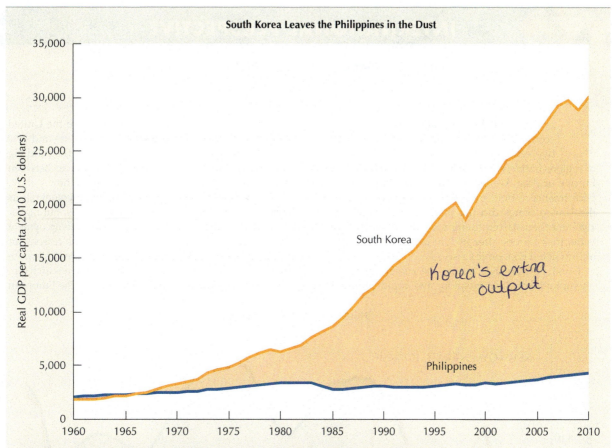

Figure 1-9 **Per-Capita Real GDP, South Korea and the Philippines, 1960–2010 in 2010 U.S. Dollars**

Per-capita real GDP in the Philippines barely grew from 1960 to 2008; the growth rate between those years was only 1.4 percent per annum. In contrast, the growth rate in Korea was 5.6 percent, enough to boost per-capita real GDP to a level fully 16 times the 1960 value.

Source: Groningen Growth and Development Center. See Appendix C-4.

1-7   Taming Business Cycles: Stabilization Policy

Macroeconomic analysts have two tasks: to analyze the causes of changes in important aggregates and to predict the consequences of alternative policy changes. In policy discussions the group of aggregates that society cares most about—inflation, unemployment, and the long-term growth rate of productivity—are called goals, or **target variables.** When the target variables deviate from desired values, alternative **policy instruments** can be used in an attempt to achieve needed changes. Instruments fall into three broad categories: **monetary policies**, which include control of the money supply and interest rates; **fiscal policies**, which include changes in government expenditures and tax rates; and a third, miscellaneous group, which includes policies to equip workers with skills they need to qualify for jobs.

How are target variables and policy instruments related to the three central macroeconomic concepts introduced at the beginning of this chapter? All three

Target variables are aggregates whose values society cares about.

Policy instruments are elements that government policymakers can manipulate directly to influence target variables.

Monetary policy tries to influence target variables by changing the money supply or interest rate or both.

Fiscal policy tries to influence target variables by manipulating government expenditures and tax rates.

INTERNATIONAL PERSPECTIVE

Differences Between the United States and Europe Before and During the Global Economic Crisis

One result of the internationalization of macroeconomics is the increased attention to the relative economic performance of major countries or regions in the world, such as the United States versus Europe or Asia. We learn from these comparisons that performance differs over time. Compared to Europe, the United States did not perform well from 1960 to 1985 but then started to improve and performed much better than Europe after 1995, at least until the 2007 start of the Global Economic Crisis.

Good performance means the achievement of low unemployment, low inflation, and rapid productivity growth. The two charts in this box compare the United States and Europe on the unemployment rate and rate of productivity growth.[a] We do not include the third big concept, the inflation rate, because differences between the U.S. and European inflation rates are minor.

The chart below shows Europe's unemployment rate as lower than the U.S. rate throughout the 1970s, but higher after 1980. In fact, in 1999 the European unemployment rate was double that in the United States. The reasons for the big increase in the European unemployment rate constitute one of the most important and exciting research topics in macroeconomics—what policies could the European

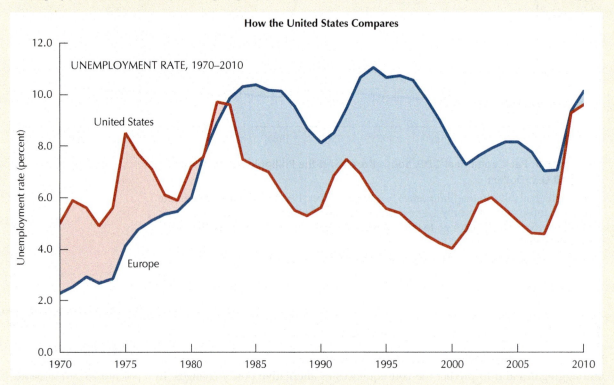

How the United States Compares

UNEMPLOYMENT RATE, 1970–2010

concepts—the unemployment rate, inflation rate, and productivity growth—are the key target variables of economic policy, the goals society cares most about.

The goal of policymakers regarding productivity growth is simple—just make productivity growth as fast as possible. There are no negatives to rapid productivity growth, and virtually every country in the world admires the growth achievement of South Korea (and some other East Asian countries) displayed in Figure 1-9 in the previous section. However, the goal of policymakers regarding the unemployment rate is not so simple. An attempt to reduce unemployment to zero would be likely to cause a significant acceleration of inflation,

countries adopt to reduce the European unemployment rate? We return to this puzzle in Chapter 10. Notice that in 2010, while Europe's unemployment rate was slightly higher than that in the United States, it had increased much less in the Global Economic Crisis period of 2008–10 than in the United States. Why? Some European nations including Germany and the Netherlands adopted a "work-sharing" policy in which people retained their jobs but worked shorter hours. Some European governments subsidized firms to retain workers. As a result, European unemployment did not rise nearly as much in 2008–10 as in the United States, but as European output slumped while workers were protected from layoffs, European productivity declined while that in the United States soared.

The chart below shows the growth rate of productivity in the United States and the same group of European countries. European productivity growth was more rapid than in the United States until 1996, after which the U.S. growth rate sped up and the European rate slowed down.

The U.S. speedup after 1995 is often attributed to its rapid adoption of computer and Internet technology, but this creates a big puzzle because there are plenty of computers and Internet use within Europe. We return to this puzzle in Chapter 12. Notice in 2008–09 that European productivity growth dropped below one percent while U.S. productivity growth revived. This occurred mainly because European firms and governments protected workers from mass layoffs to some extent, at least in comparison to the United States where American firms were panicked by the crisis and laid off millions of workers. It is not yet clear whether the impressive gains in U.S. productivity in 2008–10 will last and will augment the post-1998 advantage of the United States over Europe in its productivity growth performance.

----

[a] All data on Europe refer to the fifteen members of the European Union prior to its enlargement to twenty-five nations on May 1, 2004.

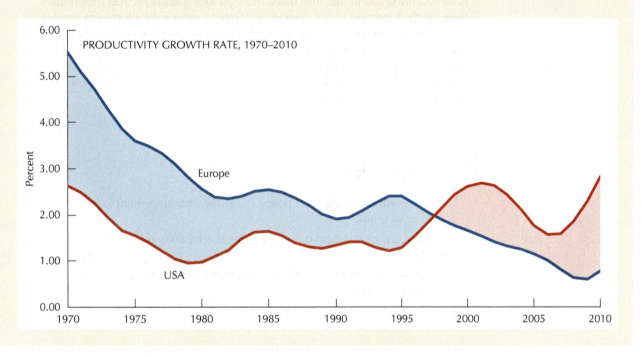

PRODUCTIVITY GROWTH RATE, 1970–2010

and moderation of inflation may be impossible if policymakers attempt to maintain the unemployment rate too low. A compromise goal for policymakers is to try to set the actual unemployment rate equal to the natural unemployment rate, since this would tend to maintain a constant inflation rate that neither accelerates nor decelerates.

The Role of Stabilization Policy

Macroeconomic analysis begins with a simple message: Either type of **stabilization policy,** monetary or fiscal, can be used to offset undesired changes

A **stabilization policy** is any policy that seeks to influence the level of aggregate demand.

in private spending. The effects of monetary and fiscal policy on the price level and on real GDP are the main subjects of Parts Two and Three of this book.

There are many problems in applying stabilization policy. It may not be possible to control aggregate demand instantly and precisely. A policy stimulus intended to fight current unemployment might boost aggregate demand only after a long and uncertain delay, by which time the stimulus might not be needed. The impact of different policy changes may also be highly uncertain. An added problem has been faced by Japan in the 1990s and by the United States in the late 1930s and since 2009. The interest rate cannot be negative, and so once monetary policy has reduced the rate to zero it loses the ability further to stimulate the economy.

GLOBAL ECONOMIC CRISIS FOCUS
New Challenges for Monetary and Fiscal Policy

The sudden collapse of the U.S. economy in the fall of 2008 created unprecedented challenges for the makers of monetary and fiscal policy. The banking and financial system almost ground to a halt, and loans were nearly impossible to obtain. Housing prices declined rapidly and many households either lost their home to foreclosure or found that they owed more on their mortgages than their houses were worth. Monetary policy reacted promptly to reduce the short-term interest rate to zero but then was stymied by its inability to reduce interest rates below zero, since the interest rate cannot be negative. Fiscal policy was also constrained by the growing public debt that resulted from deficit spending to combat the recession. Monetary and fiscal policy adopted novel and controversial strategies that we will study in Chapters 5 and 6 and elsewhere in the book.

SELF-TEST

1. Is it the task of stabilization policy to set the unemployment rate to zero? Why or why not?

2. Is it the task of stabilization policy to set the inflation rate to zero? Why or why not?

3. What are the two big problems in applying stabilization policy to control aggregate demand?

1-8 The "Internationalization" of Macroeconomics

More than ever before, macroeconomics is an international subject. The days are gone when the effects of U.S. stabilization policy could be analyzed in isolation, without consideration for their repercussions abroad. This old view of the United States as a **closed economy** described reality in the first decade or so after World War II. In the 1940s and 1950s, trade accounted for only about 5 percent of the U.S. economy, exchange rates were fixed, and financial flows to and from other nations were restricted.

A **closed economy** has no trade in goods, services, or financial assets with any other nation.

The United States has increasingly become an **open economy.** Imports now equal 17 percent of U.S. GDP. The exchange rate of the dollar has been flexible since 1973 and has fluctuated far more widely than anyone had predicted prior to that time. International financial flows are massive and often instantaneous, with computers sending messages to buy or sell stocks, bonds, and foreign currencies at the speed of light among the major financial centers of Tokyo, London, New York, and Chicago.

An **open economy** exports (sells) goods and services to other nations, buys imports from them, and has financial flows to and from foreign nations.

The growing integration of the world economy was particularly evident in the emergence of the Global Economic Crisis in 2008–09. As we will learn later in Chapter 5, the Global Economic Crisis started in the United States, but it soon spread to the rest of the world as the meltdown of U.S. financial markets spread to banks and other financial institutions in Europe and Asia.

A primary example of global integration and interdependence had emerged long before the Global Economic Crisis. Back in 2005–07 (before the recession), the United States ran a large foreign trade deficit, importing far more than it exported. Many of these imports came from China, which was happy to lend money to the United States to continue to buy those American exports manufactured in China. Why would China so eagerly lend money to the United States to buy its goods? The simple answer, to which we return in Chapter 7, is that China pursues policies that keep its exports cheap, thus providing millions of jobs for Chinese workers, even though to achieve this China must lend billions of dollars to the United States.

Summary

1. The three central macroeconomic concepts are those that most affect everyday lives. They are the unemployment rate, inflation rate, and productivity growth.

2. Macroeconomics differs from microeconomics by focusing on aggregates that are summed up over all the economic activities in the economy. Theory in macroeconomics is a process of simplification that identifies the most important economic relationships.

3. Gross domestic product (GDP) is a measure of the overall size of the economy. While it does not affect everyday life directly, the behavior of GDP helps us to understand the behavior of the three central macroeconomic concepts that do influence everyday life.

4. Neither too much nor too little real GDP is desirable. The best compromise level is called natural real GDP and is consistent with a constant inflation rate. When the economy is operating at its natural level of real GDP, it is also by definition operating at its natural rate of unemployment.

5. The topic of "business cycles" studies short-run phenomena in macroeconomics over a period of one to five years. The topic of "economic growth" studies long-run phenomena over a period lasting a decade or more.

6. While most macroeconomic analysis concerns relatively normal events, a challenge for macroeconomists is to explain how extreme and unusual events can occur. Two of these were the Great Depression of the 1930s and the German hyperinflation of 1922–23. Another challenge is to understand how the rate of economic growth can be so different between two countries like South Korea and the Philippines that are located in the same region of the world.

7. In this century, periods of high unemployment have coincided with those of low real GDP. The Great Depression clearly scored worst on both counts.

8. The three central macroeconomic aggregates, (unemployment rate, inflation rate, and productivity growth) are the main targets of stabilization policy. Stabilization policy may not be effective in improving well-being if both unemployment and inflation are too high, and stabilization policy may operate with a long delay or have effects that are highly uncertain.

9. Macroeconomics is an international subject. International repercussions influence the way fiscal and monetary policy work and how the inflation process operates. Countries around the world face the same dilemmas as does the United States. How can low output and high unemployment be cured without massive increases in government deficits and government debt?

Concepts

macroeconomics	actual real GDP	target variables
Global Economic Crisis	natural real GDP	policy instruments
unemployment rate	natural rate of unemployment	monetary policy
inflation rate	GDP gap	fiscal policy
productivity	unemployment gap	stabilization policy
aggregate	business cycles	closed economy
gross domestic product	economic growth	open economy

Questions

1. Read either an entire week of the *Wall Street Journal* or a business-oriented weekly magazine such as *Business Week* or *The Economist*. Identify three stories that deal with topics related to microeconomics and another three stories that discuss topics related to macroeconomics. Explain why you have put each story in either the microeconomics or macroeconomics category.

2. Using the quarterly data in Table A-2 for the period 1947–2010 (Appendix A), attempt to identify the recession phases and the expansion phases of the basic business cycle depicted in Figure 1-4. (Note: The official start and end of each phase of a business cycle is determined by the National Bureau of Economic Research Business Cycle Dating Committee. The committee looks at more data than simply GDP in determining when each phase occurs and dates phases by months, not quarters. Therefore your answer will only approximate the official recession and expansion phases; for more details on the way the committee determines when each phase occurs and the official dates of business cycles, go to www.nber.org/cycles/main.html.)

3. Using your answer to question 2, compare the lengths of recessions and expansions for the period 1947–1982 with the years 1983–2007. Compare the length of the 2007–09 recession with the other recessions of the post–World War II era.

4. How are the natural real GDP and the natural real unemployment rates related to the rate of inflation?

5. Between June 2003 and June 2005, U.S. unemployment fell from 6.3 percent to 5.0 percent of the labor force. The Federal Reserve, the nation's monetary policy-making authority, took active measures beginning in June 2004 to raise short-term interest rates. What might have motivated policymakers to raise interest rates and what were they hoping to accomplish?

6. In April 2000, the seasonally adjusted unemployment rate was 3.8 percent. By June 2001, the unemployment rate had increased to 4.5 percent. Yet the measures by the Federal Reserve to reduce short-term interest rates were taken in stages, and in fact the unemployment rate continued to rise. What might have motivated the policymakers' cautious behavior?

7. (a) The "big three" concepts of macroeconomics are the unemployment rate, the inflation rate, and productivity growth. Discuss which of these concepts primarily relate to the behavior of the economy (i) in the short run and (ii) in the long run.

    (b) Using Figures 1-3 and 1-5 as guides, discuss how natural real GDP is used to evaluate the behavior of the economy in both the short run and the long run.

8. Explain why productivity growth not only allows a society to have higher living standards in the form of more goods and services, but also allows it to increase the percentage of an average person's life that is spent in school, on vacation, in retirement, or in other non-work related activities.

9. Explain how the value of real GDP relative to natural real GDP can be used by policymakers to decide how to change the values of the target variables.

10. How does the performance of the U.S. economy contrast with the performance of the European economy for the periods 1960–2007 and since the start of the Global Economic Crisis?

Problems

 Visit www.MyEconLab.com to complete these or similar exercises.

1. (a) Suppose that real GDP is currently $97 billion per year and natural real GDP is currently $100 billion. Measured as a percentage, what is the GDP gap?
   (b) Suppose natural real GDP is growing by $4 billion per year. By how much must real GDP have risen after two years to close the GDP gap?
2. The sum of exports and imports as a percent of gross domestic product is sometimes used as a measure of how open an economy is. In particular, the greater the percent, the more open the economy is considered.

Use the following data to compute this measure of the openness of the United States economy in 1960, 1970, 1980, 1990, 2000, and 2009. Discuss what the data show in terms of the "internationalization" of the United States economy since 1960.

	1960	1970	1980	1990	2000	2009
GDP	2,830.9	4,269.9	5,839.0	8,033.9	11,226.0	12,880.6
Exports	98.5	175.5	351.7	600.2	1,188.3	1,490.7
Imports	114.5	236.6	344.7	673.0	1,639.9	1,853.8

◆ SELF-TEST ANSWERS

p. 7. (1) When actual real GDP is above natural real GDP, the actual unemployment rate is below the natural unemployment rate. (2) In this opposite case, the actual unemployment rate is above the natural unemployment rate. (3) There is no such thing as the natural rate of inflation. When the economy is operating at its natural rate of unemployment, the inflation rate does not change. But it does not change from whatever level is inherited from the past, and this could be zero, 10 percent per year, or 100 percent per year.

p. 10. (1) short-run, (2) long-run, (3) short-run, (4) both (the money can create jobs during a recession but also will stimulate long-run productivity growth).

p. 20. (1) Stabilization policy cannot set the unemployment rate to zero or any other rate below the natural rate of unemployment without causing accelerating inflation. (2) Stabilization policy can set the inflation rate to zero only at the cost of a recession and a substantial cost in terms of lost output. (3) The two big problems are lags and uncertainty. A policy change may affect aggregate demand only after a long and uncertain delay, and the impact of different policy changes may also be highly uncertain.

The Measurement of Income, Prices, and Unemployment

It has been said that figures rule the world; maybe. I am quite sure that it is figures which show us whether it is being ruled well or badly.
—Johann Wolfgang Goethe, 1830

Our first task is to develop a simple theoretical model to explain real output (gross domestic product, or GDP) and the price level. Before we can turn to theory in Chapter 3, however, we must stop in Chapter 2 for a few definitions. What are GDP and the price level? How are they measured? What goods and services are included in or excluded from GDP? How are private saving, private investment, the government deficit, and the current account deficit related to one another? How are the inflation rate and unemployment rate measured?

2-1 Why We Care About Income

In Chapter 1 we identified two key links between real GDP and the three central concepts of macroeconomics. First, we noted that movements in the unemployment gap are inversely related to the parallel movements of the GDP gap. Thus the key to understanding changes in unemployment (the first central concept) is the change in actual real GDP.

Second, the level and growth rate of our standard of living are measured by productivity (the third central concept), defined as the ratio of output to the number of hours worked. Output is the same as real GDP. Thus any discussion of U.S. productivity performance in comparison with the country's history or with other nations requires an understanding of the data on real GDP.

This chapter begins by asking what is included in GDP and why. We then learn about the different sectors of the economy that purchase portions of the total GDP and how that GDP is the source of different types of income. We learn how the price level and rate of inflation are measured. Finally, we learn how the unemployment rate is measured and how important components of distress caused to families by the Global Economic Crisis are not included in the official measure of the unemployment rate.

2-2 The Circular Flow of Income and Expenditure

We begin with a very simple economy, consisting of households and business firms. We will assume that households spend their entire income, saving nothing,

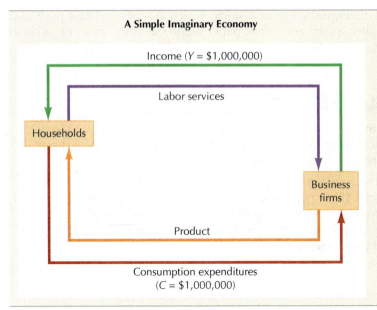

A Simple Imaginary Economy

Income (Y = $1,000,000)

Labor services

Households

Business firms

Product

Consumption expenditures
(C = $1,000,000)

Figure 2-1 **The Circular Flow of Income and Consumption Expenditures**

Circular flow of income and expenditure in a simple imaginary economy in which households consume their entire income. There are no taxes, no government spending, no saving, no investment, and no foreign sector.

and that there is no government.[1] Figure 2-1 depicts the operation of our simple economy, with households represented by the box on the left and business firms by the box on the right. There are two kinds of transactions between the households and the firms.

First, the firms sell goods and services (product)—for instance, bread and shoes—to the households represented in Figure 2-1 by the lower orange line, labeled product. The bread and shoes are not a gift, but are paid for by a flow of money (C), say $1,000,000 per year, represented by the solid red line, labeled **consumption expenditures.**

Second, households must work to earn the income to pay for the consumption goods. They work for the firms, selling their skills as represented by the upper purple line, labeled labor services. Household members are willing to work only if they receive a flow of money, usually called wages, from the firms for each hour of work. Wages are the main component of income (Y), shown by the upper green line.

Since households are assumed to consume all of their income, and since firms are assumed to pay out all of their sales in the form of income to households, it follows that income (Y) and consumption expenditures (C) are equal. For the same reason, the labor services provided in return for income are equal to the goods and services (product) sold by the firms to households in return for the money flow of consumption expenditures:

$$\begin{aligned} \text{income}(Y) &= \text{labor services} \\ &= \text{consumption expenditures}(C) \\ &= \text{product} \end{aligned}$$

Each of the four elements in the preceding equation is a **flow magnitude,** any economic magnitude that is measured per unit of time, like U.S. GDP *per*

Consumption expenditures are purchases of goods and services by households for their own use.

A **flow magnitude** is an economic magnitude that moves from one economic unit to another at a specified rate per unit of time.

---

[1] Because households do no saving, there is no capital or wealth, and all household income is in the form of wages for labor services.

A **stock** is an economic magnitude in the possession of a given economic unit at a particular point in time.

year. A flow is distinguished from a **stock,** which is measured at a particular point in time, such as the amount of paper money in your wallet or purse at noon on September 11, 2011.

◆ SELF-TEST

1. Imagine that a student named Eric purchases a haircut, priced at $10, with a $10 bill. Describe in words how the student's haircut will be included in each of the four flows of Figure 2-1.

2. Imagine that a student named Alison obtains a job as a lifeguard at a summer camp paying $8 per hour for July and August, and that the camp obtains the money to pay Alison from fees paid by parents for their children to go to the camp. Describe in words how the fees and the lifeguard job will be included in each of the four flows of Figure 2-1.

2-3   What GDP Is, and What GDP Is Not

National Income and Product Accounts is the official U.S. government economic accounting system that keeps track of GDP and its subcomponents.

The **National Income and Product Accounts** (also called NIPA, or national accounts, for short) is the official U.S. government accounting of all the flows of income and expenditure in the United States. Historical data for GDP and other macro concepts are listed in Appendix A for the United States and in Appendix B for other major nations. A guide to government data sources is provided in the box on p. 27.

Defining GDP: What's In and What's Out

In our free market economy, the fact that a good or service is sold is a sign that it satisfies certain human wants and needs; otherwise, people would not be willing to pay a price for it. So by including in the GDP only things that are sold through the market for a price, we can be fairly sure that most of the components of GDP contribute to human satisfaction. There are three major requirements in the rule for including items in the total **final product,** or GDP: *Final product consists of all currently produced goods and services that are sold through the market but not resold during the current time period.*

Final product includes all currently produced goods and services that are sold through the market but are not resold. It is the same as gross domestic product (GDP).

Currently produced.   The first part of the rule—*to be included in final product, a good must be currently produced*—helps us to define what GDP is not. GDP excludes sales of any used items such as houses and cars, since they are not currently produced. Similarly, it excludes financial transactions such as sales or purchases of bonds and stocks. Because neither the purchase nor the sale of a financial asset is included, GDP by definition excludes capital gains on assets that occur when they are sold for more than they cost to buy. GDP also excludes any transaction in which money is transferred without any accompanying good or service in return. Among the **transfer payments** excluded from national income in the United States are payments from the government to persons, such as Social Security, Medicare, and unemployment benefits.

Transfer payments are those for which no goods or services are produced in return.

Sold on the market.   The second part of the rule—*goods included in the final product must be sold on the market and are valued at market prices*—means that we

Where to Find the Numbers: A Guide to the Data

The first place to look for macroeconomic data is the appendixes in the back of this textbook. There you will find annual data covering more than a century (from 1875 on) and quarterly data since 1947 on major macroeconomic concepts. Also included are several important annual data series for Japan, Canada, and the major European nations for the period since 1960.

Time Passes and Revisions Occur: How to Cope

You will need to know where to find macroeconomic data that are not included in the textbook appendixes or data for more recent periods that were released after the textbook was printed. For these head to the Internet. There you can find the most recent and comprehensive sources of economic data.

The "Big Three" Agencies

Using the Internet is by far the easiest way to gather economic data; whether it be rather simple data, such as real GDP or the most recent Consumer Price Index, or more detailed data, such as the unemployment rate for males aged 20–24 or how much U.S. consumers spend on funerals. For these and many other series, turn to one of the Web sites of the government agencies that actually produce the data. The three most important are the Bureau of Economic Analysis (BEA, a branch of the Commerce Department), the Bureau of Labor Statistics (BLS, a branch of the Labor Department), and the Federal Reserve Board (usually called by its nickname, the Fed).

BEA: National Income Data   All the data on GDP, and related income and product series, are produced by the BEA in an organized system of tables called the National Income and Product Accounts (NIPA). These extend back to 1929 for annual data and to 1947 for quarterly data and are updated regularly on the BEA Web site **www.bea.gov**. Here you can find not only NIPA tables, but recent news releases, industry data, and international and regional series.

BLS: Labor Market, Price, and Wage Data   The BLS is a primary producer of data on employment, unemployment, consumer and producer prices, and wage rates. The BLS runs several large surveys, contacting thousands of families each month to learn about their employment and unemployment experience and contacting thousands of retail outlets to track price changes. All of the BLS data series are available at **www.bls.gov**.

The opening screen of the Bureau of Economic Analysis Web site.

The Fed: Financial Market Data   The Federal Reserve compiles data on interest rates, the money supply, and other figures describing the banking and financial system. One of the regional Feds, the Federal Reserve Bank of St. Louis, supports an online database known as FRED (**research.stlouisfed.org/fred2**). This database provides historical U.S. economic and financial data, including daily interest rates, monetary and business indicators, exchange rates, balance of payments, and select regional economic data. The Federal Reserve Board of Governors Web site (**www.federalreserve.gov**) is also useful.

The preceding list does not even include the grandfather of all statistics agencies, the Bureau of the Census, which conducts the decennial Census of Population and, every five years, economic censuses of business establishments. The Census data form the raw material for much of the BEA's work in creating the national accounts, not to mention much research by economists on both macro and micro topics. See **www.census.gov**.

International Web Sites to Know:
Org. for Economic Cooperation and Development
> **www.oecdwash.org/DATA/online.htm**
World Bank
> **www.worldbank.org/data**
International Monetary Fund
> **www.imf.org/external/data.htm**
Groningen Growth and Development Center
> **www.ggdc.net/databases/index.htm**

Many more sites are available through such search engines as google.com, yahoo.com, and ask.com.

measure the value of final product by the market prices that people are willing to pay for goods and services. We assume that a Mercedes gives 10,000 times as much satisfaction as a package of razor blades because it costs about 10,000 times as much. Excluded from GDP by this criterion is the value of personal time spent engaged in activities that are not sold on the market (often called "home production," this includes time spent cooking, mowing lawns, painting, and maintenance). Also excluded is any allowance for the costs of air pollution, water pollution, acid rain, or other by-products of the production process for which no explicit charge is made. A final exclusion in this category is illegal activity, such as sales of illegal drugs that are typically bought and sold for cash. Some other activities paid for in cash may be excluded because they are hard to measure, including household helpers who are paid in cash and whose employers do not pay social security taxes on their behalf.

But not resold.   The third part of the rule—*to be included in final product, a good must not be resold in the current time period*—further limits the inclusion of items. The many different goods and services produced in the economy are used in two different ways. Some goods, like wheat, are mainly used as ingredients in the making of other goods, in this case, bread. Any good resold by its purchaser is an **intermediate good** and is not included in GDP. Any good that is not resold is called a final good because it is sold to a final user, such as a household or the government.

An **intermediate good** is resold by its purchaser either in its present form or in an altered form.

Intermediate Goods, Final Goods, and Value Added

The opposite of an intermediate good is a **final good,** one that is not resold. Bread sold at the grocery is a final good, used by consumers, as are the many other products that consumers buy. Take a simple example of a loaf of bread that sells for $2.00. We assume that the only ingredient in the bread is wheat, which the bakery buys from the wheat farmer for $0.50 per loaf. The remaining $1.50 represents the wages of the bakery employees, the rent on the bakery building, and the profits of the owner. Only the $2.00 spent for the final good, a loaf of bread, is included in GDP.

A **final good** is part of final product because it is sold to a final user rather than being resold.

We cannot include intermediate goods in GDP, because that would be double counting. The value of the wheat is already included in the price of bread, so we don't want GDP to include *both* the $0.50 value of the wheat and the $2.00 value of the bread, since the resulting sum of $2.50 would be more than consumers pay for the bread.

Another way to compute GDP is to add up the **value added** at each stage of production, defined as the value of a firm's output minus the amount paid for intermediate goods. Assuming there are no intermediate goods involved in growing wheat, in this example the wheat farmer has a value added of $0.50 and the bread bakery has a value added of $1.50 (consisting of wages, rent, and profit). Total GDP is the sum of the value added of each firm, $0.50 for the farmer and $1.50 for the bread bakery. By definition, the final product of $2.00 is equal to value added of $2.00. GDP is equal to *both* total final product and total value added.

Value added is the value of a firm's output minus the value of the intermediate goods that the firm produces. It includes wages paid to the firm's employees, rental of buildings and equipment, and the firm's profit. By definition, total value added is equal to final product.

Table 2-1 summarizes what's in and out of GDP. Notice that sales of used assets like cars and houses do have an effect on GDP if they generate current income for used car dealers and real estate agents. Similarly, fees and commissions earned by financial institutions are included in GDP.

Table 2-1   **What's In and What's Out of GDP**

Category	What's In	What's Out
Currently Produced	Goods and Services	Sales of Used Assets*
		Sales of Financial Assets**
		Transfer Payments
Sold on the Market	Market Production	Home Production
		Environmental Pollution
		Illegal Activity
		Some Unrecorded Payments Made with Cash
Not Resold	Final Goods and Services	Intermediate Goods and Services

Notes: * Fees and commissions earned by used-car dealers and real estate agents are included in GDP
** Fees and commissions earned by financial institutions are included in GDP

What's the "Domestic" in Gross Domestic Product (GDP)?

GDP includes all final goods and services produced within the 50 states of the United States regardless of whether they are sold within the 50 states or exported. Imported goods produced in other countries are excluded from GDP. If we want to know how much income is being earned by Americans, we need an alternative concept called **gross national product (GNP).** Once we know GDP, we can calculate GNP by adding receipts of factor income (wages, rent, and profits) by Americans from the rest of the world and subtracting payments of factor income to the rest of the world:

$$\text{GNP} = \text{GDP} + \text{Factor Payments from Rest of World} - \text{Factor Payments to Rest of World} \qquad (2.1)$$

Gross national product (GNP) is GDP plus factor payments received from the rest of the world minus factor payments sent to the rest of the world.

For instance, Procter & Gamble makes Tide detergent and Crest toothpaste in factories around the world. The value of the detergent and toothpaste is included in the GDP of the countries where the foreign plants are located, from Japan to Britain, and is not part of U.S. GDP. But Procter & Gamble brings some of the profits from these plants back to the United States, and these are included in "Factor Payments from Rest of World" and raise U.S. GNP relative to GDP. Conversely, Japanese factories produce millions of cars inside the United States, and the value of these cars is included in U.S. GDP. But these factories are profitable, and some of their profits are sent back to Japan. These profits are treated as a factor payment to the rest of the world, which is subtracted from GNP and makes it smaller than GDP.

Overall, the factor payments received by the United States, such as profits earned abroad by McDonald's and Procter & Gamble, and those sent from the United States, such as profits earned by Honda and Toyota, are roughly equal in size, and so GNP is very similar in size to GDP (GNP was 0.7 percent larger than GDP in 2009). But in some other countries, such as Ireland, GNP is much smaller than GDP because many of the factories are owned by foreign-owned companies. In other countries, such as Kuwait, GNP is much larger than GDP because Kuwaiti residents own large amounts of bank deposits and other assets in other countries and receive large flows of interest and dividend income on those assets.

What's the "Gross" in Gross Domestic Product (GDP)?

Depreciation (consumption of fixed capital) represents the part of the capital stock used up due to obsolescence and physical wear.

Net domestic product (NDP) is equal to GDP minus depreciation.

In economics, **gross** refers to the inclusion of depreciation; **net** refers to the exclusion of depreciation.

GDP includes **depreciation,** which is the amount that business firms set aside to replace structures and equipment that wear out or become obsolete, like old computers that still work but do not have the speed or memory to handle today's complex software. In the national accounts (NIPA), depreciation is called "consumption of fixed capital." Since it is a cost of doing business, it must be deducted out in order to measure the net result of economic activity, which is called **net domestic product (NDP).**

> The terms **gross** and **net** usually refer to the inclusion or exclusion of depreciation. Thus the difference between "gross investment" and "net investment," or between "gross saving" and "net saving," is exactly the same as the difference between GDP and NDP.

2-4 Components of Expenditure

Types of Investment

Private investment is the portion of final product that adds to the nation's stock of income-yielding physical assets or that replaces old, worn-out physical assets.

Inventory investment includes all changes in the stock of raw materials, parts, and finished goods held by business.

The goods and services produced by business firms, which are not resold as intermediate goods to other firms or consumers during the current period, qualify by our rule as final product. But the business firm does not consume them. Final goods that business firms keep for themselves are called **private investment** or private capital formation. These goods add to the nation's stock of income-yielding assets. Private investment consists of *inventory investment* and *fixed investment*.

Inventory investment. Bread produced by the baker but not resold to consumers in the current period stays on the bakery's shelves, raising the level of the bakery's inventories. Since all the bread that is produced is included in GDP, we must define expenditure so as to include the bread, whether it is sold to consumers or whether it remains unsold on the shelf. *By including the change in inventories as part of expenditure, we guarantee that GDP (that is, total product) by definition equals total expenditure.* When inventories increase, the inventory investment component of GDP is positive. When inventories decrease, the inventory investment component of GDP is negative.

◆ SELF-TEST

Imagine that a bakery has 10 loaves of bread at the close of business on December 31, 2010. Valued at the baker's price of $2.00, the value of the bakery's inventory is $20.00. At the close of business on March 31, 2011, the baker has 15 loaves or $30.00 of bread on the shelves.

1. What is the level of the baker's inventory on December 31, 2010, and on March 31, 2011?

2. What is the change in the baker's inventories in the first quarter of 2011?

3. What is the implication of these numbers for the contribution of the baker's inventories to GDP in the first quarter of 2011?

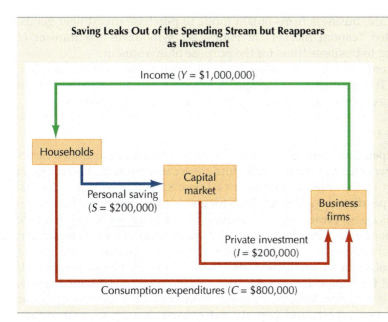

Figure 2-2 Introduction of Saving and Investment to the Circular Flow Diagram
Starting from the simple imaginary economy (Figure 2-1), we now assume that households save 20 percent of their income. Business firms' investment accounts for 20 percent of total expenditure. Again, we are assuming that there are no taxes, no government spending, and no foreign sector.

Fixed investment. **Fixed investment** includes all final goods purchased by business, other than additions to inventory. The main types of fixed investment are structures (factories, office buildings, shopping centers, apartments, houses) and equipment (refrigerated display cases, computers, trucks). Newly produced houses and condominiums sold to individuals are also counted as fixed investment—a household is treated in the national accounts as a business firm that owns the house as an asset and rents the house to itself.[2]

Fixed investment includes all final goods purchased by business that are not intended for resale.

Relation of Investment and Saving

Figure 2-1 described a simple imaginary economy in which households consumed all of their total income. Figure 2-2 introduces investment into that economy. Total expenditures on final product are the same as before, but now they are divided into consumption expenditures by households (C) and business purchases of investment goods (I). Households spend part of their income on purchases of consumption goods and save the rest.

The portion of household income that is not consumed is called **personal saving.** What happens to income that is saved? The funds are channeled to business firms in two basic ways:

Personal saving is that part of personal income that is neither consumed nor paid out in taxes.

1. Households buy bonds and stocks issued by the firms, and the firms then use the money to buy investment goods.
2. Households leave the unused income (savings) in banks and other financial institutions. The banks then lend the money to the firms, which use it to buy investment goods.

---

[2] An individual who owns a house is treated as a split personality in the national accounts: as a business firm and as a consuming household. My left side is a businessperson who owns my house and receives imaginary rent payments from my right side, the consumer who lives in my house. The NIPA identifies these imaginary rent payments as "Imputed rent on owner-occupied dwellings," which makes rent payments the most important exception to the rule that a good must be sold on the market to be counted in GDP.

In either case, business firms obtain funds to purchase investment goods. The box labeled "capital market" in Figure 2-2 symbolizes the transfer of personal saving to business firms for the purpose of investment.

In other words, saving is a "leakage" from the income used for consumption expenditures. This leakage from the spending stream must be balanced by an "injection" of nonconsumption spending in the form of private investment.

Net Exports and Net Foreign Investment

Exports are goods and services produced within one country and sold to another.

Imports are goods consumed within one country but produced in another country.

Exports are expenditures for goods and services produced in the United States and sent to other countries. Such expenditure creates income in the United States but is not part of the consumption or investment spending of U.S. residents. **Imports** are expenditures by U.S. residents for goods and services produced elsewhere and thus do *not* create domestic income. For instance, an American-made Chevrolet exported to Canada is part of U.S. production and income but is Canadian consumption. A German-made Mercedes imported to the United States is part of German production and income but is U.S. consumption. If income created from exports is greater than income spent on imported goods, the net effect is a higher level of domestic production and income. Thus the difference between exports and imports, **net exports,** is a component of final product and GDP.

Net exports and **net foreign investment** are both equal to exports minus imports. The term "net foreign borrowing" is used when net exports are negative.

Another name for net exports is **net foreign investment,** which can be given the same economic interpretation as domestic investment. Why? Both domestic and foreign investment are components of domestic production and income creation. Domestic investment creates domestic capital assets; net foreign investment creates U.S. claims on foreigners that yield us future flows of income. An American export to Japan is paid for with Japanese yen, which can be deposited in a Japanese bank account or used to buy part of a Japanese factory. The opposite occurs as well. When the United States imports more than it exports, as it has in every year since 1981, net foreign investment is negative. U.S. payments for imports provide dollars that foreign investors use to buy American factories, hotels, and other assets including bank accounts in the United States.

The Government Sector

Up to this point we have been examining an economy consisting only of private households and business firms. Now we add the government, which collects taxes from the private sector and makes two kinds of expenditures. Government purchases of goods and services (tanks, fighter planes, school-books) generate production and create income. The government can also make payments directly to households. Social Security, Medicare, and unemployment compensation are examples of these transfer payments, given the name *transfer* because they are payments from the government to the recipient without any obligation for the recipient to provide any services in return. As you learned in Section 2-3, transfer payments are not included in GDP.

Figure 2-3 adds the government (federal, state, and local) to our imaginary economy of Figures 2-1 and 2-2. A flow of tax revenue (R) passes from the households to the government.[3] The government buys goods and services (G).

---

[3] In the real world, both households and business firms pay taxes. Here we keep things simple by limiting tax payments to personal income taxes.

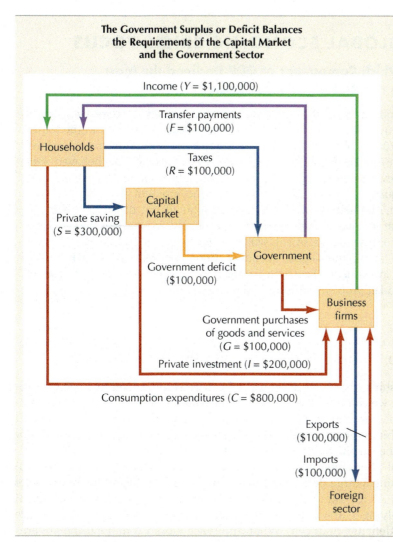

The Government Surplus or Deficit Balances the Requirements of the Capital Market and the Government Sector

Income (Y = $1,100,000)

Transfer payments (F = $100,000)

Households

Taxes (R = $100,000)

Private saving (S = $300,000)

Capital Market

Government deficit ($100,000)

Government

Government purchases of goods and services (G = $100,000)

Business firms

Private investment (I = $200,000)

Consumption expenditures (C = $800,000)

Exports ($100,000)

Imports ($100,000)

Foreign sector

Figure 2-3 **Introduction of Taxation, Government Spending, and the Foreign Sector to the Circular Flow Diagram**

Our simple imaginary economy with the addition of a government collecting $100,000 in tax revenue, paying households $100,000 in transfer payments, and purchasing $100,000 of goods and services. Its total expenditures ($200,000) exceed its tax revenues ($100,000), leaving a $100,000 deficit that is financed by selling government bonds to the households.

In addition the government sends transfer payments (F), such as welfare payments, to households, leaving a deficit that must be financed. To do this, the government sells bonds to private households through the capital market, just as business firms sell bonds and stock to households to finance their investment projects.

Also shown in Figure 2-3, in the bottom right corner, is the foreign sector. Imports are already included in consumption and investment spending, so imports are shown as a leakage by the blue arrow pointing down toward the foreign sector box. Exports are spending on domestic production, as shown by the red arrow going from the foreign sector to the business firms. To keep the diagram simple, exports equal imports.[4]

---

[4] If imports exceed exports, there is a flow equal to the difference going from the foreign sector box to the capital market box. This is the inflow of foreign capital available to finance private investment or the government deficit.

GLOBAL ECONOMIC CRISIS FOCUS
Which Component of GDP Declined the Most in the Global Economic Crisis?

The peak and trough of the business cycle were defined in Figure 1-4 on p. 9. The economy in the most recent business cycle reached its peak in the fourth quarter of 2007 (abbreviated 2007:Q4) and reached its trough (minimum level of real GDP) in 2009:Q2. The different components of GDP behaved very differently over those six quarters. Real consumption spending declined over those six quarters by only 0.8 percent. Real government spending grew by 6.6 percent. Net exports were negative throughout but declined to a much smaller negative value, which stimulated the economy. So what was the problem? It was the collapse of investment, which *fell by an amazing 31.7 percent!* As we learn more about the Global Economic Crisis, we will come back to this collapse of investment, the relative stability of consumption, and the role of financial market problems in causing the recession.

2-5 The "Magic" Equation and the Twin Deficits

The **magic equation** states that private saving plus net tax revenue must by definition equal the sum of private domestic investment, government spending on goods and services, and net exports.

The relationships displayed in Figure 2-3 can be summarized in a simple relationship that we call the "magic" equation because of its versatility in explaining central macroeconomic concepts. The **magic equation** helps us understand the relationships among investment, private saving, the government surplus or deficit, and the surplus or deficit of exports versus imports.

A central phenomenon of the current U.S. economy is that the government is running a large deficit, with government expenditures far in excess of tax revenue. At the same time, the U.S. economy imports far more than it exports, implying a large international deficit (negative net exports). How are these "twin deficits" financed? What difference would it make if the government ran a surplus while the international deficit remained the same? What would happen if the international deficit were zero while the government deficit remained large? The magic equation can help us to answer these questions.

Implications of the Equality Between Income and Expenditures

By definition, total income created (Y) is equal to total expenditure on final product (E). Why is this true by definition? Because income is created from total production, and expenditures include both the production that is sold to final users, as well as the production that is not sold (i.e., the change in inventories). We can indicate that this relationship is true by definition by using the three-bar equals sign, otherwise known as the "identity sign":

$$Y \equiv E$$

There are four types of expenditure on final product: consumption expenditures (C); private domestic investment (I); government purchases of goods and services (G); and net exports (NX):

$$E \equiv C + I + G + NX \tag{2.2}$$

The total personal income that households receive consists of the income created from production (Y) and transfer payments from the government (F). This total ($Y + F$) is available for the purchase of consumption goods (C), private saving (S), and the payment of taxes (R):

$$Y + F \equiv C + S + R$$

An equivalent expression is obtained if we subtract F from both sides:

$$Y \equiv C + S + R - F \tag{2.3}$$

Transfer payments (F) can be treated as negative taxes. Accordingly, we define net tax revenue (T) as taxes (R) minus transfers (F), converting equation (2.3) into the simpler expression:

$$\boxed{Y \equiv C + S + T} \tag{2.4}$$

Leakages and Injections

Since $Y \equiv E$, the right side of equation (2.4) is equal to the right side of equation (2.2), and we obtain:

$$
\begin{array}{rl}
C + S + T \equiv & C + I + G + NX \\
-C & \quad -C \qquad \text{subtracting } C \text{ from both sides} \\
\hline
S + T \equiv & I + G + NX
\end{array} \tag{2.5}
$$

The bottom line of (2.5) can be translated to a general rule:

> Since income is equal to expenditure, the portion of income not consumed (saving plus net taxes) must be equal to the nonconsumption portion of expenditure on final product (investment plus government spending plus net exports).

In other words, **leakages** out of the income available for consumption goods ($S + T$) must be exactly balanced by **injections** of nonconsumption spending ($I + G + NX$).

Equation 2-5 is one of the most important relationships in macroeconomics and reappears often in the next few chapters. We call it the magic equation; its more technical name is the leakages–injections identity. The importance of this relationship is that it shows how some of the most basic concepts in macroeconomics—private saving, government spending and taxes, domestic investment, and net exports—are connected *by definition*.

Leakages describe the portion of total income that flows to taxes or saving rather than into purchases of consumer goods.

Injections is a term for nonconsumption expenditures.

The Government Budget and the Twin Deficits

The magic equation shows how the funds resulting from a government budget surplus are used, and it is equally useful in showing how the government finances a budget deficit. We can arrange equation (2.5) to show the uses of a government budget surplus:

$$T - G \equiv (I + NX) - S \tag{2.6}$$

On the left side of this definition is the government budget surplus. If the left side is negative, the government is running a budget deficit. Shown on the right side is the excess of total investment, both domestic (I) and foreign (NX), over private savings (S).

If government spending is greater than net tax revenue, as has occurred in most years over the past three decades, the government is running a deficit, and equation (2.6) shows that there are three possible implications. First, the government budget deficit could make domestic investment (I) smaller than otherwise. Second, the government budget deficit requires that private saving must rise to avoid any downward pressure on the sum of domestic and foreign investment ($I + NX$). Third, if there is no increase in private saving, then to avoid a decline in domestic investment there must be more borrowing from foreigners (larger negative NX) or a decline in lending to foreigners.

We can use a numerical example from recent years to illustrate how the right-hand side of equation (2.6) changed as the government shifted from its 1993 deficit to its surplus in 2000 and then to an even larger deficit in 2010.

$$T - G \equiv (I + NX) - S$$

1993	$-1.9 \equiv (17.6 - 1.2) - 18.4$
2000	$4.3 \equiv (20.9 - 4.1) - 12.5$
2010	$-6.8 \equiv (15.5 - 3.6) - 18.8$

 various decisions

In the year 2000, there was a government budget surplus equal to 4.3 percent of GDP, which together with foreign borrowing of 4.1 percent, allows domestic investment to be 8.4 percent of GDP larger than saving. In contrast there was a government budget deficit in both 1993 and 2010. Since saving was roughly the same in the two years (18.4 vs. 18.8 percent of GDP), the much larger government deficit in 2010 compared to 1993 was financed by reduced investment (down from 17.6 to 15.5 percent of GDP) and triple the foreign borrowing (up from 1.2 to 3.6 percent of GDP).

Because the magic equation (2.5 or 2.6) is true by definition, it does not identify the direction of causation among the interrelated variables. For instance, in the year 2000 did the government run a budget surplus because domestic investment was so strong, or was investment so strong because the government ran a surplus? Did the sharp decline in investment between 2000 and 2010 cause the government to run a deficit, or did the government deficit occur for other reasons?

During most of the period since 1980, the United States has experienced "twin deficits," with a government budget deficit accompanied by foreign borrowing (negative NX). The year 2000, with its budget surplus accompanied by foreign borrowing, was the exception rather than the rule, but the year 2000 shows that the deficits are not guaranteed to be "twins."

GLOBAL ECONOMIC CRISIS FOCUS

Chicken or Egg in Recessions?

The numbers for the magic equation at the top of this page show an enormous contrast between the prosperous conditions of the year 2000 and the depressed conditions of 2010. The only similar element was net exports at around −4 percent of GDP. The most dramatic change was in the government budget, from a surplus of 4.3 percent of GDP to a deficit of −6.8 percent, a shift into deficit of 11.1 percent of GDP. The numbers show that of this epochal shift, 5.4 percent of GDP represented a decline of investment and 6.3 percent an increase in saving. Which was the chicken and which was the egg? We will learn that, while changes in government tax and expenditure policy obviously influence the budget, there is a big impact of the economy on the budget. So weak investment and strong saving both held down GDP, and hence government tax revenues.

2-6 Where Does Household Income Come From?

Income, Leakages, and the Circular Flow

An important lesson of circular flow diagrams like Figure 2-3 (see p. 33) is that the expenditures on GDP (consumption, investment, government spending, and net exports) create income, and this income is available to be spent on another round of expenditure. Households receive only part of the GDP generated by business firms; the rest leaks out of the circular flow in the form of tax revenue for government and saving that provides funds to the capital market. Recall from equation (2.5) that total leakages (taxes and saving) must by definition equal total nonconsumption spending, also called *injections*.

Table 2-2 provides a concise summary of the steps by which income travels from business firms to households. Down the left-hand side are the various

Table 2-2 Households Get What Remains After All the Leakages

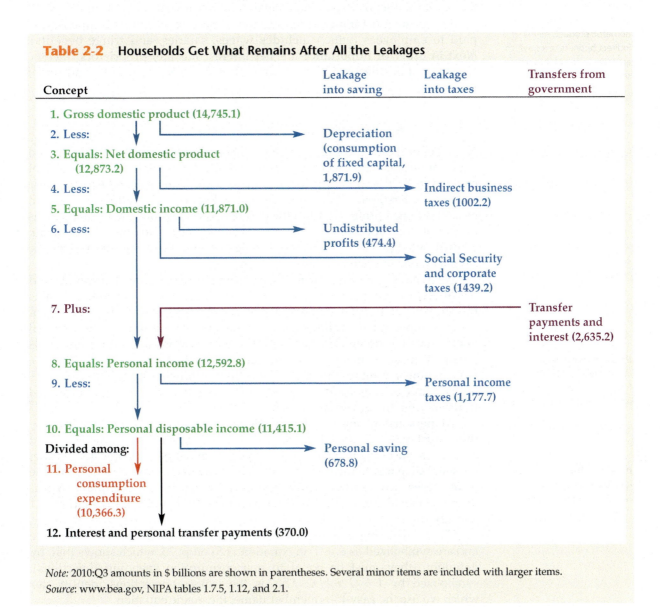

Concept	Leakage into saving	Leakage into taxes	Transfers from government
1. Gross domestic product (14,745.1)			
2. Less:	Depreciation (consumption of fixed capital, 1,871.9)		
3. Equals: Net domestic product (12,873.2)			
4. Less:		Indirect business taxes (1002.2)	
5. Equals: Domestic income (11,871.0)			
6. Less:	Undistributed profits (474.4)		
		Social Security and corporate taxes (1439.2)	
7. Plus:			Transfer payments and interest (2,635.2)
8. Equals: Personal income (12,592.8)			
9. Less:		Personal income taxes (1,177.7)	
10. Equals: Personal disposable income (11,415.1)			
Divided among:	Personal saving (678.8)		
11. Personal consumption expenditure (10,366.3)			
12. Interest and personal transfer payments (370.0)			

Note: 2010:Q3 amounts in $ billions are shown in parentheses. Several minor items are included with larger items.

Source: www.bea.gov, NIPA tables 1.7.5, 1.12, and 2.1.

concepts of total income; these differ depending on which tax and saving leakages are included. The three remaining columns identify the major types of saving and tax leakages, as well as transfer payments (which work like taxes in reverse).

Line 1 starts with GDP, the total amount of income created by domestic production. The first leakage, on line 2, is for depreciation, defined on p. 30, the amount business firms set aside for the replacement of worn-out and obsolete investment goods.

What remains after depreciation deductions is net domestic product (NDP), shown on line 3.

Next, line 4 in Table 2-2 deducts indirect business taxes, which include state and local sales and property taxes. These tax payments are not available as income to households or business firms. Only what is left over, called **domestic income** (line 5), is available to provide net income to the domestic factors of production (labor and capital) that produce current output.

Domestic income is the earnings of domestic factors of production, computed as net domestic product, minus indirect business taxes, which are taxes levied on business sales.

By far the most important portion of domestic income is compensation paid to employees (which includes wages, salaries, and fringe benefits). Next in order of importance are net interest income, proprietors' income (from small businesses like farms and shops), corporate profits, and rental income.

From Domestic Income to Personal Income

Not all of domestic income is paid out to households as personal income, and personal income also includes some receipts by households that are not counted in GDP or domestic income. Lines 6 and 7 in Table 2-2 explain these differences. First, part of domestic income is kept by corporations in the form of undistributed profits—that is, the part of corporate profits that is not paid as dividends to stockholders or as corporate taxes to the government. Undistributed profits are a type of saving leakage, providing funding for the capital market to finance investment spending.

Personal income is the income received by households from all sources, including earnings and transfer payments.

Next, large amounts flow to the government in the form of corporate and Social Security tax payments, then back from the government to households in the form of transfer payments like Social Security and unemployment benefits. Government funds also are paid out for interest on the national debt. Adjusting domestic income for these deductions and additions yields **personal income,** the sum of income payments to households (line 8). Personal income represents the current flow of purchasing power to households coming from *both* the productive activities of business firms *and* transfers from the government sector.

Personal disposable income is personal income minus personal income tax payments.

All personal income is not available to households to spend, first because they must pay personal income taxes to the government (line 9). What remains is one of the most important concepts in national income accounting, **personal disposable income** (line 10). This is available for households to use in the three ways shown at the bottom of Table 2-2: consumption expenditure, personal interest and transfer payments, and personal saving (lines 11 and 12).

The total saving and tax leakages (with transfers treated as a negative tax) are symbolized as $S + T$ in equation (2.5) on p. 35, which shows that, by definition, they must be equal to nonconsumption spending (injections), symbolized by $I + G + NX$. This is the leakages–injections identity, for which we use the easy-to-remember name, the magic equation.

2-7   Nominal GDP, Real GDP, and the GDP Deflator

Thus far, all the terms and relationships of national income accounting apply to a particular time period (a quarter or a year) and are measured at the prices actually paid by households and firms. Any economic magnitude measured at the prices actually paid is described by the adjective **nominal.** For instance, **nominal GDP** is the total amount of current product valued at the prices actually paid on the market.

Nominal is an adjective that modifies any economic magnitude measured in current prices.

Nominal GDP is the value of gross domestic product in current (actual) prices.

Real and Nominal Magnitudes

Nominal amounts are not very useful for economic analysis because they can increase either when people buy more physical goods and services—more cars, steaks, and haircuts—or when prices rise. An increase in my nominal spending on consumption goods from $40,000 in 2010 to $50,000 in 2011 might indicate that I became able to buy more items, or it could simply mean that I had to pay higher prices in 2011 for the same items purchased in 2010. Changes in nominal magnitudes hide more than they reveal. So economists focus on changes in real magnitudes, which eliminate the influence of year-to-year changes in prices and reflect true changes in the number, size, and quality of items purchased.

Real GDP and Real Output

We need a measure of real gross domestic product, or real GDP. Like any real magnitude, real GDP is expressed in the prices of an arbitrarily chosen base year. The official measures of GDP in the United States currently use 2005 as the base year. Real GDP for every year, whether 1929 or 2011, is measured by taking the production of that particular year expressed at the constant prices of 2005. For instance, 2011 real GDP measured in 2005 prices represents the amount that the actual 2011 production of goods and services would have cost if each item *had been sold at its 2005 price.*

Since prices usually increase each year, nominal GDP is higher than real GDP for years after 2005. Similarly, nominal GDP is lower than real GDP for years before 2005. You can see this regular pattern in Figure 2-4, which displays nominal and real GDP for each year since 1900. Only in 2005 are nominal and real GDP the same.

The percentage ratio of nominal GDP to real GDP is a price index called the **GDP deflator,** and this is displayed as the orange line in Figure 2-4. The GDP deflator measures the ratio of the prices actually paid in a particular year to the prices paid in the base year 2005. For instance, in 1959 nominal GDP was about 18 percent of real GDP, indicating that prices actually paid in 1959 were about 18 percent of the prices that would have been paid in 2005 for the same goods and services.

The **GDP deflator** is the economy's aggregate price index and is defined as 100 times the ratio of nominal GDP to chain-weighted real GDP.

Later on we will consider other real magnitudes, such as real consumption and the real money supply. An alternative label for real magnitudes is constant-dollar; in contrast, nominal magnitudes are usually called current-dollar. To summarize:

Alternative labels for magnitudes			
Items measured in prices of a single year like 2005	Constant-dollar	or	Real
Items measured in actual prices paid in each separate year	Current-dollar	or	Nominal

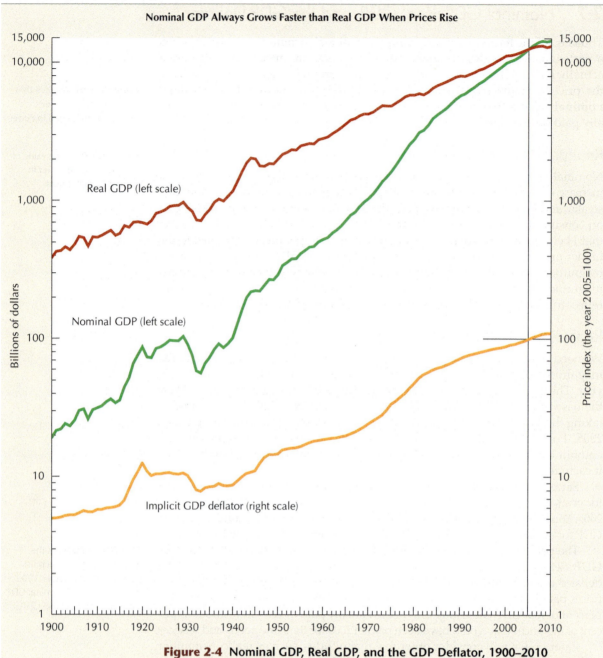

Figure 2-4 Nominal GDP, Real GDP, and the GDP Deflator, 1900–2010

Notice how the nominal GDP line lies below the real GDP line before 2005 but lies above the real GDP line after 2005. This reflects the fact that before 2005 the current prices used to measure nominal GDP were lower than the 2005 prices used to measure real GDP. After 2005, the current prices used to measure nominal GDP were higher than the 2005 prices used to measure real GDP. Notice how the nominal GDP line crosses the real GDP line in 2005, the same year that the GDP deflator attains the value of 100.

Source: Appendix Table A-1. See explanation in Appendix C-4.

How to Calculate Inflation, Real GDP Growth, or Any Other Growth Rate

Often, you will want to calculate a percentage growth rate, whether the U.S. rate of inflation, real GDP, or even your own income over a period of years. In this section we will learn a very simple formula that will allow you to calculate the growth rate of *anything* over any period, no matter how long or short, and convert it to an annual rate.

In this book we will use lowercase letters, say x, to designate the growth rate of a variable, the level of which is called the same uppercase letter X. Let's say that we have been given the value of the GDP deflator for 2008 as 108.5 and for 2009 as 109.8, and we have been asked to calculate the inflation rate for 2009. (You will find GDP deflator data for these and many other years in Appendix Table A-1 in the back of this book.)

The general formula to calculate the percentage annual growth rate of any variable X at a time period t from another period s years earlier (call this t-s) is as follows:

General Form
$$X_t = 100 \, LN(X_t/X_{t-s})/s$$
Numerical Example
$$1.19 = 100 \, LN(109.8/108.5)/1.0$$

Here LN means "natural logarithm" and is a function key found on any scientific calculator. The answer to the example is found simply by taking the ratio $109.8/108.5 = 1.0120$ and then pushing the "LN" button, which yields 0.0119, and finally multiplying that result by 100.

Exactly the same formula can be used to calculate the annual rate of inflation between two adjacent quarters. Let us take the level of the GDP deflator for the fourth quarter of 2009, abbreviated "2009:Q4" from Appendix

Table A-2, which is 109.7. The value for the next quarter, 2010:Q1, is 110.0. What is the annual rate of inflation between those two quarters?

General Form
$$X_t = 100 \, LN(X_t/X_{t-s})/s$$
Numerical Example
$$1.09 = 100 \, LN(110.0/109.7)/0.25$$

The method is exactly the same. The only difference is that now we are comparing two adjacent quarters rather than two adjacent years, and so $s = 0.25$ (one-quarter of a year) instead of $s = 1$ as before.

Our final exercise is to calculate the average annual growth rate of U.S. real GDP from 1875 to 2010, using the data in Appendix Table A-1:

General Form
$$X_t = 100 \, LN(X_t/X_{t-s})/s$$
Numerical Example
$$3.38 = 100 \, LN(13248.7/138.8)/135$$

Again, this is exactly the same formula, now with $s = 135$ since there are 135 years between 1875 and 2009. Despite the fact that real GDP in 2010 was 95 times larger than in 1875, such a long period elapsed between those two years that the annual growth rate was a mere 3.38 percent.

The extremely useful formula discussed in this box can be used for any calculation involving growth rates, not just for such macroeconomic concepts as the price level or real GDP, but to calculate the annual rate of return of an investment over any period of time, even for a single day.

Why We Care About Real GDP and the GDP Deflator

We care about real GDP because its movements create a mirror image movement in the opposite direction in the unemployment rate, one of the three key macroeconomic concepts introduced in Chapter 1. Further, we care about accurate measurements of real GDP, since they are essential to measuring productivity, or output per hour, the third of our central macro concepts.

We care about the GDP deflator because it is the basis for measuring the inflation rate. Recall from the beginning of Chapter 1 that the inflation rate is the percentage rate of increase in the economywide average price level, which we measure by the GDP deflator. To convert the GDP deflator into the inflation rate, we use the universal formula for calculating growth rates shown in the box higher up on this page.

Further, we care about the GDP deflator because very fast inflation can destroy a society, as in the German hyperinflation (see pp. 14–16). Fast inflation is bad because of the direct harm it causes, and because of the indirect harm done by measures taken to stop it. And to measure the inflation rate, we need to start with the GDP deflator.

The Appendix to Chapter 2 provides the details that you need to understand how to calculate real GDP and the GDP deflator from specific prices and quantities of individual products.

SELF-TEST

Without looking at Figure 2-4, you should now be able to answer the following:

1. Is the implicit GDP deflator greater or less than 100 percent in every year before 2005? In every year after 2005?

2. In what year is the implicit GDP deflator equal to exactly 100 percent?

2-8   Measuring Unemployment

The unemployment rate is the first of the central macro concepts introduced in Chapter 1. Families dread the financial and emotional disruption caused by layoffs, so news of an increase in the unemployment rate creates public concern and plummeting popularity ratings for incumbent politicians. Because of widespread public awareness, the unemployment rate is generally considered the most important of the central macro concepts. In this section we learn how the unemployment rate is measured.

The Unemployment Survey

Many people wonder how the government determines facts such as "the teenage unemployment rate in October 2010 was 27.1 percent," because they themselves have never spoken to a government agent about their own experiences of employment, unemployment, and time in school. It would be too costly to contact everyone in the country every month; the government attempts to reach each household to collect information only once each decade when it takes the decennial Census of Population.

As a compromise, each month 1,500 Census Bureau workers interview about 60,000 households, or about 1 in every 1,400 households in the country. Each month one-fourth of the households in the sample are replaced, so that no family is interviewed more than four months in a row. The laws of statistics imply that an average from a survey of a sample of households of this size comes very close to the true figure that would be revealed by a costly complete census.

Questions asked in the survey.   The interviewer first asks about each separate household member aged 16 or older, "What were you doing most of last week—working, keeping house, going to school, or something else?" Anyone who has done any work at all for pay during the past week, whether part-time (even one hour per week), full-time, or temporary work, is counted as employed.

For those who say they did no work, the next question is, "Did you have a job from which you were temporarily absent or on layoff last week?" If the person is awaiting recall from a layoff or has obtained a new job but is waiting for it to begin, he or she is counted as unemployed.

If the person has neither worked nor been absent from a job, the next question is, "Have you been looking for work in the last four weeks, and if so, what have you been doing in the last four weeks to find work?" A person who has not been ill and has searched for a job by applying to an employer, registering with an employment agency, checking with friends, or other specified job-search activities is counted as unemployed. The remaining people who are neither employed nor unemployed, mainly homemakers who do not seek paid work, students, disabled people, and retired people, fall in the category of "not in the labor force."

Definitions based on the interview. Despite the intricacy of questions asked by the interviewer, the concept is simple: People with jobs are employed; people who do not have jobs and are looking for jobs are **unemployed;** people who meet neither labor-market test are not in the labor force. The **total labor force** is the total of the civilian employed, the armed forces, and the unemployed. Thus the entire population aged 16 and over falls into one of four categories:

> The **unemployed** are those without jobs who either are on temporary layoff or have taken specific actions to look for work.
>
> The **total labor force** is the total of the civilian employed, the armed forces, and the unemployed.

1. Total labor force
   a. Civilian employed
   b. Armed forces
   c. Unemployed
2. Not in the labor force

The actual **unemployment rate** is defined as the ratio

> The **unemployment rate** is the ratio of the number unemployed to the number in the labor force, expressed as a percentage.

$$U = \frac{\text{number of unemployed}}{\text{civilian employed} + \text{unemployed}}$$

Example: In October 2010, the BLS reported an unemployment rate of 9.6 percent. This was calculated as the percentage ratio

$$U = 100 \times \left(\frac{\text{number of unemployed}}{\text{civilian employed} + \text{unemployed}} \right)$$

$$= 100 \times \left(\frac{14{,}843{,}000}{139{,}061{,}000 + 14{,}843{,}000} \right)$$

or

$$U = 9.6 \text{ percent}$$

The labor force participation rate is the ratio of the total labor force (civilian employed, armed forces, and the unemployed) to the population aged 16 or over. Those who do not participate in the labor force include those above age 15 who are in school, retired individuals, people who do not work because they are raising children or otherwise choose to stay at home, and those who cannot work because they are ill, disabled, or have given up on finding jobs. In June 2010 the labor force participation rate was 64.5 percent.

Flaws in the definition. The government's unemployment measure sounds relatively straightforward, but unfortunately it disguises almost as much as it reveals. The adjacent Global Economic Crisis box explains some of the flaws in the official definition of unemployment, and the dimensions of harm done by the 2007–09 recession to workers who are not officially counted as unemployed.

UNDERSTANDING THE GLOBAL ECONOMIC CRISIS

The Ranks of the Hidden Unemployed

Flaws in the Definition

The official definition of unemployment unfortunately disguises as much as it reveals. The first problem is that the unemployment rate overstates the social harm done by unemployment. But a much more serious second problem is that the unemployment greatly understates the number of people whose lives are negatively impacted by recessions and their aftermath.

1. *The unemployment rate by itself is not a measure of the social distress caused by the loss of a job.* Each person who lacks a job and is looking for one is counted as "1.0 unemployed people." But the social impact of unemployment is very serious for the head of a household responsible for feeding numerous dependents, while it is much less serious for a 16-year-old looking only for a 10-hour-per-week part-time job to provide pocket money. Further, many of the unemployed in normal times are looking for jobs not because they have been laid off but because they are young people entering the labor force for the summer between school years, women reentering the labor force after maternity leave, and people who quit their jobs voluntarily and are counted as unemployed while looking for a new job. In prosperous periods like 2007, only a minority of the unemployed had lost their jobs involuntarily.

2. *The official unemployment concept misses millions of people who are still working but nevertheless are hurt by a recession.* Millions of those still employed may be forced to work part-time when they really want to work full-time. The number of "forced part-time workers" was particularly high in 2009 and 2010.

3. *A person lacking a job must actively look for a job within the most recent four weeks.* What about people who have looked and looked for a job and are convinced that nothing is available? If they stop looking, they are not counted as unemployed. They simply disappear from the labor force, entering the category of "not in the labor force." This group of people who have given up looking for jobs has been called "discouraged workers" and the "disguised unemployed." The government now keeps track of them as a separate category called "marginally attached workers."

Hidden Victims in the Global Economic Crisis and Its Aftermath

The chart tracks two categories of people officially defined as unemployed, and two categories of people who are not so defined. The yellow area at the bottom represents the people officially counted as unemployed who do not represent a major social problem, including new-entrant youth, reentrant mothers, and people who choose to quit their jobs to look for a better job. Variations in the yellow area are fairly minor, although the relatively high levels in 1975–85 and in 2009–10 reflect a weak labor market that made it harder for entrants, reentrants, and job leavers to find a job.

The light blue area represents those people who have lost their jobs or have just completed temporary jobs, and everyone in the blue area is officially counted as unemployed. These are the most obvious victims of recessions, and you can see sharp upswings in the size of the blue area in the recessions of 1975, 1981–82, and 2008–09, and to a lesser extent in the milder recessions of 1990–91 and 2001. A common feature of the blue area is that it tends to remain relatively high even after the recession is over. Also note that the blue area never disappears.

Unemployment has always been a *lagging indicator* and stays high sometimes for many months after output stops declining (refer to Figure 1-4 on p. 9, which shows that the business cycle "trough" that ends a recession occurs when output stops declining). Notice that the blue area declined rapidly in 1984–85 but slowly in 1991–94 and 2002–04. Current forecasts suggest that unemployment will remain at near-record high levels not just in 2009–10 but for at least two or three years after that.

The two types of hidden distress caused by recessions are shown by the red and brown areas. The red area represents those forced to work part-time who desire to work full-time; it grows during recessions and shrinks only slowly during business expansions. The large number of forced part-time workers in 2009–10 leads to a pessimistic prediction for the unemployment rate after 2010. Firms can add hours of labor most easily by shifting the employees already on the job from part-time to full-time status, and the large overhang of these part-time workers will allow employers to delay any need to hire new workers

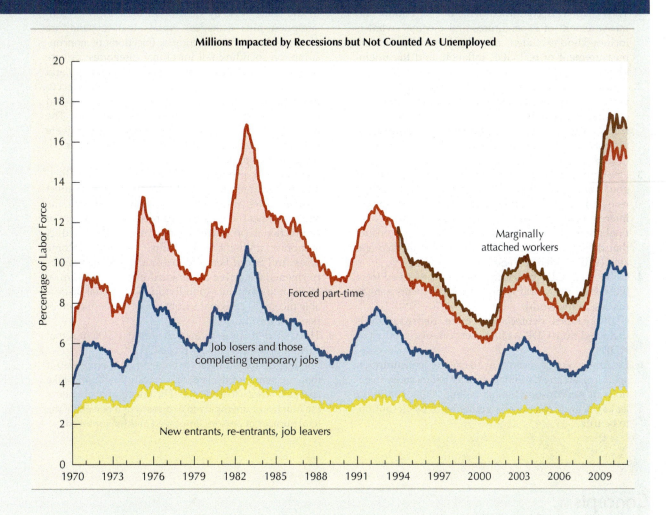

Millions Impacted by Recessions but Not Counted As Unemployed

Percentage of Labor Force

Marginally attached workers

Forced part-time

Job losers and those completing temporary jobs

New entrants, re-entrants, job leavers

from the ranks of the unemployed or marginally attached workers.

The brown area is based on data that only begin in 1994 (this is why there is no brown area in the left portion of the chart). The marginally attached workers, including those who have given up looking for jobs, grow in number during recessions but appear to be a fairly constant percentage of the labor force during recoveries and expansions. The people in the red and brown areas are victims of recessions just as surely as those in the blue area.

When people are unemployed, they lose their incomes. If they are unemployed long enough, they use up their life savings and reach borrowing limits on credit cards and other debt. What do they live on then? A great political debate emerged in 2010 over proposals to extend unemployment benefits (transfer payments to the unemployed) any further. Some who opposed extending the benefits argued that the harm done by the large federal budget deficit and growing debt outweighed the need of the unemployed for continued help. The protracted symptoms of long-term unemployment began to show some similarity to the Great Depression. We return to the great debate about how to help the unemployed and cure the economy in Chapters 5 and 6.

Summary

1. This chapter is concerned with the definition and measurement of expenditures and income—what is included and excluded, and why, as well as with the measurement of real GDP, inflation, and the unemployment rate.

2. A flow magnitude is any money payment, physical good, or service that flows from one economic unit to another per unit of time. A flow is distinguished from a stock, which is an economic magnitude in the possession of an individual or firm at a moment of time.

3. Final product (GDP) consists of all currently produced goods and services sold through the market but not resold during the current time period. By counting intermediate goods only once, and by including only final purchases, we avoid double-counting and ensure that the value of final product and total income created (value added) are equal.

4. GNP equals GDP plus factor payments received from the rest of the world minus factor payments sent to the rest of the world.

5. GDP includes depreciation. Once depreciation is deducted from GDP, we have net domestic product or NDP.

6. Leakages out of income available for consumption spending are, by definition, exactly balanced by injections of nonconsumption spending. This equality of leakages and injections is guaranteed, by definition, to be true.

7. In the same way, by definition, total income (consumption plus leakages) equals total expenditure (consumption plus injections). Injections of nonconsumption spending fall into three categories: private domestic investment (on business equipment and structures, residential housing, and inventory accumulation); foreign investment or net exports; and government spending on goods and services. The definitions require private saving to exceed private investment (domestic and foreign) by the amount of the government deficit.

8. Net domestic product (NDP) is obtained by deducting depreciation from GDP. Deduction of indirect business taxes from NDP yields domestic income, the sum of all net incomes earned by domestic factors of production in producing current output. If we deduct corporate undistributed profits, corporate income taxes, and Social Security taxes, and add in transfer payments, we arrive at personal income, the sum of all income payments to individuals. Personal disposable income is personal income after the deduction of personal income taxes.

9. The GDP deflator is defined as nominal GDP in actual current prices divided by real GDP.

10. Those aged 16 and over are counted as unemployed if they are temporarily laid off or want a job, and take specified actions to find a job. The unemployment rate is the number of unemployed expressed as a percent of the total number of persons employed and unemployed.

Concepts

consumption expenditures
flow magnitude
stock
National Income and Product
    Accounts
final product
transfer payments
intermediate good
final good
value added
gross national product (GNP)
depreciation (consumption of fixed
    capital)

net domestic product (NDP)
gross
net
private investment
inventory investment
fixed investment
personal saving
exports
imports
net exports
net foreign investment
magic equation
leakages

injections
domestic income
personal income
personal disposable income
nominal
nominal GDP
GDP deflator
unemployed
total labor force
unemployment rate

Questions

1. Explain the difference between a stock magnitude and a flow magnitude. Label each of the following as either a stock or a flow:
   (a) depreciation
   (b) saving
   (c) wealth
   (d) government debt
   (e) government deficit
   (f) current account deficit
   (g) savings
   (h) money supply
   (i) labor force
   (j) labor services
   (k) net exports
   (l) net taxes

2. Decide whether each of the following transactions is included in GDP. If the transaction is included, determine which component of final spending it represents. If the transaction is excluded from GDP, explain why.
   (a) Your local ice cream maker buys peaches to make peach ice cream.
   (b) Your local ice cream maker buys a new and improved ice cream maker.
   (c) You buy peach ice cream from your local ice cream maker.
   (d) Your local ice cream maker sells peach ice cream to a restaurant that serves peach smoothies.
   (e) Your cousin in Canada buys peach ice cream from your local ice cream maker.
   (f) You buy a used book to learn how to make peach ice cream.
   (g) You buy peaches to make peach ice cream for yourself.
   (h) You buy a new ice cream maker to make peach ice cream for yourself.
   (i) You give some of your peach ice cream to your cousin when she visits from Canada.

3. Explain whether each of the following would be included in GDP, GNP, or both of the United States.
   (a) The salary of an American who is working in Japan for Honda (a Japanese company).
   (b) The profits that Honda earns from its production of cars in Ohio.
   (c) The value of the software that Microsoft sells to Honda for use in its corporate headquarters in Japan.

4. Explain why the value of goods and services purchased by Europeans vacationing in the United States would be considered U.S. exports and the money that Americans spend traveling overseas is considered part of U.S. imports.

5. Assume that the GDP of the United States is twice as large as the GDP of China. Can you conclude, based on this information, that the average individual in the United States is two times as well off as the average individual in China? Why or why not?

6. The term "underground economy" encompasses economic activity that people do not report because it is illegal or because they hope to avoid paying taxes. Though the size of the underground economy is unknown, it may be a sizable fraction of the nation's GDP. How does the underground economy affect the accuracy of official measures of GDP, unemployment, and productivity, and complicate the tasks of policymakers?

7. Using the information contained in the box on p. 27 concerning where to find data on the economy, go to the correct Web site to get the following data for the most recent month or quarter:
   (a) interest rates on two-year Treasury notes and ten-year Treasury bonds;
   (b) the GDP deflator;
   (c) the number of people unemployed, the number of civilians employed, the number of people in the labor force, the unemployment rate, and the nonfarm payroll;
   (d) nominal and real GDP and nominal and real personal consumption expenditures.

8. (a) Savings and taxes are called leakages. From what do they leak? Where do they go? Imports are also a leakage. From what do they leak? Where do they go?
   (b) Private domestic investment and government purchases of goods and services are called injections. What are they injections into? From where do they come? Exports are an injection. What are they injections into? From where do they come?

9. When the government runs a budget deficit, funds flow from capital markets to the government as the government borrows from capital markets by selling bonds. Explain how funds flow from the government to the capital markets when the government runs a budget surplus.

10. In the national income and product accounts, personal income is calculated by subtracting from national income any income earned but not received

and adding back in any income received but not earned. Explain.

11. Four hundred tires are produced by a tire manufacturer and sold for $75 each to General Motors in December 2010. In February 2011, General Motors puts the tires on 100 newly produced cars and sells each car for $30,000. What is the contribution made to GDP in 2010 and 2011 by the transaction described? (Assume all other components of the cars are produced in 2011.)

12. Starting from the situation depicted in Figure 2-3, assume that business firms produce an additional $500,000 worth of goods, of which only $450,000 are bought during the current year. What are the new values for the following categories?
    (a) income
    (b) consumption expenditure
    (c) personal saving
    (d) investment

13. Suppose that the amount of private saving declines. Explain why at least one of the following must occur: Government saving must increase, private domestic investment must decrease, or net foreign investment must decrease.

14. If you learn that nominal GDP for 2011 is greater than nominal GDP for 2010, what do you know about changes in the level of output during this period? Changes in prices during this period? Would your answer change if real GDP had increased in 2011?

15. In late 2003 and early 2004, the Federal Reserve was concerned about the possibility of deflation, which is a general fall in prices. If deflation occurs, explain which grows faster, nominal GDP or real GDP.

16. Explain how a person who falls into the ranks of the "hidden unemployed" differs from someone who is officially counted as unemployed. Compare the Global Economic Crisis with earlier recessions in terms of the severity of "hidden unemployment" and how long people were unemployed.

17. If the government suddenly decided to include the noncivilian employed, that is, the armed forces, together with the civilian employed in the denominator of the unemployment rate, what would happen to the unemployment rate?

18. Due to a recession, ABC Enterprises' sales decline. In order to reduce losses, ABC lays off 10 percent of its labor force, including Don, Ellen, and Frank. ABC indicates that it will hire all its workers back within two months. In each of the following cases, explain if the person is employed, unemployed, or not in the labor force.
    (a) Don decides he is going to use the two months to go fishing in Montana.
    (b) Ellen questions whether ABC will really hire her back. She quickly finds another job.
    (c) Frank's wife decides she wants to go back to work, but urges him to go back to school. He agrees and resigns his position at ABC. He also decides to devote all of his efforts to school. His wife starts looking for a job to support them.

Problems

myeconlab   Visit www.MyEconLab.com to complete these or similar exercises.

*Indicates that the problem requires the Appendix to Chapter 2.

1. Use the following data to answer the following questions (all figures are in billions of dollars):

Item	Amount
Government purchases of goods and services	$1,721.6
Exports	1,096.3
Receipts of factor income from the rest of the world	382.7
Depreciation (consumption of fixed capital)	990.8
Net fixed investment	688.2
Corporate income taxes	265.2
Consumption expenditures	6,739.4
Indirect business taxes	664.6
Imports	1,475.8
Payments of factor income to the rest of the world	343.7
Inventory change	56.5
Social Security contributions	702.7
Undistributed corporate profits (retained earnings)	130.3
Government transfer and interest payments	1,366.3
Personal interest payments	286.2
Personal taxes	1,235.7

   (a) What is gross domestic product?
   (b) What is gross national product?
   (c) What is net domestic product?
   (d) What is domestic income?
   (e) What is personal income? (*Hint:* Personal interest payments are part of the category "interest and personal transfer payments" on line 12 of Table 2-2.)
   (f) What is disposable personal income?
   (g) What is personal saving?

2. Assume that gross private domestic investment is $800 billion and the government (state, local, and federal combined) is currently running a $400 billion deficit. If households and businesses are saving $1,000 billion, what is the value of net exports? Use equation (2.6) to explain your answer.

3. Orange growers sell $15 billion of their crop to orange juice processors and $6 billion of their crop to supermarkets. The orange juice processors sell their orange juice to supermarkets for $18 billion. The supermarkets sell oranges to consumers for $8 billion, orange juice to consumers for $18 billion, and orange juice to restaurants for $4 billion. The restaurants sell orange juice to consumers for $8 billion.
   (a) Calculate the amounts oranges and orange juice contribute to GDP.
   (b) Calculate the value added by orange growers, orange juice processors, supermarkets, and restaurants.

*4. Assume that a country produces only two goods, automobiles and fast PCs. In year 1, automobiles cost $20,000 each and the PCs cost $3,000 each; 1,000 automobiles and 10,000 PCs are produced. In year 2, the price of automobiles has increased to $22,000; because a new, even faster type of PC is about to be introduced, the price of fast PCs has fallen to $700. In year 2, 1,000 automobiles and 15,000 PCs are produced.
   (a) Fill in the following table.

	Year 1	Year 2
Nominal GDP (Total of current-dollar expenditures)		
Real GDP (i) at fixed year 1 prices (ii) at fixed year 2 prices		

   (b) Using the technique of chain-weighting, calculate the percentage change in real GDP between year 1 and year 2.
   (c) Calculate the GDP deflator for year 2.

5. If nominal GDP is $10,608 and real GDP is $10,400, what is the value of the GDP deflator?

6. Suppose that the GDP deflator equals 100 and real GDP equals 10,000. Calculate the value of nominal GDP.

7. Suppose that the GDP deflator equals 102.5 and nominal GDP equals 11,200. Calculate the value of real GDP.

8. Calculate percentage annual growth rates using the data that follow.
   (a) Productivity growth measures increase in output per hour of work. Output per hour was 54.0 in the first quarter of 1973, 75.4 in the first quarter of 1996, and 111.0 in the first quarter of 2010 (2005 = 100). Calculate the average annual rates of productivity growth between 1973 and 1996 and between 1996 and 2010. Using your answers, explain during which of these two periods living standards rose more quickly.
   (b) The GDP deflator was 30.7 in 1974, 43.8 in 1979, 59.8 in 1984, 69.5 in 1989, 79.9 in 1994, 86.8 in 1999, 96.8 in 2004, and 109.6 in 2009. During which five-year interval was the annual inflation rate the

highest? During which interval was the average annual inflation rate the lowest? What was the trend in inflation over the last quarter of the twentieth century? (*Hint:* The inflation rate is the annual percentage change in the GDP deflator.)

(c) In the second quarter of 2005, real GDP was 12,587.5. In the second quarter of 2006, real GDP was 12,962.5; in the third quarter of 2006, it was 12,965.9. Calculate the percentage annual growth rates between the second quarters of 2005 and 2006, and the second and third quarters of 2006. Interpret your results.

9. How long will it take real GDP to double if it grows at the following rates?
   (a) 4 percent per year
   (b) 6 percent per year
   (c) 8 percent per year

10. In 2009, civilian employment was 139,877,000 and unemployment was 14,265,000. What was the unemployment rate?

◆ SELF-TEST ANSWERS

p. **26.** (1) The payment of the $10 bill to the barber is a flow of money shown by the red line labeled consumption expenditure. The provision of the haircut by the barber for the student is shown by the orange line labeled product. The barber's income of $10 is shown by the green line labeled income, and the barber's provision of labor services to perform the haircut is shown by the purple line labeled labor services. (2) Alison provides labor services, shown by the purple line, to the summer camp, in return for which she receives income ($8 per hour for each hour she works) from the summer camp, shown by the green line. The camp fees paid by parents are part of consumer expenditures, shown by the red line, and the camp services are part of product, shown by the orange line.

p. **30.** (1)(2) Included in GDP for the first quarter of 2011 is the change in the value of the bakery's inventories between December 31, 2010, and March 31, 2011. This is $30.00 minus $20.00, or $10.00. If the level of inventories had fallen, instead of rising as in the example, inventory investment would have been negative. (3) The baker's inventory change contributes $10.00 to GDP in the first quarter of 2011.

p. **42.** (1) Less than 100 percent in every year before 2005; greater than 100 percent in every year after 2005. (2) Equal to 100 percent in 2005.

Appendix to Chapter 2

How We Measure Real GDP and the Inflation Rate

Clearly, nominal GDP is of no interest by itself. We must find some way of separating its movements into those caused by changes in real GDP and those caused by inflation. Only if we succeed in making this "split" of nominal GDP changes will we be able to identify separately the growth rate of total output, or real GDP, and the inflation rate.

How We Calculate Changes in Real GDP

Real GDP cannot be observed directly. No one can see, feel, or touch it. There's an old saying that "you can't add apples and oranges." Real GDP carries that saying to its limit, since real GDP consists not just of apples and oranges, but also computers, electricity, haircuts, restaurant meals, and thousands of other goods and services that can't be added directly. The only way to combine the different products is to place a value on each component of GDP, and that requires using the prices of the goods and services produced. However, since prices are constantly changing, our measure of real GDP and its changes will depend on which time period we choose to take the prices for this essential valuation of the components of GDP.

The table shows how the change in real GDP between year 1 and year 2 differs, depending on the prices that are used. Lines 1 and 2 show the hypothetical prices and quantities of oranges and apples used in this imaginary two-good economy. Notice that the price of oranges doubles between year 1 and year 2, while the price of apples goes up only 25 percent. As a result, the consumption of oranges drops in year 2 while the consumption of apples doubles. As you will see, the change in measured real GDP between years 1 and 2 depends on the importance we assign to the big decline in orange consumption and the big increase in apple consumption.

One approach, which was used previously to calculate real GDP in the United States, was to hold the value of all products fixed over all years at the prices of a single

Calculation of Real GDP and GDP Deflators in an Imaginary Economy Producing Only Oranges and Apples

	Year 1	Year 2
1. Prices		
a. Oranges	$0.10	$0.20
b. Apples	0.20	0.25
2. Quantities		
a. Oranges	30	20
b. Apples	10	20
3. Current-dollar expenditures		
a. Oranges (1.a times 2.a)	$3.00	$4.00
b. Apples (1.b times 2.b)	2.00	5.00
c. Total: Nominal GDP	5.00	9.00
4. Constant-dollar expenditures each year		
a. At fixed year 1 prices	$5.00	$6.00
b. At fixed year 2 prices	8.50	9.00

(continued)

	Year 1	Year 2
5. Real GDP (index, year 1 = 1.00)		
a. At fixed year 1 prices	1.00	1.20
b. At fixed year 2 prices	1.00	1.06
c. Chain-weighted (geometric mean, 5.a and 5.b)	1.00	1.13
6. Additional indexes, year 1 = 1.00		
a. Nominal GDP (3.c)	1.00	1.80
b. GDP deflator (6.a/5.c)	1.00	1.59

Sources, by line:
4.a. Year 1 same as 3c. Year 2 (.10 × 20 + .20 × 20 = 6.00)
4.b. Year 2 same as 3c. Year 1 (.20 × 30 + .25 × 10 = 8.50)
5.a. Year 2 divided by year 1 from line 4a, 6.00/5.00 = 1.20
5.b. Year 2 divided by year 1 from line 4b, 9.00/8.50 = 1.06
5.c. Year 2 is geometric mean of year 2 from the two lines above, $\sqrt{1.20 \times 1.06}$

year. The actual dollars spent on oranges, apples, and total fruit are shown on line 3 of the table. The expenditures, measured in fixed year 1 prices, are shown on line 4.a. This yields an increase in real GDP in year 2 (measured in the constant prices of year 1) of 20 percent, since the ratio of year 2 expenditures to year 1 expenditures ($6.00/$5.00) is 1.20. This gives us line 5.a, showing that real GDP, using year 1 prices, increases from 1.00 in year 1 to 1.20 in year 2.

But we get a different answer if we measure constant-dollar expenditures in each year using fixed year 2 prices. As shown on line 4.b, expenditures in year 2 increase from $8.50 to $9.00. This yields an increase in real GDP in year 2 (measured in the constant prices of year 2) of 6 percent, since the ratio of year 2 expenditures to year 1 expenditures ($9.00/$8.50) is 1.059. Why does this second method give us a lower estimate of the increase in real GDP? This occurs because year 2 prices are relatively lower for apples compared to oranges, and using year 2 prices places a lower importance on the big jump in apple consumption.

This example shows a general tendency—that choosing the prices of a later year tends to give us a lower increase in real GDP, since the later year places a lower valuation on the quantities that have increased most rapidly. This is particularly important in recent years in actual calculations of real GDP, since the prices of some goods, such as personal computers, TV sets, and telephone equipment, have been declining rapidly in contrast to continuous increases in the prices of many other goods and services.

The Chain-Weighted Calculation of Real GDP

Which is the correct measure of the increase in real GDP in this example? Is 20 percent correct or is 6 percent? The startling fact is that *there is no single answer to this question,* because the prices of each year are equally valid as alternative ways to value the quantities actually produced. A reasonable compromise is to average the two answers together. To do this, economists have long known that the best type of average is a geometric average, which is obtained by multiplying the two answers together and then taking the square root, that is:

$$\sqrt{1.20 \times 1.06} = 1.13.[1]$$

---

[1] Take a scientific calculator and check the answer for yourself. Multiplying 1.20 by 1.06 and then taking the square root yields an answer of 1.128. An alternative method to arrive at exactly the same answer is to take the natural logarithms of 1.20 and 1.06, which are 0.1823 and 0.0583, respectively, add them together (0.2406), divide by 2 (0.1203), and then take the antilogarithm (e^x) of the answer, yielding 1.128.

The United States now calculates real GDP using this technique of geometric averaging across hundreds of different types of products. The outcome is called chain-weighted real GDP, because the weights move forward from year to year. For instance, the percentage change in real GDP between 2007 and 2008 uses a geometric average of 2007 and 2008 price weights. Then the percentage change in real GDP between 2008 and 2009 shifts to a geometric average of 2008 and 2009 price weights. The resulting percentage changes are chained together into an index of real GDP, moving forward and backward from the base year of 2000.

The Implicit GDP Deflator

The method illustrated in line 5.c. of the table yields the chain-weighted measure of real GDP. The implicit GDP deflator is simply the ratio of nominal GDP to chain-weighted real GDP.

The implicit deflator, which is plotted in Figure 2-4 on p. 40, tells us the percentage ratio of prices actually charged in any single year (say, 1959) to the prices charged in the base year 2005. For instance, the implicit GDP deflator in 1959 was 18.3, the percentage ratio of actual nominal GDP ($506.6 billion) to real GDP, which is spending for the same year measured in 2000 prices (2,762.5 billion):

$$\frac{\text{implicit GDP}}{\text{deflator for 1959}} = 18.3 = 100 \times \left(\frac{506.6\text{ billion}}{2{,}762.5\text{ billion}} \right)$$

$$= 100 \times \left(\frac{\text{nominal GDP}}{\text{real GDP}} \right)$$

In words, this equation states that the implicit GDP deflator in 1959 was 18.3 because 1959 nominal GDP was 18.3 percent of the value of the 1959 real GDP. This percentage in turn reflects the fact that the average level of prices in 1959 was about one-fifth of the level of the base year 2005.

The rate of inflation is simply the percentage growth rate of the chain-weighted GDP deflator. The box on p. 41 explains how to calculate the growth rate of any magnitude.

Income and Interest Rates: The Keynesian Cross Model and the *IS* Curve

An honest man is one who knows that he can't consume more than he has produced.
— Ayn Rand, 1966

Our introduction to macroeconomics in Chapter 1 distinguished two main groups of issues: those that concern *short-run* business cycles and those that concern the economy's *long-run* growth rate. This chapter begins a two-part unit, spanning Chapters 3–10, that develops the theory of business cycles and examines the potential role of monetary and fiscal policy in dampening the amplitude of these cycles. Thus we will be concerned with the *short-run* behavior of the economy for the next several chapters and will return to the sources of *long-run* growth starting in Chapter 11.

3-1 Business Cycles and the Theory of Income Determination

As we learned in Chapter 1, a business cycle refers to the alternation of periods of rapid or slow growth in real GDP. In this chapter we start to learn about the origins of business cycles; we put together into a simple economic model the numerous factors that contribute to economic volatility.

The Volatile Business Cycle: The Global Economic Crisis Follows the Great Moderation

The goals of monetary and fiscal policy are to dampen business cycles and move toward an ideal world in which real GDP grows steadily from one quarter to the next. The real world as shown in Figure 3-1 is far from that ideal world. Plotted along the red line are changes in real GDP compared with the same quarter one year earlier. The four-quarter growth rate of real GDP has been as high as 12.6 percent in 1950 and as low as −3.9 percent in 2009.

Our first impression from Figure 3-1 is of relentless volatility in GDP growth, with a repeated pattern of ups and downs. Yet if we look more closely, we see that during the period between 1985 and 2007 real GDP growth showed remarkable steadiness, with only two mild recessions in 1990–91 and in 2001. The period of relatively steady growth during the 1986–2007 period has been called the "Great Moderation," and macroeconomists have debated its causes. Were shocks to the economy smaller, was policy managed better, or both?

Complacency about the Great Moderation was dashed after 2007 when the economy tumbled into the worst recession since the 1930s. The scale of the economic disaster that we call the Global Economic Crisis raised doubts whether

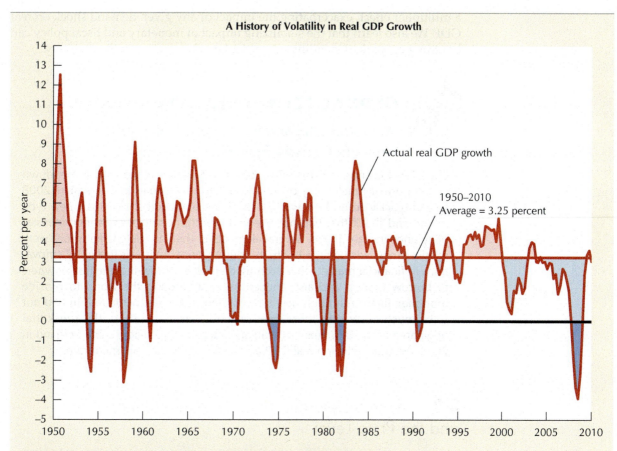

Figure 3-1 Real GDP Growth in the United States, 1950–2010
The shading shows that the growth in real GDP (plotted as the change from four quarters ago) can be divided up into three types of performance. The shaded red periods are when the actual growth rate was faster than the 61-year average of 3.25 percent. The shaded light blue periods are when the actual growth rate was slower than 3.25 percent but greater than zero. The shaded darker blue periods indicate periods of negative real GDP growth.

there had been any fundamental improvement in monetary or fiscal policy during the period of the Great Moderation. It seemed plausible in retrospect that the economy performed well in 1985–2007 because shocks were moderate, and that in 2008–09 the economy was hit by a set of new unanticipated shocks.

In this chapter we begin the process of identifying what some of those shocks may be. Among the candidates are changes in consumer confidence and business optimism, changes in prices of residential homes and in prices on the stock market, and changes in foreign demand for goods and services produced in the United States. These shocks to **aggregate demand** (also known as **demand shocks**) are the basic source of business cycle volatility.

Monetary and fiscal policy are intended to stabilize the economy but sometimes can be the source of additional shocks, due for instance to monetary policy decisions that set interest rates too high or too low, and fiscal policy changes, particularly in military expenditures. The model of income determination developed in this chapter and the next shows that demand shocks have

Aggregate demand is the total amount of desired spending expressed in current (nominal) dollars.

A **demand shock** is a significant change in desired spending by consumers, business firms, the government, or foreigners.

a multiplier effect, exacerbating the impact of any given demand shock on real GDP. We also learn that the stabilizing impact of monetary and fiscal policy can be strong or weak, depending on particular relationships in the economy.

GLOBAL ECONOMIC CRISIS FOCUS

What Were the Shocks That Made the 2008–09 Economic Crisis So Severe?

The Global Economic Crisis originated in U.S. financial markets. A meltdown in the normal functioning of these markets that began in September 2008 spread quickly around the world. This financial market shock was a new type of demand shock that had not been an important source of economic instability since the late 1920s. Several elements of the financial market shock were relatively new, including a boom in housing prices that was fueled by innovations in financial markets that both made it easy for low-income homeowners to borrow money, and also enticed investors around the world to provide mortgage finance through new types of financial investments that turned out to be much riskier than these investors had believed. In short, this shock that originated in the U.S. financial markets sharply reduced aggregate demand in 2008–09, thus reducing real GDP and raising the unemployment rate.

3-2 Income Determination, Unemployment, and the Price Level

Unemployment is the mirror image of business cycles in real GDP, or more precisely of changes in the gap between actual and natural real GDP (see Chapter 1, Figure 1-2). When that gap rises into positive territory as the economy expands, the unemployment rate falls; when that gap becomes negative as the economy slides into a recession, the unemployment rate rises. *Thus the key to understanding the causes of fluctuations in unemployment is to develop a theory of fluctuations in real GDP.* The unemployment rate was so high in the years after 2008 because the real GDP gap was so negative.

Income Determination and the Price Level

Shocks to aggregate demand can change either real GDP, the price level (GDP deflator), or both. Later we will learn that the division of changes in aggregate demand between changes in real GDP and the price level depends both on shocks to aggregate demand and to **aggregate supply,** the amount that firms are willing to produce at a given price level. In order to focus on changes in aggregate demand, we will make a bold but extremely useful simplifying assumption: *The price level is fixed in the short run.* Because the price level is fixed, *all changes in aggregate demand automatically cause changes in real GDP by the same amount in the same direction.*

Aggregate supply is the amount that firms are willing to produce at any given price level.

$$\text{Changes in Real GDP} = \frac{\text{Changes in Aggregate Demand}}{\text{Fixed Price Level}} \tag{3.1}$$

Many features of the real world support our assumption that the price level is fixed in the short run and that changes in aggregate demand are translated directly into changes in real GDP. Prices in restaurants are printed on menus that are expensive to reprint. Price labels for many products on supermarket shelves are changed infrequently. Prices in mail-order catalogues are set for the entire season until the next catalogue is printed. The most important cost for many business firms is the cost of the wages and salaries paid to workers, and the wage or salary level usually changes only once each year, and some wages are set by labor union contracts that last for as long as three years.

True, the prices of vegetables at the supermarket and of gasoline at the pump can change from day to day, but we gain insight by adhering to the useful simplification that all prices are like those in mail-order catalogues, fixed for a set period of time. Once we have used this simplification to learn about shocks to aggregate demand and the potential role of monetary and fiscal policy in stabilizing the economy, we then will be ready to allow the price level to change in response to aggregate demand and aggregate supply shocks.

What We Explain and What We Take as Given

Any theoretical model in economics sets limits on what it tries to explain. The limited number of variables to be explained are called **endogenous variables.** The large number of variables that are taken as given and are not explained are called **exogenous variables.**

In macroeconomic theory we begin with a short list of endogenous variables and treat most as exogenous. Gradually, we move some from the exogenous list to the endogenous list as our theory becomes more realistic. In the first part of Chapter 3, we develop a simple model that explains only two endogenous variables, consumption and real GDP. All the other important macroeconomic variables are not explained, that is, they are treated as exogenous variables.

Throughout our study of business cycles, the key instruments of monetary and fiscal policy will continue to be treated as exogenous, or taken as given. These include the money supply, government spending, and tax rates. Also taken as exogenous is the real GDP of foreign nations that determine the quantity of U.S. exports, as well as potential causes of demand shocks, such as changes in consumer and business confidence, and changes in the willingness of financial institutions to grant credit. Now we turn to the simplest version of the theory of income determination that treats only consumption and income (or real GDP) as endogenous and everything else as exogenous.

Endogenous variables are those explained by an economic theory.

Exogenous variables are those that are relevant but whose behavior the theory does not attempt to explain; their values are taken as given.

3-3 Planned Expenditure

Our study of national income accounting in Chapter 2 identified four types of expenditure on GDP. By definition, total expenditure on GDP (E) is equal to the sum of these four components: consumption (C), investment (I), government spending on goods and services (G), and net exports (NX).

$$E \equiv C + I + G + NX \qquad (3.2)$$

The Consumption Function

At the beginning, we treat only consumption spending (C) as endogenous, or explained by the theory, and treat the other three types of planned spending as exogenous. An obvious way to explain consumption is that people spend more when their incomes go up and vice versa. The income that matters for consumption decisions is income after taxes, or disposable personal income. This can be written as total real income (Y) minus personal taxes paid (T), or $Y - T$.[1]

How do households divide their disposable income between consumption and saving? Households consume a fixed amount that does not depend on their disposable income, plus a fraction of each dollar of disposable income:

An **autonomous magnitude** is independent of the level of income.

$$C = C_a + c(Y - T) \tag{3.3}$$

The **marginal propensity to consume** is the dollar change in consumption expenditures per dollar change in disposable income.

The fixed amount is called **autonomous** consumption, abbreviated (C_a), and this is completely independent of disposable income. The amount by which consumption expenditures increase for each extra dollar of disposable income is a fraction called the **marginal propensity to consume,** abbreviated (c). This equation (3.3) says, in words, that consumption spending (C) equals autonomous consumption (C_a) plus the marginal propensity to consume times disposable income [$c(Y - T)$]. Another name for this last term is **induced consumption.**

Induced consumption is the portion of consumption spending that responds to changes in income.

The consumption function can also be shown graphically, as in Figure 3-2. The thick red line shows on the vertical axis the amount of consumption for

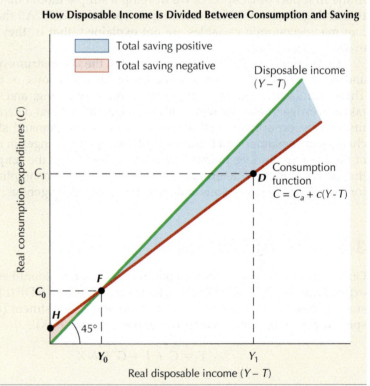

Figure 3-2 A Simple Hypothesis Regarding Consumption Behavior

The red line passing through F and D illustrates the consumption function. It shows that consumption is the marginal propensity to consume (c) times (C_a) disposable income plus an autonomous component of that is spent regardless of the level of disposable income. The blue-shaded area shows the amount of positive saving that occurs when income exceeds consumption; the pink area shows the amount of negative saving (dissaving) that occurs when consumption exceeds income.

How Disposable Income Is Divided Between Consumption and Saving

Total saving positive
Total saving negative

Disposable income $(Y - T)$

Real consumption expenditures (C)

Consumption function $C = C_a + c(Y - T)$

Real disposable income $(Y - T)$

---

[1] The notation T in this chapter continues, as in Chapter 2, to mean "total taxes minus transfer payments."

alternative values of disposable income (measured along the horizontal axis). The line slopes upward from point H to point F to point D, because higher real disposable income along the horizontal axis raises real consumption expenditure along the vertical axis. When income $(Y - T)$ is zero, consumption is a positive number (C_a).

For instance, autonomous consumption (C_a) might be $500 billion at point H. Let's assume the marginal propensity to consume (c) is 0.75. If income at point Y_0 is $2,000 billion, then consumption at point F is $500 billion plus 0.75 times $2,000 billion, or $2,000 billion. Similarly, if income at point Y_1 is $8,000, then consumption is 500 plus 0.75 times 8,000, or $6,500 billion at point D.

SELF-TEST

1. If a person's disposable income is zero, what is that person's level of consumption spending in equation (3.3)?

2. How can that person consume a positive amount with a zero disposable income? Think of yourself—what options are open to you to buy something even if you have no income?

Induced Saving and the Marginal Propensity to Save

The simplest way to show the amount of saving is to use a graph like Figure 3-2. The thick green line shows the amount of disposable income in both a horizontal and a vertical direction; this line is often called the "45-degree" line. Since the thick red line shows the consumption function, the distance between the two lines indicates the total amount of saving.

To the right of point F, total saving is positive because disposable income exceeds consumption; this is indicated by the blue shading. To the left of point F, total saving is negative because consumption exceeds disposable income; this is indicated by the pink shading. How can saving be negative? Individuals can consume more than they earn, at least for a while, by withdrawing funds from a savings account, by selling stocks and bonds, or by borrowing. Negative saving is quite typical for many college students who borrow to finance their education.

The blue shaded vertical distance between the green and red lines represents personal saving (S), that is, the difference between disposable income and consumption:[2]

$$S = Y - T - C = Y - T - C_a - c(Y - T)$$
$$= -C_a + (1 - c)(Y - T) \tag{3.4}$$

---

[2] Be careful to distinguish "savings" (with a terminal "s"), which is the *stock* of assets that households have in savings accounts or under the mattress, from "saving" (without a terminal "s"), which is the *flow* per unit of time that leaks out of disposable income and is unavailable for purchases of consumption goods. It is the flow of *saving* that is designated by the symbol S. For review, see the definitions of flows and stocks on pp. 25–26.

This *saving function* starts with the definition of saving as personal disposable income minus consumption; then it substitutes the consumption function from equation (3.3). The last line simplifies the saving function, which now states that personal saving equals minus the amount of autonomous consumption $(-C_a)$ plus the **marginal propensity to save** $(1 - c)$ times disposable income $(Y - T)$.

Marginal propensity to save is the change in personal saving induced by a $1 change in personal disposable income. It can be abbreviated as $1 - c$ or as s.

◆ SELF-TEST

1. Can you derive a general expression showing how the level of consumption and disposable income at point *F* depend on autonomous consumption (C_a) and the marginal propensity to consume (c)?

2. If disposable income in Figure 3-2 is between points Y_0 and Y_1, then is saving positive or negative?

Autonomous Consumption, the Interest Rate, Asset Values, and Financial Markets

Thus far we have seen that the total amount of consumption spending will change if there is a change in income, but also if any factor causes a change in autonomous consumption (C_a). What are these factors? One of the most important is the interest rate; as we learn in the last part of this chapter, autonomous consumption rises when the interest rate falls and vice versa. Low interest rates in 2001–04 stimulated consumption of automobiles and houses. Similarly, the increase of interest rates in 2004–06 put a squeeze on consumer purchases of cars and houses, and by 2007 many households that could not afford the higher interest rates charged on their mortgages were "foreclosed" by banks, meaning that they were forced to move out of their homes due to their inability to pay the higher monthly mortgage interest payments.

The second major factor affecting autonomous consumption is **household wealth.** This consists of all the assets of households, particularly the market value of houses, stocks, bonds, and bank accounts, minus any mortgage loans, credit card balances, or other liabilities. When wealth increases, households can spend more even if their income is fixed, thus boosting autonomous consumption and reducing saving.

Household wealth is the total value of household assets, including the market value of homes, possessions such as automobiles, and financial assets such as stocks, bonds, and bank accounts, minus any liabilities, including outstanding mortgage and credit card debt, automobile loans, and other loans.

The third major factor affecting autonomous consumption is the set of financial market institutions that determine whether a household finds it easy or hard to get loans to buy houses, cars, and other major purchases like large flat-screen TVs. Loans were very easy to obtain in 2001–06 for reasons that we will study in Chapter 5. Then conditions in financial markets turned around radically in 2007–08, making loans difficult or impossible to obtain. Since purchases of houses and cars are much too expensive for households to pay cash for the entire purchase, loans from financial institutions are crucial to the functioning of the industries that supply houses, cars, and other "big-ticket" items.

GLOBAL ECONOMIC CRISIS FOCUS

Financial Market Instability as the Main Cause of the Global Economic Crisis

The Global Economic Crisis originated in U.S. financial markets. During the period 2001–07, financial innovations made it much easier for low-income families to obtain mortgage loans. Rising housing prices allowed families at all income levels to raise the size of the mortgage indebtedness on the basis of the increased value of their homes, and they obtained large amounts of cash ("cashing out" through home equity withdrawal) by paying off a mortgage for say $200,000 and replacing it with a new mortgage of $250,000. When housing prices came crashing down after 2006, borrowers could no longer refinance their mortgages and often found themselves "under water," owing more than their home was worth. This was just one element in the financial market instability that created the largest negative demand shock since the 1930s.

3-4 The Economy In and Out of Equilibrium

Until now, we have seen that the level of consumption spending depends both on autonomous consumption and on disposable income. But so far we have no idea what the level of income will actually be. We need an extra element, besides the consumption function, to construct our theory of income determination.

This extra element is the distinction between planned (i.e., desired) spending and unplanned (i.e., unwanted spending). Recall that the four components of total expenditure are consumption *(C)*, investment *(I)*, government spending on goods and services *(G)*, and net exports *(NX)*. Copying equation (3.2) from page 57, we can write:

$$E \equiv C + I + G + NX$$

Of these four components of E, we assume that spending on C, G, and NX is always the planned amount. Only investment can be either planned (I_p) or unplanned (I_u).

The key extra element in our theory of income determination is that business firms will adjust production until unplanned investment is eliminated. If unplanned investment is positive ($I_u > 0$), output will be reduced. If unplanned investment is negative ($I_u < 0$), output will be increased. There is no pressure for change in output only when the economy is in equilibrium, which occurs only when output (Y) equals planned expenditure (E_p), that is when Y = E_p. Thus, output must be equal to:

$$E_p = C + I_p + G + NX \qquad (3.5)$$

The four components of expenditure in equation (3.5) are exactly the same as in equation (3.2), except that we use a subscript p for investment. We do not need a subscript p for C, G, or NX, since the actual amount of spending is always the amount planned.

How Changes in Wealth Influence Consumer Spending

We have seen that there are three main factors that can alter autonomous consumption (C_a). These are changes in interest rates, in household wealth, or in the ease or difficulty of obtaining loans from financial markets. If any of these factors raise autonomous consumption, it reduces the personal saving rate, that is, the ratio of the amount households save to their disposable personal income. In this box we learn more about household wealth and see that its fluctuations help to understand why households do not always save a fixed fraction of their disposable income. This implies that variations in household wealth can create an *aggregate demand shock* that aggravates business cycle fluctuations.

Household wealth is defined in the text as the value of household assets minus household liabilities. The left graph plots the components of household wealth since 1970 as a percentage of disposable income. The upper blue line shows "twin peaks" in the ratio of total assets to disposable income first in 1999 and again in 2006. The upward movement of the blue line in the late 1990s

reflects the "dot.com" stock market bubble. The sharp decline in wealth in 1999 to 2002 echoes the collapse of stock prices during that period, while the second upward movement from 2002 to 2006 reflects the combined impact of a revival in the stock market plus the sharp rise in house prices during that period.

Changes in stock prices are often measured by the Standard and Poor's 500-stock index. By this measure the percent log increase in stock prices was 60 percent between February 2003 and October 2007, followed by a decline of 71 percent from then until the monthly trough in March 2009. Adding to instability in household wealth was the sharp 82 percent increase in the Case-Shiller house price index between January 2000 and April 2006, followed by a 40 percent decline from then until the housing price trough in May 2009.

To obtain household net wealth or net worth, we must subtract out the amount that households owe in the form of debt on home mortgages, auto loans, credit cards, and other forms of credit. The red line in the

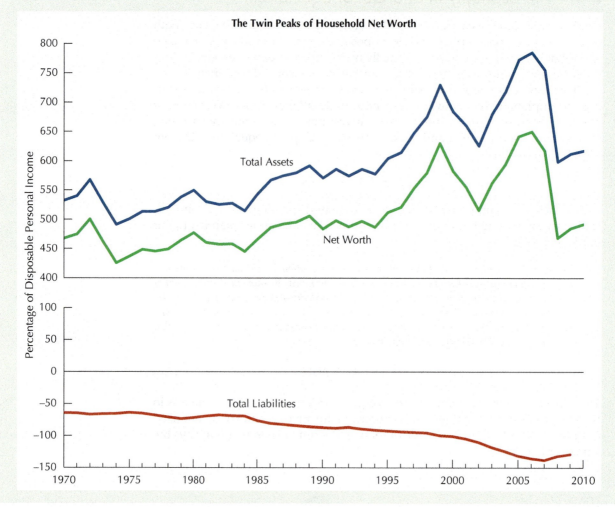

The Twin Peaks of Household Net Worth

bottom frame of the graph shows that household liabilities have become steadily larger over the past three decades, rising from 70 percent of disposable income in 1984 to 138 percent in 2007 and then declining slightly to 129 percent in 2009. Because liabilities are *subtracted* from total assets in order to compute net worth, the red line displays the percentage of liabilities to disposable income as an ever-growing negative number.

When we subtract the red line from the blue line, we obtain the green net worth line, which mimics the twin peaks of the blue total asset line. Between 2006 and 2009 the net worth ratio to disposable income fell from 650 to 490 percent. Put another way, if households had the same net worth ratio as in 2006, in 2009 their net worth would have been $1.7 trillion higher than it actually was. That difference comes out at $149,000 per household! No wonder that this enormous loss of wealth dragged down consumer spending in 2008–10.

The right graph plots the same green net worth line against the personal saving rate, with the values of the net worth ratio shown along the right vertical axis. Whenever an increase in asset prices raises autonomous consumption, as in the late 1990s and 2003–06, then we would expect the personal saving rate to decline. And this is just what is shown in the same graph, where the personal saving rate is plotted against the left scale.

The saving rate declined from a peak of 10.9 percent in 1982 to 1.4 percent in 2005. As we have seen, a rising value of household net worth tends to increase autonomous consumption relative to income, and so the stock market boom of the late 1990s contributed to this decline in the saving rate. Then the housing bubble of 2001–06 created further increases in household wealth, contributing to the decline of the saving rate between 2000 and 2005. Rising housing prices allowed people to refinance their mortgages, withdrawing cash that would allow them to increase their consumption spending even if their income had not increased.

Finally the party came to an end in 2006 when housing prices stopped rising and began to fall, and further after October 2007 when stock prices began their precipitous decline of 50 percent. Households could no longer raise their consumption faster than the increase in their disposable income by "cashing out" through mortgage refinance. Since the conditions of easy credit that had lowered the household saving rate before 2007 had ended, it was not surprising to find that the tighter credit conditions and ending of "cash-out mortgage equity withdrawal" raised the saving rate in 2008 and 2009. Now consumption was growing slower than personal disposable income, worsening the 2008–09 recession and then holding back the pace of the recovery that began in 2009. Just as our theory predicts, the personal saving rate bounced back as a result of the sharp decline in household net worth, from 1.4 percent in 2005 to 5.9 percent in 2009 and 5.9 percent again in 2010.

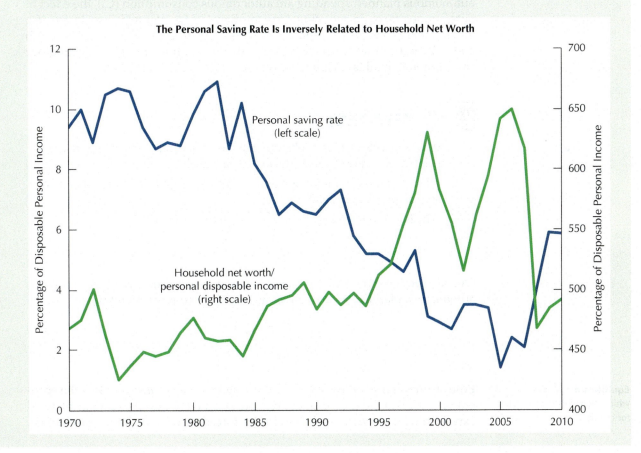

The Personal Saving Rate Is Inversely Related to Household Net Worth

The next step is to combine the consumption function from equation (3.3) with the definition of planned expenditure from equation (3.5):

$$E_p = C_a + c(Y - T) + I_p + G + NX \qquad (3.6)$$

In words, this states that planned expenditure equals autonomous consumption, plus induced consumption, plus the fixed values of planned investment, government spending, and net exports.

A **parameter** is a value taken as given or known within a particular analysis.

The word **parameter** means something that is taken as given, including not only exogenous variables but also fixed elements of a function. In the case of the consumption function, there are two such fixed elements (C_a and c), and we will take both as given. In addition, the three components of planned expenditure other than consumption (I_p, G, and NX) can be considered as both exogenous variables and parameters.

Autonomous Planned Spending

It helps to simplify the subsequent analysis if we take all the elements of equation (3.6) that do not depend on total income (Y) and call them *autonomous planned spending* (A_p):

$$A_p = E_p - cY = C_a - cT_a + I_p + G + NX \qquad (3.7)$$

In words, this states that autonomous planned spending consists of all the components of planned spending that do not depend on income, that is, excluding induced consumption (cY). To summarize, the five components of autonomous planned spending are autonomous consumption (C_a), the effect of autonomous taxes in reducing consumption ($-cT_a$), planned investment (I_p), government spending (G), and net exports (NX). In comparing equations (3.6) and (3.7), notice that we have replaced the tax component (T_a), reflecting our assumption that all taxes are autonomous.

 SELF-TEST

1. Why is I_p written with a p subscript, but the other components of autonomous planned spending (C_a, $-cT_a$, G, and NX) are not?
2. Why does the (cT_a) term appear with a minus sign but all the other sums appear with a plus sign?
3. Why is T_a multiplied by c but the other terms are not?

Overall, we have learned that total planned expenditure (E_p) has two parts, autonomous planned spending (A_p) and induced consumption (cY).

$$E_p = A_p + cY \qquad (3.8)$$

When Is the Economy in Equilibrium?

Equilibrium is a state in which there exists no pressure for change.

Equilibrium is *a situation in which there is no pressure for change.* When the economy is *out of equilibrium*, production and income are out of line with planned expenditure, and business firms will be forced to raise or lower production.

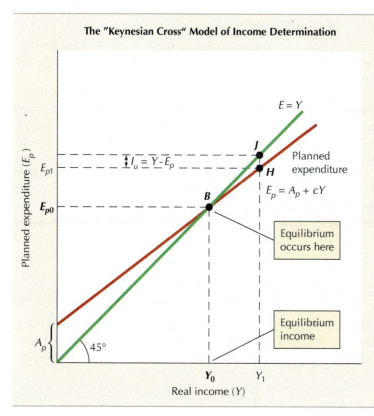

The "Keynesian Cross" Model of Income Determination

Planned expenditure (E_p)

E_{p1}

$I_u = Y - E_p$

E_{p0}

A_p

45°

$E = Y$

J

H

Planned expenditure

$E_p = A_p + cY$

B

Equilibrium occurs here

Equilibrium income

Y_0 Y_1

Real income (Y)

Figure 3-3 How Equilibrium Income Is Determined

The economy is in equilibrium at point B, where the red planned expenditure (E_p) line crosses the 45-degree income line. At any other level of income, the economy is out of equilibrium, causing pressure on business firms to increase or reduce production and income.

When the economy is *in equilibrium,* production and income are equal to planned expenditure, and on the average, business firms are happy to continue the current level of production.

This idea is illustrated in Figure 3-3. The thick green line, as in Figure 3-2, has a slope of 45 degrees; everywhere along it the level of income plotted on the horizontal axis is equal to the level of expenditure plotted on the vertical axis. Hence the green line is labeled $E = Y$. The red line is the total level of planned expenditures (E_p) given by equation (3.8), namely, A_p plus cY.

The "Keynesian Cross" Model In and Out of Equilibrium

Only where the green and red lines cross at point B is income equal to planned expenditure, with no pressure for change. Because the economy is in equilibrium at the crossing point of the green 45-degree line and the red planned expenditure line, this theory of income determination is often called the "Keynesian Cross" model after the great English economist John Maynard Keynes. We learn more about Keynes in Chapter 8, where you will find his photo on p. 249.

The economy is in equilibrium at point B in Figure 3-3 because households and business firms want to spend E_{p0} when income is Y_0. And this amount of income is created by the E_{p0} of production of the goods and services that households and firms want to buy.[3]

---

[3] Note that the horizontal axis in Figure 3-3 is income (Y) rather than disposable income ($Y - T$) as in Figure 3-2. This reflects our assumption that taxes are autonomous and are included in A_p on the vertical axis.

What Happens Out of Equilibrium?

The economy is out of equilibrium at all points other than *B* along the 45-degree line. For instance, at point *J*, income is Y_1. How much do households and business firms want to spend when income is Y_1?

The vertical position of the red E_p line at point *H* shows that planned expenditures fall short of income (shown along the green line) by the distance *JH*. Since the amount *J* is being produced but only *H* is being purchased, the remaining production is being accumulated as **unintended inventory investment,** which is the same thing as unplanned investment (I_u). Production and income will be cut until this discrepancy disappears and the unwanted inventory buildup ceases $(I_u = 0)$. This occurs only when the economy arrives at *B*. Only at *B* are businesses producing exactly the amount that is demanded.

Unintended inventory investment is the amount business firms are forced to accumulate when planned expenditure is less than income.

At point *J*, as in every situation, income and actual expenditure are equal by definition:

$$\text{income } (Y) \equiv \text{expenditure } (E)$$
$$\equiv \text{planned expenditure } (E_p) +$$
$$\text{unintended inventory investment } (I_u) \qquad (3.9)$$

By contrast, the economy is in equilibrium only when unintended inventory accumulation or decumulation is equal to zero $(I_u = 0)$. When we substitute $(I_u = 0)$ into the equation (3.9), we obtain the economy's equilibrium situation:

$$Y = E_p \qquad (3.10)$$

Table 3-1   Comparison of the Economy's "Always True" and Equilibrium Situations

	Always true by definition	True only in equilibrium
1. What concept of expenditure is equal to income?	Actual expenditure including unintended inventory accumulation	Planned expenditure
2. Amount of unintended inventory investment (I_u)	Can be any amount, positive or negative	Must be zero
3. Which equation is valid, (3.9) or (3.10)?	(3.9) $Y = E = E_p + I_u$	(3.10) $Y = E_p$
4. Where does the economy operate in Figure 3-3?	Any point on 45-degree income line (example: point *J*)	Only at point *B* where E_p line crosses 45-degree income line
5. Example in Figure 3-3 of nonequilibrium and equilibrium situations.	At point *J*, $Y_1 = E_{p1} + I_{u1}$	At point *B*, $Y_0 = E_{p0}$

Table 3-1 summarizes the differences between what is always true and what is true only in equilibrium.

SELF-TEST

1. What happens in Figure 3-3 when income is an amount less than Y_0?
2. Describe the forces that move the economy back to equilibrium at *B*.

Determining Equilibrium Real GDP

How do we calculate the equilibrium level of real GDP? We have already used one method by drawing the Keynesian Cross diagram as in Figure 3-4. However, it is much faster to calculate equilibrium real GDP using a simple equation. We start with the definition of equilibrium in equation (3.10), that income (Y) is equal to planned expenditure (E_p), and we combine it with the definition from equation (3.8) that planned expenditure is equal to autonomous planned spending (A_p) plus induced consumption (cY):

$$Y = A_p + cY$$

Then we subtract induced consumption from both sides of this equation and obtain:

$$(1 - c)Y = A_p \tag{3.11}$$

Because the marginal propensity to save equals 1.0 minus the marginal propensity to consume ($s = 1 - c$), we can rewrite (3.11) as

$$sY = A_p \tag{3.12}$$

This states that **induced saving** (sY) equals autonomous planned spending. Now it is easy to solve for equilibrium income by dividing both sides of equation (3.12) by the marginal propensity to save (s):

$$Y = \frac{A_p}{s} \tag{3.13}$$

Induced saving is the portion of saving that responds to changes in income.

3-5 The Multiplier Effect

Our conclusion thus far that equilibrium income occurs at point B in Figure 3-3 depends on the assumption that autonomous planned spending is a particular amount designated A_{p0}. To illustrate the effect of a change in A_p, we shall assume that business firms become more optimistic and increase their investment spending from A_{p0} to a higher amount A_{p1}.

Calculating the Multiplier

We can use equation (3.13) to calculate the equilibrium level of income in the new and old situations. Note that only A_p changes; there is no change in the marginal propensity to save (s).

$$\begin{array}{lll} \text{Take new situation} & Y_1 = \dfrac{A_{p1}}{s} \\[2ex] \text{Subtract old situation} & Y_0 = \dfrac{A_{p0}}{s} \\[1ex] \hline \\[-1ex] \text{Equals change in income} & \Delta Y = \dfrac{\Delta A_p}{s} & (3.14) \end{array}$$

The top line of the table calculates the new level of income. The second line calculates the original level of income. The change in income, abbreviated ΔY, is simply the first line minus the second. The **multiplier** (k) is defined as the ratio of the change in income (ΔY) to the change in planned autonomous spending (ΔA_p) that causes it:

$$\text{multiplier } (k) = \frac{\Delta Y}{\Delta A_p} = \frac{1}{s} \tag{3.15}$$

The **multiplier** is the ratio of the change in output to the change in autonomous planned spending that causes it. It is also 1.0 divided by the marginal propensity to save.

In Figure 3-4 we can see why the multiplier (k) is $1/s$. Figure 3-4 reproduces from Figure 3-3 the original situation, with planned autonomous spending at its original level of A_{p0}.

Because only 25 percent of extra income is saved, income must rise by $1/s$ times the rise in A_p to generate the required extra amount of induced saving. In terms of the line segments:

$$\text{multiplier } (k) = \frac{\Delta Y}{\Delta A_p} = \frac{RJ}{RB} = \frac{1}{s} \left(\text{since } s = \frac{RB}{RJ} \right)$$

Example of the Multiplier Effect in Action

How does the magic of the multiplier work? An answer is provided by a real-life example. Let us consider Southwest Airlines' decision in 2010 to increase planned investment with the purchase of $4 billion of Boeing 737 aircraft. Initially the $4 billion of new investment spending would raise income by the $4 billion earned by Boeing workers in Seattle, where the aircraft plant is located. But, using our previous example of a marginal propensity to consume (c) of 0.75, the Boeing workers would soon spend 0.75 of the $4 billion, or $3 billion, on goods and services at Seattle stores. The stores would have to reorder $3 billion of additional goods, causing production and income to rise at plants all over the country that supply the goods to the stores in Seattle. Workers at these supplying plants also have a marginal propensity to consume of 0.75, adding another $2.25 billion of spending and income. So far, in the first three rounds of spending, income has gone up by $4.0 billion plus $3.0 billion

Figure 3-4 The Change in Equilibrium Income Caused by a $500 Billion Increase in Autonomous Planned Spending

The increase in autonomous planned spending (A_p) is shown by the increase in the vertical intercept of the red planned expenditures line from A_{p0} to A_{p1}, as shown in the lower left corner of the diagram. The upward shift in the red line moves the equilibrium position where the red planned expenditures line crosses the green 45-degree line from point B to point J. This change in A_p has a multiplier effect, raising real income from Y_0 to Y_1.

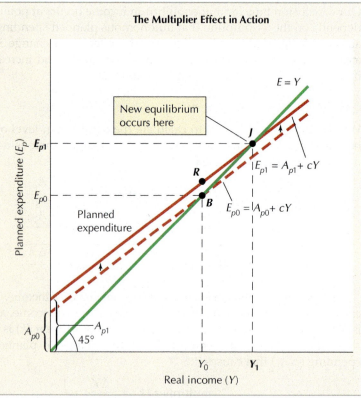

The Multiplier Effect in Action

plus $2.25 billion, or $9.25 billion. But the process continues, as induced consumption is increased in each successive round of spending. Eventually, the total increase in income will be four times the initial increase in planned investment, or $16 billion (= $4 billion times 1/0.25).[4]

3-6   Sources of Shifts in Planned Spending

Is a multiplier expansion or contraction of output following a change in autonomous planned spending desirable or not? In Chapter 1 *natural real GDP* was defined as the desirable level of real GDP. Thus, whenever actual real GDP declines below natural real GDP, this creates job losses for workers and an increase in unemployment, just as occurred recently in 2008–09. Policymakers attempt to avoid any decline in actual real GDP below natural real GDP.

What might cause actual real GDP to decline below the desired level? A drop in planned investment, a major component of A_p, can be and has been a major cause of actual real-world recessions and depressions. In the Great Depression, for instance, fixed investment dropped by 81 percent, and this contributed to the 27 percent decline in actual real GDP between 1929 and 1933.

The most important point of this section is that there are five components of autonomous planned spending, as in equation (3.7), and any of these can change. Real GDP can increase or decrease through a multiplier response to changes in autonomous consumption, planned investment, and net exports, an example of the "demand shocks" that create business cycles. At least in principle, if it can act fast enough, the government can offset any undesirable shift in autonomous consumption, planned investment, or net exports by creating an offsetting movement in autonomous planned spending *in the opposite direction* through its control over government spending and autonomous taxes.

---

[4] It is possible to use an algebraic trick to prove that the sum of ΔA_p plus the induced consumption at each round of spending is exactly equal to the multiplier $\dfrac{1}{1-c}$ times ΔA_p. The first round of consumption is $c\Delta A_p$. The second is c times the first, $c(c\Delta A_p)$, or $c^2 A_p$. Thus the total ΔY is the series of all the infinite number of rounds of spending:

$$\Delta Y = \Delta A_p + c\Delta A_p + c^2\Delta A_p + \cdots + c^\infty \Delta A_p \tag{a}$$

Factor out the common element ΔA_p on the right-hand side of equation (a):

$$\Delta Y = \Delta A_p(1.0 + c + c^2 + \cdots + c^\infty) \tag{b}$$

Multiply both sides of equation (b) by $-c$:

$$-c\Delta Y = \Delta A_p(-c - c^2 - \cdots - c^\infty) \tag{c}$$

The difference between lines (b) and (c) is

$$(1 - c)\Delta Y = \Delta A_p \tag{d}$$

We can neglect the c^∞ term, since any fraction raised to the infinity power is zero. Dividing both sides of equation (d) by $(1 - c)$, we obtain the familiar:

$$\Delta Y = \frac{\Delta A_p}{1 - c} = \frac{\Delta A_p}{s}$$

Government Spending and Taxation

Equation (3.7) states that autonomous planned spending equals the sum of its five components. It also implies that the *change* in autonomous planned spending equals the sum of the *change* in each of the same five components. We can state this as an equation if we insert the "change" symbol, Δ, in front of each element in equation (3.7). The only remaining element without a Δ symbol is the marginal propensity to consume (c), which we are assuming to be fixed:

$$\Delta A_p = \Delta C_a - c\Delta T_a + \Delta I_p + \Delta G + \Delta NX \tag{3.16}$$

In sum, the five causes of changes in A_p are:

1. A \$1 change in autonomous consumption (C_a) changes A_p by \$1 in the same direction.
2. A \$1 change in autonomous tax revenue (T_a) changes A_p by c (the marginal propensity to consume) times \$1 *in the opposite direction.*
3. A \$1 change in planned investment (I_p) changes A_p by \$1 in the same direction.
4. A \$1 change in government spending (G) changes A_p by \$1 in the same direction.
5. A \$1 change in net exports (NX) changes A_p by \$1 in the same direction.

Once the change in A_p has been calculated from this list, our basic multiplier expression from equation (3.14) determines the resulting change in equilibrium income:

$$\Delta Y = \frac{\Delta A_p}{s} \tag{3.14}$$

The multiplier, as written in equation (3.15), is *1/s*. If the marginal propensity to save *(s)* is for example equal to 0.25, then the multiplier is 4.0. A \$1 change in any component of A_p on the list above will raise Y by four times as much.

SELF-TEST

1. Notice that there is no Δ in front of the *c* in equation (3.16). Why?
2. Notice that there is no Δ in front of the *s* in equation (3.14). Why?
3. How is *s* defined in terms of *c*?

Fiscal Expansion

Let's say that in Figure 3-4 the higher real income level Y_1 is the desired level but the economy is stuck at Y_0, which is too low. Say the desired level of real income at Y_1 is \$8,000 billion and the actual level at Y_0 is only 6,000. To stimulate the extra \$2,000 of real income, policymakers can use the multiplier formula. If the multiplier is 4.0, policymakers need to raise planned autonomous spending by ¼ of \$2,000 billion. *Thus, an increase in government expenditures of \$500 billion will deliver the required boost to real income and real GDP of \$2,000 billion because the multiplier is assumed to be 4.0.* If the multiplier were higher, less extra government spending would be needed. If the multiplier were lower, more extra government spending would be needed.

The needed increase in A_p can also be achieved by a cut in tax revenue. Since a reduction in autonomous taxes ΔT_a is multiplied by the marginal propensity to consume, 0.75 in our example, then to achieve an increase in A_p of \$500 billion, tax revenue must be reduced by \$500 billion divided by 0.75, or \$667 billion.

The Government Budget Deficit and Its Financing

Any change in government expenditure or tax revenue has consequences for the government's budget. The government budget surplus has already been linked to other key magnitudes in Section 2-5 on p. 35 as the magic equation. Tax revenue minus government expenditure, $(T - G)$, by definition equals investment plus net exports minus private saving.[5]

$$T - G \equiv I + NX - S$$

Similarly, the change in the left side of the magic equation must balance the change in the right side:

$$\Delta T - \Delta G \equiv \Delta I + \Delta NX - \Delta S \tag{3.17}$$

When the government boosts its spending, autonomous consumption, investment, and net exports are fixed ($\Delta C_a = \Delta I = \Delta NX = 0$) and that tax revenue remains at zero ($\Delta T = 0$). Thus the only elements of (3.17) that are changing are ΔS and ΔG. The value of ΔG is the fiscal stimulus. But what is the value of ΔS? Saving changes by the marginal propensity to save times the change in disposable income, $\Delta S = s(\Delta Y - \Delta T)$. Using this expression for saving, we can substitute the numbers for this example into equation (3.17) and obtain:

$$\Delta T - \Delta G = \Delta I + \Delta NX - s(\Delta Y - \Delta T)$$
$$0 - \Delta G = 0 + 0 - s(\Delta Y - 0)$$

The increase in output induces extra saving. Each extra dollar of saving is available for households to purchase the government bonds that the government must sell to finance its government budget deficit. The payoff of this government deficit is the boost in income needed to raise income to its desired amount.

The Tax Multiplier

As an alternative to stimulating the economy by raising government spending by \$500 billion, it could choose to reduce autonomous taxes by \$667 billion. As we have seen, these two actions have exactly the same effect, which is to boost autonomous planned spending by \$500 billion and to raise income through the multiplier effect by \$2,000 billion.

The tax multiplier is $-c/s$ or -3.0 in our example, compared to a multiplier of $1/s$ or 4.0 for government spending and the other components of autonomous planned spending. The tax multiplier is less simply because taxes are not part of expenditures; taxes change expenditures only by the amount they change consumption.

---

[5] See equation (2.6) on p. 35. Page 36 also provides examples of the real-world values of the magic equation for the years 1993, 2000, and 2010.

SELF-TEST

1. If government spending is reduced by $500 billion and the marginal propensity to save is 0.25, how much does total saving change?
2. What is the government doing when it runs a surplus, and how do private savers react?
3. If taxes are raised by $667 billion and marginal propensity to save is 0.25, how much does saving change? How do private households pay for the higher taxes?

The Balanced Budget Multiplier

In the previous example, the government could boost income by $2,000 billion either by raising government spending by $500 billion or by cutting taxes by $667 billion. Yet either method would create a large increase in the government deficit, which may be undesirable. Yet, surprisingly, the government can stimulate the economy even if it needs to maintain a balanced budget. To see this, we simply add the multipliers for government spending ($k = 1/s$) and that for a change in taxes (*tax change multiplier* $= -c/s$):

$$\text{Balanced budget multiplier} = \frac{1}{s} + \frac{-c}{s} = \frac{1-c}{s} = 1.0 \qquad (3.18)$$

This states that the multiplier for a balanced-budget fiscal expansion is always 1.0, no matter what the value of *c!* Why? The positive multiplier occurs because one dollar of government spending raises autonomous planned expenditure by exactly one dollar, whereas the extra dollar of taxes only reduces autonomous planned expenditure by *c* times one dollar, and *c* (the marginal propensity to consume) is normally substantially less than unity. Thus, the government can achieve any desired increase in income and real GDP by a sufficiently large increase in government spending accompanied by exactly the same increase in tax rates.[6]

3-7 How Can Monetary Policy Affect Planned Spending?

Thus far fiscal policy seems to be the only tool that the government can use to fight against demand shocks caused by changes in autonomous consumption, planned investment, and net exports. Where does monetary policy fit in? Now we are ready to drop our simplifying but unrealistic assumption that autonomous consumption and planned investment are exogenous. In the next two sections we learn how and why interest rates can influence planned autonomous spending, raising spending when interest rates are low as in years such as 2001–04 and cutting spending in years when interest rates are high such as 1981 and 1989.

---

[6] The appendix to this chapter shows that this simple expression for the balanced budget multiplier does not apply to a more realistic world in which tax revenues and imports depend on income.

Functions of Interest Rates

Interest rates help the economy allocate saving among alternative uses. For savers, the interest rate is a reward for abstaining from consumption and waiting to consume at some future time. The higher the interest rate, the greater the incentive to save. For borrowers, the interest rate is the cost of borrowing funds to invest or buy consumption goods. At a higher interest rate, people will borrow fewer funds and purchase fewer goods.

Interest rates are central to the role of monetary policy. Since the government, through the Federal Reserve Board (the Fed), can influence the interest rate, it can affect the cost of borrowed funds to private borrowers.

Types of Interest Rates

Banks offer a variety of interest rates on checking and savings accounts. Some types of accounts allow customers to earn interest instantly; others require customers to leave funds on deposit for a year or more. The phrase "short-term interest rate" refers to interest that is paid on funds deposited for three months or less; "long-term interest rate" refers to interest on funds deposited for a year or more.

In addition to short-term interest rates on bank deposits, there are short-term interest rates that apply to funds borrowed by the government (the Treasury bill rate), by businesses (the commercial paper rate), and by banks (the federal funds rate). Similarly, in addition to long-term rates on bank deposits, there are long-term interest rates that apply to funds borrowed by the government (the Treasury bond rate), by businesses (the corporate bond rate), and by households (the mortgage rate).

The hallmark of a good theory is its ability to spotlight important relationships and to ignore unnecessary details. For most purposes, the differences between alternative interest rates fall into that category of detail, in contrast to the important overall *average* level of interest rates. Thus "the" interest rate discussed in this chapter can be regarded as an average of all the different interest rates listed in the previous paragraph.

3-8   The Relation of Autonomous Planned Spending to the Interest Rate

Business firms attempt to profit by borrowing funds to buy investment goods—office buildings, shopping centers, factories, machine tools, computers, airplanes. Obviously, firms can stay in business only if the earnings of investment goods are at least enough to pay the interest on the borrowed funds (or to attract enough investors to warrant a new issue of stock). The lower the interest rate, the more investment goods firms will buy. The higher is the interest rate, the fewer investment goods firms will buy.

Autonomous consumption (C_a) depends on the interest rate, just as does planned investment spending. Households will buy new cars more often—and will purchase bigger and more expensive cars—if the interest rate is low because this reduces the monthly payment for any given car. Similarly, high interest rates on car loans will force some households to buy smaller cars or to buy a used car instead of a new car. Overall, both planned investment and autonomous consumption are negatively related to the interest rate.

A Central Explanation of Business Cycles Is the Volatility of Investment

Figure 3-5 displayed at the bottom of page 75 shows that both planned autonomous spending and real income depend negatively on the interest rate. This negative relationship allows monetary policy to change interest rates as needed to stabilize the economy. Yet Figure 3-5 contains another lesson. An economic downturn can happen if there is a decline in autonomous planned spending at a given interest rate, shifting leftward both the A_p demand schedule and, with a multiplier effect, shifting leftward also the *IS* curve. What could cause sharp leftward movements in the A_p demand schedule and the *IS* curve? We have already learned that auto-nomous consumption (Ca) can be reduced not just by a higher interest rate (which moves the economy northwest along a given A_p demand schedule), but also by a *leftward shift* in the A_p demand schedule caused by lower consumer confidence, lower household net worth, and greater difficulty of obtaining credit from financial institutions. Planned investment (I_p) is even more fragile, prone to more volatility than any other component of GDP or aggregate expenditures.

Total investment varies widely between 12 and 20 percent of GDP. When investment rises or declines as a share of GDP, this has a multiplier effect. In recessions investment typically declines far more than GDP, and through the multiplier effect a sharp downturn of investment drags down consumption expenditures as well.

The graph on the opposite page displays the ratio of total investment to GDP in two recessions, that which started in mid-1981 and that which started in late 2007. The line plotted shows the percentage ratio of total investment to GDP as a fraction of its ratio in the initial quarter of the recession. The span plotted in the graph goes from four quarters before the business cycle peak to 12 quarters after. This is why both the blue and red lines in the graph are equal exactly to 100 in the quarter on the horizontal axis marked as "zero" quarters after the peak.

The big message of the graph is that the ratio of investment to GDP fell drastically in both recessions, thus driving down the rest of the economy through the multiplier effect. In the 1981–82 recession shown by the blue line, the ratio of investment to GDP by the fifth quarter had fallen to 78 percent, that is, a decline of 22 percent from the peak. The collapse of investment in the most recent recession starting in late 2007 was even worse. In the 2007–09 recession as shown by the red line the ratio of investment to GDP had fallen to 69 percent, that is, a decline of 31 percent from the peak.

Clearly, the volatility of investment implies that shifts in the *position* of the *IS* curve are as important as the slope of the *IS* curve. The sharp declines of the investment-to-GDP ratio, as shown in the graph for 1981–82 and 2007–09, suggest that understanding investment behavior is the key to understanding the business cycle.

There is another interesting aspect of the red line compared to the blue line. While both lines plotting the investment-to-GDP ratio decline rapidly and then recover, notice how much faster is the recovery in the 1980–84 business cycle than in 2006–10. The distinct feature of the recent recession is that it has been deeper and has lasted longer than the worst previous recession in 1981–82, as shown on the graph.

Why was the collapse of investment in 2006–10 so severe? We have already learned one cause, the unsustainable bubble of housing prices that boosted residential construction (a part of total investment) during 2001–06. When the housing price bubble collapsed in 2006–07, investment in residential houses and condominiums declined precipitously. Building of residential structures fell by 75 percent between 2006 and 2009.

Another factor contributing to the collapse of investment was the financial market "meltdown" that created a sense of panic for almost every business firm, not just

The Demand for Autonomous Planned Spending

You learned earlier that there are five components of autonomous planned spending (A_p): planned investment, autonomous consumption, government spending, the effect of autonomous taxes on consumption, and net exports. We have now seen that planned investment and autonomous consumption both depend on the interest rate; both types of spending are stimulated by a lower interest rate.

In Figure 3-5 we plot the relationship of the components of autonomous planned spending on the horizontal axis to the interest rate on the vertical axis. The total amount of government spending, the effect of autonomous taxes on consumption, and net exports ($G - cT_a + NX$) do not depend on the interest rate and so are plotted as a black vertical line in Figure 3-5.

Total autonomous planned spending also consists of autonomous consumption (C_a) and planned investment (I_p), both of which depend negatively on the interest rate, so *the amount of these two components added to the first three*

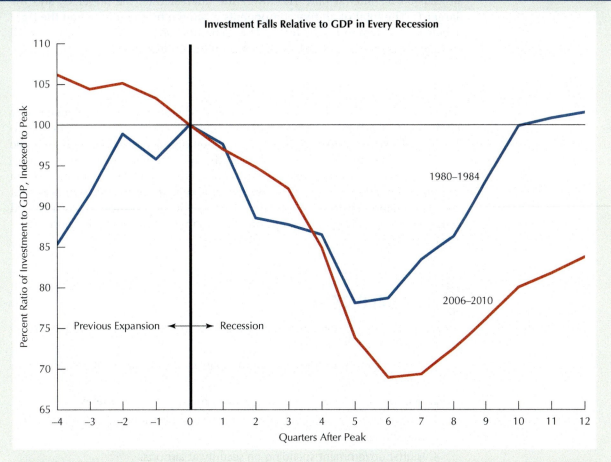

Investment Falls Relative to GDP in Every Recession

y-axis: Percent Ratio of Investment to GDP, Indexed to Peak

1980–1984

2006–2010

Previous Expansion ← → Recession

x-axis: Quarters After Peak

in the United States but in foreign countries as well. What caused this financial market panic? We will return in Chapter 5 to explore the changes in financial markets that contributed to the sharp leftward shift of the autonomous planned spending and *IS* curves in Figure 3-5. The weak recovery of investment after 2009

poses a dilemma for policymakers, because, as we will learn in the next two chapters, the ability of monetary and fiscal policy to offset weakness of investment may be limited. In fact, in the Great Depression total investment fell by 74 percent from 1929 to 1933 and did not return to its 1929 level until 1941.

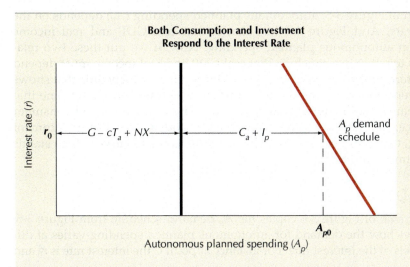

Both Consumption and Investment Respond to the Interest Rate

Interest rate (r)

r_0

$\leftarrow G - cT_a + NX \rightarrow$ $\leftarrow C_a + I_p \rightarrow$

A_p demand schedule

A_{p0}

Autonomous planned spending (A_p)

Figure 3-5 Relation of the Various Components of Autonomous Planned Spending to the Interest Rate

The vertical black line shows that three components of autonomous planned spending do not depend on the interest rate. These are government spending (G), the effect of autonomous taxes ($-cT_a$), and net exports (NX). The sloped line shows that autonomous consumption (C_a) and planned investment (I_p) depend inversely on the interest rate. Hence, the total demand for autonomous planned spending, as shown by the "A_p demand schedule," also depends inversely on the interest rate.

depends on the interest rate. The lower the interest rate, the larger C_a and the larger I_p. The total of all five components is shown by the red line on the right labeled "A_p demand schedule." This schedule shows that the total of all autonomous planned spending depends on the interest rate.

Shifts in the A_p Demand Schedule

The A_p demand schedule will shift to the right whenever there is a change in any component of planned autonomous spending. Increases in government spending or net exports and reductions in autonomous tax revenues will shift the schedule to the right. Anything that raises the amount of autonomous consumption or planned spending at a given interest rate, for instance, an increase in consumer confidence or business optimism about future profits, will also shift the A_p demand schedule to the right. Changes in any component of planned autonomous spending in the opposite direction will shift the A_p demand schedule to the left.

 SELF-TEST

Explain how the A_p demand schedule will shift to the left, right, or not at all in response to the following events:

1. A reduction in auto imports from Japan as the quality of American-built cars improves.
2. The stimulus to housing given by lower mortgage interest rates.
3. Higher taxes levied by the government in an attempt to reduce the budget deficit.
4. Higher government spending on security at airports.
5. A reduction in household net worth due to a sharp decline in house prices.

3-9   The *IS* Curve

As shown in Figure 3-5, autonomous planned spending (A_p) depends on the interest rate. And Figure 3-4 has shown that real GDP and real income depend on autonomous planned spending. Now, if we put these two relationships together, we conclude that real GDP and real income must depend on the interest rate. In this section we derive a graphical schedule that shows the different possible combinations of the interest rate and real income that are compatible with equilibrium, given the state of business and consumer confidence, the marginal propensity to save, and the level of government spending, taxes, and net exports. This schedule is the **IS curve,** which stands for Investment and Saving.

The **IS curve** is the schedule that identifies the combinations of income and the interest rate at which the commodity market is in equilibrium; everywhere along the *IS* curve the demand for commodities equals the supply.

How to Derive the *IS* Curve

The left frame of Figure 3-6 copies the A_p demand schedule from Figure 3-5. This shows how the demand for autonomous planned spending varies at different levels of the interest rate. For instance at point C the interest rate is r_0 and

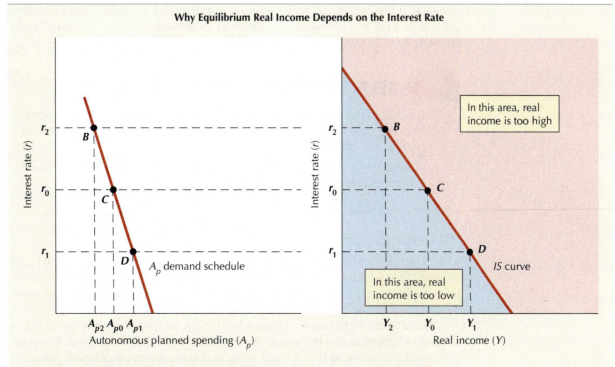

Figure 3-6 Relation of the *IS* Curve to the Demand for Autonomous Spending
In the left frame, the "A_p demand schedule" shows that the demand for autonomous planned spending depends on the interest rate. The right frame displays the *IS* curve, which shows that real GDP also depends negatively on the interest rate. Point *B* in the right frame is at a horizontal position equal to point *B* in the left frame times the multiplier. The same is true for points *C* and *D*.

the level of autonomous planned spending is A_{p0}.[7] At point *D* the lower interest rate r_1 stimulates a higher level of autonomous planned spending labeled A_{p1} on the horizontal axis.

We have already learned in Figure 3-4 and in equation (3.14) that a higher level of A_p raises output by that amount times the multiplier ($\Delta Y = k\Delta A_p$). In the right frame of Figure 3-6 the vertical axis is the same interest rate as in the left frame, while the horizontal axis is real income and output.

If in the left frame the interest rate would decline from point *C* to point *D*, then autonomous planned spending would rise from A_{p0} to A_{p1}. How much would real income respond? We have already learned that the output response is equal to the increase in autonomous planned spending times the multiplier. So a reduction of the interest rate from point *C* to point *D* in the right frame raises output from Y_0 to Y_1. Because the multiplier is larger than 1.0, and in fact is 4.0 in our example in this chapter, the horizontal increase in *Y* in the right frame is much greater than the horizontal increase in A_p in the left frame. For

---

[7] For instance, let us assume that the equation of the A_p demand schedule in the left quadrant of Figure 3-6 is:

$$2{,}500 - 100r$$

Thus, when the interest rate is at 10 percent at point *C*, the level of autonomous planned spending along the A_p demand schedule is $2{,}500 - (100 \times 10) = 1{,}500$. If the multiplier is 4.0, then the level of real income in the right frame along the *IS* curve at point *C* is 4 times 1,500, or 6,000.

instance, if the horizontal increase in A_p in the left frame is 500 and the multiplier ($k = 1/s$) is 4.0, then the horizontal increase of output (Y) in the right frame will be 2000, or 4.0 times as much.

◆ **SELF-TEST**

1. Describe what happens to the interest rate, autonomous planned spending, and income when the economy moves from point *C* to point *B* in both frames of Figure 3-6.

2. At what point in the right frame of Figure 3-6 does the economy operate if the interest rate is r_1 in the right frame?

What the *IS* Curve Shows

The *IS* curve shows all the different combinations of the interest rate (r) and income (Y) at which the economy's market for commodities (goods and services) is in equilibrium, which occurs only when income equals planned expenditures. At any point off the *IS* curve the economy is out of equilibrium.

Notice in the right frame of Figure 3-6 that the area southwest of the *IS* line is shaded in light blue and the area to the northeast is shaded in light red. The positions on the *IS* curve at *B, C, D,* and other points represent equilibrium positions where real income and output are just right, given the interest rate, to generate enough planned expenditure to equal that level of income.[8] However, points in the blue-shaded area are not equilibrium points. For any given income level like Y_0 at point *C*, any position lower than *C* would have a lower interest rate, and this would raise planned expenditure above that income level and result in negative unplanned investment, forcing firms to raise production. Any position in the light red area above point *C* would have a higher interest rate, lower planned expenditure, and insufficient demand to avoid positive unplanned investment and a cut in production. In short, there is pressure for change in the amount produced at any point in the blue- and red-shaded areas that are off the *IS* curve.

3-10 Conclusion: The Missing Relation

The *IS* curve is like a menu, providing us with innumerable combinations of interest rates and income that are consistent with equilibrium in the commodity market. But which item on the menu should we choose? There is not enough information here to make a choice. We need to find another relationship to link income and the interest rate in order to tie down the economy's position along the *IS* curve. In the familiar language of elementary algebra, we have two unknowns but only one equation. In the next chapter, we supply the missing equation and arrive at a complete theory of how income and the interest rate are determined.[9]

---

[8] We call the *IS* schedule a "curve," even though we have drawn it as a straight line, because in the real world the relationship might be a curve. Also the term "*IS* curve" has been familiar to generations of economists since its invention by the late Sir John Hicks in a classic article, "Mr. Keynes and the Classics: A Suggested Interpretation," *Econometrica,* vol. 5 (April 1937), pp. 147–59.

[9] Despite its name, the *IS* curve has no unique connection with investment (*I*) or saving (*S*). It shifts whenever there is a shift in the A_p demand schedule, which can be caused by a change in government spending, in taxes or transfers, or in net exports, as well as by changes in business and consumer confidence.

Learning About Diagrams: The *IS* Curve

Since the *IS* curve is so important and useful, we pause here to study it more closely. (A full algebraic treatment of the *IS-LM* model is given in the Appendix to Chapter 4.)

Diagram Ingredients and Reasons for Slope

The vertical axis is the interest rate and the horizontal axis is the level of income.

The *IS* curve takes information from two other graphs, the A_p demand schedule and the equilibrium between induced saving and autonomous planned spending. Because A_p depends on the interest rate, and because equilibrium income is a multiple (k) of A_p, equilibrium income becomes a negative function of the interest rate.

The horizontal position (equilibrium income) along the *IS* curve is equal to the horizontal position along the A_p demand schedule times the multiplier k.

The *IS* curve slopes down because income is a multiple of A_p, and A_p depends negatively on the interest rate.

The *IS* curve becomes flatter, the more responsive is A_p to the interest rate, and the larger the multiplier. The *IS* curve becomes steeper, the less responsive is A_p to the interest rate, and the smaller the multiplier.

What Shifts and Rotates the *IS* Curve?

The *IS* curve is equal to the interest-dependent level of A_p times the multiplier (k). Anything that shifts the A_p demand schedule will shift the *IS* curve in the same direction. The factors that shift the *IS* curve to the right include an increase in business or consumer confidence, an increase in household wealth, an increase in the willingness of financial institutions to grant loans, an increase in government spending or net exports,

and a decrease in taxes (or increase in transfers). Opposite changes will shift the *IS* curve to the left.

A rightward shift in the A_p demand schedule causes a rightward shift in the *IS* curve by an amount equal to the A_p shift times the multiplier.

The multiplier (k) transforms the A_p demand schedule into the *IS* curve. An increase in the multiplier (due, for instance, to a smaller marginal propensity to save) rotates or twists the *IS* curve outward around its intercept on the vertical interest rate axis. Thus the higher the multiplier, the flatter the *IS* curve.

Anything that makes investment or consumption demand less sensitive to the interest rate (for instance, a tendency for firms to pay for investment goods with internal funds rather than borrowed funds) rotates or twists the *IS* curve upward around its intercept on the horizontal income axis. Thus the less sensitive the response of autonomous spending to the interest rate, the steeper the *IS* curve.

What Is True of Points That Are Off the *IS* Curve?

The entire area to the left of each *IS* curve is characterized by too low a level of production and income for the economy to be in equilibrium. There is undesired inventory decumulation (negative unplanned investment, I_u).

The entire area to the right of each *IS* curve is characterized by too high a level of production and income for the economy to be in equilibrium. There is undesired inventory accumulation (positive unplanned investment, I_u).

At any point off the *IS* curve there is pressure for business firms to adjust production until the economy returns to the *IS* curve.

The missing relation between real income and the interest rate (in addition to the *IS* curve), occurs in the "money market," a general expression for the financial sector of the economy. The operation of the money market provides the crucial missing link that explains how the interest rate is determined. At the beginning of the next chapter, we will learn how the money market creates a second, positively sloped relationship between real income and the interest rate. We will learn that the Fed, through its control of the money supply, can shift this positive relationship back and forth and offset some or all of the effects of the demand shocks (such as changes in business and consumer confidence) that shift the position of the *IS* curve. We will also learn how monetary and fiscal policy can be used together to determine both the interest rate and the level of real income.

Summary

1. This chapter presents a simple theory for determining real income. Important simplifying assumptions include the constancy of the price level.

2. Disposable income is divided between consumption and saving. The amount of consumption per dollar of disposable income is a fixed amount called autonomous consumption (C_a) plus the marginal propensity to consume (c) times personal disposable income, that is, income after taxes. Anything that boosts autonomous consumption must reduce the ratio of personal saving to personal disposable income.

3. The ratio of personal saving to personal disposable income declined drastically from over 10 percent in 1984 to just 1.4 percent in 2005. This resulted mainly from the increases of stock market and housing wealth that many households enjoyed in the late 1990s and particularly in the 2003–07 interval. The collapse of stock and housing prices after 2007 raised the personal saving rate back to its level of the early 1990s.

4. Output and income (Y) are equal by definition to total expenditures (E), which in turn can be divided up between planned expenditure (E_p) and unintended inventory accumulation (I_u). We convert this definition into a theory by assuming that business firms adjust production whenever I_u is not zero. The economy is in equilibrium, with no pressure for production to change, only when there is no unintended inventory accumulation or decumulation ($I_u = 0$).

5. Autonomous planned spending (A_p) equals total planned expenditure minus induced consumption. The five components of autonomous planned expenditure are autonomous consumption (C_a), planned investment (I_p), government spending (G), net exports (NX), and the effect on consumption of autonomous tax revenue ($-cT_a$).

6. Any change in autonomous planned spending (ΔA_p) has a multiplier effect: An increase raises income and induced consumption over and above the initial boost in A_p. Income must increase until enough extra saving has been induced ($s\Delta Y$) to balance the injection of extra autonomous planned spending (ΔA_p). For this reason, the multiplier, the ratio of the change in income to the change in autonomous planned spending ($\Delta Y/\Delta A_p$), is the inverse of the marginal propensity to save ($1/s$).

7. The same multiplier is valid for a change in any component in A_p. Thus, if private spending components of A_p are weak, the government can raise its spending (G) or cut taxes (T) to maintain stability in A_p and thus in real output.

8. Interest rates allocate the supply of funds available from savers to alternative borrowers. Not only do private households and firms borrow in order to buy consumption and investment goods, but the government also borrows to finance its budget deficit.

9. Private autonomous planned spending (A_p) depends partly on the interest rate. The higher the interest rate, the lower is A_p.

10. Private autonomous planned spending (A_p) can shift up at any given interest rate in response to greater optimism by consumers or business firms, in response to higher household wealth, and in response to a greater willingness by financial institutions to grant loans.

11. The *IS* curve indicates all the combinations of the interest rate and real income at which the economy's commodity market is in equilibrium. At any point off the *IS* curve, the commodity market is out of equilibrium.

Note: Asterisks designate Concepts, Questions, and Problems that require the Appendix to Chapter 3.

Concepts

aggregate demand	marginal propensity to consume	unintended inventory investment
demand shock	induced consumption	induced saving
aggregate supply	marginal propensity to save	multiplier
endogenous variables	household wealth	*IS* curve
exogenous variables	parameter	*marginal leakage rate
autonomous magnitude	equilibrium	*automatic stabilization

Questions

1. Explain the distinction between exogenous variables and endogenous variables. Explain the distinction, if any, between a parameter and an exogenous variable. For the most complete model used in this chapter, which of the following variables are endogenous? Which are exogenous?
   (a) autonomous taxes
   (b) consumption

(c) marginal propensity to consume
(d) exports
(e) net exports
(f) GDP
(g) price level
(h) interest rate
(i) investment
(j) tax revenue
(k) disposable income
(l) saving
(m) foreign trade surplus (deficit)
(n) government budget surplus (deficit)

2. Why do we distinguish between autonomous consumption and induced consumption?

3. Explain how the increases of house prices from 2000 through April 2006 and stock prices from 2003 through 2007 and then the collapse of those prices following their peaks affected household wealth, consumption expenditures, and the personal saving rate over the course of the last decade.

4. Explain why inventories would tend to rise just before the start of a recession and again tend to rise once businesses become more confident that the economy is expanding.

5. What moves the economy toward equilibrium when unintended inventory investment is positive? negative?

6. Assume that there is an increase in autonomous investment of $100 billion. Will the effect on the level of equilibrium real GDP be greater with a relatively high or a relatively low marginal propensity to consume? Explain.

7. Explain why government action that increases the deficit is expansionary fiscal policy. What about action that decreases the surplus?

8. Explain why the *IS* curve slopes down and to the right. Explain the difference between a movement along the *IS* curve and a shift of the *IS* curve.

9. Explain how the rise and fall of the investment-GDP ratio from 1980–84 and 2006–10 shifted the *IS* curve. Using the data presented in the box on pages 74–75, compare how much the *IS* curve shifted during each recession and the period following the end of each recession.

10. Explain how each of the following will shift the *IS* curve.
    (a) The decline in sales of American agricultural products to foreign countries resulting from a strong U.S. dollar in the early to mid-1980s.
    (b) The collapse in consumer confidence that occurred in the fall of 1990 following the rapid rise in energy prices after Iraq's invasion of Kuwait in August 1990.
    (c) The drop in business confidence following the collapse of the stock market and the Internet bust in 2000.
    (d) The increased reluctance by some banks to make car and housing loans following the financial crisis of 2007–08.

11. One of the hypotheses for the increased stability of the U.S. economy since 1985 is that demand shocks have become smaller and less important. Explain why a demand shock can be thought of as a shift of the *IS* curve. Then discuss the hypothesis concerning demand shocks and the increased stability of the U.S. economy in terms of shifts of the *IS* curve.

The following three questions assume knowledge of the Appendix to Chapter 3.

*12. Given a consumption function of the form $C = C_a + c(Y - T)$ and $T = T_a + tY$, write the formula for the expanded consumption function. Write the formula for the expanded saving function that is implied by the stated consumption function.

*13. How would your answer in question 6 change if the alternatives read with a relatively high or with a relatively low marginal leakage rate? Explain.

*14. When all taxes and net exports are autonomous, the balanced budget multiplier is one. Find the balanced budget multiplier when all taxes are autonomous, but net exports have an autonomous and induced component. Is this new balanced budget multiplier less than, greater than, or equal to one?

Problems

 Visit www.MyEconLab.com to complete these or similar exercises.

1. Consider an economy in which all taxes are autonomous and the following values of autonomous consumption, planned investment, government expenditure, autonomous taxes, and the marginal propensity to consume are given:

   $C_a = 1,400 \quad I_p = 1,800 \quad G = 1,950 \quad T_a = 1,750 \quad c = 0.6$

   (a) What is the level of consumption when the level of income (Y) equals $10,000?
   (b) What is the level of saving when the level of income (Y) equals $10,000?
   (c) What is the level of planned investment when the level of income (Y) equals $10,000? What is the level of actual investment? What is the level of unintended inventory investment?
   (d) Show that injections equal leakages when income (Y) equals $10,000.
   (e) Is the economy in equilibrium when income (Y) = $10,000? If not, what is the equilibrium level of income for the economy described in this question?

(f) Is there a surplus or deficit in the government budget at the equilibrium level of income? How much?

2. Consider an economy in which taxes, planned investment, government spending on goods and services, and net exports are autonomous, but consumption and planned investment change as the interest rate changes. You are given the following information concerning autonomous consumption, the marginal propensity to consume, planned investment, government purchases of goods and services, and net exports:

$$C_a = 1,500 - 10r \quad c = 0.6 \quad T = 1,800$$
$$Ip = 2,400 - 50r \quad G = 2,000 \quad NX = -200$$

(a) Compute the value of the marginal propensity to save.

(b) Compute the amount of autonomous planned spending, A_p, given that the interest rate equals 3.

(c) Compute the equilibrium level of income, given that the interest rate equals 3.

(d) Suppose that autonomous consumption changes by 4 percent for any change in household wealth and that the decline in the housing market from 2006–09 and the drop in stock market from 2007–09 reduce household wealth by $3 trillion. Compute the decline in consumption that results from the decline in household wealth.

(e) Calculate the new amount of autonomous planned spending, A_p, and the new equilibrium level of income, given that the interest rate equals 3.

(f) Using your answers to parts c–e, compute the value of the multiplier.

(g) Fiscal and monetary policymakers can respond to the decline in household wealth by taking actions that restore income to its initial equilibrium level. Fiscal policymakers can increase government spending or cut taxes or do both. Monetary policymakers can reduce interest rates. Given the values of the multiplier, the tax multiplier, and the balanced-budget multiplier, compute by how much:

Government spending must be increased in order to restore the initial equilibrium level of income, given no change in taxes or the interest rate.

Taxes must be cut in order to restore the initial equilibrium level of income, given no change in government spending or the interest rate.

Government spending and taxes must be increased in order to restore the initial equilibrium level of income, given no change in the government budget balance or the interest rate.

The interest rate must be reduced in order to restore the initial equilibrium level of income, given no change in government spending or taxes.

3. Consider an economy in which taxes, planned investment, government spending on goods and services, and net exports are autonomous, but consumption and planned investment change as the interest rate changes. You are given the following information concerning autonomous consumption, the marginal propensity to consume, planned investment, government purchases of goods and services, and net exports:

$$C_a = 1,500 - 20r \quad c = 0.6 \quad I_p = 2,450 - 60r$$
$$G = 1,980 \quad NX = -200 \quad T = 1,750$$

(a) Compute the value of the marginal propensity to save.

(b) Compute the amounts of autonomous planned spending, A_p, when the interest rate equals 0, 2, 4, and 6.

(c) Compute the equilibrium levels of income when the interest rate equals 0, 2, 4, and 6. Graph the *IS* curve.

(d) Suppose that policymakers decide to reduce the number of troops in Afghanistan, which results in a reduction of government spending of $80 billion. Compute the new amounts of autonomous spending, A_p, when the interest rate equals 0, 2, 4, and 6.

(e) Compute the equilibrium levels of income when the interest rate equals 0, 2, 4, and 6 and graph the new *IS* curve.

(f) Suppose that a government expansion of health care causes its spending to increase by $160 billion from $1,960 to $2,120. Compute the new amounts of autonomous spending, A_p, when the interest rate equals 0, 2, 4, and 6.

(g) Compute the equilibrium levels of income when the interest rate equals 0, 2, 4, and 6 and graph the new *IS* curve.

(h) Suppose that initially the interest rate equals 4 and the economy is in equilibrium at natural real GDP, which equals 10,900. If monetary policymakers want to maintain income at natural real GDP, explain by how much they will change the interest rate as a result of either the Afghanistan troop reduction or the expanded health care.

*4. Assume an economy in which the marginal propensity to consume, c, is 0.8, the income tax rate, t, is 0.2, and the share of imports in GDP, nx, is 0.04. Autonomous consumption, C_a, is 660; autonomous taxes, T_a, are 200; autonomous net exports, NX_a, are 300; planned investment, I_p, is 500; and government spending, G, is 500.

(a) What is the value of autonomous planned spending (A_p)?

(b) What is the value of the multiplier?

(c) What is the equilibrium value of income (Y)?

(d) What is the value of consumption in equilibrium?

(e) Show that leakages equal injections.

(f) Suppose government expenditures decline by 150. Describe the economic process by which the new equilibrium value of Y is attained.

(g) What is the new equilibrium value of Y?

5. Consider an economy in which taxes, planned investment, government spending on goods and services, and net exports are autonomous, but consumption and planned investment change as the interest rate changes. You are given the following information concerning autonomous consumption, the marginal propensity to consume, planned investment, government purchases of goods and services, and net exports: $C_a = 1{,}400 - 15r$; $c = 0.5$; $I_p = 2{,}350 - 35r$; $G = 1{,}940$; $NX = -200$; $T_a = 1{,}600$.

(a) Compute the value of the multiplier.

(b) Derive the equation for the autonomous planned spending schedule, A_p.

(c) Derive the equation for the IS curve, $Y = kA_p$.

(d) Using the equation for the IS curve, calculate the equilibrium levels of income at interest rates equal to 0, 3, and 6.

(e) Using your answers to part d, calculate the slope of the IS curve, $\Delta r / \Delta Y$.

(f) Suppose that autonomous consumption rises by $40 billion, so that $C_a = 1{,}440 - 15r$. Explain whether this increase in autonomous consumption is caused by a rise or fall in consumer confidence. Derive the new equation for the IS curve.

(g) Using the equation for the new IS curve, calculate the new equilibrium levels of income at interest rates equal to 0, 3, and 6.

(h) Using your answers to parts d and g, explain whether the IS curve shifts to the left or right when autonomous consumption rises. Explain why the horizontal shift of the IS curve equals the multiplier times the change in autonomous planned spending.

6. The purpose of this problem is to study how the slope of the IS curve changes as the multiplier changes and the responsiveness of autonomous planned spending to interest rate changes. Initially, use the same information as given in problem 5.

(a) Suppose that the marginal propensity to consume increases from 0.5 to 0.6. Compute the new value of the multiplier.

(b) Derive the equation for the new autonomous planned spending schedule, A_p.

(c) Derive the equation for the new IS curve, $Y = kA_p$.

(d) Using the equation for the new IS curve, calculate the new equilibrium levels of income at interest rates equal to 0, 3, and 6.

(e) Using your answers to part d, calculate the slope of the new IS curve, $\Delta r / \Delta Y$.

(f) Given that $c = 0.6$, suppose that the equation for planned investment expenditures is now $I_p = 2{,}350 - 45r$. Derive the equation for the new autonomous planned spending schedule, A_p.

(g) Derive the equation for the new IS curve, $Y = kA_p$.

(h) Using the equation for the new IS curve, calculate the new equilibrium levels of income at interest rates equal to 0, 3, and 6.

(i) Using your answers to part h, calculate the slope of the new IS curve, $\Delta r / \Delta Y$.

(j) Using your answers to part e of problem 5, and parts e and i of this problem, explain whether the IS curve gets flatter or steeper as (1), the multiplier increases, and (2), the responsiveness of autonomous planned spending to the interest rate increases.

*7. Consider an economy in which consumption, taxes, and net exports all change as income changes. In addition, consumption and planned investment change as the interest rate changes. You are given the following information concerning autonomous consumption, the marginal propensity to consume, planned investment, government purchases of goods and services, and net exports: $C = C_a + 0.85(Y - T)$; $C_a = 225 - 10r$; $I_p = 1{,}610 - 30r$; $G = 1{,}650$; $NX = 700 - 0.08Y$; $T = 100 + 0.2Y$.

(a) Compute the value of the multiplier.

(b) Derive the equation for the autonomous planned spending schedule, A_p.

(c) Derive the equation for the IS curve, $Y = kA_p$.

(d) Using the equation for the IS curve, calculate the equilibrium level of income at an interest rate equal to 3.

(e) At the equilibrium level of income at an interest rate of 3, show that leakages equal injections.

◆ SELF-TEST ANSWERS

p. 59. (1) $C = C_a$ in the general linear form, $C = 500$ in the numerical example. (2) Your options are to borrow, reduce your savings account, and sell stocks, bonds, or any other assets you may own.

p. 60. (1) At point F consumption and disposable income are equal. Thus consumption, $C_a + c(Y - T)$, equals disposable income, or $Y - T$. Setting these two equal, we can subtract $c(Y - T)$ from $Y - T$ to obtain $C_a = (1 - c)(Y - T)$. Dividing by $1 - c$, we obtain the answer that disposable income $(Y - T)$ is equal to $C_a/(1 - c)$ and so is consumption. (2) Saving is positive.

p. 64. (1) We write planned investment as I_p with a p subscript, to reflect our assumption that *consumers, the government, and exporters and importers are always able to realize their plans,* so that there is no such thing as autonomous unplanned consumption, autonomous unplanned tax revenues, unplanned government spending, or unplanned net exports. Only business firms are forced to make unplanned expenditures, as occurs when investment (I) is not equal to what they plan (I_p), but also includes unplanned inventory (I_u). (2) cT_a appears with a minus sign because an increase in taxes will reduce, rather than increase, autonomous planned spending by the amount of the tax times the fraction of the tax that would have been consumed rather than saved. (3) T_a is multiplied by c because taxes are not part of GDP. A change in taxes only alters GDP if it alters consumption. The effect on consumption is given by $-T_a$ times the marginal propensity to consume.

p. 66. (1) Planned expenditure shown by the red line exceeds income, forcing firms to reduce their inventories in order to meet demand. (2) Firms increase production to replace their depleted inventories, and this raises real income (Y).

p. 70. (1) We are assuming that the marginal propensity to consume does not change. (2) When we assume the marginal propensity to consume does not change, the marginal propensity to save will not change either.[a] (3) $s = 1 - c$.

p. 72. (1) Income will decline by 2,000 and saving will decline by one quarter of 2,000, the exact amount of the decline in government expenditures. (2) Tax revenues exceed government spending. Private savers no longer purchase government bonds. Private saving will equal the amount by which total investment exceeds the government surplus. (3) If taxes are raised by $667 billion, saving declines by exactly $667 billion. Private households pay for the higher taxes by reducing their level of saving.

p. 76. (1) A reduction of imports raises net exports and shifts the A_p demand schedule to the right. (2) A change in interest rates moves the economy *along* the schedule but does not shift it. (3) Higher taxes reduce consumption and thus shift the A_p demand schedule to the left. (4) Higher government spending shifts the A_p demand schedule to the right. (5) A reduction in household net worth reduces autonomous consumption and shifts the A_p demand schedule to the left.

p. 78. (1) When the economy moves from point C to point B in the left frame of Figure 3-6, the interest rate increases from r_0 to r_2 and the level of planned autonomous spending declines from A_{p0} to A_{p2}. The multiplier effect of this increase in A_p causes real income to decline by a multiple of the decrease from A_{p0} to A_{p2}. In the right frame this multiplier effect is shown by the larger leftward movement from Y_0 to Y_2. Notice that the horizontal distance between point C and point B in the right frame is substantially greater than the horizontal distance between C and B in the left frame, due to the multiplier. (2) The economy operates at point D in the right frame if the interest rate is r_1.

[a] Using the calculus formula for the change in a ratio, the change in income when both A_p and s are allowed to change is

$$\Delta Y = \Delta A_p/s - A_p\Delta s/s^2$$

Equation (3.14) in the text simply sets Δs equal to zero in this expression.

Appendix to Chapter 3

Allowing for Income Taxes and Income-Dependent Net Exports

Effect of Income Taxes

When the government raises some of its tax revenue (T) with an income tax in addition to the autonomous tax (T_a), its total tax revenue is:

$$T = T_a + tY \tag{1}$$

The first component is the autonomous tax, for which we continue to use the symbol (T_a). The second component is income tax revenue, the tax rate (t) times income (Y). Disposable income ($Y - T$) is total income minus tax revenue:

$$Y_D = Y - T = Y - T_a - tY = (1 - t)Y - T_a \tag{2}$$

Leakages from the Spending Stream. Following any change in total income (Y), disposable income changes by only a fraction ($1 - t$) as much. Any change in total income (ΔY) is now divided into induced consumption, induced saving, and induced income tax revenue. The fraction of ΔY going into consumption is the marginal propensity to consume disposable income (c) times the fraction of income going into disposable income ($1 - t$). Thus the change in total income is divided up as shown in the following table.

Fraction going to:	
1. Induced consumption	$c(1 - t)$
2. Induced saving	$s(1 - t)$
3. Induced tax revenue	t
Total	$(c + s)(1 - t) + t = 1 - t + t = 1.0$

As in equation (3.10) on p. 66, the economy is in equilibrium when income equals planned expenditures:

$$Y = E_p \tag{3}$$

As before, we can subtract induced consumption from both sides of the equilibrium condition. According to the preceding table, income (Y) minus induced consumption is the total of induced saving plus induced tax revenue. Planned expenditure (E_p) minus induced consumption is autonomous planned spending (A_p). Thus the equilibrium condition is

induced saving + induced tax revenue = autonomous planned spending (A_p) (4)

From the table just given, equation (4) can be written in symbols as:

$$[s(1 - t) + t]Y = A_p \tag{5}$$

The term in brackets on the left-hand side is the fraction of a change in income that does not go into induced consumption—that is, the sum of the fraction going to induced saving $s(1 - t)$ and the fraction going to the government as income tax revenue (t). The sum of these two fractions within the brackets is called the **marginal leakage rate**. The

The **marginal leakage rate** is the fraction of income that is taxed or saved rather than being spent on consumption.

85

equilibrium value for Y can be calculated when we divide both sides of equation (5) by the term in brackets:

$$Y = \frac{A_p}{s(1 - t) + t} \tag{6}$$

Income Taxes and the Multiplier

The change in income (ΔY) is the change in autonomous planned spending (ΔA_p) divided by the marginal leakage rate:

$$\Delta Y = \frac{\Delta A_p}{s(1 - t) + t} \tag{7}$$

The multiplier ($\Delta Y / \Delta A_p$) is 1.0 divided by the marginal leakage rate. The multiplier was $1/s$ when there was no income tax. Now, with an income tax:

$$\text{multiplier} = \frac{1}{\text{marginal leakage rate}} = \frac{1}{s(1 - t) + t} \tag{8}$$

Thus raising the income tax rate reduces the multiplier and vice versa. This gives the government a new tool for stabilizing income. When the government wants to stimulate the economy and raise income, it can raise income in equation (6) and the multiplier in equation (8) by cutting income tax rates. This occurred most recently in 2001, 2003, 2008, and 2009. And, when the government wants to restrain the economy, it can raise income tax rates, as occurred most recently in 1993.

The Government Budget

The government budget surplus is defined as before; it equals tax revenue minus government spending, $T - G$. Substituting the definition in equation (1), which expresses tax revenue (T) as the sum of autonomous and induced tax revenue, we can write the government surplus as:

$$\text{government budget surplus} = T - G = T_a + tY - G \tag{9}$$

Automatic stabilization is the effect on the government budget deficit or surplus of the change in tax revenues when income rises or falls.

Thus the government budget surplus automatically rises when the level of income expands. This consequence of the income tax is sometimes called **automatic stabilization.** This name reflects the automatic rise and fall of income tax revenues as income rises and falls. When income rises, income tax revenues rise and siphon off some of the income before households have a chance to spend it. Similarly, when income falls, income tax revenues fall and help minimize the drop in disposable income. This is why the presence of an income tax makes the multiplier smaller.

Autonomous and Induced Net Exports

The theory of income determination in equation (6) states that equilibrium income equals autonomous planned spending (A_p) divided by the marginal leakage rate. When the United States trades with nations abroad, U.S. producers sell part of domestic output as exports. Households and business firms purchase imports from abroad, so part of U.S. expenditure does not generate U.S. production.

How do exports and imports affect the determination of income? We learned in Chapter 2 that the difference between exports and imports is called net exports and is part of GDP. When exports increase, net exports increase. When imports increase, net exports decrease. Designating net exports by NX, we can write the relationship between net exports and income (Y) as:

$$NX = NX_a - nxY \tag{10}$$

Net exports contains an autonomous component (NX_a), reflecting the fact that the level of exports depends mainly on income in foreign countries (which is exogenous, not explained by our theory) rather than on domestic income (Y). Net exports also contains an induced component $(-nxY)$, reflecting the fact that imports rise if domestic income (Y) rises, thus reducing net exports. The meaning of nx can be stated as "the share of imports in GDP."

Because we now have a new component of autonomous expenditure, the autonomous component of net exports (NX_a), we can rewrite our definition of A_p as the following in place of equation:

$$A_p = C_a - cT_a + I_p + G + NX_a \tag{11}$$

Because imports depend on income (Y), the induced component of net exports $(-nxY)$ has exactly the same effect on equilibrium income and the multiplier as does the income tax. Imports represent a leakage from the spending stream, a portion of a change in income that is not part of the disposable income of U.S. citizens and thus not available for consumption. The fraction of a change in income that is spent on net exports (nx) is part of the economy's marginal leakage rate.

Types of leakages	Marginal leakage rate
Saving only	s
Saving and income tax	$s(1 - t) + t$
Saving, income tax, and imports	$s(1 - t) + t + nx$

Full Equations for Equilibrium Income and the Multiplier

When we combine equation (6), equation (11), and the table, equilibrium income becomes:

$$Y = \frac{A_p}{\text{marginal leakage rate}} = \frac{C_a - cT_a + I_p + G + NX_a}{s(1 - t) + t + nx} \tag{12}$$

The change in income then becomes

$$\Delta Y = \frac{\Delta A_p}{\text{marginal leakage rate}}$$

where $\Delta A_p = \Delta C_a - c\Delta T_a + \Delta I_p + \Delta G + \Delta NX_a$ and the marginal leakage rate is the same as the denominator of equation (12).

The Balanced Budget Multiplier

The balanced budget multiplier may be generalized from equation (3.18) in Chapter 3 by replacing s in the denominator by the marginal leakage rate:

$$\text{balanced budget multiplier} = \frac{1 - c}{\text{marginal leakage rate}}$$

Strong and Weak Policy Effects in the *IS-LM* Model

Money is always there, but the pockets change.
 —Gertrude Stein

4-1 Introduction: The Power of Monetary and Fiscal Policy

The last chapter examined the determinants of the demand for commodities, that is, the goods and services that make up total real GDP. We learned that the economy is in equilibrium when total output or real GDP is equal to what households, business firms, the government, and foreigners want to buy, that is, planned expenditures. When any of the determinants of planned expenditures change, business firms will react by raising or reducing output, and the economy will experience business cycles rather than smooth and steady growth of real GDP.

The last chapter summarized the relationship between equilibrium real GDP and the interest rate in a downward-sloping graphical schedule called the *IS* curve. Everywhere along the *IS* curve, the commodity market is in equilibrium and there is no unplanned inventory accumulation or decumulation. The position of the *IS* curve depends on the components of planned autonomous spending and the multiplier, and its slope depends on the multiplier and the responsiveness of planned spending to changes in the interest rate.

However, this single graphical schedule, the *IS* curve, cannot determine two unknown variables: real GDP and the interest rate. We cannot determine real GDP without knowing the value of the interest rate, and the reverse is true as well: We cannot determine the interest rate until we have determined real GDP.

To determine *both* real GDP and the interest rate simultaneously, we need a second, separate relationship between them. This second relationship, called the *LM* curve, is provided by the money market, where the supply of money controlled by the Federal Reserve Board interacts with the demand for that money by households and business firms. The economy's equilibrium real GDP and its equilibrium interest rate are simultaneously determined at the intersection of the *IS* curve and the *LM* curve, where both the commodity market and money market are in equilibrium.

4-2 Income, the Interest Rate, and the Demand for Money

The money market is a general expression for the financial sector of the economy. In reality, the financial sector consists of many assets in addition to money, including short-term debt of corporations and the government, as well as bonds, stocks, and mutual funds. In this chapter we will limit our attention to the segment of the financial sector generally referred to as "money." In the next chapter we will look more closely at a wider range of assets in the financial sector.

The **money supply** (M^s) consists of two parts: currency and checking accounts at banks and thrift institutions. The money supply may be considered to be a policy instrument that the Fed can set exactly at any desired value, just as we have been assuming that the government can precisely set the level of its fiscal policy instruments—that is, its purchases of goods and services and tax revenues.

The theory developed in this chapter establishes a link between the money supply, income, and interest rates. The hypothesis that links the money supply, income, and the interest rate states that *the amount of money that people demand in real terms depends both on income and on the interest rate.* Why do households give up interest earnings to hold money balances that pay no interest? The main reason is that at least *some* holding of money is necessary to facilitate transactions.

> The **money supply** consists of currency and transactions accounts, including checking accounts at banks and thrift institutions.

Income and the Demand for Money

Funds held in the form of stocks or bonds pay interest but cannot be used for transactions. People have to carry currency in their pockets or have money in their bank accounts to back up a check before they can buy anything. (Even if they use credit cards, they need money in their bank accounts to keep up with their credit card bills.) Because rich people make more purchases, they generally need a larger amount of currency and larger bank deposits. Thus, the demand for **real money balances** increases when everyone becomes richer—that is, when the total of real income increases.

> **Real money balances** equal the total money supply divided by the price level.

Changes in real income alter the demand for money in real terms—that is, adjusted for changes in the price level. Let us assume that the demand for real money balances (M/P) equals a fraction h of real income (Y):

$$\left(\frac{M}{P}\right)^d = hY$$

The superscript d means "the demand for."

If real income (Y) is the amount Y_1, the demand for real money balances $(M/P)^d$ will be hY_1, as shown in Figure 4-1 by the vertical line (L') drawn at $(M/P)^d_0$. The line is vertical because we are assuming initially that the demand for real balances $(M/P)^d$ does not depend on the interest rate (r).

The Interest Rate and the Demand for Money

The L' line is unrealistic, however, because individuals will not hold as much money at a 10 percent interest rate as at a zero interest rate. Why? Because the interest rate plotted on the vertical axis is paid on *assets other than money,* such as bonds and savings certificates. The higher the reward (r) for holding interest-earning financial assets (that are not money), the less money will be held.

In Figure 4-1 the downward slope of the L_1 line through points F and D indicates that when the interest rate rises from zero to interest rate r_1, people cut down their money holdings to the amount shown at point D. When the interest rate is even higher at r_0, their money holdings are cut even further to the amount shown at point F. The new L_1 line can be summarized as showing that the real demand for money is a fraction h of income minus f times the interest rate:

$$\left(\frac{M}{P}\right)^d = hY - fr$$

Figure 4-1 The Demand for Money, the Interest Rate, and Real Income

The vertical line L' is drawn on the unrealistic assumption that the demand for real money balances does not depend on the interest rate but rather is a fixed fraction h of real income, that is, $(M/P)d_1 = hY_0$. The alternative downward sloping L_1 curve has the same level of income and the same horizontal intercept $(M/P)d_1 = hY_0$. But as the interest rate rises from zero to point D to point F the demand for real balances decreases. The shaded area shows the amount shifted into other assets, an amount that grows as the interest rate rises, leaving a smaller and smaller amount that is held as money.

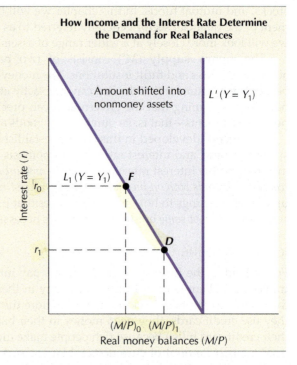

How Income and the Interest Rate Determine the Demand for Real Balances

A change in the interest rate moves the economy up and down its real money demand schedule, whereas a change in real output (Y) shifts that schedule to the left or right, as shown in Figure 4-2. At any given interest rate, the change in the amount of money demanded is given by

$$\Delta\left(\frac{M}{P}\right)^d = h\Delta Y$$

Figure 4-2 Effect on the Money Demand Schedule of a Decline in Real Income

The L_1 line is copied from Figure 4-1 and shows the demand for real balances at different rates of interest, assuming that real income is fixed at the level Y_1. A decline in real income from Y_1 to Y_0 causes the demand for real money to decline by a fraction h of the decline of income. Everywhere along the new L_0 line the demand for money at any given interest rate is lower than along the old L_1 line.

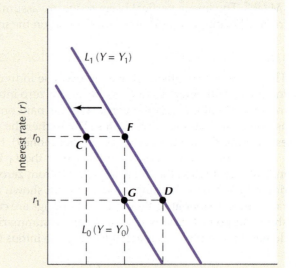

A Drop in the Level of Income Shifts the Money Demand Schedule to the Left

Between points F and C, the interest rate is the same, output falls from Y_1 to Y_0 and the demand for money declines by h times the decline of income.

SELF-TEST

1. What are the two determinants of the real demand for money?
2. What is the effect of each determinant on the real demand for money?
3. Does a change in either determinant shift the *IS* curve?

Other Factors That Shift the Demand for Money Schedule

Thus far we have allowed for only one factor, real income, that shifts the money demand schedule as in Figure 4-2. In reality, there are several other factors besides real income that can shift that schedule. Recall that we use the word "money" in this chapter to include currency and checking accounts and treat all other assets, including savings accounts, stocks, and bonds, as "nonmoney assets." Here we introduce some of these additional shift factors and return at the end of this chapter to examine their impact on the determination of income and interest rates.

Wealth. If people become wealthier by saving a lot or through higher prices on their houses and holdings in the stock market, then some of that wealth may be held in the form of extra holdings of money. In reality, however, most increases in wealth are held in nonmoney assets such as savings accounts, stocks, and bonds. Recall from Chapter 3 (p. 60) that higher wealth also raises autonomous consumption and shifts the *IS* curve to the right.

Expected future inflation. If people expect the price level to rise rapidly in the future, they know that their money will buy less in the future and will try to hold as little as possible. They will try to convert their money into nonmoney assets that will rise in price as a result of high inflation, including stocks and houses.

Payment technologies. Any technological development that alters how people pay for goods and services, or the ease of switching between money and nonmoney assets, can influence the demand for money. For instance, ATM cash machines now are everywhere, enabling people to carry less cash because it is so easy to obtain extra cash when it is needed. Before the invention of ATMs, people had to carry more cash because money could be obtained only in person at a bank branch during business hours. Equally important was the invention of credit cards that allow most transactions to be paid for without using currency at all. Both ATM machines and credit cards reduced the demand for money at any given interest rate.

4-3 The *LM* Curve

Thus far we have learned that the supply of money (M^s) is controlled by the Fed, and that the real quantity of money demanded by households ($M/P)^d$ depends on both income and the interest rate. Now we can tie these two relationships together by assuming that the money market is always *in equilibrium* (a situation where there is no pressure for change), with the real supply of money equal to the real demand for money. This equilibrium condition for the money market allows us to derive a relationship called the *LM curve*.[1] To achieve equilibrium in the money market, the real supply of money (M^s/P) must equal the demand for real money ($(M/P)^d$):

$$\frac{M^s}{P} = \left(\frac{M}{P}\right)^d = hY - fr \tag{4.1}$$

The supply of money does not depend on the interest rate, so M^s/P is drawn in the left frame of Figure 4-3 as a vertical line. The two money demand schedules, L_0 and L_1, are copied from Figure 4-2.

How to Derive the *LM* Curve

The sloped money demand line in the left frame (L_1) assumes an income value of Y_1 and crosses the vertical money-supply line at point F. Looking to the right frame, the same interest rate is designated by point F and this point is plotted at the horizontal position Y_1 on the horizontal axis.

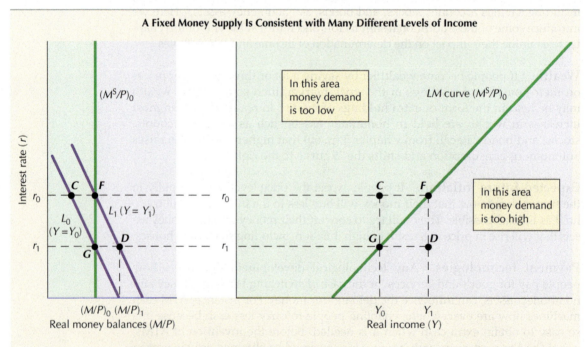

A Fixed Money Supply Is Consistent with Many Different Levels of Income

Figure 4-3 Derivation of the *LM* Curve

In the left frame the L_0 and L_1 schedules are copied from the previous figure. The vertical M^s/P line shows the available supply of money provided by the government. The money market is in equilibrium where the supply line (M^s/P) crosses the demand line (L_0 or L_1). When income is Y_1, equilibrium occurs at point F, plotted again in the right frame. When income is Y_0, equilibrium occurs where L_0 crosses M^s/P at point G, also plotted in the right frame. The *LM* curve or schedule shows all combinations of Y and r consistent with equilibrium in the money market.

---

[1] The name of the *LM* curve comes from two words "liquidity" (L) and "money" (M). Liquidity is a feature of money lacking for most other assets, namely the ability to obtain full value instantly, in contrast to a nonliquid asset like a house that can only be sold over an uncertain amount of time for an uncertain price. Hence, the letter "L" has traditionally been used to discuss the demand for money, as in Figures 4-1 and 4-2.

Learning About Diagrams: The *LM* Curve

The *LM* curve is as important and useful as the *IS* curve, introduced in Section 3-9. This box explains the slope of the *LM* curve and what makes it shift and rotate its position.

Diagram Ingredients and Reasons for Slope

The vertical axis is the interest rate and the horizontal axis is the level of income (same as the *IS* curve).

The *LM* curve shows the different combinations of the interest rate and income consistent with setting the demand for money equal to a *fixed* supply of money. Since the demand for money is fixed everywhere along the *LM* curve, but income increases as we move to the right, "something" must happen to offset the higher demand for money that results from higher income. That something is the higher interest rate, which induces people to shift out of money into nonmonetary assets, freeing up more of the fixed available money to be used for the higher level of transactions.

Along any given *LM* curve, the level of real money balances (M^s/P) is fixed, but real income (Y) varies. The ratio of real income to real balances is called the *velocity* of money (V):

$$\text{velocity } (V) = \frac{Y}{M^s/P} = \frac{PY}{M^s}$$

The right-hand expression states that velocity is also equal to nominal income (PY) divided by the nominal money supply (M^s). The higher the interest rate, the higher is velocity. Why? If r increases, people want to hold less money. But the money supply is fixed. To maintain equilibrium in the money market, there *must be an increase in income* to induce households to hold the fixed existing quantity of money. Anything that can cause the economy to move up and down along a fixed *LM* curve achieves a change of velocity by altering Y while M^s/P is fixed.

What Shifts and Rotates the *LM* Curve?

The *LM* curve is drawn for a fixed real supply of money (M^s/P). A higher nominal supply of money (M^s) will shift the *LM* curve to the right, and a lower nominal supply of money will shift the *LM* curve to the left. An increase in the price level (P) will shift the *LM* curve to the left, and vice versa.

Just as the *LM* curve shifts to the right when the money supply *increases* or when the price level *declines*, it will shift to the right when there is a decline in the demand for money due to a change in any determinant other than the interest rate and real income (which are already on the vertical and horizontal axis, respectively). These factors, as discussed in the text, are a reduction in the interest paid on money, a reduction in wealth, an increase in expected inflation, or technological innovations such as ATMs and credit cards.

Anything that makes the demand for money less sensitive to the interest rate makes both the money demand schedule, $L(Y)$, and the *LM* curve steeper (rotating it upward around its horizontal intercept). Anything that makes the demand for money less responsive to changes in income will make the *LM* curve flatter and also shift it outward.

What Is True of Points That Are Off the *LM* Curve?

The entire area to the left of the *LM* curve has an excess supply of money because income is lower than that needed to create a sufficient demand for money to match the supply.

The entire area to the right of the *LM* curve has an excess demand for money because income is higher than required to match the demand for money to the fixed supply.

At any point off the *LM* curve there is pressure for interest rates to change. For instance, when there is an excess demand for money, people try to obtain money by selling bonds and other financial assets, and this pushes up the interest rates on bonds and other financial assets.

Similarly, at point G in the left frame the money supply is equal to the money demand curve L_0 drawn for an income value of Y_0. In the right frame point G is plotted at the same interest rate and the income level Y_0, which is lower than Y_1.

What the *LM* Curve Shows

The line connecting points G and F in the right-hand frame of Figure 4-3 is called the **LM curve.** The *LM* curve represents all combinations of income (Y)

The **LM curve** is the schedule that identifies the combinations of income and the interest rate at which the money market is in equilibrium; on the *LM* curve the demand for money equals the supply of money.

and interest rate (*r*) where the money market is in equilibrium—that is, where the real supply of money equals the real demand for money.

At any point off the *LM* curve, say point *D*, the money market is not in equilibrium. The problem at *D* and all other points in the purple shaded area is that the demand for real money exceeds the available supply. At point *C* and all other points in the green shaded area there is an excess supply of money that exceeds the demand.

How does the economy adjust to guarantee that the given supply of money created by the government is exactly equal to the demand when the money market is out of equilibrium, as at point *D*? The economy might achieve money market equilibrium from point *D* by increasing the interest rate. This would move it to point *F*, cutting the demand for money. Or, instead, income might fall while the interest rate remains fixed. This would cause a movement to point *G* and would also cut the demand for money. Or some other combination might occur, with a partial drop in income and a partial increase in the interest rate. Which of these possibilities actually occurs depends on the slope of the *IS* curve, as we see in the next section.

SELF-TEST

Describe how the demand for money changes when the economy moves between the following two points in Figure 4-3.

1. From point *D* to point *F*
2. From point *D* to point *G*
3. From point *C* to point *F*
4. From point *C* to point *G*

4-4 The *IS* Curve Meets the *LM* Curve

Now we are ready to examine the economy's general equilibrium, which takes account of behavior in both the commodity and money markets. We do this by bringing together the IS_0 curve from Figure 3-6 and the LM_0 curve from Figure 4-3.

Equilibrium in the commodity market occurs only at points on the *IS* curve. Figure 4-4 copies the IS_0 schedule from Figure 3-6. At any point off the IS_0 curve, for instance *G* and *F*, the commodity market is out of equilibrium. *C*, *D*, and E_0 all represent different combinations of income and the interest rate that are compatible with commodity-market equilibrium. At which equilibrium point will the economy come to rest? The single IS_0 schedule does not provide enough information to determine *both* income and the interest rate. *Two* schedules are needed to pin down the equilibrium values of *two* unknown variables.

The *LM* curve provides the necessary additional information, showing all combinations of income and the interest rate at which the money market is in equilibrium for a given real money supply. Figure 4-4 copies the LM_0 schedule from Figure 4-3. At any point off the LM_0 curve, for instance points *C* and *D*,

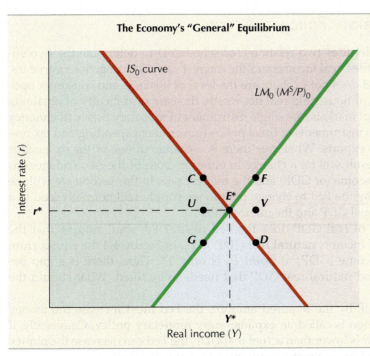

The Economy's "General" Equilibrium

Figure 4-4 **The *IS* and *LM* Schedules Cross at Last**

The IS_0 schedule is copied from Figure 3-6, the LM_0 schedule is copied from Figure 4-3. Only at the point E_0 is the economy in general equilibrium, with the conditions for equilibrium attained in both the commodity market (along *IS*) and the money market (along *LM*). At points *U*, *V*, *G*, and *F*, the commodity market is out of equilibrium. At points *U*, *V*, *C*, and *D*, the money market is out of equilibrium.

the money market is out of equilibrium. Equilibrium in the money market occurs only at points such as *G*, *F*, and *E**, each representing combinations of income and the interest rate at which the real demand for money is equal to the real money supply.

How does the economy arrive at its **general equilibrium** at point *E**? If the commodity market is out of equilibrium and involuntary inventory decumulation or accumulation occurs, firms will step up or cut production, pushing the economy in the direction needed to reach *E**. If the money market is out of equilibrium, there will be pressure to adjust interest rates. Either way, the economy arrives at *E**.

General equilibrium is a situation of simultaneous equilibrium in all the markets of the economy.

GLOBAL ECONOMIC CRISIS FOCUS

Causes of a Leftward Shift in the *IS* Curve

The *IS-LM* model helps to sort out the causes of business cycles and particularly the sources of the Global Economic Crisis 2008–09. By far the most important cause of business cycles is a host of factors that can shift the *IS* curve to the left, thus causing a recession. Recall that private sector demand shocks can shift the *IS* curve to the left, thus causing a recession. Among these shift factors are the effect on autonomous consumption of changes in consumer optimism, household net wealth, and the difficulty of obtaining loans from financial institutions. Even more important are the effects of business optimism and pessimism on planned investment, including the influence of the ease of obtaining mortgage loans for residential structures and commercial loans for nonresidential structures.

4-5   Monetary Policy in Action

The *IS-LM* model uses two relations (or schedules) to determine the two en-dogenous variables, real income and the interest rate. The exogenous variables, which the model does not explain, are the level of business and consumer opti-mism, the level of household real net worth, the ease or difficulty of obtaining loans on financial markets, the single instrument of monetary policy (the money supply), the two instruments of fiscal policy (government spending and tax rev-enues), and net exports. Whenever there is a change in one of the exogenous variables, the result will be a change in either or both of the two endogenous variables, real income (or GDP) and the interest rate. In this section we will see that a decision by the Fed to change the money supply will normally lead to a change in both real GDP and the interest rate.

What level of real GDP does the Fed desire? We shall assume that the desired level of income, natural real GDP, is Y_1. In Figure 4-4 the equilibrium level of real income (GDP) at point E_0 is only Y^*. Thus, there is a gap be-tween actual and natural real GDP that needs to be filled. What should the Fed do?

To raise GDP by the required amount, the Fed must increase the money supply. This action is called an **expansionary monetary policy.** Conversely, if natural real GDP is lower than actual real GDP, the Fed can decrease the money supply. This is an example of a **contractionary monetary policy.**

An **expansionary monetary policy** is one that has the effect of lowering interest rates and raising GDP.

A **contractionary monetary policy** is one that has the effect of lowering GDP and raising interest rates.

Normal Effects of an Increase in the Money Supply

Will an increase in the money supply increase real income, reduce the interest rate, or both? If the *IS* and *LM* curves have the "normal" shapes displayed in Figure 4-4, the answer is both.

Figure 4-5 repeats the initial LM_0 curve of Figure 4-4. Also repeated is the IS_0 curve of Figure 4-4. The economy's general equilibrium, the point

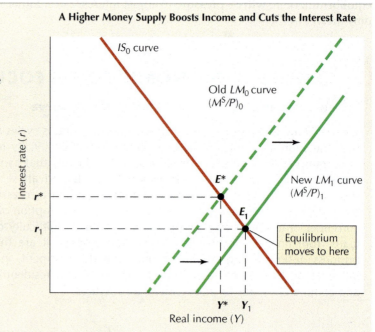

Figure 4-5 The Effect of an Increase in the Money Supply with a Normal *LM* Curve

The real money supply rises from $(M_s/P)_0$ along the old LM_0 curve to $(M_s/P)_1$ along the new LM_1. In order to maintain equilibrium in both the commodity and money markets, equilibrium income must rise and the equilibrium interest rate must fall, as indicated by the movement from E^* to E_1.

A Higher Money Supply Boosts Income and Cuts the Interest Rate

where both the money and commodity markets are in equilibrium, occurs at point E^*.

Assume that the Fed now raises the nominal money supply. As long as the price level stays fixed at 1.0, the real money supply increases by the same amount. The *LM* curve shifts to the right. How can the economy generate the increase in the real demand for money needed to balance the new higher supply?

Finding themselves with more money than they need, individuals transfer some money into savings accounts and use some to buy stocks, bonds, and commodities. This raises the prices of bonds and stocks and reduces the interest rate. The lower interest rate raises the desired level of autonomous consumption and investment spending, requiring an increase in production. Only at point E_1, are both the money and commodity markets in equilibrium. Compared to the starting point E^*, the increase in the real money supply has caused both an *increase* in real income and a *reduction* in the interest rate.

The *LM* Curve Can Also Be Shifted by Changes in the Demand for Money

So far we have interpreted the rightward movement of the *LM* curve in Figure 4-5 as being caused by an *increase* in the money supply. But exactly the same rightward shift in the *LM* curve can be caused by *reduction in* the demand for money. Some of the factors that could reduce the demand for money at a given interest rate and level of real income were introduced on p. 91. These include a decrease in wealth, an increase in expected future inflation, and new payment technologies such as ATMs and credit cards that reduce the need for people to carry currency in their purses and wallets. Any of these changes would shift the *LM* curve to the right and the opposite changes would shift the *LM* curve to the left.

If the Fed wants to avoid a change in real GDP and the interest rate when these shifts in money demand occur, then it needs to change the money supply in the same direction. Thus if the invention of ATMs and credit cards reduces the demand for money, the Fed must reduce the supply of money by the amount needed to keep the *LM* curve from shifting to the right.

4-6   How Fiscal Expansion Can "Crowd Out" Private Investment

In the last section we examined the effects on real income and the interest rate of changes in monetary policy by shifting the *LM* curve along a fixed *IS* curve. Now we shall do the reverse and shift the *IS* curve along a fixed *LM* curve. The original *IS* curve is copied from Figure 4-4 and is labeled in Figure 4-6 as the "old IS_0 curve."

Expansionary Fiscal Policy Shifts the *IS* Curve

An expansionary fiscal policy taking the form of an increase in government purchases shifts the *IS* curve to the right. The horizontal distance between the old and new *IS* curves represents not just the effect of the higher government expenditures in raising A_p but also the multiplier effect that shifts the *IS* curve rightwards by a multiple of A_p ($\Delta Y = k\Delta A_p$).

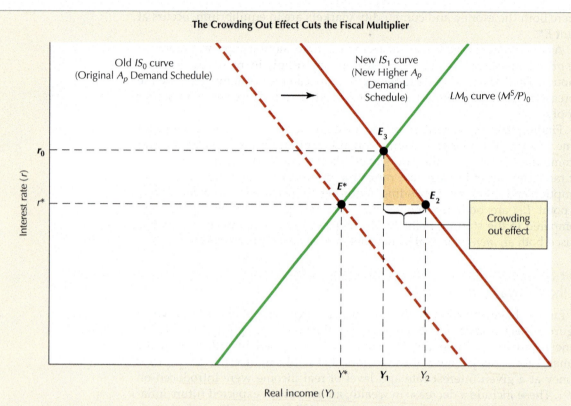

Figure 4-6 **The Effect on Real Income and the Interest Rate of an Increase in Government Spending**
Along the original IS_0 curve, the economy's equilibrium occurs at point E^*. An increase in government spending shifts the IS curve rightward to IS_1. The economy's equilibrium slides up the LM curve from point E^* to E_3. If the interest rate had not changed, as was assumed in the multiplier formula of Chapter 3, the economy would have shifted rightwards to position E_2 instead of rising to E_3. As the chart is drawn, half of the Chapter 3 multiplier from E^* to E_2 is wiped out by the crowding out effect due to the need to keep the economy on the LM curve, that is, to maintain equilibrium in the money market.

Figure 4-6 demonstrates that the effect of an expansional fiscal policy on real income is overstated by our original Chapter 3 multiplier ($k = 1/s$). This full fiscal multiplier would move the economy from E^* in Figure 4-6 straight rightwards to E_2. Instead, the interest rate rises and income increases less. The reason the interest rate must rise is that the rightward IS shift increases income, which increases the demand for money, but by assumption the real supply of money is held constant along the LM curve.

The Crowding Out Effect

The **crowding out effect** describes the effect of an increase in government spending or a reduction of tax rates in reducing the amount of one or more other components of private expenditures.

Some economists and journalists use the phrase **crowding out effect** to compare points such as E_2 and E_3 in Figure 4-6. The difference in real income between points E_2 and E_3 results from the investment and consumption spending crowded out by the higher interest rate. Point E_2, used in calculating the size of the crowding out effect, is a purely hypothetical position that the economy cannot and does not reach. Actually, far from being crowded out, total private spending is higher in the new equilibrium situation at E_3 than at the original situation at E^*. Not only does the increase in government spending boost GDP directly, but it has a multiplier effect that raises consumption and investment. However, there are two offsetting effects that explain why the new equilibrium point E_3 has a lower income than at point E_2.

The higher interest rate reduces autonomous consumption and planned investment by enough to offset most (but not all) of the increase of induced consumption stimulated by the added government expenditures. Without the increase of interest rates, we would be back in the model of Chapter 3 in which an increase of government spending would increase induced consumption without any offset at all in the amount of autonomous consumption or planned investment.

Can Crowding Out Be Avoided?

The fundamental cause of crowding out is an increase in the interest rate that is required whenever income rises and the supply of money is fixed while the demand for money responds positively to an increase in income. To offset the increase in the demand for money caused by higher income, it is necessary for the interest rate to rise by enough to offset the effects of higher income on the demand for money.

The simplest way to avoid crowding out would be for the Fed to increase the money supply, thus allowing the *LM* curve to shift rightward by the same amount as the *IS* curve. Another possible exception to crowding out would be if the demand for money did not depend on income. Other hypothetical situations in which crowding out would be avoided are when the *IS* curve is vertical (that is, the interest responsiveness of spending is zero) or when the *LM* curve is horizontal (that is, the interest responsiveness of the demand for money is infinite).

In the next section we will examine the situations in which monetary policy and fiscal policy are unusually strong or weak, and we will study interactions between the two types of policy. Can weak monetary policy be offset by strong fiscal policy, or vice versa?

GLOBAL ECONOMIC CRISIS FOCUS

How Monetary Policy Can Be Ineffective in the *IS-LM* Model

The next section provides a theoretical analysis of situations in which monetary or fiscal policy might be very weak or very strong. This is highly relevant to the Global Economic Crisis of 2008–09 because the Fed lost its control of interest rates once the federal funds rate reached almost zero in December 2008. The United States was also unable to use monetary policy to stimulate the economy during the last half of the Great Depression in 1935–40. Japan was not able to use monetary policy to stimulate its economy during much of the past 20 years. The theoretical analysis in the next sections helps us to understanding the Global Economic Crisis, and we continue this theme in the box on pp. 102–03 and in Chapter 5.

4-7 Strong and Weak Effects of Monetary Policy

We have already seen the effect of a normal monetary stimulus in Figure 4-5. The increase in the money supply requires that the economy adjust in order to raise the demand for money. This task of raising money demand is shared in Figure 4-5 between the higher level of income (which raises money demand) and the lower interest rate (which also raises money demand).

But there is the possibility that the effects of a monetary stimulus on income may be greater or lower than shown in Figure 4-5. It is possible that monetary policy may become so weak that it loses its ability to raise output. We will also see that the effects of fiscal policy on output may be strong, weak, or nonexistent.

Strong Effects of Monetary Expansion

The outcome depends on the slopes of both the *IS* and *LM* curves. With the normal slopes shown in the top frame of Figure 4-7, the economy moves from point E^* to point E_1. The higher money supply boosts income from Y^* to Y_1 and lowers the interest rate from r^* to r_1. The economy's equilibrium moves from E^* to E_1, just as in Figure 4-5. Higher income and lower interest rates suffice to boost the demand for money by the amount needed in order to match the assumed higher supply of money that the Fed has created.

What would it take for the impact of the same increase in the money supply to differ from this normal case? In one variant, monetary expansion has an unusually strong effect on income. This occurs when the *LM* curve is steep (due to a low interest responsiveness of the demand for money). Shown in the bottom frame of Figure 4-7 is the same starting place at E^*, and exactly the same *IS* curve as in the top frame. But now the old and new *LM* curves are vertical, indicating the extreme case of a zero interest responsiveness of the demand for money. The same increase in the money supply as in the top frame moves the *LM* curve to "new *LM*" (note that the horizontal shift in the *LM* curve in both the top and bottom frames is the identical distance marked from E^* to E_2). As a result, the economy moves from point E^* to point E_4 in the bottom frame. Income increases twice as much in the bottom frame as in the upper frame, while the interest rate falls twice as much.

Why does monetary policy exert a greater stimulus in the bottom frame? In both frames the money supply increases by the same amount, and so does money demand. But in the bottom frame the demand for money is totally insensitive to a reduction in the interest rate, *so all the "work" of boosting money*

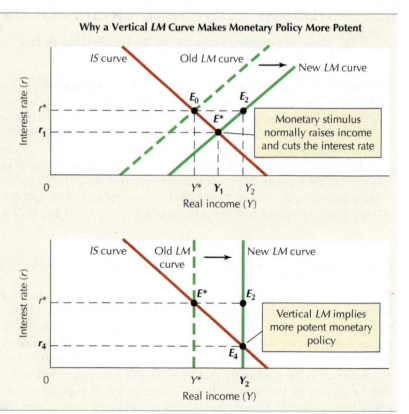

Figure 4-7 The Effect of an Increase in the Money Supply with a Normal *LM* Curve and a Vertical *LM* Curve

The top frame shows the normal effect of an increase in the real money supply, which is to raise real income and to reduce the interest rate. In the bottom frame, the *LM* curve is vertical, and the same increase in the real money supply leads to a greater drop in the interest rate and a greater increase in real income.

demand must be achieved by higher income. Since the lower interest rate offers no help in boosting money demand, income must rise further than in the top frame. And, to maintain commodity-market equilibrium along the fixed *IS* curve, a greater drop in the interest rate is needed to achieve the required boost in income.

Weak Effects of Monetary Policy

The Fed boosts the money supply when it believes that income is too low. But in some circumstances the effects of monetary policy are so weak that the policy cannot boost real income sufficiently to reach the desired level Y_1. This section reviews two such cases. First, changes in the interest rate may have only weak effects on autonomous planned spending (A_p). Second, money demand might be extremely sensitive to changes in the interest rate, which weakens the Fed's ability to reduce the interest rate.

Steep *IS* curve. The first case is shown in the top frame of Figure 4-8. The zero interest responsiveness of A_p implies that the *IS* curve is vertical. This situation occurs when business firms are so pessimistic about the future that they choose not to boost investment spending in response to lower interest rates. As a result, a lower interest rate does not raise equilibrium income. Income is "stuck" at point Y^* in response to the same rightward shift in the

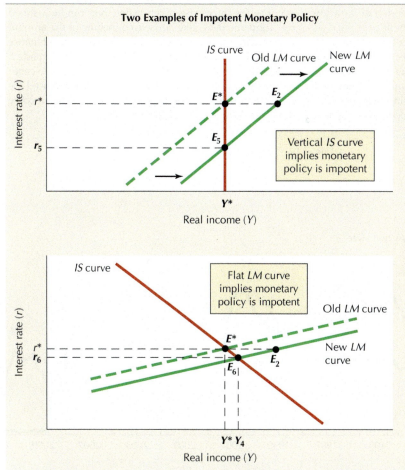

Two Examples of Impotent Monetary Policy

Figure 4-8 Effect of the Same Increase in the Real Money Supply with a Zero Interest Responsiveness of Spending and with a High Interest Responsiveness of the Demand for Money

In the top frame, the higher money supply does not stimulate expenditures because expenditures are assumed to be independent of the interest rate—that is, the *IS* curve is vertical. In the bottom frame, the *LM* curve is so flat that the same increase in the money supply (as in the top frame of this figure and in both frames of Figure 4-7) hardly reduces the interest rate at all, and so real income hardly increases at all.

UNDERSTANDING THE GLOBAL ECONOMIC CRISIS

How Easy Money Helped to Create the Housing Bubble and Bust

Monetary policy is carried out by the Federal Reserve System (or the "Fed" for short). Roughly every six weeks, an important meeting is held by the Federal Open Market Committee (FOMC). At precisely 2:15 P.M. Eastern time, an announcement is issued as to whether the FOMC has decided to raise, reduce, or leave unchanged the federal funds rate, an interest rate that banks charge each other for lending or borrowing bank reserves (see Chapter 13).

In our textbook model of Chapters 3 and 4, there is only one interest rate. In reality, there are two major interest rates, the federal funds rate controlled by the Fed, and the rate of 10-year government bonds, shown by the purple line in the figure. The 10-year bond rate is set in a daily auction at the Chicago Board of Trade and is only indirectly influenced by the Fed, but is extremely important as it is the basis on which interest rates on home mortgages are set. The traders who set the 10-year bond rate are influenced by their *expectations* about the future course of Fed policy; the longer the traders expect the Fed to keep the federal funds rate at a low level, the lower the 10-year bond rate will go.

In the left frame the green line plots the federal funds rate and the purple line plots the Treasury 10-year bond rate. The green line displays a series of sustained peaks and valleys in the federal funds rate, with prominent valleys in 1991–94, 2002–04, and starting in December 2008. The purple line shows that the 10-year bond rate wiggles a lot month to month but overall does not rise and fall by as much as the federal funds rate. Nevertheless, the federal funds rate clearly has an influence on the 10-year bond rate, as following each sharp decline in the green line we notice a marked decline in the red line.

How the Fed Fueled the Housing Price Bubble, 2003–06

In the text, a reduction in the interest rate achieved by the Fed stimulates spending, as the *LM* curve moves rightward along the downward-sloping *IS* curve, as in Figure 4-5. As an example, the decline in the federal funds rate in 2001–03 allowed auto companies to offer lower interest rates on auto loans. In response, auto purchasers raced to showrooms to buy cars. Lower mortgage rates allowed more home buyers to qualify for mortgages, or allowed them to buy bigger homes, stimulating new home construction, a part of real GDP.

A "bubble" in the price of an asset like housing can occur when prices rise much faster than can be justified by "fundamentals" like household income or the amount of rent charged for an apartment. The Fed's maintenance of a low 1.0 percent federal funds rate in 2002–04 made it so easy for people to finance houses that they were eager to buy houses and condos, and their eagerness caused the ratio of housing prices to personal disposable income almost to double between 2000 and 2006.

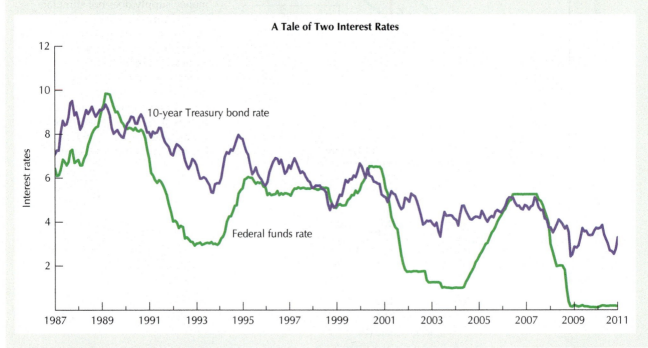

A Tale of Two Interest Rates

Housing prices surged and many new units, particularly condominiums, were bought not as residences but as speculative investments, as buyers placed bets that prices would keep rising and that the newly bought units could easily be "flipped," that is, sold quickly at a higher price to a new buyer. The Fed's low Treasury bill rate policy made it easy for lending institutions to borrow at low short-term rates and issue long-term mortgages at much higher rates. The profits created a new feeding frenzy in the mortgage broker industry, where brokers hungry for lucrative commissions and fees were "looking under every rock" for borrowers. A "sub-prime" mortgage sector developed in which low-income households were enticed into taking out loans that required minimal down payments and virtually no verification of employment or income.

The essence of a bubble is that eventually the merry-go-round has to end because housing prices cannot rise forever relative to household income. Not only was the practice of buying and "flipping" condos dependent on ever-rising prices, but so was the unprecedented amount of home mortgage refinancing or "re-fi." The Fed's low-interest rate policy allowed many homeowners to refinance their mortgages (repaying the old loan with a new loan, usually involving an increase in the amount borrowed). When interest rates stabilized in 2003, re-fi's continued due to the rise in house prices, since the higher the price of a house, the more the owner can borrow against it.

The Bubble Burst, and Residential Construction Collapsed

The merry-go-round began to slow down when the Fed raised the federal funds rate in stages from 1.0 percent in mid-2004 to 5.25 percent in mid-2006. This made granting loans less profitable for lending institutions, and so they raised their rates above the level that the sub-prime borrowers could afford. Gradually the rise in house prices slowed, stopped in mid-2006, and began its plunge.

Once house prices were falling, many households suddenly found that they were in trouble and began to cut back sharply their consumption spending. Speculators who had bought condos in order to flip them at higher prices found themselves instead stuck with condos worth less than the mortgage debt borrowed against them (this is called being "under water"). Households could no long obtain cash from their mortgages when house prices were falling rather than rising. As 2006 turned into 2007 and 2008, the decline in house prices became steeper and many homeowners found that they could not keep up with their monthly mortgage payments.

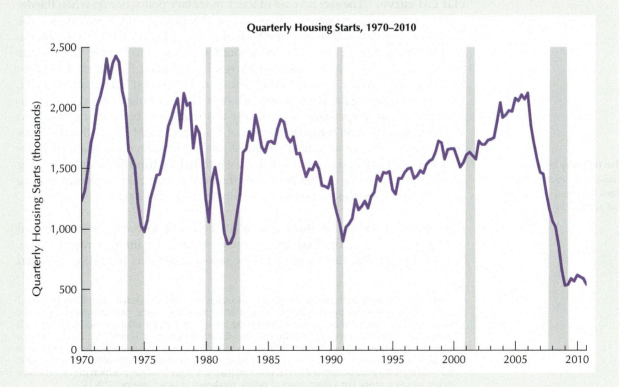

Quarterly Housing Starts, 1970–2010

The right graph shows that the result of the housing price bubble was an enormous upswing and subsequent sharp drop in residential investment, one of the major components of planned investment and planned autonomous spending (A_p). When residential construction collapses as it did after 2006, it creates a sharp leftward shift in the A_p demand curve and in the *IS* curve. The residential housing cycle of 2000–09 is a classic example of how volatility of investment is the most important single driver of the overall business cycle.

The right graph of housing starts provides some insight into the behavior of housing investment over the past four decades. It is not unusual for residential investment to crash by up to 50 percent, as occurred from 1972 to 1975 and from 1978 to 1982. The largest housing crash in American history since the Great Depression of the 1930s occurred between late 2006 and mid-2009

when housing starts fell from 2.1 million in early 2006 to only 0.5 million in early 2009, a remarkable decline of 76 percent.

By allowing the housing bubble to take place, the Fed is indirectly responsible for the catastrophe of the Global Economic Crisis. In the next chapter we tackle the difficult question, what alternative actions should the Fed have taken to avoid the debacle? Even though the housing price bubble was occurring, other aspects of the economy were weak, thus leading the Fed to keep the federal funds rate low in 2002–04 as it did. We will learn that the Fed's big mistake was limiting itself to a single policy instrument, its control of the federal funds rate. Housing markets in most other countries did not suffer the same instability as is recorded for the U.S. housing industry in the right graph. What did other countries do differently and can the United States learn from them?

LM curve that occurs in the top frame of Figure 4-7. The only effect of the higher money supply in the top frame of Figure 4-8 is a lower interest rate as the economy moves from point E_0 down vertically to point E_5. Since real income is stuck at Y^*, all the work of boosting money demand now must be achieved by a lower interest rate.

Flat *LM* curve. The second case of weak monetary policy occurs when the demand for money is extremely responsive to the interest rate, which makes the *LM* curve very flat, as shown in the bottom frame of Figure 4-8. Once again, the money supply goes up by the same amount as before, and the *LM* curve shifts horizontally by the distance shown between E_0 and point E_2. But now, because the *LM* curve is so flat, the economy's equilibrium position hardly moves at all, from E_0 to E_6. Before the interest rate falls enough to stimulate an increase in autonomous planned spending, it is already low enough to boost money demand and falls no further. In the extreme case of a horizontal *LM* curve, the Fed loses control over both output and the interest rate, which remain unchanged in response to a higher money supply. This case is called the **liquidity trap,** signifying a loss of control by the central bank over the interest rate. Some economists have suggested that Japan experienced a liquidity trap in 1998–2002.[2]

The **liquidity trap** is a situation in which the central bank loses its ability to reduce the interest rate.

Zero lower bound. A third reason the Fed may lose its power over real output can occur if the Fed has already pushed the interest rate to zero, because the interest rate cannot decline below zero. This limitation is called

---

[2] Normally an increase in the money supply reduces the interest rate because people try to get rid of the excess money by purchasing bonds and other financial assets, thus raising the price of bonds and other financial assets and reducing the interest rate. In the extreme (and hypothetical) case of the "liquidity trap," people are convinced that the prices of bonds and other financial assets are unusually high and are likely to fall, so they hold on to the extra money and refuse to buy any financial assets. As a result, the Fed (or the Bank of Japan) loses control of the interest rate, and the *LM* curve becomes a horizontal line that no longer shifts its position in response to a higher money supply. For a discussion of policy weakness in Japan, see pp. 110–11.

the "zero lower bound." Why is that? When the interest rate is positive, you pay the bank interest in return for borrowing money. But if the interest rate were negative, the bank would pay you interest for being so kind as to borrow money. *At a negative interest rate, the demand for loans would become infinite!* The box on pp. 110–11 discusses three historical examples when monetary policy lost its power due to the interest rate being at zero.[3]

◆ SELF-TEST

1. If the demand for money is independent of the interest rate, is the *LM* curve vertical or horizontal?

2. Does an increase in the money supply have strong or weak effects when the *LM* curve is steeper than normal?

3. When is it flatter than normal?

4-8   Strong and Weak Effects of Fiscal Policy

As with monetary policy, the effect of a fiscal policy stimulus on real income depends on the slopes of the *IS* and *LM* curves. Fiscal policy is strong when the demand for money is highly interest-responsive, as illustrated in the top frame of Figure 4-9. With this extreme case of a horizontal *LM* curve, the multiplier becomes just the simple multiplier (*k*) of Chapter 3. There is no crowding out effect, since the interest rate remains constant.

The opposite situation occurs when the interest responsiveness of money demand is zero, which makes the *LM* curve vertical. An increase in government spending shifts the *IS* curve to the right in the bottom frame of Figure 4-9, exactly as in the top frame by the identical distance from E^* to E_2, but real income cannot increase without throwing the money market out of equilibrium. Why? An increase in real income would raise the demand for money above the fixed money supply.

But because of the zero interest responsiveness of money demand, no increase in the interest rate can keep money demand in balance with the fixed money supply and a higher level of income. Thus as long as the money supply is fixed, real income cannot be any higher than its initial position at Y^*. In this case the only effect of a fiscal stimulus is to raise the interest rate. The crowding out effect is complete, with the higher interest rate cutting autonomous *private* spending by exactly the amount by which government spending increases, leaving total autonomous spending unchanged.

Which diagram is the most accurate depiction of the effects of expansionary fiscal policy with a fixed real money supply—the "normal" case depicted in Figure 4-6 or the extreme cases shown in Figure 4-9? Numerous historical episodes suggest that the original analysis of Figure 4-6 is accurate—the crowding out effect is partial rather than complete or nonexistent. Furthermore, statistical

---

[3] The zero lower bound only applies to the nominal (or actual) interest rate. It does not apply to the "real interest rate," which is the nominal interest rate minus the inflation rate. For instance, the nominal interest rate could be at its zero lower bound but the inflation rate could be 2 percent, implying a negative real interest rate of minus 2 percent. The real interest rate is defined on p. 321.

Figure 4-9 Effect of a Fiscal Stimulus When Money Demand Has an Infinite and a Zero Interest Responsiveness

In the top frame, an infinite interest responsiveness means that the interest rate is fixed, and no crowding out can occur. In contrast, the same fiscal stimulus has no effect on income when the interest responsiveness is zero (bottom frame), because then a higher interest rate releases no extra money to support higher income, and the income level is completely determined by the size of the real money supply. Since the fiscal stimulus causes no growth at all in income from E_0 to E_8, crowding out is complete.

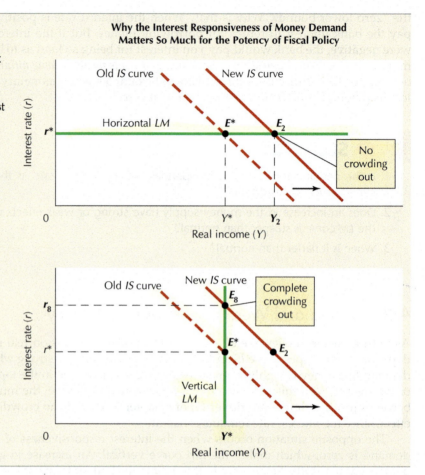

Why the Interest Responsiveness of Money Demand Matters So Much for the Potency of Fiscal Policy

evidence shows that the interest responsiveness of the demand for money is neither zero nor infinity. For this reason we should regard Figure 4-6 as giving a reliable example of the effects of expansionary fiscal policy, while Figure 4-9 depicts two artificial and extreme cases rather than realistic possibilities.

Summary of Crowding Out

The fundamental cause of crowding out is an increase in the interest rate caused by a fiscal policy stimulus. Crowding out can be avoided only if there is no upward pressure on the interest rate when the *IS* curve shifts rightward; with a fixed money supply this requires a horizontal *LM* curve as in the top frame of Figure 4-9. In this frame, there is zero crowding out. Another possibility, as we shall see in the next section, is for the Fed to maintain the interest rate constant by raising the money supply by the necessary amount. This avoids crowding out even if the *LM* curve has the normal positive slope.

Crowding out can be either partial or complete. If there is any increase in real income in response to the fiscal policy stimulus, crowding out is partial, as is shown in Figure 4-6. If there is no increase in income at all in response to the fiscal policy stimulus, then crowding out is complete. This occurs in the bottom frame of Figure 4-9, where there is absolutely no increase in income at the new point E_8, as compared with the initial point E^*.

SELF-TEST

Indicate whether crowding out is zero, partial, or complete in the following cases:

1. Zero interest responsiveness of autonomous planned spending.
2. Zero interest responsiveness of the demand for money.
3. Infinite interest responsiveness of the demand for money.

4-9   Using Fiscal and Monetary Policy Together

So far we have used the *IS-LM* model to examine, first, the effects of a monetary expansion and, second, the separate effects of a fiscal expansion. Yet the two types of policy do not always work in isolation. The Fed's monetary policy, formed on the "west side" of Washington, may strengthen or dampen the fiscal policy formed on the "east side" of Washington.[4]

The Fiscal Multiplier Depends on the Monetary Response

How does the response of income to a fiscal policy stimulus (the fiscal multiplier) depend on the Fed? The basic idea is simple: The more the Fed *expands* the money supply, the larger is the fiscal multiplier; the more the Fed *contracts* the money supply, the smaller is the fiscal multiplier. If the Fed contracts the money supply enough, the fiscal multiplier could even be negative.

Three cases are shown in Figure 4-10. In the upper left frame, we repeat the standard case from Figure 4-6. When the Fed holds the money supply constant, the *LM* curve remains at its original position. A fiscal stimulus consisting of either an increase in government spending or a tax cut shifts the *IS* curve rightward to the "new *IS* curve." Because the money supply is fixed, the higher demand for money created by rising income forces interest rates higher, crowding out some investment and consumption spending. The economy goes from point E_0 to E_3 just as in Figure 4-6.

In the upper right frame is a second possibility. If the Fed's goal is to keep the interest rate fixed, the money supply must be allowed to change passively whenever there is a shift in the *IS* curve. If the Fed allows the money supply to change by the amount needed to keep the interest rate constant at r^*, it must shift the *LM* curve rightward. The result of the fiscal stimulus is now the same as the Chapter 3 multiplier (k), which ignored the money market and the impact of interest rate changes. The economy goes from E_0 to E_2, the same as the new equilibrium position in the top frame of Figure 4-9. When trying to stabilize the interest rate and allowing the money supply to respond passively to any change in the *IS* curve, the Fed is said to "accommodate" fiscal policy. In effect, the east side of Washington has taken control of the west side.

The Japanese dilemma discussed in the box on pp. 110–11 shows that there is another advantage to using monetary and fiscal stimuli together—that the

---

[4] Monetary policy is formulated in the Federal Reserve building, about seven blocks west of the Washington Monument. Fiscal policy is formulated not just in the White House (near the Washington Monument) but in the Capitol and nearby Senate and House office buildings, which are about fifteen blocks east of the Washington Monument.

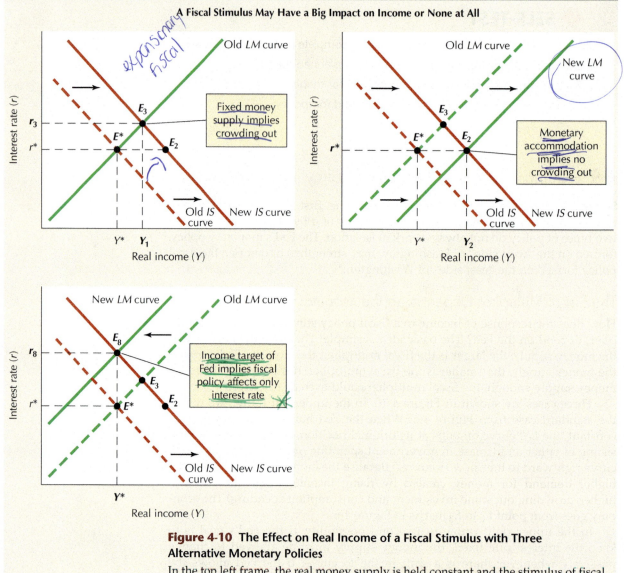

A Fiscal Stimulus May Have a Big Impact on Income or None at All

Figure 4-10 **The Effect on Real Income of a Fiscal Stimulus with Three Alternative Monetary Policies**

In the top left frame, the real money supply is held constant and the stimulus of fiscal policy on real income is partly crowded out (as in Figure 4-6). In the top right frame, the Fed maintains a fixed interest rate, which eliminates the crowding out effect (as in the top frame of Figure 4-9). In the bottom left frame, the Fed attempts to maintain a constant level of real income by shifting *LM* to the left whenever *IS* shifts to the right, implying complete crowding out; in this case, fiscal policy influences only the interest rate, not real income.

required fiscal deficit can be financed by money creation, thus avoiding any need for an increase in the national debt held by households, banks, and business firms. This implication of the *IS-LM* model applies equally to the United States as it struggles to recover from the 2007–09 Global Economic Crisis.

The Monetary-Fiscal Mix and Economic Growth

Returning to Figure 4-10, the bottom left frame shows that the *IS-LM* model contains an important lesson about economic growth. By changing the mix of monetary and fiscal policy, government policymakers can alter the interest rate without any need for a change in real income. In general, the lower the interest rate for any given level of real income or real GDP, the larger the fraction of that real GDP that will consist of real investment and the smaller the fraction that will consist of real consumption. Higher investment tends to boost economic growth.

Let us see in the bottom left frame of Figure 4-10 how the government can cause the interest rate to vary without changing the level of real income from its initial level Y^*. If the Fed wants to maintain income at Y^*, it can respond to a fiscal stimulus *by moving the* LM *curve in the opposite direction from the movement in the* IS *curve*. Thus, if government spending is increased, the Fed must reduce the money supply. In the bottom left frame of Figure 4-10, the economy moves from E^* to E_8 (the same position shown in the bottom frame of Figure 4-9). When the Fed behaves this way, fiscal policy no longer has any control over the level of income and affects only the interest rate. The effect of fiscal policy is to raise the interest rate from r^* to r_8, because the Fed has reduced the money supply by enough to maintain the initial level of income Y^*.

This illustrates an important point about monetary and fiscal policy. Once the government has decided on the desirable level of income, it can achieve that level of income with many different interest rates. We can assume that points E^* and E_8 share not only the same level of output, but also the same unemployment rate. What are the differences?

Point E_8 offsets the fiscal policy stimulus, assumed to be a higher level of government spending, by reducing the money supply. In contrast, point E^* has a higher real money supply (shown by the fact that the LM curve is farther to the right) but a tighter fiscal policy (shown by the fact that the IS curve is farther to the left). The higher interest rate at E_8 crowds out planned investment and autonomous consumption below that at point E^*, in order to make room for a higher level of government spending.

The two points E^* and E_8 are said to differ in the mix of monetary and fiscal policy. Point E^* has a **policy mix** of "easy money, tight fiscal," while point E_8 has the opposite policy mix of "tight money, easy fiscal." Which mix should society prefer? At E^*, investment is higher; thus the economy is building for the future, and its future level of productivity growth will be higher. At E_8, government spending is higher than at E^*, and investment is lower. Should society prefer the faster output growth of point E^* or the higher level of public services of point E_8?

The **policy mix** refers to the combination of monetary and fiscal policy in effect in a given situation. A mix of tight monetary and easy fiscal policy leads to high interest rates, while a mix of easy monetary and tight fiscal policy leads to low interest rates.

This is a central question of macroeconomics. Its solution depends on whether the government spending consists largely of government consumption (national defense, police, and fire protection) or government investment (highways and school buildings). If the extra government spending at point E_8 consists of government consumption, then the choice between points E_8 and E^* depends on society's taste for present consumption of goods and services (at E_8) versus future consumption, since a high investment strategy at E^* yields higher consumption only in the future. If the extra government spending at E_8 consists of government investment, then the choice depends on whether there is a higher payoff for society from government investment (of which there is more at E_8) as compared with private investment (of which there is more at E^*). The same criteria are relevant if the fiscal stimulus takes the form of a tax cut that can stimulate either private investment or consumption, depending on the types of taxes that are cut.

Summary of Monetary-Fiscal Interactions

By working together, monetary and fiscal policy can be more effective than if they are operated independently. A fiscal stimulus accompanied by a monetary expansion is more effective than a fiscal stimulus carried out in the presence of a

INTERNATIONAL PERSPECTIVE

Monetary Policy Hits the Zero Lower Bound in Japan and in the United States

We have seen that monetary policy loses its effectiveness in three situations—when the *IS* curve is vertical as in the top frame of Figure 4-8, when the *LM* curve is nearly horizontal as in the bottom frame of Figure 4-8, or when the interest rate controlled by the Fed reaches the zero lower bound. This third factor has rendered monetary policy nearly impotent in three important historical episodes. Two involve the United States, one in the late 1930s and the second in the current recession and weak recovery. The third involves Japan, which experienced a "lost decade" of slow income growth, and the Japan malaise has persisted for more than a decade.

The three examples illustrated in this box provide nightmare scenarios in which the economy is on its knees, unemployment is high and real GDP growth is sluggish, yet the central bank (Fed or Bank of Japan) is powerless to revive the economy. This is no hypothetical theory. The near-zero interest rates and the sluggish GDP growth are recorded in the data for everyone to see.

Example #1: The United States Economy, Prostrate in 1935–40

The unemployment rate in the Great Depression remained above 10 percent from 1930 to 1940 and only fell below 10 percent as a result of government spending

for rearmament in 1940–41. The first chart shows that monetary policy could do nothing, as it hit the zero lower bound for interest rates way back in 1935. There was nothing further for monetary policy to do once the short-term interest rate had hit zero.

Example #2: Japan Since 1992

The low level of the Japanese short-term interest rate since 1995 is shown in the second graph. Monetary policy could not push interest rates appreciably lower, yet fiscal policymakers felt constrained in achieving a large fiscal stimulus. Why? They resisted further deficit spending because the ratio of public debt to GDP in Japan had already exceeded 100 percent, far higher than the equivalent U.S. number in 2010 (see box on p. 171).

However, numerous critics of Japanese policy point to the *IS-LM* model as suggesting a way out of the Japanese policy dilemma. As shown in the top right frame of Figure 4-10 on p. 108, a combined monetary and fiscal policy stimulus that shifts the *LM* and *IS* curves rightward by the same amount can boost real GDP without any need for a decline in interest rates. Also, with such a combined policy, there is no need for a further increase in the national debt held by the public, since to

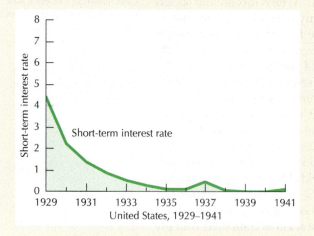

United States, 1929–1941

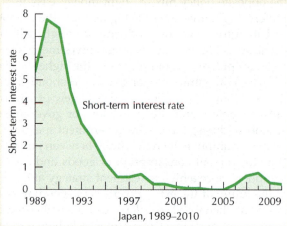

Japan, 1989–2010

fixed or shrinking money supply. This can be seen in the difference between the upper left and upper right frames of Figure 4-10, where the crowding out evident on the left is eliminated on the right by the increase in the money supply. Stagnation in Japan since 1995 (discussed in the box above) is ample evidence that both monetary and fiscal policy can be paralyzed when they ignore the possibility of working together.

achieve its monetary expansion, the central bank can buy the government bonds issued as a result of the increased fiscal deficit. Government bonds owned by the central bank remain inside the government and are not a debt of the government to domestic or foreign individuals or financial institutions.

Example #3: The United States Since 2009

The federal funds rate controlled by the Fed has been close to zero since January 2009, as shown in the third graph. This has eliminated any ability of the Fed to stimulate economic activity by reducing short-term interest rates. As we shall see in the next chapter, the Fed has experimented with unconventional policies called "quantitative easing" to attempt to reduce long-term interest rates such as those displayed in the graph on p. 102.

Why Do Governments Resist the Combined Power of Monetary and Fiscal Policy?

The three episodes all have one thing in common. There is a policy solution that policymakers at the time could not perceive but would have raised economic activity, including the United States in 1935–40, Japan in 1998–2006, and the United States since 2009. This solution is to engineer a massive fiscal policy

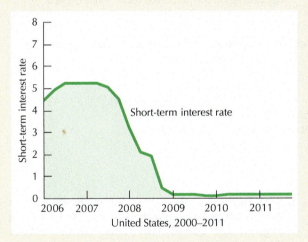

United States, 2000–2011

stimulus funded by a simultaneous monetary policy stimulus. This combined monetary–fiscal policy expansion is exactly what is illustrated by the upper right frame of Figure 4-10. The *IS* and *LM* curves shift rightward together.

This type of combined policy response solves all policy dilemmas at once. Is the central bank worried because it cannot lower the interest rate? No, because it can still buy up the government securities issued to fund the growing public debt.

Should the public worry that the public debt is increasing? No, because the only part of the public debt that matters is that held outside the government. When a fiscal policy stimulus is financed by the Fed buying government bonds, as occurs whenever there is a simultaneous rightward shift of the *IS* and *LM* curves as in the upper right frame of Figure 4-10, there is no increase of interest rates and no crowding out.

In fact, debates about fiscal stimulus in the United States in 2010 and 2011 were ill-informed. There was too much worry about the rise in the public debt and the interest burden it would place on future American taxpayers. But that was an entirely false worry. As long as the additional fiscal deficits are financed by Fed purchases of government bonds (as implied by the simultaneous rightward shift of the *IS* and *LM* curves), the national debt can be increased without limit with no added burden of future taxpayers to pay interest on the debt.

A traditional worry is that fiscal deficits paid for by the Central bank will be inflationary. This is also a false claim, as is evident in many episodes of economic history, including the failure of the 2001–07 Bush administration deficits to ignite any inflation at all, after subtracting the effects of food and energy prices. Despite fiscal deficits and a zero federal funds rate in 2010, there was no acceleration of inflation. Instead, inflation (i.e., "core inflation" stripped of food and energy prices) slowed down in this period.

In Chapter 5 we will return to these themes. How can the economy be revived after the Global Economic Crisis? At the zero lower bound, the response of fiscal policy is crucial, but how large must that fiscal stimulus be?

In 2010–11 the United States faced a similar dilemma, as the economic recovery appeared to be too weak to achieve the swift decline in the unemployment rate that was needed. Is the U.S. economy in the early phase of a "lost decade" as occurred in Japan and during the Great Depression on a larger scale? We return to this issue in the next chapter.

Summary

1. The main functions of money are its use as a medium of exchange, a store of value, and a unit of account.
2. The real quantity of money that people demand depends both on real income and on the interest rate. Equilibrium in the money market requires that the real supply of money equal the demand for real money balances.
3. The *LM* curve represents all the combinations of real income and of the interest rate where the money market is in equilibrium.
4. An increase in the money supply raises real income and reduces the interest rate when the *IS* curve has its normal negative slope and the *LM* curve has its normal positive slope.
5. A fiscal expansion raises real income and the interest rate, causing crowding out if the money supply is held constant and both the *IS* and *LM* curves have their normal slopes.
6. Monetary policy has a relatively strong effect on real income when the interest responsiveness of the demand for money is relatively low (steep *LM* curve). Monetary policy is weak when the interest responsiveness of the demand for money is very high (flat *LM* curve), or when the interest responsiveness of autonomous planned spending is very low (steep *IS* curve).
7. The normal effect of a fiscal policy stimulus, consisting either of an increase in government spending or a reduction in tax rates, is to raise both real income and the interest rate. The fiscal multiplier is lower than the Chapter 3 multiplier (k) due to partial crowding out of planned investment and autonomous consumption.
8. A fiscal stimulus has a relatively strong effect on real income when the interest responsiveness of the demand for money is relatively high (flat *LM* curve) or the interest responsiveness of autonomous spending is relatively low (steep *IS* curve). A fiscal stimulus has a relatively weak effect with the opposite pattern of interest responsiveness (steep *LM* curve or flat *IS* curve).
9. The effect of a fiscal stimulus on income (fiscal multiplier) is greatest, and there is no crowding out effect, if the Fed is attempting to stabilize interest rates, since this requires that the money supply passively accommodate the fiscal stimulus (the *LM* curve must move to the right by exactly the same distance as the *IS* curve).
10. An intermediate fiscal multiplier, with partial crowding out, occurs when the Fed maintains a constant real money supply, the original case of Figure 4-6.
11. The fiscal multiplier is zero when the Fed stabilizes real income, moving the *LM* curve in the opposite direction from the *IS* curve.
12. By varying the monetary-fiscal mix, government policymakers can maintain a given level of real income with many different interest rates. An "easy money, tight fiscal" mix yields a low interest rate and stimulates private investment. A "tight money, easy fiscal" mix yields a higher interest rate, less private investment, and some combination of additional government consumption, government investment, or private consumption, depending on the particular fiscal policy chosen.

Note: Asterisks designate Concepts, Questions, and Problems that require the Appendix to Chapter 4.

Concepts

money supply	general equilibrium	crowding out effect
real money balances	expansionary monetary policy	liquidity trap
LM curve	contractionary monetary policy	policy mix

Questions

1. Describe the automatic adjustment that will take place in the economy when the current position of the economy is off the *IS* curve.
2. Describe the automatic adjustment that will take place in the economy when the current position of the economy is off the *LM* curve.
3. Why is the distinction between autonomous expenditure and induced expenditure crucial to an understanding of the crowding out effect?
4. Under what circumstances could government spending (federal, state, and local) be crowded out? Do you think this is likely to be the case?
5. What happens to the velocity of money (defined in the box on p. 93) when the economy moves along a given *LM* curve? Why does velocity behave this way?
6. Use Figure 4-4 to identify a point where each of the following situations occurs and how the economy will adjust:
   (a) planned spending exceeds income and there is an excess supply of money
   (b) unintended inventory investment is positive and the real demand for money is less than the real supply of money

(c) unintended inventory investment is negative and there is an excess demand for money

(d) planned spending is less than income and the real demand for money exceeds the real supply of money

7. Discuss how the Fed's monetary policy from 2002–04 fueled the housing bubble and how its change in policy from mid-2004 to mid-2006 contributed to the bursting of the housing bubble.

8. A change in which of the following would cause the *LM* curve to shift? To rotate? To both shift and rotate? Which do not affect the position or slope of the *LM* curve? (See the box on p. 93.)

(a) nominal money supply (M^s)

(b) responsiveness of the demand for money to the interest rate

(c) responsiveness of the demand for money to income

(d) business and consumer confidence

(e) interest rate (r)

(f) In 2001, many countries in Europe switched from their own currencies to the euro. In each country, the prices of goods and services and nominal amounts in checking accounts were adjusted in proportion to the amount a unit of each currency could be converted into the euro.

(g) People switch from using checks to using debit cards to buy goods and services.

(h) People switch from using checks to using credit cards to buy goods and services.

9. During the 1980s, the size of the federal government debt became so large that servicing the interest payments became a significant portion of total federal expenditure. In response, many representatives and senators felt that the federal deficit needed to be reduced. If government spending (G) becomes negatively sensitive to changes in the interest rate, what effect does this have on the amount of autonomous consumption and planned investment that is crowded out? If autonomous taxes (T_a) become positively sensitive to changes in the interest rate, what effect does this have on the amount of autonomous consumption and planned investment that is crowded out?

10. Suppose that private sector spending is highly sensitive to a change in the interest rate. Compare the effectiveness of monetary and fiscal policy in terms of raising and lowering real GDP.

11. Suppose that the demand for money is highly insensitive to a change in the interest rate. Compare the effectiveness of monetary and fiscal policy in terms of raising and lowering real GDP.

12. Suppose Congress raises autonomous taxes. How will this tax increase affect real income? The interest rate? Consumption? Planned investment?

13. The "Great Moderation" from 1985–2007 could have been due to either smaller demand shocks when compared to the period prior to 1985 or a better response by monetary policymakers between 1985 and 2007 to the same demand shocks that occurred prior to 1985. Evidence to determine which of these arguments is correct may be found by examining the behavior of the interest rate during the "Great Moderation." If the "Great Moderation" was due to smaller demand shocks, then less variation in real GDP would have been accompanied by less variation in the interest rate as well. On the other hand, if the "Great Moderation" was due to better response by monetary policymakers to the same demand shocks that occurred previously, then the decline in the variation of real GDP would have been accompanied by an increase in the variation of the interest rate. Evaluate these arguments using the *IS-LM* model.

14. Suppose that the Fed is not worried about inflation, but is convinced that unemployment is too high. Use the *IS-LM* model to explain what actions the Fed is likely to take to ensure that very little private sector spending is crowded out by a tax cut aimed at reducing unemployment.

15. You learned in Chapter 1 that inflation speeds up when actual real GDP exceeds natural real GDP. Suppose that policymakers believe actual real GDP exceeds natural real GDP and fear that inflation will rise. Compare the effects on private sector spending of the following two policies: (a) only monetary policymakers are able to take actions to bring actual and natural real GDP in line with one another; (b) monetary and fiscal policymakers are able to jointly adopt a "tight money, tight fiscal" policy mix in an effort to reduce actual real GDP relative to natural real GDP.

16. Assume that the Federal Reserve Board has decided to maintain the level of real GDP at the current level. If Congress passes a $50 billion decrease in personal taxes, what action, if any, would the Fed have to take? Describe the effect of the actions of Congress and the Fed on:

(a) the interest rate

(b) the composition of output

(c) the future growth rate of the GDP

17. Evaluate the following argument using the *IS-LM* model: When consumer and business confidence are high and the economy is booming, the interest rate is high. Therefore, during a recession the Fed could promote a higher level of income if it used monetary policy to raise the interest rate.

18. Explain how the zero lower bound for the interest rate controlled by the Fed has an impact on the effectiveness of monetary policy. Discuss what mix of monetary and fiscal policy can be used to increase economic activity when the zero lower bound is reached. Finally, evaluate the validity of the arguments presented against that policy mix when the zero lower bound is reached.

Problems

myeconlab   Visit www.MyEconLab.com to complete these or similar exercises.

1. You are given the following equation for the real demand for money: $(M/P)^d = .25Y - 50r$.
   (a) Compute the demand for money for each of the following interest rates when income is equal to $11,940, $12,000, $12,060, $12,120, and $12,180:

   $$r = 4.4 \quad r = 4.7 \quad r = 5.0 \quad r = 5.3$$
   $$r = 5.6 \quad r = 5.9 \quad r = 6.2$$

   (b) Given your answers to part a, graph the demand for money curves when income equals $11,940 and income equals $12,180.
   (c) Suppose the real money supply, M^s/P, equals $2,750. Given your answers to part a, find the interest rates and levels of real income at which the money market is in equilibrium. Use these combinations of the interest rate and real income to graph the *LM* curve, given that the real money supply equals $2,750. Label this curve LM_0.
   (d) Suppose the real money supply increases to $2,780. Given your answers to part a, find the new combinations of the interest rates and real income at which the money market is in equilibrium. Use these combinations to graph the new *LM* curve, given that the real money supply now equals $2,780. Label this curve LM_1.
   (e) Suppose the real money supply decreases to $2,720. Given your answers to part a, find the new combinations of the interest rates and real income at which the money market is in equilibrium. Use these combinations to graph the new *LM* curve, given that the real money supply now equals $2,720. Label this curve LM_2.

2. You are given the following information for the commodity market, in which taxes, planned investment, government spending on goods and services, and net exports are autonomous, but consumption and planned investment change as the interest rate changes:

   $$C_a = 2,180 - 20r \quad c = 0.6 \quad I_p = 2,400 - 60r$$
   $$G = 2,000 \quad NX = -300 \quad T = 1,800$$

   The money market is described in problem 1.
   (a) Compute the values of the marginal propensity to save, s, and the multiplier, k.
   (b) Derive the equation for the autonomous planned spending A_p.
   (c) Derive the equation for the *IS* curve, $Y = kA_p$, and graph the *IS* curve when the interest rate equals 4.7, 5.0, 5.3, 5.6, and 5.9.
   (d) Using your answers to part c of problem 1 and part c of this problem, explain at what interest rate and at which level of real income the commodity and money markets are both in equilibrium.

(e) In the first half of 2003, the Fed changed monetary policy because unemployment was too high and it feared any additional decline in the rate of inflation would result in deflation. Suppose that natural real GDP equals $12,060 and the equilibrium in part c is similar to economic conditions in the first half of 2003. Using your answers to parts d or e of problem 1 and part c of this problem, explain how the Fed should change the real money supply in order to move real income to natural real GDP in an effort to reduce unemployment and avoid a further reduction in the inflation rate.

3. The money and commodity markets are as described in problems 1 and 2 and the real money supply equals $2,750, so that the economy's equilibrium is initially the same as in part d of problem 2.
   (a) During the Congressional election of 2010, Party A proposes to increase government spending on roads and bridges by $120 billion and to pay for that spending by raising taxes by that amount. If Party A's proposal were to be enacted, derive what the new equations for autonomous planned spending, A_p, and the *IS* curve, $Y = kA_p$, would be. Graph that new *IS* curve when the interest rate equals 4.7, 5.0, 5.3, 5.6, and 5.9.
   (b) Using your answer to part a, explain at what interest rate and at which level of real income the commodity and money markets would both be in equilibrium under Party A's proposal.
   (c) During the same campaign of 2010, Party B proposes to cut taxes by $80 billion and not change government spending. If Party B's proposal were to be enacted, derive what the new equations for the autonomous planned spending, A_p, and the *IS* curve, $Y = kA_p$, would be. Graph that new *IS* curve when the interest rate equals 4.7, 5.0, 5.3, 5.6, and 5.9.
   (d) Using your answer to part c, explain at what interest rate and at which level of real income the commodity and money markets would both be in equilibrium under Party B's proposal.
   (e) Explain how the economy would be similar and different under the proposals of Parties A and B.

4. The money and commodity markets are as described in problems 1 and 2 and the real money supply equals $2,750, so that the economy's equilibrium is initially the same as in part d of problem 2.
   (a) In an effort to reduce oil consumption, fiscal policy makers decide to increase government spending on research and development of alternative energy sources by $48 billion. Derive the new equations for the autonomous planned spending, A_p, and the *IS* curve, $Y = kA_p$, given the increase in energy

spending. Graph that new IS curve when the interest rate equals 4.7, 5.0, 5.3, 5.6, and 5.9.

(b) Using your answer to part a, explain at what interest rate and at which level of real income the commodity and money markets are both in equilibrium, given the increase in energy spending.

(c) Using your graph of the new IS curve and your answer to part b, compute how much real income is crowded out by the increase in energy spending. Using your equation for autonomous planned spending, compute how much autonomous private sector spending is crowded out by the increase in energy spending.

(d) Suppose that the Fed wants to prevent any crowding out from the increase in energy spending. Using your answer to either part d or e of problem 1, explain how the Fed should change the real money supply in order to avoid the crowding out effect. For the Fed to be willing to do this without risking a rise in the inflation rate, explain what the smallest level of natural real GDP could be.

(e) Suppose that natural real GDP equals $12,000 and that the Fed does not want the increase in energy spending to cause a rise in the inflation rate. Using your answer to either part d or e of problem 1, explain how the Fed should change the real money supply in order to avoid a rise in the inflation rate.

*5. Assume the following equations summarize the structure of an economy.

$$C = C_a + 0.85(Y - T)$$
$$C_a = 260 - 10r$$
$$T = 200 + 0.2Y$$
$$(M/P)^d = 0.25Y - 25r$$
$$M^s/P = 2,125$$
$$I_p = 1,500 - 30r$$
$$G = 1,700$$
$$NX = 500 - 0.08Y$$

(a) Compute the value of the multiplier.
(b) Derive the equation for the autonomous planned spending schedule, A_p.
(c) Derive the equation for the IS curve.
(d) Calculate the slope of the IS curve, $\Delta r/\Delta Y$. (Hint: Use the equation of the IS curve to compute $\Delta Y/\Delta r$. Then use the fact that the slope of the IS curve, $\Delta r/\Delta Y$, equals the inverse of $\Delta Y/\Delta r$.)
(e) Derive the equation for the LM curve.
(f) Calculate the slope of the LM curve, $\Delta r/\Delta Y$. (To do this, use the same hint as in part d.)
(g) Compute the equilibrium interest rate (r).
(h) Compute the equilibrium real output (Y).

*6. Using the information given in problem 5, compute the new equilibrium real output and interest rate

(a) if government spending increases by 160. What is the amount of autonomous spending that is crowded out by this expansionary fiscal policy?
(b) if G equals 1,700 but the real money supply increases by 100.

*7. Using the information given in problem 5, compute by how much the Fed must increase the money supply if it wants to avoid the crowding out of the expansionary fiscal policy described in part a of problem 6. What will be the new value of real GDP?

*8. Suppose that the real demand for money in the economy changes to $(M/P)^d = 0.2Y - 75r$ and the real money supply changes to $M^s/P = 1,431.9$ but the structure of the commodity market is the same as in problem 5.

(a) Derive the equation for the new LM curve and verify that the equilibrium interest rate and real output are the same as you computed in parts 5g and 5h, respectively.
(b) Calculate the slope of the new LM curve, $\Delta r/\Delta Y$.
(c) Compared to the money demand curve given in problem 5, has money demand become more or less responsive to a change to the interest rate? Is the LM curve steeper or flatter as a result? How does this change in the interest responsiveness of money demand alter the amount by which real output will change following an expansionary change in fiscal or monetary policy?
(d) Compute the new equilibrium interest rate and real output if government spending increases by 160.
(e) Compute the new equilibrium interest rate and real output if G equals 1,700 but the real money supply increases by 100.
(f) How and why do the answers in parts d and e differ from problem 6a and 6b, respectively? Is your prediction in part c confirmed?

*9. Suppose that autonomous consumption and planned investment in the economy described in problem 5 change to $C_a = 470 - 15r$ and $I_p = 1,700 - 60r$. All other aspects of the structure of the commodity and the money markets are as described in problem 5.

(a) Derive the equation for the new IS curve and verify that the equilibrium interest rate and real output are the same as you computed in parts 5g and 5h, respectively.
(b) Calculate the slope of the new IS curve, $\Delta r/\Delta Y$.
(c) Compared to problem 5, have autonomous consumption and planned investment become more or less responsive to a change in the interest rate? Is the IS curve steeper or flatter as a result? How does this change in the interest responsiveness of autonomous spending alter the amount by which real output will change following an expansionary change in fiscal or monetary policy?
(d) Compute the new equilibrium interest rate and real output if government spending increases by 160.

(e) Compute the new equilibrium interest rate and real output if G equals 1,700 but the real money supply increases by 100.

(f) How and why do the answers in parts d and e differ from problem 6a and 6b, respectively? Is your prediction in part c confirmed?

*10. Assume the following equations summarize the structure of an economy.

$$C = C_a + 0.8(Y - T)$$
$$C_a = 260 - 10r$$
$$T = 200 + 0.2Y$$
$$(M/P)^d = 0.25Y - 25r$$
$$M^s/P = 2,000$$
$$I_p = 1,900 - 40r$$
$$G = 1,800$$
$$NX = 700 - 0.14Y$$

(a) Derive the equation for the *IS* curve.

(b) Derive the equation for the *LM* curve.

(c) Compute the equilibrium interest rate (r) and real output (Y).

(d) Suppose consumer and business confidence decline, resulting in decreases in the amounts of autonomous consumption and planned investment by 40 and 60, respectively. Derive the new equation for the *IS* curve and compute the new equilibrium interest rate (r) and real output (Y).

(e) Suppose that natural real GDP equals the amount of real output that you computed in part c. Compute the amount of a cut in autonomous taxes that would be necessary in order to overcome the declines in consumer and business confidence and restore real output to natural real GDP.

(f) Suppose that instead of fiscal policy, monetary policy is used to restore real output to natural real GDP. Compute by how much the Fed would have to increase the money supply in order to do so.

(g) Compute the amounts of autonomous consumption and planned investment associated with each of the policies described in parts e and f. Explain which policy is likely to result in a higher rate of growth in real output over the long run.

 SELF-TEST ANSWERS

p. 91. (1) The levels of income (Y) and the interest rate on assets other than money (r) are the two determinants of the real demand for money, $(M/P)^d$. (2) An increase in Y raises the real demand for money, and an increase in the interest rate reduces the real demand for money. (3) Neither determinant shifts the *IS* curve, because the axes of the *IS* curve diagram are these very determinants, Y and r.

p. 94. (1) From point D to point F the level of income is constant but the demand for money declines as the interest rate moves upward from r_1 to r_0. (2) From point D to point G the interest rate is constant but the demand for money declines as income declines from Y_1 to Y_0. (3) From point C to point F the interest rate is constant but the demand for money increases as income increases from Y_0 to Y_1. (4) From point C to point G the level of income is constant but the demand for money increases as the interest rate declines from r_0 to r_1.

p. 105. (1) If the demand for money is independent of the interest rate (the variable on the vertical axis), then the *LM* curve is vertical. (2) An increase in the money supply has strong effects when the *LM* curve is steeper than normal, as occurs in the bottom frame of Figure 4-7. (3) An increase in the money supply has weak effects when the *LM* curve is flatter than normal, as occurs in the bottom frame of Figure 4-8.

p. 107. (1) Zero crowding out, because the increase in the interest rate caused by a fiscal policy expansion does not have any effect in reducing planned investment or autonomous consumption; (2) complete crowding out, the case shown in the bottom frame of Figure 4-9; (3) zero crowding out, the case shown in the top frame of Figure 4-9.

Appendix to Chapter 4

The Elementary Algebra of the *IS-LM* Model

When you see an *IS* curve crossing an *LM* curve, as in Chapter 4, you know that the equilibrium level of income (Y) and the interest rate (r) occurs at the point of crossing, as at point E_0 in Figure 4-4. But how can the equilibrium level of income and the interest rate be calculated numerically? Wherever you see two lines crossing to determine the values of two variables such as Y and r, exactly the same solution can be obtained by solving together the two equations describing the two lines.

In the Appendix to Chapter 3, we found that equilibrium income is equal to autonomous planned spending (A_p) divided by the marginal leakage rate, so that the autonomous spending multiplier (k) is equal to the inverse of the marginal leakage rate ($k = 1/\text{MLR}$).

$$\text{multiplier} = k = \frac{1}{\text{marginal leakage rate}} = \frac{1}{\text{MLR}} \tag{1}$$

In this appendix we shall continue using the same example as in Chapters 3 and 4, namely $k = 4.0$.

Once we have determined the multiplier from equation (1) above, we can write real income simply as:

General Linear Form | Numerical Example

$$Y = kA_p \qquad\qquad Y = 4.0A_p \tag{2}$$

In Section 3-7, the assumption was introduced that autonomous planned spending A_p declines when there is an increase in the interest rate (r). If the amount of A_p at a zero interest rate is written as (A_p'), then the value of A_p can be written:

General Linear Form | Numerical Example

$$A_p = A_p' - br \qquad\qquad A_p = A_p' - 100r \tag{3}$$

Here b is the interest responsiveness of A_p; in our example there is a \$100 billion decline in A_p per one percentage point increase in the interest rate. Substituting (3) into (2), we obtain the equation for the *IS* schedule:

General Linear Form | Numerical Example

$$Y = k(A_p' - br) \qquad\qquad Y = 4.0(A_p' - 100r) \tag{4}$$

Thus, if A_p' is 2,500 and $r = 0$, the IS_0 curve intersects the horizontal axis at 10,000.

The *LM* curve shows all combinations of income (Y) and the interest rate (r) where the real money supply (M^s/P) equals the real demand for money ($M/P)^d$, which in turn depends on Y and r. This situation of equilibrium in the money market was previously written as equation (4.1) in the text:

General Linear Form | Numerical Example

$$\left(\frac{M^s}{P}\right) = \left(\frac{M}{P}\right)^d = hY - fr \qquad\qquad \left(\frac{M^s}{P}\right) = 0.5Y - 200r \tag{5}$$

In this example, where h is the responsiveness of real money demand to higher real income, 0.5 here, and f is the interest responsiveness of real money demand, there is a

$200 billion decline in real money demand per one percentage point increase in the interest rate. Adding fr (or $200r$) to both sides of (5), and then dividing by h (or 0.5), we obtain the equation for the *LM* schedule when M^s/P is 2,000:

General Linear Form   Numerical Example

$$Y = \frac{\frac{M^s}{P} + fr}{h} \qquad\qquad Y = \frac{2,000 + 200r}{0.5} \qquad (6)$$

We are assured that the commodity market is in equilibrium whenever Y is related to r by equation (4) and that the money market is in equilibrium whenever Y is related to r by equation (6). To make sure that both markets are in equilibrium, both equations must be satisfied at once.

Equations (4) and (6) together constitute an *economic model*. Finding the value of two unknown variables in economics is very much like baking a cake. One starts with a list of ingredients, the *parameters* (or knowns) of the model: A_p, M^s/P, b, f, h, and k. Then one stirs the ingredients together using the recipe instructions, in this case equations (4) and (6). The outcome is the value of the unknown variables, Y and r. The main rule in economic cake-baking is that the number of equations (the recipe instructions) must be equal to the number of unknowns to be determined. In this example, there are two equations and two unknowns (Y and r). There is no limit on the parameters, the number of ingredients known in advance. Here we have six parameters, but we could have seven, ten, or any number.

To convert the two equations of the model into one equation specifying the value of unknown Y in terms of the six known parameters, we simply substitute (6) into (4). To do this, we rearrange (6) to place the interest rate on the left side of the equation, and then we substitute the resulting expression for r in (4). First, rearrange (6) to move r to the left side:[1]

$$r = \frac{hY - \frac{M^s}{P}}{f} \qquad (6a)$$

Second, substitute the right side of (6a) for r in (4):

$$Y = k(A_0 - br) = k\left[A_p' - \frac{bhY}{f} + \frac{b}{f}\left(\frac{M^s}{P}\right)\right] \qquad (7)$$

Now (7) can be solved for Y by adding $kbhY/f$ to both sides and dividing both sides by k:

$$Y\left(\frac{1}{k} + \frac{bh}{f}\right) = A_p' + \frac{b}{f}\left(\frac{M^s}{P}\right)$$

---

[1] First multiply both sides of (6) by h:

$$hY = \frac{M^s}{P} + fr$$

then subtract M^s/P from both sides:

$$hY - \frac{M^s}{P} = fr$$

Now divide both sides by f:

$$\frac{hY - \frac{M^s}{P}}{f} = r$$

Equation (6a) is then obtained by reversing the two sides of this equation.

Finally, both sides are divided by the left term in parentheses:

$$Y = \frac{A'_p + \dfrac{b}{f}\left(\dfrac{M^s}{P}\right)}{\dfrac{1}{k} + \dfrac{bh}{f}} \tag{8}$$

Equation (8) is our master general equilibrium income equation and combines all the information in the *IS* and *LM* curves together; when (8) is satisfied, both the commodity market and money market are in equilibrium. It can be used in any situation to calculate the level of real income by simply substituting into (8) the particular values of the six known right-hand parameters in order to calculate unknown income.[2]

Because we are interested primarily in the effect on income of a change in A'_p or M^s/P, we can simplify (8):

$$Y = k_1 A'_p + k_2\left(\frac{M^s}{P}\right) \tag{9}$$

All we have done in converting (8) into (9) is to give new names, k_1 and k_2, to the multiplier effects of A'_p and M^s/P on income. The definitions and numerical values of k_1 and k_2 are:

General Linear Form   Numerical Example

$$k_1 = \frac{1}{\dfrac{1}{k} + \dfrac{bh}{f}} \qquad\qquad k_1 = \frac{1}{\dfrac{1}{4.0} + \dfrac{100(0.5)}{200}} = 2.0 \tag{10}$$

$$k_2 = \frac{b/f}{\dfrac{1}{k} + \dfrac{bh}{f}} = \left(\frac{b}{f}\right)k_1 \qquad\qquad k_2 = \frac{100(2.0)}{200} = 1.0 \tag{11}$$

Using the numerical values in (10) and (11), the simplified equation (9) can be used to calculate the value of real income:

$$Y = k_1 A'_p + k_2\left(\frac{M^s}{P}\right) \tag{12}$$

$$= 2.0(2{,}500) + 1.0(2{,}000)$$

$$= 7{,}000$$

This is an example of how the value of income can be calculated for a specific numerical example. With this equation it is extremely easy to calculate the new value of Y when there is a change in A'_p caused by government fiscal policy or by a change in business and consumer confidence, and when there is a change in M^s/P caused by a change in the nominal money supply. Remember, however, that the definitions of k_1 and k_2 in (10) and (11) do depend on particular assumptions about the value of parameters $b, f, h,$ and k.

The main point of Sections 4-8 and 4-9 is that changes in fiscal and monetary policy may have either strong or weak effects on income, depending on the answers to these questions.

1. How does the effect of a change in A'_p on income, the multiplier k_1, depend on the values of b and f (the interest responsiveness of the demand for commodities and money)?

---

[2] A parameter is taken as given or known within a given exercise. Parameters include not just the small letters denoting the multiplier (k), and the interest and income responsiveness of planned autonomous expenditures and money demand ($b, h,$ and f), but also autonomous planned expenditures at a zero interest rate (A'_p) and the real money supply (M^s/P). Most exercises involve examining the effects of a change in a single parameter, as in A'_p or in M^s/P.

2. How does the effect of a change in M^s on income, the multiplier k_2, depend on the values of b and f?

Example: Let us raise M^s/P from 2,000 to 3,000. We know, using (10), that the value of k_1 is 2.0. Using (11), the value of k_2 is 1.0. Thus, using equation (9), income is

$$Y = k_1 A_p' + k_2\left(\frac{M^s}{P}\right)$$

$$= 2.0(2,500) + 1(3,000)$$

$$= 8,000$$

Using equation (6a), we learn that the interest rate in the new situation is

$$r = \frac{[(0.5)(8,000) - 3,000]}{200} = 5.0$$

This example, in which an increase in the money supply raises real income and reduces the interest rate, is shown in the top frame of Figure 4-7. The bottom frame of the same figure shows the alternative income if the *LM* curve is vertical, which happens when the interest responsiveness of the demand for money is zero ($f = 0$).

$$k_1 = \frac{1}{\dfrac{1}{k} + \dfrac{bh}{f}} = \frac{1}{\dfrac{1}{4} + \dfrac{100(0.5)}{0}} = 0$$

$$k_2 = \frac{h}{\dfrac{f}{k} + bh} = \frac{100}{\dfrac{0}{4} + 100(0.5)} = 2.0$$

Thus, in the bottom frame of Figure 4-7, the new equilibrium situation at point E_4, illustrated there without specific numbers, is as follows when the real money supply rises from 3,500 along the old *LM* line to 4,500 along the new *LM* line:

$$Y = k_1 A_p' + k_2\left(\frac{M^s}{P}\right) = 0(2,500) + 2.0(4,500) = 9,000$$

We cannot solve for the interest rate using (6a), since the denominator (f) is zero. Instead, we can use equation (4) to solve for the interest rate along the *IS* curve. When (4) is solved for the interest rate, we obtain the general expression:

$$r = \frac{A_p' - Y/k}{b} = \frac{2,500 - 9,000/4}{100} = \frac{250}{100} = 2.5$$

This lower interest rate is depicted by point E_4 in the lower frame of Figure 4-7. In short, a comparison of the top and bottom frames of Figure 4-7 shows that a given increase in the money supply (a \$1,000 billion change in the numerical example) has double the effect when $f = 0$ as when $f = 200$.

Financial Markets, Financial Regulation, and Economic Instability

Atoms or systems into ruin hurl'd, and now a bubble burst, and now a world.
—Alexander Pope, *An Essay on Man, 1733*

5-1 Introduction: Financial Markets and Macroeconomics

Households around the world have been devastated by the Global Economic Crisis. Their real incomes have declined while their chances of losing a job have increased and their chances of finding a new job have greatly diminished.

U.S. economic activity reached its peak in late 2007, and the downturn started in earnest in September 2008 with a financial crisis that originated on Wall Street in New York City. Monetary and fiscal policy reacted swiftly and undertook both standard policy actions and also unprecedented decisions that may have averted a repeat of the Great Depression of the 1930s. While macro-economists frequently disagree, there is a growing consensus that the policy response in the fall of 2008 and in 2009 was swift, strong, and appropriate.

Yet more than two years after the 2008 financial crisis, these aggressive policy measures have failed to bring the economy of the world or of the United States back to normal. In the United States in late 2010 nearly half of the unem-ployed had been without jobs for 6 months or more, and 1.5 million people had been without a job for more than two years. Tens of millions of people had seen their finances shattered, their dreams of retirement postponed, and the benefits of their college education eroding due to the difficulty of finding any job at all, much less the good jobs traditionally obtained by college graduates.

Integrating Financial Markets into the *IS-LM* Model

At first glance the *IS-LM* model introduced in the two previous chapters offers an easy solution to a downturn. If the intersection of the *IS* and *LM* curves is too far to the left, with inadequate output that is insufficient to generate the necessary num-ber of jobs that people desire, there is a simple solution. Monetary policymakers can move the *LM* curve to the right while fiscal policymakers can move the *IS* curve to the right. While we learned in Chapter 4 that in extreme situations mone-tary policy can be impotent, or fiscal policy can be impotent, we also learned that there is no limit to their power when they are used together in tandem.

Yet the reality of economic stagnation and high unemployment in 2010 and beyond raises fundamental questions about the *IS-LM* model. What is missing? This chapter introduces fundamental causes of macroeconomic instability that can originate in financial markets. Part of the impact of financial markets on the economy comes through the wealth effect. We have already learned in Chapter 3 that a decline in real household wealth reduces autonomous consumption, raises saving, and pushes the *IS* curve to the left. A decline in real wealth can occur not

121

only as a result of a stock market crash and pricking of a housing bubble, as in 2007–08, but also if households borrow too much and raise the ratio of their debts to their incomes to unprecedented levels, as also occurred at the same time.

In addition to the wealth effect on autonomous consumption, Chapter 3 also introduced the financial market as a separate cause of changes in autonomous consumption and hence in the *IS* curve. When financial markets make it very easy to borrow, the *IS* curve shifts to the right, and vice versa. In 2002–06 loans to buy houses and cars were easy to get, moving *IS* to the right, but in 2008–10 these loans were much harder to obtain, shifting *IS* quite far to the left.

In addition to its impact on the *IS* curve, a financial crisis changes the interpretation of the *LM* curve. A crisis typically raises the interest rates charged for loans to households and corporations far above the federal funds rate set by the Fed. In this chapter we move beyond the simplifying *IS-LM* assumption that there is just one interest rate. When the economy is in trouble, as in the fall of 2008, market participants believe that all loans are riskier than before and raise the rate charged for loans far above the interest rate set by the Federal Reserve (hereafter the "Fed"). The impact of risk on the *LM* curve is a second channel by which a financial crisis can reduce real GDP.

Bubbles, Risk, and Leverage

The Global Economic Crisis is remarkable because it did not have multiple origins around the world but rather started in a relatively small part of the U.S. financial market, that for so-called *subprime mortgages* granted to borrowers with low incomes and poor credit histories. To understand how problems in such a small part of the financial market could have such monumental consequences, we begin in this chapter by learning how banks have traditionally operated and how the mortgage market worked in more normal times. Then we will examine how financial markets changed after 2000 to develop innovations in mortgage markets that ultimately contributed to its instability and ultimate crash.

Financial crises are nothing new and indeed they have been documented over the past 800 years.[1] A feature of some financial crises is a price *bubble* in which the price of an asset, for instance stocks or houses, soars far above "fundamentals" like corporate earnings or household incomes. The chapter examines similarities and differences among three important bubbles and their aftermath, of which the most recent was the 2000–06 housing bubble, its subsequent collapse, and the financial crisis that it caused.

A common theme of this chapter is that there are several culprits to blame for the Global Economic Crisis. Some critics say that the Fed was to blame by keeping interest rates too low for too long in 2002–04. Others blame financial innovations that increased *risk* and *leverage*, two new concepts defined and examined below. Still others blame lax regulation that allowed risky financial innovations to occur to such an extent that they undermined the ability of monetary and fiscal policy to stabilize the economy.

 ## 5-2 CASE STUDY

Dimensions of the Global Economic Crisis

Before we try to understand the causes of the Global Economic Crisis, we should begin by examining some measures of its severity. First we compare

---

[1] For the history of financial crises going back 800 years, see the much heralded recent book, Carmen M. Reinhart and Kenneth S. Rogoff, *This Time Is Different.* Princeton University Press, 2009.

measures of the output gap for the United States, Europe, and Japan, and this provides convincing evidence that the crisis has been worldwide, not just limited to the United States. Next we examine several measures of distress in the U.S. labor market, showing that by some measures the U.S. labor market in 2010 was in the worst shape since the Great Depression of the 1930s.

The Worldwide Economic Downturn

It is unusual for all regions of the world economy to experience a simultaneous and synchronized business cycle. Yet this is exactly what happened in 2008–09, as output in every economy tumbled downward together. A key measure of the impact of any economic downturn is the output gap, that is, the percent log ratio of actual to natural real GDP.[2] When actual real GDP is exactly equal to natural real GDP, the output gap is zero. In prosperous times when actual real GDP is above natural real GDP, the output gap is positive. And in downturns like 2008–09, the output gap is negative.

Figure 5-1 compares the output gap of the United States with those of Europe and of Japan.[3] The output gap is set equal to zero in 2007, a normal year without much evidence of excess supply or excess demand. While these three economic units displayed differing behavior before 2007, their uniform decline in the output gap after 2007 is remarkable. The three lines tumble downwards like a waterfall. The simultaneity in the downward movement provides support for the view that there was a common set of causes for the Global Economic Crisis.

Another striking fact is that there is little difference in the forecast recovery of the output gap in the United States, Europe, and Japan in 2010 and 2011.

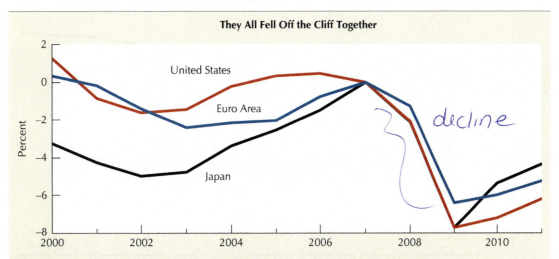

Figure 5-1 The Log Percent Output Gap for the United States, the Euro Area, and Japan, Index with 2007 = 0, 2000–2011

The graph shows that the output gap was slightly above zero in the United States in the three years leading up to the business cycle peak year of 2007. The gap for the Euro Area before 2007 was negative and for Japan even more negative. However, after 2007 the three output gaps simultaneously collapsed by about the same amount and recovered only slowly after the trough in 2009.

Source: OECD *Economic Outlook.*

---

[2] The GDP gap was defined on p. 6 of Chapter 1. The "output gap" is a synonym for the "GDP gap."

[3] Here and elsewhere in the book, "Europe" refers to the member nations of the Euro currency area.

Thus the first unique property of the Global Economic Crisis is that it struck all countries at the same time. The second unique property is that for all nations recovery is weak and a full return of the output gap from large negative percentages back to zero appears likely to take many years, not just a year or two as in previous recession episodes. Subsequently at the end of the chapter we will ask why the crisis, which originated in the U.S. market for residential mortgages, spread so swiftly to other countries.

The Unique Severity of the Economic Crisis in the United States: 2007–11 Compared to 1981–85

So far we have learned that the United States shares with Europe and Japan both the simultaneous sharp free-fall of the output gap and a lamentably slow recovery in 2010 and 2011. Useful perspective for the United States is provided by a comparison between the post-2007 recession and early recovery with the cyclical episode of 1981–85 that had previously ranked as the worst U.S. downturn since the Great Depression.

While the 1981–85 recession and recovery had very different causes than that of 2007–11, its magnitude was similar, at least in the recession phase. Figure 5-2

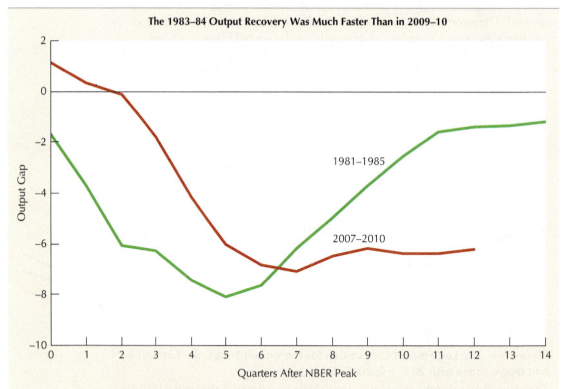

Figure 5-2 The Log Percent Output Gap for the United States in Two Episodes, 1981–85 and 2007–10

Both lines plot the output gap for the United States. The green line begins in the peak quarter of the previous expansion, 1981:Q3, and the red line begins in the most recent business cycle peak quarter, 2007:Q4. The green line shows that the output gap started lower than in 2007, and the recovery after quarter 5 (1982:Q4) was much faster. The red line exhibits a rapid decline between quarters 2 and 7 (2009:Q3) and then a sluggish recovery.

Source: NIPA Table 1.1.6 and author's calculations.

shows the quarterly output gap in both episodes starting in the peak quarter of the previous expansion, 1981:Q3 in the earlier episode and 2007:Q4 in the most recent event. The green line for 1981–85 starts at a negative value and declines to a low point of −8.2 percent in the fifth quarter of the recession, while the red line for 2007–11 starts at a positive value and falls faster and longer, reaching a low point of −7.1 percent in the seventh quarter of the recession.

But in the recent recession the employment gap fell even further to −7.3 percent in the worst quarter of 2009:Q4. What gives the recent recession the title as the worst since the 1930s is not the output gap comparison of Figure 5-2, or the depth to which the employment gap fell in Figure 5-3, but the widely predicted likelihood that the employment gap will continue to be negative for five or more years after 2010. In contrast, the employment gap jumped rapidly in the 1981–82 recession from its worst value of −5.1 percent in 1983:Q1 to −1.4 percent in 1984:Q2, only five quarters later.

The weakness of the economic recovery in 2010–11 also helps to explain why so many unemployed people could not find new jobs, again very much unlike the recovery of 1983–84. The starkest contrast between the two

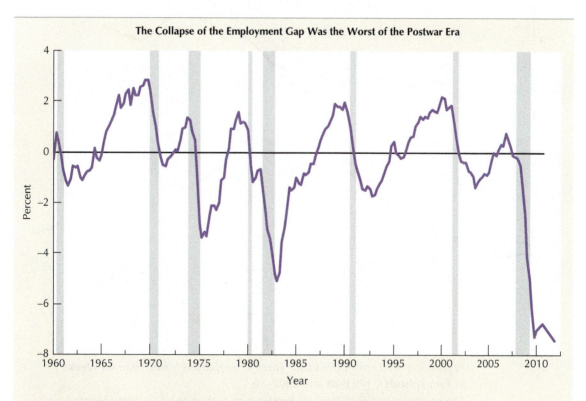

Figure 5-3 The Log Percent Employment Gap for the United States, 1960–2010

The employment gap is the log ratio of actual employment relative to the level of employment that would occur if the economy were operating with a zero output gap. The sharp declines in the employment gap in recessions reflect mainly rising unemployment but also falling labor force participation as people become discouraged and give up looking for jobs. The precipitous decline in the employment gap that occurred in 2008–09 was the worst in the postwar era and substantially greater than in the previous worst recession of 1981–82.

Source: bls.gov and author's calculations.

cyclical episodes is in the ever-increasing length of unemployment spells in 2010–11. In Figure 5-4 the green line for 1981–85 shows that those unemployed more than 26 weeks (or 6 months) peaked roughly two years after the cyclical peak at 2.6 percent of the labor force and then declined in the subsequent year and a half to just 1.1 percent. In contrast, the red line for 2007–11 shows that this percentage had not yet peaked in late 2010, almost three years after the peak, and was roughly double the level of the same percentage back in 1983–84.

What makes the post-2009 economic recovery in the United States so notable as to justify the frequent attention in this book to the causes and solutions to the Global Economic Crisis? Figure 5-4 provides the key contrast to

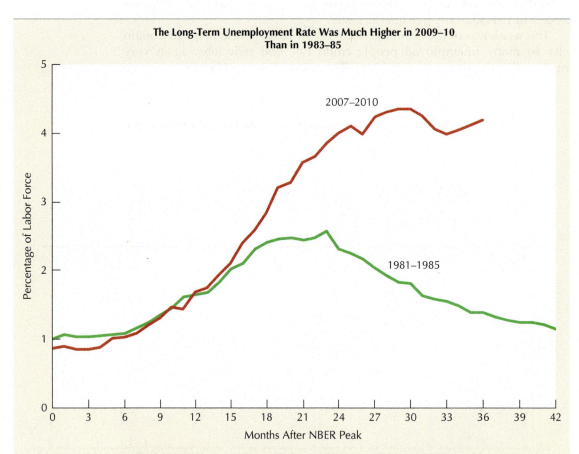

Figure 5-4 Percent of the Labor Force Unemployed More Than 26 Weeks in Two Episodes, 1981–85 and 2007–10

The percent of the labor force unemployed more than 26 weeks was about the same at the beginning of the 1981–82 recession as at the beginning of the 2007–09 recession. For the first 16 months this percentage grew by about the same amount in both recessions, from about 1 percent to about 2 percent. But then in the earlier recession the percentage leveled off and declined almost back to 1 percent, whereas in the recent recession the percentage continued to rise until it reached above 4 percent.

Source: bls.gov.

earlier major recessions. Three years after the previous business cycle peak, long-term unemployment was getting worse, not better. Millions had been unemployed more than one year. Desperation and pessimism set in among these millions that they would ever again be able to find jobs that used their education and accumulated work experience. Those who found jobs often could do so only by accepting wage rates that were half or less of their previous pay rates. The hopeless struggle to find jobs had no postwar precedent and began in some respects to resemble the decade-long Great Depression of the 1930s.

The post-2008 economic crisis is the most important macroeconomic event since the Great Depression. The rest of this chapter develops a unified analysis of its causes and links that analysis to the *IS-LM* model of Chapters 3 and 4. The search for solutions begins in this chapter and continues in subsequent chapters. ◆

5-3 Financial Institutions, Balance Sheets, and Leverage

Some households and firms currently spend more than they earn and need to borrow funds. Others currently earn more than they spend and need a place to keep their savings. Financial markets perform the essential function of channeling funds from those with surplus funds (savers) to those in need of funds (borrowers). In this section we learn the basics of how banks and other financial institutions are able to create loans to households and business firms by several multiples of the equity (or net worth) of the institution.

Financial Institutions and Financial Markets

Funds are channeled from savers to borrowers, either directly or indirectly. The direct channel is through **financial markets,** exchanges where securities or financial instruments are bought and sold. Financial markets provide direct finance when borrowers issue securities directly to savers. The securities, such as General Motors stock or bonds, are a liability or debt of the borrower (General Motors) and an asset of the saver.

The indirect channel operates through **financial intermediaries,** such as Citibank, which issue liabilities in their own names. The intermediaries balance their liabilities (for example, savings accounts) with assets (for example, loans).

What determines whether savers channel their funds through financial markets or through intermediaries? The simple answer is that savers are only willing to purchase securities through the direct channel—that is, via financial markets—from borrowers *large enough* to have established a reputation for paying back borrowed money. Most large business firms and units of government issue securities directly through financial markets.

But most individuals and small businesses cannot do so because they do not have established reputations: Individuals may be willing to entrust their savings to Citibank, but they are unlikely to accept IOUs issued by other individuals like themselves. Financial intermediaries *spread risk* and

Financial markets are organized exchanges where securities and financial instruments are bought and sold.

Financial intermediaries make loans to borrowers and obtain funds from savers, often by accepting deposits.

Figure 5-5 **The Role of Financial Intermediaries and Financial Markets**

Shown on the left are the savers—any economic unit with surplus funds. The arrows show where savers send their funds—they can be held as currency, deposited in a financial intermediary, or used to purchase a money market instrument, stocks, or bonds directly from the financial markets. Financial intermediaries both purchase financial market instruments and also lend to borrowers. So borrowers have two sources of funds, shown by the two red arrows pointing to the "Borrowers" box: loans from intermediaries and funds that come from issuing financial market instruments.

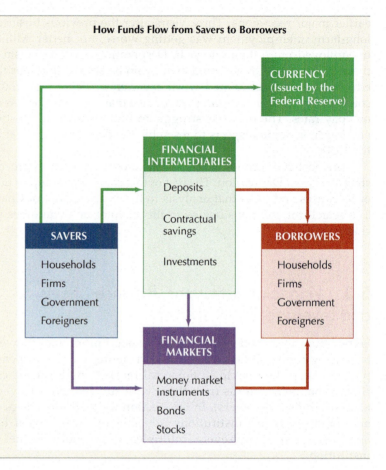

How Funds Flow from Savers to Borrowers

collect information efficiently. Thus Citibank makes loans to many borrowers, only a small fraction of whom will fail to repay their loans. To cover the losses from borrowers who do not repay, Citibank sets aside a contingency fund and adds the cost of this fund to the rates charged to borrowers. Because Citibank is large enough to hire specialists to assess credit risks, it is less risky for it to lend to individuals than it is for individuals to lend to each other.

Figure 5-5 illustrates the role of financial markets and institutions. The blue box on the left represents savers, and the red box on the right represents borrowers. The green box represents the financial intermediaries, and the purple box represents the financial markets. The lines connecting the boxes indicate the flows of funds from savers to borrowers. Notice that financial intermediaries not only provide funds directly to borrowers (loans to individuals) but also purchase financial market instruments. Banks and other intermediaries hold billions of dollars worth of bonds, mostly issued by the government, in addition to loans granted directly to borrowers.

Balance Sheets and Leverage

Every economic unit has a balance sheet that sums up that unit's assets and liabilities. If assets are greater than liabilities, the economic unit has a positive net worth, and if assets are less than liabilities, the economic unit has a negative net worth. Most households have a positive net worth, and this tends to increase with age as households save for their retirement. Older people in their 60s typically

Table 5-1

The Initial Balance Sheet of the First Reliable Bank

(Millions of dollars)

Assets		Liabilities	
Loans and Investments	910	Deposits	900
Reserves (including cash)	90		
Total Assets	1000	*Total Liabilities*	900
		Equity (Net Worth)	100

have a much higher net worth than people in their 20s, and indeed many young people have a negative net worth when their meager assets are swamped by large liabilities for student loans.

Just as each household has a balance sheet, so does every corporation. The balance sheet of the hypothetical First Reliable Bank is shown in Table 5-1. The assets are shown on the left; these are the assets that the bank owns, including mortgages, car loans, and loans to business firms. The liabilities are shown on the right; these are the amounts that the bank owes to others.

The difference between total assets and total liabilities is shown on the lower right as the bank's **equity,** which is the same as net worth. Notice that the vertical line separating the assets from the liabilities joins together with the horizontal line under the words "Assets" and "Liabilities" to form the shape of the letter "T." Thus balance sheets are also called "T-accounts." The First Reliable Bank has $1,000 million in assets and $900 million in liabilities, and so its bank equity is $100 million. Bank equity is the same thing as its net worth and is sometimes called "bank capital."

> **Equity** is the difference between the assets and liabilities of an economic unit and is the same as "net worth."

The assets of any bank consist mainly of loans of all types. Most banks also have investments in government debt and private securities, for instance, mortgage-backed securities. Any "security" is a promise for the borrower to pay back a certain amount of interest each year, and the value of these promises can change over time as market conditions change. When borrowers are impacted by a recession and lose their jobs, the value of the securities they have issued declines.

Banks tend to reduce their loans and raise their investments when they perceive that loans involve a substantial **risk** that the borrower may not be able to repay the loan. In such times banks turn to investments that they believe to be safe, including bonds issued by the U.S. government. As we shall see later, banks also believed that mortgage-backed securities issued by private institutions were safe, but the housing meltdown greatly reduced the value of many of these securities.

> **Risk** is the probability that a given investment or loan will fail to bring the expected return and may result in a loss of the partial or full value of the investment.

The other type of bank asset is the cash in its vaults that is held in anticipation of depositor withdrawals and the bank's reserves that it is required to hold at the Fed to meet the Fed's mandatory reserve requirements. The bank sets aside 10 percent of deposits to hold as cash and reserves, and so it holds $90 million in cash and reserves because that is 10 percent of its deposits of $900 million. The assets of the First Reliable Bank in Table 5-1 are divided up into $910 million of loans and investments and the remaining $90 million in cash and reserves, summing to the $1,000 million in total assets.

The bank's main liability is the deposits that it owes to its depositors. Some of these deposits are checking and ordinary savings deposits and can be withdrawn at any time. To meet such unexpected withdrawals, the bank may maintain cash and reserves at the Fed in excess of the Fed's formal reserve requirements. Other deposits cannot be withdrawn before a fixed term, for instance one year or three years. The longer the term of the deposit, the higher the interest rate that is paid on it.

In addition to being subject to the Fed's reserve requirements, the bank is also required to maintain a capital requirement, which is the ratio of its equity to the value of its total assets. In the example of the First Reliable Bank, the capital ratio is the amount of equity ($100 million) divided by total assets ($1,000 million), or 10 percent.

Leverage: A Central Ingredient in the Financial Market Meltdown

Leverage is the ratio of the liabilities of a financial institution to equity capital. Leverage increases when banks develop methods to grant more loans with their existing equity capital.

Banks make profits by making loans at an interest rate higher than that which they pay to depositors. The more loans that banks grant per dollar of bank equity, the higher the bank's rate of return on that equity. The word **leverage** in the broadest sense means "making the most out of the least," in this case making the bank's loans and investments as large as possible relative to the bank's equity. The example of the First Reliable Bank leverage is the $900 million of liabilities divided by the $100 million of equity, or 9-to-1. Similarly, if a homeowner buys a $300,000 home with a 5 percent down payment ($15,000) and borrows the rest ($285,000), the leverage ratio is 285/15 or 19-to-1.

A common feature of leverage is that it magnifies profits when the value of an investment is increasing and reduces profits or even wipes out equity when investment values are falling. For the homeowner, if the price of the house rises from $300,000 to $350,000, the loan is still $285,000 but now the equity has grown to $65,000, representing a $50,000 profit on an original investment of only $15,000. But if the price of the house were to decline only 5 percent from $300,000 to $285,000, the equity would be wiped out. If the house price were to decline further to, say, $250,000, the house would be worth $35,000 less than the value of the loan and equity would be negative. The homeowner would be said to be "under water," owing more than the home is worth.

The key element that creates these wide swings of profit and loss on equity is that *the value of the loan stays fixed while the market price of the asset can freely rise or fall*.[4] The household example can be easily adapted to the case of the bank. Flexible asset prices can change the value of the bank's investments without causing any change in its deposits. If loans and investments were to rise in our example from $910 million to $1,010 million, this increase in assets of $100 million would boost equity (net worth) by $100 million, because bank liabilities have not changed. The bank's 11 percent return on its loans and investments (100/910) *has been magnified* into a 100 percent gain on its equity (100/100). Whenever the value of investments rises, banks make a much greater percentage return on equity than the percentage increase in the asset's value, due to the power of leverage.

But leverage can also create a disaster if the values of investments fall instead of rise. The magnification we observed in the previous paragraph works as investment values decline. Table 5-2 illustrates the condition of the First Reliable Bank after a reduction in the value of its loans and investments from the initial $910 million to $800 million, a 12 percent loss. Banks have seen the value of their loans and investments decline since 2007 for several reasons. Banks that had lent

---

[4] We ignore here that most home mortgages require the borrower gradually to pay down the principal, i.e., the amount borrowed. But "interest-only" mortgage loans are also available that do not require any repayment of principal.

Table 5-2

The New Balance Sheet of the First Reliable Bank

After a Decline in Loan and Investment Values to $800 Billion

(Millions of dollars)

Assets		Liabilities	
Loans and Investments	800	Deposits	900
Reserves (including cash)	90		
Total Assets	890	*Total Liabilities*	900
		Equity (Net Worth)	−10

money to firms that went into bankruptcy often lost most or all of the value of the loans they had extended to the now-bankrupt firms. And banks found that their investments in mortgage-backed securities lost value when borrowers stopped making loan payments due to job loss and other factors.

Bank Insolvency and Deposit Insurance

Whatever the causes of the decline in the value of the bank's loans and investments, the consequences are clear. Assets have declined by $110 billion while liabilities have not changed at all, causing the original $100 million of equity to be wiped out and replaced by negative equity of −$10 million. A bank or other financial institution is insolvent when its equity or net worth reaches zero or turns negative. When this occurs, the bank is said to have "failed."

Should depositors constantly monitor the condition of their bank to make sure it has adequate equity? During the economy's collapse at the beginning of the Great Depression in 1929–32, thousands of banks failed as depositors feared for the solvency of the banks and rushed to the front door to withdraw their money (this is called a **bank run**). But no bank holds cash in its vaults adequate to meet the demands of depositors, because it must use the funds from most of its deposits to make loans and investments if it is to make a profit and stay in business. When the cash in the vault ran out, the rest of the depositors at the end of the line were out of luck. Millions of Americans lost their life savings as a result of bank failures in 1930–32, and this made the Great Depression even deeper and more prolonged.

One of the first acts of the Roosevelt New Deal in 1933 was to establish the Federal Deposit Insurance Corporation (FDIC) to insure bank deposits against loss. The guarantee offered by the FDIC now offers depositors full protection of the value of their deposits up to $250,000. The insurance is paid for by regular insurance premiums made by all banks in the system.

The FDIC not only insures bank deposits but also is responsible for shutting down a bank when it becomes insolvent. In 2009 there were 140 bank failures and the number in 2010 was expected to be even larger. In contrast in 2007, prior to the Global Economic Crisis, there were only three bank failures.

A **bank run** takes place when the customers of a bank fear that the bank will become insolvent. Customers rush to the bank to take out their money as quickly as possible to avoid losing it.

Nonbank Institutions: The Wild West of Finance

While the Fed regulated the required reserves and leverage ratios of banks, it could not prevent them from making risky investments, such as granting too many construction loans for condominiums in local housing markets that were

Table 5-3

The Balance Sheet of the Exotica & Toxic Fund

(Millions of dollars)

Assets		Liabilities	
Investments	350	Borrowing	340
Total Assets	350	*Total Liabilities*	340
		Equity (Net Worth)	10

already overbuilt with too many condos. Further the financial market contains not just banks but many other types of "nonbank" financial institutions that make risky investments while funding them not primarily with deposits but with funds borrowed from other financial institutions including both domestic and foreign sources of funds. The nonbank institutions included two major New York City institutions that failed in 2008, Bear Stearns in March and Lehman Brothers in September. The collapse of Lehman set off the Global Economic Crisis.

Table 5-3 displays the balance sheet for the hypothetical "Exotica and Toxic" Fund, which specialized in buying risky investments. Many of these were mortgage-backed securities, which were later described as "toxic assets" because the securities were backed by pools of individual mortgages taken out by people who could not afford them. Some of these mortgage borrowers had incomes too low to qualify for a regular mortgage and found that they could not handle the monthly payments when one or more family members was laid off from a job.

There are three main differences between the bank in Table 5-1 and the nonbank institution in Table 5-3. First, the nonbank does not hold any reserves, because it is not regulated by the Federal Reserve or any other government entity. Second, it obtains the funds to buy investments not by attracting deposits but rather by borrowing. Third, it holds minimal equity. Because Table 5-3 shows liabilities of $340 million and equity of only $10 million, the leverage ratio is 34 to 1. A mere 10 percent rise in the value of the investments would boost total assets from $350 to $385 million, but this would cause equity to soar from $10 million to $45 million, an enormous rate of return.

But, as turned out to be true in 2007–09, even a 10 percent decrease in the value of investments from $350 to $315 million would wipe out all the equity and leave a negative equity of −$25 million.

The higher the leverage, the greater the profits when asset values increase but the more quickly firms tumble into negative equity positions and go insolvent when asset values decrease.

◆ SELF-TEST

1. In Figure 5-5 are bonds and stocks sold by financial intermediaries or financial markets?

2. Is a bank's equity part of its assets or its liabilities?

3. Is leverage the ratio of (a) assets to liabilities, (b) loans to equity, (c) deposits to loans, or (d) liabilities to equity?

5-4   A Hardy Perennial: Bubbles and Crashes

The past century has witnessed two tragic implosions of aggregate demand, first the Great Depression that began in 1929 and second the Global Economic Crisis that began in 2008. The common feature of these crises was that they were preceded by an asset price **bubble.** Such a bubble is defined as a situation when asset prices rise significantly relative to "fundamentals" and then collapse as when a soap bubble is pricked with a pin.

> An asset **bubble** is a sustained large rise in the price of an asset relative to its fundamental value, followed by a collapse in prices that eliminates most or all of the initial price gain.

The most common types of bubbles are in stock prices and house prices. A stock price bubble occurs when stock prices rise far above the factor that creates the underlying value of stocks, namely corporate profits. If corporate profits increase by 20 percent over a multiyear interval while stock prices increase by 100 percent, then it is likely that a stock price bubble is occurring.

The most important stock price bubbles in the past century were those of 1927–29 and of 1996–2000. The stock market bubble of the late 1920s was followed by the Great Depression, a full decade during the 1930s when the unemployment rate remained above 10 percent. The stock market bubble of the late 1990s was followed by a collapse in which stock prices dropped by half, but there was no major business cycle calamity. Thus bubbles do not always create major business cycles.

A bubble can also occur in the price of housing. Housing bubbles can be identified by examining the ratio of housing prices to the closest alternative, which is the price of renting a dwelling unit. The 2000–06 U.S. housing price bubble was unique in postwar U.S. history and was followed by its collapse, which helped to create the Global Economic Crisis.

Two Bubbles Examined: Stock Prices 1996–2000 and House Prices 2000–06

Figure 5-6 illustrates the stock price bubble of the late 1990s. The graph shows the ratio of stock prices to corporate profits over the four decades since 1970. The data are expressed relative to the value in 1995, which was a turning point between low and high stock market valuations.

Stock prices were depressed in the 1970s and 1980s, because macroeconomic performance was abysmal with high unemployment and high inflation.

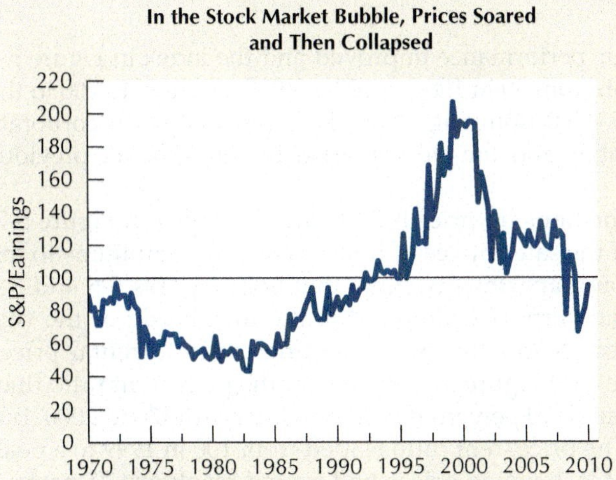

In the Stock Market Bubble, Prices Soared and Then Collapsed

Figure 5-6 Ratio of S&P 500 Stock Price Index to Earnings of S&P 500 Companies, 1970–2010, Index with 1995 = 100, 1970–2010

The graph displays the price/earnings ratio for the S&P 500 stock price index. Stock prices were depressed between 1973 and 1994, with two decades below the 1995 ratio that is set equal to 100. Then the price-earnings ratio doubled between 1995 and 2000, followed by a collapse in 2000–03. The revival in 2004–07 was only a pale shadow of the late 1990s bubble, and then stock prices collapsed again to a ratio in early 2009 not seen since 1987.

UNDERSTANDING THE GLOBAL ECONOMIC CRISIS

Two Bubbles: 1927–29 in the Stock Market Versus 2000–06 in the Housing Market

The most destructive bubble of all was the soaring of stock market prices in the late 1920s, followed by a crash that reduced stock prices by almost 50 percent within the single month of October 1929. The Great Depression that followed between 1930 and 1940 was marked most notably by an unemployment rate above 10 percent for 11 straight years. The collapse of the 1927–29 stock market bubble revealed many other aspects of excess leverage in financial markets of the late 1920s, just as the collapse of the housing bubble in 2006–07 revealed the role of excess leverage in the decade that followed the year 2000.

What were the similarities and differences between the financial bubble of the late 1920s and that of 2000–06? A common theme is increased leverage. In the 1920 stock market bubble, individual investors could borrow 90 percent of the price of any stock they purchased, putting down only 10 percent. In contrast over the past several decades only 50 percent could be borrowed. Thus leverage on the stock market in the 1920s was 9-to-1 in contrast to 1-to-1 in the modern era. This high leverage exacerbated the rise in the stock market but also its subsequent collapse in October 1929.

Similarly in the housing bubble of 2000–06, a similar feature was the steady erosion of down payment requirements on houses from 20 or 10 percent down to 5, 3, or even 1 percent. This increase in leverage increased the chances that a modest decline in house prices could wipe out the value of a homeowner's equity.

Another parallel is between the increased leverage of 2000–06 and the similar phenomenon in 1927–29 when financial market leverage also increased. A prominent feature of the late 1920s was a financial superstructure based on ever-higher leverage, as corporations were established to buy other corporations with borrowed money. Also similar in the 1920s and the 2000–06 period were large profits by investment bankers and a stimulus to consumer demand taking the form of capital gains on equities in the late 1920s and the form of mortgage equity "cash-out withdrawal" during the housing price bubble of 2000–06.

The U.S. commercial real estate boom of the 1920s was every bit as much of a bubble as the residential housing boom of 2001–06. More office buildings greater than 250 feet tall were constructed in New York City between 1922 and 1931 than in any other ten-year period before, or since. An innovation of the 1920s was speculative building with no tenant committed up front to occupy the building. The securities that financed the construction boom were just as toxic as in the past decade. Bond sellers courted retail investors. Mortgage-backed securities are nothing new but proliferated in the late 1920s. Issues of the securities counted on ignorance of the retail buyers of the risks inherent in these securities. Widening yield spreads on these risky securities starting one year before the 1929 stock market crash were an early warning signal of the impending financial debacle.

There were important differences between the institutions and regulations of the late 1920s and of this decade. A glaring difference was that prior to 1933 there was no deposit insurance, leaving a trail of disaster as bank failures beginning in 1930 caused lifetime savings of many American households to evaporate, thus exacerbating the Great Contraction of 1929–33. Another and

---

Gradually macroeconomic performance improved and the index in Figure 5-5 soared, rising in the graph from 50 in 1984 to 100 in 1995 and then to 200 in the year 2000. But that 1995–2000 doubling of stock prices relative to corporate earnings was unsustainable, and the stock market bubble (like all previous bubbles) collapsed.

The dimensions of the housing price bubble are displayed in Figure 5-7, which shows the ratio of the sales prices of houses and condominiums to the price of renting houses and apartments. Note that both Figures 5-6 and 5-7 are drawn with the same vertical scale, so that the magnitude of the two bubbles can be compared. Normally the house price ratio to rental prices fluctuates relatively little, and Figure 5-7 shows that the price/rent ratio fluctuated only between 95 and 120 percent during the interval 1970 to 2000. But then the bubble began. The price/rent ratio leaped from 100 in 1999 to a peak of 174 in early 2006. That is, housing prices had soared by almost 75 percent faster than rents had increased over that seven-year period.

perhaps the most important difference was in the response of monetary policy to financial collapse, with the Fed's indifferent neglect in 1930–32 contrasting with its aggressive post-2007 responses.

Viewed more broadly, a more basic similarity between the 1920s and the period between 1995 and 2006 was the view that permanent prosperity had arrived, and that the good times should be allowed to roll. The underpinning of this benign environment in the 1920s was the excitement created by the development of radio together with the delayed but growing impact of the two great inventions of the late nineteenth century, electricity and the internal combustion engine. Similar excitement was generated in the late 1990s by the invention of the Internet.

Indirectly the result of this general contentment with the macroeconomic environment was to blind policy-makers and risk-takers of the possibility of bad outcomes. Just as the stock market mania of the late 1920s led gullible investors to ignore unsustainable price-earnings ratios, so the housing bubble of 2000–06 led both homeowners and the financial community to disregard the growing and unsustainable ratio of housing prices to income. In this sense macroeconomic success led to macroeconomic failure.

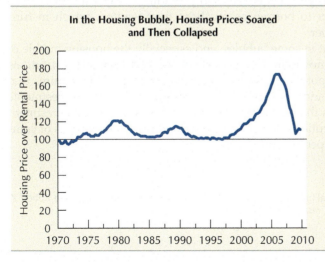

In the Housing Bubble, Housing Prices Soared and Then Collapsed

Figure 5-7 Ratio of Housing Price Index to an Index of Rents of Houses and Apartments, Index with 1995 = 100, 1970–2010

The graph displays the ratio of the S&P/Case-Shiller Housing Price Index to an index of rents charged for apartments and houses. The ratio is expressed as an index number with 1995 = 100. From 1970 to 2000 the ratio was relatively constant, but after 1999 the ratio soared from 100 to a maximum of 173 in early 2006. Then the housing bubble was pricked, and the price/rent ratio declined almost to where it had started ten years earlier.

Yet, just as in the stock market bubbles of 1927–29 and 1996–2000, the high prices could not be sustained. Instead prices crashed and created unprecedented financial stress and even disaster both for the ordinary people who held mortgages on properties whose value had collapsed, and for rich investors who had purchased securities backed by mortgages that were soon revealed to be unsound. The iron law of leverage went into action—the greater the leverage ratio, the higher were profits on the way up but the more quickly financial institutions became insolvent on the way down.

Why Do Bubbles Occur?

The origin of bubbles starts with an outside shock that changes perceptions of profit opportunities. The invention of the Internet in the mid-1990s created unbounded optimism about the profit prospects of newly formed Internet companies (later called the "dot.coms"). This was the foundation of the boom and collapse of the stock market displayed in Figure 5-6. Similarly, the housing bubble of 2000–06 illustrated by Figure 5-7 was fueled by two factors, the very low interest rates engineered by the Fed's easy monetary policy, and the financial innovations that allowed credit extended to mortgage finance to be multiplied many times over.[5]

Once the starting impetus to a bubble is established, it takes on a life of its own. Prices, whether of stocks or houses, begin to increase. Any time that prices increase and are expected to increase further, speculators want to borrow money in order to increase leverage and make the highest possible profits from the price increases.

Any bubble creates the same incentives to borrow as much as possible as long as potential investors expect the bubble to continue. The lower the down payment and the larger the fraction borrowed, the greater the profit and the greater the risk of future loss and insolvency. Thus leverage fuels bubbles, creating a more explosive mix and greater economic damage when the bubble inevitably collapses. Thus a second fundamental ingredient in a bubble is a ready supply of credit. The housing bubble of 2000–06 was fueled by the Fed's policy of maintaining low interest rates, together with large capital flows to the United States from foreign countries. The Fed often defends its monetary policy for the bubble period by pointing to a worldwide "saving glut" as the source of the funds that fueled the bubble. In truth, both the Fed's own policy and the inflow of foreign funds played coequal roles in providing the credit necessary to allow the house buyers to borrow as much as they wanted, which in turn pushed prices ever higher.

The third ingredient in some bubbles, and especially the housing bubble of 2000–06, is financial innovation. Innovation encouraged financial institutions that were attracted by potential profits to increase leverage. This requires that they are willing to take additional risk that returns on new types of investments may turn out to be less than expected. The process was driven by investment banks and related institutions that created, sold, and traded new types of complex securities that few people understood.

---

[5] The classic book on financial bubbles over the centuries is Charles P. Kindleberger and Robert Z. Aliber, *Manias, Panics, and Crashes.* John Wiley, 2005.

5-5   Financial Innovation and the Subprime Mortgage Market

Financial innovations in the period 1999–2007 included many aspects of financial markets, but the most important innovations were those that helped to destabilize the housing market and thus to cause the housing price bubble and its subsequent collapse.

Securitization

Perhaps the most important financial innovation was the "mortgage-backed security." In earlier eras banks that granted mortgage loans would continue to own them as assets on their balance sheet and would have a strong interest in granting such loans only to credit-worthy stable borrowers. However, in the new era the banks that originated mortgages did not hold on to them. Instead they sold the mortgages (that is, they sold both the mortgage debt and the borrower's signed contract promising to pay a certain amount of interest and principal until the loan was paid off, typically in 15 or 30 years).

The process by which the originating bank sold off the mortgages to large financial institutions is called **securitization,** which led to increasingly complex "securitized" pools of loans promising high returns with low risk. Thus in the United States ballooning mortgage loans to riskier borrowers, initially caused by low interest rates and a government policy of encouraging home ownership for borrowers of dubious repayment capacity, provided the basis for an ever larger inverted pyramid of structured products.

Securitization is the process of combining many different debt instruments like home mortgages into a pool of hundreds or thousands of individual contracts, and then selling new financial instruments backed by the pool, for instance mortgage-backed securities, to investors.

The Subprime Mortgage Market

Another financial innovation was in part created by the profit opportunities made possible by the Fed's policy of maintaining very low short-term interest rates in 2002–04. Mortgage specialists called "mortgage brokers" were offered lucrative fees by large mortgage banks, of which the most notorious were Countryside and Washington Mutual. These banks spurred mortgage brokers to find willing borrowers, driven by the large profits that could be made by granting mortgages at interest rates of 4 or 5 percent when short-term money to finance those mortgages could be obtained (thanks to Fed policy) for only 1 percent or a bit higher.

As the mortgage brokers worked through their rolodexes looking for mortgage customers, they had to dip further into a group of borrowers who had low incomes, unsteady jobs, and poor credit ratings. So eager were the large mortgage banks to make loans and so eager were the mortgage brokers to earn fees, that traditional lending standards began to evaporate. Borrowers no longer had to verify income or employment. These risky loans came to be nicknamed "NINJA loans," standing for "No Income No Job No Assets."

This **subprime** mortgage market thrived as long as the Fed kept short-term interest rates low, and the granting of home loans to risky borrowers was in harmony with overall government policy to extend the right of homeownership to as many people as possible. But once the Fed began to raise the short-term rate in mid-2004, the interest rates on many subprime mortgages began to "reset" to higher rates. Borrowers who could barely afford the initial monthly payments began to fall behind on their payments, and the road was paved toward subsequent foreclosure (losing a home due to failure to keep up with mortgage payments).

In the **subprime** mortgage market borrowers typically have some combination of low incomes, unstable employment histories, and poor credit records.

Why Did Investors Buy the Risky Subprime Mortgage-Backed Securities?

Investors were misled about the riskiness of these innovative new securities by unrealistically optimistic ratings provided by the rating agencies. Either because of plain ignorance or a desire to make additional profits, the rating agencies like Moody's and Standard and Poors gave many securities "AAA" ratings even though they were backed by highly risky mortgages taken out by people with poor credit histories and unstable employment.

Why were financial institutions willing to take on so much risk? One answer is ignorance, due to the fact that there had never been a previous housing price bubble and thus no experience with the disastrous financial consequences of a collapse in housing prices. Another answer is more sinister, simple greed for additional short-term profits that would be made possible (as long as housing prices continue to soar upward) by making risky investments with borrowed money. Since firms made more profits if they made ever-more risky investments, and because executives and traders were given immense personal bonuses based on the performance of their firm or their department within that firm, thousands of managers and employees of large financial firms were mesmerized with their chase for the last dollar of bonus income.

The End of the Housing Bubble and the Onset of the Financial Crisis

But the underlying assumption of all this profit-driven taking of risk overlooked the basic driver of the process, and this was rising housing prices, which could not continue forever. Why not? The first reason is clear in the interest-rate graph in Figure 5-10 on p. 143. Between mid-2004 and mid-2006 the Fed raised the federal funds rate sharply from 1.0 percent to 5.25 percent. This in turn caused financial institutions to raise interest rates on some types of mortgages that had adjustable rates rather than fixed rates. These adjustable rate mortgages typically had lower interest rates than fixed-rate loans and were attractive to people who were trying to cut corners in obtaining mortgages.

Soon families found the interest rate on their mortgages soaring, and they then faced the choice of defaulting on their mortgage or squeezing other household expenses. Similar families with low or uncertain incomes and low credit ratings, who might have found mortgages easily in 2003–04, found it increasingly difficult to find affordable mortgages in 2005–06. The reduction in housing demand was enough to slow down the rate of increase in housing prices, as shown in Figure 5-7. Suddenly the "flippers," who owned condominiums for the sole purpose of making money from ever-higher prices, became fearful that the game was over and tried to sell, but everyone else was also trying to sell. Housing prices began to plummet.

Once housing prices began to decline, the game was over. The new mortgage-backed securities had been backed by the collateral of steady and regular mortgage payments by the households who had taken out the original mortgages before they were securitized. When these households fell behind or stopped paying entirely, the value of the securities began to decline. That happened not just to households with their homes now worth less than their mortgage debt, but to large financial firms that found themselves insolvent because the value of their assets now declined below the amount their had borrowed to buy these assets. And those who made those loans now suddenly learned that their loans were not secure.

In summary the 2000–06 housing bubble was fueled by investor overoptimism that housing prices would go up forever, by a ready supply of funds from the Fed's easy money policy in 2002–04, from foreign investors eager to find high-yielding investment vehicles in the United States, and finally by a set of financial innovations that encouraged institutions to originate risky mortgages and sell them through the process of securitization. When housing prices finally declined in 2006–10, household consumption was curtailed and many financial firms reached or neared insolvency and suddenly stopped making loans both to households and business firms. The worst financial crisis since the 1930s was at hand. We learn later in this chapter about the monetary policy response to the emerging crisis and in Chapter 6 about the fiscal policy response.

 SELF-TEST

1. How did securitization change the ownership of residential mortgages?
2. Why does higher leverage make bubbles worse, adding to the price increase and also the price collapse at the end of the bubble?
3. Why were investors so eager to buy risky mortgage-backed securities? (a) High interest rates on these securities compared to alternatives, (b) ignorance, (c) overly optimistic credit ratings.

5-6   The *IS-LM* Model, Financial Markets, and the Monetary Policy Dilemma

We are now ready to combine our previous analysis of the *IS-LM* model with new elements required to understand the Global Economic Crisis and the difficulties it has posed for the traditional tools of monetary policy. The first element relevant to the crisis is the familiar net wealth effect on consumption first introduced in Chapter 3. As we learned there, a sharp decline in household net worth reduces autonomous consumption and raises the saving rate, and indeed we have seen how much the saving rate increased in 2008–10. This decline in net worth and increase in saving shifts the *IS* curve to the left. ✳

Added to this familiar net wealth effect on the *IS* curve were two factors that made the leftward shift of the *IS* curve more severe than in previous recessions. The first factor was a financial innovation, the unusual ease of refinancing mortgages during the housing bubble period, when millions took advantage of rising house prices to take out a new larger mortgage. As an example, consider a homeowner who buys a $250,000 house, takes out a $200,000 mortgage, and pays for the rest with a $50,000 down payment. When rising prices boost the home's value from $250,000 to $300,000, the homeowner can refinance, replacing the $200,000 mortgage with a larger $250,000 mortgage. The homeowner will then receive a check for the $50,000 difference from the bank, so-called "cash-out refinancing." All of this extra cash propelled a consumption boom and the decline in the saving rate during 2000–07 shown on p. 63, temporarily pushing the *IS* curve rightward. But when housing prices began to fall in 2006, cash-out refinancing became impossible and this artificial prop to consumption was removed, aggravating the leftward shift in the *IS* curve.

The second new factor is to remove a simplification in our previous discussion of the *IS-LM* model. Until now we have assumed that there is a single interest rate controlled by the Fed at which consumers and business firms can freely borrow. But in reality there is not just a single federal funds short-term interest rate. Also relevant is the long-term government bond rate, already introduced on p. 102, which sets the basis for setting mortgage interest rates. The third relevant interest rate is the interest rates at which corporations can borrow, and this is always higher than the long-term government bond rate. To allow for these different interest rates, we must allow the *LM* curve controlled by the Fed to differ from the *LM* curve faced by potential borrowers of home mortgages and corporate debt.

A notable feature of a major financial crisis that results from the end of a bubble is a widespread fear that financial institutions will become insolvent and corporations will go bankrupt. The interest rates at which corporations can borrow shoot up relative to safe government debt to compensate investors for the feat that some corporate borrowers may not repay their loans. We will learn that this increase in the relative interest rate of corporate debt compared to government debt is called the risk premium and can substantially undermine the Fed's ability to stimulate the economy with monetary policy.

Monetary Policy Confronts a Normal Negative *IS* Shock

To understand unusual aspects of the Global Economic Crisis, we begin with a standard *IS-LM* graph as shown in Figure 5-8. The economy is initially in equilibrium at point E^*, the crossing point of the "Initial *IS* Curve" and the "Initial *LM* Curve." Real income is Y^*, assumed to be the desirable natural level of output, and the interest rate is r^*.

Now a demand shock occurs that shifts *IS* leftward to the "New Recession *IS* Curve." This leftward shift could be caused by consumer or business pessimism, a decline in household net wealth, a decline in government military spending, or a decline in exports. Initially the economy moves from E^* to point A, and real income declines from Y^* to point Y_A. The Fed has no problem

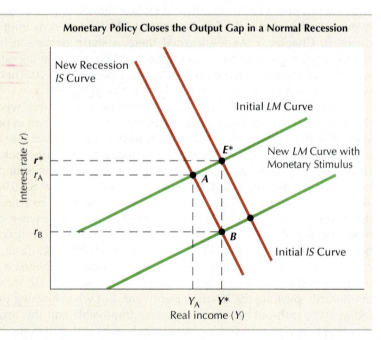

Figure 5-8 A Negative Demand Shock Followed by a Monetary Policy Stimulus

The economy is initially in equilibrium at point E^* where the interest rate is r^* and the desired natural level of real income is at Y^*. A negative demand shock shifts the *IS* curve leftward to the "New Recession *IS* Curve," and the economy initially moves from point E^* to point A. However, a prompt monetary policy stimulus that shifts the *LM* curve rightward is capable of bringing real income and output back to its initial amount Y^* at point B, where the interest rate has declined to r_B.

Monetary Policy Closes the Output Gap in a Normal Recession

returning the economy to the natural level of output at Y^*, as it can simply reduce interest rates by enough to move the economy to point B from point A.

The situation in Figure 5-8 might describe a mild and brief recession like that of 2001, when real GDP barely fell at all. By reducing interest rates rapidly the Fed brought the recession to an end after a few months.

Monetary Policy Confronts an Unusually Big Negative *IS* Shock

A close inspection of Figure 5-8 shows that it is a special case. The *IS* and *LM* curves are drawn so that the leftward movement of the *IS* curve leaves the bottom part of the *IS* curve to the right of the natural level of output Y^*. If the leftward shift of *IS* is larger, then even a zero interest rate may not be capable of bringing the economy back to the natural level of output.

This unhappy possibility is shown in Figure 5-9. Here the negative demand shock is much bigger. The negative wealth effect at the end of the housing bubble may be supplemented by a second negative wealth effect coming from the collapsing stock market. The end of the housing bubble dries up the market for cash-out refinancing, further reducing autonomous consumption. Banks and nonbank financial firms may stop making loans entirely as they near or reach insolvency. As a result the "New Crisis *IS* Curve" moves far enough to the left so that the bottom of that *IS* curve intersects the zero interest rate axis at point D, with output Y_D below the desired output level Y^*.

Even though the Fed has pushed the *LM* curve down, the interest rate cannot go below zero, due to the zero lower bound for interest rates (as defined and explained in Chapter 4 on p. 104). The *LM* curve is shown with a kinked shape, positively sloped to the right of point D and flat at a zero interest rate to the left of point D. Monetary policy is no longer able to boost real income and output higher than Y_D. Something else must be done to shift the *IS* curve back to the right. The obvious possibility is a fiscal stimulus, a topic to which we return in the next chapter.

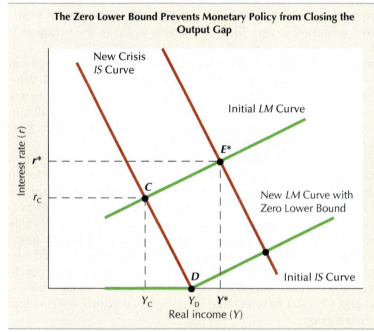

The Zero Lower Bound Prevents Monetary Policy from Closing the Output Gap

Figure 5-9 An Unusually Large Negative Demand Shock Cannot Be Fully Offset by Monetary Policy

The economy is initially in equilibrium at point E^* where the interest rate is r^* and the desired natural level of real income is at Y^*. A very large negative demand shock shifts the *IS* curve leftward to the "New Crisis *IS* Curve," and the economy initially moves from point E^* to point C. However, a monetary stimulus can only reduce the interest rate to zero at point D, where real income level Y_D is below the desired output level Y^*.

The Term Premium and the Risk Premium

As if the situation in Figure 5-9 were not bad enough, the Fed in its struggle to revive the economy faces a constraint beyond its control. Even though the Fed has the ability to push the short-term federal funds rate down to zero, as it did for several years after January 2009, no consumer, mortgage borrower, or corporate borrower can obtain a zero interest rate loan. There are two reasons. First, most consumers and business firms want loans for a much longer term than the overnight loans for which the federal funds rate is relevant, and the interest rate naturally must be higher on average for long-term loans than for short-term loans. Second, consumer and business loans are risky because they might not be paid back in full, and the interest rate must be higher on this risky private debt than on government debt.

The top frame of Figure 5-10 displays the values since 1987 of three interest rates. For two of these the graph is identical to that on p. 102 in Chapter 4. The lower green line plots the short-term federal funds rate. The upper purple line exhibits the interest rate for 10-year maturity government debt, also called the "10-year Treasury bond rate." Notice that, despite all its small wiggles, the long-term rate is more stable over the business cycle than the short-term rate and does not exhibit the marked sharp downturns and upturns that mark the beginning and end of easy money policy by the Fed, as occurred during the rate decline of 2001–02, the rate increase of 2004–06, and the rate decline of 2008–09.

Notice also that the long-term bond rate on average is substantially above the average short-term federal funds rate over this period. The tendency of the long-term bond rate to be higher than the short-term interest rate consistently over an average of many years is called the **term premium.** This means that while the Fed can push the short-term rate down to zero as it did in 2009–10, it cannot force the long-term bond rate to be zero or anything close to zero. Notice that in years like 1989, 2000, and 2006–07, the green line was briefly above the purple line and the term premium was negative. This can occur when investors in long-term bonds believe that the high short-term rate is temporary, and that they will be better off investing in the slightly lower long-term bond rate because it will apply for the following ten years, whereas the short-term rate is very likely to decline again in the future as it had in the past.

The **term premium** is the average difference over a long period of the interest rate on long-term bonds and the interest rate on the short-term federal funds interest rate.

Why do investors require a higher average interest rate on long-term bonds? The answer is simple, the ten-year bond does not pay back its full principal for ten years, and the next ten years are highly uncertain. Investors worry that the short-term rate might rise substantially in the future, as it did in 2004–06. And they also worry that inflation might rise at some point in the next ten years, eroding the purchasing power of their government bonds.

Many borrowers want to take out loans that are fully paid off 10, 20, or 30 years in the future. But borrowers in the private economy cannot borrow for 10 years as cheaply as the federal government. Why? The government has the power to repay its debt fully in U.S. dollars, while no household mortgage borrower or corporate bond borrower can guarantee that its loan is completely safe with zero chance of default. Homeowners sometimes stop paying their mortgage payments when they encounter personal or financial difficulties, and corporate bankruptcies in the future may greatly reduce the value of corporate debt. Just in the past decade such firms as United Airlines, Delta Airlines, General Motors, and Chrysler have entered bankruptcy in which stockholders have lost all of their money.

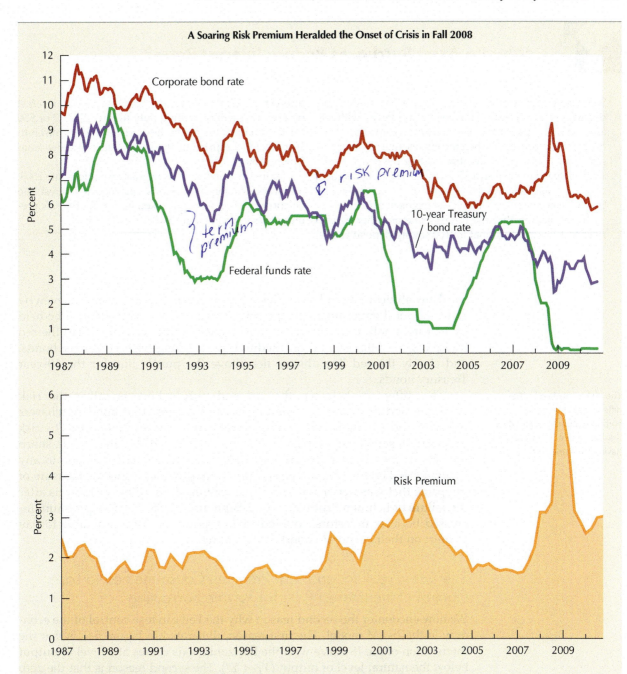

A Soaring Risk Premium Heralded the Onset of Crisis in Fall 2008

Figure 5-10 **The Federal Funds Rate, the Ten-Year Treasury Bond Rate, and the BAA Corporate Bond Rate, 1987–2010**

The green and purple lines in the top frame are copied from the graph on p. 102. The red line is the interest rate on BAA (medium-grade) corporate bonds. The difference between the purple and green lines is the term premium and is usually (but not always) positive. The difference between the red and purple lines is the risk premium and is shown separately as the orange line in the bottom frame.

Why Do Asset Purchases Reduce Interest Rates?

Securities or bonds promise to pay back a fixed number of dollars, say $5 per year. If the bond lasts forever, without any need to pay back the amount borrowed, then the bond is worth $100 when the interest rate on other assets is 5 percent. Why? Because holding the bond worth $100 will pay out interest of $5, but so will holding another asset such as a savings account, where a deposit worth $100 will receive an annual interest payment of $5.

Now imagine that the interest rate on other assets rises to 10 percent, so that a $100 saving deposit earns

interest of $10. People receiving $5 per year in interest on the bond will be willing only to pay $5/0.10 or $50 for the bond. Thus as the interest rate goes from 5 to 10 percent, the price of the bond will plummet from $100 to $50.

For instance, in the financial market panic in late 2008, investors sold corporate bonds, causing the interest rate on corporate bonds to skyrocket, increasing the risk premium as shown in Figure 5-10.

Thus all debt issued by entities other than the U.S. government, even by state and local governments, is perceived as being less safe and will be held by investors only if it provides a higher interest rate. In Figure 5-10 the red line plots the interest rate on medium-quality long-term corporate bonds, and clearly the red line always lies above the purple line for the 10-year Treasury bonds.

The **risk premium** is the difference between the corporate bond rate and the risk-free rate of Treasury bonds having the same maturity.

The difference between the red and purple lines is called the **risk premium** and measures the amount of extra interest that bond purchasers require to be willing to hold home mortgages or corporate bonds. The risk premium is shown separately in the bottom frame of Figure 5-9. Its sharp increase in the fall of 2008 and early 2009 was far beyond its value in any earlier period on the graph. The risk premium provides a specific measure of the panic that was pervasive in the financial markets in the six months after the failure of Lehman Brothers in mid-September 2008. The risk premium increased because investors doubted that corporations would be able to pay interest on their corporate bonds outstanding.

The Term Premium and Risk Premium Cause the Fed to Lose Control of the Interest Rate for Private Borrowing

We now encounter the second reason why the Fed can lose control of the economy in the *IS-LM* model. The first reason, illustrated in Figure 5-9, is that the intersection of the *IS* curve with the horizontal axis comes at a level of output below the natural level of output $(Y_D < Y^*)$. The second reason is that the zero federal funds rate achieved by the Fed is irrelevant to household and business borrowers, who face a far higher rate.

Figure 5-11 incorporates the term premium and the risk premium into the *IS-LM* model. The "New Crisis *IS* Curve" and the "New *LM* Curve with Zero Lower Bound" are copied from Figure 5-9, as is their crossing point D and the level of output (Y_D) that occurs at a zero interest rate. However, autonomous consumption and planned investment cannot be financed by borrowing at zero; lenders grant loans only at a much higher interest rate that incorporates both the term premium and the risk premium.

The term premium is the distance between the lower *LM* curve and the middle *LM* curve, which shows the amount by which the long-term government bond

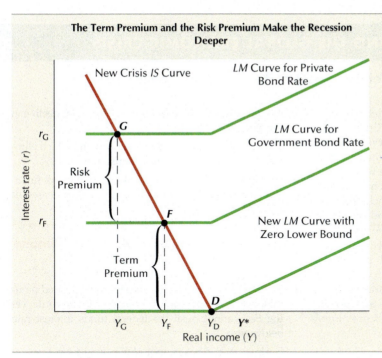

The Term Premium and the Risk Premium Make the Recession Deeper

Figure 5-11 The Risk Premium and Term Premium Make a Bad Situation Even Worse

This graph qualifies the previous Figure 5-9. In that graph the economy winds up at point D and is prevented from reaching the desired output level Y^*. While the Fed can push the short-term interest rate down to zero, households and business firms cannot borrow at a zero rate and so the economy cannot achieve point D. If the risk premium is zero, the borrowing rate is the same as the long-term government bond rate and the economy operates at point F. But if the risk premium is higher than zero, the economy operates at point G and the level of real income and output Y_G falls far below the desired level Y^*.

rate lies above the short-term federal funds interest rate. If households and private firms could borrow at the long-term government bond rate, then the economy would be in equilibrium at point F with an interest rate r_F and output level Y_F. This would be the economy's equilibrium position if the risk premium were zero.

But we know from the data in Figure 5-10 that there was a sharp increase in the risk premium in late 2008 and early 2009. A hypothetical increase in the risk premium from zero to a large amount as shown in Figure 5-11 would push the economy toward an even higher borrowing rate and an even lower level of output. The new equilibrium point is at G where the interest rate is r_G and the output level is Y_G, far below Y_F and even further below the desired natural level of output Y^*.

Thus we have come up with several reasons why the Global Economic Crisis became the largest economic downturn of the postwar era. The box summarizes these causes and distinguishes between issues involving the *IS* curve and those involving the *LM* curve. What can policymakers do about the dilemma posed in Figure 5-11? In the rest of this chapter and the next we consider past policy actions and a menu of future policy options.

 SELF-TEST

1. Why does the *IS* curve shift further to the left in Figure 5-9 than in Figure 5-8?

2. Why is monetary policy unable to achieve the desired natural level of output (Y^*) in Figure 5-9?

3. Why is real income and output lower at point G in Figure 5-11 than at point D in Figure 5-9?

UNDERSTANDING THE GLOBAL ECONOMIC CRISIS

The *IS-LM* Summary of the Causes of the Global Economic Crisis

In this section we have used the *IS-LM* model to sort out the main causes of the Global Economic Crisis. These begin with the negative slope of the *IS* curve itself and the net wealth effect as a factor shifting the *IS* curve, both introduced in Chapter 3. The *IS* curve was pushed further to the left than usual due to additional negative factors introduced in this chapter. These include the simultaneous end of the housing bubble and decline in stock market prices, the end of cash-out mortgage refinance, and the near shutting-down of credit as over-leveraged banks and nonbank financial institutions neared or reached insolvency and bankruptcy.

New factors introduced in this section that raise the interest rate paid for loans by households and private firms include the term premium and the risk premium.

Causes That Pushed the *IS* Curve Far to the Left

1. The negative wealth effect from the collapse of the housing bubble

2. The negative wealth effect from a 50 percent decline in the stock market

3. The end of cash-out mortgage refinancing which eliminated a previous stimulus to consumption

4. Growing unwillingness of banks and nonbank financial institutions to grant loans at all, as they neared or reached insolvency

Causes That Prevented a Monetary Stimulus from Eliminating the Output Gap

1. The intersection of the *IS* curve with the desired natural level of output requires a negative interest rate, yet the Fed cannot push the federal funds interest rate below zero.

2. Business and firms cannot obtain long-term loans at the short-term interest rate controlled by the Fed. They must pay the long-term interest rate.

3. The higher the risk premium, the higher is the actual borrowing rate.

5-7 The Fed's New Instrument: Quantitative Easing

The tools of monetary policy are called the "instruments," as in a surgical scalpel and forceps. The primary target of Fed policy is to keep the economy operating at the desired natural level of output, Y^* in the diagrams of Chapters 4 and 5.[6] Stated another way, the Fed's goal is to minimize the difference between actual real income or output and the natural level of output. We have previously called that difference the "output gap" (see Chapter 1, p. 6), and so another way of stating the Fed's goal is to minimize the output gap.

Thus far, the Fed's only instrument has been its ability to control the federal funds interest rate, and indeed since January 2009 it has maintained the federal funds interest rate at zero in order to stimulate the economy. But in the previous section we have learned that the Fed's primary instrument of controlling the federal funds rate is not enough to maintain the economy at the desired natural level of output with a zero output gap. Instead the output gap can tumble into negative territory and the Fed cannot stop that tumble once it has reduced the federal funds rate to zero.

The frustration of the Fed is summed up in the *IS-LM* diagrams in the last section. The Fed faces two basic limitations. The first is that it cannot reduce the

---

[6] Subsequently we shall learn that the Fed cares not only about the output gap but also about inflation. The *IS-LM* model assumes fixed prices and ignores inflation. This is an acceptable simplification in this chapter, because inflation was subdued during the Global Economic Crisis of 2008–10. Hence we do not introduce inflation at this stage. Instead, the Fed is assumed to have a simple target of minimizing the output gap.

interest rate below zero, this is the so-called "zero lower bound." If the horizontal intercept of the *IS* curve occurs at an output level below the desired natural level of output (e.g., Y_D in Figures 5-9 and 5-11), then the Fed's interest rate policy cannot eliminate the output gap.

The second frustration of the Fed is that it does not set the interest rate that matters for private borrowing, particularly the mortgage interest rate paid by households and the corporate bond rate paid by business firms for medium-term and long-term loans. As we learned in Figure 5-11, the term premium and the risk premium elevate the interest rates actually paid by real-world borrowers far above the federal funds rate that is controlled by the Fed. Is there anything the Fed can do to reduce the term premium and the risk premium in order to push the economy southeastward from the depressed equilibrium position *G* in Figure 5-11?

The Fed's Balance Sheet

The starting point in any explanation of the Fed's operation is its balance sheet, as set out in Table 5-4 with real-world data for January 2, 2008, that is, prior to the beginning of the Global Economic Crisis. The assets of the Fed are primarily government securities, as shown on the left side of the table. There are also other assets, including gold held by the Fed.

The liabilities of the Fed are better known. The Fed issues all of the U.S. dollar currency. Look at a $1 bill; above George Washington's portrait are the words "Federal Reserve Note." In Table 5-4 currency is by far the largest liability of the Fed. The other liabilities are mainly bank reserves, which the banks hold on deposit with the Fed primarily to meet reserve requirements. In January 2008 in Table 5-4, there were $44.4 billion of reserves of which $42.1 billion were required and only $2.3 billion were excess. The amount of required reserves is calculated by the Fed by multiplying the required reserve ratio on certain types of bank deposits by the total amount of those types of deposits.

Subsequently in Chapter 13, we will learn the details of how the Fed uses its balance sheet to change the federal funds rate, its primary policy instrument. The amount of currency can be taken as exogenous. Banks allow depositors to redeem as much as they want in currency, so the total amount of currency is decided by the public (including foreign holders of the dollar), not the Fed.

Table 5-4

The Balance Sheet of the Federal Reserve

(Billions of dollars, January 9, 2008)

Assets		Liabilities	
Government Securities	740.7	Currency	828.9
Other Assets	185.3	Total Reserves	44.4
		Required Reserves	42.1
		Excess Reserves	2.3
		Other Liabilities	52.7
Total Assets	926.0	*Total Liabilities*	926.0

The total amount of currency is quite stable from week to week. Since the Fed's assets must balance its liabilities, whenever the Fed buys government securities and enlarges the asset side of its balance sheet, it also automatically makes its liabilities larger (since assets must always equal liabilities). If the Fed wants the interest rate to decline, it increases bank reserves by making its assets larger, buying government securities. Banks react to their extra reserves by increasing lending, stimulating spending in the economy.

As we will learn in Chapter 13, the Fed's creation of reserves in normal times is a gift to banks, allowing them to increase their assets, liabilities, and profits by a multiple of the Fed's reserve creation. The Fed can take away this gift when it wants to raise the interest rate, selling securities and reducing bank reserves, thus requiring banks to reduce their loans and investments.

How the Fed Uses Quantitative Easing

Quantitative easing occurs when a central bank purchases assets with the intention not of lowering the short-term interest rate, which is already at zero, but with the purpose of increasing bank reserves.

We have seen that the Fed cannot push the federal funds rate below zero. Since the Global Economic Crisis began in September 2008, the Fed has attempted to lessen the impact of the crisis by new methods called **quantitative easing.** In these operations the Fed buys up not just government securities but also a wide variety of private securities. The aim of these asset purchases is not to reduce the short-term interest rate, which is already zero, but to raise bank reserves and support the markets in the government and private securities that the Fed chooses to buy.

In the autumn of 2008 the financial markets of the world appeared on the brink of collapse. Many securities could not find a buyer. The Fed stepped in and bought massive amounts of securities, including short-term private commercial paper (short-term debt of corporations) in addition to other securities issued by the private sector. Uniquely among economic institutions in the United States, the Fed has the ability to buy any security it wishes to buy, because it can pay for that security by creating bank reserves.[7]

We can see how the Fed's quantitative easing has radically changed the Fed's balance sheet if we compare the balance sheet for mid-2010 in Table 5-5 with the balance sheet for January 2008 that we have already discussed in Table 5-4. The

Table 5-5

The Balance Sheet of the Federal Reserve

(Billions of dollars, August 11, 2010)

Assets		Liabilities	
Government Securities	938.3	Currency	947.9
Mortgage-backed Securities	1119.5	Total Reserves	1090.9
Other Assets	275.2	Required Reserves	65
		Excess Reserves	1025.8
		Other Liabilities	292.2
Total Assets	2331.0	*Total Liabilities*	2331.0

---

[7] As we shall learn in more detail in Chapter 13, the Fed pays for the security it purchases by writing a check on itself. The bank selling the security deposits that check in its reserve account at the Fed, thus creating extra bank reserves equal to the amount of the security purchase.

most striking fact evident in comparing Table 5-5 with Table 5-4 is that both assets and liabilities have exploded, reaching 2.5 times in August 2010 the initial value of January 2008.

Let us look first at Table 5-5 to see how assets increased from early 2008 to mid-2010. Holdings of government securities increased substantially from $741 to $938 billion. "Other" assets increased also from $185 to $275 billion. But these increases were swamped by the huge increase in Fed holdings of mortgage-backed securities (MBS), which rose from nothing to $1,119 billion.

Quantitative Easing and the Term and Yield Premiums

Why would the Fed want to buy more than $1 trillion of MBS? The only answer must be that the Fed feared in late 2008 and early 2009 that the market for MBS would dry up and create bankruptcies for many financial firms that held MBS. The Fed bought the MBS in order to create a demand for these securities to balance the retreat of private market investors.

Another way to interpret the Fed's purchase of securities is that it was trying to reduce the interest rates that it does not control directly. By purchasing long-term government securities the Fed is trying to reduce the term premium. By purchasing MBS or other private securities, it is trying to reduce the risk premium. If the Fed is successful in reducing these premiums, it can move the economy's equilibrium in Figure 5-11 southeast down the *IS* curve from point *G* and raise the level of real income and output above Y_G.

The evolution of the Fed's balance sheet between January 2008 and August 2010 is shown in Figure 5-12. The top frame shows the major types of assets and the bottom frame shows the major types of liabilities. Notice that the thin black line on top in each frame is exactly the same; both show a doubling from less than $1,000 billion to more than $2,000 billion within just a few weeks in the fall of 2008. Since then there have been minor fluctuations, but the total of both assets and liabilities was still above $2,300 billion in August 2010.

The top frame shows that the composition of the Fed's assets has shifted over 2009 and 2010. Initially the jump in assets took the form of a wide variety of private assets shown by the orange area, including short-term commercial paper issued by corporations, and the amount of government securities held was actually lower in early 2009 than in early 2008. However, during the year 2009 the Fed gradually shifted its holdings of private assets from the miscellaneous "other" category to MBS as shown by the shrinkage of the orange area and growth of the blue area.[8] Comparing the overall increase in assets between January 2008 and August 2010, as shown in Tables 5-4 and 5-5, we see that the total increase of about $1,400 billion was divided up into a $1,100 billion increase in MBS, a $200 billion increase in government securities, and a $100 billion increase in other assets.

The liabilities side of the Fed's balance sheet shows the same overall increase but the components are more stable. The green and yellow areas showing currency and required reserves grew steadily but slowly. By far the largest share of the growth in total liabilities is excess reserves, as shown by the red area.

These huge amounts of excess reserves are highly unusual. Normally banks lend out their excess reserves or use them to purchase investments that pay interest higher than the Fed pays on reserves. The existence of more than $1 trillion of excess reserves in August 2010 underlines the weakness of the economy and the

---

[8] Most of the Fed's holdings of mortgage-backed securities (MBS) are those issued by the two large quasi-government mortgage organizations, Fannie Mae and Freddie Mac.

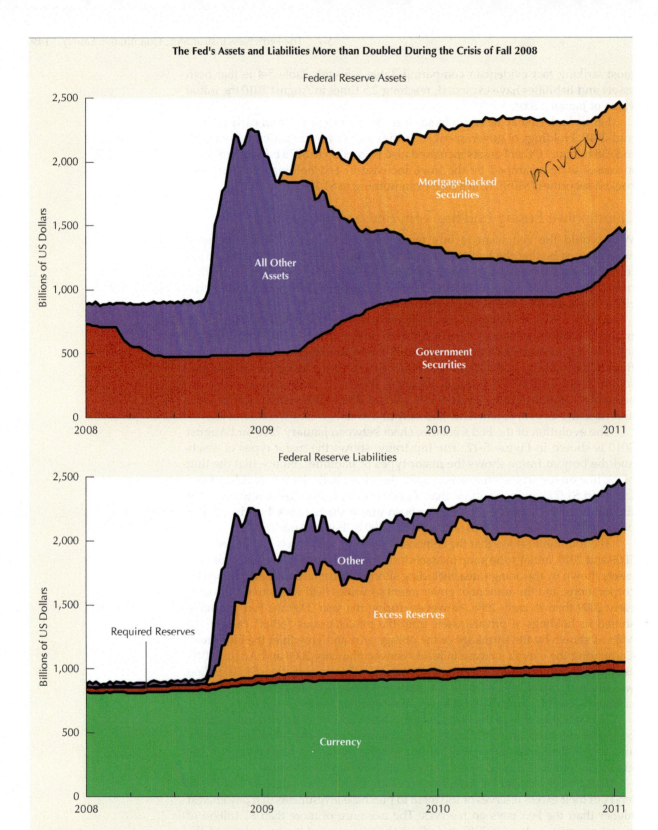

Figure 5-12 Major Components of Federal Reserve Assets and Liabilities, January 2008 to December 2010

The top frame shows total assets in billions and the three components government securities (purple), mortgage-backed securities (blue), and other assets (orange). The bottom frame shows total liabilities and the four components, which are dominated by currency (green) and excess reserves (red).

Fed's difficulty in stimulating it. Because interest rates on other assets are so low, banks refuse to use their excess reserves to buy investments. Because the economy is weak and loans are perceived to be very risky, bankers are refusing to lend out their excess reserves as they normally would.

The only other comparable period when excess reserves were so large was in the Great Depression decade of the 1930s. For instance, excess reserves in 1938 were about 5 percent of nominal GDP, as compared to 7 percent of nominal GDP in mid-2010.[9] This is one of many respects in which the Global Economic Crisis resembles the Great Depression more closely than it does the previous postwar recessions in the United States.

5-8   How the Crisis Became Worldwide and the Dilemma for Policymakers

The Global Economic Crisis was caused most directly by the 2000–06 U.S. housing bubble and its collapse after 2006. In turn the causes of the housing bubble can be divided up into three underlying causes, each of which interacted with the other. First was the Fed's maintenance of unusually low interest rates in 2002–04.[10] Second was financial innovations, which included securitization, subprime mortgages, leverage, and increased risk of default. Third was a failure of government regulators to keep ahead of the financial innovations and limit the amount of leverage.

How a Small Part of the U.S. Mortgage Market Caused the Global Economic Crisis

Why did the apparently minor financial problems that started in the market for U.S. subprime mortgages multiply its impact into a significant downdraft on world real GDP and a collapse in worldwide stock market valuations? The losses of financial institutions on mortgages granted to the U.S. subprime housing market have been estimated at $250 billion. But between 2007 and 2009 the decline in world GDP amounted to 20 times more than the initial $250 billion shock, and the loss in the world's stock markets between 2007 and the winter of 2009 had reached 100 times the initial shock. What were the mechanisms that caused such an enormous *amplification* of the initial subprime mortgage shock?

We have learned that financial innovations, particularly the development of securitization, fostered an increase in leverage, made possible by gaping holes in the regulatory patchwork quilt that allowed large financial institutions to increase leverage by reducing their equity (net worth) as a share of total assets. This excess leverage guaranteed that any future loss in the value of assets, as occurred at the end of the housing bubble, would push some institutions toward insolvency.

Amplification Mechanisms

The first multiplier mechanism to spread the U.S.-born crisis around the world was the dramatic jump of the interest rate risk premium that we have already examined in Figure 5-10. Costs of finance increased even for the most credit-worthy

---

[9] Nominal GDP is from Appendix Table A-1 in this book. Excess reserves from Milton Friedman and Anna J. Schwartz, *A Monetary History of the United States 1867–1960*, Princeton University Press for NBER, 1960, Table 19 on p. 460 and Table A-2 on p. 740.

[10] Subsequently in Chapter 14 we will develop a measure called "Taylor's Rule," which provides an estimate of the unusual nature of low interest rates in 2002–04.

firms, forcing firms both in the United States and in the rest of the world to cut costs drastically, including labor, inventories of raw materials, imported materials and goods, and investment projects.

In some cities construction on office towers was halted midway, leaving half-completed buildings to mar the urban landscape, and everywhere residential projects to build low-rise and high-rise condominium projects were suspended. In many suburban housing developments isolated houses may be occupied by their owners, but they are surrounded by miles of vacant terrain when developers abandoned projects.

Unlike the early 1930s deposit insurance protected depositors from worries that their bank might close its door and fail, thus causing their life savings to evaporate. Deposit insurance continued to protect depositors from fear. But many banks and most nonbank institutions had liabilities that consisted not of deposits but of short-term loans from other financial institutions. Such loans were part of the way that so many financial institutions increased their leverage compared to what had been common in the past. As we learned earlier on p. 131, the higher the leverage ratio, the sooner an institution will become insolvent when the values of its investments or loans starts to decline.

Suddenly when the risk premium jumped in late September 2008, providers of uninsured short-term "wholesale" loans started to monitor closely the possibility of bank insolvency and to restrict lending to suspect institutions. Further compounding the implosion was the difficulty of placing market valuations on securities of unknown riskiness, thus increasing uncertainty and the fear of insolvency. Runs and uncertain valuations were complementary and interacting sources by which the subprime mortgage crisis in the United States was amplified to have such a large impact on the rest of the world.

Foreign Investors and the Dollar Shortage

Amplification from the United States across national borders was fostered by increased foreign investments held by banks in Europe and Japan, including U.S. subprime mortgage-backed securities (MBS). As the value of MBS fell, foreign banks were forced to stop lending to all borrowers deemed potentially risky. Why were foreign banks and other investors willing to invest in such risky securities backed by the mortgage payments of dubious low-income borrowers? The answer is a combination of ignorance and misinformation. U.S. credit-rating agencies gave unwarranted high ratings to toxic securities that misled foreign investors as to their safety.

The world quickly developed a shortage of dollars. Foreign banks and other institutions had invested heavily in dollar-denominated mortgage-backed securities as had U.S. financial institutions. But the foreign banks often paid for these relatively high-yielding mortgage-backed securities with short-term low-interest dollar loans. When the U.S. credit markets froze after the failure of Lehman Brothers in mid-September 2008, many foreign institutions found that they could not renew their dollar loans, exacerbating the crisis. Thus ironically, even though the crisis originated in the United States, there was not a run on the dollar but rather a rush into the dollar. We shall see in Chapter 7 that the exchange rate of the dollar increased during the worst months of the crisis. We shall also see why some countries, for instance those in Eastern Europe, were hurt by the crisis more than others, including China and several other Asian countries.

Weighing the Causes: Why Did Canada Perform Better?

This chapter has developed a cast of characters responsible for creating the Global Economic Crisis. These characters include the makers of Federal Reserve policy, particularly its chairman Alan Greenspan, the mortgage brokers and mortgage banks who originated the subprime mortgages, the gullible subprime borrowers who signed up for loans they could not afford, the financial institutions who developed securitization of home mortgages and chased the profit opportunities offered by steadily increasing leverage, the credit rating agencies who put gold-star credit ratings on toxic securities, and finally the regulators who let all of this happen without stepping in.

But which of these characters was the most important? A fascinating test of hypotheses about the causes of the U.S. financial meltdown resides north of the border in Canada. Banks in Canada did not write subprime loans, did not create toxic securities, did not have a subprime mortgage crisis, and did not even have a housing bubble. What were the differences?

Because of the large share of the U.S. market in the demand for Canadian exports, the Canadian economy has always been viewed as an appendage of the American economy. But several factors over the past few years insulated Canada from the worldwide crisis. Some of these were not enlightened regulation but rather the good luck to be an economy heavily dependent on exports of raw materials in an environment of a worldwide increase in commodity prices. Nevertheless, commodity prices cannot explain why in the spring of 2010 employment in Canada was 2 percent higher than at the beginning of 2007, while in the United States it was 6 percent lower.

The institutional and regulatory environment of Canadian banks was a crucial difference. Banks were much more conservative in their lending than U.S. banks. Tighter lending standards prevented the emergence of a housing price bubble comparable to that in the United States. In Figure 5-7 the ratio of housing prices to housing rents collapsed in the United States by about 40 percent between 2006 and 2009, while in Canada the same ratio was flat.

There was no subprime loan or foreclosure crisis in Canada, nor a collapse of major financial institutions. Canada's independent Financial Consumer Agency has a mission of preventing the emergence of subprime borrowing. Since Canadian monetary policy typically has echoed that of the United States, and interest rates in Canada closely tracked those in the United States, an argument can be made that it was a U.S. regulatory failure rather than lax U.S. monetary policy that was the core element in the 2008 breakdown of U.S. financial markets.

The elements of Canadian regulatory prudence are straightforward. Banks face high capital requirements and their leverage is limited. Their assets cannot exceed 20 times their true equity capital, whereas in 2006–07 some American and European banks reached 40 times. Down payments for home purchases are 20 percent, in contrast to the United States where down payments reached nearly zero at the height of the bubble. Similarly there are limits on the percentage of home equity that can be withdrawn when a mortgage is refinanced. Five large banks with a single bank regulator dominate Canadian financial markets.

There are other aspects to the Canadian institutional environment that help to prevent housing bubbles and excess lending. Mortgage interest is not deductible on income tax returns. Instead of giving a subsidy up front, the tax system allows tax deductibility of housing capital gains. Down payment requirements mean that it is less likely that homeowners will find themselves "under water," owing more than their house is worth. And, under

Canadian law, borrowers cannot walk away from their debts because banks can claim their other nonhousing assets to obtain repayment of legal debt. This set of regulations and the virtual monopoly of the large Canadian banks in the mortgage markets make mortgages profitable so that the banks have no incentive to package and sell them, and so mortgage securitization did not happen.

The Canadian model can be questioned. Canadian banks have been viewed as sleepy and slow to innovate. Yet in a world in which financial innovation has proved to be so counterproductive, one can question whether innovation is a virtue.

The Policy Dilemma

For more than two years the world's policymakers have been struggling to turn the tide and to return the world to vigorous economic growth. The recession reached bottom in many countries in mid-2009, but the recovery since then has been slow and halting. What should policymakers do?

We have studied closely in this chapter the dilemma of monetary policy. Its primary tool of controlling the short-term federal funds interest rate has been ineffective ever since the federal funds rate reached zero in January 2009. The zero lower bound makes it impossible for the nominal interest rate to fall below zero, and thus the Fed has lost the use of its primary instrument.

Thus the Fed has been forced to use a second and more novel tool called quantitative easing. Even though the Fed cannot reduce the federal funds rate below zero, it hopes to reduce the term premium and risk premium by buying both government securities and mortgage-backed securities. Has this been effective? Apparently the Fed has had some success with this policy, but there is no agreement on the magnitude of the reduction in the term premium and risk premium that the Fed has achieved.[11]

But even if quantitative easing has a modest effect in pushing the economy southeast along the *IS* curve from the depressed equilibrium point *G*, it cannot deal with the fundamental source of the problem. The economy is at point *G* primarily because the *IS* curve is so far to the left. Factors that have shifted the *IS* curve leftward include the negative wealth effects of the collapse of the housing bubble, the overhang of high consumer debt that forces consumers to retrench, and the reluctance of banks to make loans, which causes banks to "sit" on $1 trillion of excess reserves.

The inability of the Fed to do anything substantial to bring the economy back to normal evokes two earlier episodes with many similarities, the Great Depression decade of the 1930s in the United States and the "lost decade" in Japan between 1992 and 2002. Because of the failure of monetary policy to revive the economy in the late 1930s, early postwar textbooks tended to downplay the relevance of monetary policy. That era developed several sayings to summarize the Fed's inability to revive the economy.

> You can lead a horse to water, but you can't make him drink.
>
> You can stuff the banks with money, but you can't make them lend.

What can be done?

The hints of the solution are provided in the upper-right corner of Figure 4-10 on p. 108. Even if monetary policy or fiscal policy is weak, there is no limit on their ability to bring the economy back to the desired natural level of output if they work together. The problem in Figure 5-11 is that the *IS* curve is too far to the left, and the government can push the *IS* curve to the right by some combination of reductions in taxes, increases in transfer payments, and increases in expenditures on goods and services.

We turn in the next chapter to fiscal policy and its own dilemmas. While there is no limit on the ability of fiscal policy to push the *IS* curve to the right at least in principle, there are both economic and political problems. Economists dispute whether the fiscal multipliers in the real world are remotely as large as

---

[11] A positive assessment of the effectiveness of the Fed's policies in reducing the term premium is provided in Taeyoung Doh, "The Efficacy of Large-Scale Asset Purchases at the Zero Lower Bound," *Federal Reserve Bank of Kansas City Economic Review*, Second Quarter 2010, pp. 5–34.

in our analysis of Chapter 3. The next problem is that a fiscal stimulus raises the government deficit and creates more debt, although we shall see that when the Federal Reserve purchases the debt issued from the fiscal stimulus, there is no necessary increase in the public debt held outside the government. Finally, the political problem is that any fiscal stimulus is controversial. There is political bickering about the form of the stimulus (e.g., tax cuts vs. expenditure increases) and also about whether a fiscal stimulus represents an unwelcome expansion of government's role in the economy and in society.

Summary

1. This chapter supplements the *IS-LM* model by adding the effects of financial markets, financial innovations, leverage, risk, and asset price bubbles.
2. The Global Economic Crisis occurred simultaneously in the United States, Europe, and Japan, and with about the same effect on the output gap. In the United States the harmful effects of the crisis were greater for employment and unemployment than for output.
3. Financial institutions and financial markets exist to channel funds from savers to borrowers.
4. Banks make profits by giving loans and making investments that earn higher interest rates than the rates that they pay to their depositors. The ability of banks to make loans is limited by reserve requirements and requirements on bank equity capital.
5. The leverage ratio is the ratio of liabilities to equity. The higher the leverage ratio, the higher the percentage return on equity when asset prices go up and the more rapidly equity is wiped out (and the institution becomes insolvent) when asset prices go down.
6. Important asset bubbles were in the stock market in 1927–29 and 1996–2000, and in the housing market in 2000–06. Bubbles are created by optimism, easy credit, excess leverage, and lax regulation of leverage ratios.
7. Important financial innovations that fueled the housing bubble were securitization of mortgage loans, an increased willingness to grant loans to subprime borrowers, and the unrealistically high credit ratings placed on risky mortgage-backed securities.
8. Financial markets can exacerbate an economic downturn in the *IS-LM* model. Factors pushing the *IS* curve to the left since 2007 have included the collapse of the housing bubble, a decline in stock prices by one-half between 2007 and 2009, a reluctance of financial institutions to lend, and the end of cash-out mortgage refinancing.
9. Factors pushing up the *LM* curve relevant for household and business firm borrowing include the term premium and the risk premium. Even if the Fed reduces the federal funds rate to zero, neither households nor firms can borrow at that rate.
10. The Fed reacted to the crisis not only by pushing the federal funds rate to zero, but also by buying more than $1 trillion of nongovernment securities. This quantitative easing may have had a minor effect but cannot by itself push the *IS* curve to the right.

Concepts

financial markets	leverage	subprime
financial intermediaries	bank run	term premium
equity	bubble	risk premium
risk	securitization	quantitative easing

Questions

1. Use the information contained in the case study of Section 5-2 to discuss why it is appropriate to use the term Global Economic Crisis to describe the economic events of the period 2007–10.
2. Compare and contrast the severity of the downturns of the U.S. economy in 1981–82 and 2007–09 and how quickly the economy recovered following those declines in economic activity.
3. Explain what a bank's assets and liabilities are, the risk that a bank faces, and how its equity is protection against that risk.
4. Explain what leverage is and under what circumstances leverage can either result in large profits for a bank or cause the bank to become insolvent.
5. Explain how a non-bank financial institution is different from a bank in terms of assets, liabilities, and equity.

6. Explain what an asset bubble is and discuss what causes an asset bubble to develop.

7. Discuss what the bubbles in stock and commercial real estate prices in 1927–29 and house prices in 2000–06 had in common and how they differed in terms of speculation, leverage, financial innovation, regulations, and the Fed's response to the bursting of those bubbles.

8. Explain what mortgage-backed securities are and what the subprime mortgage market is. Discuss how the combination of these two financial innovations and low interest rates from 2001–04 contributed to the development of the housing bubble. Finally, explain why a rise in interest rates from 2004–06 burst the housing bubble and brought on the financial crisis of 2007–08.

9. Explain what the term premium and risk premium are and why they cause the interest rates that affect the cost of borrowing by households and businesses to differ from the federal funds rate.

10. Discuss what assets and liabilities are contained in the balance sheet of the Federal Reserve System. Explain what quantitative easing is, how it affects the Fed's balance sheet, and how the use of quantitative easing is intended to affect the term and risk premiums. Finally, discuss the evidence that indicates that the Fed engaged in quantitative easing during and following the financial crisis in the fall of 2008.

11. Explain how the crisis in the relatively small U.S. subprime mortgage market was amplified into the Global Economic Crisis. What dilemma does the Global Economic Crisis pose for monetary policy makers?

12. Explain what aspects of the Canadian banking system and mortgage markets helped prevent the development of a housing bubble in that country in the last decade.

Problems

 Visit www.MyEconLab.com to complete these or similar exercises.

1. Suppose that the equation for autonomous planned spending, A_p, is $A_p = 6,200 - 200r$ and the value of the multiplier, k, is 2.5.
   (a) Derive the equation for the *IS* curve, $Y = kA_p$. Graph the *IS* curve for interest rates between 0 and 8, with intervals of one-half of a percentage point.
   (b) Suppose the equation for the *LM* curve is $Y = 13,500 + 100r$. Use this equation to explain the level of income at which there is a zero lower bound on the federal funds rate, the interest rate that the Fed controls.
   (c) Graph the *LM* curve for interest rates between 0 and 8, with intervals of one-half of a percentage point.
   (d) Suppose that the term premium is 1.0 percentage point and the risk premium is 2.0 percentage points. With Figure 5-11 as a guide, use the *LM* curve with the zero lower bound and the term premium and risk premium to graph the *LM* curve for the government bond rate and the *LM* curve for the private bond rate at interest rates between 0 and 8, with intervals of one-half of a percentage point.
   (e) Use the graphs of the *IS* curve and the three *LM* curves to explain what the equilibrium interest rates for the federal funds rate, the government bond rate, and the private bond rate are and what the equilibrium level of income is.

2. Suppose that a collapse of housing and stock prices reduces real wealth. That reduction in real wealth reduces autonomous planned spending by 800 billion at every interest rate.
   (a) Derive the new equations for autonomous planned spending, A_p, and the *IS* curve, $Y = kA_p$. Graph the new *IS* curve for interest rates between 0 and 8, with intervals of one-half of a percentage point.
   (b) Use the graph of the new *IS* curve and the graphs of the three *LM* curves from part (d) of problem 1 to explain what the new equilibrium interest rates are for the federal funds rate, the government bond rate, and the private bond rate and what the new equilibrium level of income is.
   (c) Suppose that the collapse of housing and stock prices creates a crisis in financial markets and that the risk premium increases from 2 percentage points to 3 percentage points. Explain why the financial crisis would lead to a rise in the risk premium.
   (d) Use the new risk premium to graph the new *LM* curve for the private bond rate for interest rates between 0 and 8, with intervals of one-half of a percentage point.
   (e) Use the graph of the new *LM* curve for the private bond rate, together with the *IS* curve from part (a) of this problem and the *LM* curve for the private bond rate, to explain how the financial crisis affects the equilibrium private bond rate and the equilibrium level of income.

3. Suppose that the financial crisis causes the Fed to adopt quantitative easing. The quantitative easing reduces the term premium to 0.5 percentage points

and reduces the risk premium to its pre-crisis level of 2.0 percentage points.

(a) Explain how quantitative easing would reduce the term premium and the risk premium.

(b) For interest rates between 0 and 8, with intervals of one-half of a percentage point, graph the new *LM* curve for the government bond rate and the new *LM* curve for the private bond rate, given the Fed's quantitative easing.

(c) Use the graph of the new *LM* curves for the government and private bond rates, together with the *IS* curve from part (a) of problem 2 to explain what the new equilibrium interest rates for the government and private bond rates are and what the new equilibrium level of income is.

(d) Discuss how your answers to part (e) of problem 1 and part (c) of this problem illustrate how monetary policy alone may not be capable of leading an economy out of as deep a downturn as the one of the Global Economic Crisis.

◆ SELF-TEST ANSWERS

p. 132. (1) Financial markets. (2) Neither, it is the difference between its assets and its liabilities. (3) (d) the ratio of total liabilities to equity

p. 139. (1) Prior to securitization, the bank originating the mortgage would hold on to it as an asset on its balance sheet. If the mortgage defaulted, the bank suffered the loss, thus making it very careful in the mortgage application process. With securitization the originating bank sells the mortgage to a financial institution, which packages it with thousands of others and sells the mortgage-backed security to investors. Thus the bank has no incentive to be careful about the credit-worthiness of borrowers, and investors are ignorant of the risks involved. (2) The higher the leverage ratio, the larger the percentage profit when the price of an asset increases. Thus the pursuit of profit causes banks to issue more loans, which increases the prices people are willing to pay for houses. The reverse occurs when

the bubble collapses. (3) All of the factors (a), (b), and (c) contributed to this key element in the global financial meltdown.

p. 145. (1) The leftward *IS* shift in Figure 5-8 is caused by the net wealth effect of the decline in housing prices. The further leftward shift in Figure 5-9 is caused by the additional net wealth effect of the decline in the stock market, by the reluctance of banks to lend, and by the end of cash-out mortgage refinance. (2) The *IS* curve intersects the vertical interest rate axis at zero at an output level below Y^*. The interest rate cannot be negative, so point D is the maximum output level that can be reached as long as this is the relevant *IS* curve. (3) They are lower because the term premium and risk premium raise the interest rate at which households and firms can borrow far above the zero short-term interest rate set by the Fed.

The Government Budget, the Government Debt, and the Limitations of Fiscal Policy

6-1 Introduction: Can Fiscal Policy Rescue Monetary Policy from Ineffectiveness?

Chapter 4 ended with the optimistic message that, while either monetary or fiscal policy might be ineffective if used by themselves, a *combined* stimulus that coordinates a monetary and fiscal policy expansion is guaranteed to bring the economy back to the desired natural level of real GDP, as long as the coordinated monetary and fiscal expansion is large enough. Does this theoretical result apply to the depressed economies of the United States, Europe, and Japan? What are the obstacles to a coordinated expansion of monetary and fiscal policy?

In the last chapter we learned that there are two crucial reasons why monetary policy by itself may be unable to bring the economy back to the desired natural level of real GDP after a very large negative demand shock such as that which hit the world economy in the fall of 2008. The first reason is that the traditional monetary policy instrument of reducing the short-term interest rate is hamstrung by the existence of the zero lower bound, the impossibility of a negative nominal interest rate. The second reason is that the Fed does not directly control the interest rate at which households and business firms can obtain loans. The interest rate for these borrowers is much higher than the federal funds rate, due to the term premium and the risk premium.

The *IS-LM* model sums up the weakness of monetary policy in a nutshell. In a depressed economy like that of 1938 or 2010, the *IS* curve is simply too far to the left, and the Fed cannot force banks to lend at rates below those set by the term premium and risk premium. Thus, the *IS-LM* model when applied to 1938 or 2010 turns the spotlight to fiscal policy. Can fiscal policy provide enough stimulus to move the *IS* curve far enough to the right to return the economy to the desired natural level of real GDP?

This chapter introduces the basic tools needed to answer this question. We start with an analysis of the side-effects of a budget deficit, including the traditional "crowding out" effect already introduced in Figure 4-6 on p. 98. Deficits also raise the public debt, and if the deficits are large enough, they raise the ratio of the public debt to GDP. We also learn that it is possible for fiscal deficits to occur, thus stimulating the economy, without raising the public debt held by the private sector of the economy.

In this chapter we come closer to understanding why the Great Depression lasted for a full decade between 1929 and 1941, and we also learn why the economy was so weak in 2010 and beyond. There was a stark contrast between the destructive passivity of monetary policy in 1930–32 and the bold aggressiveness of 2008–09 that prevented the 2008 crisis from turning into another Great Depression. Yet the inability of monetary policy to push the economy to a full recovery in 1935–39 had a striking resemblance to the weakness of monetary policy in propelling a robust recovery in 2009–2010. Not only did monetary policy have weak effects, but the fiscal stimulus was not nearly large enough either in 1935–39 or 2009–11. In the late 1930s, despite the Roosevelt New Deal and its much-publicized innovations to create jobs, total government spending hardly budged as a share of GDP, and the same was true in 2009–10 despite the Obama stimulus plan. What scale of coordinated monetary and fiscal expansion might be necessary in 2011 and beyond to bring the American economy back from its deep slump to the desired natural level of real GDP? The answer is clouded in uncertainty, but this chapter makes a beginning at sorting out the relevant issues.

6-2   The Pervasive Effects of the Government Budget

In this section we examine several adverse effects of persistent deficits that in the early 1990s eventually created the political will to end the deficits and push the government budget into surplus. However, this political will to convert the government budget deficit into a surplus, as was achieved in 1998–2001, was short-lived. The transition from the budget surplus of 1998–2001 to the persistent and growing deficits after 2001 combined four factors. First, during 2001–03 tax revenue was reduced by a political philosophy that favored tax cuts. Second, in part due to the shock of the September 11, 2001 attacks, defense spending increased substantially. Third, the Global Economic Crisis starting in 2008 greatly reduced government revenues while also raising transfer payments, especially for unemployment benefits—we learn in this chapter to call these tax and transfer effects the *automatic stabilizers*. Fourth, a relatively large fiscal stimulus in 2008–10, consisting of tax cuts, transfer increases, and increases in government spending, further increased the budget deficit.

Crowding Out of Net Exports

The *IS-LM* model in Chapter 4 emphasized that a fiscal expansion, taking the form of an increase in government spending or a reduction in tax rates, is likely to crowd out domestic private investment. But, in addition, a fiscal expansion may crowd out net exports. We can review the magic equation (2.6) in Chapter 2 on p. 35 (here renumbered as equation (6.1)) to see why one or the other type of crowding out must occur:

$$T - G \equiv (I + NX) - S \qquad (6.1)$$

On the left-hand side of this definition is the government budget surplus $(T - G)$. On the right-hand side is the excess of total investment, both domestic (I) and foreign (NX), over private saving (S). This means that a government surplus is available to finance an excess of domestic investment over private saving $(I - S)$ or to lend to foreigners (positive NX).

When the quantity on the left-hand side is negative (T smaller than G), the government is running a deficit. Then equation (6.1) indicates that there are only three ways for the government deficit to be financed. First, private saving can go up. Second, domestic private investment can go down; this is the crowding out effect that we examined in Figure 4-6 on p. 98. Third, foreign investment can go down, and if it drops far enough and becomes negative, we call it foreign borrowing.

Impact on Future Generations

Persistent government budget deficits have another implication as well. A deficit raises the public (or national) debt, while a surplus reduces the public debt. Future generations, including current college students reading this book, will be obliged to pay higher taxes than otherwise would be necessary so the government can pay interest on its debt.

Clearly, a persistent budget deficit has pervasive consequences on domestic investment, foreign investment or borrowing, and the wealth of citizens in the future. A persistent surplus reverses these effects. However, it will take many years of surpluses to offset fully the impact of the deficits that have already occurred. This is ample motivation to study closely the causes and effects of the budget deficit.

It seems obvious that a government deficit must increase the government debt. However, there is one exception to this rule. When the Fed "accommodates" a fiscal policy expansion financed by deficit spending, the Fed buys up the government debt that is issued. While the government debt held by the Fed increases, the government debt held by private households, firms, financial institutions, and foreigners does not increase. One of the most important lessons of this chapter is that the ability of the Fed to buy up government debt provides latitude in the conduct of fiscal policy that would otherwise be missing.

6-3 CASE STUDY

The Government Budget in Historical Perspective

Throughout history the largest government budget deficits have been incurred as a result of wars, when government expenditures increased more than government tax revenues. Governments choose not to pay the full cost of wars through taxation for fear that heavy taxes will demoralize citizens when their utmost efforts are needed for war production.

The top frame of Figure 6-1 plots U.S. government expenditures (including transfer payments) and revenues as a percentage of natural GDP, for the century between 1900 and 2010. The difference between expenditures and revenues is shaded: Red shading indicates a government budget deficit and green shading indicates a government budget surplus. Included is not just the federal government budget but also the budgets of the state and local governments.

Wars and the Increasing Size of Government

Five facts stand out in the top frame of Figure 6-1. First, government expenditures exhibit a marked spike in war years, with World War II having a much greater impact than World War I. Second, tax revenues also exhibit a spike in wartime, but a smaller spike than expenditures, so deficits increase in wartime. Third, the size of government has increased in the years since World War II, as compared with the years before 1940, with real expenditures averaging about 26 percent of GDP between 1950 and 1980 and 32 percent between 1981 and 2010. Fourth, expenditures increased more than revenues during the 1980s, leading to a persistent budget deficit except for 1998–2001. Fifth, revenues were stable at 28 to 30 percent during the 1980s and 1990s before briefly soaring to 33 percent in 2000 and then declining back to only 25 percent in 2009 and 2010.

The middle frame shows the government budget deficit and surplus. The areas in red and green shading in the middle frame are identical to the corresponding areas in the top frame. Here the tendency of wars to create deficits is even more evident. The 1980–97 and 2002–10 deficits pale in comparison with the gigantic deficits of World War I and World War II. To compare more clearly the recent deficits, the period 1970–2010 is magnified in the bottom frame.

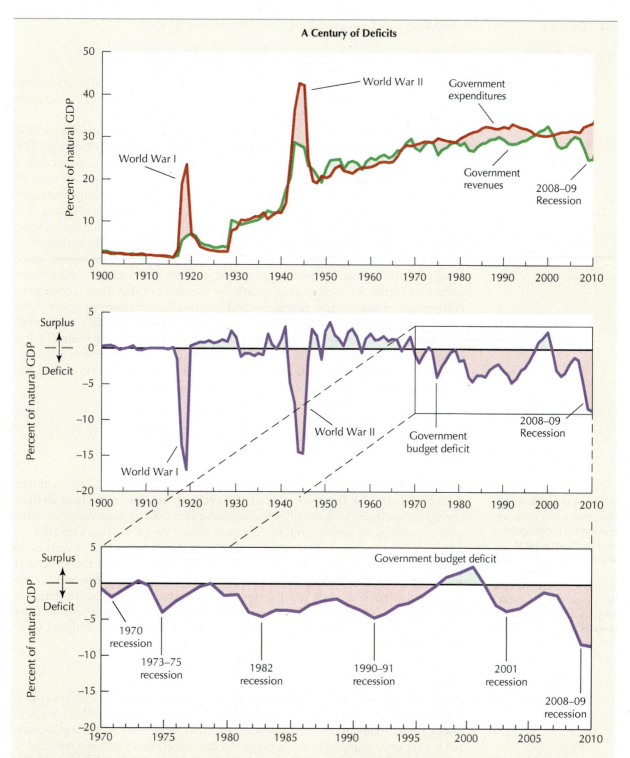

Figure 6-1 Real Government Expenditures, Real Government Revenues, and the Real Government Budget Deficit, 1900–2010

The top frame compares government expenditures and revenues (for federal, state, and local government) as a share of natural GDP, and shows the dramatic effects of wars and also the gradual increase in the expenditure share in the 1970s and 1980s and its decline in the 1990s, followed by the temporary bulge of revenue in 1999–2000 and its collapse in 2002–10. The middle frame shows the government budget surplus and deficit for the century, and the bottom frame is a blowup of the experience of the 1970–2010 period.

Source: Bureau of Economic Analysis, *Historical Statistics of the United States: Millennial Edition.* Details in Appendix C-4.

The Effect of Recessions

During a recession, government revenues decline and transfer payments increase. Notice in the bottom frame how deficits occurred during or soon after the recessions of 1970, 1975, 1982, 1990–91, 2001, and 2008–09.

If government deficits had frequently been associated with recessions in the past, why did the deficits of 1980–97 and 2002–10 create so much controversy? The answer is visible in the bottom frame of Figure 6-1. Each previous recession deficit episode has a sharp V shape, and the government budget deficit quickly went to zero as the economy recovered after the recession. But as the economy recovered after the 1982 recession, the *government budget deficit did not disappear but remained large.* The major budget deficits after 1982 occurred in peacetime, not in wartime, and in a situation of economic recovery and expansion rather than recession.

The recession of 2008–09 caused by far the largest budget deficit since World War II. The size of the budget deficit, evident in the middle and bottom frames of Figure 6-1, was caused mainly by the effect of this deep recession in cutting government tax revenues and increasing of transfer payments, especially unemployment benefits. As we shall see subsequently, the deficit also was made larger by fiscal stimulus and bail-out programs instituted by the outgoing Bush administration in 2008 and by the incoming Obama administration in 2009. In the next section we learn how to distinguish the effects of the economy on the budget and of the budget on the economy. ◆

6-4 Automatic Stabilization and Discretionary Fiscal Policy

The **cyclical deficit** is the amount by which the actual government budget deficit exceeds the **structural deficit**, which in turn is defined as what the deficit *would be* if the economy were operating at natural real GDP. The **cyclical surplus** and **structural surplus** are the same as the deficit concepts with the signs reversed.

In this section we distinguish between two types of change in the government budget deficit. The first type, called the **cyclical surplus** or **cyclical deficit,** occurs *automatically* as a result of the business cycle. Recessions cause government revenues to shrink and the cyclical deficit to grow; this condition is followed by recoveries and expansions that cause government revenues to grow and the cyclical deficit to shrink. The second type is called the **structural surplus** or **structural deficit;** this is the surplus or deficit that remains after the effect of the business cycle is separated out. The structural surplus or deficit is calculated by assuming that current levels of government spending and tax rates remain in effect, but that the economy is operating at natural real GDP rather than the actual observed level of real GDP.

Automatic Stabilization

Recall from Chapters 2 and 3 that the symbol T stands for "net" tax revenues, that is, total tax revenues minus government transfer payments. If net tax revenues (T) rise when income is high and fall when income is low, we can express net tax revenue as equal to the average net tax rate (t) times real income (Y):[1]

$$T = tY \tag{6.2}$$

This implies that the government budget can be written as

$$\text{budget surplus} = T - G = tY - G \tag{6.3}$$

---

[1] Note that t is now the average ratio of total tax revenue to GDP, whereas in the Appendix to Chapter 3 the same symbol t was used for the marginal income tax rate.

The government budget deficit is simply a negative value of the surplus, as defined in (6.3). The purpose of writing the government budget surplus or deficit in this way is to distinguish two main sources of change in the surplus or deficit: (1) **automatic stabilization** through changes in Y, and (2) **discretionary fiscal policy** through changes in G and t.

When real GDP increases in an economic expansion, the government surplus automatically rises as more net tax revenues are generated (that is, gross tax revenues rise and transfer payments such as unemployment benefits fall). The higher surplus (or lower deficit) helps to stabilize the economy, since the extra net tax revenues that are generated by rising incomes leak out of the spending stream and help restrain the expansion. Similarly, tax revenues drop and transfers rise in a recession, cutting the leakages out of the spending stream and helping dampen the recession.

The automatic stabilization effect of real income or GDP (Y) on the government surplus or deficit is illustrated in Figure 6-2. The horizontal axis is real income and the vertical axis is the government budget surplus and deficit. In the green area above the zero level on the vertical axis, the government runs a surplus, with tax revenues exceeding expenditures. In the red area below zero, the government runs a deficit, with expenditures exceeding tax revenues. Along the horizontal black line separating the green and red areas, the government budget is balanced, with expenditures exactly equal to tax revenues.

The purple upward-sloping BB_0 schedule is the **budget line**, which illustrates the automatic stabilization relationship between the government budget and real income when other determinants of the budget in equation (6.3) are constant, that is, at the assumed values G_0 and t_0. The budget line BB_0 has a slope equal to the tax rate t_0. In Figure 6-2 the budget line BB_0 is drawn so that the government runs a balanced budget at point A, when real income is equal to natural real GDP (Y^N). If real income were to fall from Y^N to Y_0, the economy would move from point A to point B, where the government is running a deficit because its tax revenues have fallen by $t_0 \Delta Y$.

Automatic stabilization occurs because government tax revenues depend on income, causing the economy to be stabilized by the change in tax revenues from the spending stream when income rises or falls.

Discretionary fiscal policy alters tax rates and/or government expenditures in a deliberate attempt to influence real output and the unemployment rate.

The **budget line** shows the government budget surplus or deficit at different levels of real income.

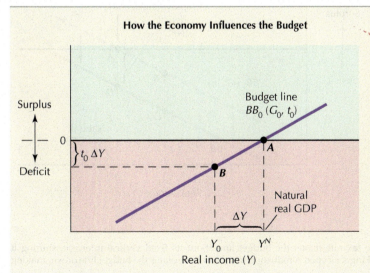

How the Economy Influences the Budget

Figure 6-2 The Relation Between the Government Budget Surplus or Deficit and Real Income

In the green area, the government budget is in surplus, while in the red area, the government budget is in deficit. The budget line BB_0 shows all the levels of the government budget surplus or deficit that are compatible with a given level of government expenditures (G_0) and tax rates (t_0). The BB line slopes upward to the right, because as we move rightward from B to A, the higher real income (Y) raises tax revenues ($t_0 Y$), thus increasing the surplus or reducing the deficit by the amount $t \Delta Y$.

Discretionary Fiscal Policy

The second source of change in the government budget deficit comes from alterations in government spending (G) and in the tax rate (t). It is evident from equation (6.3) that a decline in government spending (G) reduces the budget deficit, while a decrease in the tax rate (t) raises the deficit. How do such discretionary changes affect the budget line? Figure 6-3 copies the budget line BB_0 from Figure 6-2. The initial budget line BB_0 is drawn on the assumption that government spending is G_0. An increase in government spending from G_0 to G_1 shifts the purple budget line downward for any given level of real income, since at a given level of income the government spends more and has a higher deficit at G_1 compared with the original spending level G_0. The new budget line is shown in the position BB_1.

Find point C along the new budget line BB_1. This shows that at the new higher level of government spending (G_1), the budget would have a large deficit at a real income level of Y_0. There are three ways to reduce the deficit. One way, shown by a movement from C to D, would be to increase real income to Y^N through an expansionary monetary policy. The second way, shown by a movement from C to B, would be to reduce government spending. A third way, not shown separately, would be to increase the tax rate (t_0), which would also shift the budget line upward.[2]

Figures 6-2 and 6-3 show that "the budget can affect the economy" and the "economy can affect the budget." An increase in government spending or a reduction in tax rates moves the *IS* curve of Chapter 4, altering real GDP. These same changes move the economy in Figures 6-2 and 6-3 to the right, altering real GDP, while also shifting downward the *BB* line.

The reverse effect, the impact of the economy on the budget, is shown by *the slope* of a given *BB* curve. When real GDP increases for some reason not related to fiscal policy (such as a change in monetary policy or consumer

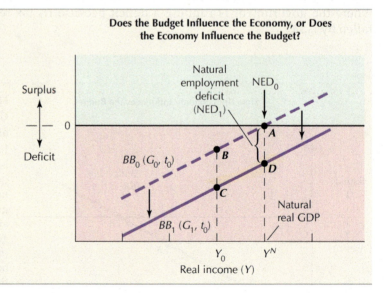

Figure 6-3 Effect on the Budget Line of an Increase in Government Expenditures

The upper budget line BB_0 is copied from Figure 6-2 and assumes a value for government spending of G_0. The lower budget line BB_1 assumes that the level of government spending has increased to G_1, thus reducing the government budget surplus or increasing the government budget deficit at every level of real income.

Does the Budget Influence the Economy, or Does the Economy Influence the Budget?

Surplus

Deficit

0

Natural employment deficit (NED$_1$)

NED$_0$

BB_0 (G_0, t_0)

B

A

D

C

BB_1 (G_1, t_0)

Natural real GDP

Y_0 Y^N

Real income (Y)

---

[2] An increase in the tax rate *rotates* the budget line about its fixed vertical intercept, shifting it upward while making it steeper. A reduction in the tax rate rotates the budget line down, making it flatter.

confidence), the economy moves northeast along a given *BB* curve. When real GDP decreases for some reason not related to fiscal policy, the economy moves southwest along a given *BB* curve.

GLOBAL ECONOMIC CRISIS FOCUS

Automatic Stabilization and Fiscal Stimulus in the Crisis

Figure 6-3 neatly summarizes the two reasons why there was such a sharp increase in the government budget deficit in 2008–10, as shown in Figure 6-1. Starting in 2007 the economy started at a position like *A*, with output at the desired natural level of real GDP. The sharp decline in actual real GDP below natural real GDP pushed the economy down the original BB_0 budget line toward the southwest to point *B*. The movement from *A* to *B* represents the powerful effect of automatic stabilization in automatically increasing the budget deficit. Then the fiscal stimulus measures detailed later in this chapter caused the budget line to shift downwards from BB_0 to BB_1, and the economy wound up at a point like *C*. The deficit was high both because of automatic stabilization and the fiscal stimulus.

The Natural Employment Surplus or Deficit

Since the actual budget surplus or deficit cannot identify discretionary fiscal policy changes, how can we summarize the effect of fiscal policy on the economy? In Figure 6-3 the more expansionary budget line BB_1 has a *lower* vertical position than the original budget line BB_0. Thus its expansionary effect can be summarized by describing the vertical position of the budget line at some standard agreed-upon level of real income, for instance, when real income is equal to natural real GDP (Y^N).

The budget surplus or deficit at the natural level of real GDP is called the **natural employment surplus (NES)** or the **natural employment deficit (NED).** It is defined as the government budget deficit that *would occur if* actual real GDP (*Y*) were equal to natural real GDP (Y^N). If we substitute natural real GDP (Y^N) for actual real GDP in equation (6.3), we can define the natural employment surplus as:

$$\text{natural employment surplus} = tY^N - G \tag{6.4}$$

The natural employment deficit is simply a negative value of the surplus in (6.4) and changes when there is a change in government spending (*G*), the tax rate (*t*), or natural real GDP (Y^N) itself. Our terminology "natural employment deficit" helps us to remember that *this is the government budget deficit when the economy is operating at natural real GDP.*

In Figure 6-3 there is a different natural employment surplus or deficit for each of the two budget lines shown. For the original budget line BB_0, the natural employment deficit is abbreviated NED_0. The value of NED_0 is zero, since along BB_0 the government budget is in balance at Y^N. For the new budget line BB_1, the natural employment deficit is NED_1 and is shown by the distance *AD*, since along BB_1 the government deficit is the amount *AD* when the economy is operating at Y^N.

We can now review the major budget concepts with the help of Figure 6-3. The actual budget deficit is shown by the economy's actual vertical position

The **natural employment surplus** or **deficit** is government expenditures minus a hypothetical figure for government revenue, calculated by applying current tax rates to natural real GDP rather than actual real GDP. This is the same concept as the structural surplus or deficit defined on p. 162.

along the appropriate *BB* line in the figure, for instance at points like *B* or *C*. The natural employment deficit is the deficit along each budget line measured at the natural level of real GDP, as at points like *A* and *D*. *Structural deficit* is another name for the natural employment deficit.[3] The cyclical deficit is the difference between the actual deficit and the natural employment deficit, the vertical distance between *A* and *B* along budget line BB_0, and the vertical distance between *D* and *C* along budget line BB_1. Automatic stabilization is represented by the slope of the budget line, since higher tax revenues and lower transfer payments cause a greater amount of real income to leak out of the spending stream whenever real income expands.

 **SELF-TEST**

How would the following be shown in Figure 6-3 and what effect would each of these have on the natural employment deficit?

1. More spending for highway repair?
2. An increase in the Social Security tax rate?
3. An increase in Social Security benefits?
4. A recession as in 2008–09 that increases the unemployment rate from 5 to 10 percent?

The Actual and Natural Employment Deficits: Historical Behavior

How have actual and natural employment deficits differed since 1970? The purple line in Figure 6-4 displays the actual government budget outcome, copied from Figure 6-1. The natural employment surplus or deficit is shown by the orange line.

The orange line isolates the structural component of the budget deficit. The distance between the purple and orange lines represents the cyclical component of the deficit. When the purple line is underneath the orange line, as in 1975–77, 1980–85, 1991–95, 2002–05, and 2008–10, the economy is weak, as shown by the blue shading. When the purple line is above the orange line, the economy is prosperous, with actual real GDP greater than natural real GDP, as shown by the pink shading.

The orange line in Figure 6-4 shows that the government ran a natural employment deficit (NED) in every year between 1970 and 2010 except the four years 1998–2001. The brief disappearance of the NED in 1998–2001 was the result of a booming economy, a temporary upsurge of stock market prices that generated unprecedented government revenue from the capital gains tax, and an increase of income tax rates.

The orange line shows that the natural employment budget was in deficit continuously after 2001. The initial switch from surplus to deficit in 2002–05 was due to the collapse of the late 1990s stock market bubble, the Bush tax cuts on both incomes and capital gains, and growing military expenditures to

---

[3] The Congressional Budget Office uses the term "standardized budget deficit" for the same concept as the "natural employment" or "structural" budget deficit.

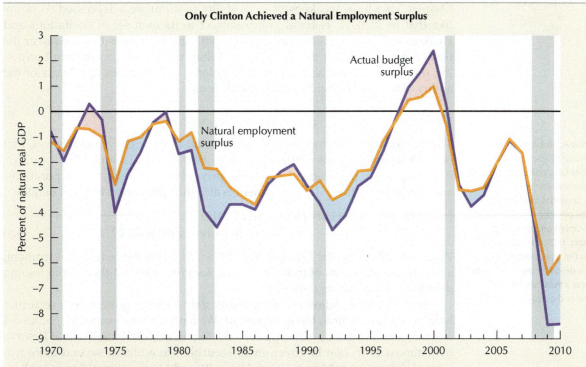

Figure 6-4 A Comparison of the Actual Budget and the Natural Employment Budget, 1970–2010

The orange "natural employment surplus" line lies above the purple "actual surplus" line in years when the economy is weak and lies below when the economy is strong. A natural employment deficit occurred in all years except in 1998–2001.

Source: Bureau of Economic Analysis and Congressional Budget Office. Details in Appendix C-4.

fight the wars in Iraq and Afghanistan. The NED became even larger after 2007 as a result of the fiscal stimulus programs designed to dampen the impact of the Global Economic Crisis, including tax cuts by both the Bush and Obama administrations, bail-outs of financial firms and auto companies, and increased expenditures on a wide variety of projects. The large blue shaded area in 2009–10 shows the additional cyclical deficit due to the automatic stabilizers.

6-5 Government Debt Basic Concepts

We have now learned about government spending, taxes, transfers, and the government deficit. All these are *flows*, measured over a period of time such as a quarter or a year. In contrast such concepts as assets, liabilities, net worth, and debt are *stocks*, measured at an instant of time such as midnight on December 31. (*Review:* The distinction between flows and stocks was introduced on pp. 25–26 in Chapter 2.) Until this point in the chapter we have focused on the fiscal deficit, the flow. Now we turn to basic concepts involving government debt, the stock.

The primary goal of this chapter is to examine fiscal policy as an instrument that can come to the rescue of monetary policy, which we learned in

Chapter 5 has basic weaknesses in its ability to stimulate a depressed economy like that in 2010–11. Is fiscal policy subject to its own set of limitations and weaknesses? The most obvious problem with fiscal policy is that the larger the fiscal deficit, the larger the public debt. What harm does government borrowing imply for current and future generations, and what are the limits of the ability of the government to run fiscal deficits?

Defining the Public Debt, Gross Versus Net

The **public debt** is the total amount of bonds and other liabilities (also called "securities") that the government has issued. These securities are held not only by private households and corporations and by foreign investors, but by some agencies within the government itself. A fiscal deficit increases the debt whereas a fiscal surplus decreases the debt.

The **public debt** is defined as the total amount that the government owes, that is, the total amount of securities (i.e., liabilities) that it has issued to all entities, including other government agencies, private households and corporations, and foreign investors. The public debt is also the cumulation of fiscal deficits:

$$\text{Debt (end of 2011)} = \text{Debt (end of 2010)} + \text{Fiscal deficit } (\textit{during the year } 2011) \tag{6.5}$$

When we talk about the U.S. public debt, we focus on the federal government, since the constitutions of most states and localities prevent them from issuing debt to cover operating deficits.

Notice that the definition of the public debt includes government securities held by agencies within the government. We have already learned in Tables 5-4 and 5-5, and in Figure 5-12 on pp. 147–50, that in mid-2010 the Federal Reserve held almost $1 trillion in government securities. In addition several more trillions of dollars are held by the Social Security and Medicare trust funds to allow them to meet their future obligations when the retirement of the baby boom generation raises the number of benefit recipients relative to the number of workers paying payroll taxes.

The **gross debt** is the total public debt, whether it is held inside or outside of the government. The **net debt** subtracts out debt held inside the government, including government securities held by the Federal Reserve and the trust funds of Social Security and Medicare.

The discussion in this section of the future burdens of the public debt does *not* apply to the debt held inside the government in these agencies. The **gross debt** is the total that the government owes, whereas the **net debt** subtracts from the gross debt the amount that the government owes to itself, that is, the securities owned by the Federal Reserve and the trust funds. Only the net debt is of concern, because the interest on the net debt must be paid by future taxpayers. In contrast, the interest earned on debt held within the government is returned to the government. For instance, the Fed returns billions of dollars each year to the Treasury from the interest it earns on its vast holdings of government securities.

The Future Burden of the Government Debt

Each extra dollar of fiscal deficit raises the gross public debt by one dollar. Some of this extra debt may be purchased by the Fed or the government trust funds. We ask in this section whether additional dollars of *net* public debt are harmful. How do we assess the impact on the well-being of future generations implied by these extra dollars of net public debt?

Government investment projects, such as the construction of highways, schools, and public universities, generate a future return, consisting of the benefits to future generations created by the project. Whether or not the net public debt is a burden depends partly on whether the extra dollars of net public debt pay for government expenditures on investment goods or for consumption goods. There is no burden if the government deficit finances productive government investment projects. In this case, the government acts just like a private corporation, say Dell Computers, which pays for much of its new plant and equipment by selling bonds to the public.

But there is a burden if the extra dollars of net public debt pay for consumption goods that yield no future benefits. Such expenditures would include, for instance, ammunition fired at target practice by soldiers or groceries purchased by recipients of Social Security benefits. These consumption expenditures have value for their recipients at the current time but not in the future.

True Burdens of the Net Public Debt

The true burden on future generations is created by government spending that is financed by deficits rather than tax revenues and pays for goods that yield no future benefits, or benefits less than their social opportunity cost—for example, meals currently consumed by members of the armed forces. Nothing is generated in the future as a rate of return; all benefits accrue in the present. The government must pay interest to keep bondholders happy, just as Dell must pay interest, yet in current government deficit-financed consumption there is no future benefit or income to pay the interest. Future taxpayers are forced to hand over extra payments to the government to cover the interest cost on the debt, and the taxpayers receive no benefit in return. Similarly, investment projects such as highways may impose a burden if their benefits are less than their social opportunity costs, such as for a little-used highway.

6-6   Will the Government Remain Solvent?

How can we tell if a government budget deficit in the United States or in some other country is too high? What matters is not whether the deficit is zero, but rather the criterion of stabilizing the ratio of the outstanding nominal federal debt (D) to nominal GDP (PY). The federal deficit can be quite large, yet the D/PY ratio can nevertheless remain stable instead of rise.

The nominal government budget deficit is equal to the change in the debt (ΔD). How large can the deficit be and keep the debt-GDP ratio, D/PY, constant? It will remain constant as long as the *growth rate* of the debt-GDP ratio is zero.

Thus, our task is to determine what size deficit will keep the growth rate of the debt-GDP ratio equal to zero. We begin by noting that the growth rate of the debt-GDP ratio (D/PY) is the difference between the growth rate in debt (d) and the growth rate in nominal GDP ($p + y$)[4]:

$$\text{Growth Rate of } \frac{D}{PY} = d - (p + y) \qquad (6.6)$$

For stability in the debt-GDP ratio, we need the growth rate of debt (d) equal to the growth rate of nominal GDP ($p + y$):

$$d = p + y \qquad (6.7)$$

---

[4] Lowercase letters represent the growth rates of the levels represented by uppercase letters. Thus, d is the growth rate of D. We use the rule that the growth rate of a product like PY is the growth rate of the first component plus the growth rate of the second component ($p + y$). The growth rate of a ratio, say A/B, is the growth rate of the numerator minus the growth rate of the denominator ($a - b$). Thus, the growth rate of the ratio D/PY is $d - (p + y)$.

When we multiply both sides of equation (6.7) by the size of the debt (D), we obtain the allowable deficit (that is, addition to debt) that is consistent with keeping the debt-GDP ratio constant:

General Form

Numerical Example

$$dD = (p + y)D \qquad (0.05)(\$9{,}000 \text{ billion}) = \$450 \text{ billion} \qquad (6.8)$$

This simple expression (6.8) leads to a surprising conclusion: *The debt-GDP ratio remains constant if the deficit equals the outstanding debt times the growth rate of nominal GDP.* In the numerical example, federal government net debt in late 2010 is about \$9,000 billion. When multiplied by an assumed growth rate of nominal GDP of 5 percent, the allowable deficit is \$450 billion. The actual deficit was much higher than that in 2009–10, which explains why the debt-GDP ratio was growing rapidly during this period, as we see in the graph on p. 173.

The Solvency Condition

The rapid rise in the debt-GDP ratio in 2008–10 and beyond was the centerpiece of a great debate among politicians and commentators about the feasibility of a further fiscal policy stimulus beyond the Obama administration's 2009–10 initial stimulus programs. The "deficit hawks" pointed to the rapid rise in the ratio of net public debt to GDP and argued that the deficit had to be brought down to keep the debt-GDP ratio from exploding. That ruled out any further fiscal policy stimulus. The "deficit doves" countered that the situation of high unemployment and weak demand required a larger fiscal response. In effect, fiscal policy was the only tool left given the weakness of monetary policy.

The government budget deficit can be divided into two parts, the basic deficit and interest on the net outstanding public debt. In turn the basic deficit equals tax revenues minus transfer payments and government expenditures other than interest payments. In 2010 the high budget deficit reflected the sum of a high basic deficit and interest payments on the large net debt.

But even in a hypothetical situation in which the basic debt is zero, the burden of interest costs could cause the ratio of net debt to GDP to grow without limit unless the "solvency condition" is satisfied. This condition states that *the government can meet its interest bill forever by issuing more bonds without increasing the debt-GDP ratio only if the economy's nominal growth rate ($p + y$) equals or exceeds its actual nominal interest rate.* Let us return to the example used above in which the net debt is roughly at its late 2010 level of \$9,000 billion. The government can run a \$450 billion deficit without increasing the debt-GDP ratio as shown in equation (6.8). How much of that deficit must be used to pay the government's interest bill? If the interest rate is 5 percent, the same as the assumed growth rate of nominal GDP, then the interest bill is (0.05) times \$9,000 billion, or \$450 billion. Thus the government can pay its entire interest cost by issuing \$450 billion in new bonds without raising the debt-GDP ratio, assuming hypothetically that the basic deficit is zero.

What is the relevance of the solvency condition for the real world of 2010–11? When the interest rate is equal to the growth rate of nominal GDP, then the basic deficit must be zero to keep the debt-GDP ratio from rising. If, however, the average interest rate paid by the government on its debt is well below the growth rate of nominal GDP, as was true in 2010–11, then there is room for the government to run a basic deficit. However, the ratio of that basic

INTERNATIONAL PERSPECTIVE

The Debt-GDP Ratio: How Does the United States Compare?

As shown in this graph and again in Figure 6-5 on p. 173, the U.S. debt to GDP ratio jumped upward from 36 percent in 2007 to 64 percent in 2010 as a result of the Global Economic Crisis and recession and as a result of the fiscal stimulus and bail-out programs instituted in 2008–10. How does this experience compare with other countries? The figure displays debt-GDP ratios for the United States and Japan and for two European countries, Germany and Italy.

The ratio for Italy is much higher than in the United States and has been above 50 percent since the early 1980s. A notable feature of Italian politics is that political support is splintered among numerous parties. It is possible to form a government only through a coalition among several parties. The necessary political compromises tend to prevent tough action to raise taxes or cut spending. Nevertheless the high debt-GDP ratio is not as serious a problem as it might appear. Italy offsets its government deficit with a very high private saving rate. As we have already learned in equation (2.5) on p. 35, high domestic saving allows a government deficit to be financed without borrowing from foreigners.

Japan's ratio of debt to GDP was only 12 percent as recently as 1991 but by 2010 had spiraled upward to 122 percent. Notice that the increase in the Japanese ratio in 2008–10 was even faster than in the United States. Japan's economic performance since the early 1990s has been plagued by sluggish economic growth and continuously falling prices (the inflation rate of the GDP deflator was negative in every year between 1999 and 2010). As a result nominal GDP did not grow at all; its average annual growth rate between 1995 and 2010 was -0.2 percent per year, much less than the U.S. growth rate of 4.6 percent per year. The absence of growth in nominal GDP together with massive fiscal deficits (reaching greater than 10 percent of GDP in 1998) explains why the Japanese debt-GDP ratio exploded as it did.

Germany is often regarded as a model of fiscal prudence. Its debt-GDP ratio hardly grew at all between 1970 and 1994 but then began a fairly steady upward creep from 19 percent in 1994 to 53 percent in 2010. Notice that the German ratio did not increase nearly as much between 2007 and 2010 as it did in the United States or Japan. This occurred because neither Germany nor Italy instituted fiscal stimulus programs on the scale of the 2009–10 Obama stimulus.

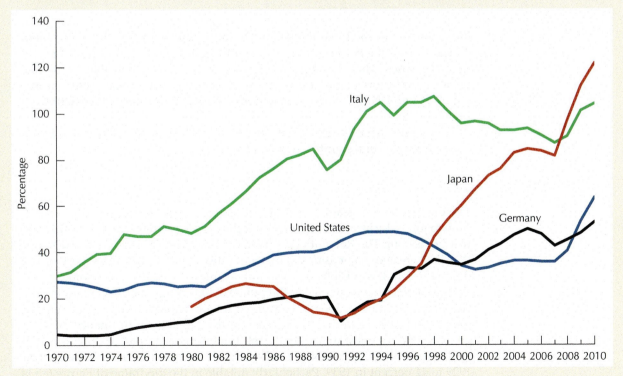

Source: Economic Report of the President and OECD *Economic Outlook*. Details in Appendix C-4.

deficit to GDP must be no larger than the difference between the nominal GDP growth rate and the nominal interest rate, and the basic deficit in 2010–11 was much higher than that. As a result, the ratio of net debt to GDP was rising rapidly, as shown in Figure 6-5 on the next page.

◆ SELF-TEST

Calculate the allowable deficit that would keep the debt-GDP ratio stable, the interest cost of the debt, and whether the government can finance its entire interest cost by issuing new bonds without increasing the debt-GDP ratio.

	Nominal GDP Growth Rate (percent)	Nominal Interest Rate (percent)	Total Net Debt ($ billions)	Total Interest Cost ($ billions)	Allowable Deficit ($ billions)	Is Interest Cost Equal or Below Allowable Deficit? (yes/no)
1	5	3	9000	_____	_____	_____
2	3	5	9000	_____	_____	_____
3	4	4	12000	_____	_____	_____
4	5	3	12000	_____	_____	_____

6-7 CASE STUDY

Historical Behavior of the Debt-GDP Ratio Since 1790

We have now learned that the debt-GDP ratio increases when the government deficit exceeds the borderline value given by equation (6.8). And the debt-GDP ratio decreases when the government deficit is smaller than that borderline value. In the history of the United States, which events were responsible for causing the debt-GDP ratio to rise, and under which circumstances did the debt-GDP ratio decline?

Figure 6-5 exhibits the ratio of net debt to GDP since 1790. From this figure we can draw several significant generalizations.

Wars and Depressions

The most consistent feature of the historical record is the tendency of the debt ratio to jump during wars and to shrink during succeeding years until the next war breaks out. The Revolutionary War, the Civil War, World War I, and World War II all created major jumps in the debt ratio, while in most other periods the debt ratio fell. Less visible, but also important, is the effect of economic recessions and depressions in raising the public debt through the effect of automatic stabilization (which reduces government revenue automatically as the output ratio Y/Y^N falls, requiring an increase in the public debt to finance ongoing government expenditures). The most important example of this was the decade of the Great Depression, when the debt ratio rose from 16 percent in 1929 to 44 percent in 1939. Particularly notable in the top frame of Figure 6-5 is

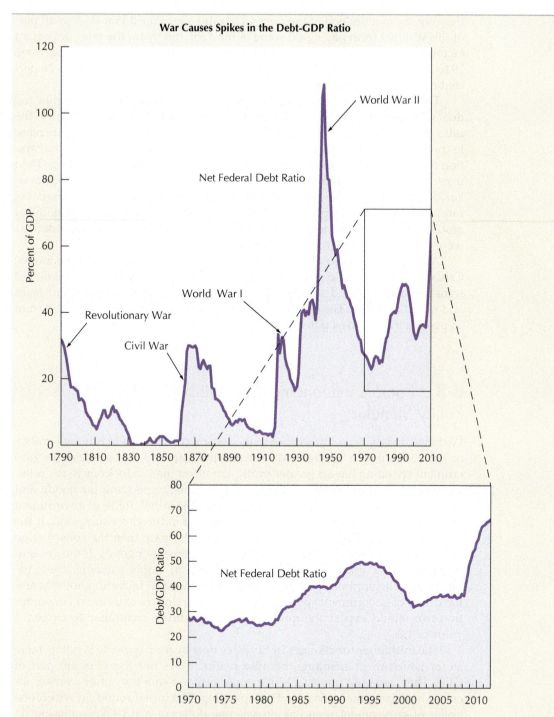

Figure 6-5 The Ratio of U.S. Net Federal Government Debt to GDP, 1790–2010

The ratio of debt to GDP has ranged widely throughout U.S. history, rising during wartime and falling between wars. During peacetime periods, the debt-GDP ratio increased during the Great Depression decade of the 1930s and during the high-deficit period of 1981–93. The shift of the federal budget from deficit to surplus caused the debt-GDP ratio to decline sharply after 1995, but then a shift back into deficits after 2001 caused the ratio to stabilize. The ratio then exploded after 2008 as a result of huge deficits caused by the Global Economic Crisis and stimulative fiscal policies designed to combat that crisis.

Sources: Historical Statistics of the United States: Millennial Edition and Federal Reserve Bank of St. Louis FRED database. Details in Appendix C-4.

the very sharp reduction of the debt-GDP ratio after World War II. A small part of this resulted from paying off some of the debt, but by far the most important factor was the growth of nominal GDP, which grew by a factor of 12 between 1946 and 1980, thus allowing the debt-GDP ratio to decline from 109 to 26 percent over the same interval.

The bottom frame of Figure 6-5 magnifies the scale in order to plot the debt-GDP ratio from 1970 to 2010. As in the top frame, the blue line refers to the ratio of net debt to GDP. The most notable feature of the ratios was its increase in the 1981–92 period. This resulted from the Reagan and first Bush administration measures that cut income tax rates and increased military spending. Then from 1993 to 2001 the ratio declined as a result of prosperity and the stock market boom, supplemented by Clinton administration policies that raised tax rates and cut military spending. The net debt ratio stayed relatively stable at around 35 percent during 2003–07, as the Bush administration budget deficits were cancelled out by growth in nominal GDP.

After 2007 the ratio exploded due to the impact of the Global Economic Crisis on the automatic stabilizers, which reduced tax revenue and increased transfer payments, and also by fiscal policy stimulus measures that cut taxes and raised transfers. The net debt to GDP ratio jumped sharply increased from 36 percent in 2007 to 64 percent in 2010. ◆

6-8 Factors Influencing the Multiplier Effect of a Fiscal Policy Stimulus

We have already been introduced to the central distinctions involving a policy of fiscal stimulus or restraint. We learned in Chapter 3 that increases in government spending have a greater multiplier effect than reductions in tax rates. The reason is simple—every dollar of government spending on goods and services is a dollar of GDP, and we expect that the initial dollar of government spending on GDP will stimulate extra dollars of induced consumption. If the government spending dollars are spent on road repair, then the construction workers have extra income that they spend on consumer goods. If the government spending goes for salaries of teachers in public schools, then the increased consumption spending by teachers lifts GDP. Including both the initial dollar of government spending and the extra dollars of induced consumption, we would expect the government expenditure multiplier to exceed a value of 1.0.

The multiplier for changes in tax rates or transfer payments is not as large as for government spending, because neither taxes nor transfers are part of GDP. They can only boost GDP if people respond to a tax cut or transfer increase by raising their consumption spending. The initial round, in which one dollar of government spending creates one dollar of real GDP, is missing. In this section we learn more about the advantages and disadvantages of different kinds of fiscal stimuli.

The Crowding Out Effect: Leakages from the Spending Stream

The initial government spending multiplier introduced early in Chapter 3 was 1.0 divided by the marginal propensity to save (MPS). So if the MPS were equal to 0.25, the multiplier would be $1.0/0.25 = 4.0$. But 4.0 is clearly too high for the multiplier, because it ignores important "leakages" that prevent all of the initial government spending from generating additional rounds of increased purchases of domestically produced goods and services.

Income taxes.   Households do not receive a full dollar of extra after-tax income from one extra dollar of GDP. The first leakage from their income is into income taxes paid to the federal government and some states and local governments. A related leakage is the increase in payroll taxes for Social Security and Medicare, which are levied on each extra dollar of labor income up to a ceiling. Sales taxes rise when consumers buy more, further reducing the after-tax multiplier effect.

Imports.   Over each of the past four decades, an increasing share of American consumer spending has been spent on imported products. Sometimes imports are cheaper; sometimes they are more innovative. Most electronic goods either are entirely imported or, if assembled in the United States, have many of the most important components manufactured in foreign countries. But each extra dollar of fiscal stimulus spent by consumers on imported goods and services fails to raise either production or jobs in the domestic economy. In 2010 the share of extra consumption that was spent on imports was particularly large, and as a result a robust recovery of domestic demand translated into surprisingly small increases in domestic production.

Corporate profits.   Both income taxes and imports are identified as leakages in the Appendix to Chapter 3, which calculates how much lower is the multiplier when the effect of income taxes and imports is taken into account. Another important leakage is corporate profits. A fiscal stimulus may raise induced consumption, and some of this extra spending may occur on domestically produced goods and services. But, at least initially, firms do not hire extra workers or pay them higher wages, so much of the additional revenue flows to corporate profits. And only a small fraction of corporate profits raises household incomes as is necessary for households to buy more consumer goods.[5]

Because of these leakages the multiplier for government spending may not be 4.0 as in the main text of Chapter 3 but rather a much lower number like 2.0 or 1.5.[6]

The Crowding Out Effect: Higher Interest Rates

The classic crowding out effect of fiscal policy was already illustrated in Figure 4-6 on p. 98. A fiscal policy expansion that occurs when the money supply is fixed raises the interest rate. This causes a negative response of

---

[5] By definition a dollar increase in corporate profits can (a) go to the government through the corporation income tax, (b) go to households as corporate dividend payments, and (c) stay in the corporate vaults as retained earnings. Neither (a) nor (c) has any effect on household income at all. Dividends (b) are adjusted upwards very slowly in response to higher corporate profits. The main way in which higher corporate profits raise household incomes in the short run is through the bonus payments and stock options of top executives, but many of these individuals are sufficiently well off that they have a very low marginal propensity to consume. In sum, most of the increase in corporate profits represents a "leakage" out of the spending stream.

[6] Using equation 12 in the Appendix to Chapter 3 on p. 87, if we set the marginal propensity to save (s) at 0.25, the income tax rate (t) equal to 0.2, and the ratio of imports to real GDP (nx) at 0.1, the marginal leakage rate is $s(1 - t) + t + nx$, or $0.25(0.8) + 0.2 + 0.1 = 0.5$. The multiplier is then 1.0 divided by the marginal leakage rate or $1.0/0.5 = 2.0$.

interest-sensitive spending, particularly business investment, residential construction, and consumer durable goods purchases. This further reduces the multiplier.

As we learned in Figure 4-10 on p. 108, this type of crowding out effect can be avoided if the central bank raises the money supply, thus pushing the *LM* curve to the right at the same time as the fiscal stimulus is pushing the *IS* curve to the right. The only reason for interest rates to go up is an insufficient money supply, and the Fed's control over the federal funds' short-term interest rate gives it the power to avert the interest-rate mechanism of crowding out.

Whenever the Fed boosts the money supply in order to support a fiscal stimulus, *the Fed is buying government securities issued as a by-product of the stimulus.* Because of the Fed's securities purchases, the net public debt does not go up. The government does not have to sell any securities to any other economic entity except the Fed. This type of cooperative monetary and fiscal expansion is sometimes called a **helicopter drop** of money. This counts as fiscal policy because the government counts the money floating down to the eager population as a transfer payment.

The interest-rate crowding out effect becomes less important when the economy is weak and the Fed is holding the short-term interest rate at zero, the so-called zero lower bound of Chapter 5. The Fed can maintain the zero short-term interest rate, and there will be no investment-stifling increase in the borrowing rates faced by business firms and consumers as long as neither the term premium nor risk premium increase. Thus in a year like 2010 the federal government can conduct a fiscal stimulus without any necessity for interest rates to rise.

> A **helicopter drop** is a figurative phrase to describe a combined monetary and fiscal policy expansion. A fiscal stimulus creates a larger deficit, and the government has to sell bonds to pay for the deficit. But instead of selling those bonds to the private sector, it sells them to the Fed. The Fed's assets and liabilities increase but the net public debt does not increase.

The Crowding Out Effect: Capacity Constraints

Economists have found that it is difficult to use statistical techniques to measure the crowding out effect. Throughout history many of the sharpest fiscal expansions have occurred at the beginning of wars, as in 1940–42 for World War II, 1950–51 for the Korean War, and during 1965–66 during the Vietnam War period. In each of these three cases the fiscal expansion occurred when the economy was close to full capacity, operating at or above the desired natural output level. In these episodes fiscal multipliers may have been quite low because government purchases literally pushed aside private purchases. For instance in the United States six months before Pearl Harbor, firms were planning to *reduce* auto production (a negative multiplier) because of shortages of steel and other components for which government weapons purchases had a higher priority.[7]

An important lesson of this section is that the case for stimulative fiscal policy is much stronger when the economy is weak, as in 2009–10, than when it is strong. In a weak economy interest rates are low, so it costs relatively little to pay the interest on the government debt. The Fed can buy up the securities issued to pay for the fiscal stimulus programs, yet higher inflation, the traditional downside of expansive Fed policies, is no threat because of the economy's weakness. In contrast when the economy is strong with actual real GDP at or above natural real GDP, fiscal multipliers are small due to the

---

[7] See Robert J. Gordon and Robert Krenn, "The End of the Great Depression 1939–41: Policy Contributions and Fiscal Multipliers," NBER working paper 16380. September 2010.

crowding out and capacity constraint effects. Yet this contrast represents an opportunity rather than a problem. Fiscal stimulus is only needed when the economy is weak and is inappropriate when the economy is strong, at which point monetary and fiscal restraint is needed, not stimulus.

SELF-TEST

For each of the following examples, indicate whether the multiplier for an increase in government expenditures is made larger or smaller:

1. A high personal income tax rate
2. A low share of consumption going to imports
3. A high share of corporate profits in GDP
4. Decision by the Fed to buy all the bonds issued as a result of higher government spending
5. A high level of capacity utilization

6-9 CASE STUDY

The Fiscal Policy Stimulus of 2008–11

The standard textbook analysis of Chapter 3 states that the government expenditure multiplier for tax changes is lower than for changes in government expenditures. That chapter's appendix shows that the multiplier for *both* government spending and tax changes is substantially lower due to leakages into income taxes and imports. And in the previous section we have added corporate profits as another type of leakage. We also have discussed higher interest rates and capacity constraints as additional reasons why the real-world multipliers might be smaller than their textbook simplification.

Widely Different Multipliers for Different Types of Fiscal Policy

Modern econometric models can include all of these different factors together and sort them out. A prominent recent model produced the estimates of fiscal multipliers as displayed in Table 6-1. As we look down the multiplier column, we notice that the multipliers range from 1.74 to 0.32.

Why do we care about the multiplier of different types of fiscal policy? One dollar of government spending or tax cuts raises the fiscal deficit by one dollar, yet the effects on GDP are clearly very different. The most effective policy would be a temporary increase in food stamps; the second most effective would be an extension of unemployment insurance. The least effective fiscal policy, shown at the bottom of Table 6-1, would be to reduce corporate tax rates, with a multiplier of 0.32.

There is a systematic reason why these multipliers differ. If the government spends a dollar that goes directly into the pocket of a household, that will make the most difference to a low-income household living from paycheck to paycheck or to an unemployed person who has no paycheck at all. This is why the programs with the highest multipliers, listed at the top of Table 6-1, are those that directly target poor people (food stamps) or unemployed people (extension of unemployment benefits).

Table 6-1 Multiplier Estimates for Selected Types of Fiscal Stimulus

Measures with Relatively High Multipliers	
Expenditures	
Temporary Increase in Food Stamps	1.74
Extending Unemployment Insurance	1.61
Increased Infrastructure Spending	1.57
General Aid to State Governments	1.41
Taxes	
Job Tax Credit	1.30
Payroll Tax Holiday	1.24
Across the Board Tax Cut	1.01
Measures with Relatively Low Multipliers	
Taxes	
Make Bush Dividend and Capital Gains Cuts Permanent	0.37
Make Bush Income Tax Cuts Permanent	0.32
Cut in Corporate Tax Rate	0.32

Source: Alan S. Blinder and Mark Zandi, "How the Great Recession Was Brought to an End," Moody's Analytics working paper, July 27, 2010. Table 11, p. 16.

The lowest multipliers by the same reasoning are those where the benefits flow mainly to rich people who already have incomes high enough so that they can spend what they want. The three bottom lines in the table with multipliers of only 0.32 to 0.37 involve tax cuts that mainly benefit individuals and families in the top 10 percent or even the top 1 percent of the income distribution.

What difference is made by the estimated multipliers in Table 6-1? According to these numbers a $100 billion increase in the federal deficit that increases the federal debt by $100 billion would have very different effects on real GDP and therefore on employment. A $100 billion increase in food stamps would boost GDP by $174 billion and raise the public debt by $100 billion. In contrast a reduction in the corporation income tax would boost GDP by only $32 billion while raising the public debt by same $100 billion. Since the reason for the fiscal stimulus is to raise GDP by as much as possible per dollar of spending, the high multiplier types of stimulus in Table 6-1 should be used and the low multiplier types of stimulus should not be used.

The Weak Effects of the Tax Cuts

The main components of the 2008–11 fiscal stimulus measures are listed in Table 6-2, where their total amounts are expressed as a percentage of GDP. The first two items in the table are tax cuts and rebates instituted by the Bush administration in the spring of 2008 and as part of the Obama stimulus measures in the spring of 2009. Lower- and middle-income households have received tax rebate checks, paid less in payroll taxes, and benefited from tax credits to purchase homes and appliances.

Table 6-2 Size of Fiscal Stimulus Measures in 2008–10

	Percent of GDP
Tax Cuts and Rebates	
2008 Bush Tax Cuts and Rebates	1.2
2009 Obama Stimulus Tax Cuts	1.4
Expenditure Increases, all from 2009–11 Obama Stimulus	
Infrastructure and Related Spending	1.1
Transfers to State and Local Governments	1.2

Transfers to Persons of which:
    Unemployment Benefits (1.6)
    2010 extensions of unemployment benefits (0.4)
	2.3

Other components	0.4
Total Stimulus, 2008–11	7.6

Source: Adapted from Table 10 in the same source as used for Table 6–1.

The peak month for output and employment was December 2007, and initially the decline into the recession of 2008–09 was quite moderate. Even so, as early as April 2008, the Bush administration devised a set of tax rebates and tax cuts that added up to 1.2 percent of GDP, or about $170 billion. Then a year later the Obama stimulus program included another 1.4 percent of GDP in additional tax cuts. Were these effective?

To see whether the tax rebates and cuts were effective, we can compare the behavior of personal disposable income, which goes up by the amount that taxes are cut, with personal consumption expenditures. If consumption jumps by most or all of the increase in disposable income following a tax cut, then we can infer that the tax cut was effective. If consumption does not respond positively, then we can conclude that the tax cut was ineffective.

Figure 6-6 shows the behavior of personal disposable income and personal consumption expenditures from early 2007 to mid-2010. Each number plotted represents the value in a particular quarter above or below the value of the same variable in 2007:Q4. Thus all three lines come together at zero in 2007:Q4. Note that the Bush tax cuts and rebates caused real disposable income to jump about 2.5 percent in 2008:Q2 relative to 2007:Q4, but consumption did not rise at all. Instead consumption remained at the same level as in 2007:Q4, and subsequently it began to decline.

Why did the tax stimulus fail to boost consumption? In a separate study based on telephone interviews, three-quarters of respondents said that they would save the stimulus payments or use them to pay down credit card debt and other types of debt.[8] The survey evidence suggests that only about one-third of the tax stimulus resulted in extra consumption, but in Figure 6-6 consumption failed to increase by even that small amount because of other factors putting

---

[8] Claudia Sahm, Matthew Shapiro, and Joel Slemrod, "Household Response to the 2008 Tax Rebate: Survey Evidence and Aggregate Implications," NBER Working Paper 15421, October 2009.

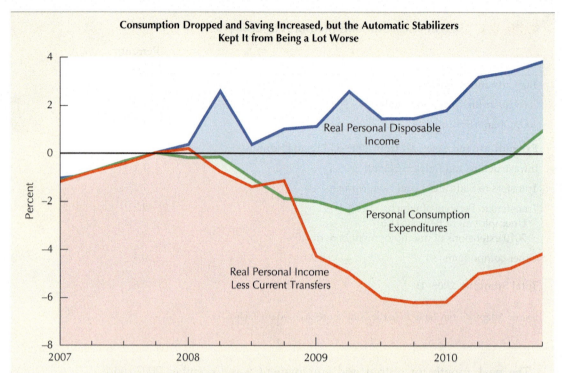

Figure 6-6 The Role of the Automatic Stabilizers in the Recession of 2008–09
All lines show the change in a particular variable as compared to the fourth quarter of 2007 (2007:Q4). The blue line shows that Real Personal Disposable Income never declined in the recession and was particularly high in 2008:Q2 and 2009:Q2, the quarters when the Bush and Obama tax cuts had their major impact. The green line shows that Personal Consumption Expenditures fell relative to Personal Disposable Income, which by definition means that the Personal Saving Rate increased. The effect of automatic stabilizers is shown by the vertical distance between the blue line and the red line, which shows how much taxes fell and transfers rose as part of the normal automatic stabilization role of fiscal policy.

downward pressure on consumption, such as declining net worth due to falling stock and house prices.

The same fate awaited the Obama tax cuts, most of which had their impact on disposable income in 2009:Q2. But once again consumption failed to respond positively. The turnaround in consumption spending shown by the green line in Figure 6-6 occurred one quarter after the tax cuts in 2009:Q3 and could possibly be cited as representing a delayed and partial impact of the tax cuts.

Contribution of the Automatic Stabilizers

We have seen that the two jumps in disposable income in spring 2008 and spring 2009 did not boost consumption. But there is another less recognized aspect to the disposable spending line in Figure 6-6. Despite the largest recession since the Great Depression, real disposable income *never fell below its value at the previous business cycle peak quarter of 2007:Q4.* How was disposable income immunized from the decline in income that occurred as millions lost their jobs and corporate profits collapsed?

The answer is given by the blue and green shaded areas in Figure 6-6 that extend between the blue disposable income line on the top to the red "personal income less current transfers" line at the bottom. The red line shows how much personal income before taxes would have dropped if changes in transfers were excluded. In 2009:Q3 the blue line had risen by 1.4 percent since 2007:Q4 while the red line had dropped by 6.0 percent, a distance of 7.4 percent indicated by the blue and green shading.

This 7.4 percent difference is accounted for by four elements:

1. Tax rebates and cuts that were part of the fiscal stimulus
2. Transfer increases that were part of the fiscal stimulus
3. Reductions in tax revenues due to the automatic stabilizers
4. Increases in transfers due to the automatic stabilizers

We have already discussed the tax cuts and rebates listed in the first two lines of Table 6-2. The same table shows that transfers to persons were increased as part of the Obama stimulus program by 2.3 percent of real GDP. Most of these transfers consisted of the extension of unemployment benefits from an eligibility period of 26 weeks, which is the time limit of these benefits in normal times, to 99 weeks. The extra transfers flowing to the unemployed were a major factor in boosting disposable income, and as we learned in Table 6-1 these extensions of unemployment benefits have relatively large multiplier effects. Most unemployed workers spend their benefits immediately, and without this form of fiscal stimulus unemployed workers and their families would have been forced to drastically cut their spending.

But a large part of the blue and green areas in Figure 6-6 is explained not by the Bush or Obama stimulus programs, but by the normal operation of the automatic stabilizers. As real incomes declined in 2008 and 2009, tax collections fell for personal, payroll, sales, and corporate taxes. Transfer payments also increased due to higher unemployment benefits and also because more people who could not find jobs decided to sign up for Social Security benefits at the earliest possible age.[9] ◆

6-10   Government Spending and Transfers to States/Localities

Our explanation of the Obama stimulus program has now covered the first two lines of Table 6-2, the tax rebates and tax cuts, and the line recording higher transfers to persons. An additional component was infrastructure and other spending, amounting to 1.1 percent of GDP, and transfers to state and local governments, amounting to 1.2 percent of GDP. The total of the Bush and Obama stimulus programs adds up to 7.6 percent of GDP, as shown on the bottom line of Table 6-2.

The infrastructure spending component has an important weakness, the very slow pace at which projects can be authorized and the money can actually be

---

[9] The increase in the unemployment rate automatically generated additional benefit payments within the normal 26-week eligibility rule, and this is counted as an automatic stabilizer. The extra payments created by an extension from 26-week to 99-week eligibility is counted as part of the Obama stimulus program.

UNDERSTANDING THE GLOBAL ECONOMIC CRISIS

Comparing the Obama Stimulus with FDR's New Deal

As we have seen in this section the best estimates of the Bush and Obama fiscal stimulus impact are quite low. In early 2011 the economy was still struggling, with unemployment near 9 percent and an anemic rate of recovery in real GDP. As the 2008–09 recession was followed by continuing high unemployment, analogies with the Great Depression were becoming more common. In that decade unemployment remained above 10 percent for eleven straight years between 1930 and 1940.

The decade of the 1930s was very different than the post-2007 period in many respects, but there were a few common features. As we learned on p. 110, the short-term interest rate was roughly zero in the last half of the 1930s, just as the short-term interest rate has been zero in the United States since the beginning of 2009. Another similarity is that Roosevelt's New Deal failed to reduce unemployment below 10 percent until shortly before the beginning of World War II. While the Obama fiscal stimulus program was large enough to keep unemployment from becoming worse, as of early 2011 it had not succeeded

in reducing the unemployment rate appreciably below 9 percent.

Franklin Roosevelt, universally known as "FDR," instituted numerous programs that directly stimulated employment. The Works Progress Administration (WPA) built roads, dams, bridges, and many post offices that still provide services today. The Civilian Conservation Corps hired unemployed people aged 18 to 24 to help build and restore America's natural resources, ultimately planting nearly three million trees and constructing more than 800 parks, including many of the national and state parks that people take for granted today.

Yet all of this government-generated activity could not end the Great Depression. Why? It has long been recognized that the answer was "not enough." More than 50 years ago an MIT professor calculated that FDR's New Deal never did succeed in creating a natural employment deficit, in contrast to the large natural employment deficit of the United States in 2009–10 as plotted in Figure 6-4 on p. 167.[10]

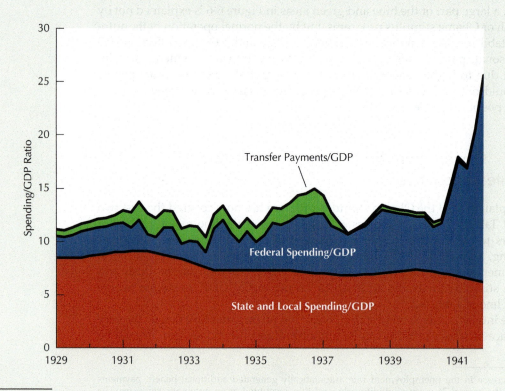

---

[10] E. Cary Brown, "Fiscal Policy in the Thirties: A Reappraisal," *American Economic Review,* vol. 46 (December 1956).

The first graph shows how FDR's New Deal failed to raise the ratio of government spending (including federal, state, and local) in natural GDP, shown by the sum of the red and blue areas in the first graph. The green area is transfer payments minus payroll taxes. Spending as a share of natural GDP was actually lower in 1940:Q2 than at the beginning of 1934, despite the substantial increase in federal spending between those dates. Transfers were no help, as a sharp rise in payroll taxes for Social Security in 1937–38 cancelled out any stimulus coming from transfer payments. Indeed it appears that fiscal policy was quite restrictive in 1937–38 and not very expansive in 1939–40.

The Great Depression came to an end due to an explosion of government spending that began in mid-1940 and caused the ratio of government spending to real GDP to jump from 11.4 percent in 1940:Q2 to 25.6 percent in 1941:Q4. That is, before the Pearl Harbor attacks, government spending had more than doubled as a share of GDP and had eliminated the real GDP gap several months before Pearl Harbor.[11]

The second graph shows the same concepts for 1980–2010, that is, the percentages of government spending and transfers to natural GDP. The most startling aspect of the second graph is that the total share of government spending to natural GDP (shown by the top of the blue area) declined steadily from 2003 to 2010, and the Obama stimulus was too small to reverse that trend. The 2008–09 recession accelerated the decline in the share of state and local government spending to natural GDP, which declined from 11.6 in 2007:Q4 to 10.5 percent in 2010:Q4. During the same period federal government spending rose from 7.0 to 7.7 percent, not enough to keep the total from declining from 18.6 to 18.2 percent.

The big difference between the 2008–09 recession and the Great Depression years prior to 1940 was the behavior of transfer payments. Between 2007:Q4 and 2010:Q2 the ratio of transfer payments (net of payroll taxes) to natural GDP went up from 5.3 to 8.0 percent, an enormous 50 percent increase. This notable increase combined the automatic stabilizers that boosted unemployment compensation and reduced payroll taxes with the stimulus measures that extended the period of eligibility for unemployment compensation. In contrast, in the Great Depression tax rates were low and transfer payments almost nonexistent, and the automatic stabilizers were far weaker in the 1930s than in 2008–09.

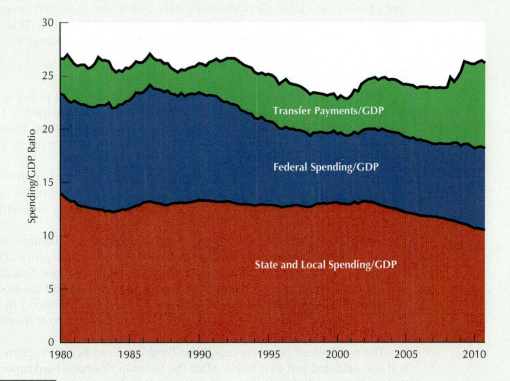

---

[11] Robert J. Gordon and Robert Krenn, "The End of the Great Depression 1939–41: Policy Contributions and Fiscal Multipliers," NBER working paper 16380, September 2010.

spent. As of June 2010 only $56 billion of a planned $147 billion in infrastructure spending had occurred. Another important weakness of the spending is that many projects, like road resurfacing, pay contractors who use lots of heavy machinery but very few workers. Critics of the Obama spending priorities suggest that many more jobs could have been created at less cost by new versions of the FDR New Deal job-creation programs described in the box on pp. 182–83.

Finally, transfers to state and local governments were necessary because most states and localities are required to balance their budgets. Thus when their tax revenues decline in a recession, they are forced to fire teachers, eliminate school programs like art and music, and even lay off police and fire employees. Federal transfer payments to states and localities can be thought of as a "defensive stimulus," helping to save jobs rather than to create new jobs.

Overall Fiscal Stimulus Impact

The effectiveness of the Bush and Obama fiscal stimulus programs is mixed. Hundreds of billions of dollars were spent on tax cuts and rebates that appear to have had quite small impacts in dampening the 2008–09 decline in real GDP. Infrastructure spending, whatever its effectiveness, was rolled out so slowly that by mid-2010 only about 40 percent had been spent. According to the multipliers in Table 6-1, the most effective components of the Obama stimulus program were aid to state and local governments and the extensions in the time duration of unemployment benefits.

As a measure of overall effectiveness a recent study has concluded that the combined Bush and Obama stimulus programs raised real GDP by a few percent in each year between 2008 and 2011, adding up to a cumulative impact of 7.8 percent of one year's GDP. Since the budgetary cost of the combined programs in Table 6-2 was 7.6 percent, the overall multiplier was 7.8/7.6 or 1.03. This is much smaller than the textbook multipliers that were discussed in Chapter 3.

Unconventional Stimulus Through Bailouts

So severe was the 2008–09 recession that monetary and fiscal policy were not enough. In this section we consider additional policies that helped reduce the downward free fall of the economy in that crisis autumn of 2008. These novel measures have been called "financial policies," and here we refer to them by their nickname "bailout policies."

The bailout policies do not fit neatly into the traditional definitions of monetary or fiscal policy. The bailout policies were carried out by both the Federal Reserve and Treasury in cooperation with each other and with other government agencies.

In the fall of 2008 the bankruptcy of the Wall Street firm Lehman Brothers created a financial panic on Wall Street that had no precedent in postwar history. The risk premium spiked upwards (see p. 143), lending from one financial firm to another dried up, many financial firms became insolvent, and the stock market crashed. Nearly every financial institution faced the likelihood of failure. The commercial paper market (consisting of short-term loans to corporations to build inventories and buy supplies) came close to shutting down.

The core bailout plan was called the Troubled Asset Relief Program (TARP) and was initiated just two weeks after the Lehman Brothers' bankruptcy. Since its inception the TARP has been controversial. Perhaps its greatest success was in lending government money to financial institutions that were on the brink of insolvency due to insufficient equity capital (see the normal and abnormal bank balance sheets in Tables 5-1 and 5-2 on pp. 129–31). The TARP and related programs also helped to prevent the liquidation of General Motors and Chrysler Motors, which would have caused hundreds of thousands of lost jobs not just in those companies but in their network of suppliers. One measure of the success of the TARP program was the sharp reduction in the risk premium. As shown in Figure 5-10 on p. 143, the risk premium leapt upwards from 1.9 percent in mid-2007 to 5.5 percent in the winter of 2009, but by mid-2010 was back down to 2.7 percent.

One of the few careful studies to assess the bailout policies concludes that the bailout policies were a major success. Without them, real GDP in 2010 would have been about 5 percent lower and the 2010 unemployment rate would have been 12.5 percent instead of 9.8 percent.

The TARP program initially allowed up to $700 billion (5 percent of GDP) to be used, but that amount proved to be unnecessary. As the financial markets stabilized many banks repaid the government loans and in some cases the government actually made a profit on its TARP intervention. It has been estimated that the ultimate budgetary cost of the TARP and other bailout programs will be just $100 billion, much less than originally planned and much less than the total cost of the fiscal stimulus programs summarized in Table 6-2. The multiplier effects have been enormous, since the cost was less than 1 percent of GDP but the impact in raising real GDP (or keeping it from falling further) amounts to at least 5 percent of real GDP in 2010, another 5 percent in 2011, and so on.

Despite its success, the TARP and related bailout programs continue to be controversial for several reasons. First, the economic analysis that demonstrates their large benefits and low cost has not been widely publicized. Second, the bailouts of the financial institutions seemed to reward those who had created the crisis in the first place, like giving candy to a child who misbehaves.

In a broader sense the TARP was a policy failure because it was perceived to be unfair. It revived Wall Street without reviving Main Street. It allowed the largest Wall Street financial firms to absorb failing firms, thus becoming even bigger. Top executives at large financial firms continued to be paid salaries, bonuses, and stock options in the multi-millions, and this understandably seemed deeply unfair to the public in view of the 25 million of unemployed and underemployed people who lost their jobs due to the crisis. Only a small fraction of the millions of homeowners facing the loss of their homes through foreclosure, often through no fault of their own due to rising unemployment, had received permanent modification of their mortgages.

6-11   Conclusion: Strengths and Limitations of Fiscal Policy

This chapter has introduced the basic concepts of fiscal policy, including budget deficits and the public debt. Budget deficits can change both because of the operation of the automatic stabilizers, that is, the effect of changes in the output gap on tax revenue and transfer payments, and also because of discretionary changes in fiscal policy in the form of changes in tax rates, and spending programs for transfers and spending on goods and services. The economy affects the budget, and the budget affects the economy.

A central theme of this chapter has been that fiscal policy is available to supplement monetary policy, especially in situations like 2009–10 when the Fed has lost its ability to control short-term interest rates. Fiscal stimulus programs that raise the government budget deficit do not raise the net public debt if the Fed buys up the securities issued as a result of the fiscal stimulus.

Fiscal stimulus programs vary widely in their multiplier effects and timeliness. Increasing transfer payments to low-income households and to unemployed individuals generate the highest ratio of economic impact to budgetary dollar spent. General tax cuts, especially those targeted at wealthy individuals, have the lowest economic impact. Government infrastructure programs like road building have significant defects, both that they are very slow to spend the stimulus money and that many of these projects do not create substantial numbers of jobs per budgetary dollar.

The U.S. economy struggled in 2010–11 with a sluggish recovery and disappointing job growth. Pressure mounted for a new round of stimulus programs that would focus more tightly on job creation. Such measures might include increasing aid to the unemployed or reducing payroll taxes for employers who create new jobs. Few had yet suggested the most radical program of all, direct federal government hiring of individuals for public works projects following the model of FDR's New Deal. However, voices across the political spectrum differed greatly in the priority placed on stimulus policies based on the criterion of jobs created per budgetary dollar, as contrasted with alternative views that emphasized the central importance of stopping the rise in the public debt.

Different Attitudes Toward Fiscal Stimulus in the United States and Europe

While most European countries suffered a decline in output and the GDP gap during the World Economic Crisis of 2008–10, very different attitudes had developed in Europe regarding the relative importance of fiscal stimulus as contrasted with fiscal restraint to reduce the ratio of public debt to GDP. As shown in the box on p. 171 in this chapter, Italy had long experienced a debt-GDP ratio much higher than that in the United States, and so had other European nations, particularly Greece.

In 2010 a crisis occurred in which Greece was feared to be about to default on its debt, that is, to fail to make interest payments to foreigners who owned much of the debt. Greece was ultimately rescued by other European governments and international agencies, but only at the cost of a drastic fiscal adjustment. Greek-style fiscal austerity is the opposite of fiscal stimulus; taxes are raised, while transfer payments and government spending programs are cut.

Soon after the Greek crisis, a newly elected government in the United Kingdom instituted a draconian fiscal austerity program designed to reduce sharply and promptly that country's fiscal deficit. Other important European countries, including France, Germany, and Italy, did not institute fiscal austerity programs but also rejected the American emphasis on fiscal stimulus.

Why did European countries have such different attitudes toward fiscal stimulus? One reason is that (except for Britain) the major European countries do not control their own monetary policy but rather are part of the Euro currency, which has its monetary policy set by the European Central Bank. Thus European countries cannot sell their public debt to the central bank, while the U.S. Treasury can sell the extra debt resulting from its fiscal stimulus programs to the Fed as part of a coordinated monetary and fiscal policy stimulus.

Another central difference is the unusual role of the United States in the world monetary system, a central theme of the next chapter. The United States is able to enlarge its fiscal debt and the Fed can raise the money supply almost without limit. The unique role of the United States is that much of the rest of the world holds international reserves denominated in U.S. dollars rather than the currency of other individual nations. The next chapter introduces the main concepts of international macroeconomics, including the unique role of the dollar as an international reserve currency that, among other effects, have made China and the United States the world's most important economic partnership.

Summary

1. An increase in the government budget deficit can crowd out domestic private investment and/or require foreign borrowing to maintain the initial level of domestic foreign investment.
2. Over the past century, the government has run a budget deficit in most years, primarily because of wars and recessions. However, since 1982 the government has run a budget deficit in every year except in 1998–2001, whether there was a recession or not.
3. The actual budget surplus or deficit is what actually occurs. The natural employment surplus or deficit is the hypothetical level of the budget surplus if the economy were operating at its natural level of output. The natural employment surplus changes whenever there is a discretionary fiscal policy action to change tax rates or the amount of government transfer payments or spending on goods and services.
4. The economy affects the budget through the automatic stabilizers. When real GDP is high tax revenues rise, causing more spending to leak out of the economy to the government, and when real GDP is low tax revenues decrease, helping to offset the decline in GDP as the government takes less spending out of the economy.
5. The public debt rises when the government runs a budget deficit. The net public debt excludes securities held inside the government at the Fed or at the trust funds for Social Security and Medicare.
6. The government faces a solvency condition, which states that it cannot perpetually run a deficit in the long run if the interest rate it pays on its debt exceeds the economy's growth rate of nominal GDP.
7. Factors limiting the size of fiscal multipliers include leakages out of the income flow into taxes, imports, and corporate profits. The crowding out effect occurs if a fiscal expansion is accompanied by higher interest rates and can be avoided if the Fed maintains constant interest rates. The fiscal multiplier tends to be higher when the economy is weak and lower when the economy is strong and capacity limits are reached.
8. Fiscal multiplier differ across types of fiscal stimulus. The highest multipliers are those that send money directly to low-income households living paycheck to paycheck and to the unemployed. The lowest multipliers are for tax cuts aimed at the top percentiles of the income distribution.
9. The Obama stimulus program included tax rebates and cuts, transfer increases, and increases in government spending on goods and services. The stimulus had a relatively low impact per dollar of budget deficit created, both because the tax cuts had low multipliers and also because the government spending projects took many months for spending actually to occur.
10. A new type of policy, neither traditional monetary nor fiscal policy, was used in 2008–09. This bailout policy that rescued large financial corporations and two large automakers had a beneficial impact by preventing an even larger economic decline than actually occurred. The bailout policies are controversial because they are widely perceived to have been unfair.

Concepts

cyclical surplus
cyclical deficit
structural surplus
structural deficit
automatic stabilization

discretionary fiscal policy
budget line
natural employment surplus (NES)
natural employment
 deficit (NED)

public debt
gross debt
net debt
helicopter drop

Questions

1. You have heard that the actual government deficit for the current year is going to be $30 billion greater than in the past year. Based on this projection, what conclusions can you make regarding the government's fiscal policy?
2. Explain the distinction among the following concepts:
   (a) cyclical deficit

   (b) structural deficit
   (c) natural employment deficit
   (d) actual deficit
3. Government deficits and surpluses are expressed throughout this chapter as percents of natural GDP. Explain why it is necessary to express government

deficits and surpluses in this manner in order to compare them over time.

4. Respond to the following statements about an economy where the government budget deficit has increased during a recession.
   (a) The increase in the budget deficit indicates that policymakers have implemented expansionary fiscal policies to bring the economy out of recession.
   (b) The increase in the budget deficit indicates that fiscal policymakers have been irresponsible. They should enact restrictive policies, such as tax hikes or spending cuts, to reduce the deficit.

5. Explain whether each of the following results in a change in the cyclical deficit, or a change in the natural employment deficit, or both.
   (a) A cut in the tax rate aimed at reducing unemployment.
   (b) The rise in taxes that occurs during an expansion.
   (c) The higher defense spending associated with the Afghanistan war.
   (d) The increase in unemployment compensation due to a rise in the unemployment rate.

6. Explain why you would expect the actual government deficit to be larger than the natural employment deficit when the economy is weak.

7. The combination of tax increases, tighter spending controls, and a very strong economy helped move the U.S. government budget from deficit to surplus by the end of the 1990s. Explain how these events led from budget deficit to surplus and relate them to the concepts of discretionary fiscal policy, automatic stabilization, budget line, cyclical deficit, and natural employment deficit.

8. What is the relationship between the government's deficit and its debt?

9. The government budget went from a surplus in 2001 to a very large deficit in 2010. Discuss the events that caused this change and whether the particular event affected primarily the cyclical deficit or the natural employment deficit. Explain how the change from a government surplus to a large government deficit affected the ratio of net public debt-to-GDP.

10. What is the difference between the gross public debt and the net public debt? Explain whether the Fed's purchase of newly issued Treasury bonds affects the gross public debt or the net public debt.

11. Compare and contrast since 1990 the ratios of debt-to-GDP for Germany, Italy, Japan, and the United States.

12. We rarely hear concern about the "burden" of privately held debt, yet many people share a concern about the public debt. Why is this so? Is the concern about the public debt reasonable?

13. Many people are less concerned with the absolute size of the government debt than they are about its size relative to GDP. Such people would not worry about the size of government deficits if the ratio of government debt to GDP remained equal to some "appropriate" level.
    (a) Should people who hold this view worry about the solvency of the government?
    (b) Explain the conditions under which it is possible for the debt-GDP ratio to be a constant.
    (c) Don't people who hold the view that has just been described have to worry about the future solvency of the government?

14. Explain what is meant by a helicopter drop and under what economic conditions it is appropriate to use a helicopter drop. Explain why a helicopter drop had no impact on the size of the net public debt.

15. The fiscal stimulus programs of 2008–11 consisted of a combination of tax cuts and increases in transfer payments and government expenditures. Discuss what the evidence shows concerning the multiplier effects of the various components of the stimulus programs and why some multipliers were larger than others.

16. Explain why real disposable income never fell during the 2007–09 recession.

17. Compare and contrast the behavior of first, government spending and second, transfer payments as percent in natural GDP during FDR's New Deal and the Obama Stimulus Program.

18. Discuss what the economic successes of Troubled Asset Relief Program and other government bailouts were and explain why they were also perceived as policy failures.

Problems

 Visit www.MyEconLab.com to complete these or similar exercises.

1. Assume $Y^N = 11,600$, $t = 0.2$, and $G = 2,610$.
   (a) Compute the amount of taxes at natural real GDP.
   (b) Explain why there is a natural employment deficit. Compute the amount of the natural employment deficit in terms of both billions of dollars and as a percent of natural real GDP.
   (c) Suppose that the goal of fiscal policymakers is to reduce the size of the natural employment deficit to 1 percent of natural real GDP. Compute what

the size of the natural employment deficit must be in terms of billions of dollars in order for fiscal policymakers to achieve their goal.
   (d) Given no change in the tax rate, compute by how much fiscal policymakers must cut government spending in order to accomplish their goal.
   (e) Given no change in government spending, compute by how much fiscal policymakers must increase the tax rate in order to accomplish their goal.

(f) Given the objective of fiscal policymakers, explain what action monetary policymakers must take for the actions of fiscal policymakers to have no effect on real income.

(g) Suppose that private saving increases as the interest rate increases. Given the fiscal-monetary policy mix described in parts c–f, explain whether national saving increases by an amount that is larger than, equal to, or less than the decrease in the natural employment deficit.

2. Assume $Y^N = 10,900, Y = 10,600, t = 0.16$, and $G = 1,890$.

(a) Compute the amount of taxes at natural real GDP and actual real GDP.

(b) Compute the amount of the natural employment deficit.

(c) Compute the amount of the actual deficit. Is there a cyclical surplus or deficit? How large is it?

(d) Suppose that fiscal policy is used to increase actual real GDP to natural real GDP. This fiscal expansion requires the average tax rate to be cut to 0.14. Compute the new amount of taxes at natural real GDP.

(e) Compute the new amount of the natural employment deficit. Why are the natural employment deficit and actual deficit now equal? Why is there neither a cyclical surplus nor a cyclical deficit?

(f) Suppose that instead of fiscal policy, monetary policy is used to increase actual real GDP to natural real GDP. What are the actual and natural employment deficits? Why are these answers different from part e?

3. In 2010, a country had a nominal GDP of $15 trillion, a net public debt of $9 trillion, and a nominal interest rate of 5 percent. The country's nominal GDP is growing at 5 percent annual rate.

(a) What is the value of the net public debt/GDP ratio in 2010?

(b) What is the amount of interest paid on the net public debt in 2010? What was the interest payment as a percentage of nominal GDP in 2010?

(c) If the government issues new net debt in 2011 to cover the amount of interest paid on its net debt in 2010, what is the new level of net public debt in 2011? How much interest has to be paid in 2011 on the net public debt, assuming the nominal interest rate is still 5 percent?

(d) What is the level of nominal GDP in 2011? Compare the percentage of nominal GDP going for interest payments in 2011 to that of 2010. Compare the ratios of net public debt for the two years. Is the ratio of net public debt to nominal GDP equal in the two years? If so, why? If not, why not?

(e) Assume the nominal interest rate for the two years was actually 6 percent instead of 5 percent. How does this change affect your answers to parts b–d?

(f) Assume the nominal interest rate for the two years was actually 4 percent instead of 5 percent. How does this change affect your answers to parts b–d?

4. Suppose that nominal GDP equals $15 trillion, the current budget deficit is $600 billion, and the net public debt/GDP ratio is 80 percent. Given that the government wishes to maintain the net public debt/GDP ratio at 80 percent, explain whether the government needs to decrease its budget deficit, maintain the current budget deficit, or can increase its budget deficit if, over the next year, nominal GDP grows by: (i), 4 percent; (ii), 5 percent; and (iii), 6 percent. If the government either needs to cut its deficit or can increase it, explain by how much in each case.

◆ SELF-TEST ANSWERS

p. 166. (1) More spending for highway repair shifts the budget line *BB* down (raises the natural employment deficit, NED). (2) An increase in the Social Security tax rate moves *BB* up (reduces NED). (3) An increase in Social Security benefits moves *BB* down (raises NED). (4) A recession like that of 2008–09 moves the economy southwest down a fixed *BB* schedule (no change in NED).

p. 172. (1) 270; 450; yes (2) 450; 270; no (3) 480; 480; yes (4) 360; 600; yes.

p. 177. (1) smaller (2) higher (3) smaller (4) higher (5) smaller.

International Trade, Exchange Rates, and Macroeconomic Policy

Trade is the mother of money.
—Thomas Draxe, 1605

7-1 Introduction

This chapter connects the United States with the rest of the world. College students experience the international economy in their everyday life. Most of the clothes they wear are made in foreign countries. Most or all of their laptops, cell phones, iPods, and other electronic devices were made in foreign countries, even if they bear the labels of American-owned companies like Apple, Dell, or HP. Just as the United States buys goods and services from other countries, it exports as well. Much of the world's construction of highways and mines is made possible by Caterpillar equipment manufactured in America's heartland, and many passengers flying between cities within China, India, or Germany are riding on aircraft made in the United States by Boeing.

The importance of imports and exports in any economy is nothing new. Throughout the book we have treated the economy as "open" to trade in goods and services, as well as capital flows. We learned in Chapter 2 that foreign trade contributes to overall economic activity. GDP includes exports and subtracts imports, and we label the difference between exports and imports with the term "net exports." When net exports rise, GDP increases. When net exports decline, GDP decreases. We also learned that the higher the share of consumer spending on imports, the lower the multiplier for changes in autonomous spending, for instance, the multiplier for changes in government spending, taxes, or planned investment.

In this chapter we will learn that the United States has long had a major imbalance in its international trade, importing vastly more than it exports. This trade imbalance is paid for by foreign investment in the United States both by private individuals and firms and by foreign governments and central banks. Why are these foreigners willing to send capital to the United States to allow it to import more than it exports? A central lesson of this chapter is that the United States is in a unique position in the international macroeconomy in its ability to attract foreign private and government money to fund its appetite for imports.

What We Learn in This Chapter

After learning the basics of the U.S. balance of payments, the current account, the capital account, and international indebtedness, we then learn about the role of the foreign exchange rates and the causes of their changes. Just as the price of wheat moves up or down to balance the supply and demand for wheat, so the foreign exchange rate moves up or down to balance the supply and demand for foreign exchange.

The foreign exchange rate of the dollar responds to imbalances in flows of exports, imports, and capital movements. We shall study the determinants of the foreign exchange rate and its interrelationship with monetary policy and interest rates. Later in the chapter we shall apply Chapter 4's *IS-LM* model to the analysis of the open economy. We shall learn that the effects of monetary and fiscal policy differ greatly, depending on whether the foreign exchange rate is fixed or flexible.

The "Trilemma"

A unifying theme of this chapter is the international "**trilemma**"—that it is impossible for any nation to maintain simultaneously (1) independent control of domestic monetary policy, (2) fixed exchange rates, and (3) free flows of capital with other nations ("perfect capital mobility"). Thus fixed exchange rates and capital mobility create a new reason why domestic monetary policy may be impotent beyond those factors that we studied in Chapters 4 and 5. For instance, Europe's common currency (the euro) has stripped member nations of their ability to conduct an independent domestic monetary policy.

How is the United States affected by the trilemma? By adopting flexible exchange rates, the United States is free to pursue an active domestic monetary policy despite keeping its borders open to perfect capital mobility. But, while the United States may want to keep its exchange rate flexible, it cannot prevent foreign nations, particularly China and Japan, from keeping their exchange rates relatively or totally fixed to the dollar. Ordinarily, the tendency of the United States to run a large foreign trade deficit would cause the U.S. dollar to depreciate, but this tendency for the dollar to become weaker can be prevented when a foreign central bank, like that of China, buys up dollars to prevent the dollar from depreciating and to prevent the Chinese currency from appreciating.

In the past decade, the United States has been running extraordinarily large foreign trade deficits, financed in part by the desire of China, Japan, and other countries to keep their currencies from strengthening against the dollar. Another main theme of this chapter is to ask whether the United States can continue to live beyond its means, borrowing more and more from foreign private companies, households, and governments. Why are these foreign countries accumulating so many dollars, can this situation last forever, and will foreigners, particularly Asians, soon change their behavior and cause the dollar to crash?

> The **trilemma** is the impossibility for any nation of maintaining simultaneously (1) independent control of domestic monetary policy, (2) fixed exchange rates, and (3) free flows of capital with other nations.

7-2 The Current Account and the Balance of Payments

In this section we look more closely at several key concepts of international macroeconomics, including the balance of payments and international indebtedness. We learn that the counterpart of the flows of goods and services counted as exports and imports are offsetting capital flows.

Just as government expenditures include not just goods and services but also interest and transfer payments, so U.S. international transactions include not just flows of goods and services but also flows of income and transfer payments. The all-inclusive measure of a nation's international transactions is called its **current account**, which includes net exports as well as two additional components that are not part of GDP, net income from abroad and net unilateral transfer payments.

> The **current account** records the nation's current international transactions, including exports and imports of goods and services, net income from abroad, and net unilateral transfer payments.

Net exports. We first learned in Chapter 2 that net exports—the difference between exports and imports—is included among the expenditures in GDP, along with consumption, investment, and government spending on goods and services. We usually think of exports and imports as goods that are loaded on ships and planes and sent to and received from foreign countries, such as U.S. exports of corn or Boeing aircraft, and U.S. imports of Japanese cars and Australian wine.

But net exports also include services. U.S. exports of services include the expenditure of a Japanese family on vacation in Hawaii, including their airfare if they fly on a U.S. airline like United or Delta. Fees earned by an American management consultant on assignment in Spain is also considered a U.S. export of services. Likewise, expenditures by an American family vacationing in Europe is an import of services, as is the use by American companies of call centers and computer programmers in India.

Net income from abroad. Income receipts flowing into the United States include earnings of Americans working in other countries plus investment income (interest, dividends, and royalties) earned on assets abroad that are owned by Americans. Earnings from American-owned companies operating abroad include a Ford plant in Germany, a Procter & Gamble plant making Tide in France, or a McDonald's restaurant in China. Income payments flowing out of the United States include interest paid on a New York bank account owned by a resident of Sweden and profits sent back to Japan that are earned by the Toyota factory in Georgetown, Kentucky. Net income from abroad is the sum of income receipts from abroad minus income payments to foreigners.

Net unilateral transfers. Just as Social Security benefits are a transfer payment because they do not represent a payment for labor, so international transfer payments are gifts that do not correspond to the purchase of any good, service, or asset. The most important type of unilateral transfer is the gift of money by Americans to their relatives who live in Mexico and other countries that are the source of American immigration.

While net exports are included in GDP, net income from abroad and net unilateral transfers are not included in GDP. Net income from abroad is included in an alternative concept called gross national product or GNP (this concept was introduced on p. 29). Net unilateral transfers are excluded from both GDP and GNP, just like any other type of transfer payment.

Throughout the past two decades, the U.S. current account has been negative. To balance the perpetually negative current account, the United States must borrow from foreign firms and households, foreign governments, or both. Foreign borrowing builds up the total indebtedness of the United States to foreign nations and implies that some part of U.S. economic growth in the future is mortgaged to pay the interest payments on this debt.

The Current Account and the Capital Account

The **balance of payments** is the record of a nation's international transactions, and includes both credits (which arise from sales of exports and sales of assets) and debits (which arise from purchases of imports and purchases of assets).

The foreign trade surplus or deficit is part of the official data on the international transactions of the United States. Like any nation, the United States has a balance of payments that records these transactions. The **balance of payments** is divided into two main parts.

1. The first part is the current account, which records the types of flows that matter for current income and output. The main components of the current

account are exports and imports of goods and services, net income from abroad, and net unilateral transfer payments. Just as purchases and sales of assets are excluded from GDP, so too are they excluded from the current account.

2. The second part of the balance of payments is the **capital account,** which records purchases and sales of foreign assets by U.S. residents and purchases and sales of American assets by foreign residents.

> The **capital account** is the part of the balance of payments that records capital flows, which consist of purchases and sales of foreign assets by domestic residents, and purchases and sales of domestic assets by foreign residents.

Any category of the balance of payments can generate a *credit* or a *debit*. To keep these terms straight, think of flows of money. Any international transaction that creates a payment of money to a U.S. resident is a credit. Included are exports of goods and services, investment income on U.S. assets held in foreign countries, transfers to U.S. residents, and purchases of U.S. assets by foreigners. Debits are the opposite of credits and result from payments of money to foreigners by U.S. residents. Debits are created by imports of goods and services, investment income paid on foreign holdings of assets within the United States, transfer payments by U.S. residents to foreigners, and purchases of foreign assets by U.S. residents.

The Balance of Payments Outcome

When total credits are greater than total debits, the United States is said to run a balance of payments surplus. When this occurs, we receive more foreign money from the credits than the sum of dollars we pay out for the debits. The opposite situation, when we pay out more dollars for the debits, is called a balance of payments deficit. The overall balance of payments surplus or deficit is the sum of the balance for the current account and the capital account.

$$\frac{\text{Current account}}{\text{balance}} + \frac{\text{capital account}}{\text{balance}} = \frac{\text{balance of}}{\text{payments outcome}} \qquad (7.1)$$

Since the early 1980s, the United States has run a persistent current account deficit, because it has consistently run a deficit on its trade in goods and services and a deficit on its transfer payments as well. In the same time period, the United States has also run a persistent capital account surplus that has partly offset the current account deficit. When a nation runs a capital account surplus, households, firms, and the government *are engaged in net borrowing from foreigners* (borrowing from foreign central banks is counted not in the capital account but in the overall balance of payments surplus or deficit).

The U.S. balance of payments outcome for five different years (1970, 1980, 1990, 2000, and 2010) is presented in Table 7-1. In both 1970 and 1980, the current account was in surplus, but the capital account was in deficit by a greater amount, so the overall balance was negative. In 1990, 2000, and 2010, there was a large current account deficit that was only partly covered by a capital account surplus. As a result, the balance of payments was negative in all three of these years.

The balance of payments in the most recent year, 2010, is particularly interesting, because the capital account surplus covered less than one-half of the current account deficit. The rest of the current account deficit was financed by massive borrowing from foreign governments, as reflected in the balance of payments outcome. Several Asian countries, particularly China and Japan, increased their foreign official reserves at a very rapid rate in order to keep their currencies from strengthening against the dollar. In effect, China and Japan willingly lent hundreds of billions of dollars to the United States to allow it to import much more than it exported in 2010.

Table 7-1   **The U.S. Balance of Payments, as a Percent of GDP, Selected Years**

	1970	1980	1990	2000	2010
1. Current Account	0.2	0.1	−1.4	−4.2	−3.3
a. Trade in goods and services	0.2	−0.7	−1.4	−3.8	−3.5
b. Net income investment	0.6	1.1	0.5	0.2	1.1
c. Transfer payments	−0.6	−0.3	−0.5	−0.6	−0.9
2. Capital Account	−0.6	−0.9	0.7	3.8	−0.9
3. Balance of Payments (row 1 + row 2)	−0.3	−0.8	−0.6	−0.4	−2.4

Note: Balance on current account given in source. Balance of payments is the sum of the increase in foreign official assets minus the increase in U.S. official reserve assets. The capital account on line 2 is then calculated as line 3 minus line 1.

Source: www.bea.gov, U.S. International Transactions, Table 1. Numbers for 2010 are the average for the first three quarters expressed as an annual rate.

How is the balance of payments related to the foreign trade concepts introduced earlier, namely, net exports (*NX*) and the current account deficit? Net exports are the same as the balance of trade in goods and services, shown on line 1a of Table 7-1. The additional items on lines 1b and 1c make the current account deficit differ somewhat from net exports. The items on lines 2 and 3 show how the current account deficit was financed, mainly by a massive inflow of capital from foreigners. Part of this inflow came from the private sector of foreign countries—that is, foreign households and business firms—and is counted as the capital account surplus on line 2. The remaining inflow involved foreign central banks and is counted on line 3 as the financing that allowed the United States to run a balance of payments deficit in all years shown.

 SELF-TEST

How much is the United States borrowing from (or lending to) foreign central banks in the following three situations?

1. Current account deficit of 100 and capital account surplus of 70.

2. Current account surplus of 100 and capital account deficit of 70.

3. Current account surplus of 70 and capital account deficit of 100.

Foreign Borrowing and International Indebtedness

A current account deficit must be financed either by net borrowing from foreign firms or households (counted as a capital account surplus), or from foreign central banks (counted as a balance of payments deficit). Either way, a country experiencing a current account deficit *automatically* must increase its indebtedness to foreigners in the private sector or to foreign central banks. Similarly, a current account surplus implies a reduction in foreign indebtedness or an increase in a country's net investment surplus. This relationship can be expressed in the following simple equation:

$$
\begin{array}{c}\text{change in net international}\\\text{investment position}\end{array} = \begin{array}{c}\text{current account}\\\text{balance}\end{array} + \begin{array}{c}\text{net}\\\text{revaluations}\end{array} \qquad (7.2)
$$

There is an extra effect on the net international investment position called *net revaluations.* This breaks the tight link between the current account and the change in the net international investment position and is essential to understanding the evolution of U.S. international indebtedness since 2001.

The value of U.S. assets abroad minus foreign-owned assets in the United States, that is, the net international investment position, can change not just as a result of the current account balance but also if the value of the assets rises or falls. For instance, if the stock market in China goes up, then the value of American stock holdings in China increases, reducing American net international indebtedness. Similarly, if the American stock market goes down, there is a decline in foreign asset holdings in the United States, again reducing American net international indebtedness.

An important factor determining the dollar value of U.S. foreign assets is the exchange rate of the dollar (which we study in this chapter). If an American owns one share of stock on the French stock market worth 100 euros, then it is worth $100 when the exchange rate of the dollar is 1.0 dollars per euro. But if the exchange rate changes to 1.5 dollars per euro, then the same share of stock is worth $150, thus raising American assets held abroad. The same change in the exchange rate of the dollar will also make U.S. factories and other assets in foreign countries more valuable.

Figure 7-1 illustrates the workings of equation (7.2) for the United States during the period since 1975. The top frame displays the U.S. current account, showing its shift into large deficits during 1982–87, its recovery back to balance in 1991, and then its steady descent into unparalleled deficits exceeding −6 percent of GDP by 2006.[1]

Then after 2006 the current account deficit became smaller as the Global Economic Crisis reduced U.S. imports more than it reduced U.S. exports. The sharp decline in U.S. imports was one of the channels by which the U.S.-originated financial crisis of 2008 spread around the world; fewer imports into the United States reduced the exports of other countries and this negative demand shock helped push them into recession.

The bottom frame of Figure 7-1 displays the U.S. **net international investment position.** This shows a shift in the net investment position from a surplus during 1975–85 to a growing deficit up until 2001. Then after 2001 the net investment position jumped around without any net change; its value in 2001 was −19.2 percent of GDP and in 2009 was exactly the same −19.2 percent of GDP. How could the net international investment position remain unchanged when the United States ran a current account deficit in every year between 2001 and 2009? The answer, according to equation (7.2), is that net revaluations must

A nation's **net international investment position** is the difference between all foreign assets owned by a nation's citizens and domestic assets owned by foreign citizens.

---

[1] The current account was only briefly balanced in 1991, in contrast to persistent deficits during every other year in the interval 1983–2006. Why? Three reasons have been suggested: (1) Most important, foreign governments made large contributions to pay for the 1991 Gulf War, converting the transfer payment item in Table 7–1, line 1c, into a temporary positive item instead of the usual negative item, (2) the United States was in a recession in 1991, which reduced imports and made net exports less negative than usual, and (3) the 1990–91 reunification of Germany created a temporary economic boom in Europe that boosted U.S. exports.

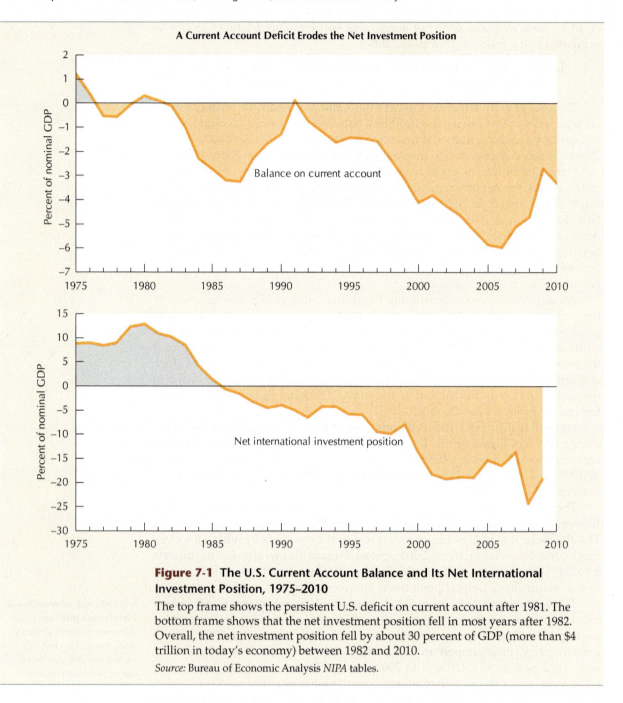

Figure 7-1 The U.S. Current Account Balance and Its Net International Investment Position, 1975–2010

The top frame shows the persistent U.S. deficit on current account after 1981. The bottom frame shows that the net investment position fell in most years after 1982. Overall, the net investment position fell by about 30 percent of GDP (more than $4 trillion in today's economy) between 1982 and 2010.

Source: Bureau of Economic Analysis *NIPA* tables.

have offset completely the effect of the current account deficits in pushing the net international investment position continuously toward a more negative value.

The United States benefits from asset revaluations when the dollar loses value. The dollar appreciated, or became more valuable, between 1995 and 2002. During this period the decline in the net international investment position was greater than could be explained by the current account deficit. Then starting in 2002 the dollar became less valuable through 2006, increasing the dollar value of American assets in foreign countries.

The fluctuations in the U.S. international investment position after 2006 reflect the sharp ups and downs in U.S. and foreign exchange rates and stock market prices during the Global Economic Crisis.

Why Is U.S. Income from Abroad Still Positive?

It would be natural to assume that the change from a positive U.S. international investment position in 1975–85 to the large negative position since then would have caused net income from abroad (the component of the current account in Table 7-1, line 1b) to become ever more negative. Yet Table 7-1 shows that net income from abroad was a positive number (1.2 percent of GDP) in 2010. How could this occur? There is only one answer to this question: *The United States must earn a much higher rate of return on the assets that U.S. residents own abroad than foreigners earn on their assets owned in the United States.*

Why does the United States earn a higher return? The most straightforward answer is that about half of the negative U.S. international investment position shown in the bottom frame of Figure 7-1 is accounted for by foreign holdings of international reserves. These are the amounts that the Bank of China, Bank of Japan, and other foreign central banks hold in U.S. dollars with the intention of stabilizing their own exchange rates. Typically, these amounts are held in very short-term U.S. government debt or in U.S. bank accounts, which earn very low interest rates for the foreign central banks. In contrast, the U.S. government holds virtually no assets in foreign countries.

The relatively high rate of return on U.S. assets held in foreign countries also can be explained by the greater propensity of U.S. investors to build factories in foreign countries and buy foreign corporations, as when Dell and Intel built factories in Ireland. Overall, most economists are surprised that the –20 percent international investment position of the United States shown in the bottom frame of Figure 7-1 has not yet implied large negative net income entries into line 1b of Table 7-1.

The International Investment Position and the U.S. Standard of Living

Even though the United States earns higher returns on its assets held in foreign countries than foreigners earn on their assets held in the United States, the inexorable arithmetic of continuing current account deficits implies a future effect on the U.S. standard of living. If the current account were to continue at the 2010 ratio of −4 percent of GDP, then with no further revaluations the international investment position of the United States would deteriorate by another 4 percent of GDP per year over the next decade. Even if the United States were to pay an interest rate to foreigners of only 3 percent on this extra 40 percent of indebtedness, that would imply 0.12 percent ($0.12 = 0.03 \times 4$ percent) of U.S. GDP would need to be diverted to foreign countries over that decade. If U.S. economic growth per person over the next decade were 1.5 percent, as many economists forecast, then the rising indebtedness to foreigners would reduce that from 1.5 minus this 0.12 percent, or to 1.38 percent per year.

The Current Account and National Saving

A current account deficit such as the United States has experienced in every year since 1991 does not happen by accident. Instead, the current account is linked together by definition with domestic saving and investment and the government budget surplus in the familiar magic equation (either equation (2.6) on p. 35 or equation (6.1) on p. 159), which is copied here:

$$T - G \equiv (I + NX) - S \tag{7.3}$$

This states in words that the government budget surplus $(T - G)$ is equal to total domestic and foreign investment $(I + NX)$ minus domestic saving. Total net exports (NX) is close to the value of the current account, and in this discussion we will treat the current account as being equal to NX.

A more useful rearrangement of equation (7.3) can be achieved by adding domestic saving (by households and business firms) to both sides of the equation:

$$S + (T - G) \equiv I + NX$$
$$NS \equiv I + NX \tag{7.4}$$

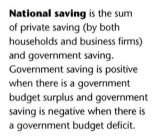

National saving is the sum of private saving (by both households and business firms) and government saving. Government saving is positive when there is a government budget surplus and government saving is negative when there is a government budget deficit.

The left side is the sum of private saving and the government surplus and is called **national saving (NS)**. This by definition is equal to national investment, which includes domestic investment (I) plus foreign investment, which is the same thing as net exports (NX).

Why would the United States run a current account deficit over a long period, as shown in the top frame of Figure 7-1? A simple rearrangement of equation (7.4) shows that foreign borrowing $(-NX)$, which is the same thing as the current account deficit, is raised by higher investment or lower national saving:

$$-NX \equiv I - NS \tag{7.5}$$

A numerical example of the components of this equation for 2010 (copied and rearranged from p. 36) is

$$3.5 \equiv 15.5 - 12.0$$

This states that net exports (NX), which is roughly the same as the current account balance, exhibited a deficit of 3.5 percent of GDP because domestic investment $(I = 15.5)$ exceeded national saving $(NS = 12.0)$. The larger the government budget deficit, the lower the national saving and hence the more likely it is for net exports and the current account to be negative. This connection between the current account deficit and the budget deficit has been called the "twin deficits."

 SELF-TEST

The economy of a small country called Importia has net exports of negative $10 billion and its net income from abroad is zero while its net unilateral transfers are zero. Which of the following statements is true?

1. Its current account deficit is negative $10 billion.
2. The sum of its capital account balance minus its balance of payments outcome is positive $10 billion.
3. The net acquisition of Importia's assets by foreigners is positive $10 billion.
4. Importia's foreign borrowing is positive $10 billion.

7-3   Exchange Rates

Nations trade goods and services within their own borders using a particular currency. Within the United States, of course, the U.S. dollar is used for transactions. Canada uses the Canadian dollar, the United Kingdom uses the pound, Japan uses the yen, Germany and France use the euro, and so on for all the other countries of the world. When an American wants to purchase a Japanese car, he or she wants to pay in dollars but the Japanese producer wants to be paid in yen.

How Exchange Rates Are Quoted

To make the preceding transaction possible, there must be a price of yen in terms of dollars, and a price of dollars in terms of yen. This price is called the **foreign exchange rate.** The foreign exchange rate of the dollar is quoted separately for every currency in the world, and these quotes are reported every day in many newspapers, as shown in Table 7-2.

The **foreign exchange rate** for a nation's currency is the amount of one nation's money that can be obtained in exchange for a unit of another nation's money.

To take an example, look at the first column at the line labeled Japan (yen). The foreign exchange rate of the yen is shown two ways, first as dollars per yen and second as yen per dollar. The first listing shows that the price of one yen is

Table 7-2   **Daily Quotations of Foreign Exchange Rates, January 12, 2011**

Currencies

U.S.-dollar foreign-exchange rates in late New York trading

Country/currency	Wed in US$	Wed per US$	US$ vs, YTD chg (%)	Country/currency	Wed in US$	Wed per US$	US$ vs, YTD chg (%)
Americas				**Europe**			
Argentina peso*	.2516	3.9746	0.1	**Czech Rep.** koruna	.05399	18.522	–1.1
Brazil real	.5977	1.6731	0.8	**Denmark** krone	.1763	5.6721	1.8
Canada dollar	1.0132	.9870	–1.1	**Euro area** euro	1.3133	.7614	1.8
1-mos forward	1.0126	.9876	–1.1	**Hungary** forint	.004772	209.56	0.7
3-mos forward	1.0112	.9889	–1.1	**Norway** krone	.1693	5.9067	1.4
6-mos forward	1.0085	.9916	–1.1	**Poland** zloty	.3419	2.9248	–1.3
Chile peso	.002038	490.68	4.9	**Russia** ruble‡	.03322	30.102	–1.6
Colombia peso	.0005355	1867.41	–2.7	**Sweden** krona	.1484	6.7385	0.3
Ecuador US dollar	1	1	unch	**Switzerland** franc	1.0348	.9664	3.4
Mexico peso*	.0828	12.0846	–2.1	1-mos forward	1.0351	.9661	3.4
Peru new sol	.3587	2.788	–0.7	3-mos forward	1.0357	.9655	3.5
Uruguay peso†	.05010	19.96	0.4	6-mos forward	1.0369	.9644	3.5
Venezuela b. fuerte	.232851	4.2946	unch	**Turkey** lira**	.6411	1.5599	1.2
				UK pound	1.5768	.6342	–1.1
Asia-Pacific				1-mos forward	1.5764	.6344	–1.1
Australian dollar	.9952	1.0048	2.7	3-mos forward	1.5755	.6347	–1.1
China yuan	.1514	6.6043	0.2	6-mos forward	1.5735	.6355	–1.0
Hong Kong dollar	.1286	7.7744	unch				
India rupee	.02221	45.025	0.7	**Middle East/Africa**			
Indonesia rupiah	.0001107	9033	0.3	**Bahrain** dinar	2.6526	.3770	unch
Japan yen	.012053	82.97	2.2	**Egypt** pound*	.1724	5.7991	–0.1
1-mos forward	.012056	82.95	2.2	**Israel** shekel	.2822	3.5436	0.5
3-mos forward	.012064	82.89	2.2	**Jordan** dinar	1.4119	.7083	unch
6-mos forward	.012079	82.79	2.2	**Kuwait** dinar	3.5480	.2818	0.1
Malaysia ringgit	.3265	3.0628	–0.7	**Lebanon** pound	.0006664	1500.60	unch
New Zealand dollar	.7629	1.3108	2.1	**Saudi Arabia** riyal	.2667	3.7495	unch
Pakistan rupee	.01167	85.690	unch	**South Africa** rand	.1463	6.8353	3.1
Philippines peso	.0228	43.898	0.6	**UAE** dirham	.2723	3.6724	unch
Singapore dollar	.7766	1.2877	0.4				
South Korea won	.0008997	1111.48	–0.9	**SDR**††	1.5271	.6548	0.8
Taiwan dollar	.03422	29.223	0.2				
Thailand baht	.03292	30.377	1.0				
Vietnam dong	.00005129	19498	unch				

*Floating rate †Financial §Government rate ‡Russian Central Bank rate **Rebased as of Jan 1, 2005 ††Special Drawing Rights (SDR); from the International Monetary Fund; based on exchange rates for U.S., British and Japanese currencies.

Source: Reprinted with permission of WALL STREET JOURNAL, Copyright © 2011 Dow Jones & Company, Inc. All Rights Reserved Worldwide.

$0.012053, or slightly more than one cent. The next listing shows that $1.00 is worth 82.97 yen. These quotations are exactly equivalent: $0.012053 per yen is the same as 82.97 yen per dollar, since $1/82.57 = 0.012053$.

It is conventional to express the foreign exchange rate of the dollar as units of foreign currency per dollar, that is, 82.97 yen per dollar, rather than the other way around. However, there are two exceptions. First, the foreign exchange rate of the dollar with the British pound is usually quoted as dollars per pound. This treatment of Britain as different goes back to the period before World War I when Britain rather than the United States was the center of the world monetary system.

The second exception is the exchange rate of the dollar versus the euro, which is the common currency of 17 nations, created in 1999.[2] This exchange rate is always quoted as dollars per euro, or $1.3133 as shown in the right column of the table. The opposite quote was that one euro was worth $0.7614.

Changes in Exchange Rates

It is very important that we pay attention to the way exchange rates are quoted. When the exchange rate is quoted as foreign currency per dollar, as in the case of the Japanese yen and most other currencies, then a higher number means that the dollar experiences an **appreciation.** The third column in Table 7-2 shows the change in the value of foreign currency per dollar between the end of the previous year, December 31, 2010, and the date of the table, which refers to January 12, 2011. We can see in the right column that the yen/dollar rate increased by 2.2 percent, indicating an appreciation. A lower number means that the dollar experiences a **depreciation.** For instance, the British pound/dollar ratio depreciated by 1.1 percent, as shown by the boldface "−1.1" in the third column on the line labeled "UK pound."

From day to day, changes in exchange rates may seem trivial. But changes can mount up to very large magnitudes over a few months or years. For the dollar, the most notable change in the last nine years has been its depreciation against the euro. When the equivalent table in the ninth edition of this textbook is compared to Table 7-2 in the current edition, the euro/dollar rate skidded from 1.1410 on February 19, 2002, to the value of 0.7614 shown in this section. This represents a depreciation in the value of the dollar of 33 percent. Alternatively, the dollar-to-euro ratio changed from $0.8764 to $1.3133, representing an appreciation of the euro against the dollar of 50 percent.

7-4 The Market for Foreign Exchange

When a U.S. tourist steps into a taxi at the Frankfurt airport, the driver will expect to be paid in euros, not U.S. dollars. To obtain the needed euro currency, the tourist must first stop at the airport bank or ATM and buy euros in exchange for U.S. dollars. Banks that have too much or too little of given types of foreign money can trade for what they need on the foreign exchange market. Unlike the New York Stock Exchange or the Chicago Board of Trade,

An **appreciation** is an increase in the value of one nation's currency relative to another nation's currency. When the dollar can buy more units of a foreign currency, say the euro, the dollar is said to appreciate relative to that foreign currency.

A **depreciation** is a decline in the value of one nation's currency relative to another nation's currency. When the dollar can buy fewer units of a foreign currency, say the British pound, the dollar is said to depreciate relative to that foreign currency.

---

[2] Which are the 17 countries that use the euro as their common currency? These are four countries with relatively large populations (France, Germany, Italy, and Spain), the three "Benelux" countries (Belgium, Netherlands, and Luxembourg), and ten relatively small countries, Austria in the center of Europe, seven nations on the periphery of Europe (Estonia, Finland, Greece, Ireland, Portugal, Slovakia, and Slovenia), and two island-nations (Cyprus and Malta).

where the trading takes place in a single location, the foreign exchange market consists of hundreds of dealers who sit at desks in banks, mainly in New York, London, and Tokyo, and conduct trades by phone and by computer keystrokes.

The results of the trading in foreign exchange are illustrated for four foreign currencies in Figure 7-2. Each section of the figure illustrates the exchange rate, expressed as units of foreign currency per U.S. dollar. The data plotted are monthly, so they do not show additional day-to-day movements. As is obvious from each section of the figure, major changes occurred during the years plotted. The exchange rates of the dollar against these four currencies have truly been flexible, rising and falling—often substantially—during each month.

Despite the quite different behavior of the four currencies displayed in Figure 7-2, we can see several interesting similarities in recent years. The chart for Canada shows the trends most clearly. The dollar appreciated consistently between 1995 and 2002, then depreciated until 2008, with a brief interruption in late 2005 and early 2006. But then when the global financial crisis occurred, the dollar appreciated strongly against all currencies besides the Japanese yen. As has often occurred before in crises, foreign investors tend to shift funds to the "safe haven" of the U.S. dollar, thus causing the dollar to appreciate in the worst months of the 2008–09 crisis. The upper-left graph for Canada shows most clearly that after the 2008–09 safe haven effect vanished, the U.S. dollar continued to depreciate against the Canadian dollar until it reached an exchange rate of 1-to-1.

Why People Hold Dollars and Euros

The factors that determine the foreign exchange rate and influence its fluctuations can be summarized on a demand–supply diagram like those used in elementary economics to analyze many problems of price determination. In Figure 7-3, the vertical axis measures the price of the dollar expressed in euros. The horizontal axis shows the number of dollars that would be demanded or supplied at different prices.

Currencies such as the U.S. dollar and the euro are held by foreigners who find dollars or euros more convenient or safer than their own currencies. For instance, sellers of goods or services may be willing to accept payment in dollars or euros, but not in the Argentine peso or the Malaysian ringgit. Thus a change in the preference by holders of money for a currency such as the dollar will shift the demand curve for dollars and influence the dollar's exchange rate.

All currencies have a demand that is created by a country's exports and a supply generated by a country's imports. For instance, purchases of U.S. exports automatically create a demand for the dollar. So, too, do funds paid by foreigners who invest in U.S. factories, who send to the United States dividends and interest payments on U.S. overseas investments, and who are attracted to put money into U.S. savings accounts and government securities. Thus the demand curve for dollars D_0 in Figure 7-3 is labeled with two of the items that create the demand (U.S. exports, capital inflows). In the same way, the supply curve of dollars S_0 depends on the magnitude of the items that generate payments by U.S. citizens to foreigners—mainly U.S. imports and capital outflows.

What explains the slopes of the demand and supply curves as drawn in Figure 7-3? The demand curve D_0 will be vertical only if the price elasticity of European demand for U.S. imports is zero, that is, completely insensitive to changes in price. If the price elasticity of demand is negative, then the demand

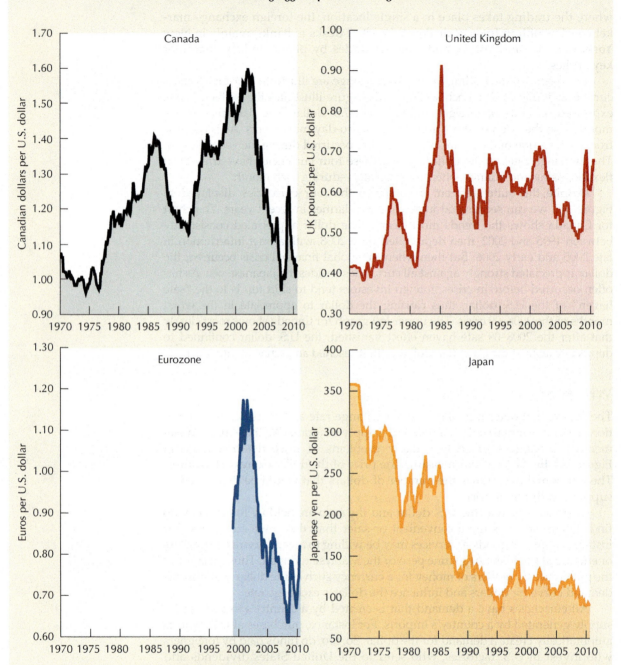

Since 1970 the Dollar Has Zigzagged Up and Down Against Other Currencies

Figure 7-2 Foreign Exchange Rates of the Dollar Against Four Major Currencies, Monthly, 1970–2010

Each foreign exchange rate is expressed as units of foreign currency per dollar. Note that the euro began only in early 1999. While the exchange rate histories of the four currencies differ, common features are the appreciation of the dollar from 1980 to 1985, its subsequent depreciation until the late 1980s, the appreciation from 1995 to 2002, and then the depreciation from 2002 to 2008. The value of the dollar showed a sharp but temporary appreciation in late 2008 and early 2009 as investors pushed funds into dollars because of their fears and their traditional trust of the U.S. dollar as a "safe haven."

Source: Federal Reserve Bank of St. Louis FRED database.

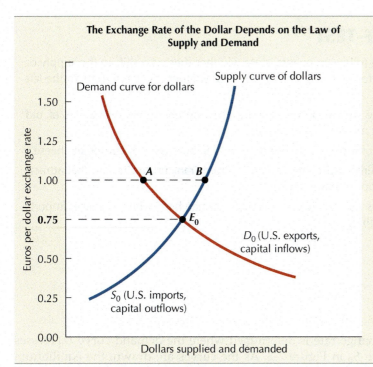

The Exchange Rate of the Dollar Depends on the Law of Supply and Demand

Figure 7-3 Determination of the Price in Euros of the Dollar

The demand curve D_0 slopes downward and to the right, reflecting the increased demand for dollars induced by depreciation (a lowering in the dollar's price). The supply curve S_0 is assumed to slope upward, although this does not always occur (see text). The equilibrium price of the dollar in the diagram is assumed to be €0.75, at the crossing point of the D_0 and S_0 curves.

curve will be negatively sloped, as shown. For instance, consider a U.S. machine costing $10,000, which would require European buyers to pay 10,000 euros if the exchange rate were 1 euro per dollar (as at point A in the figure). If the exchange rate were to drop to 0.75 euros per dollar (as at point E_0), the cost of the same machine would drop to 7,500 euros. If the European demand for such machines were to increase from 10 machines to 11 in response to the lower price, the European demand for dollars would increase from $100,000 to $110,000 (since the price in dollars is still unchanged, $10,000). In short, a depreciation in the dollar along the demand curve from A to E_0 boosts the demand for dollars (plotted on the horizontal axis) and accounts for the negative slope of the demand curve.

The analysis for the supply curve S_0 is different. Here the supply curve will be vertical if the price elasticity of the U.S. demand for European imports is minus 1.0. Only in this situation are U.S. expenditures on imports in dollars independent of the exchange rate.[3] Only if the price elasticity is greater than unity (in absolute value) will the supply curve slope positively, as drawn in Figure 7-3.

---

[3] The price elasticity of demand, a concept used in every elementary economics course, is defined as

$$\text{elasticity} = \frac{\text{percentage change of quantity}}{\text{percentage change of price}}$$

When the elasticity is –1.0, the percentage change of quantity is equal to and opposite in sign from the percentage change of price, so that revenue (= price × quantity) does not change. A depreciation of the dollar causes a given percentage increase in the price of European machines imported into the United States, provided their price in euros does not change. If the number of machines purchased drops by the same percent, then total dollar expenditures do not change, and the supply curve is vertical.

◆ SELF-TEST

For each of the following events, state whether there is a shift in the supply or demand curve for dollars in Figure 7-3, and whether the curve shifts to the left or right:

1. An increase in the desire of European households to buy DVDs of old Hollywood movies.

2. Popularity of Mexican cheese reduces U.S. purchases of European cheese.

3. American Airlines discontinues a flight from Frankfurt to Chicago that attracts mainly European passengers.

4. U.S. citizens start producing imitation German beer, which displaces imports of the real thing.

How Governments Can Influence the Foreign Exchange Rate

The foreign exchange rate is determined where the demand curve D_0 crosses the supply curve S_0 in Figure 7-3. As the curves are drawn, the equilibrium exchange rate is 0.75 euros per dollar at point E_0. At a higher exchange rate, say 1.00 euros per dollar, the supply of dollars exceeds demand by the distance AB. The supply of dollars created by U.S. imports and by capital outflows exceeds the demand for dollars created by U.S. exports and capital inflows. In order to induce foreigners to accept U.S. dollars, U.S. citizens will have to accept a lower exchange rate, 0.75 euros per dollar.

But some countries are not willing to accept a depreciation in the dollar from 1.00 euros at point A to 0.75 euros at point E_0. Some countries want to maintain an exchange rate that prevents this depreciation of the dollar, since this would mean an appreciation of their currencies, making their exports more expensive to sell to the rest of the world. How do foreign governments manipulate the exchange rate of the dollar to prevent an appreciation of their own currencies and a depreciation of the dollar?

Let us imagine in Figure 7-3 that the European Central Bank (ECB) wants to maintain the exchange rate at 1.0 euros per dollar instead of allowing the dollar to decline to the equilibrium exchange rate of 0.75 euros. A more expensive dollar would imply a cheaper euro, allowing Europe to sell more exports to the rest of the world. What the ECB must do to maintain an exchange rate of 1.0 euros per dollar is to buy dollars, adding its own demand by an amount AB to the market demand for dollars shown at point A. How does the ECB purchase the needed number of dollars shown by the distance AB? It sells euros. The ECB, like any central bank, has the ability to create an unlimited amount of its own currency. In short, a government that wants to prevent a depreciation of the dollar (and a corresponding appreciation of its currency against the dollar) must buy dollars. This is the real-world situation today in which China and Japan are buying massive numbers of dollars to keep their currencies from appreciating. As we have seen, this is recorded as the negative balance of payments item for the United States in the bottom line of Table 7-1 on p. 194.

7-5   Real Exchange Rates and Purchasing Power Parity

Nominal and Real Exchange Rates

For most issues in macroeconomics, we adjust variables for the effects of inflation. Real GDP is a more meaningful gauge of economic activity than nominal GDP. The level of saving and investment are related to the real interest rate, not to the nominal interest rate. Similarly, we shall see that it is the **real exchange rate** that determines net exports, not the nominal exchange rate.

The real exchange rate is equal to the nominal foreign exchange rate adjusted for the difference in inflation rates between two countries. The definition can be written as a formula, where we express the real exchange rate (e) as equal to the nominal exchange rate (e') times the ratio of the domestic price level (P) to the foreign price level (P^f):

$$e = e' \times P/P^f \qquad (7.3)$$

$$\frac{\text{Real exchange}}{\text{rate}} = \frac{\text{nominal exchange}}{\text{rate}} \times \frac{\text{ratio of domestic price level}}{\text{to foreign price level}}$$

To understand this relationship, let us assume that in 2011 the nominal and real exchange rates of the Mexican peso are both 10 per dollar, and the price level in both countries is 100:

$$10 \text{ pesos}/\$ = 10 \text{ pesos}/\$ \times (100/100)$$

$$\frac{\text{Real exchange}}{\text{rate}} = \frac{\text{nominal exchange}}{\text{rate}} \times \frac{\text{ratio of domestic price level}}{\text{to foreign price level}}$$

Then, let us assume that in 2012, the Mexican economy experiences a rapid inflation, causing the Mexican price level to double from 100 to 200, while the U.S. price level remains fixed at 100. If the nominal exchange rate were to remain at 10 pesos per dollar, the real exchange rate would fall by half:

$$5 \text{ pesos}/\$ = 10 \text{ pesos}/\$ \times (100/200)$$

In such a case, we would say that the dollar has experienced a *real depreciation* against the peso, since one dollar buys only half as many pesos when adjusted for differences in national price levels. The opposite would be true as well; the Mexican peso would have experienced a *real appreciation*.

Normally, countries that experience unusually high inflation, as in this example, find that their nominal exchange rate depreciates while their real exchange rate remains roughly unchanged. For the real exchange rate to remain unchanged in this example, the nominal exchange rate of the peso would have to jump from 10 to 20 pesos per dollar (this is a nominal appreciation of the dollar and a nominal depreciation of the peso).

$$10 = 20 \times 100/200$$

This final example is quite realistic. Countries with unusually rapid inflation, as has been experienced by Mexico, Argentina, Brazil, and other Latin American countries at various times over the past several decades, witness a nominal depreciation of their currency without any major change in the real exchange rate. (We return to the causes and consequences of rapid inflation in Chapter 10.)

We care about the real exchange rate, not the nominal exchange rate, because it is a major determinant of net exports. When the real exchange rate appreciates,

The **real exchange rate** is equal to the average nominal foreign exchange rate between a country and its trading partners, with an adjustment for the difference in inflation rates between that country and its trading partners.

imports become cheap for domestic residents to purchase, while exports become expensive for foreigners to purchase. The result is a squeeze on domestic profits and layoffs of domestic workers. In the opposite situation, when the real exchange rate depreciates, domestic profits improve and companies are eager to hire workers.

◆ **SELF-TEST**

Assume that the price level in 2011 in both the United States and Europe is 100, and that both the real and the nominal exchange rates of the euro are 0.75 euros per dollar. Now imagine that in the year 2012 the U.S. price level has increased from 100 to 110, while the euro price level remains fixed at 100, and the nominal exchange rate changes to 0.65 euros per dollar.

1. What is the real exchange rate of the dollar in the year 2012?
2. Has the dollar experienced a real appreciation or depreciation?
3. Following this change what would you expect to happen to U.S. exports to Europe? To U.S. imports from Europe?

The Theory of Purchasing Power Parity

The most important determinant of exchange rates is the fact that in open economies the prices of traded goods should be the same everywhere after adjustment for customs duties and the cost of transportation. This is called the **purchasing power parity (PPP) theory** of the exchange rate.

> The **purchasing power parity (PPP) theory** holds that the prices of identical goods should be the same in all countries, differing only by the cost of transport and any import duties.

This theory implies that the real exchange rate (e) should be constant. We can set the real exchange rate at a constant value of unity in equation (7.3) on p. 205:

$$1 = e' \times P/P^f \qquad (7.4)$$

$$\frac{\text{Fixed real}}{\text{exchange rate}} = \frac{\text{nominal exchange}}{\text{rate}} \times \frac{\text{ratio of domestic price level}}{\text{to foreign price level}}$$

By swapping the left-hand and right-hand sides of equation (7.4), and solving for e', we emerge with the PPP theory of exchange rates:

$$e' = \frac{P^f}{P} \qquad (7.5)$$

This states that if the foreign price level P^f increases faster than the domestic price level (P), there is an increase in P^f/P and the nominal exchange rate must appreciate if PPP is to prevail.

PPP and Inflation Differentials

Another way of writing equation (7.5) is to express the exchange rate and the two prices in terms of rates of growth.[4]

$$\Delta e'/e' = p^f - p \qquad (7.6)$$

$$\frac{\text{Growth rate of nominal}}{\text{exchange rate}} = \frac{\text{Growth rate of foreign price level}-}{\text{Growth rate of domestic price level}}$$

---

[4] The growth rate of a ratio such as P^f/P is equal to the growth rate of the numerator P^f minus the growth rate of the denominator (P).

Here the term $\Delta e'/e'$ is positive when there is an appreciation of a currency. The same term is negative when there is a depreciation of a currency. The term $p^f - p$ is the **inflation differential** between foreign and domestic inflation. When this differential is positive, the PPP theory of exchange rates expressed in equation (7.6) states that $\Delta e'/e'$ is positive and the exchange rate of the domestic currency appreciates.

The PPP theory contains an essential kernel of truth: Nations that allow their domestic inflation rate (p) to exceed the world rate will experience a depreciation of their exchange rate, and vice versa. But there are numerous exceptions to the relationship, because the demand for and supply of foreign currency depend on factors other than the simple ratio of domestic and foreign aggregate price indexes.

The **inflation differential** is foreign inflation minus domestic inflation; the PPP theory of exchange rates predicts that when this differential is positive the domestic country's nominal exchange rate appreciates and when this differential is negative the nominal exchange rate depreciates.

Why PPP Breaks Down

The "Big Mac" International Perspective box on pp. 208–09 shows that the PPP equation relating the change in the exchange rate to the inflation differential does not work well for most industrialized nations; for example, in 2010, the dollar was overvalued against 12 of the countries shown in the "Big Mac" table and undervalued against the other 29 countries. There are numerous reasons why PPP breaks down. They all have a single fact in common—for any given inflation differential between two nations, there are numerous factors that can cause major appreciations and depreciations in the exchange rate without altering the inflation differential. Some of these factors are:

1. A nation may invent new products that other countries want to import, such as the Internet software developed by U.S. firms in the 1990s. Such inventions may cause the dollar to appreciate without any change in the inflation differential.

2. A nation may discover new deposits of raw materials that it can sell to other nations, thus raising the demand for its currency. For instance, in the late 1970s the British began producing oil from the North Sea, causing the exchange rate of the pound to appreciate.

3. The exchange rate depends not just on exports and imports but on the demand for a currency by foreigners. Customers from all over the world send funds to Switzerland and other countries for deposit in banks and other financial institutions, often to avoid taxes or to hide the proceeds from criminal activity. The higher demand for the Swiss franc and other such currencies causes them to appreciate.

4. The theory of PPP is based on the comparison of the exchange rate with an economywide price index in two countries, but that price index may include types of economic activity that are not traded (for example, building construction and retail services). There is no mechanism that forces prices of nontraded goods and services to be the same across countries.

5. For any given inflation differential, government policy can cause a currency to depreciate when the government makes large foreign transfers. Governments can also interfere with free trade by subsidizing exports or taxing imports. Finally, a government may try to prevent its currency from appreciating by buying foreign currency, as did Japan and China in this decade (see pp. 214–15).

As we shall see later in Figure 7-4, the U.S. real exchange rate has not remained constant, as assumed in the PPP equation (7.4), which suggests that PPP is not a good description of U.S. exchange rate behavior.

INTERNATIONAL PERSPECTIVE

Big Mac Meets PPP

If PPP worked perfectly, goods would cost the same in all countries after conversion into a common currency. An interesting test of PPP has been constructed by the *Economist* magazine, which for many years has collected data on the prices of Big Mac hamburgers in the United States and in numerous foreign countries. In the month covered by the table, the Big Mac cost an average of $3.73 in four American cities. According to PPP, the cost in other countries should be $3.73 times the exchange rate of the other currency per dollar. To understand this table taken from *The Economist*, we will take the example of a single country, Sweden.

The *actual* exchange rate of the Swedish kroner was 7.37 kroner per dollar. Multiplying the American Big Mac price of $3.73 by the actual exchange rate of 7.37, a Big Mac in Sweden should have cost 27.49 kroner. However the actual price in Sweden was 48.4 kroner, a much higher price indicating an overvaluation of the Swedish kroner.

Stated another way, if the relative prices of Big Macs in Sweden and the United States were representative of all goods, a dollar would have the same purchasing power as 13.0 kroner (the Big Mac Swedish price of 48.4 kroner divided by the U.S. price of $3.73), not the mere 7.37 kroner available on the foreign exchange market. The foreign exchange market appears to overvalue the Swedish kroner by 76 percent (13.0 − 7.37)/7.37.

As shown in the right-hand column of the table, there are 12 countries including Sweden that have currencies that are overvalued (+) against the dollar. These countries include the relatively rich countries of western Europe, including the euro zone, Denmark, Sweden, Switzerland, and a few others. American college students can anticipate that visits to these countries will be very expensive compared to the prices they would pay for restaurant meals in the United States. However, 29 other countries have currencies that are undervalued (−) against the dollar.

In China, Hong Kong, Sri Lanka, and the Ukraine, a Big Mac costs about half the U.S. price of $3.73 when calculated at the market exchange rate. College students can look forward to cheap restaurant meals in those and other countries marked as undervalued.

When other currencies are overvalued against the dollar, like those in Europe, the dollar is undervalued against them. The extent of over- or undervaluation of the U.S. dollar changes through time. As shown in Figure 7-2, the dollar appreciated from 1995 to 2001 against most currencies and then depreciated between 2002 and 2010. When the dollar was at its peak in 2001 it was overvalued relative to the euro area, in contrast to its undervaluation against the euro in 2010 as shown in the table.

7-6   Exchange Rate Systems

A balance of payments deficit like the one experienced by the United States in 2011 means that more dollars are flowing abroad as a result of the current account deficit than are coming back in the form of capital inflows from foreign private investors. As a result, there is a net outflow of dollars. Two basic systems have been developed to handle a surplus or deficit in the balance of payments, like the deficit that the United States ran in 2010 (Table 7-1, p. 194, line 3). The difference between these systems lies in whether the foreign exchange rate of the dollar is allowed, month after month, year after year, to change freely (say, from 0.75 euros per dollar this month to 0.65 euros per dollar next month) or is held fixed (at, say, 0.75 euros per dollar).

In a **flexible exchange rate system,** the foreign exchange rate is free to change every day in order to establish an equilibrium between the quantities supplied and demanded of a nation's currency.

Flexible Versus Fixed Exchange Rates

Flexible exchange rate system.   Under a "pure" version of the **flexible exchange rate system,** an outflow of dollars would act just like an excess supply of any commodity—the price would go down until an equilibrium price is established. The balance of payments deficit would be eliminated by a decline in the foreign exchange rate of the dollar sufficient to raise exports and cut

Cash and Carry: The Hamburger Standard

	Big Mac Prices		Implied PPP[a] of the dollar	Actual dollar exchange rate July 2nd	Under (−)/over (+) valuation against the dollar, %
	in local currency	in dollars			
United States[b]	$3.73	3.73			
Argentina	Peso 7.00	1.78	1.88	3.93	−52
Australia	A$4.35	3.84	1.17	1.13	+3
Brazil	Real 8.71	4.91	2.33	1.77	+31
Britain	£2.29	3.48	1.63[d]	1.52[d]	−7
Canada	C$4.17	4.00	1.12	1.04	+7
Chile	Peso 1,750	3.34	469	524	−10
China	Yuan 13.2	1.95	3.54	6.78	−48
Colombia	Peso 8,200	4.39	2,196	1868	+18
Denmark	Dkr 28.5	4.90	7.63	5.81	+31
Egypt	Pound 13.0	2.28	3.48	5.70	−39
Euro Area[c]	€ 3.38	4.33	1.10[e]	1.28[e]	+16
Hong Kong	HK$14.8	1.90	3.96	7.77	−49
Indonesia	Rupiah 22,780	2.51	6,102	9,063	−33
Israel	Shekel 14.9	3.86	3.99	3.86	+3
Japan	¥320	3.67	85.7	87.2	−2
Lithuania	Litas 7.30	2.71	1.96	2.69	−27
Malaysia	Ringgit 7.05	2.19	1.89	3.21	−41
Mexico	Peso 32.0	2.50	8.57	12.8	−33
Norway	Kroner 45.0	7.20	12.1	6.25	+93
Pakistan	Rupee 210	2.46	56.3	85.5	−34
Philippines	Peso 102	2.19	27.3	46.5	−41
Russia	Rouble 71.0	2.33	19.0	30.4	−38
Saudi Arabia	Riyal 10.0	2.67	2.68	3.8	−29
Singapore	S$4.23	3.08	1.13	1.37	−18
South Africa	Rand 18.5	2.45	4.94	7.54	−34
South Korea	Won 3,400	2.82	911	1204	−24
Sweden	Skr 48.4	6.56	13.0	7.37	+76
Switzerland	SFr 6.50	6.19	1.74	1.05	+66
Thailand	Baht 70.0	2.17	18.8	32.3	−42
Turkey	Lire 5.95	3.89	1.59	1.53	+4
Ukraine	Hryvnia 14.5	1.84	3.88	7.90	−51

[a]Purchasing-power parity; local price divided by price in United States
[b]Average of New York, Chicago, Atlanta, and San Francisco
[c]Weighted average of prices in euro area
[d]Dollars per pound
[e]Dollars per euro

Sources: McDonald's: *The Economist*, July 22, 2010.
More recent versions of the Big Mac Index can be found at http://www.economist.com/markets/bigmac/

imports, as occurred in the United States following the huge 1985–87 decline in the value of the dollar. In addition, for reasons explained later, a decline in the exchange rate tends to stimulate larger private capital inflows. Although the exchange rates have varied widely since 1973, the current system of flexible exchange rates still is not a pure one. If it were, the United States could not run a balance of payments deficit as it did in 2010, as shown in Table 7-1. Instead, today's system is a mixture of flexible and fixed exchange rates.

Fixed exchange rate system.   During the post–World War II era prior to 1973, most major countries maintained a **fixed exchange rate system.** Under this system, central banks agreed in advance to finance any surplus or deficit in the balance of payments. To do this, central banks maintained foreign exchange reserves, mainly in gold and dollars. The banks stood ready to buy or sell dollars as needed to maintain the foreign exchange rate of their currencies.

Workings of the Fixed Exchange Rate System

In the 1950s and 1960s, the German central bank (Bundesbank) maintained a rate of 4.0 marks per dollar. If an excess supply of dollars entered Germany (due, for instance, to higher U.S. imports of Volkswagens) and threatened to put downward pressure on the rate to, say, 3.5 marks per dollar, the Bundesbank could intervene by purchasing the excess dollars and adding them to its **foreign exchange reserves.** Similarly, if an excess demand for dollars (due, for instance, to exports of Boeing jet planes to Lufthansa, the German airline) put upward pressure on the rate to, say, 4.5 marks per dollar, the Bundesbank could intervene by selling dollars from its reserves, thus satisfying the excess demand for dollars.

Clearly, there is a flaw in this system. What if a country were to keep increasing its imports, paying for them by drawing down its reserves? Eventually it would run out of reserves, like a family whose bank balance has fallen to zero. Under the fixed exchange rate system, such an event would cause a crisis, and the country would be forced to reduce, or **devalue,** its exchange rate. An example occurred in 1994, when Mexico was forced to devalue the peso, thus making it less valuable in relation to the dollar. By doing so, Mexico intended to make Mexican exports less expensive and more attractive to foreign purchasers, thus increasing the demand for the peso. An example in the opposite direction occurred in 1969 when Germany's reserves of dollars were growing rapidly, and it decided to **revalue** the mark (that is, increase the value of the mark) by 5 percent.

Characteristics of the Flexible Exchange Rate System

Under the old, fixed exchange rate system, changes in the exchange rate were very infrequent. The word *devaluation* was used for a decline in the value of a country's currency and the word *revaluation* was used for an increase in the value of a country's currency. In today's flexible exchange rate system, different terms are used. A *depreciation* of the foreign exchange rate occurs when a country's currency decreases in value in terms of other currencies. An *appreciation* in the foreign exchange rate occurs when a country's currency increases in value in terms of other currencies.

The current system is not a pure flexible exchange rate system because the Fed and foreign central banks do not allow the dollar to fluctuate with

---

In a **fixed exchange rate system**, the foreign exchange rate is fixed for long periods of time.

Foreign exchange reserves are government holdings of foreign money used under a fixed exchange rate system to respond to changes in the foreign demand for and supply of a particular nation's money. Such reserves are also used for intervention under a flexible exchange rate system.

Under the fixed exchange rate system, a nation **devalues,** or reduces the value of its money expressed in terms of foreign money, when it runs out of foreign exchange reserves. A nation **revalues,** or raises the value of its money, when its foreign exchange reserves become so excessive that they cause domestic inflation.

complete freedom. The system is not pure because central banks have practiced **intervention.** Foreign central banks, particularly those of China and Japan, have "propped up" the value of the dollar by buying massive amounts of it, thus artificially inflating the demand for dollars and keeping the dollar's foreign exchange rate higher than it otherwise would have been. In the period 1986–2009, *foreign central banks increased their dollar reserves by more than $4 trillion as a result of their intervention.*

> **Intervention** occurs under the flexible exchange rate system when domestic or foreign central banks buy or sell a nation's money in order to prevent unwanted variations in the foreign exchange rate.

Other terms are used to describe flexible exchange rate systems. A "clean" system is one that is pure, without any intervention by central banks. A "dirty," or "managed," flexible exchange rate system is one with frequent intervention by central banks. Why is the current system so dirty? Central banks in China and Japan fear a possible collapse of the dollar, which would make American exports more competitive and reduce the American demand for imports. Such circumstances would create layoffs and factory closings in foreign countries, something governments want to avoid.

The Exchange Rate of the Dollar Since 1980

Since the flexible exchange rate system began in 1973, the dollar has experienced substantial volatility. Figure 7-4 shows the changes in both the nominal and real exchange rates of the dollar since 1980. Displayed is the effective exchange rate of the dollar, which weights the dollar's exchange rate against an

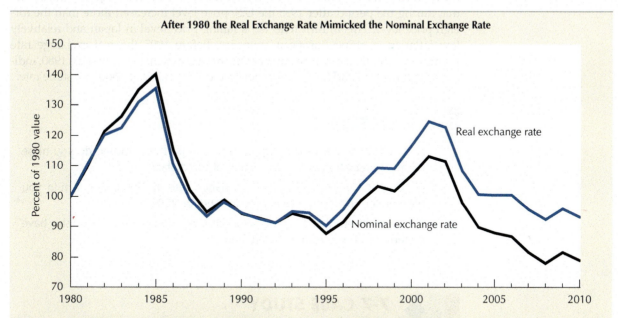

Figure 7-4 Nominal and Real Effective Exchange Rates of the Dollar, 1980–2010

Except for a minor difference after 1995, the real and nominal exchange rates for the United States followed essentially the same path. This means that the inflation differential between the United States and other nations was very small compared to the highly variable ups and downs of the nominal exchange rate. This implies that the real exchange rate should have mimicked the movements of the nominal exchange rate, which it did.

Source: Federal Reserve Board of Governors *H.10 Foreign Exchange Rates.*

average of the euro, British pound, Japanese yen, and other currencies, with each country weighted in proportion to its importance in American foreign trade. The base year for the effective exchange rate is 1980, so any period (such as 1985) with an exchange rate greater than 100 indicates that the dollar was stronger than in 1980. Any period with an exchange rate less than 100 (such as 1995) indicates that the dollar was weaker than in 1980.

Let us first examine the nominal exchange rate of the dollar, the black line in Figure 7-4. From 1980 to 1988, international economics was dominated by the effect of the enormous appreciation of the dollar, which peaked in February 1985, and the depreciation of equal magnitude that followed in 1985–87. The strong dollar exacerbated the U.S. recession of 1981–82 and slowed the pace of economic recovery in 1984–85.

From 1988 to 1995, the dollar fluctuated within a relatively narrow range but then began a sharp appreciation against most currencies after 1995. This strength of the dollar was the counterpart of the weakness of several currencies, particularly in Asia during the late 1990s and the weakness of the euro from its inception in early 1999 until early 2002. Then, after 2004, the dollar depreciated again and by 2010 was below its 1995 level in nominal terms, although not in real terms.

Has the real exchange rate behaved differently than the nominal effective exchange rate? As shown in Figure 7-4, between 1995 and 2001 the real exchange rate appreciated somewhat more rapidly than did the nominal exchange rate. And then between 2002 and 2010 the real exchange rate depreciated somewhat less than the nominal exchange rate. The gap between the two lines in Figure 7-4 indicates that during the period after 1995 the U.S. price level increased more than the foreign price level. This in turn reflected a falling price level in Japan and relatively low inflation in some European countries. Before 1995 the real exchange rate mimicked virtually every movement of the nominal exchange rate since 1980, indicating that the U.S. and foreign price levels have increased at about the same rate.

SELF-TEST

1. As a college student planning a trip to Europe this summer, do you hope for an appreciation or a depreciation of the dollar?

2. Looking at the plot of the real exchange rate in Figure 7-4, would you have preferred to travel to Europe in 1995 or 2001?

3. If a German student had the same choice, when would he or she have preferred to travel to the United States?

7-7 CASE STUDY

Asia Intervenes with Buckets to Buy Dollars and Finance the U.S. Current Account Deficit—How Long Can This Continue?

The United States escapes the ironclad logic of the trilemma that no nation can simultaneously operate an independent domestic monetary policy while maintaining fixed exchange rates and allowing perfectly mobile international capital movements. The United States escapes this logic by maintaining flexible exchange rates with its trading partners, including the euro area, Britain, Japan, and many other nations. But the U.S. cannot *force* other nations to maintain flexible exchange rates between their currencies and the dollar. Instead, other nations can subvert the U.S. intention to maintain flexible exchange rates *by taking actions to fix the value of their currencies to the dollar.*

China is the world's leading example of a country that can unilaterally convert the dollar's flexible exchange rate into a virtually fixed exchange rate. During the decade between 1995 and 2005, the Chinese maintained an absolutely fixed exchange rate. The dollar exchange rate of the Chinese yuan during that decade was never higher than 8.33 or lower than 8.27. However, after 2005 the Chinese allowed their currency to appreciate and the dollar to depreciate. Over the period between mid-2005 and mid-2008, the dollar depreciated from 8.27 to 6.83 yuan, a depreciation of about 18 percent. However after that the Chinese fixed the exchange rate, which never varied between 6.79 and 6.83 between July 2008 and August 2010.

How do we know that the equilibrium exchange rate is far lower than 6.8 yuan per dollar? This is because the situation of China versus the United States is just like the situation depicted in Figure 7-3 by the distance *AB* in which the central bank buys up billions of dollars to keep the dollar from depreciating from 1.0 to 0.75 euros per dollar. The new element after 2005 was that the Bank of China slightly decreased its purchases of dollars from the amount needed to keep the yuan absolutely fixed at 8.27 yuan per dollar, to smaller purchases that allowed the yuan to appreciate slowly, and the dollar to depreciate slowly, from 8.27 to 6.8 yuan per dollar.

Why does China pursue this policy? By fighting against an appreciation of the yuan, China receives all the benefits of any currency that has a relatively low exchange rate (as we saw on p. 208, a Big Mac in China costs 48 percent less than in the United States). With a low exchange rate, Chinese exporters can sell their goods at cheaper prices in the U.S. market, and higher volumes of exported goods allow Chinese business firms to employ more workers, helping to propel the remarkable economic growth of China that we examine in Chapter 11. Hong Kong is an even more extreme example, having fixed its exchange rate against the dollar at 7.8 Hong Kong dollars per U.S. dollar for more than three decades. Several other Asian nations also purchase dollars to keep their exchange rates from appreciating, particularly Japan, which has succeeded in keeping its exchange rate within the range of 105 to 123 yen per dollar between 2000 and early 2008. Finally between then and late 2010 the Japanese allowed the dollar to depreciate from 105 to 80 yen per dollar.

A remarkable aspect of this situation is that the United States is uniquely positioned to take advantage of the willingness of other nations to finance its current account deficit. The United States has been called "the country in the center" due to the attractiveness of U.S. dollars as the currency in which most nations prefer to hold their international reserves. Despite the depreciation of the dollar and appreciation of the euro in 2002–08, Asian nations continue to keep most of their international reserves in dollars. Thus, in essence, the United States can "print money" that Asians willingly hold in order to finance its U.S. current account deficit. Ironically, it was this same ability to print international money in the 1960s under the former Bretton Woods system that led to the breakdown in 1971 of fixed exchange rates. Many commentators are worried that the current system is equally unsustainable and must inevitably lead to a collapse of the U.S. dollar exchange rate at some point in the future—the near future according to pessimists and the far future according to optimists.

How Large Are the Reserves and Which Countries Hold Them?

Figure 7-5 displays foreign official holdings of dollars as a percent of U.S. GDP. These are the dollar reserves of nations such as China, Japan, and other countries (mainly in the Middle East and Asia).[5] As of 1995, these reserves were little more than 5 percent of U.S. GDP. But then the dollar reserves began to explode, soaring to almost 10 percent in 2002 and then to almost 30 percent in 2010.

Why Do the Asians Subject Themselves to Disastrous Capital Losses?

The U.S. government views this buildup of Asian dollar reserves with an attitude of "benign neglect." Why not, since the huge purchases of dollar securities, much of which is U.S. government debt, helps to support the U.S. stock and bond markets and allows the U.S. federal government to support tax cuts and expenditure increases without the sharp increase in domestic U.S. interest rates that would otherwise occur. But for Asian countries this is a raw deal, because the hundreds of billions of dollars that the Asians are spending of their own currencies to buy dollars could be used to raise the living standards

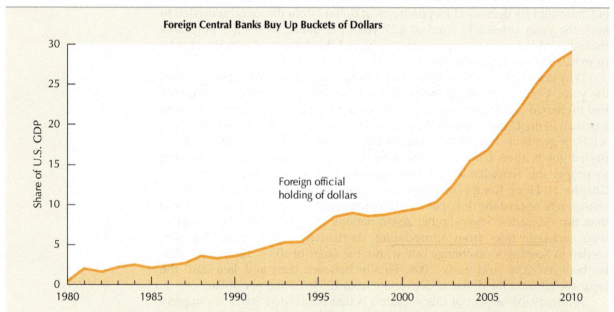

Figure 7-5 Foreign Official Holdings of Dollar Reserves as a Percent of U.S. GDP, 1980–2010

Shown is the percentage ratio of foreign official holdings of dollar reserves to U.S. GDP. The rapid growth of these reserves since 1995 is the counterpart of the decline in the U.S. international investment position shown in the bottom frame of Figure 7-1. By 2010 foreign official holdings of dollar reserves were substantially larger than the U.S. negative investment position shown in the bottom frame of Figure 7-1.

Source: Department of Commerce. See Appendix C-4.

---

[5] These data show the increase in the official balances that finance the U.S. balance of payments deficit. They take foreign official holdings of dollar assets and subtract U.S. holdings of official international reserves.

of millions of their own inhabitants through investment in their domestic economies.

The Asian central banks are pouring their own funds into a currency, the dollar, on which they make capital losses. While China can buy enough dollars to keep its yuan/dollar exchange rate fixed, it cannot prevent the flexible exchange rate between the dollar and other currencies (such as the euro, the British pound, and the Swiss franc) from depreciating. Thus the buying power of Chinese and Japanese dollar reserves in the world economy sinks each year that the dollar depreciates, as it did between 2002 and 2008.

The Asian strategy of stabilizing their currencies against the dollar creates an economic dilemma for the European nations in the euro area. From 2001 to 2010, the euro has appreciated by more than 50 percent against the dollar, making European exports more expensive. But the Asian policies make the European dilemma worse. If China keeps its currency pegged to the dollar, and the euro appreciates by 50 percent against the dollar, then *automatically* the euro appreciates by 50 percent against the Chinese yuan. Cheap Chinese exports flood not only the United States but also Europe, costing not just American but also European jobs. The willingness of the Bank of China to allow the yuan to appreciate by 18 percent between 2005 and 2008 took a bit of pressure off the Europeans, but not much. The yuan would have to appreciate far more to reach its equilibrium exchange rate against the dollar and the euro.

Asian policies make the European dilemma worse

Can this situation continue? The Asian nations and the United States both seem to be trapped in a symbiotic relationship. One journalist drew an analogy with a small shopkeeper:

> This is an absurd situation, like a shopkeeper lending ever larger amounts of money to an important customer who is also a profligate spender, so that he can maintain consumption. The customer signs ever-increasing amounts of IOUs, and the shopkeeper has decreasing faith in these. But he cannot sell them so long as he retains his dependence on keeping the customer happy.[6] ◆

7-8 Determinants of Net Exports

Now we are ready to fit the foreign exchange rate into the *IS-LM* model of income determination developed in Chapters 3–5. The analysis proceeds in two steps. First, we allow net exports, previously assumed to be exogenous, to depend both on income and on the exchange rate. Second, we allow the exchange rate to depend on the interest rate. The combined effect of these two steps is to introduce an additional channel by which interest rates affect total expenditures.

Net exports (*NX*), as we learned in Chapter 2, is an aggregate that equals exports minus imports, and it is a component of total expenditure in GDP, along with consumption (*C*), investment (*I*), and government spending (*G*):

$$E = C + I + G + NX \tag{7.7}$$

A $200 billion increase in net exports provides just as much of a stimulus to income and employment as a $200 billion increase in consumption, investment, or government spending. A $200 billion decrease in net exports can

---

[6] Quotes in this section are from Kathy Wolfe, "Asia Ponders Exit Strategy from the Dollar," *Executive Intelligence Review*, February 20, 2004.

offset much of the stimulus to expenditures provided by expansionary monetary and fiscal policy.

Net Exports and the Foreign Exchange Rate

Clearly, fluctuations of net exports play an important role in the fluctuations of total real expenditures. Determining the ups and downs of net exports are real income and the foreign exchange rate.

Effect of real income. We can indicate the dependence of net exports (NX) on income as

$$NX = NX_a - nxY \tag{7.8}$$

Here, NX_a is the autonomous component of net exports (determined mainly by foreign income), nx is the fraction of a change in income that is spent on imports, and Y is real income.[7] If we ignored changes in the foreign exchange rate, then equation (7.8) would adequately explain net exports. For the given level of foreign income that determines the autonomous component (NX_a), net exports would be low in economic expansions when income is high, causing a large volume of imports, and net exports would be high in recessions when income is low, causing a small volume of imports.

Effect of the foreign exchange rate. When the exchange rate appreciates against foreign currencies, U.S. exports become more expensive in terms of foreign currencies, so exports tend to decline. Also, the lower dollar prices of imports attract American customers, and the quantity of goods imported into the United States rises. With exports down and imports up, the appreciation of the foreign exchange rate causes a drop in net exports. This is just what happened in the United States during 1995–2001. The appreciation of the dollar and the collapse of net exports are shown in Figure 7-6.

The striking fact that stands out in Figure 7-6 is the strong negative relationship between net exports and the real exchange rate. The rise in the real exchange rate between 1980 and 1985 was accompanied by a continuous decline in net exports. The 1985–88 depreciation of the dollar led to a sharp jump in net exports after 1987, and the 1996–2001 appreciation contributed to the collapse of net exports in 1998–2001.

Notice that the historical mirror-image relationship between the real exchange rate and real net exports broke down after 2002. We would have expected the depreciation of the dollar between 2002 and 2008 to revive net exports, but it did not. Why? Figure 7-6 neglects the relationship between net exports and income shown in equation (7.8). Net exports tend to move down (in a negative direction) when U.S. income is rising relative to those of other nations. Indeed, we learned in Chapter 5 that 2003–07 were the years of the housing bubble and excess U.S. consumer borrowing and spending. The spending frenzy of American consumers sucked up huge inflows of imports, while weak economic growth in many of America's trading partners held back the growth of U.S. exports.

The tables were turned in 2008–09 when the U.S. economy suffered a sharp recession, and imports declined more than exports, thus boosting net exports.

---

[7] This equation is identical to equation (10) in the Appendix to Chapter 3, p. 86.

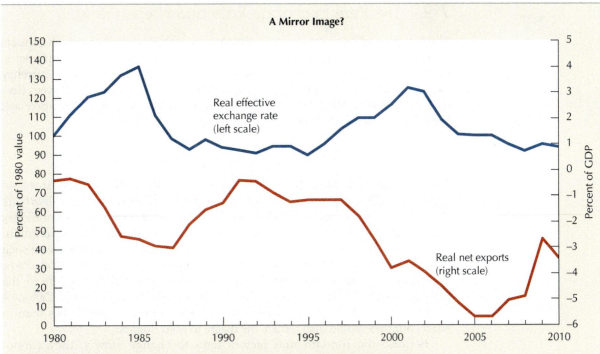

Figure 7-6 U.S. Real Net Exports and the Real Exchange Rate of the Dollar, 1980–2010

The two lines display a striking mirror-image relationship, indicating that an appreciating dollar tends to reduce net exports, and vice versa. The period 2003–10 is an important exception.

Sources: Bureau of Economic Analysis *NIPA Tables* and Federal Reserve Board *H.10 Foreign Exchange Rates.*

Thus Figure 7-6 shows a sharp improvement in net exports from −5.7 percent of GDP in 2006 to −2.7 percent in 2009. In short, we cannot adequately explain the ups and downs of net exports without including *both* real income and the exchange rate as causes.

We amend equation (7.8) to allow net exports (*NX*) to depend not just on income but also on the real exchange rate (*e*), which is expressed as a percentage of a base year (for instance, 1980 = 100).

General Linear Form   Numerical Example

$$NX = NX_a - nxY - ue \qquad NX = 1{,}400 - 0.1Y - 2e \qquad (7.9)$$

This equation states in words that net exports are equal to autonomous net exports (NX_a), minus a parameter (nx) times real income (Y), minus another parameter (u) times the real exchange rate (e). For any given level of income, an appreciation of the real exchange rate (as happened in the United States between 1995 and 2001) reduces net exports. For instance, if the economy is operating with actual real income at the natural real GDP level of $12,000 billion, and the real exchange rate is 100, then net exports are zero [= 1,400 − (0.1 × 12,000) − (2 × 100)]. An appreciation in the real exchange rate from 100 to 150 would reduce net exports in the example to −$100 billion [= 1,400 − (0.1 × 12,000) − (2 × 150)].

7-9 The Real Exchange Rate and Interest Rate

The foreign exchange rate is set in the foreign exchange market, which consists of bank employees all over the world buying and selling different currencies, primarily using online computer networks. When the demand for a currency like the dollar rises relative to the supply of dollars, these bank employees (foreign exchange traders) bid up the value of the dollar, causing it to appreciate. When the demand for dollars falls, its value falls, or depreciates.

The Demand for Dollars and the "Fundamentals"

The demand for dollars stems from two sources: the desire to buy American products and the desire to buy financial assets denominated in dollars (like bank deposits, U.S. government bonds, and the bonds issued by U.S. corporations). Changes in the worldwide desire to buy American products tend to occur gradually. Among the factors, sometimes called fundamentals, that might create such changes are the invention of new American products, like iPhones and iPads. A fundamental factor that could *reduce* the desire to hold dollars might be the development of new products in other countries, like Japanese-made Canon or Nikon digital cameras. Higher expected inflation in the United States than in other countries would also reduce the desire to hold dollars.

Because the fundamental factors tend to change slowly, they cannot account for much of the highly volatile movements evident in Figure 7-6 in the dollar's real exchange rate. Instead, these sharp up and down movements can be attributed to the second main source of the demand for dollars, the desire by foreigners to buy securities denominated in dollars. When U.S. securities become more attractive, the demand for dollars increases and the foreign exchange traders bid up the dollar's value. Similarly, when foreign securities become more attractive to Americans, U.S. residents supply extra dollars to the foreign exchange traders to obtain the foreign currencies they need to buy foreign securities and the dollar's value goes down.

The **interest rate differential** is the average U.S. interest rate minus the average foreign interest rate.

The relative attractiveness of U.S. and foreign securities depends on the **interest rate differential,** defined as the average U.S. interest rate minus the average foreign interest rate. When the U.S. interest rate increases and the foreign interest rate remains unchanged, the interest rate differential increases. Foreigners find U.S. securities attractive; they demand additional dollars to buy them, and the foreign exchange rate of the dollar is bid up by the foreign exchange traders.

This section has suggested that an increase in the U.S. interest rate should cause an appreciation of the dollar, and a decrease in the U.S. interest rate should cause a depreciation of the dollar. The relationship between the U.S. interest rate and the value of the dollar is demonstrated in Figure 7-7, which plots the two together for the period since 1978. The real exchange rate of the dollar is copied from Figure 7-6. The period of high interest rates after 1980 was accompanied by an appreciation of the dollar. The 1984 peak in the real interest rate came shortly before the 1985 peak in the real exchange rate. The decline in the real interest rate during 1984–89 coincided with the decline in the real exchange rate from 1985 to 1989.

The positive relationship between the real interest rate and the real exchange rate appears to have broken down after 1995. The real exchange rate appreciated by almost as much as it did in 1980–85, but the real interest rate was virtually unchanged. This new relationship reflects the role of the late 1990s U.S. stock market boom in attracting foreign capital inflows, which pushed up the value of the dollar, even though the real interest rate did not rise. After 2002, the

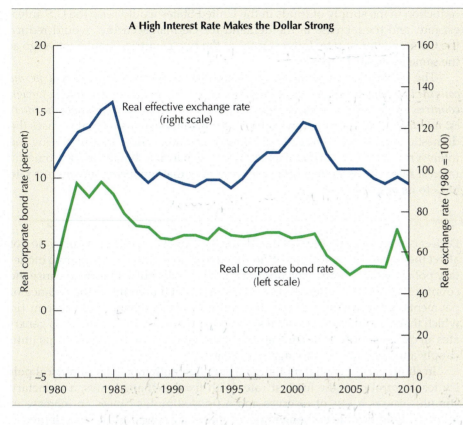

Figure 7-7 The U.S. Real Corporate Bond Rate and the Real Exchange Rate of the Dollar, 1978–2010

The real exchange rate is copied from Figure 7-6. A positive relationship between the two lines is evident, with movements in the interest rate appearing to occur prior to movements in the exchange rate. The relationship changed after 1995 as discussed in the text.

Sources: Moody's and Federal Reserve Board of Governors. See Appendix C-4.

real effective exchange rate depreciated and the real interest rate fell at the same time, repeating the experience of 1985–88. Finally in 2009 the bond rate jumped a lot due to the increase in the risk premium discussed in Chapter 5, and there was a small appreciation of the real exchange rate as investors flocked to the United States, which they viewed as a "safe haven."

 SELF-TEST

Assume that you are an American student traveling to Europe next summer. Which would you prefer assuming that you do not own any stocks?

1. A boom in the U.S. stock market?
2. A collapse in the U.S. stock market?

Interest Rates and Capital Mobility

The mechanism by which interest rates affect the exchange rate involves flows of capital between countries. **Perfect capital mobility** occurs when a resident of one country can purchase any desired assets in another country immediately, in unlimited amounts, with very low commissions and fees. The crucial implication of perfect capital mobility is that interest rates in one country are tightly linked to interest rates in other countries. Why? An American investor faced with a choice of a return of 6.0 percent at home and 6.6 percent in Germany would immediately choose to buy financial assets in Germany. This

Perfect capital mobility occurs when investors regard foreign financial assets as a perfect substitute for domestic assets, and when investors respond instantaneously to an interest rate differential between domestic and foreign assets by moving sufficient assets to eliminate that differential.

reduction in the supply of funds in the United States would raise the U.S. interest rate, and the increase in the demand for German securities would reduce the German interest rate. Interest rates in the two countries would converge at the same level, say 6.3 percent.

The implication of perfect capital mobility is profound. *Any event in one country that tends to change its interest rate (r) relative to the interest rate in foreign countries (r^f) will generate huge capital movements that will soon eliminate the interest rate differential ($r - r^f$).* As an example, a monetary expansion that reduces the domestic interest rate will generate a huge capital outflow that will bring the interest rate back to its original level. A fiscal expansion that raises the domestic interest rate will generate a huge capital inflow that will bring the interest rate back to its original level.

The Two Adjustment Mechanisms: Fixed and Flexible Rates

Perfect capital mobility implies that domestic monetary and fiscal policy do not affect the domestic interest rate. With fixed exchange rates, a stimulative monetary policy will not reduce the domestic interest rate, but will instead cause the country to lose international reserves as the capital account in the balance of payments is thrown into deficit. In a pure flexible exchange rate system (in which there are no international reserves), the monetary policy stimulus generates an excess supply of dollars, and the exchange rate of the dollar drops until supply and demand are once again in balance.

In short, perfect capital mobility implies that both monetary and fiscal policy lose control over the interest rate. With fixed exchange rates, a monetary stimulus causes a loss of reserves and a fiscal stimulus causes an increase in reserves. With flexible exchange rates, a monetary stimulus causes a depreciation of the exchange rate and a fiscal stimulus causes an appreciation of the exchange rate. The reverse events occur with a monetary policy contraction or a fiscal policy contraction.

Is Perfect Capital Mobility Relevant for the United States?

A **small open economy** with perfect capital mobility has no power to set its domestic interest rate at a level that differs from foreign interest rates.

A **large open economy** can influence its domestic interest rate.

As an analytical tool, perfect capital mobility is most relevant for a **small open economy,** too small to influence the world level of interest rates (r^f). In such an economy, because of perfect capital mobility, the small domestic capital market is swamped by capital inflows whenever there is even a minor increase in the domestic interest rate above the world interest rate (and capital outflows for even a minor decrease in the domestic interest rate).

The United States is too large to be considered a small open economy, and even under perfect capital mobility its own domestic capital market is too large for capital movements to bring its domestic interest rate into perfect equality with the foreign interest rate. We examine the case of the **large open economy** after first studying how monetary and fiscal policy work in a small open economy with perfect capital mobility.

7-10   Effects of Monetary and Fiscal Policy with Fixed and Flexible Exchange Rates

The assumption of perfect capital mobility introduces a new element into the *IS-LM* model of income determination. This is the assumption that the differential between domestic and foreign interest rates ($r - r^f$) must remain at zero. Any small change in the domestic interest rate caused by shifts in monetary and fiscal policy (or in shifts in the *IS* curve due to different levels of consumer and business optimism) will generate capital flows that will quickly bring the domestic interest rate back into line with the unchanged foreign interest rate.

The Analysis with Fixed Exchange Rates

Now we will examine the effects of a monetary and then a fiscal expansion in a small open economy with fixed exchange rates. Throughout, we will assume that the price level is fixed. These results remain valid, even if the price level is allowed to change, as long as changes in the price level occur more slowly than the speed at which capital flows in and out of the small open economy.

Monetary expansion.   As we learned in Chapter 4, a domestic monetary expansion occurs when the central bank (the Federal Reserve or "Fed" in the United States) raises the money supply, thus shifting the *LM* curve to the right. This normally reduces the interest rate and stimulates spending. But in a small open economy with perfect capital mobility, the interest rate is fixed at the level of the world interest rate. When the central bank increases the money supply, there immediately are huge capital outflows and losses of international reserves. Thus, as stated by the *trilemma* introduced at the beginning of this chapter, the Fed or any central bank loses control of the money supply when the exchange rate is fixed and capital is perfectly mobile. Thus monetary policy becomes completely impotent with fixed exchange rates.

Fiscal policy.   As usual, fiscal policy works in the opposite way from monetary policy. As we learned in Chapter 4, when monetary policy is weak, fiscal policy is strong, and vice versa. This works in the same way in a small open economy. A fiscal policy stimulus works by shifting the *IS* curve to the right, just as in Chapter 4. But this tends to raise the interest rate relative to the world interest rate and attract inflows of capital, swamping the central bank with reserves. Under a fixed exchange rate system, the central bank must respond by allowing the money supply to rise until the interest rate returns to its initial level. Thus *both* the *IS* and *LM* curves move to the right, as in the top right frame of Figure 4-10 on p. 108. Perfect capital mobility clearly makes fiscal policy very effective, since it gives fiscal policy control over the money supply, forcing the *LM* curve to amplify any movement in the *IS* curve. *Perfect capital mobility with fixed exchange rates forces monetary policy to be accommodative; in effect, fiscal policy gains control over monetary policy.*

The Analysis with Flexible Exchange Rates

In the previous section we learned that a fixed exchange rate system makes monetary policy impotent and fiscal policy very effective in changing the level of real income. In this section we learn that the opposite is true with flexible exchange rates. Monetary policy becomes extremely effective, whereas fiscal policy becomes ineffective.

When exchange rates are flexible, the central bank does nothing to prevent an exchange rate appreciation or depreciation. Thus any event that reduces the domestic interest rate will cause a capital outflow, raising the supply of domestic currency on the foreign exchange market and causing the exchange rate to depreciate. The exchange rate depreciates whenever monetary policy reduces the interest rate and appreciates whenever monetary policy raises the interest rate.

The new ingredient in the *IS-LM* model implied by flexible exchange rates was introduced in equation (7.9). An exchange rate appreciation reduces net exports and hence shifts the *IS* curve to the left (since net exports are a component of autonomous planned spending, and any change in autonomous planned spending shifts the *IS* curve). Similarly, an exchange rate depreciation raises net exports and shifts the *IS* curve to the right.

Monetary expansion. When the central bank increases the money supply with flexible exchange rates, interest rates decline, the exchange rate depreciates, and net exports rise, thus shifting the *IS* curve to the right. Hence, in a small open economy, monetary policy is very powerful since monetary policy gains control of the *IS* curve and forces it to move in the same direction as the *LM* curve.

However, as also shown in equation (7.9) on p. 217, higher income boosts imports. As a result, when the economy arrives at its new equilibrium level of output, the boost to net exports from the depreciated exchange rate is offset exactly by the reduction in net exports caused by higher income. The current account is in balance and, because the domestic interest rate is equal to the foreign interest rate, the capital account is also in balance.

We learned in Chapter 4 that the normal effect of a fiscal expansion in a closed economy is to shift rightward the *IS* curve and raise the interest rate. But now, with flexible exchange rates, the fiscal expansion and higher interest rate causes the exchange rate to appreciate. Domestic exports are made more expensive, and domestic residents start buying more imported goods. Net exports fall, and this continues until the *IS* curve shifts back to its initial position. In this situation the *LM* curve does not shift.

Domestic crowding out is replaced by international crowding out, and international crowding out is complete. The domestic interest rate and income are the same as they were initially; thus, so are domestic investment and saving. The increase in the fiscal deficit caused by the higher level of government spending is exactly offset by the decline in net exports, and the higher fiscal deficit is totally financed by foreign borrowing. *The twin deficits are identical*, and the cause of the foreign trade deficit is the fiscal deficit. To summarize these different cases:

1. With fixed exchange rates, fiscal policy is highly effective and the central bank is forced to accommodate fiscal policy actions. Monetary policy is impotent, since any increase in the money supply immediately flows abroad and fails to stimulate the domestic economy.

2. With flexible exchange rates, monetary policy is highly effective. The central bank can control the money supply and can stimulate the economy by causing the exchange rate to depreciate. This action boosts net exports until income has grown so much that (due to income-induced growth in imports) net exports return to their original level. With flexible exchange rates, fiscal policy is impotent and international crowding out is complete.

How a Large Open Economy Differs from a Small Open Economy

In contrast to a small open economy, a large open economy like the United States has substantial control over its domestic interest rate. Its large size relative to the rest of the world means that capital flows are not sufficiently powerful to push its domestic interest rate into exact equality with the world interest rate. Capital mobility is imperfect. When the domestic interest rate rises above the foreign interest rate by a fixed amount, say 0.5 percent, only a limited inflow of foreign capital will occur, not enough to eliminate the interest rate differential.

For a small open economy, the interest rate equals the world interest rate. In contrast, in a large open economy there can be a continuing capital inflow if the domestic interest rate is high enough and a continuing capital outflow if the domestic interest rate is low enough. As a result, the distinguishing characteristic of a large open economy is that the capital account is in surplus when the domestic interest rate is high and in deficit when the domestic interest rate is low. To achieve an overall balance of payments of zero, any surplus in the capital account must be offset by a deficit of exactly the same amount in the current account; this requires a high level of real income, so that imports (which depend on income) are large and the current account is in deficit. The opposite occurs when interest rates are low; the deficit in the capital account is offset by a current account surplus, caused by low income that in turn reduces imports.

We previously concluded that in a small closed economy with fixed exchange rates, monetary policy was impotent. The same is true in a large open economy. Fiscal policy is effective, but somewhat less so than in a small open economy, since the effects of a fiscal policy stimulus are divided between an increase in real income and in the domestic interest rate, instead of being entirely directed toward an increase in real income.

With flexible exchange rates, fiscal policy is impotent in a large open economy, just as in a small open economy. The prompt collapse of net exports following the 1981 shift to fiscal deficits provides a perfect example of the impotence of fiscal policy in a large open economy. Monetary policy is highly effective with flexible exchange rates, as in a small open economy. However, since higher income is accompanied by higher interest rates, there is some crowding out of domestic expenditure, and this must be offset by a larger stimulus to net exports than in a small open economy, requiring an even larger exchange rate depreciation. To summarize these contrasting cases:

1. With fixed exchange rates, fiscal policy is highly effective, but a fiscal stimulus does not increase real income as much in a large open economy as in a small open economy. Monetary policy is impotent in both a large and a small open economy.

2. With flexible exchange rates, monetary policy is highly effective and boosts income even more in a large open economy than in a small open economy. With flexible exchange rates, fiscal policy is impotent in both a large and a small open economy. International crowding out is complete.

GLOBAL ECONOMIC CRISIS FOCUS

Is the United States Prevented from Implementing a Fiscal Policy Stimulus by Its Flexible Exchange Rate?

The analysis in this section would appear to create a dilemma for policymakers in the United States, which is clearly a large open economy. Since the United States has flexible exchange rates, does this mean fiscal policy is impotent? Does a fiscal policy stimulus act to raise interest rates, appreciate the exchange rate, and cause a decline in net exports that cancels out the impact of the fiscal stimulus on GDP?

The answer is no because monetary and fiscal policy can work together, a possibility that is not included in the summary table. This possibility is shown in

(continued)

Summary of Monetary and Fiscal Policy Effects in Open Economies

	Small open economy, perfect capital mobility	
	Fixed exchange rates	**Flexible exchange rates**
Monetary policy	Impotent, no independent effect, consistent with trilemma	Strong, exchange rate impact augments direct effect of policy on domestic spending
Fiscal policy	Strong, fiscal policy gains control over money supply	Impotent, international crowding out augments domestic crowding out

	Large open economy, imperfect capital mobility	
	Fixed exchange rates	**Flexible exchange rates**
Monetary policy	Impotent, same as in small open economy	Strong, with more exchange rate effect than in small open economy
Fiscal policy	Strong, but not as effective as in small open economy	Impotent, as in small open economy

the top right frame of Figure 4-10 on p. 108 and discussed extensively in Chapter 6 (see especially p. 176). If the central bank buys the bonds issued as part of the fiscal policy stimulus, then interest rates do not need to rise at all. There is no exchange rate appreciation and no crowding out of fiscal policy.

Indeed the main changes in the exchange rate of the dollar in 2009–10 were not caused by fiscal policy but rather by attitudes toward the risk of a global economic meltdown. Widespread panic in late 2008 and early 2009 caused a flood of foreign capital to flow into the United States, which was viewed as a safe haven, thus causing a dollar appreciation that is most visible in the euro exchange rate graph in Figure 7-2 on p. 202. Another round of dollar appreciation occurred in the spring of 2010 when fear spread across the world that Greece and perhaps other European countries would fail to pay the interest on their debt. U.S. fiscal policy, working in tandem with monetary policy, can be conducted without the fear of international crowding out working through the exchange rate mechanism discussed in this section.

7-11 Conclusion: Economic Policy in the Open Economy

We have learned in this chapter that there are interactions among monetary and fiscal policy, the current account balance, and the foreign exchange rate. A unifying theme is the international trilemma, which states that countries cannot simultaneously maintain an independent monetary policy, fixed exchange rates, and free unfettered international capital movements. The implications of this analysis differ for the United States, Europe, and Asia.

The Trilemma, the United States, and the Euro

The United States has chosen to keep its exchange rate flexible and to leave to other countries the decision of whether to tie their currencies to the dollar or to let their currencies float. This means that the United States has been able to maintain control over domestic monetary policy and also has allowed free inflows of private capital that largely financed the huge increase in the U.S. current account deficit that occurred in 1998–2007. Another important factor in financing the U.S. deficit has been the willingness of foreign central banks, especially in Asia, to accumulate large stocks of dollar reserves, thus lending to the United States the remaining funds needed to pay for its current account deficit.

By adopting a single currency (the euro), thirteen nations in Europe emulate the United States by having a fixed exchange rate within the borders of the thirteen nations while allowing the exchange rate of the euro to float against other currencies. The trilemma implies that the thirteen nations thereby gave up a traditional aspect of national sovereignty, the ability to maintain independent control of domestic monetary policy. Instead, they ceded control over monetary policy to the European Central Bank, which now plays a role analogous to that of the U.S. Federal Reserve System. We return to issues raised by the introduction of the euro in Chapter 14.

Finally, we have learned that the United States and the major Asian countries, especially China and Japan, have entered into a mutually reinforcing relationship of codependence. The United States relies on Asia to finance its ever-growing current account deficit. Asian countries willingly accumulate dollar reserves in order to prevent their currencies from appreciating, thus preventing a slump in their exports and potential unemployment. The United States maintains flexible exchange rates, thus escaping from the constraints of the trilemma, while the Asian countries are in a trap in which they continue to accumulate dollar assets that not only earn a relatively low interest rate, but also decline in value as the dollar depreciates against currencies in other regions of the world, especially against the euro.

Summary

1. The current account includes net exports, net income from abroad, and net unilateral transfers. A current account deficit is balanced by some combination of private capital inflows and borrowing from foreign central banks. The balance of payments is often negative for the United States because capital inflows to the United States do not offset the large current account deficit.

2. A nation has a negative net international investment position when its assets in foreign countries are smaller than the assets of foreigners in its country. The change in the international net investment position equals the current account balance plus the net revaluation term, primarily reflecting the impact of changes in exchange rates and stock market prices on the values of assets held in foreign countries.

3. In a flexible exchange rate system, the foreign exchange rate is free to move every day. An increase in the amount of foreign currency that can be bought per unit of domestic currency is called an appreciation, and a decrease is called a depreciation.

4. In the absence of government intervention, the foreign exchange rate tends to appreciate when there is increased demand for a currency due to higher exports or capital inflows. The exchange rate tends to depreciate when there is an increased supply of a currency due to higher imports or capital outflows.

5. The real exchange rate remains constant if changes in the nominal exchange rate are exactly offset by the differential between domestic and foreign inflation. The purchasing power parity theory of long-run exchange rate determination predicts that the real exchange rate will remain constant.

6. The real exchange rate can change for many reasons not taken into account by the PPP theory. These include differences between nations in the rate of technological change, their comparative rates of discovery of natural

resources, and the balance of flows of capital and government transfer payments between them.

7. Exchange rates between nations were largely fixed until 1973. Since then there has been a mixed "impure" flexible exchange rate system, under which central banks practice intervention to prevent undesired movements in exchange rates. Some countries, especially in Asia, have attempted to fix their exchange rates versus the U.S. dollar and have accumulated large quantities of U.S. dollars in the form of international reserves, thus allowing the United States to run a larger current account deficit than would otherwise have been possible.

8. Net exports, the difference between exports and imports, depend both on income and on the real exchange rate. In turn, the real exchange rate depends on the real interest rate. An increase in the real interest rate causes an appreciation of the real exchange rate, as foreign investors find domestic securities more attractive and bid up the exchange rate in order to buy them.

9. In a small open economy with fixed exchange rates, fiscal policy is highly effective and monetary policy is completely impotent. With flexible exchange rates the policy roles are reversed, since monetary policy is highly effective and fiscal policy is impotent.

10. In a large open economy with fixed exchange rates, monetary policy is impotent, but fiscal policy is effective (although less so than in a small open economy). With flexible exchange rates monetary policy is highly effective (even more so than in a small open economy), but fiscal policy is impotent.

Concepts

trilemma	appreciation	foreign exchange reserves
current account	depreciation	devalue
balance of payments	real exchange rate	revalue
capital account	purchasing power parity	intervention
net international	(PPP) theory	interest rate differential
investment position	inflation differential	perfect capital mobility
national saving	flexible exchange rate system	small open economy
foreign exchange rate	fixed exchange rate system	large open economy

Questions

1. Explain the difference between a credit and a debit in the balance of payments.

2. Distinguish between the current account and the capital account in the balance of payments.

3. Four international transactions are listed below. For each, determine whether it is a credit or a debit in the U.S. balance of payments, whether it is a current account or capital account transaction, and whether it increases or decreases the size of the U.S. balance of payments deficit.
   (a) Japan buys rice from the United States.
   (b) Ford Motor Company builds an automobile plant in Russia.
   (c) A German insurance company buys U.S. government bonds.
   (d) U.S. residents vacation in Asia.

4. Suppose that the current account deficit equals $600 billion. Explain if the change in net foreign investment position will be larger or smaller than $600 billion in each of the following cases.
   (a) Initially, the value of U.S.-owned assets overseas is $3 trillion and of foreign-owned assets overseas in the United States is $4 trillion. The value of U.S.-owned assets overseas rises by 10 percent, but the value of foreign-owned assets in the United States increases by only 5 percent.

   (b) The number of yen required to buy a dollar increases from 110 to 115.

5. The net international investment position of the United States was 19.2 percent of GDP in both 2001 and 2009. Explain how this was possible in light of the rather large current account deficits between 2001 and 2009.

6. Figure 7-1 shows that the U.S. net international borrowing has become a larger percentage of GDP since 1990. Yet net investment income from the rest of the world has remained a positive, though declining, share of output. Explain how this is possible.

7. Explain what national saving is and whether a rise in the government's budget deficit adds to national saving or reduces it. Explain why a rise in the budget deficit must be met by either a reduction in domestic investment or an increase in foreign investment.

8. Find the section of the *Wall Street Journal* that contains the daily quotations of foreign exchange rates (see Table 7-2 on p. 199). Get the exchange rates in terms of currency per U.S. dollar for the day you are reading this and for one year prior to this day for each of the following currencies: Australian dollar, Canadian dollar, Indian rupee, Japanese yen, Mexican peso, Polish zloty, and the South African rand. Use these data to explain whether the U.S. dollar has appreciated or depreciated against each currency over the last year.

9. Under what conditions is the demand for foreign exchange negatively sloped?

10. Under what conditions is the supply of foreign exchange positively sloped? Negatively sloped?

11. Explain whether each of the following events would cause the nation's currency to become overvalued or undervalued relative to its implied purchasing power parity value:

   (a) Russia becomes a leading exporter of crude oil and natural gas.

   (b) Euro zone nations decide they no longer want to import American entertainment such as movies and music.

   (c) Rapid development in India's technology sector results in large inflows of funds into the Indian stock market from other countries.

12. What is a "dirty" flexible exchange rate system, and what incentives exist to transform a "clean" system into a "dirty" one?

13. Explain how China was able to maintain an essentially fixed exchange rate between its currency, the yuan, and the dollar from 1995 through 2005. Explain why China would have wanted to maintain this fixed exchange rate.

14. What is the relationship between a country's foreign exchange rate and its net exports? Why?

15. What is the relationship between a country's interest rate and its foreign exchange rate? Why?

16. Suppose an economy's productivity growth rate increases, causing the prices of its exports to fall, the quantity of its exports to rise, and its current account balance to move from a deficit to a surplus. Using a supply and demand diagram, explain the effect of this increase in productivity growth on the country's foreign exchange rate. If the country's policymakers want to maintain the foreign exchange rate at its current value, what actions must they undertake?

17. Despite the fall of the dollar against the euro in 2004, the Japanese government was willing to buy American dollars in order to keep the value of the yen from appreciating relative to the dollar. Suppose that instead of slow growth, the Japanese economy had experienced rising inflation over the past decade. Discuss how rising inflation might have changed the Japanese government's willingness to help finance the current U.S. account deficit.

18. What is the trilemma? Explain how the United States, a large open economy, and Ireland, a small open economy and euro zone member, have dealt with the trilemma.

19. Suppose that both the Irish and American economies risk a rise in the inflation rate due to low unemployment. Given the information contained in question 18, and your answer to that question, explain what actions policymakers in each economy must take in order to reduce real GDP relative to natural real GDP in an effort to restrain a rise in the inflation rate.

20. "Perfect capital mobility with fixed exchange rates forces monetary policy to be accommodative; in effect, fiscal policy gains control of monetary policy." Explain.

21. Fiscal policymakers in a large open economy are reluctant to cut taxes or raise spending. If real GDP is less than natural real GDP, will the central bank be able to reduce unemployment? Under what circumstances?

22. For a large open economy in a pure flexible exchange rate system, it is expansionary monetary policy rather than expansionary fiscal policy that will have a negative long-term effect on private investment. Evaluate.

Problems

 Visit www.MyEconLab.com to complete these or similar exercises.

*Indicates that the problem requires the Appendix to Chapter 4.

1. Suppose a country has net exports of 40, transfer payments of 20, net investment income of −15, and a balance of payments surplus of 10. Find this country's current account balance and capital account balance.

2. You are given the following information:

Year	Current Account Balance	Change in the Net International Investment Position	Change in Foreign-owned Assets in U.S.	Change in U.S.-owned Assets Overseas
1	−500	−360	110	
2		−360	160	350
3	−380		−375	−150
4	−640	−670		−30

   (a) Compute the amount of net revaluations in each of the four years.

   (b) Compute the change in U.S.-owned assets overseas in year 1.

   (c) Compute the current account balance in year 2.

   (d) Compute the change in the net international investment position in year 3.

   (e) Compute the change in foreign-owned assets in the United States in year 4.

3. Suppose that *ex* is the exchange rate between the U.S. dollar and the Chinese yuan in that *ex* indicates the number of yuan that can be purchased with one dollar. The demand for dollars, denoted, $D_\$$, is given by the equation $D_\$ = 2,800 − 200ex$. The supply of dollars, denoted, $S_\$$, is given by the equation $S_\$ = 400 + 100ex$.

   (a) Calculate the demand for dollars and supply of dollars at exchange rates between 0 and 12 in increments of one.

(b) Graph the demand for dollars and supply of dollars against the exchange rate. What is the value of the equilibrium exchange rate?

(c) Suppose the demand for dollars increases by 300 billion at each exchange rate. Explain if the increase in demand results from a large purchase by the Chinese of a new American-made airplane or a large purchase by Americans of new lower priced Chinese-made high definition televisions. Calculate the new demand for dollars at each exchange rate and graph the new demand curve. What is the new equilibrium exchange rate, given the original supply of dollars?

(d) Suppose the supply of dollars increases by 600 billion at each exchange rate. Explain if the increase in supply results from a large purchase by the Chinese of a new American-made airplane or a large purchase by Americans of new lower priced Chinese-made high definition televisions. Calculate the new supply of dollars at each exchange rate and graph the new supply curve. What is the new equilibrium exchange rate, given the original demand for dollars?

4. (a) Suppose that there is a large purchase by Americans of new lower priced Chinese-made high definition televisions. Given your answers to problem 3, explain whether the Chinese government must buy or sell dollars and by how much if it wants to maintain the value of the yuan relative to the dollar at the level of your answer in part b of problem 3.

(b) Suppose that there is a large purchase by the Chinese of a new American-made airplane. Given your answers to problem 3, explain whether the Chinese government must buy or sell dollars and by how much if it wants to maintain the value of the yuan relative to the dollar at the level of your answer in part b of problem 3.

5. Suppose that the demand for dollars is given by the equation $D_\$ = 2,800 - 200ex$ and the supply of dollars is given by the equation $S_\$ = 400 + 100ex$. Therefore the equilibrium exchange rate is your answer to part b of problem 3.

(a) Suppose that there is a change in U.S. fiscal policy that reduces the demand for dollars by 200 billion and increases the supply of dollars by 100 billion at each exchange rate. Explain if the capital outflows are caused by a decrease in defense spending or an increase in government's health care spending. Calculate the new demand for dollars and the new supply of dollars at each exchange rate and graph the new demand and supply curves. What is the new equilibrium exchange rate?

(b) Suppose that there is a change in U.S. monetary policy that increases the demand for dollars by 400 billion and decreases the supply of dollars by 200 billion at each exchange rate. Explain if the capital inflows are caused by an expansionary or contractionary monetary policy. Calculate the new demand for dollars and the new supply of dollars at each exchange rate and graph the new demand and supply curves. What is the new equilibrium exchange rate?

6. Suppose the European demand for a U.S. machine is given by the following equation:

$$q = 240,000/p$$

Here q is the quantity of U.S. machines bought by the Europeans and p is the price, in euros, of the U.S. machine.

(a) If the exchange rate is 0.8 euros per dollar and the dollar price of the machine is $12,000, what is the euro price of the machine?

(b) According to the demand function just given, how many machines would the Europeans buy?

(c) If the dollar price of the machine remained unchanged, but the exchange rate fell to 0.625 euros per dollar, what would the euro price of the machine now be?

(d) Now how many machines would the Europeans buy?

(e) At the exchange rate of 0.8 euros per dollar, what is the quantity demanded of dollars by the Europeans?

(f) At the exchange rate of 0.625 euros per dollar, what is the quantity demanded of dollars by the Europeans?

(g) If this machine were the only U.S. export to the Europeans, draw the European demand curve for dollars. Put the dollars demanded on the horizontal axis and the euro/$ exchange rate on the vertical axis.

(h) At the exchange rate of 0.8 euro per dollar (or $1.25/euro), what is the quantity supplied of euros by the Europeans?

(i) At the exchange rate of 0.625 euro per dollar (or $1.60/euro), what is the quantity supplied of euros by the Europeans?

(j) If this machine were the only U.S. export to the Europeans, draw the European supply curve of euros. Put the euros supplied on the horizontal axis and the $/euro exchange rate on the vertical axis. (Note the inversion of the exchange rate. Although there are exceptions, it is customary to express a country's exchange rate as the number of units of foreign currency that exchange for one unit of the domestic currency.)

7. Fill in the missing information in each of the following examples.

Example	Real Exchange Rate	Nominal Exchange Rate	Domestic Price Level	Foreign Price Level
(a)		6	100	100
(b)		6	110	100
(c)		6	100	110
(d)	6		110	100
(e)	6		100	110

What conclusions regarding real and nominal exchange rates do these examples suggest?

8. In addition to its Big Mac index, *The Economist*[a] magazine started to publish a PPP index based on the price of a tall latte at Starbucks coffee shops around the world. This problem is intended to show how to use such an index to determine whether a currency is over- or undervalued. You are given the following information:

Country	Coffee price in U.S. dollars	Actual Exchange Rate
United States	1.50	
Javaland	1.20	2.35
Uppercaffina	2.25	6.00
Isle of Roast	2.70	1.65
Erehwon	.90	4.35

Calculate the implied purchasing power parity (PPP) exchange rate for each of the fictional countries and explain which currencies are over- or undervalued.

9. Suppose that the domestic price level P grows at the rate of 2 percent per quarter for five years, while the foreign price level P^f grows at the rate of 1 percent per quarter for five years. At what rate must e' change for PPP to hold?

*10. Assume the following equations summarize the structure of a small open economy with a flexible exchange rate system.

$$C = C_a + 0.85(Y - T)$$
$$C_a = 200 - 8r$$
$$T = 200 + 0.2Y$$
$$(M/P)^d = 0.25Y - 25r$$

[a] *The Economist*, January 17, 2004, p. 67, The Starbucks Index.

$$M^s/P = 2,250$$
$$I_p = 1,700 - 32r$$
$$G = 1,800$$
$$NX = 870 - 0.08Y - 200e$$

(a) Initially let foreign and domestic interest rates be equal, so that $r = r^f$, and let the foreign exchange rate (e) equal 2.
  1. Derive the equation for net exports, NX.
  2. Compute the value of the multiplier.
  3. Derive the equation for the autonomous planned spending schedule, A_p.
  4. Derive the equation for the IS curve.
  5. Derive the equation for the LM curve.
  6. Compute the equilibrium domestic and foreign interest rates (r and r^f).
  7. Compute equilibrium real output (Y).

(b) We now let the small economy's domestic interest rate diverge temporarily from the foreign interest rate. Suppose that the monetary authority attempts to reduce output by decreasing the real money supply, M^s/P, by 50 to 2,200.
  1. Derive the equation for the new LM curve.
  2. Compute the new equilibrium domestic interest rate (r).
  3. Compute the new (temporary) equilibrium real output (Y).
  4. Given the decrease in the real money supply, compute the level of real output that equalizes domestic and foreign interest rates.
  5. Find the foreign exchange rate that equalizes domestic and foreign interest rates. (*Hint:* Calculate the change in net exports required to reduce output to the level that equalizes domestic and foreign interest rates. Then calculate the change in the foreign exchange rate required to change net exports by that amount.)

(c) Again we let the domestic interest rate diverge temporarily from the foreign interest rate. Suppose that fiscal policymakers decrease government spending (G) by 80 to 1,720. Assume that the value of the real money supply equals 2,250.
  1. Derive the equation for the new autonomous planned spending schedule, A_p.
  2. Derive the equation for the new IS curve.
  3. Compute the new equilibrium domestic interest rate (r).
  4. Compute the new (temporary) equilibrium real output (Y).
  5. Given that there has been no change in the real money supply, compute the level of real output that equalizes domestic and foreign interest rates.
  6. Find the foreign exchange rate that equalizes domestic and foreign interest rates. (*Hint:* Calculate

by how much autonomous planned spending must change to equalize in domestic and foreign interest rates. Then calculate the change in the foreign exchange rate required to change net exports by that amount.)

(d) Based on your answers to parts b and c, compare and contrast the effectiveness of monetary and fiscal policy in a small open economy with a flexible exchange rate system.

◆ SELF-TEST ANSWERS

p. 194. (1) Balance of payments deficit of 30, which requires borrowing 30 from foreign central banks; (2) balance of payments surplus of 30, which requires lending 30; (3) same as (1).

p. 198. All of the statements are true. They all are different ways of describing the same situation.

p. 204. (1) Shifts the demand curve for dollars to the right. (2) No effect on the supply curve of dollars (people from the United States shift some of the supply of dollars from Europe to Mexico). (3) Shifts the demand curve for dollars to the left. (4) Shifts the supply curve of dollars to the left.

p. 206. (1) The real exchange rate in the year 2009 is $0.65 \times (110/100) = 0.75$ euro per dollar. (2) Since the real exchange rate was 0.75 euro per dollar in 2008, the dollar has experienced a real depreciation.

(3) U.S. exports to Europe should rise and imports should fall.

p. 212. (1) A college student going to Europe (like anyone buying foreign goods or services) hopes for an appreciation of the dollar. (2) Other things remaining the same, you would have preferred traveling to Europe in 2001 when the dollar's foreign exchange value was approximately 41 percent higher than it was in 1995. (3) For the German student, the situation is the opposite. He or she would prefer to travel to the U.S. when the dollar is weaker, as was the case in 1995.

p. 219. College students going to Europe prefer a strong dollar. This means that they prefer a booming stock market that attracts capital investment into the United States.

Aggregate Demand, Aggregate Supply, and the Great Depression

Once I built a railroad, now it's done, Brother, can you spare a dime?
—Edgar Y. ("Yip") Harburg

8-1 Combining Aggregate Demand with Aggregate Supply

In principle, shocks to aggregate demand can change either real GDP, the price level (GDP deflator), or both.[1] Up until now, in order to focus on changes in aggregate demand, we have made a bold but useful simplifying assumption: *that the price level is fixed in the short run.* This has implied that all changes in aggregate demand automatically cause changes in real GDP by the same amount in the same direction. Repeating from equation (3.1) on p. 56:

$$\text{Changes in Real GDP} = \frac{\text{Changes in Aggregate Demand}}{\text{Fixed Price Level}} \qquad (8.1)$$

Now it is time to drop the unrealistic assumption that the price level is fixed. Recall that the price level is measured by an aggregate price index like the GDP deflator. When the prices of most goods are rising, the aggregate deflator (*P*) increases, and we have inflation. When the prices of most goods are falling, *P* decreases, and we have deflation. How can we determine whether changes in aggregate demand create changes in real GDP, the price level, or both?

This chapter introduces two new elements to answer that question. First, we introduce a negatively sloped schedule relating real GDP to the price level, called the **aggregate demand (*AD*) curve.** We have already learned in Chapters 3–6 all the reasons why the *AD* curve shifts its position; here the only new element is the curve has a negative slope, reflecting the fact that a higher price level reduces the real money supply and hence reduces aggregate demand.

But the *AD* curve by itself cannot determine two unknowns, real GDP and the price level. The needed extra relationship is the **short-run aggregate supply (*SAS*) curve,** a positively sloped relationship between real GDP and the price level. Whereas the *AD* curve shows how much people want to buy, the *SAS* curve shows how much business firms are willing to sell at each price level. When the price level increases, while the costs of labor and other inputs remain stable, then business profits will increase and firms will produce more real GDP. Both real GDP and the price level are determined at the point where the *AD* and *SAS* curves intersect. We shall learn that the reason for the positive slope of the *SAS* is inherently temporary, that prices adjust while labor costs

The **aggregate demand (*AD*) curve** shows different combinations of the price level and real output at which the money and commodity markets are both in equilibrium.

The **short-run aggregate supply (*SAS*) curve** shows the amount of output that business firms are willing to produce at different price levels, holding constant the nominal wage rate.

---

[1] *Review:* The concepts "aggregate demand" and "demand shocks" were first defined in Chapter 3 on p. 55, and these definitions are also found in the glossary in the back of the book.

The **long-run aggregate supply (*LAS*) curve** shows the amount that business firms are willing to produce when the nominal wage rate has fully adjusted to any changes in the price level.

(the nominal wage) do not. Once the nominal wage rate is free to adjust in proportion to the price level, the **long-run aggregate supply (*LAS*) curve** becomes vertical.

This chapter begins by deriving the *AD* and *SAS* curves, explaining why they are sloped as they are, and what causes them to shift their position. Subsequently, we use both curves to examine differing views of economists regarding the causes of business cycles and the effectiveness of monetary and fiscal policy. We use the distinction between aggregate demand and supply to examine the causes of the Great Depression, which involve the causes of the leftward shift in the *AD* curve, the slope of the *SAS* curve, and the determinants of shifts in the *SAS* curve. The chapter ends with comparisons between the Great Depression of the 1930s and the Global Economic Crisis.

8-2 Flexible Prices and the *AD* Curve

In this section we develop the *AD* curve, which summarizes the effect of changing prices on the level of real GDP. The *AD* curve summarizes the *IS-LM* model of Chapter 4; the only new element is that the price level is now allowed to change instead of being fixed as in Chapters 3–7.

Effect of Changing Prices on the *LM* Curve

We already know that the *LM* curve shifts its position whenever there is a change in the *real* money supply. Until now, every *LM* shift has resulted from a change in the *nominal* money supply, while the price level has been fixed. The price level has been treated as a parameter, or a known variable, allowing us to concentrate on the determination of the two unknowns, real income (Y) and the interest rate (r).

However, the *LM* curve can shift *in exactly the same way* when a change in the real money supply M^s/P is caused by a change in the price level P, while the nominal money supply M^s remains fixed at a single value, say M_0^s. The top frame of Figure 8-1 illustrates three *LM* curves drawn for three values of P and M^s/P, each assuming the same nominal money supply, M_0^s. Initially the economy is at point E_0, where the *IS* curve crosses the LM_0 curve, drawn for the initial assumed price level P_0. The economy is in equilibrium with income level Y_0 and interest rate r_0. So far, everything is the same as in Chapter 4.

Now we consider something new, a change in the price level. If the price level were *lower* than P_0, say P_1, the real money supply would be *larger* (M_0^s/P_1). To maintain equilibrium in the money market, the interest rate would have to fall to r_1. This change would boost planned expenditures and cause real GDP to grow to the larger amount Y_1, so that the economy's equilibrium position would move from E_0 to point H. The reverse is true as well. A higher price level, say P_2, would reduce the real money supply and cause real GDP to shrink to the lower level Y_2, and the economy's equilibrium position would move to point J.

The bottom frame of Figure 8-1 presents the relationship between equilibrium real GDP (Y) and the assumed price level. The horizontal axis (real GDP) is the same as that in the top frame, but the vertical axis in the bottom frame plots the price level. Points J, E_0, and H in the bottom frame plot the three different assumed price levels and the corresponding level of real GDP from the

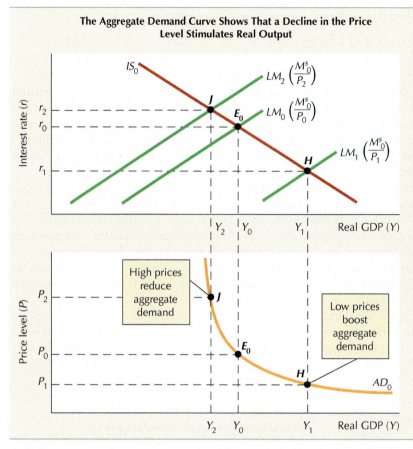

The Aggregate Demand Curve Shows That a Decline in the Price Level Stimulates Real Output

Figure 8-1 Effect on Real Income of Different Values of the Price Level

In the top frame, three different *LM* curves are drawn for three different hypothetical values of the price level. Corresponding to the three levels of the price level are three positions of equilibrium, *J*, E_0, and *H*. These three points are drawn again in the lower frame with the same horizontal axis (real income), but with the price level for the vertical axis. A drop in the price index from point *J* to E_0, and then to *H*, raises the *real* money supply and stimulates real output along the aggregate demand curve AD_0.

top frame. In this example, price level P_2 is twice as high as P_0, and P_0 is twice as high as P_1.

In the bottom frame, the aggregate demand curve (AD_0) connecting points *J*, E_0, and *H* shows all the possible combinations of *P* and *Y* consistent with the assumed level of the *nominal* money supply (M_0^s) and also with the assumed IS_0 curve. If the price level is higher, then real spending and real GDP are low, and vice versa. Because the level of real GDP along the *AD* curve is always at a point where the *IS* and *LM* curves cross in the upper frame, *everywhere along the* AD *curve both the commodity and money markets are in equilibrium.*

Why is the *AD* curve a curved line instead of a straight line? Its curvature indicates that a given decline in the price level will boost real GDP more when the price level is low than when the price level is high. This in turn occurs because a given decline in the price level creates a greater *percentage* decline in the price level, the lower is the price level. Consider reducing the price level by 0.5 from 2.0 to 1.5. This is a reduction of 0.5/2.0, or 25 percent. Reduce the price level by another 0.5 from 1.5 to 1.0. This is a reduction of 0.5/1.5, or 33 percent. Then reduce the price level by another 0.5 from 1.0 to 0.5. This is a reduction of 0.5/1.0, or 50 percent. In short, the lower the price level, the greater is the percentage reduction in the price level, and hence percentage increase in the real money supply and in real GDP, in response to a given reduction in the price level by a set amount such as 0.5.

8-3   Shifting the Aggregate Demand Curve with Monetary and Fiscal Policy

Effects of a Change in the Nominal Money Supply

The AD curve is fixed in position by the assumed value of the nominal money supply and the assumed position of the IS curve, which in turn depends on consumer and business confidence, fiscal policy, and net exports. A change in any of these assumed conditions will shift the position of the AD curve and thus change the amount of spending and real GDP at any given price level.

To understand the factors that shift the AD curve, we begin with a doubling of the nominal money supply, from M_0^s to M_1^s. The economy starts out at point E_0 in the top frame of Figure 8-2, the same position as in Figure 8-1. Doubling the money supply shifts the LM curve rightward to the new position LM_1. Since the price level has not changed, in the bottom frame the economy remains at the same vertical position as at point E_0 but moves horizontally to point H', which lies directly below point H' in the upper frame. The economy's real GDP is exactly the same at point H and H'.

But, since we drew the initial AD_0 curve on the assumption that price level P_1 is half of P_0, it follows that the price level at H' is double its value at H in the bottom frame. Similarly, every point along the new, higher AD_1

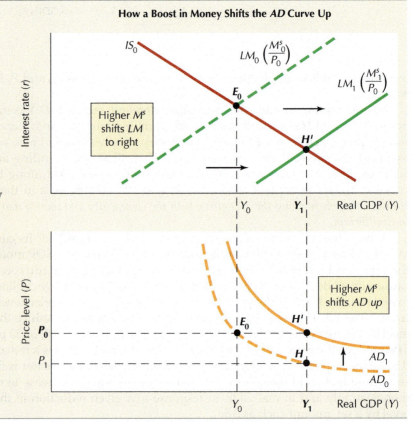

Figure 8-2 The Effect on the *AD* Curve of a Doubling of the Nominal Money Supply

In the top frame, a doubling of the nominal money supply from M_0^s to M_1^s moves the LM curve rightward from LM_0 to LM_1 and moves the economy's general equilibrium (where IS crosses LM) from point E_0 to point H'. In the lower frame, we remain at a vertical distance of P_0, since nothing has happened to the price level. The higher money supply raises real income and causes the economy's equilibrium position in the bottom frame to be at point H' rather than at point E_0. Notice that the new AD_1 curve running through point H' lies everywhere twice as high as the old AD_0 curve.

curve is twice as high as along the original AD_0 curve. *The general rule is that an increase in the nominal money supply by a given percentage shifts the AD curve vertically by the same percentage.*[2] Why? The price level must shift upward by the same percentage as the nominal money supply to keep the economy at a fixed level of real GDP. And, with a fixed IS curve as in the top frame of Figure 8-2, a constant level of real GDP requires a constant real money supply.

SELF-TEST

1. Would a steeper IS curve make the AD curve steeper or flatter?
2. Would a steeper LM curve make the AD curve steeper or flatter?

Effects of a Change in Autonomous Spending

In the last section, the IS curve remained fixed at its original position but an increase in the nominal money supply shifted the LM and AD curves. Now we reverse what is fixed and what changes. We hold fixed the nominal money supply but allow a drop in planned spending to shift the IS curve to the left. This change might occur because of a decline in consumer or business confidence, a decline in real wealth, a tightening of credit availability, a decline in government spending, an increase in tax rates, or a drop in the autonomous component of net exports.

When the IS curve shifts leftward in the top frame of Figure 8-3, the economy's equilibrium position shifts southwest from point E_0 to point F, at the crossing point of the new IS curve and the unchanged LM curve, drawn for the unchanged nominal money supply (M_0^s) and a given price level (P_0). In the bottom frame, if the price level remains at P_0, the economy shifts from point E_0 to point F. Real GDP falls from Y_0 to Y_3. The drop in planned spending creates a leftward shift in the AD curve.

Comparing the bottom frames of Figures 8-2 and 8-3, we note that the shifts in the AD curve are different. A change in the nominal money supply, as in Figure 8-2, shifts the AD curve up or down *vertically*. However, a change in autonomous spending in Figure 8-3 shifts the AD curve to the left or right *horizontally*. The decline in real GDP in the bottom frame that results from a given leftward shift in the IS curve is exactly the same, no matter whether the initial price level is low or high.

Will the reduction in planned spending reduce real income and leave the price level unchanged? Or will the reduction in planned spending reduce the price level and leave real income unchanged? Which outcome will occur? Figure 8-3 cannot tell us, because the AD curve by itself does not contain enough information to pin down both the price level and real income. To ascertain where the economy will come to rest along the numerous possible positions along the AD curve, we must find another schedule to intersect the AD curve. This is the SAS curve introduced in the next section.

---

[2] The proportional vertical movement in the AD schedule requires that all forms of real wealth double when the nominal money supply doubles.

Figure 8-3 The Effect on the *AD* Curve of a Decline in Planned Autonomous Spending

Any event that reduces planned autonomous spending by shifting the *IS* curve leftward also creates a parallel leftward shift in the *AD* curve. If the price level remains stable at P_0, the economy shifts leftward to point F and real income drops to Y_3. Another possibility is that the price level could drop to P_3, moving the economy down to point G and allowing real income to remain at the original Y_0. A drop in the price level to P_3 would increase the real money supply and shift the *LM* curve to the right in the top frame to a position that intersects the IS_1 line directly above Y_0.

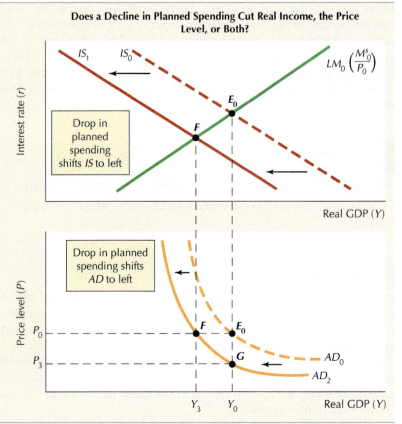

Does a Decline in Planned Spending Cut Real Income, the Price Level, or Both?

GLOBAL ECONOMIC CRISIS FOCUS

The Crisis Was a Demand Problem Not Involving Supply

The Global Economic Crisis starting in 2008 occurred primarily because of a sharp leftward shift in the aggregate demand *(AD)* curve. As we learned in Chapters 4 and 5, the crisis originated in the U.S. financial market as a result of the housing bubble, lax regulation, financial innovation, securitization, and monetary policy so stimulative that it fed the housing bubble. The crisis spread rapidly to foreign countries because of the interconnections between capital markets and the fact that many foreign banks owned mortgage-backed securities that ultimately turned out to be "toxic," backed by mortgages on which borrowers had stopped making payments.

We can tell that the aggregate supply curve (introduced in the next two sections) did not play an important role in the crisis. The inflation rate and the price level remained relatively stable, indicating that the economy remained in about the same vertical position in the bottom frame of Figure 8-4. What changed was the value of real GDP along the horizontal axis. The economy moved straight west in the crisis as between points E_0 and point F and did not move to the northwest or southwest.

Learning About Diagrams: The *AD* Curve

The aggregate demand (*AD*) curve, as drawn in the bottom frames of Figures 8-1 to 8-3, summarizes everything we have already learned about the *IS-LM* model and adds a single new ingredient, the ability of the price level to change instead of remaining fixed (as in Chapters 3–7).

Diagram Elements and Reasons for Slope

The vertical axis is the price level and the horizontal axis is the level of real GDP.

The *AD* curve shows all the possible crossing points of a single *IS* commodity-market equilibrium curve with the various *LM* money-market equilibrium curves drawn for each possible price level. Everywhere along the *AD* curve *both* the commodity (*IS*) and money (*LM*) markets are in equilibrium (as shown in Figure 8-1).

The *AD* curve slopes downward because a lower price level (*P*) raises the real money supply, thereby lowering the interest rate and stimulating planned expenditures. This stimulus requires an increase in actual real GDP (*Y*) to keep the commodity market in equilibrium. The steeper the *IS* curve, the steeper the *AD* curve.

What Shifts the *AD* Curve?

The *AD* curve is drawn for a fixed nominal supply of money (*M^s*) and a fixed set of determinants of the *IS* curve (business and consumer confidence, government spending, tax rates, autonomous net taxes, and the autonomous component of net exports).

A given percentage increase in the nominal money supply will shift the *AD* curve *vertically* upward by a similar percentage.

Anything that shifts the *IS* curve creates a parallel *horizontal* shift in the *AD* curve in the same direction. The *amount* of the horizontal shift of the *AD* curve is usually less than that of the *IS* curve, because of the crowding out effect.[a]

The following is a list of factors that will shift the *AD* curve to the right. The opposite changes will shift the *AD* curve to the left.

An increase in autonomous consumption due to
An increase in consumer optimism

An increase in stock market or housing wealth
A decrease in the interest rate due to a reduction in the demand for money caused, for instance, by the invention of credit cards
An increase in the willingness of financial institutions to lend to consumers and business firms
An increase in government spending
A reduction in either autonomous taxes or the income tax rate
An increase in the marginal propensity to consume
An increase in foreign income that raises exports
A reduction in the share of GDP spent on imports
A depreciation of the exchange rate that boosts net exports

What Is True of Points That Are Off the *AD* Curve?

The entire area to the right of the *AD* curve has an excess supply of commodities; too much is being produced relative to the demand for goods and services at that price level.

The entire area to the left of the *AD* curve has an excess demand for commodities; too little is being produced relative to the demand for goods and services at that price level.

At any point off the *AD* curve, there is pressure for change. For instance, at a point with excess production to the right of the *AD* curve, there is unplanned inventory accumulation, which places downward pressure on production. There is also downward pressure on prices as firms attempt to boost sales with lower prices.[b]

---

[a] For details, see equation (10) in the Appendix to Chapter 4. For any given change in, say, government spending, the *IS* curve shifts in the same direction by the multiplier *k*, while the *AD* curve shifts in the same direction by the multiplier k_1, defined in equation (10).

[b] The equation of the *AD* curve is the income equation (9) in the Appendix to Chapter 4.

$$Y = k_1 A'_p + k_2 \frac{M^s}{P}$$

8-4   Alternative Shapes of the Short-Run Aggregate Supply Curve

The short-run aggregate supply schedule shows how much business firms are willing to produce at different hypothetical price levels. Such a schedule of business firms' behavior can have several possible shapes. Depending on the shape, the implications of a shift in the *AD* curve are quite different. In Figure 8-4 we show a rightward shift in the *AD* curve from AD_0 to AD_1.

How will the increase in aggregate demand be divided between a higher level of real GDP and a higher price level? Three hypothetical answers, corresponding to three hypothetical aggregate supply curves, are shown in Figure 8-4. In Chapters 3–7 we assumed that the price level always remains fixed; thus we assumed that the economy moved from its initial position E_0 directly rightward to a higher level of real GDP at point E_1 along the horizontal aggregate supply curve. Thus throughout Chapters 3–7 we were assuming a horizontal aggregate supply curve like that shown in Figure 8-4.

A second possibility is that real GDP is always fixed at the level of natural real GDP. If so, the same increase in aggregate demand would have no effect at all on real GDP. Instead, business firms would simply raise the price level from P_0 to a higher price level at point E_3 along the vertical aggregate supply curve in Figure 8-4, leaving their level of production (Y) unchanged. As we shall see, natural real GDP is the only output level consistent with equilibrium in the labor market.

A third possibility is shown by the line labeled "positively sloped aggregate supply curve." If this curve were valid, then the rightward shift in the *AD* curve would cause business firms to raise *both* their prices and their level of production, moving the economy to a point like E_2. As we shall see, a point like E_2 is likely to be achieved only temporarily.

The choice among the three shapes of the aggregate supply curve in Figure 8-4 has created decades of controversy in macroeconomics. The horizontal supply curve that was assumed in our fixed-price analysis of Chapters 3–7 is very convenient but unrealistic, since it cannot explain why the inflation rate is not always zero. The vertical supply curve is a convenient shortcut for analyzing periods of very rapid inflation, since it implies that changes in the money supply mainly or entirely affect the inflation rate with minor or negligible effects on real output. The third, positively sloping alternative seems more realistic, at least for the short run.

In the next section, we shall see that the positively sloped line in Figure 8-4 is the short-run aggregate supply (*SAS*) curve introduced at the beginning of this chapter. It is valid only in the short run, a period short enough for the price

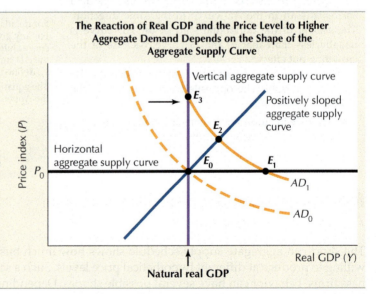

Figure 8-4 Effect of a Rightward Shift in the *AD* Curve with Three Alternative Short-Run Aggregate Supply Curves

The horizontal supply curve at the price level P_0 reflects the "fixed price" assumption of Chapters 3–7. An increase in aggregate demand that shifts the AD_0 curve to AD_1 will move the economy from its initial position E_0 to new position E_1. In contrast, if the supply curve is vertical, higher aggregate demand pushes the economy from point E_0 to E_3. An intermediate possibility is that both output and prices rise *in the short run* to a point such as E_2, and that *in the long run* the *boost* in real GDP gradually disappears until we arrive at E_3

The Reaction of Real GDP and the Price Level to Higher Aggregate Demand Depends on the Shape of the Aggregate Supply Curve

level to adjust but during which the nominal wage rate temporarily remains fixed. Also in the next section, we shall learn that the vertical line in Figure 8-4 is the long-run aggregate supply (*LAS*) curve that applies after nominal wage rates have fully adjusted to any changes in the price level.

8-5   The Short-Run Aggregate Supply (*SAS*) Curve When the Nominal Wage Rate Is Constant

We are now ready to learn why aggregate demand shocks, taking the form of changes in the nominal money supply or in any of the factors that can shift the *IS* curve, will change *both* real GDP and the price level. Will a demand shock change the price level more than it changes real GDP, or will the demand shock change real GDP more than the price level? The answer depends on the slope of the *SAS* curve.

In this section we show that the positively-sloped *SAS* curve of Figure 8-4 is based on the idea that the price level is flexible but input costs are fixed in the short run. As long as those input costs remain fixed, the positively-sloped *SAS* curve retains a fixed position. But if input costs rise, the *SAS* curve shifts up, while if input costs fall, the *SAS* curve shifts down.

What Is Held Constant Along the *SAS* Curve?

When a business firm raises the prices of the goods and services it sells, but its input costs remain constant, then the profit earned by the business firm increases. The higher profits motivate the firm to produce more. For instance, during the fall of 2010 the nation's wheat farmers were busy calculating how much more wheat to produce in response to an increase in the price of wheat that occurred in summer 2010, due to a severe drought in Russia that reduced Russian production of wheat. The key insight behind the *SAS* curve is:

Higher product price + fixed input costs => higher profits => higher output

The key input costs that are held constant along the *SAS* curve are the nominal wage rate, prices of raw materials, and the level of productivity and technology.

The nominal wage rate.   Along any given *SAS* curve the nominal wage rate is fixed. We first encountered the distinction between nominal and real variables in Chapter 2, where we learned about nominal and real GDP. The nominal wage rate is simply the actual wage rate paid (*W*). The real wage rate (*W/P*) is the nominal wage rate (*W*) divided by the price level (*P*).

Whenever the nominal wage rate increases, the *SAS* curve shifts its position upward, while whenever the nominal wage rate decreases, the *SAS* curve shifts its position downward. The assumed fixity of the nominal wage rate is a simplification to represent the fact that nominal wage rates tend to adjust very slowly to ups and downs of production over the business cycle.

The tendency of nominal wage rates to adjust slowly occurs for three main reasons.

1. First, formal or informal contracts set nominal wage rates for a considerable period of time. Most professors are paid a fixed salary for a full year, while airline pilots belonging to labor unions often have their wages

fixed for three to five years. While wages remain fixed, any increase in the product price will raise business profits, encouraging more output to be produced. For instance, in 2010 airline fares increased by 25 percent or more from 2009 but wages did not, greatly increasing airline profits and providing an incentive for airlines to add more planes and more flights.

2. Even when there are no formal contracts between workers and firms, wage rates can remain fixed for a substantial period of time. Management time is scarce, and managers lack time to think every day about what their employees' wages and salaries should be. They tend to postpone decisions about wage changes until a set time of year, perhaps once every six or twelve months.

3. Firms may be reluctant to cut wages when output declines. Wage reductions tend to reduce worker morale and work effort, and some of the firm's best workers may quit and move to other firms if wages are cut.

Prices of raw materials. Besides wages and salaries paid to workers, the next most important input cost is that of raw materials, such as energy (including electricity, coal, oil, and natural gas). The price of oil is an important source of shifts in the *SAS* curve, which shifts upward and to the left when oil prices go up as in 2007–08 and downward to the right when oil prices decline as in 2008–09.

Productivity and technology. The profit of a firm depends not just on the wage rate of a worker but on how much that worker can produce. If a counter worker at McDonalds is paid $10 per hour and serves 20 customers per hour, the labor cost per customer is $0.50. But if McDonalds redesigns work practices and installs better equipment, the worker may be able to serve 40 customers per hour, reducing the labor cost per customer from $0.50 to $0.25. An improvement in productivity, whether caused by better machines, newer technology, or reorganization of business practices, shifts the *SAS* curve downward to the right.

The Short-Run Aggregate Supply (SAS) Curve

The line connecting points *A*, *B*, and *C* in the left frame of Figure 8-5 is the *SAS* curve. It has the same appearance as the positively sloped *SAS* curve in Figure 8-4, except that now it is drawn as a curve rather than as a straight line. To the right of the label SAS_0 the assumed initial constant wage rate W_0 is listed in parentheses. If the wage rate rises above W_0 the *SAS* curve will shift its position upward. To simplify the diagram, we do not list explicitly on the graph the two other major factors that can shift the *SAS* curve that were examined previously, namely the prices of raw materials and the level of productivity and technology.

We start at point *B* where the price level is P_0 and real GDP is Y_0. What happens if the price level rises? Since the price level is plotted on the vertical axis, we know that the *SAS* curve does not shift its position. A general rule of graphs is that a change in the variable on the horizontal or vertical axis in any graph *does not cause a change in the curve or relationship, just a movement along the curve*. Thus an increase in the price level from P_0 to P_1 moves the economy from the initial point *B* to the new point *C* where real GDP is the higher level Y_1. Because the wage rate (W_0) as well as the prices of raw materials and the level of productivity and technology are fixed along the SAS_0 curve, the higher price flows straight into the profit margin of business firms, inducing them to produce more output. Similarly, the price level falls from P_0 to the lower P_2, then the economy will move downward from the initial point *B* to point *A*.

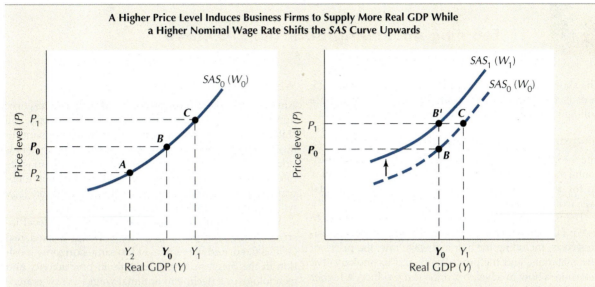

A Higher Price Level Induces Business Firms to Supply More Real GDP While a Higher Nominal Wage Rate Shifts the *SAS* Curve Upwards

Figure 8-5 The Short-Run Aggregate Supply *(SAS)* Curve for Two Different Values of the Wage Rate, W_0 and W_1

The left frame shows that along the SAS_0 curve an increase in the price level raises the level of real GDP. Since the SAS_0 curve assumes a fixed nominal wage rate (W_0), fixed prices of raw materials, and fixed productivity and technology, any increase in the price level such as that between P_0 and P_1 raises profits and induces firms to produce more real GDP. The right frame shows that when the nominal wage rises from W_0 to W_1, the entire *SAS* curve shifts upward from the initial curve SAS_0 to the new curve SAS_1.

Following an increase in the price level the nominal wage rate will not stay fixed forever. Workers can see that the price level has risen, thus decreasing the buying power of their fixed nominal wage. They will want a wage increase, but this may be delayed until the expiration of the formal or informal wage contracts or until the customary date when management considers wage increases. Firms will respond to worker demands by raising wages, both because they can afford to (since their profits have risen) and for fear that the best workers will quit and go to work for other firms.

When the nominal wage rate rises from W_0 to W_1 the SAS_0 curve shifts upward to the new higher curve SAS_1. In the right frame of Figure 8-5, we assume that W_1 exceeds W_0 by the same percentage as P_1 exceeds P_0:

$$\frac{W_1}{P_1} = \frac{W_0}{P_0}$$

Because the wage rate has risen as much as the price level, the firm's profits fall back to the original level that occurred when real GDP was Y_0. Both sides of the equation represent the equilibrium real wage at which output is constant at Y_0. Since both the wage and price level have increased, the economy's position is at point B', which shares the same real GDP as the initial point B but a higher wage and price level. The real wage is important, because the increase in the firm's profit that motivated the initial movement from point B to point C occurred because the price level increased while the wage level did not. This decline in the real wage could not last because workers would insist on enough of a wage

Learning About Diagrams: The *SAS* Curve

The short-run aggregate supply curve, abbreviated *SAS*, depicts the amount of output that business firms are willing to produce at different alternative price levels.

Diagram Elements and Reasons for Slope

The *SAS* curve is plotted with the same vertical and horizontal axes as the *AD* curve; the aggregate price level is on the vertical axis and real GDP is on the horizontal axis. Examples are shown in Figure 8-5.

The *SAS* curve slopes up because it allows the price to rise or fall while holding constant all components of business costs, including the nominal wage rate, the prices of raw materials, and the productivity and technology that determines how much each worker can produce. A higher price level raises business profits because costs are fixed, thus providing an incentive for each business firm to produce more real GDP.

The following discussion assumes that at point *B* in the left frame of Figure 8-5, the assumed wage level (W_0) along the SAS_0 curve, divided by the price level (P_0), is the **equilibrium real wage** (W_0/P_0). As usual we define an equilibrium as a situation in which there is no pressure for change. Thus at point *B* the forces of the supply and demand for labor have established a particular real wage as the equilibrium level. At a lower real wage, workers will be dissatisfied and demand a return in the real wage to its equilibrium level, and at a higher real wage firms will be dissatisfied and demand a return in the real wage to its equilibrium level.

What Shifts the *SAS* Curve?

Anything that raises business costs will shift the *SAS* curve upwards and anything that reduces business costs will shift the *SAS* curve downward. The main determinants of business costs are nominal wage rates, raw materials prices, and productivity and technology. Increases in wage rates or raw materials prices will shift the *SAS* curve upward and improvements in productivity and technology will shift the *SAS* curve downward.

When the nominal wage rate and the price level increase by the same percentage, the real wage is fixed, real GDP is fixed, and we remain at the same horizontal position in the diagram. Improvements in productivity and technology or a decline in nominal wages or raw materials prices will shift the *SAS* curve downward.

What Is True of Points That Are Off the *SAS* Curve?

Since the *SAS* curve shows the different combinations of the price level and real GDP consistent with the maximization of profits by business firms, any point off the *SAS* curve would not be chosen by these firms.

A point to the right of the *SAS* curve indicates that firms are producing too much, and that the price level is below the cost of production. Firms would boost profits by a decrease in output. Similarly a point to the left of the *SAS* curve indicates that firms are producing too little and should raise production until they get back onto the *SAS* curve.

The **equilibrium real wage rate** is the amount determined by the supply and demand for pressure; at this real wage rate there is no pressure for change in the real wage.

increase to return to the initial equilibrium real wage. Even though explicit and implicit wage contracts may keep the nominal wage fixed for a limited period, there will always be pressure for the nominal wage rate to rise whenever the real wage rate W/P is pushed below its initial equilibrium level W_0/P_0.

 SELF-TEST

Which of the following causes a movement *along* the short-run aggregate supply (*SAS*) curve, and which causes a shift in the curve? If the curve shifts, does it shift up or down?

1. A union concession that reduces the wage rate to help a firm survive foreign competition.

2. A discovery of a giant oil field in Missouri that reduces the price of oil.

3. An increase in the money supply.

4. An increase in the GDP deflator.

8-6   Fiscal and Monetary Expansion in the Short and Long Run

In Chapter 4 we examined the effect of expansionary monetary policy, assuming that the price level was fixed. We found that either a monetary or fiscal stimulus would normally raise real GDP. Now we have eliminated the previous restriction that the price level must remain fixed. As a result a monetary or fiscal expansion raises both output and the price level in the short run, but in the long run only the price level is increased while output falls back to its initial level.

In the following example we will take the specific example of a fiscal stimulus, but the same analysis applies to a monetary stimulus or indeed any factor that would shift the aggregate demand (AD) curve to the right, including an increase in real wealth, easier availability of credit in financial markets, a burst of investor optimism, or a jump in exports due to high foreign demand.

Initial Short-Run Effect of a Fiscal Expansion

In Figure 8-6, we begin in equilibrium at point B with the price level equal to P_0 and real GDP equal to Y_0. Now a fiscal stimulus is introduced, in the form of an increase in government purchases that shifts the aggregate demand curve rightward from AD_0 to AD_1. Where do we find the new equilibrium levels of output and the price index? If the price level were to remain constant, we would move straight to the right from point B to point L. But the price level

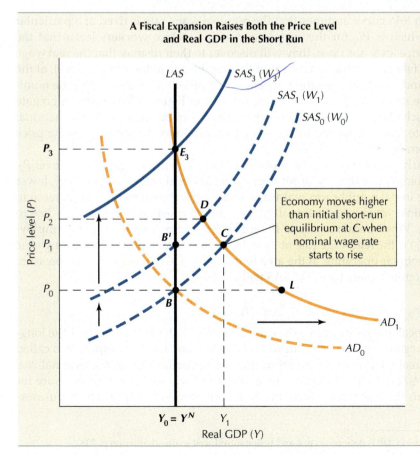

A Fiscal Expansion Raises Both the Price Level and Real GDP in the Short Run

Figure 8-6 Effects on the Price Level and Real Income of an Increase in Planned Autonomous Spending from AD_0 to AD_1

Higher planned autonomous spending shifts the economy's equilibrium position from the initial point B to point C, where both the price level and the real output have increased. Point C is not a sustainable position, however, because the real wage rate has fallen below the equilibrium real wage rate. Only at point E_3 does the actual real wage rate return to its initial equilibrium value.

cannot remain fixed, because firms will insist on an increase in the price level in order to raise their profits enough to induce them to increase the level of real GDP. In short, point L is not a point at which firms will be willing to produce.

Point C is at the intersection of the new AD_1 schedule and the SAS_0 schedule. The increase in government purchases has simultaneously raised the price level to P_1 and increased output to Y_1. This shift has occurred because higher aggregate demand has raised prices, stimulating business firms to produce more, at least as long as the wage rate fails to adjust.

Note that output has not increased by the full Chapter 4 multiplier based on a fixed price level, the horizontal distance between B and L. Instead, point C lies northwest of the constant price point L, because the higher price level at C reduces the real money supply and hence the demand for commodities. The situation illustrated in Figure 8-6 at point C would result from any stimulative factor that raises aggregate demand, as summarized in the box on p. 237. As long as the SAS curve slopes upward to the right, any of these changes will shift the AD curve rightward and simultaneously raise both output and prices to point C along the SAS_0 curve that is held fixed by the constant nominal wage W_0.

The Rising Nominal Wage Rate and the Arrival at Long-Run Equilibrium

Point C is not the end of the adjustment of the economy to the higher level of government purchases. Business firms are satisfied but workers are not because the price level has risen from P_0 to P_1, while the nominal wage rate is still stuck at W_0. The real wage rate has decreased to W_0/P_1.

Each SAS curve assumes that the nominal wage rate is fixed at a particular value, which is W_0 for the supply curve SAS_0. Once workers learn that the actual price level has risen, they will discover to their dismay that the real wage rate has fallen. To achieve a return of their real wage to the original level, at the next round of wage bargaining, workers will insist on an increase in the nominal wage rate to W_1. Just as in the right frame of Figure 8-5, the new aggregate supply schedule SAS_1 shows the consequences of an increase in the nominal wage rate from W_0 to W_1, in the same proportion as the increase of the price level from P_0 to P_1.

Clearly the economy now moves to point D, with a higher price level P_2. But at point D workers are upset once again. The real wage rate is W_1/P_2, lower than the initial equilibrium real wage rate. Again they insist on an increase in the nominal wage rate. Eventually the economy must slide up the AD_1 line to point E_3. Why? Because only at the initial level of real GDP (Y_0) and employment (N_0) is the real wage rate at its initial equilibrium value (W_0/P_0). Any time the economy is operating in the area to the right of Y_0, there is upward pressure on the nominal wage rate, and SAS will shift up.

The Long-Run Aggregate Supply Curve

The vertical line rising above the original real GDP level (Y_0) is called the long-run aggregate supply (LAS) curve. Only at this one level of output, also called natural real GDP (Y^N), is the labor market in equilibrium at the original real wage (W_0/P_0).[3] This is the only level of output where there is no pressure for change in the real wage, since this is the only level of output where business

---

[3] Natural real GDP is defined on p. 4 and is first introduced in this chapter on p. 238.

Summary of the Economy's Adjustment to an Increase in Aggregate Demand

Is the economy in short-run (SR) or long-run (LR) equilibrium in Figure 8-6 on p. 243?

Point	AD curve, initial or new?	Price level	Wage level	Output level	In SR or LR equilibrium?
B	Initial	P_0	W_0	Y^N	SR, LR
C	New	P_1	W_0	Y_1	SR
D	New	P_2	W_1	Above Y^N, Below Y_1	SR
E_3	New	P_3	W_3	Y^N	SR, LR

firms are willing to produce and where workers are content with the real wage rate. *The vertical LAS line shows all the possible combinations of the price level (P) and natural real GDP (Y^N).* It was initially defined on p. 232.

Short-Run and Long-Run Equilibrium

The economy is in **short-run equilibrium** when two conditions are satisfied. First, the level of output produced must be enough to balance the demand for commodities. This first condition is satisfied at any point along the appropriate *AD* curve. Second, the price level *P* must be sufficient to make firms both able and willing to produce the level of output specified along the *AD* curve. This can happen only along a short-run supply (*SAS*) curve specified for a particular nominal wage rate (W_0).

   The economy is in **long-run equilibrium** only when all the conditions for a short-run equilibrium are satisfied, and, in addition, the real wage rate is at its equilibrium value. In Figure 8-6, long-run equilibrium occurs only where all three schedules—*AD*, *SAS*, and *LAS*—intersect. The reason why the economy does not move immediately to its new long-run equilibrium following an *AD* shift is that adjustment takes time and there are time lags in the response of wages and prices.

Short-run equilibrium occurs at the point where the aggregate demand curve crosses the short-run aggregate supply curve.

Long-run equilibrium is a situation in which labor input is the amount voluntarily supplied and demanded at the equilibrium real wage rate.

 SELF-TEST

If the economy is to remain in long-run equilibrium, what must happen to the price level, the wage level, and the level of real GDP when the following events occur?

1. An increase in government-financed highway construction.

2. An increase in Japanese GDP that boosts U.S. net exports.

3. An increase in the U.S. money supply.

4. An increase in productivity caused by more use of computers (while the money supply is constant).

Interpretations of the Business Cycle

The preceding theory of price and output adjustment relies on an asymmetry between price and wage adjustment. In the short run, prices are flexible while the nominal wage rate is fixed. A realistic explanation of this asymmetry is that the nominal wage or salary for many types of jobs is changed only infrequently, sometimes only once per year, and in labor union contracts not for three years or more. The assumed short-run fixity of the nominal wage rate together with the flexibility of the price level implies a **countercyclical** movement of the real wage; that is, a movement in the real wage in the opposite direction from the movement in real GDP. However, statistical studies of data for the United States do not show a strong or consistent countercyclical movement of the real wage. In reality, movements in the real wage are relatively minor compared to the volatile movements of real GDP over the business cycle (see Figure 3-1 on p. 55).

A **countercyclical variable** moves over the business cycle in the opposite direction from real GDP.

An alternative view of the theory is that *both* prices and wages are fixed in the short run, and that the *SAS* curve is relatively flat. Just as the nominal wage rate is set by labor contracts and customs that alter wages only infrequently, so do many prices remain the same for long periods of time. Prices for many products are set in advance, including prices on restaurant menus and in mail-order catalogs. Firms buy supplies at prices that are fixed for long periods of time. We return to theories of wage and price rigidity in Chapter 17. There we will learn that there are good reasons for both prices and wages to adjust only slowly over time. When real GDP rises above equilibrium (or natural) real GDP, a process is set in motion that causes *both* prices and wages to rise, and there is inflationary pressure until the economy returns to a point along the *LAS* curve like point E_3 in Figure 8-6.

8-7 Classical Macroeconomics: The Quantity Theory of Money and the Self-Correcting Economy

The economy's **self-correcting forces** refer to the role of flexible prices in stabilizing real GDP under some conditions.

The classical economists who predated Keynes's *General Theory*, including Adam Smith, David Ricardo, John Stuart Mill, Alfred Marshall, and Arthur C. Pigou, believed that the economy possessed powerful **self-correcting forces** that guaranteed full employment and prevented actual real GDP (Y) from falling below natural real GDP (Y^N) for more than a short time. These forces consisted of flexible wages and prices, which would adjust rapidly to absorb the impact of shifts in aggregate demand. Because the classical economists did not believe that business cycles in real output or in unemployment were problems, they saw no need for the government to stabilize the economy with monetary or fiscal policy.

The Quantity Equation and the Quantity Theory of Money

The most important macroeconomic model developed by classical economists is the famous "quantity equation," relating the nominal money supply (M^s) and velocity (V) to the price level (P) and real GDP (Y).

$$M^s V \equiv PY \tag{8.2}$$

The quantity equation is true by definition, simply because velocity is *defined* as $V \equiv PY/M^s$. (*Note*: Velocity was first defined in the box on p. 93.)

To convert the quantity equation into a theory, classical economists assumed that any change in M^s or V on the left-hand side of the equation would be balanced by a proportional change in P on the right-hand side of the equation, with no change in real GDP (Y). Primary emphasis in this theory, called the **quantity theory of money**, was placed on the idea that changes in the money supply (M^s) cause proportional changes in the price level P. Why did the theory focus on M^s rather than V? Velocity (V) was regarded as being relatively stable and primarily determined by changes in payment methods (for instance, cash versus checks) that gradually evolved over time. Over shorter periods of two to five years, business cycles were attributed mainly to changes in the money supply.

Any theory can be analyzed in terms of the quantity equation (8.2). For instance, the *IS-LM* model of Chapter 4 examines the effect of a change in government spending, which causes a shift in the *IS* curve but not in the *LM* curve, reflecting the assumption that changes in government spending do not change the money supply. Since both M^s and P are fixed, higher government spending raises V on the left-hand side of equation (8.2) and raises Y on the right-hand side. In this sense, the analysis of shifts in planned spending in the fixed-price *IS-LM* model is the opposite of the quantity theory, linking changes of V to changes in Y, unlike the quantity theory that links changes in M^s to changes in P.

The **quantity theory of money** holds that actual output tends to grow steadily, while velocity is determined by payment practices such as the use of cash versus checks; as a result, a change in the money supply mainly affects the price level and has little or no effect on velocity or output.

Self-Correction in the Aggregate Demand-Supply Model

The approach of the old classicists, whose analytical model primarily relied on the quantity theory of money, can be translated into the aggregate demand and supply model developed in this chapter. Figure 8-7 has the same elements as Figure 8-6 but lacks a short-run aggregate supply (*SAS*) curve.

The classical economists assumed that the economy would not operate away from the long-run aggregate supply curve (*LAS*). For instance, if a decline in demand caused the *AD* curve to shift downward from AD_0 to AD_1 in

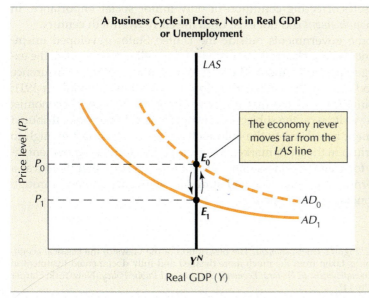

A Business Cycle in Prices, Not in Real GDP or Unemployment

The economy never moves far from the *LAS* line

Figure 8-7 Effect of a Decline in Planned Spending When the Price Level Is Perfectly Flexible

The classical economists assumed that the price level would decline whenever a drop in aggregate demand occurred. Starting from point E_0, a drop in planned spending would shift the *AD* curve from AD_0 to AD_1 and move the economy straight down to point E_1. The level of real GDP remains at Y^N, because the lower price level raises the level of real balances (M_0^s/P) by exactly enough to offset the decline in planned spending. A shift back to AD_0 would raise the price level and return the economy to the original position E_0.

Figure 8-7, the classical economists would predict that the economy would move from the initial point E_0 to the new point E_1 with only a brief interval (shown by the curved arrow on the left) during which actual real GDP would decline below natural real GDP. The price level would promptly decline from its initial level at P_0 to the new level P_1.

The classical economists took the same view of the economy's behavior in response to an increase in aggregate demand. With Y above Y^N, firms would raise nominal wage rates and prices. Wage and price increases would continue until production fell back to the Y^N level.

Because the downward and upward movement of the economy from E_0 to E_1 and back again would not involve any significant movement of real GDP (Y) away from natural real GDP (Y^N), *no business cycle in real GDP would occur.* Yet there would be a business cycle in the price level, from P_0 down to P_1 and back to P_0, and it was this movement in the price level that the classical economists attempted to explain in their early theories of the business cycle. However, classical economists did not view price movements as sufficiently undesirable to warrant the intervention of government monetary or fiscal policy.

Classical View of Unemployment and Output Fluctuations

We have seen that classical economists did not believe that real GDP could remain for more than a short period below natural real GDP (Y^N). How, then, did they explain the unemployment that occurs in real-world modern economies when people are laid off and production is cut back? Jobless individuals were sometimes written off as irresponsible, having an insufficient desire to work. Any normal person would be compelled by hunger to seek work, some classical economists thought. And most believed that if there were not enough jobs to go around, competition among workers would reduce the real wage rate until an equilibrium was obtained in the labor market.

Although some journalists and a few isolated economists (including Karl Marx and Friedrich Engels) began to suggest that unemployment was an inevitable by-product of the newly emerging industrial society of England in the mid-nineteenth century, most classical economists dismissed unemployment as a transitory, self-correcting condition of only minor social importance. In fact, the term *unemployment* did not exist until the early twentieth century.

Ironically, some governments outside the United States developed unemployment insurance before classical economists were willing to recognize the existence of prolonged unemployment. The world's first unemployment insurance system was introduced in the United Kingdom by Winston Churchill in 1911; only afterward, in 1913, was the first important book by a classical economist (Arthur C. Pigou) written on the subject of unemployment.[4] The book attributed such unemployment as existed to the failure of wages to adjust fast enough to maintain equilibrium in the labor market. Suggested cures for unemployment involved remedies for wage stickiness rather than any suggestion that there was a role for the government to intervene and stimulate aggregate demand through expansionary monetary or fiscal policy.

---

[4] This was Arthur C. Pigou's *Unemployment*. The description of the views of the classical economists in this section is taken from the much more detailed and fully documented treatment in John A. Garraty, *Unemployment in History: Economic Thought and Public Policy* (New York: Harper & Row, 1978), pp. 70–145.

8-8   The Keynesian Revolution: The Failure of Self-Correction

The Great Depression began with the stock market crash in late 1929 and by 1932 real GDP had declined by one-third and unemployment had spiraled upward beyond 20 percent. Classical economists were caught flat-footed, without any explanation for the severe and prolonged unemployment beyond the claim that for some reason real wages were too high. Economics had lost its intellectual moorings, and it was time for a new diagnosis. In this atmosphere, it was perhaps not surprising that the 1936 publication of Keynes's *The General Theory of Employment, Interest, and Money* was eagerly awaited. Its publication transformed macroeconomics, and only one year later John R. Hicks published an article in which he set out the *IS-LM* model of Chapter 4 as an interpretation of what Keynes had written.

John Maynard Keynes (1883–1946)

His *The General Theory of Employment, Interest, and Money* (1936) was one of the most influential works in economics in the twentieth century.

Monetary Impotence and the Failure of Self-Correction in Extreme Cases

We can use the aggregate demand and supply curves to illustrate Keynes's analysis of the high unemployment that bedeviled the world's economy in the 1930s. For Keynes, the economic problem could be divided into two categories: one concerning demand and one concerning supply. The demand problem was the possibility of **monetary impotence,** while the supply problem was that of **rigid wages.**

Unresponsive expenditures: The vertical *IS* curve. As we learned in Section 4-8 on pp. 105–06, increases in the real money supply (M^s/P) can have either strong or weak effects, depending on the shapes of the *IS* and *LM* curves. One case of monetary impotence occurs when the *IS* curve is vertical. Any change in the nominal money supply shifts the *LM* curve up and down along the vertical *IS* curve, leaving real GDP unaffected. Just as important, any decline in the price level (P) that raises the real money supply (M^s/P) leaves real GDP unaffected.

We examined a vertical *IS* curve in Figure 4-7; now, in Figure 8-8, we observe its implications for the aggregate demand curve. If *IS* is vertical at an income

Monetary impotence is the failure of real GDP to respond to an increase in the real money supply.

Rigid wages refers to the failure of the nominal wage rate to adjust by the amount needed to maintain equilibrium in the labor market.

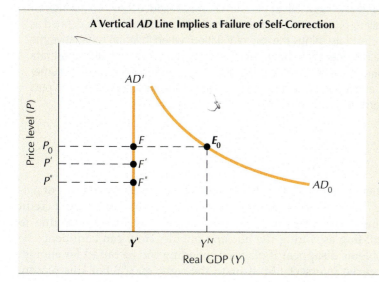

A Vertical *AD* Line Implies a Failure of Self-Correction

Figure 8-8 The Lack of Effect of a Drop in the Price Level When There Is a Failure of Self-Correction

The conditions of a failure of self-correction are either (1) a vertical *IS* curve that lies to the left of Y^N, or (2) a normal *IS* curve that intersects a horizontal *LM* curve to the left of Y^N. With a failure of self-correction, the aggregate demand schedule is a vertical line like AD', in contrast to the normally sloped AD_0 curve. Because of a failure of self-correction, the higher real money supply is unable to stimulate the economy; thus, a decline in the price level just moves the economy down from F to F' to F''.

level like Y', then a decline in P has no power to raise real GDP above Y', so the aggregate demand curve is the vertical line AD' in Figure 8-8. Shown for contrast in Figure 8-8 is a normally sloped AD_0 curve, copied from Figure 8-6.

The liquidity trap: A horizontal *LM* curve. The same problem of a vertical AD' curve may occur if there is a horizontal *LM* curve and *if the* IS *curve intersects this horizontal* LM *curve to the left of* Y^N (a nearly horizontal *LM* curve was illustrated in the bottom frame of Figure 4-8 on p. 101). In this case, an increase in M^s/P does not shift the *LM* curve down. Real GDP is stuck at, for example, point Y', where the horizontal *LM* curve crosses the normally sloped *IS* curve. Again, the aggregate demand curve is vertical, as in Figure 8-8.

Monetary impotence and a failure of self-correction arise when there is a vertical *IS* or horizontal *LM* curve. In either case, the classical cure-all of deflation cannot remedy a cyclical recession or depression. In Figure 8-8, the price level can fall continuously, from P_0 to P' to P'', yet real GDP remains stuck at Y'. The economy just moves downward vertically from point F to F' to F'', without any rightward motion, as would be needed to return the economy from the depression level of real GDP (Y') to the desired level of real GDP (Y^N).

GLOBAL ECONOMIC CRISIS FOCUS

The Zero Lower Bound as Another Source of Monetary Impotence

The "zero lower bound" was introduced in Chapter 4 (bottom of p. 104) as another source of monetary impotence. The zero lower bound refers to the fact that the nominal interest rate cannot be negative, because that would mean that banks *would pay borrowers to borrow money*, leading the demand for loans instantly to reach infinity. As we learned on pp. 110–11, in the United States during the late 1930s, in Japan in the late 1990s, and in the United States since early 2009 the nominal short-term interest rate had reached zero. Thus no matter how much the Fed raises the money supply, it cannot reduce the interest rate. In this section we are considering the effect of a falling price level in raising the real money supply, and likewise a falling price level cannot reduce the nominal interest rate. In fact a falling price level increases the *real* interest rate (which is defined as the nominal interest rate minus the rate of inflation; when inflation is negative the real interest rate is higher than the nominal interest rate). A rising real interest rate caused by a falling price level reduces the demand for interest-sensitive consumer durable goods and business investment in equipment and structures and puts further downward pressure on real GDP.

Fiscal Policy and the Real Balance Effect

The crucial problem that makes the AD' curve in Figure 8-8 lie to the left of natural real GDP (Y^N) includes some combination of low real wealth, tight credit conditions, business and consumer pessimism, and low investment due to previous overbuilding as during the housing bubble. How can confidence be revived? All problems disappear if planned spending can be raised far enough to make the *IS* curve intersect *LM* at or to the right of Y^N. For this reason,

Keynes believed that fiscal policy, which can shift the *IS* curve, is the obvious antidepression tool to use. ✳

Stabilizing effects of falling prices.

In theory at least, government action to shift the *AD* curve may not be necessary, because the *AD* curve may have a negative slope like the curve AD_0. There are two mechanisms by which lower prices raise aggregate demand, and so far we have discussed only one of them.

The **"Keynes Effect"** is a name given to the normal role of falling prices in raising the real money supply and boosting output. We have learned that the Keynes Effect disappears when there is a horizontal *LM* curve, which in turn is one of the causes of the vertical *AD* curve in Figure 8-8. Another cause of the vertical *AD* curve is the zero lower bound for the nominal interest rate, as indicated in the Global Economic Crisis Focus box on p. 250.

> The **Keynes Effect** is the stimulus to output that occurs when a lower price level raises the real money supply and thus decreases the real interest rate.

But the **Pigou Effect** or **real balance effect** can come to the rescue. The real money supply is part of household wealth, and we have seen in Chapter 3 that an increase in household wealth stimulates autonomous consumption and shifts the *IS* curve to the right. As prices fall and real money balances rise, consumers feel wealthier and spend more. This is a simple idea, that as the prices of goods from toothpaste to cars decline along with the overall price level, consumers with a given amount of money in their pockets and checking accounts can afford to buy more real goods and services.

> The **Pigou Effect** or **real balance effect** is the direct stimulus to aggregate demand caused by an increase in the real money supply and does not require a decline in the interest rate.

So far we have learned that the Keynes Effect and Pigou Effect can stabilize the economy when prices fall. Unfortunately, there are two additional effects that can destabilize the economy. These are the destabilizing effects of falling prices.

Destabilizing effects of falling prices.

Unfortunately, the stimulative effects of price deflation are not always favorable, even when the Pigou Effect or real balance effect is in operation. There are two major unfavorable effects of deflation:

- The **expectations effect** is the idea that when people expect prices to continue to fall, they tend to postpone purchases as much as possible to take advantage of lower prices in the future. This decline in the demand for commodities may be strong enough to offset the stimulus of the Pigou Effect.

> The **expectations effect** is the decline in aggregate demand caused by the postponement of purchases when consumers expect prices to decline in the future.

- The **redistribution effect** may be more important than the expectations effect. It is caused by an *unexpected deflation* that causes a redistribution of income from debtors to creditors. Why? Debt repayments are usually fixed in dollar value so that a uniform deflation in all prices, which was not expected when the debts were incurred, causes an increase in the real value of mortgage and installment repayments from debtors to creditors (banks and, ultimately, savers).[5] This redistribution reduces aggregate demand, since creditors tend to spend only a relatively small share of their added income, while debtors have nothing to fall back on and are forced to reduce their consumption to meet their higher real interest payments.

> The **redistribution effect** is the decline in aggregate demand caused by the effect of falling prices in redistributing income from high-spending debtors to low-spending savers.

During the Great Depression deflation of 1929–33, for instance, the GDP price deflator declined by 24 percent. Yet the interest income of creditors hardly fell at all, from $4.7 to $4.1 billion (current dollars). Farmers were hit worst by

---

[5] A concise discussion of the consequences of these effects on the economy's self-correcting mechanism is contained in James Tobin, "Keynesian Models of Recession and Depression," *American Economic Review* (May 1975), pp. 195–202. See also Axel Leijonhufvud, *On Keynesian Economics and the Economics of Keynes* (New York: Oxford University Press, 1968), pp. 315–31.

falling prices—their current-dollar income fell by two-thirds, from $6.2 to $2.6 billion—and many lost their farms through foreclosures as a result of this heavy debt burden. Although many factors were at work in the collapse of real autonomous spending during the Great Depression, it appears that the negative expectations and redistribution effects of the 1929–33 deflation dominated the stimulative Keynes and Pigou Effects. The International Perspective box on pp. 258–59 looks further into the puzzle of why the Great Depression was worse in the United States than in other nations.

The expectations and redistribution effects are not just ancient fossils relevant only to the 1930s. In the early and mid-1980s, falling prices of farm products, farmland, and oil reduced the income of farmers, oil producers, and employees of farms and oil companies. Many of these people were severely hurt by falling prices, especially because in the 1970s some (especially farmers) had incurred a heavy burden of debt to buy high-priced farmland. More recently Japan suffered from economywide deflation, that is, negative inflation, for twelve straight years between 1999 and 2010.

◆ SELF-TEST

Not only do falling prices and a depressed economy affect aggregate demand, but so do rising prices and prosperity.

1. Explain whether the Pigou Effect (real balance effect) stabilizes or destabilizes the economy when aggregate demand is high.

2. How does this effect occur?

3. Similarly, explain whether the expectations and redistribution effects stabilize or destabilize the economy when prices are rising.

4. Describe how these effects occur.

Nominal Wage Rigidity

Keynes attacked the classical economists on two fronts. As we have seen, his first line of attack was the possibility of a vertical AD' line that fails to intersect the LAS line, creating monetary impotence and a failure of self-correction. His second line of attack was simply that deflation would not occur in the necessary amount because of rigid nominal wages. And if little or no deflation occurred, *the debate about the relative potency of the Keynes, Pigou, expectations, and distribution effects would become irrelevant.*

We have already seen in Section 8-5 on pp. 239–42 that the theory of the SAS curve is built on the assumption that the nominal wage rate is slow to adjust to an increase in prices and output. Wages can remain fixed for relatively long periods of time because of explicit union contracts, implicit contracts in which workers and firms understand that wages are changed only infrequently, and constraints on management time that prevent them from reconsidering the correct wage rate every day or every week. In this section we examine the extreme assumption that the nominal wage rate is completely rigid and does not adjust at all as the price level declines in an economic slump.

Figure 8-9 shows the effects of rigid nominal wages. The two aggregate demand curves, AD_0 and AD_1, are copied from Figure 8-7. They have the normal negative slopes. AD_1 lies to the left of AD_0 because consumer and business

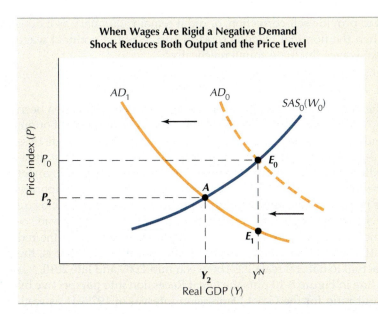

When Wages Are Rigid a Negative Demand Shock Reduces Both Output and the Price Level

Figure 8-9 Effect of a Decline in Planned Spending When the Nominal Rate Is Fixed at W_0

The short-run aggregate supply curve SAS_0 is fixed in position by the assumption of a rigid nominal wage rate, W_0. The decline in planned spending shifts the aggregate demand curve leftward from AD_0 to AD_1, and the economy moves southwest from point E_0 to point A.

pessimism or other negative factors reducing aggregate demand lowers the assumed amount of planned spending. The short-run aggregate supply curve SAS_0 is fixed in position by the fixed nominal wage rate (W_0). Starting at point E_0, the leftward shift in aggregate demand moves the economy to point A, where the new AD_1 curve intersects the aggregate supply curve SAS_0.

Keynes pointed out that the economy would remain stuck at point A even with the normally sloped aggregate demand curve AD_1. Why? If the nominal wage is completely rigid and never changes from the value W_0, then the supply curve is fixed as well at the position SAS_0. The price level would not fall below P_2. Hence the economy would not move from point A to point E_1, as required in the analysis of the classical economists.

Failure to attain equilibrium in the labor market. Keynes's assumption of a rigid *nominal* wage differs from the description of the economy's adjustment toward long-run equilibrium in Section 8-6, which assumed that there is an equilibrium *real* wage rate that equates demand and supply in the labor market.

Keynes's assumption of nominal wage rigidity fails to explain how or why the wage remains rigid. Its only virtue is that it provides an explanation of a persistent output gap, for instance the distance between Y_2 and Y^N along the horizontal axis of Figure 8-9. The persistent output gap and accompanying decade-long persistent unemployment were the two defining characteristics of the Great Depression. In the next section we turn to the causes of the Great Depression.

8-9 CASE STUDY

What Caused the Great Depression?

This case study investigates several important aspects of the Great Depression years of 1929 to 1941. Three topics are given primary emphasis. First, why was aggregate demand so low? Is there evidence to support monetary impotence or a failure of self-correction? Second, did the economy's aggregate supply curve shift downward to provide self-correction, or did it remain stationary as it does in Figure 8-9 when the nominal wage is rigid? Third, was the nominal wage rigid, and did real wages fluctuate countercyclically?

Dimensions of the Great Recession and Great Depression

The impact of the Global Economic Crisis on the U.S. economy has often been described as the "Great Recession" of 2007–09. But even after output hit bottom in June 2009 and the recession was officially over, deep economic distress remained in 2010–11. Among the symptoms of this unfortunate economic situation were the endless search for jobs by the unemployed, the underemployment represented by people who wanted full-time jobs but could find only temporary or part-time jobs not paying benefits, and the widespread trauma of foreclosure and the forced eviction of people who had lost their homes. The widespread social and economic pain was likely to last for a long time; as shown by the red line in Figure 8-10, there was no improvement in the output ratio (that is, the percent ratio of actual to natural real GDP) between mid-2009 and late 2010.

Yet the blue line in Figure 8-10 puts the Great Recession into perspective by plotting the output ratio for the Great Depression interval of 1929–41 as well.

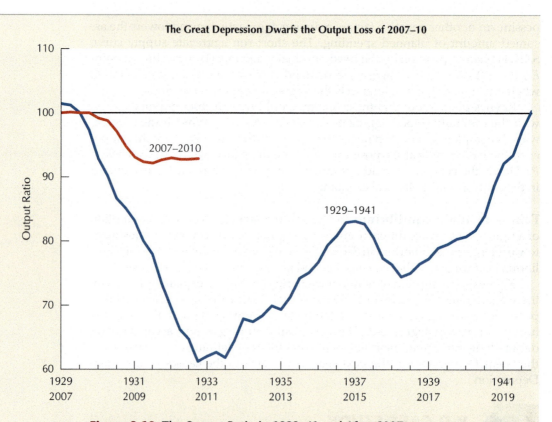

Figure 8-10 **The Output Ratio in 1929–41 and After 2007**

The graph plots the percent output ratio (Y/Y^N) during the Great Depression of 1929–41 and the Global Economic Crisis period starting in 2007. By mid-2009 the output ratio had declined from 100 percent in late 2007 to 92 percent and exhibited little recovery through the end of 2010. In contrast the decline in the output ratio during the Great Depression was much larger, declining from more than 100 percent in mid-1929 to 61 percent in late 1932. As late as mid-1940, fully eleven years after the 1929 cyclical peak, the output ratio as only about 82 percent.

In the depth of decline in the output ratio and in the duration of the low output ratio, nothing in macroeconomic history remotely compares with the Great Depression of the 1930s. Compared to the decline of the output ratio to about 92 percent in 2009–10, the same ratio declined from above 100 percent in 1929 to 61 percent at the end of 1932, dwarfing the 2009–10 episode. Even after four years of relatively steady recovery during 1933–37, the output ratio rose only to 82.7 percent in 1937:Q2 before sinking again in the recession of 1937–38. The ratio exceeded its peak 1937 value only in 1940:Q3 and did not finally return to 100 percent until the eve of the Pearl Harbor attack on December 7, 1941.

The very rapid recovery of the output ratio starting in mid-1940 can be attributed to an explosion of defense and rearmament government spending that started in June 1940, fully 18 months before the Pearl Harbor attack. During this 18-month period the ratio of total government spending (federal, state, and local) in GDP more than doubled, an example that a fiscal expansion can be powerful if it is large enough and if it occurs when the economy has plenty of excess capacity, as it did in 1940 and early 1941 (see the graph of the ratio of government spending to income in 1929–41 on p. 182).[6]

Behavior of Output, Unemployment, and Other Variables in the Great Depression

The Great Depression involved far more than the dry data of the output ratio, which is shown in column (5) of Table 8-1. This table exhibits several other features of the dismal economic performance of the American economy between 1929 and 1941. This twelve-year period is distinguished above all by the unemployment figures shown in column (7) especially by the extraordinarily high level reached by the unemployment rate (25.2 percent in 1933), and the long duration of high unemployment (ten straight years, 1931–40, with unemployment above 10 percent). An obvious puzzle is why the economy was so weak, especially between 1934 and 1939. In 1939, *the real money supply* (column 2) *was 48 percent higher than in 1929.* Yet in 1939 real GDP (column 3) *was only 10 percent higher than in 1929.* In 1939 the unemployment rate was still 17.2 percent about the same as in 1931, because the output ratio was only 80.1 percent, lower than in 1931. Thus by 1939 the economy's unemployment rate and output ratio were as bad or worse than 1931, when the economy had already experienced an unprecedented collapse in the Great Contraction that began in 1929.

The output ratio by definition is the ratio of actual real GDP to natural real GDP (Y/Y^N). To rise from its 1931 value of 82.1 percent back to a normal level of 100 percent, the numerator of the ratio (actual real GDP) needed to grow substantially faster than the denominator (natural real GDP), but it did not. Natural real GDP was growing quite rapidly in the 1930s as a result of population and productivity growth and in fact grew at a healthy annual rate of 3.6 percent between 1929 and 1941, and actual real GDP did not keep up the pace. Real GDP needed to rise by about 50 percent over the decade of the 1930s to provide sufficient jobs to workers, given the relatively rapid growth rates of population and productivity growth.

Explanations of Weak Aggregate Demand

The Keynesian interpretation that the *IS* curve shifted far to the left is supported in Table 8-1 by column (4) which shows the collapse of real fixed investment

---

[6] See Robert J. Gordon and Robert Krenn, "The End of the Great Depression 1939–41: Policy Contributions and Fiscal Multipliers," NBER Working Paper 16380, September 2010.

Table 8-1 Money, Output, Unemployment, Prices, and Wages in the Great Depression, 1929–41

Year	Money supply ($ billions)	Real money supply ($ billions, 1929 prices)	Real GDP ($ billions, 1929 prices)	Real fixed investment ($ billions, 1929 prices)	Output ratio (Y/Y^N) (percent)	GDP deflator (1929 = 100)	Unemployment rate (percent)	Long-term interest rate	Average hourly earnings (dollars)	Average real hourly earnings (1929 dollars)
	(1)	(2)	(3)	(4)	(5)	(6)	(7)	(8)	(9)	(10)
1929	26.0	26.0	103.7	14.9	102.8	100.0	3.2	3.6	.563	.563
1930	25.2	26.1	94.8	11.4	90.8	96.3	8.9	3.3	.560	.581
1931	23.5	26.7	88.7	8.0	82.1	86.3	16.3	3.3	.532	.605
1932	20.6	25.5	77.2	4.5	69.0	76.2	24.1	3.7	.485	.600
1933	19.4	24.4	76.1	3.9	65.7	74.1	25.2	3.3	.457	.575
1934	21.4	26.0	84.3	5.2	70.4	78.3	22.0	3.1	.512	.623
1935	25.3	30.4	91.9	6.7	74.1	79.8	20.3	2.8	.524	.630
1936	28.8	34.4	103.7	8.9	80.8	80.7	17.0	2.7	.534	.637
1937	30.2	35.0	109.2	11.0	82.2	84.2	14.3	2.7	.566	.656
1938	29.8	35.3	105.4	9.1	76.7	81.7	19.1	2.6	.576	.681
1939	33.4	39.8	114.0	10.9	80.1	80.7	17.2	2.4	.583	.695
1940	38.8	45.8	123.7	13.2	84.0	81.9	14.6	2.2	.597	.705
1941	45.4	51.1	144.9	15.5	95.0	87.4	9.9	2.0	.655	.737

Sources: See Appendix A. The interest rate is series B-72 in *Long-Term Economic Growth* (U.S. Department of Commerce, 1970). Average hourly earnings are from Martin N. Baily, "The Labor Market in the 1930s," in James Tobin, ed., *Macroeconomics, Prices, and Quantities* (Brookings Institution, 1983), Table 1, p. 23.

from $14.9 billion in 1929 prices in 1929 to $3.9 billion in 1933, *a decline of 74 percent.* Also shown is the incomplete recovery of real fixed investment, with a value in 1939 that was still 27 percent below the 1929 level. The failure of investment to recover fully to the 1929 level, despite a 53 percent increase in the real money supply since 1929, is consistent with either a vertical *IS* curve or a horizontal *LM* curve. Which diagnosis is more realistic?

For the *IS* curve to be vertical, a decline in the interest rate must fail to stimulate autonomous planned spending, which chiefly consists of fixed investment. As shown in Table 8-1, the interest rate declined substantially from 1934 to 1941, and yet real fixed investment in 1939 and 1940 was still below its 1929 level.

For the *LM* curve to be horizontal, an increase in the real money supply must fail to reduce the interest rate. Yet the long-term interest rate fell fairly steadily from 3.7 percent in 1932 to 2.0 percent in 1941. Thus the observations between 1934 and 1941 seem consistent with the hypothesis that the demand for money depends inversely on the interest rate. There is no sign that the interest rate hit a minimum level at any time during the latter half of the Great Depression decade. In short, the evidence is more consistent with the interpretation that the *IS* curve was vertical than that the *LM* curve was horizontal.

What pushed the *IS* curve to the left?   There was a sharp decline in both consumption and investment spending from 1929 to 1930. Part of the decline in consumption reflects the working of the multiplier, as induced consumption fell in response to a decline in autonomous planned spending. Autonomous consumption contributed to this decline in planned spending, as the crash of the U.S. stock market in October 1929 wiped out a significant proportion of the wealth of households. A decline in real wealth works the same way as the real balance effect introduced in this chapter on p. 251; higher real wealth raises autonomous consumption and lower real wealth as in 1929–30 reduces autonomous consumption.

The collapse of fixed investment documented in Table 8-1 reflects in part a hangover from excessive investment in the 1920s, particularly of residential and nonresidential structures. Excessive optimism created too much construction, much like the housing and commercial construction bubbles of 2001–06, which endowed the economy after 2007 with an enormous oversupply of residential houses, condos, office buildings, and hotels. The weakness of investment throughout the 1930s reflected the influence of overbuilding in the 1920s—why should firms build new factories and office buildings when their existing factories and office buildings were half vacant?[7]

The role of domestic and international monetary policy.   In 1927–29 the Fed pursued a restrictive monetary policy in order to cool down the stock market boom as well as the overheated construction boom. Further, the Fed's policy tightening was transmitted to foreign countries, causing an even more drastic tightening of monetary policy in those countries. As other countries fell into recession and depression, their demand for U.S. exports declined, amplifying the declines in autonomous consumption and planned investment. Starting in 1930, banks began to fail (closing their doors without enough money in the vaults to redeem deposits), and households lost their life savings.[8] After the middle of 1931, most economists agree that the primary cause of the severity of the Great Depression was restrictive monetary policy; the nominal money supply was allowed to decline by 25 percent between 1929 and 1933 (Table 8-1, column (1)).

Prices and the Output Ratio in the Great Depression

Does the behavior of output and the price level in the Great Depression support the Keynesian assumption of rigid nominal wages or the classical interpretation of a self-correcting economy? If the classicists are correct, we should find evidence of the economy's self-correcting forces at work through price deflation. Turning back to Figure 8-9, we would expect that when price deflation works in

---

[7] Many important aspects of the Great Depression and comparisons with the 1990s are contained in Robert J. Gordon, "The 1920s and the 1990s in Mutual Reflection," in Paul W. Rhode and Gianni Toniolo, *The Global Economy in the 1990s* (Cambridge University Press, 2006), pp. 161–92.

[8] The classic account stressing bank failures, the collapse of the money supply, and Federal Reserve policy errors as the root causes of the Great Depression is Milton Friedman and Anna J. Schwartz, *A Monetary History of the United States, 1867–1960* (Princeton University Press for NBER, 1963), Chapter 7. A more recent account that emphasizes international factors is Barry Eichengreen, *Golden Fetters: The Gold Standard and the Great Depression, 1919–1939* (New York: Oxford University Press, 1992). Other assessments of the role of monetary and nonmonetary factors are Barry Eichengreen, "The Origins and Nature of the Great Slump Revisited," *Economic History Review*, vol. 45, no. 2 (May 1992), pp. 213–39, and Christina D. Romer, "The Nation in Depression," *The Journal of Economic Perspectives*, vol. 7, no. 2 (Spring 1993), pp. 19–39.

INTERNATIONAL PERSPECTIVE

Why Was the Great Depression Worse in the United States Than in Europe?

The text reviews the basic causes of the Great Depression, which combined a downward shift in planned investment in response to excessive building during the 1920s with a downward shift in autonomous consumption following the stock market crash of October 1929. Augmenting these demand shocks that pushed the *IS* curve leftward was a decline in exports, due both to trade restrictions (tariffs and quotas) levied by each nation against their trading partners, and also due to declining foreign demand for exports as foreign central banks tightened monetary policy. The leftward *IS* shifts were greatly exacerbated by the perversely restrictive monetary policy pursued by the Fed, which allowed thousands of banks to fail and allowed the nominal money supply to decline by 25 percent between 1929 and 1933.

The figure shows the evolution of real GDP per person between 1920 and 1941 in the United States compared with Germany, Japan, and the United Kingdom. Real GDP per person is expressed as a percent of the 1929 value in each country. Thus, in 1933 real GDP per person had fallen to 70 percent of the 1929 value in the

United States, in contrast to 86 percent in Germany, and 94 percent in both the United Kingdom and Japan. Other countries exceeded their 1929 value by 1934, in the case of the United Kingdom and Japan, and by 1935 for Germany. In contrast, the United States just barely equaled the 1929 value by 1937, fell back into a recession in 1938, and finally exceeded the 1929 value only in 1939, fully ten years later.

Three factors help to explain why the other three countries experienced economic slumps that were less severe and shorter in duration than in the United States. These are exchange rate policy, fiscal policy, and policy toward wages and prices. The clearest contrast was in exchange rate policy. In September 1931, the United Kingdom abandoned the gold standard that fixed its exchange rate with that of the dollar. The devaluation of the British pound sterling boosted British exports and cut British imports, thus shifting the British *IS* curve to the right and initiating the recovery shown by the blue line during 1932–34. The U.S. government did not reduce the value of the dollar until 1933, and in the interval of 1931–33, the world demand for exports shifted

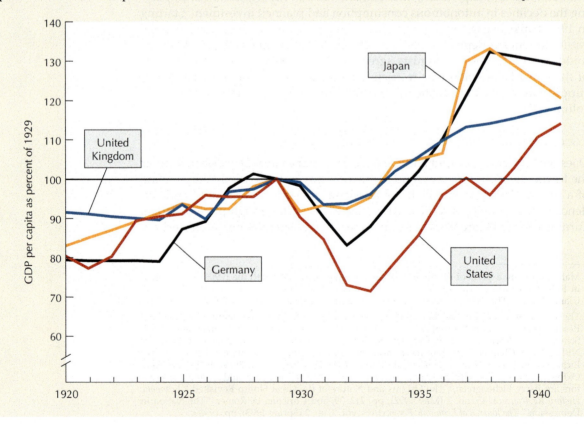

from the United States to the United Kingdom and other countries that had devalued their currencies in 1931.

The contrast between Germany and the United States lies both in fiscal policy and wage policy. The 1929–32 slump in Germany was almost as severe as that in the United States, but its recovery starting in 1933 was much faster. The new German government of Adolf Hitler took control on January 30, 1933. Soon after, the government began an ambitious policy of fiscal expansion, raising government spending drastically and financing this spending largely through budget deficits rather than higher taxes. While most of the government spending went for rearmament as Germany built its military machine that conquered most of Europe in 1939–42, some of the government spending went for housing construction and for the Autobahn, a system of limited access multi-lane freeways that anticipated the U.S. interstate highway construction of the 1950s and 1960s. By 1938, the German economy had reached a level of income per person fully 30 percent above the 1929 level. Rearmament in Japan, which invaded

Manchuria in 1931 and China in 1937, caused the path of the Japanese economy to resemble that of Germany.

Not only was fiscal expansion in the United States much more timid than in Germany or Japan, but the United States also pursued policies that attempted to push wages and prices up, thereby causing the *SAS* curve to shift upward and offset some of the impact of the recovery in aggregate demand. In contrast, the German government restricted the growth of wages. Because labor was cheap, employment grew much faster in Germany than in the United States during the 1930s.

Despite its disastrous policies that caused World War II and the Holocaust, in the narrower realm of economic policy, Germany must be given credit for its fiscal expansion that began in 1933 and implemented Keynesian economics even before Keynes's book was published. The rapid recovery of the U.S. economy in 1939–41 provides another example of the strong expansionary effects of a rightward shift in the *IS* curve (caused by higher government spending, exports, and fixed investment) when increases in nominal wages are relatively modest.

a stabilizing direction, the economy would slide down an *AD* curve to the southeast, as from point *A* to point E_1.

Now compare this theoretical diagram to a graph of the actual data plotted in the top frame of Figure 8-11. The horizontal axis is measured as the ratio of actual to natural real GDP. Starting to the right of the vertical *LAS* schedule in 1929, with a price index of 100 (on a 1929 base), the economy moved rapidly to the southwest until 1933. Then a recovery to the northeast began, interrupted briefly in 1938.

Absence of self-correction. The story of the Great Depression appears to lie in shifts in the *AD* curve to the left and then back to the right. There is no evidence at all of a movement southeast along a given *AD* curve, as would have occurred had price deflation played a major role in stimulating the recovery. Particularly important is the fact that there was no deflation between 1936 and 1940, even though Y/Y^N remained at or below 86 percent throughout that five-year interval.

Despite the absence of perfect price flexibility, the price level was not rigid during the Great Depression and did drop 26 percent between 1929 and 1933. The path from northeast to southwest to northeast reflects a regularity, as if the *AD* curve were following a well-marked highway. The bottom frame of Figure 8-11 represents a hypothetical interpretation of what happened. The *AD* curve in 1929 was close to the vertical *LAS* schedule, but by 1933 it had moved well to the left as business and consumer confidence collapsed. The actual location of the economy in 1933 suggests that the economy's aggregate supply schedule looks like SAS_0 of Figure 8-9, and so we have drawn in a positively sloped SAS_0 curve in the bottom frame of Figure 8-11.

Figure 8-11 The Price Level (*P*) and the Ratio of Actual to Natural Real GDP (*Y*/*Y*ᴺ) During the Great Depression, 1929–41

The upper frame illustrates the actual values of the implicit GDP deflator *(P)* and an estimate of the ratio of actual to natural real GDP during the Great Depression era, 1929–41. The remarkable fact in the top frame is that the economy returned almost to natural output in 1941 with a price level that was only modestly below that in 1929, despite the intervening decade that should have pushed the price level much lower. The bottom frame illustrates a hypothetical interpretation of what happened.

Source: Appendix A.

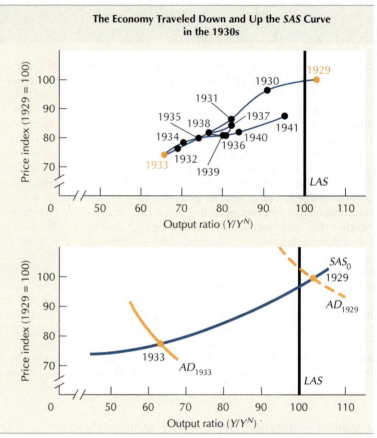

Behavior of nominal and real wage rates. The interpretation of the Great Depression contained in Figure 8-11 raises an obvious question: Why did the aggregate supply curve fail to shift downward to bring the economy to its long-run equilibrium level of output along the vertical *LAS* line at a lower price level? A fixed *SAS* curve requires a rigid nominal wage rate. Data on the nominal wage rate are included in Table 8-1, column 9.

By 1937, the nominal wage rate was back to the 1929 level, despite an unemployment rate of 14 percent. Thus, it is an exaggeration for the Keynesian model to treat the nominal wage rate as absolutely rigid. A decline did occur in 1931–33. But the nominal wage rate did not exhibit the continued decline after 1933 that would have been necessary to bring the economy back to natural real GDP through the classical mechanism of self-correction.

Policy failures after 1932. As we have seen, there was a profound failure of monetary policy in 1929–33, as banks were allowed to fail and as the nominal money supply was allowed to decline. And, as shown in the box, the failure to devalue the dollar in response to the British devaluation of 1931 prolonged the U.S. depression, in constrast to the rapid recovery of the British economy.

But policy failures did not stop with the inauguration of President Franklin D. Roosevelt in 1933. The government could have pursued an aggressive fiscal expansion but did not. It failed to understand the difference between actual and structural budget deficits, as explained in Figures 6-2 and 6-3 on pp. 163–64. It was inhibited in raising government spending and cutting taxes by its fear of budget deficits, yet these deficits were caused by the weakness of the economy, not by fiscal expansion.

Just as serious an error was the failure to understand the role of falling wages and prices in promoting a recovery; the *SAS* curve needed to shift down but instead the government tried to push the *SAS* curve up. During 1934 and 1935 the National Industrial Recovery Act (NIRA) explicitly attempted to raise wages and prices. Although the NIRA was declared unconstitutional in 1935, it was succeeded in the next several years by alternative legislation aimed at boosting prices and particularly wages. ◆

Summary

1. The aggregate demand curve shows the different combinations of real output and the price level that are consistent with equilibrium in the commodity and money markets. The position of the aggregate demand curve depends on planned spending and on the money supply.

2. A shift in aggregate demand may change the level of real output, the price level, or both. With a horizontal aggregate supply curve, only real output changes. With a vertical aggregate supply curve, only the price level changes. With a positively sloped aggregate supply curve, both real output and the price level change.

3. The short-run aggregate supply curve holds constant the costs faced by business firms, including the nominal wage, the price of raw materials, and the productivity of workers. Because costs are fixed, an increase in the price level raises business profits and creates an incentive for firms to raise output. The fact that a higher price level induces firms to produce more output explains the upward slope of the *SAS* curve.

4. Initially the economy is assumed to be in equilibrium at the natural level of real GDP where the real wage equals the equilibrium real wage. If business firms raise the price level while the nominal wage rate is fixed, the actual real wage declines below the equilibrium real wage, creating upward pressure for change in the actual nominal wage rate.

5. When the nominal wage rate rises in response to worker demands for higher wages, the *SAS* curve shifts upward.

6. In the short run, a fiscal or monetary expansion raises both real output and the price level. However, the short-run change in real output puts pressure for change on the nominal wage rate and causes the short-run aggregate supply curve to shift. This pressure for change is eliminated only when real output returns to the value that occurred prior to the fiscal or monetary expansion.

7. The economy is in long-run equilibrium only at a single level of natural real GDP, where there is no upward or downward pressure on the nominal wage rate. In the long run, any change in aggregate demand changes the price level without causing a change in real GDP.

8. Classical economists believed that cycles in aggregate demand mainly affected the price level, not real output. The economy's self-correcting forces of price flexibility protected real output from fluctuations.

9. Keynes criticized the classical economists on two grounds. The first was that the aggregate demand curve might be vertical rather than negatively sloped, due to a failure of planned spending to respond to the interest rate (vertical *IS* curve), or to a failure of a higher real money supply to lower the interest rate (horizontal *LM* curve), or both. Pigou countered that falling prices raise wealth and spending, guaranteeing a negatively sloped aggregate demand curve.

10. Keynes also criticized the classical economists because he believed that nominal wages were rigid, preventing prices from adjusting sufficiently to return real GDP to the level of natural real GDP.

Concepts

aggregate demand (*AD*) curve
short-run aggregate supply (*SAS*)
    curve
long-run aggregate supply (*LAS*)
    curve
equilibrium real wage rate

short-run equilibrium
long-run equilibrium
countercyclical variable
self-correcting forces
quantity theory of money
monetary impotence

rigid wages
Keynes Effect
Pigou Effect or real
    balance effect
expectations effect
redistribution effect

Questions

1. Explain the difference between the aggregate demand curve developed in this chapter and the demand curve for a product (for example, movies) used in microeconomics.
2. How will the AD curve be affected if, all other things remaining equal, (a) the interest responsiveness of the demand for money becomes larger? (b) the income responsiveness of the demand for money becomes larger?
3. All other things remaining equal, which of the following changes would cause the AD curve to shift to the right? To the left? Make it flatter? Make it steeper? Leave it unchanged (that is, cause a movement along the AD curve)? (*Hint:* Explain how each change affects the IS or LM curves that lie behind the AD curve.)
   (a) an increase in the nominal money supply
   (b) an increase in foreign income
   (c) an increase in the income tax rate
   (d) an increase in the marginal propensity to consume
   (e) a decrease in the responsiveness of investment to changes in the interest rate
   (f) an increase in the price level
   (g) an increase in government spending
   (h) a decrease in the exchange rate
   (i) a boom in housing prices
   (j) a decline in the availability of credit
4. Explain the importance of the assumption of fixed *nominal* wages in the determination of the short-run aggregate supply curve.
5. Describe whether the following variables increase or decrease when real GDP (Y) increases above Y_0 in the left frame of Figure 8-5.
   (a) the price level
   (b) the nominal wage rate
   (c) the real wage rate
6. Explain why an increase in the price level causes an increase in the amount of real GDP that business firms produce, given that input costs are fixed.
7. Explain why nominal wage rates adjust slowly.
8. Explain with words and diagrams how each of the following events affects the SAS curve.
   (a) technology improves
   (b) the nominal wage rate decreases
   (c) the prices of raw materials decline
9. Assume that the aggregate demand curve shifts to the right through increased government spending. Assuming that the position of the AD curve changes, how does this event affect the government budget deficit and the foreign trade deficit?
10. Predict, with the aid of the IS-LM and the SAS-AD models, the short-run and long-run results of each of the following:
    (a) a decrease in the nominal money supply
    (b) an increase in net exports that results from a depreciation of the dollar.

(*Hint:* Both models measure real GDP on the horizontal axis, so aligning the diagrams vertically will help you to see how they are related. Assume the economy is initially in long-run equilibrium at the natural real GDP [Y^N]. Also, remember that changes in the price level shift the LM curve.)

11. Is sustainable long-run equilibrium always reached when the AD and SAS curves intersect? Why or why not?
12. According to the view of the classical economists, there should have been a movement down the AD curve during the 1930s. Explain why this type of movement would require a shifting SAS curve. Did the SAS curve shift during the Great Depression in the way expected by the classical economists?
13. What is meant by the term *monetary impotence*? According to Keynes, what two conditions could lead to monetary impotence? Were either of these conditions present during the Great Depression?
14. Explain why the zero lower bound on interest rates is a source of monetary impotence during a period of deflation.
15. Use the AD-SAS model to explain how differences in exchange rate policy, fiscal policy, and policy toward wages and prices made the Great Depression worse in the United States than it was in the United Kingdom or Germany.
16. Explain the role played by the interest rate in the Pigou Effect.
17. Why does the existence of a potent Pigou Effect guarantee a negatively sloped AD curve?
18. If policymakers were trying to decrease output in a period of continuing inflation, would the existence of the Pigou Effect have any impact? Can you explain, under these circumstances, how the redistribution effect and the expectations effect might affect the economy?
19. Given the existence of a Pigou Effect, or real balance effect, what do you predict will happen to the IS and AD curves if the economy experiences an unexpected increase in autonomous exports? (Assume that the economy begins in a long-run equilibrium position where AD crosses LAS.)
20. The whole controversy regarding the location of the IS curve and the potency of the real balance effect becomes irrelevant if nominal wages are rigid downward. Why is this so? Use the AD-SAS model to explain your answer.
21. Compare how the downturn in the United States' output ratio during the Global Economic Crisis compares to the decline during the Great Depression.
22. Discuss what caused aggregate demand to collapse during the Great Depression and whether any of those were similar to why aggregate demand declined during the Global Economic Crisis.

Problems

myeconlab Visit www.MyEconLab.com to complete these or similar exercises.

*Indicates that the problem requires the Appendix to Chapter 4.

1. You are given the following equations for the aggregate demand (*AD*) and short-run aggregate supply (*SAS*) curves:

$$AD{:}\ Y = 1.25A'_p + 2.5M^s/P$$
$$SAS{:}\ Y = 11{,}250 - 20W + 1{,}000P$$

where Y is real GDP, A'_p is the amount of autonomous planned spending that is independent of the interest rate, M^s is the nominal money supply, P is the price level, and W is the nominal wage rate. Assume that A'_p equals 5,000, M^s equals 2,000, W equals 50, and natural real GDP, Y^N, equals 11,250.

(a) Use the values for the amounts of autonomous planned spending that is independent of the interest rate and the nominal money supply to derive the equation for the aggregate demand curve. Compute the amount of aggregate demand when the price level equals 2.0, 1.25, 1.0, 0.8, and 0.5. Graph the aggregate demand curve.

(b) Derive the equation for the short-run aggregate supply curve, given that the nominal wage rate equals 50. Compute the amount of short-run aggregate supply when the price level equals 2.0, 1.25, 1.0, 0.8, and 0.5. Graph the short-run aggregate supply curve.

(c) Given your answers to parts a and b, explain what the short-run and long-run equilibrium levels of real GDP and the price level are.

(d) Given your answers to part c, explain what the equilibrium real wage rate is.

(e) Suppose that autonomous planned spending increases by 800 billion so that $A'_p = 5{,}800$. Explain if this increase is the result of increased willingness of financial market firms to lend to consumers and business firms or a collapse in the housing market, which reduces household wealth and housing construction. Derive the new equation for the aggregate demand curve. Compute the new amount of aggregate demand when the price level equals 2.0, 1.25, 1.0, 0.8, and 0.5. Graph the new aggregate demand curve.

(f) Given your graphs in parts b and e, explain what the new short-run equilibrium values of real GDP and the price level approximately are. (*Note*: You can find the exact equilibrium values of the real GDP and price level by setting the equation for the new aggregate demand curve equal to the equation for the short-run aggregate supply curve and solve for the price level. Solving for the

price level requires that you find the roots of a quadratic equation.)

(g) Explain what the new long-run equilibrium real GDP and equilibrium price level are, given the increase in aggregate demand. Explain how the short-run aggregate supply curve shifts as the economy adjusts to the new long-run equilibrium. Compute the new nominal wage rate at the new long-run equilibrium price level and derive the new short-run aggregate supply curve, given the new nominal wage rate.

(h) Suppose policymakers want to prevent a rise in the price level that would otherwise result from the increase in planned spending. Explain by how much fiscal policymakers would have to reduce planned spending in order to prevent a rise in the price level. Explain by how much monetary policymakers would have to decrease the nominal money supply in order to prevent a rise in the price level.

2. Use the information given at the start of problem 1.

(a) Suppose that autonomous planned spending decreases by 1,000 billion so that $A'_p = 4{,}000$. Explain if this decrease is the result of increased willingness of financial market firms to lend to consumers and business firms or a collapse in the housing market, which reduces household wealth and housing construction. Derive the new equation for the aggregate demand curve. Compute the new amount of aggregate demand when the price level equals 2.0, 1.25, 1.0, 0.8, and 0.5. Graph the new aggregate demand curve.

(b) Given your graphs in part a of this problem and part b of problem 1, explain what the new short-run equilibrium values of real GDP and the price level approximately are. (*Note*: Again you can find the exact equilibrium values of the real GDP and price level by proceeding as you did for part f of problem 1.)

(c) Explain what the new long-run equilibrium real GDP and equilibrium price level are, given the decrease in aggregate demand. Explain how the short-run aggregate supply curve shifts as the economy adjusts to the new long-run equilibrium. Compute the new nominal wage rate at the new long-run equilibrium price level and derive the new short-run aggregate supply curve, given the new nominal wage rate.

(d) Suppose policymakers want to prevent a rise in unemployment that would otherwise result from the drop in planned spending. Explain by [1] much fiscal policymakers would have to increase planned spending in order to prevent a rise in unemployment. Explain by how much monetary policymakers would have to increase the nominal money supply in order to prevent a rise in unemployment.

*3. The *IS* and *LM* curves for the economy have the following equations:

$$IS: Y = k(A'_p - 200r)$$
$$LM: Y = 5(M^s/P) + 500r$$

where $k = 2.5$, $A'_p = 5,200$, $M^s = 1,800$, and $P = 1.0$.

(a) Find the equilibrium level of output and the equilibrium interest rate.

(b) What are the equilibrium real output and equilibrium interest rate when the price level equals 0.8? When it is 1.2? When it is 2.0? Plot the aggregate demand curve based on these answers.

(c) Suppose that natural real output [Y^N] equals 11,000. Given the aggregate demand curve from part b, determine long-run equilibrium real output, the interest rate, and the price level.

(d) Suppose that autonomous spending increases by 600 billion so that $A'_p = 5,800$. What are the equilibrium levels of real output and the interest rate when the price level equals 0.8, 1.0, 1.2, and 2.0? Plot the new aggregate demand curve.

(e) Assume an upward-sloping *SAS* curve that intersects the original *AD* curve at $Y = 11,000$ and $P = 1.0$. What will happen in the short-run to actual real output, the price level, and the real wage rate as a result of the increase in aggregate demand?

(f) Given the increase in aggregate demand, determine the new long-run equilibrium real output, equilibrium interest rate, and equilibrium price level. Explain what will happen to the nominal wage rate and the *SAS* curve as the economy adjusts to the new long-run equilibrium.

*4. A Pigou Effect is introduced into an economy similar to problem 3 by allowing A'_p to become price-dependent. We now have:

$$IS: Y = k(A'_p - 200r)$$
$$LM: Y = 5(M^s/P) + 500r$$

where $k = 2.5$, $A'_p = 4,600 + 600/P$, $M^s = 1,800$, and $P = 1.0$. As with parts a and b of problem 3, this problem aims to derive the *AD* curve.

(a) Find the equilibrium level of output and the equilibrium interest rate.

(b) What are the equilibrium real output and equilibrium interest rate when the price level equals 0.8? When it is 1.2? When it is 2.0? Plot the aggregate demand curve based on these answers.

(c) Is the *AD* curve flatter or steeper than the *AD* curve of part b of problem 3?

◆ SELF-TEST ANSWERS

p. 235. (1) When the *IS* curve is steep, an increase in the real money supply causes output to increase less than when the *IS* curve is flat, implying a steeper *AD* curve. (2) When the *LM* curve is steep, an increase in the real money supply causes output to increase more than when the *LM* curve is flat (compare the top and bottom frames of Figure 4-7). Thus, when the *LM* curve is steep, a given price reduction (which raises the real money supply) leads to a greater output increase and a *flatter AD* curve than when the *LM* curve is flat.

p. 242. (1) A union concession shifts the *SAS* curve down. (2) A discovery of a giant oil field shifts the *SAS* curve down. (3) An increase in the money supply shifts the aggregate demand *(AD)* curve upward and thus causes a movement *along* the *SAS* curve. (4) An increase in the price level causes movement *along* the *SAS* curve.

p. 245. (1)–(3) All these events cause an upward shift in the aggregate demand *(AD)* curve. In long-run

equilibrium, the price level and nominal wage level must increase by the same percentage, while the level of real GDP does not change. (4) This causes a rightward shift in both the *LAS* and *SAS* downward along the fixed *AD* curve, reducing the long-run equilibrium price level and raising real output.

p. 252. (1) The Pigou Effect stabilizes the economy when demand is high. (2) Rising prices reduce the value of real balances and real wealth, which in turn reduce consumption. (3) The expectations and redistribution effects destabilize the economy. (4) The expectations effect causes people to spend sooner, since they expect future prices to be higher. This boosts demand when demand is already high. Similarly, the redistribution effect causes income to be redistributed from savers who spend little to borrowers who spend much, thus boosting demand when demand is already high.

CHAPTER 9

Inflation: Its Causes and Cures

Why is our money ever less valuable? Perhaps it is simply that we have inflation because we expect inflation, and we expect inflation because we've had it.
—Robert M. Solow[1]

9-1 Introduction

Explaining the Inflation Rate: The Central Target of Monetary Policy

Throughout Chapters 3–7 the price level was assumed to be fixed, implying that the inflation rate was zero. In Chapter 8 for the first time the price level was allowed to rise or fall, responding to shifts in the aggregate demand (*AD*) curve and in the short-run aggregate supply (*SAS*) curve. The *AD-SAS* model implies that any event that causes a *single upward shift* in the economy's *AD* curve will cause a *single upward jump* in the price level. But **inflation** is a continuous increase in the price level, not a single jump. Thus sustained inflation requires a *continuous increase* in aggregate demand. To focus on the causes of a sustained inflation, in this chapter we will alter our *AD-SAS* model to explain the inflation rate (designated as lowercase *p*), instead of explaining the price level (designed as uppercase *P*) as in Chapter 8.

Inflation is a sustained upward movement in the aggregate price level that is shared by most products.

Inflation is important because if it continues at apparently small annual rates of change for a long time, it can cause the price level to double or triple. For instance, an annual inflation rate of 7 percent causes the price level to double in ten years and an annual inflation rate of 14 percent causes the price level to double in only five years. Rapid inflation erodes the purchasing power of the amounts parents have saved to send their children to college and of the amounts families have saved up for their retirement. Because of its insidious effects, which we investigate further in Chapter 10, a central goal of all central banks, including the U.S. Federal Reserve, is to control inflation by raising the interest rate when the inflation rate rises. Since the inflation rate is at the core of monetary policy goals, it is important that in this chapter we understand the causes of inflation and the constraints that the central bank faces in its attempt to control inflation.

We learn that an acceleration or deceleration of inflation can be caused either by shifts in aggregate demand ("demand shocks") or in aggregate supply ("supply shocks"). When supply shocks are absent, shifts in aggregate demand are the main cause of swings in real GDP and in the rate of inflation. Any attempt to sustain a level of real GDP above the natural level of real GDP will cause continuously accelerating inflation. The unfortunate corollary is that a reduction of inflation requires a transition period of recession in which

---

[1] *Technology Review* (December/January 1979), p. 31.

actual real GDP falls below natural real GDP. It is a central goal of the Fed to restrain inflation, and on repeated occasions during the postwar era, the Fed has been sufficiently concerned about accelerating inflation to institute restrictive policies that raise interest rates, in order deliberately to create a recession as needed to reduce the inflation rate. The impact of higher aggregate demand in creating inflation forces the Fed into a constant state of vigilance, to make sure that aggregate demand does not become excessive and to always be prepared to move to a restrictive monetary policy when needed.

The Volatile History of the Inflation Rate

The price level (P) is measured by the GDP deflator. The rate of inflation (p) is measured by the *percentage rate of change* of the GDP deflator, and this is plotted in the top frame of Figure 9-1. There we see that the inflation rate in the United States since 1960 has ranged from low values of around 1 percent per year in the early 1960s and again in 2009–10, to high values of 10 percent per year in 1975 and again in 1982. How can these volatile ups and downs in the inflation rate be explained? One promising hypothesis is suggested by Chapter 8, where we learned that an increase in aggregate demand raises the price level permanently, and it also raises actual real GDP temporarily above natural real GDP. We begin our search for the causes of inflation in this chapter by examining the relationship between the inflation rate and the ratio of actual real GDP to natural real GDP.

How Is Inflation Related to the Output Ratio?

The **output ratio** is the ratio of actual real GDP to natural real GDP.

The central theme of this chapter is that there is no unique relationship between inflation and the **output ratio,** that is, the ratio of actual real GDP to natural real GDP. The output ratio exceeds 100 percent when actual real GDP exceeds natural real GDP. The output ratio falls short of 100 percent when actual real GDP is less than natural real GDP.[2]

The volatile history of the output ratio is plotted in the bottom frame of Figure 9-1. There we see five periods when the output ratio soared above 100 percent (that is, the percentage amount by which actual real GDP exceeded natural real GDP). The longest period with the highest output ratio was the Vietnam-era expansion of 1966–69, and the output ratio reached its second-highest peak at the end of the economic boom of the late 1990s. Smaller values of the output ratio above 100 percent are observed in 1972–73, 1978–79, and 1988–90. Sustained periods when the output ratio was below 100 percent are observed in the early 1960s, 1974–75, 1991–94, but especially in 1982–83 and 2009–10.

Demand Shocks and Supply Shocks

Sometimes inflation and the output ratio rise or fall together. The economy's response to an upward shift in aggregate demand has already been examined in Figure 8-6; an increase in aggregate demand raises the price level and also raises the output ratio above 100 percent, but only temporarily. Soon the nominal wage rate begins to increase, and the output ratio gradually declines back to 100 percent, ending its temporary increase.

---

[2] The output ratio is closely related by definition to the GDP gap introduced on p. 6. The GDP gap is the output ratio minus 100 percent. Thus if the output ratio is 95 percent, the GDP gap is 95 − 100, or -5 percent. A synonym for the GDP gap, also introduced on p. 6, is the "output gap."

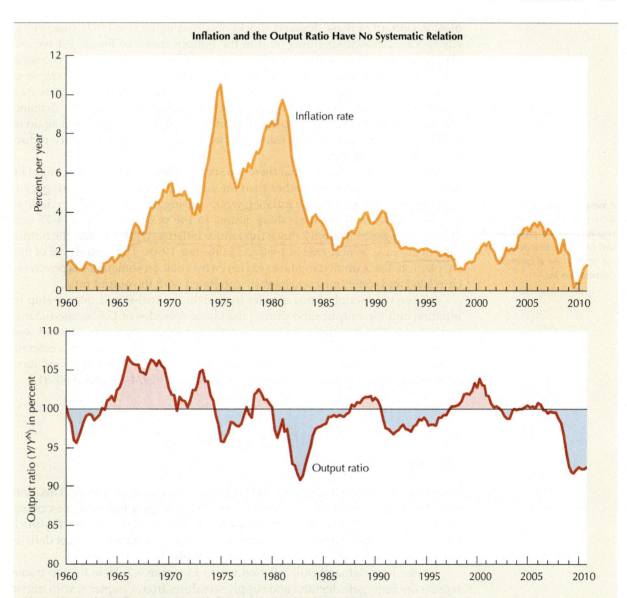

Figure 9-1 The Inflation Rate and the Output Ratio, 1960–2010

The top frame displays the inflation rate, measured as the percentage rate of change of the GDP deflator over the previous four quarters. The bottom frame displays the output ratio, that is, the percentage ratio of actual real GDP to natural real GDP. The high output ratio of 1965–69 caused inflation to accelerate during the late 1960s, and the same pattern is evident in the late 1980s. The low output ratio observed in the 1982–83 period explains part of the sharp drop in the inflation rate between 1981 and 1984, and this happened again in 2008–10. But sometimes the inflation rate and output ratio moved in opposite directions, as in 1974–75, 1979–81, and 1995–98.

Sources: Bureau of Economic Analysis *NIPA Tables* and research by Robert J. Gordon. Details in Appendix C-4.

In this chapter we are interested in changes in the growth rate of aggregate demand, which we will call a **demand shock**.[3] When a positive demand shock occurs, inflation increases and the output ratio rises temporarily. The

A **demand shock** is a sustained acceleration or deceleration in aggregate demand, measured most directly as a sustained acceleration or deceleration in the growth rate of nominal GDP.

[3] The term "demand shock" was previously defined in Section 3-1 on p. 55.

most important of these demand shocks occurred in the late 1960s, due primarily to Vietnam War spending, and in the bottom frame of Figure 9-1 we can clearly see the effect of the sustained high ratio in causing a steady acceleration of inflation between 1965 and 1970 in the top frame. A milder example of the same pattern appears in the late 1980s, when the output ratio increased above 100 percent, causing an acceleration of inflation. A negative demand shock can cause the inflation rate to fall, most notably in 1982–83 and again in 2008–10 when the deepest recessions of the postwar era caused a sharp reduction of the inflation rate.

We learn in this chapter that there is a second reason why inflation might be accompanied by a decline, rather than an increase, in the output ratio. An adverse supply shock can boost inflation while causing the output ratio to decline, as occurred when there were sharp jumps in the price of oil in 1974–75 and 1979–81. A beneficial supply shock can reduce inflation while causing the output ratio to increase, as occurred in 1986 and in the late 1990s. The central goal of this chapter is to use a unified model to explain why inflation sometimes is positively correlated and sometimes is negatively correlated with the output ratio.

We use the model of this chapter to explain the real-world relationship of inflation and the output ratio during the major episodes of U.S. economic history since 1960. Sometimes inflation accelerated when aggregate demand was strong, as in the 1960s and late 1980s. Sometimes inflation failed to accelerate when aggregate demand was strong, as in the late 1990s. Sometimes inflation accelerated when aggregate demand was weak, as in 1974–75 and 1980–81.

A **supply shock** is caused by a sharp change in the price of an important commodity (e.g., oil) that causes the inflation rate to rise or fall in the absence of demand shocks.

9-2 Real GDP, the Inflation Rate, and the Short-Run Phillips Curve

A *continuous* increase in demand pulls the price level up *continuously*. This kind of inflationary process is sometimes called demand-pull inflation, describing the role of rising aggregate demand as the factor "pulling up" on the price level. This type of inflation can be caused by large government budget deficits and excessive rates of growth of the money supply.

We see how demand-pull inflation works in Figure 9-2. Here the top frame repeats the aggregate demand and supply schedules from Chapter 8, with minor changes: For expositional simplicity, we have drawn both curves as straight lines, and we have introduced specific numbers on the vertical and horizontal axes. The horizontal axis now plots the output ratio, that is, the ratio of actual to natural real GDP. When the output ratio is 100 percent, actual and natural real GDP are equal. The economy initially is assumed to be at point E_0, where the AD_0 and SAS_0 curves cross. The initial values of the price index (P_0) and an index of the nominal wage rate (W_0) are both 1.0. The real wage rate (W_0/P_0) is initially at its equilibrium value of 1.0. The output ratio is 100 percent.

The short-run aggregate supply (*SAS*) curve has a positive slope, meaning that a higher level of output raises the price level. Each *SAS* curve is drawn for a particular nominal wage rate, shifting upward when the nominal wage rate increases, just as in Chapter 8. The long-run aggregate supply (*LAS*) curve is a vertical line at the point when the output ratio is 100 percent. As we learned in Chapter 8, there is upward pressure for an increase in the wage rate (and thus for an upward shift in the *SAS* curve), whenever the output ratio exceeds 100 percent. This occurs whenever the economy operates to the right of the vertical *LAS* curve.

Effects of an Increase in Aggregate Demand

An increase in aggregate demand shifts the AD curve upward from AD_0 to AD_1 in Figure 9-2. The economy moves initially to point E_1, where the price level is 1.03. The higher price level puts upward pressure on the nominal wage rate to rise. Everywhere to the right of the LAS curve, including point E_1, there is upward pressure on the nominal wage rate, so gradually the SAS curve will shift up. When this occurs, we move to the new SAS_1 curve, which assumes that the nominal wage rate is 3 percent higher than it was along the original SAS_0 curve.

How Continuous Inflation Occurs

What happens to the output ratio and the price level as the result of the upward shift from SAS_0 to SAS_1? There are two possibilities, both illustrated in the top frame of Figure 9-2.

A one-shot increase in aggregate demand.   The first possibility is that aggregate demand remains at the level indicated by the AD_1 schedule. Then the upward shift of the supply curve to SAS_1 shifts the economy from E_1 northwest to point D. What must happen to prevent the output ratio from declining? The aggregate demand schedule AD must shift upward by exactly the same amount as the supply schedule SAS. Thus if the nominal wage rate increases from 1.00 to 1.03, shifting supply up from SAS_0 to SAS_1, output can remain fixed *only if the demand curve shifts up* again, this time from AD_1 to AD_1'. Once

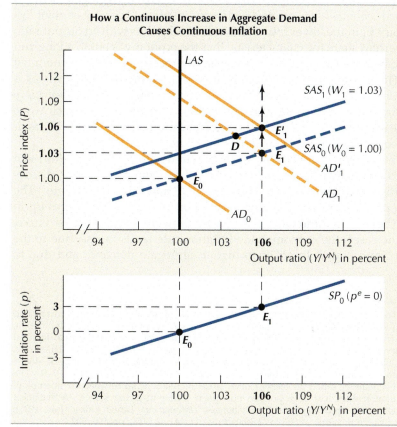

How a Continuous Increase in Aggregate Demand Causes Continuous Inflation

Figure 9-2 Relationship of the Short-Run Aggregate Supply (*SAS*) Curve to the Short-Run Phillips (*SP*) Curve

In the top frame, the economy starts in long-run equilibrium at point E_0. When aggregate demand shifts up from the AD_0 curve to the AD_1 curve, the price level moves to point E_1. The economy can stay to the right of the LAS line only if aggregate demand shifts up continuously from AD_1 to AD_1' to even higher levels of aggregate demand. The nominal wage rate adjusts upward whenever the economy is in the area to the right of LAS. Aggregate demand must keep ahead of the upward adjustment of the nominal wage rate, shown by the vertical path marked by black arrows. This continuous inflation of 3 percent per period is represented directly below in the lower frame at point E_1.

again the price level of 1.06 at point E_1' has raced ahead of the wage rate of 1.03, and there will again be upward pressure on the nominal wage rate.

A continuous increase in aggregate demand. To keep the output ratio from declining, aggregate demand must increase continuously; the economy will move straight upward along the path depicted by the black arrows in the top frame. The bottom frame shows the same process in a much simpler way. The horizontal axis is the same as in the top frame, but now the vertical axis measures not the price level but its rate of change, the inflation rate. Thus in the top frame when the price level is fixed in long-run equilibrium, as at point E_0, the percentage rate of change of prices (or inflation rate) in the bottom frame is zero, as at point E_0. The vertical axis measures the zero rate of inflation occurring at point E_0 as $p = 0$.

The maintenance of a high output ratio requires a continuous increase in aggregate demand and in the price level, as depicted by the vertical path of the black arrows in the top frame. This same process of continuous inflation in the bottom frame is illustrated by *the single point E_1*, where in each period the rate of change of the price level is 3 percent (just as in the top frame the price level rises by 3 percent between points E_1 and E_1').

The *SP* Curve

The bottom frame of Figure 9-2 differs from the top frame only by plotting the *inflation rate* rather than the price *level* on the vertical axis. In the bottom frame, the upward-sloping line connecting points E_0 and E_1 is called the *SP* line. It shows that to maintain the output ratio above 100 percent, aggregate demand must be raised *continuously* to create a *continuous* inflation (3 percent at point E_1).

Thus point E_1 in the lower frame and indeed all points with an output ratio above 100 percent share the characteristic that the economy is not in a long-run equilibrium, because the price level is constantly racing ahead of the nominal wage rate. The reason for the continuous upward pressure for higher wages is that labor contracts fail to *anticipate further inflation, and, as a result, they fail to specify in advance the wage increases needed to keep up with inflation.* Such wage contracts are said to have an **expected rate of inflation** of zero. This is abbreviated $p^e = 0$ and is included as a label on the *SP* line.

The term *SP curve* is used as an abbreviation for the term **short-run Phillips (*SP*) Curve,** which is named after A. W. H. Phillips, who first discovered the statistical relationship between real GDP and the inflation rate.[4] The *SP* curve slopes upward for the same reason that the *SAS* curve slopes up in Chapter 8. There are additional reasons for the upward slope of the *SP* curve. As output increases, the economywide inflation rate tends to rise, due to the sensitivity of raw materials prices to higher aggregate demand, and due to

The **expected rate of inflation** is the rate of inflation that is expected to occur in the future.

The schedule relating real GDP to the inflation rate achievable given a fixed expected rate of inflation is the **short-run Phillips (*SP*) Curve.**

---

[4] Phillips showed that over 100 years of British history, the rate of change of wage rates was related to the level of unemployment. Because the change in wage rates, in turn, is related to inflation, and unemployment is related to real GDP, the research of Phillips popularized the idea, depicted by the *SP* curve in Figure 9-2, that a high level of output is associated with a high inflation rate. See A. W. H. Phillips, "The Relation Between Unemployment and the Rate of Change of Money Wage Rates in the United Kingdom, 1861–1957," *Economica* (November 1958), pp. 283–99. The curve should actually be called the Fisher Curve, since the relationship between the unemployment and inflation rates had been pointed out much earlier in Irving Fisher, "A Statistical Relation Between Unemployment and Price Changes," *International Labour Review* (June 1926), pp. 785–92, reprinted in *Journal of Political Economy* (March/April 1973), pp. 596–602.

the tendency of business firms to boost prices more rapidly when aggregate demand is high.

The position of the SP curve is fixed by the rate of inflation that was expected at the time current wage contracts were negotiated (p^e), assumed in Figure 9-2 to be zero. Because the position of the SP curve depends on expectations, it is sometimes called the **expectations-augmented Phillips Curve.**

The **expectations-augmented Phillips Curve** (another name for the SP curve) shifts its position whenever there is a change in the expected rate of inflation.

◆ SELF-TEST

From what you have learned so far, try to generalize about the accuracy of the expected rate of inflation in the bottom frame of Figure 9-2.

1. In what area is actual inflation greater than expected inflation?

2. In what area is actual inflation less than expected inflation?

3. Where in the diagram does the expected rate of inflation turn out to be exactly right?

9-3   The Adjustment of Expectations

The remarkable thing about the inflation process illustrated in Figure 9-2 is that it presupposes that people never learn to *anticipate* inflation when they negotiate their labor contracts. Each period, the price level races ahead of the nominal wage rate along the path shown by the upward-pointing arrows, but people fail to build this inflation into their labor contracts *ahead of time*.

Changing Inflation Expectations Shift the SP Curve

Once negotiators anticipate inflation in advance, the short-run Phillips Curve shifts upward, as illustrated in Figure 9-3. There the lower SP_0 short-run

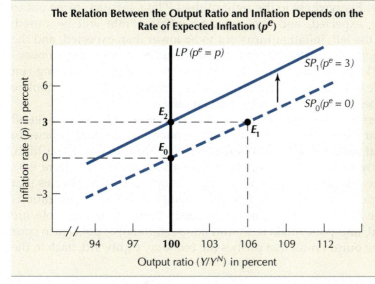

The Relation Between the Output Ratio and Inflation Depends on the Rate of Expected Inflation (p^e)

Figure 9-3 Effect on the Short-Run Phillips Curve of an Increase in the Expected Inflation Rate (p^e) from Zero to 3 Percent

The lower SP_0 curve is copied directly from the bottom frame of Figure 9-2 and shows the relation between output and inflation when no inflation is expected ($p^e = 0$). But when people begin fully to expect the 3 percent inflation, the 3 percent actual inflation yields only the level of real GDP at E_2. The short-run Phillips Curve has shifted upward by exactly 3 percent, the amount by which people have raised their expected inflation rate. The vertical LP line running through points E_0 and E_2 shows all the possible positions of long-run equilibrium where the actual and expected inflation rates are equal ($p^e = p$).

Phillips Curve is copied directly from the bottom frame of Figure 9-2. Everywhere along the SP_0 curve, no inflation is expected. At point E_0 the actual inflation rate is just what is expected—zero—and the economy is in a long-run equilibrium position with the price level completely fixed. At point E_1, no inflation is expected ($p^e = 0$) either, but the actual inflation rate turns out to be 3 percent.

When an expected 3 percent inflation occurs ($p = p^e = 3$), the long-run equilibrium position occurs at point E_2. The entire short-run Phillips Curve has shifted upward by exactly 3 percent, the degree of adjustment of the expected inflation rate. The rise of the output ratio above 100 percent has led firms to raise their prices, and workers have obtained larger wage increases in newly negotiated contracts. Now an output ratio above 100 percent cannot be achieved along the new SP_1 schedule unless the actual inflation rate exceeds 3 percent, in which case the actual inflation rate would again exceed the expected inflation rate.

The economy is in long-run equilibrium only when there is no pressure for change. Point E_1 certainly does not qualify, because the actual inflation rate of 3 percent at point E_1 exceeds the zero inflation rate expected along the SP_0 curve. There is pressure for people to adjust their erroneous expectation ($p^e = 0$) to take account of the continuing inflation. At point E_2, the pressure for change ceases, because expected inflation has been boosted enough ($p^e = 3$). Wage agreements allow *in advance* for a 3 percent inflation. This keeps employment and output unaffected by inflation.

Thus point E_2 qualifies as a point of long-run equilibrium, because expectations turn out to be correct, just as does point E_0. The only difference between points E_0 and E_2 is the inflation rate that is correctly expected, zero at E_0 versus 3 percent at E_2. Otherwise the two points share the correctness of expectations and the same output ratio of 100 percent.

The *LP* "Correct Expectations" Line

The black vertical *LP* line connects E_0 and E_2 and shows all possible points where the expected inflation rate turns out to be correct. The term *LP line* stands for *Long-run Phillips Curve* and can be thought of as the "correct expectations" line. Everywhere to the right of the *LP* line, inflation turns out to be higher than expected, and the expected inflation rate will be raised. Everywhere to the left, inflation turns out to be lower than expected, and the expected inflation rate will be reduced. The vertical *LP* line showing all possible positions of long-run equilibrium is analogous to the vertical *LAS* long-run supply schedule of Chapter 8. Its message is the same: real GDP (Y) cannot be pushed permanently away from its long-run natural level (Y^N).

What important message does the vertical *LP* line send to policymakers? It tells them that the best way to stabilize the economy is to adopt policies to keep the output ratio equal to 100 percent. If the output ratio is too high, inflation is likely to accelerate (as between points E_0 and E_1 in Figure 9-3). The appropriate response is that policymakers adopt restrictive policies that reduce the output ratio back to 100 percent. Similarly, if the output ratio is to the left of the *LP* line, then output is needlessly being wasted and jobs are being destroyed, and policymakers should adopt stimulative policies to spur a recovery in the output ratio that pushes the economy rightward, back to the *LP* line.

Learning About Diagrams: The Short-Run (*SP*) and Long-Run (*LP*) Phillips Curves

The Phillips Curve depicts the relationship between inflation and the output ratio.

Diagram Elements and Reasons for Slope

Both the *SP* curve and *LP* curve are plotted with the output ratio on the horizontal axis and with the inflation rate on the vertical axis.

The *SP* curve slopes upward because higher output boosts inflation through the same mechanisms that cause the short-run aggregate supply curve to slope upward in Chapter 8.

The *LP* curve shows the level of output when inflation is accurately anticipated ($p^e = p$). The *LP* curve is a vertical line, because accurate anticipations can occur only when the output ratio is 100 percent, that is, when actual and natural real GDP are equal ($Y = Y^N$).

What Shifts the *SP* Curve and *LP* Curve?

The crossing point of the *SP* curve with the *LP* curve shows the rate of anticipated inflation (p^e). An increase in p^e will shift the *SP* curve up, and a decrease in p^e will shift the *SP* curve down.

The *LP* curve does not shift its position. If there is an increase in natural real GDP, then actual real GDP must increase by the same amount for the output ratio to remain at 100 percent.

What Is True at Points Off the Curves?

A point below the *SP* curve represents an inflation rate below that anticipated by firms and workers. A point above the *SP* curve represents the opposite.

A point to the right of the *LP* curve but on the *SP* curve represents a situation in which actual inflation exceeds expected inflation. In such a situation, there is upward pressure on the expected rate of inflation. A point to the left of the *LP* curve but on the *SP* curve represents a situation in which actual inflation is less than expected inflation, putting downward pressure on expected inflation.

What Is True at a Short-Run Equilibrium?

The economy is at a short-run equilibrium when it is operating on its *SP* curve.

What Is True at a Long-Run Equilibrium?

The economy is at a long-run equilibrium when three conditions are met. First, it must be operating on its *SP* curve. Second, the inflation rate (p) must be equal to the growth rate of nominal GDP (x), which is required for real GDP growth to be zero. Third, the economy must be on its *LP* line along which expected inflation (p^e) is equal to the actual inflation rate (p).

SELF-TEST

Assume that the economy is initially at point E_2 in Figure 9-3. There is a decline in aggregate demand, and the output ratio declines from 100 to 94 percent.

1. What happens subsequently to the expected inflation rate?
2. What happens to the position of the *SP* curve?
3. What happens to the position of the *LP* curve?

9-4 Nominal GDP Growth and Inflation

Once we have determined the value of p^e, the expected inflation rate at the time contracts were negotiated, we know which *SP* curve applies to today's economy. But we still have a major question remaining if we are to understand the determination of the output ratio and the inflation rate: *Where will the economy's position be along the current* SP *curve?* For instance, along SP_0, will the economy be at point E_0, point E_1, or some other point?

The *SP* curve is a single relationship between the inflation rate and the output ratio. We need to find an additional relationship, because two separate relations between inflation and the output ratio are needed to pin down the values of these two unknown variables.

Our model of inflation in this chapter uses a single variable to represent the growth rate of aggregate demand, and this is the growth rate of nominal GDP. First we review the relationship between the *levels* of nominal GDP, real GDP, and the GDP deflator. Then we introduce the relationship between the *growth rates* of nominal GDP, real GDP, and the GDP deflator (the growth rate of the GDP deflator is the same thing as the inflation rate).

Starting with the *levels* of these variables, we recall from Chapter 2 that nominal GDP (X) is defined as the price level (P) times real GDP (Y):

$$X \equiv PY \tag{9.1}$$

Just as real GDP is determined in the *IS-LM* model of Chapter 4 by such factors as real government spending and the real money supply, so nominal GDP is determined by nominal government spending and the nominal money supply. In addition, nominal GDP is determined by any other *shock* to aggregate demand discussed in the preceding chapters, including changes in tax rates, autonomous net taxes, the autonomous component of net exports, real wealth, how easy or difficult it is for consumers or businesses to obtain loans from financial institutions, and finally shifts in business and consumer optimism.

In this chapter we are interested in the *growth rate* of the price level, that is, the rate of inflation, and its relation to the *growth rate* of nominal GDP. The growth rate of any product of two numbers, such as P times Y in equation (9.1), is equal to the sum of the separate growth rates of the two numbers.[5] Writing the growth rates of variables in equation (9.1) as, respectively, x, p, and y, implies

$$x \equiv p + y \tag{9.2}$$

In words, this equation says that the growth rate of nominal GDP (x) equals the inflation rate (p) plus the growth rate of real GDP (y).

If the level of nominal GDP starts out at 100, as in period 0 in Table 9-1, then a growth rate of 6 percent will bring the level to 106 in period 1. As shown in Table 9-1, several different combinations of inflation and real GDP growth are compatible with a 6 percent growth rate for nominal GDP ($x = 6$). The lesson we learn from Table 9-1 is that for any given growth rate of nominal GDP, the rate of real GDP growth will vary inversely with the inflation rate.

For instance, alternative B shows that if inflation is 6 percent, higher prices will absorb all of the 6 percent growth of nominal GDP so that nothing will remain for real GDP growth. Real GDP remains constant, then, at its initial level of 100. Inflation "uses up" all of nominal GDP growth.

In contrast, alternative C shows that if inflation is only 3 percent, then half of the 6 percent growth in nominal GDP will remain for real GDP to grow by

---

[5] The formal way to show this is to take the logarithm of the product of two terms, such as PY:

$$\log X \equiv \log P + \log Y$$

Then the derivative of both sides is taken with respect to time:

$$\frac{d \log X}{dt} \equiv \frac{d \log P}{dt} + \frac{d \log Y}{dt}$$

This is the same as the equality in equation (9.2), since x is defined as $(d \log X)/dt$ and likewise for p and y.

Table 9-1 Alternative Divisions of 6 Percent Nominal GDP Growth Between Inflation and Real GDP Growth

	Period	Level of variable			Growth rate of variable between periods 0 and 1		
		Nominal GDP (X)	Real GDP (Y)	GDP deflator (P)	Nominal GDP (x)	Real GDP (y)	GDP deflator (p)
Alternative A:							
Inflation at 9 percent	0	100	100	1.00	6	−3	9
	1	106	97	1.09			
Alternative B:							
Inflation at 6 percent	0	100	100	1.00	6	0	6
	1	106	100	1.06			
Alternative C:							
Inflation at 3 percent	0	100	100	1.00	6	3	3
	1	106	103	1.03			

3 percent, from 100 initially to 103 in period 1. Here inflation uses up only half of nominal GDP growth.

Finally, alternative A on the top line of Table 9-1 shows that if inflation is 9 percent, then nominal GDP growth of 6 percent will not be sufficient to maintain real GDP constant at 100. Real GDP growth must be *minus* 3 percent, forcing the level of real GDP to fall from 100 in period 0 to 97 in period 1. Here inflation uses up more than the available rate of nominal GDP, forcing real GDP to fall.

Example: When inflation is less than the growth rate of nominal GDP, real GDP must rise, just as in alternative C. When inflation is greater than the growth rate of nominal GDP, real GDP must fall, just as in alternative A.

		x	=	p	+	y
Years like Alternative C	1977	10.7	=	6.2	+	4.5
	1984	10.6	=	3.7	+	6.9
	2007	4.9	=	2.7	+	2.2
Years like Alternative A	1974	8.1	=	8.6	+	−0.5
	1982	4.0	=	5.9	+	−1.9
	1991	3.3	=	3.4	+	−0.1

9-5 Effects of an Acceleration in Nominal GDP Growth

The basic theme of this chapter is that the inflation rate can be either positively or negatively correlated with the output ratio, depending on the evolution of demand shocks and supply shocks. The role of supply shocks is examined later in this chapter. Now we are concerned with the role of demand shocks. As in

Figure 9-4 The Adjustment Path of Inflation and the Output Ratio to an Acceleration of Nominal GDP Growth from Zero to 6 Percent When Expectations Fail to Adjust

The economy initially is at point E_0 with actual and expected inflation of 0 percent. A 6 percent acceleration in nominal GDP growth moves the economy in the first period to point F. If the expected rate of inflation ($p^e = 0$) fails to respond to faster actual inflation (an unrealistic assumption), the economy eventually arrives at point E_3. Once we allow expectations to adjust, the economy will move to point E_4, which is both on the LP line and allows inflation to be equal to nominal GDP growth.

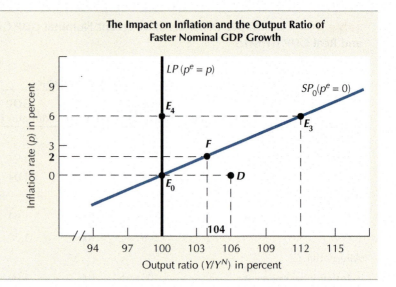

The Impact on Inflation and the Output Ratio of Faster Nominal GDP Growth

the previous section, we measure demand shocks by a single variable, that is, changes in the growth rate of nominal GDP (x).

How do changes in nominal GDP growth (x) affect real GDP (Y) and the inflation rate (p)? We shall assume that initially the economy is in a long-run equilibrium in Figure 9-4 at point E_0. The actual and expected inflation rates are both zero ($p = p^e = 0$). Thus the SP curve that applies is SP_0, which assumes $p^e = 0$, and is copied from Figure 9-3.

If nominal GDP growth is also zero ($x = 0$), then the economy can stay at point E_0, since $x = p$. Why? As we can see by subtracting p from both sides of equation (9.2), when $x = p$, the growth rate of real GDP (y) must be zero:

$$y = x - p \tag{9.3}$$

$$0 = 0 - 0 \text{ (the specific values at point } E_0)$$

As long as $x = 0$, point E_0 is a long-run equilibrium, meeting the three conditions (1) that the economy is on the SP curve, (2) that $x = p$ (so $y = 0$), and (3) that expectations are accurate ($p^e = p$).[6] These are the same three conditions listed in the box on p. 273.

Now let us assume that nominal GDP growth (x) accelerates permanently from 0 to 6 percent. What happens? The economy can no longer stay at E_0, because it is no longer true that $x = p$. Instead, the 6 percent value of x exceeds the 0 percent initial value of p, and real GDP must grow. Equation (9.3) teaches us the following key rule about the adjustment of real GDP and inflation: *Real GDP must grow; that is, the growth rate of real GDP is positive* ($y > 0$), *whenever nominal GDP growth exceeds the inflation rate* ($x > p$).

Starting from E_0, an acceleration in nominal GDP growth from zero to 6 percent will slide the economy up the fixed positively sloped schedule SP_0, since people initially expect an inflation rate of zero ($p^e = 0$). This extra 6 percent of nominal GDP growth is divided between inflation and output growth,

---

[6] In order to link equation (9.3) to Figure 9-4, we need to assume that the growth rate of natural real GDP is zero ($y^N = 0$). The Appendix to Chapter 9 loosens this assumption that the growth rate of natural real GDP is zero and allows for any rate of change of natural real GDP.

according to equation (9.3). In this example, two percentage points of the total six percentage point acceleration in x are devoted to higher inflation at point F, and the remaining four percentage points are devoted to output growth, that is, raising the output ratio from 100 to 104. Point F is a position of *short-run equilibrium*, since it is on the SP_0 curve and it also satisfies equation (9.3).

The continuing adjustment. What happens next? The economy cannot stay at point F, because *F is not a position of long-run equilibrium*. It violates two of the three requirements stated earlier for long-run equilibrium: that $x = p$ and that expectations be accurate.

Let us deal with the first of these issues. Real GDP grows whenever nominal GDP growth exceeds the inflation rate. This means that *real GDP must keep growing until inflation "uses up" all of nominal GDP growth*, that is, until inflation rises until it reaches 6 percent, the assumed permanent growth rate of nominal GDP.

While point E_3 plots 6 percent inflation, it is not satisfactory, because it fails to satisfy the second condition for long-run equilibrium—that expectations be accurate. The economy cannot stay at E_3 because this point has inflation racing along at 6 percent, while expectations of inflation (p^e) remain at zero. It is inevitable that labor contract negotiations will take the ongoing 6 percent inflation into account. As the rate of wage increase is raised to take account of the unfortunate reality of 6 percent inflation, the SP curve will shift upward.

The SP curve will stop shifting upward only when the economy reaches a long-run equilibrium, satisfying the three requirements that (1) the economy is on the SP curve, (2) $x = p$ (so the output ratio stops growing), and (3) expectations are accurate ($p^e = p$). While the first two conditions are met at point E_3, the third is satisfied only along the vertical LP line. Given the assumed growth rate of nominal GDP ($x = 6$), this occurs only at point E_4, where $x = p = 6$. Why? Only when $x = p$ does the output ratio stop growing, with $y = 0$.

To summarize this section, when the growth rate of nominal GDP accelerates (from zero to 6 percent in this example), the inflation rate must accelerate by the same amount, from zero to 6 percent. But the inflation rate does not respond instantly, because it takes time for workers and firms to raise their expected rate of inflation. During the time period when the workers and firms are gradually raising their expected rate of inflation (p^e), there is a temporary increase in the output ratio.

9-6 Expectations and the Inflation Cycle

Forward-Looking, Backward-Looking, and Adaptive Expectations

How high can real GDP be pushed by the acceleration in nominal GDP growth, and for how long? Everything depends on the speed at which p^e (the average rate of inflation expected when current wage and price contracts were negotiated) responds to higher inflation. This speed of adjustment depends on several factors.

Forward-looking expectations. First, are expectations forward-looking or backward-looking? **Forward-looking expectations** attempt to predict the future behavior of an economic variable, like the inflation rate, using an economic model. Contract negotiators with forward-looking expectations might reason, for instance, that an acceleration of nominal GDP growth from zero to 6 percent

Forward-looking expectations attempt to predict the future behavior of an economic variable, using an economic model that specifies the interrelationship of that variable with other variables.

implies 6 percent inflation in the long run, and immediately raise the expected rate of inflation to 6 percent. The growth rate of the nominal wage rate would speed up by 6 percent, and this would shift the *SP* curve directly upward by 6 percent. The economy would move *immediately* from point E_0 to point E_4, without any interval at all with the output ratio greater than 100 percent.

The rationality of backward-looking expectations. Another alternative, **backward-looking expectations,** does not attempt to calculate the implications of economic disturbances *in advance*, but simply adjusts to what has *already* happened. For instance, the backward-looking approach bases expectations of inflation on the past behavior of inflation, without any attempt to guess the future path of nominal GDP growth or its implications. There are two important reasons why rational workers and firms may form their expectations by looking backward rather than forward:

> **Backward-looking expectations** use only information on the past behavior of economic variables.

1. People may have no reason to believe that an acceleration in nominal GDP growth will be permanent. Nominal GDP growth has fluctuated up and down before, making individuals reluctant to leap to the conclusion that the change is permanent. They may prefer just to wait and see what happens.

2. Even if the acceleration of nominal GDP growth were permanent, the existence of long-term wage and price contracts and agreements, both formal and informal, would prevent *actual* inflation from responding immediately. Since people know about these contracts and agreements, they know that changes in wages and prices will adjust *gradually* to the acceleration in nominal GDP. The exact speed of adjustment cannot be predicted in advance, since it depends on many factors, including the average length of wage and price contracts and agreements. Further, *one* set of contract negotiators may have no idea whether *other* negotiators expect future nominal GDP growth to be 6 percent, 0 percent, or some other number.

> **Adaptive expectations** base expectations for next period's values on an average of actual values during previous periods.

The most popular form of backward-looking expectations, and one that has been widely studied and verified, is called **adaptive expectations.**[7] The idea is simply that when people find that actual events do not turn out as they were expected to, they adjust their expectations to bring them closer to reality. Here is a particularly simple example of adaptive expectations. Assume that the expected inflation rate is always set equal to what actually happened last period. In Figure 9-4, the acceleration of nominal GDP growth from zero to 6 percent, which raises actual inflation from zero to 2 percent as the economy moves from point E_0 to point F, would cause the next period's expected inflation rate to rise by the same amount, to 2 percent. Here is the simple relation to remember: *This period's expected inflation rate equals last period's actual inflation rate, or $p^e = p_{-1}$.*

Adjustment Loops

The economy's response to higher demand growth depends on the adjustment of expectations. In Figure 9-5, two responses are plotted. The blue line moving straight northeast from point E_0 through point F to E_3 duplicates Figure 9-4. Expectations do not adjust at all, and the economy remains on its original SP_0 curve. As before, point E_3 is not a long-run equilibrium because it is not on the *LP* line.

---

[7] The idea of adaptive expectations was first used in macroeconomics in a classic paper, Phillip Cagan, "The Monetary Dynamics of Hyperinflation," in Milton Friedman, ed., *Studies in the Quantity Theory of Money* (Chicago: University of Chicago Press, 1956), pp. 25–117.

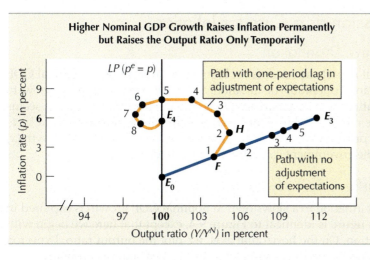

Higher Nominal GDP Growth Raises Inflation Permanently but Raises the Output Ratio Only Temporarily

Figure 9-5 **Effect on Inflation and Real GDP of an Acceleration of Demand Growth from Zero to 6 Percent**

When expectations do not adjust at all, the economy follows the blue path northeast from E_0 to E_3, exactly as in Figure 9-4. When expectations adjust fully to last period's actual inflation, the economy moves upward along the orange path going northwest from point H toward the long-run equilibrium at point E_4.

The orange line shows full adjustment with a one-period lag. In each period the SP curve shifts upward by exactly the previous period's increase in actual inflation. Because actual inflation increases by two percentage points in going from E_0 to point F, then in the next period the SP curve shifts upward by two percentage points and takes the economy northward from F to H. But then expectations adjust upward again, because at H inflation has risen above the 2 percent people expected. Eventually, after looping around the long-run equilibrium point E_4, the economy arrives there. (The appendix to this chapter shows how to calculate the exact location of the economy in every time period along this path.)

The orange path exhibits several basic characteristics of the inflation process:

1. An acceleration of demand growth (as in Figures 9-4 and 9-5) raises the inflation rate and the output ratio in the short run.

2. In the long run, the inflation rate (p) rises by exactly the same amount as x, and any increase in the output ratio along the way is only temporary. The economy eventually arrives at point E_4.

3. Following a permanent increase in nominal GDP growth (x), inflation (p) always experiences a temporary period when it overshoots the new growth rate of nominal GDP. For instance, in Figure 9-5, x increases from 0 to 6, and eventually inflation settles down to 6 percent at point E_4. But along the adjustment path, actual inflation temporarily exceeds the final equilibrium value of 6 percent inflation. Along the orange path, for instance, inflation reaches 8 percent in periods 4 and 5. Overshooting occurs along this path because the economy initially arrives at its long-run inflation rate ($p = 6$) in period 3 before expected inflation has caught up with actual inflation. The subsequent points that lie above 6 percent reflect the combined influence on inflation of (1) the upward adjustment of expectations and (2) the continued upward demand pressure that raises actual inflation above expected inflation whenever the economy is to the right of its LP line.

◆ SELF-TEST

Look at the orange adjustment loop in Figure 9-5. Why is the line from point 1 to point 2 steeper than from E_0 to point 1?

9-7   Recession as a Cure for Inflation

How to Achieve Disinflation

Disinflation is a marked deceleration in the inflation rate.

In the theoretical model summarized in Figure 9-5, an increase in nominal GDP growth causes an acceleration of inflation. Now we need to find out how to achieve **disinflation,** that is, a marked deceleration in the inflation rate. It seems obvious that the most straightforward way of eliminating inflation would be *to set in reverse* the process that created the inflation. By causing demand growth (*x*) to slow down, the government can cause inflation to decelerate.

The "Cold Turkey" Remedy for Inflation

The response of inflation to a slowdown in nominal GDP growth is explored in Figure 9-6. This figure is identical to Figure 9-4, except that here we begin with 10 percent inflation. On the horizontal axis, we plot the output ratio. Expected inflation is assumed to be 10 percent along the SP_2 line, and the economy is initially at point E_5.

The **cold turkey** approach to disinflation operates by implementing a sudden and permanent slowdown in nominal GDP growth.

In this diagram, we assume that the government introduces a policy, sometimes called **cold turkey,** that suddenly reduces demand growth (*x*) from 10 to 4 percent. If people expect inflation of 10 percent because inflation last period was 10 percent, then the economy will move initially to point K along the SP_2 schedule. The government's policy cuts inflation from 10 percent at point E_5 to 8 percent at K, but at the cost of a recession, as the output ratio falls from 100 to 96.

Notice that the move from E_5 to point K in Figure 9-6 represents an exact reversal of the adjustment from E_0 to point F in Figure 9-4. In both cases, the initial reaction of the economy to the 6 percent change in nominal GDP growth is divided into two percentage points of adjustment of inflation and four percentage points of adjustment in real GDP.

The Process of Adjustment to the New Long-Run Equilibrium

The process of adjustment finally comes to an end when inflation is equal to the new growth rate of nominal GDP ($p = x = 4$) and when the expected inflation rate has declined to its long-run equilibrium value ($p^e = 4$).

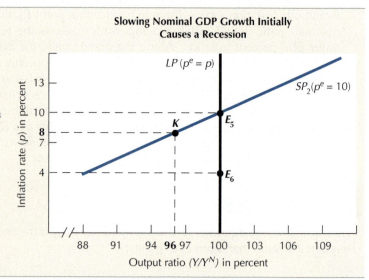

Figure 9-6 Initial Effect on Inflation and Real GDP of a Slowdown in Nominal GDP Growth from 10 Percent to 4 Percent

Initially the economy is in a long-run equilibrium at point E_5 with expected inflation (p^e) equal to the actual inflation rate (*p*) of 10 percent. When nominal GDP growth slows down suddenly and permanently from 10 percent to 4 percent, the economy initially moves to point K in the first period. Eventually the economy will reach long-run equilibrium at point E_6.

The downward spiraling loop. In Figure 9-7 the economy starts at point E_5, the same point as in the previous diagram. Nominal GDP growth, actual inflation, and expected inflation are all 10 percent at point $E_5 (x = p = p^e)$. The orange loop running southwest from point E_5 shows what would happen if the rate of nominal GDP growth (x) were suddenly slowed down from 10 percent in 1980 and prior years to 4 percent in 1981 and all future years. The economy's initial reaction is to go to the point marked 1981, with inflation of 8 percent and an output ratio that falls from 100 to 96 percent. *The point marked 1981 is exactly the same as point K in Figure 9-6.*

For 1982 and the following years, the economy follows the orange path. This downward spiraling loop, which shows the effects of a permanent deceleration of x from 10 to 4, is the *mirror image* of the upward spiraling loop in Figure 9-5, which showed the effects of a permanent acceleration of x from 0 to 6. The economy overshoots, with inflation falling temporarily below the 4 percent permanent growth rate of nominal GDP (x).

 ◆ **SELF-TEST**

1. If the slope of the *SP* curve were flatter than assumed in Figures 9-6 and 9-7, would the economy's adjustment to lower nominal GDP growth be slower or faster?

2. If the slope of the *SP* curve were steeper, would the economy's adjustment be slower or faster?

The Output Cost of Disinflation

The path depicted in Figure 9-7 displays the cold turkey approach to disinflation, that is, a sudden drop in nominal GDP growth from 10 percent in 1980 to 4 percent forever afterward. The cost of disinflation is a slump in output. What policy would avoid this decline in output? One alternative would be to do nothing and live with inflation. This would require that the economy stay permanently at point E_5 in Figure 9-7.

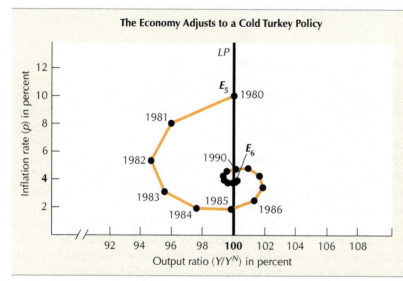

The Economy Adjusts to a Cold Turkey Policy

Figure 9-7 Adjustment Path of Inflation and Real GDP to a Policy That Cuts Nominal GDP Growth from 10 Percent in 1980 to 4 Percent in 1981 and Thereafter

The orange line between 1980 and 1981 traces exactly the same path as between E_5 and K in Figure 9-6 and shows what happens in subsequent years. The particular shape of the adjustment path assumes that nominal GDP growth suddenly slows from 10 percent to 4 percent in 1981 and remains at 4 percent forever.

INTERNATIONAL PERSPECTIVE

Did Disinflation in Europe Differ from That in the United States?

Most industrial nations have experienced relatively low rates of inflation since the mid-1990s. But before this, inflation rates were much higher and differed widely among the major nations.

The figure compares the inflation rate for the United States, beginning in 1975, with the four largest European nations—France, Germany, Italy, and the United Kingdom. Until the 1990s, Germany had the lowest inflation rate of all, and its inflation rate rose relatively little during the time of the 1979–81 oil shock. Germany's success in maintaining relatively low inflation is attributable to the relatively tight monetary policy conducted by the then German central bank, the Deutsche Bundesbank.

During the early 1980s, the other three European countries had higher inflation rates than the United States and more than double the inflation rate experienced by Germany. These countries did not follow the same tight monetary policy as did Germany; instead, monetary and fiscal policies were much looser, allowing nominal GDP to rise much faster than in Germany. In 1980, the inflation rate in Italy reached 20 percent per year; in the United Kingdom, the inflation rate was almost as high.

Clearly, something important changed after 1980. While the United States achieved a substantial disinflation between 1981 and 1986 (as shown in Figures 9-1 and 9-8), the amount by which the inflation rate fell was even greater in Italy and the United Kingdom. The key ingredient in the European disinflation was the establishment of the European Monetary System (EMS) in 1979. Member nations attempted to maintain their exchange rates within a relatively narrow band around that of the then German currency, the deutsche mark, or DM.

At first, the British and Italian exchange rates could not be held fixed for very long, since their inflation rates were so much higher than Germany's. At a fixed exchange rate, high inflation meant that British and Italian export prices rose rapidly compared to German prices, and these countries became uncompetitive. Hence, the EMS allowed for periodic adjustments of exchange rates for nations with high inflation rates. But the U.K. and Italy committed themselves to reducing inflation, primarily through tight monetary policies (aided by the decline in the real price of oil as displayed in Figure 9-8). By 1987 they had made sufficient progress and could commit to maintaining their exchange rates within a narrow band relative to the deutsche mark. However, the price of this progress was that unemployment rose to levels that were much higher than those in the United States. For instance, the unemployment rate in France never fell below 9.0 percent between 1985 and 2000 and was above 10 percent for four years straight (1996–99). Between 2000 and 2008 the French unemployment rate declined a bit but was never below 7.4 percent during a period when the U.S. unemployment rate fell as low as 4.5 percent.

The era of fixed exchange rates for the major European nations within the EMS lasted from 1987 to 1992, when it broke down. Italy, the United Kingdom, and several other countries, including Spain and Sweden, devalued their exchange rates relative to the DM, while France and several other countries maintained parity with the DM.

The sacrifice ratio. The model that generates the disinflation loop of Figure 9-7 can be used to assess the costs and benefits of a cold turkey policy compared to a policy of living with inflation. With a cold turkey policy, over the five years 1981–85, the total amount by which the output ratio falls below 100 percent is 16.3 percent. A convenient measure of the cost of disinflation is the **sacrifice ratio,** the ratio of the *cumulative* output lost to the permanent reduction in the inflation rate created by a disinflationary policy like the cold turkey approach shown in Figure 9-7. With the cold turkey policy, the sacrifice ratio is a loss of output of 16.3 percent to obtain a permanent reduction of inflation of 6 percent, or a sacrifice ratio of 2.7 (16.3/6).

The issue addressed by the sacrifice ratio is "how important is it to reduce the inflation rate permanently?" Would citizens endorse a policy of permanently reducing the inflation rate by 1 percent if they knew this would require a loss of output equal to 2.7 percent of one year's GDP, which amounts to about $400 billion for the United States in today's prices?

The **sacrifice ratio** is the cumulative loss of output incurred during a disinflation divided by the permanent reduction in the inflation rate.

The divergence of exchange rates in Italy and the United Kingdom after 1992 helps to explain why in 1994–97 inflation in those countries was substantially above that in France and Germany. However, the introduction of a single currency (the euro) in 1999 tied the exchange rate of Italy to that of France and Germany, leading to the near-convergence of Italy's inflation rate with those two countries. The United Kingdom (which refused to join the euro) maintained a slightly lower inflation rate than Italy during 2000–10, due to a restrictive type of monetary policy called "inflation targeting" that we examine in Chapter 14.

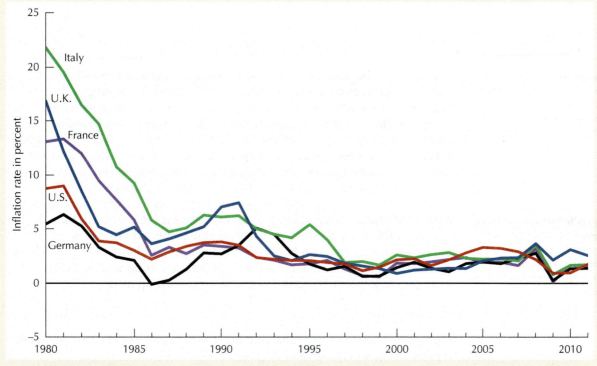

Sources: International Monetary Fund *World Economic Outlook Database*, April 2010, and Bureau of Economic Analysis *NIPA Tables*. Details in Appendix C-4.

GLOBAL ECONOMIC CRISIS FOCUS

Policymakers Face the Perils of Deflation

We can see in Figure 9-7 that any event, whether caused by policy or not, that pushes down nominal GDP growth radically can cause both a major recession and a substantial reduction of the inflation rate. In Figure 9-7 the inflation rate starts out at point E_5 with a rate of 10 percent, and it winds up at point E_6 with an inflation rate of 4 percent. It is easy to see from the graph that if the inflation rate started out at a much lower level, like 4 percent, and nominal GDP growth were reduced by the same amount as in Figure 9-7, then *the inflation rate would be pushed down so far as to enter negative territory. A negative inflation rate is called a "deflation."*

We learned in Chapter 8 on pp. 251–52 about the negative impact that deflation can have on aggregate demand. We also know from pp. 110–11 that

(continued)

Japan suffered from a continuous deflation between 1999 and 2008 during a period called "the lost decade" of Japan's very slow economic growth. Thus policymakers and commentators worry whether the United States is headed toward an era of deflation over the next few years. Unfortunately as we learned in Chapter 5, policymakers are short of ammunition to fight against a possible future deflation. Monetary policy is hobbled by the zero lower bound, and fiscal policy is mired in political squabbles.

9-8   The Importance of Supply Shocks

Demand inflation is a sustained increase in prices that is preceded by a permanent acceleration of nominal GDP growth.

So far in this chapter, we have studied **demand inflation,** which is inflation caused by an acceleration of the growth rate of nominal aggregate demand—that is, nominal GDP. Demand inflation can be caused by changes in any of the demand factors studied earlier in the book—consumer and business confidence, the money supply, real wealth, the tightness or ease of credit conditions in financial markets, government spending, tax rates, transfers, and net exports. These same factors can also cause a deceleration in nominal GDP that leads to the adjustment paths of deflation depicted in Figure 9-7.

Supply inflation is an increase in prices that stems from an increase in business costs not directly related to a prior acceleration of nominal GDP growth.

Now we turn to a second reason for changes in the inflation rate, that is, **supply inflation.** As we see in the top frame of Figure 9-8, during the decade between 1971 and 1981 the U.S. inflation rate exhibited volatile accelerations and decelerations that can be attributed to supply inflation. Shifts in supply inflation also help us understand why inflation was so low in 1986, why it was again so low in 1995–2000, and why it speeded up during 2003–07.

Types of Supply Shocks

Supply inflation stems from sharp changes in business costs that are not related to prior changes in nominal GDP growth.

Oil shocks.   The most important single cause of supply inflation in the 1970s and early 1980s in most industrialized countries in the world was a sharp increase in the price of oil, shown in the bottom frame of Figure 9-8. A sharp decline in the price of oil in 1986 reversed some of the earlier harm done by supply inflation. The rise in the real price of oil during 1990, in 1999–2000, and again in 2003–08 are other examples of an adverse supply shock, while the declines during 1996–98 and during 2009–10 provide recent examples of a beneficial supply shock.

Farm price shocks.   Supply inflation can also result from an increase in the prices of other raw materials, particularly farm products, if they are sufficiently important. Sometimes the *weather* causes supply shocks, as in the case of a crop failure that causes a sharp increase in farm prices. Usually supply shocks caused by the weather are *temporary,* lasting only a year or two, after which conditions return to normal. The OPEC oil shocks, however, were considered *permanent,* causing an increase in the real price of oil that lasted from 1974 to 1986. Many observers think that a significant part of the 2003–08 increase in real oil prices will be permanent.

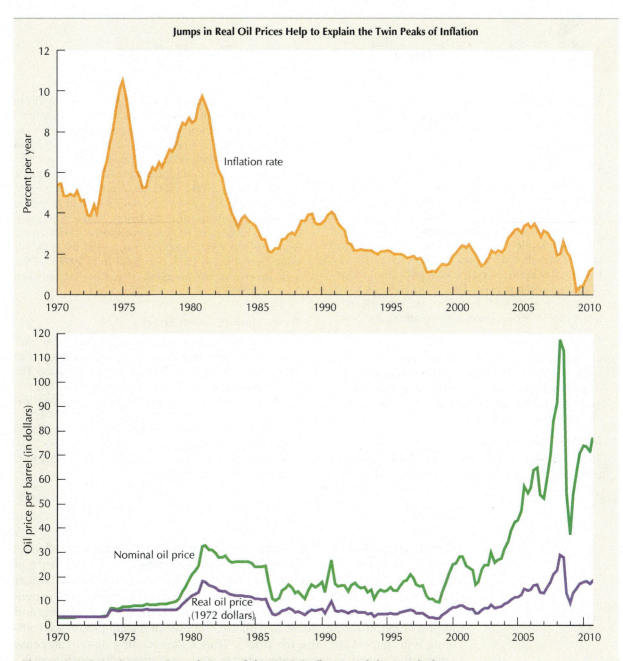

Jumps in Real Oil Prices Help to Explain the Twin Peaks of Inflation

Figure 9-8 **Four-Quarter Growth Rate of the GDP Deflator and the Level of Nominal and Real Oil Prices, 1970–2010**

The top frame displays the inflation rate since 1970; this is the same series as was plotted in Figure 9-1. In the bottom frame, the nominal price of oil is compared with the real price of oil, using 1972 as a base year. Notice the upsurge in inflation in the top frame at the times of the two oil shocks in the bottom frame, that is, in 1974 and 1979–80. Notice also the low point of inflation in 1986 when oil prices tumbled, and also the low level of inflation and oil prices in 1998. The gradual rise in the real oil price during 2003–08 caused only a modest increase in the inflation rate plotted in the top frame.

Sources: Top frame: Bureau of Economic Analysis *NIPA Tables*. Details in Appendix C-4. Bottom frame: Energy Information Administration *Monthly Energy Review*. Details in Appendix C-4.

Types of Supply Shocks and When They Mattered

This box summarizes the four types of supply shocks and when they mattered. When they were adverse they pushed the inflation rate higher. When they were beneficial they pushed the inflation rate lower.

Oil Shocks

Since 1970, the price of oil per barrel has ranged from $2 to $150. Oil shocks matter because oil prices affect all energy prices, including gasoline, heating oil, natural gas, and coal, and because past increases in oil prices have been sudden. Oil prices matter because a sharp increase filters through the rest of the economy by raising the prices of airline fares, trucking prices, and the prices of plastics and raw materials. Oil price shocks were adverse during 1973–81, beneficial during 1981–86 and again in 1995–99, and then adverse during 2003–08.

Farm Price Shocks

The prices of farm products doubled between 1972 and 1974, helping to set off the rapid inflation of the 1970s. More recently in 2005–2008, farm prices rose due to the increased demand for corn as a key ingredient in ethanol, an alternative to imported petroleum.

Import Price Shocks

When the dollar depreciates, the price of imported products rise, and this raises the price of consumer products, since so much of U.S. consumer expenditure is on imported products. Imports are excluded from GDP (because although they are part of consumer expenditures, they are not part of domestic production or GDP), nevertheless higher import prices put upward pressure on domestic prices. When Volkswagen, Mercedes, and BMW raise their prices of imported cars, this gives General Motors, Ford, and Chrysler the opportunity to raise the prices of their domestically produced cars. Import price shocks were adverse from 1970 to 1980, beneficial from 1980 to 1985, adverse from 1985 to 1987, beneficial from 1995 to 2002, and adverse again for most of the period between 2002 and 2008.

Productivity Growth Shocks

Faster productivity growth makes workers more efficient and, for any given wage rate, reduces the cost of hiring them in terms of the output they produce. The productivity growth effect on inflation does not happen month-to-month or year-to-year but over long time spans of five to ten years. Productivity growth shocks were adverse from 1965 to 1980, modestly beneficial in the early 1980s, strongly beneficial from 1995 to 2004, mildly adverse between 2004 and 2008, and highly beneficial in 2009 and early 2010.

Import price shocks. We learned in Chapter 7 that the foreign exchange rate of the dollar is flexible, appreciating or depreciating every day in terms of the number of units of foreign currency that a dollar can buy. When the dollar depreciates, it can buy less foreign currency, and imports become more expensive (*Review:* The effect of an exchange rate change on the prices of exports and imports is found on pp. 202–03). This then allows domestic producers competing with imports to raise the prices. Thus a depreciating dollar can cause higher inflation and an appreciating dollar can cause lower inflation. Figure 9-8 shows that most recently, inflation was held down during 1995–2002 by a dollar appreciation and pushed up in 2003–08 by a dollar depreciation. Previous periods with major depreciations were 1970–80 and 1985–87, and during 1980–85 there was a major appreciation that helps to explain why the inflation rate declined so much during that period in Figure 9-8.

Productivity growth shocks. When productivity growth is rapid, the amount each worker can produce grows rapidly, and it becomes cheaper to hire workers per unit that they produce. The effect of productivity growth on inflation does not come from year-to-year movements but from changes in productivity growth over longer periods of five to ten years, often labeled the "productivity growth trend." This trend slowed down from 1965 to 1980, helping to explain the high inflation of the 1980s. The trend gradually recovered after 1980, helping to explain the rapid decrease of inflation during 1980–85, but surged in 1995–2004, helping explain why inflation was so low in the late 1990s (a graph of the productivity trend for the United States is in Figure 12-5 on p. 409).

Adverse and Beneficial Supply Shocks

Supply shocks can be either *adverse* or *beneficial*. An adverse supply shock is one that makes inflation worse while causing real GDP to fall, as in the case of sharp increases in oil prices during the 1970s. A beneficial supply shock is one that reduces inflation while causing real GDP to rise, as in the case of the sharp decline in oil prices in 1986, 1997–98, and 2009.

Whether adverse or beneficial, supply shocks pose a difficult challenge for the makers of monetary and fiscal policy. Adverse supply shocks impose unpleasant choices on policymakers, who can avoid extra inflation only at the cost of lower real GDP, or vice versa. But even beneficial supply shocks may require policymakers to make choices.

Supply Shocks, the "Twin Peaks," and the "Valleys"

If demand shocks were the only cause of inflation, then we would observe periods after an acceleration of nominal GDP growth during which the output ratio would rise and the inflation rate would rise. Yet in other periods, the relationship between inflation and the output ratio would not be positive but rather negative. In the next section, we will learn to understand the source of this negative correlation as due to supply shocks that cause inflation to move sharply higher or lower, followed by a subsequent movement of the output ratio in the opposite direction. This explains the "twin peaks" of inflation in the periods 1974–75 and 1979–81. It also explains the "valleys" of low inflation in 1986 and 1997–98, both periods when the output ratio was rising.

Overall, we have seen that there are four types of supply shocks: oil, farm prices, import prices, and productivity growth. Each can be adverse or beneficial. An important reason that inflation was so high in the 1970s and early 1980s was that all four shocks were adverse during this period. Then inflation fell very rapidly after 1980, and this was due not just to tight monetary policy but to the fact that the oil, import price, and productivity growth shocks all turned from adverse to beneficial around 1980. Similarly, inflation was low despite a prosperous economy with a high output ratio between 1995 and 2000. In 2004–08, the oil price, import price, and productivity growth shocks were adverse, but inflation responded less to these shocks than in the 1970s.

The big run-up of nominal oil prices from $17 per barrel in early 2002 to $117 per barrel in 2008:Q2 was accompanied by a rise in the inflation rate from about 1.5 percent in early 2002 to 3.5 percent in early 2006. Economists have pondered why the inflation response to higher oil prices was relatively muted in 2002–06 in contrast to the sharp increase of inflation in response to the oil price increases of 1973–74 and 1979–80. One factor is that the output ratio was barely positive in 2002–07 and thus put no upward pressure on the inflation rate as had occurred with the positive output ratios of 1973 and 1979. A second factor is that workers found it harder to obtain wage increases when oil prices went up in 2002–08. Why? Since the 1970s, the bargaining position of American workers versus management has weakened, due to a marked decline in the percentage of workers unionized, to competition from low-skilled immigrant workers, and also to the effect of imports in shutting down factories that formerly provided relatively high-wage work for employees with high-school educations.

9-9 The Response of Inflation and the Output Ratio to a Supply Shock

In Figure 9-8 we examined the relationship between oil price shocks and the U.S. inflation rate. There we saw that increases in the *level* of the real price of oil caused a change in the aggregate *rate of inflation*. How can this response of the rate of inflation be explained in terms of the *SP* diagram?

Supply Shocks and the Short-Run Phillips (*SP*) Curve

To see how supply shocks can shift the *SP* curve, we use Figure 9-9. The SP_2 curve in Figure 9-9 assumes that the expected rate of inflation is 6 percent. The vertical axis plots the aggregate rate of inflation, while the horizontal axis plots the output ratio.

Supply shocks shift the *SP* schedule. As long as the real price of oil remains constant, the only factor that could make the *SP* curve shift would be a change in the expected rate of inflation (p^e). But if a supply shock changes the real price of oil, then we have a second reason why the *SP* curve might shift up.

Point E_4 in Figure 9-9 depicts a situation of long-run equilibrium. Actual inflation is 6 percent, and initially the rate of nominal GDP growth is assumed to be 6 percent. Since SP_2 assumes that expected inflation (p^e) is 6 percent, the condition $p^e = p$, required for long-run equilibrium, is satisfied.

Now let us assume that oil producers suddenly double the price of oil over the course of a year, as occurred in 1979, and let us assume that its action is sufficient *to add three extra percentage points to the inflation rate at any given level of the output ratio.* The three extra points of inflation are reflected in the upward shift of the *SP* schedule from SP_2 to SP_3. Where will the economy move along the new SP_3?

Figure 9-9 The Effect on the Inflation Rate and the Output Ratio of an Adverse Supply Shock That Shifts the *SP* Curve Upward by 3 Percent

The economy is initially at point E_4, with an output ratio of 100 percent and both actual and expected inflation rates of 6 percent. The supply shock shifts the *SP* curve upward to SP_3. The movement of the economy depends on the policy response. With an accommodating policy, the economy moves from E_4 to point N, with a neutral policy to point L, and with an extinguishing policy to point M.

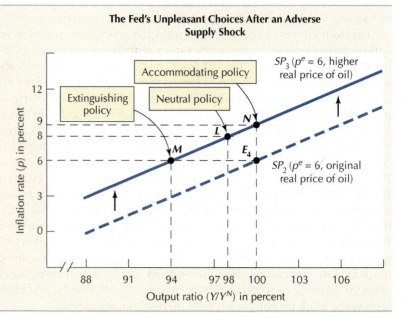

The Fed's Unpleasant Choices After an Adverse Supply Shock

Policy Responses to Supply Shocks

The response of the economy to the adverse permanent supply shock depicted in Figure 9-9 *depends on the response of nominal GDP growth*. The government can implement policy measures to alter nominal GDP growth. These policy actions determine where the economy moves along the new SP_3 schedule.

Neutral, accommodating, and extinguishing policy responses.   There are three possible policy responses. The first is called a **neutral policy.** Such a policy would attempt to keep nominal GDP growth unchanged from the original rate (6 percent). This is shown by point L in Figure 9-9. Since real GDP growth, by definition, must be equal to nominal GDP growth minus the inflation rate ($y = x - p$), *a neutral policy makes the output ratio decline by the same amount as inflation increases.* Thus, at point L, the output ratio falls by 2 percent (from 100 to 98) and inflation rises by 2 percentage points (from 6 to 8 percent).[8] The sum of -2 and $+2$ is precisely zero, the assumed zero change in the growth rate of nominal GDP.

Does the government have any way to escape the simultaneous worsening of inflation and decline in the output ratio shown at point L? It can keep the output ratio fixed only if it is willing to accept more inflation. Or, it can keep inflation from accelerating above 6 percent only if it is willing to accept a greater decline in the output ratio.

An **accommodating policy** attempts to maintain the output ratio intact at point N. To do this, inflation must be allowed to rise by the full extent of the vertical shift in SP, so that inflation jumps from 6 to 9 percent per year. This acceleration of inflation requires an acceleration of nominal GDP growth from 6 to 9 percent per year.

An **extinguishing policy** attempts to eliminate entirely the extra inflation caused by the supply shock. This requires cutting nominal GDP growth by 6 percent to zero, which is enough to take the economy to point M, where the inflation rate is 6 percent, but the output ratio has fallen from 100 to 94 percent (instead of to 98 percent at point L). Why is the extra four-point decline in the output ratio necessary? To extinguish the extra two percentage points of inflation that occur at L compared to M, the output ratio must be cut by four percentage points, since the slope of the SP curve is assumed to be 1/2 (two units in a vertical direction for each four units in the horizontal direction).

> Following a supply shock, a **neutral policy** maintains unchanged nominal GDP growth so as to allow a decline in the output ratio equal to the increase of the inflation rate.

> Following a supply shock, an **accommodating policy** raises nominal GDP growth so as to maintain the original output ratio.

> Following a supply shock, an **extinguishing policy** reduces nominal GDP growth so as to maintain the original inflation rate.

What Happens in Subsequent Periods

If the hypothetical supply shock occurs for just one period, then in Figure 9-9 the SP curve shifts down to its original position (SP_2) after one period at position SP_3. The economy would then be free to return to the original output ratio and the original inflation rate. The indirect effect on the output ratio (Y/Y^N) and on the rate of inflation would last for just one period.

But the SP curve returns to position SP_2 only if the expected inflation rate remains at 6 percent. The expected inflation rate must not respond to the increase in the actual inflation rate that occurs at points L and N in Figure 9-9. Is this plausible? The response of the expected inflation rate depends on whether people view the supply shock as temporary or permanent and on

---

[8] The text discussion of the graphical example in Figure 9-9 ignores the decline in Y^N that is likely to occur. The precise definition of a neutral policy is one involving no change in the excess of nominal GDP growth over the growth rate of natural real GDP from its initial value, assumed to be 6 percent ($x - y^N = 6$). This more precise definition is developed in the appendix to this chapter.

UNDERSTANDING THE GLOBAL ECONOMIC CRISIS

The Role of Inflation During the Housing Bubble and Subsequent Economic Collapse

We have already learned from the discussion of Figure 9-8 in the previous section that the inflation rate was surprisingly low in the late 1990s, given the high level of the output ratio shown here. The primary reason that inflation was so low, particularly in 1998 and 1999, was a set of reinforcing beneficial supply shocks, including oil prices that fell to as little as $11 per barrel in early 1999, a strong appreciation of the dollar during 1995–2002 that held down import prices, and a surprising revival of productivity growth during 1995–2004.

Inflation During the Housing Bubble Period of 2001–07

As shown in Figure 9-8 inflation was lower in 1998–99 than at any time since the early 1960s. As oil prices began to rise inflation also moved ahead moderately in 2000–01, slumped in 2002, and then began a sustained rise that lasted from 2002 until 2006. What factors caused this behavior of inflation? As usual, the outcome reflected a mix of demand and supply factors. As shown in the graph, the upward pressure on inflation of aggregate demand (as represented by the output ratio) declined markedly between 2000 and 2003, replacing upward pressure on inflation with slight downward pressure in 2001–03 and mild upward pressure in 2003–06.

Because the output ratio never rose appreciably above 100 percent in 2003–06, the main factor pushing up on inflation during those years was the adverse supply shock caused by the higher price of oil (see Figure 9-8 above). As shown in Figure 9-8, the increase in the real price of oil during 2002–08 was as large or

larger than in 1973–74 or 1979–80 but the macroeconomic disruption was not as large. Inflation did not respond as much to higher oil prices in 2002–08 as in the 1970s, and unlike the 1970s the sharply higher oil prices did not cause a recession prior to 2008. The most plausible answer to explain the smaller response of the overall inflation rate to the supply shock of 2002–08 is the diminished power of unions and the much less important role of COLAs in wage bargaining. Thus the higher oil prices of this period had very little impact on the core inflation rate.

Inflation During the Recession and Recovery, 2008–10

As shown in the graph, aggregate demand as measured by the output ratio collapsed after 2007, particularly in the last half of 2008 and first part of 2009. Part of this was the standard response of the economy to an adverse supply shock, as consumer purchasing power was drained by the oil shock in the form of a $4 price per gallon of gasoline during the summer of 2008. But there was also strong feedback from the economy to the inflation rate. Notice that the inflation rate declined sharply between 2007 and 2009, largely because of weak aggregate demand but also because oil prices plummeted after their brief peak in the early summer of 2008.

In summary inflation did not play an important role in causing the Global Economic Crisis of 2008–10. The adverse supply shock caused by rising oil prices in 2003–08 helps explain why the recovery was relatively weak, but the main causes of the crisis were those factors

whether labor contracts incorporate cost-of-living agreements (COLAs) that automatically boost wages by a percentage that is related to the inflation rate.

Why are COLAs crucial? Without COLAs, contract negotiators will recognize that it is possible for the economy to return to its original position (point E_4 in Figure 9-9) after the one-period effect of the supply shock. But with COLAs, the one-period increase of inflation (to point L or N) will be incorporated automatically into a faster growth of nominal wage rates *next period*. Contract negotiators in subsequent periods will see that COLAs have raised the rate of change of the nominal wage and will realize that this makes it impossible for the economy to return to point E_4. Their expected rate of inflation will shift up above the original 6 percent, and the SP curve will shift to a position above the original SP_2 in subsequent periods.

reviewed in Chapter 5. These include the housing bubble, excessive lending and indebtedness, financial market excesses and instability, lax regulation of financial institutions, and the fallout from the post-2006 collapse in housing prices which caused housing construction to collapse, eliminated millions of jobs in the construction industry, and through the multiplier effect pushed the rest of the economy into a recession.

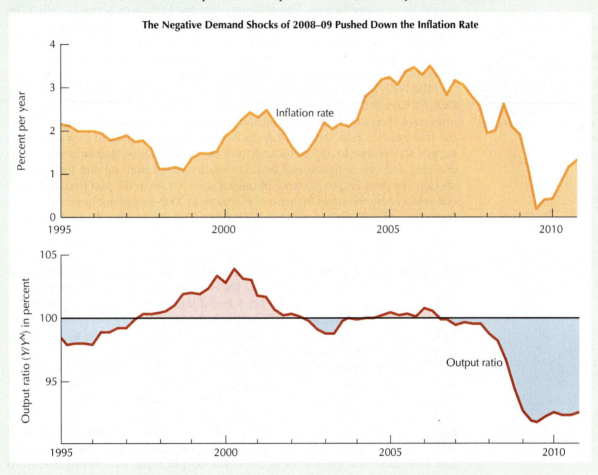

The Negative Demand Shocks of 2008–09 Pushed Down the Inflation Rate

The policy dilemma.   Thus we see that COLAs create a dilemma for the makers of monetary policy. COLAs imply that a permanent supply shock will permanently raise the inflation rate *unless an extinguishing policy response to the initial impact of the supply shock prevents any increase at all of inflation and thus prevents any increase at all in the rate of change of nominal wage rates.*

What should the Fed do when presented with this dilemma? It faces the classic trade-off between inflation and lost output. With even partial COLA protection for workers, a permanent adverse supply shock will permanently raise the inflation rate in the absence of an extinguishing policy. But this does not mean that the Fed should actually pursue such an extinguishing policy. The social costs of the loss in output may be severe, as (Y/Y^N) declines to point M in Figure 9-9, while the social costs of permanently higher inflation following a neutral or accommodating policy response may be relatively small. We examine those social costs in the next chapter.[9]

As it has faced a succession of adverse and beneficial supply shocks over the years since the 1970s, the Fed has relied on a distinction between two definitions of the inflation rate. The actual inflation rate as depicted in the top frames of Figures 9-1 and 9-8 is called the "headline" inflation rate and tends to respond positively when an adverse supply shock occurs that is due to higher oil prices or other factors. The inflation rate the Fed cares about is called the **core inflation rate** and *excludes the prices of food and energy.* Thus if the headline inflation rate rises but the core inflation rate remains unchanged, the Fed tends to ignore that extra headline inflation on the grounds that it is caused by inherently transitory movements in oil and food prices.

The Fed's target of core inflation also helps it deal with the dilemma caused by COLAs. Core inflation is primarily driven by wage increases. If COLA clauses are important, then supply shocks in oil and food prices will push up wage growth and the core inflation rate. But if COLA clauses become less important over time, then supply shocks due to higher oil and food prices will not be transmitted to wage changes, and core inflation will be relatively insulated from oil and food supply shocks. The declining importance of unions and COLAs in the past two decades is one reason why the rapid increase of oil prices in 2003–08 did not have as large an impact on overall inflation as in the 1970s when COLAs were much more common.

> The **core inflation rate** is the inflation rate for all products and services other than food and energy. The core inflation rate attracts attention because roughly a 2 percent annual rate of core inflation appears to be the inflation goal of the Federal Reserve.

Why Beneficial Supply Shocks Help Us Understand the 1990s

The great macroeconomic puzzle about U.S. economic performance in the 1990s, especially in 1996–2000, is why the economy performed so well. By early 2000, the unemployment rate had reached a lower level than in any calendar quarter since 1969, while in 1997–98 the inflation rate was lower than at any time since 1961. How could both unemployment and inflation be so low at the same time? Our analysis of supply shocks provides the answer.

The policy options in response to beneficial supply shocks like those in the late 1990s are the same as for adverse supply shocks like those of the 1970s and early 1980s. A neutral policy maintains constant nominal GDP growth, thus causing the benefits of the supply shock to be split between lower inflation and higher real GDP. An accommodating policy requires a reduction in nominal GDP growth, so that the entire impact of the beneficial shock reduces the inflation rate and none spills over to boost the output ratio. In contrast, the third policy option, an extinguishing policy, would keep the inflation rate constant and allow the full impact of the shock to boost the output ratio.

Preview: A Graphical Summary of the Role of Supply Shocks

The evolution of the U.S. economy was dominated by the effects of supply shocks in 1974–75, 1979–81, 1986, and again in 1996–2000. In the first two episodes, the supply shocks operated in an adverse direction, primarily due to sharp jumps in oil prices but also due to increases in non-oil import prices in response to a decline in the foreign exchange rate of the dollar. Accordingly, the

---

[9] The analysis of supply shocks in this chapter was introduced in two papers. See Robert J. Gordon, "Alternative Responses of Policy to External Supply Shocks," *Brookings Papers on Economic Activity,* vol. 6, no. 1 (1975), pp. 183–206, and Edmund S. Phelps, "Commodity Supply Shocks and Full-Employment Monetary Policy," *Journal of Money, Credit, and Banking,* vol. 10 (May 1978), pp. 206–21. The separate models in these two papers were merged and summarized in Robert J. Gordon, "Supply Shocks and Monetary Policy Revisited," *American Economic Review Papers and Proceedings,* vol. 74 (May 1984), pp. 38–43.

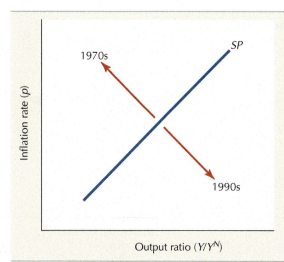

Figure 9-10 Effect of Adverse Supply Shocks in the 1970s and Beneficial Supply Shocks in the 1990s

The blue *SP* line shows the relationship between the inflation rate and the output ratio if there are no supply shocks. Adverse supply shocks, primarily increases in the real price of oil, moved the economy in an undesirable direction in the 1970s, with an acceleration of inflation and decline in the output ratio. Beneficial supply shocks, as discussed in the text, moved the economy in a desirable direction in the late 1990s, with a deceleration of inflation and an increase in the output ratio.

main response of the economy was for inflation to increase and for the output ratio to decline, as shown by the arrow marked "1970s" in Figure 9-10.

As we have seen, several supply shocks operated in the opposite (beneficial) direction during the late 1990s. These were oil prices, import prices, and productivity growth. As a result, the main response of the economy was for inflation to decrease and for the output ratio to increase, as shown by the arrow marked "1990s" in Figure 9-10.

 SELF-TEST

Imagine that the real price of oil falls by half within a single year and exhibits no change thereafter.

1. With what policy response will the inflation rate be reduced by this event in the year of the change?

2. With what policy response will the output ratio increase in the year of the change?

3. With what policy response will there be no change in the inflation rate? No change in the output ratio?

9-10 Inflation and Output Fluctuations: Recapitulation of Causes and Cures

In this chapter, we have learned that an acceleration of inflation can be caused by excessive nominal GDP growth and by adverse supply shocks. Supply inflation and demand inflation are interrelated because the extent and duration of the acceleration of inflation following a supply shock depends on the response of nominal GDP growth, which is controlled in part by policymakers.

A Summary of Inflation and Output Responses

Figure 9-11 provides a highly simplified summary of our analysis in this chapter. The figure presents four cases corresponding to (a) demand shifts

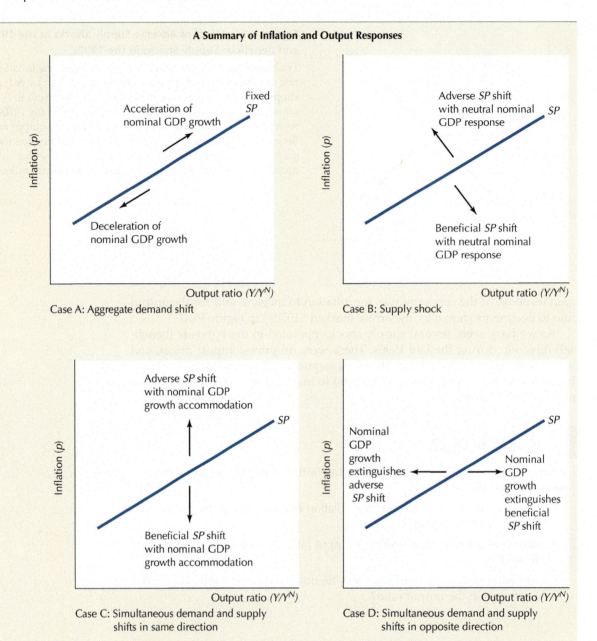

A Summary of Inflation and Output Responses

Case A: Aggregate demand shift

Case B: Supply shock

Case C: Simultaneous demand and supply shifts in same direction

Case D: Simultaneous demand and supply shifts in opposite direction

Figure 9-11 Responses of the Inflation Rate (p) and the Output Ratio (Y/Y^N) to Shifts in Nominal GDP Growth and in the SP Curve

In Case A, an aggregate demand shift moves the economy to the southwest, or to the northeast if there is no supply shift. In Case B, a supply shift moves the economy to the northwest, or to the southeast when nominal GDP growth is unchanged (a neutral policy response). Case C illustrates the northward or southward movement that occurs with an accommodative policy response to a supply shift. Case D illustrates the westward or eastward movement that accompanies a supply shift with an extinguishing supply response.

alone, (b) supply shifts alone, (c) demand and supply shifts in the same vertical direction, and (d) demand and supply shifts in opposite directions. In our discussion we identify examples from U.S. history that illustrate the four cases.

Case A: Demand shifts alone.   When we observe a marked increase in the output ratio with a modest or small increase in the rate of inflation, we can infer that there has been an increase in nominal aggregate demand growth with little if any shift in the SP curve. Expectations of inflation (p^e) remain roughly constant, and there are no supply shocks. The economy exhibited this type of response during 1963–66, when tax cuts and the beginning of Vietnam War spending, supported by monetary accommodation, boosted nominal GDP growth. A similar movement to the northeast occurred in 1987–89. Examples of a shift in a southwestern direction, with a deceleration of nominal GDP growth, occurred in the first few quarters of the 1981–82 recession, when there was a sharp decline in the output ratio with little downward response of the inflation rate, and a milder repeat of this episode in 1990–91 and 2001–02. In 2008–10 there was also a sharp decline in the output ratio with only a modest decline of the inflation rate.

Case B: Supply shifts alone.   The United States experienced a straight northwestward movement in 1973–74, when food and energy supply shocks, together with rising import prices and slowing productivity growth, sharply boosted the inflation rate, with a relatively small change in the rate of nominal GDP growth. As a result, the inflation rate and the output ratio moved in opposite directions and by about the same amount. In 1979 and 1980, a second supply shock had roughly the same impact. The most important examples of a southeast movement were caused by the 1986 collapse in the price of oil and by the beneficial supply shocks of 1996–2000 reviewed in the previous section.

Case C: Demand and supply shifts in the same vertical direction. When we observe the economy move straight north on the diagram, with an acceleration of inflation but little change in the output ratio, we can infer that there is a simultaneous demand and supply shift. For instance, between 1967 and 1969 nominal GDP growth accelerated while the SP curve shifted upward in response to accelerating inflationary expectations. As a result of this, inflation accelerated while the output ratio remained constant.

Case D: Demand and supply shifts in opposite directions.   The economy can move straight to the right when nominal GDP growth accelerates and cancels out the effect of a downward SP shift. This occurred in 1984, when the effect of falling inflation expectations in holding down the inflation rate was offset by rapid nominal GDP growth. A leftward movement can occur when nominal GDP growth decelerates while the SP curve is shifting upward. This occurred during the 1969–70 recession, when nominal GDP growth slowed while the SP curve was shifting upward as the expected inflation rate (p^e) continued its slow and delayed adjustment to the acceleration of actual inflation during 1966–69. This interpretation helps us understand why inflation in early 1971 was still as rapid as in 1969 despite an intervening decline in the output ratio. The same pattern was repeated in 1989–90.

◆ **SELF-TEST**

In Figure 9-11, which plots the inflation rate against the output ratio, it is possible for the economy to move in any direction. Can you explain why the economy would move in each possible direction:

1. North?	5. South?
2. Northeast?	6. Southwest?
3. East?	7. West?
4. Southeast?	8. Northwest?

Cures for Inflation

Just as excessive nominal GDP growth and adverse supply shocks are the fundamental causes of inflation, the basic cure for inflation is to turn these causes on their head. The reverse of fast nominal GDP growth is obviously slow nominal GDP growth. A decision to reduce the inflation rate by restricting the growth rate of nominal GDP can be both effective and costly, as in 1981–82 or, to a lesser extent, in 1990–92. Inflation can be cut markedly, but only at the cost of a substantial and prolonged slump in the output ratio and a substantial increase in the number of jobless workers.

But government policy against inflation is not limited to creating a deceleration of nominal GDP growth. Whether there are adverse supply shocks or not, the government can attempt to create beneficial supply shocks by eliminating or weakening price-raising or cost-raising legislation, and by creative tax and subsidy policy.

Sometimes government policymakers are just plain lucky, as when a beneficial supply shock occurs. The decline in oil prices in 1986 was one example of such a beneficial shock, and so was the role of several beneficial supply shocks in 1996–2000. In these episodes, it is important for policymakers to recognize their good luck and to prepare for a possible reversal in the sources of the beneficial shocks by not allowing the economy to become overstimulated. For instance, some observers think that the Fed should have raised interest rates sooner in 1998–2000 because the output ratio was too high and the stock market boom was unsustainable.

The Fed's policy responses after 2000 are in part explained by the behavior of the inflation rate. Many economists have criticized the Fed for holding down interest rates for too low and for too long in 2002–04 (see pp. 468–71), and they have claimed that this was a major cause of the housing bubble of 2001–06. Yet the Fed claims to have been worried during that period by the threat of deflation, which can have adverse consequences for aggregate demand that were reviewed in the previous chapter (pp. 251–52). As inflation speeded up in large part due to the adverse oil supply shock during the 2003–06 period, the Fed sharply raised the federal funds rate from 1.0 percent in mid-2004 to 5.25 percent in 2006–07. Thus the behavior of inflation had an influence on the responses of policymakers.

Inflation was a sideshow in the Global Economic Crisis of 2008–10. The inflation rate did not cause the crisis but mainly reacted to it, declining appreciably in response to the collapse in the output ratio. Indeed as the economy remained weak in 2010–11 with a continuation of a low output ratio and a high unemployment rate, the Fed began once again to worry about deflation.

9-11   How Is the Unemployment Rate Related to the Inflation Rate?

Economists frequently discuss the "trade-off between unemployment and inflation." Is there such a trade-off? In this section we learn that there is a strong negative correlation between the unemployment rate and the *output ratio*, and so: *Everything we have learned in this chapter about the relationship between the output ratio and the inflation rate is true in the reverse direction for the relationship between the unemployment rate and the inflation rate. Since the relationship between the output ratio and the inflation rate can be positive, negative, vertical, or horizontal, the same is true for the relationship between the unemployment rate and the inflation rate. In short, there is no systematic negative relationship between the unemployment rate and the inflation rate.*

Changes in the Unemployment Rate Are the Mirror Image of Changes in Real GDP

At the beginning of this book, we learned that the unemployment rate and inflation rate are two of the most important concepts in macroeconomics. What have we learned thus far about the unemployment rate? Beginning in Chapter 1 (see Figure 1-2 on p. 6) we learned that the unemployment rate is *inversely related* to real GDP, or more precisely, to the *output ratio* (the ratio of actual real GDP to natural real GDP). Thus we can discuss the economy's prosperity as described either by *low* unemployment or a *high* output ratio. We can describe the opposite conditions of weak aggregate demand, recessions, and job loss either by *high* unemployment or a *low* output ratio.

Throughout Chapters 3–7 of this book, we focused on explaining business cycles in real GDP, caused primarily by the ups and downs in aggregate demand. *We have not required a separate theory to explain unemployment, simply because unemployment is inversely related to the output ratio.* Any factor that raises aggregate demand—whether events in the private sector of the economy such as business and consumer optimism or an increase in foreign income that raises net exports, or an event in the government sector such as higher government spending, lower tax rates, or a higher money supply—all of these both boost the output ratio and reduce unemployment. In this section, we will take a closer look at the mirror image relationship between the unemployment rate and the output ratio.

The Unemployment Rate, the Output Ratio, and Okun's Law

The close relationship between the unemployment rate and the output ratio is illustrated in Figure 9-12. The unemployment rate is plotted on the vertical axis, and the average unemployment rate since 1965 is indicated at a vertical level of 6.0 percent. The output ratio is plotted on the horizontal axis, and the long-run equilibrium value of the output ratio is marked at 100 percent.

In Figure 9-12 we notice the cluster of prosperous years, 1965–69 and 1999–2000, in the lower right corner, with values of the output ratio well above 100 percent and unusually low unemployment rates. The contrasting situation in the upper left corner occurred in the recession years 1982, 1983, 2009, and 2010, when massive layoffs caused the output ratio to fall and unemployment to rise. The negative slope of the blue line going through the points in Figure 9-12 just reflects common sense. When sales slump, workers are laid off and the jobless rate rises. But when sales boom and the output ratio is high, some of the jobless are hired and the unemployment rate declines.

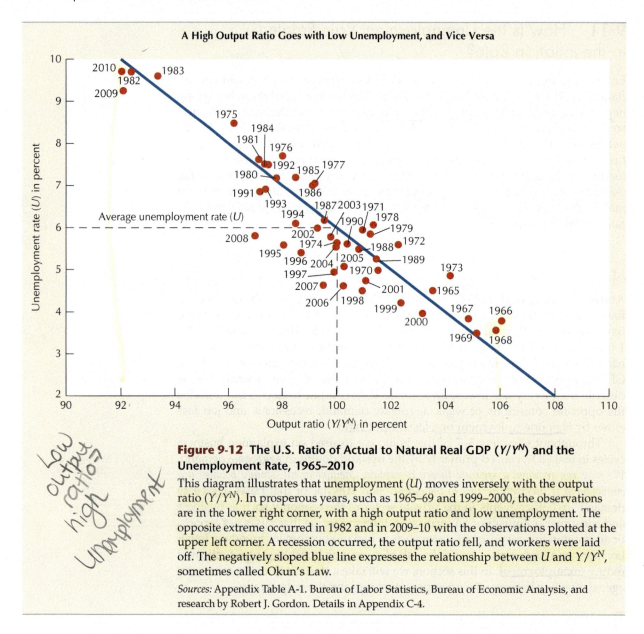

Figure 9-12 The U.S. Ratio of Actual to Natural Real GDP (Y/Y^N) and the Unemployment Rate, 1965–2010

This diagram illustrates that unemployment (U) moves inversely with the output ratio (Y/Y^N). In prosperous years, such as 1965–69 and 1999–2000, the observations are in the lower right corner, with a high output ratio and low unemployment. The opposite extreme occurred in 1982 and in 2009–10 with the observations plotted at the upper left corner. A recession occurred, the output ratio fell, and workers were laid off. The negatively sloped blue line expresses the relationship between U and Y/Y^N, sometimes called Okun's Law.

Sources: Appendix Table A-1. Bureau of Labor Statistics, Bureau of Economic Analysis, and research by Robert J. Gordon. Details in Appendix C-4.

Okun's Law is a regular negative relationship between the output ratio (Y/Y^N) and the gap between the actual unemployment rate and the average rate of unemployment.

The close negative connection between the unemployment rate (U) and the output ratio was first pointed out in the early 1960s by Arthur M. Okun, who was chairman of the Council of Economic Advisers in the Johnson administration. Because this theory has held up so well, the relationship is known as **Okun's Law.** U tends to follow the major movements in the output ratio; in addition, the percentage-point change in the unemployment rate tends to be roughly 0.5 times the percentage change in the output ratio, in the opposite direction. For instance, the downward-sloping Okun's Law line is drawn so that an output ratio of 100 percent corresponds to an average actual unemployment rate of 6.0 percent. A drop in the output ratio by 4 percentage points, from 100 to 96, would correspond to an increase in the unemployment rate of 2.0 percentage points, as indicated by the Okun's Law line going through 8.0 percent unemployment on the vertical axis and 96 percent on the horizontal axis.

Recall that the output ratio is defined as the ratio of actual to natural real GDP. When the output ratio is equal to 100 percent, the actual unemployment rate is equal to the natural rate of unemployment. Throughout much of the period plotted in Figure 9-12, the natural unemployment rate was very close to the average unemployment rate of 6.0 percent. In periods like 1965–69, the output ratio was well above 100 percent and the actual unemployment rate was well below the natural rate of unemployment. In periods like 1982–83 and 2009–10, the output ratio was well below 100 percent and the actual unemployment rate was well above the natural rate of unemployment.[10]

Notice that in Figure 9-12 that some of the observations lie underneath the blue Okun's Law line while others lie above that line. This reflects the fact that, while the diagram is drawn on the assumption that 6.0 percent unemployment corresponds to an output ratio of 100 percent, in fact the natural rate of unemployment has not been a constant value of 6.0 percent forever. Starting around 1990, the natural rate of unemployment declined, and so the unemployment rate corresponding to a 100 percent output ratio began to decline from 6.0 percent toward 5.0 percent or even less.

If you look closely at Figure 9-12, you'll notice that most of the observations lying well below the blue Okun's law line are for years between 1993 and 2010. The red dots above the blue Okun's law line are mainly for years in the 1970s and 1980s. We return to the post-1990 decline of the natural rate of unemployment on pp. 345–46 in Chapter 10.

Interpreting the Postwar History of Unemployment and Inflation

The analysis of this chapter now allows us to interpret the history of unemployment and inflation since 1960, as displayed in Figure 9-13. We have already learned that when supply shocks are absent, an increase in aggregate demand boosts the output ratio and the inflation rate. Because unemployment declines when the output ratio rises, an increase in aggregate demand creates a *negative trade-off* between unemployment and inflation. It is this negative tradeoff that restrains the Fed from allowing aggregate demand to increase so much that the unemployment rate is pushed substantially below the natural rate of unemployment.

When is the unemployment rate too low? This occurs whenever the output ratio rises above 100 percent, implying that the actual unemployment rate falls substantially below the natural rate of unemployment. As shown in Figure 9-13 by the blue line, the unemployment rate fell to its lowest level of the entire period during 1965–69, and the orange line shows the acceleration of inflation that occurred between 1965 and 1970. This was the classic period of the negative trade-off between unemployment and inflation, but once inflation expectations and wages began to ratchet upward in response to accelerating inflation, the Fed introduced restrictive policies that reduced aggregate demand, and the unemployment rate shot up in 1970–71.

A similar and milder episode of relatively low unemployment in 1988–89 also pushed up the inflation rate in 1988–90 and again elicited a restrictive response by the Fed that reduced aggregate demand and led to the recession of 1990–91. The negative trade-off between unemployment and inflation is also evident in the periods when high unemployment brought the inflation rate down, as in 1975–76, 1982–83, 1991–92, 2001–02, and 2008–10.

---

[10] *Review:* Natural real GDP and the natural rate of unemployment are both defined as a situation consistent with a constant inflation rate. See Section 1-3, pp. 4–7.

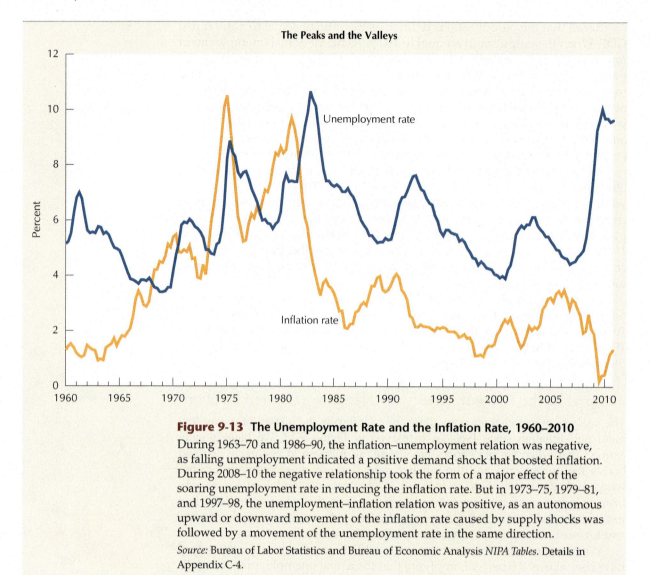

The Peaks and the Valleys

Figure 9-13 **The Unemployment Rate and the Inflation Rate, 1960–2010**

During 1963–70 and 1986–90, the inflation–unemployment relation was negative, as falling unemployment indicated a positive demand shock that boosted inflation. During 2008–10 the negative relationship took the form of a major effect of the soaring unemployment rate in reducing the inflation rate. But in 1973–75, 1979–81, and 1997–98, the unemployment–inflation relation was positive, as an autonomous upward or downward movement of the inflation rate caused by supply shocks was followed by a movement of the unemployment rate in the same direction.

Source: Bureau of Labor Statistics and Bureau of Economic Analysis *NIPA Tables.* Details in Appendix C-4.

A central theme of this chapter has been that demand shocks and supply shocks have opposing effects on the relationship between the output ratio and inflation—demand shocks create a positive relation and supply shocks create a negative relationship. The same thing is true of the relationship between unemployment and inflation, but in reverse. There is a *negative trade-off* between unemployment and inflation created by demand shocks, and a *positive relation* between unemployment and inflation created by supply shocks. This is evident in the 1970s, when sharp increases in oil prices in 1974–75 and 1979–81 created the "twin peaks" of unemployment and inflation. In each case, inflation soared first, which pushed the economy into recession. In 1975, the peak of unemployment came about six months after the peak of inflation; in 1982, the peak of unemployment came about 18 months after the peak of inflation. Thus inflation created these recessions, just as in the theoretical model of Figure 9-9 on p. 288.

Beneficial supply shocks also created a positive relation between unemployment and inflation in the late 1990s. By making possible a decline of inflation in

1997–98 despite high aggregate demand, supply shocks made it possible for the Fed to keep interest rates relatively stable, and as a result unemployment declined steadily from 1992 to 1999. These beneficial supply shocks were reversed in 2002–03, and inflation after 2003 was almost twice as high as in the late 1990s.

Implications of the Unemployment–Inflation Trade-off

As we can see from Figure 9-13, unemployment is sometimes negatively related to inflation because of demand shocks and sometimes positively related because of supply shocks. In the absence of supply shocks, however, the negative unemployment–inflation trade-off is the primary constraint that prevents the Fed from allowing aggregate demand to grow without limit. When the unemployment rate falls below the natural rate of unemployment, the Fed must raise interest rates in order to restrain the growth of aggregate demand and prevent an acceleration of inflation. Often the Fed's restrictive policies create a recession, as in 1969–70, 1981–82, and 1990–91, and the recession raises the unemployment rate and reverses the acceleration of inflation, working through the negative unemployment–inflation trade-off.

The unemployment–inflation trade-off suggests that the unemployment rate cannot be maintained below the natural rate of unemployment for any substantial length of time. To achieve a lower unemployment rate permanently, something must happen to reduce the natural rate of unemployment itself. Indeed, in the 1990s the natural rate of unemployment fell from roughly 6 percent to roughly 5 percent. In the next chapter, we will learn about both the costs of inflation and the determinants of the natural rate of unemployment, and about some of the factors that reduced the natural rate of unemployment after 1990.

Summary

1. The fundamental cause of demand inflation is excessive growth in nominal GDP. In long-run equilibrium, when actual inflation turns out to be exactly what people expected when they negotiated their labor contracts, the pace of that inflation depends only on the growth rate of nominal GDP.

2. In the short run, actual inflation may be higher or lower than expected, and real GDP can differ from long-run equilibrium natural real GDP. An acceleration of nominal GDP growth in the short run goes partially into an acceleration of inflation, but also partly into an increase in the output ratio, that is, the ratio of actual to natural real GDP. When expectations of inflation catch up to actual inflation, the economy will return to its level of natural real GDP.

3. The response of inflation to an acceleration in demand growth depends on the slope of the short-run Phillips Curve (SP) and the speed with which expectations of inflation respond to changes in the actual inflation rate. The flatter is the SP curve, the longer it takes for inflation to respond to faster nominal GDP growth, and the longer the temporary expansion of the output ratio.

4. A permanent end to inflation requires that nominal GDP growth drop to the growth rate of natural real GDP, assumed in the text to be zero. But this will cause a temporary recession in actual real GDP, the length and intensity of which will depend on the slope of the SP curve.

5. The highly variable inflation experience of the United States since the 1960s cannot be explained solely as the consequence of previous fluctuations in the growth rate of nominal GDP. Instead, supply shocks caused inflation to accelerate and decelerate independently of the influence of nominal GDP growth.

6. The main effect of an adverse supply shock is the impact on the inflation rate and on the output ratio. Policymakers cannot avoid a worsening of inflation, a decline in the output ratio, or both. An accommodating policy keeps real GDP at its previous level, but causes inflation to accelerate by the full impact of the supply shock; an extinguishing policy attempts to cancel out the acceleration of inflation, but at the cost of a reduction in real GDP.

7. There are four types of supply shocks, each of which can be adverse or beneficial. An increase in the real price of oil, the real price of farm products, the real price of imports, and a decrease in the long-term trend in productivity growth are adverse supply shocks. The reverse changes are beneficial supply shocks.

8. Accommodation would be an attractive policy if the upward shift in the *SP* curve were expected to be temporary, and if expectations of inflation did not respond to the temporary jump in the inflation rate. But accommodation may cause a permanent increase of inflation if wage contracts have cost-of-living adjustment clauses that incorporate the supply shock into wage growth.

9. The low inflation rate experienced by the United States in the late 1990s reflected in part the role of beneficial supply shocks, created by favorable developments in the medical care and computer industries, as well as the falling real prices of energy and imports.

10. Demand shocks create a negative trade-off between unemployment and inflation, and supply shocks create a positive relation between unemployment and inflation. The negative trade-off created by demand shocks explains why the Fed has used restrictive policy in several episodes to create recessions in order to control inflation.

Concepts

inflation

output ratio

demand shock

supply shock

expected rate of inflation

short-run Phillips (*SP*) Curve

expectations-augmented
    Phillips Curve

forward-looking
    expectations

backward-looking
    expectations

adaptive expectations

disinflation

cold turkey

sacrifice ratio

demand inflation

supply inflation

neutral policy

accommodating policy

extinguishing policy

core inflation rate

Okun's Law

Questions

1. Use Figure 9-1 to discuss when, since 1960, the output ratio and the inflation rate moved in the same direction and when they moved in opposite directions.

2. In what ways are the *SAS* curve and the *SP* curve similar? In what ways do they differ?

3. Explain whether each of the following events causes a movement up or down along the *SP* curve or an upward or downward shift of the *SP* curve.
   (a) an increase in the rate of money supply growth
   (b) an increase in the inflation rate expected by workers and business firms
   (c) a decrease in production costs resulting from technological improvements
   (d) a decrease in nominal GDP growth

4. If the equilibrium real wage remains constant, what happens to the nominal wage when the actual inflation rate exceeds the expected inflation rate?

5. What are the three conditions for long-run equilibrium? What happens if each of the conditions is violated?

6. In Figure 9-4, why can't the economy move from point E_0 to point *D* when the level of real GDP increases?

7. Distinguish between forward-looking and backward-looking expectations. Which type of expectations would rational workers and firms be most likely to use? Explain why.

8. Suppose that when nominal GDP growth changes, workers and firms immediately adjust their inflation expectations so that $p^e = x$. Is this an example of forward-looking or backward-looking expectations? How does it alter the adjustment loops in Figures 9-5 and 9-7? How does it affect the output cost of disinflation?

9. Suppose that workers and business firms believe that the Fed will take action to prevent demand shocks from causing a permanent change in the inflation rate.
   (a) Will the short-run Phillips Curve shift when a change in the output ratio changes the inflation rate?
   (b) For workers and business firms to continue to hold these expectations, explain what actions the Fed must take when there is a positive demand shock and when there is a negative demand shock.

10. Assume that the output ratio initially equals 100 and that natural real GDP grows by 3 percent per year. If p^e remains constant and actual real GDP rises, what happens to the rate of inflation?

11. Explain what the four types of supply shocks are and when each type had an adverse or beneficial impact on the economy.

12. What differentiates accommodating, extinguishing, and neutral policy responses to an adverse supply shock? What happens to the rate of inflation and the output ratio in each of the three cases?

13. Under what conditions would a permanent supply shock cause a temporary increase in the inflation rate? If these conditions exist, are there any permanent effects of the supply shock on the economy?

14. Explain why inflation was so low in the late 1990s and why it rose between 2002 and 2006.

15. Identify the combination of changes in nominal GDP growth and supply shocks that could account for each of the following observed changes in inflation and the output ratio.
    (a) Inflation and the output ratio both increase.
    (b) Inflation increases and the output ratio decreases.
    (c) Inflation is constant and the output ratio decreases.
    (d) Inflation decreases and the output ratio is constant.
16. What is the difference between the "headline" inflation rate and the core inflation rate? Discuss which one of these inflation rates the Fed pays the closest attention to in deciding how to react to supply shocks.

17. Explain why sharply higher oil prices in the last decade resulted in only a modest increase in the inflation rate between 2002 and 2006.
18. Explain why the correlation between the unemployment and inflation rates can be positive, zero, or negative.
19. In each of the following cases, explain whether the policymakers' response to a beneficial supply shock was accommodating, extinguishing, or neutral.
    (a) The inflation rate fell, but the unemployment rate did not change.
    (b) The inflation and the unemployment rates both fell.
    (c) The unemployment rate fell, but the inflation rate did not change.

Problems

 Visit www.MyEconLab.com to complete these or similar exercises.

1. Suppose that natural real GDP is constant. For every 1 percent increase in the rate of inflation above its expected level, firms are willing to increase real GDP by 4 percent. The purpose of this problem is to learn how to draw the short-run Phillips Curve and to understand how either a change in the expected rate of inflation or a supply shock causes it to shift.
    (a) Given that the output ratio is initially 100 and the expected inflation rate equals 3.2 percent, calculate the rate of inflation if real GDP grows by 3.2 percent.
    (b) Given that the output ratio is initially 100 and the expected inflation rate equals 3.2 percent, calculate the rate of inflation if real GDP grows by 5.6 percent.
    (c) Given that the output ratio is initially 100 and the expected inflation rate equals 3.2 percent, calculate the rate of inflation if real GDP declines by 2.4 percent.
    (d) Given that the output ratio is initially 100 and the expected inflation rate equals 3.2 percent, calculate the rate of inflation if real GDP declines by 4.4 percent.
    (e) Use your answers to parts a–d to draw the short-run Phillips Curve, given that the expected inflation rate equals 3.2 percent.
    (f) Given that the output ratio is initially 100 and the expected inflation rate equals 1.4 percent, calculate the rate of inflation if real GDP grows by 2.8 percent.
    (g) Given that the output ratio is initially 100 and the expected inflation rate equals 1.4 percent, calculate the rate of inflation if real GDP grows by 5.2 percent.
    (h) Given that the output ratio is initially 100 and the expected inflation rate equals 1.4 percent, calculate the rate of inflation if real GDP declines by 1.6 percent.
    (i) Given that the output ratio is initially 100 and the expected inflation rate equals 1.4 percent, calculate the rate of inflation if real GDP declines by 6.4 percent.
    (j) Use your answers to parts f–i to draw the short-run Phillips Curve, given that the expected inflation rate equals 1.4 percent.

    (k) Suppose that a beneficial supply shock lowers the inflation rate by 1.2 percentage points at any output ratio. Use your answers to parts f–i to draw the short-run Phillips Curve, given the beneficial supply shock.
2. Suppose that natural real GDP is constant. For every 1 percent increase in the rate of inflation above its expected level, firms are willing to increase real GDP by 1 percent. The expected rate of inflation in the current period equals the actual rate of inflation in the previous period. Initially the output ratio is 100 and the actual and expected inflation rates equal 2 percent.
    (a) Compute points on the short-run Phillips Curve when the inflation rate equals 0, 1, 2, 3, 4, and 5. Graph the short-run Phillips Curve.
    (b) What is the growth rate of nominal GDP in the economy?
    Suppose that due to baby boomers becoming eligible for Medicare, there is a permanent increase in the growth rate of the federal government's spending. That increase causes the growth rate of nominal GDP to accelerate to 4 percent.
    (c) Use the short-run Phillips Curve to explain what the rate of inflation and the output ratio are in the first period after the increase in the growth rate of nominal GDP.
    (d) Explain what the inflation rate is in the long run, given the increase in the growth rate of nominal GDP, and describe how the economy adjusts to the long-run equilibrium.
3. Use the information contained in problem 2 to answer this problem. Suppose that monetary policymakers do not want to see a permanent rise in the inflation rate result from the increase in government spending. So following the increase in government spending, they take actions to reduce the growth rate of nominal GDP.
    (a) What is the expected inflation rate in the second period? Compute points on the new short-run

Phillips Curve for the second period when the inflation rate equals 0, 1, 2, 3, 4, and 5, given the expected inflation rate in the second period. Graph the short-run Phillips Curve for the second period.

(b) If monetary policymakers wish to reduce the rate of inflation to 2 percent in the second period, what must they reduce the growth rate of the nominal GDP to in the second period and what is the output ratio at the end of the second period, given the monetary contraction?

(c) What is the expected inflation rate in the third period? Compute points on the new short-run Phillips Curve for the third period when the inflation rate equals 0, 1, 2, 3, 4, and 5, given the expected inflation rate in the third period. Graph the short-run Phillips Curve for the third period. In order to maintain an inflation rate of 2 percent in the third period, explain why the growth rate in nominal GDP would have to be greater than 2 percent in the third period. What would the growth rate of nominal GDP have to be the long run in order to maintain an inflation rate equal to 2 percent?

Suppose that monetary policymakers have been able to establish a record of maintaining inflation at 2 percent. As a result, workers and employers expect that any increase or decrease in the inflation rate is only temporary because monetary policymakers take steps to change the growth rate of nominal GDP so as to quickly restore inflation to its long-run equilibrium level of 2 percent.

(d) Given the expectation that any increase or decrease in the inflation rate is only temporary, does the short-run Phillips Curve shift up or down when the actual inflation rate deviates from the expected inflation rate?

(e) Given your answer to part d, what must monetary policymakers reduce the growth rate of the nominal GDP to in the second period in order to reduce the inflation rate to 2 percent and what is the output ratio at the end of the second period, given the monetary contraction? What would the growth rate of nominal GDP have to be in the third period in order to maintain an inflation rate of 2 percent?

(f) Explain why your answers to parts b, c, and e are different.

4. The purpose of this problem is to study the sacrifice ratio. Suppose that initially actual and natural real GDP both equal 11,000 and that the rate of inflation is 3.5 percent. Natural real GDP grows by 3 percent per year over the next five years. Actual real GDP decreases by 2 percent in the first year, but then grows by 4 percent in the second year, 5.5 percent in the third year, 4.2 percent in the fourth year, and 3.5 percent in the fifth year. Inflation in years 1–5 equals 3.1 percent, 2.2 percent, 1.6 percent, 1.3 percent, and 1.1 percent, respectively.

(a) Calculate natural real GDP for years 1–5.
(b) Calculate actual real GDP for years 1–5.
(c) Calculate the output ratio for years 1–5.
(d) Calculate the cumulative loss of output for years 1–5.
(e) Calculate the sacrifice ratio.

5. Suppose that natural real GDP is constant. For every 1 percent increase in the rate of inflation above its expected level, firms are willing to increase real GDP by 2 percent. The output ratio is initially 100 and the inflation rate equals 2 percent.

(a) Based upon the preceding information, draw the short-run Phillips Curve.
(b) What is the growth rate of nominal GDP in the economy?

An adverse supply shock raises the inflation rate associated with every output ratio by 3 percentage points.

(c) Draw the new short-run Phillips Curve.
(d) The government chooses to follow a neutral policy in response to this shock. What will be the growth rate of nominal GDP? What will be the new rate of inflation? What will be the output ratio?
(e) If the government chooses to follow an accommodating policy, what would be the new inflation rate? The output ratio? The growth rate of nominal GDP?
(f) If the government chooses to follow an extinguishing policy, what would be the new inflation rate? The output ratio? The growth rate of nominal GDP?

◆ SELF-TEST ANSWERS

p. 271. (1) Everywhere to the right of 100 percent actual inflation is greater than expected inflation (for instance, actual inflation of 3 percent at E_1 is greater than expected inflation of $p^e = 0$ along the SP_0 line). (2) Everywhere to the left of 100 percent actual inflation is less than expected inflation. (3) Only at 100 percent is expected inflation correct.

p. 273. (1) A decline in aggregate demand moves the economy to the left of point E_3, down along the SP_1 curve. (2) When real GDP declines from 100 to 94, the actual inflation rate drops to zero, and is now below the 3 percent inflation rate expected everywhere along the SP_1 curve. Eventually the expected inflation rate will decline as well, shifting the *SP* curve downward. (3) The *LP* curve remains fixed.

p. 279. Why in Figure 9-5 is the orange line from point 1 to 2 steeper than the blue line from E_0 to point 1? The line is steeper because inflation is higher at point 2 than at point 1, because the expected rate of inflation (p^e) has shifted up in response to the actual inflation that occurred at point 1. And, since nominal GDP growth (x) is the same at point 1 and point 2, but inflation (p) is higher, the growth of real GDP ($y = x - p$) must be less from 1 to 2 than from E_0 to point 1. Similarly, since inflation is even higher at point 3, real GDP growth must be even lower, and in fact is negative, going from point 2 to point 3.

p. 281. (1) The slope of the *SP* curve determines how a slowdown in nominal GDP growth is divided between a decline in the inflation rate (p) and a decline in real GDP growth (y). The flatter the *SP* curve, the larger is the decline in real GDP and the smaller is the decline in actual inflation. With backward-looking (adaptive) expectations, a smaller decline in the actual inflation rate produces a smaller decline in the next period's expected inflation rate. Smaller declines in expected inflation make the economy's adjustment path longer: It takes more time for the economy to return to long-run equilibrium. (2) Conversely, the economy's adjustment path is shorter the steeper the *SP* curve and the faster the decline in actual and, hence, in expected inflation.

p. 293. (1) The inflation rate will fall in the year of the decline in the relative price of oil, except in the case of an extinguishing policy that raises nominal GDP growth sufficiently to cancel out the oil price effect. And, if the inflation rate declines in the first year, it will also decline in subsequent years if the expected rate of inflation declines and/or if COLA agreements cause lower inflation in the first year to cause lower wage changes in subsequent years. (2) The output ratio will increase unless there is an accommodating policy that cuts nominal GDP growth by the amount of the supply stock. (3) An extinguishing policy response will prevent a change in the inflation rate. An accommodating policy response will prevent a change in the output ratio.

p. 296. *North:* an adverse supply shock accommodated by an increase in nominal GDP growth. *Northeast:* an acceleration of nominal GDP growth, causing inflation during the period prior to the adjustment of expectations. *East:* a beneficial supply shock extinguished by an increase in nominal GDP growth. *Southeast:* a beneficial supply shock accompanied by an unchanged rate of nominal GDP growth. *South:* a beneficial supply shock accommodated by a reduction in nominal GDP growth. *Southwest:* a deceleration of nominal GDP growth, causing disinflation prior to the adjustment of expectations. *West:* an adverse supply shock extinguished by a reduction in nominal GDP growth. *Northwest:* an adverse supply shock accompanied by an unchanged rate of nominal GDP growth.

Appendix to Chapter 9

The Elementary Algebra of the *SP-DG* Model

Throughout Chapter 9, we have located the short-run equilibrium rate of inflation and level of real GDP along an *SP* curve, as at point E_4 of Figure 9-9. Now we learn how to draw a second line—the *DG* line—which shows where the economy will operate along the *SP* schedule. We also learn how to calculate the inflation rate and level of real GDP without going to the trouble of making drawings of the *SP* and *DG* lines. We do this by solving together the equations that describe the *SP* and *DG* lines, just as we did in the Appendix to Chapter 4, where we learned the equivalent in algebra to the *IS* and *LM* curves. We use *SP-DG* diagrams to show that either the algebraic or graphical method leads to the same answer.

The centerpiece of our model in this appendix is the deviation of the output ratio from 100 percent. One way to write this deviation is:

$$100(Y/Y^N) - 100$$

This deviation is zero when the output ratio (Y/Y^N) equals 1.0, which occurs when actual output (Y) equals natural output (Y^N).

Calculations in the model are more accurate and straightforward when we use natural logarithms. Since the natural logarithm of 1.0 is zero, the natural log of the output ratio is zero when the output ratio is unity. Thus a second way of expressing the deviation of the output ratio from 100 percent is the "log output ratio" expressed as a percentage.

$$\hat{Y} = 100[LN(Y/Y^N)]$$

The following table shows that $\hat{Y}$ is very close in value to the deviation $100(Y/Y^N) - 100$:

Y/Y^N	$100(Y/Y^N) - 100$	$\hat{Y}$
0.90	−10	−10.5
1.00	0	0.0
1.05	5	4.9

In the rest of this appendix, a value of $\hat{Y}$ of zero corresponds to 100 on the horizontal axis of those diagrams in Chapter 9 that plot the output ratio against the inflation rate.

Equation for the *SP* Curve

The *SP* curve can be written as a relationship between the actual inflation rate (p), the expected inflation rate (p^e), and the log output ratio $(\hat{Y})$.

General Linear Form	Numerical Example	
$p = p^e + g\hat{Y} + z$	$p = p^e + 0.5\hat{Y}$	(1)

Here the z designates the contribution of supply shocks to inflation, and initially in the numerical example we assume that the element of supply shocks is absent $(z = 0)$, so that we can concentrate on demand inflation. The numerical example also assumes that the slope of the *SP*, designated g in the general linear form, is 0.5 in the numerical example. Thus $g = 0.5$ indicates that the *SP* line slopes up by one percentage point in extra inflation for each two percentage points of extra real GDP relative to natural real GDP.

We also note that when $\hat{Y} = 0$, the economy is on its vertical LP line where actual and expected inflation are equal ($p = p^e$).

In order to understand what makes the SP curve shift, we assume the expectations of inflation (p^e) are formed adaptively as a weighted average of last period's actual inflation rate (p_{-1}) and last period's expected inflation rate (p^e_{-1}), where j is the weight on last period's actual inflation rate (j must be between 0 and 1).

<table>
<tr><td>General Linear Form</td><td>Numerical Example</td><td></td></tr>
<tr><td>$p^e = jp_{-1} + (1 - j)p^e_{-1}$</td><td>$p^e = p_{-1}$</td><td>(2)</td></tr>
</table>

The numerical example assumes that $j = 1$; that is, that expected inflation depends simply on what the inflation rate actually turned out to be last period, with the subscript -1 indicating "last period." This was also assumed in drawing Figures 9-5 and 9-7.

When we substitute (2) into (1), we obtain a new expression for the SP line that depends on two current-period variables ($\hat{Y}$ and z) and two variables from last period (p_{-1} and p^e_{-1}):

<table>
<tr><td>General Linear Form</td><td>Numerical Example</td><td></td></tr>
<tr><td>$p = jp_{-1} + (1 - j)p^e_{-1} + g\hat{Y} + z$</td><td>$p = p_{-1} + 0.5\hat{Y}$</td><td>(3)</td></tr>
</table>

Equation for the DG Line

But we need more information than that contained in (3) to find both current inflation (p) and the current log output ratio ($\hat{Y}$). In other words, we have two unknown variables and one equation to determine their equilibrium values. What is the missing equation? This is the DG line and is based on the definition that nominal GDP growth (x) equals the inflation rate (p) plus real GDP growth (y), all expressed as percentages:

$$x \equiv p + y \tag{4}$$

In the theoretical diagrams of Chapter 9, the natural level of real GDP (Y^N) is constant. But now we want to be more general and allow Y^N to grow, as it does in the real world. We subtract the growth rate of natural real GDP (y^N) from each side of equation (4):

$$x - y^N \equiv p + y - y^N \tag{5}$$

Let us give a new name, "excess nominal GDP growth" ($\hat{x}$), to the excess of nominal GDP growth over the growth rate of natural real GDP ($\hat{x} = x - y^N$). We can also replace the excess of actual over natural real GDP growth ($y - y^N$) with the change in the log output ratio ($\hat{Y}$) from its value last period ($\hat{Y}_{-1}$).[1]

When these replacements are combined, (5) becomes

$$\hat{x} \equiv p + \hat{Y} - \hat{Y}_{-1} \tag{6}$$

Combining the SP and DG Equations

Now we are ready to combine our equations for the SP line (3) and DG line (6). When (6) is solved for the log output ratio $\hat{Y}$, we obtain the following equation for the DG line:

$$\hat{Y} \equiv \hat{Y}_{-1} + \hat{x} - p \tag{7}$$

---

[1] This replacement relies on the definition of a growth rate from one period to another as the change in logs (here we omit the "100" that changes decimals to percents):

$$y = \log(Y) - \log(Y_{-1})$$
$$y^N = \log(Y^N) - \log(Y^N_{-1})$$

Subtracting the second line from the first, we have

$$y - y^N = \log(Y) - \log(Y^N) - [\log(Y_{-1}) - \log(Y^N_{-1})] = \hat{Y} - \hat{Y}_{-1}$$

This says that the DG relation between $\hat{Y}$ and p has a slope of -1 and that the relation shifts when there is any change in $\hat{Y}_{-1}$ or $\hat{x}$. Now (7) can be substituted into the SP equation (3) to obtain:

$$p = jp_{-1} + (1 - j)p^e_{-1} + g(\hat{Y}_{-1} + \hat{x} - p) + z \qquad (8)$$

This can be further simplified if we factor out p from the right-hand side of (8).[2]

General Linear Form $\qquad\qquad$ Numerical Example

$$p = \frac{1}{1+g}[jp_{-1} + (1 - j)p^e_{-1} + g(\hat{Y}_{-1} + \hat{x}) + z] \qquad p = \frac{2}{3}[p_{-1} + 0.5(\hat{Y}_{-1} + \hat{x})] \qquad (9)$$

Now we are ready to use equation (9) to examine the consequences of any event that can alter the inflation rate and log output ratio in the short run and long run. One focus of Chapter 9 was the consequences of accelerations and decelerations in nominal GDP growth (x), so let us use equation (9) to reproduce the path of adjustment plotted in Figure 9-5 following an acceleration in x from zero to 6 percent per annum. Now, however, we shall perform the analysis for adjusted nominal GDP growth , thus allowing it to remain valid for any value of y^N.

Example when $\hat{x}$ Rises from Zero to 6 Percent

We start out initially with zero inflation and with an output ratio of 100 percent, as at point E_0 in Figure 9-5. This means that the log output ratio ($\hat{Y}$) is zero. We also assume that there are no supply shocks ($z = 0$). Thus our initial situation begins with:

$$p_{-1} = p^e_{-1} = \hat{x} = \hat{Y}_{-1} = 0$$

Substituting into the numerical example version of (9), we can confirm that these values are consistent with an initial value of zero inflation:

$$p = \frac{2}{3}[0 + 0.5(0 + 0)] = 0$$

Now there is an assumed sudden jump in $\hat{x}$ to 6 percent per year. What happens to inflation in the first period? Substituting $\hat{x} = 6$ into the numerical example, we have:

$$p = \frac{2}{3}[0 + 0.5(0 + 6)] = \frac{2}{3}(3) = 2$$

The new log output ratio can be found by using equation (7):

$$\hat{Y} = \hat{Y}_{-1} + \hat{x} - p = 0 + 6 - 2 = 4$$

Thus we have derived the combination of p and $\hat{Y}$ plotted at point F in Figure 9-5—that is, inflation of 2 percent and a log output ratio of 4.[3]

The adjustment continues in future periods. We can compute the values of p and $\hat{Y}$ in the next few periods by substituting the correct numbers into the numerical example

---

[2] To obtain (9) from (8), add gp to both sides of equation (8). Then divide both sides of the resulting equation by $1 + g$.

[3] In Figure 9-5 we assumed for simplicity that natural real GDP was not growing. Thus any change in real GDP became simply a shift in the output ratio, in this case a 4 percent increase from 100 to 104 in Figure 9-5.

version of (9), using a pocket calculator. These values correspond exactly to the path labeled "Path with one-period lag in adjustment of expectations" in Figure 9-5:

Period	p_{-1}	$\hat{Y}_{-1}$	$\hat{x}$	p	$\hat{Y}$
0	0.00	0.00	0	0.00	0.00
1	0.00	0.00	6	2.00	4.00
2	2.00	4.00	6	4.67	5.33
3	4.67	5.33	6	6.89	4.44
4	6.89	4.44	6	8.07	2.37

Exercise 1: Using the same numerical example, calculate what happens for the first four periods when the economy is in an initial long-run equilibrium at point E_5 in Figure 9-6, with $x = p = p^e = 10$ and $\hat{Y} = 0$, and suddenly the adjusted growth rate of nominal GDP ($\hat{x}$) falls to a new permanent value of zero. How is your answer changed if the coefficient of adjustment of expectations is assumed to be $j = 0.25$ instead of $j = 1.0$?

[*Hint:* This requires that you substitute $j = 0.25$ and $g = 0.5$ into the General Linear Form version of equation (9).]

Learning to Shift the *SP* Curve and *DG* Line

In this section we learn how to draw graphs in which the *SP* curve and *DG* lines are accurately shifted, so that the economy's adjustment path can be traced out. In an example we will see how to trace out the path in Figure 9-5 marked "Path with one-period lag in adjustment of expectations," showing how the economy reacts to a permanent six percentage point acceleration in nominal GDP growth.

Shifting the *SP* Curve

The two *SP* curves plotted in the left frame of Figure 9-14 are based on the Numerical Example of equation (1), repeated here for convenience:

$$p = p^e + 0.5\hat{Y} \qquad (1)$$

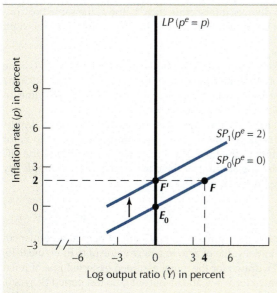
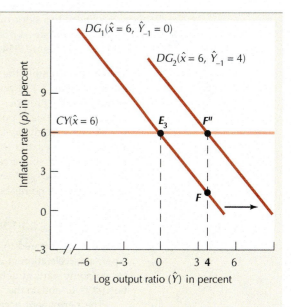

Figure 9-14

The lower SP_0 curve assumes that $p^e = 0$. Thus it shows that inflation (p) is zero when $\hat{Y} = 0$. When $\hat{Y}$ is 4, inflation is 2 percent. In our numerical example, the inflation rate in period 1 is shown by point F on SP_0. If $j = 1$, so the expected rate of inflation always equals last period's actual rate of inflation ($p^e = p_{-1}$), then there is an easy rule for drawing the new SP line for the subsequent period:

> **Rule for shifting SP when $j = 1$:** If the economy is at point F in period 1, then the SP curve for period 2 can be drawn as intersecting the LP line at the same vertical coordinate as point F, shown by the point F'.

Thus in the example the SP curve for period 2 is SP_1, shown as having the same slope as SP_0, but intersecting LP at point F'. The vertical coordinate of the point where SP intersects LP tells us what expected rate of inflation (p^e) is being assumed along that SP. Along SP_1, for instance, p^e must be 2 percent, since the vertical coordinate of point F' is 2 percent.

Shifting the *DG* Line

The *DG* lines plotted in the right frame of Figure 9-14 are based on equation (7), repeated here for convenience:

$$\hat{Y} \equiv \hat{Y}_{-1} + \hat{x} - p \tag{7}$$

Since p and $\hat{Y}$ are on the two axes, to plot a *DG* line we need to know the values of $\hat{x}$ and $\hat{Y}_{-1}$. The DG_1 line in the right frame of Figure 9-14 assumes that $\hat{x} = 6$ and $Y_{-1} = 0$. This line has a slope of minus 45 degrees, sloping down one percentage point vertically for every percentage point in the horizontal direction.

When the economy is at point F in period 1 in our example, with an inflation rate of 2 percent and an output ratio of $\hat{Y} = 4$, we must draw a new *DG* line for period 2. To develop a general rule for shifting *DG*, we draw a horizontal line, *CY*, which stands for "constant output." The *CY* line is always horizontal, and its vertical coordinate is the assumed growth rate of $\hat{x}$, in this case 6 percent. It shows that if inflation were equal to $\hat{x}$, then by equation (7) the output ratio would be constant, $\hat{Y} = \hat{Y}_{-1}$, hence the name constant output, or *CY* line. Now we can write a general rule for shifting *DG*:

> **Rule for shifting *DG*:** Start from the economy's position in period 1, point F in this example. Then draw a horizontal *CY* line at a vertical coordinate corresponding to the assumed value of $\hat{x}$, in this case 6 percent. Then the *DG* line for period 2 will be a line with a slope of minus 45 degrees intersecting the *CY* line at the same horizontal coordinate as point F. This point of intersection is labeled point F'' in the right frame of Figure 9-14.

Thus in the example the *DG* line for period 2 is DG_2, shown as parallel to the DG_1 line but intersecting *CY* at point F''. Note that the rule also applies to the DG_1 line. Since the economy in the previous period (period 0) was at a log output ratio of 0, the DG_1 line intersects the *CY* line at point E_3 which has a horizontal coordinate of 0.

Another, equivalent way to remember the rule for shifting the *DG* line is simple. When $\hat{x}$ increases, the *DG* line shifts up *vertically* by the amount of the change in $\hat{x}$, for example, up by six percentage points to the line DG_1. But when $\hat{Y}_{-1}$ increases, the *DG* line shifts to the right *horizontally* by the amount of the change in $\hat{Y}_{-1}$, for example, by four percentage points between the lines DG_1 and DG_2.

Tracing the Economy's Adjustment with Shifts in *SP* and *DG*

Now we are prepared to draw a graph tracing the economy's adjustment to a permanent 6 percent acceleration in $\hat{x}$, from an initial value of zero to a new value of 6. In Figure 9-15, the economy starts at point E_0 on SP_0 drawn for the initial assumed expected rate of inflation ($p^e = 0$), and on the DG_0 line drawn for $\hat{x} = 0$ and an output ratio last period ($\hat{Y}_{-1}$) of 0.

The permanent acceleration of $\hat{x}$ fixes the *CY* line at a vertical position of 6. We draw a new DG_1 line intersecting *CY* directly above point E_0. The *SP* does not shift in

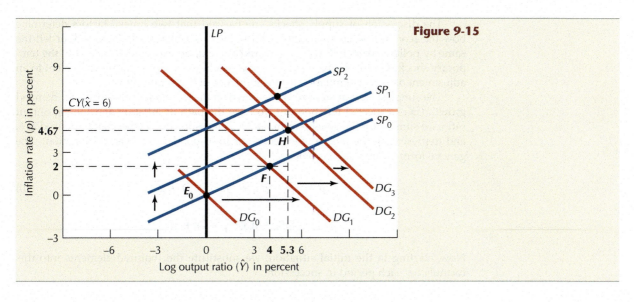

Figure 9-15

period 1, because expectations of inflation adjust with a one-period lag. Thus in period 1 the economy moves from E_0 to F, with an inflation rate (p) of 2.0 percent and an output ratio ($\hat{Y}$) of 4.0 percent. Then in period 2 both SP and DG shift. We draw the new SP_1 line, as in Figure 9-15, as intersecting the LP line at the same vertical coordinate as point F. We draw a new DG_2 line, as in Figure 9-15, as intersecting the CY line at the same horizontal coordinate as point F. The two new lines, SP_1 and DG_2, intersect at point H, where the inflation rate (p) is 4.67 percent and the log output ratio is 5.33 percent. This is the same as the economy's position in period 2, calculated by the algebraic method in the preceding section.

The adjustment in period 3 is also shown in Figure 9-15. A new SP_2 curve is drawn as intersecting the LP at the same vertical coordinate as point H. A new DG_3 line is shown as intersecting the CY line at the same horizontal coordinate as point H. The economy's new position in period 3 is at the intersection of the SP_2 curve and DG_3 labeled in Figure 9-15 as point I. Inflation has now risen to 6.89 percent and the log output ratio has fallen to 4.44 percent.

The general principles developed in this section can be used to show the economy's adjustment to either a shift in $\hat{x}$ or a supply shock. General characteristics of the adjustment process, shown in the example of Figure 9-15, are as follows:

> The SP line always shifts up in the subsequent period when the economy's position in the current period is to the right of LP, and it shifts down when the economy is to the left of LP. The DG line always shifts to the right in the subsequent period when the economy's current position is below the CY line, that is, when inflation is less than $\hat{x}$. And the DG line shifts to the left in the subsequent period when the economy is above the CY line. Thus, in the example of Figure 9-15, the DG line drawn for period 4 would intersect the CY line at the same horizontal coordinate as point I and thus would be to the left of the DG_3 line.

The Consequences of a Supply Shock

We have examined the effect on inflation of an acceleration of growth in nominal GDP. But another source of inflation may be a supply shock, such as an increase in the relative price of food or energy. Let us assume that we start in long-run equilibrium at point E_4 in Figure 9-9, with $\hat{x} = p = p^e = 6$ and $\hat{Y} = 0$. Initially the supply-shock variable z is equal to zero. But now let us assume there is a jump in the relative price of oil that boosts z to a value of 3 for two periods, followed by a return after that to $z = 0$.

The discussion of supply shocks emphasized that two crucial factors determine how the economy reacts to a supply shock. First, is $\hat{x}$ increased, decreased, or left the same by policymakers following the shock? Second, do expectations adjust to the temporary shock? Cost-of-living adjustment clauses in wage contracts are equivalent to an adjustment of expected inflation for the influence of the supply shock.

The simplest case to analyze is one in which there is no response of either demand growth ($\hat{x}$) or expected inflation (p^e). To trace the path of inflation and the log output ratio, we simply use the general formula (9) with assumed to be permanently fixed at 6, and (representing the failure of expectations to respond at all to actual inflation). The general form for this case becomes:

$$p = \frac{1}{1+g}[p^e_{-1} + g(\hat{Y}_{-1} + \hat{x}) + z] \tag{10}$$

$$= \frac{2}{3}[p^e_{-1} + 0.5(\hat{Y}_{-1} + \hat{x}) + z]$$

Now, starting in the initial situation, we substitute the required elements into this formula for each period in succession.

Period	p^e_{-1}	$\hat{Y}_{-1}$	$\hat{x}$	z	p	$\hat{Y}$
0	6	0.00	6	0	6.00	0.00
1	6	0.00	6	3	8.00	−2.00
2	6	−2.00	6	3	7.33	−3.33
3	6	−3.33	6	0	4.89	−2.22
4	6	−2.22	6	0	5.26	−1.48
5	6	−1.48	6	0	5.51	−0.99

This adjustment path shows what would happen to the economy with a two-period supply shock of $z = 3$, with a neutral aggregate demand policy that maintains steady excess nominal GDP growth, and with no response of expectations to the effects of the supply shock. A good example of this is the temporary 1990–91 oil shock after the Iraqi invasion of Kuwait. In period 1 the inflation rate jumps from 6 to 8, exactly duplicating the movement from point E_4 to point L in Figure 9-9. In the next period, inflation diminishes somewhat, since the position of the DG line depends on the current period's starting value of $\hat{Y}$, which has fallen from 0 to −2. Thus the intersection of DG and SP slides southwest down the stationary SP_3 line to $p = 7.33$ and $\hat{Y} = -3.33$. Then the supply shock ends, z returns to its original zero value, and the economy gradually climbs back up the SP_2 line to its long-run equilibrium position, $p = 6.0$ and $\hat{Y} = 0$.

Exercise 2: What rate of adjusted nominal growth should policymakers choose if they want to pursue an accommodating policy? An extinguishing policy? (*Hint:* An accommodating policy means that $\hat{Y}$ remains fixed at 0, which requires that $\hat{x} = p$. Substitute p for $\hat{x}$ in equation (10) and, in addition, note that $\hat{Y}_{-1} = 0$, thus obtaining $p = p^e_{-1} + z$. For an extinguishing policy, take (10) and set the left-hand side (p) equal to 6; then solve for the required $\hat{x}$.)

Exercise 3: For a neutral policy response, calculate the adjustment path of inflation and $\hat{Y}$ in the first four periods when expectations respond fully to the extra inflation caused by the supply shock. That is, assume now that $j = 1$ instead of $j = 0$ as in the previous exercise. Next, maintaining the assumption that $j = 1$, calculate the same adjustment path when the policy response is accommodative. (See the hint for Exercise 2.) How would you describe the disadvantages of an accommodative policy when $j = 1$?

The Behavior of the Unemployment Rate

The unemployment rate (U) is very closely related to the log output ratio ($\hat{Y}$), as we learned from Okun's Law and Figure 9-12 on pp. 297–99. Corresponding to the natural level of real GDP (Y^N), defined as the level of real GDP at which expectations of inflation turn out to be accurate, there is a natural rate of unemployment (U^N). When real GDP is above Y^N, and inflation is accelerating, we also find that the actual unemployment rate (U) is below the natural rate of unemployment (U^N). This relationship can be written:[4]

<table>
<tr><td>General Linear Form</td><td>Numerical Example</td><td></td></tr>
<tr><td>$U = U^N - h\hat{Y}$</td><td>$U = U^N - 0.5\hat{Y}$</td><td>(11)</td></tr>
</table>

How is this relationship to be used? First, we must determine the value of the natural rate of unemployment. In the United States in the 1980s this appeared to be approximately $U^N = 6.0$ percent. Then we take alternative values for $\hat{Y}$ and substitute these values into equation (11). Here are two examples:

Example 1: $\hat{Y} = -6$

Since $U^N = 6.0$, we use (11) to determine the unemployment rate:

$$U = 6.0 - 0.5(-6) = 9.0$$

In other words, there is an unemployment rate of 9.0 percent.

Example 2: $\hat{Y} = 6$

$$U = 6.0 - 0.5(6) = 3.0$$

The unemployment rate is 3.0 percent. Thus we see that for every six percentage points by which $\hat{Y}$ exceeds 0, the unemployment rate lies three percentage points below U^N, the natural unemployment rate of 6.0 percent. And for every six percentage points by which $\hat{Y}$ falls short of 0, the unemployment rate lies three percentage points above the natural unemployment rate of 6.0 percent.

There is also a simple short-cut way of calculating the *change* in the unemployment rate from last period (U_{-1}) to this period (U).[5]

<table>
<tr><td>General Linear Form</td><td>Numerical Example</td><td></td></tr>
<tr><td>$U = U_{-1} - h(y - y^N)$</td><td>$U = U_{-1} - 0.5(y - y^N)$</td><td>(12)</td></tr>
</table>

Thus, starting with $U_{-1} = 6.0$, a value of $y - y^N$ of 1.0 will cause the unemployment rate to fall to $U = 5.5$ percent.

Exercise 4: Go back through the previous exercises and calculate the unemployment rate for each period corresponding to that period's value of $\hat{Y}$.

---

[4] *Caution:* In the Appendix to Chapter 4 we used h to designate the income responsiveness of the demand for money.

[5] How can (12) be derived from (11)? Let us write down (11) and then subtract from it the value of (11) for last period:

$$U = U^N - h\hat{Y}$$

$$-U_{-1} = U^N_{-1} - (-h\hat{Y}_{-1})$$

If there is no change in U^N from one period to the next, then this difference is:

$$U - U_{-1} = -h(\hat{Y} - \hat{Y}_{-1})$$

But now we can substitute $y - y^N$ into this expression

$$U - U_{-1} = -h(y - y^N)$$

To see why this substitution is valid, look back at footnote 1 in this appendix on p. 307.

The Goals of Stabilization Policy: Low Inflation and Low Unemployment

The government fighting inflation is like the Mafia fighting crime.
—Laurence J. Peter

This book began by introducing three major concepts of macroeconomics—unemployment, inflation, and growth in per person output—that are linked to the three major goals of macroeconomic policy, namely, to achieve low unemployment, low inflation, and rapid growth in per person output. In Chapter 1 we learned why growth in output per person is desirable. Simply put, economic growth produces more goods and services, and more is better, allowing society to have everything it now produces and more, without the need to sacrifice something currently produced.

Now we inquire into the two other major goals of economic policy, beginning with low inflation in the first part of this chapter and ending with low unemployment in the last part. As we learned in Chapter 9, in order to achieve a lower inflation rate by restrictive monetary or fiscal policies, policymakers must be willing to accept a transition period during which the output ratio is lower and the unemployment rate is higher. Is the goal of achieving lower inflation worth the cost of lost jobs in the period during which inflation is reduced? This depends on the costs of inflation—just what is it that society loses if inflation proceeds at a rate of 5 percent per year instead of 2 percent?

In the last part of the chapter we inquire into the costs of unemployment. Is unemployment of a teenager seeking a part-time job as costly to individuals and society as unemployment of an adult head of household? Why can't the unemployment rate be pushed down to zero percent? Why are some people unemployed even in a prosperous economy?

GLOBAL ECONOMIC CRISIS FOCUS

Inflation Versus Unemployment in the Crisis

By far the most important problem facing the contemporary United States and many other countries is persistently high unemployment. Except for periodic ups and downs of oil prices, inflation is nowhere in sight. In fact, policymakers instead of worrying about a positive inflation rate are worried that the inflation rate might decline below zero, becoming negative. A situation with a negative inflation rate is called a *deflation* and, as we learned in Chapter 8 on pp. 251–52, can depress aggregate demand through the expectations and redistribution effects.

(continued)

We begin this chapter by studying the costs of a high and positive rate of inflation for two reasons. First, we need to understand the harm done by inflation if we are to comprehend why restraining inflation is, along with maintaining low unemployment, one of the twin goals of monetary policy. Second, the goal of fighting high inflation led monetary policy in past historical episodes, most notably 1979–81, deliberately to create unemployment.

As we compare the two deepest recessions of the postwar era, in 1981–82 and 2007–09, we can see that their causes were entirely different, and as a result their cures are different as well. Since the 1981–82 recession was caused by tight monetary policy that succeeded in curing the inflation problem, the cure for the recession was straightforward. In 1982 monetary policy was eased and the economy took off like a rocket, with very rapid growth in real GDP during 1983–85. But the causes of the 2007–09 recession, as we learned in Chapter 5, were not tight monetary policy but rather the collapse of a housing bubble and the breakdown in financial markets. And as we learned in Chapters 5 and 6, the hangover from the recent recession in the form of persistently high unemployment cannot be easily cured either by easy monetary or fiscal policy.

10-1 The Costs and Causes of Inflation

Inflation is widely viewed as a social evil, although the degree of its seriousness is debated. At one extreme, inflation is considered as serious a problem as unemployment. This view was popularized by Arthur Okun, who defined the "misery index" as the sum of the inflation and unemployment rates. This index implies that the social value of a reduction of inflation by one percentage point (say from 3 to 2 percent) exactly offsets the social cost of an increase in the unemployment rate by one percentage point (say from 6 to 7 percent), leaving the economy with an unchanged level of "misery."

Others think that the harm done by inflation is minimal. James Tobin has written that "inflation is greatly exaggerated as a social evil." Many economists like Tobin do not regard the benefits of lower inflation as worth the sacrifice of lost output and jobs necessary to achieve it.

In Chapter 9 we learned that the basic cause of inflation is excessive growth in nominal GDP. In this chapter we ask why governments inflate; that is, why do they allow excessive nominal GDP growth to occur? We then examine the costs of inflation, asking whether they are serious enough to warrant stopping inflation, even though doing so may require policies that cut output and cause millions to lose their jobs.

Any debate about the costs of inflation must distinguish between moderate (crawling) inflation and extreme inflation, usually called **hyperinflation.** One traditional definition of hyperinflation is an inflation rate of 50 percent per month, or 12,975 percent per year.[1] We shall use as our definition an inflation

Hyperinflation is a very rapid inflation, sometimes defined as a rate of more than 22 percent per month, or 1,000 percent per year, experienced over a year or more.

---

[1] Why is a 50 percent monthly inflation equivalent to an annual rate of 12,975 percent? This occurs because of compounding. Starting at 100, after one month prices are up to 150, after two months they are at 225, after three months they are at 338, and after twelve months they are at 12,975. Although these simple geometric changes are widely cited in the literature, they become increasingly misleading at high rates of inflation; a better measure is the logarithmic price change, which in this example is 40.5 percent per month, or 487 percent per year. See problems 1 and 2 at the end of the chapter.

rate of 1,000 percent per year or above; a rate of 1,000 percent per year (or 22 percent per month) afflicts a society with all the problems usually associated with hyperinflation. Argentina, Brazil, Nicaragua, Peru, and Poland all suffered from inflation rates of over 1,000 percent per year for one or more years in the late 1980s or 1990s.[2] The African country of Zimbabwe experienced a hyperinflation of 5,000 or more percent per year in 2006–09.

Everyone agrees that hyperinflation is a severe plague, and we will learn how economic policymakers have managed to stop hyperinflations in several specific cases. Before turning to hyperinflation, we will examine the social costs of moderate inflation, such as that experienced by the United States. We will see that there are quite different costs associated with an inflation that is fully anticipated (crawling along at roughly the same rate year after year) and an inflation that is a "surprise," changing in an unpredictable way.

10-2   Money and Inflation

In Chapter 9 our model of inflation showed that a permanent increase in the growth rate of nominal GDP would lead to a permanent increase in the inflation rate. Since nominal GDP growth is so important in determining the inflation rate, we need to understand its determinants.

Definitions Linking Money, Velocity, Inflation, and Output

A convenient starting point for understanding the determinants of inflation is provided by the quantity equation of Section 8-8:

$$M^s V \equiv X \equiv PY \tag{10.1}$$

This equation is familiar; it duplicates equation (8.2) on p. 246. The right side of the equation states that nominal GDP (X), by definition, is equal to the price index, or the GDP deflator (P), multiplied by real GDP (Y). The left side states that nominal GDP is also equal, by definition, to the money supply (M^s) multiplied by velocity (V).[3] Thus nominal GDP must rise if there is an increase in either the money supply or in velocity.

Equation (10.1) is a good beginning, but it concerns the price *level*. How can we convert equation (10.1) into a relationship that shows the determinants of the rate of *inflation*, that is, the rate of change of the price level? As we learned in Chapter 9, the growth rate of any product of two numbers, such as P times Y in equation (10.1), is equal to the sum of the separate growth rates of the two numbers. This allows us to take equation (10.1), a relationship among *levels* (written as uppercase letters), and restate it as a relationship among *growth rates* (written as lowercase letters):

$$m^s + v \equiv x \equiv p + y \tag{10.2}$$

---

[2] The 1,000 percent cutoff for episodes of "extreme" inflation is suggested in R. Dornbusch et al., "Extreme Inflation: Dynamics and Stabilization," *Brookings Papers on Economic Activity*, 1990, no. 2, pp. 1–84.

[3] Why is the left side true by definition? As we learned in Chapter 4 in the box on p. 93, velocity is defined as $V \equiv PY/M^s$, or $V \equiv Y/(M^s/P)$. This definition is repeated in Chapter 8 on p. 246.

In words, this states that the growth rate of the money supply (m^s) plus the growth in velocity (v) equals the growth rate of nominal GDP (x), which in turn equals the sum of the inflation rate (p) and the growth rate of real GDP (y). The formula immediately allows us to classify the determinants of inflation, when we rewrite equation (10.2) with inflation on the left side:

$$p \equiv x - y \equiv m^s + v - y \tag{10.3}$$

If we are interested in the long-run determinants of inflation, we can assume that the growth rate of real output (y) is fairly constant, roughly fixed by the growth rate of the population and of productivity. This leads to the same conclusion that we reached in Chapter 9: *In the long run, the inflation rate equals the excess growth rate of nominal GDP, that is, the difference between nominal GDP growth and the long-run growth rate of real GDP.*

The right-hand terms in equation (10.3) provide additional insight into the causes of inflation. In the long run, the inflation rate must equal the excess growth rate of money plus velocity, relative to the long-run growth rate of real GDP.[4]

Thus, to understand the determinants of inflation, we need to know what determines the excess growth of money plus velocity. The growth rate of the money supply is controlled by the central bank (in the United States by the Federal Reserve, in Canada by the Bank of Canada, and by similar institutions in other countries). Velocity changes whenever there is a change in real GDP relative to the real money supply (M^s/P). In Chapter 4 we learned that anything that shifts the *IS* curve will change velocity, including changes in business and consumer confidence, credit conditions in financial markets, government spending, tax rates, autonomous net taxes, autonomous net exports, or the foreign exchange rate. Further, if the demand for money changes for reasons independent of changes in income, then velocity will change. For instance, velocity would increase following the introduction of credit cards that allow households to economize on their holdings of money.

While the growth rate of velocity can be highly volatile in the short run, over the long run velocity growth tends to be quite stable. For the United States, the average annual growth rate of velocity has been almost exactly zero over the past five decades.[5] Thus if we assume $v = 0$ in equation (10.3), the determinants of inflation become extremely simple: *In the long run, the inflation rate equals the excess growth rate of the money supply, that is, the difference between the growth rate of the money supply and the long-run growth rate of real GDP. If the central bank allows the money supply to grow rapidly, rapid inflation will result. The key to attaining zero inflation is for the central bank to allow the money supply to grow no faster than the long-run growth rate of real output.*

---

[4] In the Appendix to Chapter 9, we subtracted the long-run growth rate of natural real GDP (y^N) explicitly from both nominal and real GDP growth. Applying the same subtraction to equation (10.3), we have

$$p \equiv (x - y^N) - (y - y^N) \equiv (m^s + v - y^N) - (y - y^N)$$

This states that in the long run when $y - y^N$ is zero, inflation equals the excess growth of nominal GDP relative to that of natural real GDP, and inflation also equals the excess growth of money plus velocity relative to that of natural real GDP.

[5] The velocity of the money supply concept M2 (defined in Chapter 13) was 1.73 in 1960 and 1.91 in 2007, for an average annual growth rate of 0.2 percent.

SELF-TEST

Assume that over a decade the growth rate of the money supply is constant at 5 percent per year, and the growth rate of velocity is constant at 3 percent per year. In the first half of the decade, the growth rate of output is 4 percent per year; then, because of a slowdown in productivity growth, it is only 2 percent for the last half of the decade. The growth in money and in velocity are not affected by the productivity growth slowdown.

1. What is the inflation rate in the first half of the decade?
2. What is the inflation rate in the last half of the decade?
3. What is the nominal GDP growth rate in the first half of the decade?
4. What is the nominal GDP growth rate in the last half of the decade?

Why Do Central Banks Allow Excessive Monetary Growth?

The previous section identified excessive monetary growth as the fundamental cause of inflation *in the long run*. If the growth rate of velocity is zero in the long run, then excessive nominal GDP growth and excessive monetary growth are identical. Why do governments and central banks allow excessive monetary growth to occur?

Four basic factors examined below can lead to excessive nominal GDP and monetary growth. As shown in Chapter 9, a permanent increase in nominal GDP growth leads to a *temporary* increase in output along with a *permanent* increase in the inflation rate. A permanent decrease in nominal GDP growth leads to a *temporary* decrease in output along with a *permanent* decrease of the inflation rate. This analysis underlies the first reason governments cause inflation.

Reason 1: Temptation of demand stimulation.   Governments and central banks may set off inflation when they attempt to raise output and reduce unemployment. While Chapter 9 indicated that such policies can boost inflation with only a temporary benefit to output, governments may think (erroneously) that the benefits of higher output will last forever or (perhaps correctly) at least long enough to benefit the government at the next election. In some countries, the central bank is controlled directly or indirectly by the government. Even in the United States, with its relatively independent central bank, it is widely believed that the Fed boosted monetary growth in 1972 to help reelect President Nixon.

Reason 2: Fear of recession and job loss.   The corollary to the first reason is the fact that stopping inflation usually causes a temporary drop in output and loss of jobs. Thus an implication of the first reason for higher inflation is that governments are reluctant to stop inflation once it gets started: An economy must sacrifice a substantial amount of lost output in order to reduce the inflation rate permanently. The size of this output sacrifice is highly controversial and differs among countries. One estimate for the United States is that a permanent decrease in the inflation rate of one percentage point would require a one-time loss of 4.7 percent of a year's GDP, or about $700 billion. The sacrifice required in some countries may be higher, in others lower.

INTERNATIONAL PERSPECTIVE

Money Growth and Inflation

quation (10.3) in the text ($p \equiv m^s + v - y$) states that the inflation rate (p) is equal to the rate of monetary growth (m^s) plus the difference between velocity growth and real GDP growth ($v - y$). If this difference is positive, then inflation exceeds the rate of monetary growth, and vice versa.

The graph plots the inflation rate over the period 1990–2009 against the rate of monetary growth for 15 countries. The diagonal 45-degree line shows all the points with equal rates of inflation and monetary growth, that is, with $v = y$. In most of the low-inflation countries, the plotted points lie below the 45-degree line, indicating that velocity growth was less than real GDP growth. For instance, in the United States, velocity growth was roughly zero, less than output growth of about 3 percent per year. These plotted points illustrate that the relationship between inflation and monetary growth is relatively close, supporting the theme of the

text that the key to understanding inflation is to understand why some governments choose much higher rates of monetary growth than others.

Compared to previous decades, the incidence of very rapid inflation in the period shown in the graph, 1990–2009, was substantially less than in previous decades. For instance, Brazil had an inflation rate of more than 400 percent per year from 1990 to 1998, but then inflation suddenly came to almost a halt, with Brazil's inflation rate of only about 7 percent from 1999 to 2009. The average inflation rate from 1990 to 2009 shown in the graph is about 60 percent, an average of very fast inflation before 1998 and much slower inflation after 1998. Why did inflation subside after the 1990s? Clearly, Brazil and other formerly high-inflation countries have learned to manage the growth of their money supplies and have cut back the fiscal deficits that previously made rapid monetary expansion necessary.

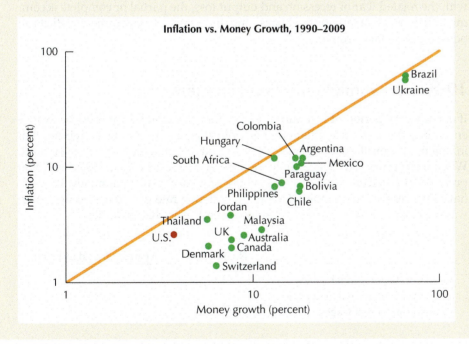

**Inflation vs. Money
Growth, 1990–2009**

Sources: International Monetary Fund World Economic Report, April 2010, and International Financial Statistics database.

Politicians and central banks may be reluctant to impose this sacrifice on citizens, and as a result inflation tends to persist year after year.

Reason 3: Adverse supply shocks.   Chapter 9 also introduced adverse supply shocks as a cause of higher inflation. When higher food or oil prices raise business costs, the inflation rate rises unless the central bank introduces an extinguishing policy that offsets the extra inflation with a massive recession.

Any sharp increase in the price of oil, such as those that occurred in 1973–74, 1979–80, and 2005–08, poses a distasteful choice for central banks. An extinguishing policy reaction can offset extra inflation only at the cost of extra unemployment. An accommodative policy calls for the central bank to "print the extra money to pay for the inflation," and this is likely to create a permanent upsurge of inflation following an adverse supply shock. Even a neutral policy, which leaves the growth rate of nominal GDP and the money supply unchanged, will cause a temporary upsurge of inflation.

Reason 4: Financing government deficits by printing money. In our analysis of the *IS-LM* model of Chapter 4, we learned that governments can run deficits (by boosting expenditures or cutting taxes) in two ways. First, they can hold the real money supply steady and issue bonds to pay for the deficit, which usually requires an increase in the interest rate. Or they can hold the interest rate steady by raising the money supply sufficiently, a policy previously described as monetary accommodation of a fiscal stimulus. However, many countries lack markets in which the government can sell bonds; in such countries virtually the only source of finance for government deficits is an increase in the money supply (often called financing deficits by "printing money"). Thus governments with excessive spending or insufficient tax revenues can cause inflation (p), according to equation (10.3), by boosting the growth rate of the money supply (m^s).

In summary, we have learned that the basic reasons why central banks allow excessive monetary growth are the temptation of demand stimulation together with the related fear of recession and output loss, the partial or complete accommodation of adverse supply shocks, and the effect of government deficits in boosting monetary growth.

10-3 Why Inflation Is Not Harmless

If a temporary period of lost output and higher unemployment must be experienced in order to reduce inflation, then policymakers need to be convinced that inflation is harmful. At first glance, worry about inflation may appear misplaced. When inflation is zero, wages may increase at 2 percent a year. When inflation proceeds at 6 percent annually, wages may grow at 8 percent annually. Workers have little reason to be bothered about the inflation rate (p) if the growth in their wages (w) always stays the same distance ahead, as in this example:

	No inflation	6 percent annual inflation
Growth rate of nominal wages (w)	2	8
Growth rate of price deflator (p)	0	6
Growth rate of real wages ($w - p$)	2	2

However, even if real wage growth is unaffected by inflation, it is still possible for inflation to impose substantial costs on society. Inflation is felt primarily by owners of financial assets. The distinction between surprise and fully anticipated inflation is central to understanding the costs of inflation and the suggested methods for reducing those costs. In this section we distinguish between nominal, expected real, and actual real interest rates. Using this distinction, we will learn that four conditions are required for inflation to be harmless, and why all four conditions are unrealistic.

Nominal and Real Interest Rates

Even in countries with moderate inflation, people learn the difference between nominal and real interest rates.

The **nominal interest rate** (i) is the rate actually quoted by banks and negotiated in financial markets.

The **expected real interest rate** (r^e) is what people expect to pay on their borrowings or earn on their savings after deducting expected inflation ($r^e = i - p^e$). It is the interest rate determined in the market for goods and services and is what matters for the investment and saving decisions of firms and households.

The **actual real interest rate** (r) is the nominal interest rate minus the actual rate of inflation ($r = i - p$).

The nominal interest rate can differ greatly in two countries with different inflation rates, or in one country at different moments in history. But investment and saving decisions will be the same in the two situations as long as the expected real interest rate is the same, and as long as all other determinants of investment and saving besides the expected real interest rate are held constant.

Consider two situations, both with a real expected interest rate (r^e) of 3 percent. In the first situation, expected inflation is zero and the nominal interest rate is 3 percent:

General Form   Numerical Example
$$r^e = i - p^e \qquad r^e = 3 - 0 = 3 \qquad (10.4)$$

In the second situation, there is an expected inflation rate of 6 percent and a nominal interest rate of 9 percent. The real interest rate is the same value, 3 percent:

General Form   Numerical Example
$$r^e = i - p^e \qquad r^e = 9 - 6 = 3 \qquad (10.5)$$

Why is the incentive to save and invest the same in each situation? In the second situation, savers face the prospect that one year later prices will be higher by 6 percent, but they receive an interest rate on their saving of 9 percent, of which 3 percent compensates them for their willingness to save (just as in the zero-inflation situation), while the additional 6 percent compensates them for inflation, that is, the fact that goods they plan to consume with their saving will be 6 percent more expensive one year later. Investors react similarly; the fact that they can sell their products for 6 percent more after one year of 6 percent inflation compensates them for having to pay a nominal interest rate of 9 percent.

Four Conditions Necessary for Inflation to Be Harmless

The above example creates the impression that inflation does not matter, since the nominal interest rate will adjust to maintain the same incentives for savers and investors at a 6 percent inflation rate as at a zero inflation rate. However, the example makes several important assumptions, none of which is validated in the real world:

1. Inflation is universally and accurately anticipated.
2. An increase in the expected inflation rate raises the market nominal interest rate (i) for both saving and borrowing by exactly the same number of percentage points.

The **nominal interest rate** is the market interest rate actually charged by financial institutions and earned by bondholders.

The **expected real interest rate** is the nominal interest rate minus the expected rate of inflation.

The **actual real interest rate** is the nominal interest rate minus the actual inflation rate.

3. All savings are held in bonds, stocks, or savings accounts earning the nominal interest rate (i); no one holds money in accounts with an interest rate held below the market nominal interest rate.

4. Only real (not nominal) interest income is taxable, and only the real cost of borrowing is tax deductible.

Violation of Condition 1: Interest Rates in a Surprise Inflation

Now let us violate condition 1 in the preceding summary list of four conditions, that is, that inflation is accurately anticipated. In several episodes in the United States, such as in 1966–69, 1973–74, 1978–80, and 1987–90, the actual inflation rate accelerated well above the rate expected by most people.

Now imagine that at the beginning of the year, everyone expects zero inflation and savers are offered an interest rate of 3 percent, but at the end of the year, the price of goods jumps by 6 percent. Savers' hopes have been dashed, because their savings have been eroded by an **unanticipated inflation.**

Unanticipated inflation occurs when the actual inflation rate (p) differs from the expected (or anticipated) inflation rate (p^e).

When actual inflation ($p = 6$ percent in the example) differs from expected inflation ($p^e = 0$ in the example), the actual real interest rate differs from that which was expected. In the example, a 3 percent real interest rate was expected ($r^e = 3$), but after the fact (*ex post facto*) the actual real interest (r) turned out to be much less, *minus* 3 percent.

$$\begin{array}{cc} \text{General Form} & \text{Numerical Example} \\ r = i - p & r = 3 - 6 = -3 \end{array} \qquad (10.6)$$

Deflation hurts debtors.   The basic case against unanticipated inflation, then, is that it redistributes income from creditors (savers) to debtors without their knowledge or consent. Conversely, an unanticipated deflation does just the opposite, redistributing income from debtors to creditors, as we learned in Section 8-8 on pp. 251–52. Throughout history, farmers have been an important group of debtors who have been badly hurt by unanticipated deflation. The

GLOBAL ECONOMIC CRISIS FOCUS

The Housing Bubble as Surprise Inflation Followed by Surprise Deflation

We do not have to go back to the Great Depression to find effects of surprise inflation or surprise deflation. Much more recently the great U.S. housing bubble created winners and losers, often the same people. As housing prices soared from 2000 to 2006, homeowners with mortgage debt benefited and often reacted to the surprise increase in housing prices by refinancing, that is, raising the amount they had borrowed.

But then the collapse of the housing bubble after 2006 brought home prices crashing down so much that many homeowners found that their homes were worth less than their mortgage debt. In the modern saying introduced in Chapter 5, these homeowners were "under water." Like the farmers of the Great Depression, millions of American homeowners in recent years have lost their homes to foreclosure when they can no longer afford to make the payments on their mortgage loans.

interest income of savers hardly fell at all between 1929 and 1933, but farmers, badly hurt by a precipitous decline in farm prices, saw their nominal income fall by two-thirds, from $6.2 to $2.1 billion. Because their nominal income fell by so much but their nominal interest payments did not fall, many farmers were unable to purchase seed, fertilizer, and other necessities. As a result, many lost their farms through foreclosures of their mortgage loans.

Gainers from surprise inflation.   Clearly, all savers lose from a surprise inflation. Who gains? The gainers from unanticipated inflation are those who are heavily in debt but have few financial assets, owning mainly physical assets whose prices rise with inflation. Private individuals who have just purchased houses with small down payments are among the classic gainers from an unanticipated inflation. The farmers who lose in a surprise deflation are winners in a surprise inflation.

Violation of Condition 2: Expected Inflation and the Fisher Effect

We have previously defined the expected real interest rate (r^e) as the nominal interest rate (i) minus the expected inflation rate (p^e). The same relation can be rearranged to show that the nominal interest rate is the sum of the expected real interest rate and the expected inflation rate:

$$i = r^e + p^e \qquad (10.7)$$

Thus the nominal interest rate can rise either if the expected real interest rate rises or if the expected inflation rate rises.[6] Among a group of nations that have roughly the same expected real interest rate, we would expect those that have a history of rapid inflation to have high nominal interest rates. This relation between expected inflation and the nominal and real interest rate is called the **Fisher equation,** so named for the famous Yale University economist Irving Fisher (1867–1947).[7] The implication that a one percentage point increase in the expected inflation rate causes a one percentage point increase in the nominal interest rate is called the **Fisher Effect.**[8] The corollary to the Fisher Effect is that the expected real interest rate is independent of changes in the expected inflation rate. *The Fisher analysis predicts that nations with rapid monetary growth will experience both rapid inflation and high nominal interest rates.*

The second condition for inflation to be harmless stated that an increase of the inflation rate by a given number of percentage points raises the nominal interest rate by the same number of percentage points. Restated, the real interest rate must not be affected by the inflation rate. If the Fisher Effect was always a

Irving Fisher (1867–1947)

Fisher, a pioneering mathematical economist, developed theories on interest rates, intertemporal choice, and money and prices. His work forms the basis of much of today's macroeconomics.

The **Fisher equation** states that the nominal interest rate equals the expected inflation rate plus the expected real interest rate.

The **Fisher Effect** predicts that a one percentage point increase in the expected inflation rate will raise the nominal real interest rate by one percentage point, leaving the expected real interest rate unaffected.

---

[6] The *IS-LM* model of Chapter 4 showed how real output and the real interest rate were determined. Recall that in the *IS-LM* model, the real interest rate rises as a result of any event that shifts the *IS* curve to the right (higher government spending, lower tax rates, etc.) or any event that shifts the *LM* curve to the left (a reduction in the supply of money or an increase in the demand for money).

[7] Fisher also popularized other important ideas in economics, including the theory that deflation feeds on itself, by cutting the buying power of debtors (for example, farmers in the Great Depression).

[8] More sophisticated analyses show that an increase in the inflation rate tends to reduce the real interest rate, so that the nominal interest rate does not rise one-for-one with the inflation rate. This is sometimes called the Mundell Effect, stemming from a famous paper by 1999 Nobel Prize winner Robert Mundell, "Inflation and Real Interest," *Journal of Political Economy*, vol. 71 (June 1963), pp. 280–83.

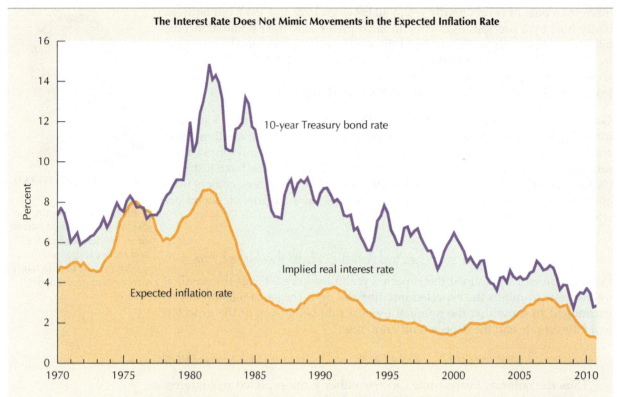

The Interest Rate Does Not Mimic Movements in the Expected Inflation Rate

Figure 10-1 **The 10-Year Treasury Bond Rate and the Expected Rate of Inflation, 1970–2010**

The purple line plots the 10-year Treasury bond rate, the same interest rate as was plotted in the box on pp. 102–04. The orange line plots an estimate of the expected rate of inflation, the average annual change over three years in the GDP deflator. The green shading between the two lines shows the expected real interest rate. Notice that in 1975–76 the expected inflation rate soared but the interest rate barely responded, pushing the expected real interest rate down to zero. In contrast, the expected real interest rate rose in the 1980s when the expected inflation rate was decreasing. Notice that the expected real interest rate almost reached zero in early 2009 as the nominal interest rate fell sharply while the expected inflation rate declined slowly.

Sources: Federal Reserve Board, Selected Interest Rates, and Bureau of Economic Analysis *NIPA Tables.*

realistic description of the real world, then the real interest rate would be independent of the inflation rate, and the second condition would be valid.

However, in the real world, the Fisher Effect is frequently violated. Figure 10-1 plots the nominal interest rate on 10-year Treasury bonds against an estimate of the expected rate of inflation, a three-year average of the rate of change of the GDP deflator, expressed as an annual rate. The green shading between the two lines shows the implied expected real interest rate. Clearly, the expected real interest rate changes when there is a sudden increase or decrease in expected inflation, implying that the second condition for inflation to be harmless is violated in the real world. This is especially evident in 1975–76, when the nominal interest rate failed to respond to an upsurge of expected inflation, driving the real interest rate to zero. The opposite occurred in the early 1980s, when the nominal interest rate increased by more than the upsurge of inflation, due partly to the tight monetary policy

The Wizard of Oz as a Monetary Allegory

The famous movie *The Wizard of Oz*, originally produced in 1939 and an annual television ritual for several decades, is based on a 1900 book (*The Wonderful Wizard of Oz*) by L. Frank Baum. Recently, economists have recognized that the book is an allegory for the major economic and political issues in the late nineteenth-century United States, the battle over free silver, which involved a debate about whether deflation or inflation was desirable.[a]

The three decades after the Civil War (1865–95) were characterized by a steady deflation that reduced the overall price level by about 40 percent and the price of farm products by about 55 percent. As we have learned in this chapter, inflation benefits borrowers at the expense of savers, and deflation does the opposite, benefiting savers at the expense of borrowers. Some of the losers from the 1865–95 deflation were farmers (who not only were debtors but also were particularly hard hit by the decline in farm prices).

The main cause of the deflation was slow monetary growth, which in turn was due to the gold standard (which essentially limited the growth in the money supply to growth in the supply of gold). Farmers and other borrowers supported the free coinage of silver, which, if adopted, would have boosted the money supply and, perhaps, converted the deflation into an inflation. The gold standard was seen as benefiting the eastern United States, home of the creditors and savers.

What are some of the references in the book? Dorothy represents America; her dog Toto represents the Prohibition Party (the name is short for "teetotaler"); and Oz is the abbreviation for ounce (as in ounce of gold or silver). Dorothy's house lands on the Wicked Witch of the East (stronghold of the gold standard), who dries up completely, leaving only her silver shoes (symbolizing the triumph of silver, but changed to ruby slippers in the movie); the yellow brick road (symbol of the gold standard) leads to the Emerald City (Washington, D.C.). The Scarecrow is the western farmer; the Tin Woodsman is the workingman whose joints are rusted due to

unemployment in the depression of the 1890s; and the Cowardly Lion is William Jennings Bryan, leader of the free-silver movement (a lion, as the symbol of one of America's greatest orators; a coward, because he later retreated from support of free silver after economic conditions improved in the late 1890s). In the end, the Wicked Witch of the West melts when Dorothy pours a bucket of water on her, symbolizing the power of water (rain) in solving the problems of the western farmers, and the Wizard is unmasked as an ordinary man who, like a dishonest politician, has been fooling the people.

_____

[a] This box is a very brief summary of Hugh Rockoff, "The 'Wizard of Oz' as a Monetary Allegory," *Journal of Political Economy*, vol. 98 (August 1990), pp. 739–60. Readers interested in the full richness of the references in the *Wizard of Oz* should consult this fascinating article. An easy introduction to the movie and the late nineteenth century references can be found at en.wikipedia.org/wiki/the_wonderful_wizard_of_oz.

pursued by the Fed in 1980–82 in order to bring down the rate of inflation. This was the cold turkey policy discussed in Chapter 9, p. 280.

Violation of Condition 3: Money Does Not Pay Interest

The third condition for inflation to be harmless is that all assets pay the nominal interest rate. But there are many assets and many interest rates, and a significant number of assets pay an interest rate below the interest rate on 10-year Treasury bonds displayed in Figure 10-1. At the extreme is currency, which pays no interest at all, and checking accounts, which pay virtually no interest. Since currency and checking accounts account for most of the core definition of the money supply (see pp. 425–27), we will explore in this section the consequences of the fact that money pays no interest, thus violating the third condition.

The market rate of interest is not paid on money for two main reasons. First, currency pays no interest. Second, bank deposits enjoy the protection of deposit insurance, and customers are willing to accept lower interest rates on deposits because they are protected from loss by deposit insurance. The fact that the market rate of interest is not paid on money has several consequences for society.

People demand money for its convenience services.   The main reason that a fully anticipated creeping inflation imposes welfare costs on society is that people do not desire money for itself, but rather for the **extra convenience services** that it provides. Inflation causes people to hold less money, so they suffer inconvenience. Money provides convenience to the consumer because purchases can be made instantly. If no money were held (that is, no currency and no checking accounts), then the consumer would have to suffer the inconvenience of going to the bank to make a savings deposit withdrawal, or—even less convenient—to sell a stock or bond before the purchase could be made.[9]

The **extra convenience services** of money are the services provided by holding one extra dollar of money instead of bonds.

People hold currency even though it pays no interest. The reason they are willing to hold currency paying zero interest, instead of holding a certificate of deposit paying 3 percent interest, *must be* that the money provides them with at least 3 percent more convenience services than the certificate. How is this related to inflation? When the inflation rate increases, the nominal interest rate on all assets other than currency tends to increase. If the inflation rate rose by 5 percent, then the nominal interest rate on certificates would rise from 3 percent to 8 percent, that is, to a rate 5 percent higher than before. Thus people would cut back on their money holdings until the extra convenience services of money rose from 3 to 8 percent. They would hold less cash in their pockets, retain cash only for those expenditures where only cash is accepted (as for taxi rides and cash-only restaurants), and would hold less cash for nonessential purposes.

The shoe-leather cost of inflation.   The effect of higher inflation and higher interest rates in causing people to hold less cash is sometimes called the **shoe-leather cost** of inflation. Why? Higher interest rates cause people to hold less cash in their pockets at any given moment, so they must go more often to the bank or nearest cash machine to obtain cash by making withdrawals from savings accounts and other interest-paying assets. The inconvenience and loss of productive time that people suffer while making these trips to the bank figuratively wear out their shoes, hence the saying shoe-leather cost.

The **shoe-leather cost** of inflation occurs when inflation raises interest rates, thus inducing people to keep more of their funds in interest-bearing bank accounts and less in pocket cash, thus requiring more frequent trips to the bank or ATM machine to obtain needed pocket cash.

Financial deregulation has allowed the banking system to pay interest on most types of checking accounts. Thus it is only currency (and the nonpayment of interest on bank reserves at the Federal Reserve banks) that accounts for money's shoe-leather costs. Taking account of the payment of interest on bank checking accounts, it has been estimated that the value of convenience services lost from a 10 percent inflation in the United States is just 0.25 percent of GDP, or about $35 billion at 2008 prices. This loss is very small in comparison to the

---

[9] While credit cards are an alternative to currency and checking accounts for many purchases, there are still many small purchases that require the use of currency and many large purchases that require the use of checks, such as making the down payment on a house.

costs of the recession that would be needed to eliminate permanently a 10 percent fully anticipated inflation, which has been estimated at 4.7 percent of GDP per 1 percent permanent reduction of inflation, or 47 percent of GDP for a 10 percent permanent reduction of inflation.

In addition to the shoe-leather costs of inflation are its **menu costs.** These are any costs of changing prices, such as printing new menus or catalogues. The faster prices rise, the more often firms will be required to print new menus and catalogues. When inflation is very rapid, prices in menus and catalogues inevitably fall behind, causing movements in relative prices such as increases in daily auction prices of corn and wheat relative to slow-moving prices of restaurant meals and catalogue apparel. Changes in relative prices interfere with the efficient operation of the economy, for instance, unfairly transferring real income from restaurant owners to customers and to farmers.

A **menu cost** is any cost of changing prices, such as the cost of printing new menus or catalogues.

Clearly the Internet has reduced menu costs for some kinds of goods. For instance, Amazon can change prices on the books, music, and electronic goods that it sells every hour or every minute if it wants to do so. But other goods and services are still sold at prices that are posted for substantial periods of time, including restaurant meals, haircuts, fares on local bus and rapid transit lines, and postage stamps.

SELF-TEST

Assume that financial deregulation occurs and allows payment of interest on checking accounts.

1. What effect does this event have on the shoe-leather costs of fully anticipated inflation?
2. What effect does this have on holdings of money per dollar of nominal GDP?
3. What effect does it have on velocity?

Violation of Condition 4: Taxes Are Levied on Nominal Interest, Not Real Interest

The fourth condition for inflation to be harmless is that only real interest is taxable. But in every nation, tax rules are based on nominal interest, both interest earned as part of income and interest paid that is tax deductible (e.g., home mortgages). The following example shows how inflation (*p*) reduces the after-tax real interest rate when nominal interest rate is taxed, even if the nominal interest rate obeys the Fisher Effect and rises by as much as the inflation rate.

We consider an example with a tax rate (*t*) of 30 percent, or 0.3. Initially, the inflation rate is zero and the nominal interest rate is 3 percent, so the real interest rate is 3 percent. But when the inflation rate jumps to 10 percent, even if the nominal interest rate jumps to 13 percent, the real after-tax interest rate declines rather than staying constant.

General Form

After-tax real interest = after-tax nominal interest − inflation rate

After-tax real interest = $i(1 - t) - p$

Numerical Example

(a) $2.1 = 3(1 - 0.3) - 0$
(b) $-0.9 = 13(1 - 0.3) - 10$

In this example, line (a) shows that the after-tax real interest rate with zero inflation is 2.1 percent, that is, the nominal interest rate of 3 percent, times the 0.7 fraction that the saver is allowed to keep after the tax rate of 0.3 is paid, minus the zero percent rate of inflation. Line (b) shows that when inflation rises from zero to 10 percent, the after-tax real interest rate falls to *minus* 0.9 percent, that is, the nominal interest rate of 13 percent, times the 0.7 fraction that the saver is allowed to keep, minus the 10 percent rate of inflation. Comparing the two examples, an increase in the inflation rate from zero to 10 percent reduces the after-tax real interest rate from 2.1 percent to *minus* 0.9 percent. Thus, the fourth condition for inflation to be harmless, that inflation has no effect on the real after-tax interest rate, is violated. As a result, savings and investment decisions are distorted by inflation, which encourages people to borrow more and save less.

10-4 Indexation and Other Reforms to Reduce the Costs of Inflation

There is a strong case for the institution of reforms that can cut substantially the costs imposed by inflation. These reforms fall into three categories: the elimination of government regulations that redistribute income from savers to borrowers, the creation of an indexed bond to give savers a secure place to save, and a restatement of tax laws to eliminate the effects of inflation on real tax burdens. The first two of these reforms have already been achieved, the third has not.

Deregulation of Financial Institutions

Much of the distortion caused by the U.S. inflation of the 1970s resulted from federal government-imposed interest rate ceilings on commercial banks and savings institutions. Financial deregulation solved this problem. By 1985, all regulations on the payment of interest on checking, savings, and time-deposit accounts had been lifted. Since then, inflation has had a smaller redistributive effect than in the past, since all individuals, rich and poor alike, are able to receive a return close to the market rate of interest on their savings accounts. Checking accounts still pay a very low rate of interest to compensate banks for the cost of clearing checks.

Even if all checking and savings accounts paid a nominal interest rate that included a full inflation premium, savers would still suffer an erosion of purchasing power on their pocket cash. Inflation would still cause people to incur shoe-leather costs as they work harder to keep their cash balances at a minimum.

Indexed Bonds

Even though the lifting of government interest rate ceilings on savings and checking accounts has substantially cut the costs of inflation, many economists recommended that the government issue an indexed bond that would fully protect savers against any unexpected movements in the inflation rate. Finally, in 1997, the U.S. government responded to these recommendations by issuing an indexed bond, called *TIPS*, which stands for "Treasury Inflation-Protected Securities."

The Indexed Bond (TIPS) Protects Investors from Inflation

Following the lead of Canada, the United Kingdom, and other countries, the U.S. Treasury introduced inflation-indexed bonds to investors in 1997. These bonds protect the savings of investors from being eroded by unanticipated increases in the inflation rate. The indexed bond introduced in the United States is called TIPS, for Treasury Inflation-Protected Securities.

Unlike a conventional bond, an indexed bond promises to pay its holder a fixed real rate of return. An indexed bond maintains its promised real rate of return even if inflation suddenly accelerates by 5, 10, or even 20 percent relative to the inflation rate that was expected when the saver purchased the bond.

For the U.S. Treasury's 10-year indexed bond, semi-annual interest payments are calculated by adjusting the principal for inflation (using the Consumer Price Index or CPI) and applying the fixed real interest rate (determined at the auction at which the bonds were first issued) to the inflation-adjusted principal.

The benefits for the U.S. Treasury are several. Indexed bonds can reduce the risk premium that the government must pay to savers who fear that their returns on bonds will be eroded by future unanticipated inflation. By eliminating the risk of loss from future unanticipated inflation,

the Treasury can reduce its average borrowing costs, thus reducing the interest component of the federal government deficit. An additional benefit is that the process of issuing indexed bonds provides information about the inflation expectations of investors, measured as the difference in market-determined interest rates on conventional and indexed bonds of the same maturities.

The figure in this box plots the 10-year Treasury bond (which is not inflation-protected) and the 10-year TIPS. The green shading shows the real interest rate based on the expectations of those who buy TIPS, and the orange shading shows the inflation rate expected by those investors. There was a decline in the expected real interest rate from 2.7 in 2001–03 to 2.1 percent in 2004–07, while between the same two time intervals the implied expected inflation rate rose from 1.8 to 2.4 percent. Part of this increase of expected inflation rate reflected the increase in inflation due to higher oil prices during this period (see pp. 284–87). During the recession period of 2008–09, the real interest rate declined from 2.1 to 1.6 percent while expected inflation declined from 2.4 to 1.8 percent. By early 2011 the real interest rate (yield on the TIPS bonds) had declined to 1.0 percent, the lowest in the history of the TIPS going back to 1997.

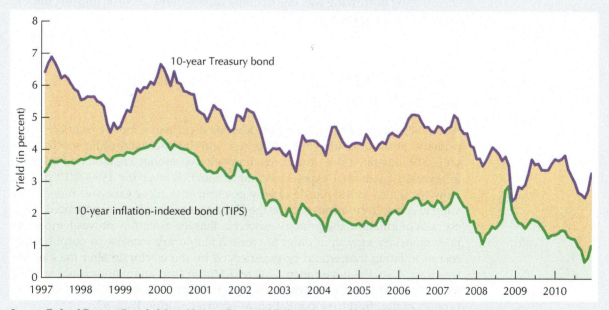

Sources: Federal Reserve Board, *Selected Interest Rates,* and Federal Reserve Bank of Cleveland. Details in Appendix C-4.

An **indexed bond** pays a fixed real interest rate; its nominal interest rate is equal to this real interest rate plus the actual inflation rate.

An **indexed bond** protects savers from unexpected movements in the inflation rate by paying a fixed real interest rate (r_0) plus the actual inflation rate (p). Thus the saver's nominal interest rate would be

General Form	Numerical Example
$i = r_0 + p$	(a) $3 = 3 + 0$
	(b) $13 = 3 + 10$

In numerical example (a), savers would receive a 3 percent return if the inflation rate were zero. If inflation suddenly accelerated to 10 percent, as in example (b), savers would find that the nominal return (i) rose to 13 percent, and they would be just as well off as if there had been no inflation. The box on p. 329 discusses the performance of TIPS since they were introduced in 1997.

Indexed Tax System

Another important reform made effective in 1985 is the partial indexation of the personal income tax system. This now raises the dollar amounts of tax credits, exemptions, standard deductions, and tax rate brackets each year by the amount of inflation that has been experienced. Without an indexed tax system, inflation would raise individual incomes and push taxpayers into higher tax brackets.

But the government must do more to achieve a fully inflation-neutral tax system. It must end present rules that discriminate against savers and favor borrowers and instead tax real rather than nominal interest and capital gains. Just as savers should be taxed only on real interest income and real capital gains, borrowers should be allowed to deduct from their taxable income only the real portion of the interest they pay on loans. These reforms would eliminate the present effect of inflation in the U.S. tax system of discouraging saving and encouraging borrowing and spending. The bias in the tax system toward encouraging borrowing was one of many causes of the 2000–06 housing bubble discussed in Chapter 5.

10-5 The Government Budget Constraint and the Inflation Tax

At the beginning of this chapter we identified excessive money creation as the primary cause of inflation in the long run, and the International Perspective box on p. 319 illustrated the close correlation between money creation and inflation in several nations that experienced rapid inflation over the 1990–2010 period. Now we return to the puzzle of why governments allow excessive money creation to occur. In countries such as the United States that have experienced modest rates of inflation, the primary answer is that the government was tempted to raise monetary growth in order to create a temporary increase in output at the cost of inflation that would be experienced by the electorate after the election was over. Also, the government was reluctant to stop an inflation, once started, for fear of the temporary period of high unemployment that would be a by-product of the effort to stop inflation, as occurred during 1982–83.

But in countries that have experienced rapid inflation or hyperinflation, the reason for excessive money creation is almost always large government deficits. By definition, government spending must be financed by some combination of tax revenues, bond creation, or money creation. When there are political obstacles to raising sufficient tax revenue, and in countries that do not have active bond markets, the government has no option other than money creation, that is, turning on the printing press.

A household must withdraw its savings or borrow if its expenditures exceed its income; the same is true of the government. The options open to the government for financing its expenditures are summarized in the **government budget constraint.** This divides government spending into two parts, spending on goods and services (G) and spending on interest payments (iB), where i is the nominal interest rate on government bonds and B is the dollar amount of government bonds outstanding. Government revenue sources are tax revenue net of transfer payments (T), the issuance of additional bonds (ΔB), and the issuance of additional government monetary liabilities (ΔH). Government monetary liabilities, which consist of currency held by the public and bank reserves, are often called high-powered money and are abbreviated H. Both B and H are part of the government debt; the only difference is that bonds pay interest and high-powered money does not.

> The **government budget constraint** relates government spending to the three sources available to finance that spending: tax revenue, creation of bonds, and creation of money.

The Government Budget Constraint Equation

The government budget constraint can be expressed in a simple formula:

$$\underbrace{G - T}_{\text{basic deficit}} + \frac{iB}{P} = \frac{\Delta B}{P} + \frac{\Delta H}{P} \tag{10.8}$$

In words, this equation states that the government's basic deficit (G - T) plus its real interest expense (iB/P) equals the real increase in bonds ($\Delta B/P$) plus the real increase in high-powered money ($\Delta H/P$). Why are three of the terms in equation (10.8) divided by P but G - T is not divided by P? This is because G and T have been defined as real inflation-adjusted variables through this book going back to Chapter 2, whereas B and H are *nominal* variables that must be divided by P to express them in real terms.

Bond Creation Versus Money Creation

Despite the fact that the U.S. federal government moved into surplus between 1998 and 2001, it moved back into deficit after 2001; for many years before 1998, it ran a deficit. Most other industrialized countries have run a government budget deficit rather than a surplus throughout the past two decades, without the interruption of a surplus as the United States enjoyed in 1998–2001. How are governments able to finance these deficits? There are two methods. These are the issuance of additional government bonds, represented by ΔB, and the issuance of additional high-powered money, represented by ΔH. When the government raises H, the total nominal money supply (M) increases.

An increase in H raises aggregate demand more than an increase in B, because a higher H raises the money supply and eliminates the crowding out effect of Chapter 4. Because a deficit financed by H is more stimulative to the economy, the government may want to finance its budget deficit by issuing more H when the economy is weak and by issuing more B when the economy is strong.

Indeed, the economy was weak in 2009–10, and this called for exactly the policy suggested in the previous paragraph. When the economy is weak, the government should finance its deficit by raising H rather than B. This is the famous policy of a "helicopter drop" of money discussed previously on p. 176.

UNDERSTANDING THE GLOBAL ECONOMIC CRISIS

How a Large Recession Can Create a Large Fiscal Deficit

Over the past several decades the U.S. federal budget has run both a basic deficit and a basic surplus. Here we see how different were the basic deficits in a year of prosperity (2000) versus a year of deep economic slack (2010).

Compare the following four situations, where the federal government deficit is expressed as a share of GDP. In the first event (1992) the federal government ran a negative basic surplus (i.e., a deficit) that was amplified by high-interest costs, boosting the basic deficit of −0.7 percent of GDP to a total of −4.7 percent. In the second event (2000), the government ran an unusually high basic surplus of 5.0 percent, which even after deducting 2.6 percent of GDP paid out as interest

costs, left a remaining surplus of 2.4 percent. The late 1990s were extremely unusual in the extent of surplus in the federal government budget, both the basic surplus and the total surplus.

The contrast between the third and fourth situations, 2007 versus 2009, provide an example of the impact of the Global Economic Crisis on the budget surplus. The basic surplus was roughly zero in 2007, but then 2.2 percent of GDP in interest costs needed to be deducted, leading to a negative surplus (deficit) of −2.1 percent. Then the basic surplus tumbled into negative territory in 2009, with a negative basic surplus of −8.9 percent of GDP and a total negative surplus of −10.7 percent.

	Basic Surplus	−	Interest Cost	=	Total Surplus
1992	−0.7	−	4.0	=	−4.7
2000	5.0	−	2.6	=	2.4
2007	0.1	−	2.2	=	−2.1
2009	−8.9	−	1.8	=	−10.7

In the United States, the size of the government deficit is determined by the administration and Congress, while the choice between bond and money creation is made by the Federal Reserve. Since the Fed controls ΔH, and since there is a large, well-organized market for government bonds, the Fed can respond to a larger government deficit by raising ΔH, reducing ΔH, or leaving ΔH unchanged. However, not every nation is able to choose between bond and monetary finance of government deficits. Developed nations such as the United States, Japan, Canada, and the more prosperous European nations have sophisticated capital markets where the government can sell bonds. But less developed nations lack these markets, so their governments have little latitude to finance their government deficits by selling bonds. As a result, in many countries a higher government deficit *automatically* requires raising ΔH, which boosts the growth rate of the money supply and (according to equation (10.3) on p. 317) the rate of inflation.

Effects of Inflation

Inflation may seem to aggravate the government's problem of financing its basic deficit, since according to the Fisher Effect, inflation raises the nominal interest rate (i) that appears on the left-hand side of equation (10.8). However, inflation also eases the government's problem. This is not evident in equation (10.8), where the inflation rate (p) does not appear. However, we can slightly rearrange equation (10.8) by multiplying the first term on the right-hand side by B/B and the second term by H/H. This converts (10.8) into:

$$G - T + \frac{iB}{P} = \left(\frac{\Delta B}{B}\right)\frac{B}{P} + \left(\frac{\Delta H}{H}\right)\frac{H}{P} \tag{10.9}$$

The term $\Delta BB/BP$ is the percentage change in bonds ($\Delta B/B$) times the amount of real bonds outstanding (B/P), and the term $\Delta HH/HP$ is the percentage change in high-powered money ($\Delta H/H$) times the amount of real high-powered money (H/P) outstanding. Clearly, if B/P and H/P are to remain stable, then the percentage growth rate of B, represented by a lowercase b, and the growth rate of H, designated by a lowercase h, will each have to equal the inflation rate (p):

$$\Delta B/B = b = \Delta H/H = h = p \qquad (10.10)$$

This equation says simply that the growth rate of bonds (b) and the growth rate of high-powered money (h) equal the rate of inflation. If that is true, then the real value of bonds (B/P) and the real value of high-powered money (H/P) will remain fixed. That is, the numerator of each ratio (B/P and H/P) will grow at the same rate as the denominator when $b = h = p$.

Why Inflation Is Tempting to Governments

Our aim is to determine the nature of the government's budget constraint that would keep the real value of bonds and high-powered money fixed. Since equation (10.10) gives the condition ($b = h = p$) that will allow this situation to persist, we need to substitute the inflation rate (p) into equation (10.9), replacing the term there for the growth rate of bonds ($\Delta B/B$) and also replacing the term for the growth rate of high-powered money ($\Delta H/H$). In arriving at this final statement of the government budget constraint, we also move the term representing real interest payments (iB/P) from the left-hand side of equation (9.9) to the right-hand side of equation (10.11):

$$G - T = \frac{pH}{P} - \frac{(i-p)B}{P} \qquad (10.11)$$

basic deficit   =   seignorage   −   real interest
                    or   on bonds
                    inflation tax

The first term on the right-hand side of equation (10.11), namely (pH/P), represents the inflation rate times real high-powered money, that is, the revenue that the government receives when it creates just enough H to maintain fixed the real quantity of high-powered money (H/P). This revenue that the government gets from inflation is called **seignorage.** Think of this simply as the revenue the government receives when it prints money. From the point of view of private households and firms that must add to their nominal quantity of H enough to keep real H/P constant, this same revenue is called the **inflation tax.**

Stated simply, if pH/P were the only term on the right-hand side of equation (10.11), it would indicate the amount of the deficit that the government could run by creating the right amount of nominal high-powered money (H) that would be consistent with keeping the real quantity of high-powered money constant. If the inflation rate is not zero, then this amount is not zero, and the government can run a deficit and still maintain real high-powered money constant. Subsequently we will see that the inflation tax is a cost of inflation to households, the exact counterpart of the benefit that inflation provides to the government.

Inflation does not eliminate the government's obligation to pay interest on its outstanding bonds held by private households and firms. But the second right-hand term [$(i - p)B/P$] in equation (10.11) illustrates that the government only has to worry about paying the *real* interest expense of servicing the bonds.

Seignorage is the revenue the government receives from inflation and is equal to the inflation rate times real high-powered money.

The **inflation tax** is the revenue the government receives from inflation and is the same as seignorage, but viewed from the perspective of households.

While it pays bond holders the nominal interest rate (i), bond holders have to give part of i back to the government to purchase sufficient additional bonds to keep their real bond holdings (B/P) constant.

An Example Showing That the Government Gains

To see how this works in an example, imagine that we start with $100 of bonds, a 5 percent inflation rate per year, an 8 percent nominal interest rate, and a 3 percent real interest rate. The government must pay $8 in interest. But, to keep the real quantity of bonds (B/P) constant, the government sells $5 in new bonds to the public, raising the value of outstanding bonds to $105. The government's net interest expense is just $3 (the real interest rate of 3 percent times the original $100 of bonds). Why? Because the government *pays* $8 in interest but *receives* $5 as a payment by the public for the new bonds.[10]

Thus the government benefits from inflation in two ways. First, it obtains an extra source of revenue, called seignorage or the inflation tax. The government can then lower ordinary taxes or increase spending more than it could otherwise. Second, the government may gain if inflation raises the nominal interest rate by less than inflation itself. Sharp increases of inflation, particularly such as those during the oil shock periods of the 1970s, are often accompanied by an increase in the nominal interest rate of less than one-for-one, thus reducing the real interest rate. And, as shown in equation (10.11), it is the real interest rate that matters for government finance.

◆ SELF-TEST

Assume that after centuries of a zero budget deficit and a zero debt, the nation of Abstinia runs a one-year deficit equal to 1 percent of GDP, which it finances by creating H/P equal to 1 percent of GDP.

1. If inflation over the next decade occurs at 5 percent per year, what must be true of the basic deficit and the level of H for Abstinia to end the decade with the same level of H/P equal to 1 percent of GDP?

2. What is the answer to the same question if the inflation rate over the next decade is 10 percent per year?

10-6   Starting and Stopping a Hyperinflation

We have already defined hyperinflation as an inflation rate of 1,000 percent or more per year. If an inflation of 1,000 percent per year were to occur in the United States, a Big Mac would increase in price from around $2.50 to $2,500![11]

---

[10] To simplify the presentation, both equation (10.11) and the numerical example in this paragraph neglect the taxation of interest earnings, which further reduces the government's net real interest expense.

[11] The text oversimplifies to state that a 1,000 percent per year inflation will raise the price of a Big Mac over one year from $2.50 to $2,500. Using the natural logarithm formula in the growth rate box in Chapter 2 on p. 41, we can calculate the amount by which a $1 price would rise after one year of 1,000 percent annual inflation. First we convert the 1,000 percent inflation back from a percent value to a decimal value ($1000/100 = 10$). The price by the end of the year can be calculated as $P_1 = e^{(1000/100)} = 22026$. This can be checked with the growth rate formula, where the annual growth rate between an initial value of 1.0 and a final value of 22026 over one year is $x = 100 \times \text{LN}(22046/1)/1 = 1,000$. Thus with 1,000 percent per year continuous inflation, the price of the Big Mac would rise from $2.50 to $55,065.

Table 10-1 **Annual Rates of Inflation in Selected High Inflation Countries, 1975–2010**

	1975–80	1980–86	1986–90	1990–95	1995–2000	2000–2010
Argentina	206	300	1,192	423	0.5	9
Bolivia	16	1,969	67	13	7	5
Brazil	50	142	1,077	1,419	17	7
Israel	61	157	24	14	7	2
Mexico	20	61	76	19	22	5
Nicaragua	23	246	5,841	528	11	8
Peru	46	95	2,342	1,341	8	3
Poland	9	37	188	132	15	3

Sources: International Monetary Fund, World Economic Outlook Database, April 2003 and April 2010.

Clearly, such an inflation rate would be disruptive if wages and salaries did not grow as rapidly, and if interest rates on savings accounts were less than the inflation rate.

As shown in Table 10-1, in 1986–90 four of the listed countries experienced annual inflation rates that averaged over 1,000 percent per year. In all of those countries, inflation was more rapid than it had been in the previous period. In fact, all of these countries (excepting Argentina) had inflation rates below 100 percent in the first period shown, 1975–80.

In the next period (1990–95) two of these countries—Brazil and Peru—continued to experience an annual inflation rate above 1,000 percent, while in Argentina the inflation rate fell to 423 percent per year. In sharp contrast was the period 1995–2000 in which none of the countries had inflation rates above 25 percent per year, and an even more dramatic event occurred in the most recent period, 2000–10, when none of the countries had an inflation rate above 9 percent. Clearly, macroeconomic policies improved markedly after 1995, and each country succeeded in limiting growth in its money supply, thus preventing hyperinflation.

Since there are more than 100 countries for which records are available, the fact that only four countries experienced inflation rates greater than 1,000 percent per year over the periods shown in Table 10-1 suggests that hyperinflations are unusual events. But, like the Great Depression of the 1930s, such unusual events are nevertheless worth studying for what they can teach us about macroeconomic behavior, and because the memory of these events may continue to influence economic theories and the beliefs of policymakers.

Costs of an Anticipated Hyperinflation

We have previously reviewed the inconvenience (or shoe-leather) cost of inflation that occurs because the interest rate paid on money is zero. The inconvenience cost of inflation becomes much larger in a hyperinflation, like that which occurred in Germany in 1922–23. In 1919 a farmer sold a piece of land for 80,000 marks as a nest egg for old age. All he got for the money a few years later was a woolen sweater. As the following account reveals, fifty years later elderly Germans could still recall the terrible days in 1923.

People were bringing money to the bank in cardboard boxes and laundry baskets. As we no longer could count it, we put the money on scales and weighed it. I can still see my brothers coming home Saturdays with heaps of paper money. When the shops reopened after the weekend they got no more than a breakfast roll for it. Many got drunk on their pay because it was worthless Monday.[12]

How a Hyperinflation Begins

Wage indexation calls for an automatic increase in the wage rate in response to an increase in a price index. It is the same as cost-of-living agreements (see Section 17-9).

What factors cause a hyperinflation to take off?[13] The first factor is familiar from Chapter 9. There we learned that accommodation of an adverse supply shock by more rapid nominal GDP growth can cause inflation to accelerate. What converts a mild acceleration into a hyperinflation is frequent (for example, monthly) **wage indexation.** Such indexation sets off a rapid inflationary spiral in which wage indexation leads to wage increases, which set off further price increases, which make a nation's goods less attractive to foreigners, in turn reducing the demand for its currency and causing a depreciation of the exchange rate, which in turn raises import prices and acts as a further supply shock. For instance, Argentina, Brazil, and Israel all had experienced relatively rapid inflation in the late 1970s and had in place systems involving frequent wage indexation. This system facilitated the countries' transition to more rapid inflation in the 1980s (although Israel never reached the hyperinflation stage). The combination of supply shocks, monetary accommodation, and frequent wage indexation is an "unholy trinity" that can lead to hyperinflation. In a hyperinflation, wage indexation occurs more frequently, aggravating the destructive power of the unholy trinity.

The other classic cause of hyperinflation is deficit financing, particularly as a result of wars (when government spending rises far more than revenues from conventional taxes). Hyperinflations do not generally occur while wars are being fought, since price controls are often used to suppress the inflationary pressure caused by deficit financing (a situation called "repressed inflation").[14] But when price controls are lifted after wars, the consequence of deficit finance can cause an explosion of monetary growth. Classic postwar hyperinflations far exceeded the rate of 1,000 percent per year, or 22 percent per month, that defines a hyperinflation. The average *monthly* inflation rate during the German hyper-inflation of 1922–23 was 322 percent, while the "mother of all hyperinflations" occurred in Hungary between August 1945 and July 1946, when the average monthly inflation rate was 19,800 percent! (See pp. 14–16 for more on the 1922–23 German hyperinflation.)

In thinking about hyperinflations, we should not be satisfied with the simple conclusion that a supply shock or a government budget deficit causes hyperinflation, as if the supply shock or budget deficit was totally exogenous. Instead, the essence of a hyperinflation is its cumulative dynamic character, best characterized as a vicious circle. Hyperinflation can create continuous supply shocks if there is a flight from a nation's currency that causes a real exchange rate depreciation. Hyperinflation can cause the real budget deficit to worsen by giving citizens a strong incentive to delay paying their taxes as long as possible. Government must then finance the growing budget deficit by an ever-increasing rate of monetary growth. The labor market also adapts to

---

[12] Alice Segert, "When Inflation Buried Germany," *Chicago Tribune*, November 30, 1974.

[13] This section summarizes several of the important conclusions of the Dornbusch *et al.* source cited in footnote 2.

[14] However, during the U.S. Civil War, prices doubled in the North and toward the end of the war rose at a near-hyperinflationary rate in the South.

hyperinflation by increasing the frequency of wage indexation, pouring more fuel on the inflationary fire.

How to End a Hyperinflation

The steps a government must take to end a hyperinflation are sometimes called a stabilization strategy. The key ingredient is to achieve a sharp reduction in the budget deficit by cutting government expenditures and subsidies and by raising taxes. In countries where tax evasion is a tradition, this fiscal reform may involve shifting to a broad-based tax that is easy to enforce, like the value-added tax.[15] At least in the short run, it is necessary to cut through the wage-price spiral by introducing some type of controls on wages, often called an **incomes policy.** This policy may involve reducing the frequency of wage indexation or obtaining an agreement between firms and workers to reduce real wages.

> **Incomes policy** is an attempt by policymakers to moderate increases in wages and other income, either by persuasion or by legal rules.

One by one, the nations that have experienced hyperinflation have achieved successful stabilizations, including Bolivia in 1985, Argentina in 1991–92, and Brazil, Nicaragua, and Peru in 1995–96. The successive failures of past attempts at reform, particularly in the cases of Argentina and Brazil, suggest that stopping a hyperinflation is a complex and difficult task. Much depends on the **credibility** of the government, that is, the public's belief that budget deficits and monetary growth are really going to stop. It may take several dramatic actions all at once to achieve credibility. The monumental achievement of stopping inflation in Argentina in 1991 required a drastic plan that combined every possible ingredient—fiscal correction, suspension of indexation, a fixed exchange rate, and international support. Unfortunately, Argentina's achievement was only temporary; as a result of poor control of fiscal deficits, by 2002 Argentina was once again a land of crisis, with a devalued currency and a soaring inflation rate of 26 percent. This inflation rate was brought down to 4 percent in 2004, only as a result of a catastrophic recession that reduced real GDP by 20 percent between 2000 and 2002. Argentina's inflation rate then bounced back to 9.1 percent, on average, during 2005–10.

> **Credibility** is the extent to which households and firms believe that an announced monetary or fiscal policy will actually be implemented and maintained as announced.

10-7 Why the Unemployment Rate Cannot Be Reduced to Zero

Thus far in this chapter we have concentrated on the causes and costs of inflation. The other major goal of macroeconomic policy (besides achieving as high a growth rate as possible in output per person) is to maintain the unemployment rate as low as possible. The analysis of unemployment appears to be simpler than that of inflation, because everyone agrees that more jobs are better. The only obstacle to reducing the unemployment rate to zero, according to our analysis of Chapter 9, is that too high an output ratio (which causes too low an unemployment rate) would cause the inflation rate to accelerate, thus exacerbating the costs of inflation.

In the rest of this chapter, we learn some of the other reasons (besides higher inflation) why maintaining too low an unemployment rate is undesirable. There

---

[15] A value-added tax, which does not exist in the United States, is common in Europe and was introduced in Canada in 1991. This tax has the same effect as a universal sales tax on all goods and services and is collected on the value that is added at each stage of production, that is, a firm's sales minus its expenditures on materials and supplies (which have already been taxed).

are good reasons why the overall unemployment rate is not zero, and these emerge from the efficient operation of a well-functioning economy. While excessively low unemployment is undesirable, excessively high unemployment causes devastating consequences for workers and families. The Global Economic Crisis brought with it persistently high U.S. unemployment in 2009, 2010, and beyond. The last part of this chapter examines the multiple dimensions of the weak labor markets in recent years.

The Actual and Natural Rates of Unemployment

At the beginning of the book, we were introduced to the concept of the natural rate of unemployment. The word "natural" describes exactly the same situation for unemployment as it does for output, an economy with a constant rate of inflation in the absence of supply shocks (see Section 1-3 on pp. 4–6). When the actual and natural rates of unemployment are equal, so also are the actual and natural levels of real GDP equal, the output ratio is 100 percent, and both the output gap and unemployment gap are zero.

Figure 10-2 plots the actual and natural rates of unemployment since 1980. The actual and natural rates of unemployment were roughly equal in 1980,

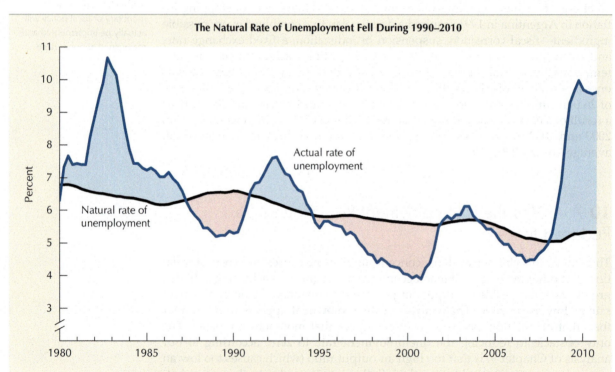

Figure 10-2 The Actual Unemployment Rate and the Natural Rate of Unemployment, 1980–2010

The actual unemployment rate was higher than the natural rate of unemployment, that is, the unemployment gap was positive, in 1981–86, 1992–95, 2002–04, and after 2007. The actual unemployment rate was lower than the natural rate of unemployment, that is, the unemployment gap was negative, in 1987–91. The natural rate of unemployment declined from 6.6 percent in 1990 to 5.1 percent in 2007.

1987, 1991, 1995, 2001, 2004, and early 2008. When the actual unemployment rate was above the natural rate, especially in 1981–86, 1991–95, and 2008–10, the inflation rate tended to decrease. When the actual unemployment rate was below the natural rate, especially in 1988–90, 1997–2001, and 2005–07, the inflation rate tended to increase, although in the late 1990s there was hardly any increase in the inflation rate due to the effect of beneficial supply shocks.

Between the late 1980s and 2007, the natural rate of unemployment (the black line in Figure 10-2) declined from 6.6 percent to 5.1 percent. Later in this chapter we will examine some of the reasons for this decline. By the year 2007 it was possible to maintain the actual unemployment rate at 5.1 percent without creating pressure for higher inflation, whereas in 1990 the unemployment rate would need to be maintained at about 6.6 percent to avoid pressure for higher inflation. This improvement is good for everyone, but still we must explain why it is not possible for the natural rate of unemployment to be zero instead of roughly 5 percent.

Distinguishing the Three Types of Unemployment

The difference between the actual rate of unemployment and the natural rate of unemployment, designated in Figure 10-2 by red and blue shading, is called **cyclical unemployment.** In Figure 10-2, cyclical unemployment is negative and the economy is prosperous when the shading is red, and cyclical unemployment is positive and the economy lacks job openings when the shading is blue. You will find the same color shading in Figure 1-6 on p. 12, which displays the actual and natural unemployment rates for a much longer period going back to 1900.

> **Cyclical unemployment** is the difference between the actual unemployment rate and the natural rate of unemployment.

Why is the natural rate of unemployment a number like 5 percent, rather than zero? When the economy is operating at the natural rate of unemployment, it experiences two types of unemployment. One is called **turnover unemployment,** sometimes also called frictional unemployment. Turnover unemployment occurs in the normal process of job search by individuals who have voluntarily quit their jobs, are entering the labor force for the first time, or are reentering the labor force. Any economy can expect to have a moderate amount of turnover unemployment.

> **Turnover unemployment** is another name for frictional unemployment. It is one of the two components of the natural rate of unemployment.

Mismatch unemployment is the second component of the natural rate of unemployment. Sometimes also called structural unemployment, it occurs when there is a mismatch between the skill or location requirements of job vacancies and the present skills or location of members of the labor force. For an unemployed individual, mismatch unemployment tends to last much longer than turnover unemployment, since more time is required for people to learn new skills or to move to new locations.

> **Mismatch unemployment** is another name for structural unemployment. It is one of the two components of the natural rate of unemployment.

To summarize, the actual unemployment rate is divided up into cyclical, turnover, and mismatch unemployment. When the actual unemployment rate is equal to the natural rate of unemployment, then cyclical unemployment is zero and all unemployment is accounted for by the turnover and mismatch components. Cyclical unemployment can be eliminated by stimulative monetary or fiscal policy that expands the economy when cyclical unemployment is positive and by restrictive monetary or fiscal policy that reduces aggregate demand when cyclical unemployment is negative. In the remainder of this chapter, we are concerned with the remaining two types of unemployment, turnover and mismatch, and the factors that tend to make them high or low.

10-8 Sources of Mismatch Unemployment

Vacancies and Unemployment in an Imaginary Economy

We can better understand the mismatch component of the natural unemployment rate (U^N) if we think of an imaginary society in which U^N is zero. All jobs are completely identical in their skill requirements, and all are located at exactly the same place. All workers are completely identical, with skill requirements perfectly suited for the identical jobs, and all workers live in the same location as the jobs. We can imagine a 10-mile-high combined factory-office-apartment highrise with very fast elevators at the corner of State and Madison streets in Chicago.

In this imaginary economy it is impossible for vacancies and unemployment to exist simultaneously. Why? Imagine that initially some workers are unemployed, and that the government pursues expansive monetary and fiscal policies that stimulate aggregate demand. Additional jobs open up, but the unemployed workers are in exactly the right place and possess the right skills, so that they instantly zoom up or down the speedy elevators in the 10-mile-high building to the job's location. Each job vacancy disappears immediately, and unemployment disappears instantly.

Quickly all the unemployed find jobs. Any further job vacancies caused by an additional demand stimulus will not disappear because there are no available jobless people to fill them. Further aggregate demand stimulus will just expand the number of job vacancies. The unemployment rate will remain at zero percent.

Skill differences among jobs can cause structural unemployment. To be slightly more realistic, let us now assume that there are two types of jobs and workers in the 10-mile-high building, typists and computer programmers. As the economy expands, it gradually uses up its supply of trained computer programmers. Once all the computer programmers have jobs, all of the unemployment consists of jobless typists. If the government further stimulates aggregate demand, we assume that an equal number of job vacancies is created for programmers and typists. The typist vacancies disappear immediately as available typists are carried by elevator to fill the job openings. But there are no computer programmers left, and so the programmer job openings remain. *Vacancies and unemployment exist simultaneously because firms refuse to hire typists to fill programmer vacancies.* The costs of training are just too high.

In reality, the actual economy is divided into numerous separate labor markets that differ in location, working conditions, and skill requirements. Any increase in aggregate spending generates job openings in some labor markets, while many people remain unemployed in other markets. Some unemployed are able to fill developing job vacancies. But others are prevented from qualifying by the cost of moving to the locations of the job openings, by the cost of acquiring the required skills, and even by the "cost of information" involved in finding out what jobs are available.

Vacancies and upward pressure on wage rates. In the imaginary economy, with all jobs and workers alike and located at the same place, policymakers could use aggregate demand stimulus to push the unemployment rate to zero. There would be no job vacancies and no tendency for firms to boost wage rates to fill empty job slots. Thus it would be possible to experience zero unemployment without upward pressure on wages.

But in the real-world economy, with numerous separate labor markets, vacancies and unemployed workers can coexist. There may be unfilled job openings for hotel workers in Iowa, while aircraft factory workers may be unemployed in Seattle. Structural or mismatch unemployment exists. Any attempt to use aggregate demand policy to push the total unemployment rate to zero will create numerous job vacancies for the types of skills that are in short supply and in the locations where labor is scarce. Firms will be desperate to fill these job vacancies and will boost wage rates, hoping to steal workers away from other firms. Higher wages will raise business costs and cause price increases. *Thus a situation with a low unemployment rate and lots of job vacancies maintained by rapid demand growth is one in which the inflation rate will continuously rise, exceeding the inflation rate of the previous year.*

Causes of and Cures for Mismatch Unemployment: Mismatch of Skills

All groups in the labor force, including adult men, adult women, and teenagers, are victims of mismatch between their own skills and locations and the skill and location requirements of available jobs. Why does this worker-job mismatch occur? We begin with causes of skill mismatch, add some suggested policy remedies, and then turn to the causes of and remedies for location mismatch.

Lack of job training. Vacant jobs often have specific skill requirements. Sometimes firms are willing to train workers when the skills are specific to the particular job; for example, an administrative assistant needs to know the filing system in a particular office. But some training, for example, how to use a personal computer, is general in nature. Firms may be unwilling to train employees in general skills for fear that the employees will quit before the firm's training investment can be repaid. Yet schools may not be able to provide the training because they lack either the equipment or properly trained instructors.

Solutions for low skills fall into three basic categories: better public education, subsidies for firms to train workers, and government-financed training programs. Better public education is essential, particularly for students from disadvantaged backgrounds, since training subsidies and programs will not work if teenagers and young adults cannot read or perform arithmetic.

Inflexibility of relative wages. Elementary economics teaches that a surplus of a commodity develops when its price is too high. In the same way, high unemployment of some groups, particularly teenagers, signals an excessive real wage for that group. In the United States there is a uniform minimum wage for both adults and teenagers, but teenage unemployment is higher than adult unemployment, and some people have proposed a lower minimum wage for teenagers.

Discrimination. Some employers will not hire women, minorities, or teenagers. Such discrimination stems from long-standing customs and from social pressure. We observe that most administrative assistants, secretaries, elementary school teachers, and nurses are women, and that minority workers are sometimes pushed into relatively unpleasant occupations. For instance, many workers in slaughterhouses that process cattle and chickens are recently arrived Hispanic immigrants from Mexico and Central America.

Several Western European nations have helped to reduce discrimination against women by subsidizing maternity leaves and providing subsidized child care, thus allowing women with children to maintain more stable job records. A case could be made for similar subsidies in the United States.

GLOBAL ECONOMIC CRISIS FOCUS

The Crisis Raises the Incidence of Structural Unemployment

Cyclical unemployment (the same concept as the "unemployment gap") soared upward in 2008–10, as we saw in Figure 10-2 on p. 338. Unlike the previous worst postwar recession in 1981–82, when the economy recovered very fast and cyclical unemployment declined rapidly in 1983–84, the economy's recovery in 2010–11 was much more sluggish. Millions of people found that, after losing their previous jobs, they could not find new jobs. Millions of people found themselves unemployed for 26, 52, or even 99 weeks.

In mid-2010 more than 1.4 million Americans had been unemployed for 99 weeks, roughly two years. Congress at least temporarily recognized their plight by extending unemployment benefits to this group, sometimes called the "99-ers." Yet as unemployment for this group stretched from two years into three, serious social consequences emerged. One of these was the gradual erosion of worker skills. Workers who were laid off in 2008 and had not been employed since then, for instance, missed out on the launch in 2009 of Windows 7 and in 2010 of Microsoft Office 2010, basic tools for office workers.

And the 99-ers were steadily becoming older and ever more subject to age discrimination. Some worried, even at ages as young as 50, that they might never be employed again because of their loss of skills and because of the "hole" created by long-term unemployment on their resumes. Long-term unemployment in the United States in 2010–11 began to resemble the double-digit average unemployment rate in Europe after 1985 (see pp. 350–51), and economic analysts were increasingly worried that high unemployment in the United States might last for five or ten years instead of rapidly disappearing as in 1983–84.

10-9 Turnover Unemployment and Job Search

We have now examined the sources of mismatch unemployment, one of the two components of the natural unemployment rate. A second component is turnover unemployment. What is the difference between mismatch and turnover unemployment? The barriers that stand between vacant jobs and workers unemployed due to mismatch are serious and require substantial investments in training or moving. But the barriers that stand between vacant jobs and those unemployed due to turnover are relatively minor, involving the costs of job search for a relatively short period in the local community for a suitable job.

One way of differentiating mismatch and turnover unemployment is the length of unemployment episodes ("spells"). Let us consider the year 2005, when the actual unemployment rate was quite close to the natural rate of unemployment, as we can see in Figure 10-2 on p. 338. In that year, if we rank all the unemployed by how many months they were unemployed, the median (the middle person) was unemployed for only 2.1 months. However, some of the unemployed suffered from long spells of unemployment lasting in some cases eight months or even a year, and those long spells brought the average number of months unemployed to 4.2 months. To understand how the mean could be double the median, consider a simplified example of ten unemployed people, eight of whom have spells of two months each while the remaining two people have spells of twelve months each. The median is clearly 2.0, but the mean is the sum of all the months of unemployment ($8 \times 2 + 2 \times 12 = 40$), divided by ten people, or an average of 4.0 months.

The fact that half of the unemployed found jobs quite rapidly, in less than two months, suggests that turnover unemployment is quite important. But the presence of long spells of unemployment for some people, making the average length of a spell double that of the median length, suggests that mismatch unemployment is also important. Thus, turnover and mismatch unemployment are not in conflict; they both occur at the same time, to different people.

Reasons for Turnover Unemployment

As we learned in Section 2-8 on pp. 42–43, Census Bureau workers ask a number of questions in order to determine whether individual household members are unemployed. These questions allow the unemployed to be broken down into five groups:

1. Persons laid off who can expect to return to the same job.

2. Persons who have lost jobs to which they cannot expect to return.

3. Persons who have quit their jobs.

4. Reentrants who are returning to the labor force after a spell of neither working nor looking for work.

5. New entrants who have never worked at a full-time job before but are now seeking employment.

Turnover unemployment consists primarily of individuals in categories 3, 4, and 5, although reentrants and new entrants may spend a long time in futile search if their skills and location are mismatched with job vacancies.

Some reasons for unemployment are concentrated in particular demographic groups. For instance, job loss tends to be most concentrated among adult males. Reentry unemployment is felt mainly by adult females, teenagers, and college students. New entry unemployment, of course, is mainly experienced by teenagers and college-age youth.

The data shown in Table 10-2 highlight several aspects of the labor market in the difficult situation of August 2010, when the overall unemployment rate

Table 10-2   **Unemployment Rates by Reason, Sex, and Age in December 2010**

	Unemployment Rate				Percentage of Group Unemployment			
	Adult Men	Adult Women	Teenagers	All Groups	Adult Men	Adult Women	Teenagers	All Groups
Job losers	7.0	4.6	3.5	5.8	75.3	56.8	14.5	61.7
Job leavers	0.5	0.6	0.6	0.6	5.4	7.4	2.5	6.4
Reentrants	1.5	2.5	7.8	2.2	16.1	30.9	32.2	23.4
New entrants	0.3	0.4	12.3	0.8	3.2	4.9	50.8	8.5
Total for group	9.3	8.1	4.2	9.4	100.0	100.0	100.0	100.0

Source: Bureau of Labor Statistics, *Employment and Earnings,* December 2010, Table A-32. ftp://ftp.bls.gov/pub/suppl/empsit.cpseea32.txt.

was a very high 9.6 percent and the labor market was exceptionally weak, with few job openings for millions of unemployed workers. Even though high unemployment in August 2010 was dominated by cyclical unemployment (a positive unemployment gap), there were some notable differences between the major demographic groups.

For instance, as shown in the right half of Table 10-2, 73 percent of adult men were unemployed because they had lost their jobs, as were 58 percent of adult women, while only 14 percent of teenagers were unemployed for this reason.

The economics of job refusal. The basic reason for turnover unemployment is explained by the theory of "search" unemployment, which develops the idea that an unemployed person may sometimes do better to refuse a job offer than accept it! Why? Imagine a teenager who quits school and begins to look for her first job. She walks down the street and soon encounters a restaurant displaying a sign "Dishwasher Wanted." An inquiry provides the information that the dishwasher opening is available immediately and pays $7.00 per hour. Will the teenager accept the job without further search? Refusal may benefit the teenager if she is able to locate a job with higher pay, say $9.00 per hour, or better working conditions.

Job search theory treats unemployment as a socially valuable, productive activity. Unemployed individuals "invest" in job search. The cost of their investment is the cost of the search itself plus the loss of wages that could be earned by accepting a job immediately. The payoff to their investment is the prospect of earning a higher wage and/or better working conditions for many months or years into the future. Because people do not always want the first available job and prefer to search, the only ways for the government to bring down turnover unemployment are (1) to provide better employment agencies that provide information that shortens the period of job search; (2) to lessen job search by reducing the motivation for quitting, reentry, and initial entry; or (3) to change the economic incentives that unnecessarily prolong the search, particularly unemployment benefits and high taxes on the income of the employed, both of which cut the net earnings of taking a job immediately rather than remaining unemployed. The invention of Internet job-finding services has helped to reduce the cost of search and hence the natural rate of unemployment.

SELF-TEST

Would the following events raise or lower the amount of turnover unemployment?

1. A change in rules allowing the unemployed to earn unemployment benefits for one year instead of the present six months.

2. A reduction in the personal income tax rate.

3. A decrease in the fraction of the working-age population consisting of teenagers.

4. An increase in the price of telephone calls.

The Human Costs of Recessions

In assessing the costs of reducing inflation by creating a temporary recession, we need to consider not only the hundreds of billions of dollars of lost output, but also the human costs of recessions. The basic difference between the costs of unemployment and inflation is that the unemployment of a household head hits the family like a hammer, whereas the costs of inflation are milder and spread more broadly across the entire population.

The human costs of unemployment are tragic. Researchers have found that with every 1 percent increase in the U.S. unemployment rate, 920 more people commit suicide, 650 commit homicide, 500 die from heart and kidney disease and cirrhosis of the liver, 4,000 are admitted to state mental hospitals, and 3,300 are sent to state prisons. In total, a 1 percent increase in unemployment is associated statistically with 37,000 more deaths, including 20,000 heart attacks. Unemployed workers are also more likely to experience dizziness, rapid heart beat, troubled sleep, back and neck pain, and high blood pressure.[16]

Common among the psychological costs of unemployment is a sense of being condemned to uselessness in a world that worships the useful. Just as serious are the long-term consequences. Many people have been deprived of medical insurance as a consequence of unemployment, since such insurance is a job benefit typically paid in part or wholly by employers. Physical and mental health deteriorates, and this is exacerbated by alcoholism. The health of children also suffers, particularly when parents take out their frustration and rage on their children in the form of child abuse.

Just as recessions and high unemployment create social and health problems, so a sustained period of low unemployment can alleviate some of these same problems. The prosperity of the U.S. economy in the late 1990s and the reduction of the unemployment rate to the lowest levels in 30 years revealed numerous examples of what the late Arthur M. Okun called the "high pressure" economy.[17] Among the most notable beneficiaries of the high-pressure economy of the late 1990s were young black men with little education and few skills. In the low-unemployment economy of the late 1990s, many black men aged 16 to 24 with a high school education or less, and many saddled with prison records, were working in greater numbers, earning bigger paychecks, and committing fewer crimes than in the early 1990s. Thus beneficiaries of the prosperous economy were not only the young black men themselves, but also—because of the decline in the crime rate—those who might otherwise have become the victims of crimes that did not occur. In fact, studies showed that crime dropped most in those cities where unemployment was the lowest.[18]

Why Did the Natural Rate of Unemployment Decline After 1990?

Figure 10-2 on p. 338 showed that the natural unemployment rate declined from 6.5 percent in the mid-1980s to less than 5.0 after the year 2000. This decline contributed to the prosperity of the late 1990s, because a given actual unemployment rate created less inflationary pressure than would have occurred a decade earlier. In addition, the beneficial supply shocks discussed in Chapter 9 (see pp. 290–92) held down the inflation rate despite the fact

---

[16] Barry Bluestone and Bennett Harrison, *The Deindustrialization of America* (New York: Basic Books, 1982), Chapter 3.

[17] Arthur M. Okun, "Upward Mobility in a High-Pressure Economy." *Brookings Papers on Economic Activity*, vol. 4 (1973, no. 1), pp. 207–52. See also Lawrence F. Katz and Alan B. Krueger, "The High-Pressure U.S. Labor Market of the 1990s," *Brookings Papers on Economic Activity*, vol. 30 (1999, no. 1), pp. 1–65.

[18] Sylvia Nasar with Kristen B. Mitchell, "Booming Job Market Draws Young Black Men into Fold," *New York Times*, May 23, 1999, p. 1.

that the actual unemployment rate dipped below the natural rate of unemployment during 1996–2001. Together, the decline in the natural rate and the beneficial supply shocks prevented the inflation rate from rising and thus allowed the Fed to keep interest rates at relatively low levels without any need for the sharp increases in interest rates that had occurred in the 1980s.

Several factors worked together to bring down the natural rate of unemployment after 1990. First, teenagers and young adults always have higher unemployment rates than older workers, because they spend time looking for work between periods in school. The fraction of teenagers in the total population fell in the 1980s and 1990s. This factor can explain perhaps one-third of the decline in the natural rate of unemployment since the late 1980s.[19] Second, by 2000 the population of inmates in prison, mostly young males, had quadrupled since 1985, and some of these inmates would have been unemployed if they were not in prison.

Third, the growth of temporary help agencies helped firms fill vacancies faster and helped workers find jobs faster, reducing both turnover and mismatch unemployment. Fourth, the invention of the World Wide Web made it easier for the labor market to match vacancies and job seekers. Taken together, these and other factors operating in labor markets help to explain why the natural rate of unemployment declined after 1990, allowing the economy to remain prosperous without the rising inflation that would have forced the Fed to raise interest rates more than it did.

10-10 The Costs of Persistently High Unemployment

The Global Economic Crisis hit the U.S. labor market perhaps harder than any other relatively rich nation. As shown in the box in this section, between 2007 and 2010 the unemployment rate in the major European economies increased by half or less than half as much as the huge spike of the U.S. unemployment rate from 4.5 percent in mid-2007 to 9.5 percent in mid-2010.

Yet the real problem of high unemployment in 2010 was not the level that had been reached by the official unemployment rate, but its persistence. While the level of real GDP reached a trough in June 2009, the unemployment rate hardly budged over the following 18 months. The unemployment rate was 9.5 percent in June 2009, and yet was still 9.4 percent in December 2010, as shown in Table 10-2.

Dimensions of Persistent Unemployment

The unemployment problem was more severe in 2010–11 than in the previous peak years of unemployment 1982–83 for a simple reason. That 1981–82 recession had been caused by very tight monetary policy aimed at conquering an ongoing inflation rate of 10 percent or more. The Fed's determination to fight inflation witnessed the unprecedented ascent of the federal funds interest rate controlled by the Fed to 19 percent in May 1981. It was no surprise that the economy tumbled into the worst postwar recession to date in 1982, but it was equally unsurprising that the relaxation of monetary tightness beginning in mid-1982 allowed the economy to leap forward to regain its unconstrained level of demand. The unemployment rate fell from 10.7 percent in the trough

---

[19] See Lawrence F. Katz and Alan B. Krueger, "The High-Pressure U.S. Labor Market of the 1990s," *Brookings Papers on Economic Activity*, 1999, no. 1, pp. 1–65.

quarter of 1982:Q4 to a mere 7.4 percent in 1984:Q2, a very rapid decline of 3.3 percentage points off the unemployment rate in only six quarters.

Yet the makers of monetary policy, as we learned in Chapter 5, have no similar tools to create a rapid revival of the economy following the devastating recession of 2007–09. That recession was not caused by tight money and we have learned that it cannot be cured by a stimulative monetary policy. Between the official trough of the recession in 2009:Q2 and 2010:Q3, the unemployment rate did not decline at all, remaining in both periods at a historically high level of 9.5 percent over this five-quarter interval. As of late 2010, prospects for future economic growth were mediocre, implying a continuation of high unemployment for several years into the future.

The weakness of the U.S. economic revival in 2010–11 evokes memories not just of the Great Depression of the 1930s (see pp. 110–11 and 253–61), but also Japan's "lost decade" that now has lasted for almost two decades, and two decades of high European unemployment registered between 1985 and 2005 as plotted in the graph at the beginning of this book on p. 18.

Will There Be a "New Normal"?

The weakness of the post-2009 economic recovery makes the future path of the unemployment rate highly uncertain. Two of many possible scenarios are illustrated in Figure 10-3. The blue line to the left of the vertical bar shows the actual unemployment rate through the end of 2010. The brown line shows the estimated value of the natural rate of unemployment through late 2010 and a forecast that assumes no change in the natural rate of unemployment after that.

The continuation of the blue line after 2010 makes the optimistic projection that the actual unemployment rate declines almost as rapidly as in 1983–85 and reaches the unchanged "optimistic" natural rate of unemployment at the end of 2014. But another much more pessimistic scenario is shown as well. The purple line shows a pessimistic projection that raises the natural rate of unemployment gradually from about 5 percent in early 2009 to 8 percent in late 2014 and thereafter. And the orange line shows the pessimistic prediction that the actual unemployment rate will decline only to 8 percent by late 2014 and remain at that value forever afterwards.

What factors lead some commentators to favor the pessimistic forecast, which some have called the "New Normal"? This nickname reflects the frequent reference to the natural rate of unemployment as the "normal" unemployment rate. Thus the "New Normal" pessimistically predicts that the natural rate will rise to a new level higher than has been observed in the United States at any time in the last half-century.

What might cause the pessimistic scenario to happen? The case centers on mismatch or structural unemployment, which we examined in Section 10-8. The longer workers remain jobless, the more likely they are to lose their skills. This is particularly true in white-collar jobs, which involve a lot of interaction with computers, because computer software is constantly changing. By this argument some office workers who lost their jobs in 2008 would be unable by 2011 to qualify for the job that they previously occupied.

Another pessimistic point is the experience of Europe (see p. 18) where the unemployment rate remained at or about 10 percent for most of the years between 1985 and 1998. In that period a popular theory was called "hysteresis," the idea that if the actual unemployment remains high for long enough, the natural rate of unemployment will rise to equal the actual rate, the opposite of the

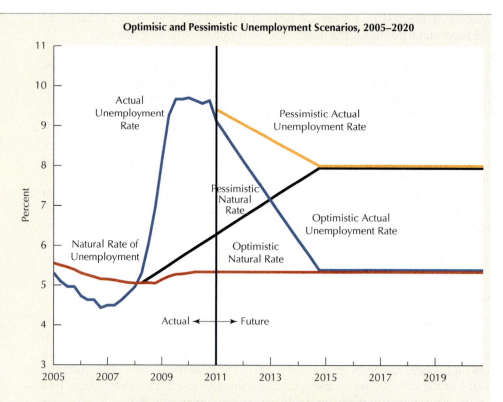

Figure 10-3 The Actual Unemployment Rate and Natural Unemployment Rate, 2005–10, and Both Optimistic and Pessimistic Forecasts for 2011–20.

The blue line shows the actual unemployment rate through 2010 and an optimistic forecast that reduces the unemployment rate to about 5 percent by the end of 2014. The brown line shows the natural rate of unemployment through 2010 and a forecast that assumes the natural rate remains at its 2010 value forever. A much more pessimistic forecast of the unemployment rate is shown by the orange line after 2010 and of the natural rate of unemployment is shown by the purple line.

Source: Bureau of Labor Statistics and research of Robert J. Gordon.

optimistic forecast in Figure 10-3 where the actual unemployment rate declines until it equals the unchanged natural rate of unemployment.

Which side is correct, the optimists or the pessimists? The optimists point to Figure 10-2 on p. 338, which shows that even though the actual unemployment rate remained above the natural rate for seven years between 1980 and 1986, the natural rate of unemployment did not rise but rather remained roughly constant. And the pessimists respond that monetary policy had much greater power to propel a rapid recovery in 1983–85 because it has pushed interest rates so high in 1980–81. In contrast, the Fed lost its power to reduce the short-term interest rate once the Fed had pushed it down to zero in early 2009.

The Costs of Persistent Unemployment

The number of unemployed people in the United States in January 2011 by the official definition was almost 15 million people, and as we learned from the figure on p. 45, millions more are not counted as unemployed because they have given up looking for work or are employed only part-time because they cannot find full-time work. Often part-time jobs do not include medical and retirement benefits.

Of those officially defined as unemployed, almost half have been unemployed for more than six months. About 1.5 million have been unemployed for more than two years, the so-called "99'ers" whose unemployment benefits have run out after a congressionally imposed limit of 99 weeks. Many of these long-term unemployed thought of themselves as securely in the middle class, only to find that after many months of unemployment their savings are depleted and they are unable to keep up with house and car payments. Some have become cut off from the world by being unable to pay for Internet service and must rely on local public libraries to use the Internet to search for jobs.

Local food pantries and shelters report that prosperous families who once donated money or food now arrive in need of food and other support. One local food shelter arranged for homeless people who had cars but no homes to sleep in their cars in a safe area behind the shelter. The director of a local food pantry described the situation:

> Once you start losing the income and you've run through your savings, then your car is up for repossession, or you're looking at foreclosure or eviction. We're a food pantry, but hunger is only the tip of the iceberg. Life becomes a constant juggling act when the money starts running out. Are you going to pay for your medication? Kids are going back to school now, so they need clothes and school supplies. The people we're seeing never expected things to turn out like this. Not in the United States. The middle class is quickly slipping into a lower class.[20]

There are additional effects of prolonged unemployment. Young people cannot start careers and their future resumes will be "scarred" by long periods of inactivity. Undergraduates who received their degrees in 2009 and 2010 are unlucky compared to those who received their degrees in 2007 and earlier years. Young people without jobs cannot afford to get married, have children, and are often forced to move back in with their parents. And the young are not alone in social distress. Those who are above age 50 and lose their jobs are subject to age discrimination, a belief that they are slower to learn new technologies and methods of production. As 2010 stretched into 2011, more and more unemployed Americans in the 50s and 60s began to worry that they might never find a job again.

---

[20] Bob Herbert, "We Haven't Hit Bottom Yet," *New York Times*, September 25, 2010.

UNDERSTANDING THE GLOBAL ECONOMIC CRISIS

Why Did Unemployment Rise Less in Europe Than in the United States After 2007?

We have already seen in a graph on p. 18 that European unemployment was much higher than in the United States between 1985 and 2007. But in the Global Economic Crisis starting in 2008 the decline in real GDP in Europe was similar to or larger than the United States, but the increase of the unemployment rate was substantially less. The adjacent chart magnifies the differences in the behavior of the unemployment rate by displaying the data only for a single decade, 2000–10. Shown are quarterly average unemployment rates for the United States, United Kingdom, France, Germany, and Italy.

The red line is the United States. We see that the unemployment rate drifted down from a peak of 6.2 percent in 2003 to 4.5 percent in 2007:Q2. After that it rose slowly at first but then very rapidly through mid-2009, but then displayed virtually no decline through the end of 2010. The total rise of the unemployment rate in the United States between early 2007 and late 2009 was a full 5.5 percentage points, that is, from 4.5 percent in 2007:Q2 to 10.0 in 2009:Q4.

As is clear from the graph, the increases in the unemployment rate were much less in Europe. Over the same 2007:Q2 to 2009:Q4 period when the American unemployment rate rose by 5.5 percentage points, the increase in the United Kingdom and Italy was about 2.4 points, that in France 1.5 points, and in Germany was an astounding *decline* of 1.1 percentage points.

How did Germany succeed in reducing its unemployment rate while the unemployment rate in most other countries, particularly the United States, was rising rapidly? This achievement was not because real GDP declined less in Germany than in the United States.[21] Rather,

it was because Germany instituted innovative policies to minimize the unemployment created by the drop of GDP.

The German achievement combines a different style of management relations with labor than in the United States, as well as specific policy interventions. The German government works explicitly on the decisions that firms make in the face of falling demand and the need to reduce output. Should the firms cut jobs or the working hours of the existing workers? The German government encourages companies to reduce hours per worker as contrasted with the American practice of fully laying people off. In place of laying off, let us say, 25 percent of their workers as in the United States, German firms are bribed by the German government to keep everyone on the payroll but to reduce the hours of all workers by 25 percent, for example, from 40 to 30 hours per week. The German government pays firms a certain amount of government subsidies to encourage them to adopt these "work-sharing" policies, and this in turn reduces the funds the government needs to provide for unemployment benefits to those who have been laid off fully and have lost their jobs.

The benefits are obvious. First, employees who retain their connection with the firm are more likely to maintain their consumption because they anticipate that they will be the first to be rehired when economic conditions improved. Second, firms retain their most skilled workers and can use the "down time" for training, maintenance of machines, and reorganizing the production process. Third, workers still have the dignity of being able to tell their friends and neighbors that they are employed rather than jobless. They do not have to spend their weeks in futile job searches.

10-11 Conclusion: Solutions to the Inflation and Unemployment Dilemma

Both inflation and unemployment are costly, but economists differ widely in their assessment of the relative costs. All agree that a steady inflation is less costly than a highly variable surprise inflation. And all agree that a hyperinflation is far more costly than a steady creeping inflation of, say, 3 percent per year. But there the agreement stops. Some economists consider it important to

---

[21] According to the *OECD Economic Outlook*, May 2010, Table 10, the output gap in Germany declined between 2007 and 2009 by almost exactly the same amount as in the United States.

There are many other differences between American and German labor markets, including the greater continuing importance of unions in Germany and the greater sense of cooperation between labor unions and management, fostered by legal requirements that corporate board of directors include substantial numbers of union leaders. While every European country has different institutions and all are not the same as Germany, on average European countries concur with German policymakers that the best way to respond to a sharp recession in aggregate demand is to share hours across workers who keep their jobs, rather than the American practice of retaining a privileged group of employees working their usual hours with an unlucky group of people who lose their jobs and suffer the social and economic devastation of unemployment as described in Section 10-10.

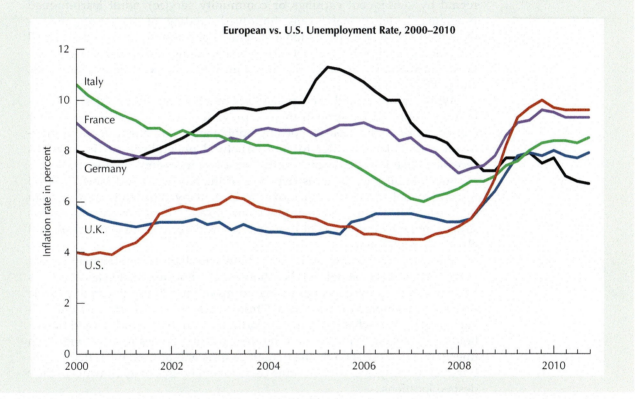

reduce the inflation rate to zero, whereas others consider the costs of a steady 3 percent inflation to be trivial.

As we have seen also in this chapter, the costs of turnover unemployment are quite low, and turnover unemployment usually lasts only a few weeks. But the costs of mismatch unemployment can be very large, leading to family breakdown, mental illness, loss of health insurance, and an erosion of job skills. For this reason, many economists believe that the costs of mismatch unemployment swamp the costs of a steady creeping inflation of, say, 3 percent.

We have learned that four options are available to reduce the costs of inflation: (1) restrictive monetary and fiscal policies that reduce output and raise unemployment temporarily, (2) price and wage controls, (3) cost-reducing policies such as reducing the burden of financial regulation, and (4) issuance of an indexed bond like TIPS and reform of the tax system to make it inflation-neutral.

What are the corresponding options to reduce the unemployment rate? There is little need for policies to reduce turnover unemployment. Responsibility for the avoidance of cyclical unemployment lies mainly with the Fed. This leaves mismatch unemployment, which results from a mismatch of job openings and available unemployed workers by skill and location. Research suggests that migration of workers between states and regions quickly eliminates unusually high or low unemployment rates in particular states without the need for government intervention.

Thus the main focus for policymakers is reducing the natural rate of unemployment by reducing the mismatch of jobs and workers by skill. Numerous programs have been suggested to help reduce the job-worker skill mismatch. Among these are widely available student loans for college (to be repaid by subsequent earnings or community service), adult learn-to-read programs, better prenatal care, improved funding of such programs as Operation Headstart, and national standards and testing to raise the overall educational level of U.S. schools. The choice among such programs goes beyond macroeconomics, into such disciplines as labor economics, sociology, and political science.

While monetary and fiscal policy face much greater difficulties in stimulating output and job growth than in previous business cycles, some other consequences of the 2000–06 housing bubble and subsequent financial meltdown also make it harder to cure structural unemployment. In previous recessions like 1981–82, known as the "rust-belt recession" because it disproportionately hit the old industrial cities of the Northeast and North Central regions, people were able to move. Indeed many thousands moved from depressed Michigan to full-employment Texas with its many prosperous firms generating employment in industries as diverse as oil exploration and electronic equipment.

But in 2009–10, many of those in states with high unemployment cannot move because they cannot sell their houses. The housing bubble and bust has left many unemployed people unable to make their house payments. While they may be tempted to "walk away" from "under water" mortgages with balances higher than what the house is worth, many of these workers and households are trapped. If they default on their existing homes in areas with high unemployment, the stain on their credit records will prevent them from qualifying for mortgages or even in some cases to rent houses or apartments in their desired locations.

Not only is it harder to cure mismatch unemployment in the current economic conditions, but also the option to move is much less feasible than in 1981–82. Several of the traditional high-growth states that previously welcomed migrants, including California, Nevada, and Florida, have some of the worst problems in dealing with the aftermath of the housing bubble. There are no construction jobs, obtaining a mortgage is very difficult, and local residents still face the possibility of additional declines in the values of their houses.

Since cures for mismatch unemployment by location are postponed by the housing crisis, attention then turns to solutions for the mismatch of skills. Priorities include government provision of student loans to make it possible for more low-income students to attend college, training grants for people to improve and update their skills, and an increased attention to measures that might reduce the cost inflation that currently plagues higher education as much as it does medical care.

Summary

1. In the long run the inflation rate equals the excess growth rate of nominal GDP, that is, the difference between nominal GDP growth and the long-run growth rate of real GDP.

2. Money growth equals the growth rate of nominal GDP minus the growth rate of velocity. Since velocity is not greatly affected by inflation, the long-run inflation rate equals the growth rate of the money supply minus the long-run growth rate of real GDP.

3. Governments allow excessive monetary growth for several reasons: (1) the temptation to boost demand before an election, (2) the output loss required to stop inflation, (3) adverse supply shocks require extra monetary growth if higher unemployment is to be avoided, and (4) inflation provides the government an added opportunity to finance expenditures without resorting to unpopular taxes.

4. The costs of unanticipated inflation are primarily felt by savers, while the benefits of such inflation primarily accrue to borrowers. Unanticipated deflation works in the opposite direction, benefiting savers while hurting borrowers.

5. The Fisher Effect is the one-for-one increase in the nominal interest rate in response to an increase in the expected rate of inflation, implying that the real rate of interest is unaffected by inflation.

6. In an ideal world, with inflation-neutral taxes and an operative Fisher Effect, fully anticipated inflation would affect only holders of money earning less than the market interest rate, particularly holders of currency. The struggle by such holders to reduce their holdings of money is the shoe-leather cost of inflation and becomes particularly important in a hyperinflation.

7. In practice, the Fisher Effect has not been validated, so that the real interest rate tends to drop even when inflation accelerates over a sustained period. This implies that even an anticipated inflation redistributes income and wealth from savers to borrowers.

8. The government budget constraint states that government spending and interest payments on government bonds must be financed by some combination of conventional taxes, money finance (the inflation tax), and bond finance. In many countries, bond finance is not feasible, so that an upsurge of expenditures or a decline in conventional tax revenues implies increased reliance on money finance, implying a higher inflation rate.

9. A hyperinflation can begin with the unholy trinity of adverse supply shocks, monetary accommodation, and frequent wage indexation. A hyperinflation can also result from a shock that sharply boosts government spending or cuts conventional tax revenue.

10. Reforms to reduce the cost of inflation include decontrol of financial institutions (which had largely occurred in the United States by the mid-1980s), indexed bonds, and an indexed tax system.

11. The main reason for high unemployment in the United States is that the natural rate of unemployment is not zero but in the vicinity of 5.0 percent. Roughly half of the natural unemployment rate consists of turnover unemployment; the rest consists of mismatch unemployment.

12. Mismatch unemployment is caused by an imbalance between the high skill requirements of available jobs and the low skills possessed by many of the unemployed. In an economy with flexible relative wages, the unskilled would be able to find jobs more easily but would receive lower wage rates. Any real cure for the problems of the unskilled—whether high unemployment, or low wages, or both—requires an increase in their skills and better matching of their locations with the locations of available job openings.

13. Turnover unemployment is another component of the natural rate. The barrier that maintains turnover unemployment is the absence of perfect information, making necessary an investment in job search to locate job openings that offer higher wage rates or better working conditions.

14. Policy solutions to reduce turnover unemployment include an improved employment service to provide better information, as well as changes in the present system of unemployment compensation, which provides a subsidy to workers who turn down job offers and continue to search or to remain at home awaiting recall to their old jobs.

15. The big problems after the Global Economic Crisis of 2008–09 involve the increased difficulty of reducing both cyclical unemployment and mismatch (or structural) unemployment. The obstacles to reducing cyclical unemployment were the main topics of Chapters 5 and 6. The obstacles to reducing mismatch unemployment are profound, both because the housing crisis makes it difficult to sell houses and condominiums when workers need to move to obtain better jobs, and because training programs may not be fruitful in reducing mismatch unemployment when there are no jobs available for those who are retrained.

Concepts

hyperinflation	actual real interest rate	Fisher Effect
nominal interest rate	unanticipated inflation	extra convenience services
expected real interest rate	Fisher equation	shoe-leather cost

menu cost
indexed bond
government budget constraint
seignorage

inflation tax
wage indexation
incomes policy
credibility

cyclical unemployment
turnover unemployment
mismatch unemployment

Questions

1. What is the misery index? What major criticism or criticisms can you make of it?
2. Distinguish between a hyperinflation and a moderate (crawling) inflation.
3. Do you agree that, as measures of the inflation rate, simple percentage changes become increasingly misleading at high rates of inflation? Why or why not?
4. What does "excess nominal GDP growth relative to natural real GDP growth" mean? Under what conditions is it equal to the inflation rate?
5. What are the four main reasons for inflation? Explain how each results in an excessive growth rate of nominal GDP.
6. Explain the distinction among the following: the nominal interest rate, the expected real interest rate, and the actual real interest rate. Which of these interest rates is the most relevant to saving and investment decisions? Which of the rates has the greatest impact on determining the distribution of income?
7. What determines the winners and losers in an unanticipated inflation? Using your answer as a starting point, explain why the major redistributional effect of unanticipated inflation is to transfer real wealth from the rich to the middle class.
8. How is the nominal interest rate affected in each of the following cases?
   (a) The money supply growth rate slows.
   (b) Velocity rises.
   (c) The expected real interest rate falls.
   (d) Real GDP growth rises.
9. Distinguish between the Fisher equation and the Fisher Effect. Which one is true by definition, and which one provides a testable hypothesis? Use Figure 10-1 and the figure in the box on p. 329 to explain whether the data support or refute the hypothesis.
10. Explain what the shoe-leather costs of inflation and the menu costs of inflation are. Compare how these costs change as the rate of inflation rises.
11. Explain why taxing real interest and real capital gains as opposed to nominal interest and nominal capital gains, but allowing the deduction of nominal interest rather than real interest, would still result in too little saving and too much borrowing and spending.
12. Explain term by term the government budget constraint of equation (10.8).
13. "In the steady state, the government benefits from inflation." Explain.
14. What are the two ways of financing a government deficit? Explain the conditions under which the financing of the deficit would be inflationary.
15. Explain the relationship between wage indexation and hyperinflation.
16. What should a government do to stop a hyperinflation?
17. Explain why people want to hold money up to the point where extra convenience services are equal to the nominal interest rate. How can this observation help us understand the net social loss to society of an inflation?
18. "Policymakers may reduce temporarily the natural rate of unemployment by pursuing an expansionary monetary policy." Do you agree with this statement? Explain your answer.
19. How can vacancies and unemployed workers coexist? If policymakers pursue an expansionary policy to increase real GDP, what will happen to the number of unemployed workers? What will happen to the number of vacancies as real output increases?
20. Explain how your answer to question 19 helps us understand why wages tend to rise faster as real output increases.
21. Explain why the length of unemployment episodes is one way of distinguishing between mismatch and turnover unemployment.
22. Explain the benefits of turnover unemployment. Compare and contrast the difficulty of reducing unemployment due to a mismatch of skills as opposed to a mismatch of location. Finally, discuss what impact being able to obtain information concerning employment opportunities over the Internet is likely to have on turnover unemployment, unemployment due to a mismatch of skills, and unemployment due to a mismatch of locations.
23. Explain how persistently high unemployment can cause a rise in the amount of structural unemployment.
24. Explain why monetary policy caused first, a rise in the unemployment rate in 1981–82 and second, a rapid decline in the unemployment rate from late 1982 through mid-1984.
25. Discuss what is meant by the "new normal" and what underlies such a pessimistic view of the future path of the unemployment rate.
26. What are the human costs of persistently high unemployment?
27. Explain why the unemployment rate did not rise as much in Germany as it did in the United States during the Global Economic Crisis.
28. Explain how the collapse of the housing bubble has made solving the problem of high mismatch unemployment more difficult.

Problems

Visit www.MyEconLab.com to complete these or similar exercises.

1. Let P_0 be the initial price level (say, a price index such as the CPI). Let p be the inflation rate per period.
   (a) If P_t is the price at the end of period t, show that

   $$P_t = P_0(1 + p)^t$$

   (b) If $P_0 = 1.00$ and $p = 50$ percent per month, calculate P_{12}.
   (c) Given P_{12}, calculate the percentage change from P_0, that is, the annual rate of inflation when the monthly rate is 50 percent.

2. If inflation is a continuous process (that is, prices rising daily or even hourly, as in a hyperinflation), calculating inflation rates at discrete intervals (such as months, quarters, and years) may be misleading. We desire a continuous analogue to the equation in problem 1. In

   $$P_t = P_0 e^{pt}$$

   let e represent the base of natural logarithms, p the instantaneous rate of inflation, and the other variables remain as defined earlier.
   (a) Prove that p is the instantaneous rate of inflation in the preceding equation. *Note:* This requires the use of calculus. You're trying to prove the following:

   $$p = (1/P_t)(dP_t/dt)$$

   (b) The logarithmic price change is given by

   $$p = (ln\ P_t - ln\ P_0)/t$$

   Derive this equation from the immediately preceding one.
   (c) If $P_0 = 1.00$, $P_{12} = 129.75$, and the time interval between these periods is twelve months, find p, using the log price change formula.
   (d) For (c), you should have gotten $p = 40.5$ percent per month. Now calculate the instantaneous rate of inflation *per year* equivalent to the instantaneous rate of inflation of 40.5 percent per month. *Hint:* Use the equation for log price change, but this time let $P_1 = 129.75$ and $t = 1$.

3. Suppose that the growth rate of the money supply is 5 percent per year, the velocity of money is constant, and natural real GDP grows by 3 percent per year. Finally assume that in the long run, actual and natural real GDP grow at the same rate.
   (a) What is the rate of inflation in the long run?
   (b) Suppose that a beneficial productivity growth shock, such as the one from 1995–2004, causes the growth rate of natural real GDP to increase to 3.5 percent per year. Given no change in the growth rate of the money supply in the long run, what is the new rate of inflation in the long run?

(c) Given the increase in the growth rate of natural real GDP to 3.5 percent per year and supposing that monetary authorities wish to maintain the inflation rate in the long run at the same level as in part a, what action do they need to take?
(d) Suppose that an adverse productivity shock, such as the one from 1965–1980, reduces the growth rate of natural real GDP to 2.5 percent per year. Given that the growth rate of the money supply equals 5 percent per year in the long run, what is the new rate of inflation in the long run? Supposing that monetary authorities wish to maintain the inflation rate in the long run at the same level as in part a, what action do they need to take, given the decline in the growth rate of natural real GDP?
(e) Given the effects of the productivity shocks on the growth rate of natural real GDP, what is an argument in favor of maintaining the growth rate of the money supply at 5 percent and what is an argument in favor of maintaining the inflation rate at a constant level?

4. Bill borrows $200,000 for three years from Larry and agrees to pay Larry 8 percent interest, compounded annually. The entire amount of the loan plus interest will be paid at the end of the third year. The price level at the time of the loan is 1.00.
   (a) What is the amount that Larry will receive at the end of the third year? If the price level is 1.00 at the end of the third year, what is the real value of the payment received by Larry?
   (b) Assume that the inflation rate in the economy is 3 percent per year for each of the three years. What is the price level at the end of the third year? What is the real value of the payment received by Larry?
   (c) Again, assume that the inflation rate in the economy is 3 percent per year for each of the three years. In this case, however, Larry had indexed the loan to protect himself from inflation. What would be the nominal interest rate for each year of the loan? What is the nominal amount of the payment received by Larry at the end of the third year? What is the real value of the payment?

5. Suppose that the nominal interest rate before taxes equals 8 percent, the rate of inflation equals 3 percent, and the tax rate equals 25 percent.
   (a) Suppose that nominal interest is taxed. What are the after-tax nominal and real interest rates?
   (b) Suppose that the inflation rate increases to 6 percent. What is the new nominal interest rate necessary to maintain the same after-tax real interest rate as in part a?

(c) Suppose that the tax system is reformed so that real interest is taxed. What is the real interest rate before taxes that yields the same after-tax real interest rate as in part a?

(d) Suppose that the Fisher Effect holds. What are the nominal interest rates, given that real interest is taxed and the inflation rates equal 3 and 6 percent?

6. Suppose the relationship between H/P and p is given by

$$H/P = 8 - 0.8p$$

Here, H/P is real high-powered money, in billions of dollars, and p is the rate of inflation, in percent. Define the inflation elasticity of real high-powered money, η, as

$$\eta = -\%\Delta(H/P)/\%\Delta p = -(p/[H/P])(\Delta[H/P]/\Delta p)$$

(a) If the current rate of inflation is 5 percent, what are H/P, pH/P, and η?

(b) If p falls to 4 percent, what are H/P, pH/P, and η?

(c) If p rises to 6 percent, what are H/P, pH/P, and η?

(d) On the basis of these calculations, can you formulate a relationship between pH/P and η?

7. Suppose that the amounts of real government spending, G, equals 700, real high-powered money, H/P, equals 1,500, and real government bonds, B/P, equals 2,000. The rate of inflation equals 5 percent and the nominal interest rate equals 7.5 percent.

(a) What is the amount of seignorage (inflation tax)?

(b) What is the real interest rate?

(c) What is the real interest on bonds?

(d) Using equation (10.11), what is the amount of taxes that keeps the real value of bonds and high-powered money fixed?

(e) Suppose that rate of inflation decreases to 4 percent. What is the new amount of seignorage?

(f) Suppose that the Fisher Effect holds. Given the lower inflation rate, what is the amount taxes must be raised or the amount government spending must be cut in order to keep the real value of bonds and high-powered money fixed?

8. Suppose that the natural rates of unemployment is 4.8 percent for adult males, 4.5 percent for adult females, and 13.4 percent for teenagers. Fifty-five percent of the labor force consists of adult males, 30 percent is made up of adult females, and the rest consists of teenagers.

(a) What is the natural rate of unemployment for the entire labor force?

(b) Suppose that the portion of the labor force that consists of adult females rises from 30 to 40 percent, but the adult male and the teenage portions decrease to 50 and 10 percent, respectively. What is the new natural rate of unemployment for the entire labor force and why has it changed?

(c) Suppose that government policies, a reduction in discrimination, the development of Internet employment services, as well as other factors reduce the natural unemployment rates for adult males, adult females, and teenagers to 4.3 percent, 4.0 percent, and 12.5 percent, respectively. What is the new natural rate of unemployment for the entire labor force?

(d) Monetary authorities monitor labor market conditions in making policy decisions concerning interest rates and the money supply. What do your answers to parts b and c suggest concerning the data monetary authorities are likely to monitor in conducting monetary policy? *Hint*: How might the Fed have acted differently in the 1990s if it did not have some indication that the natural rate of unemployment was declining over the course of that decade?

9. The purpose of this problem is to show how the unemployment rate depends on both the number of people who become unemployed in any month and the amount of time they are unemployed. Suppose that the size of the labor force is 160 million people.

(a) During any month when the output gap is zero, two million people become unemployed, and they remain unemployed for four months before finding work. Compute the number of unemployed people in any month when the output gap is zero and the natural rate of unemployment.

(b) Suppose that a mild recession causes three million people to become unemployed in any month, but the amount of time it takes them to find work remains at four months. Compute the number of unemployed people during any month in this recession and the unemployment rate during this recession.

(c) Suppose that a more severe recession also causes three million people to become unemployed in any month but that the number of months that it takes to find work increases to eight months. Compute the number of unemployed people during any month in this recession and the unemployment rate during this recession.

(d) Suppose that when the economy recovers from the severe recession and the output gap returns to zero, the number of people who become unemployed during any month falls back to two million. However the severe recession caused a decline in the skills of workers, and as a result it now takes people five months to find work. Compute the number of people now unemployed in any month when the output gap is zero and the new natural rate of unemployment.

◆ SELF-TEST ANSWERS

p. 318. (1) The inflation rate in the first half of the decade is 4 percent per year. (2) For the last half it is 6 percent per year. (3) Nominal GDP growth is 8 percent in the first half and (4) also 8 percent in the last half.

p. 327. (1) Financial deregulation, which allowed the payment of interest on checking accounts, made the demand for money (that is, checking accounts plus currency) less responsive to an increase in the interest rate. Hence an increase in the nominal interest rate caused by higher inflation causes less shifting away from money than prior to deregulation, thus reducing the shoe-leather cost of fully anticipated inflation. (2) It raises the ratio of the money supply to nominal GDP. (3) It reduces velocity (PY/M^s).

p. 334. (1) If inflation occurs at 5 percent per year for a decade, then the price level grows at 5 percent per year. To keep H/P constant, H must grow at 5 percent per year. Seignorage, the pH/P term in equation (9.11), is equal to 5 percent ($p = 0.05$) times 1 percent of GDP ($H/P = 0.01$ times GDP), or 0.05 percent of GDP. Thus the government must run a basic deficit of 0.05 percent of GDP in order to end the decade with a fixed level of H/P. (2) The basic deficit must be 0.10 percent of GDP.

p. 344. (1) An extension of the time to earn unemployment benefits would reduce the cost of refusing a job and hence would extend the period of search and raise the turnover unemployment rate. (2) A reduction in the personal income tax rate would raise the cost of refusing a job, since it would increase the after-tax pay for any given pretax wage rate, and hence would reduce the period of search and the turnover unemployment rate. (3) Fewer teenagers would imply less turnover, since teenagers often engage in search unemployment when they look for after-school or summer employment, or work during years off from school. (4) A higher price of phone calls would raise the cost of search and hence would reduce the amount of search and reduce the turnover unemployment rate.

The Theory of Economic Growth

In essence the question of growth is nothing new but a new disguise for an age-old issue, one which has always intrigued and preoccupied economics: the present versus the future.
—James Tobin[1]

11-1   The Importance of Economic Growth

As we learned in Chapter 1, a fundamental task of macroeconomics is to determine the sources of economic growth. By economic growth we usually mean the growth rate of real GDP per person (or per capita). The achievement of rapid economic growth is one of the most (if not *the* most) important distinguishing features of a successful economy. The fact that the U.S. economy grew more rapidly than those of the industrialized nations of Europe during the century between 1850 and 1950 allowed Americans to enjoy a higher standard of living than most residents of Europe throughout the postwar era.

Welfare Gains from Growth

The profound importance of growth comes from the power of compound arithmetic. Even apparently small differences in growth rates make a huge difference in the standard of living over, say, a period of fifty years. Consider an average income of $45,000 in 2010. At a growth rate of 2 percent, that income would grow over fifty years to $122,300 in the year 2060. At a growth rate of 2.5 percent, that income would grow to $157,100 in 2060, a difference of $34,800, or more than three-quarters of the initial income level!

Thus the welfare gains resulting from even minor increases in the rate of economic growth are enormous. In the oft-quoted words of Nobel Prize–winning University of Chicago economist Robert E. Lucas, Jr., "the consequences for human welfare are simply staggering. Once one starts thinking about them, it is hard to think of anything else."[2] This is true because small differences in the rate of economic growth can make a huge difference in the welfare of the average citizen when compounded over 50 or 100 years.

The newly industrializing countries of Asia (China, India, Korea, Taiwan, Hong Kong, and Singapore) are widely admired for their success in achieving very rapid economic growth over the past forty years. Although Korea had about the same level of real income per capita as the Philippines in 1965, by 2010 (thanks to its stunning achievement of rapid economic growth), Korea's real income per capita was *six times* that of the Philippines.[3]

---

[1] "Economic Growth as an Objective of Government Policy," *American Economic Review*, vol. 54 (May 1964), p. 1.

[2] Robert E. Lucas, Jr., "On the Mechanics of Economic Development," *Journal of Monetary Economics*, vol. 22 (July 1988), p. 5.

[3] See Figure 1-9 on p. 17.

The Great Questions of Economic Growth

By far the most important reason to study economic growth is the great and growing chasm between standards of living in the world's rich and poor countries. By "rich" we mean North America, much of Europe, Japan, some of the successful Asian countries, and Australasia. By "poor" we mean many of the rest. In between, there are middle-income countries like most former members of the Soviet Bloc, which are neither rich nor poor. As is illustrated by the contrast between Korea and the Philippines, only a few decades of fast growth were necessary for Korea to leave the ranks of the poor and join the rich nations, while the Philippines remains mired in poverty. What secrets did the Koreans discover? What kept the Philippines from benefiting from the same methods? After we learn about the theory of growth in this chapter, we turn in the next chapter to the puzzle of rich versus poor.

The Next Two Chapters

Economic growth has always been a central topic in macroeconomics. We now begin a two-chapter discussion of economic growth and other issues related to the long-run evolution of the economy. In this chapter we examine the simple theory of economic growth and its relation to growth in population and in the capital stock. To address puzzles that the simple theory cannot explain, we broaden the approach to include other types of investments that tend to favor growth, including education, research, and development.

Chapter 12 begins by taking a closer look at the success of rich nations and the failure of poor nations. Simple growth theory suggests that poor nations should grow more rapidly, yet some succeed while others fail. Why? We introduce the role of political and other noneconomic factors that may promote or retard growth, including crime, corruption, absence of property rights and a reliable legal system, and the geographical disadvantages suffered by some nations.

11-2   Standards of Living as the Consequence of Economic Growth

The Poor United Kingdom

In 1870, average real GDP per person in the United Kingdom was 37 percent higher than in the United States. But by 2010 average real GDP per person in the United States was 32 percent higher than that in the United Kingdom. How was this possible? Faster **economic growth,** meaning a higher average annual growth rate of natural real GDP per person, allowed the United States first to catch up to the United Kingdom in 1906 and then from 1916 to 1950 to move ahead of the United Kingdom. Although the United Kingdom kept pace with the United States after 1950, the United Kingdom was never able to close the gap. This was a race between the tortoise and the hare, in which the tortoise never caught up.

In economics, **economic growth** is the study of the causes and consequences of sustained growth in natural real GDP per person.

The gap between the average real GDP per person in the two countries makes an enormous difference in their relative standards of living. The comparisons are made in a way that holds constant the prices of goods and services in

INTERNATIONAL PERSPECTIVE

The Growth Experience of Seven Countries Over the Past Century

The accompanying figure shows the level of per person GDP in seven leading industrial countries for selected years over the past 140 years. The figures are expressed in 2010 U.S. dollars and are based on a careful study that bases the prices actually paid by inhabitants of other countries on the average paid in all industrialized countries. The table summarizes some of the most important information contained in the figure, including the values, in 2010 U.S. prices, of per person GDP in both 1870 and 2010, as well as the growth rates of per person GDP during selected intervals. In the table, countries are listed in order of 2010 per person GDP. Several major conclusions can be drawn from an inspection of the figure and companion table:

1. All nations have enjoyed substantial growth in per person GDP: in the United States it increased by a factor of almost 13, from $3,714 in 1870 to $47,133 in 2010.

2. The figure is plotted on a logarithmic scale. This means that the slope of each line indicates the economic growth rate; a steep line means fast growth and a flat line indicates slow growth. For all countries, 1955–73 was the period of fastest growth, and all countries have experienced a growth slowdown since 1973.

3. Differing growth rates among countries have led to changes in relative positions. Japan had the most rapid growth, particularly between 1955 and 1973, when it reached the incredible rate of 7.9 percent per annum. Japan overtook Italy in 1971 and the United Kingdom in 1980.

4. The United Kingdom's loss of relative position has been continuous over the entire century. From 1870 to 1973, the United Kingdom had a growth rate at the bottom of the group. The United Kingdom was overtaken by the United States in 1906, by France and Germany in 1960, and by Japan in 1980.

5. Japan's malaise, the "lost decade" that has now extended for almost two decades, shows up in the graph as well. While Japan had overtaken the United

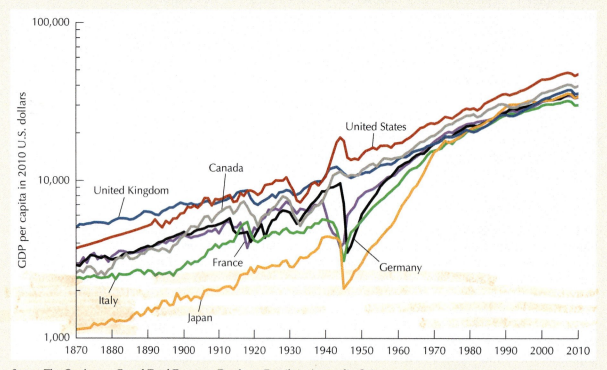

Source: The Conference Board Total Economy Database. Details in Appendix C-4.

Kingdom in 1980 and both Germany and France by the mid-1980s, by 2000 these countries had caught up with Japan again. After 2000 the United Kingdom surged ahead of Japan while France and Germany stayed even with Japan's per-person real income.

6. The United States is something of a "has-been" in the growth race, owing its high living standard to its superior growth performance before 1950. In particular, the United States gained an advantage in its freedom from wartime destruction as compared to some European nations.

Types of Economic Change

The figure displays not only the process of economic growth that raises the standard of living decade after decade, but two types of shorter-term movements. The first of these is wartime destruction, which is clearly visible in the sharp drop in the living standards of Germany and Japan from 1940 to 1950. Making up for wartime destruction explains much of the rapid economic growth in these two countries in the 1950s and early 1960s.

The second type of short-term economic change is the business cycle. The data for each country are annual, so the alternation of business recessions and expansions is visible, most notably during the depression years of the 1930s. The figure also highlights the unique nature of the Great Depression in the United States and Canada, where per person real GDP declined much more than in the other countries, as discussed in the box on pp. 258–59.

Level and Growth Rate of Per Capita Real GDP in 2010 Dollars for Seven Countries, 1870–2010

	Level in 2010 U.S. dollars		Average annual growth rate in percent				
	1870	2010	1870–2010	1870–1913	1913–1955	1955–1973	1973–2010
United States	3,714	47,133	1.81	1.80	1.72	2.37	1.67
Canada	2,598	39,844	1.95	2.24	1.56	2.91	1.59
United Kingdom	5,038	35,660	1.40	1.01	1.14	2.36	1.68
Japan	1,133	34,176	2.43	1.47	1.69	7.87	1.75
France	2,926	33,770	1.75	1.44	1.36	4.04	1.43
Germany	2,905	34,226	1.76	1.59	1.10	4.03	1.61
Italy	2,412	30,108	1.80	1.25	1.41	4.57	1.55

the two countries.[4] Thus the average American can purchase all the goods and services bought by the average U.K. resident and still have 32 percent more left over for additional spending. And this difference is the result of a seemingly puny and insignificant difference in the U.S. economic growth rate between 1870

---

[4] The "bible" for comparisons of living standards across nations, as in the table and figure in the International Perspective box in this section, is an immense body of data collected by economists at the University of Pennsylvania. See Robert Summers and Alan Heston, "The Penn World Table (Mark 5): An Expanded Set of International Comparisons, 1950–88," *Quarterly Journal of Economics* (May 1991), pp. 1–41. The latest version of the data is available at pwt.econ.upenn.edu. This was released in September 2010, and covers the years 1950–2007. As a simple example of what the Penn project involves, let us assume that if Japanese output is translated from yen to dollars at today's exchange rate, Japanese output per person is $60,000 while U.S. output is just $40,000. If every good in Japan costs twice as many dollars to buy as the same goods in the United States, then the true Japanese standard of living must be divided by 2 and becomes $30,000 ($60,000/2), or just 0.75 of the U.S. standard of living. The Penn project makes such comparisons of the cost of living for many different goods in 188 countries over a long period of time and can easily be accessed at the Web site listed above. Another excellent source of economic growth data can be found by searching for "Conference Board Total Economy Database."

and 2010: 1.81 percent per year for the United States as compared to 1.40 percent for the United Kingdom. *Minor differences in economic growth rates sustained over a long period build up into substantial differences in relative living standards.*

Economic Growth: Something for Nothing?

It is easy to see why economic growth is such a fascinating topic. High rates of economic growth make it possible to have more of everything—higher health spending and welfare benefits, with plenty left over for more private consumption of goods and services. In contrast, a society with a low rate of economic growth suffers continual strife as difficult choices must be made about the allocation of a slow-growing pie. In this unfortunate "zero-sum" society, more spending on health or education may mean higher taxes or a cut in Social Security benefits. No wonder that exploration of economic growth has moved to the forefront as a central topic of macroeconomics.

11-3 The Production Function and Economic Growth

The traditional theory of economic growth (often called the "neoclassical" theory) has filled many academic journals with highly mathematical articles. Yet the basic ideas are very simple. The theory divides output growth into two categories: (1) growth of **factor inputs,** such as labor and capital, and (2) growth in output relative to growth in factor inputs. Thus the theory converts the question of how to achieve faster output growth into two subquestions: how to achieve faster growth in factor inputs, and how to achieve faster growth in output relative to inputs.

The economic elements that directly produce real GDP are **factor inputs.**

Throughout most of this book we have examined the causes and consequences of changes in the ratio of actual real GDP to natural real GDP, which we have called the output ratio (Y/Y^N). But now we are interested in changes in economic conditions over long periods during which the output ratio may be expected to be roughly constant. Thus our theory of economic growth refers to the growth of natural real GDP.

The Production Function

How much real GDP (Y) can be produced at any given time? This depends on the total available quantity of the two main factor inputs, capital (K) and labor (N), and also the behavior of output per average available factor input, which the neoclassical theory calls A (for the "autonomous" growth factor).[5]

The **production function** is a graphical or algebraic relationship that shows how much output can be produced by a given quantity of factor inputs.

The **production function** states the relationship between Y, A, K, and N:

$$Y = AF(K, N) \tag{11.1}$$

In words, real GDP (Y) equals an autonomous growth factor (A), expressed as an index, multiplied by a function of an index of capital input (K) and labor input (N). The appendix to this chapter provides background information on the general functional form used in equation (11.1) and a popular numerical example often used to illustrate the workings of the production function.

---

[5] The use of the symbol A in this context and the decomposition of real GDP growth into growth in labor, capital, and the "residual" A date back to the seminal paper by Robert M. Solow, "Technical Change and the Aggregate Production Function," *Review of Economics and Statistics,* vol. 39 (August 1957), pp. 312–20. The symbol A stands for autonomous growth factor and should not be confused with A_p, the symbol for autonomous planned spending in Chapters 3–4.

Output per person and the capital-labor ratio.   We need to isolate those factors that determine the increase in per person real GDP, which can be written as follows when the production function is divided through by the amount of labor input (N).[6]

$$\frac{Y}{N} = Af\left(\frac{K}{N}\right) \tag{11.2}$$

This important relationship states that there are just two sources of growth in the standard of living, or real GDP per person (Y/N). These are the autonomous growth factor (A), and the ratio of capital to labor input (K/N), or "capital per person." (In this chapter we simplify by treating "persons" and "employment" as synonyms, ignoring changes in the ratio of employment to the population.)

Equation (11.2) is the per person version of the production function. It is illustrated in Figure 11-1. This production function is drawn by assuming that the autonomous growth factor is fixed at A_0. Each successive addition to the per person stock of capital (K/N) yields less and less of an increase in per person output (Y/N). In the diagram, point B represents one possible level of production, with capital input per person $(K/N)_0$ producing output per person $(Y/N)_0$.

SELF-TEST

1. Why is the production function a curved line instead of a straight line?

2. What happens to the ratio of output to capital (Y/K) as more capital per person is accumulated?

3. What happens to Y/K if the level of capital per person declines?

The production function in Figure 11-1 is just a start toward an adequate theory of economic growth. So far our analysis tells us simply that the main sources of growth in the standard of living are an autonomous factor (A) and growth in capital per person (K/N). But this does not explain why these two sources of growth differ among countries or among historical eras. We do not yet know why the autonomous growth factor in Figure 11-1 is A_0 rather than some other amount, nor do we know what determines the level of K/N.

Our study of what determines the autonomous growth factor is deferred until later. Here, we focus on the determinants of growth of capital per person (K/N). We begin by reviewing the basic relationships between investment, the growth in capital, and saving.

---

[6] How can equation (11.2) be derived from equation (11.1)? There are two intermediate steps. First, we multiply and divide K by N in equation (11.1):

$$Y = AF(NK/N, N) \tag{11.1'}$$

If the function F displays constant returns to scale (see appendix to this chapter), then there is a unit elasticity of Y with respect to a given percentage increase in both N and K. This fact allows us to factor out the N term and rewrite equation (11.1') as follows:

$$Y = ANf(K/N, 1) \tag{11.1''}$$

Notice here that we have given a new name (f) to the function. Equation (11.2) in the text is obtained by dividing through both sides of (11.1'') by N.

Figure 11-1 A Production Function Relating Per Person Output to Per Person Capital Input

The production function shows how much output per person can be produced by different amounts of capital per person. One possible position for the economy is point B, but other positions are possible as well. We cannot tell from this diagram how large the economy's per person capital stock will be. The slope of the production function is the marginal product of capital ($\Delta Y/\Delta K$), showing the extra amount produced by raising capital, when the amount of labor is held constant.

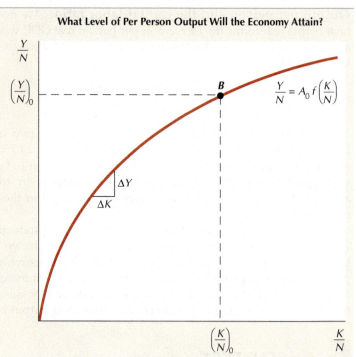

What Level of Per Person Output Will the Economy Attain?

Saving and Investment in the Steady State

How is K/N related to total national saving? This relationship is important, since it represents the link between the government's fiscal policy, private saving decisions, and the long-run growth of output per person.

We will first study an economy that has no technical change, implying that the autonomous growth factor (A in equation 11.2) is constant, so that the economy stands still at a point like B in Figure 11-1. The economy is at a fixed vertical position at point B when Y and K grow at the same rate, implying that the ratio Y/K is fixed. This situation is called a **steady state.** When we add the additional assumption that there is no technical change, then the growth rates of Y and K are also equal to the growth rate of labor input (N), implying that the ratio K/N is fixed.

> A **steady state** is a situation in which output and capital input grow at the same rate, implying a fixed ratio of output to capital input.

As in previous chapters, we use lowercase letters to designate growth rates, including the growth rate of output ($y = \Delta Y/Y$), the growth rate of capital ($k = \Delta K/K$), and the growth rate of labor input ($n = \Delta N/N$). Thus the condition for a steady state with no technical change in which capital per person (K/N) is constant, can be written as

$$k = n \qquad (11.3)$$

In commonsense terms, equation (11.3) states the condition necessary for the economy to stand still at a point like B in Figure 11-1, since equal growth rates of k and n imply that the ratio K/N is fixed. The growth rate of capital can also be written as the change in capital (ΔK) divided by capital itself (K):

$$\frac{\Delta K}{K} = k = n \qquad (11.4)$$

Now we link the growth rate of capital to the two types of investment (I), net investment that causes the capital stock to increase (ΔK), replacement investment that replaces old capital that becomes worn out or obsolete (dK) where d is the fraction of the capital stock (say 0.10) that is replaced each year due to wear and tear and obsolescence.

$$I = \Delta K + dK = \left(\frac{\Delta K}{K} + d \right)K = (n + d)K \qquad (11.5)$$

Here we obtain the third term by dividing and multiplying the second term by K, and then we obtain the fourth term using equation (11.4) to replace $\Delta K/K$ by n.

Now we are ready to relate investment to total national saving, and here we will use the symbol S to represent national saving (in contrast to Chapters 3–7 where the symbol S represented private saving). If we assume that net exports are zero, total *national* saving (S) equals private investment (I).[7]

$$S = I \qquad (11.6)$$

When we define a lowercase s as the ratio of saving to GDP ($s = S/Y$), then we can replace the left side of equation (11.6) by sY and replace investment on the right side by equation (11.5), yielding

$$sY = (n + d)K \qquad (11.7)$$

Our last step is to divide both sides of equation (11.7) by the amount of labor (N), and we now have our central relationship that links the vertical axis (Y/N) of Figure 11-1 to the horizontal axis (K/N).

$$\frac{sY}{N} = (n + d)\frac{K}{N} \qquad (11.8)$$

In words, equation (11.8) states that total national saving per person equals capital per person times the growth rate of capital plus the fraction of capital that must occur as replacement investment.

 SELF-TEST

There are five components of equation (11.8): s, Y/N, K/N, n, and d.

1. Which of these components changes its value as we move to the left or right along the production function in Figure 11-1?

2. For those components that do not change, suggest at least one factor that determines the value of that component.

11-4   Solow's Theory of Economic Growth

Can an increase in the ratio of national saving to output (s) create a permanent increase in the growth rate of output? The answer is no. This was the most surprising result of the "neoclassical" theory of economic growth originally

---

[7] We can repeat here a version of the magic equation, equation (2.6) on p. 35, which shows the relation of national saving ($S + T - G$) to private investment (I) and net exports (NX):

$$S + (T - G) = I + NX$$

When S is redefined to include both private saving and government saving, we have:

$$S = I + NX$$

This is the same as equation (11.6) in the text, where NX is set equal to zero.

Robert M. Solow (1924–)

Solow, 1987 Nobel Prize winner, invented both the modern theory of economic growth and the standard method for empirically distinguishing the roles of capital and technological change in the growth process.

developed in the 1950s by MIT's Robert M. Solow,[8] a theory for which he was awarded the Nobel Prize in 1987. We have already developed the major building blocks of Solow's theory. These are the per person production function of equation (11.2) and Figure 11-1, and the relationship between saving and steady-state investment in equation (11.8).

Solow's Insight

The algebra of equation (11.8) had been worked out in the 1940s by Sir Roy Harrod, an English economist, and Evsey Domar, who later taught at MIT. In their Harrod-Domar model of economic growth, all of the elements of equation (11.8) are constant. But then, why does the left side of equation (11.8) equal the right side? This equality seems an unlikely coincidence, since the elements of equation (11.8) depend on totally unrelated factors. The ratio of national saving to output (s) on the left-hand side of the equation is determined by the saving decisions of households, business firms, and the government. And the growth rate of labor input (n) and depreciation rate (d) on the right-hand side of equation (11.8) are determined by totally different considerations—birth rates, death rates, immigration, and the rate at which old capital wears out or becomes obsolete.

What Solow did was to marry the per person production function of equation (11.2) to the saving-investment relation in equation (11.8). Once again, on the left-hand side of equation (11.8), we have total national saving per person, which is the national saving rate (s) times output per person (Y/N), and this, in turn, is given by the per person production function of equation (11.2). On the right-hand side of equation (11.8), we have the amount of steady-state investment per person, that is, the amount of investment needed to equip each new population member with the same capital per person as the existing population, and to replace worn-out or obsolete capital.

The Solow Model in Pictures

The two sides of equation (11.8) can be plotted separately, as in Figure 11-2. In the left frame, the upper red line is a copy of the per person production function from Figure 11-1, plotting the output-labor ratio (Y/N) as a function of the capital-labor ratio (K/N). When we multiply this line by the fixed saving rate (s), we obtain the blue line, national saving per person (sY/N). The distance between the two lines indicates consumption per person. The right-hand frame plots steady-state investment per person, which rises steadily to the right, since a larger K/N raises the amount of investment needed to equip new population members and replace worn-out and obsolete capital.

Now in Figure 11-3 we put together the two parts of Figure 11-2, omitting for clarity the per person production function. The steady state occurs at point E_0, where the capital-labor ratio is $(K/N)_0$. Why is this a steady state? At any point to the left of E_0, say point C, saving and investment are higher than the investment required to maintain (K/N) at a fixed level. This extra investment makes (K/N) grow, moving the economy rightward from point C

---

[8] Robert M. Solow, "A Contribution to the Theory of Economic Growth," *Quarterly Journal of Economics*, vol. 70 (February 1956), pp. 65–94.

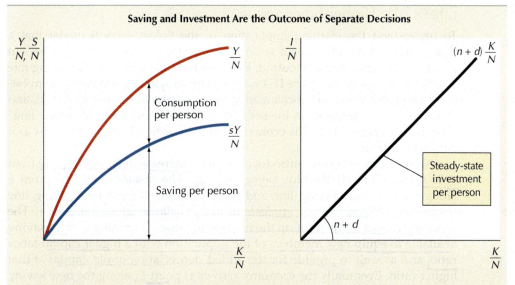

Figure 11-2 Output, Saving, and Steady-State Investment Per Person

The upper curved red line in the left frame copies the per person production function from Figure 11-1. Multiplying it by the saving rate (s) produces the lower curved blue line showing per person saving. Consumption per person is the distance between the two lines. The right frame shows steady-state investment per person, the amount needed to replace old capital and equip new workers for each capital-labor ratio (K/N).

to the steady-state equilibrium E_0. Similarly, starting at point D, saving and investment are below the required amount, meaning that not enough is being invested to equip new members of the population and replace worn-out and obsolete capital. Hence starting from point D, the economy moves leftward back down the blue line to the steady-state equilibrium at point E_0.

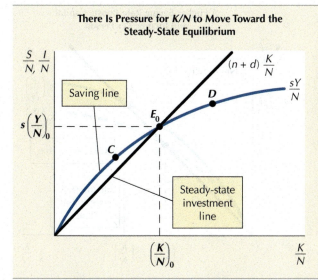

Figure 11-3 Equilibrium of Saving and Investment in the Solow Growth Model

This figure superimposes the two frames of Figure 11-2. The saving line crosses the steady-state investment line at point E_0. At any point to the left, like C, saving and actual investment exceed steady-state investment (the amount needed to keep K/N constant), and accordingly K/N grows until the economy reaches point E_0. At any point to the right, like D, saving and actual investment are less than steady-state investment and K/N shrinks back to E_0. Only at E_0 is per person saving just the right amount to equip new members of the population with $(K/N)_0$ and replace worn-out and obsolete capital.

Effects of a Higher Saving Rate

To understand the startling implication of the Solow growth model that a change in the ratio of national saving to output does not create a permanent change in the growth rate of output, let us see how an increase in the saving rate affects the economy. In Figure 11-4 we begin by copying the steady-state investment line (which remains unchanged in the examples of Figures 11-2, 11-3, and 11-4, but could change as in the self-test on p. 365) and the "old saving line" directly from Figure 11-3. The economy's initial position is at point E_0, just as it was in that figure.

Now in Figure 11-4 we introduce a sudden increase in the saving rate from s_0 to s_1, which shifts the blue saving line up. The distance between point F along the new blue saving line and point E_0 along the old blue saving line represents *additional saving available to fuel growth in capital per person.* The economy moves to the right up the new saving line, since there is extra saving available to equip new members of the population with a higher capital-labor ratio, and as well to provide for the added depreciation of old capital at that higher ratio. Eventually the economy arrives at point E_1 along the new saving line. But once at E_1, the capital-labor ratio is fixed at the new higher ratio, per person saving and output are fixed, and the growth in output is once again equal to the growth rate of labor input (at E_1 as at E_0, $y = k = n$).

Thus the saving rate matters, but not as people had believed prior to the development of Solow's model. An increase in the saving rate raises the standard of living, since the higher capital-labor ratio at E_1 produces a higher output-labor ratio. To achieve this higher standard of living, the growth rate of output is *temporarily* raised above the growth rate of N. But the higher saving rate does not create a permanently higher growth rate of output, which depends only on population growth. In the steady state Y/N is fixed, so that Y and N must grow at the same rate. Intuitively, the extra saving finances only a higher *level* of the capital stock per person (K/N), not continuing *growth* in the capital stock per person. The extra saving is "eaten up" by the extra replacement investment implied by the higher capital stock, and the extra net investment required to equip each worker with the higher level of capital stock per person.

Figure 11-4 The Effect of a Higher Saving Rate on Capital and Income Per Person

The lower "old saving line" is copied from Figure 11-3. A higher saving rate implies the higher "new saving line." The economy's position immediately jumps from E_0 to F. Now saving and actual investment are above steady-state investment, and so K/N grows until the economy reaches point E_1.

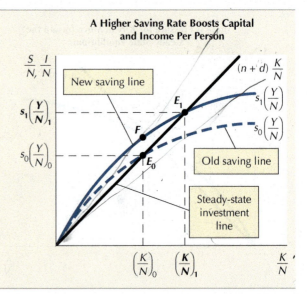

A Higher Saving Rate Boosts Capital and Income Per Person

SELF-TEST

Explain the effect of a reduction in the rate of population growth (n) on the following:

1. The growth rate of output.
2. The capital-output (K/Y) ratio.
3. The capital-labor (K/N) ratio.

One aspect of this theory may seem puzzling. We learned in Chapter 3 that an increase in the saving rate (s) depresses the economy by reducing consumption spending. How can we be so sure here that an increase in the saving rate will stimulate the growth of per person capital? The answer is that *the Solow model is intended for long-run analysis* (decades, not months or years) *and assumes continuous full employment and flexible prices*. Thus, when the saving rate rises in this model, consumption and the price level both decline. The interest rate falls by enough to stimulate sufficient investment to guarantee that saving and investment will remain equal along the economy's path between E_0 and E_1.

Clearly, in addition to responding to a change in the saving rate (s), the economy must also adjust to the other parameters in equation (11.8), namely the rate of population growth (n) and the depreciation rate (d). An increase in either the rate of population growth or the depreciation rate will make the black line rotate up and to the left around the origin of the diagram, moving the economy's equilibrium down and to the left. Faster population growth reduces the economy's standard of living (Y/N) and its capital-labor ratio (K/N). In the new steady state, Y/N and K/N are lower and remain constant, but the growth rates of y and k are more rapid, reflecting the new higher population growth rate. A higher depreciation rate causes the same decline in Y/N and K/N without any change in the growth rates y and k, which remain equal to unchanged population growth.

11-5   Technology in Theory and Practice

At first glance, the Solow growth model seems to contain a major flaw. As presented thus far, the model implies that the permanent growth rate of output should be the same as the growth rate of the population, and that the standard of living (Y/N) should be fixed. How, then, does the theory explain the sharp increase in the standard of living shown in the box on pp. 360–61 that has occurred over the past century in each of the major industrialized nations?

Two Types of Technological Change

Solow used two methods to make the model consistent with history. Both methods introduce an added element into the story: growth in technology in all its forms, including better schooling, improved organization, better health care, and all the fruits of innovation and research. The two methods for introducing technological change into the Solow growth model are to assume (1) that technology makes each worker more efficient, and (2) that technology shifts the production function relating per person output to per person capital.

Labor-augmenting technological change. This approach leaves our previous discussion of the Solow growth model, including the diagrams, completely intact. We simply need to adopt a broad definition of growth in "labor input." Instead of just counting the number of bodies at work, we count effective labor input, taking into account improved education and the storehouse of technology that makes today's workers more efficient than workers a century ago. We now interpret N as effective labor input, and n as the growth rate of effective labor input. In the steady state, output can grow at 3 percent ($y = 3$) if effective labor input grows at 3 percent ($n = 3$), leaving the ratio of output to effective labor input (Y/N) fixed. Now K/N remains fixed if the capital stock grows at 3 percent. Effective labor input growth of 3 percent exceeds population growth of, say, 1 percent, allowing the standard of living (Y per person) to grow at 2 percent.[9]

Neutral technological change. One problem with the first approach is that it assumes that technology only makes workers more efficient, with no impact on capital input. A more realistic assumption is that technology makes *both* labor and capital input more efficient. This "neutral" type of technological change simply means that the autonomous growth factor (A) in equations (11.1) and (11.2) grows over time. Here we copy equation (11.2) and renumber it for convenience:

$$\frac{Y}{N} = Af\left(\frac{K}{N}\right) \tag{11.9}$$

If education, innovations, and research raise the value of A every year, then per person GDP can increase steadily. The growth rate of per person GDP ($y - n$) is

General Form	Numerical Example	
$y - n = a + b(k - n)$	$y - n = a + 0.25(k - n)$	(11.10)

Here a is the growth rate of the autonomous growth factor, and b is the elasticity of output with respect to capital input, assumed to be 0.25 in the numerical example. An economy might, for instance, have values of $a = 1.5$ and $k - n = 2$, which would be consistent with a steady state in which

$$y - n = a + b(k - n) = 1.5 + 0.25(2) = 2.0$$

In this example, there is a steady state, because per person output and per person capital are growing at the same rate, allowing Y/K to remain fixed. After introducing neutral technological change into the diagrams of the Solow growth model, the production function shifts upward steadily, thus shifting the saving line up and to the right along a fixed steady-state investment line. Y/N and K/N rise in the steady state, but at the same rate.

---

[9] Labor-augmenting technical change can be introduced into our original production function from equation (11.1) by defining effective labor input as a technological factor (A) times the population:

$$Y = F(K, AN)$$

When A enters in this form, it is sometimes called "Harrod-neutral" technical change.

SELF-TEST

Calculate the percentage growth rate of real GDP per person ($y - n$) from the numerical example of equation (11.10), assuming that b always equals 0.25, for the following combinations of the rates a, k, and n:

a	k	n	$y - n$
0	0	4	———
0	4	4	———
4	0	0	———
4	4	4	———

The "Solow Residual"

Soon after Solow developed his theory of growth, he applied the theory to the measurement of the autonomous growth factor (a) in equation (11.10). His idea was to turn equation (11.9) around so that a could be calculated from the other components:

$$a = (y - n) - b(k - n) \qquad (11.11)$$

Since data were available on the growth rates of output (y) and of both capital and labor input (k and n), the only trick in determining the value of a was to identify the elasticity b. Here Solow's idea was to apply the theory of profit maximization in a competitive firm. Solow pointed out that such firms would also set the return on capital equal to the marginal product of capital, which implies that the elasticity b can be measured by the share of capital income in total GDP.[10]

Solow's finding was controversial. Fully seven-eighths of the growth in output per hour of work ($y - n$) over the period he studied (1909–57) was attributed to "technical change in the broadest sense," including education, research, innovations, and other improvements, while only the remaining one-eighth was attributed to growth in the capital stock per hour of work ($k - n$). But this is not a very satisfactory outcome. Knowing that some mysterious a factor was important in the growth process does not tell us, for instance, what caused a to grow more slowly during 1973–95 or more rapidly after 1995.

Some skeptics believe that a should not be given a name like "technological change," which implies we know precisely what determines a. They suggest that we call a instead the **residual** or, more frankly, "the measure of our ignorance." Government agencies like the U.S. Bureau of Labor Statistics, which now routinely calculate a, describe a as the growth in **multifactor productivity,** or total factor productivity. In recent years macroeconomists have come to describe a as **Solow's residual.**

The simplified version of Solow's growth model summarized in the previous section (Figures 11-2, 11-3, and 11-4) illustrated one key implication of his model, that a change in the saving rate would cause only a temporary, rather than a permanent, increase in the growth rate of output per unit of labor input. That simplified version could not explain steady growth of output—a defect that we have remedied in this section by introducing technological change.

The **residual** is a label sometimes applied to multifactor productivity.

The **multifactor productivity,** or total factor productivity, is the growth rate of output per hour of work, minus the contribution to output of the growth in the quantity of other factors of production per hour of work, notably capital but sometimes including energy, raw materials, or other factors of production.

Solow's residual is the growth in multifactor productivity. It is the same as residual.

---

[10] Let r be the rate of return to capital. Then competitive firms will set r equal to the marginal product of capital (MPK). The share of capital in GDP is rK/Y, which competitive firms will set equal to (MPK)(K/Y), which is equal to the elasticity of output with respect to capital, (dY/dK)(K/Y) = (dY/Y)(dK/K).

And we have seen that Solow's own empirical research identified technological change (broadly defined) as a much more important source of economic growth than increases in capital input per unit of labor input. However, the Solow growth model has received substantial criticism. In the next section we identify several puzzles that his model cannot explain, and in the following section, we learn about recent developments in growth theory.

11-6   Puzzles That Solow's Theory Cannot Explain

In recent years economists have become increasingly dissatisfied with Solow's neoclassical theory of economic growth, for two primary reasons. First, the theory makes economic growth depend primarily on "Solow's residual," which remains unexplained. Thus we are left with very little understanding of why the world's standard of living stagnated until the industrial revolution that occurred around the year 1800, why it grew rapidly from then until the early 1970s, and why in some countries like the United States the standard of living grew slowly in the 1970s and 1980s but then accelerated after 1995. Second, we are left with little understanding of differences among nations—why some are rich and some remain poor, and why some grow rapidly while others stagnate.

The critics of neoclassical growth theory go beyond claiming that the theory provides an inadequate explanation of growth. They point to widely observed phenomena in the world that *conflict* with the predictions of the theory. In this section we review these conflicts.

Conflict 1: Income Per Capita Varies Too Much Across Countries

Real income per capita in a rich country like the United States is more than ten times as high as in a poor country like India or Bangladesh. Yet this fact conflicts with the neoclassical theory. Why? The theory states that there are only two reasons for differences in per capita income. One reason could be a difference in saving rates, since, as shown in Figure 11-4, an increase in the saving rate raises income per capita (Y/N). Another could be a difference in the slope of the steady-state investment line ($n + d$). However, even very large differences in the saving rate or rate of population growth cause only small variations in per capita income, not the large variations observed in the world. To take one example, quadrupling the saving rate and reducing the rate of population growth by two-thirds would boost per capita income only from 1.0 to 1.7, whereas in the real world we observe countries differing in per capita income by magnitudes on the order of 1.0 to 10.0.[11]

---

[11] To see this, let us combine equation (11.8) with the Cobb-Douglas production function (explained in the appendix to this chapter):

$$s\left(\frac{Y}{N}\right) = (n + d)\left(\frac{K}{N}\right) \tag{i}$$

$$\left(\frac{Y}{N}\right) = \left(\frac{K}{N}\right)^{b} \tag{ii}$$

By solving equation (ii) for (K/N), substituting into equation (i), and simplifying, we obtain:

$$\left(\frac{Y}{N}\right) = \left(\frac{s}{n + d}\right)^{\frac{b}{1-b}} \tag{iii}$$

Using as examples $s = 0.1$, $n = 0.03$, $d = 0.07$, and $b/(1 - b) = 1/3$, we can calculate that $Y/N = 1^{1/3} = 1$. Quadrupling the saving rate to 0.4 would raise Y/N from 1 to $4^{1/3} = 1.59$. Reducing the rate of population growth from 0.03 to 0.01 (assuming the saving rate remains at 0.4) would raise Y/N further from 1.59 to $(0.4/0.08)^{1/3} = 1.7$.

A flaw in the neoclassical theory is to assume that all countries have the same production function (equation (11.9)). Poor countries are assumed to operate at the same level of technology and knowledge as rich countries. To see that the production function is at fault, consider a specific version of equation (11.9) called the Cobb-Douglas production function (see the appendix to this chapter).

General Form $\qquad$ Numerical Example

$$Y/N = (K/N)^b \qquad Y/N = (K/N)^{0.25} \qquad (11.12)$$

Here we set the autonomous growth factor (A) equal to unity to simplify the exposition.

To see what difference in K/N would be needed to explain a ten-fold difference in per capita income, we can solve for K/N:

General Form $\qquad$ Numerical Example

$$K/N = (Y/N)^{1/b} \qquad K/N = (Y/N)^{1/0.25} \qquad (11.13)$$

Let us take the value of Y/N for the poor nation to be 1 and the value of Y/N for the rich nation to be 10. Substituting 10 for the rich nation's Y/N in the numerical example, we see that the rich nation's K/N must be equal to $(Y/N)^{1/0.25}$ or 10^4, which is 10,000. Yet there is no evidence of such huge differences among nations in K/N. In fact, a regular feature of real-world economies is a roughly constant ratio of K/N, not ratios of K/N that are hugely greater in rich countries than poor countries (by 10,000/10 or 1,000 times greater in the example).

Conflict 2: Poor Countries Do Not Have a Higher Rate of Return on Capital

The neoclassical theory describes the difference in per capita income between poor countries and rich countries simply as a result of differing levels of per capita capital, which in turn result from differences in the three parameters that appear in equation (11.8)—the saving rate (s), population growth rate (n), and depreciation rate (d). As shown in Figure 11-5 a poor country is at a position like point P, with a low capital-labor ratio $(K/N)_P$, while a rich country is at a position like point R, with a high capital-labor ratio $(K/N)_R$.

But this leads to an unrealistic implication. The slope of the per person production function in Figure 11-5 is the marginal product of capital ($\Delta Y/\Delta K$), and this is much higher on the left side of the diagram for the poor country than on the right side of the diagram for the rich country. A simple numerical example shows that the marginal product of capital should be as much as 4,000 times higher in a poor country as in a rich country when per capita income is ten times as high.[12] The implied high marginal product of capital in the poor country implies that the rate of return on capital in poor countries should be much higher than in rich countries, *and that there should be massive flows of capital from rich countries to poor countries to earn this higher rate of return.* Yet we do not observe high rates of return on capital, or massive capital inflows, in many of the poorest

---

[12] With the Cobb-Douglas production function, the marginal product of capital (MPK) is

General Form $\qquad$ Numerical Example

$$MPK = b(K/N)^{b-1} \qquad MPK = 0.25(K/N)^{-0.75}$$
$$= b(Y/N)^{(b-1)/b} \qquad MPK = 0.25(Y/N)^{-3.0}$$

Thus, if Y/N is ten times greater in a rich country, the marginal product of capital in the numerical example would be 0.25 times 10^{-3} or 1/4,000 times smaller.

Figure 11-5 A Production Function Relating Per Person Output to Per Person Capital Input

The per person production function is the same as in Figures 11-1 and 11-2. The poor country has a capital-labor ratio of $(K/N)_P$ and produces at point P. The rich country has a capital-labor ratio of $(K/N)_R$ and produces at point R. The marginal product of capital is given by the slope of the production function, $\Delta Y/\Delta K$. Because of the curvature of the per person production function, this slope is clearly larger for the poor country than for the rich country. The text discusses reasons why this diagram makes the erroneous prediction that the marginal return to capital is higher in poor countries than in rich countries.

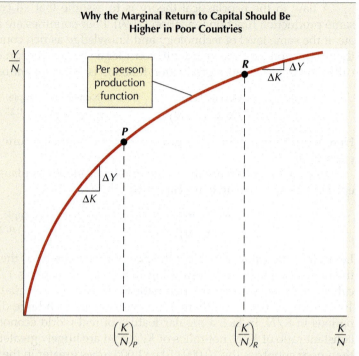

Why the Marginal Return to Capital Should Be Higher in Poor Countries

countries of the world. Some less-developed countries enjoy substantial inflows, but others do not.

How can we explain why the rate of return on capital in very poor countries is not substantially higher than in rich countries? The poor countries may not be operating on the same production function as the rich countries, unlike the single production function drawn in Figure 11-5.

Conflict 3: Convergence Has Not Been Uniform

The neoclassical model predicts that poor nations should "converge" to the income levels of the rich. That is, nations that are initially poor should have faster growth rates than nations that are initially rich. This occurs for three reasons. First, nations that are below their steady-state growth paths (for instance, at point F in Figure 11-4) will grow faster until they reach the steady state (at point E_1 in Figure 11-4). Second, as noted, the neoclassical model predicts that the rate of return is much higher in poor countries, causing capital to flow from rich to poor countries and thus boosting the capital stocks of poor countries. Third, whatever the barriers that prevent poor countries from fully utilizing the production technology, the passage of time should allow poor countries to learn how to use the productive techniques of the rich countries.

Economists have devoted much attention in recent years to the issue of convergence, and the subject is controversial.[13] There has been convergence among

---

[13] A pioneering study of cross-country differences in growth rates is Robert J. Barro, "Economic Growth in a Cross Section of Countries," *Quarterly Journal of Economics*, vol. 106 (May 1991), pp. 407–33. Another influential study is N. Gregory Mankiw, David Romer, and David N. Weil, "A Contribution to the Empirics of Economic Growth," *Quarterly Journal of Economics*, vol. 107 (May 1992), pp. 407–37. For an illuminating survey of this literature, see Jonathan Temple, "The New Growth Evidence," *Journal of Economic Literature*, vol. 37 (March 1999), pp. 112–56. A less technical introduction is contained in Robert J. Barro, *Determinants of Economic Growth: A Cross-Country Empirical Study* (Cambridge, Mass.: MIT Press, 1997), Chapter 1.

the major industrialized countries; for example, Japan has caught up substantially to the per capita income levels of Europe and the United States, as shown in the box on pp. 360–61. There has also been convergence among the income levels of states within the United States and among regions within Western Europe. However, in the world at large, convergence has not been uniform. Many nations of Africa and some of the poorer nations of Asia have fallen further behind the advanced countries over the past fifty years, and the relative income levels of major Latin American nations have fallen relative to Western Europe and the United States. We need to go beyond neoclassical growth theory to understand the persistent differences between rich and poor nations. We return to the facts about convergence in the next chapter (see pp. 392–97).

11-7 Human Capital, Immigration, and the Solow Puzzles

If the neoclassical model cannot explain differences in per capita income by observed differences in capital per person, then what explanation remains? One of the most promising is to recognize that most of the income that labor receives in the rich countries is not a reward to "pure" labor (that is, just the fact that someone is alive) but rather to the education that people have acquired. Education makes a tremendous difference in the incomes that people receive. Management consultants with an MBA degree are typically paid double the salary earned by those with no more than an undergraduate degree, who in turn receive double or more the typical earnings of high-school graduates, who in turn earn substantially more than high-school drop-outs.

What Is Human Capital?

Economists use the term **human capital** to refer to the value over one's lifetime of the extra earnings made possible by education. A 20-year-old planning to work for 45 years might be able to make $6 million in the future with an MBA degree, but someone of that age might be limited to a lifetime income of only $600,000 if he or she drops out of school with only an elementary-school education, thus limiting the available job options to menial jobs like digging ditches and washing dishes. The difference between $6 million and $600,000, or $5.4 million, is said to be the "human capital" that the MBA degree-holder has accumulated. Another person who stops his or her education with an undergraduate degree might be expected to make $3 million in the future and to acquire $2.4 million in human capital (the difference versus the alternative of a mere elementary-school education). For society as a whole, the value of human capital is the sum of the human capital of each inhabitant.

> **Human capital** is the value, for a person or for society as a whole, of the extra future earnings made possible by education.

The name "human capital" was given to the value of education in order to reflect the parallels between investing in education and investing in physical capital, that is, structures and equipment like computers and forklifts. Investment in physical capital requires that money be spent in order to earn a future return, in the form of the extra profits that can be made after the structure is built or the equipment is purchased. Similarly, investment in human capital requires an expenditure of money on education and the sacrifice of income that could otherwise be earned by working instead of going to school. This expenditure is made in order to earn a higher income in the future, and the rate of return on the cost of education can be stated on a percentage basis in just the same way as the rate of return on the cost for a firm of buying a new computer.

How Does Human Capital Raise Total Output?

An economy like the United States that contains many educated people can produce more output and a higher standard of living than an economy like many in Africa where most inhabitants have had little education. Thus human capital (H) becomes a factor of production, just like physical capital (K), and the production function, instead of using equation (11.1), can be written as:

$$Y = A\, F(K, H, N) \tag{11.14}$$

In words, this states that real GDP (Y) equals an autonomous growth factor (A), expressed as an index, multiplied by a function of an index of physical capital (K), human capital (H), and labor (N). Now labor is interpreted as the productive capability of the population *if* everyone had dropped out of school after elementary school (sometimes called "brute force" labor, capable only of digging ditches), while all the extra earnings of the population above that educational level are included in human capital input (H).

Human Capital and the Solow Puzzles

The inclusion of human capital goes a long way toward repairing the inability of the Solow neoclassical model to explain differences between the rich and poor countries. Let us write the per person production function in the Cobb-Douglas form of equation (11.12), making only a single change, namely, to add human capital per person (H/N) as an extra determinant of output per person (Y/N):

General Form	Numerical Example
$Y/N = (K/N)^b (H/N)^c$	$Y/N = (K/N)^{0.25}(H/N)^{0.65}$

$\qquad\qquad\qquad\qquad\qquad\qquad\qquad\qquad\qquad\qquad\qquad$ (11.15)

This states that output per person equals physical capital per person (K/N) raised to the power b, which is 0.25 as before, and human capital raised to the power c, which is assumed to be 0.65. Instead of labor making a contribution to output of $(1 - b)$ or 0.75, the contribution of uneducated labor (N) is now $1 - b - c$, or only 0.10 (which equals 1.0 minus 0.25 minus 0.65).

As we saw in the preceding discussion of equations (11.12) and (11.13), the basic reason that the Solow neoclassical model cannot explain observed differences between rich and poor nations is that the exponent on capital ($b = 0.25$) is so small. If capital is so unimportant, then why should poor countries lag so far behind rich countries? But now we have introduced human capital as an additional difference between rich and poor countries, and the sum of the exponents on the two types of capital ($b + c$) is now 0.9, not 0.25. If we replace $1/0.25$ in equation (10.13) by $1/0.9$, we find that a rich nation having 10 times the per person income (Y/N) as a poor nation needs to have only $10^{1/0.9}$ or about 12.6 times as much combined physical and human capital as the poor nation. This is much more plausible than the implication of equation (10.13) in the model without human capital that the rich nation needed to have 10,000 times as much physical capital as the poor nation.[14] In the same way, if the exponent on total capital is 0.9 rather than 0.25, it is no longer necessary for the

---

[14] This insight is one of the contributions of the article by Mankiw, Romer, and Weil cited in the previous footnote.

rate of return on investment in capital (both physical and human) to be much lower in rich countries than in poor countries (this was the second conflict discussed in this section).[15]

The Immigration Puzzle

Thus the addition of human capital to the Solow neoclassical growth theory goes a long way toward explaining the conflicts introduced in the previous section. Rich countries differ from poor countries not just because they have many more structures and lots more equipment, but because their inhabitants are much better educated than those in poor countries. Yet the human capital explanation runs into a problem when we consider the immigration of an unskilled person from a poor country to a rich country. To be specific, let us consider a poorly educated Guatemalan who crosses the Rio Grande and soon finds a job in the United States paying, say, $10 per hour in contrast to the $1 per hour that he earned in Guatemala. Yet the first day on the job, there has been no change in the former Guatemalan's human capital. What is it about the process of production in a rich country that allows a recent immigrant to have a much higher marginal product and earn a much higher wage than was previously possible in Guatemala?

Let us say that the Guatemalan's new job is with a landscaping service that mows the lawns of well-to-do Americans. The task of mowing the lawn (using physical capital consisting of a gas-powered lawn mower) takes virtually no education. What enables the Guatemalan to earn $10 per hour is that there are Americans who themselves are rich enough to be able to afford to pay to have their lawn mowed instead of mowing it themselves. Thus the immigration puzzle comes down to this: *every factor* that makes the United States a richer country than Guatemala contributes to the ability of the new immigrant to earn much more. As we will see in the next chapter, there are many factors not included in a production function like equation (11.14) that help to explain the immigration puzzle—differences between rich and poor countries include additional factors beyond physical and human capital, among them cultural attitudes toward work, climate and geography, how well the legal system protects property rights, the presence or absence of crime and corruption, and infrastructure in the form of highways, airports, and a well-functioning electricity supply and telephone system.

11-8   Endogenous Growth Theory: How Is Technological Change Produced?

Ever since the development of Solow's neoclassical growth model in the 1950s, economists have been uneasy about several of its implications. We have now reviewed several implications of the model that conflict with important facts about the real world. As we have seen, a primary problem is that technical change (*a*, the autonomous growth factor) is *exogenous*, dropping from the sky totally unexplained. Thus a nation desiring to boost its growth rate of output gains no insight into how to achieve a higher level and growth rate of *A*.

---

[15] Go back to footnote 12 on p. 373 and substitute $b = 0.9$ in place of $b = 0.25$. The bottom line of the numerical example becomes:

$$MPK = 0.9(Y/N)^{-0.1/0.9}$$

If Y/N in the rich country is 10 times higher, then the marginal product of capital in the rich country should be 0.9/1.29 or about 0.7 times that in the poor country, not 1/4,000 as in the example of footnote 12 based on $b = 0.25$.

Since the late 1980s there has been an explosion of activity in what is now called "endogenous growth theory," so named because it attempts to explain technical change as the outcome of market activity in response to economic incentives rather than just assuming that technical change drops exogenously from the sky. The chief inventors of endogenous growth theory are Paul Romer of Stanford University and his Ph.D. thesis adviser at the University of Chicago, Robert E. Lucas, Jr. (also the inventor of the new classical macroeconomics and pictured in Chapter 17). Much of the writing on endogenous growth theory is highly technical; here we summarize some of the main ideas at a nontechnical level.[16] As the early ideas of Romer and Lucas continue to be subjected to critical reviews and reconsidered, the theory is still evolving.

The Production of Ideas

Endogenous growth theory begins from the awkward fact that, as we have seen, the standard of living in many advanced countries is as much as ten times higher than that in many less-developed countries. But if technical change is freely available to all nations, then *all* of this huge superiority in standards of living must be attributable to a capital-labor ratio that is higher by a factor of 10,000. This would imply very little capital in less-developed countries and a huge rate of return to additional investment, since this would be guaranteed to bring these countries up toward the level of advanced nations. As a consequence, we should observe massive flows of capital from advanced countries to poor countries, but in fact we do not.

As we have seen, one solution to this puzzle is to introduce human capital as a key source of difference between rich and poor nations. But consideration of immigration leads to basic problems for the human capital approach, as it does for the concept of "effective labor" in the neoclassical model. Both of these models imply that immigrants to a rich country from a poor country with, say, 1/10 the output per person and 1/10 the human capital per person, upon arrival in the rich country should earn only 1/10 as much as native citizens. But many immigrants to the United States and other rich countries soon achieve the same high average standard of living as native residents.

Endogenous growth theorists thus have been led to focus on what are the characteristics of a rich society that not only make its native residents rich but also seem automatically to equip immigrants from poor countries with much higher incomes than they earned before. They have built models in which the key to growth is the development of ideas for new goods. To solve the incentive problem of how these ideas get produced, the models rely on monopoly power that is reinforced by patents and copyrights. International trade also plays an important role, since each country can concentrate on developing the ideas to produce a few new goods and then trade them with other countries, so that consumers can enjoy all of the new goods produced anywhere in the world. For instance, American households enjoying DVD movies are benefiting from early research that took place in Europe and the United States,

---

[16] Frequently cited academic papers include Paul M. Romer, "Increasing Returns and Long-Run Growth," *Journal of Political Economy*, vol. 94 (1986), pp. 1002–37; the same author's "Endogenous Technological Change," *Journal of Political Economy*, vol. 98 (1990), pp. S71–103; and Robert E. Lucas, Jr., "On the Mechanics of Economic Development," *Journal of Monetary Economics*, vol. 22 (1988), pp. 3–42. The summary in this section is partly based on Paul M. Romer, "Increasing Returns and New Developments in the Theory of Growth," in W. A. Barnett, et al., eds., *Equilibrium Theory and Applications* (Cambridge University Press, 1991), pp. 83–100.

together with product development in Japan and Korea that made the DVD player inexpensive to buy and relatively repair-free.

When the concept of ideas is applied broadly, it helps explain not only the introduction of new goods but also the development of better production techniques and higher quality in older goods like automobiles and household appliances. Rich countries use ideas and techniques that produce more and better goods per person. Furthermore, most of these ideas won't work without associated investment in physical capital and human capital. Even if a poor country like Bangladesh obtained piles of instruction manuals for making automobiles and personal computers, these manuals would be useless without educated people, factories, and equipment. This approach simultaneously explains why poor people clamor to migrate to rich countries, and also why poor nations are so eager for foreign investment by companies from rich countries, companies that can bring with them the required equipment and educated engineers and managers.

Empirical Studies and Policy Implications

As endogenous growth theory has developed, so has research on a wide variety of rich and poor countries, looking for correlations between growth rates and other variables. The conclusion is that faster growth is associated with a higher rate of investment by either the private or government sector, a lower share in GDP of government consumption spending, higher school enrollment rates, greater political stability, and lower fertility (that is, fewer children per female of childbearing age). And if the influence of all these factors is taken into account, a poor country tends to grow more rapidly than a rich country.

Unfortunately, all these factors are not the same in rich and poor countries. Poor countries have lower rates of investment, lower school enrollment rates, higher fertility rates, and less political stability. The implication of this research is that government policies can affect growth rates by taxing consumption, subsidizing investment and research, and shifting resources from government consumption to government investment.

Overall, endogenous growth theory has taken economists a long way from the original Solow model, with its pessimistic implications that a higher national saving rate alters economic growth only temporarily, and that technological change is exogenous, falling from the sky with no potential for policy effects.[17] However, endogenous growth theory is incomplete, because still omitted are numerous additional factors that contribute to growth and help to explain the growing gap between the rich and poor countries. We return to these additional factors, some of them noneconomic, in the next chapter.

11-9 Conclusion: Are There Secrets of Growth?

The theory of economic growth has come a long way since the original Solow growth model, which tended to minimize the role of capital accumulation and maximize the role of an unexplained rate of technological change. An important

---

[17] Readable overviews of endogenous growth theory are provided in a symposium in the Winter 1994 issue of the *Journal of Economic Perspectives*. See especially Paul Romer, "The Origins of Endogenous Growth," pp. 3–32, and Robert M. Solow, "Perspectives on Growth Theory," pp. 45–54. This complex literature has been summarized for lay economists such as college economics majors by David Warsh in his book *Knowledge and the Wealth of Nations: A Story of Economic Discovery* (New York: Norton, 2006). Chapters 1 and 2 provide a fascinating glimpse inside the economics profession.

development in the new growth theory has been to broaden the definition of capital, so that it includes research and development and human capital (that is, education). In the next chapter, we will broaden the concept of capital further to include government-financed infrastructure (for example, highways and airports), and more generally, the "capital" needed to protect liberty and property rights.

Despite these developments, however, much remains unexplained. Those studying the success of some fast-growing nations and the failure of other nations find it difficult to tie a record of success to particular economic theories. Columbia economist Joseph Stiglitz argues that it is necessary to go far beyond traditional economic theories and into political science to understand what happened in the successful countries of East Asia and elsewhere:

> No single policy ensured success, nor did the absence of any single ingredient ensure failure. There was a nexus of policies, varying from country to country, sharing the common themes that we have emphasized: governments intervened actively in the market, but used, complemented, regulated, and indeed created markets, rather than supplanted them. Governments created an environment in which markets could thrive. Governments promoted exports, education, and technology; encouraged cooperation between government and industry and between firms and their work-ers; and at the same time encouraged competition. The real miracle of East Asia may be political more than economic: Why did governments undertake these policies? Why did politicians or bureaucrats not subvert them for their own self interest?... The recognition of institutional and individual fallibility gave rise to a flexibility and responsiveness that, in the end, must lie at the root of sustained success.[18]

The verdict of Stiglitz in the preceding quote is humbling for economists, because it implies that the successful countries had a particular talent for "just doing the right thing," and the definition of the right thing varied across countries.

We take a more systematic look in the next chapter at the key sources of economic growth.

Summary

1. Divergences between the economic growth rates of individual nations, sustained over long periods of time, can create substantial differences in living standards. Although Britain had the highest level of real GDP per capita in 1870 among the major industrialized nations, by 1996 Britain was at the bottom as a consequence of its slow rate of economic growth in the twentieth century.

2. The production function explains real GDP as depending on the quantity of factor inputs (capital and labor) and on an autonomous growth factor that reflects the influence of research, innovation, and other factors. An increase in the growth rate of real GDP per person requires either an increase in the growth rate of capital per person or an increase in the growth rate of the autonomous growth factor.

3. National saving is the sum of government saving (which equals the government surplus or deficit) plus private saving. National saving equals private investment, which is equivalent to the change in the capital stock plus the investment expenditures required to replace capital goods that wear out or become obsolete.

4. In the absence of technological change, an equilibrium called the "steady state" occurs when output, capital, and labor input are all growing at the same rate. If per person saving exceeds steady-state investment per person, the capital-labor ratio will grow until the per person steady-state investment is high enough to halt the growth in the capital-labor ratio. At this point, the economy reaches a new steady state with a constant capital-labor ratio.

---

[18] Joseph E. Stiglitz, "Some Lessons from the East Asian Miracle," *World Bank Research Observer*, vol. 11, no. 2 (August 1996), pp. 151–77.

5. In the Solow model of economic growth, the economy's growth rate of output in the long run depends only on its rate of population growth or, more broadly, on the growth rate of "effective" labor input (which takes account of improvements in education, skills, and technology). An increase in the saving rate does not change the economy's steady-state growth rate of output.

6. One of the two types of technical change is called labor-augmenting technical change, which makes each worker more efficient. In this case, a steady state involves a constant ratio of output and capital to effective labor input. Technical change, better skills, and more education make effective labor input grow faster than the population growth rate, thus allowing both output and capital to grow more rapidly than the population.

7. The second type of technical change is called neutral technical change, which makes both labor and capital more efficient. In this case, neutral technical change allows both output and capital to grow faster than the population, and now the definition of the steady state changes so that both output and capital grow at the same rate, which is faster than the rate of population growth.

8. There are three facts that conflict with the predictions of the Solow growth theory. First, income per capita varies too much across countries. Second, poor countries do not have a higher rate of return on capital as the theory predicts. Third, poor countries have not uniformly converged to the income level of rich countries, as the theory predicts.

9. These facts that conflict with the Solow theory are partially eliminated when human capital, that is, the value of education, is introduced as an additional source of differences in output per capita between rich and poor countries. Yet human capital raises an additional question as to why immigrants to rich countries are able to earn so much more than in poor countries when their educational attainment is not altered by the act of immigration.

10. Endogenous growth theory emphasizes the interactions among the production of ideas, investment in physical capital, and investment in human capital (education) to explain why poor countries cannot instantly boost their standard of living up to the level of rich countries. It takes many years of investment in physical and human capital for the ideas developed in the rich countries to benefit the poor countries.

11. Solow's growth model states that an increase in the national saving rate cannot permanently boost the growth rate of output, but there are two reasons to believe that this theoretical result is misleading. First, the strong relationship between saving rates and growth rates in different countries over long periods of time suggests that saving and growth are related in a way not explained by the Solow growth model. Second, endogenous growth theory suggests several ways in which a higher rate of saving and investment might generate faster growth in ideas, human capital, and physical capital.

Concepts

economic growth	steady state	Solow's residual
factor inputs	residual	human capital
production function	multifactor productivity	

Questions

1. In terms of the great questions of economic growth discussed at the beginning of this chapter, why do the presented theories of economic growth concentrate on the growth of output per person as opposed to total output?

2. If the production function is characterized by constant returns to scale, what happens to real GDP (Y), capital per person (K/N), the ratio of output to capital (Y/K), and output per person (Y/N) when labor and capital inputs both double? What happens when labor and capital inputs double and the autonomous growth factor (A) also doubles?

3. What is the "steady state" in the Solow growth model? How is it reached from some other initial situation in which the conditions required for the steady state are not satisfied?

4. Explain what an increase in the depreciation rate, d, means. Using a graph like Figure 11-3, explain the effect of an increase in the depreciation rate on the steady-state capital-labor ratio and steady-state income per person. Again using a graph like Figure 11-3, explain how the savings rate must change in order for a rise in the depreciation rate to have no effect on the steady-state capital-labor ratio and steady-state income per person. Finally, discuss why your explanations make intuitive sense.

5. Assuming the autonomous growth factor (A) remains unchanged, explain why the gains in output per worker associated with an increase in the capital-labor ratio inevitably fall following increases in the level of investment.

6. What is the most important implication of the Solow growth model? Does it imply that an increase in the rate of private saving is useless as a means to increase the standard of living in the long run?

7. Explain why, in spite of the suggested steady-state outcome of Solow's model, the national saving rate is treated in this chapter as playing such an important role in determining the rate of economic growth.

8. Many people advocate policies to raise the U.S. national saving rate (s). According to the Solow growth model, should a low saving rate be a matter of national concern? What policies might be implemented to raise it?

9. Explain the difference between labor-augmenting technological change and neutral technological change. Explain into which category of technological change each of the following examples falls:
   (a) Development of a new microprocessor that allows for faster computers that enable architects to design buildings in less time.
   (b) A new operating system that enables programmers to use their existing computers to write and test programs in less time.

10. The record of economic growth in the leading industrialized countries over the past century hardly represents the steady state described and predicted by the Solow model. Explain what the "Solow residual" is and how it is used to account for the long-term improvement in output per person in these countries over the past century. Explain what problem the "Solow residual" presents for economic growth theory.

11. Explain the difference between productivity as defined on p. 2 in Chapter 1 and multifactor productivity as defined in this chapter. Explain why productivity as defined in Chapter 1 must increase if multifactor productivity rises and why productivity can increase without an increase in multifactor productivity.

12. Explain why the facts that (i) poor countries do not seem to have higher rates of return on capital, and (ii) the gaps between the per capita income of rich and poor countries have not narrowed significantly are puzzles for the Solow growth model.

13. What is endogenous growth theory? What weaknesses of the Solow growth model led to its development?

14. Distinguish between *human capital* and *physical capital*. Why are both important to a country's economic growth?

15. What is endogenous growth theory and what puzzles associated with the Solow growth model does it attempt to resolve?

16. What does endogenous growth theory, as well the empirical studies based on it that attempt to explain economic growth differences between countries, suggest concerning how government policies influence economic growth? What do these studies suggest about the ability of poor countries to catch up with living standards in rich countries?

Problems

myeconlab Visit www.MyEconLab.com to complete these or similar exercises.

*Indicates that the problem requires the Appendix to Chapter 11.

1. (a) Using the data presented in the International Perspective box (pp. 360–61), compute the per capita real GDP of Germany, Japan, Canada, France, the United Kingdom, and Italy relative to the United States in 1870 and 2010.
   (b) For the country whose per capita real GDP rose relative to the United States between 1870 and 2010, discuss when the increase occurred.
   (c) For each of the countries whose per capita real GDP fell relative to the United States between 1870 and 2010, discuss when the gap between standards of living, as measured by per capita real GDP, narrowed and when it widened.

2. You are given the following information concerning the relationship between the capital-labor ratio and output per person in eight situations:

Capital-labor ratio

A	B	C	D	E	F	G	H
0	10,000	20,000	22,000	23,512	25,000	30,000	30,260

Output per person

A	B	C	D	E	F	G	H
0	19,102	23,518	24,200	24,688	25,416	26,560	26,629

(a) Suppose that the savings rate, s, equals 0.1; the population growth rate, n, equals 0.01; and the depreciation rate, d, equals 0.1. Calculate the amounts of savings per person and steady-state investment per person at each of the capital-labor ratios given in the table above. Calculate the values of the steady-state capital-labor ratio and steady-state output per person.

(b) Suppose that the population growth rate, n, decreases to 0.005, but there are no changes in the savings and depreciation rates. Calculate the new amount of steady-state investment per person at each of the capital-labor ratios given in the table above. Calculate the new steady-state values of the capital-labor ratio and output per person.

(c) Suppose that the savings rate, s, increases to 0.125, but the population growth and depreciation rates are the same as in part a. Compute the new amount of savings per person at each of the capital-labor ratios given in the table above. Then explain the new steady-state values of the capital-labor ratio and output per person.

3. Assuming that the United States' output is characterized by a Cobb-Douglas production function with constant returns to scale and that the elasticity of output with respect to the capital input equals 0.25, consider the following five cases, where n equals the growth rate of labor, k equals the growth rate of capital, and a equals the growth rate of the autonomous growth factor.

Case I:	$n = 1\%$	$k = 3\%$	$a = 2.5\%$
Case II:	$n = 2\%$	$k = 3\%$	$a = 0.75\%$
Case III:	$n = 1\%$	$k = 4\%$	$a = 2.4\%$
Case IV:	$n = 3\%$	$k = 3\%$	$a = 0\%$
Case V:	$n = 0\%$	$k = 0\%$	$a = 3\%$

(a) In each case, what is the rate of growth of output?
(b) In each case, what is the rate of growth of per person output?
(c) Assuming that the autonomous growth factor is a "neutral" type of technological change, which case or cases are consistent with steady-state growth?

4. Using equation (11.10), derive a formula for the steady-state growth rate of income per person and the capital-labor ratio in terms of the autonomous growth factor, a, and elasticity of output with respect to the capital input, b. (*Hint*: let c equal the steady-state growth rate of income per person and the capital-labor ratio and solve equation (11.11) for c in terms of a and b.) Use this formula to discuss how the steady-state growth rate of income per person and the capital-labor ratio change due to an increase in (i), the autonomous growth factor, and (ii), the elasticity of output with respect to the capital input.

5. Suppose that the elasticity of output with respect to the capital input, b, equals 0.3.
   (a) If the country's income has been growing at 3.1 percent per year over the past 25 years, while the labor input has been growing at 1.5 percent per year and the capital input has been growing at 2.5 percent per year, what part of the total growth is accounted for by autonomous growth factor?
   (b) Suppose that over the next 25 years, the retirement of the baby boomers causes the growth rate of labor to fall to 1.0 percent per year. Given your answer to part a for the autonomous growth factor and given no change in the growth rate of capital, compute the new steady-state growth rate of income. What does this new steady-state growth of income imply concerning the ability of the country to pay the higher medical care costs associated with the retirement of the baby boomers?

(c) Suppose that the country wanted to maintain its 3.1 percent per year growth of income, given the retirement of the baby boomers. Given the autonomous growth factor that you computed in part a, compute what the growth rate of capital would have to be in order for the country to achieve that goal. What would have to happen to the savings rate in the country for it to be able to maintain a 3.1 percent per year growth of income?

*6. Consider an economy characterized by the following production function: $Y = AK^{1/3}N^{2/3}$, with a capital stock of $3,000 billion and current net investment of $120 billion.
   (a) If the growth rate of autonomous factors is zero and the growth rate of labor is 1 percent, what is the current growth rate of per person output? Is this a steady-state situation?
   (b) If the government wanted to increase the growth rate of per person output by an extra percentage point through tax and subsidy policies that affected capital growth alone, by what percentage would it have to raise investment?
   (c) In the unlikely event that the government successfully stimulated the required investment, at what rate of growth in output would the economy arrive in the steady state according to the implications of the Solow growth model? Does the text accept this assumption? Why or why not?

*7. You are given the production function $Y = AK^{1/3}N^{2/3}$, where $A = 4$.
   (a) Convert the production function to a function relating Y/N to K/N.
   (b) Consider two countries that have access to the same technology and have the same quality of labor and capital, as well as the same production function, given above. Suppose that one country has per-person output ten times as high as the second country. To what factor is the difference attributable? Quantify the difference between the countries with respect to that factor.

*8. You are given the production function $Y = AK^{1/4}H^{1/4}N^{1/2}$, where $A = 4$. The population growth rate n is 0.025, the depreciation rate d is 0.075 (both physical and human capital depreciate at the same rate), and the growth rate of autonomous factors is zero. Investment I is the sum of two components, investment in physical capital I_K and investment in human capital I_H. The fraction of GDP that goes to physical capital investment is $s_K = 0.05$ and the fraction of GDP that goes to human capital investment is $s_H = 0.05$.
   (a) Convert the production function to a function relating Y/N to both K/N and H/N.
   (b) Consider two countries that have access to the same technology and have the same quality of labor and capital, as well as the same production function, given above. Suppose that one country

has per-person output 10 times as high and a physical capital-labor 100 times as the second country. To what other factor is the difference attributable? Quantify the difference between the countries with respect to that factor.

(c) Find the steady-state physical capital-labor ratio and the steady-state human capital-labor ratio.

(d) Find the steady-state per person output.

*9. Suppose that the production function for an economy is given by $Y = AK^bH^cN^{1-b-c}$. The marginal product of physical capital, MPK, is given by the formula $bAK^{b-1}H^cN^{1-b-c}$ and the marginal product of human capital, MPH, is given by the formula $cAK^bH^{c-1}N^{1-b-c}$. It is assumed that each unit of each factor is paid its marginal product. Find the shares of both physical and human capital in GDP (in each case the total payment to the factor divided by output).

◆ SELF-TEST ANSWERS

p. 363. (1) Y/K declines as K/N increases. This result follows from diminishing returns to capital per person in the per person production function (equation 11.2). Because additions to output per person decrease in size with constant increases to capital per person, output per person grows more slowly than capital per person, and the ratio of output to capital declines. This can be seen by drawing a straight line from the origin (lower-left corner) of Figure 11-1 to point B. The slope of this line is the Y/K ratio. As K/N increases, we move to the right along the production function, and the slopes of lines from the origin to points on the production function decrease. (2) Y/K declines as K/N increases. (3) Y/K rises as K/N declines.

p. 365. (1) As we move left along the production function of Figure 11-1, both Y/N and K/N decline, but Y/N declines by proportionately less so that the ratio Y/K rises. This result follows from the curvature of the production function. As we move right along the production function, both Y/N and K/N rise, but Y/N rises by proportionately less so that the ratio Y/K declines. The other components of

equation (11.8) are fixed, namely s, n, and d, and they are not introduced into the graphical analysis until Figure 11-2. (2) The saving-income ratio (s) is related to the interest rate and wealth; the population growth rate (n) depends on fertility decisions, health, and immigration; the depreciation rate (d) depends on the longevity of capital.

p. 369. (1) A decline in the growth rate of population (n) causes the growth rate of output (y) to decline by exactly the same amount, after which the economy reaches a new steady state. But the lower rate of population growth raises the standard of living (Y/N). Be sure that you can explain why: Start from point E_0 in Figure 11-3, assume that the old saving line remains valid, and rotate the steady-state investment line downward to the right, as required by the decline in the growth rate of population (n). (2) As the steady-state investment line shifts downward, K rises relative to Y, and (3) K rises relative to N.

p. 371. The following are the growth rates of real GDP per person ($y - n$) corresponding to the four blanks: -1.0, 0.0, 4.0, 4.0.

Appendix to Chapter 11

General Functional Forms and the Production Function

Until this point, we have used only "specific linear" forms for the behavioral equations. For instance, the demand for money in the Appendix to Chapter 4 on p. 117 was written as:

$$\left(\frac{M}{P}\right)^d = hY - fr$$

This equation can be stated in words as: The real demand for money $(M/P)^d$ is equal to a positive number (h), times real GDP (Y), minus another number (f), times the interest rate (r). The equation tells specifically how the real demand for money depends on real GDP and the interest rate.

The production function can also be written in a specific form called the Cobb-Douglas production function.[1]

General Linear Form	Numerical Example
$Y = AK^b N^{1-b}$	$Y = AK^{0.25} N^{0.75}$

In words, this states that real GDP (Y) is equal to an autonomous growth factor (A), multiplied by a geometric weighted average of an index of capital (K) and of labor (N). The weights, b and $1 - b$, represent the elasticity (or percentage response) of real GDP to an increase in either factor.[2] For instance, in our numerical example if all variables are indexes initially at 1.0, a 4 percent increase in labor input will cause a 3 percent increase in real GDP. Initially:

$$1.0 = 1.0(1.0^{0.25}\, 1.0^{0.75})$$

After a 4 percent increase in labor input:

$$1.03 = 1.0(1.0^{0.25}\, 1.04^{0.75})$$

Thus the elasticity of real GDP with respect to a change in labor input is 0.75 ($= 3/4$).

Several other characteristics of the production function are evident. First, an equal percentage increase in both factors, capital and labor, raises real GDP by the same percentage. This characteristic, called *constant returns to scale*, occurs because the sum of the weights (b and $1 - b$) is unity. When both factor inputs increase by 4 percent, we have

$$1.04 = 1.0(1.04^{0.25}\, 1.04^{0.75})$$

after a 4 percent increase in both K and N.

A second characteristic is the direct one-for-one response of real GDP to the autonomous growth factor A. If A increases by four percentage points, while capital and labor input remain fixed at 1.0, real GDP increases by the same four percentage points

$$1.04 = 1.04(1.0^{0.25}\, 1.0^{0.75})$$

after a 4 percent increase in A.

The Cobb-Douglas production function is only one of many ways in which real GDP might be related to A, K, and N. Often in economics we want to make the simple

---

[1] The function is named after an Amherst mathematics professor, Charles W. Cobb, and a University of Chicago economics professor (later U.S. senator), Paul H. Douglas, and is described in a book by the latter, *The Theory of Wages* (New York: Macmillan, 1934), especially Chapter V.

[2] *Elasticity* is a term introduced in most elementary economics courses and refers to the percentage change in one variable in response to a 1 percent change in another variable.

statement that "Y is related to A, K, and N," but without restricting the particular form of the relationship. To accomplish this, we sometimes use a *general functional form*. An example of such a general form for the production function is:

$$Y = F(A, K, N)$$

In words, this states simply that real GDP (Y) depends on an autonomous growth factor (A), an index of capital input (K) and an index of labor input (N). The capital letter F and the parentheses mean *depends on*, and any alphabetical letter can be used.

Why is it interesting to know simply that one variable depends on others? By writing an alternative equation, one could state the *alternative hypothesis* that there is no role for an autonomous growth factor:

$$Y = F(K, N)$$

This states that real GDP depends *only on* capital and labor input.

Sometimes it is desirable to make a specific assumption about the form in which one variable enters, but not the others. This occurs in equation (11.1) on p. 362 in the text, which states that the elasticity of real GDP with respect to the autonomous growth factor is unity, but does not restrict the form of the relationship between real GDP and the other inputs, capital and labor:

$$Y = A\, F(K, N)$$

Without further information one cannot look at these general functional forms and learn whether the assumed relationship is positive or negative. The positive relationship between real GDP and both capital and labor inputs can be written in either of two ways:

$$\text{Method 1:} Y = AF(K,N)$$
$$(+)(+)$$
$$\text{Method 2:} Y = AF(K,N); F_K > 0, F_N > 0$$

The terms to the right of the semicolon in method 2 can be put into these words: The response of real GDP to a change in capital input (F_K) and in labor input (F_N) is positive (>0).

Exercise: Consider a general functional form for the demand for money:

$$\left(\frac{M}{P}\right)^d = L(Y, r)$$

State in words what this function states about the relationship between the real demand for money ($M/P)^d$ and real GDP (Y) and the interest rate (r). Use both methods 1 and 2 to write down the facts that the real demand for money depends positively on real GDP and negatively on the interest rate.

The Big Questions of Economic Growth

Few problems are more fascinating, more important, or more neglected than the rates at which development proceeds in successive generations in different countries.
—Wesley Mitchell, 1927

12-1 Answering the Big Questions

More than half of the world's population lives on less than $4,000 per year, well below one-tenth of the $48,000 average level of per-person income in the United States. This startling level of inequality of the average income level across countries is much greater than the degree of inequality within a single country like the United States. Many theoretical models, like the Solow neo-classical growth model examined in the last chapter, predict that poor countries would steadily *converge* to the income levels of the rich countries. But this has not happened; the ratio of income per person in the richest countries to that of the poor countries has barely changed in the past 50 years.

Why Are We So Rich and They So Poor?

There is no more important question in economics than understanding the success of some countries in becoming relatively rich and the failure of other countries that have remained so poor. As expressed by Harvard economist David Landes, "Why Are We So Rich and They So Poor?"[1] Some countries, like the United States, Britain, and France, have remained at or near the frontier of income per person throughout the past century. Some other countries, like Asia's "Four Tigers" (Korea, Taiwan, Hong Kong, and Singapore), have achieved very rapid growth and within only one generation have transformed themselves from a group of poor nations to a group of rich nations, achieving the convergence predicted by the Solow growth model. The "BRIC" countries (Brazil, Russia, India, China) are also growing rapidly. But a third group of countries, including Pakistan, Bangladesh, and numerous countries in Africa and Latin America, have failed to converge. In many cases, their income per-person was below 10 percent of the U.S. level in 1960 and remains there today.

The Solow growth model of Chapter 11 provides a partial answer to the first basic question about economic growth. Countries with a higher level of income per person have a higher level of capital per person, which they achieve by saving and investing. The weakness of the Solow model is that it predicts differences between rich and poor nations in both capital per person and the rate of return on capital that are several orders of magnitude greater than is true in the

---

[1] David S. Landes, "Why Are We So Rich and They So Poor?" *American Economic Review Papers and Proceedings* (May 1990), pp. 1–13.

data. This weakness is partially remedied, as we have seen on pp. 375–77, by including human capital as well as physical capital in the analysis and by assuming that much of the income earned by labor is actually a reward to human capital rather than pure physical exertion. Yet even then we are left with questions, starting with the need to explain why an immigrant from a poor country to a rich country is able to achieve such a big jump in income without any immediate change in his human capital (i.e., educational attainment).

A bigger question is why some countries are so much more productive than others in using the capital that they have. In this chapter we broaden our investigation of the sources of economic growth in several directions. We will see that people will not start businesses or invest in those businesses if they cannot earn a decent return on their investment. Economic growth requires a political environment that creates incentives for investment, requiring a legal system that protects property rights and protection of ordinary citizens against corruption, bribery, theft, and confiscation of the returns on their investments. Even in a crime-free environment, political decisions can influence the incentives to invest and the productivity of those investments, including regulations on the trading of securities, on the protection of ideas through patent rights, and on the costs and difficulty of hiring and firing workers. Growth also requires investment in **infrastructure,** including some types of capital that benefit society as a whole and are often provided by government investment, including highways, airports, telephone systems, and electricity supply.

Infrastructure consists of types of capital that benefit society as a whole, including highways, airports, trains, waterways, ports, telephone networks, and electricity grids.

What Creates a Growth Miracle?

We have divided nations into the rich, the poor that have remained poor, and an intermediate group of countries, including Asia's Four Tigers, that have sprinted ahead from the ranks of the poor to the ranks of the rich. The BRIC countries, most of which started out poorer than the Four Tigers, have surged ahead recently, in some cases at even faster rates than the Four Tigers. The experience of such countries that have sustained growth rates of 5 percent or more for several decades—often called a "growth miracle"—is illustrated by the comparison of Korea versus the Philippines on pp. 16–17. Such sustained rates of growth create unbelievable changes in the standard of living of ordinary citizens; for instance, a 5 percent growth rate sustained for four decades is sufficient to boost per-capita real income by a factor of 7.4, from $2,500 to $18,500.

The Solow theory suggests that all nations should eventually converge to the level of the world's technological leader, which for most of the past century has been the United States. The achievements of the fast-growing miracle economies could simply be dismissed as an automatic process if it were not for the fact that their achievements are so unusual; in fact, many other countries that started out poor 50 years ago are still just as poor, with income levels less than one-tenth of the United States. We can learn a great deal by studying the experience of the miracle nations as well as those countries that failed, especially by contrasting them as in this chapter.

The Mechanism of Growth

In addition to questions about the success or failure of poor countries in catching up to the technological frontier established by the rich countries, there is the separate question of the frontier itself. What determines the rate at which the frontier advances? Is it saving and investment, technological change, education, or other factors? As we shall see, growth would grind to a halt without a continuing stream of new inventions, and maintaining the flow of inventions and new ideas requires incentives to inventors to make the large, up-front investments needed to create new computer chips, smart phones, software, medical technology, drugs, and other novel products.

12-2 The Standard of Living and Concepts of Productivity

In Chapter 11 we used the concepts of "output per person," "productivity," and "output per hour" interchangeably, using the symbol Y/N. As before, the growth rate of a ratio is the difference between the growth rates of the numerator and denominator, so the growth rate of these concepts was designated as $y - n$.

Distinguishing the Standard of Living from Labor Productivity

However, it is possible for the growth rate of the population to differ from the growth rate of labor input. To maintain intact our previous development of the Solow growth model, we will continue to use the symbol N (growing at rate n) for the population, and we introduce a new easy-to-remember symbol H (growing at rate h) for the growth rate of labor input (total hours of work). Factors that could cause labor input to grow faster than the population ($h > n$) include a movement of women into the labor force, as happened in the 1970s and 1980s. Another cause of $h > n$ would be a decline in the birth rate that initially reduces growth in the number of children; this would immediately reduce the rate of population growth and only later reduce the growth of labor input (which only counts those aged 16 and above). Factors that could cause labor input to grow more slowly than the population ($h < n$) include a rise in the unemployment rate or a decline in the labor-force participation rate, and the upcoming retirement of the baby boom generation, which will reduce the number of hours of labor input without initially reducing the population.[2]

Economic growth refers to an improvement in the **standard of living,** defined as output per capita or member of the population *(Y/N)*. **Labor productivity** is defined as output per hour of work *(Y/H)*, using the same definition of output. The growth rate of the standard of living is $y - n$, while the growth rate of labor productivity is $y - h$. Thus the difference between the growth rate of the standard of living and that of labor productivity is

$$y - n - (y - h) = h - n \qquad (12.1)$$

The **standard of living** is real GDP per member of the population, or "real output per capita."

Labor productivity is real GDP per hour of work, or "real output per hour."

Therefore, whenever hours grow faster than the population ($h > n$), the standard of living grows faster than labor productivity, and vice versa.

The distinction between n and h is worth making when examining differences between the United States and other countries. As shown in the figure on p. 360, European countries still lag well behind the United States in their output per capita, but several of the leading European nations have almost caught up to the United States in their level of labor productivity, or output per hour. The reason that productivity in Europe has grown faster than the standard of living is clear from equation (12.1)—hours of work in Europe have grown more slowly than the population. Over the two decades before 2007, Europeans

---

[2] The labor force, defined on p. 43, is the sum of employment plus unemployment. The labor-force participation rate is the ratio of the labor force to the working-age population, aged 16 and older. The labor-force participation rate in the United States in December 2010 was 64.5 percent.

chose to take longer vacations than are typical in the United States, their average unemployment rate rose, and their labor-force participation rate declined. Europeans retire at earlier ages than Americans. These events prevent the European standard of living from catching up to the United States even as the productivity gap has vanished for some European nations. For Western Europe as a whole, by 1995 productivity had reached 91 percent of the United States but since then has dropped back to about 83 percent. We return to contrasts between Europe and the United States in the last section of this chapter.

Multifactor Productivity (Solow's Residual)

A second concept of productivity is important in the study of economic growth. Already defined in Chapter 11, this is multifactor productivity (MFP), which is sometimes called "Solow's residual" after Robert M. Solow, the Nobel-prize winning inventor of neoclassical growth theory. The concept of MFP differs from labor productivity in that it expresses the amount of output produced relative to *both* labor and capital inputs; in contrast, labor productivity expresses the amount of output produced relative to labor input only. The contribution that capital makes to output is measured by the elasticity of output to capital (b), which we will continue, as in Chapter 11, to assume is 0.25 in our numerical examples. The elasticity of output to capital and labor input together is unity (1.0), and so the elasticity of output to labor is the remaining amount not attributable to capital ($1 - b$), or 0.75 in the numerical example.

The growth rate of MFP (for which we use, as before, the symbol a) can be written as the growth rate of output (y) minus the contribution of capital (bk) minus the contribution of labor hours $[(1 - b)h]$:

$$a = y - bk - (1 - b)h \tag{12.2}$$

Thus, to measure the growth rate of multifactor productivity, we need to know four facts: the growth rates of output, capital, and labor (y, k, and h), and the elasticity of output with respect to capital (b). As Robert Solow showed in the 1950s in part of the work that earned him the Nobel Prize in economics, this elasticity can be measured by the share of capital in national income, including corporate profits, depreciation, rent, interest, and the portion of the income of the self-employed that is attributable to capital.[3]

How are the growth rates of multifactor productivity (a) and labor productivity ($y - h$) related to each other? Equation (12.2) can be rearranged to show their relationship.[4]

General Form   Numerical Example

$$a = (y - h) - b(k - h) \qquad 2.25 = (4 - 1) - 0.25(4 - 1) \tag{12.3}$$

In words, the growth rate of multifactor productivity is equal to the growth rate of labor productivity minus b times the growth in the ratio of capital input to labor input.[5] Since growth in the ratio is almost always positive, the growth of MFP is almost always slower than that of labor productivity.

---

[3] Solow's idea of linking the elasticity of output to capital with capital's share in national income is explained in Chapter 11, footnote 10, on p. 371.

[4] Equation (12.3) is identical to equation (11.11) on p. 371, except for the replacement of the symbol n, used in Chapter 11 to denote the growth rate of both population and labor hours, with the more precise symbol h, which is used in this chapter to designate the growth rate of labor hours. As we learned in equation (12.1), the growth rate of the population can differ from the growth rate of labor hours.

[5] The growth of the ratio of capital input to labor input is often called "capital deepening."

SELF-TEST

The definition of MFP growth in equation (12.3) has five elements: y, a, k, h, and b.

1. Assuming that b always equals 0.25, any of the four remaining elements can be calculated if the other three are known. Fill in the blanks:

y	a	k	h
—	4	4	1
4	3	4	—
3	0	—	1

2. For each example in the table above, which is higher: labor productivity growth or MFP growth? Why should this be the case?

How the Real Wage Is Related to Productivity

If labor productivity (Y/H) grows slowly, the real wage (W/P) tends to grow slowly. We have already learned in equation (12.2) that an ingredient in the measurement of multifactor productivity (MFP) is labor's share in national income $(1 - b)$. This central concept, called labor's share, can be defined in a way that connects labor productivity with the real wage:

$$\text{Labor's share} = 1 - b = \frac{WH}{PY} = \frac{W/P}{Y/H} \qquad (12.4)$$

The first expression states that labor's share is equal to the total compensation of labor [the nominal wage rate (W), times the quantity of labor input (H)], divided by total income in nominal terms (PY). The second expression states that this is exactly the same as the real wage divided by labor productivity.

Equation (12.4) helps us see that if labor's share in national income is constant, then the real wage must grow at the same rate as labor productivity. As usual, we employ lowercase symbols to represent growth rates, and we can use the familiar relationship that the growth rate of any ratio equals the growth rate of the numerator minus the growth rate of the denominator. This implies that the growth rate of labor's share equals the growth rate of the real wage $(w - p)$, minus the growth rate of labor productivity $(y - h)$:

$$\text{Growth rate of labor's share} = (w - p) - (y - h) \qquad (12.5)$$

This leads us to a very important conclusion about the growth rate of the real wage. If labor's share is constant (so that the growth rate of labor's share is zero), then *the growth rate of the real wage must be exactly equal to the growth rate of productivity.*

Condition if the growth rate of labor's share is zero

$$w - p = y - h \qquad (12.6)$$

Labor's share of national income in the United States has been virtually constant for the past 50 years. As a result, the real wage has grown at the same rate as labor productivity.

12-3   The Failure of Convergence

If almost half of the world's population still lives in countries with output per capita that is less than one-tenth the level of the United States, then this implies that these countries have failed to converge to the U.S. standard of living. Yet convergence is just what is predicted to occur by the Solow neoclassical growth model studied in the last chapter. First, let us review why the Solow model predicts convergence; then we will look at the facts.

The Theoretical Prediction of Convergence

The simple Solow model with no technical change does not actually explain economic growth. It predicts that a country with a given per-person production function and given saving rate (s) will have a fixed level of labor productivity (Y/N) and capital per worker (K/N).[6] For instance, in Figure 12-1 we have copied the equilibrium in the Solow model from Figure 11-3, where the economy operates at point E_0 with a capital stock per hour of $(K/N)_0$ and a level of saving equal to $s(Y/N)_0$. How does the Solow model explain how a poor nation might be operating at point P with a much lower level of capital per hour $(K/N)_P$ and level of saving $s(Y/N)_P$?

Clearly, such an economy must not be in its long-run equilibrium, because its level of saving per person at point P exceeds its investment requirements shown at point A, that is, the amount of investment $(n + d)(K/N)_P$ needed to provide for population growth and depreciation. Since actual investment equals saving and is in excess of investment requirements, the capital-labor ratio will grow steadily until the economy reaches long-run equilibrium at point E_0. According to the Solow model, the only difference between rich nations and poor nations is that the poor nations have a lower capital-labor ratio K/N. Since there is no difference in the per-person production function between rich and

---

Figure 12-1 Saving, Investment, and Capital Per Hour in Long-Run Equilibrium for a Poor Nation

The blue saving line and black investment requirements line are copied from Figure 11-3. The long-run equilibrium point is shown at E_0. The only reason given by the Solow growth model for the low output per hour $(Y/N)_P$ of poor nations is their low level of capital per hour $(K/N)_P$, and their economies operate at the point labeled P. Because their saving and investment per hour at P exceed their investment requirements for population growth and depreciation, shown at A, there is sufficient excess investment to boost the K/N ratio up to the equilibrium value $(K/N)_0$.

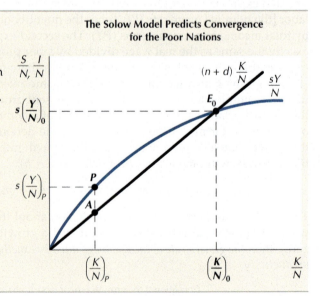

The Solow Model Predicts Convergence for the Poor Nations

---

[6] In this section there is no need to distinguish between the population (N) and hours of labor input (H), so we return to the notation of Chapter 11 in which the symbol (N) stands for both the population and the hours of labor input.

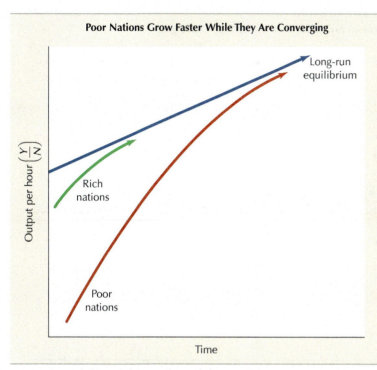

Poor Nations Grow Faster While They Are Converging

Output per hour $\left(\frac{Y}{N}\right)$

Long-run equilibrium

Rich nations

Poor nations

Time

Figure 12-2 Output Per Hour of Rich and Poor Nations During the Period of Convergence

Both the rich and poor nations are assumed to start off with an equilibrium level of capital per hour (K/N) that is below equilibrium, but the poor nations begin much below the rich nations. Because all nations initially have investment in excess of requirements for population growth and depreciation, they all grow faster than the equilibrium path until they catch up. Since the poor nations start further back, it takes them more time to converge to the equilibrium path, and their growth rates are faster during this time period.

poor nations, the process of saving in excess of investment requirements will automatically cause the poor nations to converge to the same equilibrium point E_0 as the rich nations.

Does technological change alter the convergence prediction of the Solow model? No, because technology is assumed to be freely available to all countries. Thus the model continues to assume that the only reason for nations to be poor is that they start at a level of the capital-labor ratio (K/N) that is well below the equilibrium value. As shown in Figure 12-2, the equilibrium level of labor productivity (Y/N) can steadily increase, but the Solow model predicts that rich countries and poor countries alike will eventually converge to the same equilibrium value. The rich countries reach the equilibrium value earlier because they started with a higher capital-labor ratio and thus required a shorter period of saving and investment.

A key empirical prediction of the Solow model is that the poorer the nation, that is, the lower its labor productivity (Y/N) in an initial period of time, the faster the growth of its labor productivity. We can see this in Figure 12-2, where the arrow labeled "Poor nations" rises at a steeper slope than the arrow labeled "Rich nations." Thus the Solow model would predict that there would be a *negative* relationship between a nation's initial level of Y/N and its subsequent growth rate ($y - n$). In short, poor nations should uniformly exhibit faster growth rates of labor productivity and per-capita output than rich nations. After rich and poor nations converge to the long-run equilibrium path, their growth rates should be identical.

Facts About Convergence

Data on rich and poor countries refer to output per person. Extensive research has been carried out by Robert Summers and Alan Heston of the University of Pennsylvania to improve the comparability of real output data across countries.

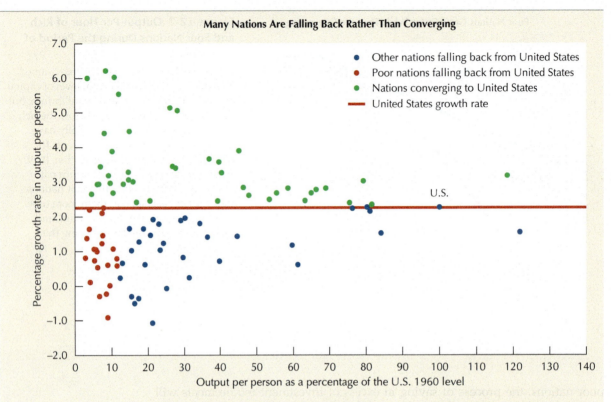

Figure 12-3 Output Per Worker Relative to the United States in 1960 and the Growth of Output Per Person, 1960–2007

The convergence hypothesis suggests that the poorest nations, those on the left of the diagram, will have the fastest rates of growth. The dots should slope downward to the right and all dots should be above the horizontal line, which represents the growth rate of the United States. The low correlation of the growth rates and levels and the substantial number of red dots, showing poor countries with growth rates below that of the United States, are evidence contradicting the convergence hypothesis.

Source: Alan Heston, Robert Summers, and Bettina Aten, Penn World Table Version 6.3, Center for International Comparisons of Production, Income, and Prices at the University of Pennsylvania, August 2009.

The Summers-Heston data measure real output per person at a common set of prices for all nations, and this tends to improve the standing of poor nations markedly compared to the crude alternative of comparing GDP across nations using foreign exchange rates.[7]

Despite these corrections for common prices, many nations remain very poor. This is shown in Figure 12-3, which has one dot for each of 98 nations. The horizontal position of each dot represents real output per worker in 1960 as a percentage of the United States, and the vertical position represents the growth rate of real output per worker from 1960 to 2007. The extent of world-wide poverty in 1960 is shown by the number of dots to the left of 10 percent on the horizontal axis; in each of these nations (31 of the 98), real output per

[7] Robert Summers and Alan Heston, "The Penn World Table (Mark 5): An Expanded Set of International Comparisons, 1950–1988," *Quarterly Journal of Economics*, vol. 106 (May 1991), pp. 327–68. The latest data are available at pwt.econ.upenn.edu/php_site/pwt_index.php.

worker in 1960 was less than 10 percent of the U.S. level. Among these poor countries, those that grew slower than the U.S. after 1960 are shown by red dots. *These are the poor countries that failed to converge.*

Recall that the Solow model predicts faster growth in poor nations than in rich nations, indicating that the slope of the dots in Figure 12-3 should be negative, slanting downward from left to right. Indeed, there are green dots at the upper left corner of the diagram; among the fast growing nations that started out relatively poor in 1960 are China, Korea, Hong Kong, Singapore, and Taiwan. These four nations all registered growth rates in the vertical direction of 5.0 percent or higher. Within this hard-charging group, the growth leaders for 1960–2007 are China and Taiwan, tied at 6.0 percent, followed by South Korea at 5.5, and Hong Kong tied with Singapore at 5.1 percent.

However, the overall correlation of the dots in Figure 12-3 is zero. There are far more countries having growth rates below the U.S. rate, shown by the red and blue dots, than having growth rates above the U.S. rate, shown by the green dots. There are even a few rich nations that failed to converge. Among these, shown in the second section of Table 12-1, are New Zealand, Venezuela, and Argentina. The next section of the table lists Japan, Hong Kong, and South Korea, nations that were initially poor but converged rapidly. Poor nations that slipped back, the opposite direction of convergence, included Bolivia in Latin America, as well as Cameroon and Mali in sub-Saharan Africa. Any country with an average growth rate below the U.S. growth rate of 2.3 percent per year wound up with an average level of output per person relative to the United States that was *worse* in 2007 than in 1960, the opposite of convergence. About two-thirds of the nations plotted in Figure 12-3 experienced the opposite of convergence. Some others, including the examples shown in the bottom section of Table 12-1, made no progress, exhibiting roughly the same growth rates as the United States over the 1960–2007 period.

While the prediction of convergence seems to be a failure of the Solow model, this verdict needs to be qualified. Among the rich nations, the required negative correlation between the initial income level and subsequent growth rate was quite strong, with few exceptions. This verdict is valid for the 1960–2007 period examined in Figure 12-3. What seems to go wrong with the prediction of convergence refers to the poor countries. When the poor countries are included, as in Figure 12-3, the negative correlation disappears, and there appears to be no systematic relationship between the initial 1960 level of real GDP relative to the United States and the subsequent growth rate.

Solutions Suggested by the Solow Model

The reason the Solow model suggests convergence is that it assumes unrealistically that all nations have the same per-person production function, saving rate, growth rate of the population, and depreciation rate. We have already seen in Figure 11-4 on p. 368 the Solow model's prediction that an increase in the saving rate can temporarily *raise* the growth rate of output and capital per person. In the same diagram, an increase in the rate of population growth (n) would *reduce* the growth rate of output and capital per person.[8] Thus one valid explanation

---

[8] Turn back to Figure 11-4 on p. 368. Imagine tilting the black investment requirements line labeled $(n + d)(K/N)$ upward. This will cause the equilibrium point E_0 to move downward and to the left, reducing the equilibrium levels of Y/N and K/N. Thus an increase in the rate of population growth (n) will reduce the equilibrium levels of Y/N and K/N, just as an increase in the saving rate (s) will have the opposite effect.

Table 12-1 **Examples of Countries Displaying Convergence, Anti-Convergence, or Neither (Levels and Growth Rates in Percent)**

Country	Output per person relative to the United States		Growth rate of output per person, 1960–2007	
	2007	1960	Actual	Relative to U.S.
Rich countries that converged				
Austria	84	66	2.8	0.5
Italy	67	55	2.7	0.4
France	69	63	2.5	0.2
Rich countries that failed to converge				
New Zealand	59	84	1.5	−0.7
Venezuela	28	61	0.6	−1.7
Argentina	36	60	1.2	−1.1
Poor countries that converged				
Hong Kong	101	26	5.1	2.9
Japan	71	37	3.7	1.4
South Korea	56	12	5.5	3.3
Poor countries that fell back				
Bolivia	9	19	0.6	−1.7
Cameroon	6	13	0.7	−1.6
Mali	3	5	1.1	−1.2
Poor countries that made no progress				
Syria	7	7	2.1	−0.2
Ghana	4	4	2.2	−0.1

Source: Alan Heston, Robert Summers, and Bettina Aten, Penn World Table Version 6.3, Center for International Comparisons of Production, Income, and Prices at the University of Pennsylvania, August 2009.

for the failure of poor countries to converge is that, with either a lower saving rate (low *s*) or higher rate of population growth (high *n*), their equilibrium growth path is not the single path depicted by the blue line in Figure 12-2 but rather is a lower path as shown by the lower blue line in Figure 12-4. Thus the puzzle of why some poor countries do not fully converge to the output per person level of the rich nations can be explained by any combination of lower saving rates or faster rates of population growth.

What government policies can achieve a higher saving rate or a lower rate of population growth? The first method to increase saving is to reduce the taxation of saving, for instance by shifting from a progressive income tax to a progressive consumption tax that exempts saving from taxation. Most studies suggest that such policies have only a small impact on saving. A more effective method of raising national saving is for the government to switch from a budget deficit to a budget surplus by some combination of raising taxes and reducing government spending. As for reducing the rate of population growth, the government could

Poor Nations May Never Catch Up

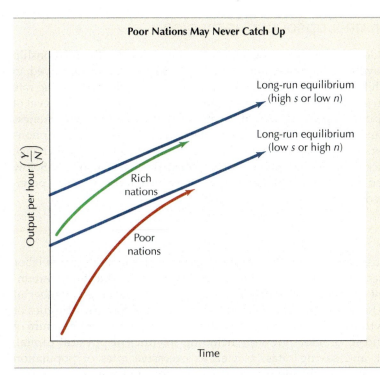

Figure 12-4 The Effect of a Low Saving Rate or High Rate of Population Growth on Output Per Person

The upper blue line shows the long-run equilibrium growth path for the rich nations. Two factors could cause the long-run path to be lower for the poor nations—either a lower saving rate (s) or a faster rate of population growth (n).

try to educate people about the benefits of birth control. An extreme example of such a policy was the "one-child" policy of China that was enforced by the political dictatorship of that country.

Does the empirical evidence support the Solow model's prediction that a higher investment rate allows nations to achieve a higher standard of living? The relationship between the investment rate (the share of investment in GDP) and the standard of living across many nations is very weak. Poor countries have investment ratios ranging all the way from 2 percent to 25 percent relative to GDP. Similarly, rich countries have investment rates ranging from 12 to 30 percent. Thus the Solow model ultimately cannot explain the failure of at least half of the poor countries to converge over the past few decades. We turn in the next two sections to alternative explanations of the continuing gap between the rich and poor countries.

 SELF-TEST

The Solow growth model makes predictions both about the level of per-person output and its growth rate.

1. What is the long-run effect of an increase in the saving rate on the level of per-person output and capital?

2. What is the long-run effect of an increase in the saving rate on the growth rate of output per capita?

3. What is the long-run effect of an increase in the rate of population growth on the level of per-person output and capital?

4. What is the long-run effect of an increase in the rate of population growth on the growth rate of output per capita?

12-4   Human Capital and Technology

The Solow model as developed in Chapter 11 cannot explain the relationship between the levels and growth rates of output per capita, as displayed in Figure 12-3. While the Solow model, as in Figure 12-4, can allow the saving rate and population growth rate to differ, thus yielding a lower equilibrium level of output per capita for poor nations, it seems to assume much more likeness between poor and rich nations than is true in fact. In particular, its assumptions that the per-person production function and the rate of technological change are identical across poor and rich countries seem dubious. Also, the Solow model as treated so far in this chapter neglects the role of human capital, previously introduced in Section 11-7 on pp. 375–77.

Human Capital and Economic Growth

Perhaps the most basic flaw in the simple Solow model is to assume that labor input is identical across rich and poor countries. In fact, educational attainment (the number of years of education achieved by an average member of the population) is vastly different between rich and poor countries. Studies of economic growth usually find that poor nations fall short in every measure of factors that tend to promote growth, including insufficient physical capital, human capital, and saving rates, as well as excessive rates of population growth. But, to use an old phrase, "correlation does not imply causation." Perhaps the sources of low growth are themselves *endogenous*, that is, caused by low growth itself. Poor countries simply cannot afford to engage in high levels of investment in physical and human capital. Further, for poor countries to achieve the lower fertility rates needed to achieve lower rates of population growth may require education, the crucial growth factor that poor nations cannot afford.

Does Technological Change Require Human Capital?

The Solow model assumes that the rate of technological change is the same in every country, *and that the best available technology is freely available to all countries*. This explains why in Figure 12-2 we have drawn the upper blue long-run equilibrium line as the same for rich and poor countries alike. The different levels for rich and poor countries of the blue long-run equilibrium lines in Figure 12-4 are caused solely by different saving rates and rates of population growth, not different growth rates of technological change.

Yet this is surely an unrealistic assumption in the Solow model. Modern technology often requires modern equipment and software. Thus both investment and technological change require educated workers, that is, a previous investment in human capital. If workers are illiterate, how can they use personal computers and the Internet as fruitfully as in countries where all workers can read and write, and where most workers are familiar with personal computers? As a skeptic suggested, "If you unloaded a pile of Dell computers and Microsoft software on a pier in Bangladesh, would that create the long-awaited convergence of the Bangladeshi standard of living to the level of the United States?" Bangladesh and many other poor countries do not have sufficient numbers of educated workers who know how to use modern computers and software, rendering modern technology inaccessible, in contrast to the assumption of the Solow model that it is freely available everywhere.

Importing Technological Change Through Foreign Investment

Most research and development takes place in the rich countries, especially in the United States, western Europe, and Japan. China has increasingly been doing new research rather than just copying ideas from the rich nations. Poor countries are unable to afford large investments in research and development activities, so what can they do to acquire the technical knowledge being developed by the rich nations? Three main methods are available. First, engineers in poor countries may try to copy modern products made in rich countries. However, this is very difficult and often impossible for the most advanced products, including computer chips. A second method is to purchase imported machinery that embodies the latest technology. Developing nations have been importing the latest technology since the early nineteenth century, when American firms imported British steam engines. A third method is to obtain investment by foreign firms, which open factories in the poor country based on the latest technology. Mexican economic growth has been spurred in the past decade by American investment, and Singapore's inclusion as one of Asia's four fast-growing "tigers" has been heavily dependent on foreign investment, mainly by Japanese and American companies. More recently, rapid economic growth in China has been propelled by foreign investment, not just from Japan and the United States, but from neighboring Hong Kong and Taiwan.

"Not so fast," economics ministers in many poor countries might respond if shown this list of three channels by which they might obtain modern technology. "Our people are not sufficiently educated to copy the latest techniques, we cannot afford to pay for imported modern machinery, and our countries are not attractive as locations for foreign investment." This hypothetical comment from the poor countries brings us to the heart of the development problem that they face. Everything depends on everything else, and some countries are in a "vicious" circle in which they are too poor to improve the educational level of their citizens or to obtain modern technology, two prerequisites to growth.

The view that "everything is endogenous" and that some poor countries are caught in a "poverty trap" makes the prospects for growth seem hopeless for many poor countries. Yet this ignores the fact that many other poor nations have succeeded in launching themselves on the path to convergence, as shown by the many green dots in Figure 12-3 on p. 394. Perhaps not every growth-inducing factor is endogenous, and there are some other factors that governments can influence, that is, convert into an exogenous growth-promoting influence. The next section discusses two important factors that governments can influence, the political/legal environment and infrastructure investment, and one that they cannot influence, the geographical location of their countries.

12-5   Political Capital, Infrastructure, and Geography

Recently economists have made substantial progress toward identifying fundamental, underlying sources of growth that help us understand why some countries "take off" on a path toward convergence, while other countries remain mired at extremely low levels of income. The most basic of these sources is the legal and political environment. The free market system requires that entrepreneurs who are taking risks by starting a new business have a high probability of making a decent profit to reward them for their effort and for the risk they are taking that their business may fail. The legal system must protect the right to own property and must protect it from thieves; the tax system must be fairly administered; and the opportunity to start a business must be open, not limited to relatives or cronies of corrupt dictators.

The second major factor that involves government decisions is infrastructure investment in such crucial factors of production as highways, airports, ports, telephone networks, and electricity systems. Among the many remarkable aspects of China's growth has been its ability to plan infrastructure to be ready in advance of economic growth; in contrast India has fallen behind in creating infrastructure and still suffers from periodic electricity blackouts.

Unfortunately, a third factor, geography, impairs the growth opportunities of some nations but cannot usually be influenced by government policy.[9]

Political and Legal Determinants of Costs and Returns

In most countries, permits must be purchased in order to start a business and construct a building. In advanced countries like the United States, these permits are easily obtained, and their price is only a small fraction of the overall cost of starting the business. But in other countries, the permits may be very expensive, there may be long delays in obtaining them, and, more important, officials may expect bribes. In Russia some investors have reported that as many as ten different agencies each expected a bribe in order to grant permission for new projects. In another example, the cost of starting a small business in Peru was estimated to be 32 times the monthly minimum wage, an impossible sum for an average worker or even a relatively well-off citizen. Not surprisingly, Peru is one of the growth failures shown in Figure 12-3 that barely registered positive growth in output per person during 1960–2007, and its output per person fell back from 24 percent of the U.S. level in 1960 to 15 percent in 2007.

There are a wider variety of factors that can influence the expected returns from starting a business. First, the country must have relatively free trade so that products manufactured in that country can be exported. Governments obtain access for their exports to other countries by having relatively low barriers to trade for imports into their countries.

Second, those who develop new ideas must be protected by a strong patent system, such as that in the United States that protects inventors for a substantial period of time from having their new ideas copied by imitators. Patents are essential to give potential inventors the incentive to develop new products and techniques. Just as important is what has been called "diversion," which includes the problem of theft (both "outside" robberies and theft by managers or workers), very high levels of taxation levied by governments, or "protection money" like that paid to the Mafia in gangster movies. Any kind of diversion reduces the expected profits on a business investment both directly and indirectly, by forcing business firms to invest in such anti-diversion activities as security systems.

Overall, even if there is no diversion at all, it still is difficult for most people in poor countries to start their own businesses. Typically in poor countries, inequality is high, with most of the income earned by a small number of rich people. The remaining people find it difficult to start a business because they are poor, lack education about how to run a business, and often do not qualify for credit.

---

[9] Parts of this section are based on Charles I. Jones, *Introduction to Economic Growth*, 2d ed. (New York: Norton, 2001), Chapter 7. See also Robert E. Hall and Charles I. Jones, "Why Do Some Countries Produce So Much More Output per Worker than Others?" *Quarterly Journal of Economics*, vol. 114 (February 1999), pp. 83–116.

INTERNATIONAL PERSPECTIVE

A Symptom of Poverty: Urban Slums in the Poor Cities

College students may find it hard to believe that billions of people, as shown in Figure 12-3 on p. 394, had a standard of living in 1960 below 10 percent of the U.S. level and were even further behind in 2004. How can people survive when the GDP per person in their country is so low? Many of the world's poor live in rural villages in primitive homes with no electricity or running water, similar to American farm families in 1875 but with much less land per person. More interesting are the conditions of life of poor people in poor countries who have chosen to move from their rural villages to the city.

In most poor countries, the large cities are surrounded by urban slums, occupied by thousands and even millions of people. Sometimes the slums are in the middle of the cities as in the case of Kibera, an area of about one square mile located in the middle of Nairobi, Kenya, populated by between 600,000 and 1 million people (nobody knows for sure). In 1960, Kenya, a former British colony, had an income per person of 12 percent of the U.S. level; by 2007, this had fallen back to 5 percent, due to the fact that Kenya registered a growth rate of per-person income of *exactly zero* between 1960 and 2007.

Kibera is an "informal" settlement, meaning that legally it does not exist. The government provides nothing. There are no basic services, no schools, no hospitals, no running water, no lavatories. Many people make money by privately providing such services to the inhabitants, often extracting bribe money. Residents must use privately owned latrines, paying the equivalent of about four American cents for the privilege. Permission to put up a shack costs about $70—but provides no legal deed or other printed document proving ownership. Most shacks are owned by an elite group that rents them out, but the renters have no security of tenure and can be kicked out on a landlord's whim.

Shacks are packed so densely that many can be reached only on foot, because there is no room for roads. There is dust in the dry season and mud in the wet season. Low-hanging roofs of jagged corrugated iron can wound people who accidentally collide with them. Litter is everywhere, including the "flying toilet," plastic bags thrown out from their doorways. The stench is ever-present.

The uneducated and unskilled people of Kibera have no choice but to provide cheap labor—which is convenient for the upper-income inhabitants of the surrounding Nairobi. Those lucky enough to have jobs must walk to them.

The misery of slums is pervasive in poor countries. In gigantic Mumbai (formerly Bombay), India, perhaps half of the 16 million residents live in slums. Less than half of the slum dwellers have running water and some of that is contaminated. Housing units have no lavatories, and hundreds of people have to use a single outdoor lavatory. Everywhere there is the stench of sewage. But India is making economic progress more rapidly than such tropical African countries as Kenya. India's urban slum dwellers are starting to earn enough money to rent apartments and buy TV sets and mobile phones. Still, life is hard. Because Mumbai is so large, most workers have to commute to work on overcrowded roads and trains, with sometimes 700 passengers crammed into (or holding onto) train cars intended for 100 passengers.

Why do urban residents endure such conditions? What else can they do? In India, the agricultural economy grows very slowly while the urban economies grow rapidly, allowing India to reach economic growth rates in recent years of close to 8 percent. Many agricultural laborers are essentially slaves, so deeply in debt that they have to do the bidding of the landowner; cities with their slums may seem to offer more opportunities.

Anyone who has experienced the slums of Kenya, India, or other poor countries and knows the United States finds the contrast incredible. American dwelling units have twice as much interior space and four times the outdoor space as typical dwelling units even in Europe's rich countries. Cities in rich countries have problems, but they are of a different magnitude than those of cities in poor countries. Most people would agree, for instance, that New York City's traffic congestion and Los Angeles's underdeveloped and underfunded public transportation system are issues that pale in comparison to Kibera's absolute lack of basic human services and Mumbai's poor sanitation system.[a]

---

[a] For more on urban slums, see a special survey in the *Economist*, May 5, 2007.

The amount of diversion in a country is determined by government policy and the type of legal system that is provided by a country's constitution. Sometimes the diversion is created by the government itself, as when dictators in Indonesia and some African countries give lucrative contracts to businesses owned by a dictator's relatives. Not only must diversion be minimized, but government policies must also be *predictable*. Countries with reputations for frequent changes in government, whether by political coups or constitutional changes, will have low expected returns to investment due to the high risks of locating a business there.

An interesting aspect of economic development is the colonial origins of a particular country's legal system. Former colonies of the United Kingdom, such as the United States, Canada, Australia, India, and Singapore, have a legal system based on common law dating back to medieval England. Former colonies of France and Spain, including most of Latin America, have a legal system dating back to the Napoleonic Codes. Studies have found that legal protections for shareholders and creditors are stronger in the English-based legal systems than in the French-based systems. As a result, countries with English-based legal systems tend to have better developed capital markets in which it is easier for new small companies to finance investment projects and develop their businesses.[10]

Why Do Governments Tolerate and Even Engage in Diversion?

It seems obvious that theft and corruption would impede economic growth by reducing the expected returns to investment, both by domestic citizens and foreign firms, which can choose from a wide variety of countries for the location of investment projects. Why then do governments tolerate these forms of diversion, and why do some governments engage directly in diversion through bribe taking and corruption? Douglass North, the 1993 Nobel prizewinner in economics, points out that government officials may want to maximize their own power and their own monetary incomes rather than being "benevolent social planners" who attempt to maximize the welfare of everyone in society. North's notion takes one step further the conventional economic precept that individuals try to maximize utility and firms try to maximize profits. Government bureaucrats may deliberately take bribes and tolerate theft by Mafia-type organizations in order to maximize income and power or minimize the nuisance of trying to get rid of offenders.[11]

MIT economist Daron Acemoglu and Harvard economist James Robinson attempt to go further and determine the political environment that encourages or discourages government activities that minimize diversion:

> Political elites may block technological and institutional development, because of a political replacement effect. Innovations often erode elites' incumbency advantage, increasing the likelihood that they will be replaced. Fearing replacement, political elites are unwilling to initiate change, and may even block economic development.... It is only when political competition is limited and also their power is threatened that elites will block development.[12]

Empirically, the presence or absence of diversion helps explain not only economic growth but also the values of other determinants of growth like investment rates and education.[13] Just as education is often called "human capital," as

[10] See Rafael La Porta, Florencio Lopez-de-Silanes, Andrei Shleifer, and Robert Vishny, "Law and Finance," *Journal of Political Economy*, vol. 106, 1998, pp. 1113–55.

[11] Douglass C. North, *Structure and Change in Economic History* (New York: Norton, 1991).

[12] Daron Acemoglu and James A. Robinson, "Economic Backwardness in Political Perspective," *American Political Science Review*, February 2006, vol. 100, pp. 115–31. See also Daron Acemoglu, Simon Johnson, and James Robinson, "Institutions as the Fundamental Cause of Long-run Growth," in P. Aghion and S. Durlauf eds., *Handbook of Economic Growth* (Elsevier, 2005).

[13] See the article by Hall and Jones cited in footnote 9. See also Jeffrey D. Sachs and Andrew Warner, "Economic Reform and the Process of Global Integration," *Brookings Papers on Economic Activity*, 1995, vol. 26, no. 1, pp. 1–95.

in the analysis of Chapter 11, in the same way we can refer to a healthy political and legal environment that discourages diversion as "political capital." Since it is a key ingredient both in growth and in fostering other growth-inducing factors like investment in physical capital and human capital, the presence of political capital may be the key to understanding why some countries succeed and others fail at achieving economic growth.[14]

Physical Infrastructure

The capital of Costa Rica, a country in Central America, is San Jose, which is located in the center of the country. To reach either the Atlantic or Pacific Ocean from San Jose, it is necessary to drive on two-lane winding roads, and it often takes three hours or more to drive 60 miles. American tourists sometimes return from Costa Rica by changing planes at the Dallas–Fort Worth International Airport, where outside their airplane window they see seven runways and many miles of taxiways and surrounding multilane expressways. In the immediate vicinity of this airport, there are probably more cubic yards of concrete than in all of Costa Rica.

Infrastructure is any type of capital not owned by the individual business firm that makes the firm's production more efficient. Good highways allow trucking firms to produce more output with the same number of trucks; airports with multiple runways allow airlines to minimize delays; fast railways provide a better transport option than airplanes over distances shorter than 200 miles; ports with many docks help shipping firms to avoid waiting time; well-functioning telephone networks help people communicate easily without waiting for dial tones or having their phone calls interrupted; and a grid providing ample amounts of electricity avoids the inefficiency created by blackouts and brownouts.

Countries differ in how much of their infrastructure is financed by the government. In France, the highways, airports, ports, railroads, telephone network, and electricity grid are all entirely or partly owned by the government. In the United States, infrastructure is owned by a mix of private companies and governmental organizations.

How is physical infrastructure related to growth? In some poor countries, the value of a business investment is reduced by poor highways and airports, by the absence of railroads, by telephone systems in which it takes months for a telephone to be installed and in which dial tones may be delayed, and by electricity systems that have inadequate capacity. Like political capital, physical infrastructure is crucial for growth, and its quantity can be influenced by government decisions.

Geography

If income per capita is plotted on a map of the world, it quickly becomes apparent that rich countries lie in temperate zones and many poor countries lie in tropical zones. Of the 30 economies classified as high income, only two (Hong Kong and Singapore) lie in the tropical zone, and these two small countries have only 1 percent of the total population of the rich countries. Otherwise, all of the rich countries, including those in North America, Western Europe, Northeast Asia, the Southern Cone of Latin America, and Australasia, are located outside

---

[14] A comprehensive introduction to the problem of low economic growth in poor countries is William Easterly, *The Elusive Quest for Growth* (Cambridge, MA: MIT Press, 2002).

INTERNATIONAL PERSPECTIVE

Institutions Matter: South Korea Versus North Korea

There is no better example of the power of institutions as a critical determinant of economic growth than the example of North Korea and South Korea. As we have seen in Figure 1-9 on p. 17, South Korea has experienced remarkable growth since 1960 and in that graph has left the Philippines "in the dust." The success of South Korea is also evident in Table 12-1 on p. 396,

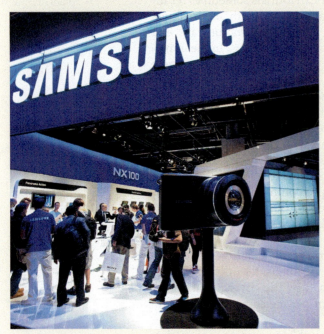

where South Korea achieved a growth rate between 1960 and 2007 of 5.5 percent per year, leaping from 12 percent to 56 percent of the level of U.S. income per person. Correspondingly, South Korea is one of the four green dots in the upper left corner of Figure 12-1, representing the countries that started furthest behind the United States that have grown the fastest since 1960 (the others are China, Hong Kong, and Taiwan).

The two Koreas make an excellent case study. A unified Korea had been a colony of Japan since 1910, and both north and south portions were in identical conditions of economic poverty when World War II ended. After the Korean War ended in a stalemate in 1953, the Korean peninsula was divided into two countries, South Korea and North Korea. Following the divide, the southern half of the peninsula prospered and became an economic powerhouse, competing with Japan in many industries. Among the South Korean products familiar to Americans are Samsung mobile telephones and Hyundai and Kia automobiles. South Korea achieved its success by a combination of emphasis on education, particularly in math and science, and a government policy of encouraging exports and fostering large corporations such as Samsung and Hyundai that became dominant in their industries by producing technologically advanced products at relatively low prices.

The contrast with North Korea could not be greater. In the north, a rigid version of Soviet-style

the tropics. In addition to being located in the tropics, another predictor of poverty is lack of access to sea-based trade. Countries that are both tropical and landlocked, including Mali in Africa (Mali appears as a nonconverging country in Table 12-1 on p. 396), are among the very poorest in the world.

The leading scholar of the role of geography in economic development is Jeffrey Sachs of Columbia University. Sachs proposes four hypotheses regarding the role of geography in the growth performance of poor countries.[15]

1. Technologies developed in the temperate zones may not be applicable to tropical areas, where insects may transmit different diseases than are common in the temperate zones, and where the soil and weather are not suitable for agricultural techniques common in rich countries.

---

[15] This section is based on Jeffrey D. Sachs, "Tropical Underdevelopment," NBER Working Paper 8819 (February 2001). His five hypotheses regarding tropical underdevelopment have been reduced to four to simplify the exposition.

communism that continues today was imposed: All property is owned by the government and there is no incentive for individual initiative or effort other than coercion. North Korea started out in 1953 at the same economic level as South Korea, with the same level of education and per-person income. Also, both were culturally and racially homogeneous.

In the 1960s and 1970s, North Korea did experience significant economic growth, occurring mainly in state-owned manufacturing and bolstered by aid from its communist allies China and the Soviet Union. But per capita income began to decline in the 1980s, then fell precipitously through the 1990s to a current level of around $1,000 per person, perhaps 4 or 5 percent of the level of South Korea.

Floods, droughts, and economic mismanagement resulted in a famine in North Korea during the mid-1990s, with deaths estimated at between 300,000 and 800,000 people per year. A 2006 survey estimated that one out of three North Koreans was malnourished and anemic because of the famine's lingering effects. Matters have been made worse by an enforced "personality cult" and the nuclear weapons mania of the dictator Kim Jong Il, the son of the first dictator, Kim Il Sung.

Foreign estimates suggest that, under Kim Jong Il, North Korea may spend as much as one-quarter of its low level of GDP on its military, further reducing resources for other economic development and needed human services. Recently, several countries, including China and the United States, have tried to use food aid as a bargaining chip to persuade North Korea to end its program of developing nuclear weapons. It is unclear if such efforts will change the North Korean dictator's policies.

Source: http://en.wikipedia.org/wiki/North_Korea

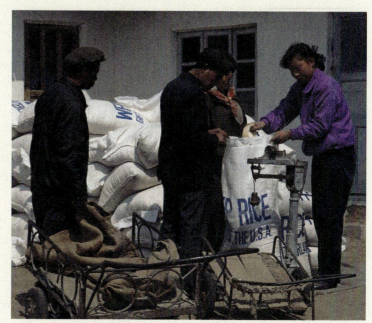

2. Technological innovation in any region often involves high development costs and low production costs, as in the case of Microsoft Windows, where hundreds of millions may be spent in development, but producing each copy costs only a few cents. Thus the bigger the market, the quicker the initial investment will be recouped and the higher the total profits will be. Small economies in tropical regions may be too small to justify any significant investment in technological innovation.

3. Poor productivity in rural agriculture in tropical countries and the prevalence of tropical diseases directly affect population growth—recall in the Solow model that a lower rate of population growth boosts the standard of living and stimulates a transition to a higher capital-labor ratio. As rich countries developed, the rapid growth of agricultural productivity produced a surplus of food and encouraged families to move from farm to city, where the cost of raising children was higher. This encouraged a "demographic transition" to lower birth rates, lower death rates, and a lower rate of population growth.

4. Most tropical countries were conquered and included in the empires of temperate-zone countries like Britain, France, Germany, and Belgium. Colonial domination impeded the process of economic growth by neglecting the formation of human capital through primary and higher education and by limiting economic activity to agriculture and mining, where most of the profits enriched landlords and absentee owners of the colonial power.

The four factors suggested by Sachs do not imply that economic growth for tropical countries is impossible, but the barriers to a growth "take-off" are surely raised by the impediments that he mentions. The box on p. 407 looks further into the puzzle of why some countries in the tropical zone are growth success or "miracle" stories and many others are not.[16]

Integrating the Exogenous Factors in Economic Growth

We can use the phrase "exogenous factors" as a common label for political capital (minimizing theft-like sources of diversion), infrastructure capital, and geography. These factors are exogenous not in the sense that they are fixed and immutable but rather that they are external to the decision-making process of individual households and firms. How should we integrate these exogenous factors into the theories of economic growth studied in Chapter 11?

After we added human capital (H) to the production function linking output (Y) to physical capital (K), labor input (N), and an autonomous growth factor (A) representing technological change, we obtained equation (11.14) on p. 376, rewritten here:

$$Y = AF(K, H, N) \tag{12.7}$$

Here we interpret labor (N) as "brute force" labor, earning the kinds of wages of people doing unskilled jobs suitable for those with an eighth-grade education, while all the extra earnings of the population above that education level are included in human capital (H). In this section we have introduced three new exogenous determinants of growth: political capital (P), infrastructure capital (R), and geography (G). The three new factors enter into the production process in different ways. Infrastructural capital is just like physical capital and enters in the same way. Political capital affects the productivity of the entire production process and enters as a determinant of the previously autonomous growth factor A, as does geography. Technology (T) is also a determinant of A.

Putting these ideas together, our "final" equation that explains the puzzles of economic growth is

$$Y = A(G, P, T)F(K, R, H, N) \tag{12.8}$$

This states in words that output depends on two functions, A and F. The first function (A) depends on the positive or negative role of geographical location (G), the amount of political capital in a country (P), and the level of technology (T). This function (A) is multiplied by the traditional production function (F), which depends on physical capital (K), infrastructure capital (R), human capital (H), and labor input (N).

---

[16] A delightfully readable introduction to the role of geography in economic development is David S. Landes, *The Wealth and Poverty of Nations* (New York: Norton, 1998), Chapter 2.

INTERNATIONAL PERSPECTIVE

Growth Success and Failure in the Tropics

The text examines Jeffrey Sachs's hypothesis that geography is an important determinant of success in achieving economic growth. A tropical location is associated with poor health and low productivity in agriculture. These disadvantages are compounded when a country is landlocked, with no border on a seacoast. Most of the world's nations that are landlocked and located in the tropics are among those that have failed to begin the process of growth that leads to convergence with the rich countries. Mali, listed in Table 12-1, is among those plotted in the lower left corner of Figure 12-3 (see pp. 394–95).[a]

Yet one of the fastest growing countries in the past three decades has been Botswana, an African country that is both tropical and landlocked. What are the secrets of Botswana's success?

In Botswana one political party is dominant. This, together with a legacy of laws and contract procedures dating back to the British colonial period, has allowed the political elite to pursue sensible policies. Foreign investment, mainly by mining companies, is encouraged. Bribery and political corruption have not been a problem. Botswana's biggest problem is a disease that is not limited in its effects to the tropics—around 30 percent of its adults are infected with HIV, the virus that causes AIDS. Through its success in achieving economic growth, Botswana is able to provide free AIDS drugs to anyone who needs them. Overall, Botswana's experience supports the importance of political capital as a key ingredient in economic growth.

Other success stories among tropical nations include Singapore, Thailand, Malaysia, and Hong Kong. These nations have the advantage of not being landlocked, and both Singapore and Hong Kong have the best natural ports in the region. Sachs singles out two common features of these tropical success stories. First, these nations all stressed the improvement of public health early in the development process. Singapore and Hong Kong have the advantage of being islands, where control of tropical diseases is easier. Second, these nations adopted policies to encourage activities other than agriculture. Their governments adopted policies to attract foreign firms to establish manufacturing plants oriented toward exporting most of their output.

The problems of economic development in the tropics, including tropical diseases and poor land, were long ago recognized by the European settlers of the nineteenth century. Despite the colonialization of Africa by Britain, France, Belgium, and Portugal, relatively few European settlers came to live in tropical Africa, choosing to emigrate to the more temperate United States, Canada, Australia, New Zealand, Argentina, and South Africa. Thus, tropical Africa was deprived of the benefits of European culture and education. Most of the Europeans who came to tropical Africa came to exploit raw materials and agricultural products, taking the profits back to Europe and leaving the African natives in a state of poverty.

Unfortunately, the examples of Botswana and the successful nations of Southeast Asia are of only limited relevance for the poorest countries in sub-Saharan Africa. In these countries, the conditions of rampant disease and poor agricultural land are so severe that substantial foreign aid is needed from the rich countries, especially to provide drugs that help control both AIDS and diseases like malaria that are specific to the tropics.

---

[a] This box is based in part on Jeffrey D. Sachs, "Tropical Development," NBER Working Paper 8119 (February 2001), and on "Economics Focus: The Tropical Exception," *Economist* (March 30, 2002). Readers interested in Botswana can read an update at en.wikipedia.org/wiki/Botswana.

The more comprehensive theory of growth depicted in equation (12.8) helps us to understand many of the puzzles involving the continuing inability of poor nations to take off on a sustainable growth path that would ultimately lead to convergence with the rich countries. The geographical factor suggests that some poor countries may never converge; the political factor helps explain why some countries are not attractive locations for foreign investment; and the technological factor itself depends on a set of determinants that are not included in the equation.

One of the growth puzzles posed in Chapter 11 asked about the "immigration puzzle." Without any change in his or her educational attainment *(H)*, an immigrant to the United States from Guatemala can obtain a wage at least ten times higher. This difference is too high to be explained simply by differences in physical capital per person. But now we have learned that there is a long list of factors that allow everyone in the United States to be more productive than in Guatemala, including geography, political capital, and infrastructure. Further, even though the immigrant's human capital does not change simply through the act of immigration, the *average* level of human capital of other members of the population is much higher in the new country (the United States) than in the original country (Guatemala). Because the United States has much larger quantities of these factors that favor economic growth, the mere act of moving from one country to another can drastically change the demand for the labor of the unskilled Guatemalan. In the United States, many people have incomes sufficiently high to make them willing to pay $10 per hour for lawn-mowing services, while in Guatemala, almost no one has an income high enough to pay anything to have his or her lawn mowed.

12-6 CASE STUDY

Uneven U.S. Productivity Growth Across Eras

Up to this point, the chapter has focused on the need to explain why some nations remain so poor while the standard of living in rich countries is many times higher and continues to advance. For citizens of rich countries like the United States, a question closer to home is why the pace of economic growth varies so much over eras. Growth in productivity was substantially faster during 1900–72 than during 1972–95. After 1995 the growth rate picked up, only to slow down again after 2004.

The long-term growth rate of productivity matters a lot for the future standard of living of every student reading this book. For instance, for a student aged 20 today, productivity will double in 23 years if its growth rate is 3 percent per year but will take 69 years to double if its growth rate is only 1 percent per year.[17] Thus we care a lot about whether the future growth in productivity will be slow as in 1973–95 or fast as in 1995–2004.

---

[17] A simple rule allows us to calculate how long it would take for something to double in size if its growth rate is x percent per year. We start with the growth rate formula in the box on p. 41 $x = 100 * LN(X_t/X_{t-s})/s$, where x is the growth rate, s is the number of years between the beginning year and the end year, X_t is the value in the end year, and X_{t-s} is the growth rate in the beginning year. We multiply each side of this formula by s, divide by x, replace X_t by the number 2 (since the quantity doubles from the beginning year to the end year), and replace X_{t-s} by the number 1. The resulting formula is $s = 100 * LN(2/1)/x$. Since the natural log of 2 is 0.693, the formula becomes $s = 69.3/x$. This "rule of 70" (since 69.3 is close to 70) allows us to calculate the number of years it takes anything to double if its growth rate is x.

The Four Eras of Postwar U.S. Productivity Growth

The rapid advance in the U.S. standard of living in the first half of the twentieth century was fueled by growth in labor productivity that averaged slightly below 2 percent per year. In this section we focus on the more recent history since 1960. The red line in Figure 12-5 shows the annual growth rate of actual labor productivity (real GDP divided by hours of work in the total economy) over the period since 1960. Because growth in actual productivity is so erratic, zigging and zagging up and down every few years, we also display as a green line the "trend" in labor productivity growth that smooths out the zigzags.

The green trend line shows that the productivity trend in the 1960s was considerably better than the 2 percent historical average achieved in the half-century before 1950. The trend reaches 2.7 percent in 1961–62 and then steadily slows down to only 1.3 percent in 1979. The period of relatively slow productivity growth, between 1.3 and 1.6 percent, extends over the two decades between 1976 and 1995. Then beginning in 1995 the trend exhibits a strong revival, reaching 2.4 percent in 2002 before slipping back to 1.8 percent in 2006–10.

We can simplify the evidence in Figure 12-5 by referring to four eras of productivity growth since 1960, described as "fast," "slow," "fast," and "uncertain."

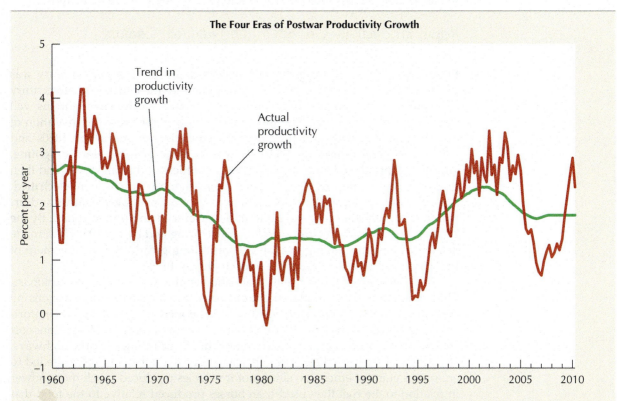

Figure 12-5 Growth Rate of Labor Productivity in the United States, 1960–2010

The zigzag red line shows the annual growth rate of labor productivity in the total U.S. economy over the previous eight quarters. The green line shows the long-term trend in productivity growth, smoothing out the zigzags in order to give a smoother estimate of the average performance of productivity growth over different eras.

Source: Bureau of Economic Analysis and Bureau of Labor Statistics. Details in Appendix C-4. Please note that the productivity data used in this chart and this section of the text refer to productivity in the total economy, not the frequently cited data for the nonfarm private business sector.

Back in the 1960s, economists and policymakers assumed that productivity growth of close to 3 percent would last forever, but it did not. The slowdown in productivity growth continued throughout the 1960s and 1970s, reaching a low point in 1979–80 as shown by the green line. Overall the "slow" period lasted from the mid-1970s to the mid-1990s.

Then productivity growth revived during the late 1990s, the heyday of the "dot.com" boom in which the Internet was invented and Web surfing became a near-universal pastime. Much to the surprise of many observers, rapid productivity growth continued until 2004, even though the dot.com stock market and investment booms collapsed in 2000–02. The productivity trend (the green line in Figure 12-5) declined after 2004 but not all the way back to the growth rate of the slow period. Thus we label this fourth era of productivity growth "uncertain" instead of either "slow" or "fast."

Our discussion in this section is divided into four sections corresponding to the four eras. We first ask why productivity growth was rapid in the 1960s and indeed through most of the twentieth century before 1960. Then we identify the factors that caused productivity growth to slow down after the early 1970s and the factors that caused the revival in 1995–2004. This section concludes with some speculative comments about the future of U.S. productivity growth, the key determinant of how rapidly the American standard of living will rise in the future.

Rapid Productivity Growth in the Twentieth Century Until the 1970s

Productivity growth during the first two-thirds of the twentieth century was propelled by the monumental "Great Inventions" of the late nineteenth century that were so important that they continued to spawn additional inventions well into the twentieth century. The most important of these were the invention of electricity in the 1870s and the internal combustion engine in the 1880s and 1890s. The initial impact of electricity was to make possible electric lighting, which was introduced almost immediately in offices and retail stores, and then gradually into homes. By 1930 68 percent of American homes were electrified. Another early application of electricity was to make possible elevators and urban transit, both streetcars and rapid transit overhead and underground. By the 1920s electricity had revolutionized manufacturing and by the 1950s had made residential air-conditioning available, contributing greatly to the movement of industry and households from the north to the south.[18]

The invention of the internal combustion engine was no less revolutionary. This made possible the replacement of horse-drawn carriages and wagons by cars, trucks, busses, and airplanes that became increasingly efficient, comfortable, and powerful over the first half of the twentieth century. Motor transport spawned numerous complementary innovations, including airports, highways, suburbs, and supermarkets. The replacement of the horse and the mule led to enormous gains of efficiency, since motor vehicles produced much more power in relation to the fuel they used than horses produced relative to the food that they ate.

In addition to electricity and the internal combustion engine, the "big two" of the Great Inventions of the late nineteenth century, there were many other inventions. These included the telephone, the motion picture, and chemicals.

---

[18] A comparison of the impact of the Internet to the great inventions of the late nineteenth century is provided in Robert J. Gordon, "Does the New Economy Measure Up to the Great Inventions of the Past?" *Journal of Economic Literature*, vol. 14, no. 4 (Fall 2000), pp. 49–74.

The twentieth century brought the first commercial radio station in 1920 and the first demonstration of commercial television in 1939. One of the less known inventions was Pasteur's "germ theory of disease" (1869), which led directly to massive investments in reservoirs and urban water and sanitation equipment. Very few houses and apartments had indoor plumbing in 1890, but by 1950 indoor plumbing was almost universal. Similarly central heating became standard during the same period.

This list of inventions accumulates to an enormous change in the standard of living of the average American between 1890 and 1950. While there have been many inventions since then, most notably mainframe computers in the 1950s followed by jet air travel in the 1960s, personal computers in the 1980s, and the Internet in the 1990s, these made less of a difference to everyday life than electric light, elevators, air-conditioning, motor vehicles, air travel, telephones, motion pictures, radio, and television. The development of indoor toilets and clean water helps to explain a startling fact: *The annual improvement in life expectance was three times faster between 1900 and 1950 as it was from 1950 to 2000.*

Sources of the Productivity Growth Slowdown from the 1970s to 1995

1. **Demographic changes.** The 1970s and 1980s witnessed large increases in the population of teenagers and of the share of females who had jobs instead of staying home. The influx of these relatively inexperienced workers reduced the average efficiency of the workforce. Furthermore, because their wages were less, labor became cheap relative to physical capital (which we designated K in Chapter 11). Growth in capital slowed, growth in the labor force rose, and the result was much slower growth in the ratio of capital to labor (K/N).

2. **Raw materials and energy.** The late Michael Bruno of Hebrew University and Jeffrey Sachs of Columbia University stressed the direct effect of the higher relative prices of energy and raw materials (the "supply shocks" of Chapter 9).[19]

   Higher energy prices induced firms to use less energy, and this reduced the productivity of the other factors of production, capital and labor. More recent research by William Nordhaus of Yale University identifies particular energy-dependent industries that bore the brunt of the slowdown in productivity growth, including oil and gas extraction, motor vehicles, electricity generation, pipelines, and air transportation.[20]

3. **Infrastructure.** Section 12-5 and equation (12.8) on p. 406 included infrastructure capital as an important source of growth. Rich nations differ from poor nations by spending more on education, sewers, highways, airports, and other types of infrastructure investment. Of particular importance was the timing of the construction of the interstate highway system between 1958 and 1972, overall a period of high productivity growth. Once the basic interstate system was completed in the early 1970s, there were no longer further benefits equivalent to the one-time-only improvement in productivity that came from substantial increases in the speeds at which truck drivers could travel.

---

[19] Michael Bruno and Jeffrey Sachs, *Economics of Worldwide Stagnation* (Cambridge, MA: Harvard University Press, 1985).

[20] William D. Nordhaus, "Retrospective on the 1970s Productivity Slowdown," NBER Working Paper 10950 (December 2004).

The Productivity Growth Revival, 1995–2004

The historical record in Figure 12-5 on p. 409 shows how productivity growth revived after 1995. As recently as 1997–98, economists had been struggling to explain "Solow's paradox" as set forth a decade earlier by Robert M. Solow (the inventor of the Solow growth model): "We can see the computer age everywhere except in the productivity statistics." But by 1999 and 2000, economists suddenly looked up from their word processors to discover that before they had satisfactorily explained Solow's paradox, it had been rendered obsolete by the post-1995 productivity revival. Suddenly the economy was awash not only in computers, but also in productivity growth.

The sudden revival of productivity growth, after years in which Solow's paradox accurately captured the lack of productivity payoff from computers, appeared to vindicate Stanford economist Paul David, who had predicted years earlier that the benefits of computers were being delayed, but after some period would finally begin to boost economywide productivity. His "delay hypothesis" was based on the historical example of electricity, which was invented in the 1880s but had its big productivity payoff four decades later in the 1920s. Enthusiasts treated the New Economy as a fundamental industrial revolution as great or greater in importance than the Great Inventions of the late nineteenth century.

Causes of the Productivity Growth Revival

1. **The production and use of computers.** Initially it appeared that most of the productivity growth revival could be explained by the production of computers and other high-tech equipment, but by 1999–2000 the productivity revival had continued long enough and was big enough to require additional explanations. It appeared that productivity growth had increased not just in firms *producing* the high-tech equipment but also in several sectors of the economy that were heavy *users* of the equipment, including the securities industry (where daily trading totals of four billion shares per day became commonplace) as well as wholesale and retail trade.

2. **Continued revival after the collapse of computer investment.** The "dot.com" investment boom collapsed after 2000. Investment in computers and software declined sharply as a share of GDP and indeed throughout the 2000–10 decade never regained the share of 1999–2000. Thus analysts who had attributed the post-1995 productivity growth revival to computers were astonished when, as shown by the red line in Figure 12-5, actual productivity growth in 2001–04 was actually faster than in the dot.com era of 1995–2000. Why did this happen?[21]. One reason was that the simultaneous collapse of the stock market and of profits in 2000–02 led business firms to cut costs more vigorously than in previous postwar recessions. Layoffs were severe, and employment continued to decline in 2002–03 even after output had started to recover. With output growing and jobs shrinking, productivity (output per hour) soared.[22]

---

[21] This section summarizes part of Robert J. Gordon, "Exploding Productivity Growth: Context, Causes, and Implications," *Brookings Papers on Economic Activity*, no. 2 (2003) pp. 207–98.

[22] The hypothesis that declining profits led to both the slump of employment and the boom of productivity growth has recently been supported in a cross-industry empirical study. See Stephen D. Oliner, Daniel E. Sichel, and Kevin J. Stiroh, "Explaining a Productive Decade," *Brookings Papers on Economic Activity*, 2007, no. 1, pp. 81–152.

3. **Production of more output with fewer employees.** In addition to the profit squeeze and associated cost cutting, another hypothesis centers on *intangible capital,* types of investment that are not included in the government's definition of computer and software investment. While the use of the Web was introduced in the late 1990s, computers did not become truly effective until old business practices were changed and employees were retrained to use the computers in new ways. In short the benefits of the invention of the Internet spilled over from the late 1990s into the 2001–04 period even though the government's measure of computer investment declined sharply. A perfect example is the airport electronic kiosk that provides you with a boarding pass without the need for an airline employee to be present; these became prevalent not in the dot.com era of the late 1990s but during 2001–04.[23]

Productivity Growth After 2004 and in the Future

Figure 12-5 shows that productivity growth slowed down markedly after 2003–04, both in the actual growth rate numbers along the red line and the estimated productivity growth trend along the green line. Was this a temporary hiatus in the post-1995 productivity growth revival or an ominous cloud on the horizon?

Over the years 2005–07, economists became more pessimistic about future productivity growth. Some pessimists suggested that the post-1995 revival had come to an end and was by its nature a "one-time-only" event rather than the start of decade after decade of rapid productivity growth. One argument was that the mid-1990s marriage of the personal computer and communication, resulting in the Internet and the World Wide Web, clearly stimulated productivity growth in the late 1990s but could only be invented once.

A second argument is that, while inventions continue with the iPod, iPhone, iPad, and others, these are mainly beneficial to consumers and have a relatively small impact on business productivity. A third argument is that, as we have suggested about the 2001–04 productivity boom, the apparent causes were inherently temporary. The crash in stock markets and profits caused extreme cost cuts and job layoffs that temporarily boosted productivity growth, but once hiring resumed productivity growth declined sharply. Similarly, the intangible capital hypothesis holds that the benefits of the 1990s computer investment boom were delayed, but only for so long.

As of late 2010, the future growth of productivity is highly uncertain. Optimists point to the sharp upturn in the actual (red) line in 2009. But pessimists point to the parallel with 2001–04. The economic crisis of 2008–09, including the collapse of profits and the stock market, echoed what happened eight years earlier. Because firms cut costs so drastically, they overreacted in laying off workers more than was justified by the decline in output, and measured productivity growth bounced up. But in 2010–11 productivity growth had slowed sharply after the 2009 spurt, just as it did in 2005–07 after the 2001–04 upsurge.

Over a longer period of 10 or 20 years, future U.S. growth in real income per capita is likely to be slower than over the 20 previous years 1987–2007 for two main reasons.[24] First, the impending retirement of the baby boom

---

[23] See Susanto Basu et al., "The Case of the Missing Productivity Growth, or Does Information Technology Explain Why Productivity Accelerated in the United States but not in the United Kingdom?" *NBER Macroeconomics Annual 2003,* pp. 9–63.

[24] The analysis in this section is based partly on Robert J. Gordon, "Revisiting Productivity Growth Over the Past Century With a View of the Future," NBER Working Paper 15834, March 2010.

generation (those who were born in 1947–63) will reduce the number of workers relative to the number of retired people. Since hours of work per person (including the entire population aged from 16 to above 100 in age) will fall, this means by definition that income per person will grow more slowly than productivity.

The second underlying cause of slower future growth, not just in the standard of living but in productivity itself, is the end of a century-long increase of an increase in the educational attainment of Americans. Steadily as elementary education spread in the late nineteenth century, as high school education became universal between 1910 and 1940, and then as millions went to college after World War II, the average number of years of education of the American population marched steadily higher. But this progress stopped around 1990. The average number of school years completed by Americans stopped increasing. Yet other nations that had long remained behind caught up and surged ahead. Why?

There are two basic answers. The first is that American higher education has a "cost disease" almost as pernicious as that of medical care. Many elite universities enroll the same number of students as 30 years ago but at much higher real cost, that is, the nominal cost adjusted for economy-wide inflation. Among the components of higher cost are faculty salaries, no-teaching leaves given to faculty as part of faculty recruiting, extra buildings despite the same number of students, and the costs of maintaining those buildings (light, heat, janitors). The second reason is the problems that students and their parents have in financing the higher cost of college education. Federal aid for scholarships is less generous than previously, and budget problems of state governments have caused rapid increases in tuition at state universities that previously charged only modest tuition. In short, many young Americans are not going to college because they and their parents cannot afford it, and they do not want to burden themselves with six-digit student loans.

As we learned above in equations (12.7) and (12.8) on p. 406, human capital (H), i.e., education, is an input into the production function that makes each worker more productive. The slowdown in the growth of human capital in the United States since 1990 is one of several reasons to be pessimistic about future growth in the standard of living, even if the pace of innovation remains as rapid as it was over the past two decades.

GLOBAL ECONOMIC CRISIS FOCUS
Lingering Effects of the 2007–09 Recession on Long-Term Economic Growth

Another reason to be pessimistic is the lingering effects of persistently high unemployment caused by the recession of 2007–09, which looks likely to continue for several more years after 2010. The millions suffering from long-term unemployment, which persists year after year, begin to lose their job-related skills. Their human capital begins to erode. This slows the growth in the H that appears in the production functions of equations (12.7) and (12.8).

And investment is relatively low because factories are empty and office buildings are partly vacant, so there is little profit to be made by building new

(continued)

factories and office buildings. This causes the growth in physical capital *(K)* to slow down as well.

The pros and cons of alternative stimulative macroeconomic policies were discussed above in Chapters 5 and 6. Now we learn that the search for successful macroeconomic policies matters not just for the task of bringing down the unemployment rate but also of offsetting the negative effects of the recession and its aftermath on long-term economic growth.

Thus the outlook is for relatively slow long-term growth over the next two decades, due to the retirement of the baby boomers, the rising cost of higher education as a barrier to the creation of human capital, and the lingering effects of the 2007–09 recession in retarding the growth of human and physical capital. Are there any policies that could help offset this tendency toward slower growth?

The retirement of the baby boomers is a problem because it reduces the ratio of the population of working age relative to the population of retired people who are not working. A partial solution available to policymakers is to encourage immigration of young people, particularly those with high skills. The rising relative cost of higher education calls for policies to restrain the cost disease, which is difficult to achieve since many of the universities with rapidly rising costs are private institutions with their own large endowments. A useful policy would be for the federal government to administer income-contingent loans, a program in which those going into lower-paid occupations like school teaching and nursing would pay back less than the full amount of their loans but those who make high incomes in finance or business would pay back more than the full amount. Finally, cures for persistent unemployment and low investment call for stimulative macroeconomic policies, as discussed above in Chapters 5 and 6. ◆

SELF-TEST

Explain how each of the following contributed to fast or slow growth in labor productivity and to which era the factor most clearly applies (pre-1970, 1970s to 1995, 1995 to 2004, after 2004).

1. Increase in female labor-force participation
2. Completion of the interstate highway system
3. Retirement of the baby boom generation
4. Invention of the Internet and World Wide Web

12-7 CASE STUDY

The Productivity Growth Contrast Between Europe and the United States

American travelers to several of the more prosperous European countries, including France, Germany, and Sweden, notice interesting differences. For instance, it is much less common in Europe for supermarkets to employ baggers in addition to checkout cashiers. Parking lots are more likely to be fully automated than to employ attendants. Valet parking services are rarely seen. The bus boy occupation—clearing and setting tables—that is so prevalent in American restaurants at the middle-price and high-price level is largely absent in similar restaurants in these European countries.

These observations are symptoms of a broader set of differences in the evolution of the economies of the United States and leading European nations over the past three decades. While the United States lagged behind Europe's growth rate of productivity in the 1973–95 period, it has surged ahead with substantially faster productivity growth than Europe since 1995. And over the entire period between the mid-1980s and the onset of recession in 2007 the United States also had a much superior record in achieving growth in jobs and maintaining a relatively low unemployment rate.

Europe Catches Up, Then Falls Back

We have already examined on p. 19 a graph that contrasts the *growth rate* of labor productivity in the United States compared to Europe, slower before 1995 and faster since 1995. In contrast Figure 12-6 shows the *level* of labor productivity in the United States compared with Europe. During the long period when American productivity was growing slowly, Europe caught up from 60 percent of the American level in 1970 to 88 percent in 1995. During this period, Europeans emphasized policies that made labor expensive to employ. As a result, in Europe employment grew slowly but productivity grew rapidly as firms tried to minimize their use of labor input to avoid its high cost. The United States during this period was pursuing policies that made it cheap for firms to hire unskilled labor, leading to many low-wage jobs but also leading to the slow productivity growth.

After 1995 productivity growth in the United States revived, as we learned in Section 12-6. This occurred not because the United States changed its policies that encouraged the employment of low-skilled labor, and indeed immigration increased steadily throughout the 1990s. What changed in the United States was the invention of the Internet and the World Wide Web, an invention dominated by American-owned firms like Microsoft, Apple, and Intel. While Europe adopted these new innovations in its manufacturing and service industries, it did not do so as rapidly as the United States, and as a result the ratio of European to American productivity slipped back from 88 percent in 1995 to 84 percent in 2001.

Different Institutions in Europe and the United States

The long period during 1973–95 of slow productivity growth and rapid employment growth in the United States compared to Europe reflected systematic differences in institutions and policies. The United States has relatively weak labor unions, a relatively low and declining real minimum wage, and substantial competition for low-skilled jobs from legal and illegal immigrants. In some countries like France it is very expensive to hire low-skilled workers, because of a high minimum wage and high payroll taxes that finance government-supported medical care and old-age pensions.

As these differences in labor market policies fostered a catching up of European productivity toward the U.S. level in 1973–95, Europe suffered from

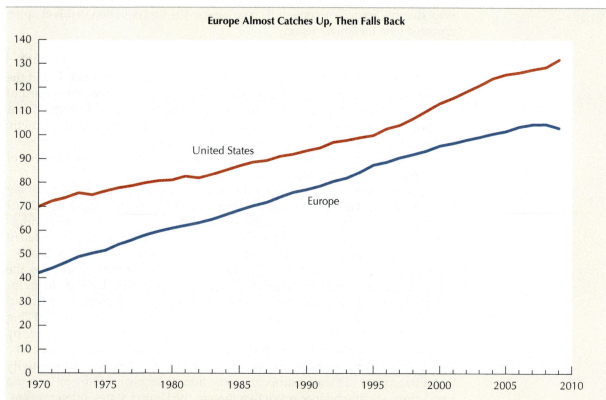

Figure 12-6 **Level of Labor Productivity in Europe and the United States, 1970–2010**

The level of productivity in the United States is displayed as an index number with 1995 = 100. The level of productivity in the 15 members of the pre-2004 European Union is displayed as an index number with 1995 = 88, based on data showing that in 1995 European productivity was roughly 12 percent below that of the United States. By 2001 the level of productivity in Europe slipped back relative to the United States to a ratio of 78 percent.

Source: Groningen Growth and Development Center, *Total Economy Database*. Details in Appendix C-4.

the lack of employment growth that was the counterpart of a strong productivity performance. Employment stagnated, unemployment was high, the average duration of unemployment was much longer than in the United States, job prospects for young people were bleak, labor-force participation languished, and many workers were encouraged to retire at young ages compared to the United States. Europeans also reacted to the scarcity of jobs by taking longer vacations than in the United States, in effect spreading the available work among more people.

How Could Europe Be So Productive Yet So Poor?

As a result, the European standard of living remained at around 70 percent of the U.S. level, even though the productivity ratio reached 88 percent in 1995.

Why did this occur? We come full circle back to the first equation in this chapter, repeated here for convenience:

$$y - n - (y - h) = h - n. \tag{12.1}$$

Here the growth rate of output is y, the growth rate of labor hours is h, and the growth rate of the population is n. The reason that the European standard of living ($y - n$) grew more slowly than labor productivity ($y - h$) is that labor hours per member of the population ($h - n$) experienced negative growth. Long vacations, high unemployment, low labor-force participation, and early retirement meant that Europeans worked many fewer hours per member of the population than occurred in the United States.

Why did Europe fall behind, with its ratio of labor productivity declining from 88 percent of the U.S. level in 1995 to 84 percent in 2001 to 78 percent in 2010? There are two reasons: The first centered on differences between service industries in Europe and the United States, and the second related to the very different responses of European labor markets to the Global Economic Crisis after 2007.

Important new research has identified the service sector in Europe as the source of Europe's ongoing failure to catch up to the level of U.S. productivity. The European problem centers on wholesale and retail trade, where the United States has achieved big productivity gains as large new stores (often called "big boxes") have been constructed in suburbs and at freeway interchanges by Walmart, Target, Home Depot, Best Buy, and other nationwide retailers. The European retailing industry has not participated in the "big box" productivity boom because of differing European institutions. European zoning or land use regulations are much more restrictive than in the United States, often preventing development of the big boxes, and there is substantial political pressure in Europe to preserve small, inefficient stores in the city center. More generally in Europe, differences in national customs and languages make it harder for retailers to expand across all of Europe, and regulations make it more difficult to start new businesses.

However, the decline in European productivity relative to the U.S. level in 2007–10 does not shine a favorable light on U.S. institutions. Faced with roughly the same sharp decline in output as in the United States, European firms responded very differently. In place of the mass layoffs in the United States, which cut labor input relative to output and raised productivity, in Europe mass layoffs were avoided, particularly in Germany, the largest European country. To create an incentive for firms to retain workers, the government encouraged firms to reduce the hours of workers, say from 40 to 20 hours per week. Yet the worker's salary was not cut in half but was largely maintained, thanks to government subsidies to this "work-sharing" set of policies. By avoiding mass layoffs, Germany and to some extent other European countries have avoided much of the human tragedy of long-term unemployment that has afflicted the United States, but at the cost of stagnant productivity.

To summarize, during the 1970–95 period Europe's productivity level increased rapidly from 60 to 88 percent of the U.S. level, but the same factors that raised productivity growth also reduced labor input per member of the population, causing the living standard in Europe to stagnate relative to the United States. Since 1995 Europe has fallen back, due in large part to its inefficient and overregulated service sector. A further decline in European productivity in 2007–10 resulted as European policies attempted to avoid the mass layoffs that occurred in the United States. ◆

12-8 Conclusion on the Great Questions of Growth

This chapter takes us considerably further toward an understanding of economic growth than did the simple theories examined in Chapter 11. We have learned that the achievement of economic growth requires more than simply saving and investment in physical capital and then sitting back to wait for the fruits of exogenous and automatic technological progress. Economies do not obtain technical progress for free, but only through a costly process of research, development, and invention. Without a continual stream of important inventions since the year 1800, continuing investments in steam engines and wooden plows would have left productivity little better than it was in that year. Most of today's standard of living relies on inventions of products and processes, including the railroad, internal combustion engine, and electricity, that did not exist in 1800.

Poor countries can obtain technological innovations that originated in rich countries by copying the innovation, by importing it, or by encouraging investment by foreign firms that bring technology with them. But some poor nations are better able than others to obtain technology through these channels. We have seen that governments can encourage growth by promoting education, by building political capital that minimizes diversion (including theft, bribes, and corruption), and by developing infrastructure capital. Yet even the most enlightened governments still face special obstacles to growth if their countries are located in the tropics. This makes the growth achievement of such tropical East Asian countries as Thailand and Singapore especially impressive.

Closer to home, American students may sympathize with the continuing struggle of poor nations, but they also are interested in the outlook for their own standard of living. Will their standard of living stagnate or double within a single generation? For two decades between 1973 and 1995, the growth in U.S. productivity was much slower than before 1973, and growth in real wages stagnated. While some explanations of this productivity slowdown period are unconvincing, it appears that differing labor market institutions constitute a unifying theme explaining faster productivity growth in Europe than in the United States over 1973–95, combined with slower European growth in employment and hours of labor input.

The post-1995 U.S. productivity revival has occurred despite labor market institutions that make it easy for American firms to hire low-skilled labor. The first phase of the revival through the year 2000 represented the beneficial effects on productivity of the New Economy boom in high-tech computer and telecommunications investment. The surprising American further revival in productivity growth in 2002–04, despite the collapse of New Economy investment, resulted in part from a collapse in profits that unleashed unusually savage cost cutting as firms were forced to produce more output with fewer workers. Another related explanation is that many new business practices were made possible by the pervasive spread of computers and invention of the World Wide Web, and that learning by business firms made possible by high-tech investment in the 1990s carried over to make possible faster productivity growth during 2002–04.

Productivity growth slowed markedly after 2004, and despite a temporary burst of productivity growth in 2009, projections of future growth over the next two decades were pessimistic for three reasons. First, the retirement of the baby boom generation will reduce the ratio of the working-age population to the retired population that no longer works. Second, cost inflation in higher education is steadily making higher education more expensive, thus reducing the growth of human capital, a crucial ingredient in long-term economic growth. Third, the lingering effects of the 2007–09 recession in the form of long-term unemployment and reduced investment will restrain the growth rate of human and physical capital for years to come.

Summary

1. The big questions of economic growth are the continuing income gap between the rich and poor countries, the sources of growth "miracles" of formerly poor countries, and the cause of productivity growth slowdowns and revivals within the group of rich nations.

2. The standard of living is output per person or per capita, labor productivity is output per hour, and multifactor productivity is output per weighted input of labor and capital together. The growth rates of labor productivity and of the real wage are equal if labor's share in the national income remains constant.

3. While convergence of poor countries to the income levels of rich countries is predicted by the Solow growth model of Chapter 11, it has not happened in fact for many poor countries. While the Solow model predicts that poor nations should grow faster than rich nations, fully half of the poor nations in 1960 grew more slowly than the United States from 1960 to 1990.

4. Poor countries typically invest a smaller share of their incomes than rich countries and have low amounts of human capital. Yet low investment in physical and human capital may be as much a consequence of poverty as a cause of it. Low levels of education prevent the poorest countries from utilizing advances in technology developed by the rich nations.

5. Poor countries can obtain modern technology by copying it, by importing machinery embodying modern technology, or by attracting foreign investment of firms that bring modern technology with them. Each of these methods confronts obstacles, since modern technology is hard to copy, some countries are too poor to import it, and some countries are unattractive as locations for foreign investment.

6. Impediments to growth that handicap many poor countries include "diversion" (crime, bribery, corruption), inadequate infrastructure (poor highways, inadequate telephone systems), and geographical handicaps, particularly location in the tropics and lack of access to ports on an ocean.

7. U.S. productivity growth was rapid before 1970, slow from the early 1970s to 1995, rapid between 1995 and 2004, and slow again after 2004. Rapid growth before 1970 can be explained by the Great Inventions of the late nineteenth century, particularly electricity and the internal combustion engine, and all the further inventions in the twentieth century that they made possible.

8. Slower productivity growth in 1973–95 is explained in part by an increase in the labor supply of inexperienced teenagers and women, and the consequent decline in the capital-labor ratio. Other causes of slowing growth included higher energy prices, reduced investment in infrastructure, and the diminished role of the Great Inventions that had made possible rapid growth earlier in the century.

9. More rapid growth between 1995 and 2001 was due to the invention of the Internet and the related investment boom in computer hardware and software. Continuing productivity growth in 2001–04, despite the collapse of the investment boom, can be attributed to delayed learning about how to use the computers and software, together with aggressive cost cutting to reduce labor input.

10. Three factors suggesting the possibility of slow future growth include the retirement of the baby boom generation, the growing difficulty of Americans in paying for higher education, and the lingering effects on human and physical capital of the 2007–09 recession and its aftermath.

11. The level of productivity in Europe increased toward the U.S. level up to 1995 but since then has fallen behind. Europe has been slower to apply the benefits of the computer revolution, due to the small size of its retail outlets and heavy regulation that prevents U.S.-style development of "big box" retailers. Europe also sacrificed productivity by adopting measures to protect jobs during the Global Economic Crisis.

Concepts

infrastructure   standard of living   labor productivity

Questions

1. What is the significance of the modifier "multifactor" in "multifactor productivity"?
2. Under what conditions will labor's share of national income grow? Decline? Remain constant over time?
3. Does the empirical evidence validate the predictions of the Solow model regarding convergence? Explain.
4. Is it true that a high investment rate is a precondition for convergence?
5. What is the relationship between real wages and labor productivity? How would real wages and labor productivity be affected by:
   (a) an increase in the quantity of other productive factors (such as capital, energy, and raw materials) used in production;
   (b) a decline in the size of the workforce resulting from lower rates of population growth and immigration?
   Is the cause-and-effect relationship between real wages and productivity the same in each case?
6. Explain what is meant by *diversion*. Discuss why governments tolerate or engage in diversion.
7. "Because each factor of production is paid its marginal product, the fraction of the population engaged in research and development is economically optimal." Comment.
8. Discuss what the difference between the legal systems of former colonies of the United Kingdom and those of France and Spain, as well as the difference in the growth rates of North and South Korea, suggest concerning the importance of political capital in determining economic growth.
9. What is *infrastructure* and why is it important for economic growth? Suppose that in order to finance additional infrastructure spending, a country has to raise taxes on other inputs that contribute to economic growth. In principle, what is the rule for how high taxes should be raised in terms of financing additional infrastructure spending? What might be some of the practical difficulties in implementing this rule, particularly in poor countries?
10. What role does Professor Jeffrey Sachs suggest geography plays in explaining the growth performance of poor countries? What does the International Perspective box on p. 407 suggest concerning the role of government in overcoming the potential barrier against economic growth that geography presents?
11. What is the "immigration puzzle" described in Chapter 11? How does the expanded model of economic growth described in equation (12.8) help to solve this puzzle?
12. What were the "Great Inventions" of the late nineteenth century, and how did they contribute to the rapid growth of productivity and living standards in the first two thirds of the twentieth century?
13. Discuss how the reasons for the post-1995 revival of productivity growth were different for the 1995–2000 period as contrasted to the 2000–04 period.
14. Explain why the growth in real income per capita over the next 10 to 20 years is likely to be slower that it was from 1987–2007.
15. "Restrictive monetary policy will lower the rate of labor productivity growth. Restrictive fiscal policy, on the other hand, will raise it." Is this statement true, false, or uncertain? Explain.
16. Convinced that strong measures must be taken to stimulate productivity growth, Senator Progrowth introduces a bill to increase federal government spending on education by $150 billion. Why might those who agree with the senator about the importance of economic growth nonetheless question the wisdom of this legislation?
17. Explain why labor productivity in Europe declined relative to the labor productivity in the United States after 1995.

Problems

 Visit www.MyEconLab.com to complete these or similar exercises.

*Indicates that the problem requires the Appendix to Chapter 11.

1. Calculate the growth rates of output (y) and labor productivity ($y - h$) in each of the following scenarios. Assume that the share of capital in total income (b) is 0.25.

(a)

y	a	k	h	$y - h$
—	2.5	2	1	—
—	2.0	2	1	—
—	1.5	2	1	—
—	1.0	2	1	—

(b)

	y	a	k	h	$y-h$
	—	2.5	2.0	1	—
	—	2.5	1.5	1	—
	—	2.5	1.0	1	—
	—	2.5	0.5	1	—

(c)

	y	a	k	h	$y-h$
	—	2.5	2.0	1.0	—
	—	2.5	2.0	1.5	—
	—	2.5	2.0	2.0	—
	—	2.5	2.0	2.5	—

Based on your calculations, what happens to output growth and labor productivity growth as MFP growth declines, capital input growth declines, and labor input growth increases, holding the other variables constant? Are these the results you would expect? Why or why not?

2. Suppose that in Country 1 the growth rates of multifactor productivity (a), capital (k), and labor (h) are 2.5, 3, and 1 percent per year, respectively, and that capital's share of output (b) equals 0.25. Initially output per hour equals 40 in Country 1 and 10 in Country 2.

   (a) Calculate the labor productivity growth rate in Country 1.

   (b) Calculate output per hour in Country 1 at the end of ten, twenty, and thirty years.

   (c) Suppose that the labor productivity grows four times as fast in Country 2 as it does in Country 1 for the first ten years, three times as fast for the second ten years, and twice as fast for the third ten years. Calculate output per hour in Country 2 at the end of ten, twenty, and thirty years.

   (d) Calculate Country 2's output per hour as a percentage of Country 1's output per hour at the end of ten, twenty, and thirty years. Are these calculations consistent with the predictions of the Solow growth model?

3. (a) Suppose labor productivity and the GDP deflator are growing at 2 percent per year. For labor's share of income to remain constant, how fast must nominal wages be increasing?

   (b) Suppose that labor productivity growth declines to 1.2 percent per year. What happens to labor's share of income if the growth rates in nominal wages and the GDP deflator are unchanged? Suppose that the Fed keeps the rate of inflation constant. What must the new growth rate of nominal wages be for labor's share of income to remain constant?

   (c) Suppose that labor productivity growth improves to 3 percent per year. What happens to labor's share of income if the rates of growth in nominal wages and the GDP deflator are unchanged? Suppose that the Fed keeps the rate of inflation constant. What must the new growth rate in nominal wages be for labor's share of income to remain constant?

4. You are given the following information concerning the initial cost of capital of starting a business, the licensing fees and other permits costs of starting the business, and income per capita in three countries, one rich and two poor.

	Country A	Country B	Country C
Initial capital costs	$10,000	$1,000	$1,000
Licensing fees and other permit costs	200	100	200
Income per capita	20,000	2,000	2,000

   (a) Suppose that a business earns a 10 percent annual return on the combined costs of initial capital and licensing fees and other permits. Compute the annual income earned by a business in each country.

   (b) Compute the licensing fees and other permit costs as a percent of income in each country.

   (c) Compute how long (in years) that it takes in each country for a business to earn enough to pay the licensing fees and other permit costs to start a business.

   (d) Based on your answers to parts b and c, discuss how much of a barrier licensing fees and permit costs are to starting a business in these three countries. If your job is to suggest reforms in each of the poor countries that would encourage new businesses, how should any reforms take into account that these licensing fees and other permits are a source of government revenues in these countries?

5. A business firm has a choice of two countries in which to undertake a project. The governments of Country 1 and Country 2 are honest and corrupt, respectively, in the sense that unlike Country 2, there is no diversion in Country 1. The startup costs of the two projects are $2 million and $2.1 million in Country 1 and Country 2, respectively. Neither project will yield any profits this year. The profits in Country 1 over the next two years equal $1.050 million and $1.764 million. The profits in Country 2 over the next two years equal $1.260 million and $1.9845 million. The interest rate equals 5 percent.

   (a) Show that the firm is better off undertaking the project in Country 2 if there is no diversion there.

   (b) For the firm to continue to undertake the project in Country 2, what is the maximum amount of diversion that Country 2 can force the firm to pay?

*6. You are given the production function $Y = AK^{1/5} R^{1/5} H^{1/5} N^{2/5}$, where K represents physical capital, R represents infrastructure capital, and H represents human capital. Convert this to a function relating Y/N to K/N, R/N, and H/N. Now consider two countries that have access to the same information on technology, the same quality and quantity of labor and capital of each type, as well as the same production function given above. Both countries are geographically similar. However, the first country, Country 1, has per person output ten times as high as the second country, Country 2. The only relevant difference between the two countries is that the same fraction of the capital of each type in Country 2 is diverted to unproductive activity, while there is no diversion in Country 1. Find the fraction of the per person capital of each type that is being diverted. In this problem, N represents the number of hours of labor.

7. Suppose that in Country 1 the growth rates of multi-factor productivity (a), capital (k), labor (h),

and population (n) are 3, 3.4, 1, and 1 percent per year, respectively, and that capital's share of output (b) equals 0.25. The growth rates of capital (k), labor (h), and population (n) are 3.8, 1, and 2 percent per year, respectively, in Country 2, while capital's share of output (b) is the same as in Country 1.

(a) Calculate the growth rates of labor productivity, output, and output per capita in Country 1.

(b) If Country 2 is to have the same growth rate of output per capita as Country 1, calculate Country 2's growth rates of multifactor productivity, labor productivity, and output. (*Hint:* What must the growth of output be in Country 2 for it to have the same rate of growth in output per capita as Country 1?)

◆ SELF-TEST ANSWERS

p. 391. (1 and 2) $y = 5.75$; $n = 0$; $k = 9$. In each case labor productivity growth ($y - n$) exceeds MFP growth (a), because in each case the growth of capital per worker ($k - n$) is positive. The growth of capital per worker increases the growth of output relative to labor input, which is what labor productivity growth measures, but it does not increase the growth of output relative to *all* inputs, which is what MFP growth measures.

p. 397. (1) An increase in the saving rate increases the level of per-person output and capital. (2) An increase in the saving rate has no effect on the growth rate of output per capita in the long run. (3) An increase in the rate of population growth reduces the level of per-person output and capital. (4) An increase in the rate of population growth has no long-run effect on the growth rate of output per capita.

p. 415. (1) The increase in female labor-force participation occurred mainly in the 1973–95 period of slow productivity growth. Initially before they gained work experience, females were initially of relatively low skill and

decreased productivity. Their entry also reduced the ratio of capital to labor (*K/H*). (2) The interstate highway system was largely complete by 1973 in the sense that motor vehicles could travel from coast to coast without encountering a traffic light. The interstate highway system greatly increased the productivity of truck drivers and thus contributed to fast growth before 1973 and slower growth afterwards. After 1973 its further development mainly consisted of suburban ring roads designed to reduce traffic congestion rather than the fundamental achievement of spanning a continent. (3) The retirement of the baby boom generation will occur during the period 2012–30 and will reduce the ratio of working hours to the population, thus reducing growth in per capita income relative to productivity. (4) The invention of the Internet and World Wide Web occurred in the late 1990s and generated a major investment boom in computer hardware and software, which in turn appears to explain why productivity growth revived after 1995.

Money, Banks, and the Federal Reserve

Money is what the state says it is. The state claims the right not only to enforce the dictionary, but also to write the dictionary.
— John Maynard Keynes, 1925

13-1 Money as a Tool of Stabilization Policy

We have learned in Chapters 4, 5, and 6 that monetary and fiscal policies are the tools of stabilization policy. The aim of these policies is to stabilize the economy's business cycles and minimize the volatility of swings of actual real GDP away from the level of natural real GDP, thus achieving a GDP gap of zero. We first encountered the sharp contrast between unsuccessful and successful stabilization policies in the graphical contrast of two fictitious countries, "Volatilia" and "Stabilia," in Figure 1-3 on p. 8.

Over the three decades before 2007 monetary policy emerged as the major tool of stabilization policy. Monetary policy conquered double-digit inflation in the late 1970s, albeit at the cost of a negative output gap that lasted from 1980 to 1986. Between the mid-1980s and 2007 macroeconomic performance improved notably, with shallower and less frequent recessions, a phenomenon called the "Great Moderation" (as we learned at the beginning of Chapter 3 on p. 54–56). There was a debate about whether the Great Moderation was caused by the decreased severity of demand and supply shocks or the increased effectiveness of monetary policy.

In contrast fiscal policy was rarely used for stabilization purposes during the period from the early 1970s until the Global Economic Crisis struck in 2007–08. Nobody asked whether the Great Moderation had been caused by the improved application of fiscal policy, due to its lack of use. The tables turned as a result of the Crisis. After the federal funds rate had been lowered to zero in early 2009, monetary policy ran out of ammunition. A traditional fiscal policy stimulus was introduced in early 2009, consisting of a package of tax cuts, and increases of transfer payments and government spending on infrastructure projects (see pp. 177–81). Just as important was a novel combination of monetary and fiscal policy implemented in late 2008, in which both the Federal Reserve and the Treasury provided bailout funds to keep the financial system from collapsing.

In this chapter we learn more about money and monetary policy. We start with the definition of the money supply, the determinants of the money supply, and the determinants of money demand. We discuss the components of the two most common definitions of the money supply, M1 and M2. In Chapter 4 the *IS-LM* model assumed for simplicity that the Federal Reserve could control the money supply precisely, while we learn in this chapter why the Fed prefers to control the short-term interest rate instead of directly targeting the money supply.

One reason that the Fed does not target the money supply directly is the multiple definitions of the money supply. As we learned in Chapter 5 on pp. 127–28, financial markets and financial intermediaries have a wide variety of assets and liabilities, and the relative attractiveness of these varies over time. Thus different definitions of the money supply may grow at quite different rates over time.

We will learn that a reliable, or stable, demand for money is required for changes in the money supply to lead to predictable changes in the aggregate demand (*AD*) curve, and thus in nominal GDP. We will see that, unless the demand for money is stable, the *LM* curve will shift unpredictably, which in turn will translate into unpredictable shifts in the *AD* curve and therefore in nominal GDP.

Next we turn to the major theories of the demand for money. These theories explain why the demand for money is related to income, to the interest rate, and to other variables, and why the demand for money appears to be stable at some times and unstable at others. We conclude this chapter by learning why the instability of the demand for money has led the Fed to focus on interest rates rather than the money supply in its attempt to stabilize the economy.

13-2 Definitions of Money

In Chapter 4 we learned that households and firms value money for its usefulness in carrying out transactions and that they value bonds for the interest they pay. In the previous section we were introduced to a wide range of assets that pay interest. These assets differ in their time to maturity, in their risk of default, and in many other dimensions. Deciding whether a financial asset should be considered a bond or a part of the money supply is not always easy because the asset may pay interest and may also be used to carry out transactions. Faced with this practical difficulty, the Federal Reserve compiles several measures of the money supply. The two most important of these are **M1,** which corresponds roughly to the medium-of-exchange function of money, and **M2,** which adds to M1 some but not all assets that can be used solely as a store of value. Financial deregulation has blurred the former distinction between M1 and M2, the distinction between the medium-of-exchange and store-of-value functions of money, by allowing interest to be paid on some checkable deposits and allowing checks to be written on some non-M1 categories of M2.

The M1 Definition of Money

Table 13-1 shows the various components of the Fed's M1 and M2 definitions of the money supply. Each of the categories of assets in M1 can be used directly for transactions.

1. **Currency** (cash) includes coins and paper currency, consisting of notes ranging in denomination from $1.00 to $100.00, that is held outside the Fed and vaults of depository institutions.

2. **Transactions accounts** include demand deposits and other deposits on which checks can be written.

3. **Traveler's checks** outstanding have been purchased from a bank or other financial institution but have not yet been used for purchases.

M1 is the U.S. definition of the money supply that includes only currency, transactions accounts, and traveler's checks.

M2 is the U.S. definition of the money supply that includes M1; savings deposits, including money market deposit accounts; small time deposits; and money market mutual funds.

Table 13-1 Components of the M1 and M2 Measures of the Money Supply, October 2010 ($ billions)

	Component of M1	Component of M2
Currency	903.9	
Transactions accounts		
Demand deposits	494.7	
Other checkable deposits	385.9	
Traveler's checks	4.7	
Equals M1	1,789.2	1,789.2
Savings deposits, including money market deposit accounts		5,255.1
Small-denomination time deposits		978.8
Money market mutual funds (retail only)		729.3
Equals M2		8,752.4

Source: Federal Reserve Board *Money Stock Measures,* www.federalreserve.gov/releases/h6/Current/

The M2 Definition of Money

The major components of M2 are:

1. **M1.** Everything included in M1 is also included in M2.
2. **Savings deposits** include passbook savings accounts, as well as savings accounts that allow deposits and withdrawals to be made by mail or on the Internet. Included in this category are *money market deposit accounts* that allow the writing of a limited number of checks per month, pay a rate of interest comparable to money market mutual funds (category 4 that follows), and because they are deposits, qualify for deposit insurance.
3. **Time deposits** with balances under $100,000 are included in M2. These are more commonly called "certificates of deposit" and they have maturities ranging from six months to several years.
4. **Money market mutual funds** allow an unlimited number of checks over a certain minimum value to be written. Unlike mutual funds that invest in stocks and bonds and experience daily changes in value, money market funds maintain a fixed principal amount.

Which financial market instruments are excluded from the M2 definition of the money supply? Comparing Table 5-5 on p. 128 with Table 13-1, we can see that M2 mainly consists of liabilities of depository institutions and investment intermediaries (money market mutual funds but not stock or bond mutual funds). None of the capital market instruments are included in M2.

Money Supply Definitions and the Instability of Money Demand

Because M2 omits several financial assets, for example stock and bond mutual funds, the demand for M2 may shift unpredictably when these omitted assets become more attractive relative to the assets that are included in M2. The demand for M1 is even more likely to be unstable, because some of the checkable deposits that are included in M1 are very similar to some of the assets, like money market deposit accounts, that are excluded from M1.

The availability of these close substitutes creates severe difficulties for *monetarists*, who endorse a constant growth rate rule (CGRR) for *"the* money supply." To implement the CGRR, they have to decide which money supply measure should have its growth rate held constant. The notion of a stable money demand function that links "money" to "income" is a central theme of the theories of the demand for money that we shall survey later in this chapter. The school of thought called *monetarism* developed by *monetarists* has largely become obsolete due to shifts in the demand for assets that are included in M1 or M2 or excluded from either definition of the money supply.

 SELF-TEST

For each of the following, state whether the event raises or lowers the demand for M1 and whether it raises or lowers the demand for M2:

1. The introduction of money market mutual funds.
2. The invention of credit cards.
3. The introduction of money market deposit accounts.
4. Increased demand for equity mutual funds resulting from a boom in the stock market.

13-3   High-Powered Money and Determinants of the Money Supply

Regardless of what definition of the money supply we select, the basic mechanism for "creating" the money supply is the same. In this section we show how the Fed and depository institutions "create" money and learn that the Fed's actions have a multiplier effect on the money supply. Though the Fed can control the longer-run average growth rate of the money supply, we will see that in practice the Fed cannot always control the money supply precisely over shorter periods.

Money Creation on a Desert Island

The role of the Fed in the money supply process is best understood by starting with a simple banking system where there is no Fed. We begin with the First Desert Island Bank, which is started by a banker who receives a deposit of 100 gold coins. Initially the bank holds the gold as an asset and has deposits of 100. However, the banker is missing an opportunity to make a profit: 100 gold coins earn no interest sitting in the vault. Because the depositor rarely withdraws more than 10 coins, the banker decides to keep "reserves" equal to just 10 percent of total deposits and to grant loans equal to the remaining 90 percent of total deposits.

Required Conditions for Money Creation

Depositing and lending the coins start the process of money creation. Suppose the loan of 90 coins is redeposited in the bank by a merchant, say, a used-raft dealer, who sold a raft to the person who borrowed the 90 coins. This raises total deposits to 190, consisting of the initial deposit of 100 and the new deposit of 90. Because the used-raft dealer has redeposited the 90 gold coins that were borrowed to pay for the raft, the bank again has the original 100 gold coins.

At this point, the banker again decides to hold as reserves 10 percent of "total" deposits. Since the banker decides to hold only 10 percent of 190 for reserves, the remaining "excess" reserves of 81 gold coins can be loaned out.

The banker can continue making loans of excess reserves until total deposits equal 1,000. At that point, the banker's actual reserves (100) equal required reserves (100 = 10 percent of 1,000) and excess reserves equal zero. Thus the original deposit of 100 gold coins leads to the creation of 1,000 units of money, all in the form of bank deposits. The First Desert Island Bank has succeeded in creating an additional nine units of money for every gold coin that it initially received.

How has this magic occurred? Four conditions are necessary for the banker to turn 100 gold coins into a money supply of 1,000.

1. **Equivalence of coins and deposits.** Paper receipts representing ownership of bank deposits, that is, checks, must be accepted as a means of payment on a one-for-one basis. In other words, checks must be treated as equivalent to payment of gold coins.

2. **Redeposit of proceeds from loans.** Any consumer or business firm receiving a cash or check payment must deposit it into an account at the same bank. We assumed in the example that the used-raft dealer redeposited the 90 gold coins received as the proceeds of the first loan.

3. **Holding of cash reserves.** The bank must hold some fraction of its reserves in the form of cash (10 percent in gold coins in this example).

4. **Willing borrowers.** Someone must be willing to borrow from the bank at an interest rate that covers the bank's cost of operation. If the First Desert Island Bank stopped lending its excess reserves, the process of money creation would stop.

The Money-Creation Multiplier

High-powered money is the sum of currency held outside depository institutions and the reserves held inside them. It is the same as monetary base.

When these four conditions are met, then the entire process of money creation can be summed up in a simple equation. We let the symbol H denote **high-powered money,** that is, the type of money that is held by banks as reserves. In the example, H consists of the 100 gold coins, which are high-powered because they generate the multiple expansion of money by the First Desert Island Bank. A synonym for high-powered money is the "monetary base."

The symbol D represents the total bank deposits. The symbol e represents the fraction of deposits that banks hold as reserves. In equilibrium, the *demand* for high-powered money to be held as reserves (eD) equals the *supply* of high-powered money (H):

e=fraction of deposits held as reserves

General Form	Numerical Example	
$eD = H$	$0.1(1,000) = 100$	(13.1)

The same equation can be rearranged (dividing both sides by e) to determine the amount of deposits (D) relative to the quantity of high-powered money (H) and the bank reserve-holding ratio (e):

General Form	Numerical Example	
$D = \dfrac{H}{e}$	$1,000 = \dfrac{100}{0.1}$	(13.2)

Comparison with income-determination multiplier. The money-creation multiplier is $1/e$, or $1/0.1 = 10$ in the numerical example. This is the second usage of the word *multiplier* in this book. In Chapter 3 we examined the factors that determined the income-determination multiplier. In its simplest version, that multiplier in Chapter 3 was

$$\frac{\text{income-determination}}{\text{multipler } (k)} = \frac{1}{\text{marginal propensity to save } (s)}$$

An increase in autonomous planned spending (A_p) is "multiplied" because spending creates income, a fraction of which *leaks out* into saving and taxes and the remainder of which goes into additional spending. The multiplier process ends only when the total of extra induced leakages equals the original increase in A_p.

The intuition behind the money-creation multiplier is the same. An increase in high-powered money (H) is multiplied in equation (13.2) because the initial deposit of H becomes reserves, a fraction of which *leaks out* into required reserves and the remainder of which is lent out and comes back as additional deposits of the households and business firms that receive the loan proceeds. The money-creation multiplier process continues until the extra induced leakages into required reserves equal the original increase in H.

Comparison with real-world conditions.   In reality, some of the four conditions required to obtain the simple money-creation multiplier may not hold.

Condition (2) required that any seller receiving a payment from the proceeds of a loan redeposit it into the bank. If not, the multiplier process of money creation cannot occur at that bank. If the cash is redeposited at another depository institution, then the second institution will find itself with excess reserves, allowing the multiplier process to proceed. Thus condition (2) can be revised to apply to, say, all the banks within the United States. As long as sellers who receive loan proceeds in the form of either cash or checks redeposit the funds in a U.S. bank, the money-creation multiplier in equation (13.2) remains valid for the U.S. banking system as a whole.

Cash holding.   The money-creation multiplier is changed, however, if households or businesses want to hold not only checkable deposits but some pocket cash as well. Imagine that everyone wants to hold a fixed fraction (c) of his or her deposits, say 15 percent, in the form of cash.[1] This demand for currency adds an extra amount (cD) to the total demand for high-powered money. In a revised desert island example, the demand for gold coins, the only form of high-powered money, might be 10 percent of deposits for bank reserves ($eD = 0.1D$), plus 15 percent of deposits for pocket cash ($cD = 0.15D$).

In practice in the real world, high-powered money (H) is equal to the liabilities of the Federal Reserve, namely bank reserves and currency. The demand for bank reserves (eD) plus the demand for currency (cD) equals the total supply of high-powered money (H):

General Form	Numerical Example
Demand = Supply	Demand = Supply
$eD + cD = H$	$0.1D + 0.15D = 100$

---

[1] The cash fraction c has nothing whatsoever to do with the marginal propensity to consume (c) of Chapter 3. Nor does the reserve holding ratio (e) have anything to do with the foreign exchange rate (e) of Chapter 7. At this stage we have run through the alphabet and are asking some letters to perform double duty. See the guide to symbols provided on the inside back cover.

or

$$(e + c)D = H \qquad 0.25D = 100 \qquad (13.3)$$

Dividing both sides by $(e + c)$, we can solve for deposits:

$$D = \frac{H}{e + c} \qquad D = \frac{100}{0.25} = 400 \qquad (13.4)$$

In words, total deposits equal the supply of high-powered money (H) divided by the fraction of deposits that leaks into reserves (e) plus the fraction that leaks into cash (c).

Remember that the total money supply (M) includes not only deposits (D) but also currency:

$$M = D + cD = (1 + c)D \qquad (13.5)$$

Substituting for D in (13.5) from (13.4), we obtain

$$M = (1 + c)D = \frac{(1 + c)H}{e + c} = \frac{1.15(100)}{0.25} = 460 \qquad (13.6)$$

The **money multiplier** is the
ratio of the money supply to
high-powered money, that is,
M/H. There is a separate money
multiplier for each definition of
the money supply.

The ratio of the money supply (M) to high-powered money (H) is called the **money multiplier** (M/H). In equation (13.6), the money multiplier is equal to $(1 + c)/(e + c)$. In the next two sections we will learn that the money multiplier is volatile due to additional factors omitted from (13.6).

Gold Discoveries and Bank Panics

The supply of money depends only on the three terms that appear in equation (13.6): the supply of high-powered money (H), the cash-holding ratio (c), and the ratio of reserves to deposits (e). When only gold can serve as high-powered money (H), the total supply of money depends on the demand for and supply of gold. Because a sustained increase in monetary growth causes higher inflation in the long run, gold discoveries have caused some episodes of inflation. For instance, inflation was higher immediately following the gold discoveries in California in 1848 and in Alaska in 1898.

Before the establishment of the Federal Reserve in 1913 and the introduction of federal deposit insurance in 1934, the U.S. economy was at the mercy of capricious changes in the money supply, stemming not only from the influence of gold discoveries on the growth of H but also from episodes in which the cash-holding ratio (c) and the reserve ratio (e) fluctuated dramatically. During banking panics, which occurred about once a decade and culminated in the serious panic of 1907, depositors feared for the safety of their deposits and withdrew their deposits as cash. This raised the cash-holding ratio (c) and thereby lowered the money supply. To deal with the tide of withdrawals, banks began to bolster their reserves by raising the reserve ratio (e), which further reduced the money supply.[2] In the pre–Federal Reserve era, there was no way for the government to raise H to offset panic-induced increases in c and e. Panics caused a drop in the money supply and in aggregate demand, cutting both output and prices. It was the panic of 1907 that led directly to the formation of the Federal Reserve in 1914. The Fed was established to control directly two

---

[2] Notice in equation (13.6) that any increase in e reduces the quantity of money (M). Although c appears in both the numerator and denominator, an increase in c reduces the money supply as long as the reserve-holding ratio (e) is less than 1.0.

components of equation (13.6), namely high-powered money (H) and the reserves ratio (e) to offset both undesired changes in the cash-holding ratio (c) as well as any adverse events in the economy as a whole.

◆ SELF-TEST

Assume that high-powered money is 500, the fraction of deposits held as currency is 0.25, and the fraction of deposits held as reserves is 0.15. Answer the following:

1. Calculate the value of deposits and the money supply.

2. Calculate the new value of deposits and the money supply if the currency-holding fraction changes from 0.25 to 0.35.

3. Calculate the new value of deposits and the money supply if the reserve-holding fraction changes from 0.15 to 0.25 (while the currency-holding fraction remains at the original 0.25).

13-4   The Fed's Three Tools for Changing the Money Supply

Suppose the Federal Reserve wants the economy to have a given money supply M. The Fed must predict the public's desired cash-holding ratio (c), over which the Fed has no control. Then the Fed can adjust the two remaining variables in equation (13.6), high-powered money (H) and the reserve ratio (e), to make its desired M consistent with the public's chosen c. The Fed uses three tools to accomplish this task; the first two control H and the last influences e. This section helps us understand which real-world events change H and e.

The Fed's Balance Sheet

We were first introduced to the balance sheet of a commercial bank in Tables 5-1 and 5-2 on pp. 129–31. We learned there that a commercial bank has two main kinds of assets, the bank reserves it holds on deposit at the Fed and the loans that it grants to households and business firms; these earn interest for the bank. The main liabilities of a commercial bank are the deposits that households and business firms entrust to the bank. By paying a lower interest rate on deposits than it receives on its loans, the bank has enough left over to pay its employees, cover its other expenses, and earn a profit.

Likewise, the Fed has a balance sheet, to which we were first introduced in Tables 5-4 and 5-5 on pp. 147–48. Traditionally the Fed's main asset has been its holdings of U.S. government bonds. Starting in late 2008 the Fed attempted to stabilize financial markets by buying a wide variety of private assets, including commercial paper (short-term debt of corporations) and private securities backed by residential home mortgages ("mortgage-backed securities").

In this section we return to the simpler form of the Fed's balance sheet that summarizes normal operations as they were conducted prior to 2008. In Table 13-2 the assets of the Fed consist entirely of $850 billion of government bonds. There are two types of liabilities. First is the currency that the Fed has printed and is liable to redeem at any time, hence this is called a liability of the Fed and in Table 13-3 is assumed to be $800 billion. The second type of

Table 13-2 A Simplified Version of the Fed's Balance Sheet (all values in $ billions)

Assets		Liabilities	
		Currency	800
Government Bonds	850	Bank Reserves	50
Total Assets	850	Total Liabilities = Monetary Base (High-Powered Money)	850

liability is the total of reserves that the Fed holds on deposit for the commercial banks, assumed to be $50 billion. The total of its liabilities is called "the monetary base," which is $850 billion in this example. The monetary base is the same as high-powered money, and we continue to use the symbol H to designate the sum of the Fed's liabilities, which is $850 billion in Table 13-2.

What Action by the Fed Will Raise the Money Supply?

The Fed's liabilities are not the same as the money supply. The money supply consists of currency ($800 billion in Table 13-2) and checking deposits at banks. Since the banks are required to hold 10 percent of their checking deposits as reserves at the Fed, we know that the $50 billion of bank reserves in Table 13-2 must be supporting $500 billion of checking deposits (in this simplified example we ignore saving deposits, certificates of deposits, and other types of bank deposits). Thus the total money supply is the total of $800 billion of currency and $500 billion of checking deposits, a total of $1,300 billion.

The money supply (M^s) is equal to the monetary base times the amount of high-powered money (H):

$$M^s = \text{money multiplier} \times H$$

or, in this example

$$\$1,300 \text{ billion} = 1.53(\$850 \text{ billion}). \tag{13.7}$$

But the Fed may not always be satisfied with a money supply of $1,300 billion. Let us say that the Fed has decided that real GDP is too low, and to stimulate more planned spending, the Fed needs to raise the money supply. It has three tools to achieve the desired increase in the money supply.

First Tool: Open-Market Operations

The first tool is by far the most important. The Fed can change H by purchasing and selling government securities like Treasury bills. When it buys Treasury bills in the open market, the Fed (electronically) receives the Treasury bills from the seller and pays for them with high-powered money. The Fed pays for the Treasury bills it has bought simply by raising (electronically) the account balance of the seller at the seller's bank and the reserve balance of the seller's bank at the seller's bank's Federal Reserve Bank. This addition to H, brought about by the Fed's **open-market operations,** leads to an even larger increase in M through the money multiplier.

Federal Reserve monetary policy is decided by the Federal Open Market Committee at meetings scheduled eight times each year. The meetings of the FOMC are held in a large and imposing room at the Federal Reserve Board in Washington, D.C., and are attended by the seven governors of the Federal

Open-market operations are purchases and sales of government securities made by the Federal Reserve in order to change high-powered money.

Reserve Board and the twelve presidents of the regional Federal Reserve banks.[3] After its meetings, the FOMC often issues a statement indicating generally what policy it has decided to follow. The FOMC also issues a directive to the Fed's open-market manager at the Federal Reserve Bank of New York, a position held in 2011 by Brian Sack.

H is created out of thin air.   The Fed issues its instructions in terms of a target federal funds interest rate, the interest rate that banks charge each other to borrow overnight reserves. This target rate has been close to zero since January 2009. These federal funds loans are necessary because at the end of any day of business, banks may wind up with too many or too few reserves. If a bank is open until 5 p.m. and at 4:59 p.m. a depositor walks in with a deposit of $3 million and the reserve requirement is 10 percent, or $300,000, then the bank must quickly find $300,000 in extra reserves. The federal funds market allows the bank automatically, by a simple computer entry, to borrow federal funds from a bank that has a surplus, and the Fed's key federal funds interest rate is that set on these overnight loans between banks. Many other interest rates, including the prime rate that banks charge to large corporations and is the basis for most home equity loans, are pegged to the federal funds rate determined by the Fed.

Let us say that Mr. Sack's directive from the FOMC calls for continued moderate growth in the money supply, and that he has decided that the time has come for a $100 million increase in high-powered money (H). All Mr. Sack has to do is pick up the phone and buy $100 million in U.S. Treasury bills from a government bond dealer, say Goldman Sachs. H is created out of thin air when the Fed electronically gives a credit of $100 million to the reserve account at the bank, say Citibank, where Goldman Sachs has a checking account. At the same time, the Fed notifies Citibank that it should give a $100 million credit to the Goldman Sachs checking account.

This transaction has given Citibank an additional liability of $100 million of deposits and an additional asset of $100 million of reserves, which earn no interest. Suppose that Citibank chooses to hold $10 million of reserves against the additional $100 million deposit. It then has $90 million of excess reserves that it can use to make interest-bearing loans. Borrowers usually get loans so that they can spend the funds. When the proceeds of the loans are spent, some will be redeposited in a depository institution someplace. That institution will then have excess reserves that it can lend out, just as Citibank did. Note that depository institutions no longer have excess reserves once all the funds have been loaned out and they are withdrawn to be spent. Thus another way to view the money-creation process is that it continues until no depository institution has excess reserves it is willing to lend out.

By buying Treasury bills with electronic credits, Mr. Sack has "created" more high-powered money, H. Goldman Sachs transferred Treasury bills to the Fed, but Fed regulations do not permit Treasury bills to be counted toward reserves. Thus, the transfer of Treasury bills did not lower H or reserves, but the Fed's paying for the Treasury bills did raise reserves. That is why the Fed's open-market purchase produced an increase in H. Mr. Sack also created a multiple increase in the money supply. The total money supply rises each time funds are deposited. As the money-creation multiplier showed us, the money

---

[3] All twelve regional presidents attend, but only five may vote. The New York Fed president always has a vote and the other four votes are rotated. All governors are entitled to vote at every FOMC meeting.

supply is likely to rise by a multiple of the original value of Treasury bills purchased by the Fed on the open market.

Effect on interest rates. Mr. Sack's purchase influences not only the total supply of money but also the interest rate. When he buys $100 million of Treasury bills, the price of Treasury bills rises, thereby lowering the return, or interest rate, they pay.

Sometimes the Fed must engage in open-market operations even when it has no desire to raise or lower the money supply. For instance, during the Christmas shopping season, the public needs more cash for transactions and raises its desired cash-holding ratio (c). Without action by the Federal Reserve, this increase in the denominator of the money-supply equation (13.6) would reduce the money supply by a multiple of the public's cash withdrawals from deposit accounts. The Fed can prevent this decline in the money supply and the associated leftward shift of the LM curve by conducting a "defensive" open-market purchase of Treasury bills. To prevent a decline in the money supply, the Fed would raise H enough to offset the effect of the higher c.

Second Tool: Discount Rate

The **discount rate** is the interest rate the Federal Reserve charges depository institutions when they borrow reserves.

Depository institutions' incentives to borrow from the Fed increase when market interest rates rise relative to the **discount rate,** the interest rate that the Fed charges them when they borrow reserves. Depository institutions' so-called discount-window borrowings tend to be high when the interest rates they can earn on money market instruments, like Treasury bills, are substantially above the discount rate that the Fed has set.

Because $100 million in Fed loans provides banks with the same $100 million in bank reserves as a $100 million open-market purchase, the Fed can control high-powered money (H) either by varying the discount rate or by conducting open-market operations. Monetary control can be achieved with either instrument and does not require both. The primary justification for allowing discount-window borrowing at the Fed is the need for immediate help by individual banks suffering from an unexpected rush of withdrawals. Such cases are rare and can be handled individually. Many economists have criticized the Fed for keeping the discount rate low enough to induce banks to borrow substantially. The unpredictability of this borrowing reduces the Fed's day-to-day control over H.

While the discount rate mechanism of the Fed had fallen into disuse in the past few decades, it jumped back into attention as the Fed responded to the subprime mortgage crisis starting in the summer of 2007 and the more generalized financial market crisis that began in September 2008. Between summer 2007 and January 2009, the Fed reduced the federal funds rate from 5.25 to less than 0.25 percent through a series of open-market purchases. But it also used reductions in the discount rate to signal its intentions to ease monetary policy, on several occasions reducing the discount rate in between regularly scheduled meetings of the FOMC.

Third Tool: Reserve Requirements

Required reserves are the reserves that Federal Reserve regulations require depository institutions to hold.

Reserve requirements are the rules that stipulate the minimum fraction of deposits that must be held as reserves.

Unlike the desert island, where the banker chose *voluntarily* to keep 10 percent of the bank's deposits on hand in the form of gold coin reserves, in the United States all depository institutions must hold reserves equal to 10 percent of transactions balances as **required reserves.** Reserves can be held in reserve accounts at the Fed or as vault cash (currency and coin).

Reserve requirements apply only to transactions accounts. In Table 13-1 on p. 426, we see that these are the portion of the money supply definition M1 other than currency. Reserve requirements previously applied to savings accounts and some other parts of the money supply definition M2, but over the past several decades the Fed has discontinued reserve requirements on any part of M2 other than the transactions accounts. The Fed rarely changes reserve requirements, and so this is the most infrequently used of the Fed's three tools.

The main reason that the Fed retains reserve requirements is that they help the Fed control the money supply. Even without reserve requirements, depository institutions would hold some reserves. Institutions hold vault cash because customers control the depositing and withdrawing of cash and their deposits and withdrawals are somewhat unpredictable. Because the 10 percent required reserve ratio is considerably higher than most depository institutions need to satisfy their customers' cash withdrawals, depository institutions typically hold no more reserves than they are required to hold. That is, depository institutions typically face a binding reserve ratio constraint and hold few, if any, excess reserves when the required reserve ratio is high. A high required reserve ratio then means that the reserve ratio, e, stays close to it. In the absence of binding reserve requirements, however, depository institutions would have lower and less predictable (excess) reserve ratios. As we can see from equation (13.6), low and unpredictable reserve ratios unpredictably change the money-creation multiplier and the money supply by sizable amounts.[4]

In 2008–10 the Fed's aggressive purchases of both private and government securities caused its assets and its liabilities to more than double, as we saw in the comparison of Tables 5-4 and 5-5 on pp. 147–48. The Fed "paid" for its new expanded securities by increasing bank reserves far in excess of the amount that banks were required to hold. Thus the largest single component of the Fed's balance sheet, as shown in Table 5-5, is its holdings of more than $1 trillion in excess reserves. While normally banks would want to use those excess reserves to grant loans, the banks were unable to find enough credit-worthy borrowers. Banks did not bother to use their excess reserves to purchase short-term government securities, because the interest rate the banks would have earned on such securities was no higher than the interest rate the Fed was already paying the banks on reserves. By 2011 excess reserves amounted to more than 5 percent of GDP, close to the 7 percent of GDP held in excess reserves in 1938–39 in the latter years of the Great Depression.

 SELF-TEST

Be sure you can answer the following questions without looking back at the preceding text:

1. If the Fed wants to reduce the money supply, does it conduct an open-market purchase of bonds or sale of bonds?

2. Why might lowering the discount rate lead to a larger money supply?

3. If the Fed wants to raise the money supply, does it raise or reduce the reserve requirement ratio (e)?

---

[4] The Fed's control of reserve requirements was also useful during World War II. The Fed needed to expand H rapidly to buy up the huge federal government deficit caused by wartime expenditures, and in order to minimize the impact on the money supply, the Fed raised the reserve ratio e to offset some (but not all) of the increase in H.

Why the Fed Can't Control the Money Supply Precisely

This chapter focuses on two problems faced by the Fed: Why it can't control the money supply precisely, and why an unstable demand for money can break the link between changes in the money supply and changes in nominal GDP. We have now learned that the Fed can use its three instruments—open-market operations, the discount rate, and changes in reserve requirements—to achieve control of the money supply (as in equation (13.6) on p. 430). Why, then, is its control imprecise?

Multiple definitions of money. There are many types of financial assets included in M2 that are not included in M1, as we learned in Table 13-1 on p. 426. Both savings deposits and time deposits are included in M2 but excluded from M1. An increase in the attractiveness of these deposits relative to transactions accounts, for example, would raise the level of M2 relative to M1. In that case, the Fed would not be able to precisely control M1 and M2 simultaneously.

Firms and households choose the amount of currency. The Fed controls two elements in the money supply equation (13.6): high-powered money (H) and the reserve ratio (e). It does not control the ratio of currency to deposits (c), which is controlled by firms and households. If the Fed cannot predict precisely when c will change, it cannot control the money supply precisely. As we will see later in this chapter, shifts in the demand for U.S. currency by foreigners further complicate attempts to control the money supply in the United States.

Other factors. Equation (13.6) simplifies the money supply process, omitting other factors that can interfere with precise Fed control. The equation does not take into account that transactions accounts have reserve requirements, while other accounts do not. And since money market mutual funds are not actually deposits, they are also free from reserve requirements. A consequence of these differing reserve requirement ratios is that shifts of funds across accounts will change the average reserve ratio, e.

A **money-multiplier shock** is any event that causes the money multiplier to change, such as a change in the public's demand for currency relative to deposits or a shift between deposits having different reserve requirements.

Taken together, these factors make the money multiplier hard to predict and thus make it hard to control precisely the LM curve. These **money-multiplier shocks** play a central role in our discussion of monetary policy later in this chapter.

13-5 Theories of the Demand for Money

Now we turn from the determinants of the supply of money to the determinants of the demand for money. Our first aim is to understand why the demand for money depends on the interest rates available on assets that are alternatives to money. This is a central assumption in our *IS-LM* model of Chapters 3 and 4, and we need to examine the theories that explain the dependence of money demand on the interest rate. Our second aim is to understand why the demand for money might shift in response to financial deregulation or other events.

Interest Responsiveness of the Transactions Demand for Money

In the early 1950s, William J. Baumol of Princeton and New York University and James Tobin of Yale demonstrated that the transactions (that is, medium-of-exchange) demand for money depends on the interest rate.[5] The funds that individuals hold for transactions, to "bridge the interval between the receipt of income and its disbursement," can be placed either in M1 (currency and transactions accounts, which are assumed by Baumol and Tobin to pay no interest) or in savings deposits (which do pay interest but cannot be used for transactions). The higher the interest rate, the more individuals shift their transactions balances into interest-bearing savings deposits and other components of M2 that do not serve as a medium of exchange.

James Tobin (1918–2002)

Tobin, 1981 Nobel Prize winner, was one of the most articulate advocates of policy activism and the inventor of the theories of the transactions and portfolio demands for money.

Baumol analyzes the money-holding decision of a hypothetical individual who receives income at specified intervals but spends it steadily between paydays. An example is given in the left frame of Figure 13-1, where the person is assumed to be paid $900 per month ($Y$) on the first of each month. How will the person decide whether to convert all of the paycheck into currency and transactions accounts (M1), which bear no interest, or to deposit part of the paycheck in a savings deposit that pays a monthly interest rate r?[6]

Costs and benefits of holding money. The individual compares the costs and benefits of holding M1 instead of the savings deposit. The cost of M1 is its opportunity cost, the interest forgone on savings (r) when M1 is held instead of savings deposits. The main benefit of holding M1 is the avoidance of what Baumol calls the "broker's fee" of b dollars charged every time (T) cash is obtained, either by cashing the original paycheck or by obtaining cash at the depository institution. The broker's fee in real life includes the time and transportation expense required to make an extra trip to the bank to obtain cash from a savings account.

The number of times the broker's fee is incurred equals the size of the paycheck (Y) divided by the average amount of cash (C) obtained on each trip. For instance, the left frame of Figure 13-1 involves no savings account; the paycheck of $900 ($Y$) is cashed at the beginning of the month ($C = 900$), and the broker's fee is incurred only one time ($T = Y/C = 1.0$). The amount of cash held dwindles as money is spent on consumption, as shown by the green triangle in the left frame.

In the middle frame half the paycheck is cashed on the first of the month ($C = 450$); the other half is deposited in a savings deposit, shown by the blue rectangle. Interest forgone equals the interest rate times the value of the average amount held in cash, which is half the value of the cash withdrawal ($rC/2$). Why? In the first half of the month the individual starts with $450 in cash, winding up with zero on the fifteenth of the month, for an average holding of $225. Then the person converts the remaining savings deposit into cash, incurring a second broker's fee. The $450 of cash dwindles again to zero on the last day of the month. The average cash holding during the last half of

---

[5] William J. Baumol, "The Transactions Demand for Cash: An Inventory Theoretic Approach," *Quarterly Journal of Economics* (November 1952), pp. 545–56; James Tobin, "The Interest-Elasticity of the Transactions Demand for Cash," *Review of Economics and Statistics* (August 1956), pp. 241–47.

[6] Throughout this section we assume that no interest is paid on transactions accounts, in contrast to the real world, where interest is paid on some components of M1 and M2 that can be used for transactions. Our analysis remains valid as long as a higher interest rate on nonmoney assets raises the average interest rate paid on M1 less than proportionately, thus reducing the demand for M1.

The Holding of Cash Depends Inversely on the Attractiveness of Holding Savings Deposits

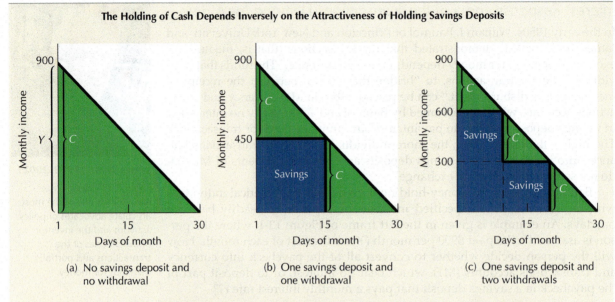

Figure 13-1 Alternative Allocations of an Individual's Monthly Paycheck Between Cash and Savings Deposits

In the left frame, the individual holds the entire paycheck in the form of cash, indicated by the green triangle, which shrinks as the paycheck is spent on consumption purchases. In the middle frame only half as much cash is held, initially and on average, because the individual finds it advantageous to hold half the paycheck in a savings account for half the month. In the right frame, even less cash is held because initially two-thirds of the paycheck is deposited in a savings account.

the month is again $225. Total interest forgone is the interest rate times $C/2$, where $C/2$ is $225 in this example.[7]

In the right frame, only one-third of the paycheck is initially cashed ($C = 300$), while the other two-thirds are deposited in the savings deposit. On the tenth and on the twentieth, withdrawals are again made, so that the broker's fee is incurred three times ($T = Y/C = 900/300 = 3$). The interest income forgone by holding cash is once again $rC/2$, or r times $150.

How many trips to the bank? How should the individual behave—as in the left frame, the middle frame, or the right frame, or should even more trips be made to the bank? The answer is that the combined cost of broker's fees (bT) and interest income foregone ($rC/2$) should be minimized:

$$\text{cost} = bT + \frac{rC}{2}$$

or

$$= b\frac{Y}{C} + \frac{rC}{2} \tag{13.8}$$

---

[7] What is the area of the green triangle in the left frame? The formula for the area of a triangle is one-half times the height, times the length, or $1/2(900)(1)$, where the length is expressed in months. This equals 450. In the middle are two green triangles, each with an area $1/2(450)(1/2)$, or $1/2(450)(1)$ for both triangles. This equals 225. On the right are three triangles, each with an area $1/2(300)(1/3)$, or $1/2(300)(1)$ for the three triangles. This equals 150.

It can be shown that the average value of the cash withdrawal (C) that minimizes cost is[8]

$$C = \sqrt{\frac{2bY}{r}} \tag{13.9}$$

This equation says that the average cash withdrawal equals the square root of the following: two times the broker's fee, times income, divided by the interest rate. A higher broker's fee (b) raises cash holdings by discouraging trips to the bank, each of which incurs the broker's fee.

Conversely, as equation (13.9) indicates, a higher interest rate on savings deposits lowers average cash holdings. The higher interest rate makes it optimal to go to the bank more frequently and make smaller withdrawals, thereby leaving more on average in the interest-earning savings accounts. The smaller withdrawals mean that, on average, cash holdings are smaller. The extra broker's fees incurred by going to the bank more frequently are compensated for by the extra interest earned on the larger savings account balances at the higher interest rate. Equation (13.9) also shows that the transactions demand for money rises with increases in income. Just as with interest rates, the Baumol model implies specifically that the transactions demand for money is related to the square root of income.[9]

> **Summary:** The Baumol-Tobin contributions are of major importance. They show that the interest sensitivity of the demand for money is based on a transactions motive that is shared by almost everyone. Their theories underpin the positive slope of the *LM* curve, which implies that changes either in private spending desires or in fiscal policy will change both real output and the interest rate, at least in the short run.

The Portfolio Approach

At about the same time as the Baumol-Tobin contributions, several articles highlighted another source of the demand for money, as a store of value. In particular, James Tobin, in another classic article, showed that people diversify their portfolios by holding several categories of assets.[10]

Tobin's contribution. Some assets, particularly those in M1 and M2, have nominal values that do not change when interest rates change and thus are

---

[8] Here elementary calculus is required. Cost is minimized by choosing C to make the derivative of cost with respect to C equal to zero:

$$\frac{\partial(\text{cost})}{\partial C} = \frac{-bY}{C^2} + \frac{r}{2} = 0$$

When this is solved for C, we obtain the square-root expression shown as equation (13.9).

[9] The Baumol theory's "square root hypothesis" of money holding can be tested against the data. In that case, both the output elasticity and the interest rate elasticity of real money demand should be one-half. Why? Let us rewrite (13.9) in exponential form:

$$C = (2bY)^{1/2}(r)^{-1/2}$$

Thus a 1 percentage point change in Y raises C by $1/2$ percent. For a more advanced treatment that allows the theoretical elasticities to differ from 1/2, see Edi Karni, "The Transactions Demand for Cash: Incorporation of the Value of Time into the Inventory Approach," *Journal of Political Economy*, vol. 81 (September/October 1973), pp. 1216–25.

[10] James Tobin, "Liquidity Preference as Behavior Towards Risk," *Review of Economic Studies*, vol. 25 (February 1958), pp. 65–86.

INTERNATIONAL PERSPECTIVE

Plastic Replaces Cash, and the Cell Phone Replaces Plastic

In 2003, the United States passed a watershed. For the first time American households used plastic cards—both debit and credit—to pay for more retail goods and services than they used cash or checks. Much of the growth in plastic card use has been in debit cards, not credit cards. The share of debit cards in total retail transactions in 2008 was 37 percent, which when added to the 22 percent share held by credit cards and 4 percent for prepaid cards, totaled a 63 percent share for plastic. The remaining 37 percent share was made up of an 8 percent share for checks and a 29 percent share for cash.[a]

The explosion of card use occurred because more people carry cards and because more retail outlets accept them. The development of "affinity cards" that provide additional benefits such as airline miles or charitable contributions has also speeded the transition from cash and checks to card purchases. Why send checks to the local plumber and electrician if they accept cards that can earn you airline miles and eventual free trips?

A novel example of a completely cashless society is the aircraft carrier U.S.S. *Harry S Truman*, which eliminated cash transactions in 2004. The Navy issued MasterCards to all 5,000 sailors aboard. Each card is loaded with a credit amount on a sailor's payday and then debited for transactions during the following month. Records show that sailors on the ship buy 250,000 soft drinks monthly. Allowing the sailors to purchase these drinks with plastic saves the effort of collecting half a ton of quarters from vending machines each month. Even contributions at Sunday chapel services can be made by swiping the card at the door of the chapel.

The aircraft carrier provides the example of a new type of plastic called the prepaid or "smart" card. An electronic credit is loaded onto the card and then purchases are deducted until the next deposit is made. Many college students are familiar with prepaid cards with which they can pay for bookstore expenses and meals at campus dining facilities. The author's prepaid card at Northwestern University is called a "Wildcard" after the school's football mascot, "Willie the Wildcat." The use of prepaid cards is proliferating at retail outlets such as the Gap and Starbucks.

The increasing use of debit cards relative to credit cards reflects the high interest rates charged on credit cards and the fear that many Americans rightly have of running up excessive debt on credit cards. Banks issuing credit cards make large profits from customers who "roll over balances" at high interest rates, and these customers in effect subsidize convenience and zero fees for the customers who pay their bills in full each month. While banks prefer that their customers use credit cards instead of debit cards, these banks nevertheless collect fees from merchants for every plastic transaction, whether made with a credit or debit card. The largest card issuer is Citigroup, parent company of Citibank, which issues 145 million cards and brings in $19 billion in revenue each year.

As the use of credit cards spreads, life gets harder for the 60 million Americans who do not have bank accounts, typically the poor and the young. It is difficult to rent a car or stay in a hotel without having a credit card, and the growing world of electronic-commerce has been built almost entirely around the ease of entering a credit card number on a computer hooked up to the Internet. Buying books from Amazon or computers from Dell over the Internet would be impossible if retailers had to wait a week or two for the checks to arrive by mail and be cleared.

The first credit card was issued in 1950 by Francis X. McNamara, who had been embarrassed to find that he lacked enough cash to pay the bill in a restaurant. Initially, he started a network of restaurant charge accounts in which customers identified themselves with a card. This network soon became Diners Club, the first credit card company. The mass use of credit cards began in 1958 with the BankAmericard, which became an association of many banks issuing cards with the same name. Its name was changed in 1976 to the familiar "Visa."

The gradual disappearance of cash has proceeded faster in some countries than others. Cash hangs on in Japan, which has almost $4,000 of currency per person, twice that of the United States. Cash is used in Japan for many transactions that in the United States would be handled by checks or plastic cards. Because street crime

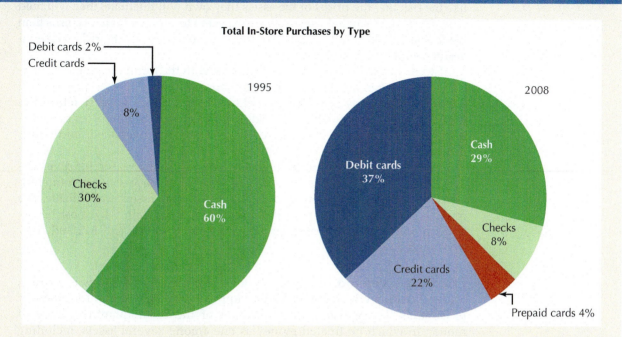

Total In-Store Purchases by Type

Debit cards 2%
Credit cards

1995

8%

Checks
30%

Cash
60%

2008

Cash
29%

Debit cards
37%

Checks
8%

Credit cards
22%

Prepaid cards 4%

is very low, Japanese housewives feel comfortable carrying large amounts of cash and routinely peel off 10,000 yen notes (about $87) to pay for their shopping. Utility bills and other invoices that Americans would handle over the Internet or by checks through the mail are paid by Japanese who go to local convenience stores and pay in cash.

The surprisingly large amount of U.S. currency outstanding, about $2,300 per U.S. resident, is not used mainly for legitimate retail transactions within U.S. borders. Some of it is used within U.S. borders by drug dealers and for cash transactions in the "underground economy" by people trying to avoid paying income taxes. Possibly as much as two-thirds of the cash in the United States is believed to be outside U.S. borders, used for transactions in many countries with a history of rapid inflation, now or in the past.

Credit cards facilitate transactions but are not considered to be "money" and are not part of any of the definitions of the money supply listed in Table 13-1 on p. 426. Credit cards are simply a very convenient and fast way of taking out a bank loan, even for $1.00 at a soft drink machine. To the extent that credit cards allow households to reduce their use of currency and checking accounts, credit cards increase the velocity of money, that is, the ratio of nominal GDP to the money supply.

Are debit cards money? With a debit card, your bank account is instantly debited when you make a transaction. In the old days you might start the month with $900 in cash, gradually spending down the $900 to $0 by the end of the month, as shown by the green triangle

in the left frame of Figure 13-1 on p. 438. If all transactions can now be made with debit cards instead of cash, then you start the month with $900 in your checking account and gradually spend down the $900 to $0 through use of your debit card. In this example, the invention of debit cards has no effect at all on the demand for money. In contrast, credit cards reduce the demand for cash and also reduce the demand for checking accounts for those who choose not to pay their full balances each month.

The next wave of the cashless society is the use of cell phones to pay for almost everything. In Japan, the traditional haven of old-fashioned cash, the use of cell phones has advanced further than almost anywhere else. In Japan, everyday transactions, from buying railway tickets to picking up groceries, already take place with customers passing their handsets over a payment receiver. When the receiver accepts the payment, it responds with the sound of a bell like an old-fashioned cash register. Using cell phones as a payment method is more convenient than using cash or having to sign a credit card receipt. And cell phones are much smarter than credit cards, as they have screens to display balances and keyboards to enter information including PIN codes. Like prepaid cards, balances are added to the cell phones before purchases are made, so no credit checks are necessary.

---

[a] Data from American Bankers Association. Some of the details in this box come from Jathon Sapsford, "Paper Losses," *The Wall Street Journal*, July 23, 2004, p. A1; Katrina Brooker, "Just One Word: Plastic," *Fortune*, February 23, 2004, pp. 125–38; and "A Cash Call," *The Economist*, February 17, 2007, p. 71.

"safe" or "riskless."[11] The prices of other financial assets, like those of stocks or long-term bonds, vary all the time and thus are "risky" assets. If investors dislike the risk that the prices of the assets they own will fluctuate, they will hold risky assets only when those assets are expected to provide higher returns than riskless assets do. Without this risk premium on risky assets, risk-averse investors would not hold them.

Faced with various safe and risky assets, with the former paying less interest than the latter, most investors compromise, diversifying their portfolios of assets. Holding only risky assets yields a high average interest return but exposes investors to much risk. Holding only safe assets eliminates risk completely but yields a low average return. A mixed, or diversified, portfolio is usually the best approach.

Although the Tobin approach gives a very appealing reason for diversifying portfolios, it does not explain why anyone holds currency or non-interest-bearing checking accounts when safe, interest-bearing assets are available. The major contribution of the portfolio approach is to explain why most households hold both safe, interest-bearing components of M1 and M2 and risky stocks and bonds.

Friedman's version. At roughly the same time that Tobin was writing, Milton Friedman developed a similar approach to the demand for money.[12] Friedman's theory was a generalization of the older quantity theory of money, in which he treated money as one among several assets, including bonds, equities (stocks), and goods. Friedman emphasized that, in principle, any category of spending on GDP could be a substitute for money and might be stimulated by an expansion of the real money supply. Because he viewed a wider range of assets as being substitutes for money than did Tobin, Friedman viewed monetary policy as having more potent effects on spending.

The portfolio approach pioneered by both Tobin and Friedman makes the demand for money a function of both income and wealth, not just income. The response of the demand for money to wealth has an implication for the efficacy of fiscal policy. A stimulative fiscal policy financed by deficit spending raises real wealth if people treat government bonds as part of their wealth. The increase in wealth, in turn, raises the demand for money and shifts the *LM* curve to the left, reducing the fiscal policy multipliers below those we calculated in Chapter 4, where the wealth effect on the demand for money was ignored.[13]

[11] "Riskless" is placed in quotes because M1 is not free of risk when prices are flexible, since inflation reduces the real value of nominal holdings of M1. This is one of the costs of inflation emphasized in Chapter 10.

[12] Friedman's approach is explained in more detail in his "The Quantity Theory of Money—A Restatement," in Friedman, ed., *Studies in the Quantity Theory of Money* (Chicago: University of Chicago Press, 1956), pp. 3–21.

[13] A formal analysis of the wealth effect in the demand-for-money function is the subject of Alan S. Blinder and Robert M. Solow, "Analytical Foundations of Fiscal Policy," in *The Economics of Public Finance* (Washington, D.C.: Brookings Institution, 1974), pp. 45–57. See also Benjamin M. Friedman, "Crowding Out or Crowding In? Economic Consequences of Financing Government Deficits," *Brookings Papers on Economic Activity*, vol 9. (1978), pp. 593–641.

SELF-TEST

Answer the following questions according to the Tobin and Friedman versions of the portfolio theory:

1. Would an increase in the supply of M1 tend to raise or lower prices in the bond market?

2. Would an increase in the supply of M1 tend to raise or lower prices in the stock market?

3. Would an increase in stock market prices raise or reduce the demand for money?

13-6   Why the Federal Reserve "Sets" Interest Rates

Pervasive deregulation and innovation in financial markets were major contributors to the frequent instability of the demand for money after the mid-1970s. In this section we use the *IS-LM* model of Chapter 4 to explain why the unpredictability, or instability, of the demand for money led the Federal Reserve to shift its policies toward setting interest rates instead of trying to control the money supply. Reports in the media and announcements from the Fed that the FOMC has decided to change interest rates often give the (incorrect) impression that the Fed sets interest rates directly. It is important to remember that the Fed can only affect the nominal federal funds interest rate indirectly. When the Fed wants to raise short-term interest rates, it undertakes open-market sales of bonds, which reduce reserves and thus the money supply. When the Fed sells the right amount of bonds, the *LM* curve shifts leftward and intersects the *IS* curve at the higher interest rate that the Fed seeks. The Fed does not care what value of the money supply is required to achieve its interest rate target.

As in Chapter 4, Figure 13-2 illustrates the working of the *IS-LM* model. We assume that the expected inflation rate is zero, so that the nominal and real interest rates are the same; both are labeled simply as the "interest rate" on the vertical axis. A constant price level is an acceptable assumption when wage and price contracts in the real world limit the flexibility of the price level in the short run. In such a case, the shifts in the *IS* or *LM* curves of Figure 13-2 mainly influence the level of real output in the first few months or quarters after the shift.

The position of the *IS* curve can be shifted by changes in business and consumer optimism, by the ease or difficulty in obtaining credit, by changes in net exports, and by changes in government spending, autonomous net taxes, and tax rates. When *commodity demand is unstable* because of swings in optimism, net exports, or government policy, the *IS* curve shifts back and forth as shown in the left-hand frame of Figure 13-2. The position of the *LM* curve can be shifted by a change in the real money supply; the LM_0 curve in the left-hand frame assumes that the real money supply is fixed.[14] The *LM* curve will also be shifted when

---

[14] A fixed real money supply (M/P) and a fixed *LM* curve can be achieved either with a constant nominal money supply (M) and a fixed price level (P), or with the money supply growing at the same rate as the price level ($m = p$).

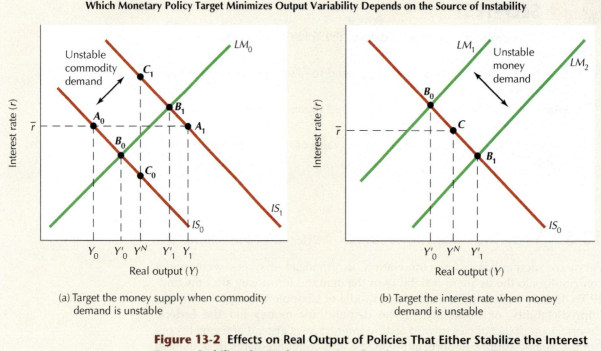

Which Monetary Policy Target Minimizes Output Variability Depends on the Source of Instability

(a) Target the money supply when commodity demand is unstable

(b) Target the interest rate when money demand is unstable

Figure 13-2 Effects on Real Output of Policies That Either Stabilize the Interest Rate or Stabilize the Real Money Supply When Either Commodity Demand or Money Demand Is Unstable

In the left frame, the demand for commodities is unstable, fluctuating unpredictably between IS_0 and IS_1. A policy that maintains a fixed real money supply and a fixed LM_0 curve leads to smaller fluctuations of output than an alternative policy that stabilizes the interest rate at r by shifting LM. A third policy, which stabilizes real GDP at Y^N, causes interest rate instability between points C_0 and C_1. In the right frame, the demand for money is unstable. In this case, a policy of stabilizing the interest rate at $\bar{r}$ will stabilize real GDP. When the real money supply is held fixed, unstable money demand shifts the LM curve from LM_1 to LM_2 and causes output to fluctuate between Y'_0 and Y'_1

the demand for money is unstable. A sudden increase in the demand for money brought on by a financial panic would shift the LM curve leftward.

Implications of unstable commodity demand. William Poole, then of Brown University and during 1998–2008 the president of the Federal Reserve Bank of St. Louis, first popularized the use of the IS-LM model to compare targeting of the money supply with the alternative of targeting the interest rate.[15] Unstable commodity demand, shown by the shifting IS curve in the left-hand frame of Figure 13-2, calls into question the wisdom of targeting the interest rate. When the real money supply is held constant and the LM curve remains fixed at LM_0, the economy moves back and forth between positions B_0 and B_1, and real output moves over the limited range between Y'_0 and Y'_1.

With unstable commodity demand, fixing the LM curve by targeting the money supply is superior to a policy of maintaining stable interest rates. When

---

[15] William Poole, "Optimal Choice of Monetary Policy Instruments in a Simple Stochastic Macro Model," *Quarterly Journal of Economics*, vol. 84 (May 1970), pp. 197–216. A little-known earlier reference is M. L. Burstein, *Economic Theory* (New York: Wiley, 1966), Chapter 13.

commodity demand is high (as along IS_1), a stable interest rate policy means that the real money supply must be allowed to rise to prevent the interest rate from increasing. The Federal Reserve must increase the money supply to accommodate the additional demand for money that occurs when commodity demand is high. The stable interest rate policy causes the economy to fluctuate between points A_0 and A_1 and it allows real output to vary over the wide range between Y_0 and Y_1.

Instead of targeting interest rates or the money supply, an alternative approach for the Fed would be to target real GDP itself. The policy of targeting real output is illustrated in the left-hand frame of Figure 13-2 by the points C_0 and C_1. Fluctuations in commodity demand would have to be offset by fluctuations in the supply of money in the *opposite* direction. If the *LM* curve can be promptly moved in the opposite direction of the shift in the *IS* curve, then the economy could remain at its natural real GDP (Y^N). And, as we learned in Chapter 9, keeping the economy at Y^N is consistent with steady inflation in the absence of supply shocks.

The analysis with unstable money demand.   The right-hand frame of Figure 13-2 assumes that commodity demand is fixed, so that the *IS* curve remains fixed at IS_0. But here the demand for money is assumed to be unstable. When the real money supply is fixed, *an unstable demand for money causes the* LM *curve to move about unpredictably between* LM_1 *and* LM_2. A constant money supply policy leads to fluctuations in the economy between points B_0 and B_1, with output varying between Y_0' and Y_1'. A superior policy is to change the money supply in order to maintain a constant interest rate. When the demand for money rises, the interest rate is prevented from rising by raising the money supply. This constant interest rate policy keeps the economy pinned to point C, with a fixed interest rate $\bar{r}$ and a fixed output level Y^N. In this diagram, an interest rate target and a natural real GDP (Y^N) target amount to the same thing.

The Choice of Targets

In the left-hand frame of Figure 13-2, an unstable demand for commodities makes a real GDP target superior to a money supply target, which in turn is superior to an interest rate target. In the right-hand frame, with an unstable demand for money, a real GDP and interest rate target are the same, and both are superior to a money supply target. If, as is likely, there is instability in both commodity and money demand, a real GDP target is superior to an interest rate target.

The Fed's decision since the early 1980s to target the interest rate reflects its view that instability in the demand for money is a more significant problem than instability in the demand for commodities. Eight times each year at meetings of the Federal Open Market Committee, it conducts a debate among the participants as to whether the current interest rate target should be maintained or should be changed up or down. In doing so, it considers the expected future behavior of its two goals, maintaining low inflation and minimizing the output gap, that is, keeping actual real GDP as close as possible to real GDP.

We will return in the next chapter to the Fed's monetary policy choices and to its two-goal approach based on trying to control inflation and the output gap at the same time. Thus, in contrast to having a single goal of controlling the money supply, the interest rate, or real GDP as in the previous discussion of Figure 13-2, instead the Fed targets the interest rate in the short-run, with the further objective of achieving its longer-term inflation and output gap goals. This approach to characterizing the Fed's interest rate decisions having the double goals of achieving low inflation and a low output gap is called the *Taylor Rule*; we will see in the next chapter how it works.

◆ **SELF-TEST**

Using the *IS-LM* model analysis of Figure 13-2, which neglects both lags and inflation, rank three types of policies (money supply rule, interest rate rule, real GDP rule) under two sets of circumstances:

1. If commodity demand is unstable, take the three policies and rank first the policy that minimizes the fluctuations in real output, rank second the policy that is next best, and rank third the policy that is worst.

2. If the demand for money is unstable, take the three policies and rank first the policy that minimizes the fluctuations in real output, rank second the policy that is next best, and rank third the policy that is worst.

Summary

1. Surplus funds from savers are channeled to borrowers by way of financial intermediaries and financial markets.

2. The United States has two major definitions of the money supply. M1 includes currency, balances in transactions accounts, and traveler's checks. M2 comprises M1 plus other assets, including savings deposits, small time deposits, and retail money market mutual funds.

3. A set of banks in a closed economy—one with no transfers of funds to the outside—can "create money" by a multiple of each dollar of cash that is initially received. This is true for a single bank on a desert island or for all banks in the United States taken together.

4. The deposit-creation multiplier is 1.0 divided by the fraction of the initial cash receipt that is held as reserves or currency. The money multiplier is then the deposit multiplier times 1.0 plus the currency-holding fraction. The money supply is equal to high-powered money times the money multiplier.

5. The Fed uses three tools for changing the money supply: open-market operations, the discount rate, and reserve requirements.

6. Several theories have been developed to explain the relation between the demand for money, income, wealth,

and the interest rate. The transactions demand for money depends on the interest rate; people will take the trouble to make extra trips to the bank and keep more of their income in savings accounts (and other interest-earning assets) when the interest rate is higher.

7. The portfolio approach emphasizes the household decision to allocate its wealth among money, savings accounts, bonds, and other assets. Any event that raises wealth, such as a stimulative fiscal policy, will tend to raise the demand for money.

8. In earlier chapters we assumed that the growth of aggregate demand could be controlled precisely by policymakers. We now recognize that in the real-world economy, policy shifts cannot instantly or precisely offset the effects on aggregate demand of shocks to *IS* or *LM* curves.

9. When commodity demand is unstable and money demand is stable, a money supply target is superior to an interest rate target, but a real GDP target is superior to both. When money demand is unstable and commodity demand is stable, both real GDP and interest rate targets are superior to a money supply target.

10. The ongoing instability of the demand for money has led the Fed to target interest rates rather than the money supply.

Concepts

M1	money multiplier	required reserves
M2	open-market operations	reserve requirements
high-powered money	discount rate	money-multiplier shock

Questions

1. What is the main distinction between the M1 and M2 definitions of money?
2. Explain why there is a different money multiplier for each definition of the money supply.
3. What is high-powered money? Explain why *both* reserves and cash held by the public are considered to be high-powered money.
4. What are the conditions required for money creation? In the Great Depression of the 1930s, many bank failures occurred in part because one or more of these conditions was no longer met. Which are the most likely candidates to explain the failure of the banking system to operate properly in the depths of the Great Depression?
5. Explain what happens when the Fed conducts an open-market purchase of $200 billion in bonds. How do the banks get involved? What is the ultimate effect on the level of high-powered money and on the money supply?
6. Explain how the money-creation multiplier is similar to the income-determination multiplier of Chapter 3.
7. Explain how each of the following events affects the money supply.
   (a) An increase in income tax rates induces the public to conduct more of its business in currency to hide earnings.
   (b) An increase in interest rates encourages the public to hold less currency.
   (c) Banks obtain discount loans from the Fed.
   (d) Increasing uncertainty about deposit withdrawals leads banks to hold on to excess reserves.
8. What are the major ways in which the supply of money can change? If it is that simple, why couldn't the Fed effectively control the money supply in the past?
9. Explain the significance of the Baumol-Tobin analysis of the transactions demand for money.
10. In what ways are the portfolio approaches developed by Tobin and Friedman similar? In what ways do they differ?
11. Money-multiplier shocks can be a source of instability in the economy. Suppose such a shock produces a decrease in the money supply. Use the *IS-LM* and *SP-LP* models to predict what will happen to real GDP, the real interest rate, the inflation rate, and the output ratio, in both the short run and the long run, if the Fed takes no action to offset the multiplier shock.
12. Many people advocate the supremacy of rules over discretion in the Fed's conduct of monetary policy, but there is less agreement as to what kind of rule the Fed should follow. A money supply rule, an interest rate rule, and a real GDP rule have all been suggested. Discuss the advantages and disadvantages of each type of rule.
13. Suppose that the Fed is able to target real GDP when there is instability in either commodity demand or the demand for money. Explain how the Fed must conduct open market operations, that is, either buy or sell government bonds, as (a) commodity demand rises and falls or (b) the demand for money increases and decreases.
14. Explain why American households have moved away from the use of cash and checks to debit and credit cards to purchase retail goods and services. Explain what effect, if any, the increased use of debit and credit cards has on the demand for money.
15. The amount of excess reserves held by U.S. banks increased to over a trillion dollars during the Global Economic Crisis. Explain what effect the increase in excess reserves had on the *e* (the fraction of deposits banks hold as reserves), the amount of high-powered money, and the money multiplier.

Problems

 Visit www.MyEconLab.com to complete these or similar exercises.

1. Given the following information for November 2010, calculate the amounts of M1 and M2 in November 2010. The amounts are in billions of dollars.

Currency	$915.0
Demand deposits	507.0
Money market mutual funds (retail only)	711.1
Other checkable deposits	405.2
Savings deposits, including money market deposit accounts	5,317.9
Small-denomination time deposits	943.3
Traveler's checks	4.7

2. Suppose the ratio of deposits that banks hold in the form of reserves is 7 percent. Suppose further that people want to hold 8 percent of their deposits in the form of cash. Then, if the Fed wants the money supply to be $6,228 billion, what is the necessary level of high-powered money?
3. Assume an economy in which the reserve ratio is 15 percent, people hold 10 percent of their deposits in the form of cash, and there are no other leakages.
   (a) Compute the value of the money multiplier.
   (b) If the current level of high-powered money is $1,500 billion, what is the money supply in this economy?

(c) How much does the money supply change if the Fed buys $30 billion of U.S. government Treasury bills from a government bond dealer? How about if banks' borrowings of reserves from the Fed decline by $6 billion?

(d) If the Fed set a target money supply of $6,424 billion, what would it have to do to achieve that target?

4. Suppose you earn and spend $2,400 per month. You receive your paycheck on the first day of the month and must decide how much of it to hold as cash or in a non-interest-earning checking account and how much to deposit in your savings account. The savings account pays 5 percent interest; however, the bank charges you $2 for each withdrawal you make during the month.

(a) What will be your average demand for money over the month?

(b) If the interest rate rose to 10 percent, what would be your average demand for money over the month? Is this change consistent with your expectations about the demand for money?

5. Suppose that the IS and LM curves for an economy are given by:

$$IS: Y = 2.5A_p' - 250r$$

$$LM: Y = 5(M^s/P) + 250r$$

where A_p' is initially 5,000, M^s is initially 2,000, and $P = 1$.

(a) Graph the IS and LM curves when the interest rate equals 3, 4, 5, 6, and 7.

(b) Use your graphs of the IS and LM curves to find the equilibrium level of income and the equilibrium interest rate.

Suppose that housing prices and the value of the dollar (the exchange rate) are both falling simultaneously, creating uncertainty as to what the future level of autonomous planned spending, A_p', will be.

(c) Explain which one of these two events would cause autonomous planned spending to fall and which one would cause it to rise.

(d) Monetary policymakers evaluate the possible effects of the declines in house prices and the value of the dollar and estimate that the most autonomous planned spending can either rise or fall by is $200 billion. Given a decline in autonomous planned spending equal to $200 billion, graph the new IS curve when the interest rate equals 3, 4, 5, 6, and 7 and label that IS curve IS'. Given an increase in autonomous planned spending equal to $200 billion, graph the new IS curve when the interest rate equals 3, 4, 5, 6, and 7 and label that IS curve IS".

(e) Suppose that the level of income you found in part a equals natural real GDP. Monetary policymakers are faced with three policy options in light

of the uncertainty concerning the future amount of autonomous planned spending. First, they could maintain the interest rate at its current level and allow real GDP to adjust as autonomous planned spending varies between $4,800 and $5,200. Second, they could maintain the real money supply at its current level and allow the interest rate and real GDP to adjust to variations in autonomous planned spending between $4,800 and $5,200. Third, they could raise and lower the money supply so as to maintain real GDP at its current level, which is natural real GDP. Use the new IS curves and the LM curve to evaluate how real GDP and/or the interest rate vary as autonomous planned spending varies between $4,800 and $5,200 under each policy option.

(f) Use your answers to part e to explain why, in terms of their effects on the inflation and unemployment rates, the first policy option is the least desirable choice, whereas the third policy option is the best choice.

(g) For each policy option, explain what actions policymakers would have to take in terms of open-market operations if autonomous planned spending falls below its current level of $5,000 or rises above its current level of $5,000.

6. Suppose that the equation for an economy's IS curve is $Y = 13,500 - 300r$. Large fluctuations in stock prices cause people to move funds in and out of assets included in M2, resulting in an unstable demand for money. Due to that unstable money demand, the demand for money fluctuates between $(M/P)^d = 0.25Y - 50r$ and $(M/P)^d = 0.2Y - 40r$. The real money supply, M^s/P, equals $2,500.

(a) Given that the demand for money is $(M/P)^d = 0.25Y - 50r$, verify that the equation for the LM curve is $Y = 10,000 + 200r$ by showing that the demand for money equals $2,400 at the following combinations of income and the interest rate: ($10,000, 0); ($10,400, 2); ($11,400, 7); ($12,000, 10). Graph these points, labeling the LM curve as LM_A.

(b) Given that the demand for money is $(M/P)^d = 0.2Y - 40r$, verify that the equation for the LM curve is $Y = 12,500 + 200r$ by showing that the demand for money equals $2,400 at the following combinations of income and the interest rate: ($12,500, 0); ($12,900, 2); ($13,900, 9); ($14,500, 10). Graph these points, labeling the LM curve as LM_B.

(c) Graph the IS curve at interest rates equal to 0, 2, 7, and 10. Use your graphs of the IS and LM curves to find the equilibrium level of income and the equilibrium interest rate when the demand for money equals $0.25Y - 50r$ and when the demand for money equals $0.2Y - 40r$.

(d) Suppose that natural real GDP equals $12,000. Use your answers to part c to explain what problem the economy faces when the demand for money equals $0.25Y - 50r$ and the problem the economy faces when the demand for money equals $0.2Y - 40r$.

(e) Suppose that monetary policymakers want to target the interest rate in order to keep real GDP equal to natural real GDP. Given that natural real GDP is $12,000, what is the interest rate that monetary policymakers must target? In order to reach this target, what must monetary policymakers set the real money supply equal to when the demand for money is $(M/P)^d = 0.25Y - 50r$ and when it is $(M/P)^d = 0.2Y - 40r$?

◆ SELF-TEST ANSWERS

p. 427. (1) This new type of account, which allows interest to be earned and checks to be written, is part of M2, and so its invention raises the demand for M2 and lowers the demand for M1. (2) As discussed on pp. 440–441, credit cards are not part of the money supply. Rather they are a quick and convenient way of obtaining a bank loan. Credit cards reduce the demand for M1 in two ways, first by reducing the need to carry currency, and second by reducing the size of checking accounts for those who choose not to pay off their entire credit card balances every month. Because M1 is part of M2, credit cards also reduce the demand for M2, including some components of M2 that are not in M1 like money market mutual funds. (3) Same as (1). (4) Equity mutual funds are in neither M1 nor M2, so the demand for both M1 and M2 will decline.

p. 431. (1) $D = H/(e + c) = 500/0.4 = 1,250$
$M = (1 + c)D = (1.25)1,250 = 1,562.5$
(2) $D = 500/0.5 = 1,000$
$M = (1.35)1,000 = 1,350$
(3) $D = 500/0.5 = 1,000$
$M = (1.25)1,000 = 1,250$

p. 435. (1) The short answer is that the Fed sells bonds when it wants to reduce high-powered money [and hence the money supply through equation (13.6)], and it buys bonds when it wants to raise the money supply. To pay for the bonds they bought, the purchasers send high-powered money to the Fed, thereby reducing the amount of H remaining in the economy. (2) Lowering the discount rate, the interest rate that they pay on their discount-window borrowings, makes it more attractive for depository institutions to borrow H from the Fed. An increased stock of H in the economy raises the money supply. (3) It reduces the reserve requirement ratio (e), which appears in the denominator of equation (13.6).

p. 443. (1) and (2) Starting from an initial equilibrium, an increase in the supply of M1 creates an excess supply of M1. According to Tobin and Friedman, M1 is a substitute for both bonds and stocks, and so some of the M1 that is in excess of the initial demand will be used to purchase bonds and stocks, causing prices to rise in both markets. (Strictly speaking, the Tobin version makes stocks and bonds a substitute only for the interest-bearing part of M1, not non-interest-bearing currency and checking deposits.) (3) The effect is ambiguous in both the Tobin and Friedman models. Since money is a substitute for stocks, an increase in the return on stocks (as occurs when stock prices go up) will reduce the demand for money. But the demand for money also depends on wealth, and an increase in wealth caused by an increase in stock market prices will raise the demand for money. The two effects go in opposite directions, and so the net effect is uncertain.

p. 446. (1) With unstable commodity demand, a real GDP rule is most capable of maintaining stable real GDP, a money supply rule comes next, and an interest rate rule is least likely to maintain stable real GDP. (2) With unstable money demand, the real GDP and interest rate rules are equally capable of maintaining stable real GDP, while the money supply rule will result in unstable real GDP.

The Goals, Tools, and Rules of Monetary Policy

Economic forecasting is the occupation that makes astrology respectable.[1]
— David Dremas, 1982

14-1   The Central Role of Demand Shocks

Unrealistic Precision of Policy Control in Previous Chapters

In earlier chapters we assumed that aggregate demand could be controlled exactly. But in the real world, life is more difficult for policymakers. Exogenous demand shocks can shift the *AD* curve and thus the level of nominal GDP, but policymakers cannot neutralize these shocks totally because nominal GDP reacts to policy changes with a lag and by an uncertain amount. As a result, many economists argue against **policy activism,** that is, the use of monetary and fiscal policy to offset exogenous demand shocks.

In this chapter we take into account those aspects of the real-world economy that make successful policy activism elusive. We contrast the real world with the idealized world of the simple *IS-LM* model (Chapter 4), where policymakers could compute the exact policy response needed to offset fully any shift in the *IS* or *LM* curves.

Policy activism purposefully changes the settings of the instruments of monetary and fiscal policy to offset changes in private sector spending.

The Economy as Supertanker

Unfortunately, policymakers cannot steer the economy back and forth as easily as a driver steers an automobile. Changing aggregate demand is much more like steering a giant supertanker. Even if the captain gives the signal for a hard turn, it takes a mile or so to see a change in the supertanker's direction, and ten miles before the supertanker completes the turn. In the same way, the real-world economy has a momentum of its own, and policy shifts cannot control aggregate demand precisely.

In this chapter we also contrast policy activism with an alternative approach based on **policy rules.** These rules call for the Fed to use its tools of monetary control, introduced in Chapter 13, to maintain a fixed growth rate or level of a particular macroeconomic variable. Early proposals called for rules to fix the growth rate of high-powered money or some measure of the money supply. Subsequent proposals for rules have focused on the inflation rate, a so-called "inflation target." Some advocate a mixed rule that targets both the inflation rate and the level of the output gap, the so-called Taylor Rule.

A **policy rule** can call for a fixed path of a policy instrument like the federal funds rate, of an intermediate variable like the money supply, or a target variable like inflation or unemployment. A rule can also call for a specified response of a policy instrument in response to a given change in a target variable.

---

[1] David Dremas, "The Madness of Crowds," *Forbes*, September 27, 1982, p. 201.

A major theme of this chapter is that both activist policy and policy rules face similar pitfalls, including lags, forecasting errors, uncertainty about responses of the economy to Fed actions, and the need to maintain credibility. The modern policy debate is less about the general merits of rules than about *which of several alternative rules should be implemented.* We also look into another monetary policy rule that has been much discussed internationally, targeting the exchange rate, and another that has been implemented in reality, namely the single European currency called the euro.

GLOBAL ECONOMIC CRISIS FOCUS

The Weakness of Monetary Policy After 2008 Reveals a More General Problem

We have previously devoted substantial attention to the reasons why the 2007–09 recession was so deep and why the subsequent recovery after 2009 was so weak. This analysis started with the theoretical prediction of Chapter 4's *IS-LM* model that with certain parameter values monetary policy could be ineffective (see especially pp. 101–05). It then went beyond the theory to examine in Chapter 5 the factors that undermined the effectiveness of monetary policy in the real-world situation of the American economy (see pp. 139–51). In this chapter we provide a more general analysis of the limitations of activist monetary policy and the difficulty of applying alternative rules. We use both the recent as well as earlier episodes to assess a variety of roadblocks to achieving the goals of monetary policy.

14-2   Stabilization Targets and Instruments in the Activists' Paradise

This section sets forth the traditional analysis of stabilization policy favored by the proponents of policy activism. We then focus on the concerns of those who advocate policy rules and oppose activism.

The Need for Multiple Instruments

Just as driving a car requires a steering wheel, accelerator pedal, and brake, so hitting two policy targets requires at least two instruments of stabilization policy. For instance, Chapter 4 showed that changes in the real money supply could not simultaneously achieve both a target level of real GDP and a target interest rate. Both monetary and fiscal policy must be manipulated to achieve an intersection of the *IS* and *LM* curves at a given combination of the interest rate and real GDP (see Figure 4-10 on p. 108).

The *IS-LM* analysis assumed that the price level was fixed. Now that we have learned to allow for inflation, we recognize that monetary policy involves control of the growth rate of a nominal variable (like high-powered money or the money supply). In the long run, when actual and natural real GDP growth are equal to each other ($y = y^N$) and the output ratio (Y/Y^N) is at 100 percent, monetary policy controls the inflation rate and fiscal policy controls the growth rate of natural real GDP, y^N. To see the relationship between fiscal policy and economic growth, review the concept of the "policy mix" on p. 109.

While monetary policy adjusts to target the output gap (and indirectly the inflation rate), fiscal policy can be adjusted to target the real interest rate. A policy mix that makes the real interest rate low will stimulate investment, which in turn will generate faster economic growth.

Monetary, fiscal, and structural employment policies. The natural rate of unemployment is beyond the control of monetary and fiscal policy. A permanent reduction in unemployment requires a permanent drop in the natural rate of unemployment, which in turn requires a separate policy instrument. That instrument is the mixture of structural employment policy tools discussed in Chapter 10, such as training subsidies and unemployment benefits.

But we have not finished adding to our list of policy instruments. Fiscal policy really consists of two types of **policy instruments:** government spending and tax rates. A given government deficit can be achieved with high spending and high tax rates or low spending and low tax rates. Thus another target of policy is the size of government spending and revenue relative to natural real GDP.

So far we are up to four instruments and four targets:

Policy instruments for monetary policy are high-powered money and the federal funds rate; for fiscal policy they are government spending and tax rates.

Instruments	Targets
Structural employment policy	Unemployment rate
High-powered money	Inflation rate
Government spending	Size of government
Tax rates	Long-run growth in real GDP per person

Figure 14-1 gives a more complete illustration of the principles of economic policy. The goal of economic policy is economic welfare, represented by the red box in the upper right corner. Economic welfare can be thought of simply as happiness, the things that individual members of society want—stable prices, full employment, and a high standard of living.

Targets, Instruments, and Structural Relations

Target variables are the economic aggregates whose values society cares most about—society's goals.

Directly to the left of the economic welfare box in Figure 14-1 we find a light red box that lists the main policy **target variables** that influence economic welfare. Some are more important than others. The distribution of income is quite different from the other targets; any policy shift that raises the income of one group at the expense of others (rich versus poor; creditors versus debtors) is bound to be controversial and lead to political conflict.

In the upper left corner of Figure 14-1 is a list of some of the policy instruments that the government can use to try to achieve its targets. Linking the green instrument box with the upper right red target box is the large blue central box, which contains the structural relations that link the variables. The *IS* and *LM* curves of Chapter 4 and *SP* and *LP* curves of Chapter 9 summarize the main relations that link money, taxes, and government spending to unemployment and inflation. But as shown in the lower left orange box, those curves can also be shifted by several exogenous factors not under the direct control of policymakers, such as a burst of business or consumer optimism, an easing of qualifications needed for obtaining credit from banks, or higher export sales (shifting the *IS* curve upward) or an adverse supply shock (shifting the *SP* curve upward).

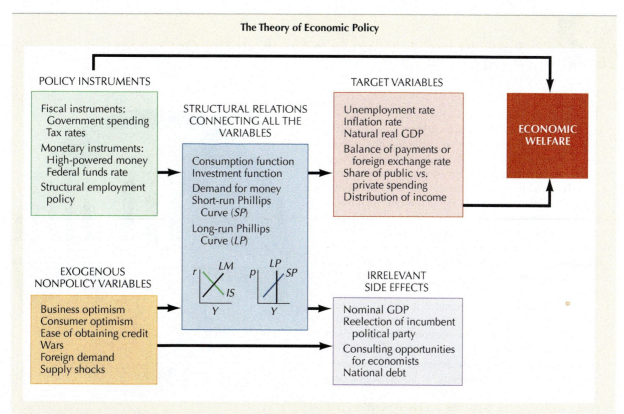

The Theory of Economic Policy

POLICY INSTRUMENTS

Fiscal instruments:
  Government spending
  Tax rates
Monetary instruments:
  High-powered money
  Federal funds rate
Structural employment
  policy

STRUCTURAL RELATIONS CONNECTING ALL THE VARIABLES

Consumption function
Investment function
Demand for money
Short-run Phillips
  Curve (*SP*)
Long-run Phillips
  Curve (*LP*)

TARGET VARIABLES

Unemployment rate
Inflation rate
Natural real GDP
Balance of payments or
  foreign exchange rate
Share of public vs.
  private spending
Distribution of income

ECONOMIC WELFARE

EXOGENOUS NONPOLICY VARIABLES

Business optimism
Consumer optimism
Ease of obtaining credit
Wars
Foreign demand
Supply shocks

IRRELEVANT SIDE EFFECTS

Nominal GDP
Reelection of incumbent
  political party
Consulting opportunities
  for economists
National debt

Figure 14-1 A Flowchart Showing the Relationship Between Policy Instruments, Policy Targets, and Economic Welfare

Both policy instruments and exogenous nonpolicy variables are fed into the structural relations that connect the exogenous (policy and nonpolicy) variables with the endogenous (target and nontarget) variables. Total economic welfare at the upper right depends on the achieved values of the target variables, and thus it depends on policymakers' decisions about the settings of policy instruments.

When the values of the exogenous and instrument variables are fed into the structural economic relations in the middle box, they produce the values of the target variables—unemployment, inflation, and the others. Other variables, shown in the lower right purple box, are also affected, but these are called irrelevant variables because they are not major determinants of economic welfare. Notice that the national debt is an irrelevant side-effect, in the sense that the size of the national debt matters only if it causes changes in the target variables; for instance, by causing inflation or by reducing natural real GDP as a result of the crowding out of private investment.

As shown in the box on the next page, one easy way to think about the rules-versus-activism debate is to note the contrast between where the two groups place their optimism and pessimism. Policy activists are pessimistic about the self-correcting powers of the private economy and optimistic about the efficacy of stabilization policy. In contrast, rules advocates are optimistic about the underlying stability of the private economy but pessimistic about the efficacy of stabilization policy.

Rules Versus Activism in a Nutshell: The Optimism-Pessimism Grid

The table in this box sorts out a wide variety of issues in debate between the policy activists and rules advocates. Activists' beliefs are presented in the top line. Activists are relatively pessimistic about the stability of the private economy. This pessimism stems from their concern that the private (that is, nongovernment) economy is subject to substantial business fluctuation. Such fluctuations are sometimes the result of a wave of business and consumer pessimism, as in the 1930s, or of a collapse of housing and other types of investments, as in 2008–09. Business fluctuations may result also from government actions, as when military spending exploded during wartime.

While the activists are pessimistic about the stability of the private economy, they are optimistic about the feasibility of stabilizing the economy through government policy. This reflects their belief that the activists' paradise, while a caricature designed to exaggerate the conditions needed for successful policy activism, nevertheless contains a kernel of truth.

As shown in the table, the activists' position is disputed on both counts by policy rules advocates. This group optimistically views the private economy as inherently self-correcting, due in part to the belief that demand disturbances are partly or largely absorbed by changes in private saving. And policy rules advocates

are pessimistic about stabilization policy, believing it can do more harm than good, due to lags, forecasting errors, uncertainty, and the other problems discussed in this chapter.

	Belief regarding automatic self-correcting properties of private economy?	Belief regarding efficacy of government stabilization policy?
Activists	Pessimistic	Optimistic
Rules advocates	Optimistic	Pessimistic

SELF-TEST

Classify the following as policy instruments or target variables:

1. The inflation rate
2. The personal income tax rate
3. The federal funds rate
4. The unemployment rate
5. High-powered money

14-3 Policy Rules

The great debate over policy rules primarily concerns monetary policy. In the 1930s, University of Chicago economist Henry Simons posed a stark contrast between a totally discretionary monetary policy and a fixed rule that takes away all discretion from the central bank.[2] In reality, there is a continuum in monetary policy between completely **discretionary policy** at one extreme and a **rigid rule** at the other extreme.

The most extreme form of a rigid rule would be for the Fed to carry out a specified set of open-market operations, for example, to buy exactly enough securities to make high-powered money (H, the sum of currency and reserves) grow by, say, 5 percent per year. However, as we learned in the last chapter (see equation (13.6) on p. 430), such an action would not lead to steady growth in the money supply, since the money supply depends not only on H but also on the reserve ratio and the public's currency-holding ratio. Even if growth in H is kept absolutely rigid, choices by the public to raise or lower its holdings of currency could lead to major swings in the money supply. Another form of a rigid rule would be for the Fed to conduct whatever open-market operations are required to maintain absolutely constant a short-term interest rate like the federal funds rate.

The best-known early proposal for a policy rule, a **constant growth rate rule (CGRR)** for the money supply, was made in the late 1950s by Milton Friedman, then at the University of Chicago. Just as maintaining a fixed growth rate for H does not ensure a fixed growth rate for the money supply, due to variations in the money multiplier (M/H), the reverse is true as well. Maintaining a CGRR for the money supply would require the Fed to manipulate H actively in order to offset changes in the money multiplier.

In addition to rules calling for a fixed growth rate of H or the money supply, many other types of rules have been proposed. Some involve not a monetary variable like H or the money supply, but rather a target variable like the price level or output. Other rules fall under the category of **feedback rules,** which systematically change monetary variables like the money supply or interest rates in response to actual or forecasted changes in target variables like inflation or unemployment. The leading example of such a feedback rule is called the Taylor Rule, discussed in Section 14-7.

The early school of thought advocating a rule for monetary policy was called **monetarism.**[3] This approach combined the key elements in the box on p. 454—optimism regarding the stability of the private economy and pessimism regarding the efficacy of discretionary policy—with a specific policy proposal advocating a CGRR for the money supply.[4] Subsequently, monetarism faded in popularity and was replaced by advocacy of rules that target the inflation rate, so called "inflation targeting," and mixed feedback rules such as the Taylor Rule.

The Positive Case for Rules

The case for rules takes two forms. One is a positive case based on the advantages of rules themselves, and the other is a negative case based on the defects of a completely discretionary policy.

Discretionary policy treats each macroeconomic episode as a unique event, without any attempt to respond in the same way from one episode to another.

A **rigid rule** for policy sets a key policy instrument at a fixed value, as in a constant growth rate rule for the money supply.

A **constant growth rate rule (CGRR)** stipulates a fixed percentage growth rate for the money supply, in contrast to the variable growth rate recommended by policy activists.

A **feedback rule** sets stabilization policy to respond in a systematic way to a macroeconomic event, such as an increase in unemployment or inflation.

Monetarism is a school of thought that opposes activist or discretionary monetary policy and instead favors a fixed rule for the growth rate of high-powered money or of the money supply.

---

[2] Henry C. Simons, *Economic Policy for a Free Society* (Chicago: University of Chicago Press, 1948). Simons originally wrote on rules versus discretion in the mid-1930s.

[3] The term *monetarism* was introduced in Karl Brunner, "The Role of Money and Monetary Policy," *Federal Reserve Bank of St. Louis Review,* no. 50 (1968), pp. 9–24.

[4] See Milton Friedman, *A Program for Monetary Stability* (New York: Fordham University Press, 1959).

The main arguments for rules as set forth by Milton Friedman are three. First, a rule insulates the central bank from political pressure, which might, for instance, take the form of pushing the central bank to overstimulate the economy in the year before an election. Second, a rule allows the performance of the central bank to be judged by the government and the public. For instance, a central bank charged with a CGRR for the money supply would be judged to be a failure if in reality the money supply gyrated wildly or grew at an average rate different from the one specified in the rule. Third, a rule reduces uncertainty since firms, workers, and consumers are able to gauge accurately what the central bank will be doing over the next several years.

However, as suggested by Stanley Fischer, formerly of MIT and now the Governor of the Bank of Israel, there are weaknesses in each of these arguments.[5] First, it is not necessarily desirable for the central bank to operate independently of political pressure; a central bank, in its attempts to achieve or maintain low inflation, might be more willing to sacrifice jobs in the short run than the general public is. The merits of the second and third arguments fail as a general support for rules, since their validity depends on what variable the central bank chooses to target. For instance, the public has no reason to care directly about the quantity of high-powered money or the money supply, since the target variables that concern the public are inflation, unemployment, and growth in productivity and in real GDP per person.

In short, it is hard to make a general case for rules without specifying the exact nature of the rule. As in the saying "there are many slips between cup and lip," there are many sources of slippage between the Fed's policy instruments, particularly open-market operations, and the most important target variables, that is, inflation, unemployment, and productivity growth. These slippages include money-multiplier shocks (Chapter 13), money demand shocks (Chapter 13), commodity demand shocks (anything discussed in Chapters 3 or 4 that can shift the *IS* curve), and supply shocks (Chapter 9).

The Negative Case for Rules

The negative case for rules consists of a criticism of activism. As shown in the box on p. 454, rules advocates are pessimistic about activist (discretionary) policy, believing that such measures can do more harm than good. Much of the rest of this chapter looks in detail at their case by examining the many reasons why the activists' optimism about policy is unrealistic—lags, uncertainty, forecasting errors, and other issues.

However, just as the merits of the positive case for rules depend on the particular type of rule being considered, so does the negative case for rules. For instance, lags and uncertainty may create so much slippage between the Fed's policy instruments and the economy's target variables that it becomes infeasible for the Fed to carry out a rule involving a target, such as the proposal that the Fed adhere to a fixed target for the inflation rate.

In recent years, the popularity of the Taylor Rule, which advocates that the central bank choose a mixed target of the inflation rate and output ratio, has caused the distinction between the rules advocates and activists to evaporate. All the obstacles to activism, such as the difficulty of controlling the money

---

[5] Stanley Fischer, "Rules versus Discretion in Monetary Policy," in Benjamin Friedman and Frank Hahn, eds., *Handbook of Monetary Economics*, vol. 2 (Amsterdam: Elsevier Science Publishers, 1990), pp. 1156–84.

supply and the long lags between changes of interest rates and the response of both inflation and the output ratio, are equally applicable to Taylor's Rule as to old-fashioned activism. We now turn to the first obstacle to either activism or Taylor's Rule: the long lags between the effects of central bank actions and the ultimate response of the economy.

14-4   Policy Pitfalls: Lags and Uncertain Multipliers

The core of Milton Friedman's case against policy activism and in favor of a monetary rule was that there are what he called "long and variable" lags between changes in monetary policy instruments and the ultimate response of target variables like inflation and unemployment. As we have seen, Friedman's arguments against activism also represent significant obstacles to modern rules like inflation targeting or Taylor's Rule. In this section we distinguish five types of lags for monetary policy and attempt to estimate the length of these lags.

The Five Types of Lags

Lags prevent either monetary or fiscal policy from immediately offsetting an unexpected shift in the demand for commodities or in the demand for money or in the impact of a supply shock. There are five main types of lags. Some are common to both monetary and fiscal policy; others are more important for one policy than the other:

1. The data lag
2. The recognition lag
3. The legislative lag
4. The transmission lag
5. The effectiveness lag

To explain the meaning of each lag and to estimate its length, let us take as an example the June 2009 end of the 2007–09 recession, the most recent recession that provides us with an example.

1. **The data lag.** Policymakers do not know what is going on in the economy the moment it happens. The index of industrial production exhibited its first significant increase during July 2009. But this news did not arrive until mid-August 2009. Typically, an economic change that starts at the beginning of one month, say July, is not fully evident in the data until the middle of the next month, so that the data lag is about 1.5 months.

2. **The recognition lag.** Policymakers do not pay much attention to changes in data that occur only for one month. The subsequent month might exhibit a reversal in the opposite direction, and frequently data are revised to change small increases into small decreases, or vice versa. Thus it was necessary to wait for the August data to confirm that industrial production had increased for two months in a row, and these data series were not released until September 2009.

3. **The legislative lag.** Although most changes in fiscal policy must be legislated by Congress, an important advantage of monetary policy is the short legislative lag. Once a majority of the Federal Open Market Committee

(FOMC) decides that a monetary policy stimulus is needed, only a short wait is necessary, since the FOMC has eight regularly scheduled meetings annually and can meet by phone anytime. This brings us to October 2009.

4. **The transmission lag.** The transmission lag is the time interval between the policy decision and the subsequent change in policy instruments. Like the legislative lag, this lag is a more serious obstacle for fiscal policy. Once the FOMC has given its order for the open-market manager to make open-market purchases, the short-term (federal funds) interest rate declines immediately.

5. **The effectiveness lag.** Most of the controversy about the lags of monetary policy concerns the length of time required for an acceleration or deceleration in the money supply to influence real output. As we have seen, Milton Friedman has argued that the effectiveness lag is long and variable.

Evidence on the Effectiveness Lag

The most difficult lag to measure, as well as the longest, is the effectiveness lag between the change in monetary policy and the response of the economy. Estimates of this lag differ for numerous reasons, including the use of different measures of monetary policy and different indicators of the economy's response.

In determining the length of the effectiveness lag, it is useful to measure the monetary policy action by the change in short-term interest rates, since the Fed can change those interest rates almost immediately after a meeting of the FOMC (thus eliminating the transmission lag). One set of estimates of the effectiveness lag is presented in Figure 14-2. This figure plots for three alternative intervals the response of real GDP to a change in the short-term interest rate, specifically the federal funds rate.[6]

As shown in Figure 14-2, the first two intervals (1961–75 and 1976–90) reveal the expected result (implied by the negatively sloped *IS* curve of Chapter 4) that real GDP declines when the federal funds rate increases. The response varies in magnitude, with the 1961–75 response substantially greater than the 1976–90 response. The main point is that the lags are long and variable, as Milton Friedman wrote long ago, even prior to the 1961 starting date of Figure 14-2.

Because the economy's response is so spread out over time, distributed over two years, it is difficult to come up with a single measure of the effectiveness lag. One sensible measure of this lag is the length of time necessary for *half of the ultimate effect to be felt*. As shown in the small boxes in Figure 14-2, this lag was 13.8 months, 14.1 months, and 24.1 months over the three intervals plotted.

It is notable that in the most recent period after 1991, not only was the lag of monetary policy very long (24 months) but also the impact on real GDP was slightly positive rather than negative. Thus the interval between 1991 and 2010 provides evidence that, not only does monetary policy impact the economy with long lags, but also and more surprisingly, *changes in the federal funds rate may not have any impact on real GDP growth at all.*

Another measure of the policy lag, one that does not rely on interest rate data, can be extracted from earlier research by David and Christina Romer of

---

[6] For those readers trained in econometrics, the details lying behind Figure 14-2 are as follows: The annualized percentage change in quarterly real GDP over the indicated intervals was regressed on a constant and lags 3 through 8 of the quarterly changes in the nominal Federal funds rate. Lag lengths of 9 quarters or greater were statistically insignificant and were omitted. The current change and the first and second lags were omitted because their coefficients are positive, indicating the presence of feedback from real GDP to the interest rate.

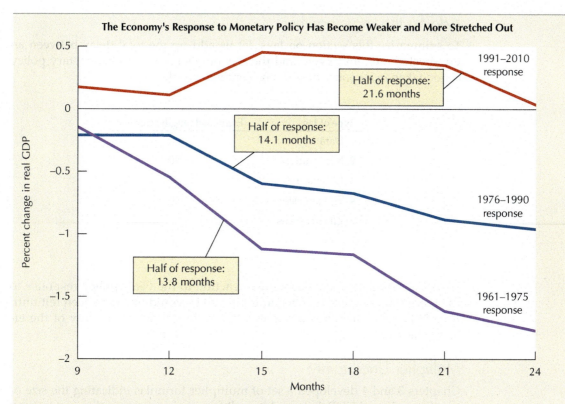

Figure 14-2 The Percent Change in Real GDP Following a 1 Percentage Point Change in the Federal Funds Rate, Three Intervals, 1961–2010

Following a 1 percentage point change in the short-term (federal funds) interest rate, real GDP changes in the opposite direction by the percentages shown by the plotted lines drawn for each of three intervals, 1961–75, 1976–90, and 1991–2010. The lines show, for instance, that after 24 months real GDP would have dropped by about 1.8 percent during the 1961–75 period, by 0.9 percent during 1976–90, but not at all in the more recent 1991–2010 interval. The boxed labels show how many months were required for half of the ultimate impact on real GDP to occur.

Source: See Appendix C-4.

the University of California, Berkeley. They read the minutes of the FOMC to identify the months when the Fed "made a decision to try to cause a recession to reduce inflation,"[7] identifying six such episodes between 1947 and 1979. They ran a statistical test similar to that in Figure 14-2 to examine the response of industrial production in the three years after the Fed's policy shift. For their six episodes, their estimated effectiveness lag averages 19 months, consistent with the lags of 14 to 24 months shown in Figure 14-2.[8]

---

[7] Christina D. Romer and David H. Romer, "Does Monetary Policy Matter? A New Test in the Spirit of Friedman and Schwartz," in O. J. Blanchard and S. Fischer, *NBER Macroeconomics Annual 1989* (Cambridge, MA: MIT Press), p. 152.

[8] Romer and Romer, ibid., Table 1, p. 153. The maximum effect of their monetary policy variable (defined as unity in one of the six months when the Fed changed policy and zero otherwise) is reached 32 months after the policy change. Half of the total effect occurs after 18.8 months. This estimate is approximate, as it omits the impact of the lagged dependent variable in their equation.

Adding the Lags Together

To summarize this section on lags, let us add up the total delay between an unexpected economic event and the economy's reaction to a monetary policy action taken in response to such an economic event.

Type of lag	Estimated length (months)
1. Data	1.5
2. Recognition	2.0
3. Legislative	0.5
4. Transmission	0.0
5. Effectiveness	19.0
Total	23.0

Thus the first half of the economy's reaction to the Fed's policy response to the economic recovery that began in July 2009 would not have been felt until June 2011 (plus or minus a few months, reflecting the variability of the effectiveness lag).

Multiplier Uncertainty

Chapters 3 and 4 developed a set of multiplier formulas indicating the size of the change in real GDP that would result from a change in a policy instrument, such as tax rates, government spending, or the money supply. But the *IS-LM* model summarized in those chapters was very simple. This section shows that we do not know nearly as much about the values of the multipliers as the simple *IS-LM* model initially led us to believe.

Dynamic multipliers are the amount by which output is raised during each of several time periods after a given change in the policy instrument.

Multiplier uncertainty concerns the lack of firm knowledge regarding the change in output caused by a change in a policy instrument.

Figure 14-2 illustrates **dynamic multipliers** that show the response of real GDP to a change in the interest rate over several intervals. We noted that the multipliers were much smaller in 1991–2010 than before 1991. Also, even for a given time period economists differ widely regarding the size of the monetary and fiscal multipliers. This **multiplier uncertainty** creates a dilemma for policymakers. Even if they could forecast perfectly that the economy needs a policy stimulus now to add 2.0 percent to real GDP four quarters from now, there remains the question as to what exact policy action should be taken. Should the interest rate be dropped today by 0.5, 1.0, or 2.0 percentage points? Any of these numbers might be correct, depending on the policy multiplier.[9]

Why Have Monetary Policy Multipliers Changed?

Three aspects of Figure 14-2 make life especially difficult for policymakers—these are the length of the lag, the change in the lag, and the change in the multiplier (that is, the total effect of an interest rate change on real GDP). We have already noted the fact that the effectiveness lag is long, with half of the effect

[9] See William Brainard, "Uncertainty and the Effectiveness of Policy," *American Economic Review*, vol. 57 (May 1967), pp. 411–25. Brainard's formula suggests that the expected gap between actual and target GDP should be closed by only a fraction of the gap, but that fraction depends on correlations that we are most unlikely to know. An earlier analysis is Milton Friedman, "The Effects of a Full-Employment Policy on Economic Stability: A Formal Analysis," *Essays in Positive Economics* (Chicago: University of Chicago Press, 1953), pp. 117–32.

taking 24 months during 1991–2007. Why is this lag longer now than it was before 1991?

Three changes in the structure of the economy since the 1960s help explain why lags are now longer and multipliers are now smaller than they were back in the 1960s. The first change concerns thrift institutions and housing. In earlier decades housing expenditures took the brunt of tight monetary policy, declining quickly in response to upward movements in interest rates. After the late 1970s this channel of influence on housing became less important, because deregulation lifted the ceilings on interest rates paid to depositors by thrifts. Also, other types of financial institutions that were not subject to interest rate ceilings began to participate more in mortgage markets, further insulating the housing sector from the impact of tightened monetary policy.

The second major change is the reduced impact of changing interest rates on consumer spending. More consumer borrowing now occurs on credit cards, but interest rates on credit cards are very insensitive to monetary policy.

The third major change was the adoption of flexible exchange rates in 1973, previously examined in Chapter 7. This added a major channel of influence of monetary policy, as changing interest rates cause changes in the foreign exchange rate and, after a long lag, changes in net exports. It takes two years or more for net exports to respond fully to changes in the foreign exchange rate.

Summary: The effectiveness lag of monetary policy has become longer, and the multiplier of real GDP response to a change in interest rates has become smaller, because the prompt channel working through housing finance has become weaker, while the time-consuming channel working through exchange rates and net exports has become stronger.

◆ SELF-TEST

For each of the following statements, indicate whether it relates to multiplier uncertainty or lags, and if your answer is "lags," indicate which of the five types of lags is most closely related to the statement:

1. Congress debated President Johnson's proposal for an income tax surcharge for 18 months, from late 1966 to mid-1968.

2. Interest rate ceilings on savings accounts were eliminated by financial deregulation.

3. A record-setting snowstorm in Washington delays publication of the Consumer Price Index by two weeks.

4. Flexible exchange rates were adopted in 1973.

14-5 CASE STUDY

Was the Fed Responsible for the Great Moderation of 1986–2007?

We have previously, particularly in Chapter 5, studied the causes of the deep recession of 2007–09 into which the economy tumbled and of the slow recovery after the end of that recession in June 2009. Clearly the macro economy remains unstable and vulnerable to demand shocks, such as the collapse of the housing bubble after 2006 and the related failure of some financial institutions and the near-failure of many others. The fact that labor market indicators, especially long-term unemployment, were weaker in 2009–10 than in the previous severe downturn of the early 1980s support the view that the economy remains vulnerable to severe shocks.

But prior to 2008, particularly during the interval 1986–2007, the economy was considerably more stable than before 1986 or after 2007. This decline in macroeconomic volatility, which turned out to be temporary, is frequently called "The Great Moderation." Since our discussion thus far in this chapter has stressed the difficulties of managing monetary policy, we face a paradox: In light of these difficulties, how did the economy succeed in achieving greater macroeconomic stability for fully two decades? One possibility is that the performance of monetary policy improved substantially; a complementary hypothesis is that the economy's stability has improved for reasons unrelated to monetary policy. Both explanations could be partly true at the same time.

One way to assess the improved stability of the economy from 1986 to 2007 is to examine Figure 14-3, which in the top frame plots the output gap (log output ratio) since 1960.[10] Clearly the economy was quite unstable, with intervals of substantial negative output gaps in the early 1960s, in 1974–77, and the two big negative episodes of 1980–86 and 2008–10. Also contributing to instability were the episodes of major positive output gaps in 1965–69 and 1972–73. But then between 1986 and 2007, the output gap was much closer to the desired level of zero. Shown in the bottom frame of Figure 14-3 is one way of summarizing the decreased volatility of the ratio, a 20-quarter moving average of the absolute value of the ratio.[11] If the ratio was always either +2 or −2 percent, the moving average of its absolute value would be 2.0. If the ratio followed the pattern 2, 0, −2, 0, averaging those numbers together would give an average of 1.0. As shown in the bottom frame, this measure of volatility was 4.4 in 1970:Q1, fell and then rose to a peak of 4.3 in 1985:Q2, and then declined to values of 2.0 percent or below from 1988:Q2 to 2009:Q3. In 2005–2007 there was a further remarkable decline to below 1.0 percent.[12] But starting in 2008 the output gap in the top frame of Figure 14-3 tumbled into deep negative territory, and by 2010 this had begun to pull the volatility measure in the bottom frame up sharply back towards its 1985 peak value.

Causes of Decreased Volatility: Smaller Demand and Supply Shocks

One hypothesis is that demand and/or supply shocks became less important and less harmful after the mid-1980s. Three types of demand shocks contributed to this improvement. Most important was the smaller size of government military

---

[10] The log output ratio is zero when actual real GDP equals natural real GDP. This concept was introduced in the Appendix to Chapter 9, p. 306. A synonym for the log output ratio is the "GDP gap" or "output gap," a concept used throughout this book and initially introduced on p. 6.

[11] The absolute value of any number is its actual value with any negative signs converted to positive.

[12] A slightly different measure of decreased volatility is considered in Olivier Blanchard and John Simon, "The Long and Large Decline in U.S. Output Volatility," *Brookings Papers on Economic Activity*, vol. 32, no. 1 (2001), pp. 135–64. Volatility measures based on four-quarter changes of real GDP show an even more pronounced reduction in volatility; see Robert J. Gordon, "What Caused the Decline in U.S. Business Cycle Volatility?" NBER Working Paper 11777, November 2005.

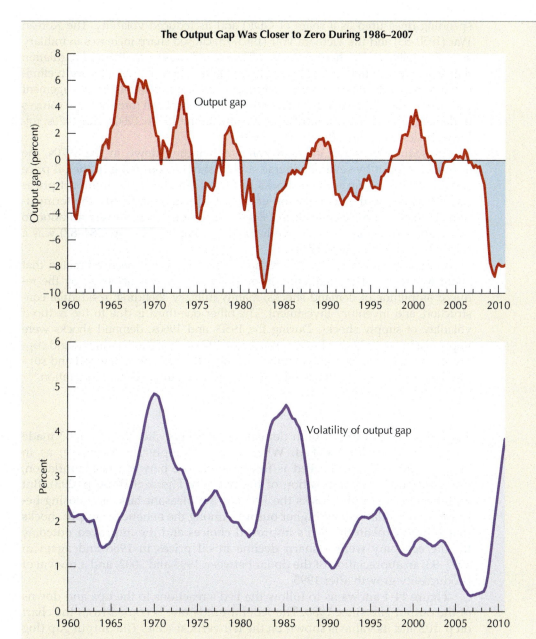

Figure 14-3 The Output Gap and the Moving Average of its Absolute Value, 1960–2010

The top frame shows the output gap in percent. During 1986–2007 the gap never exceeded +4 percent and never fell below -3 percent, in contrast to the period before 1986 when the range extended from +5.2 to -8.2 percent. This decrease in volatility is summarized by the 20-quarter moving average of the absolute value of the output gap, as shown in the bottom frame. This moving average reached peaks of 4.4 in 1970 and 4.3 in 1985, in contrast to the period between 1988 and mid-2009 when the measure never exceeded 2.0 percent and fell as low as 0.5 percent in 2007.

Source: See Appendix C-4.

spending (measured as a share of GDP) and its reduced volatility. The Korean War (1950–53) and the Vietnam War (1965–75) caused sharp increases in military spending followed by sharp decreases. The second cause was financial regulation that made residential construction more volatile; these regulations were eliminated in the early 1980s. Finally, computers and improvements in management practices reduced the volatility of inventory investment. All three of these sources of demand shocks made output more volatile in the 1950s, 1960s, and 1970s, followed by less volatility after the mid-1980s.

Subsequently as the Vietnam War was winding down in the 1970s, the economy was hit by several adverse supply shocks, consisting of the oil price shocks of 1974–75, farm price shocks in 1972–73, higher non-oil import prices in 1973–74 due to the depreciation of the U.S. dollar, and, finally, the termination of Nixon-era price controls in 1974–75. All these shocks caused inflation to shoot up, and a side effect (as we learned in Chapter 9 on pp. 284–87) was a sharp decline in the output ratio.

Comparing the periods 1950–85 and 1986–2007, it has been estimated that about two-thirds of the reduction in output volatility was achieved by the reduced amplitude of demand shocks, mainly military spending, residential construction, and inventory investment. The other one-third is due to the reduced volatility of supply shocks. During the 1950s and 1960s, demand shocks were important but supply shocks were not. From 1970 to 1985, both demand and supply shocks contributed high volatility. During 1986–2007, both demand and supply shocks exhibited greater stability and contributed to the Great Moderation.[13]

The Role of the Fed Between 1983 and 2001

The reduced volatility of both demand and supply shocks after 1983 made life much easier for the Fed. When adverse supply shocks strike, as in 1974–75 and 1979–81, the Fed is forced to choose between faster inflation, lower output, or a combination of the two (see Figure 9-10 on p. 293). But with beneficial supply shocks the Fed has the pleasant task of choosing between lower inflation and higher output. Among the beneficial supply shocks that help to explain the Fed's improved choices and the improved outcome for the economy were a sharp decline in oil prices in 1986 and again in 1997–98, an appreciation of the dollar between 1995 and 2002, and a revival of productivity growth after 1995.

Figure 14-4 allows us to follow the Fed's reactions to the ups and downs of the output gap since 1980. The federal funds rate is copied from the chart on p. 102 and its value is shown on the left vertical scale. The output gap (log output ratio) line is copied from Figure 14-3 and its value is shown on the right vertical scale.

The 1980–86 period was highlighted by a large negative output gap caused by the Fed's tight disinflationary monetary policy that caused the federal funds

---

[13] This paragraph is based on the author's NBER Working Paper cited in footnote 12. See also James H. Stock and Mark W. Watson, "Has the Business Cycle Changed? Evidence and Explanations," in *Monetary Policy and Uncertainty: Adapting to a Changing Economy*, Federal Reserve Bank of Kansas City, 2003, pp. 9–56. Another broad overview is S. Ahmed, A. Levin, and B. A. Wilson, "Recent U.S. Macroeconomic Stability: Good Policies, Good Practices, or Good Luck?" *The Review of Economics and Statistics*, vol. 86, no. 3, pp. 824–32. The role of financial deregulations and innovations is explored in K. E. Dynan, D. W. Elmendorf, and D. E. Sichel, "Can Financial Innovation Help to Explain the Reduced Volatility of Economic Activity?" *Journal of Monetary Economics*, vol. 53, January 2006, pp. 123–50.

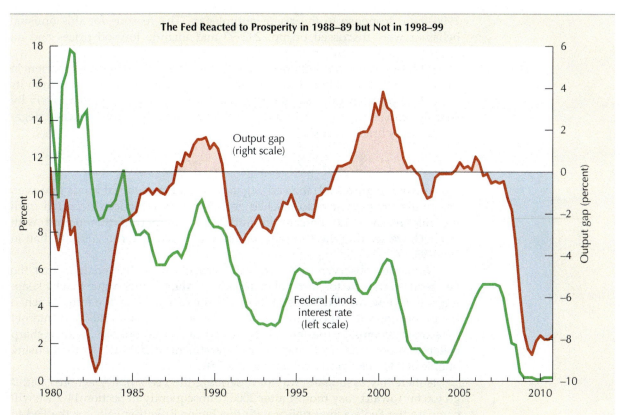

Figure 14-4 The Federal Funds Interest Rate and the Log Output Ratio, 1980–2007

Since the 1980s the Fed has tended to raise and lower interest rates in anticipation of the economy's overheating or stalling out. In the late 1980s the Fed began to raise interest rates when the log output ratio went above zero. When signals began to suggest in 1989 that the log output ratio would be falling appreciably below zero in the near future, the Fed began lowering interest rates. The Fed raised interest rates in 1994 as the log output ratio again seemed headed above zero. But after 1996 the Fed changed its behavior for reasons discussed in the text.

Source: See Appendix C-4.

rate to rise briefly almost to 18 percent. As inflation subsided the federal funds rate was allowed to decline between 1981 and 1987, but as soon as the output gap rose above zero in 1988 the federal funds rate was increased with a delay of only about six months. Then when the output gap fell below zero in late 1990, the Fed dropped the federal funds rate in a series of steps that lasted until early 1993. The Fed's actions in 1988–93 were prompt and represented steps in the right direction, that is, in the direction that stabilized the output gap.

The Fed's first mistake appears to be the sharp increase in the federal funds rate in 1994 when the output gap was still negative. This move, called at the time a "preemptive strike," reflected imperfect knowledge of the output gap. But then the Fed ignored the sharp rise in the output gap between 1996 and 2000, failing to raise the federal funds rate at all as it had done in 1988–89. Why? By far the most important reason was the behavior of inflation. As we learned from Figure 9-1 on p. 267, the inflation rate did not accelerate in

1996–99 in response to the rising output gap. The reasons for this unusual behavior were discussed on pp. 292–93 and include low oil prices and an appreciation of the dollar exchange rate.

While the Fed did briefly raise the federal funds rate for several quarters in the year 2000, it quickly reduced the rate as the output ratio declined from its early 2000 peak. In this case the Fed also, as in 1994, acted preemptively by sharply reducing the federal funds rate before the output ratio reached negative territory briefly in 2002–03.

The Fed's Controversial Easing After 2000

As shown in Figure 14-4, the Fed began to reduce the federal funds rate even before the log output ratio reached zero. Further reductions occurred until the rate reached 1.0 percent in mid-2003. Comparing this period with 1990–93, we see that the Fed reduced the rate much faster in 2001–02 than in 1990–93.

Numerous observers have argued, particularly with hindsight, that the Fed reduced the rate too fast and by too much. Many critics argue that by keeping rates so low, the Fed poured fuel on the fire of a housing boom that reached the proportions of a speculative bubble. Just as the stock market and Internet investment booms of the late 1990s turned out to be bubbles, with a sharp collapse in both the stock market and investment in 2000–03, so the housing bubble of 2003–06 led to a collapse in 2007–09.

Is there any systematic way of describing the Fed's policy actions? Did it go too far toward easy money after 2000? Subsequently in Section 14-7 we will compare the Fed's actual policy with the Taylor Rule that calls for the Fed to raise interest rates whenever inflation speeds up or whenever the log output ratio rises above zero. ◆

14-6 Time Inconsistency, Credibility, and Reputation

We have already seen that one of the advantages that Milton Friedman claimed for policy rules was that firms, workers, and consumers would be able to form accurate expectations of future policy actions. Proponents of activism saw no merit in this claim, since any good rule could be adopted by a discretionary policymaker.

Time Inconsistency

In 1977, Finn Kydland of Carnegie-Mellon University and his colleague Edward Prescott (now at Arizona State University) introduced the concept of **time inconsistency.**[14] The basic idea is that discretionary policymakers decide on policy A because it is optimal at that time, and private decisionmakers make consumption, investment, and labor supply decisions based on that policy. However, once private decisionmakers have done so, it may be optimal for

Time inconsistency describes the temptations of policymakers to deviate from a policy after it is announced and private decisionmakers have reacted to it.

---

[14] Kydland and Prescott won the Nobel Prize in economics in 2004. The original reference is Finn E. Kydland and Edward C. Prescott, "Rules Rather Than Discretion: The Inconsistency of Optimal Plans," *Journal of Political Economy,* vol. 85 (June 1977), pp. 473–92. The most influential subsequent article was Robert J. Barro and David B. Gordon, "A Positive Theory of Monetary Policy in a Natural Rate Model," *Journal of Political Economy,* vol. 91 (August 1983), pp. 589–610.

policymakers to shift to policy B, thus invalidating the expectations on which private decisionmakers acted.

The simplest example arises in the classroom. Professors want their students to learn but hate to make up tests and grade them. Time inconsistency occurs when a professor announces that there will be a tough final exam. The students respond to policy A by studying hard, but then, just before the scheduled exam time, the professor announces policy B, that the exam has been canceled.

In macroeconomics the prominent example of time inconsistency involves the Phillips Curve trade-off between inflation and unemployment. For any given unemployment rate, the actual inflation rate will be low if expectations of future inflation are low. This gives the Fed an incentive to pursue policy A, vowing to achieve low inflation. But once inflation expectations have shifted down, the Fed is tempted to shift to policy B by a monetary stimulus that reduces unemployment, even though policy B will raise inflation and invalidate the low expectations of inflation held by workers and firms.

The implication of the time inconsistency argument is that economic performance may be better, on average, if private decisionmakers know that the central bank will adhere to a rigid rule to target the inflation rate. Knowing that there is no discretion and thus no chance of a surprise monetary stimulus (policy B), expectations of future inflation will subside, making possible a lower actual inflation rate for any given unemployment rate.

Credibility and Reputation

In order to achieve the best possible economic performance, with low or even zero inflation combined with unemployment at the natural rate (U^N), it may pay a central bank to invest in its reputation. If the central bank succeeds year after year in avoiding the temptation to boost monetary growth in order to reduce unemployment (policy B), it will convince private decisionmakers that a future upsurge of inflation is unlikely. Once the actions of policymakers create this type of reputation, they are said to gain **policy credibility**.[15]

Over the past decade economists have built sophisticated models of "reputational equilibrium."[16] These lead to the conclusion that *if* the policymaker has a long time horizon and *if* the policymaker has a low discount rate, then an equilibrium with zero inflation is possible. That is, the policymaker has an incentive to produce a time-consistent policy, and private decisionmakers adjust their expectations accordingly. However, such theoretical models are not very practical for real-world situations in which governments and central bankers do not last forever and in which governments face regular election campaigns.

In order to reduce the influence of the vagaries of government political motives, many nations like the United Kingdom have granted freedom to the central bank to operate independently of the elected economic officials of the government. And many central banks in foreign countries, but not the Federal Reserve in the United States, have used their independence to adopt rules that rigidly target the inflation rate without any concern for the performance of real output.[17]

Policy credibility is the belief by the public that the policymakers will actually carry out an announced policy.

---

[15] A useful introduction is Benjamin M. Friedman, "The Use and Meaning of Words in Central Banking: Inflation Targeting, Credibility, and Transparency," NBER Working Paper 8972, June 2002.

[16] See Fischer, "Rules versus Discretion," pp. 1175–78.

[17] An important reference on the concept and implementation of inflation targeting, and a set of papers on the experience of several countries is Ben S. Bernanke et al., *Inflation Targeting: Lessons from the International Experience* (Princeton, NJ: Princeton University Press, 1999).

Implications for Rules Versus Discretion

The debate over time inconsistency focuses on the process by which private decisionmakers form expectations concerning the inflation rate. Other target variables, such as the unemployment rate, are ignored on the assumption that the natural rate hypothesis is valid, so in the long run policymakers have no power to make the actual unemployment rate deviate from the natural rate.

Like many other aspects of the rules versus discretion debate, much of the literature on time inconsistency ignores the variety of different rules that are possible. It ignores as well the many slippages that occur between the policy instrument most directly under the Fed's control and the target variable of central concern in the debate, that is, the inflation rate.

Because of these slippages, no monetary policy based on rigid control of high-powered money is likely to produce a steady inflation rate. Only a policy rule that targets the inflation rate is likely to establish policy credibility, but all the problems with activism examined in this chapter apply as well to such a policy rule. We return to inflation targeting in Section 14-8.

 SELF-TEST

Are the following statements true, false, or uncertain?

1. For any given deceleration of nominal GDP growth created by a tight monetary policy, the recession will be shorter and less severe if the central bank possesses policy credibility with the public.

2. For any given deceleration of nominal GDP growth created by tight monetary policy, the recession will be shorter and less severe if the public believes that the central bank's policy is subject to time inconsistency.

3. Policy credibility increases the merits of a "cold turkey" disinflation as compared to a policy of "living with inflation."

4. The possibility of time inconsistency strengthens the case of discretionary policy against a policy rule that targets the growth rate of high-powered money.

 14-7 CASE STUDY

The Taylor Rule and the Changing Fed Attitude Toward Inflation and Output

No matter what type of rule the Fed attempts to achieve, its short-term instrument of control is the federal funds rate, plotted as the green line in Figure 14-4 on p. 465 and in Figure 14-5 in this section. If the Fed attempts to achieve a rule for growth in the money supply, then the federal funds rate must be raised when the money supply exceeds the desired growth rate. Similarly, if the Fed wants to target the inflation rate, the federal funds rate must rise when the inflation rate exceeds the desired inflation rate.

A problem with targeting the inflation rate is that there are very long lags between an increase in the federal funds rate and a subsequent reduction in the inflation rate. Continuing increases in the federal funds rate, while the Fed

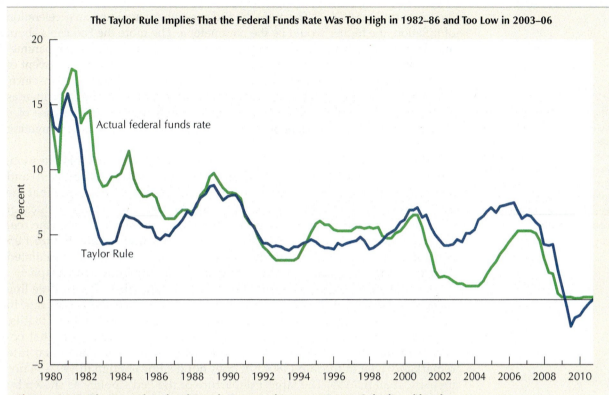

Figure 14-5 **The Actual Federal Funds Rate and Interest Rates Calculated by the Taylor Rule, 1980–2010**

The green line plots the actual federal funds rate. The blue line plots the interest rate forecast by a Taylor Rule with equal weights of 0.5 on inflation and output ($a = b = 0.5$). The accompanying text explains the major differences between the green and blue lines.

Source: See Appendix C-4.

waits for inflation to subside, may cause economic activity to falter, the output ratio to decline, and the unemployment rate to increase. The Fed may prefer to pursue two objectives at the same time, responding to *both* excessive inflation and insufficient output.

John Taylor, of Stanford University and formerly undersecretary of the Treasury, has proposed a simple rule for the Fed (or any other central bank) to follow in setting the real federal funds rate (r^{FF}).[18] The Fed would raise the real interest rate above its desired long-term value whenever inflation exceeded the desired rate and also whenever actual output exceeded natural output:

$$r^{FF} = r^{FF*} + a(p - p^*) + b\hat{Y} \tag{14.1}$$

The terms on the right-hand side are the desired real federal funds rate (r^{FF*}), a parameter (a) times the deviation of the actual rate of inflation from the desired rate of inflation ($p - p^*$), and another parameter (b) times the output gap, that is,

---

[18] John B. Taylor, "How Should Monetary Policy Respond to Shocks While Maintaining Long-Term Price Stability? Conceptual Issues," in *Achieving Price Stability*, Federal Reserve Bank of Kansas City, 1996, pp. 181–95.

the log output ratio ($\hat{Y}$).[19] The more the Fed cares about avoiding an acceleration of inflation, the higher would be the parameter *a*. The more the Fed cares about avoiding recessions and high unemployment, the higher would be the parameter *b*. If the Fed cares equally about 1 percent of excess inflation and 1 percent of insufficient output, then it would set *a* and *b* equal to each other, for instance, $a = b = 0.5$. No matter what the values of *a* and *b* are, the formula written as equation (14.1) has become known as the **Taylor Rule.** The special case of a Taylor Rule with a zero weight on output ($b = 0$) is called an "inflation targeting rule."[20]

The **Taylor Rule** calls for the central bank to move the real short-term interest rate away from its desired long-term value in response to any deviation of actual inflation from desired inflation and in response to any deviation of real GDP from natural real GDP.

How closely did the Fed follow a Taylor Rule? To answer this question, we need to assume a value for the desired real interest rate (3.0 percent) and for the desired inflation rate (2 percent per year). Let us also assume that the Fed places equal weights on inflation and output and assign values of $a = b = 0.5$. Then we can calculate the nominal federal funds rate (the real rate plus the actual inflation rate) called for by the Taylor Rule. Figure 14-5 compares the actual federal funds rate as the green line with the calculated "Taylor Rule" using values of the parameters assumed in this paragraph.[21]

Compared with the green actual rate line, the blue fixed Taylor Rule line reveals interesting differences. First, the Fed did not cut the actual rate in 1981–86 by nearly as much as the Taylor Rule would have required, that is, the Fed did not care enough about the large negative output ratio that occurred in the early 1980s. The blue Taylor Rule line tracks the actual rate remarkably well in the late 1980s but does not decline enough in 1993–94 nor increase at all in 1994. The largest departure of the Fed's policy as shown by the green line from the Taylor Rule as shown by the blue line that occurred during 2001–06. The federal funds rate was held far below the Taylor Rule rate, and many critics have blamed the Fed for keeping interest rates "too low for too long" (see pp. 102–04). The final departure of reality from the Taylor Rule was unavoidable—in 2009–10 the Taylor Rule called for the nominal interest rate to be negative, which is impossible due to the zero lower bound (pp. 104–05).

How are the departures of the Fed's actual policy from the Taylor Rule to be explained? A simple answer is that the Fed varied its policy responses, choosing different values of the coefficients *a* and *b* at different times. For instance in 1981–87 the Fed might have placed a greater "*a*" weight on bringing down inflation. And in 2001–06 the Fed might have placed a greater "*b*" weight on stimulative policy to respond to the output gap.

It is easy to redo the calculations of the blue Taylor Rule line in Figure 14-5 to allow for varying coefficients *a* and *b*. While a high assumed value of *a* in the 1981–86 period does bring actual behavior closer into alignment with the

---

[19] *Review:* The symbol $\hat{Y}$ stands for the logarithm of the ratio of actual real GDP (Y) to natural real GDP (Y^N), expressed as a percent. This concept has been called the "output gap" or "GDP gap" starting on p. 6 of this book. Whenever $\hat{Y}$ equals zero, then actual real GDP is equal to natural real GDP.

[20] On inflation targeting, see Lars E. O. Svensson, "Inflation Targeting: Should It be Modeled as an Instrument Rule or a Targeting Rule?" *European Economic Review,* vol. 46 (2002), pp. 771–80.

[21] The inflation rate is the percent change in the quarterly GDP deflator from one year earlier, the log output ratio is the same as that plotted in Figure 14-4, and the desired real interest rate is chosen to minimize the mean difference between the actual rate and the calculated fixed Taylor Rule rate. Note that there is no need for the parameters *a* and *b* to sum to 1.0.

Taylor Rule, an alternative higher *b* coefficient does not help to explain Fed behavior in 2003–06. Why? The output gap was not negative after 2003, so there was no problem for the Fed to fix. ◆

GLOBAL ECONOMIC CRISIS FOCUS

Taylor's Rule Confronts the Zero Lower Bound

The record shown in Figure 14-5 reveals a dramatic turnaround in the relationship between the actual federal funds interest rate and the Taylor Rule interest rate. Between 2001 and 2007 the actual interest rate shown by the green line was far below the blue Taylor Rule line. But then forces not directly related to monetary policy caused a collapse in the output gap, from roughly zero in late 2007 to about -8 percent in 2009 and 2010. Because the Taylor Rule calculation of the interest rate in equation (14.1) on p. 469 reduces the interest rate in response to a large negative output gap, the calculated Taylor Rule interest rate in Figure 14-5 for 2010 is about -2 percent.

Yet we have learned that it is impossible for the nominal interest rate to be negative, because this means that banks would pay you interest for borrowing money, and any intelligent borrower would ask for an infinite amount from the banks. This logical lower limit of zero on the nominal interest rate has been called throughout this book the "zero lower bound" (see pp. 104–05). Thus, in complete contrast to 2001–06 when Figure 14-5 suggests that the Fed's monetary policy was too stimulative, the same diagram for 2009–10 suggests that Fed policy was not stimulative enough.

14-8   Rules Versus Discretion: An Assessment

A central theme of this chapter is that money-multiplier shocks, money demand shocks, commodity demand shocks, and supply shocks loosen the links between the Fed's policy instruments and its targets for the economy. These shocks imply that a rigid rule for setting the growth rate of the supply of high-powered money (the only policy rule that the Fed is capable of achieving directly) may not achieve the nation's unemployment, inflation, and other targets. Similarly, these shocks may make a rule for a target variable like the inflation rate difficult to achieve.

A second theme is that some policy rules provide a **nominal anchor** for the economy. That is, these rules target a nominal variable (high-powered money, the money supply, nominal GDP, or the inflation rate) and thus automatically place a limit on the ability of inflation to accelerate. A nominal anchor is inherently desirable because it increases the chance that inflation expectations will turn out to be accurate, thus facilitating financial planning by households and firms.

A **nominal anchor** is a rule that sets a limit on the growth rate of a nominal variable, for instance, high-powered money, the money supply, the price level, or nominal GDP. A nominal anchor prevents inflation from accelerating without limit.

Rules for Policy Instruments

Table 14-1 assesses seven policy rules. The first two rules set the values of the Fed's policy instruments, either high-powered money or the federal funds interest rate. A rule for high-powered money growth provides a nominal anchor

Table 14-1 **Assessing Alternative Policy Rules**

Variable to be fixed by policy rule	Main advantages	Main disadvantages
Growth rate of high-powered money	Feasible for Fed to achieve; provides nominal anchor	May lead to variable inflation and unemployment rates
Nominal interest rate	Feasible for Fed to achieve (in short run)	*IS* curve shocks or unstable commodity demand may lead to variable unemployment rate. Does not provide nominal anchor; hence inflation can increase without bound
Growth rate of the money supply (monetarist CGRR)	Provides nominal anchor	Money supply hard to control; money demand instability may lead to variable inflation and unemployment rates
Inflation rate or price level	Provides nominal anchor; if successful, most likely to stabilize inflation expectations and avoid time inconsistency	Hard to control; requires extinguishing reaction to supply shocks, creating highly variable unemployment rate
Unemployment rate or output ratio	Avoids welfare cost of variable unemployment; allows households and firms to carry through on plans without making mistakes	Hard to control; requires accommodating reaction to supply shocks, creating highly variable inflation rate; does not provide nominal anchor
Growth rate of nominal GDP	Provides nominal anchor; splits supply shock effect between output and inflation	Hard to control
Taylor Rule (combines inflation and output targeting)	Provides the advantages of inflation targeting and a nominal anchor while reducing the variance of output and unemployment	Hard to control

but allows shocks to carry the economy away from its target. A nominal interest rate target does not provide a nominal anchor, and either a fiscal stimulus or other positive *IS* shock, or a positive commodity demand shock, can lead to explosive inflation under a nominal interest rate rule.[22]

A Rule for the Money Supply

The money supply is neither directly under the control of the Fed nor is it a target variable. For this reason it is sometimes called an "intermediate variable." A money supply rule (like the monetarist CGRR) has only two advantages. In the first place, it provides a nominal anchor; in the second (as in Figure 13-2 on p. 444), it is superior to an interest rate rule when commodity demand is

---

[22] This defect of a nominal interest rate rule was a major theme of Milton Friedman's 1967 address to the American Economic Association. A positive commodity demand shift boosts the nominal interest rate; to maintain its target, the Fed must raise the money supply; this raises inflationary expectations and boosts the nominal interest rate again; again, the Fed must raise the money supply. Soon the Fed has caused a spiral of accelerating money growth and inflation. This phenomenon occurred when the Fed accommodated the fiscal stimulus of the Vietnam War during 1967–68.

unstable but money demand is stable. Otherwise, it combines the weakness of rules for targets (they are difficult to control) with the weakness of a high-powered money rule.

Rules for Target Variables

The main target variables are inflation and unemployment. Unemployment moves inversely with the ratio of actual to natural output, so a rule that targets unemployment is similar to a rule that targets the output ratio.[23] Because inflation plus real GDP growth equals nominal GDP growth, a nominal GDP growth rule has some of the characteristics of other rules for target variables, even though nominal GDP itself is not a target variable.

Rules for target variables avoid slippage between the instruments and the targets. In particular, all target rules (if successful) prevent instability in either commodity or money demand from causing undesirable fluctuations in target variables. These rules also suffer from a common disadvantage: It is difficult to control target variables because of policy lags, forecasting errors, and multiplier uncertainty. As shown in Table 14-1, rules for target variables differ. Rules for nominal GDP growth or inflation provide a nominal anchor; rules for unemployment or the output ratio do not.

The main advantage of a nominal GDP rule is that it requires no policy response to a supply shock (defined in Chapter 9 as a "neutral policy" response). In contrast, an inflation rule requires that the effect of supply shocks on the price level be extinguished, which raises the variability of output; whereas a real GDP or unemployment rule requires that the effect of supply shocks be "accommodated," which raises the variability of inflation. Because a nominal GDP rule represents a compromise response to supply shocks and provides a nominal anchor, several economists have come to advocate that the Fed adopt such a rule.

By placing weight both on inflation and output, a Taylor Rule (as examined on pp. 468–71) is similar to a nominal GDP rule. A nominal GDP rule is the same as a Taylor Rule that places equal weights on inflation and real GDP *growth* (relative to desired values), in contrast to the traditional Taylor Rule, which targets inflation and the *level* of real GDP relative to natural real GDP (that is, the output ratio). What is the difference? Consider a deep recession like that of 1981–82. The growth rate of real GDP was rapid after early 1983, but the previous recession had created a large negative output ratio that did not return to zero until 1987. In the intervening period of 1983–87, a Taylor Rule based on the output ratio would have caused a lower interest rate than a rule based on the growth rate of output and thus would have helped to make output less variable. *This distinction suggests that a traditional Taylor Rule is superior to a nominal GDP growth rule.*

Implementing a Nominal GDP Rule or a Taylor Rule

Either a nominal GDP growth rule or a Taylor Rule that responds both to excess inflation and insufficient output avoid some of the flaws of other rules listed in Table 14-1. But both approaches are still subject to the difficulties of forecasting and long lags between changes in the instruments controlled by the

---

[23] The negative "Okun's Law" line describing the close inverse relation of the unemployment rate and the output ratio is displayed in Figure 9-12 on p. 298.

The Debate About the Euro

Ever since the end of World War II, the nations of western Europe have been moving toward closer relations. The formation of the NATO security alliance in 1949 was followed by the formation of an economic alliance, the European Economic Community, in the 1950s. During the 1960s and 1970s, a "single market" was created to permit the unfettered movement across national borders of goods and services, financial capital, and people. During the 1980s, economic policies were coordinated even more when the European Monetary System was formed to stabilize the exchange rates of its member nations. The 1992 Maastricht Treaty called for much greater economic integration in its proposal for a monetary union that would replace each member nation's currency with a single European currency.

The Euro Arrives

Finally, on January 1, 1999, the euro was created, while the franc, mark, and other European currencies disappeared from the computer screens of currency traders. Euro coins and currency began to circulate in January 2002, and the colorful French franc, German mark, and other European currencies disappeared from the purses and wallets of citizens in 12 different European countries (now 17 nations).

Politicians across Europe have sought greater economic cooperation because, in general, such cooperation seems to enhance the chances of having Europe remain prosperous and at peace. Economists as a group have been among the most vocal detractors of the EMU and the euro.

For the Euro

Some have argued that international trade within Europe would be enhanced by having a single currency, which would eliminate the costs and risks associated with exchange rates. The irony is that advances in financial markets now make it easier and cheaper than before for firms and financial institutions to manage risks associated with exchange rate fluctuations. In spite of that, it may still be expensive, especially for smaller firms and tourists, to deal with the numerous European currencies and the risks and uncertainties that they entail.

Since World War II, Germany has kept its inflation rate low. Some supported the EMU as a vehicle for other countries to "free-ride" on the German resolve and reputation for low inflation. The European Central Bank (ECB), seems to carry out monetary policy the way the German Bundesbank did, with a single goal of low inflation. Thus the euro is favored by some as a vehicle for achieving the low inflation rates that Germany achieved.

The euro is a common currency, but it may also provide fiscal discipline. Countries that have very high inflation rates sometimes adopt fixed exchange rates in order to discipline both their monetary and their fiscal policies. Among the criteria of the Maastricht Treaty for countries to qualify for inclusion in the euro were that government deficits not exceed 3 percent of GDP and that government debt not exceed 60 percent of GDP. Other entrance criteria stipulated that inflation and interest rates not diverge too widely from those of the other countries entering the euro.

The graph shows the ratio of fiscal deficits to GDP for several member countries of the euro, compared to the 3 percent goal. We see in the left part of the graph that Italy, Spain, and France were required drastically to reduce their fiscal deficits in order to achieve admission into the euro club. From 1997 to around 2002, all the countries shown in the graph were able to maintain their budget deficits below the 3 percent limit. But in 2002–06 several nations breached that limit, allowing their deficits to rise beyond the limit of 3 percent up to 4 percent. Since this was perceived as a minor infraction, no penalties were levied against these countries.

But then the Global Economic Crisis struck Europe very soon after its origination in the United States in 2007–08. Declining real GDP reduced tax revenues sharply, causing the big spikes of the ratio of the government deficit to GDP as shown in the graph. Of the countries shown, the budget deficit of Spain increased to the highest level, followed by France, Italy, and Germany.

Against the Euro

In Chapter 7 we learned about some of the important *economic* costs and benefits of a fixed exchange rate regime like the euro or its predecessor, the EMU. Recall that when a nation chooses to fix its exchange rate, it surrenders the independence of its central bank. Its central bank is committed to use its one policy instrument, the money supply, to achieve its one goal, the exchange rate. In the case of the euro, each member gives up its national currency and any independent monetary policy.

To the extent that the macroeconomic shocks that strike Europe have similar effects on all euro members and that the members have similar preferences about how best to respond to such shocks, the ECB can apply a European monetary policy to the entire group of euro countries and that policy would also be appropriate to each member nation. On the other hand, to the extent that the effects or preferences tend to be more nation-specific, nations have misgivings about the single European monetary policy.

The case for the euro flounders because centralized control of monetary policy at the European Central Bank (ECB, the equivalent for Europe of the Federal Reserve) faces obstacles that are not present within the currency union of the fifty United States. First, the common ECB monetary policy contrasts with the separate uncoordinated fiscal policies of the member euro nations. Several smaller members of the Euro zone allowed their fiscal deficits to reach unprecedented ratios of GDP, up to 12 percent for Greece in 2010. As a result there was a financial crisis within Europe that was at least temporarily stemmed when Germany and other core nations in the Euro zone agreed to bail out floundering Greece, conditional on draconian budget cuts in Greece that would send its economy reeling into an unprecedented recession.

Another reason that the Euro zone of a common currency cannot work as flexibly as the dollar zone of fifty states involves the labor market. Europeans speak many different languages, and each nation has a unique culture, in contrast to the homogenized culture of the United States. While unemployed auto workers in Michigan may readily move to Texas to find jobs, unemployed workers in southern Italy are much less likely to migrate to the Netherlands (which in 2010 had the lowest unemployment rate in Europe).

As 2010 came to a close, the Greek financial crisis was followed by a similar crisis related to excessive fiscal deficits in Ireland. There was worry that the crisis might spread to Portugal, Spain, and perhaps other members of the Euro zone. All of these crises ultimately occurred because the 1999 invention of the Euro represented a monetary union as in the United States without the fiscal U.S. union in the form of a large federal government with an almost unlimited ability to run fiscal deficits.

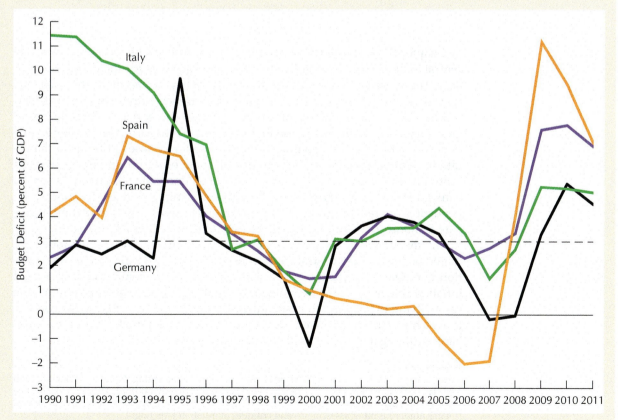

Source: OECD Economic Outlook, no. 81, Annex Table 27.

Fed and the ultimate response of inflation and output. One approach that attempts to circumvent the problem of long lags is for the central bank to target its best *forecast* of inflation and output. Thus, if the average lag between a monetary policy action and the response of inflation is two years, the central bank would respond to changes in its best forecast of inflation two years from now, rather than of inflation today.[24] Indeed, it is clear in analyzing Figure 14-5 on p. 469 that in at least two episodes the Fed relied on forecasts in implementing a policy that resembled a Taylor Rule. In 1994, the Fed's "preemptive strike" raised the federal funds rate sharply in anticipation of accelerating inflation and a positive log output ratio that did not actually occur for several years. And, in 2001, the sharpness of the Fed's interest rate reductions reflected its forecast that there would be a recession deeper than actually occurred.

In the end, we may conclude that the distinction between policy discretion and rules has been exaggerated in the literature on macroeconomic policy. As it implements a policy that seems similar to a Taylor Rule, the Fed has shown that it can change the weights on inflation and output within that rule. And in order to implement that rule, it still must choose a desired long-term real interest rate, a desired inflation rate, and it must determine the current value of natural real GDP in order to calculate the output ratio. Even in implementing a rule, there is plenty of discretion for the Fed and other central banks in deciding exactly how to implement that rule.

14-9 CASE STUDY

Should Monetary Policy Target the Exchange Rate?

In Chapter 7 we learned that when a country has flexible exchange rates, its central bank is free to set policy to attain its objectives for the domestic economy. The more expansionary the monetary policy is, the more the exchange rate is likely to depreciate. The weaker currency stimulates exports and restrains domestic purchases of imported goods and services. Thus the easier monetary policy is likely to raise that country's net exports, thereby shifting its *IS* curve to the right. By contrast, when a country chooses to fix its exchange rate in relation to some other currency or some other group of countries, its central bank surrenders the freedom to pursue domestic objectives; its central bank must use monetary policy to keep the exchange rate fixed. It cannot independently operate to attain other domestic objectives, like stimulating aggregate demand. This is a fundamental lesson of the Chapter 7 *trilemma.*

In the previous section we saw that a country's average inflation rate would be lower if the central bank were committed to a rigid rule for the inflation rate. One way for the central bank to convey its commitment to a rigid inflation rule is to fix the exchange rate. Fixing the exchange rate commits the central bank to keeping domestic interest rates in line with that of the country to which its currency is fixed, thereby precluding the possibility of the central bank adopting a more stimulative monetary policy.

---

[24] See Lars E. O. Svensson and Michael Woodford, "Implementing Optimal Policy through Inflation-Forecast Targeting," in Ben S. Bernanke and Michael Woodford, *The Inflation Targeting Debate* (Chicago and London: University of Chicago Press, 2005), pp. 19–83. The same book contains numerous other assessments and critiques of inflation targeting.

Countries do not casually inflate their economies. More often they print money out of desperation. Hyperinflations have almost always occurred among the vanquished following an international or civil war or other major calamity (Germany, Hungary, the Soviet Union, China, Nicaragua). The very high inflations in Latin America (Brazil, Argentina, Bolivia) occurred after the prices of commodities they exported collapsed, and energy prices and the interest rates they paid to foreigners soared. The very high inflations in eastern Europe and the countries of the former Soviet Union occurred during the difficult transition to market economies, when their needs for public outlays were high and their ability to generate tax revenue was low (Poland, Russia). (For more on hyperinflation and rapid inflation, see Section 10-6 on pp. 334–37).

During the 1990s many of the countries of western Europe pledged to keep their exchange rates fixed relative to each other (but not relative to the United States or Japan). This system was the precursor to the ultimate fixed exchange rate system, a single currency (the euro), discussed in the International Perspective box on pp. 474–75. ◆

Summary

1. In earlier chapters we assumed that the growth of aggregate demand could be controlled precisely by policymakers. We now recognize that in the real world economy, policy shifts cannot control aggregate demand instantly or precisely.

2. Hitting several targets of stabilization policy, such as unemployment and inflation, requires several policy instruments. The conditions required for activist policy intervention to be effective (the "activists' paradise") are quite stringent, including accurate forecasting, possession of powerful tools, absence of costs of changing policy instruments, and absence of political constraints.

3. The general case put forth by advocates of policy rules is that rules insulate a central bank from political pressure, allow the performance of the central bank to be judged, and help private decisionmakers form correct expectations. However, the strength of this case depends on which variable is being targeted by a rule.

4. Policy activists are pessimistic about the stability of the private economy, while they are optimistic about the feasibility of discretionary policy. Advocates of rules reverse the locus of their optimism and pessimism.

5. Five lags (data, recognition, legislative, transmission, and effectiveness) limit the speed at which policy can respond to a demand or supply shock. By far the longest for monetary policy is the effectiveness lag. Additional obstacles to effective activist policy, or to policy rules based on targets, are multiplier uncertainty and forecasting errors.

6. Time inconsistency suggests that discretionary policymakers may have an incentive to alter policies after private decisionmakers have reacted to previous policy announcements. To encourage decisionmakers to form low expectations of inflation, it may pay the central bank to target the inflation rate and achieve a reputation for succeeding in keeping the inflation rate low, thus establishing policy credibility.

7. The Taylor Rule combines a response to excessive inflation and to an output gap that differs from zero. The Fed appears to have followed the Taylor Rule during some periods since 1980 but not others. The Taylor Rule is superior to alternative rules examined in the chapter, including targets for the growth in the money supply or nominal GDP, and targets for the inflation rate.

8. Proposed policy rules differ in the variables they propose to target. Rules targeting policy instruments may be successful but irrelevant for the achievement of desirable outcomes for target variables like inflation and unemployment, due to slippages coming from money-multiplier shocks, money demand shocks, commodity demand shocks, and supply shocks. Rules for target variables may lead to better outcomes in principle, but may be difficult to implement successfully.

9. Fixing its exchange rate deprives a nation's central bank of discretionary monetary policy. In practice, that sometimes leads nations to redress their fiscal imbalances, as well as prevent the money growth that leads to inflation. Member nations of the euro have achieved fixed exchange rates with each other but have lost any control over monetary policy, which they have ceded to the European Central Bank.

Concepts

policy activism
policy rule
policy instruments
target variables
discretionary policy

rigid rule
constant growth rate rule (CGRR)
feedback rule
monetarism
dynamic multipliers

multiplier uncertainty
time inconsistency
policy credibility
Taylor Rule
nominal anchor

Questions

1. In the Appendix to Chapter 4, the equations of the *IS* and *LM* curves are given as follows:

$$IS: Y = k(A'_p - br)$$
$$LM: Y = [(M^s/P) + fr]/h$$

Here, $k = 1/[s(1 - t) + t + nx]$.

Let $A'_p = C'_a - T_a + I'_p + G + NX_a$, where C'_a is that part of consumption spending that is independent of both Y and r, I'_p is similarly defined, and the other terms are as defined in the Appendix to Chapter 3.
   (a) List the exogenous variables (and parameters) in this model. (See Chapter 3 to review the definition of this term.)
   (b) List the endogenous variables in this model. (See Chapter 3 to review the definition of this term.)
   (c) List the target variables in this model.
   (d) List the variables that make up the policy instruments in this model.
   (e) What is the relationship, if any, between endogenous variables and target variables in this model?
   (f) What is the relationship, if any, between exogenous variables and policy instruments in this model?
   Note: In answering this question, use only the variables in the *IS* and *LM* equations and the variables defining k and A'_p. For example, don't include a variable such as structural employment policy as a policy instrument or the unemployment rate as a target variable; they are not variables in the preceding model, even though they are listed in Figure 14-1 as a policy instrument and target variable, respectively.

2. In the *IS-LM* model of the preceding question, what are the monetary policy variables? What are the fiscal policy variables?

3. In the model of question 1, how many policy instruments are there? How many target variables? Is this consistent with the text's statement that you need as many policy instruments as target variables to achieve the desired values of the target variables?

4. What do advocates of policy rules think are the main objections to countercyclical activism?

5. Distinguish between a rigid rule and a feedback rule. Give an example of each.

6. One way of describing the rules-versus-activism debate is to compare the beliefs of each side regarding the self-correcting powers of the economy and the efficacy of stabilization policy. What does each side believe about these issues?

7. Under the constant growth rate rule (CGRR), the single target for the policymaker becomes the growth rate of the money supply. Does this statement suggest that those advocating the CGRR are not concerned with the level of real output and employment?

8. Explain why stability of the demand for money is so important to those advocating a constant growth rate rule for the money supply. What happens to the argument in favor of this rule if money demand is unstable?

9. Identify and describe the five main types of lags that affect the timeliness of monetary and fiscal policy.

10. What problems do long and variable lags present to the policymaker? If lags are long and fixed (rather than long and variable), do any problems remain?

11. Why does multiplier uncertainty create a dilemma for policymakers?

12. How is the effectiveness lag of monetary policy measured in the data shown in Figure 14-2? Using those data, compare the effectiveness of monetary policy for the periods 1961–75, 1975–90, and 1991–2010. Discuss some of the reasons why the effectiveness of monetary policy changed over time.

13. Explain how the rise in volatility in the late 1960s was different from the increases in volatility in the early 1980s and since 2007.

14. Use the various types of lags to explain why a reduction in demand and supply shocks makes it easier for the Fed to conduct monetary policy.

15. Explain why the behavior of inflation caused the Fed to react differently to a rise in the output gap in the late 1990s than it had in the late 1980s.

16. Suppose policymakers announce their intentions to lower the inflation rate and adopt policy changes to slow nominal GDP growth. Describe, in terms of the *SP* model, the effects on the economy's output ratio, unemployment rate, and inflation rate under each of the following cases.
   (a) The public finds this announcement credible, and policymakers stick to their announced policies.
   (b) The public finds this announcement credible, but policymakers abandon their announced policies and leave the growth rate of nominal GDP unchanged.

(c) The public does not find this announcement credible, but policymakers do stick to the announced policies.

(d) The public does not find this announcement credible, and policymakers abandon their announced policies and do not lower the growth rate of nominal GDP.

17. Chapter 9 described three alternative policy responses by the Fed to a supply shock: neutral, accommodating, and extinguishing. In terms of how the Fed weighs inflation against output, that is, the parameters a and b of equation (14.1), explain how each of the Fed's policy responses to a supply shock would fit into a Taylor Rule.

18. Suppose the output ratio is 100 and the inflation rate is 5 percent. Given these conditions, why will policymakers be more likely to pursue a zero inflation target if they have a long time horizon and a low discount rate rather than a short time horizon and a high discount rate?

19. Use Figure 14-5 to explain why the "zero lower bound" meant that monetary policy could not provide as much stimulus to the economy in 2010 as implied by the Taylor Rule.

20. What is a nominal anchor for the economy and what is the advantage of using a nominal anchor in choosing a target variable to be fixed by a policy instrument? Explain why a nominal GDP growth rate rule and a Taylor Rule that places equal weight on inflation and output growth each has a nominal anchor. Finally, compare a Taylor Rule that places equal weight on inflation and output growth with one that places equal weight on inflation and the output ratio.

21. If effectiveness lags are long and variable, should policymakers use the current values or their best forecasts of target variables to determine policy? In evaluating the behavior of the Fed between 1994 and 2001, does it seem more likely that current or forecasted values of inflation and output determined their policies?

22. What are the arguments for and against using monetary policy to target a currency's exchange rate?

23. What are the arguments for and against the euro?

Problems

 Visit www.MyEconLab.com to complete these or similar exercises.

1. You are given the following two IS curves that show how real GDP (Y_t) in the current time period t depends on the current interest rate and interest rates in previous periods, where r_t is the interest rate in time period t. Furthermore each time period corresponds to a quarter or three months.

$$\text{I. } Y_t = 8{,}800 - 25r_t - 25r_{t-1}$$
$$- 25r_{t-2} - 25r_{t-3} - 20r_{t-4} - 20r_{t-5}$$
$$- 20r_{t-6} - 15r_{t-7} - 15r_{t-8} - 10r_{t-9}$$

$$\text{II. } Y_t = 8{,}400 - 5r_t - 5r_{t-1}$$
$$- 5r_{t-2} - 5r_{t-3} - 5r_{t-4} - 10r_{t-5}$$
$$- 15r_{t-6} - 15r_{t-7} - 15r_{t-8} - 20r_{t-9}$$

Suppose that the Fed can set the interest rate and that for the last 10 quarters, the interest rate has been 4 percent.

(a) Verify that initially real GDP equals 8,000 for both IS curves.

(b) Suppose that the Fed lowers the interest rate to 3 percent and keeps it there for the next 10 quarters. Calculate real GDP for the next 10 quarters for each IS curve.

(c) For each IS curve, what is the total increase in real GDP?

(d) For each IS curve, how many quarters does it take for the increase in real GDP to equal one-half of the total increase?

(e) Using Figure 14-2, explain which one of the IS curves resembles the economy's response to a change in the interest rate prior to 1991 and which one resembles its response since 1991. Explain how your answer is related to the interest-rate parameters in each IS equation.

(f) Given your answers to parts b–d, explain how the changes in the monetary policy effectiveness lag and the interest-rate multiplier affects how much and how long monetary policymakers must change interest rates in response to any given demand shock.

2. Suppose that natural real GDP (Y^N) equals \$12,000, the Federal Reserve's desired real federal funds rate (r^{FF*}) equals 2.5 percent, and its desired inflation rate (p^*) equals 2 percent. Initially, an asset bubble collapses, which results in a negative demand shock. It is then followed by an upsurge in government spending that results in a positive demand shock. You are given the following combinations of actual inflation and real GDP: (1.0, \$11,400); (1.5, \$11,700); (2.0, \$12,000); (2.8, \$12,480); (2.4, \$12,240).

(a) For each level of real GDP, compute $\hat{Y} = 100(\log(Y/Y^N))$.

(b) Explain what each of the following pairs of values for the parameters a and b in equation (14.1), the equation for the Taylor Rule, means in terms of how the Fed weighs inflation against output: (0.5, 0.5); (1/3, 2/3), if real GDP is less than natural real GDP, and (2/3, 1/3), if real GDP exceeds natural real GDP; (0.0, 1.0); (1.0, 0.0). In particular, which combination might be referred to as unemployment targeting and which combination might be referred to as inflation targeting?

(c) Use the Taylor Rule as given by equation (14.1) to calculate the real federal funds rate for the given combinations of inflation and real GDP when $a = b = 0.5$.

(d) Use the Taylor Rule as given by equation (14.1) to calculate the real federal funds rate (r^{FF}) for the given combinations of inflation and real GDP when $a = 1/3$ and $b = 2/3$ if real GDP is less than natural real GDP, and when $a = 2/3$ and $b = 1/3$ if real GDP exceeds natural real GDP.

(e) Use the Taylor Rule as given by equation (14.1) to calculate the real federal funds rate for the given combinations of inflation and real GDP, when $a = 0$ and $b = 1$.

(f) Use the Taylor Rule as given by equation (14.1) to calculate the real federal funds rate for the given combinations of inflation and real GDP, when $a = 1$ and $b = 0$

(g) Use your answers to parts c–f to explain why the greater the weight the Fed places on output, the greater the variation in the real federal funds rate.

(h) Use your answers to part g and your knowledge of the monetary policy effectiveness lag to discuss how the weight the Fed places on inflation relative to output affects how long it takes for the economy's output to return to natural GDP after a demand shock, all other things being equal.

◆ SELF-TEST ANSWERS

p. 454. (1) target, (2) instrument, (3) instrument, (4) target, (5) instrument.

p. 461. (1) Legislative lag. (2) Multiplier uncertainty. (3) Data lag. (4) Both the effectiveness lag and multiplier uncertainty.

p. 468. (1) True; the public will believe that the central bank will maintain low rates of growth of the money supply and the price level. (2) False; opposite of (1). (3) True; same as (1). (4) False; time inconsistency strengthens advocates of rules involving nominal variables such as the growth of high-powered money or the inflation rate.

The Economics of Consumption Behavior

Economists become upset when they learn that we aren't spending money as they've planned for us.
—Eliot Marshall

15-1 Consumption and Economic Stability

In Chapters 4–6 and also in Chapters 13–14 we have studied the role of stabilization policy, which consists of monetary and fiscal policy. The last chapter began with a contrast between proponents of activism who believe that the economy tends to be buffeted by shocks and requires policy intervention, and proponents of rules who are more optimistic about the inherent stability of the economy and more pessimistic that policy actions can stabilize the economy. In recent years these views have merged together as most advocates of rules have adopted the Taylor rule, which calls for the Federal Reserve to change interest rates in response both to deviations of inflation from its desired inflation rate and also in response to the output gap. The Taylor rule is a more disciplined and quantitative version of policy activism.

Advocates of the Taylor rule assume that the economy is subject to numerous shocks that require a policy response, including commodity demand shocks (Chapters 3 and 4), financial market shocks (Chapter 5), supply shocks (Chapter 9), and money multiplier and money demand shocks (Chapter 13). We now return to the sources of commodity demand shocks that create instability in personal consumption expenditures (this chapter) and in domestic private investment (the next chapter). We learn in this chapter that personal consumption spending tends to be more stable than other components of GDP. We learn in the next chapter, however, that domestic private investment is quite unstable, adds to the volatility of real GDP, and requires intervention by monetary and/or fiscal policy to offset its inherent instability.

Unlike the simple Keynesian consumption function of Chapter 3, in which consumption responds instantly to changes in disposable income, in reality consumption has only a small response to income changes that households believe to be temporary. This implies that consumption is a source of stability. In recessions, consumption declines much less than total GDP and in some recessions consumption does not decline at all. In contrast, investment is more volatile than real GDP and tends to respond to *changes* in real GDP.

Forward-Looking Theories of Consumer Behavior

The focus of this chapter is a theory of consumer behavior that incorporates more sophisticated and realistic behavior than the Keynesian consumption function of Chapter 3. This theory states that consumers have **forward-looking**

Forward-looking expectations are estimates of the future values of economic variables. They are generally based on the current and past values of several variables and an economic model that accounts for their behavior.

expectations. Because consumers prefer stable as opposed to highly variable patterns of consumption, they assess whether changes in their incomes are likely to persist when deciding how much to change their consumption. Consumers behave quite differently in response to a change in disposable income that is expected to be *temporary* than they do in response to a change in disposable income that is expected to be *permanent*. Consumers can maintain their consumption when income changes temporarily by drawing down their accumulated savings. By contrast, if income is reduced permanently, consumption will fall more dramatically.

Introducing the PIH and LCH. The hypothesis that consumption depends on forward-looking expectations was developed independently in the 1950s by two economists who later won the Nobel Prize, Milton Friedman and Franco Modigliani. Friedman's version is called the **permanent-income hypothesis (PIH).** It predicts that consumption responds only to permanent changes in income, not to transitory ones. The PIH suggests that temporary changes in income will have minor effects on permanent income and, therefore, on consumption. As a result, the multiplier effect of a temporary change in autonomous spending is much smaller than the effect calculated in Chapter 3. In that case, the shifts in the *IS* curve are also much smaller than suggested in Chapter 4.

The **permanent-income hypothesis (PIH)** holds that consumption spending depends on the long-run average (or permanent) income that people expect to receive.

Modigliani's version, called the **life-cycle hypothesis (LCH),** holds that consumers attempt to smooth out their consumption spending over their lifetimes. This version also implies that transitory blips of income will cause only a small response in consumption. The LCH also implies that consumption spending depends not just on disposable income but on the real wealth of consumers as well. It implies, for instance, that major movements in stock market and housing prices affect consumption. The Modigliani version provides the theoretical foundation for our explanation in Chapter 5 of the severity of the 2007–09 recession. Household real net wealth fell precipitously not only because of the sharp declines in stock prices and in the prices of houses and condominiums, but also because consumers had taken on unprecedented levels of debt. Since net wealth equals assets minus liabilities, an extra dollar of household debt can reduce consumer spending by as much as one less dollar of household assets.

The **life-cycle hypothesis (LCH)** implies that households base their current consumption on their expected total lifetime incomes and their wealth.

 15-2 CASE STUDY

Main Features of U.S. Consumption Data

Before we study these two forward-looking theories of consumption behavior, we will examine data on aggregate consumption in the United States. Plotted in Figure 15-1 are total real consumption expenditures over the period 1960–2010, as well as the behavior of the three main components of consumption: durable goods, nondurable goods, and services. Both the total and the three components are expressed as a share of natural GDP. This removes the upward trend in overall GDP and allows us to more clearly understand both the cyclical behavior of consumption spending and also changes in the shares of the three components.

The top of the orange area in Figure 15-1 shows the share of personal consumption expenditures in natural GDP. That share fluctuates up and down over the 50 years since 1960 in response to the business cycle, but it also grows

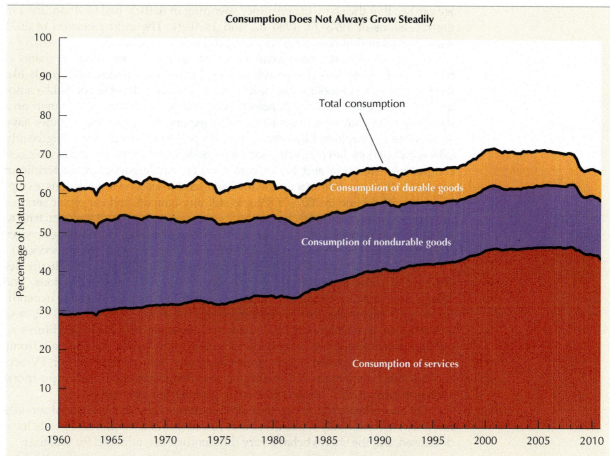

Figure 15-1 Consumer Expenditure and Its Three Components as a Share of Natural GDP, 1960–2010

This chart plots nominal personal consumption expenditures and of its three components, durable goods, nondurable goods, and services. All values are expressed as a share of nominal natural real GDP in order to control for the growing size of the economy. Note that the share of services has grown markedly and does not tend to decline in recessions. The share of nondurable goods (food, clothing, gasoline) has declined and is moderately sensitive to recessions. The top orange area shows that consumption of durable goods has remained relatively steady but is quite sensitive to business cycle fluctuations.

Source: Bureau of Economic Analysis, bea.gov, and author's calculations.

substantially. The share was 62 percent in 1960 and the same 62 percent as recently as 1984. But between 1984 and 2000 the share increased substantially. The average share during 1960–84 was 62.1 percent but had grown to a much higher 71.0 percent during 2000–07. In Chapter 3 and again in this chapter, we attribute the rise in the consumption share of natural real GDP to the effect of capital gains on stock market and housing assets in boosting consumption, particularly during the 2000–07 period of the housing price bubble. The collapse of stock prices and house prices in 2007–09 caused a sharp drop in the consumption share back from 71.0 percent in 2000–07 to 66.3 percent in 2009–10.

The sharp drop of consumer spending after 2007 is consistent with behavior in previous postwar recessions. At the top of the orange area in Figure 15-1 we can see that the share of consumer spending in natural real GDP declined in the recessions of 1973–75, 1980–82, and 1990–91. The mild recession of 2001 was unusual in that consumer spending did not decline at all.

Now we look at the three colored areas of Figure 15-1, showing the shares in natural GDP of services (the brown area on the bottom), nondurable goods like food, clothing, and gasoline (the blue middle area), and durable goods like automobiles, electronics, and appliances (the orange area on top). The brown area shows that the share of services has steadily expanded, as growing incomes have allowed more people to hire other people to perform services, including beauty salons, nail parlors, lawn mowing services, hotels, restaurants, and the two biggest components—housing and health care services. An important characteristic of services is that expenditures on them do not tend to decline in recessions, except for a modest decline in 2007–09. People still buy haircuts and car repair services during recessions, they get sick and need health care services, and they also tend to live in the same house or condo even if they are unemployed (housing services from owner-occupied housing is included in consumer expenditures on services).

The blue area shows that the share of nondurable goods has gradually declined, and these expenditures do exhibit modest declines in recessions. The orange area at the top exhibits substantial volatility in durable goods expenditures, with major declines in the recessions of 1970, 1973–75, 1980–82, and 1990–91, but especially after 2007. Why are consumer durable expenditures so volatile? Purchases of big-ticket items including autos, appliances, and electronic goods can be postponed. Many households buy new automobiles or TV sets because they want improved quality or new features; they can often postpone such purchases if their household income declines temporarily.

The chart shows that when measured in nominal terms the share of services has grown substantially while the shares of durable and nondurable goods have decreased. But the shares behave very differently when adjusted for inflation:

	1960:Q1	2010:Q4
Nominal Shares in Total Consumption		
Services	46.5	66.4
Nondurable goods	39.6	22.8
Durable goods	13.9	10.8
Real Shares		
Services	62.2	64.7
Nondurable goods	32.8	22.3
Durable goods	4.9	13.1

The top section of the table shows the changes in the share of the three components in total consumption, underscoring Figure 15-1, which shows a major increase in the share of services but a decline in the share of nondurable and durable goods. However, the long-term change between 1960 and 2010 is quite different when we calculate the shares in real terms, that is, adjusted for the different inflation rates for the three components of consumption expenditures.

As shown in the table, the share of services increased greatly in nominal terms but not in real terms. This occurred because the relative price of services increased, as haircuts, car repair, and especially medical care and college tuition became much more expensive relative to the average consumption good. The shares of nondurable goods were about the same in nominal and real terms, indicating that price inflation for nondurables was about the same as for the average of all consumer expenditures. But the real share of durable goods increased enormously in real terms, since durable goods were the diametric opposite of services. The relative prices of durable goods decreased steadily between 1960 and 2000, as newly invented types of durable goods like personal computers, smart phones, color TVs, and then high-definition TVs, tumbled in price. While the price of a haircut may have increased by a factor of 10 since 1960, and college tuition in elite private schools by a factor of 40, a sparkling high-definition color TV set can be purchased today for the same price (say $350) as a fuzzy black-and-white set with a smaller picture size in 1960. ◆

15-3   Background: The Conflict Between the Time-Series and Cross-Section Evidence

One of the major innovations in Keynes's *General Theory* was the multiplier, which followed directly from the assumptions that consumption responds to income and that the marginal propensity to consume is less than unity: "The fundamental psychological law...is that men are disposed, as a rule and on the average, to increase their consumption as their income increases, but not by as much as the increase in their income."[1]

Keynes's second innovative idea was that there is a given amount, a, that individuals will consume no matter what their income, so that it is possible for saving to be negative if disposable income is very low. Denoting consumption as C and disposable income as Y_D, the Keynesian consumption function can be written:

$$C = C_a + cY_D \tag{15.1}$$

This is identical to equation (3.3) on p. 58.

The hypothetical Keynesian consumption function and saving ratio are plotted in the top two frames of Figure 15-2. In the top frame, consumption (C) rises less rapidly than disposable income (Y_D), since the marginal propensity to consume (c) is less than 1.0. Consumption starts out greater than Y_D, equals Y_D at the income level Y_{D0}, and then is less than Y_D. Everywhere to the right of Y_{D0} the shortfall of consumption below disposable income allows room for a positive amount of saving. For instance, the income level Y_{D1} is divided into the consumption level C_1 and the saving level S_1.

Moving down to the middle frame of Figure 15-2, we find plotted the saving/income ratio, S/Y_D. To the left of the income level Y_{D0}, saving is negative; to the right of Y_{D0}, saving is positive. As income rises, according to the hypothetical Keynesian relation in the middle frame, a larger share of disposable income is saved.

The actual data plotted in the bottom frame of Figure 15-2 confirm Keynes's hypothesis for a **cross section** of Americans who were polled on their income, saving, and consumption behavior. Most people with low incomes do

A **cross section** consists of data for numerous units (for instance, households, firms, cities, or states) observed over a single period of time.

---

[1] See John Maynard Keynes, *The General Theory of Employment, Interest and Money* (New York: Macmillan, 1936), Book III. The idea of the multiplier was first introduced by R. F. Kahn, "The Relation of Home Investment to Unemployment," *Economic Journal* (June 1931), but Keynes was the first to fit the multiplier into a general economic model of commodity and money markets.

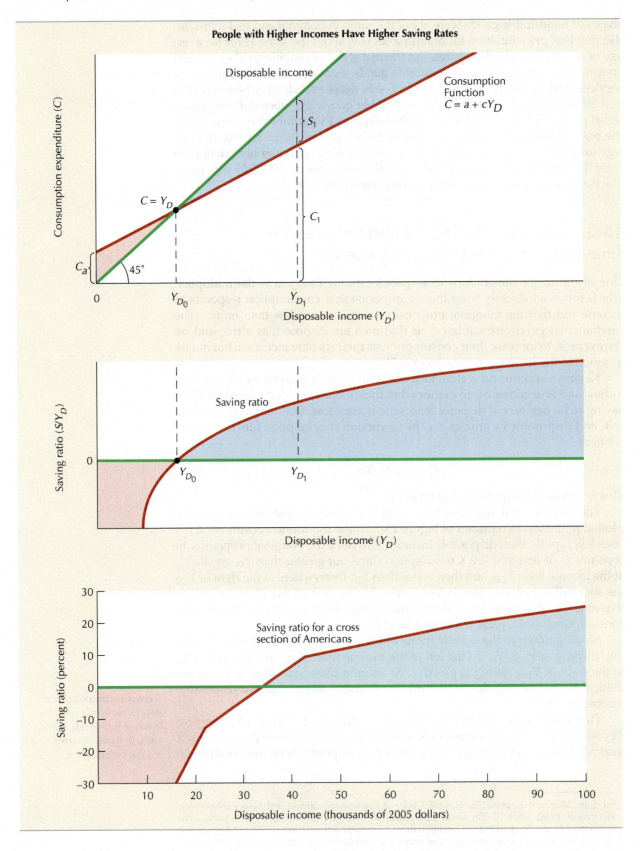

People with Higher Incomes Have Higher Saving Rates

> **Figure 15-2** The Relation Between Disposable Income (Y_D), Consumption Spending (C), and the Ratio of Saving to Income (S/Y_D)
>
> The top frame repeats the consumption function introduced in Chapter 3. At levels of disposable income below (to the left of) Y_{D0}, people consume more than their income and saving is negative, as shown by the shaded red area. To the right of Y_{D0} consumption is less than income, and the shaded blue area, which represents the difference between income and consumption, that is, the amount of saving, is a steadily growing fraction of disposable income. In the middle frame, the share of saving in disposable income is plotted as a negative fraction to the left of Y_{D0} and a positive and growing fraction to the right. The bottom frame plots actual data on the relation of saving to disposable income from a survey of consumers. Notice the close correspondence between the theoretical diagram in the middle frame and the actual data in the bottom frame.

not save at all, but instead "dissave," consuming more than they earn by borrowing or by drawing on accumulated assets in savings accounts. As we move rightward from the poor to the rich, we find that the saving/income ratio increases, just as in the hypothetical relationship of the middle frame.

The Saving Rate: Short-Run Variability, Long-Run Constancy

Implicit in Figure 15-2 is a potentially serious problem for the economy. If individuals save more as their incomes rise, then consumption spending may be inadequate to maintain actual real GDP at the desired level of natural real GDP. Keynes's concern that the saving rate would rise as the years passed seemed particularly relevant during the Great Depression of the 1930s, when the world's actual real GDP was far below its natural level for many years and investment spending was very weak. The weakness of investment spending during the Great Depression led some to argue that government spending must be used to raise output to its natural level.

But, has the saving rate, in fact, risen over time as natural real GDP has risen? Look now at Figure 15-3, which plots the actual historical **time-series** data for the average saving ratio for each major business cycle of the twentieth century. Between 1894–1896, the first observation plotted, and 2007–2010, the last observation plotted, real income per person increased by a factor of ten. Yet there is little indication that the saving ratio trended upward over the twentieth century. Instead, the saving ratio did not change dramatically between 1895 and 1980 when it began a sharp decline. The main longer-term variations in the saving ratio were the low saving ratio during the Great Depression of the 1930s and the high saving ratio during World War II, and more recently the low saving ratio since 1980 that we discuss later in this chapter.

A **time series** consists of data covering a span of time for one or more measures (for instance, disposable income or consumption spending).

Keynes's consumption function implies that the saving ratio will decline in recessions and that in cross-section data, those with higher incomes will tend to have higher saving rates. The data confirm both of these implications. Keynes's consumption function, however, does not explain why over the longer run the saving ratio is constant or even declining instead of rising as predicted. The two most important hypotheses about consumption (and thus about saving) that can account for the long-run near-constancy of the

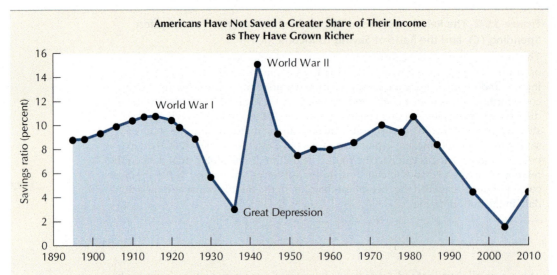

Figure 15-3 Ratio of Personal Saving to Disposable Personal Income (S/Y_D), Averages Over Business Cycles, 1894–2010

The low level of saving during the Great Depression is consistent with our theory. The high level of saving during World War II was caused by the shortages of civilian goods and services. Leaving out these two extreme periods, the ratio of saving to disposable income was fairly constant until 1980, after which it declined almost to zero in 2001–07 before rebounding in the last (incomplete) business cycle of 2007–10.

Sources: For 1887–99: Paul David and John Scadding, "Private Savings: Ultrarationality, Aggregation, and 'Denison's Law,'" *Journal of Political Economy* (March/April 1974). For 1900–32: *Historical Statistics of the United States Millennial Edition. 1933–2010: National Income and Product Accounts.* Business cycle data from NBER *Business Cycle Expansions and Contractions.*

saving ratio, as well as the short-run variability and the cross-section pattern of saving, are Friedman's permanent-income hypothesis and Modigliani's life-cycle hypothesis.

15-4   Forward-Looking Behavior: The Permanent-Income Hypothesis

A Theory of Steady Consumption

Imagine that you have a job and receive your take-home pay of $1,000 on the first day of each month. Suppose you regard your income on the first day of each month as $1,000, and your income on each of the remaining days of the month as zero. If you spend based on the simple Keynesian consumption function with a high marginal propensity to consume and a small autonomous component, you will do almost all your consumption spending on the first day of the month and consume very little over the rest of the month!

Of course people consume more steadily than that, setting aside part of their pay to buy groceries and other items during the rest of the month.

Individuals who have variable income will be happier if they consume about the same amount each day rather than allowing their consumption to change each day with their changing income.

Milton Friedman first proposed the hypothesis that individuals consume a constant fraction (k) of their expected income, which Friedman called **permanent income** (Y^P).[2]

Permanent income is the annual average income that people expect to receive over a period of years in the future.

General Form	Numerical Example	
$C = kY^P$	$C = 0.9(\$10,000) = \$9,000$	(15.2)

The marginal propensity to consume out of permanent income (k) depends on individual tastes and on the variability of income (farmers, salespeople, and others with variable income need higher saving to support themselves during bad years). In addition, k may depend on the interest rate. People may be willing to save more (and spend less) when interest rates are higher.[3]

Revising the estimate of permanent income.   The permanent-income hypothesis summarized in equation (15.2) does not say that individuals consume exactly the same amount year after year. Every year new events occur that are likely to change individuals' guesses about their permanent income. For instance, an individual might find that in good years income has increased. Gradually the individual will revise his or her estimate of average expected income upward and will increase his or her stable-consumption level.

Friedman's permanent-income hypothesis consists of the assumption in equation (15.2) that individuals consume a constant portion of their permanent income. But this is not enough, because an additional assumption is required to indicate how individuals estimate the size of their permanent income. Friedman proposed that individual estimates of permanent income for this year (Y^P) be revised from last year's estimate (Y^P_{-1}) by some fraction (j) of the amount by which actual income (Y) differs from (Y^P_{-1}):

General Form	Numerical Example	
$Y^P = Y^P_{-1} + j(Y - Y^P_{-1})$	$Y^P = 10,000 + 0.2(15,000 - 10,000)$	(15.3)
	$= 11,000$	

Adaptive expectations.   The behavior described in equation (15.3) is sometimes called the "error-learning" or "adaptive" hypothesis of expectation formation. This hypothesis implies that individuals will allow their consumption to respond modestly to changes in actual income because consumption depends on permanent income, and in turn permanent income in equation (15.3) depends only in part on this period's actual income. When we substitute (15.3) into (15.2), we obtain the following relationship between an individual's current consumption (C), this period's actual income (Y), and last period's estimate of permanent income (Y^P_{-1}):

General Form	Numerical Example	
$C = kY^P_{-1} + kj(Y - Y^P_{-1})$	$C = 0.9Y^P_{-1} + 0.18(Y - Y^P_{-1})$	(15.4)

---

[2] Milton Friedman, *A Theory of the Consumption Function* (Princeton, NJ: Princeton University Press, 1957). Milton Friedman's photo appears on p. 545.

[3] Because of the limitations of the alphabet we are once again forced to duplicate the use of letters. The k here is completely unrelated to the k used in Chapters 3 and 4 to represent the multiplier.

Exactly the same hypothesis for the formation of expectations was introduced in the Appendix to Chapter 9 in the discussion of inflation expectations (see equation (2) on p. 307). Equation (15.3) can be rewritten in the form used there.

$$Y^P = jY + (1 - j)Y^P_{-1}$$

This says that permanent income in this period is a weighted average of actual income and last period's permanent income.

Two marginal propensities to consume.   Equation (15.4) helps us see that Friedman's theory is based on a distinction between two concepts of the marginal propensity to consume (MPC). The *long-run* MPC is simply the coefficient (k) of permanent income in the original consumption function (15.2), and indeed k is the coefficient of the first term in (15.4). In our numerical example, the long-term MPC (k) is 0.9. The *short-run* MPC is the coefficient of a change in actual income, the coefficient kj (or $0.18 = 0.9$ times 0.2) in the second term in (15.4). When today's actual income (Y) increases, the second term in (15.4) shows that today's consumption goes up by the short-run MPC (kj, or 0.18).

The portion of today's income change that is not expected to be permanent is called **transitory income** in Friedman's theory. Transitory income (Y^t) is simply actual income minus permanent income:

Transitory income is the difference between actual and permanent income and is not expected to recur.

General Form	Numerical Example	
$Y^t = Y - Y^P$	$Y^t = Y - Y^P$	
$= Y - Y^P_{-1} - j(Y - Y^P_{-1})$	$= 0.8(Y - Y^P_{-1})$	(15.5)
$= (1 - j)(Y - Y^P_{-1})$		

Friedman achieves his sharp distinction between the long-run and short-run MPC by assuming that the MPC out of transitory income is zero. Thus his consumption function (15.2) could be rewritten as:

$$C = 0Y^t + kY^P \qquad (15.6)$$

Reconciling the Conflict Between Cross-Section and Time-Series Data

The motivation for Friedman's PIH was the apparent conflict between the cross-section data in Figure 15-2, where high-income people were shown to have higher saving ratios than low-income people, and the long-run near-constancy of the saving ratio shown in Figure 15-3. The PIH contends that the high saving ratios of high-income people are due to their having atypically large, positive, transitory incomes (for example, executives who received large bonuses after a good year; movie stars after the release of unusually popular films; or professional athletes, who have short-lived, high-income careers). Similarly, the PIH contends that low-income people dissave or have low saving ratios (as in Figure 15-2) because they are more likely than the average person to have actual incomes that are temporarily below their permanent incomes. (Examples of people with negative transitory income include farmers whose crops were ruined by drought, floods, or disease; executives who have just been fired; and college students who believe that their incomes will be higher in the future.) Thus, the PIH explains how, even when the longer-run savings

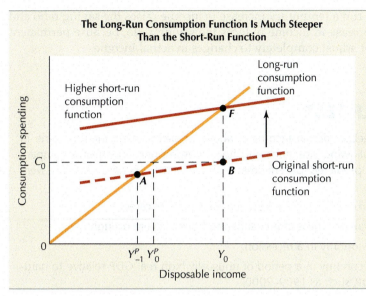

The Long-Run Consumption Function Is Much Steeper Than the Short-Run Function

Figure 15-4 **The Permanent-Income Hypothesis of Consumption and Saving**
The long-run schedule shows that consumption is a fixed fraction of income in the long run, when actual and permanent income are equal. But short-run gains in actual income, as at point B, are not fully incorporated into permanent income. Thus consumption increases only a small amount (compare points B and A), and at B most of the short-run increase in income is saved. When the same gain in income is maintained permanently, the short-run schedule shifts upward along the long-run schedule to point F.

ratio is constant across individuals and across time, cross-section data will record that high-income people have higher saving ratios.

The two consumption functions illustrated. Figure 15-4 illustrates the distinction between the long-run and short-run consumption functions. The solid orange line running through points A and F is the long-run consumption function; its slope is the long-run MPC (k, or 0.9 in our example). It is called the long-run consumption function because it indicates the level of consumption only when actual income has remained long enough at a particular level for individuals to fully adjust their estimated permanent income to the actual level.

What happens in the short run, when actual income can differ from permanent income? The flatter dashed red schedule running between A and B is the short-run schedule and plots equation (15.4). When current income (Y) is exactly equal to last period's permanent income Y_{-1}^P, the short-run schedule intersects the long-run schedule at point A. But during an unusually good year, when an individual's income is at the high level Y_0, the current estimate of permanent income (Y^P) rises above last period's estimate Y_{-1}^P by a fraction (j) of the excess of actual income over last period's estimate. And the higher value of Y^P raises consumption by k times the increase in permanent income.

Thus consumption at point B lies vertically above point A by the fraction kj (18 percent in the numerical example) times the horizontal distance between Y_{-1}^P and Y_0. With the short-run marginal propensity to consume (kj) so far below the long-run propensity (k), any short-run increase in income goes disproportionately into saving. If Y_0 comes to be regarded as permanent, the short-run consumption function will go through F.

To summarize, estimates of permanent income are continually raised as actual income outstrips previous levels, causing the relationship between consumption and income to follow the long-run schedule, as marked by the arrow in Figure 15-4. Thus in the long run the saving ratio is roughly constant.

But in the short run a temporary increase in income raises the saving ratio and a temporary decrease in income reduces the saving ratio, because permanent income does not adjust completely to changes in actual income.

SELF-TEST

Determine whether actual income is above or below permanent income in each of the following situations and how consumption and saving compare to the values predicted by Friedman's theory if the income changes were permanent:

1. A stockbroker enjoying the best year of his or her career.
2. A North Dakota wheat farmer suffering from a severe drought.
3. The U.S. economy in a recession.
4. The U.S. economy in a period of unusually high real GDP relative to natural real GDP, such as 1999–2000.

15-5 Forward-Looking Behavior: The Life-Cycle Hypothesis

About the same time that Friedman wrote his book on the permanent-income hypothesis, Franco Modigliani of MIT and collaborators devised a somewhat different way of reconciling the positive relation between the saving ratio and income observed in cross-section data and the constancy of the saving ratio observed over long periods in the historical time-series data.[4] Modigliani and Friedman both began with the perspective that individuals prefer to maintain a stable consumption pattern rather than allow consumption to rise or fall with every transitory oscillation of their income. But Modigliani carried the stable-consumption argument further than Friedman and suggested that people *would try to stabilize their consumption over their entire lifetimes.*

Because of its emphasis on the lifetime horizon of consumers, the Modigliani theory is called the life-cycle hypothesis (LCH). Since it stresses the way consumers smooth consumption over their lifetimes and save in preparation for their retirement years, the LCH falls into the category of theories based on *forward-looking expectations.* It shares with Friedman's theory the ability to reconcile a low short-run MPC with a high and stable long-run MPC. But the LCH adds a "lifetime budget constraint" to Friedman's theory, which is the condition that the consumption of households over their lifetimes equals their income plus their holdings of assets coming from sources other than work (for example, gifts from parents). This feature of the LCH provides a rigorous connection between consumption expenditures and the value of the assets held by consumers.

Franco Modigliani (1918–2003)

The 1985 Nobel Prize winner is best known for the life-cycle model of consumption behavior and for his articulate advocacy of policy activism.

---

[4] Franco Modigliani and R. E. Brumberg, "Utility Analysis and the Consumption Function," in K. K. Kurihara, ed., *Post-Keynesian Economics* (New Brunswick, NJ: Rutgers University Press, 1954). Also A. Ando and F. Modigliani, "The 'Life Cycle' Hypothesis of Saving: Aggregate Implications and Tests," *American Economic Review*, vol. 53 (March 1963), pp. 55–84.

GLOBAL ECONOMIC CRISIS FOCUS

The Modigliani Theory Helps Explain the Crisis and Recession of 2007–09

Because the Modigliani theory provides a direct channel from higher household net wealth as a cause of higher consumer spending, and from lower household net wealth as a cause of lower consumer spending, it is well suited to help us understand the Global Economic Crisis. Three factors came together in 2007–09 to cause a sharp drop in consumer spending. The first was the end of the housing price bubble, in which housing prices rose relative to rents by about 60 percent between 2000 and 2006 and then fell by almost as much between 2006 and 2010. The second was the stock market crash, which caused the S&P 500 stock market index to decline by more than half, from 1568 in mid-October 2007, to less than 700 in early March 2009. The third was the increase in household liabilities (these are debts that are subtracted from assets in calculating net worth).

A chart on p. 62 of this book illustrates the decline in household assets from 2006 to 2009 and the longer-term increase in household debt from the early 1990s to 2007. Expressed as a share of household disposable income, household assets declined from 785 percent at the end of 2006 to 599 percent at the end of 2008. Household debt increased from 91 percent in 1994 to 138 percent in 2007. Household net worth, the difference between assets and liabilities, declined as a share of disposable income from 650 percent in 2006 to 468 percent in 2008, below the 487 percent registered as long ago as 1994. This collapse in household net worth and the struggle by consumers to pay off debts helps to explain why the economic recovery in 2010–11 was so slow.

Lifetime Asset Holding: Modigliani's Asset Pyramid Illustrated

We now examine Figure 15-5, which shows how a simple version of Modigliani's theory predicts how income, consumption, saving, and asset accumulation will behave over the lifetime of the typical consumer. The horizontal axis shows various ages, with the age at retirement marked by R and the age at death marked by L. An individual is assumed to maintain a constant level of consumption (C_0) throughout life. Income, however, is earned only during the R working years. If there are no assets initially, as shown by the zero level of initial assets (A_0) in the bottom frame, then the only way individuals can manage to consume without any income during their retirement is to save during their working years. The amount saved, income minus consumption, is shown by the blue area during the period up to time R, and then the dissaving that occurs when consumption exceeds income during retirement is shown by the red area from time R through time L. In the bottom frame, the accumulation of assets occurs steadily during the working years through time R, when assets reach their maximum level A_R. Assets decline thereafter and are zero at time L.

No initial assets.   How are consumption and income related when there are no initial assets? Total lifetime consumption of C_0 per year for L years is constrained to equal total income Y_0 per year for R years:

$$C_0 L = Y_0 R \quad \text{or} \quad C_0 = \left(\frac{R}{L}\right) Y_0 \tag{15.7}$$

Figure 15-5 **The Behavior of Consumption, Saving, and Assets under the Life-Cycle Hypothesis**

Under the life-cycle hypothesis particular attention is paid to the relation between the length of the lifetime (L) and an individual's age at retirement (R). The length of the retirement period is $L - R$. In the upper frame, a constant amount (C_0) is consumed every year of one's life, as indicated by the red line. A constant amount of income Y_0 is earned each year until retirement. During the working years until R, income exceeds consumption, as shown by the saving that occurs in the blue area. Then consumption exceeds the zero income during retirement and is financed by dissaving, as shown by the red area. In the bottom frame, the green line shows the growth of assets from the initial level (A_0) to the maximum level at retirement (A_R), followed by a decline in assets back to zero at death.

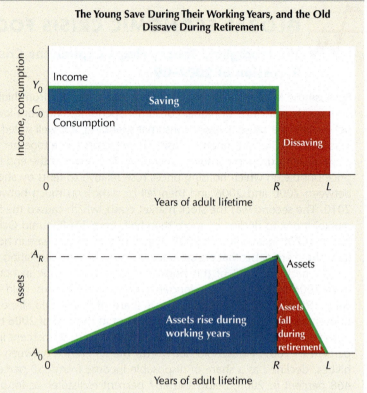

As Figure 15-5 is drawn, R is four-fifths of L, so consumption per year is limited to four-fifths of Y_0.[5]

The simple version of the life-cycle hypothesis can explain the positive association of saving and income, since the upward trend in per capita, natural real GDP raises both the saving and income of those of working age relative to those who are retired. The long-run constancy of the saving ratio can be explained by the fact that if the population in each historical era is divided into the same proportions of working and retired people, and each age group has the same saving behavior in generation after generation, then the long-run saving ratio will be constant.

The life-cycle hypothesis shares with Friedman's permanent-income hypothesis the implication that the saving ratio should rise in economic boom years and fall in recession years. A temporary increase in income today will be

---

[5] There are several simplifications in Figure 15-5 and equation (15.7) involving the treatment of interest income. Assuming that interest is earned on asset holdings at the nominal interest rate i, then total income is equal to wage income in real terms (W/P) plus real interest income (rA), where r is the real interest rate. Then (15.7) becomes

$$C_0 L = (W/P)_0 R + \sum_{t=0}^{L} rA_t$$

Thus total income increases gradually through time R and then decreases to zero, but is nevertheless positive during the retirement period. To reflect the fact that consumption depends on total income, including both wage income and earnings from the holding of assets, the symbol Y (for total real income) rather than W/P is used in (15.7) in the text. The official definition of income overstates Y, since it includes the entire income from assets, including that portion of the nominal return ($i - r$) needed to maintain intact the real value of assets.

consumed over one's entire lifetime. For instance, imagine a person who believes he has 40 years left to live and receives an unexpected increase in income this year of $4,000 that he does not expect to receive again. His total lifetime consumption goes up by the $4,000 and his actual consumption this year goes up by only 1/40 of that amount, a mere $100. In each succeeding year, an additional $100 would be spent, for a total of $4,000 over the remaining 40 years of life.

Thus, in an economic boom widely expected to be temporary, an unexpected bonus of $4,000 would lead to only $100 extra of current consumption and $3,900 extra of saving. The short-run propensity to consume would be just 0.025, or 100/4,000. By contrast, if the $4,000 income increase is expected to be maintained for each of the next 40 years, then $4,000 extra can be consumed this year and again in each of the next 39 years and the saving ratio will not rise.

The role of assets.   The Modigliani theory provides an important role for assets as a determinant of consumption behavior. Let us assume that initially a person has an endowment of assets of A_1, but plans to use these assets to raise consumption through his or her lifetime rather than to leave the assets to heirs. Then, as shown in Figure 15-6, consumption can be higher for a given level of income (Y_0), and saving can be lower, since the initial asset endowment provides more spending power. Now total lifetime consumption equals total lifetime income from work plus the available assets:

$$C_1 L = A_1 + Y_0 R$$

or

$$C_1 = \frac{A_1}{L} + \frac{R}{L} Y_0 \tag{15.8}$$

The right-hand expression shows that consumption per year (C_1) depends not just on income (Y_0); it also depends on the ratio of available assets per year of life. Figure 15-6 is oversimplified because it assumes that the initial endowment of assets is received at the beginning of the working life. In reality, however, increases in the value of assets occur throughout one's life, so one would expect the response of annual consumption to a change in asset value to be larger than is assumed in equation (15.8). Modigliani's empirical research has estimated that a $1 increase in real asset values raised annual real consumption by about $0.06, which would indicate that people use a 15-year horizon over which to spend an increase in real assets.

In Chapter 8 we learned that the economy's self-correcting forces are enhanced when real consumption spending depends on real assets or real wealth. If a drop in spending cuts the price level, the level of real wealth is raised, which helps arrest the decline in spending.[6] In the other direction, if an increase in spending raises the price level, the level of real wealth declines, which helps dampen the original stimulus to spending. We return to the relationship between real wealth and consumption behavior in Section 15-8.

Thus, ironically, Modigliani's life-cycle hypothesis supports the optimism of rules advocates regarding the stability of the private economy, even though Modigliani was a prominent critic of policy rules. Private spending is stabilized because transitory increases in disposable income, those that are not

---

[6] Review the Pigou, or real balance, effect discussed in Section 8-8 on pp. 251–52.

Figure 15-6 Consumption, Saving, and Assets Under the Life-Cycle Hypothesis When There Is an Initial Stock of Assets

This diagram is identical to Figure 15-5, but here there is an initial stock of assets, A_1, in contrast to the initial stock of zero in the previous diagram. If we continue to assume that dissaving during retirement runs the stock of assets down to zero, then the existence of A_1 makes more total consumption possible with a smaller amount of saving. This is shown by an upward shift from the previous level of consumption (C_0) to a new higher level (C_1). The blue saving area is now smaller, as is the blue area in the bottom frame, which shows the increase in assets due to saving.

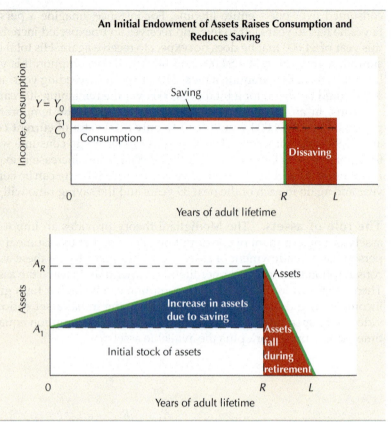

An Initial Endowment of Assets Raises Consumption and Reduces Saving

expected to last very long, have only a modest influence on current consumption. In addition, the real-asset effect stabilizes the economy because higher prices cut the real value of assets and dampen spending. Overall, life-cycle considerations reduce the current marginal propensity to consume, cut the multiplier, and insulate the economy from unexpected changes in investment, net exports, or other types of spending.

 SELF-TEST

Assume that an adult is making a consumption plan and anticipates a life of 40 more years, 30 of which will be spent in work and 10 in retirement.

1. If income during the working years is $50,000, and the endowment of initial assets is zero, what will annual consumption expenditures be during the working years? During the retirement years?

2. What will be the average propensity to consume (C/Y) during the working years?

3. Now, assume instead that initial assets are $200,000. What will annual consumption expenditures be during the working years? During the retirement years?

4. What will be the average propensity to consume during the working years?

15-6 Rational Expectations and Other Amendments to the Simple Forward-Looking Theories

In recent years consumption behavior has been one of the most active areas of research in macroeconomics. Much attention has been directed toward the implications of households using more sophisticated methods of forming their expectations about their future incomes than the simple adaptive expectations method shown in equation (15.3). The contrast between the predictions of the resulting theory and the actual cyclical behavior of consumption has highlighted the role of several additional factors that are not part of the pure PIH or LCH theories: liquidity constraints, consumer durables, bequests, and uncertainty.

Rational Expectations

Recall from equation (15.3) that in its original Friedman formulation, the PIH is combined with the adaptive or error-learning method of calculating permanent income. Thus when actual income increases, people only *gradually* revise upward their estimate of permanent income. Though it provides a simple and convenient approximation to how households might form their expectations about their future incomes, the adaptive expectations hypothesis may be too simple. Among its drawbacks are that it mechanically extrapolates the past and that it does not explicitly allow for the effects of variables other than income on expectations of future income.

The **rational expectations** hypothesis suggests that people use a more sophisticated method of forming their expectations about their future incomes. Rational expectations assume that expectations of future events are formed using *all* the information available. Thus rational expectations imply that all the information that can be gleaned from the past and even from credible announcements about the future, like tax cuts that have been enacted but that have not yet taken effect, will be used to form estimates of permanent income. As a result, only *new* information will change estimated permanent incomes, which implies that consumption will change only if *unanticipated* events occur. Previously expected events provide no news and therefore no revisions to permanent income and no change in consumption.

Is consumption too volatile or too smooth? A controversy has developed over the empirical implications of the rational expectations version of the PIH. Everything depends on how consumers view the nature of new information about income. If a change in current income provides no information about income in the future, then estimates of permanent income change very little, and the marginal propensity to consume out of this change in current income should be close to zero.[7] However, our case study (Section 15-2) showed that consumption displayed visible responses to the decline of income in the 1974–75, 1980–82, 1990–91, and 2007–09 recessions. This points toward the conclusion

Rational expectations are forecasts of future economic magnitudes based on information currently available about the structure and past performance of the economy and future government policies.

---

[7] In this case it can be shown in a specific mathematical model that the MPC would be $r/(1 + r)$, where r is the real rate of interest. Thus, depending on the asset used to measure r, the MPC would be between zero and 0.07. This result is developed in the excellent but mathematically advanced survey by Andrew B. Abel, "Consumption and Investment," in B. M. Friedman and F. Hahn, eds., *Handbook of Monetary Economics* (Amsterdam: Elsevier Science Publishers, 1990), pp. 725–78.

UNDERSTANDING THE GLOBAL ECONOMIC CRISIS

Did Households Spend or Save the 2008 Economic Stimulus Payments?

The first signs of the Global Economic Crisis began to become apparent in 2006 when housing prices started to decline in the United States, thus bursting the American housing bubble. Financial markets reacted in the late summer of 2007 when market participants began to doubt whether some of the mortgage-backed securities issued in the previous four years against subprime loans would warrant their "Triple-A" ratings or would suddenly lose value due to the inability of low-income borrowers to make mortgage payments.

Fearing a recession (that in retrospect began in December 2007), the Bush administration and Congress in February 2008 passed the Economic Stimulus Act (ESA), a classic example of a fiscal policy stimulus. The total fiscal stimulus of $100 billion consisted of sending payments by check or electronic transfer to most of the

that actual consumption responds too strongly to changes in actual income, that is, it is *excessively volatile* relative to the prediction of the theory.[8]

However, another possibility is that changes in current income provide a good prediction of changes in future income. For instance, a person who loses a high-paying job may have very good reason to predict that future income will be lower, perhaps for many years. In the extreme case, if it were true that estimates of permanent income always responded by one dollar to any change in current income of one dollar (that is, $j = 1$ in equations (15.3) and (15.4)), then the marginal propensity

---

[8] The rational expectations approach to the study of consumption behavior was introduced in Robert E. Hall, "Stochastic Implications of the Life Cycle-Permanent Income Hypothesis: Theory and Evidence," *Journal of Political Economy*, vol. 86 (December 1978), pp. 971–87. The excess volatility argument is usually credited to Marjorie Flavin, "The Adjustment of Consumption to Changing Expectations about Future Income," *Journal of Political Economy*, vol. 89 (October 1981), pp. 974–1009. A collection of Hall's essays on consumption is Robert E. Hall, *The Rational Consumer* (MIT Press, 1990).

130 million households in the United States, a massive undertaking. Thus the average payment per household was $100 billion divided by 130 million, or about $770 per household. Single households received less and couples received more.

The key question about any fiscal stimulus program is how large was the multiplier effect? The size of the multiplier is particularly important for tax cuts, since those benefiting from lower taxes may not spend more on personal consumption expenditures that are included in GDP, but they may instead keep money in their bank accounts or use their check to pay off old auto loans and credit card balances.

Previous studies had focused on the response of consumer expenditures on nondurable goods and services. Indeed, the leading study of the 2008 ESA found that only about 12 to 30 percent of the ESA payments were spent on nondurable and service expenditures during the first three months after the payments were received. However, the impact of the ESA payments was much higher when spending on durable goods, including new vehicles, is included. Total consumption expenditures including durables, nondurables, and services constituted 50 to 90 percent of the ESA payments. Overall, total consumer expenditures were raised by roughly 1.8 percent in 2008:Q2 and by 0.8 percent in 2008:Q3 as a result of the stimulus payments.[a]

To interpret these results, we need to recall that GDP data are presented at annual rates. If consumption expenditures were actually $2,500 billion in 2008:Q2, these are multiplied by 4.0 and stated as $10,000 billion at an annual rate. Thus the results of this study suggest that consumer expenditure was increased by $2500 billion times 1.8 percent in 2008:Q2 ($45 billion) plus $2500 billion times 0.8 percent in 2008:Q3. This is a total of $65 billion in spending from $100 billion in federal payments to households, implying a marginal propensity to consume of 0.65, not far below the 0.75 assumed in the examples of Chapter 3.

Other studies of the 2008 ESA payments find smaller effects. One survey found that only about 20 percent of respondents indicated that they had spent their ESA payment, while the others saved it or used it to reduce debt. A second survey found that 30 percent spent the payment, 18 percent saved it, and the remaining 52 percent used it to pay down debt.[b] Overall, it appears that tax rebates such as the ESA payments are less effective in raising real GDP than the alternative policy of spending the same number of dollars on real government purchases of goods and services, which automatically raise real GDP. If policymakers prefer to make payments to individuals, these are likely to be more effective and have a higher multiplier effect if they take the form of transfer payments to the unemployed (by extending unemployment benefits) or to low-income households by, for instance, increasing food stamp allowances. The unemployed and low-income households are more likely to spend the government payments immediately than middle-income households benefiting from an across-the-board tax rebate such as the 2008 ESA payments.

---

[a] See Jonathan A. Parker et al., "Consumer Spending and the Economic Stimulus Payments of 2008," working paper, Northwestern University, September 2010.

[b] Matthew D. Shapiro and Joel Slemrod, "Did the 2008 Tax Rebates Stimulate Spending?" *American Economic Review Papers and Proceedings*, vol. 99 (May 2009), pp. 374–79.

---

to consume out of current income would be k (simply because the marginal propensity to consume out of permanent income is k). But the data show clearly that consumption is smoother than current income. So by this contrasting approach, actual consumption is *too smooth* relative to the prediction of the theory.[9]

Thus far the debate over the cyclical behavior of consumption has not been settled. However, the initial conclusion that consumption was too volatile led to the realization that the simple versions of the PIH and LCH we have just reviewed, as well as the rational expectations updating of these theories, omit several important aspects of consumption behavior. Until these issues are adequately integrated into the theory, it is unlikely that the question of whether consumption is too volatile or too smooth will be resolved.

---

[9] See Angus Deaton, "Life-Cycle Models of Consumption: Is the Evidence Consistent with the Theory?" in T. F. Bewley, ed., *Advances in Econometrics Fifth World Congress* (New York: Cambridge University Press, 1987), pp. 121–48.

Consumer Durables

Both the permanent-income hypothesis and the life-cycle hypothesis are based on the desirability of maintaining a roughly constant level of enjoyment over time from consumption goods and services. If there is an increase in permanent income, people will not only want to increase their expenditures on services and nondurable goods, but will also want to increase their enjoyment of the services of durable goods. For consumer services and nondurable goods, such as haircuts and doughnuts, the enjoyment and the consumer spending occur at about the same time. Consumer durable goods are different. A television set is purchased at a single instant in time but produces enjoyment for many years thereafter. Thus the PIH and LCH suggest that it is not purchases of consumer durable goods that are kept equal to a fixed fraction of permanent income, but rather the flow of services (enjoyment) received from consumer durables. Consumers can keep the service flow at the same fixed fraction of permanent income by keeping the *stock* of consumer durable goods at the same fixed fraction of permanent income.

The essence of a durable good is that it provides service for many periods. New cars, for example, have service lives of ten years or more. Like any long-term asset, a durable good costs far more to purchase than the service it provides each period. A new car that sells for $25,000, for example, may provide only $2,500 worth of service each year. Thus, when a household decides that its higher permanent income warrants its annually consuming another $2,500 of car services, expenditure initially rises by $25,000. As a result, expenditures for durables may surge temporarily as consumers raise their stocks of durables in proportion to the increase in their permanent incomes.

As a result of the upsurge in purchases of consumer durables, total consumption expenditures may *rise* as a fraction of income when actual income rises, even though the PIH and LCH predict that consumption should *fall* as a fraction of income when actual income rises. Both the PIH and LCH predict that the saving ratio *falls* with higher income when consumer durables are counted as consumption expenditure but *rises* with higher income when consumer durables are counted as saving. Realization of the procyclical nature of consumer durable expenditures limits research on the validity of the PIH and LCH to consumer expenditures *excluding* durables—that is, including just services (haircuts) and nondurables (doughnuts).

Behavior of consumer durable expenditures in recessions. Both the PIH and LCH predict that in a recession, when income exhibits a transitory decline, households should maintain their consumption expenditures *by cutting back on the ratio of saving to disposable income* (S/Y^D). However as shown in the following table, data for postwar recessions indicate that the saving ratio increased slightly between the peak and trough quarters of ten recessions between 1953–54 and 2007–09. While the saving ratio did decline on average in the previous nine recessions, it increased sharply in 2007–09. This occurred because of a factor ignored by the PIH but emphasized by the LCH, namely the wealth effect on consumption. Household wealth fell sharply in 2008 due to the stock market crash and end of the housing bubble, and households reacted by cutting their consumption (as is evident in Figure 15-1 on p. 483) and by raising their saving.

In both 2007–09 and in the nine earlier recessions, there was a decline in consumer durable spending. As a result the ratio of the sum of saving and consumer durable spending to disposable income $[(S + C^D) / Y^D]$ has declined on average in all ten recessions, as shown in this table.

Averages for Ten Recessions, 1953–54 to 2007–09, in percent

Ratio to disposable income	Peak	Trough	Peak to trough change
Personal saving	7.5	7.9	+0.4
Consumer durable expenditures	8.8	8.0	−0.8
Sum of personal saving and consumer durable expenditures	16.4	15.9	−0.5

Liquidity Constraints

The simple version of the LCH in Figure 15-5 assumes that consumption is constant over the lifetime and that labor inc1ome is constant until the date of retirement. Actually, however, labor income tends to rise with age, peaking a bit after age 50. To achieve a constant level of consumption throughout their lifetimes, young people would need to borrow during their low-income years and repay the loans later in high-income years. But banks generally will not allow young people to borrow all they would like, which implies that the consumption expenditures of young people are subject to a **liquidity constraint.** A liquidity constraint may afflict people of any age who are suffering from a transitory loss of income; for instance, banks may be unwilling to lend to a farmer who is close to bankruptcy after a year of poor growing weather, even though the weather can be expected to be better in the future.

A **liquidity constraint** prevents households from borrowing as much as they wish, even though there is sufficient expected future income to repay the loans.

People whose consumption can go no higher than their *current income* because of the unavailability of loans will have a much higher marginal propensity to consume in response to temporary changes in income than is predicted by the PIH or LCH theories. Economists have attempted to measure the importance of this so-called excess sensitivity of consumption to current changes in income. The consensus is that households whose consumption is subject to liquidity constraints account for about 15 percent of aggregate income. These households have MPCs out of transitory income of about 1. The remaining unconstrained households behave roughly as predicted by the LCH: They have negligible MPCs out of transitory income.[10] Thus liquidity constraints do not seem to be prevalent enough to seriously weaken the implication of the LCH (and PIH) that the short-run MPC will be much lower than the long-run MPC.

15-7   Bequests and Uncertainty

In both of our diagrams of the LCH (Figures 15-5 and 15-6), individuals are assumed *to consume all of their lifetime savings during retirement.* Their assets dwindle to zero on the date of death, and nothing is left in the form of bequests

---

[10] Estimates that the share of aggregate income accruing to liquidity-constrained households has been as high as 50 percent can be found in John Y. Campbell and N. Gregory Mankiw, "Consumption, Income, and Interest Rates: Reinterpreting the Time Series Evidence," *NBER Macroeconomics Annual 1989* (Cambridge, MA: The MIT Press), pp. 185–216.

INTERNATIONAL PERSPECTIVE

Why Do Some Countries Save So Much?

While the world saving rate has remained relatively stable over the past few decades, saving rates differ by large amounts across countries and have fluctuated greatly within many countries. In general, saving rates in industrialized countries have been both lower and more stable than they have been in developing countries. National saving rates for industrialized countries have averaged about 15 percent since 1970, but they have averaged more than 25 percent in developing countries. In individual industrial countries, the national saving rate has typically fluctuated within a 10 percentage point range.

The Life-Cycle Model and Dependency Ratios

We have learned that consumption, and thus saving, responds to a number of factors: the stage of the life cycle, interest rates, wealth, and expectations about future income. The life-cycle model suggests that saving rates are lower for the young, who have recently embarked on their working lives, and for the retired, who have left the labor force. Workers, especially those near their peak earnings years, have considerably higher saving rates. That means that countries with higher dependency ratios, that is, with larger fractions of the population not working, would save less.

Over the next few decades, dependency ratios are expected to rise in developed countries (especially Japan), where the number of retired people will increase markedly as life expectancy continues to rise and the huge baby-boom generation retires. By contrast, dependency ratios are expected to fall in developing countries, which now have populations with low average ages. Over the next few decades, large numbers of young people in developing countries will move from being students to being workers, but relatively few people in those countries will attain retirement age.

Saving and Economic Growth

In Chapter 11 we learned that an increase in the private saving rate can increase the rate of economic growth temporarily. But much of the causality runs in the opposite direction, from growth to saving rather than from saving to growth. Sustained increases in growth are associated with permanent increases in the rate of saving; in fact, an increase in the growth rate of 1 percent per annum can raise the private saving rate by as much as 1 percent.

Why does a higher growth rate tend to raise the saving rate? Look back at the top frame of Figure 15-5 on p. 494, which shows the lifetime pattern for a household that saves during the working years and spends all that saving during retirement. If a country has no economic growth, then there is no difference between the income of working people, say aged 40 today, and the income that today's 70-year-old retired people earned 30 years ago when they were aged 40. But if a country is growing rapidly, as in the case of Korea, then today's 40-year-old workers have much higher incomes than today's retired people had 30 years ago, and so the saving by people of working age is much greater than the dissaving of today's retired people, who were saving out of much smaller incomes 30 years ago.

Government Deficits and Private Saving

Do increased government deficits lead to increased private saving? Some economists have suggested that an increase in the government deficit would generate an equal increase in private saving, which would offset the expected future tax burden associated with the increased deficit. The very low level of U.S. private saving in 2003–07 accompanying large government deficits provides evidence that deficits do not boost private saving.

Interest Rates and Consumer Credit

Higher interest rates may either raise saving by providing people with a higher income level (some of which will be saved) or may lower saving by making less saving necessary to achieve a target level of saving for purposes such as retirement. There is no consensus in the economic literature on which effect is stronger. In the United States, the saving rate was lower in the 1990s than in the 1980s, which may have been partly due to a decline in the real interest rate over that period. However, as we shall see later in the chapter, the biggest reason for the decline in the U.S. saving rate was the large capital gains earned by American households on their holdings of equities on the stock market and on their ownership stake in their homes.

Forward-looking consumers will raise their current spending, and thus reduce their saving out of current income, in response to an increase in their expected future incomes. One reason why consumers might raise their spending less than their permanent or life-cycle incomes justify, and thus may raise their saving by more, is the inability to borrow on the basis of expected future incomes. Today's college students are experts on this phenomenon. An economics major may expect a relatively high income after graduation, but few financial institutions will lend today's student more than just a small fraction of that expected future income. In the same way, the household saving rate will tend to be low in countries like the United States where consumer credit is relatively easy to obtain and high in countries like Italy where consumer credit is harder to obtain.

Cross-Country Differences in Saving

The bar chart displays the 2001–10 household saving rate for seven countries, ranging from 10.6 percent for Germany down to 1.4 percent for Australia. How can these differences be explained? In this chapter we explore several explanations of differences across nations in their household saving rates. The LCH suggests that countries with faster economic growth will save more, because they have more households in the high-saving working age groups and fewer retirees.

The most notable aspect of the bar chart is the low saving rates of the United States and Australia. The experience of these two countries supports the view that capital gains on the stock market and housing raise consumption and depress saving. These two nations enjoyed substantial gains in stock market and housing wealth over the decade ending in 2007, whereas in high-saving nations such as Germany and Italy, there has been much less accumulation of household wealth in the form of capital gains on stocks and housing equity, so German and Italian households need to save more by abstaining from consumption. We return subsequently in this chapter to discussing alternative measures of U.S. household saving that take account of wealth accumulation.

The relatively low saving rate of Japan, only 3.5 percent, is surprising in light of Japan's history as a high-saving country. Part of the decline in saving directly results from Japan's economic slump since the early 1990s (see pp. 110–11). As suggested by the permanent-income hypothesis, households reduce their saving in response to higher unemployment or lower incomes that they believe to be temporary. Young Japanese, unable to afford their own housing, are returning to live with their parents and are able to consume all of their income without the need to save up for their own houses. Formerly many Japanese received semiannual bonuses, which they put into savings accounts, but economic hard times have caused firms to cut these bonuses drastically. Finally, interest rates on saving accounts in Japan are in many cases below 1 percent, providing no incentive to save.

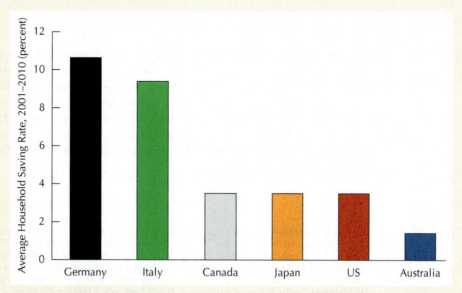

Source: OECD Economic Outlook 88, November 2010, Annex Table 23. Rates are predicted by OECD and may differ from actual outcomes.

to heirs. In fact, however, people do leave bequests. It has been claimed that about 80 percent of asset accumulation by U.S. households is transmitted to heirs rather than used for consumption during retirement.[11] This evidence seems to deny that the appropriate horizon to describe consumer behavior is the lifetime.

The Role of Bequests

The existence of bequests has been interpreted as support for a striking theory of fiscal policy, often called the Barro-Ricardo equivalence theorem. This theory was developed by Robert J. Barro of Harvard University, using ideas originally suggested by the early nineteenth-century British economist David Ricardo.[12] People are expected to leave bequests because they care about their children. Any event that leaves their children worse off will lead members of the present generation to increase saving in order to leave a larger bequest to their children. A prime example of such an event would be a deficit-financed tax cut that raises the taxes that must be paid by future generations (to pay the interest and principal on the bonds issued to finance the debt). According to the Barro-Ricardo theorem, such a tax cut would not stimulate consumption because people would save all of the increase in their after-tax income in order to raise their bequests.

The Barro-Ricardo theorem has been criticized because it is contradicted by the facts. Most important, the U.S. household saving rate did not increase at all following the Reagan tax cuts of the 1980s or the Bush tax cuts of 2001–03, as the theorem would have predicted. In fact, as we shall see in Figure 15-7 on p. 507, the saving rate in 2006–07 fell to its lowest level since the Great Depression. Thus it seems likely that the mere existence of bequests does not validate the kind of behavior postulated by the theorem—specifically the refusal of current households to raise their consumption in response to a tax cut.

Motives for Bequests

If parents do not adjust their bequests for every current event that changes their heirs' future tax liabilities, why does a large fraction of personal saving eventually flow to children in the form of bequests? Many think that the central issue is the uncertainty of the age of death. Benjamin Franklin's observation that "in this world nothing can be said to be certain, except death and taxes" omits the fact that the *timing* of death is quite uncertain. Contrary to the assumption of Figures 15-5 and 15-6, households cannot know the lengths of their lifetimes.

---

[11] Laurence J. Kotlikoff and Lawrence H. Summers, "The Role of Intergenerational Transfers in Aggregate Capital Accumulation," *Journal of Political Economy*, vol. 89 (August 1981), pp. 706–32. This finding is very controversial. A lengthy scholarly debate on the Kotlikoff-Summers findings is contained in Franco Modigliani, "The Role of Intergenerational Transfers and Life Cycle Saving in the Accumulation of Wealth," and Laurence J. Kotlikoff, "Intergenerational Transfers and Savings," both in *Journal of Economic Perspectives*, vol. 2 (Spring 1988), pp. 15–40 and 41–58, respectively.

[12] Robert J. Barro, "Are Government Bonds Net Wealth?" *Journal of Political Economy*, vol. 82 (November/December 1974), pp. 1095–1117.

By this interpretation, *much saving is life cycle in nature, but only for a part of the lifetime and for medical care that does not occur for everyone.* Many people die before expensive nursing care treatment becomes necessary and thus have substantial wealth "left over" that goes as bequests to the children. By this interpretation, bequests are primarily involuntary and are made because parents do not want to lose control of their assets and their living conditions prior to death.

Implications for the LCH theory. The interpretation of bequests as primarily involuntary leaves the main predictions of the LCH intact. The only adjustment to the LCH is that the relevant horizon for most households extends beyond the actual age of death (as assumed in Figures 15-5 and 15-6) to the *oldest conceivable age of death.* For instance, a 25-year-old may have a future life expectancy of 50 years, with 75 the most probable age of death, but may base consumption and saving decisions on the outside chance of living until age 90.

This amended version of the LCH would operate just like the version depicted in Figure 15-6, except the extended lifetime (L^*, say 90) replaces the most probable lifetime (L, say 75). Use of L^* instead of the lower L would imply an even lower MPC for temporary changes in income, and would imply that increases in wealth from the stock market would be consumed over the extended period until L^*. If parents are unwilling to move out of their homes (and are also unwilling to sell their homes to their children and pay them rent), then the gains parents make from higher housing prices may not be consumed over the lifetime but may be largely ignored and lead to a larger bequest.

Why Retirees Cut Their Consumption So Much

Looking back at Figure 15-5 on p. 494, the LCH predicts that consumption is maintained at a fixed level throughout a person's working life and retirement years. But a growing body of evidence suggests that retirees consume much less than working people who are otherwise the same in terms of income and family characteristics.

Why do people cut their consumption after they retire? First, many people react to retirement by moving, because they are no longer tied to the location of their job, and they often move into smaller dwellings. Second, many retirees have paid off the mortgages on their homes, even if they do not move. Third, retirees can eliminate consumption expenses previously required by work, including job-related clothing, automobile and fuel expenses required by commuting, and business-related meals eaten outside the home. Fourth—perhaps a minor factor—retirees have more leisure time and can spend more time searching for bargains, thus reducing the cost of everyday household necessities.[13]

Does the decline in consumption after retirement, in contrast to the steady retirement depicted in Figure 15-5, invalidate the LCH? Not at all, because all

---

[13] Two papers provide an illuminating analysis of the drop in consumption after retirement. See Michael Hurd and Susann Rohwedder, "Some Answers to the Retirement-Consumption Puzzle," NBER working paper 12057, February 2006 and John Ameriks, Andrew Caplin, and John Leahy, "Retirement Consumption: Insights from a Survey," NBER working paper 8735, January 2002.

of the reasons for lower consumption after retirement are anticipated by households long in advance of retirement. All the predictions of the LCH, including the effect of higher stock market or housing wealth in raising consumption and reducing saving, and the lack of response of consumption by working-age households to temporary changes of income, are still valid for households that plan their retirement consumption in advance, no matter whether that consumption is planned to equal working-age consumption or whether it is planned in advance to be lower.

◆ SELF-TEST

Imagine that, in order to reduce the federal budget deficit, the government institutes a $1,000 increase in the yearly personal income tax paid by every household. The tax increase is announced to be permanent. What would the following theories predict to be the effects on consumption?

1. Permanent-income hypothesis
2. Life-cycle hypothesis with certain lifetime
3. Life-cycle hypothesis that explains bequests as resulting from uncertain lifetimes
4. Barro-Ricardo equivalence theory

15-8 CASE STUDY

Did the Rise and Collapse of Household Assets Cause the Decline and Rise of the Household Saving Rate?

Early in this book in the graph on p. 63 we saw that the household saving rate (that is, household saving divided by personal disposable income) declined from the early 1980s through 2007 and then increased. For convenience, this graph is repeated on the next page as Figure 15-7. The blue line plots the personal saving rate since 1970. The rate was above 10 percent as recently as 1984 and was still above 7 percent in 1992, yet it fell to a mere 1.4 percent in 2005. Why did it decline so much between 1984 and 2005? And then the saving rate increased to 5.9 percent in 2009. What created this turnaround?

What do the theories of this chapter predict as possible causes of the decline and then partial recovery of the saving rate? The prediction of the Friedman permanent income hypothesis goes in the opposite direction of the decline in the saving rate in the 1990s, since the PIH would predict that households would have viewed the rapid income growth of the 1990s to be at least partially transitory and would have increased their saving rate accordingly, yet in fact households reduced their saving rate in the 1990s.

The Modigliani life-cycle hypothesis is more successful in predicting the decline in the saving rate through 2005 and then the increase from then until 2009. As we have learned, the Modigliani theory makes consumption depend not only on lifetime income but also on real assets. Allowing for consumer debt, consumption depends not on real assets but real net worth (i.e., assets

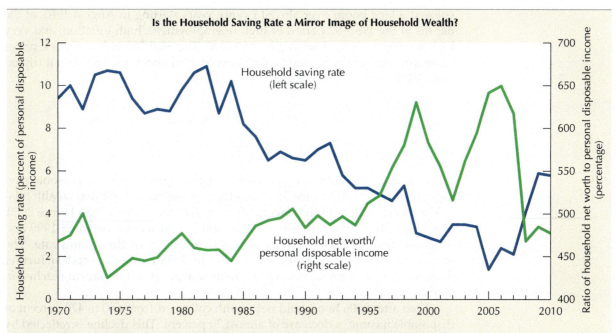

Figure 15-7 The Household Saving Rate and the Ratio of Household Net Worth to Personal Disposable Income, 1970–2010

Sources: Federal Reserve Board *Flow of Funds Accounts* and Bureau of Economic Analysis *NIPA Tables*. Details in Appendix C-4.

minus liabilities). The extraordinary boom in the stock market that occurred in the late 1990s created huge gains in real household wealth and substantially boosted consumption relative to income, thus by definition depressing the percentage of disposable income saved by households.

The Explosion and Then Collapse of Household Net Wealth

The most relevant measure of wealth for explaining household consumption and saving behavior is a series on household net worth, compiled by government statisticians at the Fed.[14] Figure 15-7 shows the ratio of net worth to disposable income as the green line that is compared to the household saving rate shown as the blue line. There is a clear negative correlation between the two lines, with low wealth and a high saving rate between 1974 and 1985, followed by an initial upward jump in wealth and decline in the saving rate between 1985 and 1989, and then a second larger jump in wealth and decline in the saving rate between 1995 and 2000. The negative correlation continued after 2000, with a third jump in wealth in 2003–06 that brought the saving rate to its postwar low point in 2005, followed by a collapse in wealth and recovery of the saving rate in 2007–09.

What triggered the three big jumps in household net worth? Clearly the cause of the first two jumps was the behavior of the stock market, which

---

[14] The data can also be found at www.econstats.com/fof/index.htm. The data displayed in Figures 15-7 and 15-8 are also found in table B.100 at this Web site. The data include not just households but also nonprofit institutions such as hospitals and universities.

enjoyed a long boom over almost twenty years starting in August 1982, at the depths of the 1981–82 period of high unemployment, high inflation, and very high interest rates, and ending in mid-2000. The S&P 500 index of stock prices more than doubled from 160 to 335 between 1984 and 1989, and then it tripled from 460 in 1994 to 1,427 in 2000.[15]

Capital Gains and Losses on Houses Reinforce the Negative Correlation Between Household Net Wealth and the Personal Saving Rate

Between 2000 and 2005 the negative relationship between the personal saving rate (blue line in Figure 15-7) and the ratio of household real wealth relative to personal disposable income (green line) are weaker than before 2000. The graph shows that the sharp reduction in real wealth between 1999 and 2002 was accompanied by only a modest recovery of the saving rate. The sharp recovery of net wealth from 2002 to 2006 created a modest further decline in the household saving rate to its low point of 1.4 percent reached in 2005.

Then after 2006 household net wealth collapsed from 650 to 470 percent of disposable income, a decrease of almost 30 percent. This decline is reflected by the financial crisis of 2007–09 that caused a stock market crash even more severe than in 2000–02, but more important the pricking of the house price bubble. Just as the Modigliani LCH theory would predict, the collapse of net worth created a strong recovery of the household saving rate from 1.4 percent in 2005 to 5.8 percent in 2010.

Few relationships in macroeconomics work as well as that depicted in Figure 15-7. By 2009–10 the saving rate had risen back to almost 6 percent, which was the average saving rate of 1992–94. And, remarkably, the real wealth ratio, the green line in Figure 15-7, in 2009–10 had returned almost exactly to the same ratio as in 1992–94.

The Separate Roles of Financial and Housing Real Net Wealth

Further understanding of what happened after 2000 is provided in Figure 15-8, which displays the ratio of total household assets to disposable income, divided between financial assets (including volatile stocks and stock mutual funds) as shown by the green area, and "tangible assets" consisting mainly of the value of household ownership of houses and condominiums. The red area representing tangible assets grew between 1998 and 2005 from 211 to 305 percent before collapsing between 2005 and 2009 back from 305 percent to 212 percent. Thus households were whipsawed by a 45 percent increase in tangible assets, with its temptation for households to borrow against the value of their houses and go ever further into debt, followed by a collapse of the value of these tangible assets back to the level of 1998. But while the value of the assets decreased, the value of the debts was fixed by contracts and did not decrease. And this led to the epidemic of foreclosures and "under water" mortgages discussed in Chapter 5. ◆

---

[15] S&P index values are averages of daily closing prices for each year.

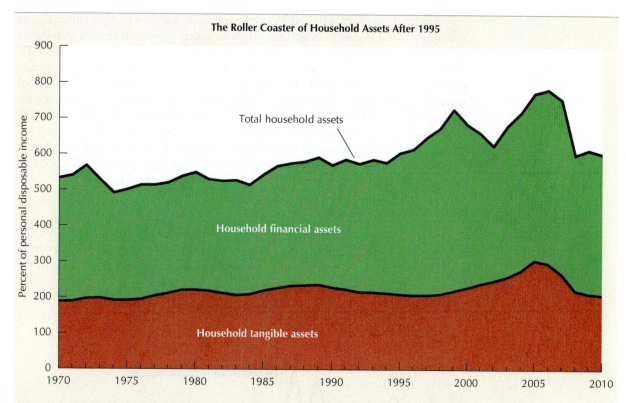

Figure 15-8 **Components of Household Assets as a Ratio to Personal Disposable Income, 1970–2010, in Percent**

The red section shows the ratio of household tangible assets, primarily consisting of the value of owner-occupied homes, to disposable income. This ratio rose in the late 1970s, in the late 1980s, and especially during 2000–06 before collapsing after 2006. The green section shows the ratio of household financial wealth, including direct holdings of stocks and stock mutual funds, to disposable income. This ratio rose in the late 1980s and especially during 1994–2000. The total ratio shown by the top of the green area fell sharply from 2000 to 2002 and recovered from 2002 to 2007, before collapsing from 2007 to 2009.

Sources: Federal Reserve Board *Flow of Funds Accounts* and Bureau of Economic Analysis *NIPA Tables*. Details in Appendix C-4.

15-9 Why the Official Household Saving Data Are Misleading

When we say the household saving rate was 5.8 percent in 2010 as in Figure 15-7, we are referring to the measure of saving used in the national income and product accounts (NIPA, reviewed in Chapter 2), namely personal disposable income minus consumption expenditures minus personal interest payments. However, the NIPA measure understates the true household saving rate. The most notable feature of the NIPA saving concept is that capital gains on stocks, bonds, houses, and other assets are excluded because these gains do not reflect returns from the current production of goods and services.

A second flaw is that the NIPA saving measure does not include purchases of consumer durable goods, even though these goods provide a stream of benefits in the future, for example, the benefit of being able to use a large-screen color TV set or automobile over a number of years. A third flaw is that inflation influences the real significance of the household saving rate. Households receive nominal interest returns from corporations, and the nominal interest rate rises with the inflation rate. Thus when inflation is rapid, as in the period between 1974 and 1982, household saving is overstated by receipt of nominal interest earnings, which are simply a compensation for inflation, not real income. Conversely, when inflation declines as it has since the early 1980s, household saving is understated because households receive lower nominal income but not lower real income.

Alternative Measures of Saving

Fortunately, alternative data sources are available to provide a more accurate impression of household saving behavior than the NIPA saving rate. Shown in Figure 15-9 is the NIPA series on the household saving rate compared with the

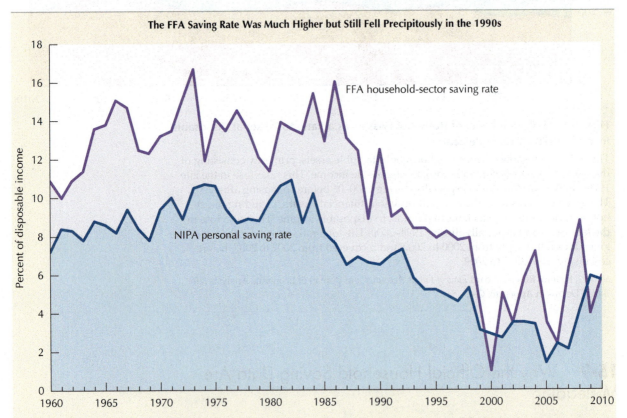

The FFA Saving Rate Was Much Higher but Still Fell Precipitously in the 1990s

Figure 15-9 Household Saving in the NIPA and Flow of Funds Accounts, 1960–2010

The blue line is copied from Figure 15-7 and shows the NIPA measure of the personal saving rate. The purple line shows an alternative saving rate compiled by the Federal Reserve Board. The Fed measure is usually higher than the NIPA measure because it includes purchases of consumer durables. Both the measures plotted here exclude the influence of capital gains and losses on household net wealth.

Sources: Federal Reserve Board *Flow of Funds Accounts* and Bureau of Economic Analysis *NIPA Tables.* Details in Appendix C-4.

equivalent saving rate from the "Flow of Fund Accounts" (FFA), which differ by including net investment in consumer durables. Here we see that in most years the FFA measure is substantially larger than the NIPA saving rate by an average of 3.6 percent over the full period 1960–2010.

However, during the period 2000–2010 the FFA measure hardly differed at all from the NIPA measure, with a difference over that period of only 1.2 percentage points. This implies that the FFA measure had declined even more from its pre-1990 values than had the NIPA measure. The decline in both measures is misleading, though, because the FFA measure like the NIPA measure excludes the effect of capital gains.

Figure 15-10 shows an alternative measure of saving defined in terms of increases in household wealth (including financial assets and housing equity) relative to total income including capital gains. Clearly the adjustment makes an enormous difference. First, the alternative "gains-inclusive saving rate" is much more volatile than either the FFA or NIPA measures; for instance, it jumped from 6 percent in 1994 to 37 percent in 1995, and it collapsed from 47 percent in 2005 to −158 percent in 2008. Second, the broader measure contradicts the implication of

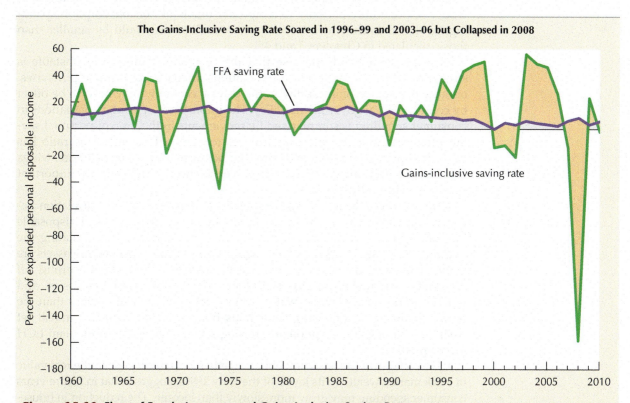

Figure 15-10 **Flow of Funds Accounts and Gains-Inclusive Saving Rates, 1976–2010**

The Fed measure of the saving rate is shown by the purple line and is copied from Figure 15-9. The volatile green line measures the change in household net wealth expressed as a percent. When stock prices rise rapidly, as in 1994–2000 and 2003–06, the change in household net wealth is a large positive fraction of personal disposable income. But when stock prices and housing values crash, as in 2007–09, the change in household net wealth can be a big negative number, about −160 percent for the year 2008 as shown in the chart.

Sources: Federal Reserve Board *Flow of Funds Accounts* and Bureau of Economic Analysis *NIPA Tables*. Details in Appendix C-4.

the NIPA that household saving nearly disappeared in 2005–06. In contrast the gains-inclusive saving rate was actually *higher* after 1995 than before 1985. The gains-inclusive saving rate averaged 24 percent in 1996–2007, substantially higher than its average of 16 percent over the earlier period 1960–85. In contrast, the FFA concept of saving declined over the same intervals from 14 to 5 percent. Thus the entire story of a decline in personal saving appears to result from the exclusion of capital gains from the conventional NIPA and FFA measures of household saving.[16]

15-10 Conclusion: Does Consumption Stabilize the Economy?

If all consumption spending consisted of nondurable goods and services, the permanent-income hypothesis and life-cycle hypothesis both would strengthen the case of those who advocate policy rules and are optimistic that the private economy is basically stable if left alone by the government. Consumption would respond only partially to temporary bursts of nonconsumption spending, so that the economy's true short-run multipliers would be smaller than those calculated in Chapters 3 and 4.

On the other hand, the case that the economy is inherently unstable is strengthened by the pro-cyclical fluctuations in consumer durable purchases, because this source of instability in the private economy may need to be offset by countercyclical government policy. The importance of erratic fluctuations in consumer spending is summarized by movements in the ratio of personal saving plus consumer durable expenditures to personal income. This ratio has fluctuated over a wide range during the postwar years. Part of these swings may reflect movements in consumer confidence, which are an important source of shifts in the *IS* curve.

The main conclusion of this chapter is the strong negative correlation between household real net wealth and the ratio of saving to personal disposable income. Increases in net wealth boost consumption, partly by facilitating the granting of new mortgage and home equity loans to consumers whose assets are rising. However, decreases in net wealth reduce consumption, cutting off the ability to borrow against assets. Millions of households face foreclosure, and millions of others are "under water" (owing more on their mortgages than the reduced value of their houses). These households react to a reduction in real net wealth by cutting consumption and raising saving, just as the Modigliani LCH theory predicts.

The collapse of the housing bubble, together with the decline in the real value of stock market wealth to its levels of the early 1990s, suggests that in future years consumer spending may grow more slowly than income. The reduction in household assets and the hangover of high consumer debt combined to reduce household net wealth by about 30 percent in 2010 from the peak level of 2005–06. This ends the long-term trend shown in Figure 15-1 on p. 483 that consumer spending steadily rose as a fraction of natural GDP from 1984 to 2000.

---

[16] For a comprehensive analysis of differences in saving rate concepts, see Marshall B. Reinsdorf, "Alternative Measures of Personal Saving," *Survey of Current Business* (September 2004), pp. 17–27. This article can also be found at www.bea.gov/bea/ARTICLES/2004/09September/PersonalSavingWEB.pdf.

Summary

1. A major area of dispute between policy activists and advocates of policy rules concerns the stability of private spending decisions. Friedman's permanent-income hypothesis (PIH) and Modigliani's life-cycle hypothesis (LCH) are based on the assumption that individuals achieve a higher level of total utility (enjoyment) when they maintain a stable consumption pattern than when they allow consumption to rise or fall with every transitory fluctuation in their actual income. Individuals can achieve the desired stable consumption pattern by consuming a stable fraction of their permanent or lifetime income.

2. If all consumption consisted of nondurable goods and services, both the PIH and the LCH would strengthen the case of those who advocate policy rules, who claim that the private economy is basically stable if left alone by the government. Consumption would respond only partially to temporary fluctuations of nonconsumption spending, so that the economy's short-run multipliers would be smaller than the simple theoretical multipliers of Chapters 3 and 4.

3. Both the PIH and the LCH can reconcile the observed cross-section increase in the saving ratio for higher incomes with the observed long-run historical constancy of the aggregate saving ratio.

4. Both hypotheses have important implications for fiscal policy. For example, a tax change announced as permanent should cause a bigger change in permanent income, and hence in consumption expenditures, than another equal-sized tax change announced as temporary. Thus temporary tax changes introduced to implement an activist fiscal policy may be rendered ineffective by offsetting movements in the saving ratio.

5. Numerous criticisms of the PIH and LCH have emerged in recent years. A large share of saving seems to be used not for consumption during retirement, but for bequests to children. Households may save more than they need, because they are uncertain about the date of death. People cut their consumption spending when they retire, conflicting with the LCH assumption that consumption is stable over the lifetime. Liquidity constraints imply that perhaps 15 percent of income is earned by households for whom the short-run marginal propensity to consume is much higher than implied by the PIH or LCH.

6. An additional consideration in explaining observed consumption and saving behavior is that consumer durable expenditures should be treated as a form of saving, not as current consumption. Sharp increases in income tend to go mainly into saving, which means that consumer durable expenditures treated as a form of saving may be very responsive to transitory income changes. Thus the PIH and LCH may be valid, but consumer durable purchases are still a source of instability in the private economy.

7. The puzzle of the decline in the U.S. household saving rate during the 1992–2007 period can be traced partly to the stock market boom of this period, as well as steady increases in housing prices. The National Income and Product Accounts concept of the saving rate excludes capital gains and adjustments for inflation and thus greatly understates increases in household wealth during the 1990s and most earlier decades.

8. The jump in the household saving rate in 2007–09 reinforces the LCH theory that saving moves inversely to real net wealth, since wealth declined sharply in 2007–09 as a result of the stock market crash and end of the housing bubble.

Concepts

forward-looking expectations	cross section	transitory income
permanent-income hypothesis (PIH)	time series	rational expectations
life-cycle hypothesis (LCH)	permanent income	liquidity constraint

Questions

1. Discuss how the consumption of durable goods, nondurable goods, and services as shares of natural GDP has changed since 1960. Discuss how and why the consumption of durable goods, nondurable goods, and services as shares of natural GDP changes during recessions.

2. Explain how and why there is a difference between how the nominal shares of durable goods, nondurable goods, and services in total consumption expenditures changed from 1960 to 2010 as opposed to when those shares are measured in real terms.

3. The saving ratio was remarkably stable between 1895 and 1980. When we examine cross-section data, however, we find that the saving ratio tends to rise as income rises. How can these two observations be reconciled?

4. Why is a distinction made between a short-run marginal propensity to consume and a long-run marginal propensity to consume in the permanent-income hypothesis (PIH)?

5. Is permanent income permanent? If not, what causes it to change?

6. How does the existence of assets affect consumption and income in the life-cycle hypothesis (LCH)?

7. What is likely to happen to the household saving rate in the United States and other industrialized economies as the proportion of the population that is retired rises? What are some ways that this effect on the saving rate could be reversed?

8. In each of the following cases, explain whether permanent income would change and if so, how much it would change initially if permanent income is calculated using adaptive expectations or rational expectations.

   (a) Due to increased health care costs, Food-2-Go reduces its work force by 10 percent. In order to maintain its output, it requires the employees it retains to work overtime on a regular basis. (Answer this question for both the workers retained and the workers let go by Food-2-Go. Assume that when workers let go by Food-2-Go get new jobs, they will earn less than they earned at Food-2-Go.)

   (b) An unusually snowy winter forces a ski resort to offer its help overtime pay in order to provide the extra services demanded by the extra skiers it has that season.

   (c) A person receives a promotion that she was expecting. However, the salary that she earns in her new job is much more than she was expecting.

9. Does the fact that many individuals leave bequests (i.e., do not consume their entire income over their lifetimes) invalidate the LCH?

10. Both the LCH and the PIH predict that the marginal propensity to consume out of transitory income is quite small (perhaps, even zero). Nevertheless, we observe many younger families spending a fairly large percentage of their transitory incomes. Is this observation consistent with the two hypotheses?

11. The PIH and LCH suggest that consumer durable expenditures should be considered separately from expenditures on nondurables and services. Why? How does this distinction alter the appearance of saving and consumption behavior? Why do some economists argue that consumer durable expenditures should be treated as saving rather than consumption?

12. Discuss whether studies of what consumers did with their 2008 Economic Stimulus Act (ESA) payments are consistent with the PIH and the LCH hypotheses. Use the concept of a liquidity constraint to explain why providing transfer payments to the unemployed is likely to have a higher multiplier effect than an across-the-board tax rebate program, like the ESA, which provides the same total amount of payments to individuals as the aid to the unemployed does.

13. Explain why a rapid increase in economic growth can cause an increase in the savings rate.

14. Does a decline in consumption by retirees invalidate the LCH? Explain why retirees can reduce their consumption when compared to groups that are similar in terms of income.

15. Discuss whether the collapse of the national income and product accounts (NIPA) personal saving rate during the 1990s is consistent with the PIH.

16. The NIPA personal saving rate fell from 1992 to 2005 and then rebounded. Discuss whether these changes are consistent with the LCH.

17. Explain why the NIPA personal saving rate does not accurately measure the household saving rate.

18. Compare and contrast the behavior of the capital gains-inclusive saving rate since 1985 with those of the NIPA and Flow of Funds Accounts (FFA) personal saving rates over that same period.

Problems

 Visit www.MyEconLab.com to complete these or similar exercises.

1. Assume that consumption and permanent income are derived as shown in equations (15.2) and (15.3). In those equations, let $k = 0.8$ and $j = 0.5$. Assume that 2010 actual income of $30,000 equals permanent income.

   (a) What would be the permanent income for 2011, 2012, and 2013 if actual income for those three years were $36,000, $45,000, and $30,000, respectively?

   (b) What would be consumption spending in those three years?

   (c) What would be the short-run marginal propensity to consume in each of those three years?

   (d) Using the distinction between permanent income and transitory income, explain why the short-run marginal propensity to consume would differ from the long-run marginal propensity to consume in 2011.

2. You are given the following information concerning income, transitory income, and permanent consumption:

Income	Transitory income	Permanent consumption
6,000	0	4,500
6,880	−120	5,250
8,020	20	6,000
8,955	−45	6,750
10,200	200	7,500

(a) Calculate the amount of permanent income at each level of income.

(b) Calculate the long-run marginal propensity to consume, k.

(c) Assuming that the marginal propensity to consume out of transitory income equals 0, compute the short-run marginal propensities to consume at income levels of $6,000, $6,880, $8,020, $8,955, and $10,200.

(d) Explain how the short-run marginal propensities to consume differ from the long-run marginal propensity to consume.

3. The marginal propensity to consume out of permanent income equals 0.9 and the marginal propensity to consume out of transitory income equals 0.1. Suppose that there is an emergency increase in government spending of $200 billion to repair infrastructure. The spending takes place within a year. The spending increase is financed by a one-time increase in taxes. Prior to the increase in government spending, permanent income equals $9,600 billion and transitory income equals zero.

(a) Compute the amounts of consumption expenditures and private saving prior to the tax increase.

(b) Compute the amount of changes in consumption expenditures and private saving, given that the tax increase lasts for only one year.

(c) Compute the initial change in aggregate demand that results from this combination of increases in government spending and taxes.

4. Again assume that the marginal propensity to consume out of permanent income equals 0.9 and the marginal propensity to consume out of transitory income equals 0.1. However, instead of a one-time increase in taxes, the infrastructure spending is financed by issuing a ten-year bond at the beginning of the first year. Taxes are then raised in each of the ten years to raise enough funds to retire the bond at the end of the ten years. Permanent income is reduced in each year by the amount of the tax increase in that year. The tax increases necessary to be able to retire the bond are: $15.33 billion in year 1; $15.79 billion in year 2; $16.26 billion in year 3; $16.75 billion in year 4; $17.25 billion in year 5; $17.77 billion in year 6; $18.30 billion in year 7;

$18.85 billion in year 8; $19.42 billion in year 9; and $20.00 billion in year 10. (*Note:* These are net tax increases in that it is assumed that the debt is purchased domestically. Therefore any interest expense paid by taxpayers is offset as income received by taxpayers.)

(a) Verify that the future value[a] of each year's tax increase in year 10 is $20 billion, given that the real interest rate the government can borrow at equals 3 percent. (*Hint:* Remember that the first year's tax increase can earn interest in years 2 through 10; the second year's tax increase can earn interest in years 3 through 10; and so on.)

(b) Compute the amounts of consumption expenditures and private saving in each of the ten years, given that the tax increase in each year results in a decrease in permanent income.

(c) Compute the amounts that the tax increases cause consumption expenditures and private saving to change in each of the ten years when compared to the amounts prior to the change in fiscal policy.

(d) Compute the initial change in aggregate demand in each of the ten years that results from this combination of changes in taxes and government spending.

(e) Compute the present discounted value[b] of the changes in aggregate demand that result from this combination of changes in taxes and government spending, given that the real interest rate the government can borrow at equals 3 percent.

(f) Explain why the expansionary effect of the change in fiscal policy is less, both in the first year and in terms of the present discounted value of the effect of the fiscal policy over ten years, when the increase in spending is financed by debt that is paid off by a permanent tax increase rather than a one-time tax increase.

(g) What value of the marginal propensity to consume out of transitory income would make the present discounted value of the one-time tax increase equal to the present discounted value of the combination of debt financing and permanent tax increases to pay off the debt?

_____

[a] The future value of some amount of money A at time t in the future, given an interest rate r, is the amount of money that a person has at time t if he sets aside the amount A today, given that it earns the interest rate r between now and t. For example, the future value of $100 in ten years, given an interest rate equal to 5 percent, is $100 $\times$ $(1.05)^{10}$ = $162.89.

[b] The present discounted value of the amount of money A at time t, given an interest rate r, is the amount of money that must be set aside today in order to have the amount of money A at time t in the future, given that it earns the interest rate r between now and t. For example, the present discounted value of $162.89 in ten years, given an interest rate equal to 5 percent, is 162.89/\left((1.05)^{10}\right)$ = $100.

5. Assume that Gina's consumption decisions are consistent with the LCH. In 2011, Gina is 25 years old, expects to earn income until she is 65, and expects to consume until she dies at age 85.
   (a) If Gina earns $30,000 per year and wishes to consume an equal amount each year, how much will she consume each year?
   (b) What is Gina's ratio of consumption to income? What is her saving ratio?
   (c) Assume that Gina has assets equal to $120,000 in 2011. Recalculate your answers for a and b.
   (d) Assume that in 2031, Gina inherits $40,000. Now what are your answers to c?

6. A recent medical school graduate age 26 will intern for seven years, making $30,000 a year. Thereafter, she will make $250,000 a year for 30 years. At age 26, she also has assets of $570,000.
   (a) In the absence of liquidity constraints, how much will she consume per year if she expects to live to age 83?
   (b) Suppose that a collapse in the stock market reduces the value of her assets at age 26 to $285,000. How much will she now consume per year if she expects to live to age 83?

7. Suppose that Jim goes to work at age 25, earns on average $40,000 a year for 40 years. He inherits $320,000 when he starts working. He expects to live to be 75.

   (a) Calculate on average how much Jim consumes per year, the ratio of his annual consumption to annual income, and his annual savings rate.
   (b) Suppose now that Jim learns that he can expect to live to be 85. If Jim does not change his retirement age, compute Jim's new annual consumption, as well as the new ratio of annual consumption to annual income, and his new annual saving rate.

8. Suppose that Alan goes to work at age 22, earns on average $60,000 a year for 43 years, and inherits $300,000 the year he starts working. He expects to live to be 82.
   (a) Calculate on average how much Alan consumes per year, the ratio of his annual consumption to annual income, and his savings rate.
   (b) Suppose that a rise in housing prices causes Alan's inheritance to increase to $480,000. If Alan does not change his retirement age, calculate Alan's new annual consumption, as well as the new ratio of annual consumption to annual income, and his annual savings rate.
   (c) Given the increase in his inheritance listed in part b, suppose that Alan decides to use the increased inheritance to finance an earlier retirement age. He does this by maintaining the same average annual consumption as in part a. At what age will Alan be able to retire?

◆ SELF-TEST ANSWERS

p. 492. (1) A stockbroker enjoying his or her best year has actual income above permanent income and consumes less and saves more than he or she would if that income were permanent. (2) A wheat farmer suffering from a drought will have actual income below permanent income and will consume more and save less than he or she would if that income were permanent. (3) When the U.S. economy is in recession, an unusually large number of people will experience below-permanent income and will consume more and save less than they would if they considered their recession-level income permanent. (4) When the U.S. economy is in a period of unusually high real GDP, a large number of people will experience above-permanent income and will consume less and save more than they would if they considered their exceptionally high income permanent.

p. 496. (1) Use the right-hand part of equation (15.7). If $A_1 = 0$, and $R/L = 30/40$, then consumption expenditures per year will be 30/40 times $50,000, or $37,500

during both the working and retirement years. (2) C/Y during working years will be $37,500/50,000, or 0.75, which of course equals R/L. (3) With initial assets of 200,000, $A_1/L = 200,000/40 = 5,000$. Consumption expenditures by equation (15.8) will then be $5,000 plus $37,500 = $42,500 during both the working and retirement years. (4) C/Y during working years will be $42,500/50,000 = 0.85$.

p. 506. (1) Since the tax increase is assumed to be permanent, it will reduce permanent income by $1,000. Consumption will fall by k times $1,000 per year. (2) According to the life-cycle hypothesis as set forth in equation (15.7), Y per year will fall by $1,000, and consumption per year will fall by R/L times $1,000. (3) According to the life-cycle hypothesis, with an uncertain lifetime L, consumption per year will fall by R/L^* times $1,000. (4) According to the Barro-Ricardo equivalence theorem, consumption will not change at all, since saving will decline by the full amount of the tax increase (reflecting the lower anticipated future tax liabilities).

CHAPTER 16

The Economics of Investment Behavior

Whatever cannot go on forever must come to an end.
   —Herbert Stein

If consumers purchased only nondurable goods and services, the permanent-income and life-cycle hypotheses predict that consumer behavior would stabilize the economy. An offsetting factor is the procyclical movement of consumer durable purchases. Although consistent with the PIH and LCH, such movement tends to aggravate booms and recessions. In this chapter we find that business fixed investment also fluctuates procyclically. Thus both durable purchases by consumers and investment purchases by businesses introduce instability into the private economy. This instability in turn supports a role for activist countercyclical monetary and fiscal policies. Such policies include the Taylor rule for monetary policy that varies the interest rate in respose to changes in the output gap that may result from the volatility of investment.

   The instability of private investment gains new relevance after the wild oscillations of the past two decades. Compared to its average annual growth rate over the period 1960–2010 of 3.2 percent, private fixed investment grew at a much faster average rate of 9.1 percent during 1996–2000 and then a decade later collapsed at an annual rate of −17.7 percent between 2007 and 2009.

16-1 Investment and Economic Stability

In Chapter 15 we found that the permanent-income and life-cycle hypotheses of individual consumption behavior explain the partial insulation of aggregate consumption spending from changes in other types of spending in the short run. But what are the sources of changes in these other types of spending? Nominal GDP in 2010 was divided among the major types of expenditures as follows:

Personal consumption expenditures	70.6%
Gross private domestic investment	12.4
Government purchases of goods and services	20.5
Net exports	−3.5
	100.0

Having already considered consumer expenditures in Chapter 15, government spending and other aspects of fiscal policy in Chapter 6, and net exports in Chapter 7, we concentrate here on private investment.

We will review a very simple theory that explains why investment spending is likely to exhibit more pronounced fluctuations than other types of spending. According to the permanent-income hypothesis, introduced in the last chapter to explain consumer expenditures, households try to maintain a constant ratio of their consumer durable stock to permanent income. This creates sudden bursts of durable purchases when an upward revision of permanent income causes the desired durable stock to increase. In this chapter we will see that investment spending on plant, equipment, inventories, and housing is driven by the same principle and therefore is also subject to sudden bursts of purchases.[1]

16-2 CASE STUDY

The Historical Instability of Investment

Total Investment Rises and Falls Dramatically and Procyclically

We begin by examining the historical record of investment spending since 1960. Figure 16-1 clearly shows that investment spending is far more variable than consumption spending (compare with Figure 15-1 on p. 483). The top line in the figure shows total gross private domestic investment (GPDI) in natural GDP. By any standard, the fluctuations in total investment are huge.

The following table shows how the GPDI share has fluctuated since 1960.

Quarters			Change in share (percentage points)	
Peak	Trough	Peak	Peak to trough	Trough to peak
1960:Q1	1961:Q1	1969:Q4	−4.2	+2.8
1969:Q4	1970:Q4	1973:Q4	−1.7	+4.6
1973:Q4	1975:Q1	1980:Q1	−5.2	+5.4
1980:Q1	1980:Q3	1981:Q3	−3.3	+2.9
1981:Q3	1982:Q4	1990:Q3	−4.9	+1.5
1990:Q3	1991:Q1	2001:Q1	−1.7	+4.1
2001:Q1	2001:Q4	2007:Q4	−1.8	+0.6
2007:Q4	2009:Q2	—	−5.8	—

Shown in the left part of the table are the dates of each successive business cycle peak and trough. We can see, for instance, that in the 1973–75 recession,

---

[1] Examples of plant and equipment investment include:

Nonresidential Plant (Structures)	Equipment
Factories	Computers
Oil refineries	Jet airplanes
Office buildings	Trucks
Shopping centers	Bar-code scanners
Private hospitals	iPhones and iPads
Hotels	Tractors

The principles developed in this chapter apply also to residential investment, construction of both single-family homes and apartment buildings.

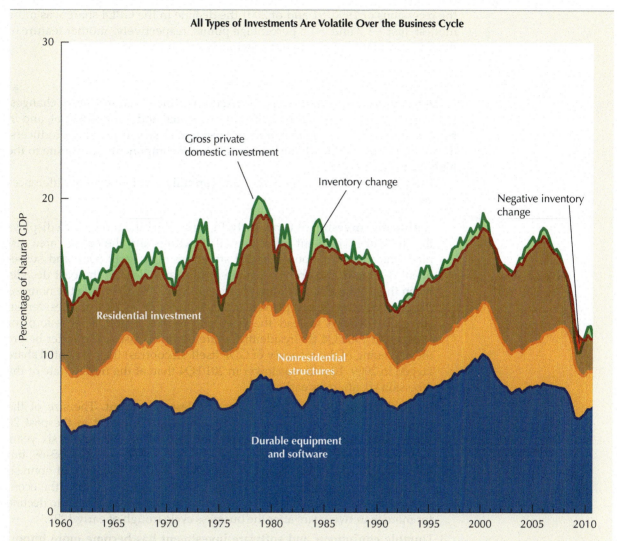

Figure 16-1 Real Gross Private Domestic Investment and Its Four Components, 1960–2010

The green line at the top of the shaded color areas shows total private domestic investment (GPDI), including both fixed investment and inventory change, while the solid brown line shows fixed investment that excludes inventory change. The shaded green areas show positive inventory change and the red areas (as in 2009) show negative inventory change when GPDI was lower than fixed investment. Investment in residential structures is shown by the shaded brown area, in nonresidential structures by the orange area, and in equipment and software by the dark blue area. Notice that the brown residential area was unusually large in 2005–06 at the peak of the housing bubble and then its collapse was unprecedented in magnitude to a mere shadow of its former value in 2009–10. Between 2006:Q1 and 2009:Q2 the share of GPDI in natural GDP declined from 18.2 to 10.2 percent, representing a decline of 44 percent.

Source: Bureau of Economic Analysis, *NIPA Tables*. Details in Appendix C-4.

the GPDI share declined by more than 5 percentage points of natural GDP and then bounced back by the same amount during the subsequent 1975–80 expansion. The share also fell by almost 5 percentage points in the 1981–82 recession and by almost 6 percentage points during the 2007–09 recession. In the recessions of 1990–91 and of 2001 the decline in the GPDI share was more modest, just −1.7 and −1.8 percentage points, respectively, another feature of the Great Moderation discussed previously on pp. 461–66.

Behavior of the Components of GPDI

GPDI is divided into two main parts: fixed investment and inventory changes. Fixed investment is further divided into residential and nonresidential, and in turn nonresidential is divided into nonresidential structures and producers' durable equipment. Clearly all four of the major components contribute to the high volatility of GPDI.

Examining the four components more carefully, we note several differences among them:

1. **Residential investment turns early.** In Figure 16-1 the brown area displays the share of investment in residential structures and the orange area displays the share for nonresidential structures. The early peak and subsequent decline in the brown area are particularly clear in the past decade, when the residential structures share peaked in 2005:Q4 while the nonresidential structures share peaked in 2008:Q2. Prior to 2000 the residential share also tended to lead the economic recovery after a recession; for instance in 1982:Q4 the residential share began its rise one quarter before the beginning of the recovery of GDP itself. In contrast the residential share lagged in 2009–10 and was lower in 2010:Q4 than at the trough date of the recession six quarters earlier.

2. **Nonresidential structures have become less important.** The size of the orange shaded area has tended to become less important in the past 20 years than before 1990. Comparing three prosperous periods of six years each, the share of nonresidential structures was 4.0 percent in 1965–69, but only 3.0 percent in 1995–99 and again in 2002–07. The recovery of nonresidential structures after a downturn tends to lag other sectors of the economy; for instance the share of nonresidential structures continued to decline for more than two years after the business cycle trough of early 1991.

3. **Durable equipment and software investment has become more important.** Comparing the same six year periods as in the previous paragraph, we find that the share of investment in durable equipment and software rose from 6.9 percent in 1965–69 to 8.7 percent in 1995–99, followed by only a partial decline to 8.0 percent in 2002–07. Also, the *relative* decline of the share of equipment and software investment is less than structures. For instance, from the quarter of the peak share to the quarter of the trough share in 2006–10, the residential structures share declined from 6.4 to 2.1, or by more than two-thirds. The nonresidential structures share fell from 4.0 to 2.5, or by about 38 percent. The equipment and software share declined even less from 8.3 to 6.7, or by just 19 percent.

4. **Inventory investment exhibits sharp but short-lived swings and has become less important.** As we learned in Chapter 3 and as we can see from the alternation of green shaded and red shaded areas in Figure 16-1, inventory changes can be either positive or negative, and the swings between positive and negative inventory changes plays a major role in the timing of the business cycle. Perhaps the most striking turnaround was when the inventory change share rose from -1.1 percent in 1982:Q4 (the trough quarter of that major recession) to +1.9 only five quarters later in 1984:Q1, for a

turnaround of 3.0 percent of GDP. The turnaround after the trough of the 2007–09 recession was almost as large, from −1.2 percent in 2009:Q2 to +0.8 percent in 2010:Q3, for a turnaround of 2.0 percentage points. While inventory change continues to contribute to the instability of the economy, it has become less important over the years, partly due to the effectiveness of computers in managing the "supply chain" of inventory replenishment. The average value of inventory change was roughly half in 1995–2007 compared to its value in the 1960s. ◆

16-3 The Accelerator Hypothesis of Net Investment

Businesses must continually evaluate whether their buildings are the right size and have the right amount of equipment. Will they have too little capacity to produce the output they expect to be able to sell in the forthcoming year, causing lost sales and dissatisfied customers? Or will capacity be excessive in relation to expected sales, wasting expenses on maintenance workers and interest costs on unneeded plants and equipment? The **accelerator hypothesis** of investment relies on the simple idea that firms attempt to maintain a fixed ratio of their stock of capital (plants and equipment) to their expected sales.

The **accelerator hypothesis** states that the level of net investment depends on the *change* in expected output.

Estimating Expected Sales

Clearly, the first key ingredient in a business firm's decision about plant investment is an educated guess about the likely level of sales. Table 16-1 provides an example of how a hypothetical firm, the Mammoth Electric Company, estimates expected output and determines its desired stock of electric generating stations. The estimate of expected sales (Y^e) is revised from the estimate of the

Table 16-1 Workings of the Accelerator Hypothesis of Investment for the Hypothetical Mammoth Electric Company

Variable	Period					
	0	1	2	3	4	5
1. Actual sales (Y)	10.0	12.0	12.0	12.0	12.0	12.0
2. Expected sales ($Y^e = 0.5Y_{-1} + 0.5Y^e_{-1}$)	10.0	10.0	11.0	11.5	11.75	11.87
3. Desired stock of electric generating stations ($K^* = 4Y^e$)	40.0	40.0	44.0	46.0	47.0	47.5
4. Net investment in electric generating stations ($I^n = K^* - K^*_{-1}$)	0.0	0.0	4.0	2.0	1.0	0.5
5. Replacement investment ($D = 0.10K_{-1}$)	4.0	4.0	4.0	4.4	4.6	4.7
6. Gross investment ($I = I^n + D$)	4.0	4.0	8.0	6.4	5.6	5.2

Note: All figures in billions of dollars.

previous year (Y^e_{-1}) by some proportion, j, of any difference between last year's actual sales outcome (Y_{-1}) and what was expected:

$$Y^e = Y^e_{-1} + j(Y_{-1} - Y^e_{-1}) \tag{16.1}$$
$$= jY_{-1} + (1 - j)Y^e_{-1}$$

This so-called adaptive or error-learning method of estimating sales expectations is exactly the same one that we encountered earlier in the formation of expectations of inflation and of permanent income.[2]

The error-learning method is illustrated in Table 16-1, where j is assumed equal to 0.5. In period 1, sales (Y^e) were expected to be $10 billion but actually turned out to be $12 billion ($Y$). The revision of expected sales in period 2 can be calculated from equation (16.1):

$$Y^e = 0.5(Y_{-1}) + 0.5(Y^e_{-1})$$
$$= 0.5(12) + 0.5(10)$$
$$= 11$$

Thus in period 2 expected sales are $11 billion, as recorded on line 2. But then another mistake is made, because in period 2 actual sales turn out to be $12 billion again instead of the expected $11 billion. Once again, expectations for the next period are revised, and they continue to be revised as long as actual sales differ from expected sales.

The Level of Investment Depends on the Change in Output

The next step in the accelerator hypothesis is the assumption that the stock of physical capital—that is, plant and equipment—that a firm desires (K^*) is a multiple of its expected sales:

General Form   Numerical Example

$$K^* = v^*Y^e \qquad\qquad K^* = 4.0Y^e \tag{16.2}$$

For example, Mammoth Electric in Table 16-1 wants a capital stock that is always four times as large as its expected sales. Notice that the desired capital stock on line 3 of the table is always exactly 4.0 times the level of expected sales on line 2. What determines the multiple v^*, which relates desired capital to expected sales? As we will see, in calculating v^*, firms pay attention to the interest rate and tax rates. Their chosen value of the multiple v^*, reflects all available knowledge about government policies and the likely profitability of investment.

Net investment (I^n) is the change in the capital stock (ΔK) that occurs each period.[3]

$$I^n = \Delta K = K - K_{-1} \tag{16.3}$$

In the example in Table 16-1, we assume that Mammoth Electric always manages to acquire new capital quickly enough to keep its actual capital stock (K) equal to its desired capital stock (K^*) in each period:

$$I^n = K - K_{-1} = K^* - K^*_{-1} \tag{16.4}$$

---

[2] The formation of expectations of inflation was the subject of Section 9-3. The calculation of permanent income was discussed in Section 15-4.

[3] This is an alternative but equivalent definition to the one we learned in Chapter 2, where net investment was defined as gross investment minus capital consumption allowances.

Equation (16.4) implies that net investment (I^n) is always equal to the change in the desired capital stock in each period, which from equation (16.2) is 4.0 times the change in expected sales:

$$I^n = K^* - K^*_{-1}$$
$$= v^*(Y^e - Y^e_{-1}) = v^* \Delta Y^e \qquad (16.5)$$

The accelerator hypothesis says that the *level* of net investment (I^n) depends on the *change* in expected output (ΔY^e). When there is an acceleration in business and expected output increases, net investment is positive. If expected output stops increasing, net investment falls to zero. And if expected output were ever to decline, net investment would become negative as businesses undertook less gross investment than the amount by which their capital stocks depreciated.

Adding replacement investment.   Total business spending on plant and equipment includes not only net investment—purchases that add to the capital stock—but also replacement purchases, which simply replace plant and equipment that has become worn out or obsolete. Line 5 of Table 16-1 assumes that each year 10 percent of the previous year's capital stock needs to be replaced. The total or gross investment (I) of Mammoth Electric, the amount recorded in the national income accounts of Chapter 2, is the sum of net investment (I^n) and replacement investment (D), and is written on line 6 of the table.

Figure 16-2 illustrates the Mammoth Electric example from Table 16-1. The level of actual sales is plotted as the top red line. Underneath, total gross

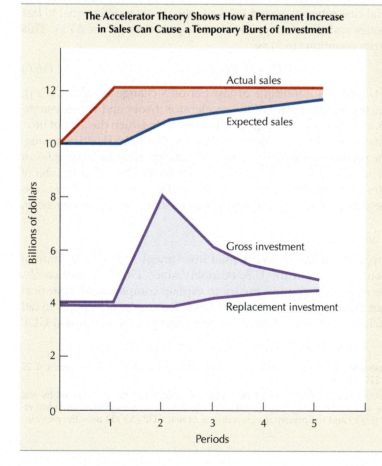

The Accelerator Theory Shows How a Permanent Increase in Sales Can Cause a Temporary Burst of Investment

Figure 16-2 The Behavior of Actual Sales, Expected Sales, Gross Investment, Net Investment, and Replacement Investment for the Mammoth Electric Company Described in Table 16-1

In period 1 actual sales increase, but expected sales are not revised until period 2. Net investment shoots up in period 2, as Mammoth Electric purchases equipment needed to service the higher expected level of sales. Expected sales continue to grow in periods 3, 4, and 5, but more slowly, so net investment actually declines from its peak in period 2.

investment is shown as the zigzag purple line that rises from $4 billion to $8 billion, only to fall in period 3 and afterward back toward the original level. Replacement investment is initially at the level of $4 billion, rising gradually as the capital stock increases. Net investment is the purple shaded area, which first increases in size and then shrinks. Overall, the accelerator theory explains why a firm's gross investment is so unstable, at first rising and then falling, even when actual sales increase permanently.

◆ SELF-TEST

1. Which is likely to be most stable from year to year—gross investment, net investment, or replacement investment? Least stable?

2. Would gross investment in long-lived types of capital (like office buildings) be more or less stable than in short-lived capital (like computers)?

16-4 CASE STUDY

The Simple Accelerator and the Postwar U.S. Economy

The relation between gross investment (I) and GDP (Y) for the economy as a whole is, according to the accelerator hypothesis, the same as for an individual firm. In the special case when expected sales are always set exactly equal to last period's actual sales and therefore $j = 1$, $Y^e = Y_{-1}$, so that $\Delta Y^e = \Delta Y_{-1}$. This allows us to rewrite equation (16.5) as

$$I^n = v^* \Delta Y_{-1} \qquad (16.6)$$

Net investment (I^n) equals a multiple of last period's change in sales (ΔY_{-1}). Equation (16.6) is the simplest form of the accelerator theory and was invented when J. M. Clark in 1917 noticed a regular relationship between the *level* of box-car production and the previous *change* in railroad traffic.[4] *This equation summarizes succinctly the inherent instability of the private economy. Any random event—an export boom, an irregularity in the timing of government spending, or a revision of consumer estimates of permanent income—can change the growth of real sales and temporarily (but significantly) change the level of net investment in the same direction.*

Assessing the Simple Accelerator

Figure 16-3 compares real net nonresidential investment (I^n) with the annual change in real output (ΔY) in the U.S. economy since 1960.[5] Unfortunately, equation (16.6) is much too simple a theory to explain completely all historical movements in net investment in the United States. True, most peak years in net investment coincided with (or followed by one year) peak years in real GDP

---

[4] J. M. Clark, "Business Acceleration and the Law of Demand," *Journal of Political Economy*, vol. 25 (March 1917), pp. 217–35.

[5] To adjust for the steady growth in the size of the economy, both I^n and ΔY are divided by real GDP (Y). Thus the actual variables plotted are the ratio of real net nonresidential fixed investment to real GDP (I^n/Y) and the percentage growth rate of real GDP ($\Delta Y/Y$) over the previous four quarters.

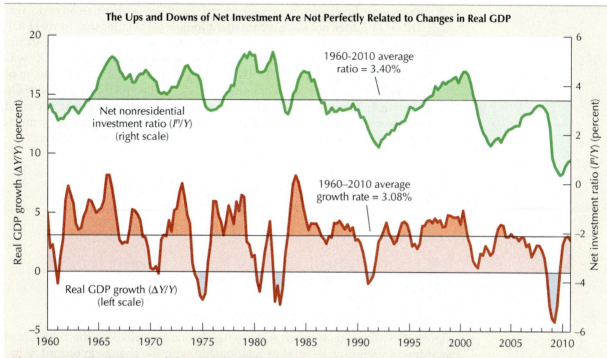

Figure 16-3 The Relation of the Net Investment Ratio (I^n/Y) to the Growth Rate of Real GDP ($\Delta Y/Y$) in the U.S. Economy, 1960–2010

The net investment ratio (I^n/Y) does not have a perfect relationship with the growth rate of real GDP ($\Delta Y/Y$). Net investment was above average during 1965–74 following above average real GDP growth between 1963 and 1973. And net investment was low in 1991–94, 2001–2005, and 2009–10 following the recession-related declines of real GDP growth in 1991, 2000–02, and 2008–09. A puzzle is why net investment was above average in 1980–82 despite low real GDP growth.

Source: Bureau of Economic Analysis, *NIPA Tables*. Details in Appendix C-4.

growth. And trough years in net investment coincided with (or followed by one year) trough years in real GDP growth, including the most recent episode in 2007–09. Furthermore, ten years of high net investment (1965–74) followed thirteen years (1961–73) in which real GDP growth rarely dipped below average.[6] Finally, low net investment in 1986–95 followed periods during which real GDP growth fell well below average. Overall, however, Figure 16-3 reveals quite an imperfect relationship.

There are three main problems with the simple accelerator theory of equation (16.6), judging from the historical U.S. data plotted in Figure 16-3:

1. Net investment does not respond instantaneously to changes in output growth, as in equation (16.6), but rather displays noticeable lags in response. These lags can be seen clearly in several episodes.

2. The lag, however, is not of uniform length, nor does net investment respond to accelerations and decelerations in real GDP growth with uniform speed. It is as if an automobile's engine responded in a split second to some movements of the accelerator but took minutes to respond to other movements.

---

[6] Average real GDP growth over the 1960–2007 period plotted in Figure 16-3 is 3.25 percent, and the average ratio of net investment to real GDP is 3.51 percent.

3. The overall level of net nonresidential fixed investment relative to real GDP (I^n/Y) does not have a consistent long-term relationship to real GDP growth ($\Delta Y/Y$). Although average real GDP growth was slower in the 1970s than it was in the 1960s, the ratio of net investment to GDP was higher in the 1970s than the 1960s. Further, despite the investment boom of the late 1990s, the overall average level of I^n/Y after 1990 was substantially lower than before 1990. In part the decline of net investment occurred because the healthy ratio of gross investment was accompanied by much higher depreciation rates of computers that rapidly became obsolete.

	Average	
Period	$\Delta Y/Y$	I^n/Y
1960s	4.3	4.0
1970s	3.2	4.2
1980s	3.0	3.9
1990s	3.0	2.9
2000–10	1.7	2.7

Prominent Features of Postwar Investment Behavior

Figure 16-3 allows us to reach some general conclusions about the behavior of investment spending, beyond its relationship with the change in output. What do we learn from a visual inspection of the net investment ratio (I^n/Y), the green line in Figure 16-3? Two main facts stand out in the figure:

1. **Variability.** As we saw earlier, gross investment is highly variable, as is the net investment ratio. The past three decades have shown that the net investment ratio can shift by as much as 3 percentage points of GDP within a short period, as between 2000:Q2 and 2002:Q4 and again between 2007:Q4 and 2009:Q4. This represents a large potential shock for the economy.

2. **Persistence.** The net investment ratio does not zigzag up and down each year but often stays relatively high or relatively low for several years in a row. The period of high net investment between 1965 and 1974 is a good example of this tendency: In every quarter from 1965 through 1974, the net investment ratio exceeded its 1960–2010 average. The persistence of low investment in the Great Depression decade was even more pronounced: The net investment ratio was negative for the entire decade 1931–40. ◆

16-5 The Flexible Accelerator

Defects of the Simple Accelerator

The simple accelerator theory of equation (16.6) depends on several restrictive and unrealistic assumptions. A more realistic version of the theory, called the **flexible accelerator,** loosens several of these assumptions.

The **flexible accelerator** theory of investment allows for gradual adjustment of sales expectations and of the capital stock. It also allows for variation in the optimal capital-output ratio.

1. The simple accelerator assumes that this period's expected output equaled last period's actual output. But the error-learning, or adaptive, hypothesis states that in general expected output is based partially on last period's actual output and partially on last period's expected output.

2. The simple accelerator assumes that the desired capital stock (K^*) equals a constant (v^*) times expected output (Y^e). But actually the desired

capital-output ratio (v^*) may vary substantially, depending on the cost of borrowing, the taxation of capital, and other factors; we will postpone until the next section a detailed consideration of the factors that change v^*.

3. The simple accelerator also assumes that firms can instantly put in place any desired amount of investment in plant and equipment needed to make actual capital this period (K) equal to desired capital (K^*). However, some kinds of capital take a substantial length of time to construct. Buildings sometimes take two or three years between conception and completion. Some types of electricity generating stations can take as long as eight years to complete.[7] Furthermore, investing very rapidly would be excessively costly because firms supplying capital goods might raise their prices. Also, rapid installation of new buildings and equipment might disrupt normal business activities.

Thus, in the real world, net investment does not always close the whole gap between desired capital and last year's capital stock; more often it closes only a fraction of it.

Determinants of Gross Investment

To summarize, the relationship between economywide gross investment and output depends on at least four major factors.

1. *The fraction of the gap between desired capital and last period's actual capital that can be closed in a single period.* The higher this fraction, the more current investment responds to the change in last period's output.

2. *The response of expected output to last period's error in estimating actual output.* The higher this response, the more expected output and hence investment respond to any unexpected change in last period's actual output.

3. *The proportion of the capital stock that is replaced each year.* For long-lived types of capital, such as office buildings, only a small fraction of the stock is replaced each year. In contrast, because computer equipment depreciates more quickly, a larger amount of computer equipment investment is required annually per dollar of equipment capital to maintain the same size computer capital stock. Firms are not forced to replace old capital on a fixed schedule. If firms delay replacement investment until expected sales are strong, total investment will respond even more than the simple accelerator model suggests.[8]

4. *The desired ratio of capital to expected output (v^*).* Investment responds more to changes in expected output in capital-intensive industries (those with a high v^*, such as electric utilities, oil refining, and chemicals) than in labor-intensive industries (those with a low v^*, such as textiles, apparel, and barber shops). Thus faster growth expected in more capital-intensive industries will spur more investment.

In the next section we investigate the determinants of the desired capital-output ratio and the policy instruments with which the government can affect the size of v^*.

---

[7] At the other extreme, a shop that opens for business today in a large city could probably obtain delivery of needed equipment—cash register, computers, mobile phones, and furniture—in a day or two.

[8] A study that confirms the procyclical behavior of replacement investment is Martin S. Feldstein and David Foot, "The Other Half of Gross Investment: Replacement and Modernization Expenditures," *The Review of Economics and Statistics*, vol. 53, no. 1 (February 1971), pp. 49–58.

Tobin's *q*: Does It Explain Investment Better Than the Accelerator or Neoclassical Theories?

Both the accelerator theory of Sections 16-3 and 16-5, as well as the neoclassical theory of Section 16-6, define a desired level of the capital stock (K^*), and then assume a gradual adjustment of the actual capital stock toward the desired level. The alternative *q* theory was developed by the late Nobel Prize winner James Tobin (who also did groundbreaking work on the demand for money and whose picture appears on p. 437). Tobin's *q* theory, instead of positing a desired level of capital and a *separate* process of adjustment, merges adjustment costs directly into the firm's single calculation of the desired rate of investment at each moment of time.[a]

Tobin's theory develops an idea of Keynes's that the attractiveness of purchasing new capital equipment depends on the market value of capital in the stock market as compared with the cost of purchasing the capital. To create a quantitative measure that reflects changes in market value relative to the purchase cost, Tobin defined his variable *q* as the ratio of the firm's market value on the stock market to the replacement cost of its capital stock. Investment, then, is an increasing function of the *q* ratio.

An example of an investment equation in the *q* theory would be the following relation between gross investment relative to the capital stock (I/K), the *q* ratio (q), and the ratio of replacement investment to the capital stock (d):

$$\frac{I}{K} = j(q - 1) + d \qquad (16.7)$$

In words, this says that the I/K ratio is equal to d when Tobin's *q* ratio is unity. If $d = 0.1$ and $j = 0.2$, then I/K would be 0.1 when *q* equals unity; I/K would rise to 0.2 when *q* equals 1.5, and I/K would fall to zero when *q* equals 0.5.

In practice, the most important source of movement in *q* is the change in the price of a firm's shares on the stock market. During 1994–2000, for example, the change in stock prices was at an annual rate of 19 percent, whereas in 2000–02 stock prices *declined* at an annual rate of 18 percent. Again in 2007–09 stock prices declined at an annual rate of 22 percent. Since stock prices are part of the numerator in *q*, such changes could change *q* by large amounts. As we have noted before, households' consumption spending might be affected by the stock market; higher stock prices might raise consumption by increasing households' wealth. Higher stock prices might also increase the amount of investment that firms undertake. Thus Tobin's *q* also

16-6 The Neoclassical Theory of Investment Behavior

One of the most important contributions to the theory of investment behavior was made in the early 1960s by Dale Jorgenson of Harvard University.[9] Jorgenson's insight was to show that the user cost of capital could be derived from neoclassical microeconomic theory by examining the decision of a profit-maximizing firm. Jorgenson then demonstrated that tax policies affected how much firms invest.

---

[9] Dale Jorgenson, "Capital Theory and Investment Behavior," *American Economic Review*, vol. 53 (May 1963), pp. 247–57. A comprehensive review of recent theories of investment is Ricardo Caballero, "Aggregate Investment," in J. B. Taylor and M. Woodford, eds., *Handbook of Macroeconomics* (North Holland, 1999), pp. 813–62.

suggests another channel through which changes in the stock market might affect aggregate demand.

Tobin's q theory of investment incorporates how the economic environment affects business firms' expectations of their future profitability. In addition to its theoretical appeal as a way to explain and forecast investment spending by firms, q has great practical appeal because it summarizes expectations about the level and riskiness of future profitability and thus makes unnecessary the exceedingly difficult job of estimating those expectations. Instead, Tobin's q theory states that we can simply look to the stock and bond markets for the valuation of the firm's expected future profitability, which is the numerator of q.

How does q fare in an empirical "horse race" with the accelerator and neoclassical models that we developed in Sections 16-3 and 16-6? A number of studies have tested the abilities of these three models to explain spending on fixed investment after the fact and also to forecast it.[b]

Empirical models have all been much better at explaining and forecasting business investment spending on *equipment*—so-called producers' durable equipment—than they have been at explaining and forecasting investment in nonresidential *structures*. The Oliner, Rudebusch, and Sichel study, for example, shows that investment spending on producers' durable equipment can be fairly well tracked by some of the models. They find that despite the theoretical and practical appeal of the q model of investment, both the accelerator and neoclassical models explain and forecast more accurately than do models based on q, with the accelerator model performing about as well as the neoclassical model. That is one reason why we presented both the accelerator and neoclassical models in this chapter—in practice neither is a clear-cut winner. (Findings similar to those reported by Oliner, Rudebusch, and Sichel emerge from the earlier time periods examined in other studies.)

Business investment in structures has proven more difficult to explain and forecast. In general, none of the models have demonstrated any significant ability to forecast movements in construction spending by business, although again, the accelerator and neoclassical models tend to outperform the q model. An example of the shortcomings of all the models was their inability to forecast, or even account for after the fact, the enormous surge in commercial real estate construction during the 1980s. The large variations in business investment in structures suggest that aggregate demand for GDP may shift importantly over time. The inability to forecast those shifts suggests that it may be difficult for policymakers to anticipate and take timely action to offset them.[c]

---

[a] Most of the references on Tobin's q theory are quite technical. For the original presentation, see James Tobin, "A General Equilibrium Approach to Monetary Theory," *Journal of Money, Credit and Banking*, vol. 1 (February 1969), pp. 15–29. A recent evaluation is contained in Martin Lettau and Sydney Ludvigson, "Time-varying Risk Premia and the Cost of Capital: An Alternative Implication of the Q Theory of Investment," *Journal of Monetary Economics*, vol. 49 (2002), pp. 31–66.

[b] See, for example, Stephen Oliner, Glenn Rudebusch, and Daniel Sichel, "New and Old Models of Business Investment: A Comparison of Forecasting Performance," *Journal of Money, Credit and Banking*, vol. 27 (August 1995), pp. 806–26, and the references cited there.

[c] A comprehensive study of the 2000–02 decline of investment and its relation to the stock market and tax policy is Mihir A. Desai and Austan D. Goolsbee, "Investment, Overhang, and Tax Policy," *Brookings Papers on Economic Activity*, no. 2 (2004), pp. 285–355. See also Stacey Tevlin and Karl Whelan, "Explaining the Investment Boom of the 1990s," *Journal of Money, Credit, and Banking*, vol. 35, 2003(1), pp. 1–22.

The User Cost of Capital

Jorgenson's theory assumes that a business firm is willing to undertake an investment project only when it expects that a profit can be made. An extra unit of capital will not be purchased unless the expected **marginal product of capital (MPK)** is at least equal to the real **user cost of capital** (u):

General Form	Numerical Example	
$MPK \geq u$	$MPK \geq 14$	(16.8)

Both the marginal product and the real user cost can be expressed as percentages. The marginal product of capital consists of the amount of extra output

The **marginal product of capital (MPK)** is the extra output that a firm can produce by adding an extra unit of capital.

The **user cost of capital** is the cost to the firm of using a piece of capital for a specifies period.

produced each year by an extra piece of plant or equipment, divided by the cost of the plant or equipment. If the purchase of an extra machine costing $100,000 allows a firm to produce $14,000 of extra output each year, then MPK would be 14 percent.[10] *The user cost of capital is the cost to the business firm of using a piece of capital for a period of time, expressed as a fraction of its purchase price. The user cost might be 14 percent, consisting perhaps of a 4 percent annual real interest rate and a 10 percent depreciation rate.*[11]

What does equation (16.8) have to do with the profitability of a business firm? When MPK is 15 percent and user cost is only 14 percent, then the extra revenue generated by a new machine exceeds its cost, and the firm's profits are increased. On the other hand, when MPK is only 13 percent and user cost is the same 14 percent, the extra revenue is insufficient to pay the costs of the new machine, and profits go down if the machine is purchased. Only if user cost falls to 13 percent or lower will the new machine be purchased.[12]

The effect of a reduction in user cost on the desired capital-output ratio is illustrated in Figure 16-4. The diminishing MPK means that each extra machine adds less output than the machine added before it, implying that the MPK curve slopes downward. Suppose each business initially faces a constant user cost u_0. Each business will then maximize its profits by choosing the capital-output ratio v^*_0, at which point the marginal benefit of the machine, its MPK, equals its marginal cost, u_0. Why? A smaller amount of capital, to the left of E_0, would mean giving up some of the profits indicated by the lighter green area that measures the difference between the marginal product of capital and the user cost. But to purchase a larger amount of capital, to the right of E_0, would cause losses. These extra units of capital have an insufficient MPK to pay for their user cost.

Tax Incentives and Investment Behavior

The user cost of capital depends not only on the depreciation rate of capital and the real interest rate that must be paid on the funds borrowed to purchase the equipment. As derived by Jorgenson, the user cost also depends on three aspects of the tax system discussed in the next section. Thus both monetary and fiscal policy can influence the user cost—monetary policy by changing the real interest rate, and fiscal policy by affecting real interest rates and by altering tax rates and the rules of the tax system.

We can use Figure 16-4 to illustrate the effect of a change in government tax policy designed to stimulate investment. Let us assume that the government changes tax rates or rules in order to cut the user cost. For instance, the tax rate that corporations pay on their profits might be cut in half, and this reduces user cost to the firm. Additional units of capital will now be purchased to bring the desired capital-output ratio rightward to v^*_1. Increased investment is required to raise the capital-output ratio to its new, higher desired level, v^*_1. The reduction in user cost has made available extra profits, indicated by the darker green area. *By using monetary and fiscal policy instruments, the user cost of capital can be*

---

[10]   As is always true in economics, the marginal product of a single input measures the extra output produced by an extra unit of that input if the quantity of other inputs is held constant.

[11]   Depreciation is part of user cost, because using a machine reduces its ability to produce and thus its value.

[12]   If this analysis seems familiar, in Section 3-9 on pp. 76–78 you learned that firms make investment decisions by comparing the rate of return to the interest rate. As we learn in this section, the user cost contains several components in addition to the interest rate.

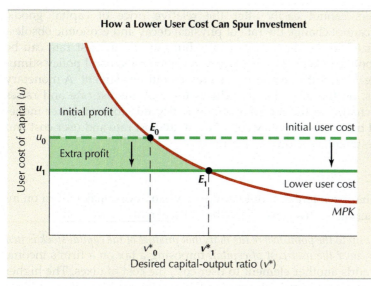

How a Lower User Cost Can Spur Investment

Figure 16-4 The Effect of a Drop in the User Cost of Capital (u) on the Desired Capital-Output Ratio (v^*)

Initially the economy is at point E_0: Firms are making a profit on their capital stock indicated by the light green area in the upper left. If the user cost falls from u_0 to u_1, the desired capital-output ratio will rise to v_1^*, the economy will move from E_0 to E_1, and the darker green area of extra profit is gained.

changed. Firms can thus be induced to adopt more capital-intensive methods of production, and the opposite is true as well. Just as an increase in the wage rate can cause firms to replace marginal workers with extra machines, an increase in capital's user cost can cause firms to substitute away from elaborate machines toward more labor-intensive techniques of production.

16-7 User Cost and the Role of Monetary and Fiscal Policy

How can government policymakers affect the user cost of capital (u)? The user cost of capital depends on several factors, which can be introduced in two steps. First, let us neglect the effect of taxation. In the absence of taxation, a capital good that is purchased at a given real price imposes three types of cost on its user.

1. *An interest cost is involved in buying a capital good.* If funds are borrowed, interest at the nominal rate (i) must be paid. Alternatively, the investor loses the interest (i) that would have been received had the funds used to buy the capital good been used instead to purchase a financial asset.

2. *Physical deterioration lessens the production ability of every capital good; in addition, some capital goods become obsolete.* The **depreciation rate** indicates the annual percentage decline in value of the capital good due to physical deterioration and obsolescence.[13]

   > The **depreciation rate** is the annual percentage decline in the value of a capital good due to physical deterioration and obsolescence.

3. *The interest and depreciation cost are adjusted by price changes for capital goods.* Rapid price increases mean that used capital goods can sometimes be resold for more than their cost when new. These price increases reduce the user cost and imply that it is a *real* interest rate that matters (the nominal interest rate minus the rate of price changes for capital goods). Conversely, declines in the prices of computers, for example, raise their user costs.

---

[13] The term "depreciation" has already been defined on p. 30 of Chapter 2. The term "depreciation rate" was already defined in the context of the Solow growth model in Chapter 11 on p. 366.

Policymakers cannot easily alter the relative price of capital goods. Similarly, they cannot change the rate of physical decay and economic obsolescence summarized in the depreciation rate. But the real interest rate can be influenced by policymakers. As we learned in Chapter 4, a fiscal policy stimulus raises the real interest rate and hence crowds out investment. A monetary policy stimulus, on the other hand, reduces the real interest rate and raises investment. A change in the monetary-fiscal policy mix toward easier monetary policy and tighter fiscal policy cuts the real interest rate and user cost and thus raises investment, as shown in Figure 16-4.

Taxation and Investment Behavior

So far taxation has been ignored. But fiscal policy can have a major effect on investment by altering the user cost. Three basic fiscal tools are available:

1. *Firms invest up to the point where the marginal product of the capital stock is just sufficient to cover the user cost of capital.* Imposing a tax on a firm's income effectively adds another element to user cost, the cost of taxes. The higher the firm's income tax rate is, the greater the effective user cost it faces. Thus a higher tax rate is likely to reduce the firm's desired capital stock, and thus investment.

2. *Firms can cut their corporate income tax by deducting the value of depreciation of plants and equipment.* The amount of depreciation they can deduct depends on tax laws and how the IRS implements them. Though the government cannot change the rate of physical depreciation or obsolescence directly, it can change the accounting rules used to calculate corporate income taxes. Liberalizing the tax rules regarding depreciation, for example, effectively reduces the corporate income tax rate. An important part of the fiscal policy package passed in December 2010 was a new temporary rule allowing businesses to deduct 100 percent of the cost of new capital investments in the year 2011.

3. *During most of the period 1962–86, a substantial part of investment in the United States was eligible for an investment tax credit.* This credit often allowed business firms to deduct 10 percent of the value of their equipment investment from their corporation income tax. Naturally this reduced the effective user cost of capital for firms making profits. The investment tax credit was rescinded in 1986 but could be reinstated if the government desired to stimulate investment. While general investment tax credits were not in effect in 2010–11, there were targeted investment credits, for instance for rehabilitation of historic buildings and for investment in alternative energy sources such as wind and solar.

These three fiscal tools provide much more flexibility in conducting stabilization policy than would be available if the government were limited to controlling the economy by varying the level of government spending and the personal income tax rate. For instance, government spending can be restrained and the personal income tax rate raised to slow down an economy that is experiencing too much aggregate demand. At the same time, any of the investment-related fiscal instruments can be liberalized if it is believed that the economy has too little investment and too much consumption.

Studies by economists suggest that changes in tax incentives probably have at least a modest effect on investment. However, such changes have numerous limitations and are not a promising instrument for an activist fiscal policy. First, changes in tax incentives are almost always subject to lengthy debate in Congress. Second, there is a substantial time lag between the passage of tax legislation and the resulting investment spending. Third, we are far from being able to estimate confidently how much investment will respond to tax incentives.

◆ SELF-TEST

1. How may tools of fiscal policy potentially affect the user cost of capital?

2. If the government wants to stimulate investment, how should it change these tools?

3. Does monetary policy also have an effect on the user cost?

16-8   Business Confidence and Speculation

Confidence and the Flexible Accelerator

In Chapters 3 and 4 the terms *business* and *consumer confidence* were used as a convenient, shorthand way to refer to factors that could change output when government spending and the money supply were fixed at a given level. In the flexible accelerator theory of investment summarized here, the confidence of business firms may influence investment spending in three ways:

1. Investment depends on what fraction of the increase in last period's actual output is incorporated into expected output, and hence into desired capital and investment. When business firms lack confidence in the future, they may refuse to extrapolate a quarter or a year of increasing output, believing instead that any increase in output is temporary.

2. The user cost of capital (u) includes the borrowing costs that business firms *expect* to have to pay if they undertake an investment project. If businesses are pessimistic, they may underestimate how much the prices of capital goods will rise and therefore overestimate the real borrowing cost they are likely to face, making their estimate of u too high and their desired capital stock too low.

3. Perhaps most important, business firms can only guess the likely marginal product of new investment projects. It is the expected marginal product that matters. If business has recently been bad, a condition experienced by many business firms in 1930–33, or as recently as 2009–10, firms may already have more capital than needed. Some present capital may be underutilized, and future capital investments may appear unprofitable, with their expected marginal products being close to zero.

Cycles of Overbuilding

Periods of business overoptimism in U.S. history have led to overbuilding, underutilized capital, and extensive pessimism. This recurring sequence played out in the years surrounding 1970, the years surrounding 1990, and most notably in the years after 2007. The housing bubble and easy credit in 2001–07 left the United States with more than a trillion dollars of unsold single-family homes, condos, as well as empty office buildings, stores, and hotels.

Investment in the Great Depression and World War II

Any event, whether political or economic, that causes a drop in business confidence can cause a sharp drop in the level of investment. In the Great Depression of the 1930s, a collapse in business confidence dropped the desired capital stock far below the actual capital stock, and business firms were so pessimistic that they did not replace depreciating capital, causing net investment to be negative year after year. The multiplier effect of the collapse of investment, together with the 1929 stock market crash and subsequent bank failures, caused consumption to decline sharply, and this fed back to a reduction in the desired capital stock and a further decline of investment spending.

The decade of the 1930s brought poverty and misery to the lives of millions of Americans. As shown in the box on pp. 258–59, the Great Depression was deeper and more severe in the United States than in any other major developed nation. The graph on the next page shows real GDP and real private domestic investment from 1929 to 1950, both expressed as an index number with 1929 equal to 100. By 1933, real GDP had declined 27 percent from its 1929 value. But even more calamitous was the decline of investment by fully 88 percent between 1929 and 1932; investment in 1932 was only 12 percent of its 1929 value!

A notable aspect of the Great Depression was not only the enormous depth of the economic decline but also its duration. Because natural real GDP grew by 53 percent between 1929 and 1941, the output ratio (actual real GDP divided by natural real GDP) remained below 100 percent until late 1941.[a] Investment briefly regained its 1929 value in 1937 and then finally soared above the 1929 value in 1940 and 1941. After 1941, the government forced business firms to stop all investment that was not essential for the war effort, and so construction of residential housing, office buildings, hotels, and nonmilitary equipment ceased. This explains the sharp drop of investment in the years 1942–45 and the instant recovery to far above 1941 levels during the first postwar years, 1946–50.

The enormous amount of underutilized capital during the 1930s brought one benefit. When the United States became involved in World War II, initially in

1940–41 as an exporter of weapons and raw materials to Britain and the USSR, and then as a full-fledged combatant after Pearl Harbor in December 1941, it was able to put back to work all those underutilized factories and equipment. They were joined by many new factories and much new equipment paid for by the government and operated by companies such as General Motors, Ford, and Chrysler. Because this government-owned, privately operated (GOPO) capital was not counted as private investment, the red line in the graph greatly understates the amount of investment that actually took place during World War II. One example of a GOPO plant was the Ford-operated factory in Willow Run, Michigan (near Ann Arbor), that produced fourteen B-24 bombers *every day* in what became known as the "world's largest enclosed room" (shown in the photo). The government financed not just gigantic new factories but also enormous amounts of industrial equipment, so much so that the

Keynes placed major emphasis on the role of business confidence in determining the level of investment. In the following passage he stresses that investment decisions are based on estimates of the future yield (or marginal product) of extra capital, estimates that may be little better than a guess. Faced with identical information and uncertainty, businesspeople may go ahead with an investment project when they feel optimistic but postpone the same project when they feel pessimistic:

The outstanding fact is the extreme precariousness of the basis of knowledge on which our estimates of prospective yield have to be made. Our knowledge of the number of machine tools (such as lathes and drill presses) in the United States actually *doubled* between 1940 and 1945.

Taken together, the underutilized old capital and the new GOPO capital help to explain how the United States was able to double its real GDP between 1939 and 1944 despite the diversion of 16 million Americans into the armed forces. This conversion of the U.S. economy into the "arsenal of democracy" also became known as the "miracle of World War II."[b]

[a] Actual and natural real GDP are listed for each year since 1875 in Appendix Table A-1 at the back of the book and are plotted since 1900 in Figure 1-6 on p. 12. For more on the relationship between actual and natural real GDP in the 1930s and 1940s, based on a new quarterly data set, see Robert J. Gordon and Robert Krenn, "The End of the Great Depression 1939–41: Policy Contributions and Fiscal Multipliers," NBER Working Paper 16380, September 2010.

[b] For more on the Willow Run plant, see en.wikipedia.org/wiki/Willow_Run and www.strategosinc.com/willow_run.htm.

The Erratic Path of Investment, 1929–50

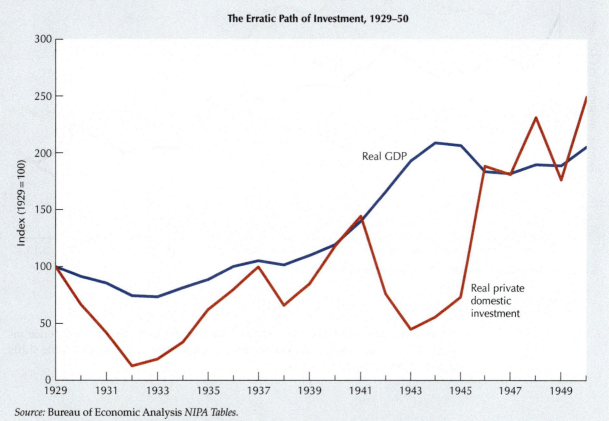

Source: Bureau of Economic Analysis *NIPA Tables.*

factors which will govern the yield of an investment some years hence is usually very slight and often negligible. If we speak frankly, we have to admit that our basis of knowledge for estimating the yield ten years hence of a railway, a copper mine, a textile factory, the goodwill of a patent medicine, an Atlantic liner, a building in the City of London amounts to little and sometimes to nothing; or even five years hence. In fact, those who seriously attempt to make any such estimates are often so much in the minority that their behavior does not govern the market.[14]

[14] Keynes, *General Theory*, pp. 149–50.

INTERNATIONAL PERSPECTIVE

The Level and Variability of Investment Around the World

For many years, investment was much lower in the United States than in Japan or Germany. And from the mid-1980s through the early 1990s, the investment gap between the United States and Japan and Germany widened. The accompanying figure shows the share of each country's GDP that is devoted to gross investment for the years 1980–2011.

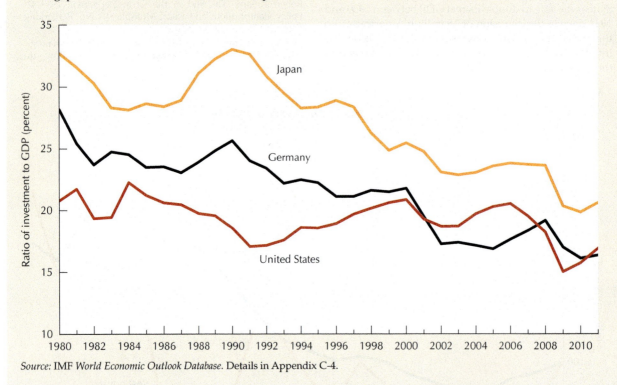

Source: IMF *World Economic Outlook Database.* Details in Appendix C-4.

Throughout this book we have treated such shifts in business confidence (as well as consumer confidence) as sources of important and unpredictable shifts in the *IS*, and thus *AD*, curves.

16-9 Investment as a Source of Instability of Output and Interest Rates

The accelerator theory resolves a favorite paradox of macroeconomics teachers. We became accustomed in Chapter 3 to associating low interest rates with high investment and high interest rates with low investment. This negative relationship between investment and interest rates has been confirmed in this chapter, because a low level of the real interest rate reduces the user cost of capital, which in turn raises the desired capital stock and hence the level of gross investment.

However, over the period 1992 to 2000, the investment ratio in the United States rose from 17.2 to 20.8 percent, and exceeded Germany's ratio in 2002–06. Japan remained ahead, but the gap between Japan and the United States fell from 15 percentage points in 1991 to approximately 4 percentage points in 2001–10.

National saving, the sum of private and government saving, always equals national investment. One reason why the investment ratio was relatively low in the United States during most of the 1970–2000 period was the low rate of U.S. national saving. During the period 1980–96 and again in 2002–11, large U.S. government deficits meant that the government surplus was negative and national saving was low. The upsurge in the U.S. investment ratio shown in the graph was made possible by heavy borrowing from foreigners, not by domestic saving.

Firms finance their investment spending in several ways. In most countries the primary source of funds for business investment in plant and equipment is retained earnings, that is, the profits that firms have not paid out in dividends but have retained inside the firms. Especially in France, Italy, and Japan, firms also rely heavily on loans from banks to finance purchases of plant and equipment. Firms in Germany, the United Kingdom, and the United States are less dependent on bank loans, obtaining relatively more of the funds they use to finance investment expenditures by issuing stocks, long-term bonds, and short-term instruments like commercial paper.

In Chapter 15 we learned that consumers sometimes face liquidity constraints, which prevent them from borrowing the full amount of funds that they would be expected to be able to repay from permanent incomes. Business firms too sometimes face liquidity constraints. Young firms, like young households, may find it difficult to borrow the amount of funds justified by their longer-term prospects. And smaller firms may find that they must reduce investment when current profits or retained earnings decline. Thus, for both households and firms, constraints on borrowing and therefore on spending may be more severe during recessions or when higher interest rates raise loan payments.

One way for firms to loosen these financing constraints may be to ally themselves with other firms. Firms in Korea sometimes belong to a *chaebol*; in Italy firms are sometimes linked by family connections; in Japan some firms belong to a group of firms called a *keiretsu*; businesses in Canada and in the United States may be owned by conglomerates; and some firms in Japan and in Germany have bankers on their boards of directors. Because the other firms in such alliances often are not in closely allied areas of business, the alliance is more likely to remain strong when one of its members may need financial support. Belonging to one of these business groups seems to provide some insulation from financing constraints, perhaps because the other firms in the group can either provide the funds needed for investment directly to a constrained firm, or can provide some assurance to an outside lender like a bank that the other firms will help repay a bank loan to the constrained firm.

Yet a predominant feature of business cycles in almost every nation is a positive correlation between business investment and interest rates. U.S. business investment fluctuates procyclically, reaching peaks in years of high output and troughs during recessions or soon afterward. But, since interest rates also fluctuate procyclically, years of low interest rates are usually associated with low investment, not high investment.

How can the positive correlation between investment and interest rates be explained? The accelerator theory provides the answer. Figure 16-6 repeats the *IS-LM* analysis of Chapter 4. The *LM* curve maintains an unchanged position whenever the real money supply (M/P) and real demand for money function are fixed. The *IS* curve fluctuates whenever there is a change in the investment purchases that business firms make at a constant real interest rate.

Causes of *IS* Shifts

We have seen that many factors can make the level of gross investment, and hence the *IS* curve, shift for a given interest rate. Among them are (1) a change

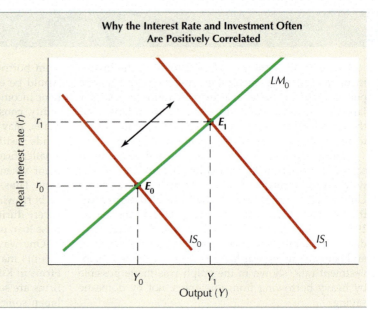

Figure 16-5 Effect on Output and the Interest Rate of a Shift in the Level of Investment Relative to the Interest Rate

Shifts in business confidence or in user cost (apart from those due to changes in the real interest rate) can shift the red IS curve back and forth between IS_0 and IS_1. The real interest rate and investment will rise and fall together. This conclusion assumes that the real money supply, which fixes the position of the LM curve, remains unchanged.

in the expected growth rate of output and thus sales, (2) a previous episode of overbuilding that makes the actual capital stock high relative to the current desired stock, (3) a shift in demand toward shorter-lived equipment, (4) a change in the relative price of capital goods, and, finally, (5) a change in fiscal incentives that alters the effective user cost of capital. A change in any of these elements shifts the level of investment that occurs at a given interest rate and, through the multiplier, shifts the IS curve and the level of total output.

Figure 16-5 illustrates two IS curves, IS_0 and IS_1. The shifts back and forth between the two IS curves reflect any one of the factors in the previous paragraph that cause an increase or decrease in gross investment. The positive relationship between investment and interest rates is explained in Figure 16-5 by the IS shifting along LM_0, which is held fixed by the fixed real money supply. That positive relationship suggests that the depressing effect of low output on investment, working through the accelerator, dominates the stimulative effect of low interest rates on investment, at least in the short run.

16-10 Conclusion: Investment as a Source of Instablity

We concluded in Chapter 15 that consumption spending on nondurable goods and services is relatively stable. Both the permanent-income and life-cycle hypotheses suggested that spending on nondurable goods and services tends to fluctuate less than disposable income. This stability bolsters the case for following a policy rule.

But this chapter tilts the balance in the opposite direction, toward the proposition of policy activists that the private economy contains sources of instability. The problem is epitomized by the accelerator theory of investment. Any event that causes a *permanent* increase in the desired capital stock—whether an increase in expected output or a reduction in the user cost of capital—causes only a *temporary* burst of investment spending. After the temporary burst, when net investment falls, economic instability is aggravated by the multiplier effect of Chapter 3.

Investment Volatility and the Taylor Rule

The multiyear cycles in fixed investment and in net exports support the activist contention that private spending is unstable. But this does not by itself mean that policy should be entirely discretionary without any tie to a rule. On the contrary, the Taylor Rule studied in Chapter 14 is based on a formula that calls for the Fed to shift to an easier monetary policy *either* when the inflation rate drops below the Fed's target for inflation, or when the output gap becomes negative.

Thus, under the Taylor Rule, the Fed is still able to ease policy in response to severe slumps of investment, as occurred in 2000–02 and particularly in 2007–09. A paradox involving the Taylor Rule for monetary policy emerged in the decade after 2000. The Fed reduced interest rates too much in 2002–04, as shown in Figure 14-5 on p. 469. But in 2007–10 the Fed did not reduce interest rates enough, since the Taylor Rule called for a *negative* nominal interest rate after 2008 yet a negative nominal interest rate is impossible as the Fed is subject to a universal law that we have called the "zero lower bound" (defined on pp. 104–05).

Summary

1. The major source of instability in consumption spending is consumer expenditures on durables, which can exhibit large fluctuations in response to income changes. This chapter adds private investment spending as an additional source of instability, with the potential of causing major changes in GDP in response to small shocks.

2. The simple accelerator theory of investment relies on the idea that firms attempt to maintain a fixed relation between their stock of capital and their expected sales. Thus the level of net investment—the change in the capital stock—depends on the change in expected output. The accelerator theory explains why the gross investment of most firms is relatively unstable, at first rising and then falling in response to a permanent increase in actual sales.

3. The flexible accelerator theory recognizes that net investment in the real world usually closes only a portion of any gap between the desired and actual capital stocks. Furthermore, the desired capital-output ratio may change, altering investment with a powerful accelerator effect.

4. The accelerator theory suggests that any event that causes a permanent increase in the desired capital stock, whether arising from an increase in expected output or from a reduction in the user cost of capital, causes only a temporary rise in investment spending.

5. Government policymakers can directly alter the user cost of capital. Fiscal and monetary policy can change the real interest rate component of user cost. Taxation can affect the user cost of capital through changes in the corporation income tax, depreciation deductions, and the investment tax credit. But the use of these policy instruments cannot eliminate all fluctuations in investment expenditures, because most policy measures operate only with lagged effects.

6. Spending on commercial construction has historically been quite variable, in part because the capital-output ratio for buildings is larger than that for other, shorter-lived types of physical capital. Because the lags between conception and completion of office buildings are long, booms and busts in spending for commercial real estate may last for several years. Changes in user costs and expected output also help explain this variability, but some of the fluctuations in construction still seem inexplicable and unpredictable.

7. Some firms face the same kinds of constraints on financing their spending that households face. Young and small firms seem particularly subject to constraints on how much investment they can undertake. In other countries around the world, firms sometimes are allied with other firms or with banks, which helps to reduce these constraints.

8. Shifts in the demand for investment spending tend to produce a positive correlation between investment and interest rates, even though the effect of higher interest rates, *ceteris paribus*, is to reduce investment spending. The former results from a shift of the *IS* curve, the latter from sliding along the *IS* curve.

9. The unpredictability of investment spending bolsters the case for the Taylor Rule for monetary policy that reacts to booms and slumps of the output ratio caused by volatile swings of investment.

Concepts

accelerator hypothesis
flexible accelerator

marginal product of
    capital (MPK)

user cost of capital
depreciation rate

Questions

1. Use the data in the case study in Section 16-2 to explain how the shares of the four components of gross private domestic investment (GPDI) in natural GDP (a), have changed since 1960 and (b), behave over the business cycle.

2. Distinguish between gross investment and net investment. Can gross investment ever be negative? Can net investment ever be negative?

3. Assume that output in the economy is growing. Does the simple accelerator model predict that net investment will also grow?

4. Discuss the role of lags in the accelerator theory. How does the existence of lags change the results of the simple accelerator model?

5. In summarizing the behavior of investment spending, the net investment ratio (I^n/Y) was described as volatile and persistent. Explain what is meant by these terms.

6. Business confidence and consumer confidence are often cited as playing a key role in the investment decision. How does business confidence enter the flexible accelerator model?

7. A capital good purchased at a given real price imposes three types of costs on its user. What are these costs? Which of these costs are subject to manipulation by policymakers?

8. What are the three tools of fiscal policy that can be used to influence the level of investment? According to the accelerator theory, are changes in these tools likely to lead to a permanent increase in the rate of investment?

9. What are the limitations to using tax incentives as a tool of activist fiscal policy?

10. Assume that the economy's output ratio equals 100 and monetary policymakers will react to any change in fiscal policy so as to prevent a rise in either the unemployment rate or the inflation rate. For each of the following changes in fiscal policy, explain what is likely to happen to the user cost of capital, the desired ratio of capital to expected output, and the level of net investment. Finally, keep in mind that any change in investment expenditures shifts the IS curve and affects aggregate demand.

    (a) Defense spending declines due to an increase in political stability across the globe.

    (b) Personal and corporate income tax rate cuts are passed in conjunction with even larger decreases in government spending.

    (c) An investment tax credit is enacted with no other changes in fiscal policy.

    (d) Federal spending on health care is increased and is only partially paid for by a higher tobacco tax.

    (e) Explain how any of your answers to parts a–d might change if the output ratio were less than 100.

11. What are the major factors that determine the relationship between gross investment and output in the economy? Briefly summarize the relationship involved.

12. Two of the functions of an economic model are to explain the behavior of economic variables and to forecast their future behavior. Using the information contained in the box on Tobin's q model, discuss how well each of the accelerator, neoclassical, and q models have explained or forecast the behavior of business spending on construction. What is the implication of this for the use of either rules-based policies or discretionary policy in efforts to stabilize the economy?

13. Use the interaction between the flexible accelerator and business confidence to explain why real private domestic investment fell so much relative to real GDP during the Great Depression. In addition, explain why real GDP rose while real private domestic investment fell during World War II.

14. According to the theory first presented in Chapter 3 and developed further in this chapter, the interest rate and investment are negatively related. Yet both business investment and interest rates tend to fluctuate procyclically, that is, are at their highest levels when the economy is at a high output level. Can you explain the paradox?

15. Using Tobin's q theory, explain what you would expect to happen to the construction of new houses as the prices of existing houses fall.

16. The procyclical nature of much investment spending tends to reduce the stability of the private economy. Suppose an investment tax credit plan is put in place under which the percentage tax credit granted to firms is negatively related to the output ratio. Would such a plan work to stabilize or destabilize the economy? Explain.

17. How does the existence of liquidity constraints affect the volatility of investment? Why might liquidity constraints be more binding on smaller firms than on larger ones and on U.S. firms than on firms in such countries as Germany and Japan?

18. Discuss how the behavior of investment described in this chapter strengthens or weakens the case for the Taylor rule.

Problems

myeconlab   Visit www.MyEconLab.com to complete these or similar exercises.

1. This problem uses the example in Table 16-1 (p. 521).
   (a) The economy will reach an equilibrium when expected sales no longer increase. What will net investment be at that point? What will gross investment be?
   (b) Assume that because of a new investment tax credit, the desired capital–expected sales ratio changes to 5. What would net investment be in periods 1–5?
   (c) When the economy reaches its new equilibrium, what will be the ultimate effect of the tax credits on investment?

2. This problem also uses the data in Table 16-1.
   (a) What would expected sales have to be in periods 3 to 5 for net investment to be constant at 4.0?
   (b) What would actual sales have to be in periods 3 to 5 to achieve a constant level of net investment?
   (c) What would actual sales have to be in periods 2 to 4 to achieve a steady 20 percent increase in gross investment in each of the periods 3 to 5?
   (d) At what rate do actual sales increase in part c?

3. This problem also uses the example in Table 16-1 (p. 521), except where noted. The flexible accelerator model states that net investment, I^n, equals a fraction, f, of the gap between the desired capital stock, K^*, and last period's capital stock, K_{-1} The capital stock in any period equals last period's capital stock plus last period's net investment. The equations that describe these relationships are

$$I^n = f(K^* - K_{-1}) \text{ and } K = K_{-1} + I^n_{-1}.$$

   (a) Assume that f equals 0.5. Calculate the amounts of the capital stock, net investment, and gross investment in periods 1–5.
   (b) Using the example in Table 16-1 and your answer to part a, discuss how net and gross investments differ between the simple and flexible accelerator models.

4. This problem also uses the example in Table 16-1 (p. 521) and the flexible accelerator from problem 3. Assume that f equals 0.5. Suppose that the desired capital-expected sales ratio, v^*, depends on the real user cost of capital, u. In particular, $v^* = 5.5 - 10u$.
   (a) Suppose that the real interest rate equals 5 percent (0.05) and that the capital stock lasts for 10 years, so that d equals 0.1. Calculate the real user cost of capital and the desired capital stock in periods 1–5. Explain why the amounts of the capital stock, net investment, and gross

investment in periods 1–5 are the same as in part a of problem 3.
   (b) Suppose that in period 1, the real interest rate falls to 3 percent (0.03) and stays at that level for periods 2–5. Given no change in the depreciation rate, compute the new real user cost of capital, and the new amounts of the desired capital stock, the actual capital stock, net investment, and gross investment in periods 1–5.
   (c) Suppose that the real interest rate equals 5 percent (0.05), but that the capital stock depreciates more quickly, so that d equals 0.2. Calculate the new real user cost of capital, and the new amounts of the desired capital stock, the capital stock, net investment, and gross investment in periods 1–5.
   (d) Use your answers from parts b and c to discuss the effect of changes in the real interest rate and the depreciation rate on the amounts of net and gross investment.
   (e) Use your answer to part b to discuss how the flexible accelerator can be used to explain why the economy's output responds with a lag to a change in monetary policy.

5. This problem uses the Tobin q model of investment. (See the box on pp. 528–29.) Suppose that the adjustment rate, j, equals 0.2 and that the depreciation rate equals 0.1. The replacement value of the AB Corporation's capital equals 10 million dollars and the market value of its stock for the next 10 periods is listed in the table below. (The market value is listed in millions of dollars.)

Period	1	2	3	4	5	6	7	8	9	10
Market value	11	12	12	11	10	9	8	8	9	10

   (a) Calculate the value of Tobin's q for the AB Corporation in periods 1–10.
   (b) Calculate the AB Corporation's investment-to-capital stock ratio in periods 1–10.
   (c) Suppose that the Tobin q's and the investment-to-capital stock ratios for all businesses behave like that of the AB Corporation during periods 1–10. Other things being equal, explain how the economy's IS curves shift during periods 2–10.
   (d) Given your answer to part c, explain how the monetary policymakers would change the interest rate in periods 2–10 if they followed either an activist policy aimed at preventing rises in either the inflation or unemployment rate or a Taylor Rule.

◆ SELF-TEST ANSWERS

p. 524. (1) Assuming, as in this section, that replacement investment is a fixed fraction of the previous year's capital stock, replacement investment is the most stable. Net investment, which depends on the *change* in expected output, is the least stable. Gross investment, the sum of net investment and replacement investment, is in-between. (2) The longer-lived is capital, the smaller is the fraction of the previous year's capital stock that needs to be replaced; hence, the smaller is stable replacement investment relative to unstable net investment. Thus we would expect gross investment in office buildings to be less stable than gross investment in computers.

p. 533. (1) The three potential tools are the corporation income tax, the value of depreciation deductions, and the investment tax credit. (2) If the government wants to stimulate investment, it can reduce the corporation income tax rate, or raise the value of depreciation deductions (by allowing business firms to take depreciation deductions earlier), or raise the percentage rate of the investment tax credit. If there is no investment tax credit, as in the United States after 1986, the government can introduce such a credit. (3) Monetary policy affects the user cost through its ability to change the real interest rate.

New Classical Macro and New Keynesian Macro

The chief cause of depressions is a want of confidence. The greater part of it could be removed almost in an instant if confidence could return, touch all industries with her magic wand, and make them continue their production, and their demand for the wares of others.
—Alfred Marshall, 1879

17-1 Introduction: Classical and Keynesian Economics, Old and New

The development of new theories in macroeconomics and the abandonment of old theories often occur in response to major macroeconomic developments. In Chapter 8 we were introduced to the classical economists whose ideas dominated macroeconomics prior to the 1930s; they believed that the price level was flexible and would shift by the amount necessary to eliminate any inadequacies in aggregate demand. We described this approach as assuming that the economy possesses "strong self-correcting properties," in the form of price flexibility, that would automatically correct any tendency for real aggregate demand to be too high or too low.

In the 1930s, a calamitous macroeconomic event, the Great Depression, brought a decade-long economic slump accompanied by double-digit unemployment rates. The Great Depression discredited the old classical approach based on flexible prices and self-correction. This epochal event created among economists, journalists, policymakers, and laypeople a receptive audience for the Keynesian revolution, based on John Maynard Keynes's influential book, *The General Theory of Employment, Interest, and Income.*[1] The Keynesian approach dominated macroeconomics until the late 1960s. The big event that undermined its dominance was the emergence at that time of significant inflation. The Keynesian theory based on rigid nominal wages had little to say about the causes of inflation.

New Classical Macroeconomics Versus New Keynesian Economics

Since the early 1970s, macroeconomics has been split between two basic explanations of business cycles. First to emerge as a challenge to the old Keynesian orthodoxy was the new classical approach originated by the late Milton Friedman, then at the University of Chicago, and Edmund S. Phelps of Columbia University.

---

[1] The late Harry Johnson examined the reasons for the success of the Keynesian revolution and developed a parallel set of reasons for the late 1960s' monetarist "counterrevolution." See his article "The Keynesian Revolution and the Monetarist Counter-Revolution," *American Economic Review,* vol. 61 (May 1971), pp. 1–14.

It was subsequently more fully developed by Robert E. Lucas, Jr., of the University of Chicago. This first approach was based on the idea that households and firms lack the full set of information needed to make their economic decisions. Later, a second strand of new classical macroeconomics emerged, based not on imperfect information but on shocks to technology and supply conditions. The second approach, the "real business cycle" model, was developed primarily by Edward Prescott of Arizona State University.

Common to all new classical models is the assumption of continuous equilibrium in labor and product markets. These markets "clear," in the sense that each worker and firm is acting as desired at the price and wage level that is expected to prevail during the period of employment or production. For Friedman, Phelps, and Lucas, business cycles emerge because workers and/or firms, while acting as desired, are doing so on the basis of incorrect information. In contrast, Prescott theorizes that business cycles emerge because a given amount of labor and capital input produces varying amounts of real GDP due to changes in the efficiency of production.

New classical macro contrasts with another recent set of theories intended in part to remedy weaknesses in the old Keynesian approach. These new theories are grouped together under the general heading of "new Keynesian" macro. Such models, examined in the second part of this chapter, accept Keynes's insight that prices and wages do not change fast enough for classical self-correction to occur. But they go beyond Keynes to examine the *reasons* why slow price and wage adjustment is often in the self-interest of workers and is consistent with profit maximization for firms. The implications of new Keynesian macro differ radically from those of new classical macro. For if prices and wages adjust slowly, no matter what the reasons, then markets do not always clear; workers are sometimes unable to obtain as many jobs as they want at the prevailing wages and prices, and firms are sometimes unable to sell as much as they would like to produce at those wages and prices.

Over the past decade macroeconomic theory has by and large rejected the new classical macroeconomics. As we shall see, the gaps of information required by the Friedman-Lucas-Phelps approach were too short in duration to explain multiyear business cycles. And the real business cycle approach was rejected for having no role of demand, nothing to say about prices and inflation, and also as having no explanation for the Great Depression. New Keynesian explanations of why prices and wages are sticky may have been useful and correct but they did not provide a full model of how the economy operates. The missing explanation needs a role for demand and supply shocks, an explanation for inflation, and a role for monetary and fiscal policy. In the last section of this chapter we will provide a brief introduction to these hybrid models that in some respects represent a blending together of new classical and New Keynesian ideas.

17-2 Imperfect Information and the "Fooling Model"

One of two related theories to introduce the new classical approach was Milton Friedman's "fooling model," developed as part of his presidential address to the American Economic Association in 1967.[2]

---

[2] Milton Friedman, "The Role of Monetary Policy," *American Economic Review,* vol. 58 (March 1968), pp. 1–17.

Distinctive Features: Market Clearing and Imperfect Information

The first distinctive feature of Friedman's model is that markets clear continuously; all actions of firms and workers are voluntary. The second distinctive feature is that business cycles can occur only if workers *inaccurately perceive the price level,* hence the label "fooling model." This feature of the Friedman model is often called "imperfect information" and is a characteristic of many modern models of the market-clearing variety.

Friedman's fooling model is asymmetric: Firms always know the current value of the price level but workers only learn the actual price level with a time lag. The economy is initially in equilibrium with actual real GDP (Y) equal to natural real GDP (Y^N). Let us consider the effects of an increase in aggregate demand caused by a monetary or fiscal expansion. Firms are willing to produce more because the high level of aggregate demand is accompanied by a higher price level (*Review:* the economy moves from point B to point C in Figure 8-6 on p. 243). The price level might rise by 10 percent and the nominal wage by 5 percent, resulting in a 5 percent reduction in the real wage that induces firms to hire more workers. But the workers do not know that the price level has increased, and they assess the 5 percent increase in the nominal wage in terms of an unchanged expected price level. They think the real wage has increased by 5 percent, and so they willingly work more. This expectational error by the workers is what makes it possible for Y to differ from Y^N; the business cycle happens only because the workers are fooled.

Sooner or later any expectational errors will be corrected, so actual real GDP cannot remain away from natural real GDP for long. As a result, Friedman's model is sometimes called a "natural rate" model, and in fact it is Friedman who is responsible for the terms "natural real GDP" and "natural rate of unemployment." It is common to describe a model with a vertical long-run supply curve (like *LAS* in Figure 8-6 on p. 243) as obeying the **natural rate hypothesis.**

Milton Friedman (1912–2006)

Friedman, a 1976 Nobel Prize winner, was the most famous proponent of policy rules (Chapter 14) and the inventor of the permanent-income hypothesis of consumption (Chapter 15).

A model obeys the **natural rate hypothesis** when shifts in nominal aggregate demand have no long-run effect on real GDP.

The Phelps Version of the Fooling Model

Simultaneously with the publication of Friedman's fooling model, Edmund S. Phelps of Columbia University developed a slightly different model in the same spirit, and he deserves equal credit for the invention of the natural rate hypothesis. In contrast to Friedman's distinction between the smart firms and the fooled workers, in Phelps's world everyone is equally fooled. Both firms and workers see the price rise in their industry and produce more, not realizing that the general price level has risen in the rest of the economy. Phelps developed one model in which firms are fooled while the workers are not. Firms see that the price of their product has increased, and they offer to hire more workers, not realizing that all other firms in the economy are experiencing the same increase in prices.

In another model, workers are isolated from information about the rest of the economy. Normally there is turnover unemployment (see Section 10-9 on pp. 342–44) as workers regularly quit one firm to go look for more highly paid work at other firms. But in a situation in which their own firm raises the wage, they stay with that firm instead of quitting. Thus the unemployment rate decreases even though, without their knowledge, all other firms in the economy have raised the wage by the same amount at the same time. The workers are

Edmund S. Phelps (1933–)

Phelps, a 2006 Nobel Prize winner, co-invented the natural rate hypothesis, pioneered the concept of the "golden rule" of economic growth, introduced the concept of imperfect information into many branches of economics, and helped to invent the analysis of supply shocks as summarized in Chapter 9.

fooled into a reduction in turnover unemployment, and the macroeconomic data register a decline in the unemployment rate.[3]

Criticisms of the Friedman and Phelps Versions of the Fooling Model

How did Friedman and Phelps justify their claim that workers will hold incorrect expectations for any significant period of time? Friedman's answer was that *firms have more accurate information than is available to workers.* Firms have this informational advantage, because they have a concentrated interest in a small number of prices of particular products and monitor them continuously. Workers, on the other hand, are interested in a wide variety of prices of the things they buy and have insufficient time to keep careful track. The workers do not immediately notice when the price level rises.

The Phelps version of the fooling model does not assume any particular informational advantage of firms over workers. *Everyone* is ignorant of what is happening in the general economy, as if they were stranded on small islands completely cut off from the rest of the world. Three telling criticisms have been directed against the assumption of imperfect information that drives both the Friedman and Phelps models. First, there is no reason to single out any particular ignorance of workers, as does Friedman and one of the Phelps models. Workers and their families buy many goods, particularly food, gasoline, and drug items, on a weekly or even daily basis, and they would discover almost immediately if the general price level had risen. Second, news about the level of prices and wages is published by the government and repeated on television newscasts every month, so any ignorance could last no longer than one month, far too short to explain multiyear business cycles. Third, if periods of high real GDP and a prosperous period of economic activity were *always* accompanied by an increase in the aggregate price level, workers and firms would learn from past episodes and realize that any period of current prosperity is doubtless accompanied by higher prices.

With realistic intelligence on the part of workers and firms, there is no room in macroeconomics for a model that bases its entire explanation of business cycles on ignorance and fooling. Any change in aggregate demand will move wages and prices up or down simultaneously and the economy will remain at its natural level of output, with no business cycles at all, just as in the classical self-correcting model of Figure 8-7 on p. 247.

17-3 The Lucas Model and the Policy Ineffectiveness Proposition

The Assumption of Rational Expectations

Despite their limitations, the Friedman and Phelps models, with their twin assumptions of market clearing and imperfect information, appealed to many economists. Preeminent among these was Robert E. Lucas, Jr., who took Friedman's model one step further by introducing an improved treatment of the way workers form their view of the expected price level (P^e). Instead of following Friedman's rather unsatisfactory assumption that workers only gradually adapted their expectations of the price level (P^e) to the actual value of the price level, allowing

Robert E. Lucas, Jr. (1937–)

Lucas, a 1995 Nobel Prize winner, is the leading developer of the new classical macroeconomics; he merged the concept of rational expectations with the assumptions of market clearing and imperfect information.

---

[3] Phelps's contributions appear in two important articles. See "Phillips Curves, Expectations of Inflation and Optimal Unemployment over Time," *Economica*, vol. 34 (August 1967), and "Money-Wage Dynamics and Labor-Market Equilibrium," *Journal of Political Economy*, vol. 76 (August 1968, Part II).

themselves to be fooled for weeks or even months, Lucas introduced the theory of **rational expectations.** Thus the **Lucas model** contains three basic assumptions: market clearing, imperfect information, and rational expectations.[4]

Expectations are rational *when people make the best forecasts they can with the available data.* It is important to recognize that these forecasts do not have to be correct, and so observing forecasting errors by individuals or professional economists does not constitute evidence against rational expectations. Instead, the theory of rational expectations argues that people do not consistently make the same forecasting errors.

For instance, the errors (or fooling) of the Friedman-Phelps model are not rational. If the observance of history suggested that any increase in employment had always been accompanied by a reduction in the actual real wage, then workers would learn that any offer of extra employment in the future would also be accompanied by a reduction in the actual real wage, causing these smart workers to refuse any such job offers. More generally, individuals should not make errors in the same direction week after week, especially in circumstances similar to those in history. The errors should be random, that is, independent of past forecasting errors.

The Lucas model, like those of Friedman and Phelps, makes output depend positively on a "price surprise," that is, a rise in the actual price level (P) relative to the expected price level (P^e). Lucas, like Phelps, relies on information barriers that apply equally to workers and firms. Lucas's firms are like small farmers who produce wheat or corn and are induced to produce more by an increase in the actual price. Information barriers prevent the farmers from learning that prices have gone up everywhere in the economy, raising their marginal cost of production and giving them no incentive to produce more.

> **Rational expectations** need not be correct but must make the best use of available information, avoiding errors that could have been foreseen by knowledge of history.
>
> The **Lucas model** is based on the three assumptions of market clearing, imperfect information, and rational expectations.

 SELF-TEST

Answer the following questions according to the Friedman-Phelps-Lucas theory of output determination:

1. Does a recession in which actual real GDP (Y) falls below natural real GDP (Y^N) require a price surprise? In which direction?

2. Does a boom in which Y rises above Y^N require a price surprise? In which direction?

3. What happens to the output gap ($Y - Y^N$) when people learn the true price level and the price surprise vanishes?

The Policy Ineffectiveness Proposition

The concept of rational expectations, which states that individuals use all available information in forming their expectations, leads to a startling prediction by Lucas and his followers. In a modern version of monetary impotence, Lucas

---

[4] Robert Lucas did not invent the idea of rational expectations, but rather receives credit for applying it to macroeconomics. The original idea was applied to microeconomic issues and was set forth in John Muth, "Rational Expectations and the Theory of Price Movements," *Econometrica,* vol. 29 (July 1961), pp. 315–35. Lucas's seminal contribution is contained in two articles. The more accessible of these is Robert E. Lucas, Jr., "Some International Evidence on Output-Inflation Tradeoffs," *American Economic Review,* vol. 63 (June 1973), pp. 326–34. A more technical article that motivates some of the assumed underlying microeconomic behavior is "Expectations and the Neutrality of Money," *Journal of Economic Theory,* vol. 4 (April 1972), pp. 103–24.

The **policy ineffectiveness proposition (PIP)** asserts that predictable changes in monetary policy cannot affect real output.

argues that *anticipated monetary policy cannot change real GDP in a regular or predictable way.* Usually called the **policy ineffectiveness proposition (PIP),** Lucas's argument for monetary impotence startled the economics profession when it was developed in the early 1970s.[5]

PIP can be understood as a corollary of rational expectations together with the theory that movements of Y away from Y^N require a price surprise ($P \neq P^e$). The central bank (the Fed) can change output only if it can find some method of creating a price surprise. However, if the public knows that an increase in the money supply raises the price level, then whenever the Fed raises the money supply there will be an increase by the same amount in *both* the actual and expected price levels, no price surprise will occur ($P = P^e$), and output will remain at the natural level of real GDP ($Y = Y^N$).

> **Summary:** The policy ineffectiveness proposition states only that fully anticipated changes in the money supply cannot affect real GDP. It does not deny that a money surprise (an unanticipated change in the money supply) can alter the level of real GDP. But it implies that the Fed faces a considerable problem in creating such a money surprise, since the Fed cannot respond to economic events in the same way it has in the past.

Problem: The Prompt Availability of Information

Although PIP created a revolution that dominated macroeconomic discussion in the late 1970s, by the end of the decade several weaknesses of PIP had been pointed out. The problem was not the Lucas contribution of rational expectations. Rather, the weakness was in the twin assumptions inherited from Friedman and Phelps, continuous market clearing and imperfect information, which made deviations of the current actual price from the expected price the *only* source of business cycle movements in real GDP. The assumption of imperfect information implies that business cycles would be eliminated if we had accurate current information about the aggregate price level.

This imperfect information aspect of the Friedman, Phelps, and Lucas models has been widely criticized. Aggregate price information is easily available with short lags of a month or two. With aggregate price information easily available, why should firms or workers take any action that might move them away from labor market equilibrium?

17-4 The Real Business Cycle Model

There now appears to be general agreement that the imperfect information theory of the business cycle is unsatisfactory, since information lags are too short to be a plausible source of multiyear business cycles.[6] New classical

---

[5] While Lucas receives the main credit for the basic ideas underlying the Lucas model, the formal case for PIP was made by Thomas J. Sargent and Neil Wallace in "'Rational' Expectations, the Optimal Monetary Instrument, and the Optimal Money Supply Rule," *Journal of Political Economy,* vol. 83 (April 1975), pp. 241–54.

[6] For instance, Robert Barro, who made important contributions to the development of the Lucas approach and PIP, was convinced by the problems addressed in the previous section that "the upshot of these arguments is that the new classical approach does not do very well in accounting for an important role of money in business fluctuations." See Robert J. Barro, "New Classicals and Keynesians, or the Good Guys and the Bad Guys," *Schweiz, Zeitschrift für Volkswirtschaft und Statistik,* Heft 3, 1989. More recently, Robert Lucas has admitted that "Monetary shocks just aren't that important. That's the view I've been driven to. There's no question that's a retreat in my views." See John Cassidy, "The Decline of Economics," *The New Yorker* (December 2, 1996), p. 55.

macroeconomists have turned to an alternative theory of the business cycle, one that still assumes continuous market clearing. Their new theory is the **real business cycle (RBC) model** of economic fluctuations.

The RBC model assumes that the origins of the business cycle lie in real (or supply) shocks rather than monetary (or demand) shocks. The main source of shifts in output lies in swings in the aggregate supply curve (both long-run and short-run), not the aggregate demand curve. The RBC approach states that fluctuations in Y are caused entirely by fluctuations in natural real GDP itself, Y^N.

What are these real (or supply) shocks that cause business cycles and account for the term "real" business cycle model? Shocks can include new production techniques, new products, bad weather, new sources of raw materials, and price changes in raw materials. Recall that the Lucas model failed to consider that information barriers are too short-lived to explain the *length* and *persistence* of actual business cycles. In contrast, the RBC approach assumes that these supply shocks are highly persistent, meaning that a favorable shock lasts several years, dies away smoothly, and is replaced by an adverse shock that lasts several years. It is important to note that the RBC theory simply *assumes* and does not explain the persistence of business cycles that undermined the Lucas approach.

In the RBC model, the economy responds to these persistent supply shocks according to the new classical assumption of continuous equilibrium. Firms produce the amount they desire at prices and wages that respond flexibly to changing economic conditions, and hire the number of workers they want; workers obtain exactly the number of hours of work that they desire at the market-determined real wage.[7] Our aggregate supply curve diagram introduced in Chapter 8 illustrates these aspects of the RBC model.

The **real business cycle (RBC) model** explains business cycles in output and employment as being caused by technology or supply shocks.

The Labor Market in the RBC Model

The top frame of Figure 17-1 exhibits the production function (F), which shows how much output can be produced by each additional worker.[8] An adverse supply shock leads to a downward shift in the production function, for instance from the usual curve F_0 to the bad shock curve F_1, implying a decline in the productivity of each worker. In the lower frame the labor demand curve, which shows the marginal product of labor, shifts down in response to the adverse supply shock from the line labeled N_0^d to the line N_1^d.

The effect of the adverse supply shock on both output and employment depends on the slope of the labor supply curve. If this slope is positive, as along the line labeled N_0^s, then a lower real wage induces workers to supply less labor (working fewer hours or leaving the labor force). Since the economy is always in equilibrium in the RBC model, the demand for labor shifts as a result of the supply shock from point B to point V. Employment falls from N_0 to N_1, while output falls from Y_0 to Y_1, seen in the upper frame.

---

[7] Two of the most influential papers in the development of the RBC approach are Finn E. Kydland and Edward C. Prescott, "Time to Build and Aggregate Fluctuations," *Econometrica*, vol. 50 (November 1982), pp. 1345–70; and Robert G. King and Charles I. Plosser, "Money, Credit, and Prices in a Real Business Cycle," *American Economic Review*, vol. 74 (June 1984), pp. 363–80. A sympathetic exposition is Bennett T. McCallum, "Real Business Cycle Models," in Robert J. Barro, ed., *Modern Business Cycle Theory* (Cambridge, MA: Harvard University Press, 1989), pp. 16–50. A less technical introduction is Charles I. Plosser, "Understanding Real Business Cycles," *Journal of Economic Perspectives*, vol. 3 (Summer 1989), pp. 51–77.

[8] We were first introduced to the production function in Figure 11-1 on p. 364. That production function related output per worker (Y/N) to capital per worker (K/N). In contrast, the production function in Figure 17-1 relates output (Y) to the number of workers (N).

Figure 17-1 Effect of an Adverse Supply Shock on Output and Employment in the Real Business Cycle Model

In the top frame, F_0 is the normal production function. In the bottom frame, N_0^d is the normal labor demand curve. An adverse movement in supply conditions, like bad weather for growing crops, shifts the production function down to F_1 and the labor demand curve down to N_1^d. In normal times the economy operates at point B in the upper and lower frames, and in bad times at point V. The decline in employment depends on the slope of the labor supply curve; if the labor supply curve were a vertical line instead of a positively sloped line like N_0^s, the economy would move to Z instead of V. Employment would remain fixed and output would fall only from Y_0 to Y_0'.

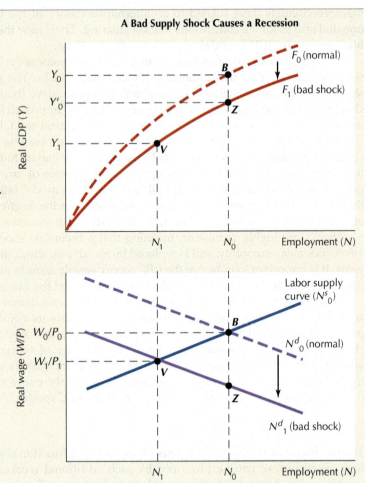

A different slope of the labor supply curve would lead to a different conclusion. Imagine that the labor supply curve, instead of being N_0^s, is a vertical line rising above N_0 through points Z and B. Then the economy's equilibrium point would be shifted downward by the adverse supply shock from B to Z. The shock would cause no change in employment, and in the upper frame there would be a much smaller decline in output, from Y_0 to Y_0'. Thus the RBC model's ability to explain why employment declines in real-world recessions requires a positive slope of the labor supply schedule, as shown by the line N_0^s.

 SELF-TEST

Answer the following questions according to the RBC theory:

1. Why does output increase in a business expansion?

2. What are examples of events that would raise output in a business expansion?

3. What are examples of events that would reduce output in a business contraction?

Labor Supply Behavior and Intertemporal Substitution

As we have seen, it is critical for the RBC model that the labor supply curve have a positive slope, as drawn in the bottom frame of Figure 17-1. The traditional microeconomic analysis of labor supply decisions stresses two conflicting effects of an increase in the real wage. A higher real wage increases the reward for work as compared to leisure (the substitution effect). But a higher real wage also raises real income and makes people want to consume more of all normal goods, including leisure, which means reducing work (the income effect). In drawing a positively sloped labor supply curve in Figure 17-1, we simply assume that the substitution effect dominates the income effect.

The RBC approach not only assumes that the substitution effect is dominant, but stresses a particular dimension of substitution that takes place over time. This type of substitution is called **intertemporal substitution.** It occurs when workers reallocate the amount of working time in response to changes in the real wage. In good times, when the real wage is high, workers choose to work more. And they take more leisure in bad times, when the real wage is low.

Students face such choices during their college years. Many students want to take one summer off to go to Europe, while planning to work in the other summers. A sophomore has two summers left before graduation. Which summer should he or she choose to go to Europe? Obviously, the summer with the best opportunities to earn relatively high wages should be chosen for work, and the European trip should be taken in the summer when high-paying jobs are scarce. This example highlights a problem in applying the theory of intertemporal substitution to the real world—how can students predict which future summer is likely to provide the most high-paying job opportunities?

Intertemporal substitution occurs when workers work more in periods of high real wages and less in periods of low real wages. It also occurs when producers raise output in periods of high prices and reduce output in periods of low prices.

17-5   New Classical Macroeconomics: Limitations and Positive Contributions

Assessment of the Real Business Cycle Model

Both the RBC model and the conventional *AD-SAS* graphical analysis of Chapter 8 agree that supply shocks can cause business cycles. Why, then, is the RBC model so controversial? The criticisms concern the unique components of the RBC analysis: the emphasis on technological shocks as the *primary* cause of business cycles, the failure to include prices or money, and the RBC interpretation of what happens in labor markets during business cycles.

Nature of technology shocks.   Critics focus on two aspects of the RBC model's treatment of technology shocks. While it is plausible that *advances* in technology may occur at an irregular pace, causing cycles in the growth rate of output, the implication that recessions are caused by *retreats* in technology ("forgetfulness") strikes most critics as implausible. Defenders of the RBC model respond that there are several types of events that have the same effect as a decay in technology, even if people do not literally forget how to produce efficiently. These include bad harvests, oil price shocks, and government regulations that require heavy investment and extra workers to reduce air and water pollution.

Perhaps a more serious charge distinguishes between the aggregate economy and the behavior of individual industries. Unlike the *IS-LM* model of Chapter 4, the RBC model does not incorporate a multiplier effect that can

INTERNATIONAL PERSPECTIVE

Productivity Fluctuations in the United States and Japan

Productivity is simply the ratio of output to inputs and measures the efficiency with which inputs are used. Labor productivity is output per unit of labor input. As we learned in Chapter 12, a more general concept, called multifactor productivity (MFP), is output per unit of total input, including not just labor but also capital, energy, and imported materials.

Interest in the RBC model is motivated by productivity shocks that vary procyclically, that is, in the same direction as the business cycle. How important are procyclical fluctuations of MFP, that is, the ratio of output to total input? The charts on the facing page show the growth rate of output and input for the United States and Japan. Whenever output grows more rapidly than input, MFP growth is positive, as shown by the red-shaded area. Whenever output grows more slowly than input, MFP growth is negative, as shown by the blue-shaded area.

In the top frame of the figure on the next page, the data for the United States show that in booms, output growth consistently increased more than input growth (defined here as a weighted average of growth in labor and capital input). MFP growth was highest when output was growing strongly, as in 1973, 1976, 1984, 1998, and 2003. In recession there are some examples in which output growth declined more than input growth, reducing MFP growth to below zero, as occurred in 1974, 1980, 1982, and 1991. However, this recession relationship changed after the 1990s. MFP growth was strongly positive in the 2001 recession, and also slightly positive in the 2007–09 recession.

In the bottom frame of the graph, the data for Japan show some striking differences. First, input growth is much smoother from year to year than in the United States, with few cycles, particularly between 1975 and 1990. Because input growth was so smooth, MFP growth was even more strongly procyclical than in the United States. But the behavior of Japanese input growth changed after 1990. Sharp declines in input

growth occurred in 1992–94, 1998–99, and 2001–02, resembling more closely U.S. input behavior.

A second difference is that MFP growth in Japan (as shown by the red shading) was consistently positive between 1976 and 1991, whereas in this period U.S. MFP growth was highly volatile, with negative growth in 1974, 1980, 1982, and 1991. After 1990 these relationships reversed. Japan suffered negative MFP growth in 1992–94, 1998–99, 2001, and 2009. In contrast for the United States every year but one experienced positive MFP growth over the entire period between 1992 and 2010. A notable sign of this change in behavior was the absence of any decline in MFP growth even in the mild recession of 2001 or the much deeper recession of 2007–09.

The changed behavior in Japan in part reflects the "lost decade" (now almost two decades) of stalled growth and depressed economic conditions that represented the "hangover" from the simultaneous stock market and real estate bubbles in Japan in the late 1980s. Between 1992 and 2010 real GDP in Japan grew only at 0.8 percent per year, as compared to 3.0 percent in the United States. A comparison of the Japanese policy dilemma of the 1990s and that of the United States in 2009–10 is provided in the box on pp. 110–11.

The procyclical behavior of MFP growth illustrated here is consistent with the procyclical technology shocks that form the basis for the RBC model reviewed in this part of the chapter. However, the observed procyclical behavior is also consistent with other theories, such as the idea that it is costly to hire and fire workers, with the result that firms adjust labor input only partially in response to fluctuations in output. It is also consistent with a widely recognized flaw in the data on capital input used in most calculations of MFP—the data reflect the total stock of capital, such as the total value of all the machines in the factor and do not adjust for the changing fraction of time that these machines are used in booms versus recessions.

magnify the impact of shocks on the economy. Therefore, to explain big recessions, the model needs big shocks. But technology is unique to particular industries. Highly distinctive technological innovations that, for instance, increase the speed of a Windows desktop computer have little impact on the productivity of coal miners. At an industry level, one would expect technological shocks (good and bad) to occur randomly, so that favorable shocks in some industries would largely cancel out adverse shocks in other industries. Any

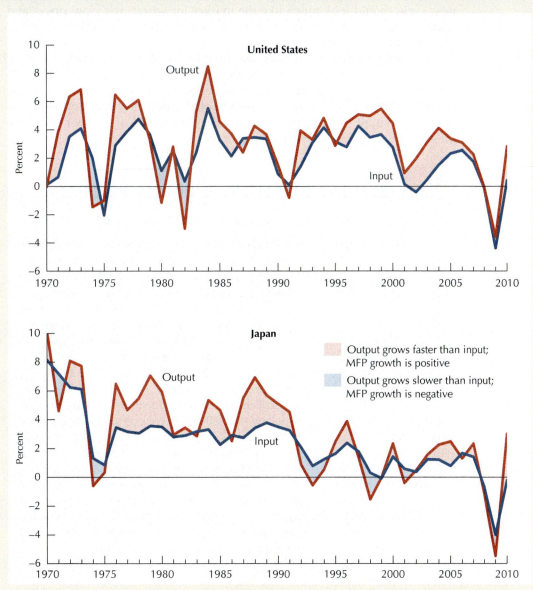

Source: United States data from the Bureau of Labor Statistics. Japan data from EU KLEMS Database, Groningen Growth and Development Center *Total Economy Database*, and OECD *Economic Outlook*. Details in Appendix C-4.

bad shock large enough to cause an economywide recession (considering that it would be partly canceled by good shocks in other industries) would be highly visible in industry data. Yet the proponents of the RBC model have as yet failed to identify any such shocks, particularly negative ones, other than the oil price shocks (see Figure 9-8 on p. 285).

The basic RBC model is based on an alternation of good and bad supply shocks, each persisting by about as long as an average U.S. business cycle. But this leads to a troublesome implication: If business cycles occur when the aggregate supply curve shifts back and forth but the aggregate demand curve remains fixed, then prices should rise in recessions and fall in booms. The business cycle should look much like the market for wheat, with low prices and high output in years of good harvests, and with high prices and low output in years with bad harvests.

The key problem is that prices are sometimes positively related to output changes, as in the Great Depression, and sometimes negatively related to output changes, as in the supply shock episodes of the 1970s and early 1980s. This suggests that business cycles are caused both by demand and supply shocks, not just by supply shocks, just as in the *AD-SAS* model of Chapter 8 and the inflation-output model developed in Chapter 9.

GLOBAL ECONOMIC CRISIS FOCUS
The 2007–09 Crisis and the Real Business Cycle Model

The Great Depression of the 1930s has always been a major embarrassment for advocates of the RBC model, since their approach forces them to interpret the massive unemployment of the 1930s as entirely voluntary and the catastrophic decline in output between 1929 and 1933 as a catastrophic adverse supply shock, an implausible episode of "forgetfulness." The Global Economic Crisis of 2007–09 raises the same questions as does 1929–33 contraction of economic activity. There was no adverse supply shock, which would have raised the price level and the inflation rate, as occurred after the oil shocks of the 1970s. Instead, inflation declined to nearly zero in 2007–09, and in 1929–33 the price level actually fell (as shown in Figure 8-11 on p. 260).

While the RBC model can explain an economic downturn only as the result of a negative shock to technology, the 2007–09 episode provides a further refutation of that approach. As shown in the graph for the United States in Figure 12-5 on p. 409, productivity growth was actually *faster* than average in 2009–10. During 2009, hours of work actually fell more than output, boosting productivity. Likewise, the Great Depression was not an era of technological forgetfulness but one of unusually rapid technical progress.[9] Both the Great Depression and Global Economic Crisis were caused by a massive downward demand shock that in part had common origins in a financial bubble (the stock market bubble of 1927–29 and the housing bubble of 2001–06).

Positive Contributions of New Classical Macroeconomics

Despite their limitations, both the Lucas and RBC versions of new classical theory have a strong appeal to a broad range of economists. What are the attractions of new classical theory?

Rational expectations: linking micro- and macroeconomics. The assumption of rational expectations appeals to economists, since it requires that

---

[9] See Alexander J. Field, "The Most Technologically Progressive Decade of the Century," *American Economic Review*, vol. 93, no. 4 (September 2003), pp. 1399–1413. Also see the book by the same author, *A Great Leap Forward: Great Depression and U.S. Economic Growth*. New Haven and London: Yale University Press, 2011.

people do not repeat their mistakes. Instead, people make the best use of all available information to guide their economic behavior. Such an approach is much more appealing than the alternative assumption that people make repeated mistakes in the same direction, period after period. The rational expectations hypothesis also has appeal because of its grounding in microeconomics. This means that the assumption of rational expectations in macroeconomics parallels the basic microeconomic assumptions of profit maximization and utility maximization.

The theory of efficient financial markets.   Many of the ideas developed by the new classical economists have been applied successfully to markets where continuous market clearing is a reasonable assumption. This is particularly true of financial markets, including the stock market, bond market, foreign exchange market, and the markets for agricultural and crude commodities, like sugar and gold. The theory of efficient markets incorporates the assumption of rational expectations. Expectations are assumed to incorporate all available information, implying that stock prices jump the instant new information is received and that there are no opportunities to make extraordinary profits on the stock market without access to inside information.

Greater understanding of economic policy.   The idea that individuals in the private part of the economy have rational expectations has improved our understanding of economic policy. Even if long-term wage and price contracts impede the flexibility of wages and prices, as discussed later in this chapter, those who negotiate contracts attempt to do so with full information on what policymakers are likely to do. For instance, wage negotiators who suspect that the government will allow rapid inflation after a supply shock are likely to demand full cost-of-living adjustments in their contracts. In contrast, past refusal of a government to allow rapid inflation following a supply shock, as in the case of the German Bundesbank in the 1970s, will increase wage negotiators' confidence that full cost-of-living protection is not necessary.

Recall that the policy ineffectiveness proposition (PIP) developed as part of the Lucas information-barrier approach implies that fully anticipated monetary policy changes have no effect at all on output. While PIP does not appear to be valid in U.S. history, a milder and more acceptable proposition is that fully anticipated policy changes have *smaller* effects than unanticipated changes. The expansionary policies pursued in the United States in the 1960s caused the output ratio to exceed 100 percent for a few years, but not permanently. In contrast, in extreme inflationary episodes (hyperinflation), radical changes in government policy seemed to halt inflation without a major decline in output.[10]

Pervasive effect on economic research.   Even if the new classical theories of the business cycle are subject to substantial skepticism, new techniques of analysis introduced by these theories have had a major influence on the way economists study variables such as consumption, investment, and the foreign exchange rate. The understanding of extreme episodes of inflation in places like Argentina and Brazil, as well as Turkey, is just one contribution of techniques

---

[10] See Thomas J. Sargent, "The Ends of Four Big Inflations," Chapter 3 in his *Rational Expectations and Inflation* (New York: Harper & Row, 1986).

introduced by new classical economists. The distinction between anticipated policy changes and policy "surprises" has improved our understanding of policy changes.

17-6   Essential Features of the New Keynesian Economics

Common Elements of the Original and New Keynesian Approaches

The adjective *new* distinguishes modern developments in Keynesian theory from the original Keynesian model developed during the Great Depression by Keynes and his followers and reviewed in Section 8-8 on pp. 249–53. The original Keynesian model combines a theory of shifts in aggregate demand (based on the *IS-LM* model of Chapter 4) with a theory of aggregate supply (based on the arbitrary assumption of a fixed nominal wage). Unlike the old and new classical models, with their assumptions of continuous equilibrium or market clearing, the Keynesian approach assumes that markets do not clear continuously. Hence the Keynesian model, either the original or the new variety, is often dubbed a **non-market-clearing model,** conveying the failure of prices to adjust rapidly enough to clear markets within a relatively short interval after a demand or supply shock. If slow price adjustment makes the return of the economy to natural output a long, drawn-out process, markets can fail to clear for years, as in 1929–41, 1980–86, or the years after 2007.

The appeal of Keynesian economics stems from the evident unhappiness of workers and firms during recessions and depressions. Workers and firms *do not act as if they were making a voluntary choice to cut production and hours worked.* A simple thought experiment is enough. Ask yourself these questions about the real world of 2010–11 when the unemployment rate was above 9 percent. Can each worker sell all the labor desired at the going wage and price? Would every worker refuse a job offer at the going wage and price? Then ask these related questions about business firms: Can each business firm sell all the output desired at today's prices? Would each business firm turn away customers at today's prices? The history of business cycles is punctuated by recessions and depressions lasting several years, during which workers and firms could not sell all the labor and output desired at the going wages and prices. Thus a theory of business cycles based on the failure of markets to clear, the new Keynesians believe, is more realistic than the new classical approach based on continuous market clearing.

In new classical models, business firms base their output level on news regarding their own price level, obtained from auction markets like the Chicago Board of Trade. In contrast, Keynesian non-market-clearing models turn the role of prices and output upside down. New Keynesian business firms base their choice of the price level on news regarding their own sales obtained by watching the ebb and flow of customers coming through the front door.

The New Keynesian Model

What, then, is the difference between the original and **new Keynesian economics?** Both assume that prices adjust slowly. But unlike the original model, which assumed a fixed nominal wage, the new Keynesian approach

In a **non-market-clearing model,** workers and firms are not continuously on their respective demand and supply schedules, but rather are pushed off these schedules by the gradual adjustment of prices.

The **new Keynesian economics** explains rigidity in prices and wages as consistent with the self-interest of firms and workers, all of which are assumed to have rational expectations.

attempts to explain the microeconomic foundations of slow adjustment of both wages and prices. The new Keynesian approach borrows—some would say steals—the concept of rational expectations from new classical economics. From traditional microeconomics, the new Keynesian approach borrows the core assumptions that firms maximize profits and workers maximize their own well-being or utility. The achievement of new Keynesian economics is to show how firms and workers make choices that maximize business profits and worker well-being at the microeconomic level, but that have adverse social consequences at the macroeconomic level.

Two distinctions are essential to the new Keynesian model. The first is between wage setting in labor markets and price setting in product markets. The second distinction is between **nominal rigidity** and **real rigidity.** Markets will not clear if something prevents the full adjustment of nominal prices, that is, prevents movements in nominal prices (P) proportionate to movements in nominal demand ($X = PY$). The first group of new Keynesian theories explains wage or price stickiness as the result of factors that make prices costly to adjust. Included in this category are **menu costs** and overlapping **staggered contracts,** which limit the flexibility of both prices and wages. These factors are said to explain *nominal rigidity,* because they deal with barriers to the adjustment of nominal prices.

New Keynesian theories also explain *real rigidities,* the stickiness of a wage relative to another wage, of a wage relative to a price, or of a price relative to another price. Theories that explain real rigidities in labor markets include the efficiency wage model, which we will examine later in the chapter. Critics note that theories of real rigidities do not explain nominal rigidity, since nothing prevents each individual agent from indexing its nominal price to nominal aggregate demand, that is, automatically changing P by the same percentage change as X, thus leaving real output (Y) unaffected. We will be particularly interested in the arguments given by new Keynesians for the absence of such full indexation, which in turn would suggest that theories of real rigidities *are* relevant to the explanation of sticky prices and wages.[11]

> A **nominal rigidity** is a factor that inhibits the flexibility of the nominal price level due to some factor, such as menu costs and staggered contracts. Such factors make it costly for firms to change the nominal price or wage level.
>
> A **real rigidity** is a factor that makes firms reluctant to change the real wage, the relative wage, or the relative price.
>
> A **menu cost** is any expense associated with changing prices, including the costs of printing new menus or distributing new catalogues.
>
> **Staggered contracts** are wage contracts that have different expiration dates for different groups of firms or workers.

17-7 Why Small Nominal Rigidities Have Large Macroeconomic Effects

A basic insight of Keynesian theory, both old and new, is that decisions of individual business firms do not always serve the best interests of society. The original Keynesian model argued that stimulative fiscal policy might be needed to avoid an economic slump resulting from some combination of monetary impotence, a failure of self-correction, and fixed wages. The new Keynesian model does not place any special emphasis on fiscal policy as opposed to monetary policy. Instead, it shows how rational profit-maximizing decisions by business firms may have adverse consequences for society.

---

[11] The best source of accessible articles on the new Keynesian version of macroeconomics can be found in a symposium in the *Journal of Economic Perspectives,* Winter 1993, vol. 7, no. 1. David Romer provides an introduction to several of the models reviewed in this chapter; Bruce Greenwald and Joseph Stiglitz contrast the "new" and "old" Keynesians; James Tobin provides new insights on the old Keynesian model; and finally Robert G. King provides an insightful bridge between the new Keynesians and the *IS-LM* model.

Price Setting by a Monopolistic Firm

The new classical and new Keynesian approaches view business firm behavior from different perspectives. In the new classical model, firms are assumed to be perfectly competitive "price takers," with no control over the price. This approach may describe farmers producing goods sold on an **auction market,** like wheat or corn sold on the Chicago Board of Trade. Such farmers choose how much to produce but have no control over price. However, the assumption of perfect competition does not apply to firms in most other sectors of the economy. Imperfect competition describes a market in which the number of sellers is sufficiently small that each firm is a price setter rather than a price taker. For instance, manufacturing firms, airlines, and many other firms can choose exactly what price to set, but they have no control over the amount sold.

The new Keynesian approach assumes that small menu costs will deter imperfectly competitive firms from constantly changing their prices and shows that menu costs do not have to be large to explain price stickiness. To see why, look at the left frame of Figure 17-2, where we review the elementary theory of price setting by a monopolist.[12] Our diagrams are particularly simple, since they assume that marginal cost is constant along the horizontal line labeled initial MC_0. There are no fixed costs, so marginal cost and average cost are the

An **auction market** is a centralized location where professional traders buy and sell a commodity or a financial security.

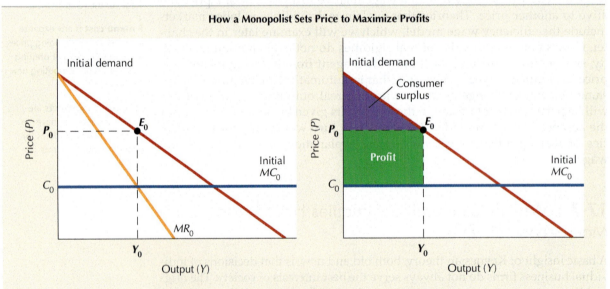

How a Monopolist Sets Price to Maximize Profits

Figure 17-2 The Price-Setting Decision of a Monopolist
In the left frame the red slanted line is the initial demand curve and the orange MR_0 line is the marginal revenue curve. The horizontal blue line is the initial marginal cost schedule MC_0. Output is chosen where MR equals MC. Price (P_0) is shown at point E_0, the intersection of the demand curve with the quantity produced. In the right frame the purple area shows the consumer surplus, the area below the demand curve and above the price level P_0. Profit is the green rectangle, the area to the left of Y_0 between P_0 and C_0.

---

[12] The presentation in this section is a simplified version of the first half of N. Gregory Mankiw, "Small Menu Costs and Large Business Cycles: A Macroeconomic Model of Monopoly," *Quarterly Journal of Economics,* vol. 100 (May 1985), pp. 529–37.

same. The quantity produced (Y_0) is determined at the point where the marginal revenue line (MR_0) intersects the marginal cost curve. The price is determined at point E_0, where the chosen quantity Y_0 intersects the initial demand curve. The right frame of Figure 17-2 shows exactly the same situation but identifies the areas that indicate the business firm's profit and the consumer surplus enjoyed by the purchasers of the product.[13]

The Firm's Response to a Decline in Demand

To understand how recessions in real output may occur, let us now examine the effects of a decline in the demand for the product. The decline is shown in the left frame of Figure 17-3 by the downward shift from the dashed red initial demand curve to the solid red new demand curve. To avoid a recession, the firm must produce the same amount as before, Y_0, which intersects the new demand curve at E_1. For unchanged output to be chosen by the profit-maximizing firm at point E_1, it is necessary that marginal cost decline by the amount shown between the initial MC_0 and required MC_1 lines. The lower blue line is called "required" because a decline in MC is needed to avoid a recession.

Will the firm avoid cutting output by reducing price from P_0 to P_1? Perhaps not, if there are menu costs, because the gain in profit by cutting price

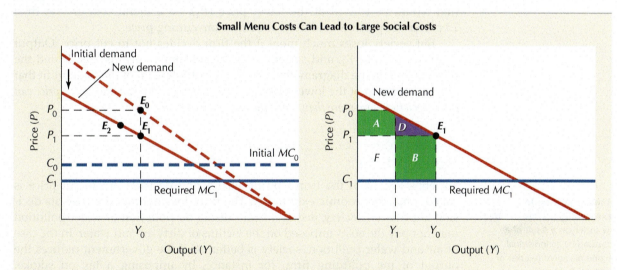

Small Menu Costs Can Lead to Large Social Costs

Figure 17-3 The Price-Setting Choice of a Monopolist Facing a Decline in Demand

In the left frame a decline in demand shifts the demand curve down from the initial demand line to the new demand line. To maintain fixed output at Y_0, the price must fall from P_0 to P_1 and marginal cost must fall to required MC_1. To decide whether or not to reduce price to the profit-maximizing level P_1, the firm weighs the gain in profit (area B minus area A in the right frame) against any menu cost that may be involved in changing price. If the firm fails to cut price below P_0, the level of output falls from Y_0 to Y_1, and society loses the area D plus B, which is much larger than B minus A.

---

[13] *Review:* When the demand curve is a straight line, the marginal revenue curve is always drawn so that it lies halfway between the demand curve and the vertical axis. The demand curve shows how much each purchaser is willing to pay for the product. At the price P_0, any purchaser whose willingness to pay is greater than P_0 enjoys a consumer surplus, reflecting the fact that the price charged is less than the willingness to pay.

may not be sufficient to cover the menu costs. Recall from the right frame of Figure 17-2 that the profit box is a rectangle lying above the MC line with its upper right corner at the equilibrium point E_0 or E_1. Comparing the two profit boxes, by lowering the price from P_0 to P_1 the firm gains the profit area marked B and loses the profit area marked A.

SELF-TEST

1. Why does area A measure the profit lost?
2. Why does area B measure the profit gained?
3. Why must the area B be greater than A?
4. What does area F represent and how does it differ from area B?

Despite the gain in profit from cutting price, the firm may choose not to cut price if the menu cost, which we can call z, is large enough. The firm cuts price if the gain in profit $(B - A)$ exceeds z, but not if z exceeds $B - A$. As drawn in Figure 17-3, the area B minus the area A is only 23 percent of the total profit that would be earned at the lower price (P_1). So a menu cost greater than 23 percent of profit would deter the firm from cutting price.

But society loses much more if the firm decides not to cut price. Output drops from Y_0 to Y_1, and society loses the consumer surplus area D and the profit area B. In the diagram, the area $D + B$ is 66 percent of the total profit that would be earned at the lower price P_1. *Thus the firm's decision not to cut price can cause society to lose more than triple the amount lost by the firm.*

The Macroeconomic Externality and the Effects of Sticky Marginal Cost

A macroeconomic externality is a cost incurred by society as a result of a decision by an individual economic agent (worker or business firm).

Society's loss from the firm's profit-maximizing decision not to cut price is called a **macroeconomic externality.** The firm does not pay the costs its decision imposes on society, just as a firm causing air pollution or water pollution may not pay the costs imposed on the victims of dirty air and water. In the case of air and water pollution, society is better off if the government reduces the output of the polluting firm, for instance, by imposing a tax on smoke. Similarly, society would be better off if all firms cut price together. Their failure to do so, even though such price cuts are in society's best interest, is called a **coordination failure** because there is no guiding invisible hand to return to the firms some portion of the amount society as a whole would gain if they were to cut their price.

A coordination failure occurs when there is no private incentive for firms to act together to avoid actions that impose social costs on society.

The analysis of Figure 17-3 assumes that the marginal cost declines instantly in proportion to the decline in demand. This is required to maintain output unchanged at the profit-maximizing price. Now let us look back at the left frame of Figure 17-3 and consider the case in which marginal cost does not decline at all and remains at the dashed blue line labeled initial MC_0. Why might marginal cost be sticky, failing to decline at all? There are many reasons, some of them discussed later in this chapter. Among these are contracts that fix wages and contracts that fix the prices of materials purchased from suppliers. If the wage paid to labor and the price paid to all suppliers remain fixed, then the *MC* line would stay fixed as well. In this case, the profit-maximizing price is at E_2, not E_1.[14]

The most important implication is that *with sticky marginal cost, menu costs are not needed at all to explain how recessions occur.* Any factor that prevents supplying firms from cutting the price of materials, or even delays such price reductions, will tend to make marginal costs sticky, implying that E_2 is the point that maximizes profit for the firm in Figure 17-3, not point E_1.

17-8   Coordination Failures and Indexation

Our discussion of the new Keynesian model has now covered a variety of factors that may inhibit the prompt adjustment of prices in response to a change in nominal GDP, thus automatically implying a response in real GDP. Leaving aside menu costs, the full adjustment of prices to a demand shock as depicted in Figure 17-3 depends on the instantaneous response of marginal cost. Following a negative demand shock, output must fall if marginal cost declines less than marginal revenue. There are two reasons why firms may rationally expect marginal cost to move differently than marginal revenue. First, marginal revenue may move with aggregate nominal demand but marginal costs may not. This would occur if a firm believes that its costs depend on many specific factors other than the perceived level of aggregate nominal demand (for example, volatile supply conditions, price changes for imported materials, changes in cost created by exchange rate movements). Second, with a fixed nominal aggregate demand, marginal cost would also remain fixed, while a local shift in demand (for example, a decline in smoking in response to new laws banning smoking in restaurants and bars) could reduce marginal revenue, providing another reason why marginal cost may move differently than marginal revenue.

The Input-Output Approach and the Absence of Full Indexation to Nominal Demand

To explain real price rigidity, the local-versus-aggregate cost distinction must apply to a world with many different firms purchasing supplies from each other. The automaker buys headlights from a firm that buys filament from a firm that buys copper from a firm that may mine copper using trucks purchased from the automaker. The input-output model emphasizes the importance of multiple buyer-supplier relations; each firm is simultaneously a buyer and a seller.[15] With only two firms, each supplying the other, firms could easily disentangle the local-versus-aggregate components of their costs. But with

---

[14] To simplify Figure 17-3, the marginal revenue line is not shown. To draw it in, find the point halfway along the horizontal axis between the vertical axis and the demand curve. Then draw a slanted line going up and to the left; it intersects the lower required MC_1 line directly above Y_0. Point E_2 lies directly above the intersection of this marginal revenue line and the higher initial MC_0 line.

[15] The input-output approach is developed in Robert J. Gordon, "What Is New-Keynesian Economics?" *Journal of Economic Literature,* vol. 28 (September 1990), see especially pp. 1150–52. A dynamic general equilibrium version of the input-output model is presented in Kevin X. D. Huang and Zheng Liu, "Production Chains and General Equilibrium Aggregate Dynamics," *Journal of Monetary Economics,* vol. 48 (2001), pp. 437–62.

thousands of firms buying thousands of components, containing ingredients from many other firms, the typical firm has no idea of the identity of its full set of suppliers. Since the informational problem of trying to guess the effect of a demand shift on the average marginal cost of all these suppliers is probably impossible to solve, the sensible firm just "waits for the next e-mail" for news of cost increases and then passes them on as price increases.

The input-output approach provides a critical contribution to understanding not just real price rigidity, but also nominal rigidity. The standard argument against the theories of real rigidity suggested previously is that they are consistent with nominal flexibility achieved through indexation to nominal demand. Yet the input-output approach emphasizes how high a fraction of a firm's costs are attributable to suppliers of unknown identity, with some unknown fraction produced in foreign countries under differing aggregate demand conditions. This environment would give pause to any firm considering nominal-demand indexation of the product price, since the failure of all suppliers to adopt similar indexation could lead to bankruptcy.

There is nothing to guarantee any confidence that supplier firms will adopt any aggregate indexation formula, for no single supplier acting alone has any incentive to do so. The rewards are too small and the penalties of acting alone are too great, *for a firm's viability depends on the relation of price to cost, not price to nominal GDP.* No individual firm has an incentive to take the risk posed by nominal GDP indexation, which would take away from the firm the required essential control of the relation of price to cost.

Coordination Failures and Daylight Saving Time

The failure of marginal cost to decline instantly and fully in response to nominal demand reflects a coordination failure. Marginal cost would drop if all workers and firms cut wages and prices together by the same percentage as nominal demand. But each is afraid to act first, since they would lose out if other workers and firms failed to act also. Daylight saving time provides a simple example of government intervention in the face of a coordination failure. All firms may want to open and close earlier in the summer to allow more time in the late afternoon for recreational activities, but none does so because each store wants to keep the same hours as other stores. By simply decreeing a shift in the clock, the government solves the failure of individual stores to coordinate their actions.

17-9 Long-Term Labor Contracts as a Source of the Business Cycle

Long-term labor contracts
are agreements between firms and workers that set the level of nominal wage rates for a year or more.

Long-term labor contracts are an important source of sticky marginal cost faced by business firms. Just as monopolistic firms impose social costs on society while maximizing profits, so too do firms and workers that enter into long-term labor contracts. Nevertheless, as the new Keynesian model emphasizes, there are good reasons why workers and firms desire such contracts. In this section, we study the features of long-term labor contracts.

Characteristics of Labor Contracts

In the United States, with few exceptions, formal labor contracts are negotiated in the union sector, which covers about 10 percent of the labor force. Industries that are heavily unionized include much of the manufacturing sector (especially autos, electrical machinery, rubber, and steel), as well as substantial parts of the construction and transportation industries (especially airlines, railroads, and trucking). Industries that tend to be nonunion include fast food and other services, retailing, and parts of manufacturing (especially apparel and textiles).

The behavior of wage rates in the union sector of the economy is more important than this 10 percent figure would suggest, since the wage rates that are negotiated in the union sector set a pattern that is imitated (although not copied exactly) by nonunion workers. One reason that unions set a pattern for nonunion wages is that nonunionized firms (such as Delta Airlines) do not want their employees to quit and join a rival unionized firm (such as American Airlines) or to vote to become unionized, and so they tend to pay wage rates similar to those in unionized firms. Indeed in 2010 Delta's flight attendants and mechanics voted down unionization, because they perceived that despite their nonunion status their wages and benefits were equal or superior to other unionized airlines.

Scheduled wage changes and COLAs. Wages negotiated under labor contracts are not completely rigid or fixed. Rather they change when a new contract is negotiated. With labor contracts, the nominal wage rate is set at the time of negotiation for the duration of the contract. Wage changes during the lifetime of the contract are allowed, but they are set in advance at the time of the negotiation. There are two types of prenegotiated changes. First, there is usually a scheduled change that takes effect in each year of multiyear contracts. Second, there is sometimes a **cost-of-living agreement (COLA)** that sets in advance the change in the nominal wage that will be allowed for each percentage point of future inflation. For instance, a contract might specify that a worker will receive a 3.0 percent increase in each of the three years of a three-year contract, plus 100 percent of the inflation that occurs in each of the three years. Thus, if the actual inflation rate turned out to be 0.0 percent in a particular year, the wage increase would be 3.0 percent. Alternatively, with an actual inflation rate of 10.0 percent, the wage increase would be 13.0 percent. A COLA contract that gives workers a fixed increase, plus 100 percent of the inflation rate, is called "full COLA protection," whereas a fixed increase plus 50 percent of the inflation rate would be "half COLA protection."

COLAs are intended to help workers maintain their real wage. Without COLAs, the real wage rate is reduced by inflation. The following table shows that a sudden change of the inflation rate from zero to 10 percent would cause a sharp decline in the real wage if the worker had no COLA protection. With full COLA protection (a nominal wage change equal to 3.0 percent plus the inflation rate), the real wage change is unaffected by inflation. With half COLA protection, the nominal wage change in the table is equal to 3.0 percent plus 0.5 times the inflation rate.

A **cost-of-living agreement (COLA)** provides for an automatic increase in the wage rate in response to an increase in the price level.

	Nominal wage change with COLA protection			Real wage change with COLA protection		
	None	Half	Full	None	Half	Full
Inflation of zero	3.0	3.0	3.0	3.0	3.0	3.0
Inflation of 10 percent	3.0	8.0	13.0	−7.0	−2.0	3.0

In this example, each of the figures for real wage change is equal to the corresponding figure for nominal wage change minus the assumed inflation rate.

◆ SELF-TEST

Under each of the following circumstances, tell whether or not the growth rate of the real wage is rigid, showing no response at all to a change in the rate of inflation.

1. With no COLA protection?
2. Half COLA protection?
3. Full COLA protection?

17-10   The New Keynesian Model Evolves into the DSGE Model

Contrast with other theories.   The new Keynesian model seems to solve the main dilemma of the other business cycle theories examined in Chapter 8 and the first part of this chapter, that is, how to explain observed business cycles without unrealistically assuming away output fluctuations (as does classical economics), assuming complete wage rigidity (as does the original Keynesian model), assuming unrealistic fooling of firms and workers (the Friedman-Phelps model), failing to explain persistent unemployment in the presence of easily available information on prices and the money supply (the Lucas information-barrier model), or requiring procyclical real wage movements and continuous labor market equilibrium (the real business cycle model).

Workers and firms in the new Keynesian model are rational, finding it *privately advantageous* to enter into long-term agreements that may have a *macroeconomic externality,* imposing employment and output losses on other workers and firms. The other approaches fail to provide an adequate theory of the business cycle, partly because they do not distinguish between the *private interest* (for instance, signing contracts) and the *collective interest* in avoiding business cycles.

Criticisms of the New Keynesian Approach

The new Keynesian model has been criticized for suggesting *too many* reasons why wages and prices are sticky. Some of these reasons, like staggered overlapping wage and price contracts, have been criticized on the grounds that business cycles were common before the rise of labor unions in the United States in the 1930s and 1940s. To explain business cycles in eras or industries where unions are not strong, we must rely on other new Keynesian explanations that do not require written contracts. Several of these, including the input-output approach, do not depend on the existence of organized labor unions.

Testing of the new Keynesian approach is in its infancy. There is as yet no agreement on which of the various sources of nominal and real rigidity have been most important. The degree of wage and price rigidity differs greatly across countries and in different historical eras. For instance, prices were more flexible before World War II in Japan and France than in the United Kingdom and United States. Prices are clearly more flexible in countries like Argentina and Brazil that have experienced high and variable inflation than in countries like the United States. Research that would explain why this is true has barely begun.

One reason that prices may be more flexible in some countries than in others can be linked to rational expectations. When firms and workers expect the government to pursue inflationary policies, they are more likely to insist on full cost-of-living protection and to invest time in trying to predict changes in government policy. They may also be unwilling to enter into long-term staggered contracts.

Building New Models That Combine Elements of New Classical and New Keynesian Macroeconomics

Much macroeconomic research in the past 15 years has been devoted to building relatively simple models that can explain all the main elements of macroeconomic behavior in a single model, based on the new classical first principles that individuals maximize their own well-being and that expectations are rational. But also included is the assumption that prices and wages are slow to adjust, giving the models new Keynesian characteristics. The goal of these models is to explain the "general equilibrium of the economy" in contrast to "partial equilibrium" models that explain only an aspect of behavior without explaining the interrelationship among the major pieces.

For instance, the Friedman permanent income hypothesis of consumption behavior explains consumption as dependent on permanent income without explaining income itself and is thus called a partial equilibrium model. The *IS-LM* model of Chapter 4 is a general equilibrium model but assumes that prices are fixed, thus providing no insight into the causes of inflation. The *SP-DG* model of Chapter 9 is a general equilibrium model that allows both output and the inflation rate to be influenced by demand shocks and supply shocks, but it does not explain where the demand shocks come from nor does it include a role for monetary policy in creating or offsetting them.

These new macro models are given the label Dynamic Stochastic General Equilibrium (DSGE). The adjective "dynamic" in the acronym DSGE refers to any model in which the passage of time is explicit, including the *SP-DG* model of inflation that appears in Chapter 9 in this book. The term "stochastic" means any model that contains random variables. "General equilibrium" describes any model that provides an explanation of the behavior of the entire economy instead just a part of the economy.

The DSGE models are usually taught only in graduate economics courses and often involve fairly advanced mathematics. Hence we only provide a brief outline here, indicating the main ingredients of these models and their relationship to several of the main models emphasized in this book. The simplest version of these models includes three equations.[16] The first is a version of the rational expectations theory of consumption reviewed in Section 15-6 on pp. 497–99. This allows consumption to depend on the interest rate and is sometimes nicknamed the *IS* equation of the DSGE model. The second equation is a version of the Phillips curve (*SP* curve) of Chapter 9, in which expectations of inflation are forward looking and formed rationally, and actual inflation depends only on expected future inflation and the output or unemployment gap. The third equation is a version of

---

[16] This description of the three-equation core DSGE model is taken from the "toy model" discussed in Olivier J. Blanchard, "The State of Macro," *Annual Review of Economics*, 2009, vol. 1, pp. 209–28. This paper may be more easily accessible as NBER Working Paper 14259, August 2008.

the Taylor Rule introduced in Section 14-7, which allows the short-term interest rate to respond to deviations of the actual inflation rate from the Fed's inflation target and also to the output gap.

The basic DSGE model builds in a gradual adjustment of inflation and wage changes to demand and supply shocks. By preventing prices and wages from adjusting instantly, it is able to reproduce realistic responses of aggregate output, inflation, and interest rates to shocks. The basic shocks that are allowed to create business cycles include shocks to consumer preferences and technology (in the consumption function), and shocks to monetary policy that occur when the Fed deviates from the specified Taylor Rule.

The earliest DSGE models, perhaps understandably in their desire to achieve rigor as simply as possible, omitted several aspects of the economy that have been instrumental in causing past business cycles. The basic DSGE model as described previously does not have a direct channel from current income to current consumption, thus ruling out liquidity constraints when households are forced to reduce expenditures when they become unemployed. There is no allowance for asset bubbles or consumer indebtedness, and so there is no explanation for the "hangover" from the 2001–06 U.S. housing bubble that led to the deep recession of 2007–09. The lack of an investment equation creates a failure to introduce the concept of overbuilding, that is an uncoordinated investment boom like those of 1927–29 or 2001–06 that endow the economy with far more square feet of residential houses, condos, and office buildings than the market can absorb. The absence of a government sector omits any discussion of fiscal policy.

Prominent macroeconomists are well aware of these limitations and have been busy in recent years building models that introduce an investment sector, or a government sector, or a financial sector that attempts to replicate the "hangover" impact of an asset bubble. The basic DSGE model has nothing to say about unemployment, and recently an explicit labor market sector has been introduced. But at least so far, these extra ingredients have been added to the models one at a time, leaving the resulting models incomplete and unable to replicate the most important historical business cycles (including the Great Depression, the supply-shock recessions of 1973–75 and 1980–82, and the Global Economic Crisis of 2007–09).[17]

Summary

1. Initially the new classical macroeconomics attempted to build a theory of the business cycle based on continuous market clearing and imperfect information. One of these theories was Milton Friedman's fooling model, in which workers are "fooled" into providing extra labor input because they do not have as prompt or complete information on the aggregate price level as do firms. Edmund S. Phelps at the same time developed theories in which *both* firms and workers have imperfect information.

2. Robert Lucas added rational expectations to the Friedman-Phelps assumptions of continuous market clearing and imperfect information. The central tool of the new classical model is the Friedman-Phelps-Lucas theory of output determination, which attributes business cycles in real output to expectational errors, also called "price surprises."

3. The central implication of the Lucas model is the policy ineffectiveness proposition, which states that monetary policy cannot affect output either through

---

[17] Perhaps the most widely cited DSGE model is Lawrence Christiano, Martin Eichenbaum, and Charles L. Evans, "Nominal Rigidities and the Dynamic Effects of a Shock to Monetary Policy," *Journal of Political Economy*, 2005, 113 (1), pp. 1–45. A promising attempt to integrate the effect of financial crises into a rigorous modeling framework is Robert E. Hall, "The Long Slump," *American Economic Review*, vol. 101 (March 2011).

an *announced* policy change or through a change that reacts to past events in a consistent and predictable way.

4. The second new classical approach is called the real business cycle (RBC) model. It explains business cycles in output as the result of slowly changing (persistent) shocks to supply conditions and technology. It explains cycles in employment as the result of intertemporal substitution by workers, who choose to work harder in periods of high real wages and enjoy more leisure in periods of low real wages.

5. The RBC model has been criticized because no one has yet identified specific technology shocks at the industry level that are large enough to explain actual recessions and depressions, except for the oil price shocks of the 1970s and 1980s. It has also been criticized for two unrealistic implications, that prices and output always move in opposite directions and that real wages vary procyclically.

6. The new Keynesian approach shares with the original Keynesian approach an explanation of business cycles based on the failure of prices to adjust sufficiently to maintain a continuous equilibrium in the labor market. The new Keynesian model differs by developing microeconomic explanations of wage and price rigidity based on rational expectations and profit-maximizing behavior.

7. Small menu costs can cause large social costs of recessions by giving profit-maximizing firms a reason not to adjust the price level to every change in demand. Sticky marginal costs imply that firms will reduce output in response to a reduction in demand, even in the absence of menu costs.

8. One source of sticky marginal costs is the role of long-term labor contracts in preventing the prompt adjustment of the nominal wage rate to changes in demand.

9. Modern macro theorizing has attempted to blend elements of the new classical and new Keynesian approaches into a new type of model known as "Dynamic Stochastic General Equilibrium" (DSGE). These models blend the new classical emphasis on rigor and rational expectations with the new Keynesian emphasis on slowly adjusting wages and prices. So far they have been able to replicate some features of real-world business cycles but have not yet been successful in capturing the key elements of the 2007–09 Global Economic Crisis.

Concepts

natural rate hypothesis	intertemporal substitution	staggered contracts
rational expectations	non-market-clearing model	auction market
Lucas model	new Keynesian economics	macroeconomic externality
policy ineffectiveness proposition (PIP)	nominal rigidity	coordination failure
real business cycle (RBC) model	real rigidity	long-term labor contracts
	menu cost	cost-of-living agreement (COLA)

Questions

1. How do the Friedman-Phelps "fooling" models differ in terms of who misperceives changes in prices and/or wages and how the labor market clears?

2. Explain how the Friedman-Phelps "fooling" model predicts that an expansionary monetary policy can lead to increased output in the short run, while the Lucas model suggests that such a policy would have no effect on real output.

3. In what ways are the Friedman-Phelps "fooling" model and the Keynesian model similar? In what ways do they differ?

4. In what ways are the Friedman-Phelps "fooling" model and the Lucas model similar? In what ways do they differ?

5. A firm has the choice of hiring either permanent or temporary employees when it needs to expand its output. If the firm hires temporary workers, it does not have to pay severance costs if it lets the workers go, which it will have to pay if it lays off anyone hired on a permanent basis. On the other hand, the wage rate paid to temporary workers exceeds the wage rate paid to permanent workers. The firm knows that the Fed follows a Taylor Rule and weighs equally the inflation rate and the output ratio. Given that the firm has rational expectations, discuss what the firm must consider in deciding whether to hire temporary or permanent workers when it sees its sales rise as the economy expands. How will its decision be affected if (a) the unemployment rate has just started falling or (b) the economy has been expanding for a number of years?

6. The policy ineffectiveness proposition (PIP) asserts that anticipated monetary policy cannot change real GDP in a regular or predictable way. Suppose that a monetary policymaker not only accepts the PIP, but is interested in adopting monetary policies that stabilize the economy. Explain what monetary polices this policymaker would advocate.

7. Explain why critics of the Friedman-Phelps and Lucas models argue that those models fail to provide a satisfactory explanation of business cycles.

8. How does an adverse supply shock affect the production function? What is the effect of an adverse supply shock on the demand for labor?

9. Explain why in a real business cycle (RBC) model, the price level and output move in opposite directions. Is that consistent with what happened in the Great Depression and the Global Economic Crisis of 2007–09? What other problems do the Great Depression and the Global Economic Crisis of 2007–09 present in terms of the RBC model providing a satisfactory explanation of business cycles?

10. What is meant by intertemporal substitution? How is the slope of the labor supply curve related to the ability of a real business cycle model to explain the real-world behavior of the real wage rate and employment over the course of the business cycle?

11. Discuss the positive contributions that the New Classical theory made to macroeconomics.

12. Compare the growth rates of input, output, and multifactor productivity in Japan and the United States since 1970.

13. What was the important assumption made with respect to wage rates in the original Keynesian model? How does the new Keynesian model differ in its approach to that assumption?

14. "Classical and new classical firms choose output, but new Keynesian firms choose price." Explain.

15. Explain why it is believed that greater pressure is placed on employment and output in response to shifts in aggregate demand under a situation of long-term staggered labor contracts than would be the case under shorter-term, uniform-expiration-date contracts.

16. What is a macroeconomic externality? How do long-term agreements impose a macroeconomic externality on the economy? What other sources of macroeconomic externalities are identified in this chapter?

17. In what ways are the original Keynesian model and the new Keynesian model similar? In what ways do they differ?

18. What is meant by the terms *nominal* and *real rigidities?* If nominal rigidities could be completely removed from the U.S. economy, would that solve the problem of output and employment fluctuations during business cycles?

19. Is it possible for there to be a business cycle without fluctuations in employment and output? Which, if any, school(s) of thought suggested that this would be the normal case?

20. What are the similarities and differences between the new Keynesian model and the new classical and real business cycle models?

21. The new Keynesian model relies on the concept of co-ordination failure to explain why demand and supply shocks lead to undesirable output and employment fluctuations. What role does this suggest for government stabilization policy? Is this a point with which the new classical model agrees? Why?

22. Explain what is meant by each of the four terms in a Dynamic Stochastic General Equilibrium (DSGE) model. What features of the New Classical and New Keynesian models are included in a DSGE model?

23. Explain which portions of the material previously discussed in this text are reflected in the three equation DSGE model discussed at the end of this chapter. What kind of a shock to this simple model would explain the behavior of interest rates during the period 2002–04?

24. Discuss some of the possible features that the simple three equation DSGE model discussed at the end of this chapter is lacking in order to be able to fully explain the events leading up to and including the Global Economic Crisis of 2007–09 and possible policy responses to the crisis.

Problems

 Visit www.MyEconLab.com to complete these or similar exercises.

1. You are given the following two forecasts of the price levels by persons A and B, as well as the actual price level for the next ten periods. Initially, the price level is 100.

Period	1	2	3	4	5	6	7	8	9	10
Person A	102	104	106	109	112	116	119	122	122	127
Person B	103	103	106	112	114	118	120	121	126	126
Actual	102	104	107	110	114	117	120	123	125	128

(a) For each person, calculate the difference between the actual price level and that person's forecast of the price level.

(b) In terms of how rational expectations are described in this chapter and your answer to part a, which person's forecasts are most consistent with the concept of rational expectations?

2. Suppose that the equation for the aggregate demand is $Y = \$9{,}000 + M^s/P$, where M^s is the nominal money supply and P is the price level. Initially the nominal money supply equals \$3,000. In addition, suppose that the expectations of firms and workers are rational in the sense defined on p. 547.

(a) Calculate points on the aggregate demand curve when the price level equals 0.8, 1.0, 1.2, 1.25, and

1.5, given the initial value of the nominal money supply.

(b) Suppose that natural real GDP equals $12,000 and that the short-run supply curve is given in the table below, where the price surprise equals $P - P^e$ and P^e is the expected price level:

Price surprise	−0.2	0.0	0.2	0.25	0.5
Real GDP	11,900	12,000	12,100	12,125	12,250

Given that the expected price level is initially 1.0, explain why the economy is in long-run equilibrium when the price level equals 1.0 and real GDP equals $12,000.

(c) Suppose that the real exchange rate declines and as a result, aggregate demand increases. Also assume that the decline in the real exchange rate will persist over time. As a result of this decline, the new equation for the aggregate demand is $Y = \$9,600 + M^s/P$. Given no change in the nominal money supply, calculate the points on the new aggregate demand curve when the price level equals 0.8, 1.0, 1.2, 1.25, and 1.5, given the initial value of the nominal money supply. Using the table given in part b, explain what the new equilibrium price level and level of real GDP are in the short run, given the price surprise induced by the decline in the real exchange rate.

(d) Monetary policymakers respond to the decline in the real exchange rate in one of three ways: (i) they do nothing and leave the nominal money supply as is; (ii) they change the money supply so as to return the price level to its level as given in part b; or (iii) they change the money supply so as to maintain the price level as determined by your answer to part c. For each of these cases, assume that this is how monetary policymakers have behaved in the past and this is how firms and workers expect them to behave in response to the decline in the real exchange rate. Calculate what the long-run equilibrium price level is and what the expected price level is under each response by monetary policymakers. Calculate by how much monetary policymakers must change the nominal money supply for the expectations of firms and workers to be realized.

3. Suppose that instead of persisting as is assumed in problem 2, the decline in the real exchange rate is only temporary in that after the initial change in the price level that you found in part c of problem 2, aggregate demand returns to its original level.

(a) Given that monetary policymakers, firms, and workers all recognize that the decline in the real exchange rate is only temporary and given the three policy responses described in part d of problem 2, again calculate what the long-run equilibrium price level is and what the expected price level is under each response by monetary policymakers. Again calculate by how much monetary policymakers must change the nominal money supply for the expectations of firms and workers to be realized.

(b) Compare your answers to part d of problem 2 with those of part a of this problem and explain why they are different.

(c) Explain what data or other factors that monetary policymakers, firms, and workers might analyze in attempting to determine if the decline in the real exchange rate is temporary or will persist. Finally, suppose that monetary policymakers are better able than firms and workers to determine if a change in the real exchange rate is temporary or will persist and that firms and workers know this. Given your answer to part d of problem 2 and part a of this problem, explain how once monetary policymakers have determined whether the change in the real exchange rate is only temporary or will persist, they could signal their finding to firms and workers.

4. Suppose that the equation for the aggregate demand is $Y = 7,000 + 2,400/P$. In this real business cycle model, the equation for natural real GDP is $Y^N = 9,000 + \text{technology shock}$. The technology shocks for periods 1–6 are given below.

Period	1	2	3	4	5	6
Technology shock	−400	−80	0	1,000	400	0

(a) Calculate the points on the aggregate demand curve when the price level equals 0.75, 0.80, 1.00, 1.20, 1.25, and 1.50.

(b) Compute the price level and real GDP in periods 1–6. Describe the cyclical behavior of real GDP and the price level in this real business cycle model.

5. Using Figures 17-2 and 17-3 as a guide, assume a price-setting monopolist firm with no fixed costs and constant marginal cost (MC_0) of $3.00 faces an original demand curve $P = 10 - 0.1Y$.

(a) What is the equation of the firm's marginal revenue curve MR_0? (Recall that for a linear demand curve, MR is twice as steep as demand.)

(b) What quantity will the firm produce to maximize profits? What price will it set to ensure that it sells all that it produces? (Hint: Recall that profit is maximized when $MC_0 = MR_0$.)

(c) At the profit-maximizing price, what is the firm's total revenue? Total cost? Profit?

(d) What is the value of consumer surplus? (Hint: Recall that the area of a triangle equals one half the area of the rectangle formed by its two sides.)

6. Now assume that the firm described in problem 5 faces a fall in demand such that the new demand curve is $P = 8 - 0.08Y$.
   (a) What is the equation for the firm's new marginal revenue curve (MR_1)?
   (b) If the firm is to maintain its original level of output (Y_0), what must happen to its marginal cost of production? What is the "*required*" marginal cost (MC_1)? (*Hint:* Set Y in MR_1 equal to Y_0.)
   (c) At what price on the new demand curve can the firm sell the original quantity of output?
   (d) If MC remains at \$3.00, and there are no *menu costs,* what output would the firm choose to produce to maximize profits? What price will it set? (*Hint:* Find the quantity and price associated with point E_2 in Figure 17-3.)
   (e) If the firm maintains the original price, what is the maximum quantity that it can sell, given the new lower level of demand? (*Hint:* Find Y_1 in Figure 17-3.)
   (f) Calculate the profits lost and gained if the firm chooses to reduce the price from the original price to the new lower price associated with the original quantity. (*Hint:* Calculate the values for area A and area B in Figure 17-3 as they apply to this problem.)
   (g) What is the maximum value for *menu costs* under which we could expect this firm to maintain its original output (assuming that it could reduce its marginal costs to the required level)?
   (h) If *menu costs* are greater than \$22.00, and marginal costs cannot be reduced below \$3.00 due to contractual input prices, would the firm seek to maximize profits by choosing the solution found in problem 6(d) (that is, where $MC_0 = MR_1$)?

◆ SELF-TEST ANSWERS

p. 547. (1) Yes, there must be a price surprise when Y falls below Y^N in a recession. When the price level is surprisingly low, firms conclude that the current period is a bad time to produce (since they receive an unrewardingly low price for their product). Hence, they reduce production voluntarily. (2) Yes, there must be a price surprise and the price level must be surprisingly high. (3) The output gap must vanish when the price surprise disappears.

p. 550. (1) A business expansion is explained by RBC theory as the result of a favorable or beneficial supply shock, which makes factors of production unusually productive. Employment increases as workers add more hours and accept more jobs in the belief that the higher real wage, paid out by firms as a result of high productivity, makes the period an attractive one in which to expend extra work effort. (2) Examples are new inventions or discoveries of new oil reserves. (3) Examples are a drought that reduces agricultural output of an adverse energy supply shock.

p. 560. (1) and (2) If a price P_0 is charged, profit is the area between P_0, the new demand curve, and the "Required MC_1" line, that is, the sum of the rectangles A and F. If a price P_1 is charged, then profit is the area between P_1, the new demand curve, and the "Required MC_1" line, that is, the sum of the rectangles F and B. Since F is in common to both situations, shifting from a price of P_0 to a price of P_1 means losing the profit rectangle A and gaining the profit rectangle B. (3) Why is B greater than A? Because E_1 is the position that maximizes profit with the new demand curve and the required MC_1 line. Thus total profits must be greater when producing at E_1 than at E_0 (given the reduction in demand), so the amount of profit gained by cutting the price from P_0 to P_1 must be positive. (4) F represents the profit earned in both situations, whereas B represents the extra profit earned when the price is reduced.

p. 564. (1) With no COLA protection, the growth rate of the real wage will be reduced by an increase in the rate of inflation, especially when the faster inflation is caused by an adverse supply shock. (2) With half COLA protection, the growth rate of the real wage will be reduced less than with no COLA protection. (3) With full COLA protection, the growth rate in the real wage is completely unaffected by inflation. This makes the growth rate of the nominal wage rate change fully in response to the change in the inflation rate.

Conclusion: Where We Stand

Experience, some people say, is like a light on a caboose, illuminating only where we aren't going. But we scrutinize the past for its elements of prologue, and consolation.
   —George F. Will

We have now finished the formal task of learning macroeconomic theory. We have also found through the Case Study text sections, International Perspective boxes, and Global Economic Crisis special sections that macroeconomics is a subject with close ties to the real world. Many events in U.S. history illustrate important themes in macroeconomic theory. And differences between the economic performance of the United States and other nations help to clarify theory and to highlight the differences among nations that are easy to explain and those that are difficult. For instance, we learned in Chapter 10 that it is relatively easy to explain why some countries experience hyperinflation—their governments have allowed very rapid growth in the money supply; that growth in turn results from their need to finance large budget deficits. But it is relatively hard to explain why high unemployment in Europe persisted between the early 1980s and mid 2000s; this provides an example of an unsettled issue in macroeconomics.

18-1   The Evolution of Events and Ideas

Events and ideas evolve together.[1] The Case Studies and boxes in this book show how theoretical ideas can be directly applied to the understanding of historical events. But the process also works in reverse—the outcome of historical events often challenges theorists and overturns theories, leading to the evolution of new theories. Some of the central ideas of macroeconomics, including those proposed by the old Keynesians, the new classicals, and the new Keynesians, can be understood as a reaction to events. In some cases, the evolution of the economy helped to resolve a debate between different schools of thought. In other cases, events occurred that could not be understood until new theories were formulated.

   In the rest of this chapter we will review some of the events that were sufficiently important to cause a change in ideas, starting in the next section with the Great Depression. The following sections treat the post–World War II period (the postwar era), dividing it in two parts, before 1970 and after 1970, and

---

[1] The title of this section and the analysis in this chapter are in part an updated version of Robert J. Gordon, "Postwar Macroeconomics: The Evolution of Events and Ideas," in Martin S. Feldstein, ed., *The American Economy in Transition* (Chicago: University of Chicago Press, 1980), pp. 101–62.

emphasizing the performance of the domestic U.S. economy. Then we examine the effect of events in the world economy, focusing primarily on the debate between advocates of fixed and flexible exchange rates. Two final sections summarize what we know, and what we still don't know—a remaining set of macro mysteries that are the focus of continuing debate, disagreement, and research in macroeconomics.

GLOBAL ECONOMIC CRISIS FOCUS

Can Economics Explain the Crisis or Does the Crisis Require New Ideas?

The Global Economic Crisis starting in 2007 was not forecast in advance except by a few isolated and prophetic economists. It was a particular surprise because in the years leading up to 2007, macroeconomic debate had been dominated by a search for the sources of the post-1984 "Great Moderation." Monetary policy was lauded for conquering inflation and delivering two decades of economic stability with less frequent and milder recessions than before 1984.

In this chapter we focus on the interaction of events and ideas. We will ask the same questions about the Global Economic Crisis as we ask about earlier episodes, going back to the Great Depression. Which of the existing models helped to explain the event? Which theories, if any, were overturned? What aspects of the event call for a new theory of the operation of part or all of the macroeconomy?

18-2   The Reaction of Ideas to Events, 1923–47

The most dramatic and unexpected event in the macroeconomic history of the United States was the Great Depression of the 1930s, consisting of the Great Contraction of 1929–33, followed by a weak recovery that failed to bring the unemployment rate below 10 percent until the outbreak of World War II. In plotting the behavior of central macroeconomic variables in Figure 18-1, we begin in 1923, in order to contrast the highly volatile 1930s and 1940s with the placid 1920s.

The Economy's Behavior in the 1920s and 1930s

The four-frame format of Figure 18-1 allows us to examine the behavior of ten macroeconomic variables on a single page. The top frame plots nominal GDP growth and M1 growth, indicating changes in the velocity of M1 by shading. The second frame plots nominal GDP growth and the inflation rate, so that the shaded areas indicate real GDP growth. The third frame plots the output ratio and the unemployment rate, and the bottom frame plots the long-term and short-term interest rates.

Prior to the Great Depression, the dominant idea in macroeconomics was the old classical approach, based on the quantity theory of money—a theory that emphasized the strong self-correcting properties of the private economy and the tendency for changes in the money supply to influence mainly the price level rather than output (Section 8-7 on pp. 246–48). The placid 1923–29 period

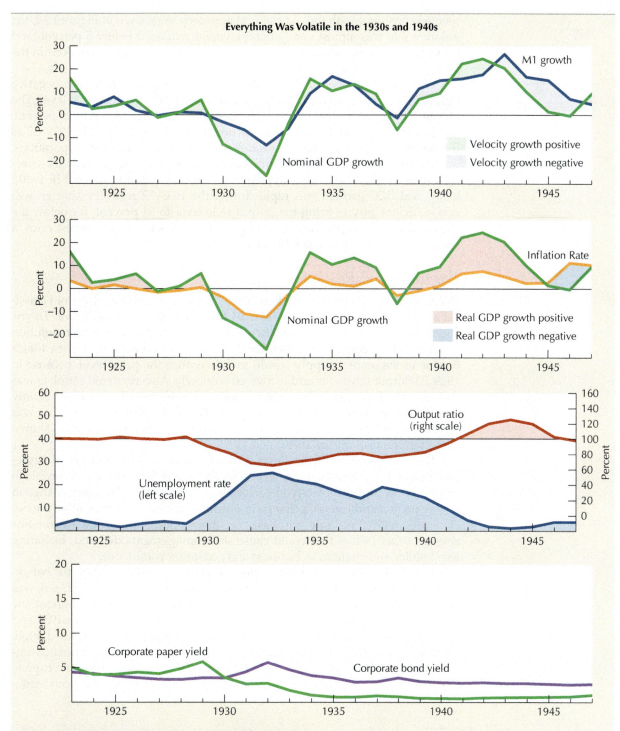

Figure 18-1 Key Macroeconomic Variables, 1923–47

These plots of annual data show the growth rates of nominal and real GDP, M1, and the GDP deflator. Also shown are the output ratio, the unemployment rate, the long-term interest rate, and the short-term interest rate. Notable features are the collapse of everything between 1929 and 1933, the weak 1933–37 recovery, the 1938 recession, and the takeoff of the economy as wartime spending began in 1940. Persistent unemployment and a continued low output ratio are the main features of the Great Depression.

Source: See Appendix C-4.

seemed consistent with the old classical approach. As shown in Figure 18-1, the inflation rate was almost zero, unemployment remained below 5 percent, and the output ratio remained near 100 percent. There were minor variations in the growth rate of nominal and real GDP and a minor recession in 1927.

Everything changed in the 1930s. Growth in everything became negative during 1930–33, including M1, nominal and real GDP, and the price level. The output ratio fell to 67 percent, and the unemployment rate soared to 25 percent. As shown in the bottom frame, the corporate bond rate jumped in 1929–32 as increasing bankruptcies made investors shy away from financing corporations.

The most notable facts about the Great Depression were not only its severity but its length. The unemployment rate was still above 10 percent in 1940.[2] While real GDP growth was rapid during the 1933–37 recovery, that growth was sufficient only to bring the output ratio back to 84 percent, far below the normal level of 100 percent. And despite very low short-term interest rates, a sharp setback occurred in the 1938 recession.

The Keynesian Revolution

Events cause the evolution of ideas. The Great Depression killed the old classical approach, stimulated John Maynard Keynes to develop his *General Theory,* and fostered the immediate worldwide acceptance of the Keynesian revolution (Section 8-8 on pp. 249–53). Rendered obsolete was the classical idea that a decline in the money supply would mainly reduce the price level, because in 1929–33 output fell so far and recovered so slowly. Also rendered obsolete was the quantity theory idea that velocity was stable, because it depended mainly on transaction practice and technology; in 1929–33 the economy's collapse was caused as much by a drop in velocity as a drop in the money supply, as shown in the top frame of Figure 18-1.

The underpinning of the Keynesian revolution was the concept of aggregate demand. Because the price level is sticky (that is, not sufficiently flexible to respond fully and completely to each change in nominal GDP), any change in aggregate demand causes a change in output and employment. Unlike the old classicals, with their sole emphasis on the money supply, the Keynesians stressed other factors that could cause shifts in aggregate demand, including fiscal policy and changes in business and consumer confidence.

The old Keynesian school of thought was heavily influenced by the behavior of the economy in the late 1930s, the time when Keynes's *General Theory* was being avidly discussed and absorbed at academic seminars throughout the United States. As shown in Figure 18-1, the money supply soared in 1939 and 1940, yet velocity growth was negative and unemployment remained high. Short-term interest rates were near zero, so that the economy could not be stimulated by further reductions in short-term interest rates. This led to the expression that monetary policy was like "pushing on a string," or "You can lead a

---

[2] There is an ongoing debate as to whether the unemployment rate in the last half of the 1930s is exaggerated, due to the counting of workers on government relief programs as unemployed rather than employed. The original critique of the official statistics is in Michael Darby, "Three and a Half Million U.S. Employees Have Been Mislaid: Or, An Explanation of Unemployment, 1934–41," *Journal of Political Economy,* vol. 84 (February 1976), pp. 1–16. A balanced assessment of the debate is contained in Robert Margo, "Interwar Unemployment in the United States: Evidence from the 1940 Census Sample," in Barry Eichengreen and T. J. Hatton, eds., *Interwar Unemployment in International Perspective* (Dordrecht, Boston, and London: Kluwer Academic Publishers, 1988), pp. 325–52.

horse to water but you can't make it drink." The only answer was stimulative fiscal policy, and the economy's prompt recovery in response to higher defense spending beginning in mid-1940 reinforced the supremacy of fiscal policy for a whole generation of economists.[3]

World War II

Macroeconomists usually omit from their analyses economic events during World War II, because government regulations skewed the normal operation of the economy. Output soared and unemployment fell almost to zero, but there was virtually no inflation, a feat made possible only because of stringent legal price controls. By 1944, government spending amounted to fully half of GDP, shifting the *IS* curve far to the right, but interest rates did not rise because the government required the Fed to "peg" the long-term government bond interest rate, printing the money to purchase any bonds that the government issued to cover its massive fiscal deficit. After the war, in 1946–47, when the price controls were lifted, inflation soared (thus reducing the real wealth of those who had patriotically purchased government bonds during the war), but interest rates remained steady, as the Fed maintained its agreement to peg long-term government bond interest rates through 1951.

> **Summary:** The big event of the interwar period was the Great Depression. This event spawned a big idea, the Keynesian revolution, with its emphasis on aggregate demand, sticky prices, and fiscal policy. The behavior of the economy during World War II seemed to support the main themes of the Keynesian revolution.

18-3   The Reaction of Ideas to Events, 1947–69

We now turn to the postwar U.S. economy. Macroeconomic behavior in the first part of the postwar period, 1948–69, is shown in Figure 18-2. Each of the four frames corresponds to Figure 18-1, but the vertical scale in the top three frames is compressed, reflecting lower volatility.

The Economy in the 1950s and a New Idea in Response

The economy's performance in the 1950s looks much better in retrospect than it did at the time. The period 1950–53 was dominated by the economic effects of the Korean War, including a brief surge of inflation in 1950–51 and very low unemployment during 1951–53. Huge increases in government spending in 1950–53 and a subsequent decrease in 1953–54 caused wide swings in the *IS* curve and high volatility in nominal GDP growth, as shown in the top two frames of Figure 18-2. The 1953–54 recession was very mild and, in retrospect,

---

[3] The stimulus of World War II began long before Pearl Harbor, due initially to military purchases by foreign countries and investment in factories producing military goods. Exports and domestic investment began to grow soon after the European war began in September 1939, and especially after the fall of France in June 1940. The United States introduced the military draft in September 1940, and as early as November 1940, there were 400,000 construction workers building military training camps for 1.4 million newly drafted soldiers. Quarterly data on the interwar economy, further examples of the pervasive effects of government defense spending in 1940–41, and estimates of fiscal multipliers are provided in Robert J. Gordon and Robert Krenn, "The End of the Great Depression 1939–41: Policy Contributions and Fiscal Multipliers," NBER Working Paper 16380, September 2010.

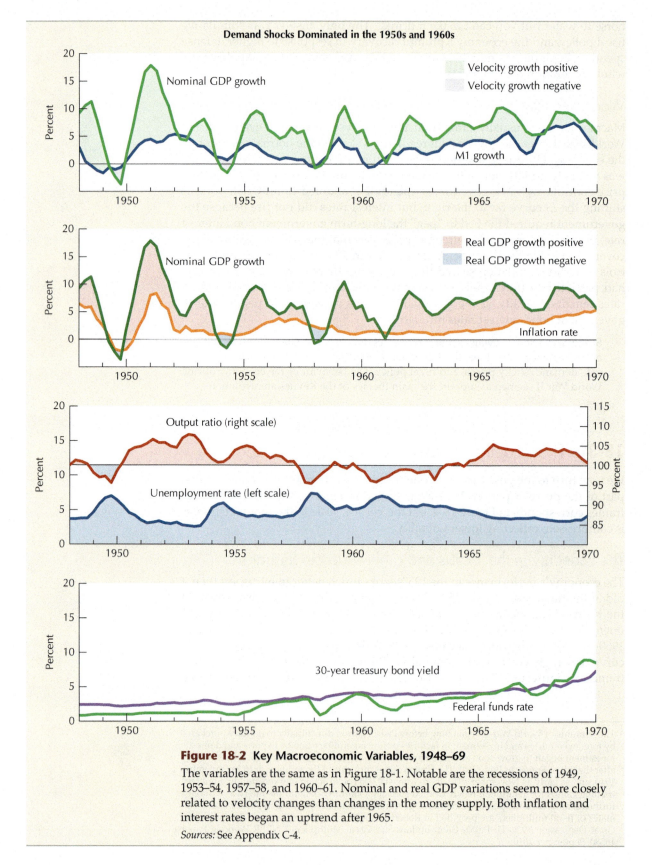

Figure 18-2 Key Macroeconomic Variables, 1948–69

The variables are the same as in Figure 18-1. Notable are the recessions of 1949, 1953–54, 1957–58, and 1960–61. Nominal and real GDP variations seem more closely related to velocity changes than changes in the money supply. Both inflation and interest rates began an uptrend after 1965.

Sources: See Appendix C-4.

exhibits the potency of easy monetary policy. A small reduction in the short-term interest rate (the federal funds rate) was sufficient to let loose a torrent of spending on housing and automobiles, causing 1955 to be a vintage year in economic annals. With both the Korean War and the threat of a renewal of the Great Depression behind them, American businesses and consumers were eager to stock up on housing and durable goods to match their newly elevated estimate of their "permanent income" (Section 15-4 on pp. 488–92).

The short-term Phillips Curve trade-off became evident in 1956–57, when inflation increased even though unemployment remained above Korean War levels.[4] In response, the Fed allowed interest rates to creep up, and this ultimately choked off the boom and brought on the sharp recession of 1957–58. Unemployment rose to the highest level yet seen in the postwar period. After a brief recovery, the economy promptly fell into another recession in 1960–61.

The main shift in ideas concerned the aggregate supply curve. Unlike the 1930s or the recession of 1949, prices did not decline at all in the recessions of 1953–54 and 1957–58. Just as U.S. economists were puzzling over the seeming inflexibility of prices, in 1958 A. W. Phillips published his famous article on the Phillips Curve, based on historical data for the United Kingdom (see Section 9-2 on pp. 268–71).

The Economy in the 1960s and a Set of New Ideas in Response

Prior to the 1990s, the longest economic expansion in U.S. economic history occurred between 1961 and 1969, shown in the third frame of Figure 18-2 by the long period of low and stable unemployment and the high output ratio. In its early phases the expansion responded to easy monetary policy, and then to massive fiscal stimulus in the form of income tax reductions in 1964–65 and, beginning in 1965, spending for the Vietnam War. While unemployment fell to the lowest rates since the Korean War, inflation steadily accelerated.

Three new ideas dominated economic discussions in the 1960s: the new economics of Walter Heller, the monetarism of Milton Friedman and others, and the natural rate hypothesis, reflecting the influence of both Milton Friedman and Edmund S. Phelps.

Of these, the new economics occurred earliest and fell out of favor fastest. When President Kennedy was inaugurated in early 1961, the economy was in recession, with unemployment at almost 7 percent. Believing that monetary stimulus was a weak tool, Kennedy's chief economic advisers (including Walter Heller, Arthur Okun, and future Nobel Prize winners Robert Solow and James Tobin) insisted that a new type of fiscal activism was necessary, consisting of changes in personal income taxes.[5] To stimulate the economy, they recommended a tax cut, which was implemented in early 1964 (with a second stage in 1965). To pay for the Vietnam War, they urged President Johnson in 1966 to enact an income tax surcharge.

Two events caused fiscal activism, later derided as "fiscal fine tuning," to fall out of favor. First was the legislative lag (Section 14-4 on pp. 457–61) which

---

[4] There were price controls in effect during the Korean War, albeit milder than the draconian controls of World War II.

[5] Kennedy's advisers viewed earlier attempts at fiscal stabilization as special events rather than as representative of a commitment to fiscal activism. The big tax increases of 1950–51, however successful, were viewed as a special event connected with the Korean War, and the 1954 tax cuts represented the expiration of temporary wartime tax increases, rather than a deliberate act of stabilization policy.

lasted 18 months before enactment of the 1968 tax surcharge. Second was the permanent-income hypothesis (Section 15-4 on pp. 488–92), which predicted that temporary tax changes would have a small multiplier effect. This prediction proved to be the case. By 1969–70, fiscal activism was discredited, and with it an underpinning of the old Keynesian school of thought.

Milton Friedman's approach was the exact opposite of the new economics; he favored rules over activism and monetary policy over fiscal policy. His approach, christened "monetarism" in 1968, advocated a constant growth rate rule for the money supply and no use at all of fiscal policy for stabilization purposes. As we learned in Section 14-2 on pp. 451–54, this approach reflected optimism that the private economy would remain stable and a pessimistic belief that activist policy would do more harm than good. Friedman's pessimism was reinforced by events of the 1960s, including long legislative lags for fiscal policy and the Fed's accommodative policy of 1964–65 and 1968, when aggregate demand was already growing too rapidly. Another event, the failure of the income-tax surcharge to slow the economy in the face of monetary stimulus in 1968, together with the impact of tight money in 1969 in ending the expansion, placed a final nail in the coffin of activist fiscal policy and left the stage open for the dominance of monetary policy over the following three decades. Only in 2001–03 was fiscal policy revived as a recession-fighting tool.

The third new idea was the most influential and long-lasting: the 1968 natural rate hypothesis, developed concurrently by Milton Friedman and Edmund S. Phelps of Columbia University (see Section 17-2 on pp. 544–46). The natural rate hypothesis took the Phillips Curve (then barely ten years old) one step further by developing the distinction between the short-run and long-run Phillips Curves (the *SP* and *LP* curves of Chapter 9). No longer could policy activists choose any arbitrary level for the unemployment rate; the microeconomic structure of labor markets decreed a particular natural rate of unemployment, and any attempt to push the actual unemployment rate below this natural rate would cause accelerating inflation.

Lo and behold, accelerating inflation was exactly what was occurring at the time the Friedman-Phelps hypothesis was unveiled in 1968. So strong was the influence of unfolding events that by 1970–71 the natural rate hypothesis had been widely accepted.

> **Summary:** The big events of the 1947–69 period were the instability of aggregate demand, due in part to the Korean and Vietnam wars, the overstimulation of the economy after 1964 by both monetary and fiscal policy, and the ensuing acceleration of inflation. Spawned in part by these events were several new ideas, including the Phillips Curve, the new economics, monetarism, and the natural rate hypothesis.

18-4 The Reaction of Ideas to Events, 1970–2010

Our summary of macroeconomic events and ideas since 1970 is based on Figure 18-3, which is arranged exactly like Figure 18-2.

Economic Behavior, 1971–82

Figure 18-3 shows that everything in the economy seemed to get worse after 1970. Notable in the diagram are the twin peaks of inflation in 1974–75 and 1980–81, and the triple peaks of unemployment in 1975, 1982–83, and 2009–10. The federal funds rate also exhibits twin peaks in 1974 and 1982–83.

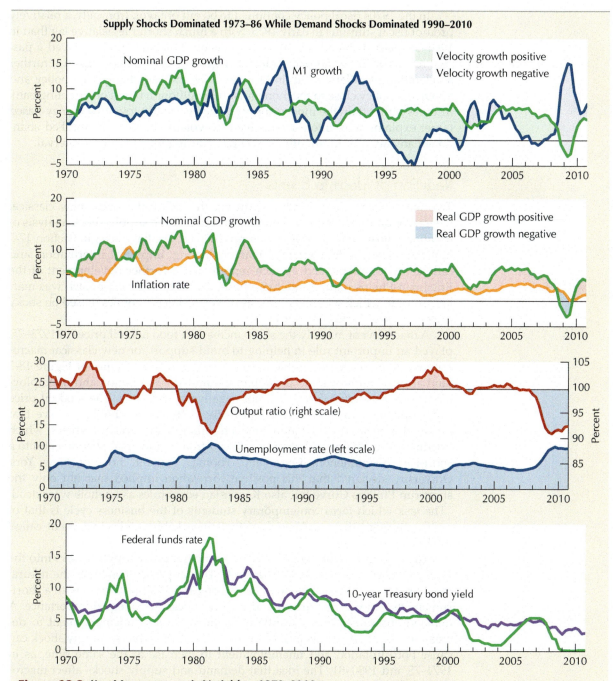

Figure 18-3 Key Macroeconomic Variables, 1970–2010

This figure duplicates the format of Figure 18-2. Evident are the positive correlation of the inflation rate in the second frame and the unemployment rate in the third frame, due largely to the supply shocks of 1973–74, 1979–81, and 1997–99. This diagram exhibits the puzzles of the twin peaks of inflation, unemployment, and interest rates in the mid-1970s and early 1980s, as well as the "twin valley" of low inflation and unemployment in 1998. The effects of the post–2009 Global Economic Crisis are clearly visible in the sharp downturns of nominal GDP and velocity in the top frame, in real GDP and inflation in the second frame, and in the third frame the sharp drop in the output ratio and rise in the unemployment rate.

Sources: See Appendix C-4.

In the 1970s fiscal policy continued to be out of favor. Ironically, a relatively prompt fiscal stimulus in early 1975, with a much shorter legislative lag than in 1966–68, helped to end the 1974–75 recession. Monetary policy played a passive role in 1975–79, allowing rapid M1 growth, which encouraged a further acceleration of inflation. But in October 1979, the Fed changed its policy and adopted a policy close to the monetarist rule (although based on targeting bank reserves rather than the money supply). The Fed's shift toward a money-based target explains why interest rates were so volatile in 1979–82; the Fed abandoned any attempt to smooth interest rates during this three-year interval.

Reaction of Ideas to Events

Two major ideas were developed during the 1970s: the Lucas new classical macroeconomics (Section 17-3 on pp. 546–48) and the supply-shock analysis of inflation adjustment (Section 9-9 on pp. 288–93). We have seen in Section 17-3 that the Lucas model combined market clearing, imperfect information, and rational expectations, and as such represented a further development of the Friedman-Phelps natural rate hypothesis. The core of this approach was market clearing, which was the antithesis of Keynesian economics (based on sticky prices and nonmarket clearing).

A macro event, namely the sharp increase in food and oil prices in 1973–75, played an important role in helping to build support for new classical macroeconomics. As is clearly visible in the second and third frames of Figure 18-3 (and also in Figure 9-13 on p. 300), in the mid-1970s inflation and unemployment were positively correlated, not negatively correlated. The food-oil price shock appeared to put another nail in the coffin of the Phillips Curve that assumed a negative correlation between inflation and unemployment, which Friedman and Phelps had already reduced from a universal phenomenon to a short-run phenomenon. Lucas and Thomas Sargent, now of New York University, declared that this positive correlation implied that not only the short-run Phillips Curve but also Keynesian economics as a whole were dead: "The task which faces contemporary students of the business cycle is that of sorting through the wreckage...of that remarkable intellectual event called the Keynesian Revolution."[6]

The second idea of the 1970s was the integration of supply shocks into the Phillips Curve analysis, as in Chapter 9. This approach combines the natural rate hypothesis (in the form of a vertical long-run Phillips Curve) with a short-run analysis in which demand and supply shocks are of equal importance. A demand stimulus can cause inflation to increase and unemployment to decrease in the short run, as in 1965–69 or 1987–90. An adverse supply shock can cause both inflation and unemployment to increase at the same time, as in 1974–75 and 1980–81. The idea that demand and supply shocks affect macroeconomic variables symmetrically helped to revive Keynesian economics.

Economic Behavior, 1982–91

After a decade (1972–82) when everything seemed to get worse, everything seemed to get better for the rest of the 1980s. The unemployment rate fell from

---

[6] Robert E. Lucas, Jr., and Thomas J. Sargent, "After Keynesian Macroeconomics," in *After the Phillips Curve: Persistence of High Inflation and High Unemployment* (Boston: Federal Reserve Bank of Boston, 1978), pp. 49–50.

10.5 percent in late 1982 to 5.0 percent in early 1989. The inflation rate fell from double digits in 1981 to just 3 percent in mid-1986. Both short-term and long-run interest rates fell from their peaks of early 1981 (see the bottom frame in Figure 18-3).

Fiscal policy fell further out of favor during the 1980s and 1990s. The Reagan-era tax cuts of 1981–83 led to fifteen years of persistent natural employment deficits. A political stalemate over the solution to the deficit problem left policymakers unable to discuss short-term fiscal policy changes and added to the skepticism about activist fiscal policy built up during the events of the late 1960s.

As we have seen, from 1979 to 1982 monetary policy attempted to target monetary growth and abandoned any attempt to stabilize interest rates, contributing to the unprecedented high level and volatility of interest rates during that period. An important legacy of high interest rates in 1979–82 was the "Volcker disinflation," which helped to return the United States from the double-digit inflation of the late 1970s and early 1980s to a more moderate inflation rate that remained below 5 percent after 1984.

However, in August 1982, surprised at the depth of the 1981–82 recession, the Fed abandoned its brief flirtation with monetarism. It announced that it would no longer hold short-term interest rates at high levels; short-term interest rates promptly fell and the stock market soared. Between 1982 and 2000, the Fed appeared to follow a Taylor Rule, responding to both inflation and the output ratio, as displayed in Section 14-7 on pp. 468–71.[7]

New Ideas of the 1980s and Early 1990s

The real business cycle (RBC) theory (Section 17-4 on pp. 548–51) was not directly a response to events. But its introduction in the early 1980s found more ready acceptance against the background of the 1973–82 period, when supply shocks seemed a more dominant source of business cycles than demand shocks. The main debate about the RBC approach does not concern the realism of supply shocks, but rather the one-sided assumption that only supply shocks matter, while demand shocks do not.

As the 1990s began, two new strains emerged in macroeconomics, although they had not yet developed into a named "theory." First was the debate over the twin deficits (Chapter 7), which reflected a belief that fiscal policy now had more of an impact on long-term economic growth and on slow productivity growth than on the business cycle. The event that inspired the twin deficits theory was the persistence of a fiscal deficit along with a current-account deficit in almost every year between 1982 and 1996.

The second new idea of the late 1980s and early 1990s was to discredit any role for monetary aggregates (like M1) in the conduct of monetary policy by the Fed. As shown in the top frame of Figure 18-3, after 1980 there was almost no connection between the growth rate of M1 and the growth rate of nominal GDP. When M1 growth exceeds that of nominal GDP, it follows that the growth

---

[7] A readable and comprehensive review of changes in monetary policy in the 1980s and 1990s, with an extensive list of references to the related literature, is Marvin Goodfriend, "Monetary Policy Comes of Age: A 20th Century Odyssey," *Federal Reserve Bank of Richmond Economic Quarterly*, vol. 83/1 (Winter 1997), pp. 1–22. A recent assessment of monetary policy is Benjamin M. Friedman, "What We Still Don't Know about Monetary Policy," *Brookings Papers on Economic Activity*, no. 2 (2007), pp. 49–71.

rate of velocity is negative, as shown by the purple shading. Years of relatively large decreases in velocity include 1985–88, 1992–95, and especially 2008–09. The wild gyrations of M1 growth did not make the economy unstable; on the contrary, the growth rate of nominal GDP was much more stable than that of M1, and this was particularly true in the years 1985–2005.

Economic Behavior, 1991–2007

The economic expansion of the 1990s began in March 1991. The expansion was unusual in at least four ways. First, the early part of the expansion was very weak. Employment barely grew in the first year, leading to the label "the jobless recovery."

The second unusual aspect of the expansion was the behavior of inflation. Instead of accelerating as it had in 1987–90, inflation exhibited a slight deceleration from 1993 to 1998. While many economists had previously believed that the natural rate of unemployment was 6 percent or above, no acceleration of inflation occurred when the unemployment rate declined below 6 percent in late 1994. As explained in Section 9-10 on pp. 293–96, beneficial supply shocks allowed inflation to decelerate through 1998.

One of these beneficial shocks was the post-1995 revival of productivity growth, ending the dismal record of slow productivity growth in the previous period 1973–95. This productivity growth revival constitutes the third unusual aspect of the expansion of the 1990s. The basic cause of the productivity growth revival was the invention of the Internet and explosion of high-tech investment in computers, software, and telecommunications equipment. Rapid productivity growth helped inflation remain low but raised questions about how long the rapid growth rate could be sustained.

The fourth unusual aspect of the expansion and the subsequent 2001 recession and recovery was the behavior of monetary policy. Compared to the hypothetical predictions of the Taylor Rule (see Section 14-7 on pp. 468–71), three aspects of monetary policy stand out as unusual over the 1994–2007 period. The first was the sharp increase in the federal funds rate from 3 to 6 percent in 1994, intended by the Fed as a "preemptive strike" to avoid an acceleration of inflation as had occurred in the late 1980s. The second was the Fed's response to the 2001 recession, when it cut the federal funds rate from 6.5 to 1.0 percent in little more than a year, lowering the interest rate to a level far below that called for by the Taylor Rule. The third unusual feature was the Fed's failure to boost interest rates in 1998–2000, when the peak interest rate of 6.5 percent was virtually the same as the 6.0 percent rate of late 1994. If the Fed had raised rates more in 1998–2000, the high-tech investment boom and bust, as well as the bubble in the stock market, might have been moderated and the subsequent recession less severe.

On the surface, the 2002–07 expansion following the 2001 recession represented a remarkable episode of economic stability. The recession was so mild that real GDP never turned negative on a year-over-year basis. Real GDP growth from 2004 to 2007 was extremely stable, as was the output ratio during that period. Repeating the 1991–92 episode, negative job growth in 2001–03 repeated the earlier "jobless recovery," but after 2003 job growth returned at a robust rate. Eight million new jobs were created between 2003 and late 2007, and the unemployment rate remained below 5 percent throughout 2006 and 2007.

GLOBAL ECONOMIC CRISIS FOCUS
Termites Were Nibbling Away at the Prosperity of 2003–07

The macroeconomic environment seemed on the surface to be unusually benign during 2003–07, with the output ratio in the third frame of Figure 18-3 quite close to 100 percent and the unemployment rate below 5 percent in 2006–07. Yet as we learned starting back in Chapter 3 (pp. 62–63) that a housing bubble fueled by excessive expansion of consumer debt and lax financial regulation pushed the saving rate down almost to zero and allowed consumption to grow more rapidly than personal disposable income. By 2006 the bubble had burst, housing foreclosures set records month after month, mortgage credit was being shut off to many borrowers, and housing starts began to plummet.

By December 2007, the official peak month of the 2001–07 business cycle expansion, the underpinnings of prosperity were rapidly unraveling. And even the relatively low unemployment rate was deceiving, as many young Americans had departed from the labor force, in large part due to the difficulty of finding a job. The labor force in December 2007 was fully 2.5 million people lower than if the labor force participation rate had remained at its value reached in 1999–2000.

New Ideas of the 1991–2007 Period

The first big puzzle involving the domestic U.S. economy was the productivity growth revival cited in the previous section. Just as economists had failed to reach a consensus about the causes of the 1973–95 productivity growth slowdown, so they had failed to converge on an explanation of the post-1995 revival and the continued strong productivity growth of 2001–04. Thus the behavior of productivity growth did not spawn any big new idea, although it motivated economists to look to the experience of other countries, for example, the failure of Europe to match the U.S. productivity achievement, in a search for explanations.

The second big puzzle was why inflation had remained so low during the expansion of the late 1990s, despite the decline in the unemployment rate to 3.9 percent, the lowest rate achieved since the 1960s. Why had the negative Phillips Curve tradeoff stopped working, in the sense that record-low unemployment rates failed to trigger the expected acceleration of inflation? What explained the even-tempered "Goldilocks economy," which was neither "too hot" nor "too cold" but rather "just right"?

The "Goldilocks" puzzle led to a new idea—that there could be regular changes in the natural rate of unemployment, often called the NAIRU (Non-Accelerating Inflation Rate of Unemployment). Macroeconomic research in the late 1990s centered on the so-called time-varying NAIRU or TV-NAIRU, an idea that was entirely an attempt to explain an empirical puzzle with no theoretical content.[8] Explanations of the decline in the TV-NAIRU during the 1990s relied on specific factual aspects of the economy, including the declining share

---

[8] See Robert J. Gordon, "The Time-Varying NAIRU and Its Implications for Economic Policy," *Journal of Economic Perspectives*, vol. 11 (February 1997), pp. 11–32, and other articles on the natural rate of unemployment (or NAIRU) in the same issue.

of teenagers and the rising share of the young male population that was in prison. This led to an ironic or even cynical explanation for the Goldilocks economy, that "we had put many of our unemployed in prison."[9]

An important new idea that developed in the 1980s and spread in the 1990s was the primacy of an inflation target as the optimal rule for central bank behavior. An inflation target was adopted in the 1990s by the Bank of England and by the European Central Bank. An inflation target is a special form of the Taylor Rule in which the short-term interest rate is set entirely to keep inflation at a particular target rate; the real interest rate is raised when inflation exceeds the target and is lowered when inflation is below the target. With inflation targeting, a *zero weight* is placed on deviations of the output ratio from 100 percent.

Finally, the old idea of short-term fiscal stabilization policy was revived during the decade 2001–10. As we have seen tax rebates were mailed out during the middle of the 2001 recession in order to stimulate the economy, and further tax cuts were enacted in 2003. Then in February 2008, Congress and the President agreed on an even larger fiscal stimulus program with such speed that it was enacted before it was even clear whether there would be a recession at all. This prompt action appeared to overturn the belief inherited from the 1960s that the legislative lag of fiscal policy was so long as to make any action impracticable.

The Global Economic Crisis of 2007–10: A Summary of Its Main Causes

We have learned throughout this book, but particularly in Chapter 5, about the causes of the Global Economic Crisis and the resulting deep recession that created the worst conditions in the U.S. labor market since the Great Depression. By now we have become familiar with the large cast of characters who created the Global Economic Crisis. On Main Street these included borrowers willing to borrow well above their ability to repay, together with a system in which mortgage brokers could make their incomes higher by finding gullible borrowers to take on mortgage debts that generated large fees for the brokers. On Wall Street the participants included the banks that pushed the mortgage brokers to dig up an ever larger quantity of low-income ("subprime") mortgage applicants, the banks and nonbank financial institutions that packaged the resulting mortgage debt into "mortgage-backed securities," and the Wall Street credit rating agencies that gave unrealistically high ratings to these risky securities.

This book has contrasted four different asset bubbles and has explained why they ended differently. The 1927–29 U.S. stock market bubble ended in the Great Depression that was made much deeper than otherwise by perversely destabilizing monetary policy. The 1987–89 Japanese stock market and real estate bubbles endowed that economy with two "lost decades" of stagnant growth and price deflation. The 1996–2000 American stock market bubble left in its wake a minor recession that pales in comparison with the U.S. Great Depression and with other previous postwar recessions. Finally, the fourth episode was the American housing bubble of 2001–06 that was still unraveling as this book went to press in early 2011, with ever more foreclosures and unsold homes.

---

[9] See Lawrence F. Katz and Alan B. Krueger, "The High-Pressure U.S. Labor Market of the 1990s," *Brookings Papers on Economic Activity*, vol. 30, no. 1 (1999), pp. 1–65.

All of these four episodes had dire macroeconomic consequences except the 1996–2000 stock market bubble. What was the difference between that episode and the others? The answer is simple—alone among the four episodes it was not based on *excess leverage*, the ratio of the assets of financial firms to their equity capital. The stock market throughout the postwar period was tightly regulated to prevent excess leverage—purchases of stocks required a 50 percent down payment requirement (compared to only 10 percent in 1927–29). Many individuals bought stocks through mutual funds in which the down payment was 100 percent of the value of the stocks.

The other three bubbles in contrast were characterized by ever-increasing leverage. By one measure leverage among nonbank financial institutions increased from 12-to-1 in the 1990s to 33-to-1 in 2005–06. Down payment requirements on residential mortgages steadily decreased as well. The higher the amount of leverage, the more quickly profits turn into losses and negative equity as asset prices decline. The larger the bubble, the more debt is created as part of the creation of the bubble and the longer it takes the financial system to clean up the mess created by the bubble.

How Did the Global Economic Crisis Change Economic Ideas?

Doubtless the most important contribution of the Crisis to economic ideas was the questioning of macroeconomic models that were based on continuous market clearing, particularly the Real Business Cycle (RBC, pp. 548–51) model. The persistent unemployment of 9.5–10 percent experienced by the United States between mid-2009 and early 2011 was consistent with the Keynesian model in which workers cannot find enough jobs at the current wage and firms cannot find enough customers at the current price. Jobs are lacking because consumers do not buy enough, and consumers do not buy enough because jobs are lacking.

In bubble episodes going back to 1927–29 and before, a counterpart of a price bubble for an asset like housing is the enthusiasm of borrowers to encumber themselves with ever-more debt. These borrowers believe in the ancient myth that prices can only go up and can never decline. When the bubble inevitably bursts and prices begin to decline, the indebted borrowers now find that the value of their assets has declined below the amount they owe to banks. They are "under water" and face foreclosure or, in some cases, "walking away" from their mortgage.

The housing market continued to be depressed in 2011 for a simple reason. Each foreclosure raised the supply of houses by one unit but did not raise the demand for housing units at all, since those who lost their houses through foreclosure in the process ruined their credit rating and could not borrow again, often for years afterward.

The fact that a bubble leaves a "hangover" of excess supply and excess debt is not a new idea, and indeed it is difficult to see that the evolution of the Global Economic Crisis created any new ideas, but rather recycling of old ideas. The evolution of the 2001–06 housing bubble involved similar financial innovations and regulatory failures as the 1927–29 stock market bubble. The fact that financial crises impede an economic recovery following a recession, by endowing the economy with a mountain of debt, is a very old idea retold recently by Carmen M. Reinhart of the University of Maryland and Kenneth S. Rogoff of Harvard University.[10]

---

[10] Carmen M. Reinhart and Kenneth S. Rogoff, *This Time Is Different: Eight Centuries of Financial Folly.* Princeton University Press, 2009.

Indeed once we accept the idea that cycles of financial excess and collapse have consequences for the real demand for goods and services, then financial bubbles and crises become yet another source of leftward and rightward movements in the *IS* curve of Chapter 4 and the Aggregate Demand Curve of Chapter 8. Macroeconomic theory thirty years ago attributed business cycles to demand and supply shocks and developed theories as to why these shocks took time to have their full impact, including such theories as the permanent income hypothesis of consumption (pp. 488–92), the accelerator theory of investment (pp. 521–24), and the long and variable lags of monetary and fiscal policy (pp. 457–61).

In short the macroeconomic theory reviewed in this book does not have to be tossed aside or overturned for us to understand the causes and consequences of the Global Economic Crisis. The core of our theory is the *IS-LM* model, which becomes the *AD-SAS* model once prices are allowed to change. Business cycles are caused by a succession of demand and supply shocks, and these shocks can be quite different in one era than in another. For instance, we learned earlier in this chapter that the most important source of aggregate demand shocks in the 1948–68 period was the volatility of government military expenditures. Then aggregate supply shocks took over as the main source of business cycles between 1973 and 1986.

The causes of the Great Depression and the Global Economic Crisis were yet another type of aggregate demand shock emanating from the financial sector. The asset bubbles of 1927–29 and 2001–06 had serious consequences that resulted from the large amount of debt created during the bubble period. The aftermath of 1927–29, the Great Depression, was catastrophic because it was accompanied by contractionary monetary policy in a world that lacked deposit insurance. The aftermath of 2001–06, the Global Economic Crisis, was severe but much smaller in magnitude than the Great Depression, because the monetary and fiscal policy reaction was highly expansionary, because deposit insurance prevented depositors from rushing to their banks to withdraw money, and because the larger size of the government sector made the automatic stabilizers (pp. 162–63) more potent.

Summary: The main events of the 1971–2010 period were the two adverse supply shocks of 1974–75 and 1979–81, which created twin peaks of inflation, unemployment, and interest rates, and the Global Economic Crisis of 2007–09, which caused output and employment to collapse and created the worst labor market conditions since the Great Depression. Monetary policy shifted from accommodation of the supply shocks of the 1970s, to the Volcker disinflation of 1979–82, to a Taylor Rule that seemed gradually to shift its emphasis from inflation targeting to stabilization of the output ratio. New ideas created by these events included the real business cycle theory, concern over the twin deficits, discrediting of monetary aggregates, and a revival of short-run stimulative fiscal policy. The Global Economic Crisis did not produce important new ideas but rather a revival of the old idea that asset bubbles and excess leverage can have long-lasting adverse consequences for the real economy.

18-5 The Reaction of Ideas to Events in the World Economy

Between the 1930s and mid-1960s, the United States was virtually a closed economy. In 1965 nominal exports and imports were barely 5 percent of GDP. But by 2010, foreign trade had become much more important, with nominal exports of 12.5 percent of GDP and nominal imports of 16.3 percent of GDP. In most other countries trade is an even larger share of GDP.

Interactions Between the World and U.S. Economies

After the Allied victory in World War II, the United States loomed large in the world economy. Its per-person GDP was far ahead of any other nation (see p. 360). Interactions between the world and the United States primarily flowed out from the United States in the form of aid programs such as the Marshall Plan (1948–53). Interactions that flowed in toward the U.S. economy consisted primarily of political events such as the Korean War, which (as we saw in Figure 18-2) destabilized the U.S. economy during the 1950–54 period.

We have described overexpansionary fiscal and monetary policies as a principal legacy of the 1960s, endowing the U.S. economy after 1970 with a higher inflation rate than would have occurred under a different policy environment. Another legacy of the 1960s was the breakdown of the fixed exchange rate Bretton Woods system, as the United States exported its inflation to other countries.

International Events Spawn Ideas: The Grass Is Greener

A simple way to summarize the international economy since the late 1960s is that the "grass is greener on the other side of the fence." This refers to the widespread enthusiasm for flexible exchange rates when the fixed (Bretton Woods) exchange rate system was breaking down, then the more recent longing for a return to fixed exchange rates, once observers noted that since 1973 flexible exchange rates were much more volatile and disruptive than had been predicted.

Flexible exchange rates had been expected to enable each country to attain monetary independence and choose the particular inflation rate that it desired. However, exchange rates turned out to be highly volatile and disruptive of the real economy, most notably when the dollar appreciated by 50 percent between 1980 and 1985, and then depreciated by the same amount between 1985 and 1987. The appreciation decimated the export markets of U.S. farms and factories. There was no doubt that businesses, jobs, and lives were disrupted by the volatility of exchange rates.

Since the late 1970s, economists and politicians have been searching for a way to return partially or completely to fixed exchange rates. The notable example is the European Monetary System, which surprised almost everyone by achieving a convergence of inflation rates within Europe (pp. 282–83). Some European countries, however, still have much higher unemployment rates than others, leading to a debate about whether the unified European currency (the euro) has now robbed individual countries of the freedom to devalue in order to revive their economies, as the United Kingdom, Italy, and other countries chose to do in 1992.

Since 1999, the exchange rates of the members of the euro have been fixed against each other. As we learned from the trilemma of Chapter 7 (pp. 191, 224–25), these nations have now lost any use of domestic monetary policy and have lost the ability (enjoyed by the U.S. Fed) to stimulate their economies when output growth is slow and the output ratio is 100 percent. Two examples of an economic "basket case" handicapped by their membership in the euro are Greece and Ireland, both of which had to be rescued in 2010 after their financial markets collapsed, leading in turn to draconian contractionary fiscal policies despite high unemployment.

International economics in the United States in the 1991–2010 period was dominated by the questions of competitiveness with Asia and the desirability of free trade, particularly with China and other East Asian countries. Questions of trade policy involve relative prices and fall within the purview of microeconomics, but there is an inevitable overlap with macroeconomics. For instance, a nation with a large trade deficit faces the alternatives of a depreciation of its foreign exchange rate or protectionist measures to reduce imports. It was universally recognized that the dollar had been propped up by the seemingly unlimited appetite of the Chinese and Japanese central banks to buy up dollars in order to keep their own currencies from appreciating. The future willingness of these central banks (and others in Asia) to buy up even more hundreds of billions of dollars was a major puzzle looming over international macroeconomics.

However, a currency depreciation and protection are not the only alternatives when a nation faces a major current account deficit, as we learned at the beginning of the book with the magic equation (also called the leakages—injections identity, see p. 35) showing that the current account balance is linked to domestic saving and investment and the government budget. An improvement in the current account deficit can be achieved by any measure that increases national saving, especially measures that reduce the government budget deficit.

> **Summary:** The main international events affecting the U.S. economy were the transition to flexible exchange rates in the early 1970s and the dislocations caused by the ups and downs of the dollar in the 1980s, its further appreciation during 1995–2002, and its subsequent depreciation during 2002–10. The unexpected volatility of exchange rates and the resulting dislocation of trade patterns led to a desire by many observers to return to some version of fixed exchange rates, as had occurred in Europe, with its adoption of the euro.

18-6 Macro Mysteries: Unsettled Issues and Debates

In their professional research papers, economists (micro and macro alike) often conclude with a section called unsettled issues or agenda for future research. This macro text also concludes by reviewing six issues where the debate is still most open and lively in macroeconomics.

The Exit Path from the Global Economic Crisis

The worst of the Global Economic Crisis was over by 2010, yet aggregate demand was still weak. In the United States the number of home foreclosures continued to climb, and consumer indebtedness continued to impede a swift recovery in consumer spending and residential construction, as had occurred in the early stages of previous economic expansions. Further the labor market indicators remained dismal, with the U.S. unemployment rate still above 9 percent at the end of 2010 and the incidence of long-term unemployment more severe than at any time since the Great Depression.

The most important economic puzzle of 2011–12 was how monetary and fiscal policy could best combat the hangover from the housing bubble and financial crisis. Monetary policy was handicapped by the zero lower bound on short-term interest rates, together with the Fed's inability to control directly the term premium and risk premium (see pp. 142–45). Further fiscal policy stimulus was handicapped both by a fear of further increases in the government deficit and by a widespread perception that the 2009–10 Obama fiscal stimulus had delivered only a weak boost to the economy. Economists have long understood that a fiscal stimulus has a larger multiplier if it consists of an increase in spending, particularly on measures that create jobs, than if it takes the form of a reduction in tax rates.

The theory of this book suggests two ways of delivering a fiscal stimulus. First, the balanced budget multiplier (pp. 69–72) theory shows that a simultaneous increase of government spending and of taxes by the same amount has a positive impact on aggregate demand. Second, if higher government spending raises the fiscal deficit, the resulting government debt can be bought by the Federal Reserve and thus remains inside the government; no future interest payments are required of current and future taxpayers. The best "exit strategy" for policymakers remained a matter of intense debate as this book went to press.

How Can Poor Countries Achieve Economic Growth?

As we learned in Chapter 12, many barriers prevent low-income countries from joining the rich countries in achieving high levels of per-capita income. The barriers holding back the poor countries are not the simple matters of physical and human capital investment, which are emphasized in Chapter 11. Many impoverished countries remain poor because their geography is unfavorable, their governments are corrupt, their legal systems do not protect property rights, and they do not encourage foreign trade. Some of the most fundamental barriers to economic growth are political, not a matter of simple economics. The ongoing success of China, India, Brazil, and other previously poor nations in achieving rapid economic growth sharpens the focus on the relative roles of political systems, institutions, and geography in holding back the nations that remain poor.

Why Productivity Growth Ebbs and Flows

A few years ago American economists were distressed about slow productivity growth, and Europeans are still puzzled as to why their productivity growth failed to duplicate the U.S. productivity revival after 1995. The European failure raises questions about the role of high-tech investment as a cause of the U.S. post-1995 revival, since European firms use the same types of computers and software as do American firms. The future growth of the American standard of living and the ability to pay for the major entitlement programs (Social Security, Medicare, and Medicaid) depend on achieving rapid productivity growth in the future. Yet the omens are not encouraging, as we can see in Figure 12-5 on p. 409. After robust growth in 1995–2004, productivity growth slowed markedly in 2005–08. The sharp jump in productivity growth in 2009 might seem a reason for optimism, but another interpretation is that this was the counterpart of financial panic, which caused many firms to cut costs more deeply than they would have in the past with a similar decline in output. Forecasts by experts spanned a wide range of uncertainty regarding productivity growth in the United States over the next two decades.

Why Did the Natural Rate of Unemployment Decline?

In 1996–2000 the United States experienced a "Goldilocks" economy, with sustained real income growth, the lowest unemployment rate since 1973, and relatively low inflation. Despite low unemployment, inflation did not accelerate in response, leading economists and the Fed governors to conclude that the natural rate of unemployment had fallen substantially since the late 1980s. But why did the natural rate decline after 1990? Many suggestions were offered, including weak labor unions, worker anxiety over the fear of losing jobs, competition for jobs from immigrants, the strong dollar, and the competition of foreign workers and markets operating through imports and global competition. The invention

INTERNATIONAL PERSPECTIVE

How Does Macroeconomics Differ in the United States and Europe?

Europe consists of a large number of economies that in the aggregate have a larger economy than the United States, but that taken individually are smaller. Five main features differentiate European from U.S. macroeconomics; these are (1) the greater emphasis on international macroeconomic issues, (2) the continuing puzzle of high European unemployment, (3) the failure of Europe to duplicate the U.S. productivity growth revival, (4) the reversed roles of monetary and fiscal policy, and (5) the greater dominance of the Keynesian school of thought.

International Emphasis

Since foreign trade in countries such as Belgium and the Netherlands accounts for more than half of GDP, it is natural that international issues that address the interaction of different economies play a greater role in European macroeconomics, while questions of stabilization policy at the national level play a lesser role. In the 1990s, European macroeconomics was dominated by debates over the desirability of moving toward a single European currency. The 1994 Maastricht Treaty set down criteria for the maximum inflation rates and deficit–GDP and debt–GDP ratios allowed for countries to enter the new European common currency (the euro) in 1999. The transition to the euro was complete in early 2002 when euro currency and coins replaced French francs and German marks.

Unemployment Puzzle Reversed

For more than two decades up to 2007, Europeans had been envious of the United States for achieving lower unemployment rates (see pp. 18–19). However the envy shifted direction in 2008–10 when the unemployment rate increased much more in the United States than in Europe even though the decline in the output ratio was similar on both sides of the Atlantic. As we learned on pp. 350–51 American firms tended to place primary emphasis on cutting costs and protecting their profits by cutting millions of jobs, while European firms tended

to retain employees while cutting their weekly hours, often maintaining worker wages with government subsidies. While the unemployment rate in the United States in 2010 was double that in 2007, the German unemployment rate was actually lower in 2010 than in 2007. The better overall performance of Europe in containing the rise in the unemployment rate masked a vast difference in the performance of individual countries, with the 2010 unemployment rate ranging from 3.5 percent in the Netherlands to over 20 percent in Spain incomes of a large number of low-income workers, who might have done better under the European system.

The Productivity Growth Puzzle

Europeans admire the U.S. productivity growth revival since 1995. Europe has not enjoyed the same type of revival and in fact productivity growth in Europe since 2000 has been *lower* than in the early 1990s. By one measure Europe slipped back from 88 percent of the U.S. productivity level in 1995 to 78 percent in 2009. Explanations of this center on some of the same factors that help to explain high European unemployment, including an excess of regulation. For instance, the U.S. has surged ahead in retailing productivity thanks to big-box firms such as Wal-Mart and Home Depot, but regulations in Europe make it much more difficult for similar stores to be established, partly because of land scarcity and regulations on land use.

Changing Roles for Monetary and Fiscal Policy

Between 1970 and 2001 short-term fiscal stabilization policy was largely ignored in favor of using monetary policy as the U.S. government's main tool to tame the business cycle. Fiscal policy emerged as a stimulus tool starting with the Bush tax cuts of 2001, 2003, and 2008, followed by the Obama fiscal stimulus of 2009–10. In Europe the roles of monetary and fiscal policy were quite different due to the adoption of the common euro

of the Internet and the development of Web-based job search sites may have reduced the time and expense previously required for unemployed workers to find new jobs.

Inflation Targeting Versus the Taylor Rule

Over the past two decades, the analysis of monetary policy has shifted from a debate between "rules versus activism" to a debate over the merits of alternative currency, which deprives the member nations of the euro of their ability to run an independent monetary policy. This leaves fiscal policy as the only available tool, but after 1994 even fiscal policy was handcuffed as nations struggled to reduce their deficits to meet the Maastricht criteria for joining the euro. In 2010 the euro experienced a confidence crisis due to the violation by member nations such as Greece and Ireland of the Maastricht deficit and debt criteria. Many critics view the euro as fundamentally flawed by attempting to combine a common currency without a common federal fiscal system. Instead fiscal policy decisions are made at the national level, and yet the euro's survival in 2010 depended on the willingness of nations with lower fiscal deficits and more responsible policies to bail out Greece, Ireland, and perhaps others in the future.

Keynesian Slant

As we learned in Chapter 17, the new classical macroeconomics consists both of Lucas's original version (combining market clearing, imperfect information, and rational expectations) and the real business cycle version (combining market clearing with an exclusion of demand shocks, thus relying entirely on supply shocks to explain business cycles). A notable difference in European macroeconomics in recent decades has been near-total lack of interest in new classical economics and common reliance on the Keynesian approach based on sticky prices of goods and services. The reason for this difference is not entirely clear; perhaps the emergence of persistent European unemployment since the 1980s prevented European macroeconomists from paying much attention to the new classicals. Perhaps the difference is political, since American new classicals tend to be more politically conservative than many Europeans. Or perhaps the answer is simpler: Lucas, Prescott, and other inventors of the new classical macroeconomics live in the United States, while Keynes lived on the other side of the Atlantic!

rules. A rule that targets the inflation rate has become the standard point of departure for debate and is used by the Bank of England and the European Central Bank. An alternative approach called the Taylor Rule targets *both* the inflation rate and the output ratio. Our analysis on pp. 468–71 suggests that the Fed uses a Taylor Rule rather than an inflation target and indeed has shifted to less emphasis on inflation and more on stabilizing the output ratio since 1990. In its reaction to the Global Economic Crisis of 2007–09 the Fed continued to place major emphasis on the declining output ratio as it adopted extremely expansionary policies, and there was no conflict with its secondary goal of controlling inflation because inflation was below its target rate and declining further. The Bank of England and the European Central Bank also adopted expansionary policies, showing that the primacy of inflation targeting could be abandoned when the decline in the output ratio became sufficiently severe.

Differences Among Countries

The science of comparative macroeconomics is only beginning to address the many differences among countries. Why did productivity growth in the United States accelerate after 2001 while that in Europe slowed down? Why do individuals in Italy and France save so much? Why is unemployment so high in Spain? Why did the unemployment rate in Germany actually decline between 2005 and 2010? Why do some countries such as Argentina and Brazil suffer from hyperinflations for a time but then enter a period of economic stability, whereas other nations cannot make the same transition, even if they implement similar policies? All these questions will remain the subject of active debate among macroeconomists for years, if not decades.

A Final Word

We have learned in this chapter about the evolution of events and ideas. Many important economic ideas respond to events, changes in economic behavior that are not compatible with previous economic theories. Virtually every theory discussed in this book has evolved in some way in response to changing macroeconomic behavior.

This book has emphasized that the United States does not stand alone. Macroeconomics makes no sense if it applies to one country but cannot explain events in other countries or differences in behavior among countries. The International Perspective boxes in this book help to introduce readers to important differences in macroeconomic behavior between the United States and other advanced countries. Some differences can be explained by our theories; others cannot. A careful study of these differences reveals some that are explained by macroeconomic theory but others that require knowledge of microeconomic theory and institutions to reach a full understanding.

As we end this book, one thing is sure. While there are many things we do not understand, there are many things that we do. Most notably, we understand a great deal about the causes and potential cures of the Great Depression and the 2007–09 Global Economic Crisis. We also understand the most important reasons why some formerly poor countries are making rapid economic progress yet others remain poor. Any reader of this book now qualifies as an instant critic of popular and media discussions of macroeconomics. Any reader is now equipped to dissect the many misleading journalistic statements about the economy appearing almost every day, and also to recognize those statements that reflect the remaining puzzles that truly qualify as macro mysteries.

Summary

1. Just as real-world events illustrate how theories work, sometimes real-world events make some theories obsolete and spur the invention of new theories. Many of the important theories discussed in this book

evolved from an attempt to understand surprising events.

2. The big event of the interwar period was the Great Depression. This event spawned a big idea, the

Keynesian revolution, with its emphasis on aggregate demand, sticky prices, and fiscal policy.

3. The big events of the 1947–69 period were the instability of aggregate demand due in part to the Korean and Vietnam wars, the overstimulation of the economy after 1964 by both monetary and fiscal policy, and the ensuing acceleration of inflation. Spawned in part by these events were several new ideas, including the Phillips Curve, the new economics, monetarism, and the natural rate hypothesis.

4. The main events of the 1970–2010 period were the two supply shocks of 1974–75 and 1979–81, which created twin peaks of inflation, unemployment, and interest rates as well as the 2007–09 Global Economic Crisis which created the weakest U.S. labor market since the Great Depression. New ideas spawned by these events included the real business cycle theory, concern over the twin deficits, and the suggestion that the natural rate of unemployment varies over time. An old idea revived by the Global Economic Crisis was that excess leverage can create asset bubbles, and that the collapse of asset bubbles endows the economy with a nasty multiyear hangover.

5. The main international events affecting the U.S. economy were the transition to flexible exchange rates in the early 1970s and the dislocations caused by the ups and downs of the dollar in the 1980s. The unexpected volatility of exchange rates and the resulting dislocation of trade patterns led many observers to desire a return to some version of fixed exchange rates.

6. The average level of unemployment includes frictional and structural unemployment. Cycles in unemployment, together with the volatility of inflation and interest rates, reflect the combined influence of demand shocks, supply shocks, and inflation inertia.

7. The most important macro mysteries subject to intense current debate are the best policies for the United States to adopt to revive the economy following the Global Economic Crisis, and the reasons why some poor countries remain poor while others are growing rapidly. Other remaining puzzles include the causes of revivals and slumps of productivity growth across eras and among nations; the sources of changes in the natural rate of unemployment; the merits of alternative monetary policy strategies including inflation targeting and the Taylor Rule, and finally the reasons for multidimensional differences in economic behavior across countries.

Questions

1. Explain how the period 1923–29 was consistent with the old classical approach and how the period 1930–33 was not.

2. How did the economy in the late 1930s seem to reinforce the old Keynesian school?

3. How did the behavior of the economy during World War II support the main themes of the Keynesian revolution?

4. Explain how the Great Depression and World War II changed economists' thinking about macroeconomic policy.

5. What events caused fiscal activism to fall out of favor by the end of the 1960s?

6. Explain how the events of the late 1960s gave rise to monetarism as an approach to macroeconomic policy.

7. Explain how the events of the late 1960s gave rise to the natural rate hypothesis and changed economists' view of the trade-off between unemployment and inflation.

8. What caused the twin peaks of unemployment and inflation in 1974–75 and 1980–82? What theoretical innovations developed to explain the twin peaks?

9. Why did both unemployment and inflation decline after 1982?

10. Discuss the events that caused the discrediting of a role for a monetary aggregate in conducting monetary policy.

11. What is meant by the "Goldilocks economy" of the late 1990s? How do you explain its main features?

12. The ideas of the Taylor Rule and inflation targeting were developed in the 1980s. Inflation targeting is a special case of a Taylor Rule. Evaluate the Fed's conduct of monetary policy during 1994–2007 in terms of whether the Fed appears to have been targeting inflation or the output ratio or a weighted average of the two as implied by the Taylor Rule.

13. Explain how the 1996–2000 stock market bubble differed from the 1927–29 stock market bubble and the 1987–89 stock market as well as real estate bubbles in Japan and the 2001–06 American housing market bubble.

14. Explain which old ideas were recycled in order to explain the Global Economic Crisis of 2007–09.

15. Discuss why events in the U.S. economy since 1929 demonstrate that any theory of how the economy works must allow for both demand and supply shocks.

16. Discuss how macroeconomic policy in the United States differs from Europe.

17. What events have led to increased interest in a return to fixed exchange rates?

18. Discuss why there is a debate concerning how monetary and fiscal policy can best be used to exit from the Global Economic Crisis of 2007–09.

19. Discuss some of the unsettled issues and debates related to long-term economic growth, both within and outside of the United States.

Time Series Data for the U.S. Economy: 1875–2010

Table A-1   Annual Data, 1875–2010

	Nominal GDP (X) (B $)	GDP deflator (2005 = 100)	Real GDP (Y) (B 2005 $)	Natural Real GDP (Y^N) (B 2005 $)	Unemploy. Rate (U) (Percent)	Natural Unemploy. Rate (U^N) (Percent)	Money Supply (M1) (B $)	Money Supply (M2) (B $)	Labor Productivity (Y/N) (2005 = 100)	Nominal Interest Rate (r) (Percent)	S&P Stock Price Index (1941–43 = 10)
1875	8.9	6.4	138.8	136.9	—	—	—	2.4	8.2	4.8	—
1876	8.6	6.1	140.4	145.7	—	—	—	2.4	8.4	4.6	—
1877	8.8	6.1	144.8	155.1	—	—	—	2.3	8.6	4.6	—
1878	8.6	5.7	151.0	165.1	—	—	—	2.2	8.7	4.5	—
1879	9.4	5.5	169.5	175.7	—	—	—	2.3	8.9	4.3	—
1880	11.0	5.8	189.6	187.0	—	—	—	2.8	9.0	4.2	—
1881	11.3	5.8	196.3	192.6	—	—	—	3.3	9.0	4.0	—
1882	12.4	5.9	208.7	198.3	—	—	—	3.6	9.1	4.0	—
1883	12.2	5.7	213.9	204.2	—	—	—	3.8	9.1	4.0	—
1884	11.9	5.5	217.8	210.2	—	—	—	3.8	9.1	4.0	—
1885	11.7	5.3	219.4	216.4	—	—	—	3.9	9.2	3.9	—
1886	12.0	5.3	226.0	222.9	—	—	—	4.2	9.3	3.7	—
1887	12.6	5.3	236.2	229.5	—	—	—	4.5	9.3	3.7	—
1888	12.7	5.4	235.1	236.3	—	—	—	4.7	9.4	3.7	—
1889	13.5	5.4	249.7	243.3	—	—	—	4.9	9.4	3.6	—
1890	13.4	5.3	253.2	250.5	4.0	4.5	—	5.4	9.2	3.7	—
1891	13.8	5.3	261.4	257.9	5.4	4.5	—	5.6	9.3	3.8	—
1892	14.3	5.2	273.8	267.7	3.0	4.5	—	6.1	9.4	3.7	—
1893	14.3	5.2	273.7	277.8	11.7	4.5	—	5.9	9.5	3.8	—
1894	13.1	4.9	265.7	288.4	18.4	4.5	—	5.9	9.6	3.6	—
1895	14.5	4.9	296.8	299.3	13.7	4.5	—	6.1	10.1	3.6	—
1896	14.2	4.9	290.0	310.6	14.4	4.5	—	6.0	9.8	3.6	—
1897	15.1	4.8	313.7	322.4	14.5	4.5	—	6.4	10.3	3.5	—
1898	15.7	4.9	321.2	334.6	12.4	4.5	—	7.3	10.5	3.4	—
1899	17.8	5.0	358.4	347.3	6.5	4.5	—	8.4	10.9	3.4	—
1900	18.5	5.1	365.4	360.5	5.0	4.5	—	9.1	11.0	3.4	6.1
1901	20.9	5.1	410.1	374.5	4.0	4.5	—	10.3	11.8	3.4	7.8
1902	21.6	5.2	417.2	389.0	3.7	4.5	—	11.3	11.5	3.4	8.4
1903	22.8	5.3	429.2	404.1	3.9	4.5	—	12.0	11.5	3.6	7.2
1904	23.9	5.4	445.5	419.8	5.4	4.5	—	12.7	12.1	3.6	7.0
1905	26.1	5.4	486.2	436.1	4.3	4.6	—	14.1	12.6	3.6	9.0
1906	28.0	5.5	506.3	453.0	1.7	4.6	—	15.3	12.6	3.6	9.6
1907	28.8	5.8	498.5	470.6	2.8	4.6	—	16.0	12.2	3.7	8.1
1908	26.6	5.7	471.2	488.9	8.0	4.6	—	15.8	12.0	3.7	7.8

Continued

	Nominal GDP (X) (B $)	GDP deflator (2005 = 100)	Real GDP (Y) (B 2005 $)	Natural Real GDP (Y^N) (B 2005 $)	Unemploy. Rate (U) (Percent)	Natural Unemploy. Rate (U^N) (Percent)	Money Supply (M1) (B $)	Money Supply (M2) (B $)	Labor Productivity (Y/N) (2005 = 100)	Nominal Interest Rate (r) (Percent)	S&P Stock Price Index (1941–43 = 10)
1909	29.8	5.9	526.2	507.8	5.1	4.6	—	17.5	12.8	3.7	9.7
1910	31.1	5.9	528.4	527.5	5.9	4.6	—	18.3	12.5	3.8	9.4
1911	32.0	5.9	545.3	548.0	6.7	4.6	—	19.4	12.6	3.8	9.2
1912	34.7	6.0	576.8	569.3	4.6	4.6	—	20.8	13.0	3.8	9.5
1913	36.4	6.1	599.5	591.4	4.3	4.6	—	21.7	13.3	3.9	8.5
1914	34.1	6.2	554.1	608.7	7.9	4.6	—	22.6	12.6	1.9	4.1
1915	36.2	6.3	574.6	626.5	8.5	4.6	12.2	24.2	13.2	4.0	8.3
1916	45.9	6.9	667.8	644.8	5.1	4.6	14.3	28.9	14.2	3.9	9.5
1917	54.9	8.2	667.6	663.7	4.6	4.6	16.7	33.7	14.0	4.1	8.5
1918	69.5	9.7	719.0	683.1	1.4	4.7	18.5	36.8	15.2	4.3	7.5
1919	77.0	11.0	698.2	703.1	1.4	4.7	21.3	42.7	15.2	4.3	9.2
1920	86.9	12.7	683.3	723.7	5.2	4.7	23.2	48.0	14.7	4.9	8.3
1921	73.0	11.1	659.3	744.9	11.7	4.7	21.0	45.2	15.8	5.1	7.2
1922	72.7	10.3	706.5	766.7	6.7	4.7	21.2	46.5	15.7	4.3	8.7
1923	85.3	10.6	805.5	789.1	2.4	4.7	22.4	50.4	16.6	4.3	8.9
1924	87.6	10.6	826.8	812.2	5.0	4.7	23.2	53.2	17.5	4.1	9.4
1925	91.1	10.8	845.4	836.0	3.2	4.7	25.1	57.9	17.2	3.8	11.6
1926	97.2	10.8	896.2	860.4	1.8	4.8	25.6	60.3	17.7	3.5	13.0
1927	96.0	10.7	901.2	885.6	3.3	4.8	25.5	61.6	17.9	3.3	15.3
1928	97.0	10.6	917.9	911.6	4.2	4.8	25.8	63.9	18.0	3.3	19.4
1929	103.6	10.6	976.9	938.2	3.2	4.8	26.0	64.2	18.8	3.5	24.7
1930	91.2	10.2	892.6	972.0	8.9	4.8	25.2	63.0	18.3	3.5	19.4
1931	76.5	9.2	835.1	1007.0	16.3	4.8	23.6	58.9	18.2	4.4	12.2
1932	58.7	8.1	725.6	1042.8	24.1	5.0	20.7	49.6	17.9	5.7	6.3
1933	56.4	7.9	716.4	1081.1	25.2	5.0	19.5	44.4	17.7	4.7	8.2
1934	66.0	8.3	794.6	1121.5	22.0	5.0	21.4	47.5	19.3	3.8	9.4
1935	73.3	8.5	864.9	1162.4	20.3	5.0	25.3	53.9	19.8	3.5	10.2
1936	83.8	8.6	978.3	1203.5	17.0	5.0	28.8	60.0	21.0	2.9	14.4
1937	91.9	8.9	1028.3	1247.7	14.3	5.1	30.2	63.0	20.8	3.0	14.4
1938	86.1	8.7	992.4	1291.2	19.1	5.1	29.8	62.7	21.7	3.5	10.8
1939	92.2	8.6	1073.2	1338.5	17.2	5.1	33.4	67.9	22.3	3.0	11.6
1940	101.4	8.7	1166.6	1386.1	14.6	5.1	38.8	76.1	23.0	2.8	10.8
1941	126.7	9.3	1365.7	1439.2	9.9	5.1	45.4	86.2	24.9	2.8	9.8
1942	161.9	10.0	1618.2	1490.9	4.7	5.1	54.1	98.2	27.4	2.8	8.7
1943	198.6	10.5	1883.0	1546.5	1.9	5.2	70.6	123.9	31.2	2.7	11.5
1944	219.8	10.8	2035.6	1601.8	1.2	5.2	83.3	147.2	34.3	2.7	12.5
1945	223.0	11.1	2011.9	1657.9	1.9	5.2	97.0	174.5	35.5	2.6	15.2
1946	222.2	12.4	1791.9	1719.4	3.9	5.2	104.1	191.1	28.6	2.5	17.1
1947	244.1	13.7	1776.2	1782.9	3.9	5.2	109.2	201.3	27.2	2.6	15.2
1948	269.1	14.5	1854.1	1842.7	3.8	5.3	109.7	204.1	28.0	2.8	15.5
1949	267.2	14.5	1844.5	1911.2	6.1	5.3	108.6	203.2	28.9	2.7	15.2
1950	293.7	14.6	2005.6	1982.1	5.2	5.3	111.5	207.9	30.8	2.6	18.4
1951	339.3	15.7	2161.4	2055.7	3.3	5.3	116.5	215.7	31.7	2.9	22.3
1952	358.3	16.0	2243.9	2139.0	3.0	5.3	122.3	227.4	32.2	3.0	24.5
1953	379.3	16.2	2347.0	2226.5	2.9	5.3	125.4	235.9	33.0	3.2	24.7
1954	380.4	16.3	2332.6	2311.6	5.6	5.3	127.3	244.2	33.6	2.9	29.7
1955	414.7	16.6	2500.2	2401.8	4.4	5.3	131.4	253.3	35.0	3.1	40.5
1956	437.4	17.2	2549.5	2488.3	4.1	5.3	133.0	257.6	34.7	3.4	46.6
1957	461.1	17.7	2601.3	2578.5	4.3	5.3	133.7	264.4	35.6	3.9	44.4
1958	467.2	18.1	2577.8	2675.6	6.8	5.3	135.2	277.3	36.4	3.8	46.2
1959	506.6	18.3	2762.3	2773.6	5.5	5.3	140.4	293.3	37.7	4.4	57.4

	Nominal GDP (X) (B $)	GDP deflator (2005 = 100)	Real GDP (Y) (B 2005 $)	Natural Real GDP (Y^N) (B 2005 $)	Unemploy. Rate (U) (Percent)	Natural Unemploy. Rate (U^N) (Percent)	Money Supply (M1) (B $)	Money Supply (M2) (B $)	Labor Productivity (Y/N) (2005 = 100)	Nominal Interest Rate (r) (Percent)	S&P Stock Price Index (1941–43 = 10)
1960	526.4	18.6	2830.7	2878.1	5.5	5.3	140.3	304.3	38.2	4.4	55.9
1961	544.8	18.8	2897.1	2988.3	6.7	5.4	143.1	324.8	39.4	4.4	66.3
1962	585.7	19.1	3072.6	3102.3	5.6	5.5	146.5	350.1	41.1	4.3	62.4
1963	617.8	19.3	3206.9	3224.1	5.6	5.6	151.0	379.6	42.6	4.3	69.9
1964	663.6	19.6	3392.1	3352.2	5.2	5.6	156.8	409.3	43.9	4.4	81.4
1965	719.1	19.9	3610.1	3486.6	4.5	5.7	163.4	442.5	45.2	4.5	88.2
1966	787.7	20.5	3845.4	3625.9	3.8	6.0	171.0	471.4	46.8	5.1	85.3
1967	832.4	21.1	3942.2	3760.3	3.8	6.2	177.7	503.6	47.6	5.5	91.9
1968	909.8	22.0	4133.2	3904.8	3.6	6.3	190.1	545.3	49.3	6.2	98.7
1969	984.4	23.1	4261.7	4053.2	3.5	6.3	201.4	578.7	49.3	7.0	97.8
1970	1038.3	24.3	4269.9	4206.7	5.0	6.2	209.1	601.5	50.1	8.0	83.2
1971	1126.8	25.5	4413.1	4372.5	6.0	6.2	223.1	674.4	52.1	7.4	98.3
1972	1237.9	26.6	4647.8	4544.8	5.6	6.1	239.0	758.2	53.8	7.2	109.2
1973	1382.3	28.1	4917.1	4720.4	4.9	6.1	256.3	831.8	55.5	7.4	107.4
1974	1499.5	30.7	4890.1	4890.3	5.6	6.2	269.1	880.6	54.6	8.6	82.9
1975	1637.7	33.6	4879.5	5071.3	8.5	6.1	281.3	963.5	56.1	8.8	86.2
1976	1824.6	35.5	5141.3	5245.7	7.7	6.2	297.2	1086.5	58.0	8.4	102.0
1977	2030.1	37.8	5377.6	5421.5	7.1	6.3	319.9	1221.2	58.9	8.0	98.2
1978	2293.8	40.4	5677.7	5602.0	6.1	6.4	346.2	1322.2	59.7	8.7	96.0
1979	2562.2	43.8	5855.0	5784.1	5.9	6.4	372.6	1425.7	59.4	9.6	103.0
1980	2788.1	47.8	5838.8	5972.0	7.2	6.5	395.7	1540.2	59.3	11.9	118.8
1981	3126.8	52.2	5987.2	6165.5	7.6	6.3	425.0	1679.3	60.1	14.2	128.1
1982	3253.2	55.4	5870.9	6380.0	9.7	6.1	453.0	1832.6	59.5	13.8	119.7
1983	3534.6	57.6	6136.1	6571.7	9.6	6.0	503.2	2056.9	62.2	12.0	160.4
1984	3930.9	59.8	6577.2	6756.9	7.5	6.0	538.6	2221.2	63.4	12.7	160.5
1985	4217.5	61.6	6849.3	6954.7	7.2	6.0	587.0	2419.0	64.4	11.4	186.8
1986	4460.1	62.9	7086.6	7150.6	7.0	6.1	666.3	2615.8	66.4	9.0	236.3
1987	4736.4	64.8	7313.3	7346.4	6.2	6.2	743.6	2786.0	66.7	9.4	286.8
1988	5100.4	67.0	7613.9	7552.8	5.5	6.3	774.8	2936.2	67.8	9.7	265.8
1989	5482.1	69.5	7885.9	7773.3	5.3	6.3	782.2	3059.7	68.3	9.3	322.8
1990	5800.5	72.2	8033.8	8004.4	5.6	6.2	810.6	3227.2	69.6	9.3	334.6
1991	5992.1	74.8	8015.1	8249.5	6.9	6.0	859.0	3346.4	70.7	8.8	376.2
1992	6342.3	76.5	8287.0	8501.2	7.5	5.8	965.9	3408.3	73.5	8.1	415.7
1993	6667.4	78.2	8523.5	8753.5	6.9	5.6	1078.4	3444.1	73.9	7.2	451.4
1994	7085.2	79.9	8870.7	9007.3	6.1	5.5	1145.2	3490.2	74.7	8.0	460.4
1995	7414.7	81.5	9093.8	9274.5	5.6	5.4	1143.0	3562.4	75.0	7.6	541.7
1996	7838.5	83.1	9434.0	9559.2	5.4	5.3	1106.8	3735.0	76.9	7.4	670.5
1997	8332.4	84.6	9854.4	9863.6	4.9	5.3	1070.2	3922.4	78.1	7.3	873.4
1998	8793.5	85.5	10283.5	10188.0	4.5	5.2	1080.7	4202.2	80.4	6.5	1085.5
1999	9353.5	86.8	10779.9	10530.8	4.2	5.1	1102.3	4512.3	83.0	7.1	1327.3
2000	9951.5	88.6	11226.0	10881.8	4.0	5.1	1103.7	4781.9	85.9	7.6	1427.2
2001	10286.2	90.7	11347.2	11228.5	4.7	5.1	1140.3	5199.0	88.4	7.1	1194.2
2002	10642.3	92.1	11552.9	11578.9	5.8	5.1	1196.3	5592.4	92.4	6.5	993.9
2003	11142.1	94.1	11840.7	11925.3	6.0	5.1	1273.5	5977.6	95.7	5.7	965.2
2004	11867.8	96.8	12263.9	12266.7	5.5	5.1	1344.2	6257.1	98.4	5.6	1130.7
2005	12638.4	100.0	12638.4	12605.5	5.1	4.9	1371.6	6523.1	100.0	5.2	1207.2
2006	13398.9	103.3	12976.3	12945.2	4.6	4.8	1374.2	6865.8	100.9	5.6	1310.5
2007	14061.8	106.3	13228.9	13295.2	4.6	4.8	1372.2	7298.5	102.5	5.6	1477.2
2008	14369.1	108.6	13228.9	13642.1	5.8	4.8	1433.1	7816.8	103.6	5.6	1220.0
2009	14119	109.6	12880.5	13987.5	9.3	5.1	1636.8	8432.1	107.2	5.3	948.1
2010	14660.2	110.7	13248.7	14341.5	9.6	5.3	1743.8	8629.3	111.0	4.9	—

Table A-2   Quarterly Data, 1947:Q1 to 2007:Q4

	Nominal GDP (X) (B $)	GDP Deflator (2005 = 100)	Real GDP (Y) (B 2005$)	Natural Real GDP (Y^N) (B 2005$)	Unemploy. Rate (U) (Percent)	Natural Unemploy. Rate (U^N) (Percent)	Money Supply (M1) (B $)	Money Supply (M2) (B $)	Labor Productivity (Y/N) (2005 = 100)	Nominal Interest Rate (I) (Percent)	Real Federal Budget Surplus (B 2005$)	Trade-Weighted Exchange Rate (Mar 1973 = 100)
1947:Q1	237.2	13.4	1772.2	1781.5	3.9	5.2	107.8	198.0	26.8	2.6	44.8	—
1947:Q2	240.4	13.6	1769.5	1792.6	3.9	5.2	109.5	200.9	27.5	2.5	38.3	—
1947:Q3	244.5	13.8	1768.0	1803.9	3.9	5.2	110.5	203.1	26.7	2.6	14.5	—
1947:Q4	254.3	14.2	1794.8	1815.2	3.9	5.3	111.0	204.9	27.8	2.8	56.5	—
1948:Q1	260.3	14.3	1823.4	1826.5	3.7	5.3	111.0	205.5	27.9	2.8	54.6	—
1948:Q2	267.3	14.4	1856.9	1838.0	3.7	5.3	110.0	204.4	27.9	2.8	35.4	—
1948:Q3	273.8	14.7	1866.9	1853.2	3.8	5.3	110.1	204.7	27.9	2.8	9.5	—
1948:Q4	275.1	14.7	1869.8	1868.7	3.8	5.3	109.7	204.2	28.1	2.8	1.4	—
1949:Q1	269.9	14.6	1843.8	1884.3	4.7	5.3	109.2	203.6	28.3	2.7	−23.2	—
1949:Q2	266.2	14.5	1837.1	1900.0	5.9	5.3	109.3	204.1	28.6	2.7	−44.9	—
1949:Q3	267.6	14.4	1857.7	1915.7	6.7	5.3	109.0	203.7	29.4	2.6	−45.1	—
1949:Q4	265.2	14.4	1840.3	1931.2	7.0	5.3	109.0	203.7	29.1	2.6	−42.3	—
1950:Q1	275.2	14.4	1914.6	1946.6	6.4	5.3	109.9	205.3	30.2	2.6	−57.7	—
1950:Q2	284.5	14.4	1972.9	1961.9	5.6	5.3	111.6	208.0	30.5	2.6	19.4	—
1950:Q3	301.9	14.7	2050.1	1983.0	4.6	5.3	112.8	209.5	31.2	2.6	92.3	—
1950:Q4	313.3	15.0	2086.2	2003.7	4.2	5.3	113.7	210.7	31.3	2.7	94.5	—
1951:Q1	329.0	15.6	2112.5	2024.2	3.5	5.3	115.0	212.5	31.3	2.7	111.1	—
1951:Q2	336.6	15.7	2147.6	2045.2	3.1	5.3	116.1	214.2	31.2	2.9	64.4	—
1951:Q3	343.5	15.7	2190.4	2066.8	3.2	5.3	117.6	217.1	32.0	2.9	34.4	—
1951:Q4	347.9	15.9	2194.1	2086.7	3.4	5.3	119.7	220.9	32.0	3.0	37.8	—
1952:Q1	351.2	15.8	2216.2	2107.5	3.1	5.3	121.3	224.1	32.1	3.0	43.5	—
1952:Q2	352.1	15.9	2218.6	2127.6	3.0	5.3	122.2	226.3	32.1	2.9	21.4	—
1952:Q3	358.5	16.1	2233.5	2148.5	3.2	5.3	123.5	229.1	32.0	2.9	6.9	—
1952:Q4	371.4	16.1	2307.2	2172.3	2.8	5.3	124.8	232.0	32.6	3.0	21.7	—
1953:Q1	378.4	16.1	2350.4	2195.3	2.7	5.3	125.3	233.7	32.8	3.1	26.7	—
1953:Q2	382.0	16.1	2368.2	2216.9	2.6	5.3	126.1	236.0	32.9	3.3	16.1	—
1953:Q3	381.1	16.2	2353.8	2237.0	2.7	5.3	126.3	237.4	33.1	3.3	21.6	—
1953:Q4	375.9	16.2	2316.5	2256.8	3.7	5.3	126.4	238.9	32.9	3.1	−19.7	—
1954:Q1	375.2	16.3	2305.5	2278.3	5.3	5.3	126.7	240.9	33.0	3.0	−20.9	—
1954:Q2	376.0	16.3	2308.4	2300.4	5.8	5.3	127.0	243.1	33.2	2.9	−12.3	—
1954:Q3	380.8	16.3	2334.4	2322.6	6.0	5.3	128.2	246.4	33.8	2.9	−8.6	—
1954:Q4	389.4	16.4	2381.2	2345.1	5.3	5.3	129.6	249.0	34.2	2.9	0.0	—
1955:Q1	402.6	16.4	2449.7	2368.3	4.7	5.3	131.0	251.8	34.8	3.0	21.3	—
1955:Q2	410.9	16.5	2490.3	2390.9	4.4	5.3	131.8	253.4	34.9	3.0	40.6	—
1955:Q3	419.4	16.6	2523.5	2413.3	4.1	5.3	132.4	254.7	35.0	3.1	28.9	—
1955:Q4	426.0	16.8	2537.6	2434.8	4.2	5.3	132.6	255.6	34.9	3.1	45.9	—
1956:Q1	428.3	17.0	2526.1	2455.5	4.0	5.3	133.1	256.3	34.5	3.1	50.1	—
1956:Q2	434.2	17.1	2545.9	2477.3	4.2	5.3	133.4	257.6	34.6	3.3	38.7	—
1956:Q3	439.2	17.3	2542.7	2498.8	4.1	5.3	133.5	258.7	34.6	3.4	44.6	—
1956:Q4	448.1	17.3	2584.3	2521.6	4.1	5.3	134.1	260.3	34.9	3.7	41.5	—
1957:Q1	457.2	17.6	2600.2	2544.1	3.9	5.3	134.4	262.5	35.3	3.7	34.7	—
1957:Q2	459.2	17.7	2593.9	2566.6	4.1	5.3	134.4	264.4	35.2	3.8	24.3	—
1957:Q3	466.4	17.8	2618.9	2590.0	4.2	5.3	134.6	266.2	35.7	4.1	24.1	—
1957:Q4	461.5	17.8	2591.3	2613.4	4.9	5.3	133.7	266.9	35.9	4.0	−9.0	—
1958:Q1	453.9	18.0	2521.2	2639.8	6.3	5.3	133.6	269.7	35.3	3.6	−18.3	—
1958:Q2	458.0	18.1	2536.6	2664.4	7.4	5.3	135.1	276.3	36.0	3.6	−46.5	—

	Nominal GDP (X) (B $)	GDP Deflator (2005 = 100)	Real GDP (Y) (B 2005$)	Natural Real GDP (Y^N) (B 2005$)	Unemploy. Rate (U) (Percent)	Natural Unemploy. Rate (U^N) (Percent)	Money Supply (M1) (B $)	Money Supply (M2) (B $)	Labor Productivity (Y/N) (2005 = 100)	Nominal Interest Rate (I) (Percent)	Real Federal Budget Surplus (B 2005$)	Trade-Weighted Exchange Rate (Mar 1973 = 100)
1958:Q3	471.7	18.2	2596.1	2687.3	7.3	5.3	136.5	281.2	36.7	3.9	−35.8	—
1958:Q4	485.0	18.3	2656.6	2711.0	6.4	5.3	138.2	284.5	37.3	4.1	−19.7	—
1959:Q1	495.5	18.3	2710.3	2735.6	5.8	5.3	139.3	287.8	37.3	4.1	17.0	—
1959:Q2	508.5	18.3	2778.8	2760.7	5.1	5.3	140.5	292.1	37.8	4.4	27.9	—
1959:Q3	509.3	18.4	2775.5	2786.1	5.3	5.3	141.5	296.1	37.8	4.5	15.3	—
1959:Q4	513.2	18.4	2785.2	2811.9	5.6	5.3	140.3	297.1	37.7	4.6	10.9	—
1960:Q1	527.0	18.5	2847.7	2837.8	5.1	5.3	139.9	298.7	38.6	4.6	62.7	—
1960:Q2	526.2	18.6	2834.4	2864.1	5.2	5.3	139.6	301.1	38.1	4.5	44.2	—
1960:Q3	529.0	18.6	2839.0	2891.0	5.5	5.3	140.9	306.5	38.1	4.3	35.4	—
1960:Q4	523.7	18.7	2802.6	2919.8	6.3	5.4	140.8	310.9	37.6	4.3	11.2	—
1961:Q1	528.0	18.7	2819.3	2947.6	6.8	5.4	141.5	316.3	38.1	4.3	12.8	117.1
1961:Q2	539.0	18.8	2872.0	2974.3	7.0	5.4	142.6	322.1	39.2	4.3	3.7	116.8
1961:Q3	549.5	18.8	2918.4	3001.8	6.8	5.4	143.4	327.6	39.7	4.4	12.7	117.7
1961:Q4	562.6	18.9	2977.8	3029.5	6.2	5.5	144.7	333.3	40.1	4.4	24.3	117.8
1962:Q1	576.1	19.0	3031.2	3058.0	5.6	5.5	145.6	340.2	40.8	4.4	12.1	118.0
1962:Q2	583.2	19.0	3064.7	3087.2	5.5	5.5	146.6	347.4	40.7	4.3	11.0	118.6
1962:Q3	590.0	19.1	3093.0	3116.8	5.6	5.5	146.5	352.8	41.2	4.3	15.7	118.7
1962:Q4	593.3	19.1	3100.6	3147.1	5.5	5.5	147.3	359.9	41.5	4.3	12.0	118.5
1963:Q1	602.5	19.2	3141.1	3177.4	5.8	5.6	148.8	367.9	41.8	4.2	20.9	118.6
1963:Q2	611.2	19.2	3180.4	3208.3	5.7	5.6	150.2	375.9	42.2	4.2	32.3	118.8
1963:Q3	623.9	19.3	3240.3	3239.5	5.5	5.6	151.7	383.6	43.0	4.3	30.1	118.8
1963:Q4	633.5	19.4	3265.0	3271.2	5.6	5.6	153.2	391.0	43.1	4.3	26.3	118.8
1964:Q1	649.6	19.5	3338.2	3303.5	5.5	5.6	154.2	397.5	43.5	4.4	9.8	118.8
1964:Q2	658.9	19.5	3376.6	3335.8	5.2	5.6	155.2	404.3	43.8	4.4	−13.8	118.8
1964:Q3	670.5	19.6	3422.5	3368.5	5.0	5.6	157.8	413.5	44.1	4.4	6.1	118.8
1964:Q4	675.6	19.7	3432.0	3400.9	5.0	5.6	159.8	422.0	43.7	4.4	15.7	118.6
1965:Q1	695.7	19.8	3516.3	3434.9	4.9	5.6	161.0	430.4	44.3	4.4	37.9	118.6
1965:Q2	708.1	19.9	3564.0	3468.6	4.7	5.6	162.0	437.5	44.6	4.4	33.7	118.8
1965:Q3	725.2	19.9	3636.3	3503.5	4.4	5.7	163.9	446.1	45.4	4.5	−2.5	118.9
1965:Q4	747.5	20.1	3724.0	3539.6	4.1	5.8	166.8	455.8	46.2	4.6	−3.5	118.8
1966:Q1	770.8	20.2	3815.4	3576.5	3.9	5.8	169.7	464.6	46.8	4.8	24.3	118.8
1966:Q2	779.9	20.4	3828.1	3609.0	3.8	5.9	171.6	470.2	46.6	5.0	16.7	118.9
1966:Q3	793.1	20.6	3853.3	3642.2	3.8	6.0	171.0	473.0	46.6	5.3	7.3	118.8
1966:Q4	806.9	20.8	3884.5	3675.9	3.7	6.1	171.5	477.7	46.9	5.4	−3.9	119.0
1967:Q1	817.8	20.9	3918.7	3709.9	3.8	6.1	173.2	485.5	47.3	5.1	−46.0	118.9
1967:Q2	822.3	21.0	3919.6	3742.5	3.8	6.1	175.6	497.1	47.5	5.3	−49.6	118.8
1967:Q3	837.0	21.2	3950.8	3776.9	3.8	6.2	179.5	510.6	47.6	5.6	−40.1	118.8
1967:Q4	852.7	21.4	3981.0	3811.8	3.9	6.3	182.4	521.4	47.8	6.0	−41.6	119.7
1968:Q1	879.8	21.7	4063.0	3849.6	3.7	6.3	184.8	530.3	48.9	6.1	−27.7	121.1
1968:Q2	904.1	21.9	4132.0	3887.4	3.6	6.4	188.0	539.1	49.3	6.3	−34.3	121.2
1968:Q3	919.3	22.1	4160.3	3923.3	3.5	6.4	191.7	549.5	49.3	6.1	6.3	121.2
1968:Q4	936.2	22.4	4178.3	3959.1	3.4	6.4	195.8	562.3	49.2	6.2	10.7	121.1
1969:Q1	960.9	22.6	4244.1	3997.9	3.4	6.3	199.3	571.9	49.6	6.7	63.6	121.3
1969:Q2	976.1	22.9	4256.5	4034.3	3.4	6.3	200.9	576.9	49.2	6.9	49.7	121.4
1969:Q3	996.3	23.3	4283.4	4072.1	3.6	6.3	201.8	580.6	49.2	7.1	23.6	122.3
1969:Q4	1004.5	23.6	4263.3	4108.4	3.6	6.3	203.5	585.6	49.0	7.5	12.7	121.0
1970:Q1	1017.1	23.9	4256.6	4146.5	4.2	6.2	205.6	587.7	49.1	7.9	−10.5	120.8
1970:Q2	1033.1	24.2	4264.3	4186.1	4.8	6.2	207.2	591.7	49.9	8.1	−66.9	120.3
1970:Q3	1050.5	24.4	4302.3	4226.8	5.2	6.2	209.9	605.1	50.7	8.2	−80.7	119.8

Continued

	Nominal GDP (X) (B $)	GDP Deflator (2005 = 100)	Real GDP (Y) (B 2005$)	Natural Real GDP (Y^N) (B 2005$)	Unemploy. Rate (U) (Percent)	Natural Unemploy. Rate (U^N) (Percent)	Money Supply (M1) (B $)	Money Supply (M2) (B $)	Labor Productivity (Y/N) (2005 = 100)	Nominal Interest Rate (I) (Percent)	Real Federal Budget Surplus (B 2005$)	Trade-Weighted Exchange Rate (Mar 1973 = 100)
1970:Q4	1052.7	24.7	4256.6	4267.3	5.8	6.2	213.7	621.3	50.2	7.9	−95.0	119.7
1971:Q1	1098.1	25.1	4374.0	4309.6	5.9	6.2	217.2	641.3	51.7	7.2	−95.2	119.4
1971:Q2	1118.8	25.4	4398.8	4351.4	5.9	6.2	221.8	666.0	51.9	7.5	−119.5	118.8
1971:Q3	1139.1	25.7	4433.9	4393.5	6.0	6.2	225.7	685.9	52.3	7.6	−114.8	116.7
1971:Q4	1151.4	25.9	4446.3	4435.7	5.9	6.1	227.8	704.4	51.9	7.3	−119.7	113.0
1972:Q1	1190.1	26.3	4525.8	4478.9	5.8	6.1	232.2	725.6	52.6	7.2	−87.1	108.4
1972:Q2	1225.6	26.5	4633.1	4523.2	5.7	6.1	236.0	743.8	53.7	7.3	−106.6	107.6
1972:Q3	1249.3	26.7	4677.5	4566.4	5.6	6.1	241.0	768.8	54.0	7.2	−64.0	108.1
1972:Q4	1286.6	27.1	4754.5	4610.6	5.4	6.0	246.9	794.4	54.4	7.1	−116.0	109.0
1973:Q1	1335.1	27.4	4876.2	4656.8	4.9	6.1	251.8	813.2	55.7	7.2	−55.5	104.0
1973:Q2	1371.5	27.8	4932.6	4700.5	4.9	6.1	254.8	826.6	55.7	7.3	−54.7	99.7
1973:Q3	1390.7	28.3	4906.3	4740.6	4.8	6.1	257.7	838.2	55.2	7.6	−37.4	97.3
1973:Q4	1431.8	28.9	4953.1	4783.7	4.8	6.2	261.0	849.0	54.9	7.7	−21.4	99.9
1974:Q1	1446.5	29.5	4909.6	4824.7	5.1	6.2	265.3	864.7	54.8	7.9	−30.2	103.6
1974:Q2	1484.8	30.2	4922.2	4867.9	5.2	6.2	267.8	875.1	54.7	8.4	−37.8	99.8
1974:Q3	1513.7	31.1	4873.5	4911.7	5.6	6.2	270.1	884.5	54.1	9.0	−36.4	102.5
1974:Q4	1552.8	32.0	4854.3	4957.1	6.6	6.1	273.4	898.0	54.6	9.0	−82.5	102.3
1975:Q1	1569.4	32.7	4795.3	5005.2	8.3	6.1	275.1	915.1	55.0	8.7	−148.2	99.4
1975:Q2	1605.0	33.2	4831.9	5050.2	8.9	6.0	279.3	948.7	55.9	8.9	−318.2	100.1
1975:Q3	1662.4	33.8	4913.3	5093.1	8.5	6.1	284.5	983.2	56.5	8.9	−188.3	104.4
1975:Q4	1713.9	34.4	4977.5	5136.8	8.3	6.1	286.4	1007.0	56.5	8.8	−187.6	105.6
1976:Q1	1771.9	34.8	5090.7	5179.4	7.7	6.1	290.6	1039.0	57.4	8.6	−156.0	105.6
1976:Q2	1804.2	35.2	5128.9	5223.6	7.6	6.2	295.6	1070.2	57.9	8.5	−142.1	106.8
1976:Q3	1837.7	35.7	5154.1	5267.9	7.7	6.2	298.6	1098.6	58.0	8.5	−150.3	106.2
1976:Q4	1884.5	36.3	5191.5	5312.0	7.8	6.3	303.9	1138.4	58.2	8.2	−156.5	107.0
1977:Q1	1938.5	36.9	5251.8	5355.7	7.5	6.3	311.2	1177.1	58.5	8.0	−127.9	107.3
1977:Q2	2005.2	37.4	5356.1	5399.2	7.1	6.3	317.3	1208.8	58.8	8.0	−110.3	106.9
1977:Q3	2066.0	37.9	5451.9	5443.4	6.9	6.3	322.3	1236.6	59.3	7.9	−124.8	106.2
1977:Q4	2110.8	38.7	5450.8	5487.8	6.7	6.4	328.6	1262.2	58.5	8.1	−125.8	103.9
1978:Q1	2149.1	39.3	5469.4	5532.8	6.3	6.4	335.6	1285.8	58.6	8.5	−123.7	100.7
1978:Q2	2274.7	40.0	5684.6	5579.1	6.0	6.4	343.9	1309.8	59.7	8.7	−69.7	99.7
1978:Q3	2335.2	40.7	5740.3	5624.9	6.0	6.4	349.8	1334.2	59.7	8.8	−53.8	94.8
1978:Q4	2416.0	41.5	5816.2	5671.2	5.9	6.4	355.3	1359.1	60.1	9.0	−41.4	93.6
1979:Q1	2463.3	42.3	5825.9	5715.9	5.9	6.4	360.3	1379.1	59.5	9.3	−20.6	94.9
1979:Q2	2526.4	43.3	5831.4	5760.9	5.7	6.4	370.3	1411.8	59.4	9.4	−20.5	96.3
1979:Q3	2599.7	44.3	5873.3	5806.9	5.9	6.5	378.4	1445.2	59.3	9.3	−33.0	94.6
1979:Q4	2659.4	45.2	5889.5	5852.9	6.0	6.5	381.1	1466.7	59.2	10.5	−52.3	96.6
1980:Q1	2724.1	46.1	5908.5	5899.3	6.3	6.5	388.1	1492.4	59.4	12.1	−73.1	96.6
1980:Q2	2728.0	47.1	5787.4	5948.2	7.3	6.5	385.9	1514.6	58.8	11.2	−122.2	96.1
1980:Q3	2785.2	48.2	5776.6	5997.3	7.7	6.5	399.3	1560.3	59.0	11.6	−148.9	93.4
1980:Q4	2915.3	49.6	5883.5	6043.2	7.4	6.5	409.4	1593.5	59.6	12.8	−127.9	95.2
1981:Q1	3051.4	50.8	6005.7	6090.2	7.4	6.4	415.0	1620.7	60.6	13.2	−83.8	98.2
1981:Q2	3084.3	51.8	5957.8	6140.8	7.4	6.3	425.8	1664.6	59.8	14.0	−90.6	104.5
1981:Q3	3177.0	52.7	6030.2	6188.9	7.4	6.3	426.9	1694.1	60.3	14.9	−103.6	109.8
1981:Q4	3194.7	53.6	5955.1	6242.4	8.2	6.2	432.1	1737.8	59.5	14.6	−154.7	106.2
1982:Q1	3184.9	54.4	5857.3	6300.8	8.8	6.2	442.4	1777.1	59.1	15.0	−191.1	110.0
1982:Q2	3240.9	55.0	5889.1	6351.4	9.4	6.1	447.1	1815.1	59.3	14.5	−198.8	114.1
1982:Q3	3274.4	55.8	5866.4	6407.1	9.9	6.1	452.1	1848.2	59.4	13.8	−263.7	118.8
1982:Q4	3312.5	56.4	5871.0	6460.9	10.7	6.1	470.3	1890.1	59.9	11.9	−320.1	120.2

	Nominal GDP (X) (B $)	GDP Deflator (2005 = 100)	Real GDP (Y) (B 2005$)	Natural Real GDP (Y^N) (B 2005$)	Unemploy. Rate (U) (Percent)	Natural Unemploy. Rate (U^N) (Percent)	Money Supply (M1) (B $)	Money Supply (M2) (B $)	Labor Productivity (Y/N) (2005 = 100)	Nominal Interest Rate (I) (Percent)	Real Federal Budget Surplus (B 2005$)	Trade-Weighted Exchange Rate (Mar 1973 = 100)
1983:Q1	3381.0	56.9	5944.0	6507.5	10.4	6.0	484.0	1993.3	60.6	11.8	−310.1	117.1
1983:Q2	3482.2	57.3	6077.6	6548.9	10.1	6.0	499.1	2044.1	62.0	11.6	−301.2	119.3
1983:Q3	3587.1	57.9	6197.5	6592.8	9.4	6.0	510.4	2076.2	62.6	12.3	−326.4	122.7
1983:Q4	3688.1	58.3	6325.6	6637.5	8.5	6.0	519.2	2113.9	62.9	12.4	−286.4	122.7
1984:Q1	3807.4	59.0	6448.3	6683.8	7.9	6.0	528.0	2159.5	62.8	12.3	−265.9	123.5
1984:Q2	3906.3	59.6	6559.6	6731.6	7.4	6.0	537.3	2205.9	63.2	13.2	−280.9	124.9
1984:Q3	3976.0	60.0	6623.3	6781.2	7.4	6.0	541.7	2234.9	63.5	13.0	−291.9	131.7
1984:Q4	4034.0	60.4	6677.3	6831.0	7.3	6.0	547.6	2284.5	63.6	12.4	−308.5	134.9
1985:Q1	4117.2	61.1	6740.3	6880.6	7.2	6.0	562.4	2353.3	63.7	12.3	−246.7	142.1
1985:Q2	4175.7	61.4	6797.3	6930.3	7.3	6.0	575.9	2395.0	63.8	11.6	−327.2	138.1
1985:Q3	4258.3	61.7	6903.5	6979.2	7.2	6.0	596.2	2445.8	64.6	11.0	−288.6	131.4
1985:Q4	4318.7	62.1	6955.9	7028.6	7.0	6.0	613.3	2481.8	65.0	10.6	−297.5	122.8
1986:Q1	4382.4	62.4	7022.8	7077.6	7.0	6.0	626.7	2518.6	65.8	9.6	−295.2	116.4
1986:Q2	4423.2	62.7	7051.0	7126.5	7.2	6.1	651.2	2585.4	66.3	9.0	−327.9	110.7
1986:Q3	4491.3	63.1	7119.0	7174.9	7.0	6.1	678.8	2650.2	66.6	8.8	−334.3	106.1
1986:Q4	4543.3	63.5	7153.4	7223.4	6.8	6.1	708.3	2709.2	66.4	8.7	−279.8	106.2
1987:Q1	4611.1	64.1	7193.0	7272.1	6.6	6.2	731.6	2751.8	66.1	8.4	−283.8	100.5
1987:Q2	4686.7	64.5	7269.5	7321.0	6.3	6.2	744.3	2775.4	66.6	9.2	−198.2	96.9
1987:Q3	4764.5	65.0	7332.6	7370.8	6.0	6.3	745.2	2792.6	66.6	9.8	−213.9	98.3
1987:Q4	4883.1	65.5	7458.0	7421.6	5.8	6.3	753.2	2824.4	67.2	10.2	−227.1	92.9
1988:Q1	4948.6	66.0	7496.6	7473.0	5.7	6.3	758.6	2874.1	67.3	9.6	−224.1	89.8
1988:Q2	5059.3	66.6	7592.9	7525.7	5.5	6.4	772.7	2929.6	67.5	9.8	−207.0	88.8
1988:Q3	5142.8	67.4	7632.1	7578.9	5.5	6.4	782.8	2957.6	67.7	10.0	−192.9	93.6
1988:Q4	5251.0	67.9	7734.0	7633.6	5.3	6.3	785.0	2983.6	68.1	9.5	−203.0	89.5
1989:Q1	5360.3	68.7	7806.6	7688.9	5.2	6.3	784.2	3000.0	67.9	9.7	−168.1	91.3
1989:Q2	5453.6	69.3	7865.0	7744.8	5.2	6.3	775.9	3020.6	68.0	9.5	−194.5	95.4
1989:Q3	5532.9	69.8	7927.4	7801.4	5.2	6.2	779.4	3078.9	68.4	9.0	−201.7	96.0
1989:Q4	5581.7	70.3	7944.7	7858.0	5.4	6.2	789.1	3139.3	68.5	8.9	−206.0	94.3
1990:Q1	5708.1	71.1	8027.7	7916.3	5.3	6.3	798.4	3184.2	69.2	9.2	−240.9	93.1
1990:Q2	5797.4	71.9	8059.6	7974.6	5.3	6.2	806.4	3210.5	69.7	9.4	−245.7	93.4
1990:Q3	5850.6	72.6	8059.5	8033.3	5.7	6.2	815.3	3244.9	70.0	9.4	−236.9	88.6
1990:Q4	5846.0	73.2	7988.9	8093.5	6.1	6.1	822.2	3269.0	69.4	9.3	−253.9	84.4
1991:Q1	5880.2	74.0	7950.2	8155.9	6.6	6.1	832.9	3309.1	69.6	8.9	−212.8	85.7
1991:Q2	5962.0	74.5	8003.8	8217.4	6.8	6.1	849.5	3347.1	70.6	8.9	−291.4	90.9
1991:Q3	6033.7	75.1	8037.5	8280.4	6.9	6.0	866.1	3359.4	71.1	8.8	−320.4	90.7
1991:Q4	6092.5	75.5	8069.0	8344.3	7.1	6.0	887.5	3370.0	71.4	8.4	−342.6	86.8
1992:Q1	6190.7	75.9	8157.6	8406.9	7.4	5.9	924.1	3398.8	72.6	8.3	−390.0	87.5
1992:Q2	6295.2	76.4	8244.3	8469.9	7.6	5.9	949.5	3401.0	73.1	8.3	−395.8	87.9
1992:Q3	6389.7	76.7	8329.4	8532.7	7.6	5.8	975.0	3404.6	73.9	8.0	−408.3	83.9
1992:Q4	6493.6	77.1	8417.0	8595.2	7.4	5.7	1014.8	3428.8	74.4	8.0	−387.0	88.8
1993:Q1	6544.5	77.6	8432.5	8659.0	7.1	5.7	1034.2	3419.5	73.9	7.7	−402.1	91.1
1993:Q2	6622.7	78.0	8486.4	8722.0	7.1	5.6	1062.9	3434.5	73.5	7.4	−352.8	88.2
1993:Q3	6688.3	78.4	8531.1	8785.4	6.8	5.6	1094.3	3451.0	73.8	6.9	−360.0	89.5
1993:Q4	6813.8	78.8	8643.8	8847.6	6.6	5.5	1122.3	3471.6	74.4	6.8	−318.8	90.8
1994:Q1	6916.3	79.2	8727.9	8911.0	6.6	5.5	1136.0	3482.0	74.8	7.2	−298.3	91.2
1994:Q2	7044.3	79.6	8847.3	8974.4	6.2	5.5	1143.2	3491.6	74.7	7.9	−254.8	89.7
1994:Q3	7131.8	80.1	8904.3	9039.3	6.0	5.5	1151.0	3493.9	74.3	8.2	−275.4	86.7
1994:Q4	7248.2	80.5	9003.2	9104.5	5.6	5.4	1150.6	3493.1	74.9	8.6	−275.4	86.1
1995:Q1	7307.7	81.0	9025.3	9171.4	5.5	5.4	1148.5	3497.4	74.7	8.3	−273.4	85.4

Continued

	Nominal GDP (X) (B $)	GDP Deflator (2005 = 100)	Real GDP (Y) (B 2005$)	Natural Real GDP (Y^N) (B 2005$)	Unemploy. Rate (U) (Percent)	Natural Unemploy. Rate (U^N) (Percent)	Money Supply (M1) (B $)	Money Supply (M2) (B $)	Labor Productivity (Y/N) (2005 = 100)	Nominal Interest Rate (I) (Percent)	Real Federal Budget Surplus (B 2005$)	Trade-Weighted Exchange Rate (Mar 1973 = 100)
1995:Q2	7355.8	81.3	9044.7	9239.8	5.7	5.4	1146.3	3530.6	74.8	7.7	−253.5	80.7
1995:Q3	7452.5	81.7	9120.7	9308.4	5.7	5.3	1144.3	3593.4	74.9	7.4	−257.4	83.1
1995:Q4	7542.5	82.1	9184.3	9378.5	5.6	5.3	1132.9	3628.3	75.5	7.0	−227.3	84.6
1996:Q1	7638.2	82.6	9247.2	9450.0	5.5	5.3	1121.5	3673.2	76.1	7.1	−235.2	86.6
1996:Q2	7800.0	82.9	9407.1	9521.4	5.5	5.3	1118.8	3717.8	77.0	7.6	−180.3	87.5
1996:Q3	7892.7	83.2	9488.9	9595.2	5.3	5.3	1103.4	3752.7	77.2	7.6	−166.3	87.2
1996:Q4	8023.0	83.6	9592.5	9670.1	5.3	5.3	1083.6	3796.2	77.3	7.2	−132.5	87.7
1997:Q1	8137.0	84.2	9666.2	9746.4	5.2	5.3	1077.4	3843.5	77.0	7.4	−109.8	92.1
1997:Q2	8276.8	84.4	9809.6	9823.6	5.0	5.3	1064.6	3887.2	77.9	7.6	−84.1	93.4
1997:Q3	8409.9	84.7	9932.7	9902.3	4.9	5.2	1069.4	3948.9	78.5	7.2	−42.0	94.7
1997:Q4	8505.7	85.0	10008.9	9981.9	4.7	5.2	1069.5	4010.0	78.9	6.9	−48.8	95.6
1998:Q1	8600.6	85.1	10103.4	10062.9	4.6	5.2	1076.5	4083.5	79.3	6.7	9.3	98.0
1998:Q2	8698.6	85.3	10194.3	10145.1	4.4	5.2	1077.2	4157.7	79.8	6.6	24.3	99.2
1998:Q3	8847.2	85.7	10328.8	10229.0	4.5	5.2	1076.9	4228.5	80.9	6.5	61.1	100.8
1998:Q4	9027.5	85.9	10507.6	10314.9	4.4	5.2	1092.0	4338.9	81.5	6.3	62.2	95.6
1999:Q1	9148.6	86.3	10601.2	10400.2	4.3	5.2	1097.4	4415.8	82.3	6.4	91.7	96.2
1999:Q2	9252.6	86.6	10684.0	10486.0	4.3	5.2	1101.5	4480.2	82.4	6.9	111.0	98.5
1999:Q3	9405.1	86.9	10819.9	10573.6	4.2	5.1	1098.3	4545.9	83.0	7.3	119.1	97.5
1999:Q4	9607.7	87.2	11014.3	10663.5	4.1	5.1	1111.9	4607.5	84.5	7.5	133.7	95.8
2000:Q1	9709.5	87.9	11043.0	10749.0	4.0	5.1	1113.0	4679.2	84.1	7.7	233.5	97.8
2000:Q2	9949.1	88.4	11258.5	10840.6	3.9	5.1	1107.6	4755.6	86.1	7.8	198.0	100.7
2000:Q3	10017.5	88.9	11267.9	10925.4	4.0	5.1	1101.3	4810.9	86.1	7.6	204.5	102.6
2000:Q4	10129.8	89.4	11334.5	11012.3	3.9	5.1	1092.7	4882.0	86.9	7.4	200.1	105.8
2001:Q1	10165.1	90.0	11297.2	11097.2	4.2	5.1	1102.7	5013.2	86.6	7.1	177.2	105.4
2001:Q2	10301.3	90.6	11371.3	11185.0	4.4	5.1	1120.4	5142.0	88.2	7.2	131.4	109.0
2001:Q3	10305.2	90.9	11340.1	11271.9	4.8	5.1	1165.0	5259.7	88.7	7.1	−114.9	108.0
2001:Q4	10373.1	91.2	11380.1	11360.1	5.5	5.1	1172.9	5381.2	90.0	6.9	−13.2	108.9
2002:Q1	10498.7	91.5	11477.9	11448.1	5.7	5.1	1191.1	5479.4	91.9	6.6	−224.6	111.6
2002:Q2	10601.9	91.9	11538.8	11535.5	5.8	5.1	1189.2	5521.3	92.0	6.7	−271.8	107.4
2002:Q3	10701.7	92.3	11596.4	11622.4	5.7	5.1	1194.1	5625.3	92.9	6.4	−284.9	103.0
2002:Q4	10766.9	92.8	11598.8	11709.4	5.9	5.1	1210.7	5743.6	92.8	6.3	−315.6	102.8
2003:Q1	10888.4	93.5	11645.8	11796.2	5.9	5.1	1234.4	5832.7	93.6	6.0	−321.5	98.0
2003:Q2	11008.1	93.8	11738.7	11882.7	6.1	5.1	1265.7	5948.1	94.8	5.3	−399.9	93.4
2003:Q3	11255.7	94.3	11935.5	11968.2	6.1	5.2	1293.6	6069.6	97.1	5.7	−478.7	93.2
2003:Q4	11416.5	94.8	12042.8	12053.9	5.8	5.2	1300.4	6060.1	97.4	5.7	−399.3	88.0
2004:Q1	11597.2	95.6	12127.6	12139.2	5.7	5.2	1318.6	6106.2	97.6	5.5	−428.0	85.4
2004:Q2	11778.4	96.4	12213.8	12224.3	5.6	5.2	1335.2	6235.3	98.5	5.9	−398.6	88.2
2004:Q3	11950.5	97.1	12303.5	12309.2	5.4	5.1	1352.3	6301.7	98.7	5.6	−372.3	86.6
2004:Q4	12144.9	97.9	12410.3	12394.0	5.4	5.1	1370.6	6385.3	98.9	5.5	−370.4	81.9
2005:Q1	12379.5	98.8	12534.1	12478.8	5.3	5.0	1370.0	6421.9	99.8	5.3	−292.5	81.4
2005:Q2	12516.8	99.4	12587.5	12563.1	5.1	4.9	1366.9	6467.0	99.6	5.1	−289.7	83.6
2005:Q3	12741.6	100.5	12683.2	12647.6	5.0	4.9	1374.0	6556.2	100.3	5.1	−286.1	84.6
2005:Q4	12915.6	101.3	12748.7	12732.2	5.0	4.8	1375.5	6647.2	100.3	5.4	−264.2	85.8
2006:Q1	13183.5	102.1	12915.9	12817.5	4.7	4.8	1380.7	6734.9	100.9	5.4	−203.1	84.9
2006:Q2	13347.8	103.0	12962.5	12902.2	4.6	4.8	1379.5	6805.5	101.0	5.9	−222.8	82.1
2006:Q3	13452.9	103.8	12965.9	12987.4	4.6	4.8	1367.7	6898.7	100.5	5.7	−207.7	81.7
2006:Q4	13611.5	104.2	13060.7	13073.7	4.4	4.7	1368.8	7024.1	101.2	5.4	−156.4	81.7
2007:Q1	13789.5	105.3	13089.3	13161.2	4.5	4.8	1367.8	7126.7	101.3	5.4	−191.4	82.0
2007:Q2	14008.2	106.2	13194.1	13249.8	4.5	4.7	1373.9	7245.5	101.9	5.6	−223.6	79.4

	Nominal GDP (X) (B \$)	GDP Deflator (2005 = 100)	Real GDP (Y) (B 2005\$)	Natural Real GDP (Y^N) (B 2005\$)	Unemploy. Rate (U) (Percent)	Natural Unemploy. Rate (U^N) (Percent)	Money Supply (M1) (B \$)	Money Supply (M2) (B \$)	Labor Productivity (Y/N) (2005 = 100)	Nominal Interest Rate (I) (Percent)	Real Federal Budget Surplus (B 2005\$)	Trade-Weighted Exchange Rate (Mar 1973 = 100)
2007:Q3	14158.2	106.7	13268.5	13339.6	4.7	4.7	1372.4	7358.9	103.0	5.8	−248.5	77.1
2007:Q4	14291.3	106.9	13363.5	13430.3	4.8	4.8	1374.5	7463.0	103.9	5.5	−258.7	73.4
2008:Q1	14328.4	107.4	13339.2	13514.5	5.0	4.8	1382.6	7606.5	103.5	5.5	−350.7	72.0
2008:Q2	14471.8	108.3	13359.0	13599.2	5.3	4.8	1392.8	7733.6	103.8	5.6	−703.0	70.8
2008:Q3	14484.9	109.5	13223.5	13684.5	6.0	4.9	1427.8	7827.6	103.5	5.7	−590.4	73.5
2008:Q4	14191.2	109.2	12993.7	13770.3	6.9	4.9	1529.2	8099.4	103.5	5.8	−622.6	81.5
2009:Q1	14049.7	109.5	12832.6	13856.6	8.2	5.0	1577.8	8351.3	104.4	5.3	−916.3	82.9
2009:Q2	14034.5	109.6	12810.0	13943.5	9.3	5.1	1624.0	8425.0	106.5	5.5	−1220.2	79.6
2009:Q3	14114.7	109.8	12860.8	14030.9	9.7	5.2	1660.9	8444.6	108.3	5.3	−1236.2	75.3
2009:Q4	14277.3	109.7	13019.0	14118.9	10.0	5.2	1684.4	8507.5	109.9	5.2	−1194.8	72.8
2010:Q1	14446.4	110.0	13138.8	14207.4	9.7	5.3	1698.7	8507.3	110.9	5.3	−1195.2	74.8
2010:Q2	14578.7	110.5	13194.9	14296.5	9.6	5.3	1711.6	8564.9	110.4	5.0	−1209.6	77.6
2010:Q3	14745.1	111.0	13278.5	14386.1	9.6	5.3	1752.3	8661.6	111.0	4.6	−1210.6	75.9
2010:Q4	14870.4	111.1	13382.6	14476.3	9.6	5.3	1812.6	8783.5	111.8	4.9	−1192.8	73.0

International Annual Time Series Data for Selected Countries: 1960–2010

Table B-1   Canada, 1960–2010

	Nominal GDP (X) (B C$)	GDP Deflator	Real GDP (Y) (B 2005 C$)	Labor Productivity (Y/N) (C$/Hr)	Unemploy. Rate (U) (Percent)	Investment Share (Percent)	Consumer Price Index (CPI) (2005 = 100)	Long-Term Interest Rate (i) (Percent)	Labor Share (wN/X) (Percent)
1960	39.7	14.1	282.5	23.4	6.5	20.1	14.5	5.2	50.7
1961	41.2	14.1	291.2	22.9	6.7	19.7	14.6	5.1	51.5
1962	44.7	14.3	311.6	23.8	5.5	20.1	14.8	5.1	51.0
1963	48.0	14.6	328.1	24.7	5.2	19.9	15.1	5.1	50.7
1964	52.5	15.0	349.3	25.5	4.4	20.4	15.4	5.2	50.6
1965	57.9	15.6	371.6	26.4	3.6	22.3	15.7	5.2	51.1
1966	64.8	16.4	396.3	26.9	3.3	23.0	16.3	5.7	51.7
1967	69.7	17.1	407.8	27.0	3.8	21.1	16.9	5.9	53.2
1968	76.1	17.8	427.7	28.4	4.5	20.9	17.6	6.7	52.9
1969	83.8	18.7	449.2	29.1	4.4	21.7	18.4	7.6	53.8
1970	90.2	19.5	462.9	30.0	5.7	19.9	19.0	8.0	54.2
1971	98.4	20.4	481.9	30.8	6.2	20.4	19.5	6.9	54.4
1972	109.9	21.6	508.2	31.7	6.2	20.6	20.5	7.2	54.7
1973	129.0	23.7	543.6	32.5	5.6	21.7	22.0	7.5	53.7
1974	154.0	27.3	563.6	32.5	5.3	23.4	24.4	8.9	53.6
1975	173.6	30.3	573.9	32.9	6.9	22.9	27.1	9.0	55.5
1976	200.0	33.1	603.7	33.2	6.9	23.2	29.1	9.2	55.7
1977	221.0	35.4	624.6	34.1	7.8	22.4	31.4	8.7	55.8
1978	244.9	37.7	649.3	34.3	8.1	21.7	34.2	9.2	54.8
1979	279.6	41.5	674.0	34.3	7.3	23.8	37.4	10.2	54.0
1980	314.4	45.7	688.6	34.6	7.3	22.6	41.2	12.3	54.3
1981	360.5	50.6	712.7	34.8	7.3	23.9	46.3	15.0	54.6
1982	379.9	54.9	692.3	35.2	10.7	19.2	51.3	14.4	55.3
1983	411.4	57.8	711.1	36.0	11.6	19.8	54.3	11.4	53.5
1984	449.6	59.7	752.5	37.1	10.9	20.5	56.6	12.7	52.8
1985	485.7	61.6	788.5	37.6	10.1	20.9	58.9	10.9	52.7
1986	512.5	63.5	807.6	37.4	9.2	21.1	61.3	9.1	53.2
1987	558.9	66.4	841.9	37.7	8.4	22.1	64.0	9.5	53.0
1988	613.1	69.4	883.8	38.2	7.4	22.8	66.6	9.8	53.1
1989	657.7	72.5	906.9	38.5	7.1	23.3	69.9	9.8	53.3
1990	679.9	74.8	908.7	38.6	7.7	20.9	73.2	10.7	54.3
1991	685.4	77.0	889.7	38.9	9.8	18.8	77.3	9.5	55.3
1992	700.5	78.1	897.5	39.8	10.6	17.8	78.5	8.1	55.4
1993	727.2	79.2	918.4	40.5	10.8	17.9	80.0	7.2	54.3
1994	770.9	80.1	962.6	41.2	9.6	18.9	80.1	8.4	52.5
1995	810.4	81.9	989.6	41.7	8.6	18.8	81.8	8.2	51.7

	Nominal GDP (X) (B C$)	GDP Deflator	Real GDP (Y) (B 2005 C$)	Labor Productivity (Y/N) (C$/Hr)	Unemploy. Rate (U) (Percent)	Investment Share (Percent)	Consumer Price Index (CPI) (2005 = 100)	Long-Term Interest Rate (i) (Percent)	Labor Share (wN/X) (Percent)
1996	836.9	83.2	1005.6	41.8	8.8	18.2	83.1	7.2	51.2
1997	882.7	84.2	1048.1	43.1	8.4	20.7	84.5	6.1	51.3
1998	915.0	83.9	1091.1	43.8	7.7	20.4	85.3	5.3	52.0
1999	982.4	85.3	1151.4	45.0	7.0	20.3	86.8	5.5	51.2
2000	1076.6	88.9	1211.7	46.2	6.1	20.2	89.2	5.9	50.6
2001	1108.0	89.8	1233.3	46.7	6.5	19.2	91.4	5.5	51.4
2002	1152.9	90.8	1269.4	47.4	7.0	19.3	93.5	5.3	51.5
2003	1213.2	93.8	1293.2	47.4	6.9	20.0	96.1	4.8	51.2
2004	1290.9	96.8	1333.6	47.6	6.4	20.7	97.8	4.6	50.9
2005	1373.8	100.0	1373.8	48.7	6.0	22.1	100.0	4.1	50.6
2006	1450.4	102.7	1412.6	49.1	5.5	23.0	102.0	4.2	51.3
2007	1529.6	105.9	1443.7	49.1	5.3	23.2	104.2	4.3	51.3
2008	1599.6	110.2	1451.2	48.9	5.3	23.1	106.7	3.6	51.2
2009	1527.3	107.9	1415.5	49.3	7.3	21.0	107.0	3.2	53.6
2010	1618.7	111.0	1458.1	49.8	7.0	21.8	108.9	3.2	—

Table B-2 Japan, 1960–2010

	Nominal GDP (X) (Tr ¥)	GDP Deflator	Real GDP (Y) (Tr 2005 ¥)	Labor Productivity (Y/N) (¥/Hr)	Unemploy. Rate (U) (Percent)	Investment Share (Percent)	Consumer Price Index (CPI) (2005 = 100)	Long-Term Interest Rate (i) (Percent)	Labor Share (wN/X) (Percent)
1960	16.1	23.1	69.6	667.7	1.7	22.5	18.6	7.5	40.2
1961	19.4	24.9	77.9	735.8	1.5	25.6	19.6	7.3	39.4
1962	22.0	26.0	84.6	797.1	1.3	25.2	20.9	7.5	41.4
1963	25.2	27.4	92.0	862.4	1.3	26.0	22.5	7.1	42.1
1964	29.6	29.0	102.3	943.3	1.2	27.2	23.4	7.2	42.0
1965	33.0	30.5	108.1	989.5	1.2	26.6	24.9	7.2	43.9
1966	38.3	32.1	119.2	1065.1	1.4	27.3	26.2	6.8	43.8
1967	44.9	33.9	132.4	1153.4	1.3	29.8	27.2	6.9	42.9
1968	53.1	35.9	148.2	1267.4	1.2	31.9	28.7	7.0	42.3
1969	62.4	37.6	165.9	1416.9	1.1	33.1	30.2	7.0	42.3
1970	74.2	43.2	171.8	1458.7	1.2	35.9	32.5	7.0	42.7
1971	81.6	45.4	179.9	1524.9	1.3	34.6	34.6	7.1	46.0
1972	93.4	47.9	195.0	1649.7	1.4	35.1	36.3	6.9	46.8
1973	113.7	54.0	210.7	1748.7	1.3	36.2	40.5	7.1	48.2
1974	135.7	65.2	208.1	1784.1	1.4	34.4	49.9	8.2	51.2
1975	150.0	69.9	214.6	1870.1	1.9	31.8	55.7	8.5	54.0
1976	168.4	75.5	223.1	1901.2	2.0	31.7	61.0	8.6	54.3
1977	187.7	80.6	232.9	1952.1	2.0	31.3	66.0	7.5	54.4
1978	206.7	84.3	245.2	2026.0	2.3	31.9	68.7	6.4	53.4
1979	224.0	86.6	258.6	2104.7	2.1	32.2	71.3	8.3	53.2
1980	242.8	91.3	265.9	2140.4	2.0	31.1	76.8	8.9	53.3
1981	261.1	94.3	277.0	2228.7	2.2	30.9	80.6	8.4	53.7
1982	274.1	95.7	286.3	2287.4	2.4	29.9	82.8	8.3	54.1
1983	285.1	96.6	295.1	2332.3	2.7	28.3	84.4	7.8	54.7
1984	303.0	98.3	308.3	2413.1	2.8	28.2	86.3	7.3	54.2
1985	325.4	99.3	327.8	2570.5	2.5	28.7	88.1	6.5	52.8
1986	340.6	101.0	337.1	2624.7	2.7	28.5	88.6	5.1	52.6
1987	354.2	100.9	350.9	2723.1	2.6	29.0	88.7	5.0	52.4
1988	380.7	101.3	376.0	2889.7	2.4	31.2	89.3	4.8	51.5
1989	410.1	103.5	396.2	3032.6	2.2	32.3	91.3	5.1	51.3
1990	442.8	105.9	418.3	3209.5	2.0	33.0	94.1	7.0	51.4
1991	469.4	108.6	432.2	3303.8	2.0	32.6	97.2	6.3	52.3
1992	480.8	110.3	435.7	3349.0	2.1	30.9	98.9	5.3	52.8
1993	483.7	110.8	436.5	3447.3	2.4	29.5	100.1	4.3	53.6
1994	488.5	111.0	440.2	3485.9	2.6	28.2	100.8	4.4	54.1
1995	495.2	110.4	448.5	3573.1	2.9	28.3	100.7	3.4	54.3
1996	505.0	109.7	460.4	3636.6	3.1	28.9	100.8	3.1	54.0
1997	515.6	110.3	467.6	3723.1	3.1	28.3	102.6	2.4	54.1
1998	504.9	110.2	458.0	3734.3	3.8	26.3	103.3	1.5	54.5
1999	497.6	108.8	457.3	3846.9	4.2	24.8	103.0	1.7	54.2
2000	503.0	106.9	470.4	3957.9	4.4	25.4	102.2	1.7	53.9
2001	497.7	105.6	471.3	4023.2	4.5	24.8	101.4	1.3	54.1
2002	491.3	104.0	472.5	4123.0	4.9	23.1	100.5	1.3	53.4
2003	490.3	102.3	479.2	4192.6	4.6	22.8	100.3	1.0	52.7
2004	498.3	101.2	492.3	4327.3	4.2	23.0	100.3	1.5	51.4
2005	501.7	100.0	501.9	4424.0	3.8	23.6	100.0	1.4	51.5
2006	507.4	99.1	512.1	4471.8	3.6	23.8	100.2	1.7	52.0
2007	515.5	98.3	524.2	4558.0	3.6	23.7	100.3	1.7	50.8
2008	505.1	97.5	518.1	4553.7	3.7	23.6	101.7	1.5	52.2
2009	474.3	96.6	491.0	4535.3	4.8	20.4	100.3	1.3	—
2010	482.7	94.8	509.5	4725.0	4.9	20.1	99.3	1.1	—

Table B-3   France, 1960–2010

	Nominal GDP (X) (B euro)	GDP Deflator	Real GDP (Y) (B 2005 euro)	Labor Productivity (Y/N) (euro/Hr)	Unemploy. Rate (U) (Percent)	Investment Share (Percent)	Consumer Price Index (CPI) (2005 = 100)	Long-Term Interest Rate (i) (Percent)	Labor Share (wN/X) (Percent)
1960	46.3	11.3	410.3	9.3	1.5	21.2	11.2	5.7	45.0
1961	50.2	11.7	430.7	9.7	1.2	21.5	11.5	5.5	46.5
1962	56.3	12.2	460.2	10.3	1.4	21.9	12.1	5.4	46.9
1963	63.2	12.9	489.3	11.0	1.6	22.2	12.7	5.3	47.8
1964	70.0	13.4	521.1	11.6	1.2	23.6	13.1	5.4	48.1
1965	75.7	13.8	546.5	12.2	1.6	23.5	13.4	6.2	48.1
1966	82.0	14.3	575.4	12.8	1.6	24.3	13.8	6.6	47.8
1967	88.7	14.7	603.9	13.5	2.1	24.4	14.1	6.7	47.8
1968	96.7	15.3	630.6	14.2	2.7	24.7	14.8	7.0	49.3
1969	111.3	16.5	676.0	15.2	2.3	25.8	15.7	8.2	49.1
1970	124.5	17.3	717.4	16.3	2.5	25.6	16.6	8.6	49.8
1971	138.8	18.4	754.9	17.2	2.8	25.4	17.5	8.4	50.4
1972	155.2	19.6	790.0	18.0	2.9	25.6	18.6	8.0	50.4
1973	178.2	21.2	841.8	19.2	2.8	26.7	19.9	9.0	50.5
1974	207.4	23.6	879.5	20.2	2.9	27.0	22.6	11.0	51.9
1975	233.4	26.8	870.9	20.7	3.7	22.9	25.3	10.3	54.4
1976	270.0	29.7	909.3	21.9	4.1	24.2	27.7	10.5	54.7
1977	304.2	32.3	941.6	22.7	4.6	23.3	30.4	11.0	55.2
1978	345.2	35.3	978.9	23.7	4.7	22.3	33.2	10.6	55.1
1979	393.6	38.8	1013.5	24.0	5.4	22.9	36.7	10.8	54.9
1980	445.2	43.2	1030.5	24.7	5.7	23.2	41.7	13.8	55.8
1981	500.8	48.1	1040.0	25.2	6.8	21.3	47.2	16.3	56.3
1982	574.4	53.9	1065.3	25.8	7.3	21.7	52.9	16.0	56.3
1983	636.6	59.1	1078.1	26.1	7.6	20.0	57.9	14.4	55.9
1984	693.1	63.3	1094.1	26.9	8.9	19.3	62.3	13.4	55.1
1985	743.9	66.9	1112.8	28.4	9.5	19.3	66.0	11.9	54.4
1986	802.4	70.4	1140.1	29.5	9.5	19.8	67.6	9.1	52.9
1987	845.2	72.3	1168.4	30.6	9.6	20.4	69.9	9.5	52.4
1988	911.2	74.6	1222.1	32.8	9.3	21.6	71.7	9.1	51.3
1989	980.5	77.0	1273.0	34.1	8.6	22.6	74.3	8.8	50.8
1990	1033.0	79.1	1306.6	33.5	8.3	22.6	76.8	9.9	51.5
1991	1070.0	81.1	1319.9	34.0	8.5	21.7	79.2	9.0	51.9
1992	1107.8	82.8	1338.0	34.7	9.4	19.9	81.1	8.6	52.0
1993	1114.7	84.1	1325.7	35.1	10.5	17.4	82.8	6.8	52.6
1994	1154.7	85.2	1355.1	36.0	10.9	18.4	84.2	7.2	51.8
1995	1194.6	86.3	1383.8	36.9	10.3	18.6	85.7	7.5	51.8
1996	1227.3	87.7	1399.2	37.1	10.8	17.7	87.4	6.3	51.9
1997	1267.4	88.6	1430.5	37.9	10.9	17.4	88.5	5.6	51.5
1998	1323.7	89.4	1480.6	38.9	10.4	18.7	89.0	4.6	51.2
1999	1368.0	89.4	1529.4	39.6	10.0	19.3	89.5	4.6	51.8
2000	1441.4	90.7	1589.2	41.0	8.5	20.4	91.0	5.4	51.9
2001	1497.2	92.5	1618.7	41.4	7.7	20.1	92.5	4.9	52.2
2002	1548.6	94.7	1635.3	42.7	7.9	19.0	94.3	4.9	52.6
2003	1594.8	96.5	1653.1	43.2	8.4	18.9	96.2	4.1	52.5
2004	1660.2	98.0	1694.0	43.4	8.8	19.5	98.3	4.1	52.2
2005	1726.1	100.0	1726.1	44.1	8.8	20.3	100.0	3.4	52.0
2006	1806.4	102.4	1764.3	45.3	8.7	21.1	101.7	3.8	51.9
2007	1895.3	104.9	1806.2	45.1	7.9	22.2	103.2	4.3	51.4
2008	1948.5	107.6	1810.1	44.8	7.4	22.0	106.1	4.2	51.6
2009	1907.1	108.2	1762.6	44.3	9.1	19.0	106.2	3.6	52.7
2010	1946.3	108.7	1791.2	44.9	9.5	19.6	107.8	3.0	—

Table B-4   Germany, 1960–2010

	Nominal GDP (X) (B euro)	GDP Deflator	Real GDP (Y) (B 2005 euro)	Labor Productivity (Y/N) (euro/Hr)	Unemploy. Rate (U) (Percent)	Investment Share (Percent)	Consumer Price Index (CPI) (2005 = 100)	Long-Term Interest Rate (i) (Percent)	Labor Share (wN/X) (Percent)
1960	150.8	22.0	684.1	8.9	1.1	—	27.2	6.3	55.0
1961	164.4	23.0	715.8	9.3	0.6	—	27.9	5.9	56.9
1962	183.6	24.5	749.2	9.9	0.6	—	28.6	6.0	56.4
1963	205.9	26.7	770.2	10.3	0.5	—	29.5	6.1	53.9
1964	228.3	27.8	821.5	10.9	0.4	—	30.2	6.2	53.1
1965	245.8	28.4	865.5	11.5	0.3	—	31.2	6.8	54.7
1966	266.1	29.9	889.7	12.0	0.3	—	32.4	7.8	54.4
1967	287.4	32.4	886.9	12.6	1.3	—	32.8	7.0	50.3
1968	312.4	33.4	935.3	13.4	1.1	—	33.4	6.7	49.7
1969	345.5	34.4	1005.1	14.3	0.6	—	34.0	7.0	50.6
1970	390.9	37.0	1055.7	14.9	0.5	33.7	35.1	8.2	53.0
1971	433.8	39.8	1088.8	15.6	0.6	32.8	37.0	8.2	54.1
1972	473.0	41.7	1135.6	16.4	0.7	32.5	39.0	8.2	55.0
1973	526.8	44.3	1189.9	17.3	0.7	32.2	41.7	9.4	56.2
1974	570.2	47.5	1200.5	18.0	1.6	28.9	44.7	10.6	57.5
1975	597.2	50.2	1190.1	18.7	3.4	26.7	47.3	8.8	57.3
1976	647.5	51.8	1249.0	19.6	3.4	28.0	49.3	8.2	57.2
1977	690.0	53.5	1290.8	20.4	3.4	27.6	51.2	6.7	57.6
1978	735.9	55.3	1329.6	21.1	3.3	27.7	52.5	6.3	57.7
1979	799.2	57.7	1384.8	21.6	2.9	29.1	54.7	7.7	57.5
1980	854.7	60.9	1404.3	22.0	2.8	28.2	57.7	8.6	58.4
1981	895.1	63.4	1411.7	22.4	4.0	25.4	61.3	10.2	58.5
1982	932.4	66.3	1406.1	22.8	5.6	23.7	64.5	9.1	57.9
1983	973.6	68.2	1428.3	23.4	6.9	24.7	66.6	8.2	56.7
1984	1021.0	69.5	1468.6	24.4	7.1	24.5	68.3	8.1	56.2
1985	1067.0	71.0	1502.8	25.1	7.2	23.5	69.7	7.2	55.9
1986	1124.2	73.1	1537.1	25.6	6.6	23.5	69.7	6.3	55.9
1987	1154.5	74.1	1558.7	26.2	6.3	23.0	69.8	6.4	56.9
1988	1217.5	75.3	1616.5	27.0	6.3	23.9	70.7	6.6	56.2
1989	1301.4	77.5	1679.5	28.1	5.7	24.8	72.7	7.1	55.0
1990	1416.3	80.1	1767.7	30.1	5.0	25.6	74.6	8.7	54.7
1991	1534.6	82.6	1858.0	31.1	5.6	24.0	75.9	8.5	55.1
1992	1646.6	86.7	1899.4	31.9	6.7	23.4	79.8	7.9	55.6
1993	1694.4	89.9	1884.1	32.4	8.0	22.2	83.3	6.5	55.4
1994	1780.8	92.1	1934.2	33.3	8.5	22.5	85.6	6.9	54.0
1995	1848.5	93.8	1970.8	34.2	8.2	22.2	87.1	6.9	54.0
1996	1876.2	94.3	1990.4	35.0	9.0	21.1	88.3	6.2	53.7
1997	1915.6	94.5	2026.3	35.9	9.9	21.1	90.0	5.7	52.8
1998	1965.4	95.1	2067.4	36.3	9.3	21.6	90.8	4.6	52.6
1999	2012.0	95.4	2109.0	36.8	8.5	21.5	91.3	4.5	52.7
2000	2062.5	94.8	2176.7	37.8	7.8	21.8	92.7	5.3	53.4
2001	2113.2	95.9	2203.7	38.4	7.9	19.5	94.5	4.8	53.1
2002	2143.2	97.3	2203.7	39.0	8.6	17.3	95.9	4.8	52.7
2003	2163.8	98.4	2198.9	39.5	9.3	17.4	96.9	4.1	52.4
2004	2210.9	99.3	2225.4	39.7	10.3	17.1	98.5	4.0	51.5
2005	2242.2	100.0	2242.2	40.3	11.2	16.9	100.0	3.4	50.4
2006	2326.5	100.4	2317.7	41.5	10.4	17.6	101.6	3.8	49.4
2007	2432.4	102.2	2379.3	41.9	8.7	18.3	103.9	4.2	48.5
2008	2481.2	103.3	2402.8	41.8	7.5	18.5	106.6	4.0	49.3
2009	2397.1	104.7	2289.4	40.9	7.8	16.5	107.0	3.2	51.1
2010	2497.6	105.3	2372.1	41.4	7.4	17.0	108.2	2.7	50.4

Table B-5   Italy, 1960–2010

	Nominal GDP (X) (B euro)	GDP Deflator	Real GDP (Y) (B 2005 euro)	Labor Productivity (Y/N) (euro/Hr)	Unemploy. Rate (U) (Percent)	Investment Share (Percent)	Consumer Price Index (CPI) (2005 = 100)	Long-Term Interest Rate (i) (Percent)	Labor Share (wN/X) (Percent)
1960	13.2	3.5	370.6	6.7	3.7	30.9	4.6	5.3	40.0
1961	14.6	3.6	401.0	7.4	3.2	31.8	4.7	5.0	40.0
1962	16.4	3.9	425.9	8.1	2.8	32.2	4.9	5.0	41.5
1963	18.8	4.2	449.8	8.9	2.4	32.0	5.2	5.2	44.1
1964	20.6	4.5	462.4	9.3	2.7	28.8	5.5	5.7	45.1
1965	22.2	4.6	477.5	10.0	3.5	26.0	5.8	5.4	44.3
1966	24.0	4.7	506.1	11.0	3.7	25.7	6.0	5.5	43.8
1967	26.5	4.9	542.4	11.9	3.4	27.0	6.2	5.6	43.8
1968	28.7	5.0	577.9	13.0	3.5	26.8	6.3	5.6	43.9
1969	31.7	5.2	613.2	14.2	3.5	28.1	6.4	5.8	43.9
1970	35.3	5.6	634.4	15.4	3.2	28.7	6.7	7.7	46.3
1971	38.5	6.0	645.9	16.1	3.3	26.3	7.1	7.0	48.8
1972	42.2	6.3	669.7	16.9	3.8	26.1	7.5	6.6	49.6
1973	50.9	7.1	717.5	18.0	3.7	27.7	8.3	6.9	49.4
1974	64.6	8.5	756.9	19.0	3.1	28.9	9.9	9.6	48.7
1975	74.0	10.0	741.1	18.7	3.4	24.4	11.5	10.0	51.2
1976	93.1	11.7	793.9	19.8	3.9	25.7	13.4	12.7	50.0
1977	113.1	13.9	814.3	20.7	4.1	23.6	15.8	14.7	50.2
1978	133.0	15.8	840.6	21.4	4.1	23.4	17.7	13.1	49.4
1979	162.8	18.3	890.7	22.5	4.4	23.8	20.3	13.0	49.0
1980	203.4	22.1	921.3	23.2	4.4	26.7	24.6	15.3	48.3
1981	243.6	26.2	929.1	23.3	4.9	24.7	28.9	19.4	49.0
1982	287.6	30.8	932.9	23.2	5.4	23.7	33.7	20.2	48.4
1983	334.8	35.5	943.8	23.4	5.9	22.2	38.6	18.3	47.7
1984	382.8	39.3	974.3	24.3	5.9	23.3	42.8	15.6	46.6
1985	429.6	42.9	1001.5	24.8	6.0	23.1	46.7	13.7	46.3
1986	475.0	46.1	1030.2	25.2	7.5	21.7	49.4	11.5	45.3
1987	519.7	48.9	1063.0	25.7	7.9	22.1	51.8	10.6	44.9
1988	577.5	52.1	1107.6	26.5	7.9	22.5	54.4	10.9	44.3
1989	634.0	55.4	1145.2	27.4	7.8	22.3	57.8	12.8	44.2
1990	701.4	60.0	1168.7	27.7	7.0	22.3	61.6	13.5	44.7
1991	765.8	64.5	1186.6	27.7	6.9	22.0	65.5	13.3	44.9
1992	805.7	67.4	1195.8	28.1	7.3	21.4	68.8	13.3	44.7
1993	829.8	70.0	1185.1	28.6	9.8	18.9	71.9	11.2	44.3
1994	877.7	72.5	1210.6	29.8	10.7	18.7	74.8	10.5	42.8
1995	947.3	76.1	1244.9	30.7	11.3	19.8	78.7	12.2	41.3
1996	1003.8	79.8	1258.5	30.6	11.3	19.2	81.8	9.4	41.4
1997	1048.8	81.8	1282.1	31.2	11.4	19.4	83.5	6.9	41.6
1998	1091.4	83.9	1300.0	31.1	11.5	19.6	85.1	4.9	39.7
1999	1127.1	85.4	1319.1	31.3	11.0	20.1	86.5	4.7	39.8
2000	1191.1	87.1	1367.8	32.0	10.2	20.7	88.7	5.6	39.2
2001	1248.6	89.7	1392.7	32.3	9.2	20.6	91.2	5.2	39.5
2002	1295.2	92.6	1399.0	32.1	8.7	21.1	93.4	5.0	39.8
2003	1335.4	95.5	1398.7	31.7	8.5	20.7	95.9	4.3	40.2
2004	1391.5	98.0	1420.2	32.1	8.1	20.8	98.1	4.3	39.9
2005	1429.5	100.0	1429.5	32.2	7.8	20.7	100.0	3.6	40.7
2006	1485.4	101.8	1458.6	32.3	6.9	21.6	102.1	4.0	41.0
2007	1546.2	104.5	1480.2	32.4	6.2	21.9	104.0	4.5	40.9
2008	1567.9	107.3	1460.7	32.0	6.8	21.1	107.4	4.7	41.9
2009	1520.9	109.6	1387.1	31.5	7.9	18.9	108.3	4.3	42.9
2010	1547.5	110.4	1401.6	31.9	8.8	19.3	109.9	3.8	—

Table B-6 United Kingdom, 1960–2010

	Nominal GDP (X) (B £)	GDP Deflator	Real GDP (Y) (B 2005 £)	Labor Productivity (Y/N) (£/Hr)	Unemploy. Rate (U) (Percent)	Investment Share (Percent)	Consumer Price Index (CPI) (2005 = 100)	Long-Term Interest Rate (i) (Percent)	Labor Share (wN/X) (Percent)
1960	26.0	6.3	411.7	7.6	2.2	19.6	6.5	5.9	58.5
1961	27.4	6.5	421.2	7.8	2.0	19.8	6.7	6.3	59.9
1962	28.7	6.7	425.6	7.9	2.7	18.3	7.0	5.8	60.4
1963	30.4	6.8	443.8	8.2	3.3	18.4	7.1	5.2	60.0
1964	33.2	7.1	468.1	8.5	2.5	21.7	7.4	5.7	59.6
1965	35.8	7.5	478.6	8.8	2.1	21.2	7.7	6.6	59.6
1966	38.1	7.8	487.8	9.0	2.3	20.7	8.0	6.9	60.0
1967	40.2	8.0	499.8	9.4	3.3	21.7	8.2	6.7	59.3
1968	43.5	8.4	520.8	9.9	3.2	22.3	8.6	7.5	58.6
1969	46.9	8.8	531.6	10.2	3.1	21.7	9.1	8.8	58.2
1970	52.0	9.6	543.5	10.6	3.1	21.0	9.7	8.6	59.0
1971	58.0	10.5	554.5	11.2	4.2	20.2	10.6	7.9	58.0
1972	64.9	11.3	574.3	11.7	4.4	19.2	11.3	8.4	58.5
1973	74.7	12.1	615.2	12.2	3.7	21.7	12.4	10.6	58.9
1974	84.6	13.9	606.9	12.2	3.7	21.4	14.3	14.2	62.2
1975	106.9	17.7	603.1	12.5	4.5	18.3	17.8	13.2	64.4
1976	126.4	20.4	619.0	13.0	5.4	19.8	20.7	13.6	61.9
1977	147.1	23.2	633.8	13.3	5.6	20.1	24.0	12.0	59.0
1978	169.6	25.9	654.4	13.7	5.5	19.8	26.0	12.1	58.4
1979	199.5	29.7	672.0	14.2	5.4	20.3	29.5	12.9	58.2
1980	233.2	35.4	657.9	14.1	6.9	17.6	34.8	13.9	59.2
1981	256.3	39.4	649.9	14.5	9.7	16.0	39.0	14.9	58.5
1982	281.0	42.3	664.2	15.2	10.8	16.6	42.3	13.1	56.6
1983	307.2	44.6	688.8	15.8	11.5	17.4	44.3	11.3	55.4
1984	329.9	46.6	707.3	15.9	11.8	18.4	46.4	11.1	55.1
1985	361.8	49.4	732.9	16.2	11.4	18.2	49.3	11.0	54.6
1986	389.1	51.0	762.4	16.9	11.4	18.1	51.0	10.1	54.7
1987	428.7	53.8	797.1	17.3	10.5	19.0	53.1	9.6	53.7
1988	478.5	57.2	837.2	17.5	8.6	21.4	55.7	9.7	53.8
1989	525.3	61.3	856.3	17.5	7.3	22.1	60.0	10.2	54.5
1990	570.3	66.1	863.0	17.8	7.1	20.2	65.7	11.8	55.4
1991	598.7	70.3	851.0	18.2	8.9	17.2	69.5	10.1	56.1
1992	622.1	73.0	852.2	19.0	10.0	16.4	72.1	9.1	55.9
1993	654.2	75.1	871.2	19.7	10.4	15.9	73.3	7.5	54.5
1994	693.0	76.3	908.5	20.2	9.5	16.6	75.1	8.1	53.3
1995	733.3	78.3	936.2	22.2	8.7	17.2	77.6	8.2	52.6
1996	781.7	81.2	963.2	22.7	8.1	16.9	79.5	7.8	51.7
1997	830.1	83.4	995.1	23.0	7.0	17.2	82.0	7.1	51.8
1998	879.1	85.3	1031.0	23.7	6.3	18.3	84.8	5.6	53.0
1999	928.7	87.1	1066.8	24.3	6.0	18.1	86.2	5.1	53.4
2000	976.5	88.1	1108.5	25.2	5.5	17.7	88.7	5.3	54.5
2001	1021.8	90.0	1135.8	25.5	5.1	17.4	90.3	4.9	55.2
2002	1075.6	92.7	1159.6	26.2	5.2	17.1	91.8	4.9	54.6
2003	1139.7	95.6	1192.2	26.9	5.0	16.7	94.4	4.5	54.1
2004	1203.0	98.0	1227.4	27.5	4.8	17.1	97.2	4.9	53.7
2005	1254.1	100.0	1254.1	27.8	4.9	17.1	100.0	4.4	54.0
2006	1328.4	103.1	1289.0	28.4	5.5	17.5	103.2	4.5	53.7
2007	1404.8	106.1	1323.6	28.9	5.4	18.2	107.6	5.0	53.5
2008	1445.6	109.3	1322.8	29.1	5.7	16.6	111.9	4.6	53.2
2009	1395.0	110.9	1258.3	28.2	7.7	13.6	111.3	3.6	55.5
2010	1468.3	114.7	1280.7	28.7	8.1	14.4	116.5	3.5	—

APPENDIX C

Data Sources and Methods

C-1   Annual Variables (Sources and Methods for Table A-1)

1. Nominal GDP (X):

    1875–1928: Data from Nathan S. Balke and Robert J. Gordon, "The Estimation of Prewar GNP: Methodology and New Results," *Journal of Political Economy*, vol. 97 (February 1989), pp. 38–92, Table 10. Linked in 1929 to:

    1929–2010: Data from U.S. Department of Commerce, Bureau of Economic Analysis. National Income and Product Accounts: Table 1.1.5 on the BEA Web site: www.bea.doc.gov

2. Implicit GDP Deflator (P):

    Same as Nominal GDP (X), except Table 1.1.9 for 1929–2010.

3. Real GDP (Y):

    Same as Nominal GDP (X), except Table 1.1.6 for 1929–2010.

4. Natural Real GDP (Y^N):

    1875–1955: Y^N is the geometric interpolation between real GDP for the benchmark years 1869, 1873, 1884, 1891, 1900, 1910, 1924, and 1949 and the value of natural real GDP in 1955 (see below).

    1955–2010: Average annual values of the natural real GDP series described in Appendix C-2.

5. Unemployment Rate (U):

    1890–1899: Lebergott's series copied from Christina Romer, "Spurious Volatility in Historical Unemployment Data," *Journal of Political Economy*, vol. 94 (February 1986).

    1900–1946: Series B1 in Long-Term Economic Growth, 1860–1970 (Washington, D.C.: U.S. Department of Commerce, 1973).

    1947–2010: Series LNS14000000 from http://stats.bls.gov, Bureau of Labor Statistics, Department of Labor. Average of quarterly values.

6. Natural Unemployment Rate (U^N):

    1890–1901: Assumed to be the same level as in 1902, 4.1 percent.

    1902–1954: U^N is the linear interpolation between the U^N values of the benchmark years of 1902, 1907,

1913, 1929, and 1949 and is calculated as $U^N = B*(U/UA)$ where UA is the published unemployment rate that adjusts for self-employment. UA equals the number of unemployed divided by the civilian labor force net of self-employed persons. The long-run equilibrium rate for UA ("B") reflects the value of UA observed in late 1954 when the economy was operating at its natural rate of unemployment. Changes in U^N before 1954 reflect only changes in the U/UA ratio.

    1955–2010: Time-varying NAIRU for chain-weighted GDP price index-based deflator with standard deviation = 0.2 from Robert J. Gordon, "Time-Varying NAIRU," *Journal of Economic Perspective*, vol. 11, pp. 11–34, extended to 2010 using unpublished research. For recent unpublished research papers on time-varying NAIRU, see http://faculty-web.at.northwestern.edu/economics/gordon/researchhome.html

7. Money Supply (M1):

    1915–1946: *Historical Statistics of the United States: Colonial Times to 1970* (Washington, D.C.: U.S. Department of Commerce, 1975), series 414. Linked in 1947 to:

    1947–1958: *Federal Reserve Bulletin* (Washington, D.C.: Board of Governors of the Federal Reserve System), various issues. Linked in 1959 to 1959–2010: Data from FRED, Federal Reserve Bank of St. Louis.

8. Money Supply (M2):

    1875–1907: Milton Friedman and Anna J. Schwartz, *Monetary Statistics of the United States* (New York: National Bureau of Economic Research, 1970), pp. 61–65. Linked in 1907 to:

    1908–1946: *Historical Statistics*, series 415. Linked in 1947 to:

    1947–1958: *Federal Reserve Bulletin* (Washington, D.C.: Board of Governors of the Federal Reserve System), various issues. Linked in 1959 to:

    1959–2010: Data from FRED, Federal Reserve Bank of St. Louis.

9. Labor Productivity (Y/N):

   1875–1946: Data computed by dividing real output from item 3 above by series A173 from *Long Term Economic Growth*, 1860–1970. Linked in 1947 to:

   1947–2010: Series PRS85006093 from http://stats.bls .gov, Bureau of Labor Statistics, Department of Labor. Average of quarterly values.

10. Nominal Interest Rate (i):

    1875–1939: The yield on corporate bonds from Robert J. Gordon, ed., *The American Business Cycle* (Chicago: University of Chicago, 1986), Appendix B.

    1940–2010: Corporate bonds (Moody's Aaa) from the Board of Governors of the Federal Reserve System.

11. S&P Stock Price Index:

    1875–1939: The index of all common stocks from Gordon, *The American Business Cycle*, Appendix B. Linked in 1940 to:

    1940–2010: Standard and Poor's Composite Index (1941–43 = 10) from the *2010 Economic Report of the President* (Washington D.C.: United States Government Printing Office, 2010).

C-2   Quarterly Variables (Sources and Methods for Table A-2)

1. Nominal GDP (X):
   1947:Q1–2010:Q4: Data from U.S. Department of Commerce, Bureau of Economic Analysis. National Income and Product Accounts: Table 1.1.5 on the BEA Web site: www.bea.gov.

2. Implicit GDP Deflator (P):
   Same as Nominal GDP (X) except Table 1.1.9.

3. Real GDP (Y):
   Same as Nominal GDP (X) except Table 1.1.6.

4. Natural GDP (Y^N):
   1947:Q1–2010:Q4: Data from Robert J. Gordon, "Exploding Productivity Growth: Context, Causes, and Implications," *Brookings Papers on Economic Activity*, 2003, no. 3, data underlying Figure 3, p. 227, updated in unpublished research.

5. Unemployment Rate (U):
   1947:Q1–2001:Q4: Series LNS14000000 from http://stats.bls.gov, Bureau of Labor Statistics, Department of Labor.

6. Natural Unemployment Rate (U^N): See Appendix C-1, line 6.

7. Money Supply (M1):
   1947:Q1–1958:Q4: *Federal Reserve Bulletin* (Washington, D.C.: Board of Governors of the Federal Reserve System), various issues. Linked in 1959 to:
   1959:Q1–2010:Q4: Data from FRED, Federal Reserve Bank of St. Louis.

8. Money Supply (M2):
   1947:Q1–1958:Q4: *Federal Reserve Bulletin* (Washington, D.C.: Board of Governors of the Federal Reserve System), various issues. Linked in 1959 to:
   1959:Q1–2010:Q4: Data from FRED, Federal Reserve Bank of St. Louis.

9. Labor Productivity (Y/N):
   1947:Q1–2010:Q4: Series PRS85006093 from http://stats.bls.gov, Bureau of Labor Statistics, Department of Labor.

10. Nominal Interest Rate (i):
    1947:Q1–2010:Q4: Corporate bonds (Moody's Aaa) from the Board of Governors of the Federal Reserve System.

11. Real Federal Budget Surplus in 2005 Dollars:
    1947:Q1–2010:Q4: Calculated by dividing the nominal federal government surplus from the U.S. Department of Commerce by the implicit price deflator using Tables 3.2 and 1.1.9.

12. Trade-Weighted Exchange Rate:
    1961:Q1–1966:Q4: Effective exchange rate (MERM) from various issues of *International Financial Statistics* (Washington, D.C.: International Monetary Fund). Linked in 1967:Q1 to:
    1967:Q1–2010:Q4: Trade-weighted exchange value of U.S. dollar versus Major Currencies from FRED, Federal Reserve Bank of St. Louis.

C-3 International Variables (Sources and Methods for Appendix B, same sources for all countries)

1. Nominal GDP (X):

   Gross domestic product (expenditures) from *Organization for Economic Cooperation and Development, National Accounts, Volume 1: Main Aggregates, and OECD Economic Outlook* no. 88, December 2010. Both are available at *OECD.Stat* online database.

2. Implicit GDP Deflator (P):

   Equals X/Y.

3. Real GDP (Y):

   Same sources as in 1. Nominal GDP.

4. Labor Productivity (Y/N):

   Real output (real GDP, Y) divided by total manhours, N (the product of total employment and hours worked per employee). Total manhours are from *The Conference Board and Groningen Growth and Development Centre, Total Economy Database,* January 2010, www.conference-board.org/economics.

5. Unemployment Rate (U):

   Unemployment rate from Bureau of Labor Statistics, *Comparative Civilian Labor Force Statistics, Ten Countries,* 1970–2009, Table 2, and International Monetary Fund *World Economic Outlook,* October 2010.

6. Investment share:

   Alan Heston, Robert Summers, and Bettina Aten, Penn World Table Version 6.3, Center for International Comparisons of Production, Income and Prices at the University of Pennsylvania, August 2009, and IMF *World Economic Outlook,* October 2010.

7. Consumer Price Index (CPI):

   International Financial Statistics Yearbook, 2010 (Washington, D.C.: International Monetary Fund, 2010). Updated using IMF *World Economic Outlook,* October 2010.

8. Long-term Interest Rate (r)

   OECD Economic Outlook, no. 88, December 2010.

9. Labor Share (wN/X):

   Calculated by dividing compensation of employees by national income in *OECD Economic Outlook No. 88,* December 2010, and *National Accounts, Volume I: Main Aggregates,* found at *OECD.Stat.*

C-4   Sources and Methods for Figures in Chapters

Please note: Many of the figures contain complete source notes. The following sources, listed in order by page number, refer to the subset of figures that require more complete or detailed source notes than can be included underneath the figures.

Some sources are abbreviated as follows:

FRB: The Board of Governors of the Federal Reserve System

BEA: U.S. Department of Commerce *Bureau of Economic Analysis*

NIPA Tables: *National Income and Products Accounts Tables* obtained from www.bea.gov

BLS: U.S. Department of Labor *Bureau of Labor Statistics*

GGDC: The Conference Board and Groningen Growth and Development Centre

Historical Statistics: *The Historical Statistics of the United States: Millennial Edition Online*

IMF: International Monetary Fund

OECD: The Organization for Economic Cooperation and Development

1. Figure 1-6 (p. 12):
   1900–2010: See Appendix C-1, lines 3–6

2. Figure 1-7 (p. 14):
   1929–41 and 1995–2010: See Appendix C, line 5

3. Figure 1-8 (p. 15):
   Thomas J. Sargent, "The Ends of Four Big Inflations," in Robert E. Hall, ed., *Inflation: Causes and Effects*, University of Chicago for NBER, 1982, Table G1, pp. 74–75

4. Figure 1-9 (p. 17):
   GDP per capita is a linear average of GK and EKS PPP GDP measures
   1960–2010: GGDC, Total Economy Database, January 2010, www.ggdc.net
   U.S. implicit GDP deflator estimates
   BEA NIPA Table 1.1.9

5. International Perspective box (pp. 18–19):
   Labor Productivity
   1960–2010: GGDC, Total Economy Database, January 2010
   EU-15 Unemployment
   1960–2010: OECD Labour Force Statistics—Summary tables Vol. 2010 release 03. SourceOECD Employment and Labour Market Statistics
   EU-15 Civilian Labor Force
   1960–2010: OECD Labour Force Statistics—Summary tables Vol. 2010 release 03. SourceOECD Employment and Labour Market Statistics
   U.S. Unemployment
   1960–2010: See Appendix C-1, line 5

6. Figure 2-4 (p. 40):
   1900–2010: See Appendix C-1, lines 1–3

7. Figure 2-5 (p. 45):
   Current Population and Employment Statistics Surveys
   1990–2010: BLS Series Ids: LNS12000000 and CES0000000001
   For accurate comparison, requires: Employment in Agriculture, Forestry, and Fishing
   1990–2010: BEA *NIPA* Table 6.8

8. Figure 3-1 (p. 55):
   Real GDP
   1950–2010: See Appendix C-2, line 3

9. Understanding the Global Economic Crisis box (pp. 62–63):
   Household total assets
   1970–2010: FRB *Z.1 Flow of Funds Accounts,* Series FL154090005.A
   Household net worth
   1970–2010: FRB *Z.1 Flow of Funds Accounts,* Series Z1/Z1/FL152090005.A
   Household total liabilities
   1970–2010: FRB *Z.1 Flow of Funds Accounts,* Series FL154190005.A
   Personal saving and disposable personal income
   1970–2010: BEA *NIPA* Table 2.1

10. Understanding the Global Economic Crisis box (p. 74–75):
    Real GDP and Gross private domestic investment
    1980–2010: BEA *NIPA* Table 1.1.6

11. Understanding the Global Economic Crisis box (pp. 102–104):
    Federal funds rate and 10-year Treasury bond rate
    1987–2011: Federal Reserve Board of Governors *H.15 Selected Interest Rates*
    Quarterly housing starts
    1970–2010: U.S. Census Bureau *Manufacturing, Mining and Construction Statistics*

12. International Perspective box (pp. 110–111):
    U.S. short-term interest rate
    1929–1941: Board of Governors of the Federal Reserve System *Banking and Monetary Statistics 1914–1941*
    2000–2011: Federal Reserve Board of Governors *H.15 Selected Interest Rates*
    Japan short-term interest rate
    1989–2010: *OECD Economic Outlook, no. 88*

13. Figure 5-1 (p. 123)
    U.S., Japan and Euro-area output gap
    2000–2011: *OECD Economic Outlook, no. 88*

14. Figure 5-4 (p. 126):
    Civilian Labor Force
    1980–2010: BLS *Labor Force Statistics from the Current Population Survey*
    Series LNS11000000

Number unemployed for 27 weeks and over
1980–2010: BLS *Labor Force Statistics from the Current Population Survey*
Series LNS13008636

15. Figure 5-6 (p. 134):
S&P Composite and Earnings
1970–2010: Robert Shiller Stock Market Data

16. Figure 5-7 (p. 134):
Rental price index
1970–2010: BEA *NIPA* Table 2.4.4
Housing price index
1970–2010: Data derived from National Association of Realtors, MacroMarkets LLC, Federal Housing Finance Agency, and Freddie Mac

17. Figure 5-10 (p. 143):
Federal funds rate and 10-year Treasury bond rate
1987–2011: Federal Reserve Board of Governors *H.15 Selected Interest Rates*
Corporate bond rate
1987–2011: See Appendix C-2, line 10

18. Figure 5-12 (p. 150):
Mortgage-backed securities, Federal agency debt securities, U.S. Treasury securities, total assets, currency in circulation, required reserves, excess reserves, and total liabilities
2008–2011: Federal Reserve *H.4.1 Factors Affecting Reserve Balances*

19. Figure 6-1 (p. 161):
Nominal GDP and Natural and Real GDP
1900–2010: See Appendix C-1, lines 1, 3 and 4
Current Receipts and Current Expenditures
1900–1928: Historical Statistics Tables Ea584, Ea585
1929–2010: BEA *NIPA* Table 3.1

20. Figure 6-4 (p. 167):
Natural Real GDP
1970–2010: See Appendix C-1, line 4
Actual Budget Surplus
1970–2010: BEA *NIPA* Table 3.1
Natural Employment Surplus from CBO, Office of Management and Budget, Table 13 Historical Budget Data

21. International Perspective box (p. 171):
U.S. debt to GDP ratio
1970–2010: Economic Report of the President, Table B-78
Italy, Germany and Japan debt to GDP ratio
1970–2010: *OECD Economic Outlook*, no. 88

22. Figure 6-5 (p. 173):
Public Debt and GDP
1790–1939: Historical Statistics Tables Ea587, Ca10
1940–2010: *Economic Report of the President: February 2010*, Table B-78

23. Figure 6-6 (p. 180):
Real Disposable Personal Income, Personal Consumption Expenditures, and Real Personal Income Less Current Transfers
2007–2010: BEA *NIPA* Table 1.1.6

24. Understanding the Global Economic Crisis box (pp. 182–183):
Federal government spending and state and local spending
1929–1941: BEA *NIPA* Table 1.1.6A
1980–2010: BEA *NIPA* Table 1.1.3
Transfer payments
1929–2010: BEA *NIPA* Table 2.1
Nominal GDP
1929–1941: See Appendix C-1, line 1
PCE Deflator
1980–2010: BEA *NIPA* Table 2.3.4
Natural Real GDP
1929–1941: See Appendix C-1, line 4
1980–2010: See Appendix C-2, line 4

25. Figure 7-1 (p. 196):
Current Account
1975–2010: BEA *NIPA* Table 4.1
Net International Investment Position
1975–2010: BEA *International Economics Accounts* International Investment Position Table 2

26. Figure 7-5 (p. 214):
Foreign Official Holding of Dollars
1980–2010: BEA *International Economic Accounts* International Investment Position Table 2

27. Figure 7-7 (p. 219):
Inflation (from personal consumption expenditures deflator)
1980–2010: BEA *NIPA* Table 2.3.4
Corporate Bond Yield
1980–2010: FRB *H.15* Moody's Yield on Seasoned Corporate Bonds, average of Aaa and Baa

28. Figure 8-10 (p. 254):
Output ratio (ratio of actual to natural real GDP)
1929–1941: Author's calculations
2007–2010: See Appendix C-2, lines 3 and 4

29. Figure 9-1 (p. 267):
Output ratio (ratio of actual to natural real GDP)
1960–2010: See Appendix C-2, lines 3 and 4
Inflation rate (from GDP deflator)
1960–2010: See Appendix C-2, line 2

30. International Perspective box (pp. 282–283):
GDP Deflator
1980–2010: See Appendix C-2, line 2
United Kingdom, France, Germany and Italy inflation rate
1980–2010: IMF *World Economic Outlook*, October 2010

31. Figure 9-8 (p. 285):
GDP Deflator
1970–2010: See Appendix C-2, line 2
Nominal oil price
1970–2010: U.S. Energy Information Administration *Domestic Crude Oil Prices*

32. Understanding the Global Economic Crisis box (p. 291):
Inflation rate (from GDP deflator)
1995–2010: See Appendix C-2, line 2

Output ratio (ratio of actual to natural real GDP)
1995–2010: See Appendix C-2, lines 3 and 4

33. Figure 9-12 (p. 298):
Real GDP, Natural Real GDP, and Unemployment Rate
1965–2010: See Appendix C-2, lines 3, 4 and 5

34. Figure 9-13 (p. 300):
GDP Deflator, Real GDP, Natural Real GDP, and Unemployment Rate
1965–2010: See Appendix C-2, lines 2, 3, 4 and 5

35. International Perspective box (p. 319):
Inflation Index
1990–2009: IMF *World Economic Outlook,* October 2010
Money Supply
1990–2009: IMF *International Financial Statistics,* September 2010

36. Box of Special Interest (p. 329):
10-year Treasury bond rate
1997–2010: FRB *H.15 Selected Interest Rates*
TIPS expected inflation estimates
1997–2010: Federal Reserve Bank of Cleveland Database

37. Figure 10-2 (p. 338):
Natural and actual unemployment rates
1980–2010: See Appendix C-2, lines 5 and 6

38. Figure 10-3 (p. 348):
Natural and actual unemployment rates (same as Figure 10-2)

39. Understanding the Global Economic Crisis box (p. 351):
U.S. Unemployment rate
2000–2010: See Appendix C-2, line 5
France, Germany, Italy, United Kingdom Unemployment rate
2000–2010: OECD *Labour Force Statistics*

40. International Perspective box (p. 322):
GDP per capita
1879–1949: OECD Development Centre *The World economy: Historical Statistics*
1950–2010: The Conference Board and Groningen Growth and Development Centre, Total Economy Database, January 2011, www.ggdc.net

41. Figure 12-5 (p. 409):
Productivity growth (Nonfarm Private Business Sector)
1960–2010: BLS *Major Sector Productivity and Costs Index* Series ID: PRS85006093
Trend line uses an average of the Hodrick-Prescott trending method with smoothing parameter 6400 and the Kalman filter with a parameter sv=16

42. Figure 12-6 (p. 417):
Labor productivity
1970–2010: GGDC, Total Economy Database, January 2011

43. Figure 14-2 (p. 459):
3-month Treasury bill rate
1961–2010: FRB *H.15 Selected Interest Rates*

Real GDP
1961–2010: See Appendix C-2, line 3
Quarterly percent change in real GDP is regressed on lags 3 through 8 of the quarterly level change in the Treasury bill rate for each of the time intervals

44. Figure 14-3 (p. 463):
Log-output ratio, log ratio of real GDP to natural real GDP
1960–2010: See Appendix C-2, lines 3 and 4

45. Figure 14-4 (p. 465):
Federal funds rate
1980–2010: FRB *H.15 Selected Interest Rates*
Log-output ratio (same as Figure 14-3)

46. Figure 14-5 (p. 469):
Federal funds rate (same as Figure 14-3)
Fixed and Variable Taylor rules calculated using weights as explained in the test on data for the Inflation rate (same as Figure 9-1 on p. 267) and on the log output ratio (same as Figure 14-3)

47. International Perspective box (p. 476):
Budget Deficit
1990–2011: OECD *Economic Outlook,* no. 88, Annex Table 27

48. Figure 15-7 (p. 505):
Personal saving and disposable personal income
1970–2010: BEA *NIPA* Table 2.1
Household net worth
1970–2010: FRB *Z.1 Flow of Funds Accounts,* Series Z1/Z1/FL152090005.A

49. Figure 15-8 (p. 509):
Household financial, tangible, and total assets
1970–2010: FRB *Z.1 Flow of Funds Accounts,* Series FL15000005.A, FL152010005.A, and FL154090005.A
Disposable personal income
1970–2010: BEA *NIPA* Table 2.1

50. Figure 15-9 (p. 510):
FAA personal saving
1960–2010: FRB *Z.1 Flow of Funds Accounts,* Series FA176006005.A
Personal saving
1960–2010: BEA *NIPA* Table 2.1

51. Figure 15-10 (p. 511):
FAA personal saving
1960–2010: FRB *Z.1 Flow of Funds Accounts,* Series FA17600605.A
Gains-inclusive saving rate function of household net worth, personal saving, and disposable personal income

52. Figure 16-1 (p. 519):
Inventory change, residential investment, fixed non-residential structures, durable equipment and software, gross private domestic investment
1960–2010: BEA *NIPA* Table 1.1.5
Natural real GDP
1960–2010: See Appendix C-2, line 4
GDP deflator
1960–2010: See Appendix C-2, line 2

53. Figure 16-3 (p. 525):
    Net nonresidential investment
        1960–2010: BEA *NIPA* Tables 1.1.5 and 5.2.5
    Real GDP
        1960–2010: See Appendix C-2, line 3
54. International Perspective box (p. 536):
    Ratio of investment to GDP
        1980–2011: IMF *World Economic Outlook*, October 2010
55. International Perspective box (p. 553):
    U.S. output growth is growth in real-value added output
    U.S. input growth is residual after output growth subtracted from multifactor productivity growth
        1970–2010: BLS *Multifactor Productivity*, Net multifactor productivity and costs table
    Japan output growth is growth rate of value added volume
    Japan input growth is residual after output growth subtracted from total factor productivity growth
    1970–2006: EU KLEMS Database, November 2009, see Marcel Timmer, Mary O'Mahony & Bart van Ark, The EU KLEMS Growth and Productivity Accounts: An Overview, University of Groningen & University of Birmingham; downloadable at www.euklems.net
    2007–2010: Estimates using input and output data and growth rates from OECD *Economic Outlook* no. 88 and GGDC, Total Economy Database, January 2011
56. Figure 18-1 (p. 573):
    Nominal GDP growth
        1923–1947: See Appendix C-1, line 1

M1 growth
    1923–1947: See Appendix C-1, line 7
Inflation rate (from GDP deflator)
    1923–1947: See Appendix C-1, line 2
Output ratio (ratio of actual to natural real GDP)
    1923–1947: See Appendix C-1, lines 3 and 4
Unemployment rate
    1923–1947: See Appendix C-1, line 5
Corporate bond yield
    1923–1947: FRB *H.15* Moody's Yield on Seasoned Aaa Corporate Bonds
Commercial paper rate
    1923–1947: FRB *Banking and Monetary Statistics 1914-1941*
    1941–1947: FRB *Supplement to Banking and Monetary Statistics (1966)*
    Both can be found in the Historical Statistics
57. Figure 18-2 (p. 576) and Figure 18-3 (p. 579):
    Nominal GDP growth
        1948–2010: See Appendix C-2, line 1
    M1 growth
        1948–2010: See Appendix C-2, line 7
    Inflation rate (from GDP deflator)
        1948–2010: See Appendix C-2, line 2
    Output ratio (ratio of actual to natural real GDP)
        1948–2010: See Appendix C-2, lines 3 and 4
    Unemployment rate
        1948–2010: See Appendix C-2, line 5
    10-year and 30-year Treasury bond rate
        1948–1963: FRB *Supplement to Banking and Monetary Statistics (1966)*
        1963–2010: *Federal Reserve Bulletin*
    Federal funds rate
        1948–2010: FRB *H.15 Selected Interest Rates*

Glossary

Accelerator hypothesis (16-3) Theory that the level of net investment depends on the *change* in expected output.

Accommodating policy (9-9) Attempt by government or central bank, following a supply shock, to raise nominal GDP growth so as to maintain the original output ratio.

Actual real GDP (1-3) The value of total output corrected for any changes in prices.

Actual real interest rate (10-3) The nominal interest rate minus the actual inflation rate.

Adaptive expectations (9-6) Prediction for next period's economic values based on an average of actual values during previous periods.

Aggregate (1-2) Total amount of an economic magnitude for the economy as a whole.

Aggregate demand (3-1) The total amount of desired spending expressed in current (nominal) dollars.

Aggregate demand (AD) curve (8-1) The graphical schedule showing different combinations of the price level and real output at which the money and commodity markets are both in equilibrium.

Aggregate supply (3-2) The amount that firms are willing to produce at any given price level.

Appreciation (7-3) A rise in the value of one nation's currency relative to another nation's currency. When the dollar can buy more units of a foreign currency, say, the euro, the dollar is said to appreciate relative to that foreign currency.

Auction market (17-7) A centralized location where professional traders buy and sell a commodity or a financial security.

Automatic stabilization (Appendix to Ch. 3, 6-4) The effect on the government budget deficit or surplus of the change in tax revenues when income rises or falls.

Autonomous magnitude (3-3) An amount independent of the level of income.

Backward-looking expectations (9-6) Predictions for next period's values based only on information on the past behavior of economic variables.

Balance of payments (7-2) The record of a nation's international transactions, both credits (which arise from sales of exports and sales of assets) and debits (which arise from purchases of imports and purchases of assets).

Bank run (5-3) Event that occurs when the customers of a bank fear that the bank will become insolvent. Customers rush to the bank to take out their money as quickly as possible to avoid losing it.

Bubble (5-4) A sustained large rise in the price of an asset relative to its fundamental value followed by a collapse in prices that eliminates most or all of the initial price gain.

Budget line (6-4) The graphical schedule showing the government budget surplus or deficit at different levels of real income.

Business cycles (1-4) Expansions occurring at about the same time in many economic activities, followed by similarly general recessions and recoveries.

Capital account (7-2) The part of the balance of payments that records capital flows, which consist of purchases and sales of foreign assets by domestic residents, and purchases and sales of domestic assets by foreign residents.

Closed economy (1-8) A nation that has no trade in goods, services, or financial assets with any other nation.

Cold turkey (9-7) An approach to disinflation that implements a sudden and permanent slowdown in nominal GDP growth.

Constant growth rate rule (CGRR) (14-3) The rule advocating a fixed percentage growth rate for the money supply, in contrast to the variable growth rate recommended by policy activists.

Consumption expenditures (2-2) Purchases of goods and services by households for their own use.

Contractionary monetary policy (4-5) Government monetary policy that has the effect of lowering GDP and raising interest rates.

Coordination failure (17-7) Result of firms neglecting to act together, due to lack of private incentive, to avoid actions that impose social costs on society.

Core inflation rate (9-9) The inflation rate for all products and services other than food and energy.

Cost-of-living agreement (COLA) (17-9) Contract that provides for an automatic increase in the wage rate in response to an increase in the price level.

Countercyclical variable (8-6) A variable that moves over the business cycle in the opposite direction from real GDP.

Credibility (10-6) The extent to which households and firms believe that an announced monetary or fiscal policy will actually be implemented and maintained as announced.

Cross-section (15-3) Data for numerous units (e.g., households, firms, cities, or states) observed at a single period of time.

Crowding out effect (4-6)   Reduction of one or more components of private expenditures due to an increase in government spending or a reduction of tax rates.

Current account (7-2)   The part of the balance of payments that includes exports, imports, investment income, and transfer payments to and from foreigners.

Cyclical deficit (6-4)   The amount by which the actual government budget deficit exceeds the structural deficit.

Cyclical surplus (6-4)   The amount by which the actual government budget surplus exceeds the structural surplus.

Cyclical unemployment (10-7)   The difference between the actual unemployment rate and the natural rate of unemployment.

Demand inflation (9-8)   A sustained increase in prices that is preceded by a permanent acceleration of nominal GDP growth.

Demand shock (3-1, 9-1)   Unexpected changes in business and consumer optimism, changes in net exports, and changes in government spending or tax rates.

Depreciation (consumption of fixed capital) (2-3)   The part of the capital stock used up due to obsolescence and physical wear.

Depreciation (of currency) (7-3)   A decline in the value of one nation's currency relative to another nation's currency. When the dollar can buy fewer units of a foreign currency, say, the British pound, the dollar is said to depreciate relative to that foreign currency.

Depreciation rate (16-7)   The annual percentage decline in the value of a capital good due to physical deterioration and obsolescence.

Devaluation (7-6)   Under the fixed exchange rate system, a nation's reduction of the value of its money expressed in terms of foreign money.

Discount rate (13-4)   The interest rate the Federal Reserve charges depository institutions when they borrow reserves.

Discretionary fiscal policy (6-4)   Alteration of tax rates and/or government expenditures in a deliberate attempt to influence real output and the unemployment rate.

Discretionary policy (14-3)   Approach that treats each macroeconomic episode as a unique event, without any attempt to respond in the same way from one episode to another.

Disinflation (9-7)   A marked deceleration in the inflation rate.

Domestic income (2-6)   The earnings of domestic factors of production, computed as net domestic product minus indirect business taxes, which are taxes levied on business sales.

Dynamic multipliers (14-4)   The amount by which output is raised during each of several time periods after a given change in a policy instrument.

Economic growth (1-4, 11-2)   Topic area of macroeconomics that studies the causes and consequences of sustained growth in natural real GDP over periods of a decade or more.

Endogenous variables (3-2)   Variables explained by an economic theory.

Equilibrium (3-4)   A state in which there exists no pressure for change.

Equilibrium real wage rate (8-5)   The real wage rate at which the labor supply and demand curves intersect, so there is no pressure for change in the real wage.

Equity (5-3)   The difference between the assets and liabilities of an economic unit. The same as net worth.

Exogenous variables (3-2)   Variables that are relevant but whose behavior economic theory does not attempt to explain and whose values are taken as given.

Expansionary monetary policy (4-5)   Government monetary policy that has the effect of lowering interest rates and raising GDP.

Expectations-augmented Phillips Curve (*SP* curve) (9-2)   A schedule relating the inflation rate to the output ratio (or unemployment rate) that shifts its position whenever there is a change in the expected rate of inflation.

Expectations effect (8-8)   The decline in aggregate demand caused by the postponement of purchases when consumers expect prices to decline in the future.

Expected rate of inflation (9-2)   Rate of inflation that is expected to occur in the future.

Expected real interest rate (10-3)   The nominal interest rate minus the expected rate of inflation.

Exports (2-4)   Goods and services produced within one country and sold to another.

Extinguishing policy (9-9)   Attempt by government or central bank, following a supply shock, to reduce nominal GDP growth so as to maintain the original inflation rate.

Extra convenience services (10-3)   The services provided by holding one extra dollar of money instead of bonds.

Factor inputs (11-3)   The economic elements that directly produce real GDP.

Feedback rule (14-3)   A rule of stabilization policy that systematically changes a monetary variable like the money supply or interest rates in response to actual or forecasted changes in target variables like inflation or employment.

Final good (2-3)   Part of final product.

Final product (2-3)   All currently produced goods and services that are sold through the market but are not resold. Same as **Gross Domestic Product (GDP).**

Financial intermediaries (5-3)   Institutions, such as banks, that make loans to borrowers and obtain funds from savers, usually by accepting deposits.

Financial markets (5-3)   Organized exchanges where securities and financial instruments are bought and sold.

Fiscal policy (1-7)   Manipulations of government expenditures and tax rates in order to try to influence target variables.

Fisher Effect (10-3)   Prediction that a one percentage point increase in the expected inflation rate will raise the nominal real interest rate by one percentage point, leaving the expected real interest rate unaffected.

Fisher equation (10-3)   Statement that the nominal interest rate equals the expected inflation rate plus the expected real interest rate.

Fixed exchange rate system (7-6)   System in which the foreign exchange rate is fixed for long periods of time.

Fixed investment (2-4)   All final goods purchased by business that are not intended for resale.

Flexible accelerator theory (16-5)   Theory of investment that allows for gradual adjustment of sales expectations and of the capital stock. It also allows for variation in the optimal capital-output ratio.

Flexible exchange rate system (7-6)   System in which the foreign exchange rate is free to change every day, to establish an equilibrium between the quantities supplied and demanded of a nation's currency.

Flow magnitude (2-2)   An economic magnitude that moves from one economic unit to another at a specified rate per unit of time.

Foreign exchange rate (7-3)   The amount of another nation's money that residents of a country can obtain in exchange for a unit of their own money.

Foreign exchange reserves (7-6)   Government holdings of foreign money used under a fixed exchange rate system to respond to changes in the foreign demand for and supply of a particular nation's money. Such reserves are also used for intervention under a flexible exchange rate system.

Forward-looking expectations (9-6, 15-1)   Predictions of future behavior of an economic variable, using an economic model that specifies the interrelationship of that variable with other variables.

GDP deflator (2-7)   The economy's aggregate price index, defined as the ratio of nominal GDP to chain-weighted real GDP.

GDP gap (1-3)   The percentage difference between actual real GDP and natural real GDP.

General equilibrium (4-4)   A situation of simultaneous equilibrium in all the markets of the economy.

Global Economic Crisis (1-1)   Crisis that began in 2007 that simultaneously depressed economic activity in most of the world's economies.

Government budget constraint (10-5)   Limitation of government spending to the three sources available to finance that spending: tax revenue, creation of bonds, and creation of money.

Gross (2-3)   Economic aggregate that includes capital consumption allowances.

Gross debt (6-5)   The total public debt, whether it is held inside or outside of the government.

Gross domestic product (GDP) (1-3)   The value of all currently produced goods and services sold on the market during a particular time interval.

Gross national product (GNP) (2-3)   Goods and services produced by labor and capital supplied by U.S. residents, whether the actual production takes place within the borders of the United States or in a foreign country.

Helicopter Drop (6-8)   A figurative phrase to describe a combined monetary and fiscal policy expansion. A fiscal stimulus creates a larger deficit, and the government has to sell bonds to pay for the deficit. But instead of selling those bonds to the private sector, it sells them to the Fed. The Fed's assets and liabilities increase but the net public debt does not increase.

High-powered money (13-3)   The sum of currency held outside depository institutions and the reserves held inside them. Same as monetary base.

Household wealth (3-3)   The total value of household assets, including the market value of homes, possessions such as automobiles, and financial assets such as stocks, bonds, and bank accounts, minus any liabilities, including outstanding mortgage and credit card debt, automobile loans, and other loans.

Human capital (11-7)   The value, for a person or for society in general, of the extra earnings made possible by education.

Hyperinflation (10-1)   A very rapid inflation, sometimes defined as a rate of more than 22 percent per month or 1,000 percent per year, experienced over a year or more.

Imports (2-4)   Goods consumed within one country but produced in another country.

Incomes policy (10-6)   An attempt by policymakers to moderate increases in wages and other income, either by persuasion or by legal rules.

Indexed bond (10-4)   A bond that pays a fixed real interest rate; its nominal interest rate is equal to this real interest rate plus the actual inflation rate.

Induced consumption (3-3)   The portion of consumption spending that responds to changes in income.

Induced saving (3-4)   The portion of saving that responds to changes in income.

Inflation (9-1)   A sustained upward movement in the aggregate price level that is shared by most products.

Inflation differential (7-5)   Foreign inflation minus domestic inflation.

Inflation rate (1-1)   The percentage rate of increase in the economy's average level of prices.

Inflation tax (10-5)   The revenue the government receives from inflation, the same as **seignorage** (the inflation rate times real high-powered money), but viewed from the perspective of households.

Infrastructure (12-1)   Types of capital that benefit society as a whole, including highways, airports, trains, waterways, ports, telephone networks, and electricity grids.

Injections (2-5)   Nonconsumption expenditures.

Interest rate differential (7-9)   The average U.S. interest rate minus the average foreign interest rate.

Intermediate good (2-3)   A product resold by its purchaser either in its present form or in an altered form.

Intertemporal substitution (17-4)   Workers work more in periods of high real wages and less in periods of low real wages. Also occurs when producers raise output in periods of high prices and reduce output in periods of low prices.

Intervention (7-6)   Under the flexible exchange rate system, the buying or selling of a nation's money by domestic or foreign central banks in order to prevent unwanted variations in the foreign exchange rate.

Inventory investment (2-4)   All changes in the stock of raw materials, parts, and finished goods held by business.

IS curve (3-9)   The schedule that identifies the combinations of income and the interest rate at which the commodity market is in equilibrium; everywhere along the *IS* curve the demand for commodities equals the supply.

Keynes Effect (8-8)   The stimulus to aggregate demand caused by a decline in the interest rate.

Labor productivity (12-2)   Real GDP per hour of work, or output per hour of work.

Large open economy (7-9)   An economy that can influence its domestic interest rate.

Leakages (2-5)   The portion of total income that flows to taxes or saving rather than into purchases of consumer goods.

Leverage (5-3)   The ratio of the liabilities of a financial institution to equity capital. Leverage increases when banks develop methods to grant more loans with their existing equity capital.

Life-cycle hypothesis (LCH) (15-1)   Conjecture that households base their current consumption on their total lifetime incomes and their wealth.

Liquidity constraint (15-6)   Occurs when households cannot borrow as much as they wish, even though there is sufficient expected future income to repay the loans.

Liquidity trap (4-7)   Situation in which the central bank loses its ability to reduce the interest rate.

LM curve (4-3)   The schedule that identifies the combinations of income and the interest rate at which the money market is in equilibrium; on the *LM* curve the demand for money equals the supply of money.

Long-run aggregate supply curve (LAS) (8-1)   A vertical line drawn at the natural level of real GDP; it shows the amount that business firms are willing to produce when the nominal wage rate has fully adjusted to any changes in the price level.

Long-run equilibrium (8-6)   A situation in which labor input is the amount voluntarily supplied and demanded at the equilibrium real wage rate.

Long-term labor contracts (17-9)   Agreements between firms and workers that set the level of nominal wage rates for a year or more.

Lucas model (17-3)   Economic model based on the three assumptions of market clearing, imperfect information, and rational expectations.

M1 (13-2)   The U.S. definition of the money supply that includes only currency, transactions accounts, and traveler's checks.

M2 (13-2)   The U.S. definition of the money supply that includes M1; savings deposits, including money market deposit accounts; small time deposits; and money market mutual funds.

Macroeconomic externality (17-7)   A cost incurred by society as a result of a decision by an individual economic agent (worker or business firm).

Macroeconomics (1-1)   The study of the major economic totals, or aggregates.

Magic equation (2-5)   Private saving plus net tax revenue must by definition equal the sum of private domestic investment, government spending on goods and services, and net exports.

Marginal leakage rate (Appendix to Ch. 3)   The fraction of income that is taxed or saved rather than being spent on consumption.

Marginal product of capital (MPK) (16-6)   The extra output that a firm can produce by adding an extra unit of capital.

Marginal propensity to consume (3-3)   The dollar change in consumption expenditures induced by a dollar change in disposable income.

Marginal propensity to save (3-3)   The change in personal saving induced by a dollar change in disposable income.

Menu cost (10-3, 17-6)   Any expense associated with changing prices, including the costs of printing new menus or distributing new catalogues.

Mismatch unemployment (10-7)   Structural unemployment; one of the two components of the natural rate of unemployment (the other being turnover, or frictional unemployment); it occurs when the present location or skills of members of the labor force do not match location or skill requirements of job vacancies.

Monetarism (14-3)   A school of thought that opposes activist or discretionary monetary policy and instead favors a fixed rule for the growth rate of high-powered money or of the money supply.

Monetary impotence (8-8)   Failure of real GDP to respond to an increase in the real money supply.

Monetary policy (1-7)   Changes made in the money supply or interest rates or both in order to try to influence target variables.

Money multiplier (13-3)   The ratio (M/H) of the money supply to high-powered money. There is a separate money multiplier for each definition of the money supply, e.g., $M1/H$ and $M2/H$.

Money-multiplier shock (13-4)   Any event that causes the money multiplier to change, such as a change in the public's demand for currency relative to deposits, or a shift between deposits having different reserve requirements.

Money supply (4-2)   Currency and transactions accounts, including checking accounts at banks and thrift institutions.

Multifactor productivity (11-5)   The growth rate of output per hour of work, minus the contribution to output of the growth in the quantity of other factors of production per hour of work, notably capital but sometimes including energy, raw materials, or other factors of production.

Multiplier (3-5)   The ratio of the change in output to the change in autonomous planned spending that causes it; also 1.0 divided by the marginal propensity to save.

Multiplier uncertainty (14-4)   The lack of firm knowledge regarding the change in output caused by a change in a policy instrument.

National Income and Product Accounts (2-3)   Official U.S. government economic accounting system that keeps track of GDP and its subcomponents.

National saving (7-2)   The sum of private saving (by both households and business firms) and government saving (the government budget surplus).

Natural employment surplus (NES) or deficit (NED) (6-4)   The government budget surplus or deficit at the natural level of real GDP.

Natural rate hypothesis (17-2)   The hypothesis that shifts in nominal aggregate demand have no long-run effect on real GDP.

Natural rate of unemployment (1-3)   The level of unemployment at which the inflation rate is constant, with no tendency to accelerate or decelerate.

Natural real GDP (1-3)   The level of real GDP at which the inflation rate is constant, with no tendency to accelerate or decelerate.

Net (2-3)   Economic aggregate excluding capital consumption allowances.

Net debt (6-5)   Gross public debt minus debt held inside the government, including government securities held by the Federal Reserve and the trust funds of Social Security and Medicare.

Net domestic product (NDP) (2-3)   GDP minus depreciation.

Net exports (2-4)   Exports minus imports.

Net foreign investment (2-4)   Equal to exports minus imports. Called "net foreign borrowing" when net exports are negative.

Net international investment position (7-2)   The difference between all foreign assets owned by a nation's citizens and domestic assets owned by foreign citizens.

Neutral policy (9-9)   Attempt by government or central bank, following a supply shock, to maintain unchanged nominal GDP growth so as to allow a decline in the output ratio equal to the increase of the inflation rate.

New Keynesian economics (17-6)   Approach that explains rigidity in prices and wages as consistent with the self-interest of firms and workers, all of which are assumed to have rational expectations.

Nominal (2-7)   An adjective that modifies any economic magnitude measured in current prices.

Nominal anchor (14-8)   A rule that sets a limit on the growth rate of a nominal variable, for instance, high-powered money, the money supply, the price level, or nominal GDP, to prevent inflation from accelerating without limit.

Nominal GDP (2-7)   The value of gross domestic product in current (actual) prices.

Nominal interest rate (10-3)   The market interest rate actually charged by financial institutions and earned by bondholders.

Nominal rigidity (17-6)   A factor that inhibits the flexibility of the nominal price level due to some factor, such as menu costs and staggered contracts. Such factors make it costly for firms to change the nominal price or wage level.

Non-market-clearing model (17-6)   Workers and firms are not continuously on their respective demand and supply schedules, but rather are pushed off these schedules by the gradual adjustment of prices.

Okun's Law (9-11)   A regular negative relationship between the output ratio (Y/Y^N) and the gap between the actual unemployment rate and the average rate of unemployment.

Open economy (1-8)   An economy that exports (sells) goods and services to other nations, buys imports from them, and has financial flows to and from foreign nations.

Open-market operations (13-4)   Purchases and sales of government securities made by the Federal Reserve in order to change high-powered money.

Output ratio (9-1)   The ratio of actual real GDP to natural real GDP.

Parameter (3-4)   A value taken as given or known within a particular analysis.

Perfect capital mobility (7-9)   A condition that occurs when investors regard foreign financial assets as a perfect substitute for domestic assets, and when investors respond instantaneously to an interest rate differential between domestic and foreign assets by moving sufficient assets to eliminate that differential.

Permanent income (15-4)   The annual average income that people expect to receive over a period of years in the future.

Permanent-income hypothesis (PIH) (15-1)   Conjecture that consumption spending depends on the long-run average (or permanent) income that people expect to receive.

Personal disposable income (2-6)   Personal income minus personal income tax payments.

Personal income (2-6)   Income received by households from all sources, including earnings and transfer payments.

Personal saving (2-4)   That part of personal income that is neither consumed nor paid out in taxes.

Pigou Effect (real balance effect) (8-8)   The direct stimulus to aggregate demand caused by an increase in the real money supply; does not require a decline in the interest rate.

Policy activism (14-1)   Active use of instruments of monetary and fiscal policy to offset changes in private sector spending.

Policy credibility (14-6)   The belief by the public that the policymakers will actually carry out an announced policy.

Policy ineffectiveness proposition (PIP) (17-3)   Assertion that predictable changes in monetary policy cannot affect real output.

Policy instruments (1-7, 14-2)   Elements that government policymakers can manipulate directly to influence target variables.

Policy mix (4-9)   The combination of monetary and fiscal policy in effect in a given situation.

Policy rule (14-1)   Requirement of a fixed path of a policy instrument like the short-term interest rate, of an intermediate variable like the money supply, or a target variable like inflation or unemployment. Also requirement of a specified response of a policy instrument to a given change in a target variable.

Private investment (2-4)   The portion of final product that adds to the nation's stock of income-yielding physical assets or that replaces old, worn-out physical assets.

Production function (11-3)   A graphical or algebraic relationship that shows how much output can be produced by a given quantity of factor inputs.

Productivity (1-1)   Aggregate output produced per hour.

Public debt (6-5)   The total amount of bonds and other liabilities (also called "securities") that the government has issued. These securities are held not only by private households and corporations and by foreign investors, but also by some agencies within the government itself. A fiscal deficit increases the debt whereas a fiscal surplus decreases the debt.

Purchasing power parity (PPP) theory (7-5)   Theory that the prices of identical goods should be the same in all countries, differing only by the cost of transport and any import (or customs) duties.

Quantitative easing (5-7)   Occurs when a central bank purchases assets with the intention not of lowering the short-term interest rate, which is already at zero, but with the purpose of increasing bank reserves.

Quantity theory of money (8-7)   Theory that actual output tends to grow steadily, while velocity is determined by payment practices such as the use of cash vs. checks, and that as a result a change in the money supply mainly affects the price level and has little or no effect on velocity or output.

Rational expectations (15-6, 17-3)   Forecasts of future economic magnitudes based on information currently available about the past performance of the economy and future government policies.

Real balance effect (Pigou Effect) (8-8)   The direct stimulus to aggregate demand caused by an increase in the real money supply; does not require a decline in the interest rate.

Real business cycle (RBC) model (17-4)   Explanation attributing business cycles in output and employment to technology or supply shocks.

Real exchange rate (7-5)   The average nominal foreign exchange rate between a country and its trading partners, adjusted for the difference in inflation rates between that country and its trading partners.

Real money balances (4-2)   Total money supply divided by the price level.

Real rigidity (17-6)   A factor that makes firms reluctant to change the real wage, the relative wage, or the relative price.

Redistribution effect (8-8)   The decline in aggregate demand caused by the effect of falling prices in redistributing income from high-spending debtors to low-spending savers.

Required reserves (13-4)   The reserves that Federal Reserve regulations require depository institutions to hold.

Reserve requirements (13-4)   Rules, which apply only to transactions accounts, that stipulate the minimum fraction of deposits that must be held as reserves.

Residual (11-5)   A label sometimes applied to **multifactor productivity.**

Revaluation (7-6)   Under the fixed exchange rate system, a nation's increase of the value of its money expressed in terms of foreign money.

Rigid rule (14-3) A rule for policy that sets a key policy instrument at a fixed value as in a constant growth rate rule for the money supply.

Rigid wages (8-8) The failure of the nominal wage rate to adjust by the amount needed to maintain equilibrium in the labor market.

Risk (5-3) The probability that a given investment or loan will fail to bring the expected return and may result in a loss of the partial or full value of the investment.

Risk premium (5-6) The difference between the corporate bond rate and the risk-free rate of Treasury bonds having the same maturity.

Sacrifice ratio (9-7) The cumulative loss of output incurred during a disinflation divided by the permanent reduction in the inflation rate.

Securitization (5-5) The process of combining many different debt instruments like home mortgages into a pool of hundreds or thousands of individual contracts, and then selling new financial instruments backed by the pool, for instance mortgage-backed securities, to investors.

Seignorage (10-5) The revenue the government receives from inflation; equal to the inflation rate times real high-powered money. Same as **inflation tax.**

Self-correcting forces (8-7) The role of flexible prices in stabilizing real GDP under some conditions.

Shoe-leather cost (10-3) Occurs when inflation raises interest rates, inducing people to keep more of their funds in interest-bearing bank accounts and less in pocket cash.

Short-run aggregate supply (SAS) curve (8-1) Graph of the amount of output that business firms are willing to produce at different price levels, holding constant the nominal wage rate.

Short-run equilibrium (8-6) The point where the aggregate demand curve crosses the short-run aggregate supply curve.

Short-run Phillips *(SP)* Curve (9-2) The schedule relating real GDP to the inflation rate achievable given a fixed expected rate of inflation.

Small open economy (7-9) An economy with perfect capital mobility and with no power to set its domestic interest rate at a level that differs from foreign interest rates.

Solow's residual (11-5) Growth in multifactor productivity. Same as **residual.**

Stabilization policy (1-7) Any policy that seeks to influence the level of aggregate demand.

Staggered contracts (17-6) Wage contracts that have different expiration dates for different groups of firms or workers.

Standard of living (12-2) Real GDP per member of the population, or output per capita.

Steady state (11-3) A situation in which output and capital input grow at the same rate, implying a fixed ratio of output to capital input.

Stock (2-2) An economic magnitude in the possession of a given economic unit at a particular point in time.

Structural deficit (6-4) What the government budget deficit would be if the economy were operating at natural real GDP.

Structural surplus (6-4) What the government budget surplus would be if the economy were operating at natural real GDP.

Subprime mortgage market (5-5) Market where borrowers typically have some combination of low incomes, unstable employment histories, and poor credit records.

Supply inflation (9-8) An increase in prices that stems from an increase in business costs not directly related to a prior acceleration of nominal GDP growth.

Supply shock (9-1) Caused by a sharp change in the price of an important commodity like oil.

Target variables (1-7, 14-2) Economic aggregates whose values society cares about—society's goals.

Taylor Rule (14-7) Calls for the central bank to move the real short-term interest rate away from its desired long-term value in response to any deviation of actual inflation from desired inflation and in response to any deviation of real GDP from natural real GDP.

Term premium (5-6) The average difference over a long period of the interest rate on long-term bonds and the interest rate on the short-term federal funds interest rate.

Time inconsistency (14-6) Policymakers' deviation from a policy after it is announced and private decision-makers have reacted to it.

Time series (15-3) Data covering a span of time of one or more measures (e.g., disposable income or consumption spending).

Total labor force (2-8) The total of the civilian employed, the armed forces, and the unemployed.

Transfer payments (2-3) Payments for which no goods or services are produced in return.

Transitory income (15-4) The difference between actual income and permanent income; it is not expected to recur.

Trilemma (7-1) The impossibility for any nation of maintaining simultaneously (1) independent control of domestic monetary policy, (2) fixed exchange rates, and (3) free flows of capital with other nations.

Turnover unemployment (frictional unemployment) (10-7) One of the two components of the natural rate of unemployment (the other being mismatch, or structural unemployment), it occurs in the normal process of job search.

Unanticipated inflation (10-3) Situation in which the actual inflation rate (p) differs from the expected (or anticipated) inflation rate (pe).

Unemployed (2-8) Persons without jobs who either are on temporary layoff or have taken specific actions to look for work.

Unemployment gap (1-3) The difference between the actual unemployment rate and the natural rate of unemployment.

Unemployment rate (1-1, 2-8) The percentage ratio of the number of jobless individuals actively looking for work or on temporary layoff divided by the total employed and unemployed in the labor force.

Unintended inventory investment (3-4) The amount business firms are forced to accumulate when planned expenditures are less than income.

User cost of capital (16-6) The cost to the firm of using a piece of capital for a specified period.

Value added (2-3) The value of the labor and capital services that take place at a particular stage of the production process.

Wage indexation (cost-of-living agreements) (10-6) An automatic increase in the wage rate in response to an increase in a price index.

Index